European Union Law

This eagerly awaited new edition has been revised after extensive user feedback to meet current teaching requirements. The first major textbook to be published since the rejuvenation of the Lisbon Treaty, it retains the best elements of the first edition – the engaging, easily understandable writing style, extracts from a variety of sources showing the creation, interpretation and application of the law and comprehensive coverage. In addition it has separate chapters on EU law in national courts, governance and external relations reflecting the new directions in which the field is moving. The examination of the free movement of goods has been restructured. Chapter introductions clearly set out what will be covered in each section, allowing students to approach complex material with confidence, and detailed further reading sections encourage further study. Put simply, it is required reading for all serious students of EU law.

Damian Chalmers is Professor of European Law at the London School of Economics and Political Science.

Gareth Davies is Professor of European Law at the Department of Transnational Legal Studies, VU University, Amsterdam.

Giorgio Monti is Reader in Law at the London School of Economics and Political Science.

European Union Law

CASES AND MATERIALS

SECOND EDITION

Damian Chalmers
Gareth Davies
Giorgio Monti

CAMBRIDGE
UNIVERSITY PRESS

CAMBRIDGE UNIVERSITY PRESS
Cambridge, New York, Melbourne, Madrid, Cape Town, Singapore, São Paulo, Delhi, Dubai, Tokyo

Cambridge University Press
The Edinburgh Building, Cambridge CB2 8RU, UK

Published in the United States of America by Cambridge University Press, New York

www.cambridge.org
Information on this title: www.cambridge.org/9780521121514

© Damian Chalmers, Gareth Davies and Giorgio Monti 2010

First published 2010

Printed in the United Kingdom at the University Press, Cambridge

A catalogue record for this publication is available from the British Library

Library of Congress Cataloguing in Publication data

ISBN 978-0-521-12151-4 Paperback

Contents

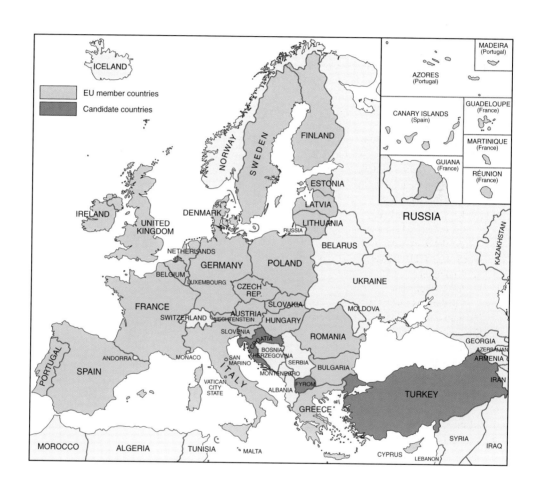

EU member countries

Candidate countries

ICELAND

NORWAY

SWEDEN

FINLAND

ESTONIA

LATVIA

LITHUANIA

RUSSIA

BELARUS

IRELAND

UNITED
KINGDOM

DENMARK

NETHERLANDS

GERMANY

POLAND

BELGIUM

LUXEMBOURG

CZECH
REP.

SLOVAKIA

UKRAINE

FRANCE

SWITZERLAND

LIECHTENSTEIN

AUSTRIA

HUNGARY

MOLDOVA

SLOVENIA

ROMANIA

CROATIA

BOSNIA
HERZEGOVINA

SERBIA

BULGARIA

PORTUGAL

ANDORRA

MONACO

SAN
MARINO

I T A L Y

MONTENEGRO

FYROM

GEORGIA

AZERBAIJAN

ARMENIA

IRAN

SPAIN

VATICAN
CITY
STATE

ALBANIA

GREECE

TURKEY

SYRIA

IRAQ

MOROCCO

ALGERIA

TUNISIA

MALTA

CYPRUS

LEBANON

RUSSIA

KAZAKHSTAN

MADEIRA
(Portugal)

AZORES
(Portugal)

CANARY ISLANDS
(Spain)

GUADELOUPE
(France)

MARTINIQUE
(France)

GUIANA
(France)

RÉUNION
(France)

Preface

The cover of this book portrays the *Myth of Europa*. The story has it that Europa, a Phoenician princess, was abducted by Zeus, the god of thunder, disguised as a bull. Zeus had been searching for a wife beautiful enough to become Queen of his native Crete. When he saw Europa he was smitten. Europa was gathering flowers by the seaside with her friends when she came upon the bull. Uncommonly gentle, the bull inspired no fear. Decking its horns with flowers, Europa climbed upon its back, whereupon the bull – Zeus – took off at a trot and dived into the sea. Europa was carried off to Crete, where she became the mother of Minos, the mythical King of Crete, who periodically demanded a tribute of young men and women of Athens to be sacrificed to the Minotaur.

This myth has not died with the ancients. In 1956, the six countries that were to sign the EEC Treaty appropriated her name to issue a set of Europa stamps to symbolise a community of interests and objectives. And today, Zeus's kidnap of Europa is depicted on the Greek 2 euro coin. The myth has been understood in a variety of ways. On one level, it is a story of virtue, innocence and romance; on another, it is a warning of violence and exclusion. As with many of the ancient myths, misunderstanding and contestation lie at its very heart. The Roman depiction on our cover is one of the first depictions and, insofar as the human participants are depicted as Romans, reminds us too that the myth has been repeatedly appropriated and reinvented. We have also here a tale with its origins in modern Lebanon, which was told by the Ancient Greeks, and which then became a central fable of Ancient Rome. Yet Europa's myth is now seen as the origin of a territory whose cultural heartland lies somewhere in central Europe, Mitteleuropa, perhaps in the modern Czech Republic, perhaps in Vienna, but certainly somewhere in a nation that became a Member State of the European Union only very recently.

In today's Europe, misunderstanding, contestation, appropriation and reinvention permeate not only its founding myth, but also its most modern institution, the European Union, the law of which is this book's subject. European Union law is often seen as embodying new ideals, new rights and new forms of welfare. Equally, however, it is portrayed as being intrusive, divisive and costly. On the one hand, EU law is said to bring an international comity and to provide a powerful counter to the narrow (and historically dangerous) parochialism that has marked so much of Europe's bloody past. On the other hand, critics point to an overweening, inflexible, even pernicious European-ness, that is intolerant of national diversity and that stymies local democracy.

The reaction to the ratification of the Lisbon Treaty exemplified this at its most extreme. The Presidents of France and Germany, Nicholas Sarkozy and Angela Merkel, have stated that it is necessary to make the European Union more democratic and to enable it to meet the challenges confronting EU citizens. By contrast, the President of the Czech President, Vaclav Klaus, announced, after ratifying the Treaty, that the Treaty marked the end of the Czech Republic as a sovereign state and seemed to incite Czechs to rise up against it. How could the same document induce such diametrically opposite and polarising reactions?

It is exactly this anxious fragility that gives European Union law its peculiar vitality and interest. It brings both a sceptical eye to the analysis of EU law and a constant demand to revisit old assumptions. As such, debates about EU law have in recent years been central in reconsidering ideas of the state and of political community, of the market, and of tradition and society.

This book owes a number of large debts. A particularly strong imprint and contribution has been left by Professors Adam Tomkins and Cristos Hadjiemmanuil, who contributed to the first edition but not to this. We miss their friendliness and vitality, but continue to benefit enormously from their insights. The efficiency, the friendliness and patience of Cambridge University Press continue as a hallmark of our relationship with them. We would particularly like to thank Elizabeth Davison and Sinead Moloney. Ila Bhate has been a consummate research assistant: friendly, helpful, enthusiastic, patient and thoughtful.

The division of responsibility for the book is as follows. Damian Chalmers wrote Chapters 1–10, 12, 14 and 17. Giorgio Monti wrote Chapters 13, 22, 23 and 24. Gareth Davies wrote Chapters 11, 16, 18, 19, 20 and 21. Damian and Giorgio co-wrote Chapter 15. In writing his chapters, Gareth drew freely on the versions written by Damian for the first edition, and would like to acknowledge this.

Finally, there are a number of personal debts. Damian Chalmers would like to thank Juliana Cardinale once again. Her support was as constant as ever, and her humour ever more sustaining. Gareth Davies wishes to thank Marjolein van Wieringen for her tolerance and good humour during the writing of his chapters. Giorgio Monti wishes to thank Ayako for her common sense and support, and Giulia for being a constant source of wonder and laughter. Giorgio and Gareth would also like to thank Damian for his invitation to join him in writing this book, as well as for his leadership and guidance throughout the writing process.

The Treaties were renumbered by the Treaty of Lisbon which came into force on 1 December 2009. We have used the new Treaty numbers throughout, but have also made reference, where possible, to their prior equivalents to help readers who are used to the old numbers. However, there is one possible point of confusion. The Treaty on European Union following the Lisbon Treaty is significantly different in its content from its predecessor, which was also known as the Treaty on European Union. To distinguish the two, we use the abbreviation 'TEU' wherever we are referring to the Treaty on European Union as currently in force, and 'TEU(M)' when referring to the Treaty on European Union in force prior to the Lisbon Treaty (the 'M' refers to the Maastricht Treaty which gave the latter treaty its famous tripartite structure). A Table of Equivalents is included for reference's sake. We have aimed to state the law as at 1 December 2009.

DC, GD, GM

Abbreviations

AFSJ Area of Freedom, Security and Justice
BER Block Exemption Regulation
BSE bovine spongiform encephalopathy
CAP Common Agricultural Policy
CESR Committee of European Securities Regulators
CFI Court of First Instance
CFSP Common Foreign and Security Policy
CISA Schengen Implementing Convention
COR Committee of the Regions
COREPER Committee of Permanent Representatives
COSAC Conference of Community and European Affairs Committees of Parliaments of the European Union
CT Constitutional Treaty
DCT Draft Constitutional Treaty
DG Directorate-General
EAW European Arrest Warrant
EC European Communities
ECB European Central Bank
ECHR European Convention on Human Rights
ECN European Competition Network
ECOWAS Economic Community of West African States
ECSC European Coal and Steel Community
ECtHR European Court of Human Rights
ECU European Currency Unit
EDC European Defence Community
EDP excessive deficit procedure
EEA European Economic Area
EEC European Economic Community
EFSA European Food Safety Authority
EFTA European Free Trade Area
EMI European Monetary Institute
EMS European Monetary System
EMU economic and monetary union
ENP European Neighbourhood Policy
EO European Ombudsman
ERDF European Regional Development Fund
ERM exchange rate mechanism

ERT European Round Table
ESC Economic and Social Committee
ESCB European System of Central Banks
ESDP European Security and Defence Policy
ESecC European Securities Committee
ESF European Social Fund
EUCFR European Union Charter of Fundamental Rights
EURATOM European Atomic Energy Community
EUROPOL European Police Office
FSA Financial Services Authority
FSAP Financial Services Action Plan
IGC intergovernmental conference
ISO International Standards Organisation
JHA Justice and Home Affairs
MCA monetary compensation amount
MEP Member of the European Parliament
MEQR measure of equivalent effect
MiFiD Markets in Financial Instruments Directive
NAAT no appreciable affectation of trade
NCA national competition authority
NCB national central bank
NGO non-governmental organisation
OHIM Office for Harmonisation in the Internal Market
OLAF European Anti-Fraud Office
OMC open method of coordination
PJCC police and judicial cooperation in criminal matters
QMV qualified majority voting
SEA Single European Act
SGEI services of general economic interest
SIA Schengen Implementing Agreement
SIS Schengen Information System
TEU Treaty on European Union
TEU(M) Treaty on European Union (Maastricht)
TFEU Treaty on the Functioning of the European Union
WTO World Trade Organization

Table of Cases

European Court of Justice: numerical order

EC Commission Competition Decisions

European Ombudsman Decisions

European Commission of Human Rights

European Court of Human Rights

EFTA Court

International Court of Justice

National Courts

European Court of Justice: alphabetical order

European Court of Justice: Opinions

Table of Treaties, Instruments and Legislation

Treaties and Analogous Instruments

EU Legislation and Policy Documents

National Legislation and Policy Documents

Table of Equivalents

TREATY ON EUROPEAN UNION

Lisbon Treaty numbers and their Amsterdam and Pre-Amsterdam equivalents (Amsterdam and Pre-Amsterdam is TEU unless specified otherwise)

Lisbon	Amsterdam	Pre-Amsterdam	Lisbon	Amsterdam	Pre-Amsterdam
1	1	A	29	15	J.5
2			30	22	J.12
3	2	B	31	23	J.13
4	10 EC	5 EC	32	16	J.6
5	5 EC	3b EC	33	18	J.8
6	6	F	34	19	J.9
7	7	F.1	35	20	J.10
8			36	21	J.11
9			37	24	J.14
10	191(1) EC	138a	38	25	J.15
11	191(1) EC	138a	39		
12			40	47	M
13	3, 5, 7, 8, 10 EC	C, D 4, 4a. 5 EC	41	28	J.18
14	189/190/192/197 EC	137, 138, 138b, 140 EC	42	17	J.7
15	4	D	43		
16	202/203/205 EC	145, 146, 148 EC	44		
17	211/214/217 EC	155, 158, 161 EC	45		
18			46		
19	220/221/224 EC	164, 165, 168 EC	47	281 EC	210 EC
20	11/11A EC		48	48	N
	27A–27E, 40–40B, 43–45		49	49	O
21	3	C			
22			50		
23			51	311 EC	239 EC
24	11	J.1	52	299(1) EC	227(1) EC
25	12	J.2	53	51	Q
26	13	J.3	54	52	R
27			55	53	S
28	14	J.4		314 EC	248 EC

TREATY ON THE FUNCTIONING OF THE EUROPEAN UNION

Lisbon Treaty numbers and their Amsterdam and Pre-Amsterdam equivalents (Amsterdam and Pre-Amsterdam is EC Treaty unless specified otherwise)

Lisbon	Amsterdam	Pre-Amsterdam	Lisbon	Amsterdam	Pre-Amsterdam
1			49	43	52
2			50	44	54
3			51	45	55
4			52	46	56
5			53	47	57
6			54	48	58
7	3 TEU	C TEU	55	294	221
8	3(2)	3(2)	56	49	59
9			57	50	60
10			58	51	61
11	6	3c	59	52	63
12	153(2)	129a	60	53	64
13			61	54	65
14	16	7d	62	55	66
15	255	191a	63	56	73b
16	286	213b	64	57	73c
17			65	58	73d
18	12	6	66	59	73f
19	13	6a	67	61	73i
20	17	8		29 TEU	K.1 TEU
21	18	8a	68		
22	19	8b	69		
23	20	8c	70		
24	21	8d	71	36 TEU	K.8 TEU
25	22	8e	72	64(1)	73l(1)
26	14	7a		33 TEU	K.4 TEU
27	15	7c	73		
28	23	9	74		
29	24	10	75	60	73g
30	25	12	76		
31	26	28	77	62	73j
32	27	29	78	63(1, 2), 64(2)	73k(1, 2), 73l(2)
33	135	116	79	63(3, 4)	73k(3, 4)
34	28	30	80		
35	29	34	81	65	73m
36	30	36	82	31 TEU	K.3 TEU
37	31	37	83	31 TEU	K.3 TEU
38	32	38	84		
39	33	39	85	31 TEU	K.3 TEU
40	34	40	86		
41	35	41	87	30 TEU	K.2 TEU
42	36	42	88	30 TEU	K.2 TEU
43	37	43	89	32 TFEU	K.4 TEU
44	38	46	90	70	74
45	39	48	91	71	75
46	40	49	92	72	76
47	41	50	93	73	77
48	42	51	94	74	78

Lisbon	Amsterdam	Pre-Amsterdam	Lisbon	Amsterdam	Pre-Amsterdam
95	75	79	147	127	109p
96	76	80	148	128	109q
97	77	81	149	129	109r
98	78	82	150	130	109s
99	79	83	151	136	117
100	80	84	152		
101	81	85	153	137	118
102	82	86	154	138	118a
103	83	87	155	139	118b
104	84	88	156	140	118c
105	85	89	157	141	119
106	86	90	158	142	119a
107	87	92	159	143	120
108	88	93	160	144	121
109	89	94	161	145	122
110	90	95	162	146	123
111	91	96	163	147	124
112	92	98	164	148	125
113	93	99	165	149	126
114	95	100a	166	150	127
115	96	101	167	151	128
116	96	101	168	152	129
117	97	102	169	153(1, 3, 4, 5)	129a
118			170	154	129b
119	4	3a	171	155	129c
120	98	102a	172	156	129d
121	99	103	173	157	130
122	100	103a	174	158	130a
123	101	104	175	159	130b
124	102	104a	176	160	130c
125	103	104b	177	161	130d
126	104	104c	178	162	130e
127	105	105	179	163	130f
128	106	105a	180	164	130g
129	107	106	181	165	130h
130	108	107	182	166	130i
131	109	108	183	167	130j
132	110	108a	184	168	130k
133			185	169	130l
134	114	109c	186	170	130m
135	115	109d	187	171	130n
136			188	172	130o
137			189		
138	111(4)	109(4)	190	173	130p
139			191	174	130r
140	121(1), 122(2), 123(5)	109j, 109k, 109l	192	175	130s
141	123(3), 117(2)	109l(3), 109f(2)	193	176	130t
142	124(1)	109m(1)	194		
143	119	109h	195		
144	120	109i	196		
145	125	109n	197		
146	126	109o	198	182	131

Lisbon	Amsterdam	Pre-Amsterdam	Lisbon	Amsterdam	Pre-Amsterdam
199	183	132	251	221(2), (3)	165
200	184	133	252	222	166
201	185	134	253	223	167
202	186	135	254	224	168
203	187	136	255		
204	188	136a	256	225	168a
205			257	225a	168a
206	131	110	258	226	169
207	133	113	259	227	170
208	177/178	130u/130v	260	228	171
209	179	130w	261	229	172
210	180	130x	262	229a	172
211	181	130y	263	230	173
212	181a	130y	264	231	174
213			265	232	175
214			266	233	176
215			267	234	177
216			268	235	178
217	310	238	269		
218			270	236	179
219	111(1, 3, 5)	109(1, 3, 5)	271	237	180
220	302, 303, 304	229, 230, 231	272	238	181
221			273	239	182
222			274	240	183
223	190(4, 5)	138(3)	275		
224	191(2)	138(3)	276		
225	192(2)	138b	277	241	184
226	193	138c	278	242	185
227	194	138d	279	243	186
228	195	138e	280	244	187
229	196	139	281	245	188
230	197(2)–(4)	140	282	8	4a
231	198	141	283	112	109a
232	199	142	284	113	109b
233	200	143	285	246	188a
234	201	144	286	247	188b
235			287	248	188c
236			288	249	189
237	204	147	289		
238	205(1, 3)	148(1, 3)	290	202	145
239	206	150	291	202	145
240	207	151	292		
241	208	152	293	250	189a
242	209	153	294	251	189b
243	210	154	295		
244			296	253	190
245	213	157	297	254	191
246	215	159	298		
247	216	160	299	256	192
248	217(2)	161	300	257/258/263	193/194/198a
249	218(2)	162(2)	301	258(1), (2), (4)	194(1), (2), (4)
250	219	163	302	259	195
			303	260	196

Lisbon	Amsterdam	Pre–Amsterdam	Lisbon	Amsterdam	Pre–Amsterdam
304	262	198	332		
305	263(2), (3), (4)	198a(2), (3), (4)	333		
306	264	198b	334		
307	265	198c	335	282	211
308	266	198d	336	283	212
309	267	198e	337	284	213
310	268/270	199/201a	338	285	213a
311	269	200	339	287	214
312			340	288	215
313	272(1)	203	341	289	216
314	272(2–10)	203	342	290	217
315	273	204	343	291	218
316	271	202	344	292	219
317	274	205	345	295	222
318	275	205a	346	296	223
319	276	206	347	297	224
320	277	207	348	298	225
321	278	208	349	299(2)–(4)	227
322	279	209	350	306	233
323			351	307	234
324			352	308	235
325	280	210	353		
326			354	309	236
327			355	299(2)–(6)	227
328			356	312	240
329			357	313	247
330			358		
331					

Electronic Working Paper Series

ARENA Working Papers: www.sv.uio.no/arena/

Constitutionalism Web (CONWeb) Papers:
www.qub.ac.uk/schools/SchoolofPoliticsInternationalStudiesandPhilosophy/
Research/PaperSeries/ConWEBPapers/

Centre for Advanced Study in Social Sciences (CEACS) Working Papers:
www.march.es/ceacs/ingles/Publicaciones/working/working.asp

Center for Culture, Organization and Politics Working Papers:
http://socrates.berkeley.edu/~iir/culture/papers.html

Jean Monnet Papers: www.jeanmonnetprogram.org/papers/index.html

European Research Papers Archive: http://olymp.wu-wien.ac.at/erpa/

European Integration Online Papers: http://eiop.or.at/eiop/

EUI Online Papers: www.iue.it/PUB/

Federal Trust Constitutional Online Papers: www.fedtrust.co.uk/constitutionalpapers

Ius Gentium Conimbrigae Working Papers: www.fd.uc.pt/hrc/pages_en/papers.htm

Lucas Pires Working Papers on Constitutionalism: www.fd.unl.pt/je/work_pap.htm

Max Planck Institut für Gesellschaftsforschung (MPIfG) Working Papers:
www.mpi-fg-koeln.mpg.de/pu/workpapers_en.html

Mannheim Zentrum für Europäische Sozialforschung (MZES) Working Papers:
www.mzes.uni-mannheim.de/frame.php?oben=titel_e.html&links=n_publikationen_e.
php&inhalt=publications/wp/workpap_e.php

Nuffield College Working Papers in Politics: www.nuffield.ox.ac.uk/Politics/papers/

Queens Papers on Europeanisation:
www.qub.ac.uk/schools/SchoolofPoliticsInternationalStudiesandPhilosophy/
Research/PaperSeries/EuropeanisationPapers/

University of Edinburgh Europa Institute Mitchell Working Papers: www.law.ed.ac.uk/mitchellworking
papers

1

European Integration and the Treaty on European Union

1 INTRODUCTION

This chapter sets out the central features of the European integration process, which provides the historical and political context for EU law. It also introduces some of the central concepts, ideas and developments in EU law.

Section 2 explores how all EU law is centred around an interplay between two central themes. The first is the addressing of many contemporary problems through a new form of transnational law. The second is the development of the ideals of Europe and European union. These ideals bestow a distinctive quality to the EU legal system and lay the ground for many of its debates. The European ideal conceives of Europe as the central place of progress, learning and civilisation, placing faith in humanity and her capacity to improve. Its dark side is its arrogance and its dismissal of 'un-European' ways of life or thought as violating these virtues. The idea of European union sets up a political community in competition with the nation-state but one, nevertheless, through which government policy is carried out.

Section 3 considers the establishment of the three Communities, the European Economic Community (EEC), the European Coal and Steel Community (ECSC) and the European Atomic Energy Community (EURATOM), by the Treaties of Paris and Rome. It sets out the central institutions: the Commission, the Parliament, the Council and the Court of Justice. It also considers the central policies established by these institutions, most notably the common market. This section also compares two developments of the 1960s that set out the two dominant models of political authority in EU law. In 1966, the Luxembourg Accords were agreed. This provided all national governments with a veto over the adoption of any law. The model was an intergovernmental one, with political authority and democracy vested in the nation-state. In 1963, in *Van Gend en Loos*, the Court of Justice declared that the EC Treaty constituted a new sovereign legal order for the benefit of its citizens. The model was a supranational one, in which authority is vested not in national institutions but the rights of European citizens.

Section 4 considers how, after a period of stagnation, European integration regained momentum with the adoption of the Single European Act (SEA) in 1986. This established the internal market: an area without internal frontiers in which there is free movement of goods, services, persons and capital. It also unlocked the decision-making processes by allowing for significant amounts of legislation to be adopted free from the national veto. The European Parliament was granted significant legislative powers for the first time.

Section 5 considers the Maastricht Treaty and the Treaty on European Union (TEU). The central mission of this treaty, signed in 1991, was to establish an economic and monetary union. However, it also established a three pillar structure. The first pillar, the EC Treaty, was dominated by supranational features, whilst the other two pillars, the Common Foreign and Security Policy and Justice and Home Affairs, were dominated by intergovernmental procedures. The TEU formalised a large number of new EU competences. It also significantly extended majority voting and the powers of the European Parliament.

Section 6 considers the Treaty of Amsterdam. Convened to deal with unfinished business from Maastricht, it was the first treaty to address increasingly popular antipathy against the European integration process. Its central policy was the establishment of the area of freedom, security and justice. The main features of this were the abolition of internal border controls between all Member States other than the United Kingdom and Ireland; the establishment of a common supranational immigration and asylum policy; and police cooperation and judicial cooperation in criminal policy. The Treaty made majority voting the dominant procedure. It also began to introduce national safeguards, most notably limited rights for national parliaments and a detailed Protocol on the subsidiarity principle, the principle which governs when the Union, acting within its competences, is better equipped to legislate than the Member States. This principle provides that the European Union should only act when Member States cannot realise their objectives acting unilaterally and by reason of the nature or scale of the action, these objectives are better realised through Union action.

Section 7 considers the enlargement of the European Union. Initially agreed between six states, the Union had grown to fifteen Member States by the mid-1990s. Almost all were prosperous and almost all came from Western Europe. The 2004 and 2007 accessions brought the number of Member States to twenty-seven with most of the new states being from Central and East Europe and having a post-communist past. This has made the Union a genuinely pan-European organisation but it has made it much more heterogeneous, posing new preferences and challenges, and raising the question of whether it is possible to have a 'one size fits all' EU law.

Section 8 considers the processes that were tried to deal with the challenges of a lack of popular enthusiasm for the Union and of enlargement. In 2000, the Treaty of Nice was agreed. This agreed limited institutional reforms to deal with the anticipated enlargements. These were perceived as insufficient. A suggestion was made to debate a wide-ranging recasting of the institutional settlement in open session by a Convention made up not just of national governments and the Commission, but also MEPs and national parliamentarians. It was to be approved by referendums across a number of Member States. This process led to the Constitutional Treaty in 2004. This was, however, rejected by referendums in the Netherlands and France.

Section 9 considers the Treaty of Lisbon, which was an attempt to rescue the process of institutional reform following the collapse of the Constitutional Treaty. The Lisbon Treaty recasts the Treaties around two treaties, the Treaty on European Union and the Treaty on the Functioning of the European Union (TFEU). Whilst special institutional arrangements are made for foreign and defence policy, all other policies are brought within a supranational framework. The Lisbon Treaty increases the powers of the Parliament and the Court of Justice and increases the areas subject to majority voting. It also introduces new safeguards to protect national autonomy. The competences of the Union are catalogued. The powers of national parliaments are increased. The subsidiarity principle is strengthened and a new principle of non-violation of national constitutional identities is established.

2 EUROPE AND THE EUROPEAN UNION

This book is about the European Union. The European Union is, amongst other things, a legal system established to deal with a series of contemporary problems and realise a set of goals that individual states felt unable to manage alone. That idea is conveyed by the word 'Union'. However, one can have a union of many things and actors. The distinctive feature of the European Union is that it claims to be a union that is *European*. Its mission is to lay claim to the development of the European ideal and the European heritage. The opening words of the Preamble to the Treaty on European Union establishing the European Union state:

> RESOLVED to mark a new stage in the process of European integration undertaken with the establishment of the European Communities,
> DRAWING INSPIRATION from the cultural, religious and humanist inheritance of Europe, from which have developed the universal values of the inviolable and inalienable rights of the human person, freedom, democracy, equality and the rule of law...

Laying claim to the ideals of Europe and the European heritage is, of course, contentious. Some may disagree with these ideals or to the European Union claiming ownership of them. Yet if one is to understand EU law, one has to realise that at its core is a constant interplay between two agendas: the development of these ideals and the government of the problems of contemporary Europe. Elements of both permeate all the chapters of this book. In some areas, there is a tension, imbalance or dysfunction between the two. In other areas, each is being revised in the light of concerns provoked by the other. However, the balance is never static. It is constantly changing as political beliefs change, the European Union's institutional settlement evolves and the challenges of the outside world alter. However, each development is not considered anew. They are considered in the light of a long legacy: be this the history of the European ideal, the institutional settlement of the European Union or a policy whose inception and development goes back many years.

Different chapters of this book consider different legal problems and goals. Yet it is worth pausing at the beginning of the book to consider some of the central elements of this European inheritance, both to understand what it means to call something European and so that we know the sort of venture upon which the European Union is embarked. If discussion of the Ancient Greeks and Charlemagne seems rather removed from that of discussion of the single European market, it is, however, worth considering what broader vision of life that market is tapping into. Does it change anything by calling itself a European market and does it change anything that has emerged within a particular trajectory of European integration?

(i) The idea of Europe

There is nothing fixed about the meaning of the term 'Europe'. It has been used for a variety of purposes, often as a form of self-justification. Its roots, like many things, are curious. The first references to 'Europe' depict it as a woman and the sun. The most famous early reference to Europe is that found in Greek mythology. Europa was a Phoenician woman seduced by the Greek god Zeus to come from Lebanon to Crete.[1] Europa was also, however, a Phoenician word that referred to the setting sun. From this, Europe was associated in Ancient Greece with the idea of 'the West'. Originally used to designate the lands to the west of Greece, usage shifted as the Ancient Greek territorial centre of gravity changed with incursions into modern Turkey and Iran. In his wars, Alexander the Great used it to denote non-Persians and it became associated with the lands in Greece and Asia Minor (today's Turkish Mediterranean coastline). Following this, the term was to lie largely dormant for many centuries. The Roman Empire and Christianity dominated in the organisation of political life, and neither had much use for the term.

Europe re-emerged as an important political idea from the eighth century AD onwards. It was here that it began to acquire many of the associations that we currently make when we use the word 'European'. In part, it became an expression of a siege mentality. The advance of Islam from the South and the East led to Europe being associated with resistance to the religion. An army of Franks, which fought against the Moors, was referred to as a 'European army'.[2] At this time Europe also became associated with the idea of Western Christianity. The Frankish Empire stretched across much of West Europe under the rule of Charlemagne in the ninth century AD. He styled himself the father of Europe and sought to impose a political

---

[1] D. De Rougemont, *The Idea of Europe* (New York, Macmillan, 1965) 6–19.
[2] D. Lewis, *God's Crucible: Islam and the Making of Europe 570–1215* (New York, Norton, 2008).

system across the region, based on communication between a large number of political and administrative centres. Alongside this, common economic practices were developed: shared accounting standards, price controls and a currency. Finally, he also sought to build a common Christian culture, which fostered learning, Christian morality, the building of churches and the imposition of a single interpretation of Christianity.[3]

These elements are all associated with a European identity. However, it was only from the twelfth century onwards that Europe was used to refer to a place whose inhabitants enjoyed a shared way of life based on Christian humanism, revolving around images of God and Christ portrayed as human.[4] Alongside particular religious beliefs, Europe also became associated with a particular form of political economy, namely that of rural trade. Increasingly, the rural town became the centre of the local economy. Trade relations between towns expanded across Europe, so that from the fifteenth century onwards, trade flourished between the Italian ports in the south and Flanders in the North, in which the role of the merchant was pivotal. The final feature of this European region was the persecution of non-Christians, be they pagans or followers of other faiths, such as Judaism or Islam. Those whose conduct offended the central values of Christianity were also maltreated, such as heretics and homosexuals, as were those perceived as socially unproductive, in particular, lepers.

Developments in the sixteenth and seventeenth centuries were to set out the dominant institutional context for the subsequent evolution of the European idea. The establishment of the modern nation-state consolidated power in centralised, impersonal bureaucracies and led to certain core policies, such as tax, law and order and foreign policy being the exclusive competence of these bureaucracies.[5] This hegemony of the nation-state over political life led to Europe acquiring new associations in the eighteenth and nineteenth centuries. It became, increasingly, an 'aesthetic category, romantic and nostalgic', associated with utopian ideals. Authors such as Rousseau and Kant saw Europe as an expression of certain ideals: be it a social contract between nations or as a form of perpetual peace. Europe was also considered to represent a shared aesthetic tradition:[6] be this a common form of high culture, institutionalised through the growth of elite tourism in Europe at that time, or that of a historical civilisation, distinguishing it from the New World and justifying its colonialism.

The final twist came in the twentieth century and derives from the United States' involvement in Europe. The role of the United States in two World Wars, the Cold War and in the regeneration of Europe after the Second World War heavily influenced European identity.[7] The idea of Europe as a historically entrenched community has been reinforced in other ways. The other association has been of Europe as the Eastern borderlands of the United States.

---

[3] The most extensive exposition is to be found in R. McKitterick, *Charlemagne: The Formation of a European Identity* (Cambridge, Cambridge University Press, 2008).

[4] J. Le Goff, *The Birth of Europe* (Oxford, Blackwell, 2005) 76–80.

[5] C. Tilly (ed.), *The Formation of Nation-States in Europe* (Princeton, NJ, Princeton University Press, 1975); G. Poggi, *The Development of the Modern State: A Sociological Introduction* (Stanford, CA, Stanford University Press, 1978); M. Mann, 'The Autonomous Power of the State: Its Origins, Mechanisms and Results' (1984) 25 *European Journal of Sociology* 185; H. Spruyt, *The Sovereign State and its Competitors: An Analysis of Systems Change* (Princeton, NJ, Princeton University Press, 1994).

[6] A. Chebel d'Appollonia, 'European Nationalism and European Union' and J. Tully, 'The Kantian Idea of Europe: Critical and Cosmopolitan Perspectives' in A. Pagden (ed.), *The Idea of Europe: From Antiquity to the European Union* (Cambridge, Cambridge University Press, 2002). Recent examples of this tradition are Z. Bauman, *Europe: An Unfinished Adventure* (Cambridge, Polity, 2004); U. Beck, *Cosmopolitan Europe* (Cambridge, Polity, 2005).

[7] G. Delanty, *Inventing Europe: Idea, Identity, Reality* (Basingstoke, Macmillan, 1995) 115–55.

For those reverting to market democracy after forty-five years of communism, a 'return to Europe' means a turn to the West and to values that are associated, unashamedly, with the United States, namely those of free markets and constitutional democracy. In today's Western Europe, Europe has acquired an alternate meaning, in that its values are similar but different to those of the United States. Although there is a shared commitment to markets and constitutional democracy, these take a different form from those in the United States. There is an emphasis on the social market and on supposedly 'European' values, such as opposition to the death penalty, which are not present in the United States.

J. Habermas and J. Derrida, 'February 15, or, What Binds Europeans Together: Plea for a Common Foreign Policy Beginning in Core Europe' in D. Levy et al., *Old Europe, New Europe, Core Europe: Transatlantic Relations after the Iraq War* (London, Verso, 2005) 5, 10–12

… the spread of the ideals of the French revolution throughout Europe explains, among other things, why politics in both of its forms – as organizing power and as a medium for the institutionalization of political liberty – has been welcomed in Europe. By contrast, the triumph of capitalism was bound up with sharp class conflicts, and this fact has hindered an equally positive appraisal of free markets. That differing evaluation of politics and markets may explain Europeans' trust in the civilizing power of the state, and their expectations for it to correct market failures.

The party system that emerged from the French revolution has often been copied. But only in Europe does this system also serve an ideological competition that subjects the socio-pathological results of capitalist modernization to an ongoing political evaluation. This fosters the sensitivies of citizens to the paradoxes of progress. The contest between conservative, liberal and socialist agendas comes down to the weighing of two aspects: Do the benefits of a chimerical progress outweigh the losses that come with the disintegration of protective, traditional forms of life? Or do the benefits that today's processes of 'creative destruction' promise for tomorrow outweigh the pain of modernity's losers?

In Europe, those affected by class distinctions, and their enduring consequences, understood these burdens as a fate that can be averted only through collective action. In the context of workers' movements and the Christian socialist traditions, an ethics of solidarity, the struggle for 'more social justice', with the goal of equal provision for all, asserted itself against the individualist ethos of market justice that accepts glaring social inequalities as part of the bargain. Contemporary Europe has been shaped by the experience of the totalitarian regimes of the twentieth century and by the Holocaust – the persecution and annihilation of European Jews in which the National Socialist regime made the societies of the conquered countries complicit as well. Self-critical controversies about the past remind us of the moral basis of politics. A heightened sensitivity to injuries to personal and bodily integrity reflects itself, among other ways, in the fact both the Council of Europe and the EU made the ban on capital punishment a condition for membership.

Since the eighth century, the idea of Europe has thus been that it is a place where there are multiple political communities with a shared way of life. This way of life is based on a commitment to progress, civilisation, learning and culture. It is based on a belief in the value of humanity and humankind's capacity to better itself and to resolve any problems. The hubristic nature of this indicates its dark sides. Europe historically posited itself as the centre of the world for all these things. It has been its job to civilise others, to spread progress or human values. There is also an intolerance of things 'non-European'. For if they are not European, there is a chance that they do not represent the good things Europe represents. At its worst, this arrogance and intolerance has led to racism and colonialism, yet it is also present in the European integration process. Time and again, the *sui generis* nature or specialness of the process is emphasised as a form of particularly enlightened cooperation between nations. There is an assumption about the desirability of the policies, as otherwise why would so many states agree to them? There is also a concern, as we shall see, that the policies should always be the very best. Opponents of integration can, thus, often be dismissed as unreasonable or nationalistic (e.g. un-European). It may be, however, that they simply disagree with the policy or the procedure, or that they believe there exist other forms of value or life beyond the European ideal.

(ii) The idea of 'European union'

Whilst related, the idea of European union has different associations from that of Europe. After all, many self-avowed Europeans oppose European union! Independent proposals for a 'united Europe' first emerged at the end of the seventeenth century. However, they were still firmly confederal in nature. Ultimate authority was vested in the state, with pan-European structures acting as little more than a fetter upon the autonomy of the states. In 1693, the English Quaker William Penn wrote *An Essay Towards the Present and Future Peace of Europe*. Penn suggested that a European Parliament should be established, consisting of representatives of the Member States. The primary purposes of this Parliament would be to prevent wars breaking out between states and to promote justice. A more far-reaching proposal was put forward by John Bellers in 1710. Bellers proposed a cantonal system based upon the Swiss model whereby Europe would be divided into 100 cantons, each of which would be required to contribute to a European army and send representatives to a European Senate.

The first proposal suggesting a Europe in which the state system was to be replaced by a system within which there was a sovereign central body came from the Frenchman Saint-Simon. This proposal was published in a pamphlet in 1814, entitled *Plan for the Reorganisation of the European Society*. Saint-Simon considered that all European states should be governed by national parliaments, but that a European Parliament should be created to decide on common interests. This Parliament would consist of a House of Commons peopled by representatives of local associations and a House of Lords consisting of peers appointed by a European monarch. Saint-Simon's views enjoyed considerable attention during the first part of the nineteenth century. Mazzini, the *éminence grise* of Italian nationalism, allied himself with Proudhon and Victor Hugo in declaring himself in favour of a United Europe. Yet, the nineteenth century represented the age of the nation-state and the relationship between that structure and that of a united Europe was never fully explored.

The balance was altered by the First World War, which acted as a stimulus for those who saw European union as the only means both to prevent war breaking out again between the nation-states and as a means of responding to increased competition from the United States, Argentina and Japan. Most prominent was the pan-European movement set up in the 1920s by the Czech Count Coudenhove-Kalergi.[8] This movement not only enjoyed considerable support amongst many of Europe's intellectuals and some politicians, but was genuinely transnational,

---

[8] N. Coudenhove-Kalergi, *Pan-Europe* (New York, Knopf, 1926). An excellent discussion can be found in C. Pegg, *Evolution of the European Idea 1914–1932* (Chapel Hill, NC, University of North Carolina Press, 1983).

having 'Economic Councils' both in Berlin and in Paris. During the 1920s, the idea of European unity received governmental support in the shape of the 1929 Briand Memorandum. This Memorandum, submitted by the French Foreign Minister to twenty-six other European states, considered the League of Nations to be too weak a body to regulate international relations, and proposed a European Federal Union, which would better police states, whilst not 'in any way affect the sovereign rights of the States which are members of such an association'. This proposal, despite being strongly confederal in that it acknowledged the authority of the nation-states, was still regarded as too radical and received only a lukewarm response from the other states.

A further shock, in the form of the Second World War, was needed to arouse greater governmental interest in the idea of a united Europe. The coming into being and development of first, the European Communities, followed by the European Union, are explored in greater depth in the rest of this chapter. It is useful to consider for a moment how the creation of this political organisation with law-making powers, with the idea of Europe as its justification and its purpose, changed the geo-political context in which the idea of Europe was formulated. On the one hand, the European Union has become an independent centre in its own right for the generation of understandings about Europe and European values and symbols. The European Union has, therefore, tried to replicate the symbols and tools of nationhood at a pan-European level, be it through the (re)discovery of European flags, anthems, Cities of Culture or common passports.[9] This understanding of Europe, as a competing alternative to the nation-state, has been replicated by 'Euro-sceptic' groups, who see Europe as a centralised, monolithic entity which crushes local communities and self-government.[10] On the other hand, the idea of European union has become a justification for national government policy, as the Union becomes a vehicle through which national governments pursue and articulate their understanding of the national interest. On such a view, Europe does not act as a competitor to the nation-state but, rather, as a vehicle through which nation-states articulate their understandings of themselves and their place in the world through asking themselves how European they are or how they relate to Europe.[11] The extract below considers the case of Finland, in which the authors argue that by placing itself within the European Union many Finns were able to resolve a prior dichotomy about whether Finland was more 'Western' or more Russian.

M. Malmborg and B. Stråth, 'Introduction: The National Meanings of Europe' in M. Malmborg and B. Stråth (eds.), *The Meaning of Europe* (Oxford and New York, Berg, 2002) 1, 20

Finland's national history has been characterized by a strong awareness of being either on the brink of Europe or on the margins of Russia or somewhere in between ... Meinander traces two basic conceptions of Finnish national identity: the Fennoman that stresses the indigenous features of Finnish culture and sees Finland as a cooperative borderland between the West and Russia, and the liberal that

---

[9] C. Shore, *Building Europe: The Cultural Politics of European Integration* (London and New York, Routledge, 2000).

[10] A flavour is provided in M. Holmes (ed.), *The Eurosceptical Reader* (Basingstoke, Macmillan, 1996).

[11] For an extremely scholarly account of this see J. Diez Medrano, *Framing Europe: Attitudes to European Integration in Germany, Spain and the United Kingdom* (Princeton, NJ, Princeton University Press, 2003).

is akin to the Russian *zapadniki* in the sense that it prescribes close integration with the Western and European cultures.[12] For the Fennomans, Russia was in a cultural sense never outside Europe, but the feeling of standing at the edge of Europe was reinforced by the Russian revolution, the Finnish civil war and the foundation of the Soviet Union, which effectively precluded any acknowledgement of the eastern layers of Finnish identity. The Finnish notion of Europe became increasingly polarized not least due to the experiences of Finland being left very much alone in the Second World War. Forced into a policy of friendly neutrality with the Soviet Union after the war Finland rediscovered its role as a mediator between East and West. The Finns began to admit that Russia, even in its Soviet manifestation, was a part of European civilization.

The accession to the EU in 1995 was supported by a feeling that the Finns had at last found an answer to two centuries of uncertainty and identity-searching. Finland had, as it were, ultimately found a synthesis of its two historical roles, to be both on the brink of Western Europe and serve as a bridge-builder toward a Europe that stretched to include Russia and Slavonic Europe. EU membership implies both an improvement of national security and an emotional homecoming.

The idea of European union has thus come to carry three associations. First, it is associated with the establishment of a political community or tier of government in competition with that of the nation-state. Any Union policy, procedure or institution is thus always evaluated for its effects on the autonomy of national administrations. Secondly, it is associated with government policies that could not be secured by the nation-state alone (e.g. environment or trade liberalisation). They are, however, policies of the governments of the day and, inevitably, they will benefit some constituencies and disadvantage others.[13] Opposition to European union is often therefore opposition to the government of the day or a dominant policy process. The third association is that European union provides a context for debates about the nature of the state and national identity. It acts as a point of comparison; but also, by joining the European Union, a state commits itself to a particular vision of political community. This vision of 'what we are' is always likely to be contentious.

3 EARLY DEVELOPMENT OF THE EUROPEAN COMMUNITIES

(i) From the Treaty of Paris to the Treaty of Rome

The origins of the current European Union lie in a crisis provoked by the establishment of the Federal Republic of Germany. In 1949, the Ruhr, then under the administration of the International High Commission, was due to be handed back to the Federal Republic, along with the Saar. French fears of emerging German industrial might were compounded by Germany's increasing share of European steel production. The French response was a plan drafted by the

---

[12] H. Meinander, 'On the Brink or In Between? The Conception of Europe in Finnish Identity' in M. Malmborg and B. Stråth (eds.), *The Meaning of Europe* (Oxford and New York, Berg, 2002).

[13] N. Fligstein, *Euro-Clash: The EU, European Identity, and the Future of Europe* (Oxford, Oxford University Press, 2008), especially ch 8.

French civil servant, Jean Monnet, which was known as the Schuman Plan, after the French Finance Minister, Robert Schuman.[14]

Robert Schuman, Declaration of 9 May 1950[15]

Europe will not be made all at once or according to a single plan. It will be built through concrete achievements which first create a *de facto* solidarity. The coming together of the nations of Europe requires the elimination of the age-old opposition of France and Germany. Any action which must be taken in the first place must concern these two countries. With this aim in view, the French Government proposes that action be taken immediately on one limited but decisive point. It proposes that Franco-German production of coal and steel as a whole be placed under a common High Authority, within the framework of an organisation open to the participation of the other countries of Europe.

The pooling of coal and steel production should immediately provide for the setting up of common foundations for economic development as a first step in the federation of Europe, and will change the destinies of those regions which have long been devoted to the manufacture of munitions of war, of which they have been the most constant victims.

The solidarity in production thus established will make it plain that any war between France and Germany becomes not merely unthinkable, but materially impossible. The setting up of this powerful productive unit, open to all countries willing to take part and bound ultimately to provide all the member countries with the basic elements of industrial production on the same terms, will lay a true foundation for their economic unification.

This Plan formed the basis of the Treaty of Paris in 1951, which established the ECSC.[16] This Treaty entered into force on 23 July 1952 and ran for fifty years.[17] It set up a common market in coal and steel, which was supervised by the High Authority, a body independent from the Member States and composed of international civil servants, which had considerable powers to determine the conditions of production and prices for coal and steel.[18] The High Authority was, in turn, supervised by a Council, which consisted of Member State representatives. The Treaty of Paris was signed by only six states: the BENELUX States (Netherlands, Belgium and Luxembourg), Italy, France and Germany. The United Kingdom had been invited to the negotiations, but refused to participate, as it opposed both the idea of the High Authority and the remit of its powers.[19]

---

[14] W. Diebold, *The Schuman Plan: A Study in International Cooperation* (Oxford, Oxford University Press, 1959).

[15] European Parliament, *Selection of Texts concerning Institutional Matters of the Community for 1950–1982* (Luxembourg, Office for Official Publications of the European Communities, 1982) 47.

[16] On the negotiations, see P. Gerbet, 'The Origins: Early Attempts and the Emergence of the Six (1945–52)' in R. Pryce (ed.), *The Dynamics of European Union* (London, Croom Helm, 1987); R. Bullen, 'An Idea Enters Diplomacy: The Schuman Plan, May 1950' in R. Bullen (ed.), *Ideas into Politics: Aspects of European History 1880–1950* (London, Croom Helm, 1984).

[17] The ECSC expired on 23 July 2002. Decision of the representatives of the Member States meeting within the Council on the consequences of the expiry of the European Coal and Steel Community [2002] OJ L194/35.

[18] A good history is D. Spierenburg and R. Poidevin, *The History of the High Authority of the European Coal and Steel Community: Supranationality in Operation* (London, Weidenfeld & Nicholson, 1994).

[19] E. Dell, *The Schuman Plan and the British Abdication of Leadership in Europe* (Oxford, Clarendon, 1995); C. Lord, '"With But Not Of"': Britain and the Schuman Plan, a Reinterpretation' (1998) 4 *Journal of European Integration History* 23.

In 1950, during negotiations for the Treaty of Paris, the Korean War began. The United States, perceiving an increased threat from Stalin's Soviet Union, pressed for German rearmament and its entry into NATO, something which was inimical to the French.[20] As a response, the French Defence Minister, Pléven, proposed a European Defence Community. There would be a European army under a European Minister of Defence, administered by a European Commissariat. Once again, Britain was invited to join, but it declined on the basis that it preferred an expansion of NATO to the establishment of a European Defence Community (EDC). Nevertheless, a treaty establishing the EDC was signed between the same six states which had signed the ECSC in 1952. However, the EDC failed. A less integrationist French government under Mendès-France assumed power and French reverses in South-East Asia made France wary about ceding military sovereignty. In 1954, the French National Assembly refused to ratify the treaty.[21]

The failure of the EDC marked a moment of considerable political fluidity. The BENELUX states were increasingly worried by the nationalist policies of the Mendès-France government in France, in particular, its attempt to upgrade bilateral relations with Germany. In 1955, the Belgian Foreign Minister, Henri-Paul Spaak, suggested that there should be integration in a limited number of sectors, notably transport and energy. This worried the Netherlands as it threatened to restrict its efficiencies, particularly in the transport sector. The Dutch government responded by reactivating the 1953 Beyen Plan, which proposed a common market that would lead to economic union. A meeting of foreign ministers was held in Messina, Italy, in 1955. The British were invited, in addition to the six ECSC Member States, but did no more than send a Board of Trade official. Despite considerable French scepticism, a Resolution was tabled, calling for an Intergovernmental Committee under the chairmanship of Spaak to be set up to examine the establishment of a common market. As a carrot to the French, it was agreed that this should be done in tandem with examining the possibility of integration in the field of atomic energy. British objections to the supranational elements required for a common market entailed that they were unable to participate in the project.

The Spaak Report, published in 1956, laid the basis for the Treaty Establishing the European Economic Community (EEC Treaty). The Report made a pragmatic distinction between matters affecting the functioning of the common market, which would require a supranational decision-making framework and some supranational supervision of Member States' compliance with their obligations, and more general matters of budgetary, monetary and social policy, which would remain within the reserved competence of the Member States. Where these policies had a significant effect on the functioning of the common market, however, Member States should endeavour to coordinate these policies. An intergovernmental conference (IGC) was convened in Venice, with the Spaak Report as the basis for negotiations. The result was the signing of the Treaties of Rome in 1957 between the Six: Germany,

[20] T. Schwartz, 'The Skeleton Key: American Foreign Policy, European Unity, and German Rearmament, 1949–54' (1986) 19 *Central European History* 369.

[21] On this ill-fated enterprise, see E. Fursdon, *The European Defence Community: A History* (London, Macmillan, 1980); R. Cardozo, 'The Project for a Political Community (1952–4)' in R Pryce (ed.), *The Dynamics of European Union* (London, Croom Helm, 1987); R. Dwan, 'Jean Monnet and the Failure of the European Defence Community' (2001) 1 *Cold War History* 141.

France, Italy and the BENELUX states. Doubts about difficulties in French ratification led to two treaties being signed, one establishing the EEC, the other EURATOM. The treaties duly entered into force on 1 January 1958.[22]

(ii) The EEC Treaty

The dominant aim of the EEC Treaty was the establishment of a common market. This can be divided into a number of different elements. The first was the customs union, which required the abolition of all customs duties or charges having equivalent effect on the movement of goods between Member States and the establishment of a common external tariff. Secondly, the common market extended beyond the customs union to include the 'four freedoms', so that restrictions on the movement of goods, workers, services and capital were also prohibited by the EC Treaty. Furthermore, a procedure was put in place for harmonising national laws whose differences were preventing the establishment and functioning of the common market. Thirdly, a competition policy was set up to ensure that private market barriers and cartels did not undermine the prohibition on state barriers. Fourthly, state intervention in the economy, such as that in the form of state aids and public undertakings, was closely regulated. Fifthly, Member States' fiscal regimes on goods were regulated so that they could not discriminate against imports. Sixthly, a common commercial policy was established to regulate the Community's trade relations with third states. Finally, provision was made for more general cooperation in the field of economic policy in order that broader economic policy-making did not disrupt the common market.

A number of other policies were established. Arguably, the most famous is the Common Agricultural Policy. At the time, agriculture accounted for about 20 per cent of the European labour force and the memory of the severe deflation in the agricultural sector during the 1930s recession had led to considerable government intervention in the sector. A separate policy was, therefore, required in order to Europeanise the system of state intervention currently in place. A further policy included in the EEC Treaty was a common transport policy. As with agriculture, this required a separate heading due to the heavy intervention by states in their transport sectors. The EEC Treaty also contained a limited social policy, whose central feature was the establishment of a principle of equal pay for work of equal value for men and women.[23] Finally, an association policy was included to provide for the economic and social development of dependent or formerly dependent territories of the Member States.

The most remarkable feature of the EEC Treaty was the institutional arrangement set up to realise these objectives. There were four central institutions. The Commission, a body independent from the Member States, was responsible, inter alia, for proposing legislation and checking that the Member States and other institutions complied with the Treaty and any secondary legislation. The Assembly, later to develop into the European Parliament, was composed, initially, of national parliamentarians. It had the right to be consulted in most fields of legislative activity and was the body responsible for holding the Commission to account. The Council was

---

[22] The literature on the negotiations is voluminous. See E. di Nolfo (ed.), *Power in Europe? Britain, France, Germany, Italy, and the Origins of the EEC, 1952–1957* (Berlin and New York, de Gruyter, 1992); E. Serra (ed.), *The Relaunching of Europe and the Treaties of Rome* (Baden Baden, Nomos, 1989).

[23] C. Barnard, 'The Economic Objectives of Article 119' in T. Hervey and D. O'Keeffe (eds.), *Sex Equality Law in the European Union* (Chichester, John Wiley, 1996) 321, 322–4.

the body in which national governments were represented. It had the power of final decision in almost all areas of EEC activity. It voted by unanimity or (in only a few areas initially) by a weighted form of voting, known as Qualified Majority Voting (QMV). Finally, the European Court of Justice was established to monitor compliance with the Treaty. Matters could be brought before it, not only by the Member States but also by the supranational Commission, or be referred to it by national courts.

(iii) De Gaulle and the Luxembourg Accords

1958 marked not only the coming into force of the Treaties, but also Charles de Gaulle becoming President of France.[24] De Gaulle was well known for his opposition to the development of any supranational organisation and for his support for a Europe of nation-states, based upon intergovernmental cooperation. As early as 1961, De Gaulle attempted to subvert the supranational qualities of the EEC Treaty through the Fouchet Plan. This proposed a European Political Community whose remit would cover not only economic, but also political and social affairs. It would be based on intergovernmental cooperation, with each state retaining a veto. This failed to gain the support of the other Member States.[25] Tensions were raised further in 1963 when De Gaulle vetoed the accession of the United Kingdom which, along with Denmark, Norway and Ireland, had applied for membership in 1961.

Matters came to a head in 1965. The Commission had made three proposals: first, increased powers for the Assembly; secondly, a system of 'own resources' so that the Communities were financially independent and not dependent on national contributions; and finally, a series of financial regulations, which would allow the common agricultural policy to make progress. France favoured the third proposal, but was strongly opposed to the first two. The Commission insisted on a 'package deal', however, where Member States accepted either all or none. When negotiations broke down, the French walked out of the Council in June 1965, refusing to take part in further EEC business. De Gaulle came under considerable domestic criticism for this drastic move.[26] Yet the Commission was also perceived as having adopted a very high-handed approach. The crisis was eventually defused in January 1966 in Luxembourg, but in a way that would cast a shadow over the development of the EEC for the next twenty years. The Luxembourg Accords, as they came to be known, were an 'agreement to disagree'. If a Member State raised 'very important interests' before a vote in the Council was taken, it was agreed that the matter would not be put to a vote. In essence, it gave every Member State a veto in all fields of decision-making.

Whilst this veto was developed at the behest of France, once in place it was subsequently deployed equally freely by all the Member States.[27] 'Very important interests' were invoked at

---

[24] An excellent overview of this period is N. Ludlow, *The European Community and the Crises of the 1960s: Negotiating the Gaullist Challenge* (Abingdon, Routledge, 2006).

[25] P. Gerbet, 'The Fouchet Negotiations (1960–2)' in R. Pryce, *Dynamics of Political Union* (London, Croom Helm, 1987); N. Ludlow, 'Challenging French Leadership in Europe: Germany, Italy and the Netherlands and the Origins of the Empty Chair Crisis of 1965' (1999) 8 *Contemporary European History* 231.

[26] On De Gaulle's Europe see W. Loth (ed.), *Crises and Compromises: The European Project, 1963–9* (Baden Baden, Nomos, 2001); C. Parsons, *A Certain Idea of Europe* (Ithaca, NY, Cornell University Press, 2003).

[27] W. Nicholl, 'The Luxembourg Compromise' (1984) 23 *JCMS* 35. For a modern perspective see J.-M. Palavret et al. (eds.), *Visions, Votes and Vetoes: Reassessing the Luxembourg Compromise 40 Years On* (Brussels, Peter Lang, 2006).

every turn, even where the interest in question was insignificant.[28] This chilled the legislative process.[29] The Commission, aware of the need for the assent of all the Member States, became a passive body reluctant to generate controversy.

Despite this, significant institutional developments did take place. At the signing of the Treaty of Rome, the Convention relating to Certain Institutions Common to the European Communities established a single Court and a single Assembly for the three Communities. In 1963, it was agreed that the other institutions, the Council and the Commission, should be merged, and this took place with the Merger Treaty in 1965.[30] In 1970, the Communities were provided with their own budget and autonomous revenue stream with the Own Resources Decision.[31] Finally, it was agreed in 1976 that there should be direct elections for the European Parliament.[32] These were first held in 1979 and have since been held at five-year intervals.

(iv) Emergence of two visions of political authority

The most significant development to take place during this time was, however, in the Court of Justice. For it was here that an alternate vision of political community – a supranational one – was first developed. It took place in *Van Gend en Loos*, arguably the most important decision ever given by that institution and one of the most revolutionary ever given by a court. The facts were arcane. Van Gend en Loos was charged an import duty on chemicals imported from Germany by the Dutch authorities. It considered this to be in breach of what is now Article 30 TFEU, which prohibits customs duties or charges having equivalent effect being placed on the movement of goods between Member States. It sought to invoke the provisions in legal proceedings before a Dutch tax court, the Tariefcommissie. The question for the Court of Justice was whether a party could invoke and rely on provisions of Community law in proceedings before a national court. The Court's answer was that it could.[33]

Case 26/62 *Van Gend en Loos* v *Nederlandse Administratie der Belastingen* [1963] ECR 1

The first question of the Tariefcommissie is whether Article [30 TFEU] has direct application in national law in the sense that nationals of Member States may on the basis of this Article lay claim to rights which the national court must protect.

To ascertain whether the provisions of an international treaty extend so far in their effects it is necessary to consider the spirit, the general scheme and the wording of those provisions.

---

[28] In 1985, they were invoked by Germany to prevent a 1.8 per cent decrease in the price of colza, a cooking oil grain. M. Vasey, 'The 1985 Farm Price Negotiations and the Reform of the Common Agriculture Policy' (1985) 22 *CMLRev.* 649, 664–6.

[29] Legislative progress has taken longer to agree, paradoxically, where there was no possibility of veto. The Accords effect seems to have been therefore mainly on the Commission's willingness to make significant legislative proposals. J. Golub, 'In the Shadow of the Vote? Decision Making in the European Community' (1999) 53 *International Organization* 737.

[30] P.-H. Houben, 'The Merger of the Executives of the European Communities' (1965) 3 *CML Rev.* 37.

[31] Decision 70/243/EEC [1970] OJ English Spec. edn (I) 224.

[32] Decision 76/287/EEC [1976] OJ L278/1. Until 1979 it consisted of representatives of national Parliaments.

[33] Here we are concerned with what *Van Gend en Loos* tells us about European constitutional law in broad terms. The details of the Court's rulings as regards supremacy and as regards direct effect are considered more fully in Chapters 5 and 7, respectively.

The objective of the EEC Treaty, which is to establish a common market, the functioning of which is of direct concern to interested parties in the community, implies that this Treaty is more than an agreement which merely creates mutual obligations between the contracting States. This view is confirmed by the preamble to the Treaty which refers not only to governments but to peoples. It is also confirmed more specifically by the establishment of institutions endowed with sovereign rights, the exercise of which affects Member States and also their citizens. Furthermore, it must be noted that the nationals of the States brought together in the Community are called upon to cooperate in the functioning of this Community through the intermediary of the European Parliament and the Economic and Social Committee.

In addition the task assigned to the Court of Justice under Article [267 TFEU][34] the object of which is to secure uniform interpretation of the Treaty by national courts and tribunals, confirms that the States have acknowledged that Community law has an authority which can be invoked by their nationals before those courts and tribunals. The conclusion to be drawn from this is that the Community constitutes a new legal order of international law for the benefit of which the States have limited their sovereign rights, albeit within limited fields, and the subjects of which comprise not only Member States but also their nationals. Independently of the legislation of Member States, Community law therefore not only imposes obligations on individuals but is also intended to confer upon them rights which become part of their legal heritage. These rights arise not only where they are expressly granted by the Treaty, but also by reason of obligations which the Treaty imposes in a clearly defined way upon individuals as well as upon the Member States and upon the institutions of the Community.

There are two remarkable features about this terse, dense passage. The first is a claim about power. It is contained in the statement that: 'the Community constitutes a new legal order of international law for the benefit of which the States have limited their sovereign rights, albeit within limited fields'. This is a vision of the EU, legally at least, as a supranational organisation that exists not merely autonomously from the national legal orders but over and above them. For the Treaty has created not merely a legal order that is independent but also one claiming to be sovereign. And if legal sovereignty is understood to be a claim to ultimate legal authority then a reversal of traditional understandings of legal authority is being asserted. National legal systems no longer form the central building block for legal authority within Europe. Rather, legal authority flows from the Treaty with national legal systems having to adapt as sub-units to it.

The second is a claim about the nature of political community within Europe. It lies in the justification: the Treaty exists to benefit not merely the governments but also the peoples of Europe. This characterises the EU legal community as a wider, more plural legal community than other international legal communities. If traditional international law governs mutual obligations between states, EU law recognises other subjects: private parties, be they EU citizens, non-EU nationals or corporations. These are to hold a direct relationship with EU law through its conferring both rights and obligations on them. It suggests that the constituent power of the

---

[34] Article 267 TFEU (ex Article 234 EC) enables national courts and tribunals to refer questions of the interpretation of Community law to the Court of Justice. The relationships between national courts and the Court of Justice are considered in detail in Chapter 7.

European Union resides at least in part in the peoples of Europe themselves. That constituent power may use the intermediary of the state to confer authority on the European Union, but it does not necessarily have to. The Court in *Van Gend en Loos* does not say this explicitly, but it clearly suggests that the founding myth of the European Union may be legally constructed so that the Union may be seen as an agreement between the peoples of Europe that binds their governments, and not simply as an agreement between the governments of Europe that binds its peoples.

It is worth setting this vision alongside the vision of political community that was presented by De Gaulle, as they represent, in reality, the two poles between which European integration has been mediated. At a press conference on 15 May 1962, he declared:

> These ideas (supranationalism) might appeal to certain minds but I entirely fail to see how they could be put into practice, even with six signatures at the foot of a document. Can we imagine France, Germany, Italy, the Netherlands, Belgium, Luxembourg being prepared on matters of importance to them in the national or international sphere, to do something that appeared wrong to them, merely because others had ordered them to do so? Would the peoples of France, of Germany, of Italy, of the Netherlands, of Belgium, or of Luxembourg ever dream of submitting to laws passed by foreign parliamentarians if such laws run counter to their deepest convictions? Clearly not.[35]

It is too crude to see this view as an expression of nationalism for nationalism's sake or an unwillingness to share power. At its heart is a vision that democracy rests upon certain social and political institutions and forms of political community which must have a certain pedigree and strength if democracy is to be sustained. Currently, these qualities exist only at the level of the nation-state. On such a view, supranationalism – be it decisions of the Court of Justice, majority voting by national governments or proposals by the Commission – is invariably a threat to democracy insofar as it limits the autonomy and power of these national institutions, and has insufficient institutions and forms of political community of its own to fall back upon.[36]

The tension between these two visions of political authority and political community permeate in an ongoing manner nearly every chapter of this book. In the 1960s and 1970s, the vesting of one vision, the Gaullist one, in the political institutions through the Luxembourg Accords, and another one, that of a pan-European political community, in the Court of Justice, led to a highly unfortunate dynamic.[37] The Court gave a series of integrationist judgments, expanding its 'constitutional' jurisprudence, developing treaty-making powers for the Community, expanding the Treaty provisions on sex equality, the economic freedoms and the competition provisions. When juxtaposed with the inertia of the legislature, this led to the development of an unplanned deregulatory bias under which national policies were prohibited or tightly restricted by the Court, without there being any substitute EU legislation available to take their place.[38]

---

35   This can be found in D. Weigall and P. Stirk, *The Origins and Development of the European Community* (Leicester, Leicester University Press, 1992) 134.

36   One of the most articulate and scholarly expositions of this is D. Miller, *On Nationality* (Oxford, Oxford University Press, 1995).

37   On how this manifested itself institutionally see J. Weiler, 'The Community System: The Dual Character of Supranationalism' (1981) 1 *YBEL* 267.

38   F. Scharpf, 'Negative and Positive Integration in the Political Economy of European Welfare States' in G. Marks *et al.*, *Governance in the European Union* (London, Sage, 1996).

Yet if this tension can give rise to difficulties, others have noted that within it lies the European Union's uniqueness and genius: namely it has to confront these poles and resolve them in a way that creates a new type of legal authority and political community.

J. Weiler, 'In Defence of the Status Quo: Europe's Constitutional Sonderweg' in J. Weiler and M. Wind (eds.), *European Constitutionalism Beyond the State* (Cambridge, Cambridge University Press, 2003) 19–22

There are, it seems to me, two basic strategies for dealing with the alien ... One strategy is to remove the boundaries. It is the spirit of 'come, be one of us'. It is noble since it involves, of course, elimination of prejudice, of the notion that there are boundaries that cannot be eradicated. But the 'be one of us', however well intentioned, is often an invitation to the alien to be one of us, by being us. Vis-à-vis the alien, it risks robbing him of his identity. Vis-à-vis oneself, it may be a subtle manifestation of both arrogance and belief in my superiority as well as intolerance. If I cannot tolerate the alien, one way of resolving the dilemma is to make him like me, no longer an alien. This is, of course, infinitely better than the opposite: exclusion, repression, and worse. But it is still a form of dangerous internal and external intolerance.

The alternative strategy of dealing with the alien is to acknowledge the validity of certain forms of non-ethnic bounded identity but simultaneously to reach across boundaries. We acknowledge and respect difference, and what is special and unique about ourselves as individuals and groups; and yet we reach across differences in recognition of our essential humanity. What is significant in this are the two elements I have mentioned. On the one hand, the identity of the alien, as such, is maintained. One is not invited to go out and, say, 'save him' by inviting him to be one of us. One is not invited to recast the boundary. On the other hand, despite the boundaries which are maintained, and constitute the I and the Alien, one is commanded to reach over the boundary and accept him, in his alienship, as oneself. The alien is accorded human dignity. The soul of the I is tended to not by eliminating the temptation to oppress but by learning humility and overcoming it.

The European current constitutional architecture represents this alternative, civilizing strategy of dealing with the 'other'. Constitutional tolerance is encapsulated in that most basic articulation of its meta-political objective in the preamble to the EC Treaty ...: 'Determined to lay the foundations of an ever closer union among the *peoples* of Europe'. No matter how close the Union, it is to remain a union among distinct peoples, distinct political identities, distinct political communities. An ever closer union could be achieved by an amalgam of distinct peoples into one which is both the ideal and/or the de facto experience of most federal and non-federal states. The rejection by Europe of that One Nation ideal or destiny is ... intended to preserve the rich diversity, cultural and other, of the distinct European peoples ...

[I]n the Community, we subject the European peoples to constitutional discipline even though the European polity is composed of distinct peoples. It is a remarkable instance of civic tolerance to accept being bound by precepts articulated not by 'my people' but by a community composed of distinct political communities ...

Constitutional actors in the Member States accept the European constitutional discipline not because, as a matter of legal doctrine, as is the case in the federal state, they are subordinate to a higher sovereignty and authority attaching to norms validated by the federal people, the constitutional demos. They accept it as an autonomous voluntary act, endlessly renewed on each occasion, of subordination, in the discrete areas governed by Europe, to a norm which is the aggregate expression of other wills, other political identities, other political communities. Of course, to do so creates in itself a different type of political community, one unique feature of which is that very willingness to accept a binding discipline which is rooted in and derives from a community of others. The Quebecois are told: in the name of the people of Canada, you are obliged to obey. The French or the Italians or the Germans are told: in the name of the peoples of Europe, you are invited to obey...

This process operates also at Community level. Think of the European judge or the European public official who must understand that, in the peculiar constitutional compact of Europe, his decision will take effect only if obeyed by national courts, if executed faithfully by a national public official with whom he belongs to a national administration which claims from them a particularly strong form of loyalty and habit. This, too, will instil a measure of caution and tolerance.

(v) The early enlargements

The United Kingdom was all too aware that the establishment of a common market left it economically isolated. Therefore, from 1956 onwards, it pushed for the establishment of a free trade area with other European States, which culminated in its setting up of the European Free Trade Area (EFTA) with Austria, Denmark, Norway, Sweden, Switzerland and Portugal in 1960. By 1961, however, states within the EEC were experiencing faster economic growth rates than Britain and the latter's failure to prevent South Africa's expulsion from the Commonwealth, following the Sharpeville massacres, brought home Britain's relative decline on the international stage.

As discussed earlier,[39] the French President, De Gaulle, vetoed the British entry in 1963. Four years later, the United Kingdom, plus Ireland, Denmark and Norway, reapplied. The application was once again vetoed by De Gaulle. This use of the veto left France increasingly isolated and French policy changed in 1969 with the resignation of De Gaulle. The Six agreed in the Hague to open negotiations with the applicants, with a view to extending membership. The United Kingdom, Denmark and Ireland formally became members on 1 January 1973.[40] However, following a referendum, where 53 per cent voted against membership, Norway did not accede to the EEC.

The next state to join was Greece. Greece applied for membership in 1975, following its establishment of a democratic government. Accession was attractive for both parties. For the Greeks, accession was not only economically attractive, but symbolised modernisation and democratic stability. For the Member States, Greece was important geo-politically during the Cold War because of its strategic location in the Aegean. Membership was, therefore, seen as tying Greece more firmly to the West. The Greek Act of Accession was completed in 1979, with Greece becoming a Member in 1981.

Like Greece, Spain and Portugal emerged from dictatorships and isolationism in the mid-1970s. They made applications to join the Communities only two years after Greece, in 1977.

---

[39] See p. 13.
[40] U. Kitzinger, *Diplomacy and Persuasion: How Britain Joined the Common Market* (London, Thames & Hudson, 1973); C. O'Neill, *Britain's Entry into the European Community, Report on the Negotiations of 1970–1972* (London, Frank Cass, 2000).

Yet, accession was more problematic in their cases. Whilst both saw the Community as a fulcrum through which to achieve economic modernisation and end their relative international isolation, the size of the agricultural sector in Spain resulted in initial French resistance to entry due to the likely negative effects on the French agricultural sector. It was, therefore, not until 1985 that an Act of Accession was signed, with Spain and Portugal becoming Members in 1986.

4 THE SINGLE EUROPEAN ACT AND BEYOND

(i) Run-up to the Single European Act

The recession of the early 1980s led national governments to confront their relative economic decline and prompted a relaunch of the integration process, as a way of combating this decline. A Solemn Declaration on European Union was adopted by the Heads of Government in 1983. This proposed few concrete reforms, but declared that there should be a 'renewed impetus' towards completion of the internal market, in particular the removal of obstacles to the free movement of goods, services and capital.[41]

This Declaration occurred against the backdrop of a number of significant developments. 1983 marked the collapse of the Keynesian economic policies which had been adopted in France. This collapse led to some convergence between national governments that economic policy-making had to focus on 'supply-side' measures which stimulated competition and trade. Market integration did both, and therefore fitted this new consensus.[42] Alongside this, since the 1970s, transnational pressure groups had begun to locate themselves in Brussels. The number of these groups expanded in the early 1980s, leading to the growth of an organised industrial constituency that was increasingly rallying for European solutions.[43] From the early 1980s onwards, major industrialists mobilised through organisations such as the European Round Table (ERT) and UNICE. These groups lobbied aggressively across Europe, arguing for the completion of the common market as a means of promoting European competitiveness.[44] Finally, direct elections had also produced a more aggressive European Parliament. Under the chairmanship of Alfiero Spinelli, it produced a draft Treaty on European Union, which proposed a fully federal Europe with common foreign, macro-economic and trade policies and a developed system of central institutions.[45]

[41] For critical comment see J. Weiler, 'The Genscher-Colombo Draft European Act: The Politics of Indecision' (1983) 6 *Journal of European Integration* 129.

[42] On the convergence of national government preferences see K. Middlemas, *Orchestrating Europe: The Informal Politics of European Union 1973–1995* (London, Fontana, 1995) 115–35; A. Moravcsik, *The Choice for Europe: Social Purpose and State Power from Messina to Maastricht* (Ithaca, NY, Cornell University Press, 1998) ch. 5; J. Gillingham, *European Integration 1950–2003: Superstate or New Market Economy* (Cambridge, Cambridge University Press, 2003) ch. 9.

[43] N. Fligstein and J. McNichol, 'The Institutional Terrain of the European Union' in W. Sandholtz and A. Stone Sweet (eds.), *European Integration and Supranational Governance* (Oxford, Oxford University Press, 1998) 59, 75–80; N. Fligstein and P. Brantley, 'The Single Market Program and the Interests of Business' in B. Eichengreen and J. Frieden (eds.), *Politics and Institutions in an Integrated Europe* (Berlin, Springer, 1995).

[44] W. Sandholtz and J. Zysman, '1992: Recasting the European Bargain' (1989) 42 *World Politics* 95, 116; M. Cowles, 'Setting the Agenda for a New Europe: The ERT and EC 1992' (1995) 33 *JCMS* 527; Middlemas, above n. 42, 136–40.

[45] [1984] OJ C77/33. For comment, see R. Bieber *et al.*, *An Ever Closer Union: A Critical Analysis of the Draft Treaty Establishing the European Union* (Luxembourg, Office for Official Publications of the European Communities, 1985).

These developments all pressed towards further European integration, but were fragmented and uncoordinated. The final piece in the jigsaw fell into place with the appointment of a new Commission in late 1984, headed by the charismatic former French Finance Minister, Jacques Delors. Delors, in lobbying for the post, had already seized upon the goal of market unity as the principal task of the new Commission to be achieved by the end of 1992. In November 1984, he gave the national governments four choices for recapturing momentum: monetary policy, foreign policy and defence, institutional reform or the internal market.[46] All agreed that the internal market was the way forward.

The Commission was instructed by the Member States to consider the practical steps necessary to realise this. In truth, the idea had been kicking around the Commission for a few years. In 1981, the German Commissioner, Karl-Heinz Narjes, had looked into the idea of creating an 'internal market' in which there were no barriers to the exchange of goods, services and labour, but this had met with opposition from the French Government in 1982.[47] The new British Commissioner, Lord Cockfield, took up Narjes' work, and in June 1985, presented the White Paper on Completion of the Internal Market to the Heads of Government at Milan.[48] The paper was a clever piece of work, suggesting that 279 measures were necessary to realise the internal market. Member States were not, therefore, committing themselves to an open-ended set of obligations, but to a finite and limited project. The project was also cast as largely a technical mission rather than having broader panoramas of greater integration.[49] For all this, the goal of the internal market was unattainable whilst unanimity voting prevailed in the Council. Any change in this was firmly opposed by Britain, Denmark and Greece. Notwithstanding this, the Italian government called for a conference to amend the Treaties. Despite their opposing stance, all three states attended. The result was the signing of the Single European Act in 1986.

(ii) The Single European Act

The principal achievements of the SEA appeared limited and modest at the time. They were described as a victory for minimalism,[50] and both the Commission and the Parliament were relaxed about the Act.[51] Much of the SEA was therefore about giving formal recognition to pre-existing policies and institutions. Provision was made for express competences in health and safety at work, economic and social cohesion, research and development and environmental protection. A Title was added on European Cooperation in the Sphere of Foreign Policy codifying intergovernmental cooperation in foreign policy. The European Council, the meetings of Heads of Government, was formally acknowledged.[52] However, there had been regular summits from 1961 and it was agreed in 1974 that these should meet twice a year to discuss

---

[46] Middlemas, above n. 42, 141.
[47] N. Fligstein and I. Mara-Drita, 'How to Make a Market: Reflections on the Attempt to Create a Single Market in the European Union' (1996) 102 *American Journal of Sociology* 1, 11–13.
[48] European Commission, *Completing the Internal Market*, COM(85)310 final.
[49] W. Sandholtz and J. Zysman, '1992: Recasting the European Bargain' (1989) 42 *World Politics* 95, 114–15.
[50] G. Bermann, 'The Single European Act: A New Constitution for the European Community?' (1989) 27 *Columbia Journal of Transnational Law* 529; A. Moravcsik, 'Negotiating the Single European Act' (1991) 45 *IO* 19.
[51] C.-D. Ehlermann, 'The Internal Market Following the Single European Act' (1987) 24 *CMLRev.* 361.
[52] Article 2 SEA. On the early evolution of the European Council, see S. Bulmer, 'The European Council's First Decade: Between Interdependence and Domestic Politics' (1985) 23 *JCMS* 89; S. Bulmer and W. Wessels, *The European Council* (London, Macmillan, 1987); J. Werts, *The European Council* (North Holland, Elsevier, 1992).

internal difficulties within the European Communities, broader issues about the future of European integration, and the place of the European Communities in the world order.

There were two reforms, which marked the SEA as possibly the most significant institutional reform of them all. The first was the commitment to establish the internal market by 31 December 1992. The internal market is now set out in Article 26(2) TFEU:

> The internal market shall comprise an area without internal frontiers in which the free movement of goods, persons, services and capital is ensured in accordance with the provisions of the Treaties.

The second was institutional reform to realise this objective. A new legislative procedure, the cooperation procedure, was introduced, which provided for qualified majority voting (QMV) in the Council and increased powers for the European Parliament.[53]

Neither reform seemed particularly radical at the time. The internal market project seemed to be no more than a restatement of the old dream of establishing a common market. In fact, it seemed a paler version, as it was unclear whether it extended to policies clearly caught by the common market, such as competition policy, commercial policy, non-discrimination and economic policy.[54] The new voting procedures did not apply to core areas such as taxation and freedom of persons, and its effect upon the Luxembourg Accords was uncertain, particularly as the United Kingdom, Greece and Denmark insisted upon a Declaration being appended to the SEA claiming that nothing within it affected Member States' rights to invoke the Accords.

However, the SEA confounded expectations and brought about the most radical change in the history of the European Union's fortunes. It changed both the legislative and political culture of the Union. In legislative terms, Member States became less tolerant of each others' attempts to invoke the Luxembourg Accords. This was reflected in the 1987 Council Decision on the 'vote to go to a vote', where it was agreed that if a simple majority of Member States voted to go to a formal vote, then a vote should be taken.[55]

The legislative processes became energised. By the end of 1990, all the measures contained in the White Paper had been formally proposed by the Commission.[56] By the end of 1992, almost 95 per cent of the measures had been enacted and 77 per cent had entered into force in the Member States.[57] Alongside this, the Commission had vastly understated the legislative output of the European Communities. Legislative output increased to 2,500 binding acts per year by 1994;[58] 53 per cent of the legislative measures adopted in France in 1991 were inspired by its Treaty obligations and 30 per cent of all Dutch legislation during the early 1990s implemented EU legislation.[59]

---

[53] This legislative procedure no longer exists as it has been completely superseded by the co-decision procedure.

[54] P. Pescatore, 'Some Critical Remarks on the Single European Act' (1987) 24 *CMLRev.* 9, 11.

[55] Council Rules of Procedure, art. 5 [1987] OJ L291/27.

[56] *Twenty Fourth Report on the General Activities of the European Communities 1990* (Luxembourg, Office for Official Publications of the European Communities, 1991) 53. For an insight into how the Commission operated during this period see G. Ross, *Jacques Delors and European Integration* (London, Polity, 1995).

[57] *Twenty Sixth General Report on the Activities of the European Communities 1992* (Luxembourg, Office for Official Publications of the European Communities, 1993) 35.

[58] W. Wessels, 'An Ever Closer Fusion? A Dynamic Macropolitical View on Integration Processes' (1997) 35 *JCMS* 267, 276.

[59] G. Mancini, 'Europe: The Case for Statehood' (1998) 4 *ELJ* 29, 40.

(iii) The road to Maastricht

This transformation in law-making discussed above brought about a change in political culture. As the technical façade of the White Paper was exposed, highly divisive questions became more salient. These included such matters as the relationship between state and market, the role of central government actors and the appropriate method to regulate non-economic public goods, such as public health or the environment.[60]

This led to tensions on three fronts: all were opposed by the British Government, which perceived them as interventionist and centralising.

The first front concerned the degree of regulation needed to complete the internal market. In a speech to the European Parliament in July 1988, the Commission President, Jacques Delors, observed that it could lead to 80 per cent of Member State economic legislation being passed as Community law. The second front concerned the social dimension of the EC. From 1986, the Commission tried to link the development of a Community social policy to the realisation of the internal market, on the grounds that some harmonisation of social legislation was necessary for the attainment of the latter. In May 1989, the Commission proposed a Community Charter of Fundamental Social Rights. This was adopted by all of the Member States, apart from Britain, at the Strasbourg European Council in December 1989.[61]

The third front was economic and monetary union (EMU). As early as 1987, the Commission indicated that due to the uncertainty generated by national currency stability, the gain anticipated for the single market could not be fully realised without some form of economic and monetary union.[62] Insofar as it was perceived to contribute to monetary stability, it also tied in with the anti-inflationary policies adopted by most Member States.[63] Monetary union was also a Trojan horse. It fitted with the aspirations of those, notably President Mitterand of France and President Kohl of Germany, who saw 1992 as being the cantilever to open the door to greater political integration. The question of economic and monetary union was, therefore, placed on the agenda of the Hanover Summit, in June 1988. At Hanover, the Heads of State asserted that 'the Single European Act confirmed the objective of progressive realisation of economic and monetary union'.[64] The Delors Committee, a committee of central bank governors chaired by the Commission President, Jacques Delors, was mandated to examine the concrete steps required to realise this goal.

In June 1989, the Delors Report on economic and monetary union was submitted to the Heads of State in Madrid.[65] This Report suggested a gradualist approach to monetary union, which was to be completed in three stages. The first stage should consist of achievement of the internal market, liberalisation of all capital movements and all Member States becoming members of the Exchange Rate Mechanism. The second stage required the establishment of an independent European Central Bank, convergence of national economies and a gradual

---

[60] J. Weiler, 'The Transformation of Europe' (1991) 100 *Yale Law Journal* 2403, 2477; R. Dehousse, 'Integration v. Regulation? On the Dynamics of Regulation in the Community' (1992) 30 *JCMS* 383.

[61] Conclusions of Strasbourg European Council, *EC Bulletin* 12–1989, 1.1.1.

[62] T. Padoa-Schipoa *et al.*, *Efficiency, Stability and Equity: A Strategy for the Evolution of the Economic System of the European Community* (Oxford, Oxford University Press, 1987).

[63] W. Sandholtz, 'Choosing Union: Monetary Politics and Maastricht' (1993) 47 *IO* 1.

[64] Conclusions of Hanover European Council, *EC Bulletin* 6–1988, 1.1.1–1.1.5.

[65] Conclusions of Madrid European Council, *EC Bulletin* 6–1989, 1.1.11.

assumption of the national central bank functions by the European Central Bank. The final stage would necessitate the European Central Bank fully taking over national central bank functions and assuming a monopoly over the money supply.[66] Faced with the opposition of all the other Member States and the threatened resignation of both her Chancellor of the Exchequer and Foreign Secretary, Mrs Thatcher grudgingly adopted the Report and it was agreed that the first stage should begin on 1 July 1990. The outmanoeuvring of Mrs Thatcher was completed at Strasbourg, where it was agreed that an intergovernmental conference should be held to amend the Treaties, with a view to economic and monetary union.

Presidents Kohl and Mitterand, the German and French Presidents, considered that economic and monetary union would not be sustainable without further political integration, and launched an initiative to that effect in April 1990.[67] In June 1990, it was agreed that a separate conference should be held on political union.[68] They culminated in the signing of the Treaty on European Union, at Maastricht, on 10 December 1991.[69]

5 THE TREATY ON EUROPEAN UNION

(i) A tripartite institutional settlement

The Treaty on European Union (TEU) was a very different Treaty from the SEA. If the latter required considerable legal integration, this was simply the byproduct of the establishment of an internal market. The TEU marked very definitely a change in tone. It created a new form of political project, which included, to be sure, an amount of arcane detail, but also marked out a new form of polity, which has its own set of political values and political communities. This shift is reflected in the first article of the current TEU, which builds on and rearticulates what was agreed at Maastricht.

Article 1 TEU

By this Treaty, the HIGH CONTRACTING PARTIES establish among themselves a EUROPEAN UNION, hereinafter called 'the Union' on which the Member States confer competences to attain objectives they have in common.

This Treaty marks a new stage in the process of creating an ever closer union among the peoples of Europe, in which decisions are taken as openly as possible and as closely as possible to the citizen.

---

[66] The German Central Bank, the Bundesbank, applied strong pressure for the Report to follow the German model of monetary policy-making as the price for its support. It was also adamant that the transition should be a gradual one. M. Artis, 'The Maastricht Road to Monetary Union' (1992) 30 *JCMS* 299.

[67] On the Franco-German role in the negotiations leading to Maastricht see C. Mazzucelli, *France and Germany at Maastricht: Politics and Negotiations to Create the European Union* (New York, Garland, 1997).

[68] Conclusions of the Dublin European Council, *EC Bulletin* 6–1990, 1.11. Political union was added as an afterthought to economic and monetary union and negotiations were not well prepared. R. Corbett, 'The Intergovernmental Conference on Political Union' (1992) 30 *JCMS* 271.

[69] The most detailed analysis of the negotiations is F. Laursen and S. Vanhoonacker, *The Intergovernmental Conference on Political Union: Institutional Reforms, New Policies and International Identity of the European Community* (Dordrecht, Martinus Nijhoff, 1992).

The Commission and the Parliament pressed for the Union to be governed by a single institutional, supranational structure. In two fields, a practice of intergovernmental cooperation had emerged that was to prove difficult to displace. The first was foreign policy. All Member States, other than the Belgians and the Dutch, wanted to keep it this way and were opposed to bringing foreign and defence policy within the EC supranational framework. The second field was that of Justice and Home Affairs, a ragbag field focused on combating international crime and policing asylum and migration of non-EU nationals. In 1985 and 1990, two agreements were signed at Schengen, in Luxembourg, between all the Member States, excluding Ireland and the United Kingdom.[70] These Conventions provided for the abolition of frontier checks between parties and a common external frontier. To realise this, the 1990 Convention provided for intergovernmental cooperation in the fields of migration of non-EU nationals, crime and policing. Whilst many Member States wanted to see this brought within the EC framework, the British, Irish, Greeks and Danes were adamant that this was an area where the national veto should be maintained.

The Union was, therefore, to be composed of three pillars. The first was that of the European Community, the second, Common Foreign and Security Policy (CFSP), and the third, Justice and Home Affairs (JHA).[71] These three pillars were, in principle, to constitute a single institutional framework.[72] The overarching, unitary provisions were weak, however. There was a unitary legal framework in that any understanding of one pillar could only be had by reference to the TEU as a whole.[73] Beyond that, only two provisions united the three pillars. The European Council was given a pre-eminent, coordinating role for all three pillars. Its position as the body with ultimate political authority and the body which was responsible for visioning and coordinating all EU activities was, for the first time, formalised.[74] In addition, the unique position of the Member States and the commitment to respect fundamental rights were recognised as a constituent element of each pillar.[75]

The institutional balance within each pillar was, however, very different. The Parliament and the Court of Justice were only minimally associated with either the second or third pillars.[76] If the EC pillar was characterised by some parliamentary and judicial controls, these were largely absent at either a national or EU level and, instead, were to be dominated by executive government. Whilst the Commission was associated quite strongly with the work of the third pillar on Justice and Home Affairs, it was almost completely excluded from the second pillar. Even between the two intergovernmental pillars, there was a mismatch, with one being more clearly Europeanised than the other. The question of legal personality was also mixed. The EC had had legal personality since 1957, and retained this. By contrast, the European Union was to have no legal personality. Whilst the EC had treaty-making powers in its field of competence, there was no equivalent power in the fields of CFSP and JHA.[77]

---

[70] This is now to be found at [2000] OJ 2000 L239/19. Iceland and Norway are also associated members.

[71] Allegedly, the idea was first suggested by a French negotiator, Pierre de Boissieu, and was constructed around the metaphor of a temple based on three pillars, Middlemas, above n. 42, 188.

[72] Article 3 TEU (M).

[73] A. v. Bogdandy and M. Nettesheim, 'Ex Pluribus Unum: Fusion of the European Communities into the European Union' (1996) 2 *ELJ* 267, 279–81; D. Curtin and I. Dekker, 'The EU as a Layered International Organization: Institutional Unity in Disguise' in P. Craig and G. de Búrca (eds.), *The Evolution of EU Law* (Oxford, Oxford University Press, 1999).

[74] Article 4 TEU (M).

[75] Article 6 TEU(M).

[76] For a reassertion of this see Case C-160/03 *Spain* v *Eurojust* [2005] ECR I-2077.

[77] D. Curtin, 'The Constitutional Structure of the Union: A Europe of Bits and Pieces' (1993) 30 *CMLRev.* 17.

There was a political price to be paid for these three pillars: a commitment to a further IGC to reconsider this in 1996.

(ii) The new competences

The EC was granted express competences in the fields of visas for non-EU nationals, education, culture, public health, consumer protection, the establishment of trans-European networks in transport, energy and telecommunications, industrial policy and development cooperation. There were two fields which evoked particular controversy.

The first was economic and monetary union. The Treaty followed the three stage structure of the Delors Report, with the third stage of economic and monetary union beginning on 1 January 1999.[78] Economic and monetary union allocated responsibility for various aspects of economic policy to different institutions. The third stage involved monetary policy becoming the responsibility of an independent European Central Bank, established in Frankfurt, which was to be exclusively responsible for authorising the issue of the new European currency, the euro, and for the setting of short-term interest rates. Constraints were also to be placed on national fiscal policy through the limiting of the size of the deficits that governments could run. A procedure was established: the excessive deficit procedure, whereby governments participating in the euro could be heavily penalised if they ran an excessive deficit. This proved too constraining for two Member States, Denmark and the United Kingdom, and Protocols were agreed reserving their right not to participate in the third stage of EMU.

The other area to prove particularly problematic was that of social policy. There was strong support amongst all Member States, apart from Britain, for an extension of the social policy provisions to all areas of labour law and social protection for workers. The British government opposed this on the grounds that this was purely a matter of national concern and it did not fit in with that government's views of a deregulated labour market. The compromise was a Protocol, which authorised all the Member States, apart from the United Kingdom, to establish an Agreement on Social Policy that would bind only those Member States, but would allow them access to existing EU machinery and resources.

(iii) The quest for Union 'democracy'

As there was a sense of putting a new political system in place, Maastricht gave far more serious consideration to the 'democratic' nature of the European Union and its need to seek political legitimacy. A variety of strategies were introduced.

The first was to increase parliamentary input into the legislative processes. A new legislative procedure was introduced, the co-decision procedure, which gave the European Parliament more powers by allowing it, in certain sectors, to veto legislation. The place of national parliaments was recognised for the first time, albeit in a fairly minimal manner. A Declaration was attached to the TEU committing governments to greater involvement of their national parliaments in the integration process and to ensuring these receive legislative proposals in

---

[78] It was initially envisaged that the third stage could begin as early as 31 December 1996 if the convergence criteria were met by sufficient Member States, Article 109j(3) EC. At the Cannes Summit, in 1995, it was agreed that the date for the third stage should be 1 January 1999, *EU Bulletin* 6–1995, 1.11.

good time. Alongside this, there was an attempt to pluralise the decision-making process. New stakeholders were introduced, most notably the Committee of the Regions which, whilst only being given consultative powers, created a voice for the European regions within the Community policy process.

The TEU was also concerned with administrative accountability. To that end, an Ombudsman was established to consider acts of maladministration by the EU institutions. Provision was also made for considering whether the decision-making procedures could be made more transparent and, for the first time, the question of freedom of information was formally acknowledged.

Most symbolic of the sentiment that a new centre for democratic participation was being created was the institution of European Union citizenship. Citizens were granted new rights to free movement and to access to social benefits in other Member States. New possibilities for democratic participation at both local and European level were created. European citizenship also created new patterns of inclusion and exclusion between Europeans and non-Europeans, insofar as these rights were only granted to Member State nationals as EU citizens. Most controversially, citizenship has traditionally been used to foster new political allegiances, as it suggests a common political identity between its members, which to some seemed to compete with that claimed by the nation-state.

The democratic turn, however, was not just about strengthening the credentials of the centre. By the time the TEU was signed, the European Union was churning out more legislation, more intensely, in more fields, than ever before. This was placing unheralded pressures on national, regional and local government. There were also concerns as to how to police and limit the activities of the Union. We have seen how special arrangements were put in place for the United Kingdom in social policy and for it and Denmark in EMU. As well as these, other Member States began to ring-fence their laws. Ireland and Denmark, thus, respectively obtained Protocols protecting their abortion law and legislation on ownership of second homes from EU law. To manage these tensions more generally, a new principle was introduced: the subsidiarity principle. In areas where both it and the Member States had powers, the Union was only to act if the objectives of the proposed action could not be sufficiently achieved by the Member States and by reason of its scale or effects the action could be better achieved by the Community.

6 THE 1990s: THE DECADE OF SELF-DOUBT

(i) Ratification of the Treaty on European Union

On 2 June 1992, the Danes voted against ratification of the TEU by 50.7 to 49.3 per cent. This shook the process to the core as the Treaty could not enter into effect unless all Member States ratified it. To boost the credibility of the ratification process, President Mitterand decided to hold a referendum in France. Although an easy 'yes' vote had been predicted, it soon became a very close contest, with only 51 per cent of the vote being in favour of ratification. The Treaty was salvaged at Edinburgh, in December 1992. The other Member States considered the Treaty to be non-negotiable, but something had to be done to allow the Danish government to say that the Treaty it was proposing for a second referendum was substantially different from the initial Treaty. The route taken was a Decision 'interpreting' the Treaty giving the Danish government guarantees about the autonomy of its citizenship and defence as well as setting out in more detail the subsidiarity principle.[79] This gave the Danish government the necessary breadth to hold a second referendum. This was duly held in May 1993, with 56 per cent voting in favour of ratification.

However, the damage had been done. The political aura of inevitable integration and the assumption of popular support for it had been tarnished. The first Danish referendum signalled the beginning of a bitter legislative fight in the British Parliament, in which ratification was fought for by both the British Labour Party and a minority of the then ruling Conservative party. The legislation was only adopted in July 1993 – a year and a half after the Treaty had been agreed – and only after the government had put a gun to its rebels' heads, by passing it as a motion of confidence, with the consequence that if it had fallen, the government would have had to resign.[80]

The drama of ratification of the Treaty was now re-enacted in the courts. Challenges to the Treaty were made before the British, French, Danish and Spanish courts.[81] It was the challenge before the German Constitutional Court, in October 1993, which was to have the most far-reaching consequences.[82] In its judgment, the German Constitutional Court placed markers on the nature and limits of European integration. It ruled that democratic legitimacy is constituted above all at a national level. Within this setting, the constitutionality of the European Union rests on its being an organisation with limited powers operated in a democratically account-able fashion. Further integration would only be possible if it did not fundamentally undermine national self-government.

The TEU entered into force on 1 November 1993 but the environment was now heavily polarised. Public support for the European Union had diminished[83] and deep divisions had emerged between national governments about which direction to take.[84] Member States had, however, committed themselves at Maastricht to a further IGC in 1996.[85] Negotiations only began in earnest in the latter half of 1996 with the Irish government presenting a draft Treaty to the other Member States in December 1996.[86] The Treaty of Amsterdam was signed on 2 October 1997.

---

[79] D. Howarth, 'The Compromise on Denmark and the Treaty on European Union: A Legal and Political Analysis' (1994) 31 *CMLRev.* 465.

[80] R. Rawlings, 'Legal Politics: The United Kingdom and Ratification of the Treaty on European Union' (1994) *PL* 254 and 367; D. Baker, A. Gamble and S. Ludlum, 'The Parliamentary Siege of Maastricht: Conservative Divisions and British Ratification' (1994) 47 *Parliamentary Affairs* 37.

[81] *R* v *Secretary of State for Foreign and Commonwealth Affairs, ex parte Rees-Mogg* [1994] QB 552 (Britain); *Re Treaty on European Union* (Decision 92–308), Journel Officiel de la République Française 1992, 5354 (France); *Re Treaty on European Union* [1994] 3 CMLR 101 (Spain).

[82] *Brunner* v *European Union* [1994] 1 CMLR 57.

[83] Opinion polls showed that those who considered the European Union a 'good thing' had dropped from 72 per cent in 1990 to 48 per cent in autumn 1996. Eurobarometer, *Public Opinion in the EU*, Report No. 46, Autumn 1996 (Luxembourg, Office for Official Publications of the European Communities, 1997).

[84] A summary of all the positions taken by the Member States at the 1996 Intergovernmental Conference can be found at http://europa.eu.int/en/agenda/igc-home/ms-doc.

[85] See p. 25.

[86] Conference of the Representatives of the Governments of the Member States, *The European Union Today and Tomorrow: Adopting the European Union for the Benefit of Its Peoples and Preparing It for the Future, A General Outline for a Draft Revision of the Treaties*, CONF 2500/96.

(ii) The Treaty of Amsterdam

(a) The Area of Freedom, Security and Justice

If the central monuments of the SEA and Maastricht were the internal market and EMU, respectively, then the Area of Freedom, Security and Justice (AFSJ) occupied a similar place for the Treaty of Amsterdam. The AFSJ is now set out in the following terms.

Article 67 TFEU

1. The Union shall constitute an area of freedom, security and justice with respect for fundamental rights and the different legal systems and traditions of the Member States.
2. It shall ensure the absence of internal border controls for persons and shall frame a common policy on asylum, immigration and external border control, based on solidarity between Member States, which is fair towards third-country nationals. For the purpose of this Title, stateless persons shall be treated as third-country nationals.
3. The Union shall endeavour to ensure a high level of security through measures to prevent and combat crime, racism and xenophobia, and through measures for coordination and cooperation between police and judicial authorities and other competent authorities, as well as through the mutual recognition of judgments in criminal matters and, if necessary, through the approximation of criminal laws.
4. The Union shall facilitate access to justice, in particular through the principle of mutual recognition of judicial and extrajudicial decisions in civil matters.

To realise the AFSJ, the Treaty of Amsterdam first integrated the Schengen Agreements into the legal framework of the TEU. A Protocol Integrating the Schengen Acquis into the framework of the European Union was adopted, which made the Schengen Acquis part of EU law.[87] Secondly, the AFSJ reallocated decision-making between the first and third pillars. Immigration, asylum and the rights of non-EU nationals were brought within EC legislative competences, whilst policing and judicial cooperation on criminal matters remained subject to the predominantly intergovernmental procedures of the third pillar. Finally, the AFSJ reoriented the EU more explicitly around certain ideals. This was marked most strongly in the new Article 6 TEU, which stated that the Union was to be founded on the 'principles of liberty, democracy, respect for human rights and fundamental freedoms, and the rule of law'. These ideals were further institutionalised in two ways First, the EC acquired a general legislative competence to combat discrimination on grounds that related to sex, race or ethnic origin, religion or belief, disability, age or sexual orientation. Secondly, provision was made for a Member State to have its rights suspended under the TEU or to be expelled from the European Union, where it was deemed that the Member State had seriously and persistently breached these ideals.

---

[87] The acquis is the name for the existing body of law that has been adopted up until now, in this instance under the Schengen procedures.

(b) Further supranational 'democratisation'

The Treaty of Amsterdam led to a significant extension of QMV. It was the first time a majority of legal bases now provided for QMV.[88] Qualitatively, QMV was extended to important new fields, including employment, countering social exclusion, equality of opportunity and treatment for men and women, public health, transparency, fraud and freedom of establishment. In terms of parliamentary accountability, it also led to a considerable extension of the European Parliament's powers. The scope of the co-decision procedure was extended considerably. The European Parliament was also, for the first time, given some involvement in the third pillar. Alongside this, more attention was paid to the role of national parliaments within the integration process. A Protocol on National Parliaments was adopted, which extended their guarantees. All consultation documents would now be sent to them and there would be a six-week period between proposals being announced and their being placed on the legislative agenda, in order to allow national parliaments to consider them. Administrative accountability was strengthened by the principle of transparency being formally incorporated into the EC Treaty with a qualified right of access to EC documents being granted to every citizen of the Union and natural or legal person having its registered office in a Member State.

(c) Differentiated integration

A new Title on Employment was added to the EC Treaty and, with a change of government in the United Kingdom, the Protocol on Social Policy was abolished, and social policy was placed on the same footing as all other first pillar policies. However, Amsterdam was more noteworthy for reflecting the multiplicity of tensions surrounding the pace, direction and form of European integration that had emerged since Maastricht. A Protocol on the Application of the Principles of Subsidiarity and Proportionality was agreed, which entrenched in Treaty law the Declarations agreed at Edinburgh that had enabled Denmark to hold a second referendum on the Maastricht Treaty.

It was clear, however, that a 'one size fits all' approach was becoming harder to manage as disagreements about the fields and intensity of the integration process became more entrenched. Provision was made, therefore, for a majority of Member States to engage, as a last resort, in 'enhanced cooperation':[89] adoption of EU laws amongst themselves where agreement was not possible involving all the EU Member States. Alongside this, country specific opt-outs proliferated at Amsterdam. The United Kingdom and Ireland obtained Protocols preserving their right to decide whether to opt-in to individual pieces of legislation on immigration, asylum and other policies concerning free movement of persons, as well as Protocols preserving their rights to impose frontier controls on persons coming from other Member States. In like vein, Denmark negotiated a Protocol stating that it would only be bound by such legislation under its general obligations in international law, as a Schengen signatory, and not by virtue of EU law.

There were also a series of soft opt-outs. A Protocol had been adopted which established a presumption of no asylum for EU nationals in other Member States. Belgium adopted a Declaration stating it would not follow this presumption but would treat each case on its merits.

---

[88] A. Maurer, 'The Legislative Powers and Impact of the European Parliament' (2003) 41 *JCMS* 227, 229.
[89] See pp. 113–16 for more detail on this.

Germany, Luxembourg and Austria sought Declarations in a different field. These states were concerned that their systems of public banking might be compromised by EU competition law, and therefore sought Declarations to the contrary.

7 RECASTING THE BORDERS OF THE EUROPEAN UNION

The shape of the European Union was modified by two events at the end of the 1980s. The success of the SEA entailed that exclusion from the world's largest trading bloc posed significant economic risks for neighbouring states. At the same time, communism collapsed in Central and Eastern Europe. Many states, previously antagonistic to the European Union, now embraced the market-orientated ideals it symbolised and saw membership as the anchor around which changes in their societies could be made.

The process of expansion began with the EFTA states (Norway, Sweden, Finland, Iceland, Austria, Liechtenstein and Switzerland). In 1991, the Treaty of Oporto was signed, establishing the European Economic Area (EEA).[90] The EFTA states were required to adopt all EU legislation in the fields of the internal market, research and development policy, social policy, education, consumer protection and environmental protection in return for access to the internal market.

In June 1993, the European Union agreed that membership be offered to Austria, Finland, Sweden and Norway.[91] Referendums were necessary in all four states prior to accession. In Austria and Finland, comfortable majorities voted in favour of membership. However, that in Sweden was narrow. The Norwegians voted narrowly against membership. The three new Member States acceded to the TEU on 2 January 1995.

More challenging was the question of possible membership of the former communist states of Central and Eastern Europe. By the early 1990s, twelve of these states had applied for membership.[92] This would almost double the size of the Union, with a corresponding reduction of political influence for existing Member States. It would create a financial burden on current members as the applicants were poorer than the Western European states and many had large agricultural populations, which could press claims for support from the EU Budget. Nevertheless, in Lisbon 1992, the European Union stated that any European state whose government was based on the principle of democracy could apply to accede.[93] A year later, at Copenhagen, the European Union went a step further and agreed that the states of Central and Eastern Europe could become members of the European Union once able to satisfy the obligations of membership. These obligations required new states to have:

- stable institutions guaranteeing democracy, the rule of law, human rights and respect for and protection of minorities;

---

[90] Although Switzerland signed the Treaty, following a referendum it decided not to ratify it. In 2002, agreements were signed between the European Union and Switzerland in the fields of free movement of persons, agriculture, transport, public procurement, mutual recognition and scientific and technological cooperation [2002] OJ L114/1. The most detailed analysis of the Treaty can be found in T. Blanchet *et al.*, *The Agreement on the European Economic Area* (Oxford, Clarendon Press, 1994).

[91] M. Jorna, 'The Accession Negotiations with Austria, Finland, Sweden and Norway: A Guided Tour' (1995) 20 *ELRev.* 131; F. Granell, 'The European Union's Enlargement Negotiations with Austria, Finland, Norway and Sweden' (1995) 33 *JCMS* 117.

[92] These were Bulgaria, Cyprus, the Czech Republic, Estonia, Hungary, Latvia, Lithuania, Malta, Poland, Romania, Slovenia and Slovakia.

[93] Conclusions of the Lisbon European Council, *EC Bulletin* 6–1992, 1.4.

- a functioning market economy as well as the capacity to cope with competitive pressures and market forces within the Union;
- the ability to assume the obligations of membership, including both adherence to the aims of the Union and adoption of all existing EU legislation;
- the legislative and administrative capacity to transpose EU legislation into national legislation and to implement it effectively through appropriate administrative and judicial structures.[94]

In 1994, it was agreed that a 'structured relationship' should be established between the European Union and the countries of Central and Eastern Europe to prepare the latter for membership. In July 1997, following the Treaty of Amsterdam, the Commission stepped up the process with the launch of its 2000 Agenda programme. In a 1,300 page document, it assessed how far the applicant states met the criteria agreed in Copenhagen. On the basis of that progress report, it recommended the opening of membership negotiations with the Czech Republic, Poland, Hungary, Slovenia, Estonia and Cyprus, with a view to accession by 2003. The discussions began in March 1998. However, limiting negotiations to a selection of applicant states proved hopelessly divisive, and in January 2000, Bulgaria, Romania, Latvia, Lithuania, Malta and Slovakia were also invited to participate. Between 1997 and 2002, the Commission published annual reports on each applicant. In Copenhagen, in December 2002, the Member States agreed that all these states, other than Bulgaria and Romania, should become Members of the European Union from 1 May 2004. These latter two states acceded to the Union on 1 January 2007, bringing membership of the Union to twenty-seven.

The expansion of the European Union from twelve states to twenty-seven in just over twelve years has not simply made the Union bigger. It has also transformed it. It can now claim to be an organisation that is genuinely pan-European rather than predominantly West European. A corollary of this is considerable diversity. Economically, the GDP per capita (even after rescaling it to account for purchasing power parity) of Luxembourg is seven times that of Bulgaria.[95] There are also significant differences in legal and political culture. Traditionally, trust in the new Member States in democratic institutions, political parties, trade unions and private enterprises is low. There are also lower levels of civic responsibility but higher levels of solidarity with the socio-economically disadvantaged.[96] This is not to be decried but, inevitably, reshapes the common political and legal space established by the European Union as new members bring in new ways of doing things.[97]

Management of this diversity has come up in relation to the question of continued enlargement. Three states have been granted candidate status: Croatia, the Former Yugoslav Republic of Macedonia (FYROM) and Turkey.

The most unproblematic has been Croatia. It was agreed to open accession negotiations in 2004 and these duly began at the end of 2005. These have passed relatively smoothly. Whilst there is a border dispute with Slovenia still to be resolved, the Commission noted at the end of

---

[94] This last condition was added at Madrid in December 1995.

[95] See http://epp.eurostat.ec.europa.eu/cache/ITY_OFFPUB/KS-SF-08-112/EN/KS-SF-08-112-EN.PDF

[96] J. Zielonka, 'How New Enlarged Borders will Reshape the European Union' (2001) 39 *JCMS* 507, 513–15.

[97] The fourth largest party in the 2009–14 European Parliament is therefore the Polish Civic Platform party and the new President, Jerzy Buzek, is one of its members. Czech and Polish Constitutional Courts have already given seminal judgments causing us to rethink our understandings of the authority of EU law. See pp. 191–3, 212–13 and 222.

2008 that negotiations had begun in twenty-one out of thirty-five Chapters, and that it hoped to publish a timetable for completion of the negotiations by the end of 2009 with the 'perspective of membership a reality'.[98] By contrast, whilst FYROM was granted candidate status only a year later than Croatia in 2005, accession negotiations have still not begun, with the Commission report in 2008 suggesting that significant progress still had to be made on all the Copenhagen criteria.[99]

Tensions have crystallised most acutely in the debate about possible Turkish membership of the European Union. Formal EU-Turkey relations go back over forty years to the signing of an Association Agreement in 1963. In 1987, Turkey applied for membership of the European Union. This application lay dormant, but fears over alienating Turkey led to a rapprochement in the mid-1990s, which resulted in the establishment of a customs union between Turkey and the European Union in 1995. It was clear that this was likely to be insufficient. In 1999, the Member States recognised Turkey's eligibility for membership and agreed this should be assessed according to the Copenhagen criteria. Turkey was pressed to reform its Criminal Code, strengthen its judiciary, secure the rights of association, expression and religion more effectively and reduce the role of the military in the government of the country. In December 2004, it was agreed that Turkey had made the necessary political reforms, and that accession negotiations would open in October 2005. In December 2006, negotiations between the Union and Turkey were disrupted over the refusal by Turkey to admit ships or planes flying the Cypriot flag into its ports or airports. This refusal was influenced by a perception that the European Union was not doing enough to improve the lot of the Turkish Cypriot community in the north of Cyprus. As a consequence, the European Union decided that there would be no negotiations in eight fields[100] and it would not consider negotiations in any field closed until this matter was resolved. Whilst negotiations have continued since, they have done so slowly, with negotiations opened on only eight out of thirty-five Chapters.

Debate about Turkish membership also goes to wider questions about the identity of the European Union. Turkey would be the largest state to join the Union since 1957. It would be the first predominantly Islamic state and would extend the Union's borders far into Asia.[101] In 2007, public surveys suggested that only 31 per cent of EU citizens were in favour of Turkish membership with 55 per cent against.[102] Analysis suggests that the economic costs or benefits of Turkish membership play only a small role. Instead, views are shaped by the perception by those opposed to Turkish membership that Turkey is too culturally different from the European Union, or the perception that the Union should be a liberal order capable of embracing all those who sign up to its values by those supportive of Turkish membership.[103] These views have as much to do with (mis)conceptions about European identity as about the nature of Turkey: whether Europe should still be seen as a Christian club, an

---

[98] European Commission, *Enlargement Strategy and Main Challenges 2008–9*, SEC(2008)674, 4.

[99] European Commission, *The Former Yugoslav Republic of Macedonia 2008 Progress Report*, SEC(2008)2695.

[100] These were free movement of goods, right of establishment and freedom to provide services, financial services, agriculture and rural development, fisheries, transport policy, customs union and external relations.

[101] European Commission, *Staff Working Paper on Issues arising from Turkey's Membership Perspective*, COM(2004)656.

[102] A. Ruiz-Jiménez and J. Torreblanca, *European Public Opinion and Turkey's Accession: Making Sense of Arguments For and Against* (Brussels, Centre for European Policy Studies, 2007) 8–9.

[103] *Ibid.* 16–23.

evangelising force for liberal values, or, as some have argued, a place not to minimise differences but to mediate between them.[104]

Another issue raised by enlargement is whether it is possible with twenty-seven states to press forward with common policies across so many different fields. Majone, in particular, has argued that this is increasingly unrealistic and that we will increasingly witness arrangements involving some Member States but not others.

G. Majone, 'Unity in Diversity: European Integration and the Enlargement Process' (2008) 33 *European Law Review* 457, 470–1

An association established to provide excludable public goods is a *club*. Two elements determine the optimal size of a club. One is the cost of producing the club good – in a large club this cost is shared over more members. The second element is the cost to each club member of a good not meeting precisely his or her individual needs or preferences. The latter cost is likely to increase with the size of the club. Therefore the optimal size is determined by the point at which the marginal benefit from the addition of one new member, i.e. the reduction in the per capita cost of producing the good, equals the marginal cost caused by a mismatch between the characteristics of the good and the preferences of the individual club members ...

Think now of a society composed, not of individuals but of independent states. Associations of independent states (alliances, leagues, confederations) are typically voluntary, and their members are exclusively entitled to enjoy certain benefits produced by the association, so that the economic theory of clubs is applicable. In fact, since excludability is more easily enforced in such a context, many goods which are purely public at the national level become club goods at the international level. The club goods in question could be collective security, policy coordination, common technical standards, or tax harmonization. In these and many other cases, countries which are not willing to share the costs are usually excluded from the benefits of inter-state cooperation. Now, as an association of states expands, becoming more diverse in its preferences, the cost of uniformity in the provision of such goods – harmonization – can escalate dramatically. The theory predicts a growing number of voluntary associations to meet the increased demand of club goods more precisely tailored to the different requirements of various subsets of more homogeneous states. It will be noted that the model sketched here is inspired by a pluralist philosophy quite different from the one-dimensional philosophy of enhanced cooperation as discussed in a previous section. It is not a question of states working closely together for the sake of the Union. Rather, the underlying idea is that variety in preferences should be matched by a corresponding variety in institutional arrangements.

... 'integration à la carte' and 'variable geometry' come closest to the situation modelled by the economic theory of clubs. The expression 'variable geometry' has been used in several meanings. In the meaning most relevant here, it refers to a situation where a subset of member states undertake some project, for instance an industrial or technological project in which other members of the Union are not interested, or to which they are unable to make a positive contribution. Since, by assumption, not all Member States are willing to participate in all EU programmes, this model combines the criterion of differentiation by country, as in multi-speed integration, and by activity or project – as in integration à la carte ...

---

[104] E. Balibar, 'Europe as Vanishing Mediator' (2003) *Constellations* 312, 332–3.

Majone presents a world in which all states can freely and equally choose between different policies. The enlargement process suggests a twist to this, however. Recent entrants have
not been able to join on an equal basis but on others' terms. The club goods described by
Majone have therefore taken the form of newer states not being allowed full access to all the
entitlements of membership. The most discussed example of this concerned free movement of
persons. Both the 2004 and 2007 entrants were subject to '2+3+2' regimes where their own
nationals would only be granted in EU law the same rights to live and work in other EU states
as other EU nationals seven years after their entry into the Union.[105] A more wide-ranging
regime was put in place for Bulgarian and Romanian accession. Both states are subject to a
Cooperation and Verification Mechanism for three years from entry under which the Commission is to monitor their legal obligations and more general performance in a number of fields.
If there is a deterioration in the economic situation in those states or the Commission considers
that they fail to meet their legal obligations or their commitments to improve performance, the
Commission may adopt measures against these states, notably suspending their rights.[106]

As well as this, entry of the new Member States to certain fields of EU policy is being closely
policed. In December 2007, all new EU Member States acceded to the Schengen Convention,
with the exception of three, Cyprus, Romania and Bulgaria, for whom provision was made to
join when ready. Membership of the euro-zone has proved more challenging. Both Slovenia
and Lithuania applied for membership from 1 January 2007. Whilst Slovenia was allowed to
join and adopt the euro as its currency, Lithuania was blocked by the Commission and other
Member States on the grounds that its level of inflation was too high. This move was perceived
as divisive and unfair by a number of the new Member States as Lithuania met all the other
criteria, which at the time was not true of a number of existing members of the euro-zone. On
1 January 2008, Malta and Cyprus also joined the euro-zone, and Slovakia on 1 January 2009,
taking its overall number to sixteen.

8 THE CONSTITUTIONAL TREATY

(i) The European Union Charter of Fundamental Rights and Freedoms and the Treaty of Nice

The achievements of the Treaty of Amsterdam were seen at the time as limited.[107] There were
two areas, in particular, that were seen as 'unfinished'. First, there had been much discussion
about whether the European Union should have its own Bill of Rights. Whilst references were
introduced to fundamental rights and provision was made for expulsion of Member States for
gross violations, a self-standing Bill of Rights was seen by some Member States as a step too
far. The second matter not addressed head on was the institutional pressures generated by possible enlargement of the Union. A Protocol was therefore signed, agreeing that a conference be

---

[105] S. Currie, '"Free" Movers? The Post Accession Experience of Accession: 8 Migrant Workers in the United
Kingdom' (2006) 31 *ELRev.* 207.
[106] Indeed, in 2008, Commission concerns with Bulgarian maladministration led it to suspend payments of €220
million structural funds to Bulgaria. European Commission, *On the Management of EU Funds in Bulgaria*,
COM(2008)496. For comment see 'The European Union and Bulgaria: The New Colonialism', *The Economist*,
19 March 2009.
[107] K. Hughes, 'The 1996 Intergovernmental Conference and EU Enlargement' (1996) 72 *International Affairs* 1;
A. Teasdale, 'The Politics of Qualified Majority Voting in Europe' (1996) *Political Quarterly* 101, 110–15.

convened at least one year before membership of the European Union reached twenty, to carry out a comprehensive review of the composition and functioning of the institutions.

Attention turned, first, to an EU Bill of Rights. The Member States, meeting at Cologne in 1999, agreed that an EU Charter of Fundamental Rights should be established cataloguing such rights. Instead of this being left to intergovernmental negotiations, a special Convention was established to agree the Charter.[108] Chaired by Roman Herzog, formerly the German President, the Convention was composed of fifteen representatives of national governments, thirty representatives of national parliaments, sixteen representatives of the European Parliament and one representative of the Commission. It met in open session, decided upon matters by consensus rather than by voting, and received extensive representations from civil society. Parliamentarians were not only more numerous in the Convention than government representatives, but also more vocal. A total of 805 amendments were put forward by parliamentarians whilst only 356 were put forward by government representatives.[109] It constituted a move away from negotiations between governments to a new form of deliberative decision-making. It was also successful in terms of its outcome: the Convention drafted the European Union Charter of Fundamental Rights and Freedoms which was wide-ranging in the entitlements it recognised. The Charter was adopted by the Convention in October 2000.

On the second matter, institutional reform, discussions began in the same month as the Treaty of Amsterdam came into force: 1 May 1999. There was agreement that negotiations should be exclusively concerned with recasting the institutional settlement so that it would function more efficiently and accommodate new states who might join the Union. Notwithstanding its technicality, this task was a challenging one, for it was a redistributive task involving reallocation of votes or influence within the EU institutions, entailing that for every winner there would be an equivalent loser.

With every state having a veto, no previous IGC had realised its ambitions for management of internal reform. This was also the case for the Treaty of Nice. The Treaty was finally signed on 11 December 2000, after over ninety hours of acrimonious, direct negotiations between the Heads of Government.[110] Even within governmental circles, the agreement was seen as limited and unsatisfactory. Agreement was not reached on many of the items for discussion: most notably the legal status of the EU Charter of Fundamental Rights and Freedoms. Instead, limited reforms were made to the four main institutions, the Commission, the Council, the Parliament and the Court of Justice. QMV was extended into thirty-one further areas, but almost all of these were procedural and were concerned with the appointment of EU officials. The reforms were not only insubstantial but the Treaties were now a confusing and incoherent mess. The Union had now a bewildering gamut of competences, governed by an array of legislative procedures, producing a range of legal instruments. There were thirty-eight combinations of 'possible voting modalities in the Council and participation opportunities of the European Parliament of which 22 were "legislative"'.[111] Whilst, therefore, there did not seem to be many

---

[108] See G. de Búrca, 'The Drafting of the EU Charter of Fundamental Rights' (2001) 26 *EL Rev.* 126.

[109] A. Maurer, 'The Convention, the IGC 2004 and European System Development: A Challenge for Parliamentary Democracy', 7 in *Democracy and Accountability in the Enlarged European Union*, Joint Conference of SWP and the Austrian Academy of Sciences, 7–8 March 2003, www.swp-berlin.org/common/get_document. php?asset_id=689 (accessed 20 July 2009).

[110] M. Gray and A. Stubb, 'The Treaty of Nice: Negotiating a Poisoned Chalice?' (2001) 395 *JCMS* 5.

[111] W. Wessels, 'The Millenium IGC in the EU's Evolution' (2001) 39 *JCMS* 197, 201.

strong reasons to vote against the Treaty of Nice, there did not seem to be many reasons to vote for it. In June 2001, the Irish voted 53.87 per cent against ratification of the Treaty of Nice.[112] A Declaration was added that nothing in the TEU affected Irish military neutrality, something that had been raised as a concern amongst a small number of Irish voters. On the basis of this, a second referendum was held in September 2002, and the Treaty of Nice was approved by 62.89 per cent of the vote.[113]

(ii) The Constitutional Treaty

Dissatisfaction with the substance and the process of Nice had emerged prior to the Irish referendum. At Nice, the Member States announced that there would be yet another IGC in 2004 to consider the significant issues that had not been resolved. These comprised delimitation of powers between the European Union and the Member States; the status of the EU Charter of Fundamental Rights; simplification of the Treaties; and setting out more fully the role of national parliaments in the European architecture. As important as the substance was the process. There was considerable dissatisfaction with this intractable process of closed negotiations between governments running up against deadlines that seemed to be brought by every IGC. In a Declaration at Nice, the Member States called, therefore 'for a deeper and wider debate about the future of the European Union' which would involve 'wide-ranging discussions with all interested parties: representatives of national parliaments and all those reflecting public opinion, namely political, economic and university circles, representatives of civil society, etc.'.[114]

This Declaration had been preceded by a significant debate between political leaders about the nature of institutional reform that had been begun by Joschka Fischer, the German Foreign Minister, at the Humboldt University in Berlin in 2000. Fischer considered that European integration had to have a *finalité*, an end-point, and that this should be a European Constitution:

> These three reforms – the solution of the democracy problem and the need for fundamental reordering of competences both horizontally, i.e. among the European institutions, and vertically, i.e. between Europe, the nation-state and the regions – will only be able to succeed if Europe is established anew with a constitution. In other words: through the realisation of the project of a European Constitution centred around basic, human and civil rights, an equal division of powers between the European institutions and a precise delineation between European and nation-state level. The main axis for such a European Constitution will be the relationship between the Federation and the nation-state.[115]

A number of Heads of Government picked up on this theme. Within two months, Jacques Chirac, the French President, talked of a 'first European Constitution'. Tony Blair, the British Prime Minister, suggested that there should be a new statement of principles about the Union. And in June 2000, Paavo Lipponen, the Finnish Prime Minister, suggested that a special Convention be established to launch a 'constitutionalisation process'.[116]

---

[112] K. Gilland, 'Ireland's (First) Referendum on the Treaty of Nice' (2002) 40 *JCMS* 527.

[113] The Treaty of Nice came into force on 2 February 2003.

[114] Declaration 23 to the Treaty of Nice on the Future of the Union.

[115] J. Fischer, 'From Confederacy to Federation: Thoughts on the Finality of European Integration', Humboldt University, Berlin, 12 May 2000, available at www.jeanmonnetprogram.org/papers/00/joschka_fischer_en.rtf (accessed July 2009).

[116] P. Norman, *The Accidental Constitution: The Story of the European Convention* (Brussels, Eurocomment, 2003) 11–24.

The debate re-emerged a year later, in December 2001, at Laeken in Belgium when Member States had to think about the preparations for the 2004 IGC. There was agreement that the institutional tinkering witnessed at Amsterdam and Nice was neither sufficient to equip the Union for the challenges it faced nor sufficient to engage popular enthusiasm. Instead, what was necessary was a process of democratic regeneration. Such an effort would not only require wide-ranging institutional reform. It was also a process that could not be managed just by an IGC. Accordingly, an extraordinary process was called for. The draft Treaty would be formulated by a Convention, named the Future of Europe Convention, which would be modelled on the Convention used to draft the EU Charter of Fundamental Rights.

Chaired by Giscard d'Estaing, the former French President, the Convention would comprise 105 members from national governments, parliaments, MEPs and the Commission. The accession states would be involved as would civil society. The Convention would meet in plenary session, with all members present, once a month. It was the final decision-making body, responsible for adopting any agreed text. Its decisions were to be taken in public by consensus rather than by vote.

The Convention opened in February 2002. Although its initial mandate was merely to identify options for the subsequent IGC, knowing that a vast majority of the Convention was willing to reach an ambitious agreement, Giscard discarded this idea at the first session stating that its purpose should be a single proposal opening the way for a 'Constitution for Europe'.[117] Sixteen months later, he presented this proposal, the Draft Constitutional Treaty, with much pomp and fanfare to the Member States. The IGC following the Convention was short. There was only one significant item in the Draft Constitutional Treaty which was subject to significant amendment. Spain and Poland were unhappy about the voting rights accorded to them in the EU law-making process. However, after a change of government in Spain and a series of small but important amendments to the text, the Member States changed their position and signed the Constitutional Treaty, at a ceremony in Rome, in October 2004.

To mark both the significance of the Constitutional Treaty and the spirit of democratic renewal, ten Member States arranged for referendums to determine whether or not they should ratify it. The first was held in Spain, where the Treaty was approved by 72 per cent of those who voted. However, in the next referendums, held in France (on 29 May 2005) and in the Netherlands (three days later, on 1 June 2005), the Treaty was roundly rejected, with 55 per cent voting against it in France and 62 per cent voting against it in the Netherlands. Analysis of the reasons for the 'No' vote in the Netherlands and France showed the Constitutional Treaty had little hold or meaning for public debate. Despite voters being reasonably well-informed about the details of the Constitutional Treaty, the reasons for their vote had little to do, in most cases, with its legal details. Opponents were protesting against globalisation, the consequences of the 2004 enlargement, fears about Turkish membership of the Union, and in the Netherlands there was anger amongst voters at the perceived power of the large Member States in the Union.[118]

---

[117] P. Magnette, 'In the Name of Simplification: Coping with Constitutional Conflicts in the Convention on the Future of Europe' (2005) 11 *ELJ* 432, 436.

[118] Flash Eurobarometer 171 and 172, *European Constitution: Post-Referendum Survey in France and in The Netherlands*. This was notwithstanding that 88 per cent of the French and 82 per cent of the Dutch still had positive perceptions of the Union in the period after the referendum. European Commission, *The Period of Reflection and Plan D*, COM(2006)212, 2.

In short, citizens did not buy into the need to create a new form of political community to which they would have loyalty and affinity and which had to be 'democratically regenerated' by them. Part of the reason is that such loyalty or affinity is challenging to generate. Bartolini has observed that it is 'an affective or emotional relationship to the organization or group that one belongs to, and makes it difficult (if not impossible) to contemplate the possibility of abandoning such a group or organization'. He notes that it is built upon the identity, solidarity and trust that exist between members of a group.[119] The development of such elements required much effort within the national context. Most notably, Bartolini has observed that the cultural, economic, coercion and politico-administrative boundaries of any modern state generally coincide and reinforce each other.[120] That is to say, there is a *national* system of law and order, a *national* community with its own myths and symbols, a *national* welfare system, a *national* economy and a *national* administration. For better or worse, this reinforcement generates common identities. By contrast, such elements are almost completely absent in the EU context.[121] To assume that they could be generated by a Convention of 105 people and a ballot was always optimistic. Instead, the absence of these elements gave the process a somewhat surreal feel with both academics and observers noting that much of the debate at the Future of Europe Convention was dominated by a disembodied, elite discourse marked by the absence of significant disagreement.[122]

By the end of June 2005, ratification of the Constitutional Treaty had reached an impasse. A significant majority of Member States, eighteen, had ratified the Treaty, with Luxembourg also having held a positive referendum. Of the remaining seven Member States, six (Czech Republic, Denmark, Ireland, Poland, Portugal and the United Kingdom), were scheduled to hold their own referendums. Of these, there was a significant chance of a 'No' vote in all bar Portugal. When combined with the French and Dutch 'No' votes, this not only suggested that there would be eight states unable to ratify the Treaty. It also suggested a scenario in which, out of the ten states holding referendums, the overwhelming majority, seven, might have voted against the project. The popular vote was out on the European Union.

9 THE LISBON TREATY

(i) The road to Lisbon

The Union was faced not with a single recalcitrant state, such as Denmark and Ireland, as with previous amending Treaties. It was instead confronted with a deep divide in which two-thirds of Member States wished to press ahead whilst one-third did not. A period of reflection was called for by the European Council which lasted until late 2006, when the Finnish government prepared the ground by engaging in a series of consultations on how to achieve institutional reform. Alongside this, a series of prominent politicians, acting under the umbrella of the organisation

---

[119] S. Bartolini, *Restructuring Europe: Centre Formation, System Building, and Political Structuring Between the Nation State and the European Union* (Oxford, Oxford University Press, 2005) 31.

[120] *Ibid.* 410.

[121] For a not dissimilar argument see P. Schmitter, 'Making Sense of the EU: Democracy in Europe and Europe's Democratization' (2003) 14 *Journal of Democracy* 71.

[122] Norman, above n. 116, 326–38; G. Stuart, *The Making of Europe's Constitution* (London, Fabian Society, 2003) 19–24. C. Skach, 'We the Peoples? Constitutionalising the European Union' (2005) 43 *JCMS* 149.

named the Action Committee for European Democracy, began to publish articles in the press indicating that the time for listening was over and that the time for action had begun.[123]

In March 2007, at the fiftieth anniversary of the Treaty of Rome, the German government obtained a commitment from the other Member States to place 'the European Union on a renewed common basis before the European Parliament elections in 2009'.[124] In other words, they had committed to a deadline for ratifying a new treaty.

The German government's strategy for reaching an agreement was to close the gap between the Member States in a highly structured manner. 'Political agreement' on the central points of disagreement was reached in closed, confidential negotiations between ministries, named 'sherpas'. Only when political agreement was reached on the main points would the second stage, an IGC, be opened. Its tasks, however, would be limited by the mandate of the political agreement, and so restricted to translating the political agreement into legal detail and resolving any ambiguities. States wishing to introduce new points or reopen old debates would run the risk of being accused of having breached the existing political agreement, and therefore of having acted in bad faith. The process was thus to be a relatively confined affair subject to few external risks or interventions. In terms of substance, the strategy involved the use of the Constitutional Treaty as a starting point, along with the question of what had to be offered to make the Treaty acceptable to those national governments constituting the recalcitrant one-third. Ultimately, for these states, the Treaty was not a question of reform, but a series of individual concessions.

The Heads of Government met between 21 and 23 June 2007 to conclude the first stage of the process. The outcome was a sixteen-page mandate that was to provide the basis for an IGC that the Heads of Government indicated was to be completed by December 2007 and was to be confined to the terms of the mandate. It also indicated that the new Treaty was to follow the text of the Constitutional Treaty unless otherwise specified by the mandate. The subsequent IGC was, consequently, highly limited. By 19 October a text had been agreed informally between the Member States. On 13 December 2007, the new text, the Treaty of Lisbon was formally signed.

The conclusion of the Treaty was a significant coup. It involved amendments to all of the articles in the TEU and to 216 provisions in the EC Treaty.[125] There were, moreover, significant differences that had to be bridged between the twenty-seven Member States, each with their own distinct agenda and constituencies. Yet this negotiating triumph came at a cost. In particular, it created a double bind. If the Treaty of Lisbon differed significantly from the Constitutional Treaty, its nature of reform was more closed and more accelerated than any other to date. There was a lack of transparency and an exclusion of national parliaments that still remains to be justified. If the Treaty of Lisbon was not substantially different from the Constitutional Treaty, that would open negotiators to charges of arrogance for ignoring the referendum results in France and the Netherlands.

---

[123] See www.iue.it/RSCAS/research/ACED/MissionStatement.shtml (accessed 18 July 2009).

[124] EU Council, Declaration on the occasion of the fiftieth anniversary of the signature of the Treaty of Rome, Brussels, 25 March 2007, para. 3.

[125] Statewatch, www.statewatch.org/news/2007/oct/eu-refrom-treaty-tec-external-relations-3-5.pdf (accessed 20 July 2009).

(ii) The Treaty of Lisbon[126]

(a) Two treaties of equal value: the Treaty on European Union and the Treaty on the Functioning of the European Union

The Treaty of Lisbon created two new treaties to replace the previous framework.[127] One, confusingly, is named the Treaty on European Union (TEU). The central items set out by it are as follows:

- the mission and values of the European Union: respect for the rule of law, the principle of limited powers, respect for national identities and upholding democracy and fundamental rights;
- the democratic principles of the Union and providing for the active contribution of national parliaments to the functioning of the European Union;
- a neighbourhood policy, whereby the Union is to develop a special relationship with neighbouring countries;
- the composition and central functions of the EU institutions;
- detailed provisions on the Union's external action in the TEU, in particular both its Common Foreign and Security Policy and its common security and defence policy;
- procedures are set out for amendment of the two Treaties;
- legal personality for the Union;
- provisions governing asymmetric integration; these include the circumstances in which a Member State may leave or be expelled from the Union and when states may engage in enhanced cooperation, the procedure whereby some Member States may develop EU legislation amongst themselves where there is not sufficient will for that legislation to be adopted by all Member States.

The second treaty is the Treaty on the Functioning of the European Union (TFEU). This sets out the explicit competences of the Union and, with the exception of external action, the detailed procedures to be used in each policy field. In legislative style, it is similar therefore to the existing EC Treaty. There is, however, one significant adaptation taken from the Constitutional Treaty: the competences and their nature are catalogued at the beginning of the TFEU.[128]

Article 3 TFEU

1. The Union shall have exclusive competence in the following areas:
   (a) customs union;
   (b) the establishing of the competition rules necessary for the functioning of internal market;
   (c) monetary policy for the Member States whose currency is the euro;

---

[126] As with discussion of other Treaty amendments in this chapter, the section below covers only the most salient features with detailed discussion left to subsequent chapters.

[127] On the Treaty of Lisbon see P. Craig, 'The Treaty of Lisbon: Process, Architecture and Substance' (2008) 33 *ELRev.* 137; M. Dougan, 'The Treaty of Lisbon 2007: Winning Minds not Hearts' (2008) 45 *CMLRev.* 617; Y. Devuyst, 'The European Union's Institutional Balance After the Treaty of Lisbon: "Community Method" and "Democratic Deficit" Reassessed' (2008) 39 *Georgetown Journal of International Law* 247. A thoughtful and detailed assessment is provided by House of Lords European Union Committee, *The Treaty of Lisbon: An Impact Assessment* (London, HL, 10th Report, Session 2007–08, 2008).

[128] The discussion is set out in more detail in Chapter 5 at pp. 206 *et seq.*

(d) the conservation of marine biological resources under the common fisheries policy;

(e) common commercial policy.

2. The Union shall also have exclusive competence for the conclusion of an international agreement when its conclusion is provided for in a legislative act of the Union or is necessary to enable the Union to exercise its internal competence, or insofar as its conclusion may affect common rules or alter their scope.

Article 4 TFEU

1. The Union shall share competence with the Member States where the Treaties confer on it a competence which does not relate to the areas referred to in Articles 3 and 6.

2. Shared competence between the Union and the Member States applies in the following principal areas:

   (a) internal market;

   (b) social policy, for the aspects defined in this Treaty;

   (c) economic, social and territorial cohesion;

   (d) agriculture and fisheries, excluding the conservation of marine biological resources;

   (e) environment;

   (f) consumer protection;

   (g) transport;

   (h) trans-European networks;

   (i) energy;

   (j) area of freedom, security and justice;

   (k) common safety concerns in public health matters, for the aspects defined in this Treaty.

3. In the areas of research, technological development and space, the Union shall have competence to carry out activities, in particular to define and implement programmes; however, the exercise of that competence shall not result in Member States being prevented from exercising theirs.

4. In the areas of development cooperation and humanitarian aid, the Union shall have competence to carry out activities and conduct a common policy; however, the exercise of that competence shall not result in Member States being prevented from exercising theirs.

Article 5 TFEU

1. The Member States shall coordinate their economic policies within the Union. To this end, the Council shall adopt measures, in particular broad guidelines for these policies. Specific provisions shall apply to those Member States whose currency is the euro.

2. The Union shall take measures to ensure coordination of the employment policies of the Member States, in particular by defining guidelines for these policies.

3. The Union may take initiatives to ensure coordination of Member States' social policies.

Article 6 TFEU

The Union shall have competence to carry out actions to support, coordinate or supplement the actions of the Member States. The areas of such action shall, at European level, be:
(a) protection and improvement of human health;
(b) industry;
(c) culture;
(d) tourism;
(e) education, vocational training, youth and sport;
(f) civil protection;
(g) administrative cooperation.

Each treaty is to have 'the same legal value'.[129] It is however unclear what this means. Is each to be interpreted in the light of the other? If that is the case, it could lead to the more detailed TFEU being given an expanded remit as a result of the broader mission of the TEU. Or does it mean that each curtails the other? In this case, many of the broader provisions of the TEU will be little more than rhetorical as they will be curtailed by the substance of the TFEU.

(b) Enhancing the democratic credentials of the Union

A different ethos permeates the Lisbon Treaty than the Constitutional Treaty. The latter was concerned to establish an autonomous pan-European constitutional democracy. The Constitutional Treaty therefore carried a number of procedures and symbols associated with constitutional democracy. At the most ephemeral level, there was provision for a European Union flag, anthem, motto and holiday. The Constitutional Treaty also contained all the tools of an autonomous European constitutional democracy. There was a primacy clause asserting the precedence of EU law over national law within the limits of the Treaty. A Bill of Rights of sorts was established with the incorporation of the EU Charter of Fundamental Rights, and EU Regulations and Directives were to become known as 'laws' or 'framework laws'. The Union was to have its own legal personality and Foreign Minister. Whilst the exact working out of these provisions resulted in much curtailed powers than those enjoyed by most liberal democratic states, they did convey the imagery of statehood.

The Treaty of Lisbon, in the words of the mandate to the IGC, abandoned the 'constitutional concept'.[130] Almost all the above provisions were removed by the Treaty of Lisbon. The provision establishing the primacy of EU law over national law and the detailed elaboration of the Charter were removed from the main text of the Treaty. A Declaration was instead attached setting out the primacy of EU law and a provision added requiring the Union to respect the rights, freedoms and principles in the Charter. Union legislative measures were to return to their traditional designation as Regulations and Directives, and the Foreign Minister was to be known as the High Representative. To be sure, sixteen Member States signed a Declaration stating that the symbols of the Union (the flag, the anthem, the motto, the provision on the

---

[129] Article 1(2) TFEU.
[130] EU Council, IGC 2007 Mandate, Brussels, 26 June 2007, para. 1.

euro as the European Union currency and the holiday) would remain as 'symbols to express the sense of community of the people in the European Union and their allegiance to it'.[131] Yet the fact that this was hidden away as a remote Declaration signed by a bare majority of states indicated constitutionalism's fall from grace.

If the constitutional conceit was abandoned by Lisbon, there was still a concern that the democratic qualities of the Union should have a more autonomous presence so that a Frankenstein should not be created which develops large numbers of laws and administers lives in an undemocratic way. This ethos is rooted around a twin set of principles.

The first is that the European Union is founded upon and must respect a set of liberal values that are shared across the Union and form part of a common identity. The nature and content of these values are set out in the first substantive provision of the TEU.

Article 2 TEU

The Union is founded on the values of respect for human dignity, freedom, democracy, equality, the rule of law and respect for human rights, including the rights of persons belonging to minorities. These values are common to the Member States in a society in which pluralism, non-discrimination, tolerance, justice, solidarity and equality between women and men prevail.

These values are not rhetorical, nor do they form some general aspirational goal. Instead, they are to be recognised by the Union, must not be violated by it, and the Union commits itself to external policing by the European Court of Human Rights.[132] The commitment to respect fundamental rights was not uncontroversial. It begs questions as to which values were to be protected and whether they would be used to bootstrap new roles for the European Union. These concerns were strongly articulated by the British and Polish governments and a Protocol was therefore added, which stated that the Charter did not extend the ability of any court to declare Polish or British measures incompatible with EU fundamental rights law. As these states had particular concerns about the development of EU social rights, the Protocol provided that Title IV of the Charter, in which most of these rights were incorporated, was only justiciable in these states insofar as the latter provided for them in national law.

The other set of principles is a more explicit commitment by the Union to democracy. The Lisbon Treaty, in particular, requires the Union to respect two forms of democracy: representative democracy and participatory democracy.[133] These principles are not just constraints that the Union must not violate. They are also a statement of its qualities. The idea of the European Union being a representative democracy was challenged before the German Constitutional Court in a challenge to the ratification of the Lisbon Treaty. Whilst allowing for the ratification of the Treaty, in that it only provided for limited powers to be conferred on the European Union, the German Constitutional Court agreed that the European Union was not a democracy when measured against national standards. It considered representative democracy, the principle of a legislator based upon one person per vote, as the heart of a democratic system. It also

---

[131] Declaration 52 to the Treaty of Lisbon on the symbols of the European Union.
[132] Article 6(1) TEU. This is dealt with in much more detail in Chapter 6 at pp. 259–62.
[133] Article 10 TEU.

considered the Union to be characterised by what it termed 'excessive federalisation'. By this, it meant the principle, as in federal systems, of equality between the constituent elements. In the case of the European Union, this meant equality of votes between the nation-states.

2 BvE 2/08 *Gauweiler* v *Treaty of Lisbon*, Judgment of 30 June 2009

280. Measured against requirements in a constitutional state, the European Union lacks, even after the entry into force of the Treaty of Lisbon, a political decision-making body which has come into being by equal election of all citizens of the Union and which is able to uniformly represent the will of the people. What is also lacking in this connection is a system of organisation of political rule in which a will of the European majority carries the formation of the government in such a way that the will goes back to free and equal electoral decisions and a genuine competition between government and opposition which is transparent for the citizens, can come about … contrary to the claim that Article 10.1 TEU Lisbon seems to make according to its wording, the European Parliament is not a body of representation of a sovereign European people. This is reflected in the fact that it, as the representation of the peoples in their respectively assigned national contingents of Members, is not laid out as a body of representation of the citizens of the Union as an undistinguished unity according to the principle of electoral equality.

281. Also in their elaboration by the Treaty of Lisbon, no independent people's sovereignty of the citizens of the Union in their entirety results from the competences of the European Union. If a decision between political lines in the European Parliament receives a narrow majority, there is no guarantee of the majority of votes cast representing a majority of the citizens of the Union. Therefore the formation, from within Parliament, of an independent government vested with the competences that are usual in states would meet with fundamental objections. Possibly, a numerical minority of citizens existing according to the ratio of representation could govern, through a majority of Members of Parliament, against the political will of an opposition majority of citizens of the Union, which does not find itself represented as a majority. It is true that the principle of electoral equality only ensures a maximum degree of exactness as regards the will of the people under the conditions of a system of strict proportional representation. But also in majority voting systems, there is a sufficient guarantee of electoral equality for the votes at any rate as regards the value counted and the chance of success, whereas it is missed if any contingent that is not merely insignificant is established.

282. For a free democratic fundamental order of a state …, the equality of all citizens when making use of their right to vote is one of the essential foundations of state order …

288. It is true that the democracy of the European Union is approximated to federalised state concepts; measured against the principle of representative democracy, however, it would to a considerable degree show excessive federalisation. With the personal composition of the European Council, of the Council, the Commission and the Court of Justice of the European Union, the principle of the equality of states remains linked to national rights of determination, rights which are, in principle, equal. Even for a European Parliament elected with due account to equality, this structure would be a considerable obstacle for asserting a representative will of the parliamentary majority with regard to persons or subject-matters. Also after the entry into force of the Treaty of Lisbon, the Court of Justice, for instance, must always be staffed according to the principle 'one state, one judge' and under the determining influence of the Member States regardless of their number of inhabitants. The functioning of the European Union continues to be characterised by the influence of the negotiating governments and the subject-related administrative and formative competence of the Commission even though the

rights of participation of the European Parliament have been strengthened on the whole. Within this system, the parliamentary influence has been consistently further developed with Parliament's being accorded the right to veto in central areas of legislation. With the ordinary legislative procedure, the Treaty of Lisbon makes a norm what is already factually decisive under the currently applicable law in many areas: in the co-decision procedure, a directive or a regulation cannot be adopted against the will of the European Parliament.

289. The deficit of European public authority that exists when measured against requirements on democracy in states cannot be compensated by other provisions of the Treaty of Lisbon and to that extent, it cannot be justified.

290. The European Union tries to compensate the existing considerable degree of excessive federalisation in particular by strengthening the citizens' and associations' rights aimed at participation and transparency, as well as by enhancing the role of the national parliaments and of the regions. The Treaty of Lisbon strengthens these elements of participative democracy aimed at procedural participation. Apart from the elements of complementary participative democracy, such as the precept of providing, in a suitable manner, the citizens of the Union and the 'representative' associations with the possibility of communicating their views, the Treaty of Lisbon also provides for elements of associative and direct democracy (Article 11 TEU Lisbon). They include the dialogue of the institutions of the Union with 'representative' associations and the civil society as well as the European citizens' initiative. The European citizens' initiative makes it possible to invite the Commission to submit any appropriate proposal on the regulation of political matters. Such an invitation is subject to a quorum of not less than one million citizens of the Union who have to be nationals of a 'significant number of Member States' (Article 11.4 TEU Lisbon). The citizens' initiative is restricted to issues within the framework of the powers of the Commission and it requires concretisation of its procedures and conditions under secondary law by a regulation...

293. Also the institutional recognition of the Member States' Parliaments by the Treaty of Lisbon cannot compensate for the deficit in the direct track of legitimisation of the European public authority that is based on the election of the Members of the European Parliament. The status of national parliaments is considerably curtailed by the reduction of decisions requiring unanimity and the supranationalisation of police and judicial cooperation in criminal matters. Compensation, provided for by the Treaty, by the procedural strengthening of subsidiarity shifts existing political rights of self-determination to procedural possibilities of intervention and judicially assertable claims of participation; this was concurringly emphasised in the oral hearing.

294. Neither the additional rights of participation, which are strongly interlocked as regards the effects of their many levels of action and in view of the large number of national parliaments, nor rights of petition which are associative and have a direct effect vis-à-vis the Commission are suited to replace the majority rule which is established by an election. They are intended to, and indeed can, ultimately increase the level of legitimisation all the same under the conditions of a *Staatenverbund* (association of States) with restricted tasks.

The view of the German Constitutional Court is not simply that the European Union is not yet sufficiently democratic. It is that it can never be fully democratic. For the Union to realise the standard of democracy set by the German Constitutional Court, it would have to turn itself into a unitary state. One would need a single legislative assembly in which representation in the dominant chamber was not allocated according seats per Member State but simply on the basis of European citizenship. As we shall see, the only directly elected body, the European Parliament, is not the dominant chamber, and there is no prospect of seats being allocated other than on a national basis. Indeed, the idea of national allocation (or excessive federalisation in the language of the German Constitutional Court) permeates all EU decision-making structures. To eradicate it is not only politically unrealistic but would create a beast unrecognisable from the current European Union.

The judgment is thus a powerful indictment of the European Union. Whilst used by the German Constitutional Court to limit the tasks which can be granted to the Union,[134] it also begs questions about the legitimacy of the European Union when acting within its aegis. For, if the Union can only look at best for what the German Constitutional Court terms 'democratic supplementation'[135] there is a challenge to justify why it should have wide-reaching authority over our lives or precedence over national laws or local traditions.

(c) Supranationalisation of the Union

The Lisbon Treaty kept the new explicit competences enumerated by the Constitutional Treaty: energy, intellectual property, space, humanitarian aid, sport and civil protection. In addition, it added a further one: that of climate change. Yet there was already competence to carry out activity here under other legal bases, and the Union had already taken significant measures in all these fields. The most important reform was not a formal extension of EU powers but an abolition of the three pillar structure established at Maastricht. All three pillars were brought into a single framework. Whilst provision was made for the Common Foreign and Security Policy to continue to be treated discretely, activities governed by the third pillar, namely policing and judicial cooperation in criminal matters, were now to be governed by the same procedures as those traditionally applied to EC activities. This reform had two important implications. The first was a significant extension of the supranational qualities and procedures of the Union to govern more extensively the sensitive fields of policing and criminal justice. The second was the extension of the so-called flexibility provision which permits legislation to be adopted to realise broad EU objectives if no more specific legal provision allows this. As the previous procedure applied only to the EC Treaty, the new procedure has a wider remit as it applies not merely to Community but to all Union activity.

Member States sought to draw some of the teeth from the unification of the pillars through the insertion of a new proviso stating that national security remains the sole responsibility of each Member State. The flexibility provision was amended so that it cannot be used as a legal base for matters relating to common and foreign security, and a Declaration was inserted stipulating that it could not be used to enable de facto amendment of the Treaties. In addition, specific provision was made for the United Kingdom and Ireland. A Protocol was introduced which amends and extends that granted at Amsterdam. In addition to being free to decide whether or not to participate in individual pieces of legislation on visas, asylum, immigration and other policies related to free movement of persons, they had now a parallel entitlement in the fields of policing and judicial cooperation in criminal justice. If either Member State chooses not to participate, it would not be bound by that legislation.

---

[134] See pp. 194–8.
[135] This term is used at para. 272 of the judgment, above n. 82.

(d) Recasting the institutional setting

The Constitutional Treaty was largely about institutional reform. Its proposals were adopted largely unscathed in the Treaty of Lisbon. QMV was extended to about fifty new areas. Provision was also made for legislative procedures based on the unanimity vote in the Council to be altered to QMV without the need for an IGC. In terms of the powers of the European Parliament, the co-decision procedure, which grants it a veto, has been applied to forty new areas. In addition, it has been granted significant powers of assent, most notably with regard to Article 352 TFEU and anti-discrimination, whereby its agreement must be obtained before any legislative proposal can become law. The Treaty of Lisbon also extended the powers granted to national parliaments. They were given additional time to consider legislative proposals and increased powers to call for a proposal to be reviewed on the ground that it does not comply with the principle of subsidiarity, which provides that EU measures should only be adopted if the objectives of the action cannot be sufficiently achieved by Member States and by reason of their scale or effects can be better realised through Union action.

This increase in QMV and European Parliament powers led to the introduction of some caveats. 'Brake' procedures were added where national governments could insist that the matter be discussed at European Council level – and therefore be subject to unanimity – if a measure touched fundamental aspects of their social security or criminal justice systems. The French government, in particular, was concerned that market liberalising measures might in some way undermine national public services. A Protocol on Services of General Interest was therefore added which stated that nothing in the Treaties affected the competence of Member States to provide, commission or organise non-economic services of a general interest.[136]

Internal reforms were also made to the EU institutions. Commission membership is slimmed down to comprise, from 2014, a number corresponding to two-thirds of the number of the Member States. The President of the Commission was also given the unilateral power to dismiss individual Commissioners. With regard to the European Parliament, the cap on the number of MEPs in the European Parliament, 732, is retained. The central change to the Council was the introduction of a new formula for QMV in which there will be a qualified majority if 55 per cent of states representing at least 65 per cent of the population vote for it, and at least four states are required to vote against a measure for it to be blocked. Finally, the European Council was finally recognised as a formal EU institution.

There were also a number of institutional innovations. First, a President of the European Council elected by the European Council for a once renewable two and a half year period is established. Her job will be to drive forward and prepare the work of that institution. Secondly, a High Representative of the European Union is established. A member of both the Council and the Commission, her duty is to represent the Union in matters relating to the Common Foreign and Security Policy and ensure the consistency of the Union's external action. Finally, provision is made for citizens' initiatives whereby the Commission is obliged to consider proposals for legal measures made by petitions of one million citizens who are nationals of a significant number of Member States.

---

[136] See pp. 1035–7.

(iii) Ratification of the Lisbon Treaty

The ratification of the Lisbon Treaty was to follow the new ethos set out by that Treaty. This was to be no big pan-European constitutional moment in which, through referendums, the peoples of Europe participated in the creation of a new pan-European constitutional democracy. Instead, ratification was to take place, discretely, through national processes, which were in most cases national parliamentary ones. Indeed, Hungary set a record by ratifying the Lisbon Treaty four days after its signature. Only one state, Ireland, was to have a referendum, and this was because it was constitutionally required to do so.

If the ethos and symbolism of the Lisbon Treaty were different from the Constitutional Treaty, for the overwhelming majority of states, the institutional detail and extension of supranational competences were not significantly so.[137] This begged the question as to what weight was being given to the referendum results in the Netherlands and France and for the promises to hold referendums in the five other states which had promised to do so and had never held a referendum.

The question was particularly challenging for two very different reasons. The first relates to the nature of the Constitutional Treaty process. As has been said, this process had (unsuccessfully) been about mobilising popular loyalty, affection and support for the European integration process. The route chosen was to garner these elements around a particular document, the Constitutional Treaty. European publics were asked to bless a text that had been developed in a civil and plural manner. This was always an optimistic strategy, but, alongside this, it conveys the message to all that this text has a significance of the highest order. If the substance of this text is now to be adopted not only through different processes but through processes that seem to fly against previous wishes, a climate of mistrust is unsurprising. The second relates to the nature of the European Union. Selling institutional reform to the public is hard work in any circumstances, as procedures seem arcane and there is no obvious large policy goal, such as the single market or EMU, around which debate can be mobilised. The European Union is particularly difficult, for, as the German Constitutional Court pointed out, its procedures are hybrid ones, oscillating between being similar but not identical to those found in national democracies and intergovernmental ones. Ratification was not therefore straightforward.

On 12 June 2008, the Irish referendum on the Lisbon Treaty was held; 53.4 per cent of the voters rejected it. Subsequent analysis of the 'No' vote suggested lack of information about the Lisbon Treaty as an important determinant, as well as concerns about perceived threats to Irish abortion laws and neutrality, as well as possible conscription to a pan-European army. None of these were countenanced by the Lisbon Treaty amendments. The only amendment that weighed heavily was the possible loss of an Irish Commissioner generated by the reduction of the Commission.[138]

In response, in December 2008, national governments agreed that they would take a Decision upon the entry into force of the Lisbon Treaty providing that the Commission would retain

---

[137] For a thoughtful comparison see House of Commons, *EU Reform: A New Treaty or an Old Constitution*, Research Paper 07/64 (London, House of Commons, 2007). Ireland and the United Kingdom obtained opt-outs from the most significant extension of supranational competences, policing and judicial cooperation in criminal matters, something not granted to them by the Constitutional Treaty.

[138] The main research for the Irish government was carried out by Milward Brown IMS, Post Lisbon Treaty Research Findings, available at http://angl.concourt.cz/angl_verze/cases.php (accessed 20 July 2009).

one Commissioner from each Member State.[139] This will, of course, prevent its being reduced to two-thirds of the number of Member States, and is, in effect, an amendment to the Lisbon Treaty. In June 2009, the Member States set out three sets of guarantees in a European Council Decision that nothing in the Lisbon Treaty would:

- affect the scope or applicability of the rights to life, protection of the family or in respect of education as set out in the Irish Constitution;
- change in any way, for any Member State, the extent or operation of EU competence in respect to taxation;
- prejudice the security and defence policy of any Member State, provide for the creation of a European army or conscription, or affect a state's right to decide whether or not to participate in a military operation.[140]

On the basis of this, the Irish government held a second referendum on 2 October 2009. The Lisbon Treaty was approved by 67 per cent of the vote. However, this was not the end of the process. The Czech government extracted a final concession before ratification. The same guarantees granted to Poland and the United Kingdom in respect of the EU Charter of Fundamental Rights were to be granted to it.

The tawdriness to the conclusion of this process contrasts markedly with the fanfare surrounding the beginning of the Future of Europe Convention; for the Heads of Government took the opportunity in the Decisions on Ireland to bring in a series of general amendments and interpretations to the Treaty of Lisbon on the size of the Commission, its ambit on taxation and its impact on national security and defence policies. In addition, at the June 2009 summit, they passed a further Solemn Declaration on Workers' Rights, Social Policy and Other Issues.[141] Whilst only repeating the wording of the Treaty of Lisbon, it emphasised the responsibility of Member States for delivery of education and health, and importance of local autonomy in the provision and organisation of services of general economic interest: a message that EU law is to interfere as little as possible in these fields as well. Whatever the substantive merits of the case, the status of these is unclear. They are not formal amendments that have gone through appropriate EU or national processes or through any form of deliberation. Their legality and relationship to the Lisbon Treaty is uncertain. And it may be that this casualness with procedure will come back to haunt the Member States if, for example, the size of the Commission is challenged before a court.

The Irish referendums carried another message for those interested in European integration. The lack of knowledge about the process and the power of the 'myths' surrounding the Treaty of Lisbon illustrated the lack of depth of popular interest in the process, and the difficulty of mobilising popular loyalty for the project. This raises doubts about how democratically legitimate the process can ever be, and raises immediate concerns to make sure that the process is properly contained.

To this end, the process was challenged before national constitutional courts, most notably those in the Czech Republic[142] and Germany.[143] Both constitutional courts focused on whether excessive powers had been granted to the Union, albeit that the bases were different. For the Czech Constitutional Court, this derived from the Czech Republic being a democratic state

---

[139] Conclusions of the Brussels European Council, 11/12 December 2008, I.2, EU Council, 17271/1/08 Rev. 1.
[140] Conclusions of the Brussels European Council, 18/19 June 2009, Annex 1, EU Council 11125/2/09/Rev. 2.
[141] *Ibid.* Annex 2.   [142] Pl ÚS 19/08 *Treaty of Lisbon*, Judgment of 26 November 2008, available at www.usoud.cz/clarek; Pl ÚS 29/09 Treaty of Lisbon II, Judgment of 3 November 2009.
[143] 2 BvE 2/08 *Gauweiler* v *Treaty of Lisbon*, Judgment of 30 June 2009.

based upon the rule of law. This entailed that unlimited powers could not be transferred to another body such as the European Union. For the German Constitutional Court, it lay in the principle of self-determination incorporated in the right of each German citizen to vote in the Bundestag (the German Parliament). This entailed that the competences central to Germany's constitutional identity were not transferred to the EU level, as the latter lacked sufficient democratic structures to safeguard this principle.

In both instances, the language used by the courts was similar in tone to that used by the national constitutional courts vetting the Maastricht Treaty. Yet this time, both courts went a step further than simply placing a marker over the integration process. Whilst allowing for ratification of the Lisbon Treaty, both expressed concerns about individual provisions, thereby holding out the possibility of future review. Both also expressed concerns about the vagueness and possibility for abuse of the simplified revision procedure. The German Constitutional Court, in particular, considered that any revision using that procedure was a formal amendment, which would be open to constitutional review and would need ratification by both German parliamentary chambers, the Bundestag and the Bundesrat. There were further concerns from both courts. The Czech Constitutional Court was unhappy about the lack of clarity surrounding the Union's treaty-making powers and the German Constitutional Court was concerned about the vagueness and breadth of the flexibility provision. Whilst these amounted to grumblings in both cases rather than opposition, these grumblings suggested that use of these procedures is likely to be subject to particular scrutiny by these courts.

This brings us to the final paradox of the Treaty of Lisbon. It started as a process intended to open up European integration to greater popular participation. It has been allowed to be realised by the most intergovernmental body of the Union, the European Council, and by national constitutional courts. The price exacted by these bodies is a far more active control over European integration in the future. The European Council has taken it upon itself to interpret the Treaties and national constitutional courts have suggested that they are more amenable to challenges to EU acts on the grounds that these are ultra vires. Neither the European Council nor the courts are majoritarian institutions. Yet, it is they who have taken on the burden of the safeguarding of the European ideal, whilst, in the case of the German Constitutional Court at least, seriously questioning its democratic credentials.

FURTHER READING

S. Bartolini, *Restructuring Europe: Centre Formation, System Building, and Political Structuring Between the Nation State and the European Union* (Oxford, Oxford University Press, 2005)

G. Delanty, *Inventing Europe: Idea, Identity, Reality* (Basingstoke, Macmillan, 1995)

M. Dougan, 'The Treaty of Lisbon 2007: Winning Minds Not Hearts' (2008) 45 *Common Market Law Review* 617

N. Fligstein, *Euro-Clash: The EU, European Identity and the Future of Europe* (Oxford, Oxford University Press, 2008)

J. Gillingham, *European Integration 1950–2003: Superstate or New Market Economy* (Cambridge, Cambridge University Press, 2003)

J. Le Goff, *The Birth of Europe* (Oxford, Blackwell, 2005)

G. Majone, *Dilemmas of European Integration: The Ambiguities and Pitfalls of Integration by Stealth* (Oxford, Oxford University Press, 2005)

K. Middlemas, *Orchestrating Europe: The Informal Politics of European Union 1973–1995* (London, Fontana, 1995)

A. Milward, *The Reconstruction of Western Europe 1945–51* (London, Methuen, 1984)

A. Moravcsik, *The Choice for Europe: Social Purpose and State Power from Messina to Maastricht* (Ithaca, NY, Cornell University Press, 1998)

A. Pagden (ed.), *The Idea of Europe: From Antiquity to the European Union* (Cambridge, Cambridge University Press, 2002)

F. Scharpf, *Governing in Europe: Effective and Democratic?* (New York, Oxford University Press, 1999)

C. Shore, *Building Europe: The Cultural Politics of European Integration* (London and New York, Routledge, 2000)

J. Zielonka, *Europe as Empire: The Nature of the Enlarged European Union* (Oxford, Oxford University Press, 2006)

2

The EU Institutions

CONTENTS

1 INTRODUCTION

This chapter looks at the institutional settlement that governs the European Union.

Section 2 considers the organisation and powers of the European Commission. An independent administration, the Commission is the central institution for proposing legislation and for securing national government compliance with that legislation. It has been delegated significant law-making powers and is responsible for many of the executive tasks of the Union.

The wide-ranging nature of the Commission's powers has led to considerable speciali-sation within the Commission and to its delegating significant administrative powers to specialised agencies. It has also resulted in the Commission being dependent on national administrations for much of the administration of the Union whilst having a responsibility for supervising the latter's performance. The consequence is an executive order with exten-sive powers, marked by specialisation and mutually reinforcing relations between differ-ent administrative actors, which escapes accountability to either pan-European or national democratic constituencies.

Section 3 considers the Council of Ministers. The Council is composed of national ministers and has the final power of decision over almost all fields of EU law. Much debate centres on the level of national influence within the Council, in particular whether a measure is decided by unanimity or by qualified majority voting (QMV) and the weighting of national votes within QMV. In practice, most Decisions are taken without a vote and this shifts the question to how influence is exercised and the quality of debate that takes place. The Council's power is lim-ited by its specialisation and by its floating membership. This has led to its being particularly dependent on the Committee of Permanent Representatives (COREPER), which prepares the Council's work, takes many of its Decisions and mediates with ministries back in the national capitals to formulate common positions.

Section 4 considers the European Council. This comprises the Heads of Government; the central roles of the European Council are to provide political direction to the Union and to resolve disputes that have otherwise proved intractable. It has historically been beset by a lack of infrastructure and a perceived lack of continuity, as the Presidency of the Council and of the European Council rotates between Member States every six months. The Lisbon Treaty creates a new fixed post of President of the European Council to prepare and to ensure follow-up to the meetings. If the European Council is to have an increased presence, its Decisions are likely to constrain and frame the workings of the rest of the institutional settlement. This will not only make the Union more of an intergovernmental and less of a supranational organisation, but, insofar as EU law constraints are likely to act less strongly on the European Council, may undermine many of the checks and balances that have been put in place.

Section 5 looks at the European Parliament. The Parliament does not have a general power of legislative initiative nor a monopoly over the adoption of laws. In addition, there are no European political parties and Members of European Parliament (MEPs) are not elected on a pan-European 'one citizen one vote' principle, but on the basis of quotas allocated to each Member State. This has led to questions about the democratic credentials of the Parlia-ment. Notwithstanding this, it is the forum where there is most open public debate about EU decision-making. The Parliament has significant powers over law-making, the Budget and holding the executive to account. In this, it has the qualities of a reviewing parliament: one in which the executive does not hold a majority and whose influence derives from its abil-ity, usually in committees, to review the proposals and activities of the executive. Whilst its formal legislative powers vary according to the nature of the legislative procedure, in all procedures Parliament has used its powers of amendment to significant effect. Similarly, it is the central institution where questions are asked, petitions considered and enquiries held about the other EU institutions.

2 THE COMMISSION

(i) The Commission bureaucracy

The Commission is often described as a single body with the sole agenda of promoting European integration. The reality is more complex. It employs more than 25,500 permanent staff, performs a wide number of tasks and has a wide array of relationships with a multiplicity of actors. Although in legal terms it is a single body, it is best to see the Commission as composed of three tiers: the College of Commissioners, the Directorates-General (DGs) and the Cabinets.

(a) The College of Commissioners

Formally, the Commission consists of twenty-seven Commissioners, with one Commissioner from each Member State.[1] These Commissioners make up the College of Commissioners. The Commission is appointed for a five-year term.[2] Once appointed, the Commissioners are allocated portfolios by the President.[3] Each Commissioner is then the primary person responsible for all the work of the Commission that falls within that policy area. The Commissioners are to be persons whose 'independence is beyond doubt'.[4] They are required not to seek or take instructions from any government or any other body and a duty is imposed on Member States to respect this principle. In addition, Commissioners must not find themselves in a position where a 'conflict of interest' arises. They must not, therefore, engage in any other occupation during their period of office. If any Commissioner fails to observe these rules, the Court of Justice may, on application by either the Council or the Commission, compulsorily retire that Commissioner.[5]

The Lisbon Treaty introduced one exception to this principle of independence. This concerns the office of the High Representative of the European Union for Foreign Affairs and Security Policy. Responsible for the conduct of the EU Common Foreign and Security Policy and its security and defence policy, she is a member of the Commission and one of the twenty-seven Commissioners.[6] However, she takes part in the work of the European Council,[7] chairs the Foreign Affairs Council[8] and acts under the mandate of the Council.[9] The intention of this 'double hat' is to create a more integrated and coordinated external policy,[10] as well as to give the Union a more salient international profile. Straddling the Commission and the Council,

---

[1] Article 17(4) TEU. It was initially anticipated that from 1 November 2014 the Commission should comprise only two-thirds that number: Article 17(5) TEU. In December 2008, as allowed by the Lisbon Treaty, the European Council took a Decision that the principle of one Commissioner from each Member State should continue after that date. EU Council, Presidency Conclusions 11 and 12 December 2008, para. 2 EU Council 17271/1/08.

[2] Article 17(3) TEU.

[3] The portfolios for the 2004–09 Commission were institutional relations and communication strategy; enterprise and industry; transport; administrative affairs and anti-fraud; justice, freedom and security; information society; environment; economic and monetary affairs; regional policy; fisheries; budget; science and research; education and culture; health and consumer protection; enlargement; development and humanitarian aid; taxation and customs union; competition; agriculture and rural development; external relations and European neighbourhood policy; internal market and services; employment, social affairs and equal opportunities; external trade; and energy. At the time of writing, they had not been allocated for the 2009–14 Commission.

[4] Article 17(3) TEU.

[5] Article 245 TFEU.

[6] Article 17(4) TEU.

[7] Article 15(2) TEU.

[8] Article 18(3) TEU.

[9] Article 18(2) TEU.

[10] Article 18(4) TEU.

she is subject to a double chain of accountability. She is appointed, by QMV, by the European Council with the agreement of the President of the Commission.[11] She is dismissed in the same manner[12] and so is the only member of the Commission who cannot be dismissed unilaterally by the President of the Commission.[13]

More generally, the independence of individual Commissioners must be seen in relative terms. Chosen because of distinguished and well-connected prior careers, they have a list of professional and political contacts, with over two-thirds chosen from a party in government at the time of appointment.[14]

> Usually, they are members – and appointees – of the major parties in their member state and continue some involvement with national politics after becoming Commissioners. Frequent trips to speak before (and to lecture to) national audiences are common. Again, the metaphor of gate-keeping is perhaps most useful: Commissioners are an easy and efficient way for the Commission to maintain a link with member state governments and domestic political systems. They will know what legislative proposals are politically acceptable in national capitals, while at the same time being in an ideal position to communicate to national elites the requirements of efficient European policy-making.[15]

Commissioners are also granted wriggle-room by only the most severe breaches of this principle being subject to sanction. In *Cresson*, the French Commissioner, Edith Cresson, had hired her dentist to be her personal adviser on a contract as a visiting scientist, notwithstanding that her chef de cabinet had seen this person as ill-qualified for any post.[16] Disciplinary proceedings were subsequently brought to withdraw some of her pension entitlements on the grounds that her actions were incompatible with her duties. The Court of Justice stated Commissioners were required to ensure that the general interest of the European Union took precedence at all times over both national and personal interests. However, slight deviations from this principle did not have to be censured. Censure was available only where the breach was of sufficient gravity. This will be the case, as was the case here, if the action by the Commissioner was manifestly inappropriate. There was little elaboration on what this phrase means, but it seems to suggest that only the most outrageous conduct will lead to legal sanction.

The other feature of the College is the principle of *collegiality*. The Commission is collectively responsible for all Decisions taken and all Commission Decisions should be taken collectively. In principle, these Decisions should take place at the weekly meetings of the Commission by a simple majority vote of the College. Meetings of each Commissioner's Cabinet (staff) occur two days before the weekly meeting. If there is agreement, it will be formally adopted as an 'A' item and there will be no formal discussion of the matter at the meeting. However, the reality is that there is little discussion within the College about the majority of the Commission's business. A 2008 study of legislative proposals between 2000 and 2004 found that only 17.4 per cent

---

[11] Article 18(1) TEU.

[12] Article 17(6) TEU.

[13] However, if the Parliament passes a motion of censure over the whole Commission, she must resign with the other Commission members: Article 17(8) TEU.

[14] A. Wonka, 'Technocratic and Independent? The Appointment of European Commissioners and its Policy Implications' (2007) 14 *JEPP* 169, 178.

[15] T. Christiansen, 'Tensions of European Governance: Politicised Bureaucracy and Multiple Accountability in the European Commission' (1997) 4 *JEPP* 73, 82; A. Smith, 'Why Commissioners Matter' (2003) 41 *JCMS* 137, 143–5.

[16] Case C-432/04 *Commission* v *Cresson* [2006] ECR I-6387.

even made it to the agenda of the meeting.[17] Of these, very few are discussed. Between 2000 and 2003, of 1,344 Decisions, there was a vote on only 11 and there was discussion on less than 3 per cent.[18]

The Commission deploys two procedures for conducting the majority of its business. The first is the 'written procedure'. Under this procedure, a proposal, a *greffe*, is adopted by the Commissioner responsible for the relevant portfolio. After the proposal has been approved by the Legal Service and associated Directorates-General, it is then circulated to the Cabinets of the other Commissioners. If there is no objection, the proposal is adopted as a Commission Decision. The 'ordinary' written procedure gives the Cabinets five working days to consider the proposal. The expedited written procedure must be authorised by the President. In such circumstances, the Cabinets are only given three working days. The second procedure is internal delegation. The Commission can delegate a straightforward 'act of management' to particular members.[19] What constitutes such an act is not clear. A Decision requiring undertakings to submit to a Commission investigation into anti-competitive practices was considered to be an act of management, which could be delegated. By contrast, a Decision finding a violation of EC competition law was not considered to be administrative in nature and was considered to be too wide a power to be delegated.[20]

(b) The President of the Commission

The President is proposed by the European Council, acting by QMV, and elected by the Parliament.[21] The only Commissioner without a portfolio, the President is the most powerful of all the Commissioners.[22] He has five important roles.

- He is involved in the appointment of the other Commissioners. With the Heads of Government, he nominates the other Commissioners, who are subject to a collective vote of approval by the Parliament and then appointed by the European Council by QMV.[23]
- He decides on the internal organisation of the Commission. This involves not only that the President allocates the individual portfolios at the beginning of the term, but that he can also shift the portfolios of Commissioners during their term of office.
- Individual Commissioners are responsible to him. The President can request individual Commissioners to resign.[24]
- He is to provide 'political guidance' to the Commission. At its most formal, this involves chairing and setting the agenda for the weekly meetings of the Commission. More substantively, it means proposing the political priorities of the Commission through pushing forward one proposal rather than another for adoption by the Commission.
- He has a roving policy brief. Although this causes tensions with the individual Commissioner concerned, the President may seek to take over a particular issue and drive Commission policy on that issue.

---

[17] A. Wonka, 'Decision-making Dynamics in the European Commission: Partisan, National or Sectoral?' (2008) 15 *JEPP* 1145, 1151.
[18] European Commission, *A Constitution for the Union*, COM(2003)548 final, Annex I.
[19] This practice was upheld in Case 5/85 *Akzo* v *Commission* [1986] ECR 2585.
[20] Case C-137/92 P *Commission* v *BASF* [1994] ECR I-2555.
[21] Article 17(7) TEU.
[22] The current President is a Portuguese national, Manuel Barroso.
[23] Article 17(7) TEU.
[24] Article 245 TFEU.

The President may be interested in the particular issue because it may be of such seminal importance to that term of the Commission or because there is strong disagreement between the Commissioner and the President over an issue. In the early 1990s, for example, Jacques Delors worked closely with the British Commissioner, Lord Cockfield, on the internal market because it was so central to the Commission's work at that time. He also intervened extensively, however, on social and environmental issues because he was unhappy with the work of the two Commissioners in those fields.[25] The President can also reserve important policy issues for himself. For example, in the mid-1990s, President Santer decided that he would assume responsibility for institutional reform. Finally, the President has an important representative role. He represents the Commission at meetings involving the Heads of Government and must account to other institutions when there is a questioning of the general conduct of the institution or a particular issue raises broader questions.

The power of the President has grown in recent times. Initially, there was no power to 'hire and fire'. Although it reflects the practice since 2004,[26] the power granted by the Lisbon Treaty for the President to fire individual Commissioners unilaterally is likely to loom over Commissioners. Awareness of it may lead them to anticipate his preferences or be particularly susceptible to his intervention. This will create particular challenges for the Commission as it reaches the end of its term. If the President wishes to be renominated, she will be especially keen to ensure her 'team' does not offend the players with the power to reappoint her, namely the national governments and the Parliament, with all the corollary implications for the independence of the Commission.

(c) The Directorates-General

The majority of Commission employees work for the DGs. DGs are the equivalent of Ministries within a national government. In the current Commission, there are forty DGs. These are divided into four groupings: policies,[27] external relations,[28] general services[29] and internal services.[30] Whilst these all fall within the portfolio of at least one Commissioner and are answerable to (at least) that Commissioner, with forty DGs and twenty-seven Commissioners, there is no neat dovetailing. Furthermore, DGs' duties are to the Commission rather than the Commissioner and individual Commissioners have complained about the autonomy they enjoy and the lack of loyalty they show.[31]

---

[25] G. Ross, *Jacques Delors and European Integration* (Oxford and New York, Oxford University Press, 1995).

[26] This is currently contained in the Code of Conduct that all Commissioners must sign on taking office. European Commission, *Code of Conduct for Commissioners*, SEC(2004)1487/2, 1.2.1.

[27] Currently these are economic and financial affairs; enterprise and industry; competition; employment, social affairs and equal opportunities; agriculture and rural development; energy and transport; environment; research; information society and media; joint research centre; fisheries and maritime affairs; internal market and services; regional policy; taxation and customs union; education and culture; health and consumer protection; justice, freedom and security.

[28] These are trade; development; enlargement; humanitarian aid; external relations and EuropeAid.

[29] These are communication; European Anti-Fraud Office; Eurostat; publications office and Secretariat General.

[30] These are personnel and administration; bureau of European policy advisers; informatics; European Commission data protection officer; infrastructures and logistics (Brussels and Luxembourg); internal audit service; budget; interpretation; legal service; translation; office for administration and payment of individual entitlements.

[31] D. Curtin and M. Egeberg, 'Tradition and Innovation: Europe's Accumulated Executive Order' (2008) 31 *West European Politics* 639, 657.

The variety of fields and roles in which the Commission is engaged results in there being little cohesion between the different DGs.[32] Put simply, the interests, backgrounds and values of those officials working for the Environment DG are likely to be very different from those working in the Competition DG. In addition to this, the work of each DG may focus on very different tasks. The bulk of the work of the Environment DG will be concentrated around the proposal and enforcement of legislation. By contrast, in the fields of education and culture the European Union has no law-making powers. The work of officials in that DG focuses on the development of programmes, administration of Community funding, and bringing different public and private actors together. This leads to different DGs having quite distinct cultures. This distinctiveness is reinforced by poor central coordinating mechanisms, which lead (arguably) to insufficient exchange between the DGs and to poor policy coherence because different DGs are often working in very different directions.[33]

(d) The Cabinets

If the College of Commissioners represents the political arm of the Commission and the DGs represent the administrative arm, between them sit the Cabinets. Formally appointed by the President, each Cabinet is the Office of a Commissioner. Composed of seven to eight officials,[34] the Cabinets act, first, as the interface between the Commissioner and the DGs under her aegis. They enable liaison between the two, and they help the Commissioner with formulating priorities and policies. They also act as the eyes and ears for the Commissioner, keeping her informed about what is happening elsewhere in the Commission. Finally, they combine with other Cabinets to prepare the weekly meetings for the College of Commissioners.

These tasks place the Cabinets in a very strong position within the Commission. The preparation of the meetings between the Commissioners forecloses a great deal of debate in the College, because in reality much is negotiated between the Cabinets. Similarly, by acting as the interface between the Commission and the DG, they inevitably become gate-keepers to the Commissioner, who must be negotiated with by DG officials wishing to put forward particular ideas. Their role is, thus, controversial. DGs have seen them at times as Machiavellian, bypassing normal procedures and sabotaging perfectly acceptable proposals.[35]

(ii) Powers of the Commission

The powers of the Commission are now systematised in a single Article.

---

[32] L. Cram, 'The European Commission as a Multi-Organization: Social Policy and IT Policy in the EU' (1994) 1 *JEPP* 195.

[33] L. Hooghe, *The European Commission and the Integration of Europe* (Cambridge, Cambridge University Press, 2001) 201–5.

[34] The President's Cabinet is larger, with eleven officials.

[35] J. Peterson, 'The Santer Era: The European Commission in Normative, Historical and Theoretical Perspective' (1999) 6 *JEPP* 46.

Article 17 TEU

1. The Commission shall promote the general interest of the Union and take appropriate initiatives to that end. It shall ensure the application of the Treaties, and of measures adopted by the institutions pursuant to the Treaties. It shall oversee the application of Union law under the control of the Court of Justice of the European Union. It shall execute the budget and manage programmes. It shall exercise coordinating, executive and management functions, as laid down in the Treaties. With the exception of the common foreign and security policy, and other cases provided for in the Treaties, it shall ensure the Union's external representation. It shall initiate the Union's annual and multiannual programming with a view to achieving interinstitutional agreements.

2. Union legislative acts may only be adopted on the basis of a Commission proposal, except where the Treaties provide otherwise. Other acts shall be adopted on the basis of a Commission proposal where the Treaties so provide.

Whilst this bringing together of the Commission's powers is very welcome, it still makes sense to consider them in the light of the different roles of the Commission, particularly as reference still has to be had to other parts of the Treaties in relation to certain powers.

(a) Legislative and quasi-legislative powers

The Commission has direct legislative powers in only two limited fields: ensuring that public undertakings comply with the rules contained in the Treaty[36] and determining the conditions under which EU nationals may reside in another Member State after having worked there.[37] It has more significant powers in the field of delegated legislation, where the Council can confer quasi-legislative powers upon it.

The remit of these quasi-legislative powers has been interpreted very broadly. Whilst the Council cannot delegate the essential elements of a policy to the Commission, it can delegate any other legal powers to the Commission.[38] The delegation of quasi-legislative powers to the Commission is also very widespread. Provision for delegation is estimated to be present in about 20 per cent of all legislation. The figure is still higher where legislation

---

Article 290 TFEU

1. A legislative act may delegate to the Commission the power to adopt non-legislative acts to supplement or amend certain non-essential elements of the legislative act.

2. The objectives, content, scope and duration of the delegation of power shall be explicitly defined in the legislative acts. The essential elements of an area shall be reserved for the legislative act and accordingly shall not be the subject of a delegation of power.

---

[36] Article 106(3) TFEU.
[37] Article 45(3)(d) TFEU.
[38] Article 290(1) TFEU. This codifies judicial practice. Joined Cases T-64/01 and T-65/01 *Afrikanische Fruchtcompanie v Council* [2004] ECR II-521.

either authorises expenditure or was adopted by QMV, with it being used in 66 per cent of all expenditure-authorising legislation and in 67 per cent of legislation adopted under the single market procedures.[39] Highly significant matters have also been delegated. The measure prompting the bovine spongiform encephalopathy (BSE) crisis, the prohibition on the export of beef and bovine products from the United Kingdom, was instigated under powers granted to the Commission to make veterinary and zootechnical checks on live animals and products with a view to the completion of the internal market.[40] The measure had huge implications for animal welfare, public health, public finances and the livelihood of farmers across the Union. These were so big that they prompted a political crisis across the Union.[41]

Since the early 1960s, the exercise of these powers has been monitored by committees composed of representatives of the national governments.[42] In certain circumstances, these committees can refer a matter to the Council, one of the primary legislative bodies in the Union, to overrule the Commission. This process, known as comitology, is dealt with in more detail in Chapter 3.[43] It is sufficient to note here that members of these committees represent governmental interests and, insofar as they are experts, also monitor the technical quality of the Commission's work. Even to secure these interests, these are quite modest controls, with an eschewal of the more rigorous types of control that are present in the United States to control similar delegated powers.[44]

Such widespread delegation raises questions of democratic accountability.[45] One justification is that the laborious nature of the primary law-making procedures can result in pressing decisions not being taken sufficiently quickly. Another is policy credibility. Primary legislatures may neither have the expertise nor be able to take a sufficiently long-term view of matters, because of fears about electoral accountability. Finally, it can be argued that the grant of legislative powers to the Commission in highly technical areas liberates other institutions, allowing them to spend more time on what 'matters'. Yet, even if these were accepted, they do not provide a blank cheque to the Commission to legislate in so many areas.[46] The Lisbon Treaty has therefore introduced increased parliamentary[47] and judicial controls.[48] It remains to be seen how effectively these will work.

---

[39] R. Dogan, 'Comitology: Little Procedures with Big Implications' (1997) 20 *WEP* 36. Similar findings are made in F. Franchino, 'Delegating Powers in the European Community' (2004) 34 *BJPS* 269.

[40] The measure was Decision 96/239/EC [1996] OJ L78/47. The principal basis for it was Directive 90/425/EEC, article 10(4) [1990] OJ L224/29.

[41] See J. Neyer, 'The Regulation of Risks and the Power of the People: Lesson from the BSE Crisis' (2006) 4 *EIOP* No. 6.

[42] The limits of comitology as a check on the Commission are perhaps reflected in its being something that was originally proposed by the Commission to garner acceptance for its proposals in agriculture. J. Blom-Hansen, 'The Origins of EU Comitology System: A Case of Informal Agenda-Setting by the Commission' (2008) 15 *JEPP* 208, 213–18.

[43] See pp. 117–24.

[44] These include time limits on delegation, appeal procedures, public hearings and requirements for explicit legislative approval. F. Franchino, 'Delegating Powers in the European Community' (2004) 34 *BJPS* 269.

[45] M. Cini, 'The Commission: An Unelected Legislator?' (2002) 8(4) *Journal of Legislative Studies* 14.

[46] G. Majone, 'Two Logics of Delegation: Agency and Fiduciary Relations in EU Governance' (2001) 2 *EUP* 103. F. Franchino, 'Efficiency or Credibility? Testing the Two Logics of Delegation to the European Commission' (2002) 9(5) *JEPP* 1; M. Pollack, *The Engines of European Integration: Delegation, Agency and Agenda-Setting in the EU* (Oxford, Oxford University Press, 2003) 101–7.

[47] Article 290(2), (3) TFEU. For further analysis see pp. 120–2 in Chapter 3.

[48] Article 263(4) TFEU. See pp. 414–15.

(b) Agenda-setting

The Commission has responsibility for initiating the policy process in a number of ways. It first decides the legislative programme for each year.[49] Secondly, in most fields, it has a monopoly over the power of legislative initiative.[50] Thirdly, it also has the power of financial initiative. The Commission starts the budgetary process by placing a draft Budget before the Parliament and the Council.[51] Finally, the Commission is responsible for stimulating policy debate more generally. The most celebrated example of this was the White Paper on Completion of the Internal Market, which set out an agenda and timetable for completing the internal market by the end of 1992.[52]

The matter will be assigned to the DG within whose field the proposal seems to fall most clearly. The DG will appoint a senior official as rapporteur. This rapporteur will be responsible to a 'management board' of senior officials within the DG. He is responsible for internal consultation with other interested DGs and for external consultation with outside parties. The external consultation will take place in expert committees, consisting of national officials and experts, and advisory committees composed of different sectional interests (e.g. industry, consumer and environmental groups and trade unions). The proposal has then to be vetted by the Commission Legal Service for its legality. It will then be adopted by a lead Commissioner with responsibility for the portfolio, who will choose whether to put it before the other Commissioners.

Very few proposals are put forward by the Commission using its own initiative. It enjoys, instead, a gate-keeper role, where different interests (national governments, industry, NGOs) come to it with legislative suggestions. Taking 1998 as an example, the Commission estimated that 35 per cent of its proposals were adapting legislation to new economic, scientific or social data; 31 per cent were because of international obligations imposed on it; 12 per cent were tasks required by the Treaty where it enjoyed no discretion; and 17 per cent were responding to requests by national governments, EU institutions or economic operators. Only 5 per cent were taken at its own behest.[53]

This results in the Commission being far more politicised than a traditional civil service. It becomes a marketplace for the development of ideas and accommodation of interests, with a variety of parties, both public and private, seeking to influence it.[54] In addition, it is both an agenda-setter and a veto-player. Nothing can happen without the Commission deciding to make a proposal in the first place and it can frame the terms of debate and legislation. It also gives the Commission significant influence in the subsequent debates. Because it can withdraw a proposal at any time, parties cannot ignore its views even after the proposal has been made. However, its power should not be overestimated. Its influence depends upon a number of variables. Central is institutional context. In areas where a unanimity vote by Member States is not required, the Commission can act as a broker between some actors and to outmanoeuvre

[49] For 2009, see European Commission, *Commission Work Programme for 2009*, COM(2008)712.
[50] The main exception is in Common Foreign and Security Policy where it has only an ancillary role. In this field initiatives or proposals may be made by any Member State, the High Representative or the High Representative with Commission support: Article 30(1) TEU.
[51] Article 314(2) TFEU.
[52] COM(85)310 final.
[53] House of Lords European Union Committee, *Initiation of EU Legislation* (22nd Report, 2007–08 Session, HL, London) 15.
[54] G. Peters, 'Agenda-Setting in the European Community' (1994) 1 *JEPP* 9.

others.[55] In some areas, it can induce other institutions to adopt its proposal as the 'lesser evil' by threatening to use other powers at its disposal, such as bringing a Member State before the Court of Justice, which would lead to more draconian consequences.[56] There is also a temporal dimension. If the Commission is impatient, its influence is weakened, as it has to accept more readily the views of the other institutions. The reverse is true if the other institutions are impatient for a measure to be adopted.[57]

The traditional justification for the Commission's powers was that its autonomy would result in its being best able to represent the common European interest.[58] Over time, this justification has come to carry less weight. The transfer of competences to the European Union has not always resulted in a corresponding transfer of powers to the Commission. Increasingly, therefore, national governments have taken an interest in agenda-setting and limiting the Commission's discretion.[59] A range of measures have also been taken to place institutional constraints on this important power.

First, the Council, through its Presidency, sets out legislative timetables of six months each, which the Commission is expected to follow. More wide-ranging, since 2002, the European Council, representing the Heads of Government, seeks to determine the legislative agenda of the Union, agreeing and revising annual and tri-annual legislative programmes every year.[60] The second measure is that both the Parliament and the Council can ask the Commission to make a proposal.[61] In 2003, the Commission gave an undertaking to 'take account' of such requests and reply 'rapidly and appropriately'.[62] The third measure is introduced by the Lisbon Treaty and is the citizens' initiative. This requires the Commission to consider petitions for proposals where these come from at least one million citizens from a significant number of Member States.[63] The details of these procedures have yet not been worked out, but it is undoubtedly intended to make the process less technocratic and more populist. In addition, there are now well-established procedures which require the Commission to consult widely and consider the impacts of a significant legislative proposal before it adopts it.[64]

It is doubtful whether this is sufficient. Formally, the Commission is the central agenda-setter for the European Union and a feature of democracies is popular contestation about future political direction. As we shall see, the democratic credentials of both the Council and Parliament can be questioned. Further, neither makes requests for initiatives that often.[65] Whilst the citizens' initiative is an attempt to open the process, there is a danger of its being captured by small interest groups, particularly as only 0.5 per cent of the EU population have to sign

---

[55] S. Schmidt, 'Only an Agenda-Setter? The Commission's Power over the Council of Ministers' (2000) 1 *EUP* 37.

[56] S. Schmidt, 'The European Commission's Powers in Shaping Policies' in D. Dimitrakopoulos (ed.), *The Changing Commission* (Manchester, Manchester University Press, 2004).

[57] M. Pollack, 'Delegation, Agency and Agenda Setting in the European Community' (1997) 51 *IO* 99, 121–4.

[58] K. Featherstone, 'Jean Monnet and the "Democratic Deficit" in the European Union' (1994) 32 *JCMS* 149, 154–5.

[59] G. Majone, *Dilemmas of European Integration: The Ambiguities and Pitfalls of Integration by Stealth* (Oxford, Oxford University Press, 2005) 51–3.

[60] See p. 77.

[61] Articles 225, 241 TFEU respectively.

[62] Interinstitutional Agreement on Better Law-Making [2003] OJ C321/1, para. 9. This duty has been strengthened by the Lisbon Treaty which now formally requires the Commission to give reasons if it does not accede to their requests: Articles 225 and 241 TFEU.

[63] Article 11(4) TEU.

[64] This is dealt with in more detail in the chapter on governance. See pp. 373–8.

[65] There are no figures from the Council but only six requests were, for example, made by the Parliament between 2004 and 2007: House of Lords European Union Committee, *Initiation of EU Legislation*, above, n.53, 27–32.

the petition; and there also remains the question of how responsive the Commission will be to these petitions. Follesdall and Hix have suggested that as the Commission holds a power, the power to initiate legislation, that is usually granted only to governments in democratic states, then one should have votes for the President of the Commission in the same way that there are votes for domestic government.

A. Follesdall and S. Hix, 'Why there is a Democratic Deficit in the EU: A Response to Majone and Moravcsik' (2006) 44 *Journal of Common Market Studies* 533, 554

...the Commission's designated role regarding the European interest should not be formulated in such a way as to imply that the content of this term is uncontested, or that the Commission is the only institution able and willing to identify and pursue it. Now that the basic policy-competence architecture of the EU has been confirmed – in terms of the regulation of the market at the European level and the provision of spending-based public goods at the national level – the role of the Commission is not fundamentally different from other political executives.

The purely Pareto-improving functions of the Commission, such as the merger control authority or the monitoring of legislative enforcement, could easily be isolated in new independent agencies. Then, the expressly 'political' functions of the Commission, in terms of defining a work programme for five years, initiating social, economic and environmental laws, and preparing and negotiating the multi-annual and annual budgets, should be open to rigorous contestation and criticism. Such criticism should not be interpreted as euroscepticism or anti-federalism, but rather as an essential element of democratic politics at the European level...

Related to these two ideas, an institutional mechanism needs to be found for generating debate and contestation about politics *in*, not only *of*, the EU. The most obvious way of doing this is contestation of the office of the Commission President – the most powerful executive position in the EU. For example, there could be a direct election of the Commission President by the citizens or by national parliaments. Alternatively, a less ambitious proposal would be for government leaders to allow a more open battle for this office without any further treaty reform. Now that the Commission President is elected by a qualified-majority vote (after the Nice Treaty), a smaller majority is needed in the European Council for a person to be nominated. This led to a dramatic increase in the number of candidates in the battle to succeed Romano Prodi and a linking of the nomination of a candidate to the majority in the newly elected European Parliament. However, the process could have been much more open and transparent – with candidates declaring themselves before the European elections, issuing manifestos for their term in office, and the transnational parties and the governments then declaring their support for one or other of the candidates well before the horse-trading began.

(c) Executive powers

The Commission is responsible for ensuring that the European Union's revenue is collected and passed on by national authorities and that the correct rates are applied. It is also responsible for overseeing and coordinating a large part of EU expenditure, be this structural, agricultural or social funds. Secondly, it is responsible for administering EU aid to third countries. Thirdly, the High Representative, who, it will be remembered, is also a Commissioner, is to represent the Union for matters relating to the Common Foreign and Security Policy. Notably, she will conduct political dialogue with third parties on the Union's behalf and express the Union's position in international organisations and at international conferences.[66] To that end, she will be assisted by a European External Action Service, which will comprise officials from the Council Secretariat of the Council and the Commission.[67] It is worth noting that there is some ambiguity about the organisations in which the High Representative is to represent the European Union. This is explicitly stated to be the case for the United Nations, the Council of Europe and the OECD.[68] The Treaties are silent on the WTO, the international organisation in which the Union has been historically most active, and it is the Commission which has traditionally represented the Union here. Finally, the Commission handles applications for membership of the European Union by carrying out an investigation of the implications of membership and submitting an opinion to the Council.[69]

(d) Supervisory powers

The Commission acts as the 'conscience of the Union'. First, the Commission enjoys certain regulatory powers. It can declare illegal state aids provided by Member States[70] or measures enacted in favour of public undertakings which breach the Treaty.[71] It has also been granted powers to declare anti-competitive practices by private undertakings illegal and to fine those firms,[72] as well as the power to impose duties on goods coming from third states, which are benefiting from 'unfair' trade practices, such as dumping or export subsidies.[73]

Secondly, it may bring Member States before the Court of Justice for breaching EU law.[74] It uses this power extensively.[75] The Commission is also responsible for monitoring compliance by Member States with judgments of the Court of Justice. It can bring those Member States which it considers to have failed to comply back before the Court to have them fined. This was done seven times in 2007.[76]

Couching it in these terms leads to the process being seen as one of enforcement. To be sure, when the matter is finally litigated before the Court that is what takes place. Yet, as the statistics show, only in a very small proportion of cases does the process get that far. Such a view also obscures the policy-choices involved in the development of local procedures to comply with, transpose and apply EU law. Instead, as Curtin and Egeberg have argued,[77] a far more synergistic relationship often emerges. The responsibility of national administrations for applying, transposing and administering EU law, with Commission responsibility for oversight

---

[66] Article 27(1), (2) TEU.
[67] Article 27(3) TEU.
[68] Article 220 TFEU.
[69] Article 49 TEU.
[70] Article 108(2) TFEU.
[71] Article 106(3) TFEU.
[72] Regulation 1/2003/EC, articles 7 and 23 respectively [2001] OJ L1/1.
[73] In relation to dumping see Regulation 384/96/EC [1996] OJ L56/1, especially articles 7–9.
[74] Article 258 TFEU.
[75] At the end of 2006, for example, the Commission had instigated proceedings in 2,518 cases. European Commission, *Twenty Fourth Annual Report on Monitoring the Application of Community Law*, COM(2007)398, 3. The number was not given for the following year.
[76] Article 260(2) TFEU. European Commission, *Twenty Fifth Annual Report on Monitoring the Application of Community Law*, COM(2008)777, 3.
[77] See also G. della Cananea, 'The European Union's Mixed Administrative Proceedings' (2004) 68 *Law and Contemporary Problems* 197; H. Hofmann and A. Türk, 'Conclusion: Europe's Integrated Administration' in H. Hofmann and A. Türk (eds.), *EU Administrative Governance* (Edward Elgar, Cheltenham, 2006).

and coordination of the process, leads to an ongoing engagement between the Commission and its national counterparts, which revolves more around resolving common interests than around antagonism. This institutional engagement and spirit generates a new executive order, which is neither simply European nor simply national.

D. Curtin and M. Egeberg, 'Tradition and Innovation: Europe's Accumulated Executive Order' (2008) 31 *West European Politics* 639, 649–50

Since the Commission does not possess its own agencies at the member state level, it (and EU-level agencies) seems to establish a kind of partnership with those national bodies responsible for the application of EU legislation as well as some involvement in the development of EU policies. Such bodies may be found among national agencies that are already somewhat detached from their respective ministerial departments.

The term 'Europe's integrated administration' takes on board the situation where in contemporary European integration processes the traditional distinction of direct and indirect administration has become blurred, with the levels being interwoven to form a more unitary pattern of 'integrated administration'. The EU level is also involved in implementing activities undertaken by member state authorities, while member states' administrations are involved in creating EU legislation and implementing acts. Case studies within five different policy fields have shown that national agencies in fact seem to act in a 'double-hatted' manner, constituting parts of national administrations while at the same time becoming parts of a multi-level Union administration in which the Commission in particular forms the new executive centre. As parts of national administrations, serving their respective ministerial departments, agency officials play a crucial role in transposition of EU legislation as well as in Council working parties and comitology committees. However, when it comes to the application of EU legislation in particular, agencies also cooperate rather closely with their respective directorates in the Commission, often by-passing their ministerial departments.

Not surprisingly, in this situation agencies may face competing policy expectations from their two 'masters' that may be hard to reconcile. A questionnaire study showed that the importance of the 'parent ministry' partly depends on its organisational capacity in the field and the extent to which the legislative area is politically contested. Obviously, the role of the Commission will tend to vary as well depending on, for example, the relative strength of the DG involved. Also, lack of knowledge and novelty make national agencies in new member states more receptive to inputs from the Commission. 'Double-hattedness' entails new patterns of cooperation and conflict in executive politics, evoking conflicts that cut across national boundaries as well. It could also be expected to lead to more even implementation across countries compared to indirect implementation, although not as even as if the Commission had its own agencies or if the application of EU law was in the hands of EU-level bodies.

The presence of such an executive order poses a number of challenges. Most fundamentally, it raises, as Curtin and Egeberg note in the remainder of their article, real questions about accountability. A world in which national administrations justify themselves to and are held to account by a Commission can not only create mixed loyalties, but also loosen the duty of those national administrations to account to other parts of their government and to their domestic constituencies. This is particularly worrisome if the relationship with the Commission is essentially a cosy one based on mutual trust, as then it becomes not so much a duty to hold oneself to account to another master as a duty not to hold oneself out too strongly to account at all.

(iii) Regulatory agencies and the Commission

The concentration of so many functions in the Commission has placed pressure on its resources. A preference has emerged for delegating specialised and time-consuming tasks to independent agencies and offices rather than for using the Commission as a repository for further regulatory competences. This preference took on a new intensity following two scandals in the late 1990s: first, the BSE scandal in which the Commission had been found to cover up knowledge relating to the risks of BSE and new variant Creutzfeldt–Jakob disease; and secondly, evidence of mismanagement by the Santer Commission. In 1999, a Task Force for Administrative Reform recommended that the Commission was administering too much and more needed to be delegated to specialised agencies.[78] This theme was taken up a year later in the Commission White Paper on Governance, which advocated the creation of independent EU regulatory agencies in any field marked by specialisation and complexity, and where a single public interest predominates.[79]

To date, twenty-two Community agencies, plus a further six executive agencies,[80] have been established. The remit of Community agencies ranges over a wide area from fundamental rights, environment and external frontiers to pharmaceuticals, trade marks and air safety. Their powers vary considerably. Some, like the European Environment Agency or the European Institute for Gender Equality, do little more than provide information and commission studies on their fields. There are two, the Office for Harmonisation of the Internal Market and the Community Plant Variety Office, which grant intellectual property rights (trade marks and plant variety rights respectively).

The most wide-ranging power granted to a number of agencies is to provide expert opinion, which will either guide other EU institutions in deciding whether to authorise a product or activity or inform legislation they wish to develop in this field. Agencies having one or both of these powers include the European Food Safety Authority (EFSA),[81] the European Aviation Safety Authority (EASA), the European Chemicals Agency (ECHA), the European Medicines Agency (EMEA), the European Railway Agency (ERA) and the European Network and Information Security Agency (ENISA). Whilst EU institutions are not bound by these Opinions in adopting legislation or granting authorisations, there is invariably a duty to consult the agency before doing this.[82] It can then depart from the agency's Opinion only on grounds of safety where it can provide an alternative, equally authoritative, contradictory opinion. This is difficult and, in practice, the Commission has always followed agency Opinions. The consequence has been that the latter has become the central institution for determining which food may be marketed in the European Union. This is not uncontroversial as it allows both the acquisition of new EU capacities and the taking of important decisions behind the cloak of 'expertise'.

[78] European Commission, *Reforming the Commission*, COM(2000)200, Part I, 6.
[79] European Commission, *European Governance: A White Paper*, COM(2001)428, 24.
[80] Executive agencies differ from other agencies in that they are more managerial in nature, being responsible for the administration of an EU programme. Their mandate is set out in Regulation 58/2003/EC [2003] OJ L11/1.
[81] The central powers of EFSA are set out in Regulation 178/2002/EC [2002] OJ L31/1.
[82] Case T-13/99 *Pfizer Animal Health* v *Council* [2002] ECR II-3305. See pp. 380–2.

M. Shapiro, 'The Problems of Independent Agencies in the United States and the European Union' (1997) 4 *Journal of European Public Policy* 262, 281–2

The standard, overt rationale for the creation of EU agencies is that they ought to be partially or wholly independent of the Commission because they are 'managerial', perform 'technical' tasks or are engaged in 'information' gathering and analysis only. In the US it may make sense to say that managerial, technical, informational functions should be separated from the regular cabinet departments or ministries because those departments are part of the Executive Branch which is political. Both in the sense that it is headed by a democratically elected President and in the sense that the President is his political party's leader. This is the get-technology-out-of-politics theme. But the separation of powers in the EU is entirely different. The Commission-Council separation is itself a supposed separation of technocracy (the Commission) from intergovernmental politics (the Council). Therefore, to assert a managerial-technical-informational rationale for separating the agencies from the Commission is, in a certain sense, absurd. It is the assertion that the technical ought to be separated from the technical.

Is all this managerial-technical-informational talk simply a smoke screen for the more fundamental argument that, because Europeans don't like the technocrats in Brussels and fear concentrating even more governance there, if we want more EU technocrats, we need to split them up and scatter them about Europe? I think the answer to this question is largely yes but not entirely.

A second motive is, I believe, a kind of 'neo-functionalism'. If currently direct routes to further political integration of the Union are blocked, following Haas's old arguments about the World Health Organisation and the UN, further growth can be achieved indirectly through the proliferation of small, limited jurisdictions, allegedly 'technical agencies' that will appear politically innocuous. That is why it is not enough to say that the agencies are not in Brussels. It must also be said that they are merely technical or informational.

A third motive is about technocracy. The member state composed management boards were no doubt a political necessity. But by stressing the technical and informational functions of these agencies, by making each highly specialised to a particular technology and by incorporating large components of scientific personnel, there is undoubtedly the hope that the technocrats will take over these agencies from the politicians. And the technocrats for each of these agencies, it is hoped will create Europe-wide epistemic communities whose technical truths transcend intergovernmental politics. As Americans say 'there is no Republican or Democratic way to pave a street', Europeans may be able to say there is no French or Greek way. Thus, while the proffered technocratic rationales do not really explain why the agencies should be independent of the Commission, they do explain why the agencies should each take a small slice of allegedly technical-informational activity. That kind of organisation is most likely, over time, to assure the internal dominance within each agency of its transnational technocrats over its national politicians.

3 THE COUNCIL OF MINISTERS

(i) Powers and workings of the Council

The Council of Ministers, alongside the European Council, is the institution that represents national governments. Its powers are rather unsatisfactorily set out in the TEU.

> **Article 16(1) TEU**
>
> The Council shall, jointly with the European Parliament, exercise legislative and budgetary functions. It shall carry out policy-making and coordinating functions as laid down in the Treaties.

In fact, ranged across the Treaties, the Council's powers are multifaceted and varied. They include the following:

- In areas of policy where responsibility lies with the Member States, such as general economic policy, the Council acts as a forum within which Member States can consult with each other and coordinate their behaviour.[83]
- It can take the other institutions before the Court for failure to comply with EU law[84] or for failure to act when required by EU law.[85]
- It can request the Commission to undertake studies or submit legislative proposals.[86]
- It prepares the work for the European Council meetings and ensures their follow-up.[87]
- It frames the Common Foreign and Security Policy and takes the decisions necessary for defining and implementing it on the basis of the general guidelines and strategic lines defined by the European Council.[88]
- It has power of final decision on the adoption of legislation in most areas of EU policy.

The last power is particularly significant. Whilst, as we shall see, it is shared with the Parliament in certain fields, it leads to the Council being perceived, as Article 16(1) TEU suggests, as the most important institution in the law-making process. The Council comprises a minister from each Member State, who is authorised to commit the government of that state on that matter.[89] Environmental ministers will, thus, sit in the Environmental Council and agriculture or fisheries ministers in the Agriculture and Fisheries Council. Since 2002, it has been agreed that more than one minister from each Member State may sit in a Council meeting, particularly where an issue crosses different ministerial portfolios.[90] Most Councils meet formally between once a month and once every two months. Prior to the Lisbon Treaty, the Council sat in nine configurations:

- General Affairs and External Relations;
- Economic and Financial Affairs;
- Justice and Home Affairs;
- Employment, Social Policy and Consumer Affairs;
- Competitiveness;
- Transport, Telecommunications and Energy;
- Agriculture and Fisheries;
- Environment;
- Education, Youth and Culture.

---

[83] Article 121 TFEU. [84] Article 225 TFEU.
[85] Article 265 TFEU. [86] Article 241 TFEU.
[87] Article 16(6) TEU. [88] Article 26(2) TEU.
[89] Article 16(2) TEU.
[90] The rules for the Council are set out in Decision 2002/682/EC, EURATOM adopting the Council's Rules of Procedure [2002] OJ L230/7. See also Decision 2009/878/EU establishing a list of Council configurations [2009] OJ L315/46.

Whilst these configurations are fewer than those which existed previously, decision-making is still perceived as fragmented by the specialised nature of the different Council configurations. Furthermore, the floating membership of each Council, with the constant changing of ministers and governments and its occasional nature (namely that it only met once a month), was felt to weaken any sense of collective identity. The Lisbon Treaty therefore provides for the European Council to adopt a Decision by QMV on all Council configurations other than General Affairs and Foreign Affairs.[91] Moreover, there is clearly a feeling that this should be urgently revisited with it being provided that, pending such a European Council Decision, the General Affairs Council may take such a Decision by simple majority vote.[92]

The other 'innovation' to enable this is the strengthening of the General Affairs Council. Since 2002, the General Affairs and External Relations Council, composed of foreign ministers, has met alternately as the General Affairs Council and as the External Relations Council. As the former, it considers matters that affect a number of EU policies and is responsible for coordinating work done by the other Council configurations, and for handling dossiers submitted by the European Council. The Lisbon Treaty formalises this by establishing two different configurations: the General Affairs Council and the Foreign Affairs Council, thereby increasing the number of configurations to ten. The former is to ensure that the different Council configurations all row in the same direction and that this direction is the one ordained by the European Council, the institution comprising the Heads of Government and State. To this end, the General Affairs Council is to secure consistency in the work of the different Council configurations and to prepare and ensure the follow-up to meetings of the European Council, in liaison with the Presidents of the European Council and the Commission.[93]

It is questionable whether this will be sufficient to overcome the current difficulties of fragmentation. The initial draft for the Constitutional Treaty proposed a permanent General and Legislative Affairs Council based in Brussels composed of Ministers of Europe, which would assume the role performed by the General Affairs Council.[94] This proposal was rejected by the national governments, who were concerned that such a Council might become too autonomous and powerful. Yet, the original initiative suggests that foreign ministers meeting every now and then in Brussels may not have the required level of interest and resources to do the job expected of them. The other concern is whether, given the jealousy that national ministers exercise over their portfolios, the General Affairs Council will have the necessary authority. Will, for example, a powerful economics minister listen to his foreign minister?

(ii) Decision-making within the Council

The first form of voting is the *simple majority* vote. Under this system, each Member of the Council has one vote, and fourteen votes are required for a measure to be adopted. This procedure is used in only a few areas, principally procedural ones, as it fails to protect national interests and undue weight is given to the interests of small states at the expense of larger ones. The only area of real significance that is subject to a simple majority vote is the decision to convene an intergovernmental conference to amend the TEU.[95] The converse of simple

---

[91] Article 236(a) TFEU.
[92] Protocol No. 10 on Transitional Provisions, Article 4.
[93] Article 16(6) TEU.   [94] Article 23(1) DCT.
[95] This is taken by the European Council, Article 48(3) TEU. The others are adoption of the Council's own rules of procedure (Articles 240(3) and 235(3) TFEU for European Council) and request for the Commission to undertake studies or submit proposals (Article 241 TFEU).

Table 2.1   Votes and population sizes of Member States

State	Votes	Population
Germany	29	82 million
United Kingdom	29	59.4 million
France	29	59.1 million
Italy	29	57.7 million
Spain	27	39.4 million
Poland	27	38.6 million
Romania	14	22 million
Netherlands	13	15.8 million
Greece	12	10.6 million
Czech Rep	12	10.3 million
Belgium	12	10.2 million
Hungary	12	10 million
Portugal	12	9.9 million
Sweden	10	8.9 million
Austria	10	8.1 million
Bulgaria	10	7.7 million
Slovakia	7	5.4 million
Denmark	7	5.3 million
Finland	7	5.2 million
Lithuania	7	3.7 million
Ireland	7	3.7 million
Latvia	4	2.4 million
Slovenia	4	2 million
Estonia	4	1.4 million
Cyprus	4	0.8 million
Luxembourg	4	0.4 million
Malta	3	0.4 million

majority voting is voting by *unanimity*. Every Member State has a veto on any legislation be-ing considered. It must actively vote against a measure for it to be vetoed; abstention is insuf-ficient. Unanimity voting is used in those areas of the TEU which are more politically sensitive. Its requirement is still widespread in the Treaty.[96] The final form of voting frequently used is that of QMV. This is a weighted system of voting, under which each Member State is allocated a number of votes. If the measure is proposed by the Commission, it requires 255 out of 345 possible votes to be adopted and at least fourteen states must vote for it. In the rare circum-stances where a measure is not proposed by the Commission, it requires 255 votes, but at least two-thirds of the Member States must vote for it. In either case, any Member State can ask to verify that states representing at least 62 per cent of the total EU population supported it. The respective votes and population sizes are shown in Table 2.1.

[96] The Annex at the end of Chapter 3 contains a list of the different legislative competences of the European Union and the procedures and voting requirements used.

The weighting of votes seeks to form a delicate balance between preserving individual national voices and reflecting the different population sizes of the Member States. Since 2004, however, the majority of EU Member States have been 'small' states with populations of less than 10 million. One has the perverse situation where the fourteen smallest Member States have a combined population of 55.4 million citizens, about two-thirds of the German population, but combined, they have 88 votes, over three times the number of votes of Germany. This is not the only anomaly, as each state's voting strength depended as much upon its perseverance in Treaty negotiations as anything else. France has, therefore, equal votes to Germany, despite having a population only two-thirds the size of the latter. An almost identical situation exists between Belgium and the Netherlands even if the latter does have one more vote. The most overrepresented states, however, are Poland and Spain. These have only two votes less than Germany, despite populations less than half its size.

The debate was hotly contested, both at the Future of Europe Convention and during the negotiations for the Lisbon Treaty. The larger Member States wished a weighting more based on population. Despite an absence of evidence that this has ever happened,[97] smaller Member States were worried that such a criterion would allow a small number of large Member States to veto any measure, as the four largest Member States comprise just over 50 per cent of the population. There was provision that existing arrangements would prevail until November 2014.

Article 16(4) TEU

As from 1 November 2014, a qualified majority shall be defined as at least 55% of the members of the Council, comprising at least fifteen of them and representing Member States comprising at least 65% of the population of the Union.

A blocking minority must include at least four Council members, failing which the qualified majority shall be deemed attained.[98]

The new formula gives greater power to the larger Member States by introducing a population requirement as a central threshold for the first time. It provides safeguards for the smaller Member States by providing that at least fifteen states must vote for it. They are protected against the large state veto by the requirement that at least four states must vote against the measure, although it must be said it is unlikely to be difficult for two large Member States to find two smaller states to join them if they try hard enough.[99]

Poland was particularly unhappy with the new formula. It benefits disproportionately from the status quo and was thus hit hard by the new weighting for QMV. A transitional regime was therefore agreed. As can be seen, the new formula does not begin to bite until 1 November 2014. Between that date and 31 March 2017, however, a Member State can ask for the existing

---

[97] M. Mattila and J. Lane, 'Why Unanimity in the Council? A Roll-Call Analysis of Council Voting' (2001) 2 *EUP* 31.

[98] This is also reproduced in Article 238(3) TFEU.

[99] On the differences in respective influence between the Treaty of Nice and the new formula see D. Cameron, 'The Stalemate in the Constitutional IGC' (2004) 5 *EUP* 373, 383.

formula to be used.[100] This is likely to lead to the existing formula prevailing until the latter date as states with a winning majority under it will want it to prevail, as will states who would wish to block a measure under it.

Perhaps even more significantly, a Decision was added indicating a new blocking minority.[100a] From 1 November 2014 to 31 March 2017, if Member States representing three-quarters of the population or of the number of states to form a blocking minority indicate their opposition to a measure, the Council shall do all in its power to reach 'a satisfactory solution' – a euphemism for resolving the matter through unanimity. Translated, that means that during that period, only 33.75 per cent of states or states representing 26.25 per cent of the EU population have to indicate their opposition to a measure for it not to be adopted. From 1 April 2017, the position is even more drastic. The figure becomes 55 per cent of the blocking minority. This means only 24.75 per cent of the states or states representing 19.25 per cent of the population have to oppose a measure for it not to be adopted. On current figures, this is eight states or three states representing 20 per cent of the population. To put this in perspective, Germany alone currently has about 17.5 per cent of the EU population. This Decision makes it significantly easier for Member States, particularly those with large populations, to block measures than under the current regime.

The debate about vote weighting may be overblown. Historically, the distinction between unanimity and QMV was seen as axiomatic to the climate of negotiation. Under unanimity, it was argued that Member States, aware of their veto, are inclined to have a heightened sense of self-interest and to look for matching concessions.[101] In circumstances where Member States do not have a veto, they are aware of the possibility of outmanoeuvring. A climate of problem-solving prevails, with Member States looking far more towards constructing common solutions and being less protective of their initial positions.[102] Whilst these differences in style may exist on occasion, more recent, empirical studies have suggested the differences to be less stark. Prior to 2004, Wallace and others calculated that votes were taken in the Council on only about 25 per cent of matters discussed, even under QMV, with the majority of voting concentrated in two sectors, agriculture and fisheries, where redistributive issues play a powerful role.[103] This figure seems to have reduced even further since 2004, with Mattila suggesting that in 2004 and 2005, 82 per cent of items decided by QMV were passed without contestation.[104] The quid pro quo for this culture of consensus is that individual concerns are, where possible, simply incorporated into the text. The 2004 enlargement led, for example, to the length of legislative documents increasing by approximately 15 per cent.[105]

---

[100] Protocol to the Treaty of Lisbon on Transitional Provisions, Article 3(2).

[100a] This is now contained in Decision 2009/857/EC relating to the implementation of Article 9C(4) TEU and Article 205(2) TFEU [2009] OJ L314/73.

[101] F. Scharpf, 'The Joint Decision Trap: Lessons from German Federalism and European Integration' (1988) 66 *Public Administration* 239. A good introduction to the different types of interaction in the Council is H. Wallace, 'The Council: An Institutional Chameleon?' (2002) 15 *Governance* 325.

[102] F. Hayes-Renshaw and H. Wallace, *The Council of Ministers* (Basingstoke, Macmillan, 1997) 256–8.

[103] M. Mattila, 'Contested Decisions: Empirical Analysis of Voting in the Council of Ministers' (2004) 43 *EJPR* 29; F. Hayes-Renshaw, W. van Aken and H. Wallace, 'When and Why the Council of Ministers of the EU Votes Explicitly' (2006) 44 *JCMS* 161, 165.

[104] M. Mattila, 'Voting and Coalitions in the Council after Enlargement' in D. Naurin and H. Wallace (eds.), *Unveiling the Council of the European Union: Games Governments Play in Brussels* (Basingstoke, Palgrave, 2008).

[105] E. Best and P. Settembri, 'Legislative Output after Enlargement: Similar Number, Shifting Nature' in E. Best *et al.* (eds.), *The Institutions of the Enlarged European Union: Change and Continuity* (Cheltenham, Edward Elgar, 2008).

In a world of consensus-seeking, the key dynamic, a study by Beyers and Dierickx suggests, is not the form of vote taken, but the presence of central players and smaller players.[106] Coalitions cluster around central players, who have the resources and networks to articulate common views and mediate between positions. These tend to be the large Member States and the Commission. Other states see themselves as having to mediate with these and rarely negotiate with other partners. Negotiations are, thus, usually driven by a few key players.

This focus on consensus has led to concerns about the quality of debate in the Council. Since 2002, parts of Council meetings have been opened to the public. This would include the initial presentation of certain legislative proposals by the Commission to the Council, the ensuing debate and the votes and explanation of votes. The form of public access was, however, of a limited kind, as it involved only the provision of a room in which the public could watch via live feed.[107] The Lisbon Treaty has opened up all deliberations and votes on legislative acts to the public.

> **Article 16(8) TEU**
>
> The Council shall meet in public when it deliberates and votes on a draft legislative act. To this end, each Council meeting shall be divided into two parts, dealing respectively with deliberations on Union legislative acts and on non-legislative activities.

This approach generates two types of response. One response sees this reform as overdue. In particular, it will allow national publics and parliaments to hold governments more fully to account and possibly generate greater interest in and understanding of the law-making process. Such a view would presumably wish this access to extend to non-legislative activities as well. The other response is to see this provision as containing risks. It may lead to grandstanding by individual ministers for the benefit of their home constituencies, thereby obstructing problem-solving. Furthermore, as it would only be the formal meetings that are made public, there is a fear that the real decision-making processes will be driven elsewhere, out of sight, with the Council becoming no more than a ratifying body designed, more than anything else, for public show.[108]

(iii) Management of the Council: the Presidency, the Secretariat and COREPER

The Presidency of the Council rotates between groups of three Member States for eighteen months at a time on the basis of equal rotation.[109] The Presidency has a number of duties:

- it arranges and chairs Council meetings and sets the agenda for them;[110]
- it represents the Council both before the other EU institutions and in the world more generally;

---

[106] J. Beyers and G. Dierickx, 'The Working Groups of the Council of the European Union: Supranational or Intergovernmental Negotiations?' (1998) 36 *JCMS* 289.

[107] Only those proposals that were governed by the ordinary legislative procedure were subject to this access.

[108] For an indication of the two views see House of Lords European Union Committee, *The Treaty of Lisbon: An Impact Assessment* (10th Report, 2007–08 Session, TSO, London) 56–47.

[109] Article 16(9) TEU, Article 236(b) TFEU. The sequence is set out in Decision 2007/5/EC, EURATOM determining the order in which the office of the President is held [2007] OJ L1/11. See also Decision 2009/881/EU on the exercise of the Presidency of the Council [2009] OJ L315/50.

[110] Decision 2002/682/EC, article 20. Each Member State will chair the Council for six months: Decision 2009/881/EU, article 1(2).

- it acts as a 'neutral broker' between other Member States in order to secure legislation;
- it sets the legislative agenda for its six-month term of office. This will be done in consultation with the Commission and the Presidencies preceding and succeeding it.

There is some debate about the power of the Presidency. It has been argued that the short term of office and the need not to appear too partisan restrict it to an essentially clerical role.[111] Certainly, these features prevent the Presidency from hijacking the agenda of the Council to further national priorities. Nevertheless, a study of eight Presidencies found that whilst these had to stay within the mandates set by their predecessors or the Commission, they have a soft power in the form of discretion to steer or shape these agendas.[112] If they had been given only a vague mandate to realise a task, they could choose, instead, to make it a priority for their Presidency. Unanticipated events, such as 9/11, also provide opportunities for agenda-setting. As they require new forms of response from the Union, reliance is placed on the Presidency to organise that response and set out the framework for future action. Conversely, they also seem to have some influence when negotiations are closed. At this moment, they have to bring views together and whilst this must be done even-handedly, empirical studies show that decisions reached during state Presidencies are usually closer to what they want than decisions taken outside them.[113]

Whilst the Presidency sets out the overall framework for Council meetings, the mundane details are carried out by the Secretariat.[114] Based in Brussels, the central functions of the Secretariat are conference organisation and committee servicing. It produces documents, arranges translation, takes notes and organises meeting rooms. It performs this role also for the European Council.[115] It also provides advice to the Council on the legality of its actions and will represent the Council before the other institutions. It will thus be the Council Secretariat who will litigate on behalf of the Council in the Court of Justice or represent the Council before Parliament committees. A new role provided by the Lisbon Treaty is that it will contribute to the External Action Service that will assist the High Representative in fulfilling her mandate.[116]

However, the central body in the preparation of Council meetings is COREPER. The formal duties of COREPER are merely to prepare the work of the Council and carry out any tasks assigned to it.[117] It has no power to take formal decisions other than ones on Council procedure.[118] It is divided into COREPER I, which is composed of deputy permanent representatives and is responsible for issues such as the environment, social affairs, the internal market and transport. COREPER II consists of permanent representatives of ambassadorial rank responsible for the more sensitive issues, such as economic and financial affairs and external relations.

---

[111] A. Tallberg, 'The Agenda-Shaping Powers of the EU Council Presidency' (2003) 10 *JEPP* 1; B. Crum, 'Can the EU Presidency Make its Mark on Interstate Bargains? The Italian and Irish Presidencies of the 2003–4 IGC' (2007) 14 *JEPP* 1208.

[112] E. Bailleul and H. Versluys, 'The EU Rotating Presidency: "Hostage Taker" of the European Agenda?', paper presented at EUSA Conference, 30 March 2005. A similar conclusion is reached by study of the Presidency of Environmental Councils: A. Warntjen, 'Steering the Union: The Impact of the EU Presidency on Legislative Activity' (2007) 45 *JCMS* 1135.

[113] R. Thomson, 'The Council Presidency of the European Union: Responsibility with Power' (2008) 46 *JCMS* 593, 604–11.

[114] Article 240(2) TFEU.

[115] Article 235(4) TFEU.

[116] Article 27(3) TEU.

[117] Article 16(7) TEU, Article 240(1) TFEU.

[118] Case C-25/94 *Commission* v *Council (FAO Fisheries Agreement)* [1996] ECR I-1469.

Each meets weekly. Successive reports have found COREPER essential both to alleviating Council workload and coordinating its work.[119]

The heart of COREPER's power lies in its setting the agenda for Council meetings and its dividing that agenda into 'A' and 'B' matters. 'A' items are technical matters, on which there is agreement. These are nodded through in the Council meeting, without discussion. 'B' items, by contrast, are considered more contentious, requiring discussion. COREPER, therefore, decides on what the Council is to decide on. An 'A' item is effectively decided by COREPER, and a 'B' item by the Council of Ministers. In this, the overwhelming majority of items are 'A' items. A study in the early 1990s found that of 500 items placed on the Agricultural Council agenda, ministers discussed only 13 per cent of them.[120]

In this, COREPER does not act as a loose cannon, but as a conduit for informing national capitals of the work of the European Union and for enabling national positions to be properly defended.[121] It is, thus, assisted by about 250 Working Groups of national civil servants. A Commission proposal is first passed to these Groups for analysis. These Groups provide Reports which set the agenda for COREPER meetings by indicating points on which there has been agreement within the Working Group (Roman I points) and points which need discussion within COREPER (Roman II points). It is best to see COREPER as the tip of complex networks of national administrations working together to agree legislation.[122] Even in this light, COREPER raises some concerns. There is disagreement about whether representatives always articulate national interests or whether they are concerned with solving problems and reaching agreement, wherever possible.[123] The other concern raised by COREPER is government by 'moonlight'. Meetings of the COREPER are not public. Its minutes are not published and it is not accountable to any parliamentary assembly. To be sure, many decisions taken in any national government are taken by civil servants, but it is the unprecedented extent of COREPER's influence that raises particular concerns about accountability and transparency.

4 THE EUROPEAN COUNCIL

The European Council comprises the Heads of Government of the Member States, its President and the President of the Commission.[124] It is a separate institution from the Council of Ministers. It is to meet at least four times per year, although additional meetings can be convened if necessary.[125] The Lisbon Treaty sets out a change of gear for the European Council. For the first time it is formally recognised as an institution of the European Union.[126] It is no longer, formally at least, confined to setting out guidelines for the Union, but is now to define its directions and priorities.

---

[119] *Report on the European Institutions by the Committee of Three to the European Council* (Tindemans Report) (Brussels, EC Council, 1979) 49–54; *Report from the Ad Hoc Committee on Institutional Affairs to the European Council* (Dooge Report), *EC Bulletin* 3-1985, 3.5.1.

[120] M. v. Schendelen, '"The Council Decides": Does the Council Decide?' (1996) 34 *JCMS* 531.

[121] F. Hayes-Renshaw, C. Lequesne and P. Lopez, 'The Permanent Representatives of the Member States of the European Union' (1989) 28 *JCMS* 119, 129–31.

[122] D. Bostock, 'Coreper Revisited' (2002) 40 *JCMS* 215, 231–2.

[123] Cf. J. Lewis, 'National Interests: COREPER' in J. Peterson and M. Shackleton (eds.), *The Institutions of the European Union* (Oxford, Oxford University Press, 2002); F. Häge, 'Committee Decision-making in the Council of the European Union' (2007) 8 *EUP* 299.

[124] Article 15(2) TEU

[125] Article 15(3) TEU.

[126] Article 13 TEU.

> **Article 15(1) TEU**
>
> The European Council shall provide the Union with the necessary impetus for its development and shall define the general political directions and priorities thereof. It shall not exercise legislative functions.

This agenda-setting is limited by the final sentence, which indicates that the European Council is not to trespass on the Commission's traditional prerogatives to propose legislation. Instead, the suggestion is that it is now to steer, direct and prompt the general course of the Union far more actively than previously. To support this enhanced role, greater organisational support is provided for it and it is made more accountable than previously.

(i) Powers of the European Council

The first set of powers enjoyed by the European Council may be described as constitution-making powers. It makes decisions about the future shape and membership of the European Union. It is the European Council, therefore, which makes the decision to suspend the membership of a state.[127] Whilst not taking the formal decision, it is the European Council which sets the criteria to be met by a state wishing to join the Union.[128] Perhaps the most important power enjoyed by the European Council is the power to instigate Treaty reform. Following the Lisbon Treaty, there are now two procedures for this. In the ordinary revision procedure, after consulting other EU institutions, it can call, by simple majority, either a convention along the lines of the Future of Europe Convention or an intergovernmental conference. These will put forward amendments which have to be ratified by all Member States in accordance with their constitutional requirements.[129]

More controversial is the simplified revision procedure. On the one hand, this allows the European Council, after consulting the other EU institutions, to amend Part III of the TFEU on Internal Policies of the European Union, although any such amendment must not increase EU competences. Any amendment cannot enter into force until ratified by all Member States in accordance with their constitutional requirements.[130] On the other, it creates what is known as a *passerelle*, which allows for amendment of the requirement of unanimity to that of QMV and adaptation of any legislative procedure to that of the ordinary legislative procedure in the TFEU and in Title V of the TEU (which governs external action).[131] Any amendment here must be notified to national parliaments and if any national parliament indicates its opposition, the amendment must be dropped.

The proponents of the simplified revision procedure argue that it is necessary to give the European Union some flexibility and responsiveness.[132] Whilst this argument can be made for QMV, as it allows the Union to take action without the shadow of the national veto, it is less convincing in the case of the ordinary legislative procedure. This gives the Parliament a

---

[127] Article 7(3) TEU.
[128] Article 49 TEU.
[129] Article 48(2)–(4) TEU.
[130] Article 48(6) TEU.
[131] Article 48(7) TEU. There is an exclusion for anything that has defence or military implications.
[132] House of Lords European Union Committee, *The Treaty of Lisbon: An Impact Assessment*, above n. 108, 37–8.

veto over legislation, and it is unclear how adding a further veto-player adds flexibility.[133] Its opponents worry that, avoiding traditional revision procedures, it could be a process for integration by stealth. In its judgment on the Lisbon Treaty, the German Constitutional Court noted that the use of the simplified revision procedure for Part III of the TFEU gave the possibility to amend 172 Articles of primary law in unpredictable ways. Whilst expressing concern over this, it reserved its full ire for the *passerelle*. It noted that with any transfer to QMV or to the ordinary legislative procedure, it would be difficult to predict the degree of power being granted to the European Union and the loss of influence for an individual Member State. Given the implications of this both for the integration process and for local democracy, the German Constitutional Court considered it an insufficient guarantee that national parliaments could simply make their opposition known. More was required. It would only be compatible with the German Basic Law if the precise amendment was approved by a German law approved by both German legislative assemblies.[134]

The second form of power enjoyed by the European Council is less controversial. These are the powers relating to organisation. Within the limits set by the Treaties, the European Council can determine the composition of the Parliament and the Commission.[135] It appoints its own President and the President of the Commission, the Commission, the High Representative, and the Executive Board of the European Central Bank.[136] To be sure, this is often done in tandem with other EU institutions but almost every non-elected office involves appointment by the Council.[137] Even judges of the Court of Justice, while not appointed by the European Council, are appointed by common accord of the governments of the Member States, which is essentially the same thing.[138]

The third form of power, alluded to more explicitly in Article 15(1) TEU, is informal agenda-setting powers. In some fields this is explicitly mandated,[139] but the European Council will agree programmes of legislation across all areas of EU policy. In such instances, a division of labour takes place, in which the European Council will usually set out broad principles and ask the Commission to develop an Action Plan to implement these principles. This role of agenda-setting transcends the formal Treaty structures and takes place in fields that fall outside formal EU competence. The pre-eminent example is the 'Lisbon process', but this is something that has nothing to do with the Lisbon Treaty. In 2000, at Lisbon, the European Council committed the Union to becoming, by 2010, 'the most competitive and dynamic knowledge-based economy in the world, capable of sustainable economic growth with more and better jobs and greater social cohesion'.[140] To do this, it recognised it would have to carry out a number of tasks that did not fall within EU competences, most notably in the fields of welfare reform and macro- and micro-economic policy. Nevertheless, every spring, under the umbrella term of the Lisbon Strategy for Growth and Jobs, the European Council sets priorities and reviews national Action Plans set by individual Member States but assessed in the light of Commission reports and guidelines that have been agreed at EU level.

---

[133] See pp. 103–5.
[134] 2 BvE 2/08 *Gauweiler* v *Treaty of Lisbon*, Judgment of 30 June 2009, paras. 311–21.
[135] Articles 14(2) and 17(5) TEU respectively.
[136] Articles 15(5), 17(7) (both President and Commission as a whole), 18(1) TEU and 283(2) TFEU respectively.
[137] The most significant exception is the Ombudsman: who is elected by the European Parliament, Article 228(1), (2) TFEU.
[138] Article 19(2) TEU.
[139] Article 68 TFEU (freedom, security and justice); Article 148 TFEU (employment).
[140] Conclusions of the Presidency, *EU Bulletin* 3-2000, 1.5.

Fourthly, the European Council has problem-solving powers. Heads of Government have the domestic authority to resolve issues which have reached an impasse within the Council of Ministers. In particularly sensitive fields, the European Council is deployed not merely where there is no resolution but where a Member State feels insufficient sensitivity is being shown to its prerogatives. In the field of Common Foreign and Security Policy (CFSP), where there is provision for QMV, a Member State may refer the matter to the European Council for 'vital and stated' reasons.[141] The other problem-solving power is the so-called 'brake procedure' introduced by the Lisbon Treaty. This allows a member of the Council to refer a legislative proposal to the European Council if it affects important aspects of its social security system[142] or fundamental aspects of its criminal justice system.[143]

Finally, the European Council has a particularly prominent role in the CFSP. It defines and identifies the strategic objectives and interests of the CFSP and sets out guidelines.[144] It also acts as a forum where Member States can consult each other about matters of general interest in this field.[145]

(ii) Organisation of the European Council

There is mismatch between the time spent by Heads of Government in the European Council and its wide-ranging tasks. For many years it was unclear whether it had the resources to discharge the more extensive responsibilities demanded of it. Thus, despite the European Council formally being pre-eminent in the Lisbon process, it was, in practice, the Commission or individual Councils that did much of the work. Since 2002, the General Affairs and External Relations Council has performed a similar role to that performed by COREPER for the Council of Ministers. This role is to ensure overall coordination of policy between the different Council of Ministers configurations and to set the agenda for the European Council. The General Affairs and External Relations Council also agrees items to be adopted without discussion and those that need further debate. If the item requires discussion, it will prepare an outline paper setting out the issues to be discussed and the options available.[146]

This has been formalised by the Lisbon Treaty, with the new autonomous General Affairs Council having this role.[147] Yet, experience since 2002 begs the question whether foreign ministers have, alongside all their other responsibilities, the authority and resources either to coordinate policy or to prepare meetings sufficiently. Alongside this, the question of continuity was a problem, as, with the rotating Council Presidencies, every six months a new Member State came forward to chair European Council meetings.

To that end, the Lisbon Treaty creates a new office, that of President of the European Council. Elected by the European Council by QMV for a two and a half year term that may be

---

[141] Article 31(2) TEU.
[142] Article 48 TFEU.
[143] Articles 82(3) and 83(3) TFEU.
[144] Articles 22 and 26 TEU.
[145] Article 32 TEU.
[146] Decision 2002/682/EC, EURATOM, article 2(3).
[147] Article 16(6) TEU. It is working with the Commission and the President of the European Council on this.

renewed once,[148] the President will sit as an additional member of the European Council.[149] Her tasks are to:

- chair and drive forward the work of the European Council whilst endeavouring to facilitate consensus and cohesion within it;
- ensure the preparation and continuity of the work of the European Council in cooperation with the President of the Commission, and on the basis of the work of the General Affairs Council;
- present a report to the Parliament after each of the meetings of the European Council;
- ensure the external representation of the Union on issues concerning its Common Foreign and Security Policy, without prejudice to the powers of the High Representative.[150]

The mission of the President has both an ex ante and an ex post dimension. Ex ante, she is to organise, coordinate and secure direction for the European Council, building alliances and facilitating agendas. Ex post, she is mandated to secure follow-up, seeing that European Council Decisions are implemented. Her success will be dependent on a number of factors. While setting the policy agenda for the European Union and building consensus around this looks like a significant task, there is no provision made for the President to have a significant administration of her own. There is also the question of her relationship with the different Member States. Since she is expected to be the handmaiden of national governments, there will inevitably be a tension between the larger Member States, which will expect her to pay more attention to their greater economic weight and larger populations, and the smaller Member States, which will expect her to treat all Member States equally regardless of size. Finally, there is her relationship with the supranational institutions, notably the Commission. They are expected to cooperate with each other, but the essential structure of the relationship is a competitive one. Each will have an agenda-setting role and will be keen to assert its preferences and prerogatives.

(iii) The European Council within the EU institutional settlement

Although recognised by the SEA,[151] the European Council is often treated as something apart from the EU institutional settlement. Its relationship to the wider institutional settlement or as part of it has not been researched in detail. This might be in part because it started as an informal summit, or because it did not conform to the same legal strictures as other parts of the Union. Even before being raised to that formal status by the Lisbon Treaty, it is a central part of the institutional settlement with significant powers.[151a]

The first question is how the exercise of European Council power shifts influence within the European Union. If it exercises a powerful guiding hand, it also has the potential to direct the Union. As the extract below illustrates, notwithstanding that voting is usually done by unanimity and sometimes by QMV, it is the body where large state influence is most to the fore.

---

[148] Article 15(5) TEU.   [149] Article 15(2) TEU.   [150] Article 15(6) TEU.   [151] Article 2 SEA.
[151a] This positioning is reflected in the European Council publishing its Rules of Procedure in the *Official Journal*: Decision 2009/882/EU adopting the European Council Rules of Procedure [2009] OJ L315/51.

J. Tallberg, 'Bargaining Power in the European Council' (2008) 46 *Journal of Common Market Studies* 685, 690–1

In Europe of today, gun-boat diplomacy is not an option and aggregate structural power affects negotiations in considerably more subtle ways. The interviews suggest that resources and capabilities rarely are actively deployed in the bargaining process. Rather, asymmetries in aggregate structural power matter indirectly, by affecting a state's range of alternatives, the resources it can commit to an issue and the legitimacy of its claims to influence.

A large home market makes a state more influential in economic negotiations, military capabilities enable a state to exercise leadership in the EU's foreign and security policy and population size grants voice in an EU conceiving of itself as a democratic community.

According to the interviewees, national executives representing structurally advantaged states are allowed greater latitude in the negotiations. Jean-Claude Juncker explains: 'If you are representing a medium-sized country, you can never say "Denmark thinks…". You can only say "I would submit to your considerations, if not…". Those who are speaking for greater Member States, by opening their mouth and by referring to their national flag, they are immediately indicating that, behind their words, you have to accept size and demography. "La France pense que…" and "Deutschland denkt…" that is something different'. Göran Persson, former prime minister of Sweden, points to a parallel dynamic: 'If you are the prime minister of a country with five to ten million people, you simply cannot monopolize 20 per cent of the time devoted to the conclusions.' Furthermore, differences in structural power are perceived to affect the legitimacy of wielding the veto. According to one prime minister, it is a simple reality of politics that 'Luxemburg can issue a veto once in a decade and Britain once per week'. By the same token, the veto of large Member States is perceived to carry more weight than that of the small or medium-sized states, according to David O'Sullivan, former secretary general of the Commission: 'The veto of Cyprus is not the same as the veto of Germany.' Interviewees also testify that large Member States may get away with tactics that otherwise are considered inappropriate, such as exploiting the inadequate preparation of an issue to push through their own proposal, or launching entirely new initiatives at the negotiation table.

As a result, the interests of the larger Member States tend to set the framework for European Council negotiations. Where the interests of France, Germany and the UK conflict, they nevertheless set the terms within which agreements must be sought. Where these states see eye-to-eye on an issue, or even have arrived at pre-agreements, it is extremely difficult to achieve outcomes that diverge from this position. Frequently cited examples in recent years of France, Germany and the UK dominating negotiations and outcomes in the European Council include the provisions on a semi-permanent president of the European Council in the 2004 Constitutional Treaty, the deal in December 2005 on the new financial perspective for 2007–13 and the political agreement in July 2007 on the subsequent Lisbon Treaty.

In the remainder of the article, Tallberg notes that the situation is not as simple as, the bigger and richer you are, the more powerful you are. He notes that the Presidency always enjoys a particular power. The personal authority of individuals matters, and on specific issues where a state has a particular interest it will acquire more authority. This simply raises further questions about how Decisions are reached and the relative legitimacy of Decisions reached in the European Council vis-à-vis those in other EU institutions, particularly when the former impact on the latter. This is addressed half-heartedly by the Lisbon Treaty. The European Council can now be subject to review by the Court of Justice[152] and the Presidents must submit reports after each meeting to the Parliament.[153] Yet it is far-fetched to imagine the circumstances in which a court would strike down a Decision by twenty-seven Heads of Government, and how seriously the latter will take any critical views of the Parliament is also open to question. More interestingly, other controls such as duties of transparency or a duty to account to national parliaments before and after any meeting are missing. The test of whether formalising the position of the European Council is simply returning decision-making to intergovernmental negotiations will be to observe whether such negotiations are developed.

5 THE EUROPEAN PARLIAMENT

(i) Composition of the European Parliament

The European Parliament was initially set up as the European Assembly and was only formally recognised as a Parliament in the Single European Act (SEA).[154] Prior to 1979, it consisted of representatives from national assemblies or parliaments. Since then, MEPs have been elected by direct universal suffrage at five-yearly intervals.[155] There are a number of features which distinguish the Parliament from its national counterparts.

The seats are not evenly distributed on the basis of population.[156] The Parliament is composed of 736 members, but citizens in smaller Member States are better represented than citizens in larger Member States. Luxembourg, with a population of 400,000 citizens, has one MEP for roughly every 65,500 citizens. Germany, by contrast, with a population of 82 million citizens, has one MEP for approximately every 828,000 citizens. The 2009 cohort of MEPs were elected before the Lisbon Treaty. This provides a different formula for future elections. The Parliament should not exceed 750 members. Representation will be on the basis of degressive proportionality, whereby the principle of per head representation is combined with the principle that the larger the population of a Member State, the lower the weighting per head. Additionally, no state should receive fewer than six MEPs and no state may have more than 96 MEPs.[157] In October 2007, the Constitutional Affairs Committee of the Parliament made a distribution of seats for each national territory on the basis of this principle and negotiations proceeded on the basis of these calculations. This was accepted with one small amendment.[158] Whilst the principle of degressive proportionality curbs the horse trading of prior times, it

---

[152] Articles 263 and 265 TFEU.

[153] Article 15(6)(d) TEU.

[154] Article 3 SEA.

[155] Decision 76/787/EEC [1976] OJ L278/1. On the history of the European Parliament since the establishment of the Common Assembly in the ECSC see B. Rittberger, *Building Europe's Parliament: Democratic Representation Beyond the Nation-State* (Oxford, Oxford University Press, 2005) chs. 3–6.

[156] The respective numbers are: Austria 17, Belgium 22, Bulgaria 16, Czech Republic 22, Cyprus 6, Denmark 13, Estonia 6, Finland 13, France 72, Germany 99, Greece 22, Hungary 22, Ireland 12, Italy 72, Latvia 8, Lithuania 12, Luxembourg 6, Malta 5, the Netherlands 25, Poland 50, Portugal 22, Romania 33, Slovakia 13, Slovenia 7, Spain 50, Sweden 18, United Kingdom 72.

[157] Article 14(2) TEU.

[158] Declaration No. 4 to the Lisbon Treaty on the composition of the European Parliament. Italy was awarded an extra seat. It was also agreed that the President of the European Parliament will count towards the total. The future allocation of seats will be 96 (Germany), 74 (France), 73 (United Kingdom, Italy), 54 (Spain), 51 (Poland), 33 (Romania), 26 (the Netherlands), 22 (Greece, Portugal, Belgium, Czech Republic, Hungary), 20 (Sweden), 19 (Austria), 18 (Bulgaria), 13 (Denmark, Slovakia, Finland), 12 (Ireland, Lithuania), 9 (Latvia), 8 (Slovenia), 6 (Luxembourg, Malta, Cyprus, Estonia).

should be noted that it is still a long way from equal representation of citizens, and Luxembourgeois votes continue to be more valuable than German ones.

There are no uniform procedures for election. Common procedures were used for the first time in the 2004 elections with MEPs elected by proportional representation. However, states can decide on the particular system of proportional representation they wish to use. They can establish constituencies as they see fit and can require parties to achieve 5 per cent of the vote before they are allocated seats.[159] Furthermore, the Parliament cannot challenge the administration of these elections even where it believes that Member States have not followed their own electoral procedures or some dubious practice has taken place. National law is taken as the exclusive basis for verifying this.[160] Finally, as mentioned previously, there are no European political parties. MEPs are elected as representatives of national political parties. This has made elections 'second order national contests'.[161] Voters vote on domestic issues and turn-outs tend to be lower than for national elections.[162] Instead, most MEPs sit in European party groupings.[163] There are seven groupings, of which the two largest are the European Peoples' Party (right of centre parties) and the Progressive Alliance of Socialists and Democrats (left of centre parties).[164] These groupings are important in the organisation of the Parliament.[165] Studies have shown that these groupings affect voting behaviour, with MEPs within groupings acting reasonably cohesively.[166] That said, voting behaviour is still considerably less cohesive than in national parliaments and party groupings are unable to affect the way national delegations cast their votes in key votes.[167]

These traits generate concerns about both the representative and deliberative capacities of the Parliament. Concerns about the former lie in the idea that a representative democracy depends upon the presence of a 'people' (*demos*) or collective sense of 'Us' to represent.[168] Without this common sense of 'Us', it is argued, there is no reason for losers of any vote to accept the view of the majority, for they do not see themselves as part of a common political community with whose decisions they must comply.[169] Concerns about the latter stem from political parties, media and civil society all being organised along predominantly national lines. This prevents a debate which is plural, transparent and vigorous.

---

[159] Decision 2002/772/EURATOM/EC, concerning the election of the members of the European Parliament by direct universal suffrage [2002] OJ L283/1.

[160] Joined Cases C-393/07 and C-9/08 *Italy v Parliament*, Judgment of 30 April 2009.

[161] M. Franklin *et al.*, 'Uncorking the Bottle: Popular Opposition to European Unification in the Wake of Maastricht' (1994) 32 *JCMS* 455, 470. On this debate see B. Crum, 'Party Stances in the Referendum on the EU Constitution' (2007) 8 *EUP* 61, 63–4

[162] Turn-out was just over 43 per cent despite voting being compulsory in some Member States.

[163] On the evolution of these see A. Kreppel, *The European Parliament and the Supranational Party System* (Cambridge, Cambridge University Press, 2002).

[164] For the 2009–14 Parliament, the groupings are European Peoples' Party (265 MEPs); Progressive Alliance of Socialists and Democrats (184 MEPs); Alliance of Liberals and Democrats for Europe (84 MEPs); the Greens and European Free Alliance (55 MEPs); European Conservatives and Reformists (54 MEPs); European United Left and Nordic Green Left (35 MEPs); Europe of Freedom and Democracy (35 MEPs). There are 27 non-attached MEPs.

[165] Membership of a grouping also entitles a national party to funding. Regulation 2004/2003/EC on the regulations governing political parties at European level and the rules regarding their funding [2003] OJ L297/1.

[166] S. Hix, A. Noury and G. Roland, 'Power to the Parties: Cohesion and Competition in the European Parliament' (2005) 35 *BJPS* 209.

[167] D. Judge and D. Earnshaw, *The European Parliament* (Basingstoke, Palgrave, 2003) 149–55.

[168] J. Weiler, 'Does Europe Need a Constitution? Reflections on Demos, Telos and the German Maastricht Decision' (1995) 1 *ELJ* 219, 225.

[169] F. Scharpf, *Governing in Europe: Effective and Democratic?* (Oxford, Oxford University Press, 1999) 7–20.

D. Grimm, 'Does Europe Need a Constitution?' (1995) 1 *European Law Journal* **282, 293–4, 296–7**

The democratic nature of a political system is attested not so much by the existence of elected parliaments ... as by the pluralism, internal representativity, freedom and capacity for compromise of the intermediate area of parties, associations, citizens' movements and communication media. Where a parliament does not rest on such a structure, which guarantees constant interaction between people and State, democratic substance is lacking even if democratic forms are present.

... At European level, though, even the prerequisites are largely lacking. Mediatory structures have hardly been even formed here yet. There is no Europeanised party system, just European groups in the Strasbourg parliament, and apart from that, loose cooperation among programmatically related parties. This does not bring any integration of the European population, even at the moment of European elections. Nor have European associations or citizens' movements arisen, even though cooperation among national associations is further advanced than with parties. A search for European media, whether in print or broadcast, would be completely fruitless. This makes the European Union fall far short not just of ideal conceptions of a model democracy but even of the already deficit situation in Member States ...

The absence of a European communication system, due chiefly to language diversity, has the consequence that for the foreseeable future there will be neither a European public nor a European political discourse. Public discourse instead remains for the time bound by national frontiers, while the European sphere will remain dominated by professional and interest discourses conducted remotely from the public. European decisional processes are accordingly not under public observation in the same way as national ones. The European level of politics lacks a matching public. The feedback to European officials and representatives is therefore only weakly developed, while national politicians orient themselves even in the case of Council decisions to their national publics, because effective sanctions can come only from them. These circumstances give professional and technical viewpoints, particularly of an economic nature, excessive weight in European politics, while the social consequences and side-effects remain in the dark. This shortcoming cannot be made up for even by growing national attention to European policy themes, since the European dimension is just what is lacking there.

If this is true, the conclusion may be drawn that the full parliamentarisation of the European Union on the model of the national constitutional State will rather aggravate than solve the problem. On the one hand it would loosen the Union's ties back to the Member States, since the European Parliament is by its construction not a federal organ but a central one. Strengthening it would be at the expense of the Council and therefore inevitably have centralising effects. On the other hand the weakened ties back to the Member States would not be compensated by any increased ties back to the Union population. The European Parliament does not meet with any European mediatory structure in being: still less does it constitute a European popular representative body, since there is yet no European people. This is not an argument against any expansion of Parliament's powers. That might even enhance participation opportunities in the Union, provide greater transparency and create a counterweight to the dominance of technical and economic viewpoints. Its objective ought not, however, to be full parliamentarisation on the national model, since political decisions would otherwise move away to where they can be only democratically accountable.

The suspicion that this assessment is a front for the idea that democracy is possible only on the basis of a homogeneous 'Volksgemeinschaft' [ethnic community] is, after all that, baseless. The requirements for democracy are here developed not out of the people, but out of the society that wants to constitute itself as a political unit. It is true that this requires a collective identity, if it wants to settle its conflicts non-violently, accept majority rule and practise solidarity. But this identity need by no means be rooted in ethnic conflict, but must also have other bases. All that is necessary is for the society to have formed an awareness or belonging together that can support majority decisions and solidarity efforts, and for it to have the capacity to communicate about its goals and problems discursively. What obstructs democracy is accordingly not the lack of cohesion of Union citizens as a people, but their weakly developed collective identity and low capacity for transnational discourse. This certainly means that the European democracy deficit is structurally determined. It can therefore not be removed by institutional reforms in any short term. The achievement of the democratic constitutional State can for the time being be adequately recognised only in the national framework.

(ii) Powers of the European Parliament

Most people consider parliaments as law-makers and their influence is often measured by their power over the making of policy and legislation. Strong parliaments are responsible for making policy and law, whilst weaker parliaments can only influence them.[170] Parliaments also exercise power over the executive. In stronger parliamentary systems, executive power is derived from the legislature. The legislature appoints the executive and sets the conditions for the exercise of its powers.[171] In weaker systems, parliaments exercise powers of scrutiny over the executive and it is accountable to them. Finally, parliaments traditionally have powers over the finances of a state. Once again, these vary according to the strength of the parliament, with the stronger parliaments having control over both revenue (money coming in) and expenditure (money going out). These are all mentioned in the description of the Parliament's powers set out in Article 14 TEU.

Article 14(1) TEU

The European Parliament shall, jointly with the Council, exercise legislative and budgetary functions. It shall exercise functions of political control and consultation as laid down in the Treaties. It shall elect the President of the Commission.

In evaluating the Parliament as a parliament, it is also worth considering it against two styles of parliament. Dann has termed these the debating parliament and the working parliament. The former, of which the British House of Commons is an example, is characterised by the government having a majority in it, and its central role being most of the time to debate government policy. On the other hand, with a working parliament, of which the US Congress is an example, the legislature is separate from the executive. It centres around reviewing the work of the executive and this is usually done by strong committees. In this regard, Dann notes that the Parliament is very much a working parliament. The extract below set outs the structure and work of the committees.

---

[170] P. Norton, *Legislatures* (Oxford, Oxford University Press, 1990) 179.
[171] P. Raworth, 'A Timid Step Forwards: Maastricht and the Democratisation of the European Community' (1994) 19 *ELRev.* 16.

P. Dann, 'European Parliament and Executive Federalism: Approaching a
Parliament in a Semi-Parliamentary Democracy' (2003) 9 *European Law Journal*
549, 564–5

First, their role in acquiring information, discussing and analysing it, and finally formulating the
political position of the European Parliament is absolutely central. The committees have the right to
interrogate the Commission and to hold hearings with special experts. Building on these instruments,
the committees can (and do) acquire specific expertise in their fields. On this basis, it is their task to
file reports for the plenary, thereby formulating and pre-determining most of the final outcomes. These
powers are a sword with two sharp sides: they not only facilitate the European Parliament's role in
legislative procedures, but also contribute to the European Parliament's ability to competently scrutinise
the executive, especially when it comes to implementation.

There is a second aspect which allows the committees to play such a pivotal part in the institution:
their internal structure. They are not only small, but also specialised and oriented in their scope
towards the division of subject matters in the Commission. Of salient importance is their special
leadership structure. This consists of a chairman and a *rapporteur*. The latter is responsible for
presenting a matter to the committee, drafting the report for the committee and arguing it in plenary
and with other institutions. Therefore a highly influential figure, he is chosen in a complicated and
hotly contested procedure. Besides, this position creates clear responsibilities, giving the committee a
distinct voice to communicate to the inside (between different committees and party groups) as well
as to the outside (to other institutions). It renders the committee especially suited to negotiate with
other institutions through an expert representative. It also contributes to the European Parliament's
chances to fit into the consensus system of the EU, where different institutions have to constantly
negotiate.

There is one more parameter to qualify a parliament as working or debating type and that is the
size and organisation of its staff: whereas the *working parliament* can acquire its expertise and level
of scrupulous scrutiny of the executive only because of the support of an extensive staff, the *debating
parliament* traditionally has very little of it. Its approach is based more on the rhetorical skill of the
single parliamentarian to surprise the government and disclose its weakness in debate than on counter-
weighing governmental bureaucracies.

Looking at the European Parliament, the staff is yet another factor which underlines its basic
nature as a working parliament. Compared to the US Congress of course, it looks petty. But
compared to all national parliaments in Europe, it has one of the largest staffs. The EP staff is
organised on different levels: on an individual level, every MEP has at least one full time assistant
which she can freely employ. On a party level, every party group in the EP is ascribed a number of
assistants according to their size and the number of languages spoken. Finally, there is the General
Secretariat of the European Parliament in Luxembourg which provides further assistance for the
parliamentarians.

Altogether, the staff of the European Parliament totals 4,100 persons. In sum: the European
Parliament is also in respect to its oversight function clearly a working parliament with well-structured
committees having prominent rights, providing an infrastructure to seriously scrutinise the executive,
and with the number and organisation of the staff displaying once again the basic character of the
European Parliament as a working parliament.

The party groups exert their strongest influence over determining the composition of Parliament committees. Although committee membership is intended to reflect the ideological and territorial composition of the full Parliament,[172] the chairs of the committees are determined by negotiation between the groups.[173] Thus, for the 2009 Parliament, there are twenty-two committees. Of these, eighteen are chaired either by a MEP belonging to the European Peoples' Party or to the Progressive Alliance of Socialists and Democrats.[174]

(a) Legislative powers of the European Parliament

On their face, the legislative powers of the Parliament seem weaker than national parliaments. The Parliament has no monopoly of adoption over any legislative proposal nor power of initiative in any significant field of policy-making. Instead, its legislative powers vary according to the legislative procedure adopted and this will depend on the policy field in question. There are two dominant procedures: the consultation procedure and the ordinary legislative procedure. Under the former, the Parliament is consulted on a proposal and has the right to propose amendments. Under the latter, in addition to these rights, the Parliament can veto any proposal. It also has the power to negotiate joint texts in a committee, the Conciliation Committee, with the Council. Bald statements of its powers do not capture the significance of its input and this is addressed in more detail in Chapter 3.

The Parliament does have, however, informal, general powers of agenda-setting under both procedures. One route is for it to request the Commission to submit a proposal.[175] The route for this is an 'Own Initiative' report. The relevant committee of the Parliament will draw up a report. The Parliament will then vote on it in plenary session, adopting a Resolution requesting the Commission to act. The request to submit a proposal is deployed in a limited manner. This is not true of the other route for agenda-setting available under both legislative procedures, which is to propose amendments to Commission proposals. Between 1999 and 2007, about 87 per cent of Commission proposals under the ordinary legislative procedure (known then as the co-decision procedure) were subject to amendment and about 54 per cent of those involving the consultation procedure.[176] The procedure involves the Parliament committee providing a report, which is then ratified by plenary session, and has been used to gain the Parliament significant influence. It is estimated that 19 per cent of its amendments under consultation[177] and up to 83 per cent under the ordinary legislative procedure are accepted. [178]

(b) Powers over the Executive

Parliament has a variety of tools to hold the other EU institutions to account. It has powers of appointment and dismissal, powers of litigation and powers of enquiry.

[172] G. Mcelroy, 'Committee Representation in the European Parliament' (2006) 7 *EUP* 5.
[173] S. Bowler and D. Farrell, 'The Organizing of the European Parliament: Committees, Specialization and Co-ordination' (1995) 25 *BJPS* 219.
[174] www.europarl.europa.eu/members/expert/committees.do?language=EN (accessed 1 August 2009). All the other groupings other than the grouping of Europe of Freedom and Democracy (the most Euro-sceptic grouping) have one chair.
[175] See p. 62.
[176] R. Kardasheva, 'The Power to Delay: The European Parliament's Influence in the Consultation Procedure' (2009) 47 *JCMS* 385, 392.
[177] *Ibid.* 394–5.
[178] European Parliament, *Activity Report for 5th Parliamentary Term*, PE 287.644, 14. Figures are only available for this procedure for the 1999–2004 period. On the reasons for this influence see pp. 105–7.

Powers of appointment and dismissal The Parliament is exclusively responsible for appointing the European Ombudsman[179] and can apply for her to be dismissed by the Court of Justice if she no longer fulfils the conditions required for the performance of her duties or is guilty of serious misconduct.[180] Of greater political significance are the Parliament's powers over the appointment of the Commission. The Parliament has a double power of approval. It must approve the President of the Commission, who has been nominated by the Heads of Government. If the nomination is accepted, it must also approve the College of Commissioners nominated by the President of the Commission and the Heads of Government.[181] Since 1999, the term of the Commission has been synchronised with that of the Parliament. This has allowed the Parliament to use its powers of assent extremely effectively. All prospective Commissioners are subject to questioning by Parliament committees before assent is given to their appointment. They must answer questions about their professional past, their views on European integration and their legislative agenda for their term in office.

That Parliament will use its power of assent if it is not satisfied with the views of individual Commissioners was demonstrated by the events of 2004. The Parliament was unhappy with three nominees, in particular. It disapproved of the Italian nomination, Rocco Buttiglione, because of his views on women and homosexuality. It was also unhappy with the Latvian nominee, Ingride Udre, because of allegations surrounding corruption in her party. Finally, it was unconvinced that the Hungarian nominee, László Kovács, had sufficient knowledge about the Energy portfolio allocated to him. When it became clear that there was not a majority for the Commission because of these nominations, Barroso, the Commission President, had to arrange for the Italian and Latvian nominations to be replaced, and Kovács was allocated the Taxation and Customs Union portfolio instead.

The Parliament also has important powers to dismiss the Commission. If a motion of censure is passed by a two-thirds majority of the votes cast representing a majority (i.e. more than 368) of the total members of the Parliament, the Commission is obliged to resign as a body.[182] This is an 'all or nothing' power. It does not allow the Parliament to criticise or dismiss individual Commissioners. Nevertheless, it was threatened against the Santer Commission in 1998 following allegations of corruption and maladministration against some of its members.[183] The Commission resigned the day before a vote would have been taken sacking the entire College. Following this, a Framework Agreement was made between the Commission and Parliament which allows the Parliament to hold individual Commissioners more to censure. Under the 2005 version of the agreement, if the Parliament expresses no confidence in an individual Commissioner, the President must either sack the individual or justify not doing so to the Parliament.[184]

---

[179] Article 228(1) TFEU.
[180] Article 228(2) TFEU.
[181] Article 17(7) TEU.
[182] Article 17(8) TEU, Article 234 TFEU.
[183] D. Judge and D. Earnshaw, 'The European Parliament and the Commission Crisis: A New Assertiveness?' (2002) 15 *Governance* 345.
[184] The agreement is available at http://ec.europa.eu/dgs/secretariat_general/relations/relations_other/docs/framework_agreement_ep-ec_en.pdf (accessed 1 June 2009).

Powers of litigation   The Parliament has unlimited powers to challenge the acts of the EI institutions before the Court of Justice as well as their failure to act where they are legally required to do so.[185] Prior to the Treaty of Nice, legal acts could only be challenged where they transgressed on the Parliament's prerogatives. Parliamentary litigation focused around securing greater institutional powers for itself. It would, therefore, litigate to try to secure those legal procedures which ensured it the greatest amount of influence and challenge legislation which delegated significant law-making powers to the Commission.[186] That strategy continues, but since the Treaty of Nice, Parliament has used its unlimited *locus standi* to challenge those acts which it cannot veto, but where it is unhappy with the policy being adopted, notably where it feels there has been a violation of fundamental rights.[187]

Powers of enquiry   EU citizens and residents of the European Union are entitled to petition the Parliament.[188] In 1987, the Parliament set up a Committee of Petitions, consisting of MEPs, to consider the petitions. In 2008, the Committee received 1,886 petitions.[189] These petitions either express views on an issue, such as human rights or animal welfare, or seek redress for a particular grievance, which may have been caused by an EU institution, national authority or private body. The process serves a number of functions. In cases where a political issue is raised, it allows the possibility for a hearing to be organised by the Parliament, thereby securing a voice for parties who might otherwise be disenfranchised. In cases where maladministration by an EU institution is alleged, the Parliament may take the matter up itself. In cases where a failure of a Member State is alleged, it will ask the Commission to take the matter up with the Member State concerned.

In addition, Parliament has the power to ask questions of or receive reports from most of the EU institutions. The European Commission, European Central Bank and Ombudsman must all submit annual reports to the Parliament.[190] In addition, the President of the European Council must report to the Parliament after each of its meetings.[191] Whilst there is no formal obligation to do so, it is also customary for the state holding the Presidency of the Council to present the proposed work of the Council during its Presidency before the Parliament. Commissioners are also required to reply to questions put by parliamentary members.[192] A convention has also grown whereby the Council will answer questions put to it by members of the Parliament.[193] A corollary of this is that the Council and the European Council have a right to be heard by the Parliament.[194] Finally, the President of the European Central Bank and members of the Executive Council may, at the request of the Parliament, or on their own initiative, be heard by the competent committees of the Parliament.[195]

[185] Articles 263 and 265 TFEU.
[186] M. McCowan, 'The European Parliament before the Bench: ECJ Precedent and EP Litigation Strategies' (2003) 10 *JEPP* 974.
[187] See e.g. Joined Cases C-317/04 and C-318/04 *Parliament v Commission (European Network and Information Security Agency)* [2006] ECR I-4721; Case C-540/03 *Parliament v Council (family reunification)* [2006] ECR I-5769.
[188] Article 20(2)(d) TEU and Articles 24 and 227 TFEU.
[189] European Parliament, *Report on the Deliberations of the Committee of Petitions during the Parliamentary Year 2008*, A6-00232/2009.
[190] Articles 249, 284(3), 228 TFEU.
[191] Article 15(6)(d) TEU.
[192] Article 230 TFEU.
[193] It is formally obliged to answer questions in the field of CFSP: Article 36 TEU.
[194] Article 230 TFEU.
[195] Article 284(3)TFEU.

(c) Financial powers of the Parliament

Parliament has significant powers over the EU Budget and, in this field, is the central player with the Council. Expenditure is set through a five-year multi-annual framework for expenditure setting out the limits on total expenditure, and ceilings for each heading of expenditure are to be set by the Council after obtaining the consent of the Parliament.[196] Annual budgets are then set each year. These have to be in balance, comply with the multi-annual framework and be based on individual institutions' estimates of expenditure. Within these constraints, the Commission sets a draft Budget, which may then be adopted by the Council. The Parliament then has the right to veto the Budget should it wish.[197]

6 OTHER INSTITUTIONS[198]

(i) The Court of Auditors

Comprising twenty-seven members appointed for a six-year term, the duty of the Court of Auditors is to audit the revenue and expenditure of the European Union.[199] The audit is to be based on the records of the Union and if necessary, performed on the spot on the premises of any body that manages EU revenue or receives any payments from the EU Budget.[200] Despite these investigative powers, it has no powers to prosecute for fraud, but is obliged to report any irregularity to the appropriate body. For these purposes, the Court of Auditors is required to liaise with national audit bodies or, where appropriate, with national departments. The Court of Auditors can submit observations or deliver opinions on specific matters at the request of the other EU institutions and it can also assist the Parliament and the Council in exercising their powers of control over the implementation of the EU Budget. However, its greatest voice comes from the annual report it publishes on EU finances at the end of each financial year.[201] The Parliament can only give a discharge to the Commission in respect of implementation of the Budget on the basis of this report.[202] These reports have been trenchant in their criticism of the management of the EU finances. In the 2008 Report, for example, on spending in 2007, the Court of Auditors found that there were insufficient controls by both the Commission and the Member States for managing the risk of irregularity and illegality in a number of fields, which included all the majority fields of expenditure.[203]

(ii) The Committee of the Regions and the Economic and Social Committee

Established to give regional authorities greater input in the decision-making process, the Committee has 344 members, appointed for a five-year renewable term.[204] Historically,

---

[196] Article 312(1), 2 TFEU.

[197] Article 314 TFEU. A process of conciliation takes place similar to that in the ordinary legislative procedure.

[198] Other EU institutions not directly involved in law-making or governing the European Union are considered in other chapters. The Court of Justice is considered in Chapter 4; the European Central Bank is considered in Chapter 17.

[199] Article 287(1) TFEU.

[200] Article 287(3) TFEU.

[201] Article 287(4) TFEU.

[202] Article 319(1) TFEU.

[203] The Annual Report can be found at [2008] OJ C286/1.

[204] Article 305 TFEU.

the Committee has just had advisory status, with its being consulted on Commission legislative proposals. In some fields this is mandatory,[205] but there still remain a number of areas with an important regional dimension, such as the internal market, competition, industrial policy and consumer protection, for which no consultation is required. The Committee has been relatively unsuccessful in this role, with its opinions carrying limited weight with the other EU institutions,[206] and the most powerful regions of the Union preferring to deal with the other EU institutions directly rather than act through the Committee.[207] The Lisbon Treaty granted the Committee of the Regions new powers as a litigator. It can now take the other EU institutions to court if it believes they violate the subsidiarity principle. This principle states that the Union must only add legislation insofar as the objectives of the measure cannot be achieved by the Member States acting unilaterally and by reason of their scale or effect can better be realised at EU level. The potential policing effect of this is mitigated by its only being able to do this in the limited fields where consultation of the Committee is mandatory,[208] and it is to be noted that the Court of Justice has yet to strike down a measure for violating the subsidiarity principle.[209]

The Economic and Social Committee (ESC) is to represent civil society within the decision-making processes. There are 344 members appointed for a five-year renewable term[210] and these are divided into three Groups: Group I comprises employers; Group II consists of employees and trade unions; Group III represents variable interests, a heterogeneous group representing farmers, small businesses, the crafts, the professions, cooperatives and non-profit associations, consumer and environmental organisations, associations representing the family, women, persons with disabilities and the academic community. The ESC's central role is to provide Opinions on legislative initiatives. In some fields, consultation with the ESC is compulsory, whilst in others it is optional. Its impact appears to be minor[211] and this, together with a perception that it is overly corporatist, led fifty-seven MEPS in 2007 to call for its abolition.[212]

[205] Most notably education (Article 165(2) TFEU); culture (Article 167(5) TFEU); public health (Article 168(4) TFEU); trans-European networks (Article 172 TFEU); and economic and social cohesion (Article 178 TFEU).

[206] R. McCarthy, 'The Committee of the Regions: An Advisory Body's Tortuous Path to Influence' (1997) 4 *JEPP* 439.

[207] T. Borzel, *States and Regions in the European Union* (Cambridge, Cambridge University Press, 2002) 73.

[208] Protocol on the application of the principles of subsidiarity and proportionality, Article 8. See also Article 263(3) TFEU.

[209] See pp. 364–5.

[210] Article 302 TFEU.

[211] Cf. S. Weatherill and P. Beaumont, *EC Law: The Essential Guide to the Legal Workings of the European Community* (3rd edn, Harmondsworth, Penguin, 1999).

[212] European Parliament, Written Declaration pursuant to Rule 116 of the Rules of Procedure by Nils Lundgren and Hélène Goudin on the abolition of the Economic and Social Committee, 0078/2007.

FURTHER READING

D. Curtin and M. Egeberg, 'Tradition and Innovation: Europe's Accumulated Executive Order' (2008) 31 *West European Politics* 639

D. Earnshaw and D. Judge, *The European Parliament* (2nd edn, Basingstoke, Palgrave, 2008)

D. Geradin *et al.* (eds.), *Regulation through Agencies in the EU* (Cheltenham, Edward Elgar, 2006)

F. Hayes-Renshaw and H. Wallace, *The Council of Ministers* (2nd edn, Basingstoke, Macmillan, 2006)

H. Hofmann and A. Türk (eds.), *EU Administrative Governance* (Cheltenham, Edward Elgar, 2006)

L. Hooghe, *The European Commission and the Integration of Europe* (Cambridge, Cambridge University Press, 2001)

M. Pollack, *The Engines of European Integration: Delegation, Agency and Agenda-Setting in the EU* (Oxford, Oxford University Press, 2003)

B. Rittberger, *Building Europe's Parliament: Democratic Representation Beyond the Nation-State* (Oxford, Oxford University Press, 2005)

A. Warntjen, 'Steering the Union: The Impact of the EU Presidency on Legislative Activity' (2007) 45 *Journal of Common Market Studies* 1135

A. Wonka, 'Decision-making Dynamics in the European Commission: Partisan, National or Sectoral?' (2008) 15 *JEPP* 1145

3

Union Law-making

CONTENTS

1 INTRODUCTION

This chapter considers the different forms of law and regulatory acts in EU law, the legislative and regulatory procedures deployed to enact them and the debate about the democratic legitimacy of the European Union. It is organised as follows.

Section 2 looks at the allocation of legislative or regulatory authority in EU law. A legal base for each field of EU law sets out the legislative procedure and legal or regulatory instruments that may be adopted in that field. In cases of contestation reference will be had to the predominant aim and content of the measure to determine the base. If the measure is inextricably and equally associated with more than one base the Court of Justice will then apply a formal hierarchy between legal bases.

Section 3 discusses the types of legislation in EU law. There are four types of binding legislative instrument in EU law: Regulations, Directives, Decisions and international agreements. Two problems to have emerged are that the legislative instruments have been used interchangeably and that there was traditionally no hierarchy between different types of legislative instrument. The latter was addressed by the Lisbon Treaty, which drew a hierarchy between legislative acts (acts adopted under the legislative procedures set out in the Treaty) and non-legislative acts. However, no hierarchy is provided between the different types of non-legislative act: delegated acts and implementing acts.

Section 4 considers the central legislative procedures. The ordinary legislative procedure grants Parliament the power of veto and Council, acting by qualified majority voting (QMV), the power of assent over any Commission proposal. Parliament rarely exercises its veto under this procedure. By contrast, it proposes extensive amendments, a significant proportion of which are accepted. Under the assent procedure Parliament has the power of assent, a requirement for it actively to approve a proposal before it becomes law. Under the consultation procedure, Parliament is merely consulted on a Commission proposal with the Council taking the final decision. Increasingly, the formal features of the legislative procedures have been blurred by the development of trilogues. These are informal meetings between representatives from the three institutions, usually taking place before the Council first considers the proposal, in which agreement is sought on the proposal.

Section 5 discusses enhanced cooperation. This enables as few as nine Member States to adopt EU laws between themselves where there is not a sufficiently high threshold for general legislation applicable across the Union. The procedural and substantial restraints on use of these procedures are stringent and no legislation has yet been adopted under them. Instead, groups of Member States have resorted to international agreements outside the structures of the Treaties. These are then either incorporated into EU law as a measure binding just those states (e.g. the Protocol integrating the Schengen Acquis) or they are subsequently made into an EU instrument as other Member States join because of the costs of exclusion (e.g. Prüm Convention).

Section 6 considers comitology. These are the procedures that govern delegated law-making by the Commission. There are four procedures: the advisory procedure, management procedure, regulatory procedure and regulatory procedure with scrutiny. Whilst their features differ, a central feature of all, other than the first one, is that a committee of national government representatives considers a draft Commission legislative act and considers whether it should be referred to the Council to adopt a different decision. In practice, almost nothing is referred and this has led to a debate about whether the interaction is an enlightened form of deliberate problem-solving, in which the different actors take on board each other's views, or whether it is simply an administrative club. In recent years, the Parliament has acquired increased powers to monitor and control the extent of delegated law-making.

Section 7 discusses the democratic deficit in the European Union. Concern about the democratic qualities of EU law-making follows a number of axes. There are, first, debates about whether the central supranational institutions have too much power at the expense of national actors. There are, secondly, concerns about whether executives and civil servants have too much power at the expense of representative institutions. Attention has, thirdly, focused on the checks and balances within the system and the efficacy of these. A final feature is the quality of public debate surrounding the EU institutions and whether it is sufficiently vigorous and plural.

2 ALLOCATION OF LEGISLATIVE PROCEDURES

The European Union has no general law-making power. Instead, its legislative powers are to be found in specific Treaty provisions, which authorise it to make laws in particular fields. Prior to the entry into force of the Treaty of Lisbon, it was possible to identify twenty-two different legislative procedures in EU law.[1] The Treaty has reduced it down to four legislative procedures, which are now set out in Article 289 TFEU.

Article 289 TFEU

1. The ordinary legislative procedure shall consist in the joint adoption by the European Parliament and the Council of a regulation, directive or decision on a proposal from the Commission. This procedure is defined in Article 294.
2. In the specific cases provided for by the Treaties, the adoption of a regulation, directive or decision by the European Parliament with the participation of the Council, or by the latter with the participation of the European Parliament, shall constitute a special legislative procedure.

The ordinary legislative procedure was known as the co-decision procedure prior to the Treaty of Lisbon. Whilst this procedure has been emphasised as being the central legislative procedure, this may be something of a misnomer. As Figure 3.1 shows, it has never been the most frequently deployed of all the legislative procedures.[2]

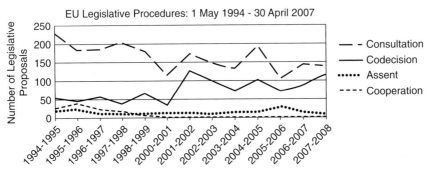

Figure 3.1   EU legislative procedures, 1 May 1994 to 30 April 2007

---

[1] *European Convention, Legislative Procedures (including the Budgetary Procedure): Current Situation*, CONV 216/02, Annex I.

[2] Figure 3.1 is taken from R. Kardasheva, *Legislative Package Deals in EU Decision-Making 1999–2007* (PhD, London School of Economics and Political Science, 2009) 16. The data was obtained from the European Parliament Legislative Observatory (OEIL). All procedures were taken into account (including procedures completed, lapsed or withdrawn and procedures under way). The period pictured runs from 1 May 1994 to 30 April 2007.

The term 'special legislative procedure' is also something of a misnomer, as, in reality, it covers two procedures. These are dealt with in more length later in the chapter but, briefly, they are the consultation procedure and the assent procedure.[3] Both the ordinary legislative procedure and the consultation procedure were extended to about forty new fields by the Lisbon Treaty. Perhaps the most interesting extension was that of the assent procedure. It was only extended to a few new competences, but these were significant ones and one, the flexibility provision in Article 352 TFEU, is one of the most frequently used. It is likely to play an increasingly prominent role alongside the other two procedures.

The choice of procedure is determined by a legal base set out in the TEU and TFEU. This legal base (e.g. Article 114 TFEU on the internal market) entitles the Union to legislate in the given field and sets out the scope for EU legislation in the area. It also determines the legislative procedures and the types of laws that can be adopted. In turn, this determines the respective powers and influences of the different EU institutions and the influence of national governments within the law-making process.[4] Often, the choice of legal base for the adoption of a provision will not be self-evident, with the different institutions seeking to use the legal basis that provides the procedure most advantageous to them. Unsurprisingly, as different procedures privilege different actors, this has led to both EU institutions and Member States vigorously litigating the choice of legal base.[5]

Prior to the Lisbon Treaty, the relationship between the three pillars had become a vexed issue as the Court of Justice had aggressively expanded the Community pillar at the expense of the other two. This led to much legislation being based on the procedures in that pillar at the expense of the procedures in the other two pillars.[6] This debate has been resolved by the abolition of the pillar structure in favour of a structure built around the two Treaties, the TEU and TFEU. The relationship between them is set out in Article 1 TEU and Article 1(2) TFEU, which both state that the Treaties are to have 'the same legal value'. This suggests that a single test will operate across the two Treaties to determine the appropriate legal base for a measure. The test used by the Court in the field of the Community pillar prior to the Lisbon Treaty, where it had to operate a single test, was to look at the predominant aim and content of the measure, and ascribe it accordingly to the appropriate legal base.[7] However, a single legal measure will often address multifarious matters (e.g. in respect of an environmental matter, single market as well as penal questions will arise). To decide that it is more about one than another is a highly contrived exercise, which inevitably involves a select foregrounding of certain features of the measure at the expense of others.

An example of the Court's reasoning is the *Recovery of Indirect Taxes* judgment. The Commission and Parliament challenged the adoption of Directive 2001/44/EC, which provided for the mutual assistance between Member States in the recovery of unpaid indirect taxation. The Council had adopted it under what is now Article 113 TFEU, which concerned

---

[3] The cooperation procedure mentioned in Figure 3.1 was abolished at Lisbon and after the coming into force of Maastricht was rarely deployed.

[4] R. Barents, 'The Internal Market Unlimited: Some Observations on the Legal Basis of Community Legislation' (1993) 30 *CMLRev*. 85, 92.

[5] H. Cullen and H. Charlesworth, 'Diplomacy by Other Means: The Use of Legal Basis Litigation as a Political Strategy by the European Parliament and Member States' (1999) 36 *CMLRev*. 1243.

[6] See, in particular, Case C-176/03 *Commission v Council (Environmental Crimes)* [2005] ECR I-7879.

[7] For a more recent restatement of the principles set out below see Case C-155/07 *Parliament v Council (EIB Guarantees)* [2008] ECR I-8103.

harmonisation of indirect taxes,[8] rather than under what is now Article 114 TFEU, the internal market provision. The latter requires the use of the ordinary legislative procedure, which provides for QMV in the Council and a veto for the Parliament. The former, by contrast, provides for a unanimity vote in the Council and a reduced role for the Parliament. If tax measures could be agreed by QMV, recalcitrant states could be outmanoeuvred and bargained down. If the process were to be subject to a veto, fiscal integration would be held hostage to the wishes of the least integrationist Member State.

Case C-338/01 Commission v Council (Recovery of Indirect Taxes) [2004] ECR I-4829

54. ...the choice of the legal basis for a [Union] measure must rest on objective factors amenable to judicial review, which include in particular the aim and the content of the measure.

55. If examination of a [Union] measure reveals that it pursues a twofold purpose or that it has a twofold component and if one of these is identifiable as the main or predominant purpose or component whereas the other is merely incidental, the act must be based on a single legal basis, namely that required by the main or predominant purpose or component...

56. By way of exception, if it is established that the measure simultaneously pursues several objectives which are inseparably linked without one being secondary and indirect in relation to the other, the measure must be founded on the corresponding legal bases...

57. However, no dual legal basis is possible where the procedures laid down for each legal basis are incompatible with each other...

58. In the present case, the procedures set out under [Article 113 TFEU], on the one hand, and that set out under [Article 114 TFEU], on the other, mean that the latter article cannot be applied...in order to serve as the legal basis for a measure such as Directive 2001/44. Whereas unanimity is required for the adoption of a measure on the basis of [Article 113 TFEU], a qualified majority is sufficient for a measure to be capable of valid adoption on the basis of [Article 114 TFEU]...

59. So far as concerns the scope of Article [114 TFEU], which the Commission and Parliament argue ought to have been used as the legal basis for the adoption of Directive 2001/44, it must be pointed out that it is clear from the very wording of Article [114(1) TFEU] that that article applies only if the Treaty does not provide otherwise.

60. It follows that, if the Treaty contains a more specific provision that is capable of constituting the legal basis for the measure in question, that measure must be founded on such provision. That is, in particular, the case with regard to Article [113 TFEU] so far as concerns the harmonisation of legislation concerning turnover taxes, excise duties and other forms of indirect taxation.

61. It must also be pointed out that Article [114(2) TFEU] expressly excludes certain areas from the scope of that article. This is in particular the case with regard to 'fiscal provisions', the approximation of which cannot therefore take place on the basis of that article...

67. ...the words 'fiscal provisions' contained in Article [114(2) TFEU] must be interpreted as covering not only the provisions determining taxable persons, taxable transactions, the basis of imposition, and rates of and exemptions from direct and indirect taxes, but also those relating to arrangements for the collection of such taxes...

76. ...it must be held that Directive 2001/44 does relate to 'fiscal provisions' within the meaning of Article [114(2) TFEU], with the result that Article [114 TFEU] cannot constitute the correct legal basis for the adoption of that directive.

---

[8] It also based it on a now defunct provision, Article 93 EC, which relates to realisation of the common market.

The Court will thus look at the predominant aim and content of a measure to decide the legal base. To ascertain this, it will look at the principles on which it is based and its ideological content rather than its effects. In *Framework Directive on Waste*,[9] the Commission challenged the adoption of the Directive under the predecessor to Article 192(1) TFEU, the environmental base, arguing that it should have been based on what is now Article 114 TFEU, the internal market provision.[10] The Court disagreed. It noted that the central tenets of the Directive were those of environmental management. Instead of securing the internal market objectives of free movement of waste, the Directive implemented the ecological principles that environmental damage should be rectified at source and that waste should be disposed of as close as possible to the place of production in order to keep transport to a minimum.

If two objectives are so inextricably and equally associated that the Court cannot ascertain the predominant purpose of a measure, it moves to a different test in which it operates a formal hierarchy between the different legal bases, looking to the relationship specified in the Treaties between each. Article 114 TFEU, the internal market provision, enjoys a precedence over Article 192(2) TFEU, the provision governing EU environmental action, on, inter alia, measures primarily of a fiscal nature, because the latter indicates that it is 'without prejudice to Article 114'. At the bottom of the pecking order of legal bases sits Article 352 TFEU, the flexibility provision that allows the Union to take measures to meet its objectives, where no other legal base provides the requisite power. This is because this provision stipulates that it can only be used where the Treaties have not provided the necessary powers elsewhere. As such, all other legal bases enjoy precedence over it.[11]

However, it will be rare that a measure pursues inextricably and equally associated objectives. In *Linguistic Diversity in the Information Society*, the Court had to consider a Decision which set up a programme to promote linguistic diversity in the information society. It had been adopted under what is now Article 173(3) TFEU, the legal base for industrial policy. The Parliament challenged this, arguing that it should have been based on what is now Article 166(5) TFEU, the legal base for culture. The Court stated that the fact that a measure had twin objectives was insufficient to bring it outside the 'predominant purpose' rule. Each component had to be equally essential to the measure and each had to be indissociable. In this instance, the predominant purpose was industrial. The beneficiaries of the programme were, almost exclusively, small and medium-sized enterprises, who might lose competitiveness because of the costs associated with linguistic diversity.[12]

Neither rule is easy to apply to particular sets of circumstances. The 'predominant aim and content' rule assumes each legal base is characterised by a distinctive set of principles, through which it is possible to identify all legislation founded on it.[13] This is rarely the case, and the Court has to engage in highly selective analysis to justify a particular legal base for a measure. The 'inextricably associated' rule, if applied literally, is so narrow that it is almost meaningless. Yet it has been applied in some cases, suggesting that, sometimes, for ulterior motives, the Court simply wishes to discard the 'predominant purpose' rule. It is wise not to be too critical

[9] Case C-155/91 *Commission* v *Council (Framework Directive on Waste)* [1993] ECR I-939.
[10] At the time the former provided only for consultation of the Parliament and unanimity voting in the Council.
[11] Case C-295/90 *Parliament* v *Council (revision of Judgment)* [1992] ECR I-4193.
[12] Case C-42/97 *Parliament* v *Council (Linguistic Diversity in the Information Society)* [1999] ECR I-869.
[13] D. Chalmers, 'The Single Market: From Prima Donna to Journeyman' in J. Shaw and G. More (eds.), *New Legal Dynamics of the European Union* (Oxford, Clarendon, 1995) 55, 69–71.

of the Court. While differing legal bases exist, uncertainty will persist and result in continued litigation. Weatherill has observed that this is a problem which is likely to remain whatever test is adopted by the Court. The underlying difficulty is the byzantine structure of the Treaties, with their proliferation of legal bases.[14]

3 EU LEGISLATION

(i) Types of legislative act in EU law

All legislative acts must be published in the Official Journal and enter into force twenty days after publication or on the date specified in the instrument.[15] The central provision setting out the types of legislative act is Article 288 TFEU.

Article 288 TFEU

To exercise the Union's competences, the institutions shall adopt regulations, directives, decisions, recommendations and opinions.

A regulation shall have general application. It shall be binding in its entirety and directly applicable in all Member States.

A directive shall be binding, as to the result to be achieved, upon each Member State to which it is addressed, but shall leave to the national authorities the choice of form and methods.

A decision shall be binding in its entirety. A decision which specifies those to whom it is addressed shall be binding only on them.

Recommendations and opinions shall have no binding force.

The provision is not exhaustive and international agreements with non-EU states, although not mentioned in Article 288 TFEU, are regarded as secondary legislation, binding both the Union and the Member States.[16] A 2004 study found Regulations were the most widely used of all, accounting for 31 per cent of all legislation. Decisions addressed to a party accounted for a further 27 per cent, with Decisions not addressed to anybody accounting for 10 per cent of all measures. Directives and international agreements each accounted for 9 per cent of all legislation.[17] The different legislative instruments have different traits.

Regulations are the most centralising of all EU instruments and are used wherever there is a need for uniformity. As they are to have general application, they do not apply to individual sets of circumstances, but to an 'objectively determined situation and produce(s) legal effects with regard to categories of persons described in a generalised and abstract manner'.[18] The other hallmark of Regulations is their direct applicability. From the date that they enter into force,

---

[14] S. Weatherill, 'Regulating the Internal Market: Result Orientation in the House of Lords' (1992) 17 *ELRev.* 299, 312–13.
[15] Article 297(1) TFEU.
[16] Article 216(2) TFEU.
[17] A. v. Bogdandy, F. Arndt and J. Bast, 'Legal Instruments in European Union Law and their Reform: A Systematic Approach on an Empirical Basis' (2004) 23 *YBEL* 91, 97.
[18] Joined Cases 789/79 and 790/79 *Calpak* v *Commission* [1980] ECR 1949.

they automatically form part of the domestic legal order of each Member State and require no further transposition. Indeed, it is normally illegal for a Member State to adopt implementing legislation because such measures might contain changes which affect the uniform application of the Regulation[19] or obscure from citizens the fact that it is the Regulation which is the direct source of their rights and obligations.[20] However, there is a caveat. In some cases, Regulations will require national authorities to adopt implementing measures. If there is such a requirement, a failure to implement the Regulation will be a breach of EU law.[21]

Directives are binding as to the result to be achieved. They leave the choice as to form and methods used to implement it to the discretion of Member States. Although, like other legislative instruments, a Directive comes into force twenty days after publication or on the date stipulated in the Directive, it will give a deadline (usually eighteen or twenty-four months after publication) by which Member States must transpose its obligations into national law.

Decisions are binding upon those to whom they are addressed. For this reason the addressee must be notified of any Decision.[22] The majority of Decisions are addressed to Member States, with only a small number addressed to private parties, with almost all of the latter being in the field of competition law, where the Commission can impose fines on parties or require them to desist from certain practices. The Lisbon Treaty introduces an amendment by stipulating that Decisions which specify those to whom they are addressed shall be binding only on them. In this, it seems to be making a distinction found in Germany, which distinguishes these types of Decisions from Decisions which have no addressee ('*Beschluss*'). If the former are seen more as directions to particular individuals, the latter impose general obligations which bind the Union as an organisational entity, and Member States as part of that entity. However, as they are not addressed to private parties, they are thought not to impose obligations on them.[23]

International agreements will only have legal effects within EU law for that part of the agreement that falls within Union competence. Their legal effects will also depend upon the phrasing of the agreement. If these agreements impose precise obligations, they will not require implementation by either Member States or EU institutions but will enter directly into force in EU and national law. More vaguely phrased provisions will necessitate implementation. Interpretation of the provisions of an international agreement will be carried out in the light of the object and purpose of that agreement. Provisions identically worded to EU law provisions may be interpreted differently, on the ground that the objective of the agreement differs from that of the Treaties.[24]

The justification for this wide array of legislative instruments is that the founders of the Treaties wanted EU law to have different legal bite in different policy fields and that in some they wished the legislator to have discretion on this matter. This rationale has been undermined by the legislative instruments being substitutable for one another. One finds Regulations which substitute for Decisions, in that they apply to individual sets of circumstances rather than generally.[25] There are, conversely, Directives which look like Regulations because they

---

[19] Case 39/72 *Commission* v *Italy (premiums for slaughtering cows)* [1973] ECR 101.
[20] Case 34/73 *Variola* v *Amministrazione delle Finanze* [1973] ECR 981.
[21] Case 128/78 *Commission* v *United Kingdom (failure to implement regulation 1463/70 on recording equipment in road transport)* [1978] ECR 2429.
[22] Article 297(2) TFEU.
[23] v. Bogdandy *et al.*, above n. 17, 103–6.
[24] The seminal case on international agreements is Case 104/81 *Hauptzollamt Mainz* v *Kupferberg* [1982] ECR 3641.
[25] See e.g. Joined Cases 41/70–44/70 *International Fruit Company* v *Commission* [1971] ECR 411.

are so detailed that they vitiate the discretion granted to Member States and must be transposed into national law verbatim.[26] Finally, Decisions without addressees act as a substitute for Directives in that they require Member States to realise certain results without specifying the means. In no instance has any of this been declared illegal.

(ii) The hierarchy of norms

The other difficulty has traditionally been that of no hierarchy of norms, where one type of instrument is taken to trump another. This is particularly problematic as 69 per cent of Regulations are delegated legislation, adopted by the Commission under powers granted to it by the other institutions.[27] The Future of Europe Convention felt that the functions of primary legislation and delegated legislation were different.[28] The function of the former should be to set out the essential elements of an area, whilst the latter's role was to fill in the detail. This was not simply for the sake of legislative clarity, but also to enable a clear separation of powers. The legislature should be focused exclusively on the central policy choices, whilst the executive should be responsible for administering the technical detail.

The Lisbon Treaty introduces a distinction, therefore, between legislative and non-legislative measures. Legislative acts are those adopted by the procedures set out in Article 289 TFEU.[29] The legislator may, however, grant to the Commission the power to take two types of measure: 'delegated' acts and 'implementing' acts. The former are described as 'non-legislative' in nature and it is safe to assume this is also true of the latter. There is thus clearly a hierarchy between them and all legislative acts. The role of delegated measures is to supplement or amend certain non-essential elements of the legislative act. The role of implementing measures is to set out uniform conditions for implementing EU legally binding acts.[30] Each must identify itself in its title as either a 'delegated' or 'implementing' measure.[31]

The distinction between delegated and implementing acts matters because the former are subject to additional controls by the Council and Parliament that the latter are not.[32] The distinction is, however, obscure. Hoffmann has observed that implementing acts are traditionally thought of as:

> rule interpretation, rule application, rule setting/evaluation, approval of funds, the extension/ new specification of funding programmes and information management. They ranged from single-case decisions to the adoption of acts 'supplementing' or 'amending non-essential elements' of a legislative act.[33]

This all fits within the definition for implementing acts set out by the Lisbon Treaty. It also fits within that for delegated acts. It is not clear how the two will be distinguished. Clearly, delegated acts are meant to have a broader sweep than implementing acts. Yet this is incredibly elastic and begs a further question: is this new concept of delegated legislation actually substituting

---

[26] Case 38/77 *ENKA v Inspecteur der Invoerrechten* [1977] ECR 2203.
[27] v. Bogdandy *et al.*, above n. 17, 99.
[28] *Final Report of Working Group IX on Simplification*, CONV 424/02.
[29] Article 289(3) TFEU.
[30] They are set out in Articles 290(1) and 291(2) TFEU.
[31] Articles 290(3) and 291(4) TFEU.
[32] Article 290(2) TFEU. See p. 121.
[33] H. Hoffmann, 'Legislation, Delegation and Implementation under the Treaty of Lisbon: Typology Meets Reality' (2009) 15 *ELJ* 482, 495.

measures by the Commission for laws that should be adopted by the Parliament and Council by virtue of their breadth, salience or importance?[34]

(iii) Soft law

Recommendations and Opinions are mentioned in Article 288 TFEU, but have no binding force. They must be viewed alongside a variety of other instruments, which include resolutions and declarations, action programmes and plans, communications by the Commission, Conclusions of the representatives of the Member States meeting in Council, guidelines and inter-institutional arrangements. These measures all come under the generic heading of 'soft law': 'rules of conduct which, in principle, have no legally binding force but which nevertheless may have practical effects'.[35] These instruments are an integral part of the Union legal order, reportedly accounting for 13 per cent of all EU law.[36] They are used for a variety of purposes.

Commitments about the conduct of institutions   These are commonly used to organise the relations between the institutions. A good example is the Joint Declaration on Practical Arrangements for the Co-Decision Procedure, which sets out the *modus vivendi* for one of the main EU legislative procedures and the institutions' understanding of their rights and duties under it.[37]

Commitments to respect certain values   Soft law, most notably Declarations, is used to commit EU institutions to pursuing certain values. Declarations are not merely commitments to future conduct, but also seek to redefine the political identity of the Union. The most obvious example is the Joint Declaration by the European Parliament, the Council and the Commission on Fundamental Rights, where the institutions were asserting for the first time that observance of fundamental rights norms was a goal of the EU institutions, thereby admitting that it was not merely concerned with economic integration, but also had an incipient civil identity.[38]

Programming legislation   The instrument, *par excellence*, for this is the Action Plan. Action Plans set out objectives and timetables for particular EU policies, which are used to justify specific legislation and which provide a wider background against which this legislation is understood and interpreted. A good example is the Commission Action Plan for European renewal in the field of freedom, security and justice, issued in 2005.[39] The Action Plan identifies ten priorities for freedom, security and justice for the period up to 2010. These include developing policies for fundamental rights and citizenship, the establishment of a common asylum area, managing migration, and developing an integrated management of the external borders of the Union. It also lists over 200 measures, some legislative and others administrative, some binding and others not, to be adopted to meet these priorities.

---

[34] For powerful criticism see *ibid.* 491–9.

[35] F. Snyder, 'The Effectiveness of European Community Law: Institutions, Processes, Tools and Techniques' (1993) 56 *MLR* 19, 32. For an exhaustive discussion see L. Senden, *Soft Law in European Community Law* (Oxford and Portland, Hart, 2004) ch. 5.

[36] v. Bogdandy *et al.*, above n. 17, 97.

[37] [2007] OJ C145/2.

[38] [1977] OJ C103/1.

[39] COM(2005)184.

Regulatory communications   In areas such as nuclear energy and competition, the Commission will issue Opinions as an informal way of indicating to undertakings whether they are complying with EU law. It will also issue notices, setting out its general enforcement policy on what infractions it will or will not pursue.[40]

Model law-making   The most controversial use of soft law is for 'model law-making', where guidelines or recommendations setting out best practice for Member States are adopted. In some areas of EU law, harmonising measures involving the setting of common standards through Regulations, Directives and Decisions are excluded. In such fields, norm-setting is done exclusively through soft law.[41] Yet, soft law is also used in many fields where there is the option of harmonising measures. The Secretariat at the Future of Europe Convention identified three circumstances where the former is likely to be preferred:

- where the area of work is closely connected with national identity or culture, e.g. culture or education;
- where the instruments for implementing national policies are so diverse and/or complex that harmonisation seems disproportionate in relation to the objectives pursued, e.g. employment;
- where there is no political will for EC legislation amongst the Member States, but there is a desire to make progress together.[42]

As it has no coercive force and no system of sanctions to underpin it, the effect of soft law on its subjects' behaviour is uncertain. It seems, at the very least, that soft law frames institutional expectations and opens actors to diverse forms of peer pressure.[43] There has been a recent fierce debate over the value of soft law. The arguments on each side have been well set out by Trubek, Cottrell and Nance.[44] Some of the criticisms of soft law they observe are that:

- it lacks the clarity and precision needed to provide predictability and a reliable framework for action;
- soft law cannot really have any effect, but is a covert tactic to enlarge the Union's legislative hard law competence;
- soft law bypasses normal systems of accountability;
- soft law undermines Union legitimacy because it creates expectations, but cannot bring about change.

---

[40] See e.g. Commission Notice on agreements of minor importance which do not appreciably restrict competition [2001] OJ C368/13.

[41] The fields include Common Foreign and Security Policy (Article 24(1) TEU); economic policy (Article 121(2) TFEU); employment (Article 148(2) TFEU); education, vocational training, youth and sport (Article 165(4) TFEU); culture (Article 167(5) TFEU); most areas of public health (Article 168(4), (5) TFEU); industry (Article 173(3) TFEU); space (Article 189(2) TFEU); tourism (Article 195(2) TFEU); civil protection (Article 196(2) TFEU); administrative cooperation (Article 197(2) TFEU).

[42] *European Convention, Coordination of National Policies: The Open Method of Coordination*, WG VI WD015, Brussels, 26 September 2002.

[43] M. López-Santana, 'The Domestic Implications of European Soft Law: Framing and Transmitting Change in Employment Policy' (2006) *JEPP* 481, 494–6.

[44] D. Trubek *et al.*, 'Hard and Soft Law in European Integration' in J. Scott and G. de Búrca (eds.), *New Governance and Constitutionalism* (Oxford and Portland, Hart, 2005).

They argue, however, that soft law has some advantages over traditional law:

- Hard law tends toward uniformity of treatment while many current issues demand tolerance for significant diversity among Member States.
- Hard law presupposes a fixed condition based on prior knowledge while situations of uncertainty may demand constant experimentation and adjustment.
- Hard law is very difficult to change yet in many cases frequent change of norms may be essential to achieve optimal results.
- If actors do not internalise the norms of hard law, enforcement may be difficult; if they do, it may be unnecessary.

From this, it would appear that much depends on the nature of the field. In areas where uniformity is not important and there is a need for experimentation, soft law would seem to have important advantages. Yet even in these fields, some of the criticisms of soft law still persist: namely the manner in which it has been used to expand EU involvement, its blurring of institutional rules,[45] and its lack of concern with asymmetries of power, so that compliance with soft law only tends to occur when it suits vested interests.[46]

4 EU LEGISLATIVE PROCEDURES

(i) Ordinary legislative procedure

(a) Central features of the ordinary legislative procedure

The ordinary legislative procedure (previously known as the co-decision procedure) is set out in Article 294 TFEU. Its central elements are set out below.

Article 294 TFEU

1. Where reference is made in the Treaties to the ordinary legislative procedure for the adoption of an act, the following procedure shall apply.
2. The Commission shall submit a proposal to the European Parliament and the Council.

First reading

3. The European Parliament shall adopt its position at first reading and communicate it to the Council.
4. If the Council approves the European Parliament's position, the act concerned shall be adopted in the wording which corresponds to the position of the European Parliament.
5. If the Council does not approve the European Parliament's position, it shall adopt its position at first reading and communicate it to the European Parliament.
6. The Council shall inform the European Parliament fully of the reasons which led it to adopt its position at first reading. The Commission shall inform the European Parliament fully of its position.

---

[45] Commission Communications have been criticised for enabling the Commission to enshrine a particular interpretation of EU law without proper judicial control. S. Lefevre, 'Interpretative Communications and the Implementation of Community Law at National Level' (2004) 29 *ELRev.* 808.

[46] See, in particular, Senden, above n. 35, 477–98.

Second reading

7. If, within three months of such communication, the European Parliament:
   (a) approves the Council's position at first reading or has not taken a decision, the act concerned shall be deemed to have been adopted in the wording which corresponds to the position of the Council;
   (b) rejects, by a majority of its component members, the Council's position at first reading, the proposed act shall be deemed not to have been adopted;
   (c) proposes, by a majority of its component members, amendments to the Council's position at first reading, the text thus amended shall be forwarded to the Council and to the Commission, which shall deliver an opinion on those amendments.
8. If, within three months of receiving the European Parliament's amendments, the Council, acting by a qualified majority:
   (a) approves all those amendments, the act in question shall be deemed to have been adopted;
   (b) does not approve all the amendments, the President of the Council, in agreement with the President of the European Parliament, shall within six weeks convene a meeting of the Conciliation Committee.
9. The Council shall act unanimously on the amendments on which the Commission has delivered a negative opinion.

Conciliation

10. The Conciliation Committee, which shall be composed of the members of the Council or their representatives and an equal number of members representing the European Parliament, shall have the task of reaching agreement on a joint text, by a qualified majority of the members of the Council or their representatives and by a majority of the members representing the European Parliament within six weeks of its being convened, on the basis of the positions of the European Parliament and the Council at second reading.
11. The Commission shall take part in the Conciliation Committee's proceedings and shall take all necessary initiatives with a view to reconciling the positions of the European Parliament and the Council.
12. If, within six weeks of its being convened, the Conciliation Committee does not approve the joint text, the proposed act shall be deemed not to have been adopted.

Third reading

13. If, within that period, the Conciliation Committee approves a joint text, the European Parliament, acting by a majority of the votes cast, and the Council, acting by a qualified majority, shall each have a period of six weeks from that approval in which to adopt the act in question in accordance with the joint text. If they fail to do so, the proposed act shall be deemed not to have been adopted.
14. The periods of three months and six weeks referred to in this Article shall be extended by a maximum of one month and two weeks respectively at the initiative of the European Parliament or the Council.

The length of this provision makes the procedure look intimidating. It is best to think of the procedure as a series of four key features.

Joint agreement   Joint adoption of legislation by the Council and Parliament can happen at three junctures during the procedure:

- First reading by the Parliament: the Commission makes a proposal. The Parliament issues an Opinion on it (the first reading). The Council can adopt the act by QMV if either the Parliament has made no amendments or it agrees with its amendments.
- Second reading by the Parliament: if there is no agreement after the first reading the Council can adopt a 'common position'. If it is adopting the Commission proposal, it does this by QMV. If it makes amendments of its own, it does this by unanimity. This common position is referred back to the Parliament for a second reading. If the Parliament does nothing for three months or agrees with the common position, the measure is adopted. Alternately, it may propose amendments. If the amendments have been approved by the Commission, they may be adopted by the Council by QMV. If, however, the Commission expresses a negative view of the Parliament's amendments, these have to be adopted by unanimity in the Council.
- Third reading: if there is no agreement following the second reading, a Conciliation Committee is established. It has six weeks to approve a joint text. This text must be adopted within six weeks, by both the Council by QMV and the Parliament, to become law.

Double veto of the Parliament   The ordinary legislative procedure grants the Parliament a veto over legislation. The veto can be exercised at the second reading if the Parliament decides to reject the common position of the Council. The other possibility is at the third reading after the Conciliation Committee has provided a joint text on which it must vote. Technically speaking, it is not a veto that is being exercised here, but Parliamentary assent. It must positively agree to it at this point for it to become law.

Assent of the Council   A measure will only become law if the Council agrees to it. The number of votes required will either be QMV or unanimity. If the measure has been approved by the Commission or by the Conciliation Committee, it will be QMV.[47] If the Council is proposing its own amendments, it must act by unanimity to adopt these amendments.

The Conciliation Committee   As mentioned under 'Joint agreement' above, this is convened following the Parliament's second reading, where the Council is unable to accept the amendments proposed by the Parliament. Modelled on the German Mediations Committee,[48] it comprises twenty-seven members from the Council and twenty-seven MEPs. The Council members vote by QMV and the MEPs by simple majority.

(b) Legislative practice and the ordinary legislative procedure

Looking at the European Parliament, the most dramatic power it enjoys appears to be the veto. However, it has made only limited use of this. Between 1 May 1999 and 1 July 2009, Parliament only used the veto three times in 916 procedures, less than 0.33 per cent of the time.[49] There are a number of reasons for this. The veto can bring the worst outcome because, often, from the Parliament's perspective, imperfect EU legislation is better than no legislation.

[47] Prior to Lisbon, there were a limited number of fields where unanimity was required in the Council, most notably culture.
[48] N. Foster, 'The New Conciliation Committee under Article 189b' (1994) 19 ELRev. 185.
[49] These statistics are from the EU Council's Consilium website, www.consilium.europa.eu/uedocs/ cmsUpload/090622-bilan_general.pdf (accessed 4 September 2009).

Regular exercise of the veto would also be bad politics. Other parties also will not communicate with the Parliament if, in the end, its position is inflexible as there is nothing to talk about. This will be true not just of the Commission and the Council, but also of lobbyists, such as those in industry and NGOs, who will no longer see it as an effective opportunity structure. For the Parliament, it is not the veto which is important, but the shadow of the veto. By threatening to thwart other parties' objectives, it can secure input for itself. They have to listen to its policy preferences and it can secure influence for itself to realise outcomes it desires. This role is reinforced by a quirk in the legislative procedure. If the Commission agrees with the Parliament, it is easier for the Council to accept parliamentary amendments than to produce its own.

Article 293(1) TFEU

Where, pursuant to the Treaties, the Council acts on a proposal from the Commission, it may amend that proposal only by acting unanimously, except in the cases referred to in paragraphs 10 and 13 of Articles 294, in Articles 310, 312 and 314 and in the second paragraph of Article 315.[50]

Acceptance of amendments proposed by the Parliament only requires a QMV in the Council, whilst it requires unanimity to produce its own. To be sure, the Commission must agree with the Parliament's suggestions but, importantly, it cannot propose amendments of its own without withdrawing the proposal and starting again. Parliament is the only institution that has the opportunity to 'improve' the text. This has led to a number of authors talking of its being a 'conditional agenda-setter'; provided it sticks within the limit of what is acceptable to the other two institutions, it can seize the agenda.[51] Statistics seem to bear this out. The last statistics prepared by any of the institutions were in 1 May 2004 by the European Parliament. It found 23 per cent of parliamentary amendments were accepted by both of the other institutions in an unqualified form. A further 60 per cent were accepted in some compromise form. In other words, 83 per cent of parliamentary suggestions are taken on in some form in the legislation.[52]

There are, however, different forms of amendment. Some just dot 'i's; others radically change policy; some clump amendments together, whilst others are put through at the behest of the Council or the Member States. Careful research by Kardasheva, which looked at 470 proposals between 1999 and 2007, found that parliamentary input was high. It amended 87 per cent of the proposals, with amendments per proposal varying from 1 to 322. Instead of looking at formal amendments, Kardasheva identified 1,567 issues raised by the Parliament (discrete matters that were not tidying up exercises) and found parliamentary success in 65.2 per cent of the cases – a high rate.[53]

---

[50] These last four provisions are budgetary provisions.
[51] G. Tsebelis, 'The Power of the European Parliament as a Conditional Agenda Setter' (1994) 88 *American Political Science Review* 128; G. Tsebelis and G. Garrett, 'Legislative Politics in the European Union' (2000) 1 *EUP* 9; G. Tsebelis, C. Jensen, A. Kalandrakis and A. Kreppel, 'Legislative Procedures in the European Union: An Empirical Analysis' (2001) 31 *BJPS* 573.
[52] European Parliament, *Activity Report for 5th Parliamentary Term*, PE287.644, 14.
[53] Kardasheva, above n. 2, 242–4.

The position of the Commission under the ordinary legislative procedure is curious. On the face of it, its influence diminishes as the procedure continues. As it plays no active role in the Conciliation Committee, it would be possible for the Council and Parliament to rearrange its proposals at that point.[54] In practice, its influence remains significant. This is because very few proposals require conciliation.[55] In the majority of instances, agreement is reached at first or second reading. At this point in the procedure, the Commission influence is considerable. Both the Council and the Parliament are working from its proposal and, in practice, it is very difficult for them to deviate from the proposal without the Commission's acquiescence. Almost all successful parliamentary amendments require the Commission's agreement. Very few are adopted by the Council where there has not been prior approval by the Commission. Earlier studies found that there was an 88 per cent probability that a parliamentary amendment would be rejected by the Council if the Commission rejected it, whilst there was an 83 per cent probability that it would be accepted if the Commission approved it.[56]

A further counter-intuitive feature of the procedure is the effectiveness of the Conciliation Committee. The Committee would appear to have little mandate, as any Decision requires the subsequent approval of both Parliament and Council and it might be thought that, by the time it meets, institutional positions would be so entrenched there would be little possibility of movement and agreement. Yet, in almost all procedures,[57] the Committee had been able to propose a joint text accepted by both the Parliament and the Council. This might be because the Council is able to behave more proactively and recapture the agenda within the Committee, as it is able to make its own amendments and accept amendments by QMV.[58] An alternative might be that, as parties are aware of each other's positions, negotiation is easier. New amendments are not continually being thrown in, but there is a stable set of issues on which discussion can proceed.[59] Whatever the reason, the effect is an increase in the influence of COREPER, as it is members of COREPER, not Council ministers, who sit in the Conciliation Committee. COREPER is not just preparing the meeting here, but also adopting the joint text.

(c) First reading and the trilogue

All the evidence discussed in the previous section suggests a picture significantly different from that provided by a simple reading of Article 294 TFEU, which would emphasise the role

---

[54] C. Crombez, 'The Codecision Procedure in the European Union' (1997) 22 *Legislative Studies Quarterly* 97.

[55] In the eighteen months to 30 June 2009 only 6 out of 203 proposals went to conciliation. EU Council, Consilium, above n. 49.

[56] G. Tsebelis *et al.*, 'Legislative Procedures in the European Union: An Empirical Analysis' (2001) 31 *BJPS* 573. For a case study see C. Burns, 'Codecision and the European Commission: A Study of Declining Influence?' (2004) 11 *JEPP* 1.

[57] Between 1 July 1999 and 30 June 2009, 112 proposals went successfully through conciliation. Only three failed. Above, n. 49.

[58] G. Tsebelis, 'Maastricht and the Democratic Deficit' (1997) 52 *Aussenwirtschaft* 26, 43–5.

[59] A. Rasmussen and M. Shackleton, 'The Scope for Action of European Parliament Negotiators in the Legislative Process: Lessons of the Past and for the Future', paper presented at 9th Biennial EUSA Conference, 31 March 2005. Rasmussen also has found that the Committee has tried to adopt positions that it knows are acceptable to both sides rather than asserting its own position. A. Rasmussen, 'The EU Conciliation Committee: One or Several Principals' (2008) 9 *EUP* 7.

of the parliamentary veto and the assent of the Council. Yet, even this understates the extent to which the balance of power is determined by a shared legislative culture, which has emerged with the evolution of the ordinary legislative procedure.

In 1999, the institutions adopted a Joint Declaration on practical arrangements for the procedure. This was updated by a 2007 Joint Declaration.[60] This Joint Declaration formalises two developments that have become a central part of institutional practice and have reshaped understandings in this area: the commitment to reach agreement at first reading and the trilogue.

The Joint Declaration commits the institutions to clear the way, where appropriate, for the adoption of the act concerned at an early stage of the procedure.[61] This is understood to mean that, wherever possible, they should try to secure agreement at first reading.[62] In the early days of this arrangement, they were only partially successful, with only about 28 per cent of the total agreed at first reading between 1 May 1999 and 30 June 2004.[63] Enlargement has had a significant effect on these figures, however. Concerns about the difficulties of getting twenty-seven states rather than fifteen to agree have led to an impetus to get agreement by first reading, so that between 1 July 2004 and 30 June 2009, 379 out of 484 dossiers, or 78.3 per cent, were agreed at first reading.[64]

This telescopes the procedure. It forecloses spaces for public debate, notably the second and third reading. It also changes the opportunity structures available as it means parties that wish to seek influence have to do so as early as possible. For first reading is no longer what it says: an opportunity for initial consideration. It is rather usually nearer to the moment of final decision. This clearly benefits parties that are well-organised, in the know and above all, have connections with the Commission, as in the period prior to first reading, the Commission's presence is particularly powerful.

This position is exacerbated by the dominance of the trilogue. Trilogues first emerged in 1995 to prepare the work of the Conciliation Committee.[65] A trilogue is composed of three parties: two or three MEPs, normally from the respective committee, a Deputy Permanent Representative, normally from the state holding the Presidency, and a senior Commission official. The job of the trilogue is to act as a forum where each side can explain its position to the other and, if possible, where agreement can be reached. They now operate at all stages of the procedure: before all the readings, after the Council common position and before the Conciliation Committee. Kardasheva has estimated that trilogues take place, in some form, on 76 per cent of Commission proposals under the ordinary legislative procedure.[66] Their value to the EU institutions is set out in the Joint Declaration.

---

[60] [1999] OJ C148/1 and [2007] OJ C145/2.
[61] *Ibid.* para. 4.
[62] *Ibid.* para. 11.
[63] European Parliament, *Activity Report for 5th Parliamentary Term*, PE287.644, 12–13.
[64] EU Council, Consilium, above n. 49.
[65] On the trilogue see M. Shackleton, 'The Politics of Codecision' (2000) 38 *JCMS* 325, 334–6; M. Shackleton and T. Raunio, 'Codecision since Amsterdam: A Laboratory for Institutional Innovation and Change' (2003) 10 *JEPP* 171, 177–9.
[66] Kardasheva above n. 2, 25.

Joint Declaration on Practical Arrangements for the [Ordinary Legislative] Procedure [2007] OJ C145/2

7. Cooperation between the institutions in the context of codecision often takes the form of tripartite meetings ('trilogues'). This trilogue system has demonstrated its vitality and flexibility in increasing significantly the possibilities for agreement at first and second reading stages, as well as contributing to the preparation of the work of the Conciliation Committee.

8. Such trilogues are usually conducted in an informal framework. They may be held at all stages of the procedure and at different levels of representation, depending on the nature of the expected discussion. Each institution, in accordance with its own rules of procedure, will designate its participants for each meeting, define its mandate for the negotiations and inform the other institutions of arrangements for the meetings in good time.

9. As far as possible, any draft compromise texts submitted for discussion at a forthcoming meeting shall be circulated in advance to all participants. In order to enhance transparency, trilogues taking place within the European Parliament and Council shall be announced, where practicable.

The growth of the trilogue has implications for the balance of power between institutions.[67] In instances, where the trilogue is successful, Parliament and COREPER are acting as genuine co-legislators. It also has implications for the democratic quality of law-making within co-decision. The trilogue is the biggest challenge to democratic legitimacy, for it centralises power in those actors who represent the Council and Parliament at the trilogue. Farrell and Héritier note, therefore, that small parties within the European Parliament are excluded by the trilogue, as they are never represented at it and the committee structure and its attendant public debates within the European Parliament are bypassed. They also noted that trilogues reinforce the power of COREPER, as they result in even less being decided by the Council of Ministers.[68] There is, in all this, a sidelining of checks and balances and a lack of formality and transparency. A division is made between formal and substantive decision-making, with the locus of substantive decision-making being hidden away. Whilst formal decision-making takes place in the Council or in parliamentary committees, in many instances substantive decisions are vested in these informal arrangements. The formal procedures do no more than rubber stamp the agreements. Only very well-connected actors have the opportunity to lobby these informal processes because only they can know where they are taking place or who is important within them. Furthermore, only they will have the resources to arbitrage between these centres of power, lobbying both central protagonists in the trilogue and other important actors in the Council, the Parliament and the Commission.

---

[67] On the trilogue see H. Farrell and A. Héritier, 'Interorganizational Negotiation and Intraorganizational Power in Shared Decision Making: Early Agreements under Codecision and their Impact on the European Parliament and the Council' (2004) 37 *Comparative Political Studies* 1184; F. Häge and M. Kaeding, 'Reconsidering the European Parliament's Legislative Influence: Formal vs. Informal Procedures' (2007) 29 *Journal of European Integration* 341.

[68] Farrell and Héritier, above n. 67, 1200–4.

(ii) Special legislative procedures

(a) Consultation procedure

The consultation procedure follows three stages:

(a) the Commission submits a proposal to the Council;
(b) the Council consults the Parliament;
(c) the Council adopts the measure, either by qualified majority or by unanimity, depending upon the field in question.

The most salient feature of the consultation procedure is the duty to consult the Parliament. In *Roquette Frères*, the Court of Justice stated that consultation was an expression of the cardinal principle of institutional balance:

> [Consultation] … allows the Parliament to play an actual part in the legislative process of the Community, such power represents an essential factor in the institutional balance intended by the Treaty. Although limited, it reflects at Community level the fundamental democratic principle that the peoples should take part in the exercise of power through the intermediary of a representative assembly. Due consultation of the Parliament in the cases provided for by the Treaty therefore constitutes an essential formality disregard of which means that the measure concerned is void.[69]

From this principle of institutional balance, the Court has crafted a number of mutual obligations between Parliament and the Council. On the one hand, the Council is obliged to reconsult Parliament if the text is amended. This ensures that the text adopted by the Council does not differ substantially from the one on which the Parliament has been consulted, unless these amendments correspond essentially to the wishes of the Parliament.[70] By contrast, Parliament must not abuse its right of consultation. In *General Tariff Preferences*,[71] the Council sought to consult Parliament on a proposal to extend the Regulation on General Tariff Preferences, which gave preferential tax treatment to imports from less developed countries, to the states which had emerged from the collapse of the Soviet Union. The request was made in October 1992 and the dossier was marked 'urgent' by the Council, but the full decision was postponed until a further debate in January 1993, on the grounds that the Parliament's Committee on Development was not happy about including these states. The Council adopted the Regulation in December 1992, without further consultation, on the grounds that the matter was urgent. The Court noted that there was a duty on the Council to consult the Parliament but, correspondingly, duties of mutual cooperation also governed relations between the EU institutions. It noted that Parliament had failed to discharge these duties by refusing to take heed of the urgency of the file and by having regard to what the Court considered to be extraneous factors.

Parliament's powers under the consultation procedure are clearly more limited than under the ordinary legislative procedure. The Council is not required to take account of the Parliament's views and the lack of leverage over the Council also harms Parliament's relations with the Commission. As Parliament's views count for so little, there are no incentives for the Commission to coordinate or even consult with it. This marginalisation is further increased by

---

[69] Case 138/79 *Roquette Frères* v *Council* [1980] ECR 3333.
[70] Case C-65/90 *Parliament* v *Council* (*Cabotage II*) [1992] ECR I-4593.
[71] Case C-65/93 *Parliament* v *Council* (*General Tariff Preferences*) [1995] ECR I-643.

the fact that the Council is not required to wait until Parliament has been consulted, before it considers a proposal. The Court has even stated that the Council is making good use of time if it considers the matter pending consultation of the Parliament.[72]

Yet, it is wrong to argue that the Parliament's presence does not matter. At the very least, parliamentary hearings bring greater transparency to the process and provide an arena for actors whose voice might otherwise have been excluded to express their views. In addition, Parliament does make significant inputs of its own. It submits amendments to about 54 per cent of proposals and about 19 per cent of its amendments are accepted – not an insignificant proportion.[73] Notwithstanding the *General Tariff Preferences* judgment, it has acquired this influence by exercising a power to delay. It does this by inviting the Commission to withdraw a proposal or to accept amendment, and when the latter refuses, referring it back to a parliamentary committee to consider its response to this.

R. Kardasheva, 'The Power to Delay: The European Parliament's Influence in the Consultation Procedure' (2009) 47 *Journal of Common Market Studies* 385, 404–5

The power to delay allows the EP [European Parliament] to enjoy important benefits in the legislative system. First, through delay the Parliament manages to force concessions from the Council and the Commission. Delay allows the Parliament to see many of its preferences incorporated in the final legislative texts. Second, delay opens the door for informal negotiations between the Council and Parliament. While informal negotiations have become a typical element of Council–Parliament legislative work under co-decision, there are few incentives for Member States to seek informal contacts in consultation. However, when the EP delays its opinion and Member States need an urgent decision, the Council has an incentive to speed up the procedure through informal contacts. Third, delay gives the consultation procedure two readings. Formally, the consultation procedure consists of only one reading. However, by delaying its final vote, the EP gains an additional reading. The EP makes its position on the Commission proposal known, but the plenary refrains from issuing an opinion. Once aware of the EP's preferences, the Council and Commission negotiate with MEPs and adjust their positions in order to speed up the decision-making process. Thus, through delay, the EP transforms the simple consultation procedure into a decision-making procedure with two readings.

However, these features exert only a limited effect upon the broader institutional settlement, which revolves around the Commission-Council axis. Both the Commission and the Council are executive-dominated and the current safeguards for national parliamentary input are weak.[74] There is still the question of which 'executive' holds the balance of power in these procedures. Everything hinges on the vote required in the Council. If a unanimity vote is required, power would seem to remain in the hands of individual national governments, as any government can veto the measure. However, the position is more complicated. Twenty-six national governments do not have the power to push through a measure if

---

[72] Case C-417/93 *Parliament v Council (consultation with Parliament)* [1995] ECR I-1185.
[73] R. Kardasheva, 'The Power to Delay: The European Parliament's Influence in the Consultation Procedure' (2009) 47 *JCMS* 385, 392–4.
[74] See pp. 126–32.

one national government resists it. Power is, therefore, concentrated in the government that is most resistant to the measure, as it holds the decision on whether or not to go forward.[75] Yet power is also strongly vested in the Commission here. As the Council can only amend its proposals by unanimity,[76] its proposals have a 'take it or leave it quality' given that it will be rare that there will be consensus on the part of, or the resources available for, the Member States to put forward an alternative proposal that secures the agreement of all of them.

(b) Assent procedure

The assent procedure is the procedure in which Parliament enjoys greatest formal powers and brings together a number of heterogeneous procedures:

- The Commission does not enjoy a monopoly of initiative. Depending on the field, a proposal can also be made by the Parliament, Member States or the European Council.
- The proposal may come direct to the Parliament. Alternatively, there may be other institutions that have either to be consulted or to give their consent to the proposal first. The procedures depend on the legal base in question.
- The Parliament will then have to consent to the measure. There are no time limits on it to do so.
- In some instances, the Council or the European Council then has to consent to the measure before it can become law.

The uniting features of all these procedures, which allow them to be classified under the assent procedure umbrella, are first that in all cases Parliament has to affirm a legislative proposal before it can be adopted. This is different from the ordinary legislative procedure in that Parliament must actively say 'yes' to a proposal whereas the latter merely gives it a veto. Secondly, it has an indefinite time in which to do this. There must be a strong majority in Parliament in favour of immediate action, therefore, if a measure is to be agreed.

The assent procedure was downplayed before the Treaty of Lisbon as it was largely used for a limited number of institutional matters related to the European Central Bank and the Parliament itself. This is no longer the case. It now governs significant fields, which include EU anti-discrimination policy,[77] significant parts of EU criminal justice policy,[78] the budget,[79] many international agreements[80] and, perhaps most prominently, the flexibility principle, which allows measures to be taken to realise Union objectives where there is no other legal base and which, historically, has been deployed about thirty times per annum.[81]

The procedure is likely to be a prominent procedure. However, it is to be wondered if, in practice, it will differ that much from the ordinary legislative procedure. Agreement will be sought to be reached after the initial proposal through a trilogue with all parties aware that the proposal requires the cooperation of each to make it law.

---

[75] On this see *Report by the Ad Hoc Group Examining the Question of Increasing the Parliament's Powers* (Vedel Report), *EC Bulletin* Supplt. 4/72; Committee of Three, *Report on the European Institutions* (Luxembourg, Office for Official Publications of the European Communities, 1980) 74–5.

[76] Article 293(1) TFEU.

[77] Article 19(1) TFEU.

[78] Articles 82, 83(1), (6), 86(1), (4) TFEU.

[79] Articles 311 and 312 TFEU.

[80] Article 218(6) TFEU.

[81] Article 352 TFEU. For a fuller list see the Annex at the end of this chapter.

5 ENHANCED COOPERATION

Enhanced cooperation grew out of a debate that emerged prior to the Treaty of Amsterdam in which deep-seated differences between Member States about both the pace and ideological direction of integration emerged. It was agreed that some Member States should not be held back from developing common laws between themselves, should they so wish, and enhanced cooperation was established to enable this. It allows EU laws to be developed by as few as nine Member States where there is not a sufficient voting threshold for general legislation. Lowering the threshold in this way intrudes on general EU law-making as it raises the possibility of a 'hard core Europe', which develops laws for itself, excluding other Member States and creating a two-tier Union.[82] To prevent this, the provisions on enhanced cooperation put in place a number of safeguards.

Article 20 TEU

1. Member States which wish to establish enhanced cooperation between themselves within the framework of the Union's non-exclusive competences may make use of its institutions and exercise those competences by applying the relevant provisions of the Treaties, subject to the limits and in accordance with the detailed arrangements laid down in this Article and in Articles 326 to 334 TFEU.

   Enhanced cooperation shall aim to further the objectives of the Union, protect its interests and reinforce its integration process. Such cooperation shall be open at any time to all Member States, in accordance with Article 328 TFEU.
2. The decision authorising enhanced cooperation shall be adopted by the Council as a last resort, when it has established that the objectives of such cooperation cannot be attained within a reasonable period by the Union as a whole, and provided that at least nine Member States participate in it. The Council shall act in accordance with the procedure laid down in Article 329 TFEU.

Article 326 TFEU

Any enhanced cooperation shall comply with the Treaties and Union law. Such cooperation shall not undermine the internal market or economic, social and territorial cohesion. It shall not constitute a barrier to or discrimination in trade between Member States, nor shall it distort competition between them.

---

[82] On the debate see A. Stubb, 'The 1996 Intergovernmental Conference and the Management of Flexible Integration' (1997) 4 *JEPP* 37; F. Tuytschaever, *Differentiation in European Union Law* (Oxford and Portland, Hart, 1999) 1–48; E. Phillipart, 'From Uniformity to Flexibility: The Management of Diversity and its Impact on the EU System of Governance' in G. de Búrca and J. Scott (eds.), *Constitutional Change in the EU: From Uniformity to Flexibility?* (Oxford and Portland, Hart, 2000).

Article 327 TFEU

Any enhanced cooperation shall respect the competences, rights and obligations of those Member States which do not participate in it. Those Member States shall not impede its implementation by the participating Member States.

The provisions suggest a total of six substantive constraints:

- there must be nine Member States;
- it must not be in a field where the Union has exclusive competence;
- the measure must only be adopted as a matter of last resort;
- enhanced cooperation must comply with other EU law;
- it must not undermine the internal market or economic or social cohesion; in particular, it must not constitute a barrier to or discrimination in trade between Member States or distort competition between them;
- it must respect the rights, competences and obligations of other Member States.

These alone would suggest enhanced cooperation could only occur in very restricted circumstances. However, additional procedural constraints have been put in place, which grant vetoes to a number of actors. Any enhanced cooperation must be notified to the Commission, which must decide whether to put forward a proposal on it, giving its reasons if it does not.[83] The Parliament and Council must then assent to it, with the Council making the Decision by unanimity.[84]

The value of the measure is further eroded to the participating states by its being deemed not to be part of the EU legislative acquis.[85] Furthermore, they do not have freedom to negotiate between themselves as they must allow non-participating states to participate in the deliberations leading up to the adoption of legislation even if they cannot vote on it.[86] Finally, non-participating states can free-ride by waiting to see the effects of the measure and then joining later. Any state that did not take part initially can apply subsequently and is free to participate subject to verification that it meets the conditions for participation.[87]

In the light of this, it is unsurprising that for all the institutional and academic energy devoted to these procedures, there has yet to be a measure adopted under them.[88] Instead, resort had been made to arrangements outside this framework, some within the EU legal framework, and in some cases outside. These arrangements have thrown up real concerns both about fragmentation of the Union and about protecting the integrity of the Union's decision-making processes.

---

[83] Slightly different procedures apply in CFSP. The proposal is notified to the Council. It obtains an Opinion from the Commission and the High Representative. Parliament is also notified. The Council then makes a Decision by unanimity with only it and not the Parliament having a veto in this field: Article 329(2) TFEU.

[84] Article 329(1), (2) TFEU.

[85] Article 20(4) TEU.

[86] Articles 20(3) TEU and Article 330 TFEU.

[87] This is to be done by Commission authorisation in all fields other than CFSP. In CFSP it is done by the Council in consultation with the High Representative: Article 331 TFEU.

[88] On the one attempt to do so, see M. O'Brien, 'Company Taxation, State Aid and Fundamental Freedoms: Is the Next Step Enhanced Co-operation?' (2005) 30 *ELRev.* 209.

The central example of 'variable geometry' within the EU legal framework, in which only some Member States participate, is the Protocol on the Schengen Acquis integrated into the framework of the European Union. The Schengen Conventions of 1985 and 1990 were international agreements concluded between thirteen of the EU-15 Member States, Norway and Iceland. They provide for the abolition of frontier checks, a common external frontier and cooperation in the fields of migration of non-EU nationals, crime and policing.[89] All Member States are currently signatory to them except Ireland, United Kingdom, Cyprus, Bulgaria and Romania.[90] The Protocol integrates the measures agreed under the Schengen Acquis into EU law. It also defines the relationship between participating and non-participating states. Article 4 of the Protocol provides that non-participants may request to take part in any part or all of the acquis, so long as all other Member States consent. This is, of course, in contrast, to the procedures on enhanced cooperation, which require simple satisfaction of the conditions of participation.[91]

In the fields covered by the Schengen Protocol, certain Member States can therefore be excluded from subsequent involvement. Yet, this begs the question of the relation between this Protocol and the general provisions on immigration, asylum, policing and frontier controls, which form part of the Treaties and to which all Member States are party. How could it be that a Member State can be excluded from a field of policy that also forms part of EU law to which it is party? The relationship between the Protocol and the rest of the Treaties was considered in two cases brought by the United Kingdom against two measures: one establishing the European Agency for the Management of Operational Cooperation at the External Borders of the Member States (Regulation 2007/2004/EC), and the other introducing common security features and biometric identifiers into passports.[92] These had been adopted under the Schengen Protocol, thereby excluding the United Kingdom, even though Article 77(2) TFEU provides for the Union to develop legislation on external borders and the United Kingdom is party to that.

Case C-77/05 *United Kingdom v Council* [2007] ECR I-11459

77. …by analogy with what applies in relation to the choice of the legal basis of a [Union] act, it must be concluded that in a situation such as that at issue in the present case the classification of a [Union] act as a proposal or initiative to build upon the Schengen acquis…must rest on objective factors which are amenable to judicial review, including in particular the aim and the content of the act…

83. It should be recalled…that both the title of the Schengen Agreement and the fourth recital in its preamble and Article 17 of the agreement show that its principal objective was the abolition of checks on persons at the common borders of the Member States and the transfer of those checks to their external borders. The importance of that objective in the context of the Schengen Agreements is underlined by the place occupied in the Implementing Convention by the provisions on the crossing of external borders, and by the fact that, under Articles 6 and 7 of that convention, checks at external borders are to be carried out in accordance with uniform principles, with the Member States having to implement constant and close cooperation in order to ensure that those checks are carried out effectively.

---

[89] For more on this see pp. 488–91 in particular.
[90] Cyprus is acceding in 2010. Romania and Bulgaria are to join when 'ready'. No date has been set.
[91] Article 331 TFEU.
[92] See also Case C-137/05 *United Kingdom v Council* [2007] ECR I-11593.

84. It follows that checks on persons at the external borders of the Member States and consequently the effective implementation of the common rules on standards and procedures for those checks must be regarded as constituting elements of the Schengen acquis.

85. Since...Regulation No 2007/2004 is intended, as regards both its purpose and its content, to improve those checks, that regulation must be regarded as constituting a measure to build upon the Schengen acquis...

This reasoning is open to criticism. It would seem that there are two possible legal bases: the Protocol and Article 77(2) TFEU. The responsibility of the Court was to mediate a conflict between these bases, which, as we have seen above, it does elsewhere. In this case it did not do this but deemed it sufficient for the matter to fall within the aegis of the Protocol for it to declare that the Protocol should prevail over other parts of the Treaty. No reasons were given for this, and it is a peculiar view of European integration, in which fragmentation and exclusion are chosen over commonality and inclusion.

The other feature to emerge is the conclusion of international agreements between limited numbers of states, who know others will subsequently join them as there will be significant exclusionary costs if they do not. Once this occurs, the international agreement is then subsequently transformed into an EU law, be it as a Regulation, Directive or Decision. This was indeed the template set out by the Schengen Protocol[93] and it was followed in 2005 by the Prüm Convention.[94] Signed between Austria, Belgium, France, Germany, Luxembourg, the Netherlands and Spain, this provides for greater exchange of DNA, fingerprint and vehicle data between security agencies than was previously possible. It is controversial at a number of levels: notably there are no common rules on collection of the data or (arguably) sufficient common rules on its protection.[95] Other security agencies were, of course, eager to have access to this pool of data as they saw it as a huge resource.

In 2008, the Prüm Convention was made part of EU law binding all Member States.[96] The difficulty with this is not simply the feeling that other states were bounced into something that, all things being equal, they might not have chosen, but also the short-circuiting of public debate. A document was agreed between seven interior ministries with little public debate in their own countries. It was then presented as a *fait accompli* to the EU legislative process in such a way that few amendments could be made, given the momentum behind the process.

---

[93] See pp. 488–91.

[94] Prüm Convention, EU Council Doc. 10900/05. For an interesting analysis, see R. Bossong, 'The European Security Vanguard? Prüm, Heiligendamm and Flexible Integration Theory', LSE/Challenge Working Paper, January 2007, available at www.2.lse.ac.uk/internationalRelations/centresandunits/EFPU/EFPUhome.aspx (accessed 5 November 2009).

[95] House of Lords European Union Committee, *Prüm: An Effective Weapon Against Terrorism and Crime?* (Session 2006–07, 18th Report, London, SO).

[96] Decision 2008/615/JHA on the stepping up of cross-border cooperation, particularly in combating terrorism and cross-border crime [2008] OJ L209/1; Decision 2008/616/JHA on the implementation of Decision 2008/615/JHA on the stepping up of cross-border cooperation, particularly in combating terrorism and cross-border crime [2008] OJ L210/12.

6 COMITOLOGY

(i) Comitology procedures

We saw in Chapter 2 that not merely 'technical', but highly significant questions are delegated to the Commission and that this delegation is also widespread.[97] In 2008 alone, the Commission undertook 2,022 measures.[98] Although this is not considered to be law-making under the Treaty, the measures are regulatory acts which still have legally binding effects and would be called delegated legislation in any other jurisdiction. The Commission adopts measures here under a set of procedures, known as comitology, in which it works in tandem with a committee of representatives of national governments whose role is to oversee it.[99] At the end of 2008, there were 270 committees in operation.[100] The role of the committee varies according to the procedure used and is set out in Decision 1999/468/EC.[101] Comitology establishes four central procedures: the advisory procedure, the management procedure, the regulatory procedure and the regulatory procedure with scrutiny. Each procedure gives the committee different powers. At the end of 2008, twenty-three advisory procedures, fifty-nine management procedures, eighty-three regulatory procedures and four regulatory procedures with scrutiny were in operation.[102] The criteria for determining which procedure is to be used is set out in article 2 of Decision 1999/468/EC.

Decision 1999/468/EC, article 2

1. Without prejudice to paragraph (2), the choice of procedural methods for the adoption of implementing measures shall be guided by the following criteria:

   (a) management measures, such as those relating to the application of the common agricultural and common fisheries policies, or to the implementation of programmes with substantial budgetary implications, should be adopted by use of the management procedure;

   (b) measures of general scope designed to apply essential provisions of basic instruments, including measures concerning the protection of the health or safety of humans, animals or plants, should be adopted by use of the regulatory procedure; where a basic instrument stipulates that certain non-essential provisions of the instrument may be adapted or updated by way of implementing procedures, such measures should be adopted by use of the regulatory procedure;

---

[97] See pp. 59–60.

[98] European Commission, *Report on the Working of the Committees during 2008*, SEC(2009)913, 6.

[99] For an excellent analysis of the evolution of comitology over the years see C. Bergström, *Comitology: Delegation of Powers in the European Union System* (Oxford, Oxford University Press, 2005).

[100] *Report on the Working of the Committees*, above n. 98, 4.

[101] [1999] OJ L184/23 as amended by Decision 2006/512 [2006] OJ L200/11. For discussion see K. Lenaerts and A. Verhoeven, 'Towards a Legal Framework for Executive Rule-making in the EU? The Contribution of the New Comitology Decision' (2000) 37 *CMLRev.* 645. There is a further procedure, the safeguard procedure, which operates in the field of external trade: article 6. Only two committees are established under it, however, and it is not discussed further here.

[102] A further 100 committees operated under a mix of procedures and were therefore difficult for the Commission to categorise. *Report on the Working of the Committees*, above n. 98, 5–6.

(c) without prejudice to points (a) and (b), the advisory procedure shall be used in any case in which it is considered to be the most appropriate.

2. Where a basic instrument, adopted in accordance with the [ordinary legislative procedure] provides for the adoption of measures of general scope designed to amend non-essential elements of that instrument, inter alia by deleting some of those elements or by supplementing the instrument by the addition of new non-essential elements, those measures shall be adopted in accordance with the regulatory procedure with scrutiny.

The procedure under which the Commission has the most freedom on paper is the advisory procedure. Under this procedure, the role of the committee is to 'advise' the Commission, with the Commission required to give 'utmost account' to the view of the committee but, having done that, being ultimately free to disregard it.

Decision 1999/468/EC, article 3

1. The Commission shall be assisted by an advisory committee composed of the representatives of the Member States and chaired by the representative of the Commission.
2. The representative of the Commission shall submit to the Committee a draft of the measures to be taken. The committee shall deliver its opinion on the draft, within a time-limit which the chairman may lay down according to the urgency of the matter, if necessary by taking a vote.
3. The opinion shall be recorded in the minutes; in addition, each Member State shall have the right to ask to have its position recorded in the minutes.
4. The Commission shall take the utmost account of the opinion delivered by the committee. It shall inform the committee of the manner in which the opinion has been taken into account.

In all the other procedures, the committee has a fire-warning role. It has to decide whether or not the Commission draft should be referred to the Council. With the management procedure, the committee, if it is unhappy with a Commission draft, can, by QMV, refer the matter to the Council. It needs a QMV majority in favour of referral. The Council then has up to three months to adopt another Decision.

Decision 1999/468/EC, article 4(3), (4)

3. The Commission shall…adopt measures which shall apply immediately. However, if these measures are not in accordance with the opinion of the committee, they shall be communicated by the Commission to the Council forthwith. In that event, the Commission may defer application of the measures which it has decided on for a period to be laid down in each basic instrument but which shall in no case exceed three months from the date of such communication.[103]
4. The Council, acting by qualified majority, may take a different decision within the period provided for by paragraph 3.

---

[103] Decision 1999/468/EC, article 8.

There was concern that the majority of committee members could disapprove of the Commission draft, but it would still be adopted. To that end, the Commission issued a Declaration on adoption of the Decision stating that, with regard to the management procedure, it would never go against 'any predominant position which might emerge against the appropriateness of an implementing measure'.[104]

This danger does not exist in the regulatory procedure, where the committee must positively agree to the Commission draft by QMV. If it fails to do this, the draft is referred to the Council, which has up to three months to take a decision of its own.

Decision 1999/468/EC, article 5(3)–(6)

3. The Commission shall, without prejudice to article 8,[105] adopt the measures envisaged if they are in accordance with the opinion of the committee.

4. If the measures envisaged are not in accordance with the opinion of the committee, or if no opinion is delivered, the Commission shall, without delay, submit to the Council a proposal relating to the measures to be taken and shall inform the European Parliament.

5. If the European Parliament considers that a proposal submitted by the Commission pursuant to a basic instrument adopted in accordance with the [ordinary legislative procedure] exceeds the implementing powers provided for in that basic instrument, it shall inform the Council of its position.

6. The Council may, where appropriate in view of any such position, act by qualified majority on the proposal, within a period to be laid down in each basic instrument but which shall in no case exceed three months from the date of referral to the Council. If within that period the Council has indicated by qualified majority that it opposes the proposal, the Commission shall re-examine it. It may submit an amended proposal to the Council, re-submit its proposal or present a legislative proposal on the basis of the Treaty. If on the expiry of that period the Council has neither adopted the proposed implementing act nor indicated its opposition to the proposal for implementing measures, the proposed implementing act shall be adopted by the Commission.

The regulatory procedure contains its own perversity, which is the difference between the voting thresholds in the committee and those in the Council. A QMV majority must actively *support* the measure in the committee for it not to be referred to the Council. By contrast, a QMV majority in the Council must actively *oppose* the measure or support an alternative for the Commission draft not to become law. This leaves a space for the Commission to adopt measures unchecked. This is best illustrated by giving an example where fourteen out of twenty-seven Member States oppose a measure. They do not make a QMV majority but they do form a blocking minority. In such circumstances, the measure would be referred by the committee as a QMV majority would not be in support. The measure could still be adopted, however, as there is not a QMV majority opposing it or formulating an alternative. A Commission measure could therefore become law even if a majority of Member States oppose it. To be sure, given the Commission's Declaration in relation to the management committee, it is unlikely it would ever

---

[104] [1999] OJ C203/1.
[105] See p. 120.

pursue the measure in such circumstances, but it may, however, where there is a substantial minority against the measure, as it can point to a simple majority being in favour.[106]

(ii) The Parliament and comitology

The other issue raised in the regulatory procedure is the role of the Parliament. The ordinary legislative procedure, of course, provides for measures to be adopted by the Council and the Parliament. The Parliament had become increasingly uneasy during the 1990s about delegating powers to the Commission that it thought would be better exercised by the ordinary legislative procedure (at that time, the co-decision procedure). It was, therefore, agreed that regulatory measures based on a parent instrument adopted under the ordinary legislative procedure would be notified to the Parliament and it could object through a Resolution if it considered they exceeded the implementing power granted by the parent instrument. Under article 8 of Decision 1999/468/EC, the Commission committed itself to reconsider the measure taking the Parliament's Resolution into account. The Decision did not require the Commission to withdraw the measure but only to give reasons for its decision. In subsequent years, Parliament continued to feel its prerogatives were being ignored and this culminated in a 2005 exchange where the Commission admitted over fifty instances where it had failed to respect Parliament's rights under comitology.[107]

Following this exchange, the regulatory procedure with scrutiny was introduced. The procedure only applies to instruments which are perceived as 'amending' their parent instruments, where the latter had been adopted under the ordinary legislative procedure. Regulatory procedure with scrutiny begins the same way as the regulatory procedure, with the Commission submitting a draft to the committee which expresses an opinion on it. The process is convoluted after that but boils down to two processes depending on whether the committee agrees with the Commission draft or not.

If the committee agrees with the draft, either the Council or Parliament can veto the draft, but only on the grounds that it is too sweeping and therefore either exceeds the implementing powers granted to the Commission or breaches the subsidiarity or proportionality principles. If they fail to act, it is adopted.[108]

If the committee disagrees with the draft, the same possibilities exist except that this time the Council can decide to oppose the measure *for any reason* and this pre-empts any consideration by the Parliament, which only looks at the draft if the Council is inclined to accept it. The Council has two months to make its opposition known and the Parliament four months after that. If they both fail to indicate their opposition, the measure will be adopted.[109]

Both the Parliament and the Council have high thresholds to meet to register their opposition: an absolute majority of members and a QMV majority respectively. However, in 2008, seven measures were vetoed by one or other of these institutions on the grounds that the

---

[106] For a case study where this happened in relation to the regulation of genetically modified organisms see D. Chalmers, 'Risk, Anxiety and the European Mediation of the Politics of Life' (2005) 30 *ELRev.* 649.

[107] K. Bradley, 'Halfway House: The 2006 Comitology Reforms and the European Parliament' (2008) 31 *WEP* 837, 842–3.

[108] Decision 2006/512/EC, article 5a(3).

[109] *Ibid.* article 5a(4). For discussion see G. Schusterschitz and S. Kotz, 'The Comitology Reform of 2006: Increasing the Power of the European Parliament without Changing the Treaties' (2007) 3 *European Constitutional Law Review* 68.

Commission was exceeding its powers, just under 10 per cent of the measures proposed for regulatory procedure with scrutiny in that year.

It is the Council that has benefited most from the procedure, not the Parliament, vetoing all but one of them.[110]

The place of these procedures has been changed by the coming into force of the Lisbon Treaty, which grants additional powers to the Council and Parliament to place constraints on the Commission with regard to delegated measures.

Article 290(2) TFEU

Legislative acts shall explicitly lay down the conditions to which the delegation is subject; these conditions may be as follows:

(a) the European Parliament or the Council may decide to revoke the delegation;

(b) the delegated act may enter into force only if no objection has been expressed by the European Parliament or the Council within a period set by the legislative act.

Both the Council and Parliament will now have the opportunity to block the measure. This power is also to exist across other areas of legislative activity, not just across the ordinary legislative procedure. The other feature of Article 290(2) TFEU is the possibility it provides to both institutions to revoke a delegation. Up until now, this could only be done through deploying the formal legislative procedures to amend the parent instrument: so if it had been adopted by ordinary legislative procedure, it had to be amended by that procedure. Article 290(2) TFEU suggests more truncated procedures may be set for revocation of a delegation, which, importantly, do not require a Commission proposal for an amendment but can be done at either of the other institutions' behest. Consequently, the Commission may be exercising its powers under the shadow of the sword with the possibility that if it does something institutionally unpopular it will suffer the consequences.

The procedure in Article 290(2) TFEU only applies to delegated acts and not to implementing acts.[111]

Article 291(3) TFEU

…the European Parliament and the Council, acting by means of regulations in accordance with the ordinary legislative procedure, shall lay down in advance the rules and general principles concerning mechanisms for control by Member States of the Commission's exercise of implementing powers.

---

[110] Seventy-one measures were adopted. *Report on the Working of the Committees*, above n. 98, 6–7.

[111] The absence of an equivalent provision to Article 291(3) TFEU in Article 290 TFEU has led some authors to suggest that comitology is prohibited for delegated measures. We disagree. The absence of such a provision does not constrain the other institutions from introducing provisions any more than its absence in the earlier Treaties, and it would be difficult to see how they could police the measures otherwise; cf. K. Lenaerts and M. Desomer, 'Towards a Hierarchy of Legal Acts in the EU' (2005) 11 *ELJ* 744, 755.

This begs the question how Article 290(2) TFEU affects the different procedures set out in Decision 1999/468/EC. Implementing measures will continue to be subject to the same comitology regime, but for delegated measures the only procedure definitely covered by Article 290(2) TFEU is the regulatory procedure with scrutiny, as the jurisdiction of both extends to amending non-essential parts of the parent instrument. For the other procedures it is opaque; and this is extremely concerning, given that the regulatory procedure with scrutiny applies to less than 2 per cent of all the committees.

(iii) Dynamics of comitology and its concerns

Despite this debate on checks and balances, it is not clear that the other institutions either have the resources to police the Commission or that the committees have the inclination to refer the matter to the Council. In 2008, the committees gave 2,185 opinions but only seven references were made to the Council.[112] The central constraints lie in the interactions between the Commission and the committee. In pioneering work, Joerges and Neyer studied the interaction between the Commission and two such committees, the Standing Committee on Foodstuffs (StCF) and the Scientific Committee on Foodstuffs (SCF). They found that comitology did not consist of national checks on Commission decision-making but was, rather, a more fluid settlement centred around deliberative problem-solving in which actors took on board each other's suggestions, and concern focused on finding the optimal solution rather than representing different interests.

C. Joerges and J. Neyer, 'Transforming Strategic Interaction into Deliberative Problem-Solving: European Comitology in the Foodstuffs Sector' (1997) 4 _Journal of European Public Policy_ 609, 618–20

Whereas the comitology system in the foodstuffs sector is far too small an arena to allow generalization, it is nevertheless indicative of how this relationship can work in practice and what its deficiencies might be. Three elements are of particular importance:

(a) The proposals which the Commission presents to the StCF are in general the result of extensive consultations with individual national administrations and independent experts. Particularly in committees like the StCF which act under qualified majority voting, proposals not only reflect the Commission's interest but also what it assumes to be in the interest of _more than a qualified majority_ of the other parties involved. This becomes of crucial importance as the effectiveness of any measure adopted depends on member states transposing the measure adequately into their national legal systems without leaving too many opportunities for evasion and – more importantly – not invoking safeguard procedures. However, in an institutional environment without effective means of hierarchical enforcement, this is only likely to happen if delegates see their own legitimate concerns acknowledged and protected in decision-making.

(b) The importance of the SCF in supporting certain arguments does not derive from any formal power to decide issues of conflict (it has only an advisory status) but from the legal fiction of its scientific expertise and neutrality. To be sure, member states are well aware that the SCF is sometimes used by

---

[112] _Report on the Working of the Committees_, above n. 98, 6–109.

the Commission as an instrument for furthering its interests and, furthermore, that its experts do not always comply with the norm of objectivity. Moreover, the bovine spongiform encephalopathy (BSE) case has highlighted the fact that even scientific institutions can easily be captured by certain interest groups and instrumentalized for political purposes by the Commission. The Scientific Veterinary Committee was not only chaired by a British scientist; the available records of attendance also show the preponderance of UK scientists and officials, meaning that the Committee tended to reflect current thinking at the British Ministry of Agriculture, Fisheries and Food. Why do member state delegates nevertheless adhere to the fiction of objective science? To understand this, one needs to consider the functions of legal fictions: scientific findings are supposed to be accepted by all the parties concerned; science-based discourses have the power to discipline arguments; and they allow a clear distinction between legitimate and illegitimate arguments in cases of conflict over competing proposals. Therefore, the fact that the opinions of the SCF have never been seriously challenged by the StCF may be grounded less in the objectivity of its opinions than in the function of scientific discourses as a mechanism that is helpful in overcoming politically constituted preferences by relying on the fiction of objective science.

(c) International negotiations concerning common solutions to problems of interdependence generally involve two modes of interaction: strategic bargaining to maximize particular utilities at the expense of others and deliberative problem-solving to maximize collective utilities. Empirically, it is important to realize that the relative intensity of both modes may vary, and identify the conditions which influence them. Whereas the mainstream literature on international negotiations does not acknowledge the possibility of deliberative problem-solving but conceptualizes international negotiations as a pursuit of domestic policy goals by different means, recent contributions to the literature on epistemic communities highlight conditions where the grip which national politicians have on delegates is rather weak. The most prominent conditions mentioned are uncertainty about the distributive effects of certain policies, long-term interaction among delegates, as well as their mutual socialization into a community with common problem definitions and collectively shared approaches to dealing with them.

Under such conditions governments may be unaware of what their preferences are, or delegates, perceiving themselves as part of a transnational problem-solving community, may be able to change their governments' perceptions of interests or even simply bypass them. The condition of high uncertainty about the distributional effects of certain policies is surely not always met; often governments have clear perceptions of the costs that certain policy options might impose on them. However, in negotiations in the StCF – and even more so in the SCF – the particular economic costs of policies cannot be explicitly discussed, and information is primarily provided on nondistributional issues. *Ceteris paribus*, therefore, the knowledge of delegates about adequate problem-solving strategies will increase with the duration of negotiations, whereas their *relative* knowledge about economic effects will decline. This change in the perceptions and preferences of delegates becomes increasingly important for shaping national preferences as their informational advantage over their national administration increases over time. It is also important to note that negotiations sometimes last for years among nearly the same set of delegates. Moreover, delegates have frequent contacts outside the sessions of the Standing Committee, and have often previously met working on the preparation of a legislative proposal in negotiations about its adoption in Council working groups. During the course of this collaboration, delegates not only learn to reduce differences between national legal provisions but also to develop converging definitions of problems and philosophies for their solution. They slowly proceed from being representatives of national interests to being representatives of a Europeanized inter-administrative discourse characterized by mutual learning and an understanding of each other's difficulties in the implementation of specific solutions.

Subsequent studies have reaffirmed this characterisation. A study of Scandinavian officials found that whilst the overwhelming majority of those sitting on the committees saw themselves as government representatives, there was also a strong perception that they saw themselves both as independent experts and as persons acting on behalf of the collective European interest. Above all, there was a strong esprit de corps and loyalty to the committee and other members of the committee, which was particularly marked amongst those who participated most intensively on the committee.[113]

Understandings of comitology as an interactive network of administrators and experts rather than as a check on the Commission's powers have provoked a fierce debate about its democratic qualities.[114] There have been two central concerns. One is that its language is too technocratic. Delicate political and social questions are reduced to questions of expertise and risk assessment.[115] The other is that its make-up is insufficiently pluralistic. Administrators may 'up their game' by having to respond to other administrators' arguments but, as Gerstenberg and Sabel artfully put it, this may only 'improve government performance and renovate the role of the bureaucrat without much changing the role of the citizen'.[116] The rights of audience or participation of private parties before these committees, for example, are notoriously unclear.[117] Joerges has observed, in defence of the processes, that they contain many checks and balances that are generally unappreciated.

C. Joerges, 'Deliberative Supranationalism: A Defence' (2001) 5(8) *European Integration online Papers (EIoP)* 8–9

…comitology…interested us because of its links not just with the bureaucracies but also with the polities of the Member States, because of its complex internal structure in which government representatives, the representatives of social interests and 'the' economy all interact. Risk regulation in the internal market seemed to us to document the weaknesses of expertocratic models adequately, because the normative, political and ethical dimensions of risk assessments resist a merely technocratic treatment. Admittedly, in the debates about the tensions between the ideals of democracy and the constraints of the 'knowledge society', Columbus' egg has not been sighted so far. My mere status as a citizen does not qualify me for a qualitatively convincing (to me at least) technical decision, nor can it be seen how 'all' the citizens affected by such decisions are really to participate in them. What is true of risk policy is present as a problem in practically every corner of modern law. And what is true of

---

[113] J. Trondal, 'Beyond the EU Membership-Non Membership Dichotomy? Supranational Identities among National EU Decision-Makers' (2002) 9 *JEPP* 468. This has been found in other surveys: see J. Blom-Hansen and G. Brandsma, 'The EU Comitology System: Intergovernmental Bargaining *and* Deliberative Supranationalism?' (2009) 47 *JCMS* 719.

[114] R. Dehousse, 'Comitology? Who Watches the Watchmen?' (2003) 10 *JEPP* 798.

[115] J. Weiler, 'Epilogue, "Comitology" as Revolution: Infranationalism, Constitutionalism and Democracy' in C. Joerges and E. Vos (eds.), *EU Committees: Social Regulation, Law and Politics* (Oxford and Portland, Hart, 1999) 339, 345–6.

[116] O. Gerstenberg and C. Sabel, 'Directly-Deliberative Polyarchy: An Institutional Ideal for Europe' in C. Joerges and R. Dehousse (eds.), *Good Governance in Europe's Integrated Market* (Oxford, Oxford University Press, 2002) 289, 320.

[117] F. Bignami, 'The Democratic Deficit in European Community Rulemaking: A Call for Notice and Comment in Comitology' (1999) 40 *Harvard International Law Journal* 451.

risk policy in an EU Member State in which (relatively) dense communicative processes guarantee the ongoing political debate is true *a fortiori* for such a polymorphic entity as the EU.

The much-maligned comitology has the advantage over agencies of the American pattern in that it structures risk policy pluralistically, that national bureaucracies have to face up to the positions of their neighbour states, and that interests and concerns in Member States cannot be filtered out. Committees can be observed closely by the wider public and such politicisation has proved to be effective. This seems to be the situation: any conceivable argument can be brought to bear in the committee system. It tends to offer *fora* for pluralistic discussions. Its links with the broader public do, however, remain dependent on the attention that an issue attracts and on the insistence of the actors concerned on public debate.

This may be so, but it requires rather a lot to be taken on trust and there is the broader question of how others would know if what was said to be happening within the committees *was* actually happening. Since 1999, there have therefore been attempts to make the procedure more transparent. Public access to the documents and discussions of the committees is granted on the same basis as to other Commission documents.[118] The Commission has established a register of draft measures placed before the committees and of the agendas and voting records of the committees.[119] Disturbingly, an independent study found that this was something of a hollow commitment: 95 per cent of draft measures and 35 per cent of agendas were not published.[120]

The Lisbon Treaty also suggested that less trust was to be placed in these procedures. It is far easier to challenge them judicially. An individual may now challenge any 'regulatory act' simply if it directly concerns her.[121] This will be the case wherever the measure directly prejudices her legal rights.[122] The consequence is that it will be relatively easy for private parties to challenge delegated legislation. It remains to be seen whether this is a panacea for opening up comitology. Litigation is notoriously ad hoc and threatens the rationales for delegation in the first place, namely policy credibility and efficiency. Furthermore, judges are also non-majoritarian actors and poor substitutes for pluralistic processes if that is the centre of the concern.

7 THE 'DEMOCRATIC DEFICIT' AND THE LEGISLATIVE PROCESS

The question of democratic legitimacy, the 'democratic deficit' in Euro-speak, has dominated debate surrounding the Union's legislative processes. Such debate typically criticises EU law-making in three ways. First, there are concerns about the quality of representative democracy. Such concerns focus both on the parliamentary input in the processes and the extent to which EU law-making undermines parliamentary democracy at a national and regional level.

---

[118] See Decision 1999/468/EC, article 7(2). On public access to the work of the Commission see pp. 384–94.
[119] *Ibid.* article 7(5).
[120] G. Brandsma *et. al.*, 'How Transparent are EU "Comitology" Committees in Practice' (2008) 14 *ELJ* 819, 833.
[121] Article 263(4) TFEU. For other legislative measures, a private party must also show that it is of individual concern to her. This is quite a restrictive hurdle to meet. See pp. 413–28.
[122] Case C-486/01 P *Front National* v *Parliament* [2004] ECR I-6289.

Secondly, there are concerns about the quality of participatory democracy. EU law-making has been accused of being insufficiently plural, of not listening to enough interested parties, and of giving too great weight to some interests. Finally, concerns have been expressed about the quality of deliberative democracy: the quality of public debate that surrounds and informs the law-making processes. Here, it is often argued that law-making processes are far too character- ised by strategic negotiation between interests rather than public debate between citizens.

(i) Representative democracy and national parliaments

Representative democracy was seen by the German Constitutional Court in its judgment on the Lisbon Treaty as central to any democratic system:

> The citizens' right to determine, in equality and freedom, public authority with regard to persons and subject-matters through elections and other votes is the fundamental element of the principle of democracy. The right to free and equal participation in public authority is anchored in human dignity...It belongs to the principles of German constitutional law that are laid down as non-amendable.[123]

A similar sentiment is expressed in Article 10(1) TEU which states that the functioning of the European Union is to be founded on representative democracy. It would seem, therefore, to be as central a filament of the Union's mission as it is to the German constitutional state. If so, it appears to fail miserably on two counts.

First, the institutions set out in the Treaty as embodying this idea are not clearly representa- tive institutions.

Article 10(2) TEU

Citizens are directly represented at Union level in the European Parliament. Member States are represented in the European Council by their Heads of State or Government and in the Council by their governments, themselves democratically accountable either to their national Parliaments, or to their citizens.

Governments, be they sitting in the Council or European Council, are not seen as representa- tive institutions. Indeed, the history of representative democracy is a history of the develop- ment of institutions to curb and hold accountable the growth of executives. Notwithstanding its direct elections, doubts can also be held over the European Parliament for the reasons given by the German Constitutional Court. Citizens are not represented equally in it. There is low interest and involvement in it. And, finally, there is little popular commitment to it.

The second reason is even more of an indictment. Administrators dominate EU law-making. It is the Commission which proposes legislation. The proposal is negotiated by national officials in COREPER and it is adopted by government ministers in the Council. Swathes of delegated legislation are adopted by the Commission with national administrators through comitology.

---

[123] 2 BvE 2/08 *Gauweiler* v *Treaty of Lisbon*, Judgment of 30 June 2009, para. 211.

The European Union seems, therefore, to violate the most central foundation of democracy as seen by itself and the German Constitutional Court. This is a swingeing condemnation. And indeed it is largely the Euro-sceptic case. The solution does not seem simply to be to increase the powers of the European Parliament, as for the reasons just outlined it can only partially alleviate concerns about representation.

The 'representative deficit' has focused in recent years, instead, on the role of national parliaments in the law-making processes.[124]

Following the Lisbon Treaty, the Treaties do provide for an increased role for national parliaments. Significantly, this is in a separate provision, suggesting that they are not to be at the heart of the Union, but are instead to remain secondary players. It outlines, inter alia, their contribution to the law-making process.

Article 12 TEU

National Parliaments contribute actively to the good functioning of the Union:

(a) through being informed by the institutions of the Union and having draft legislative acts of the Union forwarded to them in accordance with the Protocol on the role of national Parliaments in the European Union;

(b) by seeing to it that the principle of subsidiarity is respected in accordance with the procedures provided for in the Protocol on the application of the principles of subsidiarity and proportionality...

(f) by taking part in the interparliamentary cooperation between national Parliaments and with the European Parliament, in accordance with the Protocol on the role of national Parliaments in the European Union.

The first form of power is involvement in the pre-legislative and legislative processes to secure influence for individual parliaments in the decision-making process. The Protocol on the Role of National Parliaments seeks to realise this in a number of ways:

- All draft legislative acts will be sent directly to national parliaments, rather than to national governments to pass onto national parliaments.[125]
- National parliaments will also be sent the annual legislative programme, as well as any policy or legislative planning instrument.[126]
- All agendas and minutes of Council meetings will be sent to national parliaments.[127]
- An eight-week period will elapse between a draft legislative act being sent to national parliaments and its being placed on the agenda of the Council.[128]

---

[124] A. Maurer and W. Wessels (eds.), *National Parliaments on their Ways to Europe: Losers or Latecomers?* (Baden Baden, Nomos, 2001).
[125] Protocol on the role of national parliaments in the European Union, Article 2.
[126] *Ibid.* Article 1.
[127] *Ibid.* Article 5.
[128] *Ibid.* Article 4.

The central intention is that the provision of this information will allow parliaments to exercise influence over their national government in the Council in such a way that it can become a vehicle for their views. Two types of procedure have emerged for the expression of this influence. The *document-based* procedure does not mandate the national minister to take a position. Instead, on important proposals, it requires the minister not to agree to any proposal until a parliamentary committee has scrutinised it and published its findings. The other is the *mandate-based* system, whereby the national parliament authorises the government to take a position and the national government cannot deviate from that, or must provide reasons if it intends to do so.[129]

Auel and Benz have argued that the most suitable procedure depends also on the nature of government-parliament relations. They observed that in the United Kingdom, the document-based system worked well, as the party which was in government also usually had a large majority in parliament. If the mandate-based system were to be used, the party in government would just fill the committee with sympathetic MPs. However, the document-based system had allowed the parliamentary committees to be relatively non-partisan, mobilising them as points for civil society and expertise to coalesce around. In turn, this reputation enables some influence. By contrast, the mandate-based system has traditionally worked well in Denmark, as coalition governments in which all the main parliamentary parties are represented has been a feature of the post-war settlement. The mandate-based procedure allows all coalition partners as well as public debate to inform the position of the minister, thereby ensuring the position has not only parliamentary but also wider government support.[130]

For all this, the limits of each procedure indicate how difficult it is to exercise indirect influence over negotiations involving so many players. The document-based system relies on the idea of soft influence. The parliamentary committee understands that the government needs room to negotiate but rather seeks to bring out issues and interests to the fore that have not been publicly debated or thought through. Its weakness, however, lies in its lack of constraint. The mandate-based system secures a far more direct parliamentary influence on negotiations. Its problem lies in its lack of flexibility. It can lead to governments being disempowered in negotiations and awareness of this often leads the parliament to soften the mandate or use it highly selectively.

There are further difficulties, whichever procedure is used. It is often difficult for national parliaments to formulate a position. As national parliaments often have few supporting staff, contacts with the relevant minister and ministry might be minimal.[131] In this regard, it is doubtful whether the eight-week period national parliaments are given to consider drafts is sufficient to enable effective input into the process.[132] To put this in perspective, the Commission

---

[129] Austria, Belgium, Bulgaria, Cyprus, France, Germany, Ireland, Italy, Luxembourg, Netherlands, Portugal, Slovakia, Spain and the United Kingdom all adopt document-based systems. Denmark, Estonia, Finland, Latvia, Lithuania, Poland, Romania, Slovakia, Slovenia and Sweden use mandate-based systems. Other Member States use a mix of the two. COSAC, *Eighth Biannual Report: Developments in European Union Procedures and Practices relevant to Parliamentary Scrutiny* (Luxembourg, COSAC, 2007) 7–9.

[130] K. Auel and A. Benz, 'The Politics of Adaptation: The Europeanization of National Parliamentary Systems' (2005) 11 *Journal of Legislative Studies* 372.

[131] For criticisms see *Future of Europe Convention, Final Report of the Working Group IV on the Role of National Parliaments*, CONV 353/02, 4–5.

[132] House of Lords European Union Committee, *The Treaty of Lisbon: An Impact Assessment* (Session 2007–08, 10th Report, London, SO) paras. 11.50–11.53.

allows a period of eight weeks for private parties to make submissions in its consultative pro-cedures.[133] Considering that national parliaments represent a wider array of interests and are charged with more significant responsibilities, giving them the same time period to intervene seems unjustified.

In addition to influence via their national governments, all national parliaments have direct relations with the Commission. Since 2006, the latter has instigated a procedure whereby it sends its proposals directly to national parliaments, who also return their opinions straight to the Commission.[134] Between September 2006 and the end of 2008, the Commission received 368 opinions from 33 national assemblies in 24 Member States. This is an impressive num-ber, particularly as 200 opinions were given in 2008 alone.[135] However, whilst the number of opinions were substantial, four chambers (the Czech Senate, the German Bundesrat, the French Senate and the UK House of Lords) were responsible for 54 of the 200 in 2008. These are all second chambers, and their predominance suggests a danger of asymmetric representation where assemblies with stronger capacity or interest are more actively involved. The quality of opinion is also variable. The Portuguese Assembly of the Republic gave 65 opinions in 2008, but all were positive on the Commission proposal and none contained specific comments. The final observation made by the Commission was that parliamentary comments tended to follow those of the respective national governments.[136]

The second set of powers provided for national parliaments in the legislative process is to police the legislative process for compliance with the subsidiarity principle: the principle whereby the European Union is only to legislate if the objects of a measure cannot be realised by Member States acting unilaterally and could by reason of their scale or effects be better realised by EU action.[137] National parliaments seem to have a particularly important role in the process. It is the powers of national and regional parliaments that are most encroached upon by EU legislation. They seem to be among the biggest stakeholders in determining where its limits should be set.

Detailed provision is made for them in the Protocol on the application of the principles of subsidiarity and proportionality.

Protocol on the application of the principles of subsidiarity and proportionality, Article 6

Any national Parliament or any chamber of a national Parliament may, within eight weeks from the date of transmission of a draft legislative act, in the official languages of the Union, send to the Presidents of the European Parliament, the Council and the Commission a reasoned opinion stating why it considers that the draft in question does not comply with the principle of subsidiarity.

---

[133] European Commission, General Principles and Minimum Standards for Consultation of Interested Parties by the Commission, COM(2002)704, 21.
[134] European Commission, *A Citizens' Agenda:- Delivering Results for Europe*, COM(2006)211 final.
[135] European Commission, *Annual Report on Relations between the European Commission and Nation Parliaments*, COM(2009)343, 4.
[136] *Ibid.* 6.
[137] Protocol on the role of national parliaments in the European Union, Article 3.

The national parliaments of each Member State are also given two votes, which are shared out between chambers in the case of a bicameral system. Opinions suggesting a violation of the subsidiarity principle are then tallied up. If at least eighteen out of the current fifty-four votes suggest that it does (fourteen in the case of Article 76 TFEU), then the institution that proposed the measure may decide to withdraw it.

Protocol on the application of the principles of subsidiarity and proportionality, Article 7(2)

Where reasoned opinions on a draft legislative act's non-compliance with the principle of subsidiarity represent at least one third of all the votes allocated to the national Parliaments…, the draft must be reviewed. This threshold shall be a quarter in the case of a draft legislative act submitted on the basis of Article 76 TFEU on the area of freedom, security and justice.

After such review, the Commission or, where appropriate, the group of Member States, the European Parliament, the Court of Justice, the European Central Bank or the European Investment Bank, if the draft legislative act originates from them, may decide to maintain, amend or withdraw the draft. Reasons must be given for this decision.

Concern was expressed that national parliaments could issue only a 'yellow card' to the Union legislature, requiring it to reconsider a proposal, and not a 'red card', requiring it to abandon it. Criticism was also expressed that there is only optional involvement of regional assemblies, who will be consulted if the respective national parliament so decides.[138] Furthermore, national parliaments have no direct powers to protect their prerogatives under the procedures through bringing annulment actions before the Court of Justice, but must rely on national governments to do so.[139] These criticisms are, however, formalistic. It is politically inconceivable that the Commission or national governments could ignore opposition from one-third or one-quarter of national parliaments. Apart from anything else, it is doubtful whether a QMV majority will be available in many circumstances where that number do oppose.

A bigger challenge is the threshold of opposition required: that of one-third or one-quarter of national parliamentary chambers. Typically, EU legislation will not violate some bright red line drawn by all national parliaments, but will threaten some tradition, which is cherished in a particular Member State. This is regardless of whether they are measures prohibiting the use of snuff in Sweden, or imperial weights and measures in the United Kingdom, or measures allowing cheese to be marketed as feta not from Greece or beer to be marketed in Germany despite not being in accordance with German purity laws. A feature of these is that they are idiosyncratic. Their value is deeply felt in the state in question, but much less so elsewhere. It will be difficult, in such circumstances, for the national parliament of that state to persuade the parliaments in other states that there has been a breach of subsidiarity.

---

[138] For criticism, see House of Lords European Union Committee, *Strengthening National Parliamentary Scrutiny of the EU* (Session 2004–05, 14th Report, London, SO) paras. 183–203.

[139] Protocol on the application of the principles of subsidiarity and proportionality, Article 8. S. Weatherill, 'Better Competence Monitoring' (2005) 30 *EL Rev.* 23, 40.

In spite of this, the Member States decided a further procedure was necessary after the failure of the ratification of the Constitutional Treaty. The 'orange card' procedure was therefore introduced by the Lisbon Treaty.

Protocol on the application of the principles of subsidiarity and proportionality, Article 7(3)

Furthermore, under the ordinary legislative procedure, where reasoned opinions on the non-compliance of a proposal for a legislative act with the principle of subsidiarity represent at least a simple majority of the votes allocated to the national Parliaments…, the proposal must be reviewed. After such review, the Commission may decide to maintain, amend or withdraw the proposal.

If it chooses to maintain the proposal, the Commission will have, in a reasoned opinion, to justify why it considers that the proposal complies with the principle of subsidiarity. This reasoned opinion, as well as the reasoned opinions of the national Parliaments, will have to be submitted to the Union's legislator, for consideration in the procedure:

(a) before concluding the first reading, the legislator (the European Parliament and the Council) shall consider whether the legislative proposal is compatible with the principle of subsidiarity, taking particular account of the reasons expressed and shared by the majority of national Parliaments as well as the reasoned opinion of the Commission;

(b) if, by a majority of 55% of the members of the Council or a majority of the votes cast in the European Parliament, the legislator is of the opinion that the proposal is not compatible with the principle of subsidiarity, the legislative proposal shall not be given further consideration.

This new procedure seems unnecessary. It is almost inconceivable that the Commission would take forward a proposal where over half the national parliaments opposed it. As national governments are accountable to national parliaments, it is almost as unimaginable that such a proposal would receive a QMV majority in the Council. On its own terms, the procedure is somewhat bizarre. It only applies to the ordinary legislative procedure. Yet, if there is a problem with Commission discretion, surely it would generally affect the institution's role in all legislative procedures. The other odd feature is that a positive majority is needed to vote a measure incompatible with the subsidiarity principle. This is a high threshold as it means that a measure could be adopted, despite the fact that a majority of national parliaments and half the members of the Council (including all the large Member States) thought EU legislation should not be developed on the matter in question.

The Protocol looks as if it also might be the making of the Conference of Community and European Affairs Committees of Parliaments of the European Union (COSAC). Established in 1989, COSAC is a forum in which national parliaments and the European Parliament meet biannually to discuss the business of the forthcoming Council Presidency and to exchange information and best practice.[140] Since 2007, COSAC has become a more proactive and salient forum for securing the subsidiarity principle. It coordinates checks by national parliaments

---

[140] Its position is formalised in the Protocol on the role of national parliaments in the European Union, Article 10. See also Article 12(f) TEU.

where Commission proposals appear to touch particularly on national sensitivities. In 2008, three exercises were conducted on Commission proposals for legislation on terrorism; organ transplants; and amending the Framework Directive prohibiting discrimination. This led to forty-five opinions by national parliaments on the two proposals.[141] COSAC has also set itself up as a forum for national parliamentary concerns. All commit themselves to an early exchange of information through communicating any particular subsidiarity concerns to each other through COSAC.[142]

(ii) Participatory democracy and republicanism

The challenges of representative democracy for the European Union lie in its not being a single political community which can lay claim to the primary political allegiances of its members in the same way as the nation-state. It is also a community of states and this leads to many of the features that obstruct the Union's claims to representative democracy: notably the weakness of the European Parliament's credentials and the heavy presence of national administrations in EU law-making.

Those relying exclusively on this to indict the Union have to explain, however, what arrangements should then exist for dealing with transnational issues. These issues can arise in at least three ways. First, they can arise because one state imposes externalities on another, such as pollution crossing from the territory of one into the other's environment. Secondly, they can arise because we can wish to create new collective goods, such as international trade, communications or transport links, which are perceived as enriching all parties' lives. Finally, they can arise because we feel responsibilities not just to those in our national territory but to others outside: that it is unacceptable to stand by and watch the suffering of others.

Traditional arrangements have either relied on one or a few states imposing their model on others to realise these goals (the colonial or neocolonial model) or on international treaties concluded between national administrations (the Westphalian model). The former excludes every state not involved in the development of the model and does not even consider what democratic controls exist within the state enacting the model. The latter is government by bureaucratic fiat, as these treaties are invariably developed by cartels of national civil servants with possibly the odd facilitation by an international civil servant. Indeed, it is positively perverse for those who criticise the European Union because it is executive-oriented or does not sufficiently involve national parliaments to hark back nostalgically to this intergovernmental model. It leads to an even higher executive dominance and even greater parliamentary exclusion.

In the absence of a less imperfect alternative, concerns about insufficient representative democracy in the European Union point to two things. First, they suggest scepticism about what it should do. If it is harder to 'democratise' transnational decision-making than national decision-making, this points to our considering carefully when to deploy the former. Secondly, they point to the Union having to look more acutely to other sources of democratic legitimation to justify its law-making powers. These are set out in Articles 10 and 11 TEU.

---

[141] European Commission, *Annual Report*, above n. 135, 5–6.
[142] COSAC, *Tenth Biannual Report: Developments in European Union Procedures and Practices relevant to Parliamentary Scrutiny* (Paris, COSAC, 2008) 17–18.

Article 10(3) TEU

Every citizen shall have the right to participate in the democratic life of the Union. Decisions shall be taken as openly and as closely as possible to the citizen.

Article 11 TEU

1. The institutions shall, by appropriate means, give citizens and representative associations the opportunity to make known and publicly exchange their views in all areas of Union action.
2. The institutions shall maintain an open, transparent and regular dialogue with representative associations and civil society.

Three particular features of the Union enable a quality of engagement to take place in which political institutions of the Union engage with each other and with the Union's citizenry in a culture of mutual respect.

First, the Union institutionalises a principle of 'constitutional tolerance'.[143] It leads nationals of Member States to accept and acknowledge a shared destiny with strangers and the values of strangers without trying to change them. A British citizen is required to recognise that the French citizen has rights and interests that she must not impinge upon and that she brings something different, but equally valuable, to the Union political community of which the British citizen is part. This is, as Müller has observed, a potentially very deep-seated form of tolerance, for it is born out of the idea that a state must be a liberal democracy and have a particular memory of the destructiveness of conflict to be a member of the European Union. This embeds a culture where only certain claims which accept the presumptive validity of difference are politically acceptable.[144]

Secondly, the Union is built around the creation of common institutions to realise shared projects (e.g. the single market, the area of freedom, security and justice, a common environmental policy). These institutions have an elevating effect, as they require citizens to come together to realise common goods; to act and negotiate in the public interest recognising each other's needs and arguments rather than acting in a self-interested manner. They require citizens to act in a public rather than a private manner.[145]

Thirdly, the institutional settlements of the Union prevent concentrations of power and foster pluralism.[146] Power is not centred in any one set of institutions, but is spread across the supranational institutions and national governments. Each has its own constituencies and

---

[143] J. Weiler, *The Constitution of Europe* (Cambridge, Cambridge University Press, 1999) especially 332–48; M. Poiares Maduro, *We, the Court: The European Court of Justice and the European Economic Constitution* (Oxford, Hart, 1998) 166–74; J. Lacroix, 'For a European Constitutional Patriotism' (2002) 50 *Political Studies* 944.

[144] J.-W. Müller, 'A European Constitutional Patriotism? The Case Restated' (2008) 14 *ELJ* 542, 554.

[145] On the ethics of participation see R. Bellamy and R. Warleigh, 'From an Ethics of Integration to an Ethics of Participation' (1998) 27 *Millennium* 447; P. Magnette, 'European Governance and Civic Participation: Beyond Elitist Citizenship?' (2003) 51 *Political Studies* 1.

[146] N. McCormick, 'Democracy, Subsidiarity and Citizenship in the European Commonwealth' (1997) 16 *Law and Philosophy* 331; K. Nicolaidis, 'Conclusion: The Federal Vision Beyond the Federal State' in K. Nicolaidis and R. Howse (eds.), *The Federal Vision: Legitimacy and Levels of Governance in the United States and the European Union* (Oxford, Oxford University Press, 2001).

each represents different interests. This allows a voice to be given to a variety of identities and interests. The most careful analysis of Union practice is that of Héritier.

A. Héritier, 'Elements of Democratic Legitimation in Europe: An Alternative Perspective' (1999) 6 *Journal of European Public Policy* 269, 274–6

2.2.1 Mutual horizontal control and 'distrust'

At each step of the European policy process, from the first tentative drafts to the formal decision-making process, policy-making is characterized by a distrustful and circumspect observation of the mutual policy proposals made by the involved actors. The participants controlling each other are generally experts and/ or decision-makers from the different member states, responding to each other's policy proposals with counterproposals backed up by expertise. The mutual distrust signifies an enormous potential for control and a chance to hold actors accountable for individual policy moves which need to be defended in substantive terms. This is the virtuous side of the slowness, and indeed potential deadlock, inherent in the European decisional process. This phenomenon is so widespread, permeating virtually the entire fabric of the decision making process across issue areas, that individual policy examples are superfluous…

The dark side of mutual control and distrust is – considering that European decision-making does not usually rely on the majority principle – of course stalemate, where a decisional process is stalled because the participants are exclusively engaged in controlling and fending-off policy initiatives presented by other actors involved. 'Distrust leads to forgone opportunities' unless it is overcome by constructive bargaining.

2.2.2 Bargaining democracy

Fortunately, bargaining constitutes the complementary side of mutual horizontal control and distrust. It is present in all aspects of European policy-making, given the presence of actors with diverse interests and a concrete need for consensual decision-making. Consensus is achieved through negotiating in the course of which compromises are formulated, compensation payments made, and package deals struck.

Actors negotiating may be representatives from territorial units or delegates from functional organizations, such as associations. Thus, in negotiating sectoral questions, such as in regional and social policy under the 'partnership principle', delegates from functional organizations are predominantly involved. During the input phase bargaining mostly takes place at the supranational level. If legislative details need to be specified during the output phase they occur at the national/ subnational level as well. Bargaining democracy creates input-legitimation since it prevents individual interests from being outvoted and thereby forces actors to take multiple interests into account. This is reflected in the more equitable outcomes of bargaining processes. By virtue of precisely this fact it also constitutes a source of output-legitimation. The underlying process mechanism is consensus-building with the help of compromises, compensation payments, and package deals.

2.2.3 Pluralistic authorities in a 'composite polity'

The multiple political and jurisdictional authorities which exist in the European Union at the vertical and horizontal level have generated more opportunities for individual citizens and corporate actors to address an authority and voice their concern in the case of a specific policy issue. In practice, this means the opportunity to exit from a specific avenue of decision-making which has proved less than promising and to test prospects in another arena. Thus, a citizen or corporate actor may address his or her representative in parliament at the national or European level, the national or the European Ombudsman, and the national courts or the European Court of Justice. These increased opportunities at the European Union level – as compared with their nation state counterparts – create leverage to press for political action.

This model is a republic model of democracy. It is an ideal and, as with any ideal that looks for its realisation in institutional practice, institutional elements identified as having positive traits also carry a negative underbelly. Arguments can be made, therefore, countering each of these claims about EU law-making.

We turn, first, to the question of constitutional tolerance. The Union may require nationals to recognise the rights and identities of foreigners, but one has to consider the extent and nature of this duty as it only applies to foreigners 'like us'. Recognition of Europeans has undoubtedly reinforced non-recognition of 'non-Europeans', who are excluded from the powerful EU law-making regimes and not granted the same legal entitlements as EU citizens. More generally, the Union can be characterised as a cartel of elites, who act together to disenfranchise others' subjects within their respective territories.[147] This view is simplistic, but studies show that about 70 to 75 per cent of accredited interest groups are business-oriented.[148]

Similarly, it is argued that the European Union induces parties to act in a public-spirited manner to realise public projects. However, there is something speculative in this statement. The art of lobbying is a black art and Brussels is full of lobbyists acting exclusively to realise their clients' interests. It is difficult to see what public spirit is being realised here. More substantively, as Héritier points out later in the article quoted above, models concerned with day-to-day checks and balances are not well designed for setting out strategic visions and common goals, as they fragment decision-making and lead to multiple veto points.[149]

Finally, the argument that the European Union diffuses power and encourages pluralism can be turned on its head. De Areilza has noted that institutional differentiation only diffuses power where different constituencies are confined to specific institutional settings. Otherwise, it benefits two kinds of powerful interest. One is that which can arbitrate between different institutional settings: lobbying MEPs, lunching with a Commissioner, visiting the office of national governments or litigating before national courts. The transnational nature of the Union means that these are likely to be actors that are well-resourced, well-connected and transnational in scope. The other is locally vested interests, which can act as veto-players: blocking something in the Council that will undoubtedly be for the greater good, but does not favour their narrow interests. It can thus act to concentrate power and, in many circumstances, make the process more opaque.[150]

The concern with the closed nature of decision-making led to the Lisbon Treaty establishing one innovatory mechanism of participatory democracy, that of the citizens' initiative.

Article 11(4) TEU

Not less than one million citizens who are nationals of a significant number of Member States may take the initiative of inviting the European Commission, within the framework of its powers, to submit any appropriate proposal on matters where citizens consider that a legal act of the Union is required for the purpose of implementing the Treaties.

---

[147] This is the essence of the consociational model. P. Taylor, *International Organization in the Modern World: The Regional and the Global Process* (London, Pinter, 1993) ch. 1.

[148] D. Coen, 'Empirical and Theoretical Studies in EU Lobbying' (2007) 24 *JEPP* 333, 335.

[149] A Héritier, 'Elements of Democratic Legitimation in Europe: An Alternative Perspective' (1999) 6 *JEPP* 269, 277–8.

[150] J. de Areilza, *Enhanced Cooperation in the Treaty of Amsterdam: Some Critical Remarks*, Jean Monnet Working Paper 13/98, http://centers.law.nyu.edu/jeanmonnet/papers/index.html (accessed 5 November 2009).

The ethos of the citizens' initiative is to instil, albeit in a limited way, some direct democracy into the Union.[151] An advantage of initiatives is that they enable citizens to make the political system responsive to individual issues of particular interest to them. This remedies a feature of representative democracy, which requires citizens to vote for candidates who stand on a platform of issues, some of which the citizen may disagree with even if she still prefers the candidate.

The concerns about citizens' initiatives are that they can enfeeble other parts of the political settlement, which allow more space for reflection and checks and balances. This has been countered to some extent by the Commission's not being required to follow a citizens' initiative. The other concern is that they can be manipulated by special interests or are used particularly by politically engaged elites. As such, they become a vehicle for dominating the Commission's attention and agenda. However, at the moment all this is speculation. All will depend on the details of the conditions which will be set out in EU legislation[152] and how EU citizens respond to it.

FURTHER READING

C. Bergström, *Comitology: Delegation of Powers in the European Union System* (Oxford, Oxford University Press, 2005)

C. Burns, 'Codecision and the European Commission: A Study of Declining Influence?' (2004) 11 *Journal of European Public Policy* 1

R. Dehousse, 'Comitology? Who Watches the Watchmen' (2003) 10 *Journal of European Public Policy* 798

H. Farrell and A. Héritier, 'Formal and Informal Institutions under Codecision: Continuous Constitution Building in Europe' (2003) 16 *Governance* 577

H. Hoffmann, 'Legislation, Delegation and Implementation under the Treaty of Lisbon: Typology Meets Reality' (2009) 15 *European Law Journal* 482

C. Joerges and E. Vos (eds.), *EU Committees: Social Regulation, Law and Politics* (Oxford and Portland, Hart, 1999)

R. Kardasheva, 'The Power to Delay: The European Parliament's Influence in the Consultation Procedure' (2009) 47 *Journal of Common Market Studies* 385

B. Kohler Koch and B. Rittberger (eds.), *Debating the Democratic Legitimacy of the European Union* (Lanham, Rowman & Littlefield, 2007)

A. Maurer and W. Wessels (eds.), *National Parliaments on their Ways to Europe: Losers or Latecomers?* (Baden Baden, Nomos, 2001)

J-W. Müller, 'A European Constitutional Patriotism? The Case Restated' (2008) 14 *European Law Journal* 542

L. Senden, *Soft Law in European Community Law* (Oxford and Portland, Hart, 2004)

---

[151] The duties on the Commission to consult on legislative and non-legislative measures are addressed in the chapter on governance. See pp. 373–9.

[152] Article 24 TFEU.

ANNEX

Treaty on the Functioning of the European Union

Legal bases covered by the ordinary legislative procedure

Article 14: services of general economic interest

Article 15(3): limitations on citizens' right of access to documents

Article 16: rules relating to data protection

Article 18: rules to prohibit discrimination on grounds of nationality

Article 19(2): incentive measures to support action taken by the Member States to combat discrimination

Article 21(2): measures to facilitate the right of citizens to move and reside freely within the Union

Article 24: citizens' initiative

Article 33: customs cooperation

Article 43(2): common organisation of agricultural markets

Article 46: freedom of movement for workers

Article 48: measures relating to social security for Community migrant workers

Article 50(1): freedom of establishment

Article 51(2): excluding application of Chapter 2, Title IV (Right of establishment) provisions to certain activities

Article 52(2): coordinating provisions providing for special treatment of foreign nationals on grounds of public policy, public security or public health

Article 53(1): mutual recognition of diplomas, certificates, other formal qualifications, etc. and self-employment and coordination of these provisions between Member States

Article 56(2): extending provisions of Chapter 3, Title IV (Services) to third country nationals

Article 59(1): liberalisation of specific services

Article 64(2): measures on the free movement of capital

Article 75: framework for administrative measures relating to movement of capital (e.g. freezing of funds) in order to combat terrorism and related activities

Article 77(2): common visa policy; management of external borders and the free movement of third country nationals

Article 78(2): common policy for asylum, subsidiary protection and temporary protection of third country nationals

Article 79(1), (2)(b), (c), (d), (3), (4), (5): measures relating to the common immigration policy; the definition of the rights of third country nationals; removal and repatriation; combating trafficking in persons; readmission agreements

Article 79(2)(a): entry and residence, long-term visas; residence permits; family reunion

Article 81: judicial cooperation in civil matters with cross-border implications; mutual recognition and enforcement of judgments, rules of evidence, access to justice, etc.

Article 82: judicial cooperation in criminal matters having cross-border dimension with provisions for minimum rules for rights of accused, victims and admissibility of evidence

Article 83(1): minimum rules for definition of certain serious crimes

Article 83(2): minimum rules regarding definition of criminal offences in areas concerned

Article 84: prevention of crime

Article 85: structure, operation, field of action and tasks of Eurojust

Article 87(2)(a)–(c): collection, etc. of information; training of staff; common investigative techniques for police cooperation

Article 88: structure, operation, field of action and tasks of Europol

Article 91: rules relating to transport policy

Article 100: provisions relating to sea and air transport

Article 114: approximation of national provisions which have as their object the establishment and functioning of the internal market

Article 116: elimination of distorting conditions of competition in the internal market resulting from national provisions

Article 118: laws for uniform intellectual property rights

Article 121: rules for monitoring the economic policies of Member States

Article 129: amending certain provisions of the Statute of the European System of Central Banks and of the European Central Bank

Article 133: measures for the use of the euro as the single currency

Article 149: incentive measures for cooperation between Member States in the field of employment

Article 153(1)(a) (e), (h), (2): support for Member State activities in relation to workers' rights; minimum standards and cooperation for the achievement of these rights

Article 157(3): equality of men and women in the workplace

Article 164: regulations for the European Social Fund

Article 165: development of quality education and sport

Article 166: content and organisation of vocational training

Article 167: contribution to development of Member State cultures and respect for national and regional diversity

Article 168: public health, including enablement of monitoring, detecting and combating cross-border threats to health

Article 169: measures to ensure consumer protection in respect of health, safety and economic interests

Article 172: trans-European networks for transport, telecommunications and energy

Article 173: ensuring the competitiveness of industry

Article 175: necessary specific actions outside structural funds

Article 177: tasks, priority objectives and organisation of structural funds

Article 178: implementing regulations relating to the European Regional Development Fund

Article 182(1), (5): multi-annual framework programme setting out all the activities of the Union and the scientific and technological objectives of the Union; establishing the measures necessary for the implementation of the European research area

Article 188: adoption of supplementary programmes

Article 189: European space policy for promotion of scientific and technical progress, industrial competitiveness and the implementation of the Union's policies

Article 192: common environmental policy, including the setting up of general action programmes

Article 194: preservation and improvement of the Union's energy policy

Article 195: promoting the competitiveness of the Union in the tourism sector

Article 196: civil protection in the event of disasters

Article 197(2): improving administrative cooperation

Article 207(2): framework for implementing the common commercial policy

Article 209: measures for the implementation of the development cooperation policy

Article 212: financial, technical and economic cooperation, including financial assistance, to third countries excluding developing countries

Article 214: framework for humanitarian aid

Article 224: regulations for political parties at European level (including rules for their funding)

Article 257: establishment of specialised courts to hear and determine specific area disputes at first instance

Article 281: amending the Statute of the European Court of Justice at the request of the Court and after consultation with the Commission, or after a proposal with the Commission and in consultation with the Court

Article 291: rules and general principles concerning mechanisms for control by Member States of the Commission's exercise of implementing powers

Article 298: provisions for European public service

Article 322(1): financial rules determining the budget procedure and checks and balances of financial actors

Article 325: combating fraud

Article 336: staff regulations of EU officials

Article 338: measures for the production of statistics

Legal bases covered by the consultation procedure

Article 21(2): measures concerning social security or social protection in relation to the right of citizens to move and reside freely

Article 22: citizens' right to vote in municipal and European Parliament elections

Article 23: protection of EU citizens in third countries

Article 62: adoption of measures which constitute a step backwards in EU law for liberalisation of capital to and from third countries

Article 72: administrative cooperation

Article 77(3): adoption of provisions concerning passports, identity cards, residence permits, etc. for common immigration policy

Article 81(3): measures concerning family law with cross-border implications

Article 87(3): measures concerning operational cooperation between the police and other criminal law enforcement authorities

Article 89: conditions for relevant criminal law enforcement authorities of one Member State to operate in other Member States

Article 95: prohibition of discrimination in relation to transport services

Article 103: anti-competitive measures

Article 109: appropriate regulations for state aid

Article 113: harmonisation of legislation relating to indirect taxation to the extent necessary for the internal market and for avoiding distortion of competition

Article 115: approximation of laws relating to the internal market when Article 114 not deployed

Article 118: language arrangements in relation to intellectual property rights

Article 126(14): replacement of and detailed rules for application of the Protocol on the excessive deficit procedure

Article 127: conferring specific tasks upon the European Central Bank concerning policies relating to the prudential supervision of credit institutions

Article 128: harmonising the denominations and technical specifications of all coins intended for circulation

Article 129(4): adopting certain provisions of the Statute of the European System of Central Banks and of the European Central Bank

Article 140(2): reporting on Member State derogation and finding conditions for abrogation

Article 148: guidelines for employment policies

Article 150: establishment of advisory Employment Committee to coordinate employment and labour policies

Article 153(1)(c), (d), (f), (g): social security of workers; collective defence of workers; protection post contract termination

Article 160: establishing the Social Protection Committee to coordinate social protection strategies

Article 182: adoption of special multi-annual framework activity programmes

Article 188: establishment of joint undertakings or any other structure necessary for the efficient execution of EU research, technological development and demonstration programmes

Article 192(2): environmental measures relating to fiscal provisions; town and country planning, land use, quantitative management of water resources; choice between energy sources

Article 194: energy provisions of a primarily fiscal nature

Article 203: detailed rules for association of countries and territories within the Union in certain circumstances

Article 218: certain agreements between the Union and third countries and international organisations

Article 219: formal agreements for the euro in relation to currencies of third states

Article 246: appointment of Commission member if vacancy caused by resignation, compulsory retirement or death

Article 262: conferring jurisdiction on the Court of Justice in disputes relating to creation of European intellectual property rights

Article 286: adoption of list of Court of Auditors

Article 308: amendment of the Statute of the European Investment Bank

Article 311: adopting a Directive relating to the system of own resources of the Union

Article 322(2): determining methods whereby the budget revenue provided relating to the Union's own resources are to be made available to the Commission; determining measures to meet cash requirements

Article 332: decision of which bodies, if not the Member States, should bear the expenditure resulting from implementation of enhanced cooperation

Article 349: adoption of specific measures relating to listed insular regions (e.g. Canary Islands) of the Union

Legal bases covered by the assent procedure

Article 19(1): combating discrimination

Article 25: measures to strengthen citizens' rights

Article 82(2)(d): adoption of decisions on miscellaneous aspects of criminal procedure

Article 83(1): identification of other particularly serious crime

Article 86: establishment of the European Public Prosecutor from Eurojust and extending his powers

Article 218(6): association agreements; agreement on accession to European Convention of Human Rights; agreements with important budgetary implications and those governed by legislative procedures where Parliament consent needed

Article 223: election procedures for the European Parliament

Article 226: exercise of right of enquiry for suspected maladministration by EU institutions

Article 311: implementation of the Union resource system

Article 312: laying down a multi-annual financial framework

Article 329: granting authorisation to proceed with enhanced cooperation

Article 352: flexibility provision

4

The EU Judicial Order

CONTENTS

1 INTRODUCTION

This chapter considers the judicial order within the European Union, comprising the Court of Justice and national courts and tribunals, and the institutional relations of this judicial order.

Section 2 considers the Court of Justice of the European Union. The institution comprises three courts: the Court of Justice, the General Court and the European Union Civil Service Tribunal.

A feature of EU law is that there is a joint responsibility between national courts and the Union courts for the interpretation and maintenance of EU law. Section 3 considers the central institutional features of this judicial order, which is governed by Articles 267 and 274 TFEU. The Court of Justice has an exclusive responsibility to declare EU measures invalid and to provide authoritative interpretations of EU law across the Union, whilst national courts have a monopoly over the adjudication of disputes. A further feature of this order is that its only subjects are courts. Institutional relations between them are not governed by a system of appeal by individuals but a reference from a national court to the Court of Justice on a point of EU law. The Court of Justice has sought to expand the subjects of this judicial order by allowing many bodies to refer, which would be considered regulatory or administrative bodies rather than courts under national law. It also allows any body to make a reference irrespective of national precedents or hierarchies. This has created a judicial order, the relationship of which to the administration is often far from clear and which is marked by a lack of hierarchy or specialisation.

Section 4 looks at the roles played by the preliminary reference procedure, the central institutional link between courts in the Union, in securing the EU legal order and judicial order. It argues that the preliminary reference procedure is pivotal, first, to the development of EU law through national courts, which set out the emerging questions to be addressed by the Court of Justice. Secondly, it is the central form of judicial review of EU institutions through individuals challenging implementation of an EU measure before a national court, which then questions the legality of the EU measure in a reference. Thirdly, it is central to preserving the autonomy and unity of EU law. Finally, it facilitates national courts in resolving disputes that involve EU law.

Section 5 looks at how relations between the courts are managed to secure these roles. This has been done, first, through the Court holding that its judgments bind all authorities in the Union, not just the referring court. Secondly, relations between the parties are managed during the reference period through the grant of interim measures by national courts. Whilst this will be used to suspend national law wherever the effectiveness of EU law requires it, the test for suspending EU measures or national measures implementing them is more restrictive: it is only if the application is urgent and the applicant would suffer irreparable damage. Suspension must be weighed against the broader Union interest in keeping the measure in place.

Section 6 looks at how the workload of the Court of Justice has been regulated. Far more cases are referred than the Court can decide each year. The strategy for managing for this is threefold. First, national courts are prevented from referring judgments in only very limited circumstances. Secondly, the central route for managing workload is the use of Chambers by the Court of Justice so that over three-quarters of cases are decided by Chambers of three or five judges. Finally, certain cases are prioritised by the use of two procedures, the accelerated and urgent procedures. Management of relations between national courts and the Court of Justice has been only partially successful.

2 THE COURT OF JUSTICE OF THE EUROPEAN UNION

The Treaties provide for the Union to have its own Court of Justice of the European Union to ensure that the law is observed in the interpretation and application of the Treaties.

Article 19 TEU

1. The Court of Justice of the European Union shall include the Court of Justice, the General Court and specialised courts. It shall ensure that in the interpretation and application of the Treaties the law is observed.

   Member States shall provide remedies sufficient to ensure effective legal protection in the fields covered by Union law.

2. The Court of Justice shall consist of one judge from each Member State. It shall be assisted by Advocates-General.

   The General Court shall include at least one judge per Member State.

   The Judges and the Advocates-General of the Court of Justice and the Judges of the General Court shall be chosen from persons whose independence is beyond doubt and who satisfy the conditions set out in Articles 253 and 254 TFEU. They shall be appointed by common accord of the governments of the Member States for six years. Retiring Judges and Advocates-General may be reappointed.

3. The Court of Justice of the European Union shall, in accordance with the Treaties:
   (a) rule on actions brought by a Member State, an institution or a natural or legal person;
   (b) give preliminary rulings, at the request of courts or tribunals of the Member States, on the interpretation of Union law or the validity of acts adopted by the institutions;
   (c) rule in other cases provided for in the Treaties.

The Court of Justice is thus composed of three courts: the Court of Justice, the General Court and, currently, only one specialised court, the European Civil Service Tribunal.

(i) The Court of Justice

As Article 19(1) TEU makes clear, the Court of Justice is made up of twenty-seven judges, one from each Member State. These are appointed for a renewable period of six years and are required to be persons whose independence is beyond doubt and who are either suitable for the highest judicial office in their respective countries or 'jurisconsults of recognised competence'.[1] The judges elect the President from amongst themselves for a three-year term.[2] Her central responsibility is to determine the case list and allocate cases to different Chambers.[3] A new system of appointment was introduced by the Lisbon Treaty to prevent the over-politicisation of the process.[4] Previously, a panel comprising members of the Court of Justice and members of national supreme courts ruled on the suitability of candidates, and governments could only appoint candidates after consulting this Panel.[5]

---

[1] See also Article 253 TFEU. This is done on a three-yearly cycle, so that every three years half the Court is replaced.
[2] Article 253(3) TFEU. The current President is Greek, Judge Skouris.
[3] The President also chairs the Grand Chamber and is responsible for interim measures.
[4] On this debate see P. Kapteyn, 'Reflections on the Future of the Judicial System of the European Union after Nice' (2001)20 *YBEL* 173, 188–9.
[5] Article 255 TFEU. It is doubtful whether this is sufficient, however, to secure a Court that is representative of the diversity within the Union. I. Solanke, 'Diversity and Independence in the European Court of Justice' (2009) 15 *CJEL* 89.

Fears have been expressed that the ability to renew the term of office might compromise the independence of the judges. In 1993, the European Parliament proposed that judges should be elected by the Parliament for a non-renewable term of nine years, a suggestion endorsed by the Court of Justice.[6] In practice, this has not posed a problem, possibly because the Court works under the principle of collegiality, in which a single judgment is given. This prevents Member States pointing to sympathetic dissenting opinions of their national judge to undermine the authority of a judgment, with judges of the Court also arguing that it allows for a considerable exchange of views and differing national legal traditions to filter through to the judgment.[7] This has been countered by some who argue that because the judgment is built on compromise, this affects the quality of its reasoning, with the Court often seeming not to counter a point or consider a question.[8]

The Court is assisted by eight Advocates General.[9] The same procedure and conditions of appointment apply to these as to judges of the Court of Justice. The role of the Advocate General is to make, in open court, impartial and independent submissions on any case brought before the Court.[10] She acts not as a legal representative of one of the parties, but as a legal representative of the public interest. These Opinions are adopted in advance of the judgment to allow the Court sufficient time to consider them. They often provide a more detailed analysis of the context and the argument than is found in the judgment of the Court itself. However, they are not binding on the Court, although they are often referred to by the Court of Justice in its judgments. Furthermore, even when the conclusions reached are similar, it is difficult to know whether the reasoning is the same, given that the Opinion is often discursive in nature, whilst the judgment itself is very terse.

For reasons of workload, cases are rarely decided by the full Court. Indeed, it is only to sit in full session in cases of 'exceptional importance' or where it is to rule that a senior EU official (e.g. Commissioner, Ombudsman, or Member of the Court of Auditors) is to be deprived of office for not meeting the requisite conditions. In 2008, no cases were assigned to the full Court. Instead, the majority of cases are heard by Chambers of either three or five judges, with 65 judgments/Opinions being given by Chambers of three judges, and 259 by Chambers of five judges. Alongside these, a Member State or EU institution party to the proceedings can request a case to be heard by a Grand Chamber of thirteen judges. This occurred in 66 cases in 2008.[11]

---

[6] Rothley Report, European Parliament Session Doc. A3–0228/93. The Court of Justice's views are in *Report of the European Court of Justice for the 1996 Intergovernmental Conference*, Proceedings of the Court 15/95, 11.

[7] See e.g. F. Jacobs, 'Advocates General and Judges in the European Court of Justice: Some Personal Reflections' in D. O'Keeffe and A. Bavasso (eds.), *Judicial Review in European Union Law, Liber Amicorum Lord Slynn*, vol. I (The Hague, Boston and London, Kluwer Law International, 2000).

[8] W. Bishop, 'Price Discrimination under Article 86: Political Economy in the European Court' (1981) 44 *MLR* 282, 294–5.

[9] Article 252 TFEU. On the Advocates General see T. Tridimas, 'The Role of the Advocate General in Community Law: Some Reflections' (1997) 34 *CMLRev.* 1349. Also the magisterial study of N. Burrows and R. Greaves, *The Advocate General and EC Law* (Oxford, Oxford University Press, 2007).

[10] Article 252 TFEU.

[11] The rules on the full Court and the Grand Chamber are set out in Article 251 TFEU and Protocol on the Statute of the Court of Justice, Article 16. This number is greater than the 333 judgments given by the Court in 2008 as it takes no account of joinder of cases. *Annual Report of the Court of Justice 2008* (Luxembourg, Office for Official Publications of the European Communities, 2009) 90.

Whilst Article 19(1) TEU suggests a general jurisdiction for the Court of Justice over both Treaties, this is subject to three forms of exclusion:

- It has no jurisdiction in the field of the Common Foreign and Security Policy.[12]
- In judicial cooperation in criminal matters and police cooperation, it has no jurisdiction to review the validity or proportionality of operations carried out by the police or other law-enforcement services of a Member State or the exercise of the responsibilities incumbent upon Member States with regard to the maintenance of law and order and the safeguarding of internal security.[13]
- If measures are taken to expel a Member State, the Court of Justice can rule on the procedure but not the substance of the grounds for expulsion.[14]

The Court's jurisdiction is further restricted by the rules on *locus standi* which determine the circumstances in which parties can bring actions before it. Matters can come before it in a variety of ways:

- preliminary references from national courts: national courts may, or in some cases must, refer the point of EU law to the Court of Justice which is necessary to enable them to decide the dispute. The Court of Justice will give judgment on the point of EU law, which the national judge will apply to the dispute in hand;[15]
- enforcement actions brought by the Commission or Member States against other Member States: the Commission, or in rare cases another Member State, can bring a Member State before the Court of Justice for a declaration that the latter is in breach of EU law;[16]
- sanctions for failure to comply with Court judgments:[17] if a Member State fails to comply with a Court of Justice judgment, the Commission can bring it back before the Court in order to have it fined for its behaviour;
- judicial review of EU institutions by other EU institutions and judicial review of the Parliament or Council by Member States;[18]
- Opinions on the conclusion of international agreements: the Council, Parliament, Commission or any Member State can ask for an Opinion of the Court as to whether the Union has lawfully concluded a draft treaty. If the Court rules that the international agreement is illegal, it can only enter into force if the treaty is first amended;[19]
- appeals from the General Court on points of law;[20]
- the Council may confer jurisdiction on the Court with regard to disputes concerning the application of European intellectual property rights.[21]

---

[12] Article 24(1) TEU, Article 275 TFEU. It can, however, rule on the limits relative to other parts of the Treaties: Article 40 TEU.
[13] Article 276 TFEU.
[14] Article 269 TFEU.
[15] Article 267 TFEU.
[16] Articles 258 and 259 TFEU.
[17] Article 260 TFEU.
[18] Article 263(2) and 265(1) TFEU; Protocol on the Statute of the Court of Justice, Article 51. There are limited exceptions for national actions against Council exercise of delegated powers, Council measures authorising state aids and Council measures defining the common commercial policy. These go to the General Court.
[19] Article 218(11) TFEU.
[20] Article 256(1) TFEU.
[21] Article 262 TFEU.

These procedures are discussed in far more detail in subsequent chapters. Combined, they make a substantial docket. In 2008, the Court of Justice disposed of 567 cases and gave 333 judgments.[22] Despite this considerable output, it struggles to cope with the number of cases that are submitted to it: 767 cases were still pending at the end of 2008.[23]

(ii) The General Court

The General Court (formerly known as the Court of First Instance) is composed of twenty-seven judges. Unlike the Court of Justice, it is not confined to a single judge from each Member State, but must comprise at least one judge from each Member State.[24] The General Court can sit in full Court if it considers the circumstances require or because of the importance of the case.[25] It almost always sits in Chambers of three or five judges. One of the judges will act as Advocate General. A single judge can give judgments in actions brought by private parties, but the circumstances in which this can occur are extremely restricted. The case must raise only questions already clarified by established case law and must not cover certain fields, notably state aids, competition, mergers, agriculture and trade with non-EU states.[26]

The General Court's jurisdiction has expanded over the years and it now has the power to receive the following cases:

- judicial review by individuals of actions or illegal action by EU institutions or action for non-contractual damages against the EU institutions;[27]
- actions by Member States against the Commission, the European Central Bank and the European Council;[28]
- matters referred to the Court of Justice under an arbitration clause;[29]
- appeals from decisions of the Office for Harmonisation in the Internal Market.[30] This agency is responsible for the grant of the Community trademark and anybody adversely affected by its decisions can appeal these to the General Court;
- appeals from decisions of the European Civil Service Tribunal.[31]

Jurisdiction over these matters results in the General Court being the central administrative court. It has thus become the key actor in the development of administrative principles of due process. As much competition law and external trade law develops through challenges by private parties adversely affected by EU measures, it is also the central judicial institution in these fields as well as in the field of the Community trade mark, where a similar process takes place with challenges to decisions by the Office for Harmonisation of the Internal Market.

---

[22] *Annual Report*, above n. 11, 87–8.
[23] *Ibid.* 94–5.
[24] Article 19(2) TEU.
[25] Rules of Procedure of the Court of First Instance, article 14(1). Available at http://curia.europa.eu/jcms/upload/docs/application/pdf/2008-09/txt7_2008-09-25_14-08-6_431.pdf (accessed 2 August 2009).
[26] *Ibid.* article 14(2).
[27] Articles 263(4), 265(3), 268 and 340(2) TFEU.
[28] Articles 263 and 265 TFEU. Protocol on the Statute of the Court of Justice, article 51. There is a limited exception for challenges against Commission authorisation of enhanced cooperation. These go to the Court of Justice.
[29] Article 272 TFEU.
[30] Regulation 40/94/EC on the Community trade mark [2004] OJ L70/1, article 63.
[31] Article 256(2) TFEU.

In 2008, actions against EU institutions accounted for 44.2 per cent of cases and trade mark cases 31.78 per cent.[32] The General Court is struggling even more than the Court of Justice to keep up with its docket. At the end of 2008, 1,178 cases were pending and the duration of proceedings was (depending on the type of action) between 20.4 and 38.6 months.[33] These delays are so serious that they have led to decisions being overturned on the grounds that they violated the applicant's fundamental right to have the case heard within a reasonable period of time.[34] Notwithstanding this, there is also provision for it to receive preliminary rulings in fields to be specified.[35] Although, as yet, no field has been transferred under this heading, the provision is important for what it promises. For it suggests that over the years, the jurisdiction and size of the General Court could be expanded.

There is a right to appeal from the General Court to the Court of Justice within two months of notification of the decision. The appeal must be on points of law,[36] but this right to appeal exists not just for parties to the dispute but also for Member States and EU institutions where the decision directly affects them.[37] Even if the Court of Justice finds that the General Court has misapplied EU law, it will only uphold an appeal if the mistake of law relates to the operative part of the judgment. Even if EU law is misapplied in the operative part of the judgment, the appeal will not be successful if the operative part is shown to be well-founded for other legal reasons.[38] In 2008, the Court of Justice considered seventy-seven appeals and found for the appellant, fully or partially, in twenty-three of these.[39] These statistics tell only part of the story as differences on significant and controversial areas of law have emerged between the two courts.[40]

If the Court of Justice finds the appeal to be well founded, it will quash the decision of the General Court. It then has the discretion to give the final judgment or to refer the matter back to the General Court. If it adopts the latter course of action, the General Court is bound by the Court of Justice's decision on the point of law.[41] The General Court takes the view that it is only bound by the judgments of the Court where its decision has been quashed by the Court of Justice and the matter is referred back, or where the principle of *res judicata* operates, that is to say, where a dispute involving the same parties, the same subject-matter and the same cause of action had already been decided by the Court of Justice.[42] Nevertheless, the circumstances in which the General Court will not follow judgments of the Court of Justice will be rare, as this would generate considerable instability.

---

[32] *Annual Report*, above n. 11, 173, 211.

[33] *Ibid.* 179.

[34] Case C-185/95 P *Baustahlgewerbe* v *Commission* [1998] ECR I-8417; Case C-385/07 P *Grüne Punkt DSD* v *Commission*, Judgment of 16 July 2009.

[35] Article 256(3) TFEU.

[36] Article 256(1) TFEU.

[37] Protocol on the Statute of the Court of Justice, article 56.

[38] Case C-30/91 P *Lestelle* v *Commission* [1992] ECR I-3755; Case C-226/03 P *José Martí Peix* v *Commission* [2004] ECR I-11421.

[39] *Annual Report*, above n. 11, 188, 211.

[40] There have been strong differences, for example, over the rules on *locus standi* of private parties to challenge EU acts, Case T-177/01 *Jégo-Quéré* v *Commission* [2002] ECR II-2365; Case C-263/02 P *Commission* v *Jégo-Quéré* [2004] ECR I-3425.

[41] Protocol on the Statute of the Court of Justice, article 61.

[42] Case T-162/94 *NMB France* v *Commission* [1996] ECR II-427.

(iii) The European Union Civil Service Tribunal

There is provision for work of the General Court to be transferred to specialised courts. The rules on the organisation for each court are likely to be different, as they will be governed by the legislation establishing it. In all cases, members must be independent and fit for judicial office. There must also be the possibility of appeal to the General Court.[43] To date, only one has been established, the European Union Civil Service Tribunal, which hears disputes between employees of the EU institutions and the institutions themselves.[44]

3 ARCHITECTURE OF THE EU JUDICIAL ORDER

It is wrong to see the judicial application of EU law as all about the activities of the three courts set out in Article 19 TEU. These are important but, as we have seen in Chapter 1 and will see in much more detail in Chapter 7,[45] EU law gives individuals the right to invoke EU law provisions before national courts in certain circumstances and imposes a whole host of duties on national courts when this happens. These are more numerous, have greater resources and are more accessible to individual litigants. There is, thus, a shared responsibility between them and the three Union courts for the application and development of EU law. This is a shared responsibility that has been made explicit by the Treaty of Lisbon with its introduction in Article 19(1) TEU of the requirement that Member States must provide remedies sufficient to ensure effective legal protection in the fields covered by EU law.

(i) Preliminary reference procedure and the EU judicial order

If EU law provides for its administration by a judicial order that comprises not just the three Union courts but all the courts and tribunals in the Member States, there are only two provisions that govern the nature of this judicial order and the duties it imposes on the different courts.

The first is Article 274 TFEU. This grants the Court of Justice exclusive jurisdiction where the Treaties provide for the Union to be a party to the proceedings.

Article 274 TFEU

Save where jurisdiction is conferred on the Court of Justice of the European Union by the Treaties, disputes to which the Union is a party shall not on that ground be excluded from the jurisdiction of the courts or tribunals of the Member States.

---

[43] Article 257 TFEU.

[44] Decision 2004/752/EC, EURATOM establishing the European Union Civil Service Tribunal [2004] OJ L333/7. It has similar problems to the other courts with, at the end of 2008, 217 cases pending and a mean waiting time of 19.7 months: *Annual Report*, above n. 11, 220–2.

[45] See pp. 268-71.

The European Union will be a party to the proceedings where one of the EU institutions is either plaintiff or defendant. It will be a defendant in cases where judicial review or damages are being sought against an act or omission of one of the institutions. The only circumstances where it will be a plaintiff are either where one EU institution is seeking judicial review against another institution(s) or the Commission is bringing enforcement actions or an action for damages against a Member State for non-compliance with EU law.

If Article 274 TFEU sets out the scenarios on which national courts cannot rule, Article 267 TFEU sets out their relationship with the Court of Justice in the contexts where they can adjudicate.

Article 267 TFEU

The Court of Justice of the European Union shall have jurisdiction to give preliminary rulings concerning:
(a) the interpretation of the Treaties;
(b) the validity and interpretation of acts of the institutions, bodies, offices or agencies of the Union.

Where such a question is raised before any court or tribunal of a Member State, that court or tribunal may, if it considers that a decision on the question is necessary to enable it to give judgment, request the Court to give a ruling thereon.

Where any such question is raised in a case pending before a court or tribunal of a Member State against whose decisions there is no judicial remedy under national law, that court or tribunal shall bring the matter before the Court.

If such a question is raised in a case pending before a court or tribunal of a Member State with regard to a person in custody, the Court of Justice of the European Union shall act with the minimum of delay.

Two initial features of the procedure are striking. First, subject to Article 274 TFEU, national courts have a monopoly of adjudication over disputes that come before them that involve EU law. Article 267 TFEU sets out circumstances when they may or must refer points of EU law to the Court of Justice and these judgments are binding on them. It is national courts, however, who decide the dispute. They decide not only points of national law that may be pertinent but, even more centrally, they decide the facts to the dispute and, on the basis of this, they decide how to apply EU law to the dispute.[46] In *WWF*, a challenge was made to the transformation of the military airport in Bolzano, Italy, into one for commercial use because there had been a failure to carry out an environmental impact assessment.[47] The airport authorities argued that the facts presented by the national court were inaccurate and that the national court, being confined to considering questions of law, had exceeded its jurisdiction by considering these questions of fact. The Court dismissed these arguments. It noted that it was for the national court, not itself, to ascertain the facts and that it was not its role to examine whether the reference had been made in accordance with national laws on court jurisdiction and procedure.

---

[46] Case 104/79 *Foglia* v *Novello* [1980] ECR 745.
[47] Case C-435/97 *WWF* v *Autonome Provinz Bozen* [1999] ECR I-5613.

The second feature is that Article 267 TFEU is a court to court procedure, with national courts acting as gate-keepers to the Court.[48] It grants private parties no direct access to the Court of Justice, nor can they appeal decisions of the national courts to the Court of Justice. The Court has thus characterised the procedure as:

> a non-contentious procedure excluding any initiative of the parties who are merely invited to be heard in the course of this procedure.[49]

There are circumstances when the parties can, on paper at least, oblige a national court to refer.[50] In addition, they may submit written observations and may make oral representations of between 15 and 30 minutes long, depending upon the nature of the proceedings, to the Court.[51] This limited role reflects, however, their not being the centre of proceedings. Instead, centre stage is taken by the reference from the national court. This will take the form of a question or number of questions about EU law. These must be accompanied by a statement setting out the factual and legal context of the dispute.

Information Note on References from National Courts for a Preliminary Ruling, OJ 2009, C 297/1

22. …The order for reference must be succinct but sufficiently complete and must contain all the relevant information to give the Court and the interested persons entitled to submit observations a clear understanding of the factual and legal context of the main proceedings. In particular, the order for reference must:
- include a brief account of the subject-matter of the dispute and the relevant findings of fact, or, at least, set out the factual situation on which the question referred is based;
- set out the tenor of any applicable national provisions and identify, where necessary, the relevant national case-law, giving in each case precise references (for example, a page of an official journal or specific law report, with any internet reference);
- identify the European Union law provisions relevant to the case as accurately as possible;
- explain the reasons which prompted the national court to raise the question of the interpretation or validity of the European Union law provisions, and the relationship between those provisions and the national provisions applicable to the main proceedings;
- include, if need be, a summary of the main relevant arguments of the parties to the main proceedings.

This statement frames the dispute. The Court of Justice cannot look behind it and will, indeed, sometimes look to it, rather than the explicit questions set out by the national court, in providing the judgment it gives.[52]

---

[48] Private parties not allowed to appear before the national court will not, therefore, be allowed to intervene before the Court of Justice: Case C-181/95 *Biogen* v *SmithKlineBeecham* [1996] ECR I-717.

[49] Case C-364/92 *SAT Fluggesellschaft* v *Eurocontrol* [1994] ECR I-43.

[50] See pp. 174–8.

[51] Protocol on the Statute of the Court of Justice, articles 20, 23.

[52] Case C-365/02 *Lindfors* [2004] ECR I-7183. T. Tridimas, 'Knocking on Heaven's Door: Fragmentation, Efficiency and Defiance in the Preliminary Reference Procedure' (2003) 40 *CMLRev.* 9, 21–6.

The wording of Article 267 TFEU is thin. It sets out a procedure but tells us little more about the mutual relations and duties surrounding this procedure. It has been left to the Court of Justice to craft its own vision of an EU judicial order and set out this provision as the spine of that judicial order. It has done this through a three stage argument. First, it sets out that the European Union is an autonomous legal order. Secondly, an autonomous legal order requires that all courts in the Union interpret EU law in a uniform manner. Thirdly, to enable this, Article 267 TFEU provides a direct relationship between national courts and the Court of Justice. It is to be interpreted and developed in the light of the needs of the Union legal order and its need for a coordinated judicial order in which EU law is given the same effect across the Union.

This reasoning emerged in *Rheinmühlen*, in which the question arose whether national courts were prevented from being able to refer by rulings from superior courts, which would normally bind them. Rheinmühlen received a subsidy to export barley outside the Union. When he failed to do this, the German authorities sought to recover the subsidy. The Hesse Finance Court considered that the authorities were entitled to recover the full subsidy, but, on appeal, the Federal Finance Court ruled that the authorities were entitled only to recover part of the subsidy. The matter was referred back to the Hesse court, which considered that the Federal court's ruling was inconsistent with the EU Regulation on the matter. It referred the question as to whether it still had a discretion to refer, unfettered by the ruling of the superior domestic court.

Case 166/73 *Rheinmühlen-Düsseldorf* v *Einfuhr- und Vorratstelle für Getreide* [1974] ECR 33

2. [Article 267 TFEU] is essential for the preservation of the Community character of the law established by the Treaty and has the object of ensuring that in all circumstances this law is the same in all States of the Community.

   Whilst it thus aims to avoid divergences in the interpretation of Community law which the national courts have to apply, it likewise tends to ensure this application by making available to the national judge a means of eliminating difficulties which may be occasioned by the requirement of giving Community law its full effect within the framework of the judicial systems of the Member States.

   Consequently any gap in the system so organized could undermine the effectiveness of the provisions of the Treaty and of the secondary Community law.

   The provisions of [Article 267 TFEU], which enable every national court or tribunal without distinction to refer a case to the court for a preliminary ruling when it considers that a decision on the question is necessary to enable it to give judgment, must be seen in this light.

3. The provisions of [Article 267 TFEU] are absolutely binding on the national judge and, in so far as the second paragraph is concerned, enable him to refer a case to the Court of Justice for a preliminary ruling on interpretation or validity.

   This Article gives national courts the power and, where appropriate, imposes on them the obligation to refer a case for a preliminary ruling, as soon as the judge perceives either of his own motion or at the request of the parties that the litigation depends on a point referred to in the first paragraph of [Article 267 TFEU].

4. It follows that national courts have the widest discretion in referring matters to the Court of Justice if they consider that a case pending before them raises questions involving interpretation, or consideration of the validity, of provisions of Community law, necessitating a decision on their part.

It follows from these factors that a rule of national law whereby a court is bound on points of law by the rulings of a superior court cannot deprive the inferior courts of their power to refer to the Court questions of interpretation of Community law involving such rulings.

It would be otherwise if the questions put by the inferior court were substantially the same as questions already put by the superior court.

On the other hand the inferior court must be free, if it considers that the ruling on law made by the superior court could lead it to give a judgment contrary to Community law, to refer to the Court questions which concern it.

If inferior courts were bound without being able to refer matters to the Court, the jurisdiction of the latter to give preliminary rulings and the application of Community law at all levels of the judicial systems of the Member States would be compromised.

The only circumstance in which the Court of Justice will have regard to national hierarchies is where the judgment of the lower court making the reference has been overturned on appeal by a more senior national court.[53] However, this appeal must relate to a point of national law that does not relate to the reference. For the Court of Justice has held that if the decision to refer has been appealed, the lower court is not bound by that appeal. The autonomous nature of Article 267 TFEU means that it has only to draw inferences from that appeal if it wishes, and it is free to maintain or withdraw the reference in such circumstances, irrespective of the wishes of the higher court.[54]

(ii) Subjects of the EU judicial order

Within the framework of Article 267 TFEU, it is crucial to be a court or tribunal. These and the Court of Justice are the only bodies recognised by the provision. National courts and tribunals become both opportunity structures for those seeking access to the Court of Justice and independent actors in their own right with new powers to ask questions of the Court of Justice and influence the contours of EU law across the Union. This begs the question, however, of what is to be considered a court or tribunal for these purposes. Throughout the Union, a variety of professional, regulatory and arbitral bodies, which are not formally designated as courts under national law, adjudicate upon EU law. It would be problematic, in terms of the uniformity of EU law, if some were entitled to refer, but not others.

In *Broeckmeulen*, therefore, the Court of Justice ruled that the uniformity of EU law required that a Union definition be provided for what constituted a court or tribunal for the purposes of Article 267 TFEU.[55] This should be a broad definition, which should include many bodies that were not formally courts within the national legal system. Thus, the Court held that an appeal committee within the Dutch professional body, regulating entry of doctors to the profession, constituted a court because it determined individual rights under EU law, acted under governmental legal supervision and employed quasi-legal procedures. Over the years, the Court has refined the

---

[53] Case 65/81 *Reina v Landeskreditbank Baden-Württemburg* [1982] ECR 33; Case C-309/02 *Radlberger Getränkegesellschaft v Land Baden-Württemberg* [2004] ECR I-11763.
[54] Case C-210/06 *Cartesio*, Judgment of 16 December 2008.
[55] Case 246/80 *Broeckmeulen v Huisarts Registratie Commissie* [1981] ECR 2311.

qualities necessary for a body to be a court. Bodies must be independent, be established by law and have a compulsory jurisdiction, and be taking a decision of a judicial nature.[56]

The criterion of independence has been held to have an external and internal dimension.[57] Externally, the body must be protected against intervention or pressure liable to jeopardise the independent judgment of its members as regards proceedings before them. There must also be safeguards protecting its independence. In *Gabalfrisa*, the Court considered the Tribunales Ecónomico-Administrativos, which reviewed the decisions of the tax authorities in Spain, to be courts.[58] Although members of these bodies were appointed and dismissed by the minister, there was considered to be a clear separation of functions between them and the tax authority.[59] By contrast, in *Syfait*, the Court did not consider the Greek competition authority to be a court even though it was formally independent, as there were insufficient guarantees against dismissal of its members by the Minister for Economic Development.[60] Internally, the body must be impartial between the parties. It must have no organisational links with any of the parties appearing before it and no interest in the outcome of the proceedings before it.[61]

Secondly, not only must the body be deciding the Union rights of the parties, but it must also have a compulsory jurisdiction over the activities in question. This means that a private body, most notably arbitration panels, cannot be a court for the purposes of Article 267 TFEU, as parties opt-in to such arrangements.[62] The last criterion is that the body must be taking decisions of a judicial nature. This leads to bodies having a floating status in which the nature of the proceedings determines whether they will be able to refer. The Court has been unclear about what constitutes a decision of a judicial nature, preferring the opposite strategy of stating that the decision must not be of an administrative nature. Courts allocating the surname to a child,[63] or registering a company[64] have been held not to be in a position to make a reference as these are considered to be administrative decisions. By contrast, if a court hears an appeal against such a decision, its decision will be considered to be of a judicial nature.[65]

The consequence of these criteria is that a whole number of public bodies have been found to be courts, notwithstanding that they are not part of the formal judiciaries of their Member States. They include immigration adjudicators,[66] professional disciplinary bodies,[67] bodies established to review public contracts[68] and tax adjudicators.[69] Whilst a case can be made for a uniform definition of a

---

[56] See Case C-210/06 *Cartesio*, Judgment of 16 December 2008.

[57] Case C-506/04 *Wilson* v *Ordre des avocats du barreau de Luxembourg* [2006] ECR I-8613.

[58] Joined Cases C-110/98–C-147/98 *Gabalfrisa* [2000] ECR I-1577.

[59] In recent years, the Court seems to have toughened up the guarantees necessary. Case C-246/05 *Häupl* v *Lidl* [2007] ECR I-4673.

[60] Case C-53/03 *Syfait and Others* v *GlaxoSmithKline AEVE* [2005] ECR I-4609.

[61] Case C-24/92 *Corbiau* v *Administration des Contributions* [1993] ECR I-1277; Case C-516/99 *Schmid* [2002] ECR I-4573.

[62] Case 102/81 *Nordsee Deutsche Hochseefischerei* v *Reederei Mond Hochseefischerei* [1982] ECR 1095; Case C-125/04 *Denuit and Cordonier* [2005] ECR I-923.

[63] Case C-96/04 *Standesamt Stadt Niebüll* [2006] ECR I-3561.

[64] Case C-182/00 *Lutz* [2002] ECR I-547.

[65] Case C-210/06 *Cartesio*, Judgment of 16 December 2008; Case C-14/08 *Roda Golf & Beach Resort*, Judgment of 25 June 2009.

[66] Case C-416/96 *El Yassini* v *Secretary of State for the Home Department* [1999] ECR I-1209.

[67] Case 246/80 *Broeckmeulen* v *Huisarts Registratie Commissie* [1981] ECR 2311.

[68] Case C-54/96 *Dorsch* v *Bundesbaugesellschaft Berlin* [1997] ECR I-4961; Case C-92/00 *HI* v *Stadt Wien* [2002] ECR I-5553.

[69] Case C-17/00 *De Coster* v *Collège des bourgmestre et échevins de Watermael-Boitsfort* [2001] ECR I-9445.

court in that it leads to an equal possibility of reference from across the Union, the rationale for the criteria used in that definition is not clear and the Court has been attacked on two fronts.

First, a rationale for a wide definition is that it is important that any body that decides EU law rights should be able to refer. If not, individuals will have to challenge the decision before a body that can refer. This adds expense and time to the process of referral and provides a disincentive for parties to seek a referral. Such a view would allow private bodies to refer and would probably not be too worried about whether the decision is of a judicial nature, as all that matters is a denial of rights and not the manner in which this happens.[70] Such a critique is, however, open to a floodgates argument in that it would allow an extensive number of poorly trained actors to overload the Court of Justice's docket.

The other criticism, made very effectively by Advocate General Colomer, is that the current definition is too wide.[71] He argues that a strategic decision was taken in Article 267 TFEU to create a conversation between courts, which would shape the development of EU law. Administrative and regulatory agencies, independent parts of the executive but nevertheless part of it, should not be part of that conversation. Colomer also notes many practical consequences of a wide definition. It allows bodies with no legal training to formulate references and statements. It has led to restrictions being placed on referrals by courts, notably the uncertain test that they be doing something of a judicial nature. Most crucially, he argues, it allows administrative actors to disrupt stable domestic judicial hierarchies and systems of judicial precedent by making a reference if they do not agree with these.

(iii) Structure of the EU judicial order

The Union court structure is different from national systems of administration of justice. These are characterised by compartmentalisation and decentralisation. There are specialised courts for particular areas, such as tax, intellectual property law, labour law and social security, and distinctions may be made between private law courts and administrative ones. Multitiered systems of appeal result in only a very small proportion of cases reaching the more senior courts. The preliminary reference procedure, by contrast, allows all courts and tribunals within the Union, no matter how high or low, to make a reference to a single court: the Court of Justice. The Union court structure is, therefore, a flat court structure of 'first, and then equals', in which all national courts are granted equal possibilities to make a reference to the Court and no national law can disenfranchise any national court of the possibility of making a reference.

K. Alter, 'The European Court's Political Power' (1996) 19 *West European Politics* 458, 466–7

While EC law supremacy posed a threat to the influence and authority of high courts and implied a significant compromise of national sovereignty, lower courts found few costs and numerous benefits in making their own referrals to the ECJ and in applying EC law. Being courts of first instance, lower-court judges were used to having another court hierarchically above them, and to having their judgments

---

[70] G. Bebr, 'Arbitration Tribunals and Article 177 of the EEC Treaty' (1985) 22 *CMLRev.* 489.
[71] See his Opinions in Case C-17/00 *De Coster* v *Collège des bourgmestre et échevins de Watermael-Boitsfort* [2001] ECR I-9445; Case C-205/08 *Alpe Adria Energia*, Opinion of AG Colomar of 25 June 2009.

re-written by courts above. They also did not have to worry about how their individual actions might upset legal certainty or the smooth functioning of the legal system. Thus, they were more open to sending to the ECJ broad and provocative legal questions about the reach and effects of European law in the national legal order. There were also many benefits for lower courts in taking advantage of the ECJ and in invoking EC law. It allowed lower courts to circumvent the restrictive jurisprudence of higher courts, and to re-open legal debates which had been closed, and thus to try for legal outcomes of their preference for policy or legal reasons. For example, recourse to EC law allowed pro-women industrial tribunals to circumvent the Employment Appeals Tribunal and the Conservative government, to get legal outcomes which helped them to promote equal pay for men and women. Having an ECJ decision also magnified the influence of the lower-court decisions in the legal process, as the decision became part of established legal precedence, and it sometimes led to journal articles on decisions which otherwise would not have been publicly reported, but which were able to decisively contribute to the development of national law. Having an ECJ decision behind a lower-court decision also made its reversal by a higher court less likely. Thus, it actually bolstered the legal power and influence of the lower courts. For a lower court, the ECJ was akin to a second parent where parental approval wards off sanction. When a lower court did not like what it thought one parent (a higher national court) would say, or it did not agree with what one parent said, it would ask the other parent (the ECJ). Having the other parent's approval decreased the likelihood of sanctions for challenging legal precedence or government policy. If the lower court, however, did not think that it would like what that other parent might say, it could follow the 'don't ask and the ECJ can't tell' policy and not make a referral.

The different strategic calculations of national courts vis-à-vis the ECJ created a competition-between-courts dynamic of legal integration; this fed the process of legal integration and came to shift the national legal context from under high courts. The limitations on interpretation of national law created by high courts provoked lower courts to make referrals to the ECJ. This enabled lower courts to deviate from established jurisprudence or to obtain preferred new legal outcomes. In so using EC law and the ECJ to achieve outcomes, lower courts created opportunities for the ECJ to expand its jurisdiction and jurisprudence, and, in some cases they actually goaded the ECJ to expand the legal authority of EC law even further. In this respect, one can say that lower courts were the motors of EC legal integration into the national order, and legal expansion through their referrals to the ECJ.

This structure is also relatively untested. This might seem a bizarre thing to say about a procedure that was in the Treaty of Rome and has given rise to 6,318 references by the end of 2008, including many of the Court of Justice's seminal judgments.[72] Yet prior to the entry into force of the Treaty of Lisbon, restrictions were placed on the references that could be made in the fields of immigration, asylum, civil justice and policing and criminal justice. In the case of policing and criminal justice, Member States could choose whether to let their courts refer and which courts could refer.[73] In the case of the other fields, only courts against whose decision there was no judicial remedy could refer. Combined, this restricted the possibilities for reference so that in 2008, only twenty-six references were made in all these fields combined.[74]

[72] *Annual Report*, above n. 11, 106.
[73] The procedures were in Article 68 EC and Article 35 TEU(M) respectively.
[74] *Annual Report*, above n. 11, 84.

Article 267 TFEU abolishes this exception and allows any national court or tribunal to refer in these fields in just the same way as in other fields. The abolition of this exception and the exposure of these fields to the full force of EU judicial structures are likely to change the workload and salience of the Court of Justice. Many of the fields traditionally exposed to these procedure, be they environmental, financial services, transport or broadcasting law, are, of course, significant but they are for the most part played out in national ministries and regulatory agencies rather than by courts. This has led to preliminary references being concentrated in limited fields perceived as technical in nature. A study carried out between 1998 and 2003 thus found that 47 per cent of the cases decided were on agriculture, VAT or the economic freedoms.[75] By contrast, the new fields – immigration, asylum and crime – constitute the daily bread-and-butter of national judicial systems in a way that other areas of EU law (with the exception of anti-discrimination law) do not. To give one example, in the United Kingdom, 390 out of 847 of all the applications for judicial review (46 per cent) that were considered were on immigration, asylum or crime.[76] The number of cases heard in any of these fields dwarfs those in other fields of EU law. They also frequently touch on civil liberty and public order sensitivities, which leads to any decision being potentially highly contentious. It remains to be seen if the procedure will meet this challenge.

4 FUNCTIONS OF THE PRELIMINARY REFERENCE PROCEDURE

The institutional role of the Court of Justice was discussed at length at the signing of the Treaty of Nice. The Court of Justice submitted a discussion paper there to the intergovernmental conference. In this paper the Court described the goal of the preliminary reference procedure as being:

> to guarantee respect for the distribution of powers between the Community and its Member States and between the Community institutions, the uniformity and consistency of Community law and to contribute to the harmonious development of the law within the Union.[77]

Extrapolating from this, the preliminary reference procedure can be said to contribute to the development of the EU legal and judicial orders in four ways.

The first is the development of EU law. It enables the Court to develop new interpretations of EU law, resolve uncertainties, correct injustices and enunciate principles. Secondly, in its statement, the Court talks of the maintenance of the institutional balance. By this it means that EU institutions do not trespass on each other's prerogatives and that the same is also true of the relationship between EU institutions and national institutions. EU institutions do not encroach in matters that are reserved to the domestic field and national institutions respect the autonomy and rules of the Union legal system. The preliminary reference procedure secures this through judicial review by private parties. Private parties can use it to challenge national behaviour through a ruling from the Court that exposes illegality by their courts, legislature or administration. Alternatively, a reference can be made which questions the legality of actions or omissions

---

[75] D. Chalmers, 'The Court of Justice and the Constitutional Treaty' (2005) 4 *ICON* 428, 455.
[76] Ministry of Justice, *Judicial and Court Statistics 2007* (London, Statistical Office, 2008) 27.
[77] European Court of Justice, *The Future of the Judicial System of the European Union* (Luxembourg, 1999) 21. Available at www.curia.eu.int/en/instit/txtdocfr/autrestxts/ave.pdf

by the EU institutions. Thirdly, the Court talks of the preliminary reference procedure as being necessary for the uniformity and consistency of EU law.[78] This is partly about coordination. Historically, decisions of the national courts of one Member State do not bind those of another. Without the possibility of access to a court whose authority is accepted by all actors, divergent interpretations of EU law would arise in the different national jurisdictions. The reference procedure also has a circulatory power in that it makes all Union courts part of a single judicial order and legal territory. A consequence of the reference procedure is that litigation in one Member State is now equally legally significant for the legal systems of all the other Member States, insofar as the Court of Justice judgment coming out of it will affect all the judiciaries. Litigation in the Netherlands, therefore, is as important as litigation in the United Kingdom for determining how EU law will govern life in the United Kingdom. Fourthly, the preliminary reference procedure has an administration of justice function. It enables national courts to decide disputes that involve EU law by allowing them to tap into the expertise of the Court of Justice.[79]

(i) Development of EU law

The reference procedure is significant quantitatively and qualitatively. Of the 767 cases pending at the end of 2008, 395 (about 51 per cent)[80] were preliminary references and almost all the significant rulings concerning EU law, other than those concerning the remit of the powers of the EU institutions, have come via the preliminary reference procedure. National courts act, therefore, as the gate-keepers to most of the central legal questions that move the EU legal order forward. However, they do more than this, as they formulate the questions that must be addressed. In this sense, they are agenda-setters, as, whilst the Court chooses how it responds to the question, they decide and frame what the Court can adjudicate upon.

The procedure is important for the development of EU law in another sense. The monopoly of adjudication provided to national courts indicates a division of functions, in which the Court of Justice is to steer the Union legal order, setting out its fundamental principles and limits and determining the legality of Union measures, whilst national courts are responsible for its day-to-day health. For the functions of the Court of Justice are exceptional in that they will not arise in most disputes involving EU law. In these disputes, it is the national courts and national legal systems that have hegemony over development of EU law: giving it a local reality, interpreting its principles, making sense of the practical relationship between it and national law.

(ii) Judicial review of EU institutions

Article 267 TFEU allows the Court of Justice to rule on the validity of EU legislation and administrative acts of the EU institutions.[81] Typically, the individual will challenge the national

---

[78] This was picked up early on in R. Buxbaum, 'Article 177 of the Rome Treaty as a Federalizing Device' (1969) 21 *Stanford Law Review* 1041. It has also been noted in a number of extra-judicial comments made by members of the Court: G. Mancini and D. Keeling, 'From CILFIT to ERT: the Constitutional Challenge Facing the Court' (1991) 11 *YBEL* 1, 2–3; G. Tesauro, 'The Effectiveness of Judicial Protection and Co-operation between the National Courts and the Court of Justice' (1993) 13 *YBEL* 1, 17.

[79] Although see Case 166/73 *Rheinmühlen-Düsseldorf* v *Einfuhr- und Vorratstelle für Getreide* [1974] ECR 33.

[80] *Annual Report*, n. 11 above, 95.

[81] Joined Cases 133/85–136/85 *Rau* v *Bundesanstalt für Landswirtschaftliche Marktordnung* [1987] ECR 2289.

measure implementing the EU act before a national court. The national court will then refer the question of whether the EU measure, which provides the legal authorisation for the national measure, is lawful or not.

In this way, the national court acts alongside the direct action procedures, which explicitly provide for individuals to challenge the acts of EU institutions.[82] Its relationship with these provisions is a complicated one as the Court sees it as part of a system of remedies. In *Jégo-Quéré*, the Commission adopted a Regulation setting a minimum mesh size for nets. Jégo-Quéré, a French company, fished for whitebait, a very small fish. The new minimum mesh sizes were now too big to allow it to do so effectively. It could not challenge the measure before a national court, as the Commission Regulation provided for no implementing measures to be taken, with the consequence that there was no national law to challenge. It sought to challenge the Regulation directly before the Court under Article 263(4) TFEU.[83] The Court held that they lacked standing, but that there were corollary duties on national authorities to allow individuals to challenge these acts before national courts, who could then refer the matter to the Union Courts.

Case C–263/02 P *Commission v Jégo-Quéré* [2004] ECR I–3425

29. It should be noted that individuals are entitled to effective judicial protection of the rights they derive from the Community legal order, and the right to such protection is one of the general principles of law stemming from the constitutional traditions common to the Member States. That right has also been enshrined in Articles 6 and 13 of the ECHR …

30. By Articles [263 and 268 TFEU]…, on the one hand, and by Article [267 TFEU], on the other, the Treaty has established a complete system of legal remedies and procedures designed to ensure review of the legality of acts of the institutions, and has entrusted such review to the Community Courts. Under that system, where natural or legal persons cannot, by reason of the conditions for admissibility laid down in the fourth paragraph of Article [263 TFEU], directly challenge Community measures of general application, they are able, depending on the case, either indirectly to plead the invalidity of such acts before the Community Courts under Article [268 TFEU] or to do so before the national courts and ask them, since they have no jurisdiction themselves to declare those measures invalid, to make a reference to the Court of Justice for a preliminary ruling on validity …

31. Thus it is for the Member States to establish a system of legal remedies and procedures which ensure respect for the right to effective judicial protection…

32. In that context, in accordance with the principle of sincere cooperation laid down in Article [4 TEU], national courts are required, so far as possible, to interpret and apply national procedural rules governing the exercise of rights of action in a way that enables natural and legal persons to challenge before the courts the legality of any decision or other national measure relative to the application to them of a Community act of general application, by pleading the invalidity of such an act…

---

[82] On these see pp. 414–37.
[83] See pp. 424–5.

The Court of Justice thus states that there is a duty on national courts to allow individuals to challenge the legality of EU acts before them with the presumption that these will then in turn refer the question to the Court of Justice.[84] In this, the Court of Justice sees the preliminary reference procedure as the central instrument for judicial review of EU acts. For private parties are not required to meet any restrictive *locus standi* requirements to do this, whereas if they seek direct access to the Court of Justice under Article 263(4) TFEU, the requirements are highly restrictive. However, subsequently in the judgment, the Court limits the force of this position by indicating that there will be no sanction if national courts fail to do this. In particular, it will not step in to give private parties direct access to the Court under Article 263(4) TFEU.

By contrast, the preliminary reference procedure cannot be used to review an EU measure where a party had *locus standi* to challenge a measure directly before the Court of Justice under Article 263(4) TFEU but failed to bring the action within the necessary time limits. In *TWD*, a German textile company sought to challenge a 1985 Commission Decision declaring a German subsidy to it to be incompatible with the EU law on state aids by asking for a preliminary reference from a German court in 1992.[85] The applicant was only barred from bringing a direct action as the time limits for such an action, under Article 263(5) TFEU, are within two months of the Decision becoming known to it. The Court refused, stating that once the time limit had expired legal certainty required that the national court be bound by the Commission Decision and could not, therefore, raise the question of its validity.[86]

Two months is a short period and most cases are different from *TWD* as parties will not be clear whether they have standing or not. In *Atzeni*, the Court tempered the limitation, therefore.[87] It stated that the exclusion would only apply where the applicant was explicitly identified in an EU institution and clearly had standing under Article 263 TFEU. In other circumstances, where parties are not identified or only identified in a general manner, there is no time-frame on challenging an EU act before a court. Whilst the motivations behind this reasoning are clear, it still does not avoid the problem of legal uncertainty and it might be here that national courts could impose their own limitation periods provided these are not too restrictive.

(iii) Preserving the unity of EU law

The unity of the Union legal system rests on the idea that the Union legal system is an autonomous legal system that must be interpreted and applied in a uniform way across the Union.[88] This has required that the Court of Justice set out the corpus of EU law on which it can give judgments under Article 267 TFEU. If particular provisions of EU law could not be referred, both the uniformity and autonomy of the legal order would be compromised, as, without authoritative guidance, national courts would give divergent interpretations and the sense of being part of the same legal jurisdiction would be compromised.

Although Article 267 TFEU only gives the Court the power to give rulings on the Treaties and acts of the EU institutions, the Court has consequently interpreted its power more broadly

---

[84] Case 314/85 *Firma Fotofrost v Hauptzollamt Lübeck-Ost* [1987] ECR 4199. See pp. 162–3.
[85] Case C-188/92 *TWD Textilwerke Deggendorf v Germany* [1994] ECR I-833.
[86] D. Wyatt, 'The Relationship between Actions for Annulment and References on Validity after TWD Deggendorf' in J. Lonbay and A. Biondi (eds.), *Remedies for Breach of EC Law* (Chichester, John Wiley, 1997).
[87] Joined Cases C-346/03 and C-529/03 *Atzeni and Others v Regione autonoma della Sardegna* [2006] ECR I-1875.
[88] Case C-195/06 *Kommaustria v ORF* [2007] ECR I-8817.

to include anything which forms part of the EU legal order, even if it is neither a provision of the Treaties nor a piece of secondary legislation, be that international agreements to which the Union has succeeded the Member States[89] or general principles of law and fundamental rights when there was no explicit reference to these in the Treaties.[90]

A feature of international agreements and fundamental rights is that they form part of the EU legal order but they also have an existence outside it. The Court has held that it will still give rulings on such provisions, notwithstanding that they apply to situations governed by both domestic and EU law. In that regard, it will rule on a provision even where it will mostly be invoked as a matter of national law and only occasionally as a matter of EU law. In *Hermès*, the Court considered a provision of the WTO Agreement on Trade Related Intellectual Property Rights which concerned enforcement of intellectual property rights. This largely fell within national competence.[91] The Court nevertheless held that, insofar as the provision could potentially cover situations which fell within the scope of EU law, most notably where intellectual property rights generated by EU law were infringed, the provision required a uniform interpretation.

The Court has been concerned to secure not just uniformity of application of EU law but also an interpretive unity. This has led it to accept references on matters that do not fall within EU legal competences but where there is, nevertheless, a reference to EU law. Whilst it has no general power to give rulings on provisions of national law,[92] the Court will, thus, give rulings wherever the latter refers to the contents of provisions of EU law or adopts similar solutions to those found in EU law.[93]

In *Dzodzi*, a Togolese woman challenged a decision by the Belgian authorities refusing her a residence permit following the death of her Belgian husband, a situation governed exclusively by Belgian law.[94] The Belgian law stated, however, that the spouses of Belgian nationals should be treated in the same way as spouses of other EU nationals, whose treatment was governed by EU law. In other words, the standard for Belgian law was to be that set in EU law. The Court ruled it to be in the Union legal interest that it give a ruling, on the grounds that every EU provision should be given a uniform interpretation, irrespective of the circumstances in which it is to be applied, in order to forestall future differences in interpretation.[95]

This concern to secure uniform interpretation has generated its own legal uncertainties. For it raises the question of how explicit the reference to EU law must be for the Court to be able to give a reference. In *Dzodzi*, there was an explicit reference. This was not the case in *Les Vergers du Vieux Tauves*.[96] The Belgian government had transposed a Directive which restricted the

---

[89] Joined Cases 267/81–269/81 *Amministrazione delle Finanze dello Stato* v *SPI* [1983] ECR 801.

[90] See e.g. Case 11/70 *Internationale Handelsgesellschaft* v *Einfuhr- und Vorratstelle für Getreide und Futtermittel* [1970] ECR 1125.

[91] Case C-53/96 *Hermès International* v *FHT Marketing* [1998] ECR I-3603; Joined Cases C-300/98 and C-302/98 *Parfums Christian Dior* v *Tuk Consultancy* [2000] ECR I-11307; Case C-431/05 *Merck Genéricos – Produtos Farmacêuticos* v *Merck* [2007] ECR I-7001.

[92] Case 75/63 *Hoekstra* v *Bedrijfsvereniging Detailhandel* [1964] ECR 177.

[93] Case C-247/97 *Schoonbroodt* [1998] ECR I-8095; Case C-170/03 *Feron* [2005] ECR I-2299. For discussion, see S. Lefevre, 'The Interpretation of Community Law by the Court of Justice in Areas of National Competence' (2004) 29 *ELRev.* 501.

[94] Joined Cases C-297/88 and C-197/89 *Dzodzi* v *Belgium* [1990] ECR I-3673.

[95] Similar reasoning has been deployed to allow the Court to accept references on contracts that incorporate terms of EU law: Case C-88/91 *Federconsorzi* v *AIMA* [1992] ECR I-4035.

[96] Case C-48/07 *Les Vergers du Vieux Tauves*, Judgment of 22 December 2008.

taxes parent companies had to pay on dividends made by subsidiaries in other Member States. The Belgian law replicated, in parts, the language of the Directive, but the substance was wider and the Belgian law did not refer to it explicitly. It also applied to relations between Belgian parent companies and their subsidiaries, something that fell outside the Directive. The Court was asked to give an interpretation on the Belgian law in a case that involved only a Belgian parent company and its subsidiary. Notwithstanding the domestic nature of the case and the absence of an explicit reference, the Court considered it sufficient that the Belgian law was intended to transpose the Directive and there was some replication of the language. However, this is a very weak and uncertain nexus. It also loses sight of the initial rationale for intervention in such cases, namely unity of interpretation of EU law. As the Court acknowledged, the Belgian court need have only partial regard to its judgment in interpreting the provision but would also be able to look at the Belgian domestic legal context. There would be no guarantee, therefore, that its interpretation of its law would be the same as interpretations of identically worded provisions in other Member States.

The unity of EU law also has an institutional dimension in that the Court of Justice has understood it as suggesting that there needs to be one court with pre-eminent authority over the interpretation and validity of EU law.[97] This view is not uncontested by national courts.[98] We have already seen that by virtue of Article 274 TFEU, the power of judicial review over acts of the EU institutions is reserved to the Court of Justice. The Court has stated that national courts cannot declare EU measures invalid but must refer where this question arises.[99] In *Fotofrost*, a Commission Decision requiring import duties to be paid on binoculars imported from the eastern part of Germany was challenged before a Hamburg court on the grounds it conflicted with the 1957 Protocol on German Internal Trade, which allowed free trade between the two divided parts of Germany. The Hamburg court asked the Court of Justice whether it could declare the Commission Decision invalid.

Case 314/85 *Firma Fotofrost v Hauptzollamt Lübeck-Ost* [1987] ECR 4199

13. In enabling national courts, against those decisions where there is a judicial remedy under national law, to refer to the Court for a preliminary ruling questions on interpretation or validity, [Article 267 TFEU] did not settle the question whether those courts themselves may declare that acts of Community institutions are invalid.

14. Those courts may consider the validity of a Community act and, if they consider that the grounds put forward before them by the parties in support of invalidity are unfounded, they may reject them, concluding that the measure is completely valid. By taking that action they are not calling into question the existence of the Community measure.

15. On the other hand, those courts do not have the power to declare acts of the Community institutions invalid. As the Court emphasized...in Case 66/80 *International Chemical Corporation* v *Amministrazione delle Finanze* (1981) ECR 1191, the main purpose of the powers accorded to the Court

---

[97] European Court of Justice, above n. 77, 17.
[98] See pp. 191–7.
[99] G. Bebr, 'The Reinforcement of the Constitutional Review of Community Acts under the EEC Treaty' (1988) 25 *CMLRev.* 667.

by Article [267 TFEU] is to ensure that Community law is applied uniformly by national courts. That requirement of uniformity is particularly imperative when the validity of a Community act is in question. Divergences between courts in the Member States as to the validity of Community acts would be liable to place in jeopardy the very unity of the Community legal order and detract from the fundamental requirement of legal certainty.

16. The same conclusion is dictated by consideration of the necessary coherence of the system of judicial protection established by the Treaty. In that regard it must be observed that requests for preliminary rulings, like actions for annulment, constitute means for reviewing the legality of acts of the community institutions. As the Court pointed out… in Case 294/83 *Parti Ecologiste 'Les Verts'* v *European Parliament* (1986) ECR 1339, 'in Articles [263 and 268], on the one hand, and in Article [267 TFEU], on the other, the Treaty established a complete system of legal remedies and procedures designed to permit the Court of Justice to review the legality of measures adopted by the institutions'.

17. Since Article [263 TFEU] gives the Court exclusive jurisdiction to declare void an act of a Community institution, the coherence of the system requires that where the validity of a Community act is challenged before a national court the power to declare the act invalid must also be reserved to the Court of Justice.

18. It must also be emphasized that the Court of Justice is in the best position to decide on the validity of Community acts. Under Article 20 of the Protocol on the Statute of the Court of Justice of the EEC, Community institutions whose acts are challenged are entitled to participate in the proceedings in order to defend the validity of the acts in question. Furthermore, under the second paragraph of Article 21 of that Protocol the Court may require the Member States and institutions which are not participating in the proceedings to supply all information which it considers necessary for the purposes of the case before it.

19. It should be added that the rule that national courts may not themselves declare Community acts invalid may have to be qualified in certain circumstances in the case of proceedings relating to an application for interim measures; however, that case is not referred to in the national court's question.

The inflexibility and strength of the requirement on national courts to challenge the validity of EU measures was illustrated in *Schul*.[100] A Dutch court of last resort asked whether it could strike down an EU instrument when an analogous instrument based on identical principles had already been struck down. The case in question concerned a charge levied on Brazilian sugar imported into the Netherlands on the basis of a Commission Regulation. An identical pricing structure was used as in a measure in the poultry sector ruled illegal by the Court of Justice, namely the Council had suggested one pricing structure (the representative price) and the Commission had exceeded its delegated power by using a different one (cif price). The Court of Justice stated that the uniformity of EU law and its procedural rules, in which all Member States and EU institutions have the right to make observations, entailed that only it could declare Union acts invalid. This was the case even where an analogous measure had already been struck down. Analogies could be misleading in that the factual and legal context surrounding each measure would necessarily be different.

---

[100] Case C-461/03 *Schul v Minister van Landbouw, Natuur en Voedselkwaliteit* [2005] ECR I-10513.

A very slight nuancing of the situation was allowed in *IATA*.[101] IATA, the central association representing airlines, challenged Regulation 261/2004/EC, which provided for compensation and assistance to passengers in the event of being denied boarding and of cancellation or long delay to long-haul flights. The English court was sceptical of the challenge and, indeed, the challenge was eventually unsuccessful. It therefore questioned the threshold at which it must refer to the Court of Justice. The latter stated it was not required to refer simply because one party challenged the validity of a measure. It should only refer if it considers an argument as to the invalidity of a measure, brought up either by itself or by one of the parties, to be well founded.

The annual Commission studies on the application of EU law have, however, not suggested any rebellion against *Fotofrost* by national courts.[102] This is, in part, because the practical application of the *Fotofrost* judgment is rather different from its rhetoric. National courts may still suspend acts through the granting of interim relief pending a reference to the Court of Justice.[103] A compact is thereby offered, whereby national courts may provisionally suspend the application of an act provided they refer the matter to the Court of Justice for a definitive ruling. They retain their power of review but at the cost of having to make a reference.

(iv) Dispute resolution

The monopoly of adjudication granted to the national court by Article 267 TFEU suggests dispute resolution for it. However, the stipulation in Article 267(2) TFEU that it only refer when the point of EU law is necessary to give a judgment has been interpreted to mean that a reference should only take place and the Court of Justice give a judgment where the latter meaningfully contributes to the resolution of the dispute. The Court of Justice will not give a ruling, therefore, if it considers it will not be used to determine a genuine dispute before the national court. This inevitably means that it will look at the litigation before the national court to verify whether a dispute is taking place. This position was tested for the first time in the *Foglia* saga. Foglia had contracted to sell Italian liqueur wine to Novello in France with the proviso that Novello would reimburse any taxes Foglia incurred, unless these were levied contrary to Community law. Foglia sought to recover the French taxes paid from Novello, equivalent to 148,000 Italian lire, who refused on the grounds that these had been levied contrary to Community law. The matter was brought before an Italian court which was asked to rule on the compatibility of the French taxes with EC law. The case had all the hallmarks of a test case. Both Foglia and Novello argued that the taxes were illegal, the amount of tax paid was derisory and Foglia indicated that he was participating in this case on behalf of Italian traders of this wine. The Court of Justice refused to give judgment in the initial reference on the grounds that there was no genuine dispute.[104] The Italian court re-referred the matter, asking what the roles of the national court and Court of Justice were in such matters.

---

[101] Case C-344/04 *R, ex parte IATA* v *Department for Transport* [2006] ECR I-403.

[102] See e.g. European Commission, *25th Annual Report on Monitoring the Application of Community Law*, COM(2008)777, Annex VI.

[103] Case C-465/93 *Atlanta Fruchthandelsgesellschaft and others (No. 1)* [1995] ECR I-3761; Case C-334/95 *Krüger* v *Hauptzollamt Hamburg-Jonas* [1997] ECR I-4517.

[104] Case 104/79 *Foglia* v *Novello* [1980] ECR 745.

Case 244/80 *Foglia* v *Novello* (No. 2) [1981] ECR 3045

14. With regard to the first question it should be recalled, as the Court has had occasion to emphasize in very varied contexts, that [Article 267 TFEU] is based on cooperation which entails a division of duties between the national courts and the Court of Justice in the interest of the proper application and uniform interpretation of Community law throughout all the Member States.

15. With this in view it is for the national court – by reason of the fact that it is seized of the substance of the dispute and that it must bear the responsibility for the decision to be taken – to assess, having regard to the facts of the case, the need to obtain a preliminary ruling to enable it to give judgment.

16. In exercising that power of appraisal the national court, in collaboration with the Court of Justice, fulfils a duty entrusted to them both of ensuring that in the interpretation and application of the Treaty the law is observed. Accordingly the problems which may be entailed in the exercise of its power of appraisal by the national court and the relations which it maintains within the framework of [Article 267 TFEU] with the Court of Justice are governed exclusively by the provisions of Community law.

17. In order that the Court of Justice may perform its task in accordance with the Treaty it is essential for national courts to explain, when the reasons do not emerge beyond any doubt from the file, why they consider that a reply to their questions is necessary to enable them to give judgment.

18. It must in fact be emphasized that the duty assigned to the Court by [Article 267 TFEU] is not that of delivering advisory opinions on general or hypothetical questions but of assisting in the administration of justice in the Member States. It accordingly does not have jurisdiction to reply to questions of interpretation which are submitted to it within the framework of procedural devices arranged by the parties in order to induce the Court to give its views on certain problems of Community law which do not correspond to an objective requirement inherent in the resolution of a dispute. A declaration by the Court that it has no jurisdiction in such circumstances does not in any way trespass upon the prerogatives of the national court but makes it possible to prevent the application of the procedure under [Article 267 TFEU] for purposes other than those appropriate for it.

19. Furthermore, it should be pointed out that, whilst the Court of Justice must be able to place as much reliance as possible upon the assessment by the national court of the extent to which the questions submitted are essential, it must be in a position to make any assessment inherent in the performance of its own duties in particular in order to check, as all courts must, whether it has jurisdiction. Thus the Court, taking into account the repercussions of its decisions in this matter, must have regard, in exercising the jurisdiction conferred upon it by [Article 267 TFEU], not only to the interests of the parties to the proceedings but also to those of the Community and of the Member States. Accordingly it cannot, without disregarding the duties assigned to it, remain indifferent to the assessments made by the courts of the Member States in the exceptional cases in which such assessments may affect the proper working of the procedure laid down by [Article 267 TFEU] ...

28. On the one hand it must be pointed out that the court before which, in the course of proceedings between individuals, an issue concerning the compatibility with Community law of legislation of another Member State is brought is not necessarily in a position to provide for such individuals effective protection in relation to such legislation.

29. On the other hand, regard being had to the independence generally ensured for the parties by the legal systems of the Member States in the field of contract, the possibility arises that the conduct of the parties may be such as to make it impossible for the State concerned to arrange for an appropriate defence of its interests by causing the question of the invalidity of its legislation to be decided by a court of another Member State. Accordingly, in such procedural situations it is impossible to exclude the

risk that the procedure under [Article 267 TFEU] may be diverted by the parties from the purposes for which it was laid down by the Treaty.

30. The foregoing considerations as a whole show that the Court of Justice for its part must display special vigilance when, in the course of proceedings between individuals, a question is referred to it with a view to permitting the national court to decide whether the legislation of another Member State is in accordance with Community law.

Foglia was extremely contentious. The power to refuse a reference established a hierarchical element between the Court of Justice and the national court, as it granted a power to the Court of Justice to review the national court's decision to refer. The enquiry into the existence of a genuine dispute by the Court of Justice would also require it to look behind the national court's reference and examine the factual background to the dispute. There was consequently debate about whether this violated the cooperative spirit of Article 67 TFEU or transgressed unduly on the national court's monopoly over fact-finding.[105] Whatever its merits, there are severe practical difficulties in applying *Foglia*.[106] The finding of an absence of a genuine dispute requires the Court to take an independent view of the facts of the case. Without its own fact-finding powers, however, the Court has little capacity to second-guess national courts.

Within this context, the Court has accepted test cases. In *Leclerc Siplec* v *TF1 Publicité*, Leclerc Siplec challenged a refusal by TF1, one of the major French television broadcasters, to televise an advertisement which sought to persuade viewers to purchase petrol from the forecourts of Leclerc's chain of supermarkets.[107] The reason for the refusal was a French law prohibiting television advertising of the distribution sector. Both parties to the dispute were in agreement about the domestic legal situation and the need for a reference. The Court accepted the reference. It noted that what was being sought was a declaration from the national court that the French law did not comply with EU law. The parties' agreement did not make the need for that declaration any less pressing or the dispute any less real. Whilst resolution of test cases is an important part of the judicial function, it is very difficult to distinguish them from hypothetical cases. In both, there is little conflict between the immediate parties to the dispute.

Since *Foglia*, the Court has also accepted cases where the national law of one Member State is challenged in the courts of another. In *Eau de Cologne*, Eau de Cologne, a cosmetics company, agreed to supply cosmetics to an Italian company, Provide.[108] The contract contained a warranty that the cosmetics would comply with Italian law. Provide repudiated the contract on the grounds that the cosmetics did not comply with Italian labelling laws. Eau de Cologne argued that they complied with the Directive regulating the matter. Under a choice of forum provision in the agreement, the matter was brought before a German court which referred

---

[105] For differing views see A. Barav, 'Preliminary Censorship? The Judgment of the European Court in Foglia v Novello' (1980) 5 *ELRev.* 443, 451–4; H. Rasmussen, *On Law and Policy in the European Court of Justice* (Dordrecht, Martinus Nijhoff, 1986) 465–97; D. Wyatt, 'Foglia (No.2): The Court Denies It has Jurisdiction to Give Advisory Opinions' (1982) 7 *ELRev.* 186; C. Gray, 'Advisory Opinions and the Court of Justice' (1983) 8 *ELRev.* 24.

[106] G. Bebr, 'The Existence of a Genuine Dispute: An Indispensable Precondition for the Jurisdiction of the Court under Article 177 EC?' (1980) 17 *CMLRev.* 525, 532.

[107] Case C-412/93 *Société d'Importation Edouard Leclerc-Siplec v TF1 Publicité SA and M6 Publicité SA* [1995] ECR I-179. M. O'Neill, 'Article 177 and Limits to the Right to Refer: An End to the Confusion?' (1996) 2 *European Public Law* 375.

[108] Case C-150/88 *Eau de Cologne v Provide* [1989] ECR 3891.

a question on the interpretation of the Directive. The Court accepted the genuineness of the dispute despite a number of factors, notably the seemingly trivial nature of the breach and the choice of forum which allowed a German court to adjudicate upon the compatibility of Italian legislation with EU law.

The *Foglia* line of reasoning survives. Instead of being used by the Court to review the motives of the parties, it is being used to review the contents of the reference and the quality of the national court's communications.[109] The Court will refuse to give a reference not merely where the dispute is hypothetical but where the factual and legal context to the dispute has not been properly explained. In *Plato Plastik* v *Caropack*, Plato Plastik produced plastic bags in Austria which it sold to Caropack, who sold them at supermarkets. Under the contract, Plato Plastik's statutory obligation to participate in a collection and recovery scheme was transferred to Caropack. Following prosecution by the Austrian authorities, Plato Plastik asked for confirmation from Caropack that it was participating in the scheme. Caropack refused, arguing that it could not absolve Plato Plastik of its statutory duties. The Austrian court referred the question whether the Austrian scheme for the collection and recovery of waste complied with Directive 94/62/EC on packaging waste. The Commission noted that both parties agreed on the law and were using the case to have the Austrian scheme declared illegal.

Case C–341/01 *Plato Plastik* v *Caropack* [2004] ECR I–4883

26. It has consistently been held that it is solely for the national court before which the dispute has been brought, and which must assume responsibility for the subsequent judicial decision, to determine in the light of the particular circumstances of the case both the need for a preliminary ruling in order to enable it to deliver judgment and the relevance of the questions which it submits to the Court. Consequently, where the questions submitted by the national court concern the interpretation of Community law, the Court of Justice is, in principle, bound to give a ruling...

27. However, the Court has also held that, in exceptional circumstances, it should examine the conditions in which the case was referred to it by the national court...The spirit of cooperation which must prevail in the preliminary ruling procedure requires the national court, for its part, to have regard to the function entrusted to the Court of Justice, which is to assist in the administration of justice in the Member States and not to deliver advisory opinions on general or hypothetical questions...

28. The Court has accordingly held that it has no jurisdiction to give a preliminary ruling on a question submitted by a national court where it is quite obvious that the interpretation or assessment of the validity of a Community rule sought by that court bears no relation to the facts or purpose of the main action, where the problem is hypothetical or where the Court does not have before it the factual or legal material necessary to enable it to give a useful answer to the questions submitted to it...

29. In order that the Court of Justice may perform its task in accordance with the EC Treaty it is essential for national courts to explain, when the reasons do not emerge beyond any doubt from the file, why they consider that a reply to their questions is necessary to enable them to give judgment...Thus the Court has also on various occasions stressed that it is important for the national court to state the

---

[109] T. Kennedy, 'First Steps Towards a European Certiorari' (1993) 18 *ELRev.* 121; D. Anderson, 'The Admissibility of Preliminary References' (1994) 14 *YBEL* 179, 186–8.

precise reasons for which it is in doubt as to the interpretation of Community law and which led it to consider it necessary to refer questions to the Court for a preliminary ruling...

30. In the present case, the action before the national court seeks, on an application by Plato Plastik, an order that Caropack must provide the latter with confirmation of its participation in the ARA system relating to the plastic bags delivered to it. It is not manifestly apparent from the facts set out in the order for reference that the dispute is in fact fictitious...The fact that the parties to the main proceedings are in agreement as to the interpretation of the Community provisions in question does not affect the reality of the dispute in the main proceedings...

31. Consequently, the argument that the dispute is fictitious cannot succeed.

There is a duty for the national court to explain the factual and legal context and also a duty to provide reasons why it considered it necessary to make a reference. These reasons must explain the national court's doubts but they must also provide some explanation of the reasons for the choice of the EU provisions to be interpreted and of the link between those provisions and the national legislation applicable to the dispute. Whilst this may lead the Court to limit its answers to only some of the questions referred,[110] in recent years the review has been extremely light-touch. The Court has therefore stated that it will only refuse to give a reference where it is 'quite obvious' that there is no dispute, the point of law referred bears no relationship to the dispute in question or that it has not been provided with the necessary factual and legal material. The 'quite obvious' test means that if there is the slightest doubt about any of these it will give a ruling. In *Stichting Zuid-Hollandse Milieufederatie*, for example, the Court accepted a question from a Dutch court about the Directive on biocides, notwithstanding that the litigation concerned legislation on another Directive, that on plant protection, on the grounds that the two Directives were closely related and governed by similar principles.[111] Furthermore, even if the statement of the factual and legal context is thin and ambiguous or the reference is posed in general and hypothetical terms, the Court will give judgment if it thinks it can relate the reference to a particular dispute[112] and if it thinks enough of the facts are provided for it to give a sufficiently informed judgment.[113]

5 MANAGEMENT OF THE EU JUDICIAL ORDER

We have seen in the last two sections that the Court of Justice has set out an EU judicial order, comprising both EU and national courts, the structure of which is underpinned by Article 267 TFEU. This has led to a division of duties where the Court of Justice has a monopoly over the review of EU institutions and what can be referred to it whilst national courts have a monopoly of adjudication over other disputes involving EU law that come before them, albeit that a reference to the Court of Justice entitles the Court of Justice to instruct them on how to interpret the point of EU law before them.

[110] Case C-380/05 *Centro Europa 7* v *Ministero delle Comunicazioni* [2008] ECR I-349.
[111] Case C-138/05 *Stichting Zuid-Hollandse Milieufederatie* v *Minister van Landbouw* [2006] ECR I-8339.
[112] Case C-537/07 *Gómez-Limón* v *INSS*, Judgment of 16 July 2009.
[113] Joined Cases C-295/04–C-298/04 *Vincenzo Manfredi and Others* v *Lloyd Adriatico Assicurazioni SpA and Others* [2006] ECR I-6619.

All this still leaves the question of how the procedure is managed to realise these different functions and whether it successfully realises this. There are three points of management. First, there are the effects of the Court of Justice judgments on the referring court and the wider judicial order. Secondly, the reference process has to be managed by the domestic court in the period when it refers and when it gives final judgment. Finally, the circumstances under which a referral is or is not made have to be managed.

(i) Binding effects of Court of Justice judgments

A judgment given by the Court of Justice binds the referring national court.[114] However, it is free to refer the question back to the Court of Justice if it is either dissatisfied with the ruling or is unclear about the meaning of the ruling. In such circumstances, in a form of judicial 'ping pong', the Court has tended simply to reiterate or extrapolate on its prior judgment.[115] There is also no meaningful sanction that is applied against national courts that do not follow the rulings.[116] That said, national compliance is very high. A cross-country study found implementation of the Court's rulings in 96.3 per cent of the cases studied.[117] Challenges to the authority of the Court were rarely in the form of direct non-observance but rather in less direct ways. A study of Austrian courts found that a variety of devices were used to evade rulings of the Court of Justice that were unpopular with the local court. These included narrow constructions of EC legal norms, arguing that the norm does not apply to the facts, weak remedies, *a contrario* reasoning and application of domestic, rather than EU, legal norms if it would lead to the same result.[118] The Court of Justice has tried to circumvent this in some instances by sending back rulings which are so detailed that they leave national courts little room for discretion in how they decide the dispute in hand. By contrast, in other cases, they have sought to defuse conflict by sending back rulings that are sufficiently vague to allow the national court considerable discretion in deciding how to resolve the dispute.[119]

There is, however, the question of the effects of the Court's judgments on the wider EU judicial community. The doctrines of *stare decisis* and precedent do not formally exist in EU law. Judgments of the Court only declare the pre-existing state of the law.[120] However, judgments having no broader effects would be highly unsatisfactory for the development of the Union legal order. It was felt to be particularly problematic where the Court declared an EU measure illegal. If the judgment only bound the parties concerned, it would lead to the instrument being invalid for them but binding upon everybody else, albeit open to challenge by everybody else. In *ICC*, therefore, the Court ruled that a judgment declaring an EU measure illegal bound all

---

[114] Case 52/76 *Benedetti* v *Munari* [1977] ECR 163.
[115] Joined Cases 28/62–30/62 *Da Costa* [1963] ECR 37; Case 244/80 *Foglia* v *Novello (No. 2)* [1981] ECR 3045.
[116] Case C-224/01 *Köbler* v *Austria* [2003] ECR I-10239.
[117] S. Nyikos, 'The Preliminary Reference Process: National Court Implementation, Changing Opportunity Structures and Litigant Desistment' (2003) 4 *EUP* 397, 410.
[118] B. Bepuly, 'The Application of EC Law in Austria', IWE Working Paper No. 39, Available at www.iwe.oeaw.ac.at
[119] The manner in which the Court has done this has been subject to some criticism. J. Snell, 'European Courts and Intellectual Property: A Tale of Zeus, Hercules and Cyclops' (2004) 29 *ELRev*. 178.
[120] Case 61/79 *Denkavit Italiana* [1980] ECR 1205. T. Koopmans, 'Stare Decisis in European Law' in D. O' Keeffe and H. Schermers (eds.), *Essays in European Law and Integration* (Deventer, Kluwer, 1982); A. Arnull, 'Owning Up to Fallibility: Precedent and the Court of Justice' (1993) 30 *CMLRev*. 247.

courts and authorities in the Union.[121] The binding force of Court judgments interpreting EU law, by contrast, was unclear for some time.[122]

In *Kühne*, the Court resolved this by holding that the statements of the law in its judgments bound all courts and administrative authorities in the Union. Kühne exported chicken legs, with part of the chicken's back still attached, to states outside the European Union. In a judgment involving other parties, the Court of Justice had ruled that these were to be classified as 'chicken legs' for the purposes of customs classification[123] Kühne then sought reimbursement from the Dutch authorities who had previously placed its goods in a customs classification on which higher customs duties were levied. The Dutch authorities observed that the matter had previously been decided by a Dutch court, which had decided against Kühne, and could not, therefore, be reopened. Kühne argued that they were bound to reconsider the matter in the light of the earlier Court of Justice judgment.

Case C-453/00 *Kühne & Heitz v Productschap voor Pluimvee en Eieren* [2004] ECR I-837

21. The interpretation which, in the exercise of the jurisdiction conferred on it by Article [267 TFEU], the Court gives to a rule of Community law clarifies and defines, where necessary, the meaning and scope of that rule as it must be or ought to have been understood and applied from the time of its coming into force...

22. It follows that a rule of Community law interpreted in this way must be applied by an administrative body within the sphere of its competence even to legal relationships which arose or were formed before the Court gave its ruling on the question on interpretation.

23. The main proceedings raise the question whether the abovementioned obligation must be complied with notwithstanding that a decision has become final before the application for review of that decision in order to take account of a preliminary ruling by the Court on a question of interpretation has been lodged.

24. Legal certainty is one of a number of general principles recognised by Community law. Finality of an administrative decision, which is acquired upon expiry of the reasonable time-limits for legal remedies or by exhaustion of those remedies, contributes to such legal certainty and it follows that Community law does not require that administrative bodies be placed under an obligation, in principle, to reopen an administrative decision which has become final in that way.

25. However, the national court stated that, under Netherlands law, administrative bodies always have the power to reopen a final administrative decision, provided that the interests of third parties are not adversely affected, and that, in certain circumstances, the existence of such a power may imply an obligation to withdraw such a decision even if Netherlands law does not require that the competent body reopen final decisions as a matter of course in order to comply with judicial decisions given subsequent to the decision. The aim of the national court's question is to ascertain whether, in circumstances such as those of the main case, there is an obligation to reopen a final administrative decision under Community law.

---

[121] Case 66/80 *International Chemical Corporation v Amministrazione Finanze* [1981] ECR 1191; Case 314/85 *Firma Fotofrost v Hauptzollamt Lübeck-Ost* [1987] ECR 4199.

[122] For contrasting views of the Advocates General, see Advocate General Darmon in Case 338/85 *Pardini v Ministerio del Commercio con l'Estero* [1988] ECR 204; Advocate General Van Gerven in Case 145/88 *Torfaen Borough Council v B & Q* [1989] ECR 765; Advocate General Lenz in Case 103/88 *Fratelli Constanzo v Milano* [1989] ECR 1839.

[123] Case C-151/93 *Voogd Vleesimport en -export* [1994] ECR I-4915.

26. As is clear from the case-file, the circumstances of the main case are the following. First, national law confers on the administrative body competence to reopen the decision in question, which has become final. Second, the administrative decision became final only as a result of a judgment of a national court against whose decisions there is no judicial remedy. Third, that judgment was based on an interpretation of Community law which, in the light of a subsequent judgment of the Court, was incorrect and which was adopted without a question being referred to the Court for a preliminary ruling in accordance with the conditions provided for in Article [267 TFEU]. Fourth, the person concerned complained to the administrative body immediately after becoming aware of that judgment of the Court.

27. In such circumstances, the administrative body concerned is, in accordance with the principle of cooperation arising from Article [4 TEU], under an obligation to review that decision in order to take account of the interpretation of the relevant provision of Community law given in the meantime by the Court. The administrative body will have to determine on the basis of the outcome of that review to what extent it is under an obligation to reopen, without adversely affecting the interests of third parties, the decision in question.

Although *Kühne* only refers to the Court's judgment binding national administrative authorities, this has been interpreted as being binding on all national authorities. They are required to change national law as soon as possible after the judgment, making sure that they give full effect to individual rights under EU law.[124] These authorities include national judges, and they are, consequently, governed by the duties set out in the judgment.[125] Care has to be had when describing their binding effects. As the judgments are assumed to be declaring pre-existing law, their binding force applies to all relationships governed by the legal instrument since it entered into force. This poses, as the judgment acknowledges, real challenges for legal certainty. In most instances, this will be resolved by national limitation periods which will prevent disputes of a certain vintage being reopened. More challenging is the situation in *Kühne*, where a court or administrative authority has just given a decision which conflicts with a subsequent Court judgment. Legal certainty will prevent it being reopened unless four criteria are met: there is an administrative body that has the power to reopen the decision; the administrative decision in question has become final as a result of a judgment of a national court ruling at final instance; that judgment is based on a misinterpretation of EU law and the court failed to refer; the person concerned complained to the administrative body immediately after becoming aware of that decision of the Court.[126] These conditions are cumulative and restrictive. The Court has therefore held that the possibility of appeal would preclude reopening the matter.[127] It will be rare that they are met and the Court has insisted that there is no general obligation on courts to reopen cases simply because they conflict with subsequent Court judgments.[128]

---

[124] Case C-231/06 *NPO* v *Jonkman* [2007] ECR I-5149.

[125] Case C-212/04 *Adeneler and Others* v *ELOG (Ellinikos Organismos Galaktos)* [2006] ECR I-6057.

[126] However, the parties do not have to have raised it themselves before the court. Case C-2/06 *Kempter* [2008] ECR I-411.

[127] Joined Cases C-392/04 and C-422/04 *i-21 Germany* v *Bundesrepublik Deutschland* [2006] ECR I-8559.

[128] Case C-234/04 *Kapferer* v *Schlank & Schlick* [2006] ECR I-2585.

(ii) Management of the reference period and interim measures

There is a lengthy period between the time the reference is made by the national court and the adoption of a judgment by the Court of Justice. In 2008, this period was an average of 16.8 months.[129] In addition, there will be the period following the Court judgment when the matter must wait to go back before the national courts. National courts are required to manage the rights of the parties during this time through the grant of interim relief. This remedy of interim relief operates in different ways depending on whether interim relief is being sought against an autonomous provision of national law whose compatibility with EU law is being contested, or whether it is being sought against a national law implementing an EU law where the validity of the EU measure is being contested.

In the case of the former, the Court has ruled that the national court must do everything to secure the effectiveness of the Court's judgment. In *Factortame*, a challenge was made by a number of Spanish fishermen to the United Kingdom's Merchant Shipping Act 1988.[130] This Act made it very difficult for non-British boats to fish in British waters by imposing, most notably, a series of residence requirements as a precondition. The national court referred the matter to the Court of Justice. In the meantime, the House of Lords found that the applicants would suffer irreparable damage if interim relief was not granted as many fishermen would go bankrupt before judgment was delivered. As English courts had no jurisdiction to suspend the Act at that time, it referred the question whether national law should be set aside where its application would deprive a party of the enjoyment of rights derived from EU law. The Court of Justice ruled that it should. It ruled that national courts were under a duty to secure the full effectiveness of EU law. This required that they had to ensure the full effectiveness of any Court judgment on those rights. If the national court considers that the effectiveness of the final judgment might be otherwise undermined, it must grant interim relief. This works to the benefit of applicants claiming possible entitlements under EU law. They merely have to show that they would not be able to claim those rights if they won to make a strong case for interim relief.

The conditions for interim relief are much more restrictive where a reference is being sought that, in effect, challenges the validity of an EU measure. In such circumstances, the applicant must show they will suffer serious and irreparable damage and this has then to be weighed against the Union interest in not having the measure disapplied. In *Martini*, manufacturers in Italy, the Netherlands and the United Kingdom challenged Directive 2002/2/EC on the circulation and marketing of compound feeding stuffs for animals[131] This required manufacturers to indicate the quantities of feed materials used in the composition of the products with a tolerance of ± 15 per cent of the declared value and, when requested by a customer, to provide the exact percentages by weight of the feed materials making up a feeding stuff product. The Dutch court asked if the national implementing measure could be suspended pending judgment.

---

[129] *Annual Report*, above n. 11, 94.

[130] Case C-213/89 *R* v *Secretary of State for Transport, ex parte Factortame Ltd* [1990] ECR I-2433.

[131] This judgment consolidates a large number of cases, Joined Cases C-143/88 and C-92/89 *Zuckerfabrik Süderdithmarschen and Zuckerfabrik Soest* [1991] ECR I-415, Case C-465/93 *Atlanta Fruchthandelsgesellschaft and Others (No. 1)* [1995] ECR I-3761, Case C-68/95 *T. Port* [1996] ECR I-6065.

Joined Cases C-453/03, C-11/04, C-12/04 and C-194/04 *Martini* v *Ministero delle Politiche Agricole e Forestali* **[2005] ECR I-10423**

103. ...references for preliminary rulings on the validity of a measure, like actions for annulment, allow the legality of acts of the Community institutions to be reviewed. In the context of actions for annulment, Article [279 TFEU] enables applicants to request enforcement of the contested act to be suspended and empowers the Court to order such suspension. The coherence of the system of interim legal protection therefore requires that national courts should also be able to order suspension of enforcement of a national administrative measure based on a Community regulation, the legality of which is contested.

104. The Court has, however, ruled that the uniform application of Community law, which is a fundamental requirement of the Community legal order, means that the suspension of enforcement of administrative measures based on a Community regulation, whilst it is governed by national procedural law, in particular as regards the making and examination of the application, must in all the Member States be subject, at the very least, to conditions which are uniform so far as the granting of such relief is concerned and which it has defined as being the same conditions as those of the application for interim relief brought before the Court...

105. The Court has pointed out in particular that, in order to determine whether the conditions relating to urgency and the risk of serious and irreparable damage have been satisfied, the national court dealing with the application for interim relief must examine the circumstances particular to the case before it and consider whether immediate enforcement of the measure which is the subject of the application for interim relief would be likely to result in irreversible damage to the applicant which could not be made good if the Community act were to be declared invalid...

106. As the court responsible for applying, within the framework of its jurisdiction, the provisions of Community law and consequently under an obligation to ensure that Community law is fully effective, the national court, when dealing with an application for interim relief, must take account of the damage which the interim measure may cause to the legal regime established by a Community measure for the Community as a whole. It must consider, on the one hand, the cumulative effect which would arise if a large number of courts were also to adopt interim measures for similar reasons and, on the other, those special features of the applicant's situation which distinguish it from the other operators concerned...

107. In particular, if the grant of interim relief may represent a financial risk for the Community, the national court must also be in a position to require the applicant to provide adequate guarantees, such as the deposit of money or other security...

108. The unavoidable conclusion in this regard is that national administrative authorities...are not in a position to adopt interim measures while complying with the conditions for granting such measures as defined by the Court.

These different tests result in applicants whose interests are prejudiced in very similar ways being treated very differently. This injustice results because the Court is giving priority to different systemic concerns: the effectiveness of EU law in one case and the cumulative effect of interim relief and the financial risks for the Union, in the other. We might wonder why these should have such priority, why different elements are emphasised in different cases and why the Court does not think these same arguments should apply analogously to national law.

This seemingly arcane question also strongly influences the type of litigant who goes to Luxembourg, and in not altogether desirable ways. The ready availability of interim relief, together with the presence of long delays in the reference system, serves to benefit litigants who can withstand delay.[132] The victory for them is simply obtaining the reference, as it will preserve their position for a couple of years. They have only to find their legal costs and hope that the position of their opponent weakens.[133] By contrast, in the second scenario, where interim relief is less likely, the applicant's position is greatly prejudiced. She will have to bear all the costs of the Union measure, however onerous, as well as the costs of litigation.

(iii) Managing the circumstances in which national courts refer

The central mechanism for determining when a reference should be made is set out in the distinction between Article 267(2) and 267(3) TFEU. The latter states that courts against whose decision there is no judicial remedy in national law are obliged to refer, where the point of EU law is necessary to decide the dispute in hand. All other courts fall within Article 267(2) TFEU and enjoy a discretion whether to refer. The obligation to refer extends not just to the highest courts in the land but also to any other court, where the party has been denied the possibility to take the matter further because they have been denied leave to appeal to a higher court. In *Lyckeskog*, Lyckeskog was prosecuted for importing rice into Sweden without paying customs duties. He appealed to the Swedish Court of Appeal, arguing that the relevant EU Regulation allowed this where the rice was for personal use. The Swedish Court of Appeal, whose decisions could be appealed to the Swedish Supreme Court, referred the question as to whether it fell within Article 267(3) TFEU for it to refuse Lyckeskog leave to appeal.

Case C-99/00 *Lyckeskog* [2002] ECR I-4839

14. The obligation on national courts against whose decisions there is no judicial remedy to refer a question to the Court for a preliminary ruling has its basis in the cooperation established, in order to ensure the proper application and uniform interpretation of Community law in all the Member States, between national courts, as courts responsible for applying Community law, and the Court. That obligation is in particular designed to prevent a body of national case law that is not in accordance with the rules of Community law from coming into existence in any Member State.

15. That objective is secured when, subject to the limits accepted by the Court of Justice...supreme courts are bound by this obligation to refer...as is any other national court or tribunal against whose decisions there is no judicial remedy under national law...

16. Decisions of a national appellate court which can be challenged by the parties before a supreme court are not decisions of a 'court or tribunal of a Member State against whose decisions there is no judicial remedy under national law' within the meaning of Article [267 TFEU]. The fact that examination of the merits of such appeals is subject to a prior declaration of admissibility by the supreme court does not have the effect of depriving the parties of a judicial remedy.

---

[132] On the difficulties and delays with the current preliminary reference procedure see p. 178.
[133] R. Rawlings, 'The Eurolaw Game: Some Deductions from a Saga' (1993) 20 *Journal of Law and Society* 309.

17. That is so under the Swedish system. The parties always have the right to appeal to the Högsta domstol against the judgment of a hovrätt, which cannot therefore be classified as a court delivering a decision against which there is no judicial remedy. Under Paragraph 10 of Chapter 54 of the Rättegångsbalk, the Högsta domstol may issue a declaration of admissibility if it is important for guidance as to the application of the law that the appeal be examined by that court. Thus, uncertainty as to the interpretation of the law applicable, including Community law, may give rise to review, at last instance, by the supreme court.

18. If a question arises as to the interpretation or validity of a rule of Community law, the supreme court will be under an obligation, pursuant to the third paragraph of Article [267 TFEU], to refer a question to the Court of Justice for a preliminary ruling either at the stage of the examination of admissibility or at a later stage.

Lyckeskog secures the universal jurisdiction of the Court of Justice. In principle, in every case, there should be a point at which individuals are able to demand a reference from a national court because there will be a moment where either leave to appeal is refused or the case is decided by the highest court in the land, and that court falls within Article 267(3) TFEU. Notwithstanding these points, there are drawbacks to such an interpretation, as it prevents national courts stopping proceedings becoming too drawn out, or matters not being referred to the Court of Justice because the sums involved are too small or the case is of very limited importance.

The distinction is not an immutable one, however. There are circumstances both when a lower court against whose decision there is a judicial remedy must refer and when a court against whose decision there is no judicial remedy must not refer.

The former circumstance has already been addressed. All national courts must refer if they consider that an EU measure may be invalid. This derives from the dictates of the uniformity of EU law, which require that EU measures cannot be declared invalid in one national territory in the Union but remain valid elsewhere. Only the Court of Justice has the power, therefore, to declare a Union measure invalid.[134]

By contrast, national courts against whose decision there is no judicial remedy are not compelled to refer if either the doctrine of *acte éclairé* or that of *acte clair* applies. The former allows a court not to refer if a materially identical matter has already been decided by the Court of Justice. The latter states that a question need not be referred if the provision in question is so clear that there is no reasonable doubt about its application.

In *CILFIT*, a group of textile firms challenged levies imposed by the Italian Ministry of Health on wool imported by them from outside the Union. The case centred on whether wool was an animal product as a Regulation prohibited levies imposed on 'animal products'. The dispute went up to the Italian Court of Cassation, the highest civil court in Italy. The Italian Ministry of Health argued that there was no need to make a reference to the Court of Justice as the question of law, namely whether wool is an animal product, was obvious.

---

[134] Case 314/85 *Firma Fotofrost v Hauptzollamt Lübeck-Ost* [1987] ECR 4199.

Case 283/81 *CILFIT* v *Ministry of Health* [1982] ECR 341

13. It must be remembered in this connection that... in Joined Cases 28 to 30/62 *Da Costa* v *Nederlandse Belastingadministratie* [1963] ECR 31 the Court ruled that: 'Although the third paragraph of [Article 267 TFEU] unreservedly requires courts or tribunals of a Member State against whose decision there is no judicial remedy under national law... to refer to the Court every question of interpretation raised before them, the authority of an interpretation under [Article 267 TFEU] already given by the Court may deprive the obligation of its purpose and thus empty it of its substance. Such is the case especially when the question raised is materially identical with a question which has already been the subject of a preliminary ruling in a similar case.'

14. The same effect, as regards the limits set to the obligation laid down by the third paragraph of [Article 267 TFEU], may be produced where previous decisions of the Court have already dealt with the point of law in question, irrespective of the nature of the proceedings which led to those decisions, even though the questions at issue are not strictly identical.

15. However, it must not be forgotten that in all such circumstances national courts and tribunals, including those referred to in paragraph (3) of [Article 267 TFEU], remain entirely at liberty to bring a matter before the Court of Justice if they consider it appropriate to do so.

16. Finally, the correct application of Community law may be so obvious as to leave no scope for any reasonable doubt as to the manner in which the question raised is to be resolved. Before it comes to the conclusion that such is the case, the national court or tribunal must be convinced that the matter is equally obvious to the courts of the other Member States and to the Court of Justice. Only if those conditions are satisfied may the national court or tribunal refrain from submitting the question to the Court of Justice and take upon itself the responsibility for resolving it.

17. However, the existence of such a possibility must be assessed on the basis of the characteristic feature of Community law and the particular difficulties to which its interpretation gives rise.

18. To begin with, it must be borne in mind that Community legislation is drafted in several languages and that the different language versions are equally authentic. An interpretation of a provision of Community law thus involves a comparison of the different language versions.

19. It must also be borne in mind, even where the different language versions are entirely in accord with one another, that Community law uses terminology which is peculiar to it. Furthermore, it must be emphasised that legal concepts do not necessarily have the same meaning in Community law and in the law of the various Member States.

20. Finally, every provision of Community law must be placed in its context and interpreted in the light of the provisions of Community law as a whole, regard being had to the objectives thereof and to its state of evolution at the date on which the provision in question is to be applied.

Read literally, the exception is so narrow so as to be almost meaningless.[135] There will be few national judges who have the capacity to compare the nuances and context of a provision in all languages of the Union.[136] Even the Court of Justice, with all the back-up of its

---

[135] H. Rasmussen, 'The European Court's *Acte Clair* Strategy in CILFIT' (1984) 9 *ELRev.* 242; F. Mancini and D. Keeling, 'From CILFIT to ERT: The Constitutional Challenge Facing the European Court' (1991) 11 *YBEL* 1, 4. For an argument that the exception should therefore be expanded see M. Broberg, '*Acte Clair* Revisited: Adapting the Demands of *Acte Clair* to the Demands of the Times' (2008) 45 *CMLRev.* 1383.

[136] For an attempt to do so see *Cunningham* v *Milk Marketing Board for Northern Ireland* [1988] 3 CMLR 815.

translating services, has struggled to come to terms with the interpretive difficulties posed by the authenticity of all the different language versions of EU law.[137] However, to concentrate on the formal limits of *CILFIT* is to miss its significance. *CILFIT* encourages national courts to decide seemingly non-controversial or technical matters of EU law themselves. To some, this creates a lacuna in judicial protection by providing circumstances where individuals will not have access to the Court of Justice.[138] To others, the doctrine of *acte clair* acts as a valve, defusing potential conflict between the higher national courts and the Court of Justice, by allowing the former to decide matters exclusively by themselves without engaging in any overt act of judicial rebellion.[139]

The practice of many senior national courts is irregular. Whilst the Belgian Constitutional Court has made seventy-one references, the Italian and Portuguese Constitutional Courts have made only one reference each, whilst the French Constitutional Council and German Constitutional Court have never made a reference.[140] However if *CILFIT* grants national courts some leeway for decision-making, it does so in a highly distorted manner. It requires the highest national court to hide behind semantic grounds as a reason for non-referral; that is, that the matter has already been decided or that the provision is so clear that it does not require interpretation. It does not permit national courts to put forward the far stronger reasons for non-referral, namely that there are important national constitutional values at stake that they wish to decide, or that to refer might lead to an abuse of the litigation process with one party needlessly drawing out the process.

Matters changed in *Köbler*.[141] Köbler was an Austrian professor who lost bonuses, to which he would otherwise have been entitled for his length of service in the university sector, because he had spent some years working outside Austria at a German university.[142] The Austrian Administrative Court, a court of last resort, wrongly ruled that this did not breach EU law and that it was not, therefore, obliged to refer. The Court ruled that an action for damages against the state would be available where it was manifestly apparent that a court had failed to comply with its obligations under Article 267(3) TFEU. This would be the case where it was evident that neither the doctrine of *acte clair* nor that of *acte éclairé* applied. In this instance, the Court ruled it was not obviously apparent, as the Austrian court had mistakenly, but in good faith, thought that the matter was covered by a previous ruling of the Court, which had held that the treatment was lawful. It contemplated, therefore, that it fell within the doctrine of *acte éclairé*.

In principle, this adds an incentive for courts to comply with their duties under Article 267 TFEU. National courts falling under Article 267(2) TFEU are as subject to appeal when they fail to apply EU law properly, as when they misapply domestic law. There is financial redress against the state if courts against whose decision there is no judicial remedy fail to refer, where it is obvious that they should. However, the duty might still only be a paper one.[143] The redress

---

[137] For difficulties with the different language versions of EU legislation see Case C-72/95 *Aanemersbedrijf P.K. Kraaijeveld* v *Gedeputeerde Staten van Zuid-Hooland* [1996] ECR I-5403.

[138] A. Arnull, 'Reflections on Judicial Attitudes at the European Court' (1985) 34 *ICLQ* 168, 172; A. Arnull, 'The Use and Abuse of Article 177 EEC' (1989) 52 *MLR* 622, 626.

[139] J. Golub, 'The Politics of Judicial Discretion: Rethinking the Interaction between National Courts and the European Court of Justice' (1996) 19 *WEP* 360, 376–7.

[140] *Annual Report*, above n.11, 104–5.

[141] Case C-224/01 *Köbler* v *Austria* [2003] ECR I-10239.

[142] This case is dealt with in more detail in Chapter 7 at pp. 308–11.

[143] J. Komárek, 'Federal Elements in the Community Judicial System: Building Coherence in the Community Legal System' (2005) 42 *CMLRev.* 9, 12–18.

is against the state, not against the court. It is not clear, short of legislation, what the other arms of government could do to redress a decision of a senior court. The incentives do not, therefore, fall directly on the court in question. Such an action would also require a court of first instance to rule negatively on the actions of the senior court. For it would require a new action to be brought before such a court, demanding that it rule that the latter had acted illegally. It seems implausible that many lower courts would do this.

Köbler is, therefore, more important for what it symbolises. This has been well described by Davies:

> Thus national court interpretations of Community law, while sometimes creative and purposive, take place in a grey area of semi-legitimacy, a sort of tolerated but not approved practice, where the assumption seems to be that ultimately any point of law will in fact make its way to the Court of Justice. Moreover, national final courts will have no interpretive competence at all.[144]

This view is strongly at odds with that of the judges of national courts, who see themselves as responsible for the administration of all law on their territories. Moreover, as a number of commentators have observed, it obstructs the goal of creating a Union court system, in which all courts in the Union identify themselves both as Union and national courts. By denying the contribution of national judges to the development of EU law, it emasculates and infantilises them.[145]

6 THE DOCKET OF THE COURT OF JUSTICE

Over the years, a number of features have emerged which have thwarted realisation of the objectives of the Union court order and throw into question how effectively the preliminary reference is managing it.[146]

Bottlenecking   At the end of 2008, there were 767 cases pending before the Court of Justice with the mean waiting time being 16.8 months. This has come down in recent years, with 840 cases pending and a mean waiting time of 23.5 months in 2004.[147] The reduction is due to very few cases (only 56 references at the end of 2008, for example) coming from the new Member States whilst the Court's capacity has increased with the addition of judges from those states.[148] However, this is, in part, down to long delays in the administration of justice in those states which means EU law cases are only just starting to feed through (there were only 18 references from these states to the end of 2006).

This will lead to a number of consequences. Important cases will get stuck in the queue behind other cases. In terms of the judicial review of the EU institutions, as it is difficult for national courts to grant it, it will lead to illegal EU measures persisting longer than they

---

[144] G. Davies, 'The Division of Powers between the European Court of Justice and National Courts' (2004) 3 *ConWeb* 19.

[145] *Ibid.*; P. Allott, 'Preliminary Rulings: Another Infant Disease' (2000) *ELRev.* 538, 542; H. Rasmussen, 'Remedying the Crumbling EC Judicial System' (2000) 37 *CMLRev.* 1071, 1092.

[146] On the evolution of the system over the years see C. Barnard and E. Sharpston, 'The Changing Face of Article 177 References' (1997) 34 *CMLRev.* 1113; C. Turner and R. Munoz, 'Revising the Judicial Architecture of the European Union' (1999–2000) 19 *YBEL* 1, 1–32.

[147] *Annual Report*, above n.11, 94–5.

[148] *Ibid.* 104–6.

should.[149] Finally, it is unsatisfactory in relation to dispute resolution. For many litigants, the redress simply arrives too late to be of much use to them. For others, conversely, the length of the procedure becomes an advantage. The delay becomes a litigation strategy that can be used to exert undue pressure on the other side.[150]

Legal pollution   The bottlenecking does not occur because the Court of Justice is a lazy court. It gave 333 judgments in 2008.[151] This compares favourably with national supreme courts in Western Europe who typically give considerably fewer than 100 judgments per year. This workload places enormous time and organisational pressures on the Court of Justice. Deadlines are tight, translation services stretched and time for judicial debate and reflection limited.[152]

Expertise   The Court is asked to adjudicate on a startling array of cases. In many other jurisdictions, these tasks would be divided between different courts. As a set of generalists, required to do all of them, it is becoming increasingly difficult for the Court to do any of them well, particularly given the time pressures it is under.

A skewed docket   The delays and contingencies of Article 267 TFEU result in its very rarely being used by litigants who are going to court for compensation. Instead, it is used predominantly by two types of litigant. There are those interested in judicial politics. This litigant is using the courts to bring about legal reform. She is not interested in compensation, but establishing a new legal principle. The second type of litigant is interested in regulatory or fiscal politics. Where large undertakings have ongoing relations with regulatory or fiscal authorities, one of the parties may use litigation to reconfigure the long-term basis for the relationship. Often the challenge is to a relatively small tax or piece of regulation, but the motive is to change the climate in which business is done. A study found that between 1994 and 1998, these two types of litigation accounted for 66.35 per cent of all references from the United Kingdom.[153] The difficulty with this is that it leads to an imbalance. Litigation is predominantly about the overturning of national regimes by discontented constituencies which are, otherwise, too isolated to mobilise change domestically.[154] If the Court accedes to only 10 per cent of these challenges, because of the one-way nature of the case, it comes across as a body consistently opposed to the domestic status quo.

These problems have been endemic for many years and there has been an ongoing debate about how to reform the preliminary reference procedure.[155] Early suggestions focused on

---

[149] See Joined Cases C-46/93 and C-48/93 *Brasserie du Pêcheur/Factortame III* [1996] ECR I-1029, which was referred in early 1993 and only decided three years later.

[150] R. Rawlings, 'The Eurolaw Game: Some Deductions from a Saga' (1993) 20 *Journal of Law and Society* 309.

[151] *Annual Report*, above, n.11, 88.

[152] J. Weiler, 'Epilogue, the Judicial après Nice' in G. de Búrca and J. Weiler (eds.), *The European Court of Justice* (Oxford, Oxford University Press, 2001).

[153] D. Chalmers, *The Much Ado about Judicial Politics*, Jean Monnet Working Paper No. 1/2000, 34, http://centers. law.nyu.edu/jeanmonnet/papers/index.html (accessed 5 November 2009).

[154] K. Alter, *The European Court's Political Power* (Oxford, Oxford University Press, 2009) 176 *et seq.* On the case of women's rights movements in different Member States see R. Cichowski, *The European Court and Civil Society: Litigation, Mobilization and Governance* (Cambridge, Cambridge University Press, 2007) ch. 3.

[155] A. Arnull, 'Refurbishing the Judicial Architecture of the European Community' (1994) 43 *ICLQ* 296; W. v. Gerven, 'The Role of the European Judiciary Now and in the Future' (1996) 21 *ELRev.* 211; D. Scorey, 'A New Model for the Communities' Judicial Architecture in the New Union' (1996) 21 *ELRev.* 224.

either establishing a system of regional courts,[156] which would create a new judicial layer between national courts and the Court of Justice, or developing specialised courts for complex, fact-intensive areas of EU law.[157] Neither of these has found favour.[158] Debate has instead distilled down to two alternatives. One alternative was that national courts decide more cases by themselves.[159] A suggestion was made that national courts submit draft answers with their references. If the Court agrees at an early stage that the draft answer is correct, it would simply state that it did not object to the suggested interpretation.[160] The other is that the Court of Justice decides more by engaging in more efficient case-management.[161] This would involve internal organisation of the Court through increased resort to Chambers, an increase in the jurisdiction of the General Court and an expansion of the translation services.[162] It would also be possible to have a mix of these two approaches.[163]

This was considered in most depth at the Treaty of Nice. A clear preference emerged for the second approach, namely that the problems were to be addressed by efficient management of its docket and internal distribution of its workload by the Court of Justice. This has involved a fourfold strategy.

First, there is only very limited control of references from national courts by the Court of Justice. As we have seen, the Court will not give a ruling if it is quite obvious there is no legal dispute, the factual and legal context to the dispute has not been provided in sufficient detail for the Court to be able to give an answer to the question, or the question referred is clearly not relevant to the dispute.[164] It will also not give a reference where this will undermine the *locus standi* conditions set out in other provisions of the Treaties.[165] It has also been noted, however, that this has led in recent times to very few references being refused. More significant is the rule in Article 104(3) of the Rules of Procedure that allows the Court to make an order referring

---

[156] J.-P. Jacqué and J. Weiler, 'On the Road to European Union, a New Judicial Architecture: An Agenda for the Intergovernmental Conference' (1990) 27 *CMLRev.* 185.

[157] P. Kapteyn, 'The Court of Justice of the European Communities after the Year 2000' in D. Curtin and T. Heukels (eds.), *Institutional Dynamics of European Integration, Liber Amicorum Schermers* (Dordrecht, Martinus Nijhoff, 1994) vol. I, 135, 141–5.

[158] Court of First Instance, 'Reflections on the Future Development of the Community Judicial System' (1991) 16 *ELRev.* 175.

[159] See Advocate General Jacobs in Case C-338/95 *Wiener* v *Hauptzollamt Emmerich* [1997] ECR I-6495.

[160] S. Strasser, *The Development of a Strategy of Docket Control for the European Court of Justice and the Question of Preliminary References*, Jean Monnet Working Paper No. 95/3, http://centers.law.nyu.edu/jeanmonnet/papers/index.html (accessed 5 November 2009).

[161] *Contribution by the Court of Justice and the Court of First Instance to the Intergovernmental Conference* (Luxembourg, Office for Official Publications of the European Communities, 2000). See also the earlier more extensive document issued by the European Court of Justice, above n. 77.

[162] British Institute of International and Comparative Law, *The Role and Future of the Court of Justice* (London, BIICL, 1996) 126–31. This is not unproblematic as the translation unit at the Court faces considerable strains. P. Mullen, 'Do You Hear What I Hear? Translation, Expansion and Crisis in the European Court of Justice' in M. Cowles and M. Smith (eds.), *The State of the European Union, vol. V, Risks, Reform, Resistance and Revival* (Oxford, Oxford University Press, 2000).

[163] *Report by the Working Party on the Future of the European Communities' Court System* (Brussels, European Commission, 2000) (Due Report). For discussion see A. Dashwood and A. Johnston (eds.), *The Future of the Judicial System of the European Union* (Oxford and Portland, Hart, 2001); P. Craig, 'The Jurisdiction of the Community Courts Reconsidered' in G. de Búrca and J. Weiler (eds.), *The European Court of Justice* (Oxford, Oxford University Press, 2001); H. Rasmussen, 'Remedying the Crumbling EC Judicial System' (2000) 37 *CMLRev.* 1071; A. Johnston, 'Judicial Reform and the Treaty of Nice' (2001) 38 *CMLRev.* 499.

[164] See pp. 167–8.

[165] Case C-188/92 *TWD Textilwerke Deggendorf* v *Germany* [1994] ECR I-833.

to its previous case law where the question is identical to one on which it has ruled, may be clearly deduced from existing case law, or where the answer 'admits of no reasonable doubt'. Twenty such orders were given in 2008. They involve only limited time savings, however, as the Court must still hear the Advocate General before making such an order.

Secondly, the central tool for efficient management of the Court is the Chamber system. The Treaty of Nice made provision, as we have seen, for preliminary references to be made to the General Court[166] and also for its possible expansion, as it introduced the provision that it comprise 'at least' one judge from each Member State.[167] There was the possibility of its becoming the central Union court with the Court of Justice only pronouncing on broad principles which affect the unity and consistency of EU law.[168] To date, however, this has not happened. Instead, reliance is placed upon the Chambers system of the Court of Justice. Between 2004 and 2008, 84.4 per cent of cases were heard by Chambers of either three or five judges.[169] This is not a new trend.[170] However, it does result in the Court becoming increasingly fragmented with individual judges acquiring special significance in the judgments upon which they rule. This is particularly concerning when important decisions are taken by Chambers of three judges, as only two judges have to agree for a judgment to be reached.[171]

Thirdly, the Court gives priority to ruling on certain types of case, notably where delay will lead to extremely adverse consequences. It does this by two procedures:

- the 'accelerated procedure': this allows a national court to request from the President of the Court that the matter be put to the Court as a matter of exceptional urgency. In such circumstances, the case will be prioritised and the time limits for observations restricted to not less than fifteen days;[172]
- the 'urgent procedure': this procedure is implicit in the amendment made by the Treaty of Lisbon, now set out in Article 267(4) TFEU, which provides that when a reference is made with regard to a person in custody, the Court shall act with the minimum of delay. It was anticipated by Decision 2008/79.[173] This procedure can either be requested by the national court or decided by the Court of its own motion. It is even more truncated than the accelerated procedure. No minimum time limits for submissions are set. Both the written procedure and the Opinion of the Advocate General can be dispensed with. To date, Opinions of Advocates General given under this procedure have not been published.

The procedures raise a number of different concerns. One of the challenges with the accelerated procedure is the high threshold of 'extreme urgency'. It is rarely used, with only thirty-four applications between 2004 and 2008, of which only two were successful.[174] The concerns

---

[166] Article 256(3) TFEU.

[167] Article 19(2) TEU.

[168] Weiler, above n. 152.

[169] *Annual Report*, above n. 11, 89.

[170] In 1999, for example, 177 out of 235 judgments were given by the Chambers. Statistics of judicial activity of the Court of Justice in 1999, http://curia.europa.eu/jcms/jcms/Jo2_7000 (accessed 12 August 2009).

[171] On concerns as to the effects of the pressures on the organisation of the Court see C. Timmermans, 'The European Union's Judicial System' (2004) 41 *CMLRev.* 393; H. Rasmussen, 'Present and Future European Judicial Problems after Enlargement and the Post-2005 Ideological Revolt' (2007) 44 *CMLRev.* 1661.

[172] It is set out in the Court's Rules of Procedure, article 104a.

[173] [2008] OJ L24/42. The procedure is now incorporated in the Court's Rules of Procedure, article 104b.

[174] *Annual Report*, above n. 11, 97. E. de la Serre, 'Accelerated and Expedited Procedures before the EC Courts: A Review of the Practice' (2006) 43 *CMLRev.* 783.

with regard to the urgent procedure are different. Six applications were made in the ten months of its use in 2008, of which three were successful. All the cases were in the fields of asylum, immigration and criminal law, for which there were twenty-six references in 2008.[175] It may thus apply in about one-quarter of the cases in these fields. These fields are, moreover, likely to take up a significant part of the Court's time following the reforms made by the Lisbon Treaty. There is thus a risk of displacing other important areas of activity. More serious are the procedural short-cuts being taken. Whilst it can be understood that the Court may wish to dispense with written submissions, the desire to dispense with an Advocate General's Opinion leads to concerns about what space there is for reflection here. And, put simply, the decision not to publish it cannot be justified on any basis whatsoever.

The jury is still out on whether these changes will reduce the current delays. In 1999, with fifteen judges, the Court gave 234 judgments. In 2008, with twenty-seven judges, it gave 333 judgments: a lower ratio of judgments per judge. Looked at from the point of view of number of cases per judge, they seem to be offering only modest efficiency gains, therefore. If the preliminary references were to increase, either because of more references from the new Member States or because of the increased jurisdiction of the Court, then it is clear that the problem of delay will be exacerbated. If the problem is not one merely of delay, but of a structural imbalance in the type of litigation arriving at the Court, then deciding more cases is likely to exacerbate existing problems. Resolution of more cases involving an ever more eclectic array of issues is likely both to stretch the Court's expertise and to dilute its capacity to act as a constitutional court. More generally, there are real concerns about the orderly development of EU law, where there is a single court rushing out around 400 judgments per year under increasingly tight deadlines. The potential for error and self-contradiction is considerable, and it will be increasingly difficult for national legal systems to keep up with and reflect on that amount of case law.

The refusal to countenance national courts making fewer references, as the article by Komárek sets out, also suggests a poorly articulated vision of the EU judicial order. It suggests that the Court of Justice should decide on everything that matters, and that virtually everything matters. It also suggests a vision where the preliminary reference procedure does not facilitate dispute resolution, but is the process at the centre of the dispute. Finally, in letting applicants force a reference, it contains a view of national courts as either incompetent or untrustworthy.

J. Komárek, 'In the Court(s) We Trust? On the Need for Hierarchy and Differentiation in the Preliminary Ruling Procedure' (2007) 32 *European Law Review* 467, 476

The attempt to attach fundamental status to every provision of EU law is contradicting the premise that EU law has become part of national law. If it has, then EU law can no longer be treated as 'supranational' law having some special force in each instance, rather must the weight of its rules reflect their actual nature.

Preliminary ruling procedure must be seen as a deviation from normal organisation of the judicial process, not as its natural component. This is because it allows obviating the existing hierarchy amongst the courts, which plays an important role in the rationalisation of the judicial process, and delays final

---

[175] *Annual Report*, above n. 11, 98 and 84 respectively.

resolution of the dispute, thus potentially bringing an element of injustice. Again, it is a question of how we want to see the EU judicial system: whether it really comprises national courts *as* European courts, or whether we use this label only for highlighting their obligations resulting from EU law. If we see it in the former sense, then we must accept that it means to see the EU judiciary as a judicial system without qualifications. Nice labels may only hide some (of course hard) choices we must inevitably make when we perceive national courts as 'Community courts of general jurisdiction'—thus fully competent to decide questions concerning interpretation of EU law. Insisting on all courts' possibility to refer to the Court of Justice questions their competence to give effective protection to individuals without the Court of Justice's assistance. At the same time, it implies that the Court should be involved in an everyday dispute settlement whenever a question of Community law arises, regardless of its importance for the EU legal system as a whole. The result is an unreasonable distribution of the Court of Justice's judicial capacity throughout the Union judicial system.

FURTHER READING

K. Alter, *The European Court's Political Power* (Oxford, Oxford University Press, 2009)

D. Anderson and M. Demetriou, *References to the European Court* (London, Sweet & Maxwell, 2002)

G. de Búrca and J. Weiler (eds.), *The European Court of Justice* (Oxford, Oxford University Press, 2001)

D. Chalmers, 'The Court of Justice and the Constitutional Treaty' (2005) 4 *ICON* 428

R. Cichowski, *The European Court and Civil Society: Litigation, Mobilization and Governance* (Cambridge, Cambridge University Press, 2007)

A. Dashwood and A. Johnston (eds.), *The Future of the Judicial System of the European Union* (Oxford and Portland, Hart, 2001)

J.-P. Jacqué and J. Weiler, 'On the Road to European Union, a New Judicial Architecture: An Agenda for the Intergovernmental Conference' (1990) 27 *Common Market Law Review* 185

J. Komárek, 'Federal Elements in the Community Judicial System: Building Coherence in the Community Legal System' (2005) 42 *Common Market Law Review* 9

H. Rasmussen, 'Remedying the Crumbling EC Judicial System' (2000) 37 *Common Market Law Review* 1071

R. Rawlings, 'The Eurolaw Game: Some Deductions from a Saga' (1993) 20 *Journal of Law and Society* 309

T. Tridimas, 'Knocking on Heaven's Door: Fragmentation, Efficiency and Defiance in the Preliminary Reference Procedure' (2003) 40 *Common Market Law Review* 9

C. Turner and R. Munoz, 'Revising the Judicial Architecture of the European Union' (1999–2000) 19 *Yearbook of European Law* 1

5

The Authority of EU Law

CONTENTS

1 INTRODUCTION

This chapter considers the authority of EU law. It is organised as follows.

Section 2 considers the claims by the Court of Justice that sovereignty is vested in the Treaties. This places ultimate legal authority in the Treaties and makes the Court of Justice the ultimate arbiter on the meaning and consequences of this authority. This has been given limited recognition by the national governments in a Declaration attached to the Treaty of Lisbon.

Section 3 considers the implications of these claims not being fully accepted by any national constitutional court. Whilst willing to grant the Treaties significant legal authority, all see their domestic constitutions, or some part of them, as sovereign. The authority of EU law rests, therefore, in the extent to which the claims of the Court of Justice are accepted by national constitutional courts and the principles on which the latter accept it. Instead of discussing sovereignty in abstract terms of whether EU law or domestic law is sovereign, it makes better sense to consider the extent to which the four different doctrines emanating from the sovereignty of EU law have been accepted.

Section 4 considers the first of these doctrines: the precedence of EU law over all national law, including national constitutions. There is almost no instance of a national constitutional court explicitly giving priority to a national law over EU law.

Section 5 considers the second doctrine: that EU law alone should determine the quality of legal authority of different norms. In particular, it is the claim of the Court of Justice that it should determine when there is a conflict between EU law and national law and what the consequences are of such a conflict. EU law sets out three different types of relationship between Member States and the European Union: exclusive competences, shared competences, and fields in which EU law cannot exclude national legislatures from law-making. These different models give rise to differing models of integration with differing scope for EU intervention.

Section 6 considers the third doctrine, namely that EU law can determine the remit of its own authority and the activities it governs. This is contained in the doctrine of conferred powers which states, first, that only EU law can determine the limits of EU law and, secondly, that the power of the Union is to be limited and contained. The latter has been challenged by the breadth of some of the provisions of the Treaties, notably the flexibility provision, Article 352 TFEU. This doctrine has been challenged by the constitutional courts of the Member States.

Section 7 considers the fourth doctrine, the fidelity principle, set out in Article 4(3) TEU. This sets out institutional duties on actors to ensure that the Union legal system functions effectively, such as requiring Member States not to obstruct EU policies. These institutional duties have been accepted by national constitutional courts subject to their not violating domestic constitutional constraints.

2 SOVEREIGNTY OF EU LAW

(i) The sovereign claims of EU law

Within standard conceptions of international law, states remain sovereign. They may have to exercise their sovereignty subject to the international treaty obligations they have created, but the domestic legal effects of any such obligations will be a matter for the national legal orders of each state to determine:

> in the context of the internal structure of a political society, the concept of sovereignty has involved the belief that there is an absolute power within the community. Applied to problems which arise in the relations between political communities, its function has been to express the antithesis of this argument – the principle that internationally, over and above the collection of communities, no supreme authority exists.[1]

In the 1950s, it was widely assumed that this, the traditional model of international law, would apply to the European Communities. Under this model, it is the states which are masters

---

[1] F. Hinsley, *Sovereignty* (Cambridge, Cambridge University Press, 1986) 158.

of the treaties and not the other way around. This means that, collectively, states were thought to be able to change the European Communities' powers, interpret their effects or even extinguish them if they so desired. Such a model would also have meant that the European Communities could not trump states' domestic, sovereign legal processes.[2]

This model was dramatically overturned by two judgments of the Court of Justice in the early 1960s that have been the starting point ever since in debates about the legal authority of EU law. First, the Court ruled in *Van Gend en Loos* that the EC Treaty did not merely regulate mutual obligations between Member States, but established what the Court called a 'new legal order of international law for the benefit of which the states have limited their sovereign rights'.[3] This was taken further in *Costa* v *ENEL*, decided shortly afterwards. An Italian law sought to nationalise the electricity production and distribution industries. Costa, a shareholder of Edison Volta, a company affected by the nationalisation, claimed that the law breached EC law. The Italian government claimed that the matter was one of Italian law as the Italian legislation post-dated the EC Treaty and, for that reason, should be held to be the applicable law.

Case 6/64 *Costa* v *ENEL* [1964] ECR 585

By contrast with ordinary international treaties, the EEC Treaty has created its own legal system which, on the entry into force of the Treaty, became an integral part of the legal systems of the Member States and which their courts are bound to apply.

By creating a Community of unlimited duration, having its own institutions, its own personality, its own legal capacity and capacity of representation on the international plane and, more particularly, real powers stemming from a limitation of sovereignty or a transfer of powers from the States to the Community, the Member States have limited their sovereign rights, albeit within limited fields, and have thus created a body of law which binds both their nationals and themselves.

The integration into the laws of each Member State of provisions which derive from the Community, and more generally the terms and the spirit of the Treaty, make it impossible for the States, as a corollary, to accord precedence to a unilateral and subsequent measure over a legal system accepted by them on a basis of reciprocity. Such a measure cannot therefore be inconsistent with that legal system. The executive force of Community law cannot vary from one State to another in deference to subsequent domestic laws, without jeopardizing the attainment of the objectives of the Treaty set out in Article [4(3) TEU] and giving rise to the discrimination prohibited by Article [18 TFEU].

The obligations undertaken under the Treaty establishing the Community would not be unconditional, but merely contingent, if they could be called in question by subsequent legislative acts of the signatories. Wherever the Treaty grants the States the right to act unilaterally, it does this by clear and precise provisions...Applications by Member States for authority to derogate from the Treaty are subject to a special authorization procedure... which would lose their purpose if the Member States could renounce their obligations by means of an ordinary law.

---

[2] See J. Weiler and U. Haltern 'The Autonomy of the Community Legal Order: Through the Looking Glass' (1996) 37 *Harvard Int'l LJ* 411, 417–19.

[3] Case 26/62 *Van Gend en Loos* v *Nederlandse Administratie der Belastingen* [1963] ECR 1. *Van Gend en Loos* is considered in more detail in Chapters 1 and 7.

The precedence of Community law is confirmed by Article [288 TFEU], whereby a regulation 'shall be binding' and 'directly applicable in all Member States'. This provision, which is subject to no reservation, would be quite meaningless if a state could unilaterally nullify its effects by means of a legislative measure which could prevail over Community law. It follows from all these observations that the law stemming from the Treaty, an independent source of law, could not, because of its special and original nature, be overridden by domestic legal provisions, however framed, without being deprived of its character as Community law and without the legal basis of the Community itself being called into question.

The transfer by the States from their domestic legal system to the Community legal system of the rights and obligations arising under the Treaty carries with it a permanent limitation of their sovereign rights, against which a subsequent unilateral act incompatible with the concept of the Community cannot prevail.

It would be difficult to overstate the radicalism of *Costa*. The claim that EU law enjoys some form of sovereignty means that the Union's legal power cannot be seen as deriving from the Member States, but must be understood instead as being autonomous and original. Not only is this absolute authority vested in the legal power of the Union. Everything – other laws and activities covered by EU law – takes subject to it. In short, it sets the legal framework for everything else around it. This is all very well, but these claims to sovereignty are just that: claims to legal authority. Legal authority rests, however, upon a relationship, in which the level of authority is accepted not just by the party seeking it but also by the parties subject to it.

The claims of the Court of Justice must be examined critically; not simply because they may be undesirable but also because they may represent only a partial statement of the authority of EU law. *Costa* may suggest a hierarchy of laws but these '[are] not rooted in a hierarchy of normative authority or in a hierarchy of real power'.[4] 'Real power' in the Union remains firmly with the national administrations. The execution or administration of EU law is overwhelmingly a matter for domestic authorities and national governments within Member States. Administrative actors are central to securing not just enforcement but also popular awareness and acceptance of the authority of EU law. In this regard, they were silent for forty years. This could be seen as tacit acceptance but it could also be seen as a lack of active support. A survey found that only in Luxembourg was there more awareness of the Court than of any of the other EU institutions.[5] It also found very little diffuse support for the Court so that citizens would support it even where they disagreed with its decisions. In Denmark, for example, such support was as low as 9.3 per cent in the early 1990s.[6]

---

[4] J. Weiler, 'Federalism Without Constitutionalism: Europe's Sonderweg' in K. Nicolaidis and R. Howse (eds.), *The Federal Vision: Legitimacy and Levels of Governance in the United States and the European Union* (Oxford, Oxford University Press, 2000) 57.

[5] On judicial politics see K. Alter, 'The European Union's Legal System and Domestic Policy: Spillover or Backlash?' (2000) 54 *International Organisation* 489; K. Alter and J. Vargas, 'Explaining Variation in the Use of European Litigation Strategies: European Community Law and British Gender Equality Policy' (2000) 33 *Comparative Political Studies* 452.

[6] J. Gibson and G. Caldeira, 'Challenges to the Legitimacy of the European Court of Justice: A Post Maastricht Analysis' (1998) 28 *British Journal of Political Science* 63.

This was initially addressed by the Constitutional Treaty. Article I-13 provided that within the competences conferred upon the Union, EU law would have primacy over the laws of the Member States. Following the failure of the Constitutional Treaty, this provision was seen as expressing too much political enthusiasm for the principle. Instead, at Lisbon, a Declaration was attached to the Treaties.

Declaration 17

The Conference recalls that, in accordance with well settled case law of the Court of Justice of the European Union, the Treaties and the law adopted by the Union on the basis of the Treaties have primacy over the law of Member States, under the conditions laid down by the said case law.

An Opinion of the Council Legal Service was also attached, which provides only sparse information.

Opinion of the Council Legal Service, EU Council Doc. 11197/07, 22 June 2007

It results from the case law of the Court of Justice that primacy of EC law is a cornerstone principle of Community law. According to the Court, this principle is inherent to the specific nature of the European Community. At the time of the first judgment of this established case law (Costa/ENEL, 15 July 1964, Case 6/64) there was no mention of primacy in the treaty. It is still the case today. The fact that the principle of primacy will not be included in the future treaty shall not in any way change the existence of the principle and the existing case law of the Court of Justice.

A minimalist interpretation is that these documents provide a reassurance of continuity that the tradition of primacy established since *Costa* is uninterrupted.[7] A more vigorous interpretation would note that this is the first time that the *Costa* case law has been explicitly endorsed and ratified by all Member States. Such ratification perhaps not only gives the interpretation greater legitimacy, but indicates that the primacy of EU law can no longer be relegated to merely being the view of the Court of Justice. Instead, primacy now represents the political consensus as to the status of EU law. Account will have to be taken of this political vindication by all courts within the Union when they apply the principle in future. If a national constitutional court were to deny the primacy of EU law, it would correspondingly be placing itself in an institutionally isolated position.

(ii) Sovereignty of EU law and domestic constitutional settlements

If the reception of the Court of Justice's case law by national administrations was important, the position of the national constitutional or senior courts was critical. This is because all Member States commit themselves to the rule of law. This commitment carries with it two

---

[7] Case 6/64 *Costa* v *ENEL* [1964] ECR 585.

requirements: first, the requirement that all be governed by the law of the land; and secondly, that this law will be determined authoritatively by an independent judicial system at the top of which sits a constitutional or senior court, whose judgments are binding on all actors, judicial and non-judicial, within their jurisdiction. This court has the last word, therefore, on who has legal authority, the extent of that authority and its consequences for the relevant Member State.

The formal authority of EU law is predominantly governed therefore by the relationship between the Court of Justice and national constitutional courts.[8] In particular, it will be settled by the nature of the claims made by the Court of Justice and the extent to which these are accepted by national constitutional courts. One of the most striking features of the EU legal system is that, despite being the ostensible guardians of their respective *national* constitutional settlements, these national constitutional courts have been generally willing to grant EU law a variant of the authority sought by the Court of Justice that is sufficiently proximate for the EU legal order to work closely along the lines suggested by the latter almost all the time.

B. de Witte, 'Direct Effect, Supremacy, and the Nature of the Legal Order' in P. Craig and G. de Búrca (eds.), *The Evolution of EU Law* (Oxford, Oxford University Press, 1999) 196–8

Among the original Six, no special efforts were required from the courts in the Netherlands and Luxembourg, where the supremacy of international treaty provisions over national legislation was accepted prior to 1957. Of the other four countries, the courts in Belgium reacted most promptly and loyally to the European Court's injunctions. A model of what national courts can achieve in the absence of clear constitutional guidelines is the 1971 judgment of the Belgian Cour de Cassation in the *Franco-Suisse Le Ski case*. Although the Belgian Constitution was silent on the domestic effect of international or European law (or precisely because of this absence of written rules) the Supreme Court adopted the principle of primacy as it had been formulated in *Costa*, and based on the nature of international law and (a fortiori) of EC law. The other Belgian courts soon followed the same line. In France, although the text of Article 55 of the Constitution recognised the priority of international treaties even over later French laws, the courts were surprisingly slow to accept that this constitutional provision could actually be used as a conflict rule in real cases and controversies. The Cour de Cassation taking the lead of all ordinary courts decided to cross the Rubicon in the 1975 *Cafés Jacques Vabre* judgment. The Conseil d'Etat (and the administrative courts subject to its authority) followed suit much later with the *Nicolo* decision (1989), after what must have been a very painful revision of established truths. One may note that one of the arguments used by the *commissaire* Frydman, when advising the Conseil in *Nicolo* to change its views on the supremacy of EC law, was that the supreme courts of surrounding countries (even those with ingrained dualist traditions) had long recognised this supremacy.

In Italy and Germany, the actual duties imposed on national courts by *Costa* went well beyond what the mainstream constitutional doctrine, at that time, was prepared to accept in terms of the domestic

---

[8] The literature is voluminous. The two best studies on the positions of the constitutional courts across the Union are M. Claes, *The National Courts' Mandate in the European Constitution* (Oxford and Portland, Hart, 2005); A. Albi, *EU Enlargement and the Constitutions of Central and Eastern Europe* (Cambridge, Cambridge University Press, 2005).

force of international treaty law. Yet the European Court suggested, by cleverly distinguishing EEC law from 'ordinary' international law, that the German and Italian courts might, with some creativity, find the constitutional resources needed for recognising the primacy of Community law. The message, in *Costa*, was primarily addressed to the Italian Constitutional Court. This court has gradually come to recognise the supremacy of Community law over national legislation, on the basis of its special nature which distinguishes it from other international treaties. A similar evolution took place in Germany...

Greece and Ireland, when they joined, had put their constitutions in order. Article 28 of the Greek Constitution, adopted prior to accession, recognises the primacy of international conventions over any national legislation. In Ireland, given the inability of the dualist constitutional tradition to cope with the demands of membership, a special EC clause was added to the Constitution (and adapted to later Treaty revisions) vouchsafing the direct effect and primacy of Community law.

In the United Kingdom, the supremacy question floated around for many years, until the *Factortame II* judgment, where the House of Lords for the first time disapplied a later Act of Parliament for being inconsistent with the EEC Treaty...

So, by and large, 'ordinary' supremacy of Community law, that is, supremacy over national legislation and sources of national law lower in rank than legislation, seems to be accepted in most Member States (primacy over national constitutional law is quite another matter...). But there are lingering doubts, even concerning 'ordinary' supremacy, in a long-standing Member State like Denmark. That country's constitution contains no rules on the relation between Community law and national law, and the doctrine of the primacy of EC law has never been expressly accepted by the courts. Indeed, it seems that there has not been, in the twenty-five years of Danish membership, a single court case involving a conflict between EC law and a later Danish Act of Parliament.

It has also been facilitated for almost all national courts to find their own ways of accepting the authority of EU law on terms and conditions drawn from their national constitutional settlements. Three broad approaches have emerged. These approaches may be called 'European constitutional sovereignty', 'national constitutional sovereignty' and 'constitutional tolerance'. Of these, it is the third which has been most widely adopted.

(a) European constitutional sovereignty

European constitutional sovereignty is where a constitutional court of a Member State unconditionally accepts the standpoint of the Court of Justice. This has the consequence that EU law is seen as being supreme, even over the national constitution. This position has not been taken by any national constitutional court. The closest is that of the Estonian Supreme Court. Prior to Estonia joining the European Union in 2004, a referendum was held approving an Amendment Act to the Estonian Constitution. Article 2 of this Act states that the Constitution applies taking account of obligations under EU law, suggesting the latter has precedence. The Constitutional Chamber of the Estonian Supreme Court was asked to interpret this provision in a case concerning the constitutional compatibility of Estonia joining the euro. Under Article 111 of the Estonian Constitution, only the Estonian Central Bank has the right to issue currency in Estonia. The Supreme Court held that Estonia was entitled to join the euro-zone, as the Treaties take precedence over its constitution.

Opinion on the Interpretation of the Constitution No. 3-4-1-3-06, Opinion of 11 May 2006[9]

15. Pursuant to § 2 of the Constitution of the Republic of Estonia Amendment Act the Constitution applies taking account of the rights and obligations arising from the Accession Treaty. As a result of the adoption of the Constitution of the Republic of Estonia Amendment Act the European Union law became one of the grounds for the interpretation and application of the Constitution.

16. In the substantive sense this amounted to a material amendment of the entirety of the Constitution to the extent that it is not compatible with the European Union law. To find out which part of the Constitution is applicable, it has to be interpreted in conjunction with the European Union law, which became binding for Estonia through the Accession Treaty. At that, only that part of the Constitution is applicable, which is in conformity with the European Union law or which regulates the relationships that are not regulated by the European Union law. The effect of those provisions of the Constitution that are not compatible with the European Union law and thus inapplicable, is suspended. This means that within the spheres, which are within the exclusive competence of the European Union or where there is a shared competence with the European Union, the European Union law shall apply in the case of a conflict between Estonian legislation, including the Constitution, with the European Union law.

It is unsurprising that this approach has attracted so little support. It involves a constitutional court writing itself out of a job, as it surrenders its powers of judgment to the Court of Justice. Leaving aside the centralisation of power this involves, such a surrender sweeps aside all the checks and balances that constitutional courts are established to secure. The Estonian example is interesting, furthermore, because the acceptance of the Court of Justice's reasoning is not as unconditional as might appear. The Amendment Act granting EU law its authority over the constitution also has a defence provision, Article 1, which states that Estonia may only belong to the European Union in accordance with the 'fundamental principles of the Constitution of Estonia'.[10] EU law must take subject to certain constitutional provisions, which are seen as having a higher status. These are taken to include fundamental rights and retention of core competences for the Estonian state.[11] If this is so, the Estonian position is not so far from that of the courts which practise the notion of constitutional tolerance discussed below.

(b) Unconditional national constitutional sovereignty

National constitutional sovereignty is the opposite of European constitutional sovereignty. It insists upon the continuing and unconditional sovereignty of the national constitutional order. Whilst acknowledging that EU law may make special claims for itself, it denies that EU law is any different from other form of international law.

---

[9] See www.nc.ee/?id=663 (accessed 20 August 2009).

[10] The Act is available at http://proyectos.cchs.csic.es/europeconstitution/content/estonia-constitutional-provisions (accessed 20 August 2009).

[11] On Estonian judicial practice see J. Laffranque and R. D'Sa, 'Getting to Know You: The Developing Relationship between National Courts of the "Newer" Member States and the European Court of Justice, with particular reference to Estonia' (2008) 19 *European Business Law Review* 311.

Polish Membership of the European Union (Accession Treaty), Polish Constitutional Court, Judgment K18/04 of 11 May 2005

6. It is insufficiently justified to assert that the Communities and the European Union are 'supranational organisations' – a category that the Polish Constitution, referring solely to an 'international organisation', fails to envisage. The Accession Treaty was concluded between the existing Member States of the Communities and the European Union and applicant States, including Poland. It has the features of an international agreement, within the meaning of Article 90(1) of the Constitution. The Member States remain sovereign entities – parties to the founding treaties of the Communities and the European Union. They also, independently and in accordance with their constitutions, ratify concluded treaties and have the right to denounce them under the procedure and on the conditions laid down in the Vienna Convention on the Law of Treaties 1969. The expression 'supranational organisation' is not mentioned in the Accession Treaty, nor in the Acts constituting an integral part thereof or any provisions of secondary Community law.

7. Article 90(1) of the Constitution authorises the delegation of competences of State organs only 'in relation to certain matters'. This implies a prohibition on the delegation of all competences of a State authority organ or competences determining its substantial scope of activity, or competences concerning the entirety of matters within a certain field.

8. Neither Article 90(1) nor Article 91(3) authorise delegation to an international organisation of the competence to issue legal acts or take decisions contrary to the Constitution, being the 'supreme law of the Republic of Poland' (Article 8(1)). Concomitantly, these provisions do not authorise the delegation of competences to such an extent that it would signify the inability of the Republic of Poland to continue functioning as a sovereign and democratic State.

9. From an axiological perspective of the Polish Constitution, the constitutional review of delegating certain competences should take into account the fact that, in the Preamble of the Constitution, emphasising the significance of Poland having reacquired the possibility to determine her fate in a sovereign and democratic manner, the constitutional legislator declares, concomitantly, the need for 'cooperation with all countries for the good of a Human Family', observance of the obligation of 'solidarity with others' and universal values, such as truth and justice. This duty refers not only to internal but also to external relations.

10. The regulation contained in Article 8(1) of the Constitution, which states that the Constitution is the 'supreme law of the Republic of Poland', is accompanied by the requirement to respect and be sympathetically predisposed towards appropriately shaped regulations of international law binding upon the Republic of Poland (Article 9). Accordingly, the Constitution assumes that, within the territory of the Republic of Poland – in addition to norms adopted by the national legislator – there operate regulations created outside the framework of national legislative organs.

11. Given its supreme legal force (Article 8(1)), the Constitution enjoys precedence of binding force and precedence of application within the territory of the Republic of Poland. The precedence over statutes of the application of international agreements which were ratified on the basis of a statutory authorisation or consent granted (in accordance with Article 90(3)) via the procedure of a nationwide referendum, as guaranteed by Article 91(2) of the Constitution, in no way signifies an analogous precedence of these agreements over the Constitution.

12. The concept and model of European law created a new situation, wherein, within each Member State, autonomous legal orders co-exist and are simultaneously operative. Their interaction may not be completely described by the traditional concepts of monism and dualism regarding the relationship

between domestic law and international law. The existence of the relative autonomy of both, national and Community, legal orders in no way signifies an absence of interaction between them. Furthermore, it does not exclude the possibility of a collision between regulations of Community law and the Constitution.

13. Such a collision would occur in the event that an irreconcilable inconsistency appeared between a constitutional norm and a Community norm, such as could not be eliminated by means of applying an interpretation which respects the mutual autonomy of European law and national law. Such a collision may in no event be resolved by assuming the supremacy of a Community norm over a constitutional norm. Furthermore, it may not lead to the situation whereby a constitutional norm loses its binding force and is substituted by a Community norm, nor may it lead to an application of the constitutional norm restricted to areas beyond the scope of Community law regulation. In such an event the Nation as the sovereign, or a State authority organ authorised by the Constitution to represent the Nation, would need to decide on: amending the Constitution; or causing modifications within Community provisions; or, ultimately, on Poland's withdrawal from the European Union.

14. The principle of interpreting domestic law in a manner 'sympathetic to European law'...has its limits. In no event may it lead to results contradicting the explicit wording of constitutional norms or being irreconcilable with the minimum guarantee functions realised by the Constitution. In particular, the norms of the Constitution within the field of individual rights and freedoms indicate a minimum and unsurpassable threshold which may not be lowered or questioned as a result of the introduction of Community provisions.

Unconditional national constitutional sovereignty emphasises national self-determination and the need to put in place an active system of constitutional checks and balances on the development of EU law. It has only been adopted by Poland.[12] This is, in part, because unconditional national constitutional sovereignty inaccurately describes institutional practice. It is not simply that the Court of Justice has developed the filaments of a new constitutional order in its case law; it is that these doctrines have been applied, albeit pragmatically, by the overwhelming majority of national courts. To describe EU law as merely another form of international law is to dismiss not merely the views of the Court of Justice, but those of the broader Union judicial community.[13]

It is also a normatively contentious position, as it privileges the idea of the state unquestioningly. If a state began adopting, for example, racist legislation that conflicted with EU law, would this be right and would it equally be able still to claim membership of the Union legal order? It might be able to affirm national legal sovereignty but only at the expense of leaving the EU legal order.

As with the Estonian Supreme Court, the Polish Constitutional Court's judgment is, moreover, not such a strong statement of European or national sovereignty. For the judgment can

---

[12] For discussion see K. Kowalik-Bańczyk, 'Should We Polish It Up? The Polish Constitutional Tribunal and the Idea of Supremacy of EU Law' (2005) 6 *German Law Journal* 1355; W. Sadurski, '"Solange, Chapter 3": Constitutional Courts in Central Europe – Democracy – European Union' (2008) 14 *ELJ* 1, 18 *et seq.*

[13] Weiler and Haltern, above n. 2, 420–3; N. Walker, 'The Idea of Constitutional Pluralism' (2002) 65 *MLR* 317, 321–3.

read as a statement of cosmopolitan values, as it privileges all international law, including EU law, above all domestic law other than the Constitution.[14] Turned around, it accepts the primacy of EU law subject to constitutional courts (like all other national constitutional courts) and subject to its respecting international law: something which the Treaties commit the Union to do.[15] As such, albeit by a slightly different form of reasoning, it parallels the reasoning of constitutional tolerance set out below.

(c) Constitutional tolerance

The third approach is that of constitutional tolerance. This posits that while the authority and reach of EU law is ultimately for national constitutional courts to decide, these courts commit themselves to recognise the special status of EU law. However, they do so on the condition that it does not violate certain constraints of national constitutional law. Of the three approaches available to national constitutional courts, this is the position that has (thus far) been most frequently taken. This approach covers a spectrum of positions, and examples can be found, inter alia, in Denmark, Belgium, Italy, France, Czech Republic, United Kingdom and Slovenia.[16] The position of the German Constitutional Court is perhaps pre-eminent in formulating the meaning of constitutional tolerance. Articulated first in *Brunner*, a challenge to the Maastricht Treaty by a German Law Professor,[17] its most recent authoritative restatement was the judgment on the compatibility of the Lisbon Treaty with the German Basic Law.

The challenge was brought by a number of prominent parties, amongst which was Die Linke, a parliamentary group within the Bundestag (the German Parliament). The challenge focused on a number of articles of the Basic Law. It argued in the first place that there was a violation of the right to vote for members of the Bundestag, set out in Article 38, on the grounds that excessive powers had been transferred to the European Union from the Bundestag. This right to participate in representative democracy was also argued to be based on two further articles, Article 1(1) on the right to human dignity, and Article 20(2), which indicates that state authority emanates from the people and is exercised by them by means of elections and voting. This was important, as Article 79(3), the constitutional identity provision, stipulates that these two latter articles are inviolable and are not amendable. The last provision over which there was debate was Article 23(2), which provides inter alia that the German Federation will consent to such limitations upon its sovereign powers as will bring about and secure a peaceful and lasting order in Europe. The claimants claimed this provision was subject to the constraints placed on it by the other provisions.

---

[14] This has been explicitly stated by the Tribunal: Pl. 37/05 *Conformity of a Polish Statute with EU Law*, Judgment of 19 December 2006.

[15] Article 3(5) TEU.

[16] See *Carlsen* v *Rasmussen* [1999] 3 CMLR 854 (Denmark); Case 12/94, B6 *Ecole Européenne*, CA, 3 February 1994 (Belgium); *Admenta and Others* v *Federfarma* [2006] 2 CMLR 47 (Italy); Cahiers du Conseil Constitutionnel No. 17, 2004, www.conseil-constitutionnel.fr/cahiers/ (France); *R* v *MAFF, ex parte First City Trading* [1997] 1 CMLR 250 (United Kingdom); U-1-113/04 *Rules on the Quality Labelling and Packaging of Feeding Stuffs*, Judgment of 7 February 2007 (Slovenia); Pl ÚS 50/04 *Sugar Quota Regulation II*, Judgment of 8 March 2006, http://angl.concourt.cz/angl_verze/doc/p-50-04.php (accessed 22 August 2009) (Czech Republic).

[17] *Brunner* v *European Union* [1994] 1 CMLR 57.

2 BvE 2/08 *Gauweiler* v *Treaty of Lisbon*, Judgment of 30 June 2009

210. The right to vote is the citizens' most important individually assertable right to democratic participation guaranteed by the Basic Law. In the state system that is shaped by the Basic Law, the election of the Members of the German Bundestag is of major importance. Without the free and equal election of the body that has a decisive influence on the government and the legislation of the Federation, the mandatory principle of personal freedom remains incomplete. Invoking the right to vote, the citizen can therefore challenge the violation of democratic principles by means of a constitutional complaint (Article 38.1 sentence 1, Article 20.1 and 20.2 of the Basic Law). The right to equal participation in democratic self-determination (democratic right of participation), to which every citizen is entitled, can also be violated by the organisation of state authority being changed in such a way that the will of the people can no longer effectively form within the meaning of Article 20.2 of the Basic Law and the citizens cannot rule according to the will of a majority. The principle of the representative rule of the people can be violated if in the structure of bodies established by the Basic Law, the rights of the Bundestag are essentially curtailed and thus a loss of substance of the democratic freedom of action of the constitutional body occurs which has directly come into being according to the principles of free and equal election…

211. The citizens' right to determine, in equality and freedom, public authority with regard to persons and subject-matters through elections and other votes is the fundamental element of the principle of democracy. The right to free and equal participation in public authority is anchored in human dignity (Article 1.1 of the Basic Law). It belongs to the principles of German constitutional law that are laid down as non-amendable by Article 20.1 and 20.2 of the Basic Law in conjunction with Article 79.3 of the Basic Law…

218. From the perspective of the principle of democracy, the violation of the constitutional identity codified in Article 79.3 of the Basic Law is at the same time an infringement of the constituent power of the people. In this respect, the constituent power has not granted the representatives and bodies of the people a mandate to dispose of the identity of the constitution. No constitutional body has been accorded the competence to amend the constitutional principles which are essential pursuant to Article 79.3 of the Basic Law. The Federal Constitutional Court watches over this. With what is known as the eternity guarantee, the Basic Law reacts on the one hand to the historical experience of the free substance of a democratic fundamental order being slowly or abruptly undermined. However, it makes clear as well that the Constitution of the Germans, in correspondence with the international development which has taken place in particular since the existence of the United Nations, has a universal foundation which is not supposed to be amendable by positive law…

225. The constitutional mandate to realise a united Europe, which follows from Article 23.1 of the Basic Law and its Preamble…means in particular for the German constitutional bodies that it is not left to their political discretion whether or not they participate in European integration. The Basic Law wants European integration and an international peaceful order. Therefore not only the principle of openness towards international law, but also the principle of openness towards European law applies.

226. It is true that the Basic Law grants the legislature powers to engage in a far-reaching transfer of sovereign powers to the European Union. However, the powers are granted under the condition that the sovereign statehood of a constitutional state is maintained on the basis of an integration programme according to the principle of conferral and respecting the Member States' constitutional identity, and that at the same time the Member States do not lose their ability to politically and socially shape the living conditions on their own responsibility…

233. The Basic Law does not grant the German state bodies powers to transfer sovereign powers in such a way that their exercise can independently establish other competences for the European Union. It prohibits the transfer of competence to decide on its own competence (*Kompetenz-Kompetenz*)... Also a far-reaching process of independence of political rule for the European Union brought about by granting it steadily increased competences and by gradually overcoming existing unanimity requirements or rules of state equality that have been decisive so far can, from the perspective of German constitutional law, only take place as a result of the freedom of action of the self-determined people. According to the constitution, such steps of integration must be factually limited by the act of transfer and must, in principle, be revocable. For this reason, withdrawal from the European union of integration... may, regardless of a commitment for an unlimited period under an agreement, not be prevented by other Member States or the autonomous authority of the Union...

239. It is therefore constitutionally required not to agree dynamic treaty provisions with a blanket character or if they can still be interpreted in a manner that respects the national responsibility for integration, to establish, at any rate, suitable national safeguards for the effective exercise of such responsibility. Accordingly, the Act approving an international agreement and the national accompanying laws must therefore be such that European integration continues to take place according to the principle of conferral without the possibility for the European Union of taking possession of *Kompetenz-Kompetenz* or to violate the Member States' constitutional identity which is not amenable to integration, in this case, that of the Basic Law. For borderline cases of what is still constitutionally admissible, the German legislature must, if necessary, make arrangements with its laws that accompany approval to ensure that the responsibility for integration of the legislative bodies can sufficiently develop.

240. Apart from this, it must be possible within the German jurisdiction to assert the responsibility for integration if obvious transgressions of the boundaries take place when the European Union claims competences... and to preserve the inviolable core content of the Basic Law's constitutional identity by means of an identity review... The Federal Constitutional Court has already opened up the way of the *ultra vires* review for this, which applies where Community and Union institutions transgress the boundaries of their competences. If legal protection cannot be obtained at the Union level, the Federal Constitutional Court reviews whether legal instruments of the European institutions and bodies, adhering to the principle of subsidiarity under Community and Union law, keep within the boundaries of the sovereign powers accorded to them by way of conferred power... Furthermore, the Federal Constitutional Court reviews whether the inviolable core content of the constitutional identity of the Basic Law is respected... The exercise of this competence of review, which is rooted in constitutional law, follows the principle of the Basic Law's openness towards European Law, and it therefore also does not contradict the principle of loyal cooperation (Article 4.3 TEU); with progressing integration, the fundamental political and constitutional structures of sovereign Member States, which are recognised by Article 4(2) TEU, cannot be safeguarded in any other way. In this respect, the guarantee of national constitutional identity under constitutional, and the one under Union, law go hand in hand in the European legal area...

The judgment is a complex one that states a number of things and it is worth taking a moment to separate them out.

First, it asserts that sovereignty rests in the national constitution and that it is ultimately for the national constitutional court to determine the relative legal authority of EU law in accordance with national constitutional principles, which must be respected. *Gauweiler* is, however, not a bald restatement of national constitutional sovereignty.[18] It asserts that commitment to European integration is not just a matter of will but a constitutional requirement. The importance of this counter-weighing argument should not be understated. The German Constitutional Court commits itself to an openness to EU law, which will only be forgone in exceptional circumstances.

Secondly, the right to vote and the right to democratic participation for German citizens is a fundamental constitutional right. It is based on the formal right to vote for deputies in the German Bundestag, but it is also an expression of two other fundamental rights, which will be violated if it is breached. One is the right to human dignity. The other is the right of the German people, as the constituent power of the German Basic Law, to participate in the exercise of state authority, particularly by voting.[19] These principles are inviolable and European integration must take subject to them.

Thirdly, these principles might be breached in three ways. The first is if the Union breaches the principle of conferred powers (ultra vires review). This will be where it takes action that exceeds the powers conferred by the Treaties, but there is also a suggestion that it will occur if there is a breach of the principle of limited powers, and the Union seeks to exercise its powers too generally. The second is where the Union trespasses on the constitutional identity of a Member State (identity review). This will be the case where the Union legislates on a matter that is so central to the identity of a state that it should be legislated only at a national or sub-national level. Whilst ultra vires review and identity review are related, they are not the same thing. The former addresses the Union observing its own procedures and not legislating too widely. It could be violated if the Union breached its own procedures or legislated too broadly on politically uncontentious matters. Identity review is about things close to a state's heart. The Union could observe its own procedures, be legislating in a confined manner but still violate identity review by touching on a matter that was core to a state's constitutional identity. The third way in which the principle can be breached is if, even observing all this, the Union acts in an undemocratic matter. The German Constitutional Court accepted that the Union was not a representative democracy[20] but noted the presence of other substitutes and checks and balances. The Union must observe these.

3 ESTABLISHMENT OF A EUROPEAN SOVEREIGN ORDER

(i) The academic debate on the different claims to sovereign authority

The position of all national constitutional courts, whilst suggesting a disposition to accept the authority of EU law, is different from that of the Court of Justice, which argues for its sovereignty. How to mediate between these positions? For legal sovereignty clearly vests in the order that emerges from the reconciliation of these claims. To put it another way, EU law will only be sovereign to the extent that the national courts accept the Court of Justice's claims. Beyond that, national legal sovereignty will remain untouched.

---

[18] T. Schilling, 'The Autonomy of the Community Legal Order: An Analysis of Possible Foundations' (1996) 37 *Harvard Int'l LJ* 389; T. Hartley, 'The Constitutional Foundations of the European Union' (2001) 117 *LQR* 225.
[19] For criticism of this style of reasoning as too nationalistic see J. Weiler, 'Does Europe Need a Constitution? Demos, Telos and the Maastricht German Decision' (1995) 1 *ELJ* 219.
[20] See pp. 43–6.

A 'cottage industry' has developed around this question, with the two most prominent schools of thought being the pluralist school and the constitutionalist school.[21] The former sees the EU legal order and national legal orders as separate orders, which must accommodate themselves to each, whilst the latter emphasises a common set of normative principles which act as the basis for collective orientation.

Let us turn first to the pluralist school, whose earliest advocate was Neil MacCormick.

N. MacCormick, 'The Maastricht Urteil: Sovereignty Now' (1995) 1 *European Law Journal* 259, 264–5

... the most appropriate analysis of the relations of legal systems is pluralistic rather than monistic, and interactive rather than hierarchical. The legal systems and their common legal system of EC law are distinct, but interacting systems of law, and hierarchical relations of validity within criteria of validity proper to distinct systems do not add up to any sort of all-purpose superiority of one system over another. It follows also that the interpretative power of the highest decision-making authorities of the different systems must be, as to each system, ultimate. It is for the European Court of Justice to interpret in the last resort and in a finally authoritative way the norms of Community law. But, equally, it must be for the highest constitutional tribunal of each Member State to interpret its constitutional and other norms, and hence to interpret the interaction of the validity of EC law with higher level norms of validity in the given state system. Interpretative competence-competence is a feature of the highest tribunal of any normative system...

What this indicates is that acceptance of a pluralistic conception of legal systems entails acknowledging that not all legal problems can be solved legally. The problem in principle is not that of an absence of legal answers to given problems, but of a superfluity of legal answers. For it is possible that the European Court interprets Community law so as to assert some right or obligation as binding in favour of a person within the jurisdiction of the German court, while that Court in turn denies the validity of such a right or obligation in terms of the German Constitution. In principle, the same conflict is possible as between any Member State system and EC law. The problem is not logically embarrassing, because strictly the answers are from the point of different systems. But it is practically embarrassing to the extent that the same human beings are said to have and not to have a certain right. How shall they act? To which system are they to give their fidelity in action?

Resolving such problems, or more wisely still, avoiding their occurrence in the first place is a matter for circumspection and for political as much as legal judgment. The European Court of Justice ought not to reach its interpretative judgments without regard to their potential impact on national constitutions. National courts ought not to interpret laws or constitutions without regard to the resolution of their compatriots to take full part in European Union and European Community. If despite this conflicts come into being through judicial decision-making and interpretation, there will necessarily have to be some political action to produce a solution.

---

[21] It is worth noting that some argue strongly for exclusive reference to the Court's case law: J. Baquero Cruz, 'The Legacy of the Maastricht-Urteil and the Pluralist Movement' (2008) 14 *ELJ* 389. Others argue that the matter should be resolved by resort to universal principles of justice: P. Eleftheriadis, 'The European Constitution and Cosmopolitan Ideals' (2001) 7 *CJEL* 2. Neither of these arguments seems to address the exact terms of the dispute, however.

The advantages and disadvantages of a pluralistic approach lie in its intellectual elasticity. Legal authority is no longer exclusively vested in the state, but is enjoyed by a number of different institutions, which include the European Union, but also international organisations, regional government and even private organisations with strong norm-setting powers, such as professional or standardisation bodies. In such a world, there are possibilities for more diverse forms of self-government and greater checks and balances, with each order limiting the excesses of the other. Such accounts give ethical priority only to the legal order as they emphasise it is the autonomy of these legal orders that must be respected. It is not clear why we should do so, or whether all such orders are sufficiently similar in their features to make such recognition possible. Just as an elephant and a mouse are mammals but are, nonetheless, very different, so these various types of law may work in diverse ways and may be quite different beasts. Is a law passed through representative institutions really the same as a technical regulation passed by a bureaucracy such as the Commission?

Furthermore, pluralist accounts are weak on explaining the processes and norms of mutual accommodation.[22] Mutual accommodation is all very well, but there must be certain norms of mutual recognition and certain criteria for determining when it would be possible for one legal order to trump another.[23] When, for example, does something become a legal order that we must recognise? When does accommodating something in one legal order excessively violate the needs of another legal order?

Kumm seeks to address this by arguing for a common idea of constitutionalism that informs both the law of the Member States and EU law and is used to resolve disputes. He has identified four tenets central to this idea of constitutionalism. These are: commitment to the rule of law, protection of fundamental rights, federalism and a commitment to valuing the specific nature of the national community. It is these tenets, he suggests, which should be used to resolve disputes.

M. Kumm, 'The Jurisprudence of Constitutional Conflict: Constitutional Supremacy in Europe Before and After the Constitutional Treaty' (2005) 11 *European Law Journal* 262, 299–300

The *first* principle is formal and is connected to the *idea of legality*. According to the principle of the effective and uniform enforcement of EU law, further strengthened by the recent explicit commitment by Member States to the primacy of EU law, national courts should start with a strong presumption that they are required to enforce EU law, national constitutional provisions notwithstanding. *The presumption for applying EU law can be rebutted, however, if, and to the extent that, countervailing principles have greater weight.* Here there are three principles to be considered. The first is *substantive*,

---

[22] For an attempt to do so albeit by reference to constitutionalist language see M. Poiares Maduro, 'Contrapunctual Law: Europe's Constitutional Pluralism in Action' in N. Walker (ed.), *Sovereignty in Transition* (Oxford, Oxford University Press, 2003).

[23] C. Richmond, 'Preserving the Identity Crisis: Autonomy, System and Sovereignty in European Law' (1997) 16 *Law and Philosophy* 377; M. la Torre, 'Legal Pluralism as an Evolutionary Achievement of Community Law' (1999) 12 *Ratio Juris* 182; N. Walker, 'The Idea of Constitutional Pluralism' (2002) 65 *MLR* 317; N. Barber, 'Legal Pluralism and the European Union' (2006) 12 *ELJ* 306. For a response, see M. Loughlin, 'Ten Tenets of Sovereignty' in the same volume and D. Kostakopoulou, 'Floating Sovereignty: A Pathology or Necessary Means of State Evolution?' (2002) 22 *OJLS* 135.

and focuses on the effective *protection of fundamental rights of citizens*. If, and to the extent that, fundamental rights protection against acts of the EU is lacking in important respects, then that is a ground to insist on subjecting EU law to national constitutional rights review. If, however, the guarantees afforded by the EU amount to structurally equivalent protections, then there is no more space for national courts to substitute the EU's judgment on the rights issue with their own. Arguably the EU, and specifically the Court of Justice, has long developed substantially equivalent protections against violations of fundamental rights. At the very least the Constitutional Treaty, with its elaborate Charter of Fundamental Rights, should finally put an end to this issue. Even if some doubt that the Court of Justice can be trusted as an institution to take rights seriously, if the Charter of Fundamental Rights becomes the law of the land after ratification the guarantees it provides may not fall below the guarantees provided by the European Convention of Human Rights as interpreted by the ECHR. The second of the counter-principles is *jurisdictional*. It protects national communities against unjustified usurpations of competencies by the European Union which undermine the legitimate scope of self government by national communities. Call this principle the principle of *subsidiarity*. Here the question is whether there are sufficient and effective guarantees against usurpation of power by EU institutions. Much will depend on how the procedural and technical safeguards of the Constitutional Treaty will work in practice once the Treaty has been ratified. If the structural safeguards will succeed in establishing a culture of subsidiarity carefully watched over by the Court of Justice, then there are no more grounds for national courts to review whether or not the EU has remained within the boundaries established by the EU's constitutional charter. Lastly, there is the *procedural* principle of *democratic legitimacy*, the third counter-principle. Given the persistence of the democratic deficit on the European level – the absence of directly representative institutions as the central agenda-setters of the European political process, the lack of a European public sphere, and a sufficiently thick European identity even if the Constitutional Treaty will be ratified – national courts continue to have good reasons to set aside EU Law *when it violates clear and specific constitutional norms that reflect essential commitments of the national community.*

The principles elaborated by Kumm are taken from federal constitutional states and provide a nuanced matrix for resolving disputes between national constitutional courts and the Court of Justice. However, as Dani has observed, they pay only limited heed to the features of the Union:

> The choice for state constitutionalism as the EU form of power relies on a strong normative assumption: it is believed that the combination of fundamental rights protection, broad legislative powers and representative democracy devices provides the most effective and, probably, the only framework for ensuring the republican ideals of political inclusion, economic prosperity and social cohesion. In this respect, conversion narratives may be regarded not only as proofs of faith on the virtues of constitutionalism and state constitutions, but also as defences of a clear political strategy intended to preserve the European *modus vivendi*.[24]

---

[24] M. Dani, 'Constitutionalism and Dissonances: Has Europe Paid Off its Debt to Functionalism?' (2009) 15 *ELJ* 324, 343.

As Dani observes, the constitutionalist restatement is above all an ideological position that mistakes the genus and practice of European integration. On the one hand, the Union was established to deal with the consequences of state failure, namely that the states within their domestic constitutions failed to provide or could not provide certain goods to their citizens. On the other hand, an image of state constitutionalism assumes all players are pulling in a similar direction. It might be that EU policies and national policies have a different dynamic. He gives the example of industrial policy, where EU policy is about realising market integration whereas national policy is about addressing market failure. Dani argues therefore that mediation must be built around two functions: addressing state abuse when it occurs, even when it takes place within the domestic constitution, and allowing for structural dissonance, namely the possibility for significant difference in policy direction.

(ii) The ends and means for reconciling difference and moving to a European sovereign order

The Lisbon Treaty has introduced a new provision, which may be the vehicle through which the different judicial claims are mediated. For it introduces a new principle of judicial review, namely that EU law has violated the principle of self-government.

Article 4(2) TEU

The Union shall respect the equality of Member States before the Treaties as well as their national identities, inherent in their fundamental structures, political and constitutional, inclusive of regional and local self-government. It shall respect their essential State functions, including ensuring the territorial integrity of the State, maintaining law and order and safeguarding national security. In particular, national security remains the sole responsibility of each Member State.

The provision is, in part, an amalgamation of earlier provisions.[25] It also is, however, a significant extension. It synthesises them around an organising principle of self-government, which is detailed, placed at the forefront of the Treaties and subject to interpretation by the Court of Justice, which will be able to review EU measures against it. It also appears it will be a central instrument used by national constitutional courts. In *Gauweiler*, at paragraph 240 in the excerpt above, the German Constitutional Court stated that the possibility for it to review EU law to guarantee national constitutional identity went hand in hand with Article 4(2) TEU. It returned to the point at paragraph 339, where it stated:

This establishment [of the inapplicability of an EU law to Germany] must also be made if within or outside the sovereign powers conferred, these powers are exercised with effect on Germany in such a way that a violation of the constitutional identity, which is inalienable pursuant to… the Basic Law and which is also respected by European law under the Treaties, namely Article 4.2 TEU, is the consequence.

[25] There were thus individual provisions requiring the national identities of the Member States to be respected: Article 6(3) TEU(M). For requirements that EU legislation in the area of freedom, security and justice should not affect national responsibilities for the maintenance of law and order and internal security, there were Articles 64(1) EC and 33 TEU(M).

For the German Constitutional Court, if an EU measure violates its *identity* review, it will also be illegal as a matter of EU law, as it will breach Article 4(2) TEU. Interpretations of Article 4(2) TEU will become the battleground or the meeting point, where the limits of the authority of EU law lie.

In this regard, it becomes important to consider the principles underlying the provision. The different elements of the academic debate outlined earlier are all present. There is the language of legal pluralism in that the prerogatives of different legal orders should be accommodated. Not only national identities must be respected, but also the fundamental structures of regional and local self-government. There is also the language of constitutionalism, with the reference in Article 4(2) TEU to respect for constitutional structures. Finally, there is the functional reference, in that respect must be had to essential state functions and to national security being the exclusive responsibility of each Member State.

Interestingly, these different elements have proved attractive to the different constitutional courts we have considered. The German Constitutional Court has addressed the question through the language of constitutionalism and constitutional identity. It has looked at how EU law might impinge on certain fundamental rights that it sees as central to German constitutional identity. The approach of the Polish Constitutional Court, by contrast, is closer to that associated with legal pluralism. It sees EU law and domestic law as two autonomous orders in which each must accommodate the other without compromising its own integrity. Finally, for all its rhetoric, the Estonian Constitutional Court is closest to the functionalist position. It accepts the sovereignty of EU law but, nevertheless, hives off certain, undisclosed key functions that it conceives as essential to Estonian statehood. The difference in nuance between these courts suggests that different courts will seek different things from the provision. This will make a 'common' interpretation very unlikely. Instead, the European sovereign legal order will, in all likelihood, be very asymmetric, with its being interpreted as meaning one thing and having one basis in one Member State and another thing, having another basis, in another.

Thought also has to be directed to where these debates will emerge. Debates take place at the meta-level over what is sovereign and who is to decide the question of sovereignty. This is the debate that has been addressed in the judgments above. It is known as the *Kompetenz-Kompetenz* debate: who is competent to decide on the competence and authority of EU law? This is quite an abstract debate, which does not address how legal relations are actually played out. It would be perfectly possible for a national court, for example, to assert domestic sovereignty but then state that it chooses to do whatever EU law tells it.[26] The reason for this is that the *Kompetenz-Kompetenz* debate, important as it is, does not address the legal substance of sovereignty and the doctrines it gives rise to. It is in the Court of Justice's claims and the national constitutional courts' acceptance of these claims that we see more clearly the level of authority of EU law.

The sovereignty of EU law makes four central claims about its authority and this leads to four different doctrines. First, EU law takes precedence over other law unless it expressly says otherwise. It cannot be disapplied in favour of any other form of law. If not, it would not have the absolute authority mentioned above (the doctrine of the primacy of EU law). The second is that EU law alone determines the quality of its legal authority. That is to say it determines

---

[26] This is to some extent what has taken place in Spain where the Spanish Constitutional Court has stated that the Spanish Constitution is sovereign but otherwise gives full effect to the case law of the Court of Justice: *Re EU Constitutional Treaty and the Spanish Constitution* [2005] 1 CMLR 981.

when there is a conflict between it and national law and what the consequences of that conflict are. This is a slightly different quality from primacy as it goes to the circumstances of any conflict and the legal consequences of EU law prevailing. The doctrine most associated with this principle is that of pre-emption. The third concerns the remit of EU legal authority. It is for EU law to determine which activities are governed by it and to what it can apply. If it cannot do this and this were to be determined elsewhere, its autonomy would be compromised (the doctrine of conferred powers). Finally, the sovereignty of EU law establishes a rule of law, to which all public institutions within the Member States are subject, including national courts. This involves specifying a series of institutional duties setting out what such institutions must do to make the European Union work as a fully effective legal system (the fidelity principle).

The remainder of this chapter looks at how these different doctrines are played out, both by the Court of Justice and the national courts.

4 THE PRIMACY OF EU LAW

The primacy principle in which EU law takes precedence over national law was first proclaimed in *Costa*. It is most neatly illustrated by the decision in *Internationale Handelsgesellschaft*, in which the Court famously ruled that EU law takes precedence over all forms of national law, including national constitutional law. The claimant brought an action before a German administrative court challenging the validity of a Regulation. The German court considered that the Regulation violated certain provisions of the German Constitution. The view of the Court of Justice was uncompromising.

> **Case 11/70 *Internationale Handelsgesellschaft* v *Einfuhr- und Vorratstelle für Getreide und Futtermittel* [1970] ECR 1125**
>
> 3. Recourse to the legal rules or concepts of national law in order to judge the validity of measures adopted by the institutions of the Community would have an adverse effect on the uniformity and efficacy of Community law. The validity of such measures can only be judged in the light of Community law. In fact, the law stemming from the Treaty, an independent source of law, cannot because of its very nature be overridden by rules of national law, however framed, without being deprived of its character as Community law and without the legal basis of the Community itself being called in question. Therefore the validity of a Community measure or its effect within a Member State cannot be affected by allegations that it runs counter to either fundamental rights as formulated by the constitution of that State or the principles of a national constitutional structure.

The primacy of EU law applies not only to substantive conflicts, when a domestic norm conflicts with an EU law. It also has a jurisdictional dimension. It is not open to national law to determine which courts can hear conflicts. The primacy of EU law applies whenever a conflict appears before any court or body which is competent to take legal decision. In *Simmenthal*, an Italian system of fees for veterinary inspections of beef imports had already been held by the Court of Justice to breach EU law. An Italian magistrate asked the Court whether he was required to disapply the relevant Italian law. This was a power which at that time was enjoyed only by the Italian Constitutional Court as only it had the power of legislative review.

Case 106/77 *Amministrazione delle Finanze dello Stato* v *Simmenthal* [1978] ECR 629

17. … in accordance with the principle of the precedence of Community law, the relationship between provisions of the Treaty and directly applicable measures of the institutions, on the one hand and the national law of the Member States, on the other is such that those provisions and measures not only by their entry into force render automatically inapplicable any conflicting provision of current national law but – in so far as they are an integral part of, and take precedence in, the legal order applicable in the territory of each of the Member States – also preclude the valid adoption of new national legislative measures to the extent to which they would be incompatible with community provisions.

18. Indeed any recognition that national legislative measures which encroach upon the field within which the Community exercises its legislative power or which are otherwise incompatible with the provisions of Community law had any legal effect would amount to a corresponding denial of the effectiveness of obligations undertaken unconditionally and irrevocably by Member States pursuant to the Treaty and would thus imperil the very foundations of the Community…

21. … every national court must, in a case within its jurisdiction, apply Community law in its entirety and protect rights which the latter confers on individuals and must accordingly set aside any provision of national law which may conflict with it, whether prior or subsequent to the Community rule.

22. Accordingly any provision of a national legal system and any legislative, administrative or judicial practice which might impair the effectiveness of Community law by withholding from the national court having jurisdiction to apply such law the power to do everything necessary at the moment of its application to set aside national legislative provisions which might prevent Community rules from having full force and effect are incompatible with those requirements which are the very essence of Community law.

On its face, primacy of EU law is the most direct expression of its sovereignty and, insofar as the latter is contested, one would have assumed it to be particularly contingent. Whilst it is difficult to imagine any national constitutional court, with the exception of the Estonian, ever allowing *Internationale Handelsgesellschaft* to be applied over its national constitution, it is almost impossible to find any recent example of a national measure being applied by a constitutional court over an EU measure.[27]

The first reason for this is that the constraints placed on the authority of EU law by national constitutional courts are exceptional ones. In principle, they are willing to grant EU law authority subject to its not violating certain national taboos. Their assertion of national sovereignty is rather an assertion of the power to put ultimate safeguards into action rather than an assertion of regular control of the application of EU law. This was reiterated in *Gauweiler*.

---

[27] Both the Cypriot Supreme Court and Polish Constitutional Tribunal refused to comply with the European Arrest Warrant which requires states to surrender individuals wanted in another state within forty-five days, *Attorney General of the Republic of Cyprus* v *Konstantinou* [2007] 3 CMLR 42; *Re Enforcement of a European Arrest Warrant* [2006] 1 CMLR 36. In each case, this was on the basis that measures then in the third pillar did not at the time have to be applied over national measures.

2 BvE 2/08 *Gauweiler* v *Treaty of Lisbon*, Judgment of 30 June 2009

331. With Declaration no. 17 Concerning Primacy annexed to the Treaty of Lisbon, the Federal Republic of Germany does not recognise an absolute primacy of application of Union law, which would be constitutionally objectionable, but merely confirms the legal situation as it has been interpreted by the Federal Constitutional Court...

337. The Basic Law's mandate of integration and current European law laid down in the treaties demand, with the idea of a Union-wide legal community, the restriction of the exercise of the Member States' judicial power. No effects that endanger integration are intended to occur by the uniformity of the Community's legal order being called into question by different applicability decisions of courts in Member States. The Federal Constitutional Court has put aside its general competence, which it had originally assumed, to review the execution of European Community law in Germany against the standard of the fundamental rights of the German constitution..., and it did so trusting in the Court of Justice of the European Communities performing this function accordingly... Out of consideration for the position of the Community institutions, which is derived from international agreements, the Federal Constitutional Court could, however, recognise the final character of the decisions of the Court of Justice only 'in principle'...

340. The Basic Law aims to integrate Germany into the legal community of peaceful and free states, but does not waive the sovereignty contained in the last instance in the German constitution. There is therefore no contradiction to the aim of openness to international law if the legislature, exceptionally, does not comply with the law of international agreements – accepting, however, corresponding consequences in international relations – provided this is the only way in which a violation of fundamental principles of the constitution can be averted... The Court of Justice of the European Communities based its decision in *Kadi*[28]... on a similar view according to which an objection to the claim of validity of a United Nations Security Council Resolution may be expressed citing fundamental legal principles of the Community... The Court of Justice has thus, in a borderline case, placed the assertion of its own identity as a legal community above the commitment that it otherwise respects. Such a legal figure is not only familiar in international legal relations as reference to the ordre public as the boundary of commitment under a treaty; it also corresponds, at any rate if it is used in a constructive manner, to the idea of contexts of political order which are not structured according to a strict hierarchy. Factually at any rate, it is no contradiction to the objective of openness towards European law, i.e. to the participation of the Federal Republic of Germany in the realisation of a united Europe... if exceptionally, and under special and narrow conditions, the Federal Constitutional Court declares European Union law inapplicable in Germany.

The other reason why constitutional courts rarely allow national law to take precedence over EU law relates to a feature of the latter, which is that it rarely prompts judicial conflicts. For only a small proportion of EU law has traditionally been invoked before domestic courts. One study found that just five areas of law – taxation, sex discrimination, free movement of goods, free movement of workers and intellectual property – accounted for 61 per cent of all reported litigation in the United Kingdom, and that just five Directives accounted for 73 per cent of the Directives that were invoked in British courts.[29] There is a quid pro quo in which the primacy of EU law is almost always accepted but, in return, it has traditionally been confined to fields that amount to only a small proportion of what is invoked before domestic courts.

[28] Joined Cases C-402/05 P and C-415/05 P *Kadi and Al Barakaat International Foundation* v *Council* [2008] ECR I-6351.
[29] D. Chalmers, 'The Positioning of EU Judicial Politics within the United Kingdom' (2000) 23 *WEP* 169, 178–83.

5 THE QUALITY OF EU LEGAL AUTHORITY

(i) Pre-emption and different models of European integration

If the doctrine of primacy is concerned with the hierarchy between EU law and national law, it is the doctrine of pre-emption which governs the question of when there is a conflict and what the consequences of a conflict are for EU law and national law.[30] This question is not a black and white one and covers a spectrum of types of conflict. These can be categorised into three general categories.

- field pre-emption: this is where EU law is considered to have a jurisdictional monopoly over a field; national laws, irrespective of whether they conflict with EU measures, can only be enacted with the authorisation of EU law;
- rule pre-emption: there is shared jurisdiction over a policy field; national measures can be adopted but will be set aside if they conflict with EU law;
- obstacle pre-emption: Member States are free to adopt national measures but must not adopt measures which obstruct the effectiveness of EU policies.[31]

All three categories address the question of how EU law and national law are to be arranged when they govern a single policy field. The debate about their relationship to each other (e.g. when a conflict arises and the consequences of that conflict) cannot take place separately, therefore, from the substantive debate on the respective places of EU and domestic law in that policy field: namely the extent to which policy is to be determined by the European Union alone or the Member States separately. Pre-emption is therefore also a debate about the allocation of different types of EU intervention. This is reflected in Article 2 TFEU, which not only codifies the doctrine of pre-emption for the first time but also sets out the different types of competence in the Treaties and, with that, the degree of EU intervention in that field.

Article 2 TFEU

1. When the Treaties confer on the Union exclusive competence in a specific area, only the Union may legislate and adopt legally binding acts, the Member States being able to do so themselves only if so empowered by the Union or for the implementation of acts of the Union.
2. When the Treaties confer on the Union a competence shared with the Member States in a specific area, the Union and the Member States may legislate and adopt legally binding acts in that area. The Member States shall exercise their competence to the extent that the Union has not exercised its competence. The Member States shall exercise their competence again to the extent that the Union has decided to cease exercising its competence.

---

[30] R. Schütze, 'Supremacy Without Pre-emption? The Very Slowly Emergent Doctrine of Pre-emption' (2006) 43 *CMLRev.* 1023, 1033. For early analyses see M. Waelbroeck, 'The Emergent Doctrine of Community Pre-emption: Consent and Re-delegation' in T. Sandalow and E. Stein (eds.), *Courts and Free Markets: Perspectives from the United States and Europe*, vol. II (Oxford, Oxford University Press, 1982); E. Cross, 'Pre-emption of Member State Law in the European Economic Community: A Framework for Analysis' (1992) 29 *CMLRev.* 447.

[31] This categorisation is taken from the excellent analysis by Schütze, above n. 30, 1038.

3. The Member States shall coordinate their economic and employment policies within arrangements as determined by this Treaty, which the Union shall have competence to provide.
4. The Union shall have competence, in accordance with the provisions of the Treaty on European Union, to define and implement a common foreign and security policy, including the progressive framing of a common defence policy.
5. In certain areas and under the conditions laid down in the Treaties, the Union shall have competence to carry out actions to support, coordinate or supplement the actions of the Member States, without thereby superseding their competence in these areas. Legally binding acts of the Union adopted on the basis of the provisions in the Treaties relating to these areas shall not entail harmonisation of Member States' laws or regulations.

The provision addresses the different but related tasks of determining when there is a conflict between EU law and national law and the quality of EU intervention in a particular field. Pre-emption, as an instrument for precluding national legislation, is only really addressed in the first two paragraphs, where the Union has exclusive or shared competences.[32] Instead, most of the provision is about setting out the scope of Union policy-making within the different fields, namely whether there should be a common policy, an EU policy complementary to national policies or any EU policy at all. The provision, therefore, is not just concerned with setting out a relationship between EU and national law, but also provides five different models of integration.

Possibly because it has been addressed at length by policy-makers in the making of the Treaties, it is the only doctrine where national constitutional courts have not intervened and where the authority of Court of Justice judgments is completely uncontested.

(ii) Exclusive competence

In fields of exclusive competence, only the Union may legislate, with Member States being able to legislate only if authorised by the Union or to implement EU measures. From a national perspective, this is the most draconian of competences as it involves a complete surrender of jurisdiction to the Union. There is *a priori* field pre-emption by the Union in these fields. For that reason, the fields of exclusive competence are rather limited. They comprise: the customs union; the competition rules necessary for the functioning of the internal market; monetary policy for the Member States whose currency is the euro; the conservation of marine biological resources under the common fisheries policy; and the common commercial policy.[33]

The philosophy or model of integration here is one of dual federalism. The European Union and Member States are co-equals with a division of power into mutually exclusive spheres, with the Union governing some and Member States others.[34] It is worth considering why we

---

[32] This has led some to argue that concerns about competence creep by the Union are perhaps overstated in most areas of policy. S. Weatherill, 'Competence and Legitimacy' in C. Barnard and O. Odudu (eds.), *The Outer Limits of European Union Law* (Cambridge, Cambridge University Press, 2009).
[33] Article 3 TFEU.
[34] R. Schütze, 'Dual Federalism Constitutionalised: The Emergence of Exclusive Competences in the EC Legal Order' (2007) 32 *ELRev*. 3.

would wish for such a model. One argument is that the competence simply does not exist unless there is an exclusive competence. There can be no customs union, therefore, without a single external tariff or single monetary policy without a single currency. The challenge with this argument is that it does not explain why the Union should preclude Member States from legislating when it has not set up the policy. A customs union does not exist without a common external tariff, but that is the case whether there are twenty-seven different tariffs or there are no tariffs at all. Another argument is a functional one. It argues that exclusivity is necessary for the policy to function optimally. The Court of Justice, for example, argued that exclusivity was necessary for the common commercial policy as different trade policies would compromise defence of a common Union interest.[35] The challenge to such an argument is that it is the argument which justifies common action in the first place. EU action is justified on the basis that it would enable a policy to function better, but this, as an advantage, has to be balanced against other advantages such as local autonomy.[36]

The justification for this model is further compromised by the fact that the central difference between exclusive competences and shared competences is that the Union has not legislated. In both cases, if it has legislated, Member States are precluded from legislating. In the absence of EU legislation, Member States are not precluded from legislating. Under this model, they simply need Union authorisation. The grant of wide authorisations led, in practice, to a *modus vivendi* where competence is effectively shared, with many national regimes still in place in fields such as fisheries and the common commercial policy, albeit placed under a duty to justify themselves to the Union.[37]

(iii) Shared competence

Fields of shared competence allow Member States to legislate to the extent that the Union has not legislated. The model is one of cooperative federalism, in which a shared responsibility is granted to both actors to realise a common policy. There is no fixed division here but they work together to realise this common goal, with the balance of responsibilities determined by the terms, limits and presence of EU legislation.[38] This model of integration applies to: the internal market; social policy; cohesion policy; agriculture and fisheries, excluding the conservation of marine biological resources; environment; consumer protection; transport; trans-European networks; energy; freedom, security and justice; and common safety concerns in public health matters.[39]

The modalities of shared competence were set out in *Commission* v *United Kingdom*. Here, the Commission brought an action against a British requirement that cars could be driven on British roads only if they were equipped with dim-dip lights.[40] The relevant Directive did not impose this as a requirement and, furthermore, it provided that any car which met its stipulations should be able to be driven on the roads. The Court of Justice found the British

[35] Opinion 1/75 *Re Understanding on a Local Costs Standard* [1975] ECR 1355.
[36] For a critique see Schütze, above n. 34.
[37] For example, national export restrictions have been allowed to be maintained in the field of the common commercial policy on such wide grounds as public policy: Case C-70/94 *Werner* [1995] ECR I-3189.
[38] R. Schütze, 'Co-operative Federalism Constitutionalised: The Emergence of Complementary Competences in the EC Legal Order' (2006) 31 *ELRev.* 167, 168–9.
[39] Article 4(2) TFEU.
[40] Case 60/86 *Commission* v *United Kingdom (dim-dip lighting devices)* [1988] ECR 3921.

requirement to be illegal. It stated that the intention of the Directive was to regulate exhaustively the conditions for lighting devices on cars. As this was now exhaustively regulated by EU law, Member States were prohibited from imposing additional requirements.

This relationship makes sense where there is a pressing need for uniformity with the conditions governed by EU legislation. Within the context of the internal market, the maintenance of differing national regimes can lead to distortions of competition and trade restrictions, with the consequence that the harmonisation process would be robbed of much of its effect. Even there, such a rule does create a regime which is both monolithic and inflexible; in which it is impossible to maintain national provisions that impose higher standards; and in which the only way of adapting legislation to new risks and technologies is through amending the EU legislation in question.[41]

In the other fields of shared competence, the need for uniformity seems less pressing and the ethos of cooperative federalism is that the relationship between EU and national law should be fluid and not fixed *a priori*. Some concession for this is made in Article 4 TFEU which provides for parallel competences in the fields of research and development, space, development and humanitarian aid. In these fields, the Union will be able to develop legislation, but that legislation will not prevent Member States enacting their own legislation, provided, one assumes, that it does not conflict with the EU legislation.[42]

In addition, in a number of areas of shared competence special provision is made for minimum harmonisation.[43] Here, Member States are not prevented from enacting more restrictive provisions. Litigation focuses on when the national legislation is more restrictive. In *Deponiezweckverband Eiterköpfe*, a landfill operator was refused permission to fill two sites with waste.[44] The reason was that the waste exceeded German limits on the proportion of organic waste that could be disposed of in landfill sites. By contrast, the Directive (on which the German law was based) set limits only for biodegradable organic waste. The operator argued that the national legislation was, therefore, unlawful. The Court of Justice disagreed. It stated that what was central was that the German legislation pursued the same objective as the Directive, namely the limitation of waste going into landfill. Insofar as it set limits for a wider range of waste, it was more stringent than the EU Directive and was, therefore, permissible.

No mention is made, however, of minimum harmonisation in Article 2(2) TFEU and the Court will, undoubtedly, have to address its relationship to the more specific provisions that provide for it. More generally, a case can be made for minimum harmonisation even in other fields, where it is felt that there are strong national public interests that should be allowed to be protected. This can be done by the relevant legislative instrument, which can provide for specific measures to be exempted or for more restrictive national measures to be permitted. However, this is not the default position and there can often be legislative oversight, in that the relationship between a new EU measure and a particularly important domestic public interest is not considered.

---

[41] S. Weatherill, 'Beyond Preemption? Shared Competence and Constitutional Change in the European Community' in D. O'Keeffe and P. Twomey (eds.), *Legal Issues of the Maastricht Treaty* (London, Chancery, 1994) 13, 18–19.

[42] Article 4(3), (4) TFEU.

[43] Notably criminal justice (Article 82(2) TFEU); social policy (Article 153(2)(b) TFEU); public health legislation on organs and blood (Article 168(4)(a) TFEU); consumer protection (Article 169 TFEU); environment (Article 193 TFEU).

[44] Case C-6/03 *Deponiezweckverband Eiterköpfe* [2005] ECR I-2753.

The Court has been sensitive to this and has departed from its standard position in circumstances where EU legislation fails to protect public interests that were previously safeguarded by national legislation. It has, on occasion, interpreted EU legislation narrowly, so that it is not deemed to regulate the field covered by national law, thereby allowing the national legislation to remain in place.[45] If this is not possible, in extreme circumstances, the Court will refuse to disapply the national legislation. *Commission v Germany* is an example.[46] Member States were required by Directive 79/409/EEC to designate the most suitable habitats in their territory for certain species of wild bird. Once designated, these habitats were to be preserved and appropriate steps taken to prevent their deterioration. The Directive envisaged no circumstances in which measures could be taken to reduce the size of the special protection areas and there was no provision for minimum harmonisation, as the Directive was based on Article 352 TFEU, the flexibility provision. Germany wished to build a dyke across one of its designated areas in the Leybucht region. It argued this was necessary for good ecological reasons. The coast would be washed away otherwise. Despite there being no provision, the Court held that it could reduce the size of the special protection area. It could do this, the Court ruled, because, exceptionally, there was in this case a general interest (protection of the coastline), which was superior to that represented in the Directive. The Court therefore ruled that the dyke could be built but must involve the smallest disruption possible to the protection area that was necessary to secure the coastline.

(iv) Other fields of competence

The three final types of competence relate to fields where the Union has no formal legislative competence and where, in a conflict between EU measures and national laws, national law is to have formal precedence. Each prescribes a different level of intervention for the Union.

The coordination of economic and employment policies set out in Article 2(3) TFEU suggests that the competence of the Union is limited to that of aligning national policies. It is not there to generate an independent policy of its own but to prevent Member States disrupting each other with their own policies. By contrast, the Union is to have its own Common Foreign and Security Policy. This is explicitly mentioned by Article 2(4) TFEU and is emphasised by the Treaties in the statement that it is moving towards framing a common defence policy, suggesting that the latter is not to be common, whereas the former is.

A Common Foreign and Security Policy suggests an independent Union policy, but does not confer the right to exclusivity, so this EU foreign and security policy is to sit alongside national ones, but commonality implies that the latter must operate within its framework. This relationship is not to be governed by pre-emption or adjudication, however. Finally, fields of supporting, coordinating and supplementing action set out in Article 2(5) TFEU sit in between these two positions. The Union is to do more than align. Yet it is unclear to what extent this can emerge into a common, autonomous policy. Union action must not only align national performance, but also improve it by supporting and supplementing actions. This implies some autonomy in considering what this improvement might mean, but it does not suggest sufficient autonomy to provide for different policy directions or priorities.

---

[45] Examples of this include Case C-11/92 *R v Secretary of State for Health, ex parte Gallaher Ltd* [1993] ECR I-3545.
[46] Case C-57/89 *Commission v Germany (conservation of wild birds)* [1991] ECR I-883.

Whilst Article 2 TFEU is quite clear about the different levels of intervention involved in each type of competence, there are no checks to secure this. Thus, to take one example, whilst Union competence is confined to coordinating national employment policies, Article 145 TFEU indicates that it and the Member States have to work towards a coordinated strategy for employment and particularly for promoting a skilled, trained and adaptable workforce and labour markets responsive to economic change. Whilst this does not increase Union powers, it does suggest certain normative requirements that could be interpreted as the basis for an EU policy.

A further criticism is of the *a priori* decision that there should be no EU legislation in these fields. One can understand concerns about competence creep, but these are fields where the Union and Member States acknowledge a shared purpose, in which there will be common action. To exclude EU legislation is to exclude a policy tool which may, in exceptional circumstances, be very useful. It is a dogmatic thing to do and perhaps concerns about competence creep could have been more easily addressed through establishing exceptional procedures, which would put in place checks and balances to ensure that this does not take place.

6 LIMITS OF EU LEGAL AUTHORITY

(i) Doctrine of conferred powers

A feature of the sovereignty of EU law is that EU law has the power to determine the remit of its authority and over which fields of activity it exercises that authority.[47] This also goes to the substantive power of the Union. If it exercises sovereign authority in very confined, technical fields, its power is very different and it is a very different beast than if it exercises that power over wide-ranging and politically significant fields of activity. Indeed, part of the secret of the reception of *Van Gend en Loos* and *Costa* was that the former concerned a very arcane tax on a specialised product, whilst in the latter the Court did not strike down the Italian law because it found no violation of EU law.

The remit of EU legal authority is governed by the principle of conferred powers which is set out in Article 5 TEU.

> ### Article 5 TEU
>
> 1. The limits of Union competences are governed by the principle of conferral...
> 2. Under the principle of conferral, the Union shall act only within the limits of the competences conferred upon it by the Member States in the Treaties to attain the objectives set out therein. Competences not conferred upon the Union in the Treaties remain with the Member States.

Alongside this, reference is made to the same principle in Article 1 TFEU.

> ### Article 1(1) TFEU
>
> This Treaty organises the functioning of the Union and determines the areas of, delimitation of, and arrangements for exercising its competences.

---

[47] Opinion 1/91 *Re European Economic Area* [1991] ECR I-6079.

The principle of conferred powers expresses two complementary ideals.

The first is that it is the Treaties and only the Treaties that determine the material remit of EU legal authority. These Treaties, rather than any other consideration, determine what the European Union can and cannot do. EU institutions cannot act beyond them because they wish to, but, equally, informal political accommodation by national governments cannot determine the limits of EU law. They have to act within the parameters of the Treaties in determining the remit of EU law.

However, Article 5(2) TEU adds a twist by stating that Union competences are not conferred by the Treaties alone but by the 'Member States in the Treaties'. This suggests that the Treaties govern the powers of the Union and the obligations, responsibilities and powers it imposes on the subjects of EU law. They do not, however, found the European Union in some more profound sense. The power to establish it, change it or terminate it rests with the Member States. This self-evident political point is given further force by the provisions on admission and exit of Member States. Whilst there is a Union procedure for admission involving the three legislative institutions and requiring consent by both the Parliament and the Council for admission, the Treaties make clear that the conditions of admission and any adjustments to the Treaties are a matter not for the EU institutions, but between the applicant state and the other Member States.[48] The situation where a state wishes to leave the Union is even more stark. Whilst there is again a Union procedure to be followed, the Treaties make clear that the power to withdraw is for that Member State alone in accordance with its constitutional requirements.[49]

More axiomatically, the idea that it is the Treaties which determine the remit of EU legal authority is the doctrine that has been most contested by national constitutional courts. Whilst they would all accept that the Union cannot act beyond the limits of the powers set by the Treaties, there is a general belief that it is the domestic constitutional settlement which determins the remit of EU law, as the limits of any transfer are, above all, a matter of domestic constitutional law. This was expressed by the German Constitutional Court in *Gauweiler* above[50] but was articulated most forcefully by the Polish Constitutional Tribunal in its judgment on Polish accession to the European Union, where it denied that EU law had competence to determine its own limits.

Polish Membership of the European Union (Accession Treaty), Polish Constitutional Court, Judgment K18/04 of 11 May 2005

Member States maintain the right to assess whether or not, in issuing particular legal provisions, the Community (Union) legislative organs acted within the delegated competences and in accordance with the principles of subsidiarity and proportionality. Should the adoption of provisions infringe these frameworks, the principle of the precedence of Community law fails to apply with respect to such provisions.

---

[48] Article 49 TEU.

[49] Article 50 TEU. See G. Majone, *Dilemmas of European Integration: The Ambiguities and Pitfalls of Integration by Stealth* (Oxford, Oxford University Press, 2005) 209–16, especially 214–16.

[50] 2 BvE 2/08 *Gauweiler* v *Treaty of Lisbon*, Judgment of 30 June 2009 at para. 233.

The remit of EU law is therefore a field in which the Court of Justice makes assertions that are subject to contradiction by national constitutional courts. The consequence is that the former is making a prima facie case for the authority of EU law, which is then policed by the latter.

The second ideal is that of limited government. The European Union is to operate only in specific, confined fields. This was given concrete expression in the Treaty of Lisbon, which set out a catalogue of powers for the Union. The central provision, Article 2 TFEU, set out above, enumerates the fields of activity in which the Union has legal competence, the features of its legal authority in each of these fields, and the degree of Union intervention that is to take place. Articles 3 to 7 TFEU then set out which fields of activity fall within which type of competence.[51] The intention is that by specifying the different competences and their qualities in such a specified and concrete form, there will be less possibility for competence creep. The Union will be confined by the details of these provisions.[52]

The principle of limited government is also one that requires these limits to be clearly defined. This has not been articulated by the Court of Justice but has begun to be picked up by national constitutional courts. The Czech Constitutional Court, in particular, has made something of it. In ruling on the compatibility of the Lisbon Treaty with the Czech Constitution,[53] it stated that the following principle guided the limits of the powers which could be transferred to the Union and could be exercised by the Union:

93. The guiding principle is undoubtedly the principle of inherent, inalienable, non-prescriptible, and non-repealable fundamental rights and freedoms of individuals, equal in dignity and rights; a system based on the principles of democracy, the sovereignty of the people, and separation of powers, respecting the cited material concept of a law-based state, is built to protect them.

From this, it went on later in its judgment to state:

135. However, the constitutional law limits for the transfer of powers contained in...the Constitution also indicate the need for clearer delimitation (and thus also definiteness and recognizability) of the transferred powers, together with sufficient review, which the Czech Republic, as a sovereign state, can exercise over the transfer of powers.

This led the Czech Constitutional Court to express particular concern over one provision, Article 216 TFEU. This grants the Union treaty-making powers wherever, inter alia, this is necessary to realise one of its objectives within the framework of its powers. The Czech Constitutional Court considered this a very vague formulation, and expressed concern about its lack of clarity. However, it held that it was not sufficiently unclear for the Lisbon Treaty to be held unconstitutional.[54]

---

[51] For these see pp. 40–2 in Chapter 1 and pp. 206–11 above.

[52] For debate see S. Weatherill, 'Competence Creep and Competence Control' (2004) 23 *YEL* 1; P. Craig, 'Competence: Clarity, Conferral, Containment and Consideration' (2004) 29 *ELRev.* 323; F. Mayer, 'Competences – Reloaded? The Vertical Division of Powers in the EU after the New European Constitution' (2005) 3 *ICON* 493.

[53] Pl ÚS 19/08 *Treaty of Lisbon*, Judgment of 26 November 2008 http://angl.concourt.cz/angl_verze/doc/pl-19-08.php (accessed 25 August 2009).

[54] At paras 184–6.

(ii) Flexibility provision

The Treaties contain numerous powers which have been expressly conferred upon the European Union, but in extraordinarily wide and undefined terms. Article 114 TFEU, for example, allows the Union to adopt measures for the approximation of national laws, which have as their object the 'establishment and functioning of the internal market'. Similarly, Article 192 TFEU allows for an astonishingly broad array of measures to be adopted in the field of environmental protection. The most problematic of these provisions, however, is the 'flexibility' provision, Article 352 TFEU.

Article 352(1) TFEU

If action by the Union should prove necessary, within the framework of the policies defined by the Treaties, to attain one of the objectives set out in the Treaties, and the Treaties have not provided the necessary powers, the Council, acting unanimously on a proposal from the European Commission and after obtaining the consent of the European Parliament, shall adopt the appropriate measures. Where the measures in question are adopted by the Council in accordance with a special legislative procedure, it shall also act unanimously on a proposal from the Commission and after obtaining the consent of the European Parliament.

Article 352 TFEU is significantly wider than its predecessor, Article 308 EC. The latter granted legislative powers whenever this was necessary to realise *Community* objectives. The new provision, by contrast, with the absorption of the Community into the Union, applies to a more extensive, ambitious set of objectives: those of *Union* objectives. The new provision is particularly controversial given the latitude with which the earlier provision was interpreted.[55]

R. Schütze, *From Dual to Cooperative Federalism: The Changing Structure of European Law* (Oxford, Oxford University Press, 2009) 136–8

What are the objectives of the European Community? The Treaty did not clearly define what its 'objectives' are. Its opening provisions refer to the – similar but not identical – concepts of 'tasks' and 'activities'. One influential current in the European law literature during the 1970s suggested that Article 308 could only be used to fill gaps inside those areas in which the Community had already been given a *specific* competence. Outside the expressly enumerated fields, it was impossible to assume the existence of an 'objective' since the Community legislator was not meant to regulate those areas in the first place. According to this view, Article 308's scope was to find a limit in the jurisdictional boundaries set by the 'activities' of the Community – a position which linked the notion of 'objective' in Article 308 to the areas listed in Article 3 EC. A gap in the Treaty could be identified only by comparing the extent of the specific legal entitlements *within* a policy field and the *specific* aims of the Community policy within that area.

---

[55] Most particularly with the German Länder who saw EU law encroaching on their autonomy in a manner that not even the German federal authorities were able to do. 'Forderungen der Länder zur Regierungskonferenz 1996', Drucksache 667/95 (Beschluß), 15 December 1995, 12–21.

A second academic camp favoured a much wider application of Article 308. This position was premised on a two-layered understanding of the enumeration principle, which draws on a conceptual distinction between *jurisdiction* and *competence*. Article 308 could be used to fill any gap between the Treaty's *aims* and its *powers*. The perhaps most comprehensive manifesto of this expansionist rationale argued that Article 308 was 'designed to bridge the discrepancy between the Community's jurisdiction – as defined by its objectives – and a partial *or complete absence of powers for their realisation*'. The provision would create a 'gap-less system of competences for achieving all Community objectives'. The Community's jurisdiction and its competence would, thus, coincide. Wherever a matter fell into the scope of the Treaty, the Community would have a legislative competence – at least a subsidiary one under Article 308 EC. The Community's competence was the sum of its objectives...

By the end of the 1970s, Article 308 had been allowed to tap into the global objectives of the Community set out in Article 2 EC. Ever since, conceptual limits to the Community's competence became hard to identify. If the Community could act to promote – for example – closer relations between the states, such a competence would be devoid of internal boundaries as all *common* legislation will, by definition, diminish legislative disparities and thereby increase the legal proximity between the Member States.

The textbook illustration for the dramatic expansion of Europe's competence sphere on the basis of Article 308 EC is provided by the Community's environmental policy. Stimulated by the political enthusiasm of the Member States after the Paris Summit, the Commission and the Council faced the legal problem that environmental policy was not an official Community activity. There was therefore no specific legal title offered by the Treaty. The way out of this dilemma had been suggested in the 1972 Paris Communiqué. It called on the Community institutions to make the widest possible use of all provisions of the Treaties, including Article 308. The Member States had thus themselves proposed an extensive interpretation of the Treaties' objectives to cause a 'small revision' of the Treaty by means of Article 308.

This 'constitutional' spirit would overcome the Treaty's textual boundaries. It can be gauged by the following commentary, in which Usher neatly captured the interpretative climate of legislative free style that would replace the missing Treaty amendment:

'[T]hose responsible for drafting Community environmental legislation appear to have found their own route for solving this dilemma. By about 1980, as exemplified in Council Directive 80/68 on the protection of ground water against pollution by certain dangerous substances, the recitals justify making use of [Article 308 EC] on the grounds of the necessity for Community action in the sphere of the environmental protection and improvement of the "quality of life", a phrase which is found neither in the recitals to the Treaty nor in its general introductory provisions... Nevertheless, over the years, the phrase the 'raising of the standard of living' was linked to improving the "quality of life" and by the time this Directive was adopted it could be stated that legislation was justified in terms of [Article 308 EC] on the basis that it improved the quality of life, *as if that were a Treaty objective.*' [56]

[56] J. Usher, 'The Gradual Widening of European Community Policy on the Basis of Articles 100 and 235 of the EEC Treaty' in J. Schwarze and H. Schermers (eds.), *Structure and Dimensions of European Community Policy* (Baden Baden, Nomos, 1988) 32–3.

It is not simply that this provision has been interpreted ambitiously. It has also been used extensively. De Búrca and de Witte reported, in 2002, that it had, by that date, served as the legal basis for about 700 EC legal acts.[57] In like vein, Schütze has observed that the provision has traditionally been deployed for about 30 legislative acts per annum.[58] The veto granted to national governments present in Article 352 TFEU and in its predecessor, Article 308 EC, has not been a sufficient safeguard to curb its use. This begs the question as to whether the even wider provision in Article 352 TFEU is closer to a general law-making power with insufficient constraints.

The Treaty of Lisbon has responded to this with the introduction of a number of constraints. Some of these are procedural. An extra veto player has been added in the form of the European Parliament and Article 352(2) TFEU requires all proposals based on the provision to be brought to the attention of national parliaments for them to consider whether these comply with the subsidiarity principle.[59] Article 352 TFEU introduces some new substantive constraints as well.

Article 352(3), (4) TFEU

3. Measures based on this Article shall not entail harmonisation of Member States' laws or regulations in cases where the Treaties exclude such harmonisation.
4. This Article cannot serve as a basis for attaining objectives pertaining to the common foreign and security policy and any acts adopted pursuant to this Article shall respect the limits set out in Article 40(2) TEU.[60]

Article 2 TFEU, it will be remembered, lists three fields where the Union does not have legislative competence. One of these is Common Foreign and Security Policy.[61] Article 352(2) TFEU repeats this, although it is worth noting that many fields of foreign policy are governed by the TFEU and it does have power to harmonise in these fields. These include trade and financial relations, sanctions, development and humanitarian aid. It can also not be used in some fields. The other two fields are those areas of employment and economic policy where the Union can only adopt guidelines and fields of coordinating, supplementary and supporting action. Article 352 TFEU cannot therefore be used in the fields, for example, of protection of human health, industry, culture, tourism or education.

So what can Article 352 TFEU be used for? Declaration 41 to the Lisbon Treaty states that the objectives pursued by Article 352 TFEU and mentioned in that provision refer to the objectives in what is now Article 3(2), (3) and (5) TEU.[62]

---

[57] G. de Búrca and B. de Witte, 'The Delimitation of Powers between the EU and its Member States' in A. Arnull and D. Wincott (eds.), *Accountability and Legitimacy in the European Union* (Oxford, Oxford University Press, 2002) 217.

[58] R. Schütze, 'Organized Change towards an "Ever Closer Union": Article 308 EC and the Limits to the Community's Legislative Competence' (2003) 22 *YBEL* 79.

[59] For more on this see pp. 361–7.

[60] This is a curious paragraph as it states that 'the implementation of the policies listed in Articles 3–6 TFEU shall not affect the application of the procedures and the extent of the powers of the institutions set out in the Chapter on CFSP'. It does not refer to Article 352 TFEU but the intent is that Article 352 TFEU must not trespass on the procedures there.

[61] Article 2(4) TFEU.

[62] The Declaration is confusing as it refers to the numbering of the Treaties before they were renumbered. Under the old numbering Article 2 was what is now Article 3, and this is referred to in the original Declaration. There was also, confusingly, reference to an Article 3(5) which did not exist in either Treaty in the original numbering. This is assumed to be the current Article 3(5) TEU.

Article 3(2), (3), (5) TEU

2. The Union shall offer its citizens an area of freedom, security and justice without internal frontiers, in which the free movement of persons is ensured in conjunction with appropriate measures with respect to external border controls, asylum, immigration and the prevention and combating of crime.

3. The Union shall establish an internal market. It shall work for the sustainable development of Europe based on balanced economic growth and price stability, a highly competitive social market economy, aiming at full employment and social progress, and a high level of protection and improvement of the quality of the environment. It shall promote scientific and technological advance.

    It shall combat social exclusion and discrimination, and shall promote social justice and protection, equality between women and men, solidarity between generations and protection of the rights of the child...

5. In its relations with the wider world, the Union shall uphold and promote its values and contribute to the protection of its citizens. It shall contribute to peace, security, the sustainable development of the Earth, solidarity and mutual respect among peoples, free and fair trade, eradication of poverty and the protection of human rights, in particular the rights of the child, as well as to the strict observance and the development of international law, including respect for the principles of the United Nations Charter.

This is the first time that an attempt has been made to confine Article 352 TFEU, but it still allows for an aggressive deployment. The objectives are wide-ranging, including social justice, intergenerational equity, full employment and the eradication of poverty. Declaration 42 is intended, however, to prevent this. It states that Article 352 TFEU:

cannot serve as a basis for widening the scope of Union powers beyond the general framework created by the provisions of the Treaties as a whole and, in particular, by those that define the tasks and the activities of the Union. In any event, this Article cannot be used as a basis for the adoption of provisions whose effect would, in substance, be to amend the Treaties without following the procedure which they provide for that purpose.

At one level, this Declaration does no more than reiterate an earlier ruling of the Court of Justice that the provision cannot be used to amend the Treaties.[63] Yet the use of such detailed language and the emphasis by twenty-seven governments carries with it a powerful message. The procedure is not to be used expansively, and far more thought must be given to the limits of Union competence in the course of its deployment.

It will be interesting to see how much heed is given to this by the Court of Justice. In *Kadi*, the Court considered the question of when a measure pursued objectives related to the operation of the internal market (now set out in Article 3(3) TFEU). The facts were that, following the 9/11 attacks, the UN Security Council adopted Resolutions requiring states to freeze all the assets and funds of anyone it believed to be associated with Osama Bin Laden. The list of persons whose assets were to be frozen was updated by a UN Sanctions Committee. In 2001, Kadi and Al Bakaraat were put on this list and their assets frozen. The Union implemented the Resolution by a Regulation. This was based on Article 352 TFEU and two provisions that are

---

[63] Opinion 2/94 *Re Accession of the Community to the ECHR* [1996] ECR I-1759.

now succeeded by Article 215 TFEU, which provides sanctions, including interrupting economic and financial relations, to be taken against non-EU states. The challenge was that these referred exclusively to relations with non-EU states, and there was no mention of sanctions on private actors in them.[64] Whilst the Regulation allowed funds for food, medical treatment, mortgages and professional fees, it was otherwise sweeping. It was essentially a Regulation that determined what property an individual could have and whether they could have any property at all. Kadi challenged this before the General Court, who upheld the Regulation. The Court of Justice allowed the appeal on the grounds that the Regulation violated fundamental rights. Another of the grounds of appeal was that the Union did not have the competence to adopt the Regulation. This was dismissed by the Court of Justice.

Joined Cases C–402/05 P and C–415/05 P *Kadi and Al Barakaat International Foundation* v *Council* [2008] ECR I-6351

224. In this regard it may be recalled that... Article 352 TFEU, being an integral part of an institutional system based on the principle of conferred powers, cannot serve as a basis for widening the scope of [Union] powers beyond the general framework created by the provisions of the [TFEU] as a whole.

225. The objective pursued by the contested regulation may be made to refer to one of the objectives of the [Union] for the purpose of Article 352 TFEU, with the result that the adoption of that regulation did not amount to disregard of the scope of Community powers stemming from the provisions of the [TFEU] as a whole.

226. Inasmuch as they provide for [Union] powers to impose restrictive measures of an economic nature in order to implement actions decided on under the CFSP, [Article 215 TFEU is] the expression of an implicit underlying objective, namely, that of making it possible to adopt such measures through the efficient use of a [Union] instrument.

227. That objective may be regarded as constituting an objective of the Community for the purpose of Article [352 TFEU]...

229. Implementing restrictive measures of an economic nature through the use of a [Union] instrument does not go beyond the general framework created by the provisions of the [TFEU] as a whole, because such measures by their very nature offer a link to the operation of the common market, that link constituting another condition for the application of Article [352 TFEU]...

230. If economic and financial measures such as those imposed by the contested regulation, consisting of the, in principle generalised, freezing of all the funds and other economic resources of the persons and entities concerned, were imposed unilaterally by every Member State, the multiplication of those national measures might well affect the operation of the common market. Such measures could have a particular effect on trade between Member States, especially with regard to the movement of capital and payments, and on the exercise by economic operators of their right of establishment. In addition, they could create distortions of competition, because any differences between the measures unilaterally taken by the Member States could operate to the advantage or disadvantage of the competitive position of certain economic operators although there were no economic reasons for that advantage or disadvantage.

---

[64] This has since been rectified by the Treaty of Lisbon which introduces an entirely new provision allowing sanctions to be taken against non-state actors, Article 75 TFEU.

The key part of the reasoning is in paragraph 226, where the Court identifies the measures as having an economic nature. This allows it to make the link with the operation of the internal market. Any economic measure by its nature can be said to affect the competitive position of operators by granting or denying them a benefit. Whether it in fact does so is another matter, and the test is a notional one. It is beyond credulity that freezing the assets of a couple of hundred individuals distorts competition in any significant way in the world's largest economic bloc.

If the link with the internal market is interpreted so creatively in *Kadi* and still found to fall within the doctrine of conferred powers, this begs the question what will fall within the other fields, such as social justice or the area of freedom, security and justice. Housing law could, for example, fall within the former, whilst family and criminal law are clearly related to the latter. This raises the paradox that fields not mentioned in the Treaties are more at risk from Union intrusion than fields where provision is made only for supporting, coordinating or supplementary actions, as Article 352 TFEU involvement in the latter is excluded.

(iii)   Protection of national constitutional identities

It also suggests that the Union may operate under a form of conferred powers, but this is very far from the model of limited powers or a model for determining what is sacred from a national point of view and what is not, both matters of concern for national constitutional courts. This led the German Constitutional Court in its assessment of the Lisbon Treaty to state that Article 352 TFEU had relaxed the doctrine of conferred powers, as the provision served 'to create a competence which makes action on the European level possible in almost the entire area of application of the primary law'.[65] If it were used, the German Constitutional Court added, this would require both German parliamentary chambers to approve formally any proposal under it before Germany would be able to agree to a proposal under it.

Even this was not sufficient: the German Constitutional Court went on to rule that there were a series of fields where Article 352 TFEU could not be used.

---

2 BvE 2/08 *Gauweiler v Treaty of Lisbon*, Judgment of 30 June 2009

251. Even if due to the great successes of European integration, a joint European public that engages in an issue-related cooperation in the rooms of resonance of their respective states is evidently growing…, it cannot be overlooked, however, that the public perception of factual issues and of political leaders remains connected to a considerable extent to patterns of identification which are related to the nation-state, language, history and culture. The principle of democracy as well as the principle of subsidiarity… therefore require to factually restrict the transfer and exercise of sovereign powers to the European Union in a predictable manner particularly in central political areas of the space of personal development and the shaping of the circumstances of life by social policy. In these areas, it particularly suggests itself to draw the limit where the coordination of circumstances with a cross-border dimension is factually required.

---

[65] 2 BvE 2/08 *Gauweiler v Treaty of Lisbon*, Judgment of 30 June 2009, paras. 326–7.

252. What has always been deemed especially sensitive for the ability of a constitutional state to democratically shape itself are decisions on substantive and formal criminal law, on the disposition of the police monopoly on the use of force towards the interior and of the military monopoly on the use of force towards the exterior, the fundamental fiscal decisions on public revenue and public expenditure, with the latter being particularly motivated, inter alia, by social-policy considerations, decisions on the shaping of circumstances of life in a social state and decisions which are of particular importance culturally, for instance as regards family law, the school and education system and dealing with religious communities.

For the German Constitutional Court, the European Union cannot pass legislation in five central fields of domestic life: the central features of criminal law, the deployment of the use of force, central budgetary issues, the central issues of social policy, and culturally important fields, in particular religion, education and family life. This is the most extensive and most explicit list of national reserved powers ever put forward. It has already been criticised. For example, why not include civil law or monetary laws, both of which have historically been important to state formation?[66]

This might be because the judgment takes the current status quo as the point of departure. The position of the Union is taken as a given but the German Constitutional Court has fired a shot across the bows about the fields into which it must not enter. This has been presaged by two decisions discussed below from France and Italy, which, whilst less clearly formulated, suggest that it must not trespass either on national constitutional symbols or the scope of national constitutional rights.

The issue of constitutional symbols was addressed by a 2005 Decision of the French Constitutional Council, in which it had to rule on the compatibility of the Constitutional Treaty with the French Constitution. Article 1 of the French Constitution provides that France is a secular republic. This has been interpreted as banning any display of religious symbols in schools, including the wearing of the cross or the veil by pupils. Article II-70 of the failed Constitutional Treaty provided that anyone may manifest their religious belief in public. There seemed, therefore, to be a straightforward conflict. However, the French Constitutional Council stated that the EU provision was intended to have the same scope and meaning as Article 9 ECHR, which allows restrictions to be imposed on the display of religious belief on grounds, inter alia, of public policy. This has been interpreted to give considerable weight to the principle of secularism in national constitutional traditions, leaving national authorities a considerable margin of discretion as to how to reconcile freedom of religion with secularism. On this basis, the Constitutional Council considered there to be no conflict between the Constitutional Treaty and the French Constitution.[67]

---

[66] D. Halberstam and C. Möllers, 'The German Constitutional Court says "*Ja zu Deutschland!*"' (2009) 10 *German Law Journal* No. 8.

[67] *Re EU Constitutional Treaty and the French Constitution*, French Constitutional Court [2005] 1 CMLR 750. For a similar style of reasoning by the Greek Constitutional Court, albeit in relation to the public status of universities, see M. Maganaris, 'Greece: The Principles of Supremacy of Community Law – The Greek Challenge' (1998) 23 *ELRev.* 179.

Whilst nothing is explicitly stated about the limits of EU law, the French Constitutional Council adopted an aggressive and some might say counter-intuitive interpretation of a Treaty provision and indicated that the Court of Justice would have to follow it. It was, in other words, asserting its hegemony over the meaning of the French constitutional order, and indicating that it would only tolerate Court of Justice involvement insofar as it took French understandings of that order as a given.

The other field where the Union must not trespass is that of constitutional rights or fundamental rights. As we shall see in the next chapter, the Court of Justice has stated that it is competent to rule on fundamental rights questions that fall within the aegis of EU law, and for that purpose has developed an autonomous EU law of fundamental rights. Following the Treaty of Lisbon, nothing must be done to restrict or adversely affect the rights set out in national constitutions.[68]

National constitutional courts have contested the Court of Justice's position. In the 1970s, both the German and the Italian constitutional courts indicated that they would not apply provisions of EU law that failed to respect the fundamental rights and values set out in their respective national constitutions.[69] In more recent times, some leeway has been given to the Court of Justice with both the German and Czech Constitutional Courts stating that, as EU law now contained sufficient fundamental rights guarantees of its own, they would not actively review EU legislation provided this general level of protection was maintained.[70]

However, they have never gone so far as to suggest that Court of Justice judgments bound them on fundamental rights and there is no instance of a national constitutional court accepting a judgment by the Court suggesting it had misinterpreted its constitution. National constitutional courts' monopoly over interpreting the meaning of rights set out in their constitutions was most explicitly stated in *Admenta*, a ruling by the Italian State Council.[71] The judgment concerned a 1991 law that allowed pharmaceutical companies to own municipal pharmacies in Milan. This was ruled unconstitutional on the grounds that, inter alia, it violated article 32 of the Italian Constitution, protecting the right to health insofar as it generated a conflict of interest in those selling the medicines. It was argued that this restriction violated EU law and it clearly fell within the aegis of EU law.[72] However, the State Council stated that under Italian law there were protected areas of law that existed outside EU law and in which Italian law was sovereign. One of these areas was fundamental rights. Even if the matter conflicted with EU law, this was not an issue, as fundamental rights were reserved for national law. There was no need for a referral, therefore, as in its view the matter was decided exclusively by the Italian Constitution.

Perhaps the most interesting question is whether the protection of national constitutional identities involves not just limits on the exercise of EU powers but some scrutiny of the democratic qualities of the Union. This was addressed in most detail in Pl US 50/04.[73] The Czech

---

[68] European Union Charter of Fundamental Rights, Article 53. See p. 242.

[69] See, respectively, *Internationale Handelsgesellschaft* [1974] 2 CMLR 540 and *Frontini v Ministero delle Finanze* [1974] CMLR 386. This has also been stated by the Czech Constitutional Court, Pl ÚS 50/04 *Sugar Quota Regulation II*, Judgment 8 March 2006, http://angl.concourt.cz/angl_verze/doc/p-50-04.php (accessed 22 August 2009).

[70] (1986) 73 BVerfGE 339 *Wünsche Handelsgesellschaft (Solange II)* [1987] 7 CMLR 225; Pl ÚS 66/04 *European Arrest Warrant*, Judgment of 3 May 2006, http://angl.concourt.cz/angl_verze/doc/pl-66-04.php (accessed 22 August 2009).

[71] *Admenta and Others v Federfarma* [2006] 2 CMLR 47.

[72] It was eventually held to fall within EU law but be lawful in Case C-531/06 *Commission v Italy*, Judgment of 19 May 2009.

[73] Pl US 50/04 *Sugar Quota Regulation II*, http://angl.concourt.cz/angl_verze/doc/p-50-04.php.

Constitutional Court annulled a series of government measures organising the sugar market on the grounds that competence for these had been transferred to the Union. In the judgment, it reflected on the relationship between EU and Czech law:

> In the Constitutional Court's view, this conferral of a part of its [the Czech Republic's] powers is naturally a conditional conferral, as the original bearer of sovereignty, as well as the powers flowing therefrom, still remains the Czech Republic, whose sovereignty is still founded upon Art. 1 para. 1 of the Constitution of the Czech Republic. In the Constitutional Court's view, the conditional nature of the delegation of these powers is manifested on two planes: the formal and the substantive planes. The first of these planes concerns the power attributes of state sovereignty itself, the second plane concerns the substantive component of the exercise of state power. In other words, the delegation of a part of the powers of national organs may persist only so long as these powers are exercised in a manner that is compatible with the preservation of the foundations of state sovereignty of the Czech Republic, and in a manner which does not threaten the very essence of the substantive law-based state. In such determination the Constitutional Court is called upon to protect constitutionalism (Art. 83 of the Constitution of the Czech Republic). According to Art. 9 para. 2 of the Constitution of the Czech Republic, the essential attributes of a democratic state governed by the rule of law, remain beyond the reach of the Constituent Assembly itself.

This formulation, repeated subsequently,[74] not only qualifies EU legal sovereignty as something that cannot extinguish the core functions of the Czech state. The Czech Constitutional Court will also intervene whenever the Union does not act according to the principles of a 'democratic law-based state'. The basis for this is that the constitutional identity of the Czech state rests upon these foundations and there can be no derogation whatsoever from these principles.

This test is more multifaceted than that in *Gauweiler*. The latter utilises a dualist logic in which representative democracy exists only at the national level and the majority of power must, correspondingly, be exercised there. As a consequence, the European Union is permitted to exercise only limited powers. The relationship between the logics of these two spheres is unexplored, with the consequence that no reason is provided why any power should be transferred to the Union, as any transfer is necessarily undemocratic. To maintain the stability of the reasoning, important notions such as national representative democracy and limited powers are left untested. Something called 'representative democracy' is taken as a sine qua non for democracy and, in like vein, the Union's extensive powers are assumed to be limited.

The reasoning of the Czech Constitutional Court, by contrast, is a unitary one. The idea of a democratic law-based state is not so troubled by a transfer of power to another democratic law-based state. The constitutional state acts as a fulcrum that both mediates power between, and provides a check on, other levels of government – a central republican principle. In addition, the idea of a democratic law-based state becomes a constitutive principle of all government. It can call for the transfer of competences between levels of government where one level is unable to meet the needs of its constituents. It also acts as a basis for each to review the actions of the other according to a common legal ethical syntax. Defined in such broad terms, it is not confined to questions of fundamental rights, but covers all questions that trouble

[74] Pl US 66/04 *European Arrest Warrant*, http://angl.concourt.cz/angl_verze/doc/pl-66-04.php.

public lawyers: checks and balances, principles of representation, accountability, deliberation and participation.

7 THE FIDELITY PRINCIPLE

A requirement on Member States simply not to breach EU law would be insufficient to secure the full effectiveness of the EU legal system. States are different from private actors in that they must not only comply with the law but are also under a positive duty to secure law and order within their territories. All legal systems confer responsibilities upon public bodies to ensure that the law is generally applied, policed and accessible, and that there are sufficient remedies for breach of the law. Known in the United States as the 'fidelity principle', the requirement is that 'each level and unit of government must act to ensure the proper functioning of the system of governance as a whole'.[75] In EU law, the principle is set out in Article 4(3) TEU.

Article 4(3) TEU

Pursuant to the principle of sincere cooperation, the Union and the Member States shall, in full mutual respect, assist each other in carrying out tasks which flow from the Treaties.

The Member States shall take any appropriate measure, general or particular, to ensure fulfilment of the obligations arising out of the Treaties or resulting from the acts of the institutions of the Union.

The Member States shall facilitate the achievement of the Union's tasks and refrain from any measure which could jeopardise the attainment of the Union's objectives.

The provision applies not only to the Member States, but also to the EU institutions, which must cooperate with national bodies to secure the full effectiveness of EU law.[76] It introduces two important modifications on its pre-Lisbon predecessor, Article 10 EC. First, it introduces the idea of 'mutual respect'. This suggests a countervailing principle, under which each institution must not only assist each other but must not transgress upon the prerogatives of the other. This would imply, for example, that if the duty of cooperation currently imposes a responsibility on national courts not to assess a potentially anti-competitive practice being considered by the Commission,[77] there may be a corollary obligation on the Commission to leave to national authorities assessment of practices more appropriately considered by them.[78] Secondly, the duty of cooperation applies to tasks that 'flow from the Treaties'. This is a more open-ended concept than the previous duty, which merely applied to tasks arising from fulfilment of Treaty obligations. Notably, it suggests that the duty of cooperation applies to projects such as the Lisbon Agenda, whose ambitions both build upon and extend beyond the Treaties.

The fidelity provision carries both negative and positive obligations for the EU institutions. The negative obligation is that these must not simply not take measures that conflict with substantive EU laws but also must not adopt measures which obstruct the effectiveness of EU

[75] D. Halberstam, 'The Political Morality of Federal Systems' (2004) 90 *Virginia L Rev.* 101, 104.
[76] Case 2/88 *Zwartveld* [1990] ECR I-3365.
[77] Case C-344/98 *Masterfoods* v *HB Ice Cream* [2000] ECR I-11369.
[78] This is already established by the Commission Notice on cooperation within the network of competition authorities [2004] OJ C101/43, para. 8.

policies in more indirect ways. The positive obligation is to take a number of measures that contribute to the realisation of Union policies. These negative and positive obligations are now set out in turn.

The central negative obligation is that once EU institutions have indicated a point of departure for common action, Member States are under a duty to abstain from any measure which could frustrate realisation of the objectives in the common action. In the field of external relations, if the Commission has been authorised to conclude an international agreement, therefore, Member States cannot enter independent bilateral agreements of their own on the subject in hand with the non-EU state concerned unless this is done with the cooperation of the EU institutions.[79] Internally, this duty applies with most force to Directives which have come into force but whose deadline for transposition has not yet expired. Whilst national authorities have until the latter date to adopt implementing legislation, the Court has indicated that they are under a duty prior to that to abstain from any measure that would compromise the objectives of the Directive.[80] The national legislature cannot pass legislation that would conflict with the Directive, and national courts, where this choice is open to them under national law, are not free to adopt interpretations that would conflict with it.

The positive obligations are multiple. First, national institutions are required to secure legal certainty for EU law. The Court of Justice has stated that Member States must implement their obligations 'with unquestionable binding force and with the specificity, precision and clarity necessary to satisfy that principle'.[81] Mere administrative practice will not be enough to meet a state's obligations. Measures must be in place which, whilst not necessarily legislation, are sufficiently binding that they cannot be changed at will. Such measures must be public so that citizens are able to identify their rights.[82]

Secondly, Member States must actively police EU law. In *Commission* v *France*, French farmers launched a violent campaign targeting the importation of Spanish strawberries.[83] Their action involved threatening shops, burning lorries carrying the goods and blockading roads. The French government took almost no action either to stop these protests or to prosecute offences committed as a result of them. While the acts stopping the import of Spanish strawberries were performed by *private* actors – the farmers – and while the relevant provision of EU law, Article 34 TFEU, imposed obligations only on *states* not to prevent the free movement of goods, the Court ruled that France had breached EU law. The state was required to adopt all appropriate measures to guarantee the full scope and effect of EU law. In taking measures that were manifestly inadequate, France had failed to do this. The requirement to police EU law, however, is not an absolute one: a Member State does not have to police EU law if this would result in public disorder which it could not contain. Similarly, it must not police EU law in such a way that it violates fundamental rights and civil liberties.[84]

Thirdly, Member States must penalise infringements of EU law under conditions, both procedural and substantive, that are analogous to those applicable to infringements of national law

---

[79] Case C-266/03 *Commission* v *Luxembourg* [2005] ECR I-4805.

[80] Case C-212/04 *Adeneler and Others* v *ELOG (Ellinikos Organismos Galaktos)* [2006] ECR I-6057. This is dealt with in much more detail on pp. 298–300.

[81] Case C-159/99 *Commission* v *Italy (conservation of wild birds)* [2001] ECR I-4007.

[82] Case C-313/99 *Mulgan and Others* [2002] ECR I-5719. The principle of legal certainty also requires that if Member States amend a law to comply with EU law, the amending measure must have the same legal force as the original measures: Case C-33/03 *Commission* v *United Kingdom (VAT on road fuel)* [2005] ECR I-1865.

[83] Case C-265/95 *Commission* v *France (Spanish strawberries)* [1997] ECR I-6959.

[84] Case C-112/00 *Schmidberger* v *Republic of Austria* [2003] ECR I-5659.

of a similar nature and importance.[85] In addition, national courts must ensure that, irrespective of the situation for breaches of national law, penalties for breach of EU law are effective, proportionate and dissuasive.[86] In *Berlusconi*,[87]Advocate General Kokott set out what these criteria mean:

> 88. Rules laying down penalties are *effective* where they are framed in such a way that they do not make it practically impossible or excessively difficult to impose the penalty provided for and, therefore, to attain the objectives pursued by Community law.
>
> 89. A penalty is *dissuasive* where it prevents an individual from infringing the objectives pursued and rules laid down by Community law. What is decisive in this regard is not only the nature and level of the penalty but also the likelihood of its being imposed. Anyone who commits an infringement must fear that the penalty will in fact be imposed on him. There is an overlap here between the criterion of dissuasiveness and that of effectiveness.
>
> 90. A penalty is *proportionate* where it is appropriate (that is to say, in particular, *effective* and *dissuasive*) for attaining the legitimate objectives pursued by it, and also necessary. Where there is a choice between several (equally) appropriate penalties, recourse must be had to the least onerous. Moreover, the effects of the penalty on the person concerned must be proportionate to the aims pursued.

Finally, Member States are under a duty to notify the Commission if they have any problems applying or enforcing EU law. In this regard, they cannot use Commission reservations, conditions or objections as a basis for derogating from EU law.[88]

Article 4(3) TEU has been described as an overarching provision 'drawing all relevant institutions into the job of effectively sustaining [Union] policy'.[89] This is true. However, the provision extends beyond that. It sets out the expectations of what a state must be capable of to sustain the obligations of membership. It set outs responsibilities of comity but, above all, it sets out expectations about the commitments and resources that states must both have and commit – be these effective judicial systems, proactive, well-resourced, non-corrupt policing or a clear and universal rule of law – for membership of the European Union.

For all this, the institutional actors, be they administrative, legislative or judicial, see themselves and are seen by EU law as domestic actors. This is significant because it suggests that they are embedded in a series of domestic constraints and relationships that shape who they are and which they cannot ignore. The heavy reliance of the Union on national authorities to apply and enforce EU law has, moreover, been seen by comparative scholars as an important democratic counterweight, which can curb the Union imposing excessive or repressive demands on local actors.[90]

---

[85] Case C-180/95 *Draehmpaehl* v *Urania Immobilienservice* [1997] ECR I-2195. They must also penalise them in an equivalent manner to breaches of other EU law provisions which are of a similar importance. Case C-460/06 *Paquay* v *Société d'architectes Hoet & Minne* [2007] ECR I-8511.

[86] Case 68/88 *Commission* v *Greece* [1989] ECR 2965; Case C-326/88 *Hansen* [1990] ECR I-2911; Case C-167/01 *Kamer van Koophandel en Fabrieken voor Amsterdam* v *Inspire Art* [2003] ECR I-10155.

[87] Joined Cases C-387/02, C-391/02 and C-403/02 *Berlusconi and Others* [2005] ECR I-3565.

[88] Case C-105/02 *Commission* v *Germany* [2006] ECR I-9659.

[89] S. Weatherill, 'Beyond Preemption? Shared Competence and Constitutional Change in the European Community' in D. O'Keeffe and P. Twomey (eds.), *Legal Issues of the Maastricht Treaty* (London, Chancery, 1994) 31. See also J. Temple Lang, 'Community Constitutional Law: Article 5 EEC Treaty' (1990) 27 *CMLRev.* 645.

[90] G. Bermann, 'Taking Subsidiarity Seriously: Federalism in the European Community and the United States' (1994) 94 *Colum. L Rev.* 331, 399; E. Young, 'Protecting Member State Autonomy in the European Union: Some Cautionary Tales from American Federalism' (2002) 77 *NYU L Rev.* 1612, 1736.

This ethos seems to be shared by national constitutional courts who have indicated that domestic actors' institutional duties under EU law are subject to those placed on them by the constitution and must not violate the constitution. Normally, this is done not by the constitutional court challenging EU law directly but rather by stating that the domestic implementing measure is illegal. Two examples will suffice to illustrate this.

In the first, the Hungarian Constitutional Court considered a 2004 Hungarian law which fined anybody engaged in speculation in agricultural products in the period prior to Hungarian accession to the European Union.[91] Speculation was assumed to have taken place where agricultural contracts were entered into after 1 January 2004 or where there was a sudden jump in the size of a farmer's inventories. The law was based on an EU Regulation designed to prevent profiteering as a consequence of the subsidies that would accrue to Hungarian farmers from EU membership and which would be based on the volume of their production. The difficulty was that both the Regulation and the Hungarian law came into force on 1 May 2004 and, therefore, were retroactive in that they punished acts that were lawful at the time they were committed.

Notwithstanding the identical phrasing of the EU Regulation and the Hungarian statute, the Constitutional Court treated it as a wholly internal matter. The Court made no reference to EU law. Instead, the Hungarian law was found to violate Article 2(1) of the Hungarian Constitution on the grounds that it violated the principle of legal certainty as it punished activities retroactively and there was no reason that those engaging in the activity could have known at the time that it would be punished.

The second example concerns consideration by the German Constitutional Court of the German law implementing the European Arrest Warrant.[92] The latter provided for the quasi-automatic surrender by a Member State to another Member State of somebody sought by the latter for the commission of a series of listed crimes. The surrender had to take place even if it were a surrendering state's own national, even if there were joint jurisdiction over the alleged criminal activities and even if these would not have been a crime in the surrendering state. Article 16(2) of the German Basic Law prohibited extradition of a German national, but provided an exception for extradition to other EU states, provided this complied with other constitutional requirements.

The German Constitutional Court found the German implementing measure violated a number of these. It found the possibility that a German national could be surrendered for an offence committed on German territory unconstitutional as it excluded a citizen's right to associate herself with a free, democratic polity, whose laws she had violated. The Constitutional Court also found insufficient judicial safeguards in the measure, as it considered any surrendering court would need to have all the facts before it in each case to make a proper assessment and to consider whether the fundamental rights of the individual would be respected in the requesting state. Finally, the German Constitutional Court considered that there was a breach of the principle of non-retroactivity insofar as a German could now be tried for something done in Germany which at the time was not illegal under German law.

---

[91] Decision 17/04 (V. 25) AB, www.mkab.hu/en/enpage3.htm (accessed 25 August 2009).
[92] *Re Constitutionality of German Law Implementing the Framework Decision on a European Arrest Warrant* [2006] 1 CMLR 16.

Both the German and Hungarian Constitutional Courts do not question directly the supremacy of EU law. Yet the domestic measures in both cases, particularly the Hungarian, accurately reflected the EU measure. In both cases, the constitutional courts refused to look at the wider EU context and the effects its ruling would have on the general operation of EU law. In this, there was an implicit suggestion that if EU law did not take account of the principles important to them, they would not have much regard for it. As Komárek has suggested, this debate is not, however, just about how amenable national constitutional courts are to EU law.[93] There is another issue, which is the distortion of institutional relations within the domestic settlement. In the Hungarian case, there was the problem of the legislature riding roughshod over both private autonomy and the power of judicial review. In the German case, there was the issue of German courts extraditing without sufficient regard to the relationship between German citizens and the political settlement. The defiance by the constitutional courts was therefore as much about protecting the checks and balances within their constitutional settlement as it was about asserting hegemony.

FURTHER READING

A. Albi, *EU Enlargement and the Constitutions of Central and Eastern Europe* (Cambridge, Cambridge University Press, 2005)

A. v. Bogdandy and J. Bast, 'The European Union's Vertical Order of Competences: The Current Law and Proposals for its Reform' (2002) 39 *Common Market Law Review* 227

M. Claes, *The National Courts' Mandate in the European Constitution* (Oxford and Portland, Hart, 2005)

M. Dani, 'Constitutionalism and Dissonances: Has Europe Paid Off its Debt to Functionalism?' (2009) 15 *European Law Journal* 324

J. Komárek, 'European Constitutionalism and the European Arrest Warrant: In Search of the Limits of "Contrapunctual Principles"' (2007) 44 *Common Market Law Review* 9

D. Kostakopoulou, 'Floating Sovereignty: A Pathology or Necessary Means of State Evolution' (2002) 22 *Oxford Journal of Legal Studies* 135

M. Kumm, 'The Jurisprudence of Constitutional Conflict: Constitutional Supremacy in Europe Before and After the Constitutional Treaty' (2005) 11 *European Law Journal* 262

R. Schütze, *From Dual to Cooperative Federalism: The Changing Structure of European Law* (Oxford, Oxford University Press, 2009)

N. Walker (ed.), *Sovereignty in Transition* (Oxford and Portland, Hart, 2003)

J. Weiler, 'Does Europe Need a Constitution? Demos, Telos and the Maastricht German Decision' (1995) 1 *European Law Journal* 219

---

[93] J. Komárek, 'European Constitutionalism and the European Arrest Warrant: In Search of the Limits of "Contrapunctual Principles"' (2007) 44 *CMLRev.* 9. For debate on this case law see also O. Pollecino, 'European Arrest Warrant and Constitutional Principles of the Member States: A Case Law-Based Outline in an Attempt to Strike the Right Balance between Legal Systems' (2008) 9 *German Law Journal* No. 10.

6

Fundamental Rights

CONTENTS

1 INTRODUCTION

This chapter considers EU fundamental rights law. It is organised as follows.

Section 2 considers Article 6 TEU, which sets out three dimensions to EU fundamental rights law. First, it describes a tension, because it grants the European Union an autonomous fundamental rights law, but these rights are to be derived from external sources, namely national constitutional traditions, the European Convention for the Protection of Human Rights and Freedoms (ECHR) and the European Union Charter of Fundamental Rights and Freedoms ('Charter'). Secondly, Article 6 TEU prescribes an institutional sensitivity to EU fundamental rights law. It is not to be used to enlarge Union competences. Finally, Article 6 TEU places the Union more firmly within the European human rights order by providing for the Union to accede to the ECHR.

Section 3 considers the rights contained within EU fundamental rights law. On the one hand, there are general principles of law derived from national constitutional traditions and the ECHR. These are non-codified and comprise civil rights, rights of defence, economic rights law and principles such as non-discrimination, legal certainty and proportionality. On the other, there is the Charter, which contains six types of right regarded as fundamental: rights to human dignity, freedoms, equality rights, solidarity rights, rights to justice and citizenship rights. Though wide-ranging, the Charter does not include certain important social rights. It makes a distinction between rights and principles, with the latter being judicially enforceable only in relation to legislation implementing them.

Section 4 considers the level of protection offered by EU law to the holders of these rights. Historically, as the ethos for protection of EU fundamental rights law has been unclear, debate has been shrouded in uncertainty about what level of protection would be appropriate. In recent years, there has been a formalistic deference to the norms set by national constitutions or the ECHR. This fails to question the processes of these settlements sufficiently and has resulted in the Court of Justice not engaging sufficiently with the ethical issues surrounding some of the cases.

Section 5 considers the institutions bound by EU fundamental rights law. EU institutions are bound by it but Member States are only bound where they implement Union measures. As this test does not cover all national measures, it gives actors the possibility to arbitrage by bringing measures within the aegis of EU law to test their fundamental rights ramifications. The other challenge of this test is that it is differently formulated from the one prior to the Lisbon Treaty, which covered national measures falling within the field of some areas of EU law. The application of EU fundamental rights law to national measures is one of the most contentious fields of EU law, because it requires the Union to be a 'community of values'. Yet, if national laws depart from these common values, pivotal choices made by national actors are called into question. The most wide-ranging challenge by national actors is the Protocol on the Application of the Charter to Poland and the United Kingdom, which provides that the Charter does not extend the ability of any court to find any of their laws incompatible with fundamental rights.

Section 6 considers the accession of the European Union to the ECHR, which was made possible by the Lisbon Treaty. Historically, this debate has taken place within the context of the Union becoming a more central actor for the protection of fundamental rights. The Treaties seek to restrict this by stating that accession will not affect Union competences or national derogations from the ECHR. The current level of protection demanded by the ECHR of the Union is lower than that for states, meaning a breach will only be found where the actions are manifestly deficient. It is to be seen whether accession will change this.

Section 7 considers the establishment of the Union fundamental rights policy. Historically, EU law has only required actors not to violate fundamental rights rather than to promote them. This was long argued to be insufficient and in 2007, a European Union Fundamental Rights Agency was established. This has the power to publish reports, collect data on fundamental rights and to issue opinions for the EU legislature. However, its remit to do this has been restricted by the EU institutions.

2 FUNDAMENTAL RIGHTS AND THE SCHEME OF THE TREATIES

Article 2 TEU states that respect for human dignity, freedom, equality and human rights are the values on which the European Union is founded. Notwithstanding this foundational status, references to fundamental rights are scarce and oblique in the Treaties. There is no catalogue of rights nor any direct statement on the legal bite of these rights or which actors are bound by them. However, the central provision is Article 6(1) TEU.

Article 6 TEU

1. The Union recognises the rights, freedoms and principles set out in the Charter of Fundamental Rights of the European Union of 7 December 2000, as adopted at Strasbourg, on 12 December 2007, which shall have the same legal value as the Treaties.

   The provisions of the Charter shall not extend in any way the competences of the Union as defined in the Treaties.

   The rights, freedoms and principles in the Charter shall be interpreted in accordance with the general provisions in Title VII of the Charter governing its interpretation and application and with due regard to the explanations referred to in the Charter, that set out the sources of those provisions.

2. The Union shall accede to the European Convention for the Protection of Human Rights and Fundamental Freedoms. Such accession shall not affect the Union's competences as defined in the Treaties.

3. Fundamental rights, as guaranteed by the European Convention for the Protection of Human Rights and Fundamental Freedoms and as they result from the constitutional traditions common to the Member States, shall constitute general principles of the Union's law.

This provision is, above all, a reference point marked by a series of allusions, all of which require further explanation.

The first point to note about Article 6 TEU is that EU fundamental rights law is based on a paradox. On the one hand, the sources for its fundamental rights come from outside the Treaty. Article 6(1) TEU refers to the Charter as one source and two further sources are provided in Article 6(3) TEU, the ECHR and national constitutional traditions. The norms governing the interpretation and application are also externally inspired. The third sentence of Article 6(1) TEU makes clear that these norms, partially at least, are to be governed by the principles set out in Chapter VII of the Charter. On the other hand, these instruments are not constitutive of the fundamental rights in EU law. They 'recognise', 'guarantee' or 'set out' these rights. These rights are seen as having a separate independent existence so that these instruments neither provide an exhaustive catalogue nor determine the formal legal status. This is done by EU law, which gives these rights, freedoms and principles (rather than the instruments in which they are contained) the same legal status as the Treaties.

The tension between this formal autonomy and substantive dependence was set out in *Kadi*. As will be remembered,[1] Kadi had been placed on a list by a UN Security Council Committee that alleged he was linked to Al Qaeda and severely curtailed the financial resources available to him. As a matter of international law, the UN Security Council Resolution establishing this

---

[1] See pp. 217–19.

Committee was binding on the European Union. Kadi argued, successfully, that it violated his fundamental rights. In particular he claimed that his being placed on the list violated the right to be heard and the right to effective judicial protection, as he had no way of challenging the basis on which he had been placed there.

Joined Cases C-402/05 P and C-415/05 P *Kadi and Al Barakaat International Foundation v Council* [2008] ECR I-6351, Advocate General Poiares Maduro, Opinion of 23 January 2008

44. ...the Court should be mindful of the international context in which it operates and conscious of its limitations. It should be aware of the impact its rulings may have outside the confines of the [Union]. In an increasingly interdependent world, different legal orders will have to endeavour to accommodate each other's jurisdictional claims. As a result, the Court cannot always assert a monopoly on determining how certain fundamental interests ought to be reconciled. It must, where possible, recognise the authority of institutions, such as the Security Council, that are established under a different legal order than its own and that are sometimes better placed to weigh those fundamental interests. However, the Court cannot, in deference to the views of those institutions, turn its back on the fundamental values that lie at the basis of the [EU] legal order and which it has the duty to protect. Respect for other institutions is meaningful only if it can be built on a shared understanding of these values and on a mutual commitment to protect them. Consequently, in situations where the [Union's] fundamental values are in the balance, the Court may be required to reassess, and possibly annul, measures adopted by the [EU] institutions, even when those measures reflect the wishes of the Security Council.

The Court

281. In this connection it is to be borne in mind that the [Union] is based on the rule of law, inasmuch as neither its Member States nor its institutions can avoid review of the conformity of their acts with the basic constitutional charter, the [Treaties], which established a complete system of legal remedies and procedures designed to enable the Court of Justice to review the legality of acts of the institutions...

282. It is also to be recalled that an international agreement cannot affect the allocation of powers fixed by the Treaties or, consequently, the autonomy of the [EU] legal system, observance of which is ensured by the Court by virtue of the exclusive jurisdiction conferred on it by Article [19(3) TEU], jurisdiction that the Court has, moreover, already held to form part of the very foundations of the [Union]...

283. In addition, according to settled case law, fundamental rights form an integral part of the general principles of law whose observance the Court ensures. For that purpose, the Court draws inspiration from the constitutional traditions common to the Member States and from the guidelines supplied by international instruments for the protection of human rights on which the Member States have collaborated or to which they are signatories. In that regard, the ECHR has special significance...

284. It is also clear from the case law that respect for human rights is a condition of the lawfulness of [EU] acts... and that measures incompatible with respect for human rights are not acceptable in the [Union]...

285. It follows from all those considerations that the obligations imposed by an international agreement cannot have the effect of prejudicing the constitutional principles of the [Treaties], which include the principle that all [Union] acts must respect fundamental rights, that respect constituting a condition of their lawfulness which it is for the Court to review in the framework of the complete system of legal remedies established by the [Treaties].

There is a subtle but important difference between the reasoning of the Court of Justice and the Advocate General. The Court's position is highly formal. It emphasises both the autonomy of EU fundamental rights law and its central contribution to the idea of legality in the Union. The Advocate General, by contrast, looks at the substantive interplay of norms. He acknowledges that the Court has to engage with a variety of external sources to understand what fundamental values are, whilst taking responsibility for delivering a statement of EU law.

The second point to note about Article 6 TEU is its institutional sensitivity. The second sentence of Article 6(1) TEU states that the Charter shall not extend in any way the competences of the Union as defined in the Treaties. The Member States are aware that assertions of values by supreme courts in federal systems are not just statements about the value of these values, but also claims to a central competence to regulate them. Statements by the US Supreme Court allowing abortion in certain circumstances or prohibiting segregation in education are thus not just articulating political values. They are regulating abortion or certain dimensions of education at the expense of local authorities. There is therefore a particular sensitivity to judicial activism here. This is not merely expressed in general terms in Article 6 TEU but, as we shall see, certain Member States have a particular sensitivity over certain values being asserted aggressively against them.

The third feature to emerge from Article 6 TEU is the presence of external constraints on EU fundamental rights law. The requirement in Article 6(2) TEU for the Union to accede to the ECHR is a new requirement. It imposes an external accountability and, arguably, the presence of a higher law of fundamental rights. If the Court of Justice is to comply with the judgments of the European Court of Human Rights, this raises questions both about its relationship to that court and the relationship between EU law and the ECHR. Accession to the ECHR has other implications, however. Until now only states could accede to the ECHR. This possibility existed not only because states, with their considerable powers, can easily violate fundamental rights, but also because they allocate values. They set out a standard of what is right and wrong within a society. Allowing the Union to accede to the ECHR is therefore a double admission. It is a body that takes decisions, which increasingly affect human rights, but it is also a body that is increasingly involved in setting out visions of what is right and wrong for EU citizens.

3 THE SUBSTANCE OF EU FUNDAMENTAL RIGHTS LAW

Although it is the Charter which is mentioned first in Article 6 TEU, while national constitutional traditions and the ECHR are mentioned almost only as an afterthought as general principles of law in Article 6(3) TEU, the Charter builds on these, refers to them and is to be interpreted in the light of them.

(i) National constitutional traditions and the ECHR in EU fundamental rights law

The original Treaties contained no system of fundamental rights protection. The relatively limited scope of the EEC Treaty, with its focus on instituting a common market, provided limited opportunities for possible conflicts. If they did arise, states expected their national constitutions to be the best guarantee of protection of fundamental rights. The early case law of the Court of Justice reflected this line of thinking. In a series of judgments through to the mid-1960s, it refused to countenance arguments that the EU institutions had violated some right protected in national constitutions.[2] The Treaties contained no reference to these fundamental rights and, in the light of this, the Court resisted implications that it was responsible for the protection of these rights.

These assumptions were changed by *Van Gend en Loos* and *Costa v ENEL*.[3] The supremacy of EU law meant that national constitutional provisions could no longer be used to safeguard fundamental rights in all circumstances, as any EU legal provision took precedence over them. These judgments not only created this lacuna in protection, but also begged the question as to why this should be so. Even if the common market were to bring many benefits to the citizens of Europe, these were certainly not sufficient to legitimate the Treaties to such a degree that its citizens would be willing for it to exercise constitutional authority over them.[4] Human rights have, by contrast, since the Second World War, acquired 'symbolic pre-eminence' as an instrument for polity legitimation. They were a particularly powerful symbol in the context of European integration, for they were something archetypically European. They represented a common heritage, with the Union, as a self-styled European organisation, as the natural guardian of that heritage.[5] Protection of human rights offered a legitimation for EU constitutional authority that market integration did not.

A softening of the Court's case law emerged towards the end of the 1960s. In *Van Eick*, the Court stated that those administering EU institution staff disciplinary procedures were 'bound in the exercise of [their] powers to observe the fundamental principles of the law of procedure'.[6] The Court was more explicit in *Stauder*.[7] The case concerned a Commission Decision designed to reduce EU butter stocks, which allowed butter to be sold at a lower price to people who were on certain social welfare schemes. In order to claim the butter, the beneficiaries had to produce a coupon which, in the German and Dutch version of the Decision, had to indicate their name, whereas this was unnecessary in the French and Italian versions. Stauder, a German national, challenged the requirement that his name be on the coupon, claiming that it violated his right to respect for privacy. The Court indicated that the more liberal French and Italian version should be adopted because in this way the Decision would not prejudice the 'fundamental human rights enshrined in the general principles of [EU] law and protected by the Court'. In other words, if there were two legitimate interpretations of an EU law provision, the Court would adopt the one that did not violate fundamental rights.

Human rights still occupied no more than a second-order status. *Van Eick* and *Stauder*, whilst stressing the consonance between EU law and established notions of fundamental rights, did not grant these fundamental rights an organic status which would allow them to be used both as a basis for steering the actions of EU authorities and as a ground for judicial review. National courts were still, therefore, left with a choice between refusing to apply EU law and neglecting fundamental liberties enshrined in their national constitutions.[8] The matter came to

---

[2] Case 1/58 *Stork v High Authority* [1959] ECR 17; Joined Cases 36/59–38/59 and 40/59 *Geitling v High Authority* [1960] ECR 423; Case 40/64 *Sgarlata v Commission* [1965] ECR 215.

[3] Case 26/62 *Van Gend en Loos v Nederlandse Administratie der Belastingen* [1963] ECR 1; Case 6/64 *Costa v ENEL* [1964] ECR 585.

[4] A. Williams, *EU Human Rights Policies: A Study in Irony* (Oxford, Oxford University Press, 2004) 139.

[5] *Ibid.* 133–4.

[6] Case 35/67 *Van Eick v Commission* [1968] ECR 329.

[7] Case 29/69 *Stauder v City of Ulm* [1969] ECR 419.

[8] U. Scheuner, 'Fundamental Rights in European Community Law and in National Constitutional Law' (1975) 12 *CMLRev.* 171, 173–4.

a head in *Internationale Handelsgesellschaft*. There, a Regulation had awarded Internationale Handelsgesellschaft, a German trading concern, a licence to export maize on condition that it put down a deposit which would be forfeited if it failed to export the maize within the time stipulated in the licence. The latter failed to export the maize and, upon forfeiture of the deposit, challenged the Regulation before the administrative court in Frankfurt. The administrative court considered that the Regulation violated the provisions in the German Constitution protecting the freedom to trade. It therefore asked the Court of Justice whether the Regulation was valid.

Case 11/70 *Internationale Handelsgesellschaft* v *Einfuhr- und Vorratstelle für Getreide und Futtermittel* [1970] ECR 1125

3. Recourse to the legal rules or concepts of national law in order to judge the validity of measures adopted by the institutions of the [Union] would have an adverse effect on the uniformity and efficacy of [EU] law. The validity of such measures can only be judged in the light of Community law. In fact, the law stemming from the Treaty, an independent source of law, cannot because of its very nature be overridden by rules of national law, however framed, without being deprived of its character as [EU] law and without the legal basis of the [Union] itself being called in question. Therefore the validity of [an EU] measure or its effect within a Member State cannot be affected by allegations that it runs counter to either fundamental rights as formulated by the constitution of that State or the principles of a national constitutional structure.

4. However, an examination should be made as to whether or not any analogous guarantee inherent in [EU] law has been disregarded. In fact, respect for fundamental rights forms an integral part of the general principles of law protected by the Court of Justice. The protection of such rights, whilst inspired by the constitutional traditions common to the Member States, must be ensured within the framework of the structure and objectives of the [Union]...

The judgment establishes that fundamental rights form an integral part of EU law, although the Court went on to rule that there had been no violation of the fundamental right to trade in this instance. However, the genesis of EU law fundamental rights law was tainted due to its emergence within the context of a dispute about the supremacy of EU law. Disgruntled, Internationale Handelsgesellschaft pursued the matter further, before the German Constitutional Court.[9] The latter noted that at that time there was no catalogue of fundamental rights in EU law and the European Parliament did not have legislative powers. This prevented any assessment by it as to whether fundamental rights protection in EU law was similar to that within the German Basic Law. In the light of this, it ruled that in the case of a conflict between EU law and fundamental rights set out in the Basic Law, it would be the latter and not EU law that would take precedence. This challenge to the supremacy of EU law was supported by the Italian Constitutional Court, which also held that supremacy of EU law would not prevail where EU law violated fundamental principles of the Italian Constitution (including fundamental rights).[10]

Although apparently confrontational, the decisions of the German and Italian Constitutional Courts allowed the possibility of a dialectic to emerge. The implication of their judgments was

---

[9] *Internationale Handelsgesellschaft* v *Einfuhr- und Vorratstelle für Getreide und Futtermittel* [1974] 2 CMLR 540.
[10] *Frontini* v *Ministero delle Finanze* [1974] 2 CMLR 372.

that if EU law developed a sufficiently rigorous fundamental rights doctrine of its own, they would not apply their own constitutional norms, for the threat to fundamental rights would be averted by EU law putting in place its own checks, so that a conflict should (in theory at least) never happen. By 1986, in *Solange II*,[11] the German Constitutional Court considered this to be the case and reversed its approach to the review of Union acts in the light of fundamental rights. Though no catalogue of fundamental rights had yet been established, the German Constitutional Court considered that the protection of fundamental rights granted by the Court of Justice had reached a level that substantially coincided with that granted by the German Basic Law. As long as that was the case, the German Constitutional Court would no longer review the validity of specific Union acts in the light of national fundamental rights.

This has led to the accusation that the motivations for the development of fundamental rights were not those relating to protection of human dignity, but ulterior ones. They were to do with inducing national constitutional courts to accept the supremacy of EU law and, in particular, the ideological objectives of market integration.[12] Member States concerned about the liberalisation of the economy were to be soothed by the parallel development of a culture of rights in EU law.[13] Little direct evidence is offered to support this analysis, and it would not explain why the Court of Justice has looked at sources other than national constitutions to determine the content of EU fundamental rights law. In *Nold*, the Court stated that international human rights treaties were another source of fundamental rights in EU law.[14] Following *Nold*, the Court has recognised a number of human rights treaties as sources. Most importantly, in *Rutili*, it referred to the ECHR.[15] Whilst the Court has indicated that the ECHR has a particular status,[16] it has also looked broadly and in an open-ended way to incorporate other international human rights treaties as sources of fundamental rights: the International Covenant on Civil and Political Rights,[17] the UN Convention on the Rights of the Child,[18] the Community Charter of Fundamental Social Rights of Workers, and the European Social Charter.[19]

Relying on national constitutional traditions and international human rights treaties, the Court has recognised a number of categories of different rights.

Civil rights   These include the right to respect for family and private life;[20] protection of the child;[21] freedom of religion;[22] freedom of trade union activity;[23] freedom of expression;[24]

---

[11] Decision of the Bundesverfassungsgericht of 22 October 1986, *Wünsche Handelsgesellschaft (Solange II)* [1987] 3 CMLR 225.

[12] J. Coppell and A. O'Neill, 'The European Court of Justice: Taking Rights Seriously' (1992) 29 *CMLRev.* 669.

[13] J. Weiler and N. Lockhart, '"Taking Rights Seriously" Seriously: The European Court and Fundamental Rights Jurisprudence, Part I' (1995) 32 *CMLRev.* 51; J. Weiler and N. Lockhart, '"Taking Rights Seriously" Seriously: The European Court and Fundamental Rights Jurisprudence, Part II' (1995) 32 *CMLRev.* 579.

[14] Case 4/73 *Nold v Commission* [1974] ECR 491.

[15] Case 36/75 *Rutili v Ministre de l'Intérieur* [1975] ECR 1219.

[16] Case C-299/95 *Kremzow v Austria* [1997] ECR I-2629.

[17] Case 374/87 *Orkem v Commission* [1989] ECR 3283.

[18] Case C-540/03 *Parliament v Council (family reunification)* [2006] ECR I-5769.

[19] Case 24/86 *Blaizot v Belgium* [1988] ECR 379; Case 149/77 *Defrenne II* [1978] ECR 1365.

[20] Case 136/79 *National Panasonic* [1980] ECR 2033; Case C-249/86 *Commission v Germany (migrant workers)* [1989] ECR 1263.

[21] Case C-540/03 *Parliament v Council (family reunification)* [2006] ECR I-5769; Case C-244/06 *Dynamic Medien Vertriebs GmbH v Avides Media AG* [2008] ECR I-505.

[22] Case 130/75 *Prais* [1976] ECR 1589.

[23] Case 175/73 *Union Syndicale* [1974] ECR 917.

[24] Case C-260/89 *Elliniki Radiophonia Tiléorassi AE and Others v Dimotiki Etairia Pliroforissis* [1991] ECR I-2925; Case C-250/06 *United Pan-Europe Communications Belgium and Others* [2007] ECR I-11135.

protection of personal data;[25] access to basic data held about oneself;[26] equality;[27] protection from discrimination on grounds of sexual orientation;[28] the right to choose one's place of residence;[29] the right to free and informed consent before any medical procedure and the right to human dignity;[30] freedom from torture or subjection to inhuman and degrading treatment.[31]

Economic rights   Normally subject to provisos which may be imposed in the public interest and which restrict their exercise, these include the right to trade;[32] the right to own property;[33] and the right to carry out an economic activity.[34]

Rights of defence   These include the right to an effective judicial remedy;[35] the presumption of innocence;[36] the right to be informed in a criminal trial of the nature and cause of accusation against one;[37] the right to legal assistance and the right for all lawyer-client communications prepared for the purpose of defending oneself to be confidential;[38] the right to be heard in one's own defence before any measure is imposed;[39] and protection from self-incrimination.[40]

General principles of law   These include the principles of non-discrimination,[41] proportionality,[42] legitimate expectations[43] and non-retroactivity.[44] The meaning of these principles is discussed further in Chapter 10.

Most of these rights also find some reflection, as we shall see, in the Charter. However, the Lisbon Treaty poses some questions about their future development. Hitherto, this has been an organic process whereby the Court looks to sources it considers authoritative wherever these seem germane.[45] In some instances these are national constitutional traditions, in others the ECHR, and in yet other cases, other international human rights treaties. This is important because national constitutions are entrenched and the ECHR is a product of the post-Second World War era. As human rights have evolved since then, new international treaties have been concluded to reflect this. The Lisbon Treaty seems to preclude EU law, for the first time, from looking at these, as it suggests that, from now on, regard can only be had to national constitutional traditions and the ECHR. It would be a pity if this were the case.

[25] Case C-101/01 *Lindqvist* [2003] ECR-12971; Joined Cases C-465/00, C-138/01 and C-139/01 *Österreichischer Rundfunk* [2003] ECR I-4919.
[26] Case C-553/07 *College van Burgemeester en Wethouders van Rotterdam v Rijkeboer*, Judgment of 7 May 2009.
[27] Case C-43/75 *Defrenne v Sabena* [1976] ECR 455.
[28] Case C-117/01 *KB v National Health Service Pensions Agency* [2004] ECR I-541.
[29] Case C-370/05 *Festersen* [2007] ECR I-1129.
[30] Case C-377/98 *Netherlands v European Parliament and Council (Biotechnology Directive)* [2001] ECR I-7079.
[31] Case C-465/07 *Elgafaji v Staatsecretaris van Justitie*, Judgment of 17 February 2009.
[32] Case 240/83 *ADBHU* [1985] ECR 531.
[33] Case 44/79 *Hauer* [1979] ECR 3727.
[34] Case 230/78 *Eridania* [1979] ECR 2749.
[35] Case 222/84 *Johnston v Chief Constable of the Royal Ulster Constabulary* [1986] ECR 1651.
[36] Case C-344/08 *Rubach*, Judgment of 16 July 2009.
[37] Case C-14/07 *Weiss v Industrie- und Handelskammer Berlin* [2008] ECR I-3367.
[38] Case 155/79 *AM & S Europe Ltd v Commission* [1982] ECR 1575.
[39] Case 17/74 *Transocean Marine Paint v Commission* [1974] ECR 1063.
[40] Joined Cases 374/87 and 27/88 *Orkem & Solvay v Commission* [1989] ECR 3283.
[41] Case C-144/04 *Mangold* [2005] ECR I-9981.
[42] Case 11/70 *Internationale Handelsgesellschaft v Einfuhr- und Vorratstelle für Getreide und Futtermittel* [1970] ECR 1125.
[43] Joined Cases C-37/02 and C-38/02 *Di Lenardo and Dilexport* [2004] ECR I-6911.
[44] Case 63/83 *R v Kent Kirk* [1984] ECR 2689.
[45] As new Members joined the Union, fundamental rights evolved to incorporate their distinctive forms of human rights: F. Bignami, 'Creating European Rights: National Values and Supranational Interests' (2005) 11 *CJEL* 241.

(ii) European Union Charter of Fundamental Rights and Freedoms

The Charter emerged out of a two-fold impetus at the end of the 1990s. On the one hand, there was a desire to accord social rights the same status as other rights, notably civil liberties.[46] On the other, there was agreement that the fundamental rights in EU law should not be hidden away in the case law of the Court of Justice but should be more visible. In 1999, at the Cologne European Council, it was agreed therefore that a charter of fundamental rights should be established. The European Council believed that this charter should be an amalgam of rights. It should include the rights contained in the ECHR and those present in the constitutional traditions common to the Member States. It should also include the rights set out in the EU citizenship provisions, and economic and social rights as contained in the European Social Charter and the Community Charter of the Fundamental Social Rights of Workers.

This charter was to be drafted by a novel method, a Convention. This would be composed of representatives from national governments, the Commission, the European Parliament and national parliaments. Other EU institutions were to be given observer status. Human rights groups, regional bodies, trade unions and wider civil society were invited to make contributions.[47] Deliberations were to be held in public. The draft of the Charter was adopted by the Convention in October 2000 and was unanimously approved by the European Council at the Biarritz European Council. The question of the legal status of the Charter was to be left open. Moreover, this was not just a formal question. As this excerpt from Clapham presciently notes, debates about rights can confer legitimacy upon a political system and generate feelings of political community, but they can also polarise opinions and generate dissensus.

A. Clapham, 'A Human Rights Policy for the European Community' (1990) *Yearbook of European Law* **309, 311**

Talking about human rights may sometimes bestow identity on Community citizens. This has a subjective dimension with citizens finding they have rights in common; as well as containing an objective perspective with the discovery of a common concern about the rights of others (inside or outside the Community). Where these rights move beyond 'God-given' or 'self evident' rights they result in an intense 'contract' or relationship with the right giver. Should the Community realize its role in distributing rights to Community citizens it could expect some increased loyalty. However such a symbiotic relationship could only occur should the Community respond to the demands of its citizens rather than reinforcing rights which are primarily geared to its own objectives.

Clearly, rights have an important role to play in the process of European integration, but, it must be said that they may well operate as a double-edged sword. Not only are they a cohesive force but they may well be divisive. Should the Community move to tackle questions such as divorce, contraception, abortion, blasphemy, surrogacy, etc., rights might no longer be handy tools for integration but vehicles of division and disintegration. Furthermore, not only will moral diversity have to be tolerated in the move towards unity, but it is clear that effective rights to challenge Community decisions or provisions could well slow up or completely ensnare new initiatives or progress at the Community level.

---

[46] Report of the Expert Group on Fundamental Rights, *Affirming Fundamental Rights in the European Union: Time to Act* (Brussels, European Commission, 1999) (Simitis Report).

[47] For discussion see G. de Búrca, 'The Drafting of the EU Charter of Fundamental Rights' (2001) 26 *ELRev.* 126: O. de Schutter, 'Europe in Search of its Civil Society' (2002) 8 *ELJ* 198, 206–12.

Leaving the status of the Convention open allowed the possibility of a wider array of rights being incorporated. It could always be argued that as these rights were not being made into 'legal' rights but only enunciated as statements of principle, their precise consequences did not have to be thought through. However, this did mean that substantive disagreement crystallised around the question of whether the Charter should have legal status or not.[48] As a consequence, at the Nice European Council, agreement on the legal status and consequences of the Charter could not be reached. Instead, it was 'proclaimed' by the Council, the Commission and the Parliament, with its final status to be resolved by the Constitutional Treaty.

This led to a period of hiatus. The Charter was not a formal legal instrument but it was an authoritative statement of the rights considered to be fundamental in the Union. Advocates General and the General Court began referring to it as a source of fundamental rights.[49] Under the Constitutional Treaty, it was inserted in Part II of the Treaty. This set out the provisions of the Charter but also constrained their remit and meaning in a manner that did not apply to other provisions of the Treaty.[50] Following the failure of the Constitutional Treaty in 2006, the Court of Justice also began to refer to the Charter as a source of fundamental rights.[51] In this, there has never been exclusive reliance on the Charter. The Court has always referred to it and an alternative source, invariably an international human rights treaty, as the basis for a right. Equally importantly, the Charter is not seen as a constitutive document but a statement of rights that are seen, in EU law at least, as fundamental.

This approach has been continued in Article 6(1) TEU, which states that the Union recognises the rights, freedoms and principles as set out in the Charter. The Charter was reproclaimed by the three EU institutions following the signing of the Lisbon Treaty.[52] It sets out its rights and principles under six headings, of which the central ones are set out below.

Rights to human dignity   Right to life; integrity of the person; prohibition of torture or inhuman and degrading treatment; prohibition of slavery or forced labour; prohibition on cloning or eugenics (articles 1–5).

Freedoms   Right to liberty and security; respect for private and family life; protection of personal data; right to marry and found a family; freedom of thought, conscience and religion; freedom of expression and information; freedom of assembly; freedom of the arts and sciences; right to education; freedom to choose an occupation and right to engage in work; freedom to conduct a business; right to asylum; right to property (articles 6–19).

Equality   Equality before the law; non-discrimination on sex, race, colour, ethnic or social origin, genetic features, language, religion or belief or political opinion, disability, sexual

---

[48] C. McCrudden, *The Future of the EU Charter of Fundamental Rights*, Jean Monnet Working Paper 13/01, http://centers.law.nyu.edu/jeanmonnet/papers/index.html (accessed 19 November 2009).

[49] See respectively Case C-173/99 *R* v *Secretary of State for Trade and Industry, ex parte BECTU* [2001] ECR I-4881, Advocate General Tizzano; Case T-177/01 *Jégo-Quéré* v *Commission* [2002] ECR II-2365.

[50] These constraints have been replicated by the Lisbon Treaty.

[51] Case C-540/03 *Parliament* v *Council (family reunification)* [2006] ECR I-5769; Case C-432/05 *Unibet* v *Justitiekanslern* [2007] ECR I-2271; Case C-275/06 *Promusicae* v *Telefónica de España* [2008] ECR I-271; Case C-12/08 *Mono Car Styling* v *Odemis*, Judgment of 16 July 2009; Joined Cases C-322/07 P, C-327/07 P and C-338/07 P *Papierfabrik Koehler* v *Commission*, Judgment of 3 September 2009.

[52] The full text of the Charter can be found at [2007] OJ C303/1. The consolidated version differs from the 2000 version in that it includes some institutional amendments that had been included in the Constitutional Treaty.

orientation, birth; cultural, religious and linguistic diversity; equality between men and women; rights of the elderly, integration of persons with disabilities (articles 20–26).

Solidarity   Workers' right to information and consultation; right of collective bargaining; protection in the event of unfair dismissal; right to placement services; fair and just working conditions; prohibition on child labour; right to social security; right to health care; protection of the family; high level of environmental and consumer protection; access to services of general economic interest (articles 27–38).

Citizens' rights   Right to vote and stand in municipal and European Parliament elections; right to good administration; right to access to documents; right to refer matters to European Parliament and petition Ombudsman; freedom of movement and residence; right to diplomatic protection (articles 39–46).

Justice   Right to an effective remedy and a fair trial; presumption of innocence; right not to be tried or punished twice for same offence; principle of legality and proportionality of criminal offences (articles 47–50).

Few of these rights are absolute and many are conditioned by exceptions. Article 52(1) of the Charter sets out limits on how these exceptions may be invoked:

Charter, article 52(1)

Any limitation on the exercise of the rights and freedoms recognised by this Charter must be provided for by law and respect the essence of those rights and freedoms. Subject to the principle of proportionality, limitations may be made only if they are necessary and genuinely meet objectives of general interest recognised by the Union or the need to protect the rights and freedoms of others.

The rights were taken from three sources: rights recognised in the EU Treaty, rights recognised in the constitutions of the Member States, and international human rights treaties concluded by the Member States.[53] There are a number of noteworthy features.

First, the Charter incorporates a wider array of rights and freedoms possibly than any other human rights treaty. There are, thus, not just civil, political, economic and social rights, but protection of cultural and ecological interests as well. It can be seen as ambitious and nuanced, therefore, in what it considers humans need for a good life. However, there is also a concern about an inflation of the language of rights. The right of free access to a placement service is worthwhile no doubt (article 29 of the Charter) but it can hardly be seen as on the same level as the prohibition on slavery (article 5 of the Charter). To be sure, it might be argued that inclusion in a single document does not mean that they are being equated, but there is the question as to why they should be placed together at all and whether this might lead to phenomena such as similar methods of interpretation being applied to both.

Secondly, in the field of social rights, in particular, certain key rights are missing.[54] The right to nationality, the right to decent pay, the right to work and the right to housing are all not

---

[53] CHARTE 4473/00, 11 October 2000.

[54] J. Kenner, 'Economic and Social Rights in the EU Legal Order: The Mirage of Indivisibility' in T. Hervey and J. Kenner (eds.), *Economic and Social Rights under the EU Charter of Fundamental Rights* (Oxford, Hart, 2003) 1, 16–18.

included.[55] Certain other rights (for example, the right to marry, the right to collective bargaining, the right of workers to information and consultation, the right to protection against unfair dismissal, the right to social security and health care) are to be recognised only in accordance with the rules laid down by national or EU laws. National laws are to determine the content of these rights, so that instead of acting as a basis for review of EU and national practices, these are turned around to justify even egregious practices.[56]

Thirdly, the Charter suggests the indivisibility of these rights. Social, civil, political and environmental rights should all be treated equally as fundamental rights. Yet, it introduces this at the expense of introducing another distinction: that between rights and principles.

Charter, article 52(5)

The provisions of this Charter which contain principles may be implemented by legislative and executive acts taken by Institutions, bodies, offices and agencies of the Union and by acts of Member States when they are implementing Union law, in the exercise of their respective powers. They shall be judicially cognisable only in the interpretation of such acts and in the ruling on their legality.

Some provisions will be protected more absolutely than others. All institutional behaviour falling within the aegis of the Charter can be judicially reviewed against provisions that contain rights. By contrast, courts will only be able to look at principles in cases where institutions are implementing these principles rather than at activities that cut across them. The justification is that the sheer breadth of the Charter prevents a 'one size fits all' approach to protection. Courts are arguably not well-suited to determining the substance of wide-ranging socio-economic or environmental rights, e.g. when a right to sustainable development warrants protection, or when the level of health provision is so low that it violates the right of access to health care. More partial judicial control might be a price worth paying for having these recognised.

However, even if one accepts this ethos, the distinction was not considered at the original drafting of the Charter but only addressed subsequently: first, in the Constitutional Treaty, and then in the modified Charter proclaimed in 2007. As a consequence, the fundamental question of which provisions articulate rights and which principles was unaddressed. There are only three provisions which explicitly use the word 'principle': those on the principle of equality between men and women (article 23), sustainable development (article 37) and on the need for legality and proportionality of criminal offences (article 49). Of these, only the provision on sustainable development would seem in any way to generate problems with judicial enforcement. Reliance cannot be had therefore on the terminology of the Charter. Instead, it may be that provisions whose content is dependent upon their realisation by national or EU law would be considered to be principles.[57] Yet, many of the provisions to be implemented by national

---

[55] Albeit that the right to 'housing assistance' is provided for in article 34(3).

[56] D. Ashiagbor, 'Economic and Social Rights in the European Charter of Fundamental Rights' (2004) 1 *European Human Rights Law Review* 62.

[57] For example, the right to marry (article 9); the right to found educational establishments (article 14(3)); workers' right to information and consultation within their undertaking (article 27); the right to collective bargaining (article 28); social and housing assistance (article 34); the right to protection in the event of unjustified dismissal (article 30); and the right to health care (article 35).

law describe themselves as 'rights'.[58] There are also provisions where the Union commits itself to respect certain values in its policies, such as a high level of environmental protection or consumer protection or respect for services of a general economic interest.[59] These provisions would not seem to confer free-standing rights, but act merely to orient the policy in question. However, the question is surrounded by ambiguity.

4 STANDARD OF PROTECTION OF FUNDAMENTAL RIGHTS

It is all very well the Union developing a plethora of rights but this means little if they are just paper rights with no substance, which offer individuals little protection. Yet, if EU law is to demand a certain level of protection or a particular balance between different values, there must, at the very least, be a certain ethos which informs us why that level of protection or balance is adopted. Indeed, that is also the view of the Court of Justice. Since *Internationale Handelsgesellschaft*, it has indicated that EU fundamental rights law is to be interpreted according to an autonomous reasoning with the meaning of particular rights determined in the light of broader Union objectives.

There has been academic debate about the logic supporting this reasoning. Some authors have argued that it should be centred around the Western liberal tradition of protecting individual autonomy, so EU law should provide the standard which would secure the individual as high a level of protection as that offered by any Member State.[60] Others have convincingly argued that this is too formal and individualistic a conception of fundamental rights. Fundamental rights articulate basic choices about the structure of state and society. The Union should develop its own model here according to EU conceptions of right and wrong.[61] Commentary on the nature of such a model is, however, disappointingly vague. It has been argued that a feature might be a greater insistence on social rights and more scepticism of 'market rights' than in the United States.[62] Others have suggested that Europe's history of tragic events, most notably the Holocaust, would involve the development of a common set of choices concerned to avoid the suffering and pain associated with Europe's past and to give a voice to those suffering equivalent injustices today.[63]

It is not clear how such visions would inform the interpretation of rights across the board, and the Court has eschewed such an approach, with it being difficult to discern any general philosophy. Williams has argued that this lack of substance and intellectual vacuity is having powerful delegitimating effects by reducing the language of fundamental rights to a series of empty labels.[64]

[58] All the provisions mentioned above n. 57 (e.g. the right to marry, etc.), with the exception of article 34 on the right to housing assistance, do this.

[59] Articles 36, 37 and 38 respectively.

[60] L. Besselink, 'Entrapped by the Maximum Standard: On Fundamental Rights, Pluralism and Subsidiarity in the European Union' (1998) 35 *CMLRev*. 629.

[61] J. Weiler, 'Fundamental Rights and Fundamental Boundaries: On Standards and Values in the Protection of Human Rights' in N. Neuwahl and A. Rosas, *The European Union and Human Rights* (The Hague, Martinus Nijhoff, 1995) 51, 52–3; M. Avbelj, *The European Court of Justice and the Question of Value Choices*, Jean Monnet Working Paper 6/04, http://centers.law.nyu.edu/jeanmonnet/papers/index.html (accessed 19 November 2009).

[62] C. Leben, 'Is there a European Approach to Human Rights?' in P. Alston (ed.), *The EU and Human Rights* (Oxford, Oxford University Press, 1999) 69–98.

[63] K. Günther, 'The Legacies of Injustice and Fear: A European Approach to Human Rights and their Effects on Political Culture' in P. Alston (ed.), *The EU and Human Rights* (Oxford, Oxford University Press, 1999) 117–46.

[64] See also I. Ward, 'Making Sense of Integration: A Philosophy of Law for the European Community' (1993) 17 *Journal of European Integration* 101, 128–9 and 132–3.

A. Williams, *EU Human Rights Policies: A Study in Irony* (Oxford, Oxford University Press, 2004) 159–60

As the concern of the Community's institutions was to stave off criticism on the one hand and gain authenticity on the other, the phrase 'human rights' was used without regard to its full meaning or possibilities. Using the language of rights as a mythic construct was considered sufficient to justify the potential detractors of the Community and its Project. The resulting indeterminacy of human rights, the repeated failure to constitutionalise any definition of the term, ensured that the field was open to interpretation. Thus, the possibility of different human rights, discourses, practices and definitions emerging in different arenas inspired by different sources of law and philosophy became apparent. The most significant demonstration of the potential for variance was at the external/internal divide. In both realms, the failure to define what the Community meant by human rights or how they should be applied and promoted in any coherent fashion determined that other forces could influence their evolution.

...the mythic nature of the narrative has presented a debilitating factor in any attempt to rectify a perceived bifurcation. Due to its lack of substance, its lack of certainty, the narrative of founding principle has become a vapid construction, a wistful statement repeated as law without any certain content or appreciation of practice. It ignores the 'considerable differences' between the attitudes of the Member States to rights. It has been incapable of providing a framework for any kind of consistent human rights activity. Instead, the myth has lost its vitality and relevance and has left human rights to the vagaries of context and inherent discrimination.

The recognition of the Charter by the Lisbon Treaty alters this. Within the Charter, one can find four guiding principles that will inform the standard of protection by EU fundamental rights law.

The first is that there should be no undermining of the protections offered to the individual by either international treaties or national constitutions.

Charter, article 53

Nothing in this Charter shall be interpreted as restricting or adversely affecting human rights and freedoms as recognised, in their respective fields of application, by Union law and international law and by international agreements to which the Union or all the Member States are party, including the European Convention on Human Rights and Fundamental Freedoms, and by the Member States' constitutions.

Whilst this provision sets the context as to how EU fundamental rights should be interpreted, its guiding force is limited. It asserts a principle of non-violation. International treaties and national constitutions are to set out a 'bed of rights', below which the Union must not go. It is left to the other provisions to set out what the Union should do beyond this, and the more detailed relationship between EU fundamental rights and the ECHR and the national constitutions.

The second principle is that courts should have regard to the Explanations drawn up by the Secretariat to the Convention on the Charter in interpreting particular provisions.

> **Charter, article 52(7)**
>
> The explanations drawn up as a way of providing guidance in the interpretation of the Charter of Fundamental Rights shall be given due regard by the courts of the Union and the Member States.[65]

The purpose of this is to restrict judicial creativity, with the courts developing unanticipated interpretations with far-reaching consequences. It sets out a doctrine of original intent. However, this provision's significance is undercut by the Secretariat's Explanations being silent on the scope and content of each right, as they do no more than state its source (e.g. a particular international human rights treaty). However, this provision does encourage adjudicators to be backward-looking in their interpretation of the Charter. For the Explanations invariably seek to locate individual provisions as simply the culmination of the existing case law of the Court of Justice or existing international treaties. Over time there is thus a real danger that undue prominence will be given to dated interpretations, rather than to interpretations that meet the demands of an evolving society.

The third principle is more significant. It requires interpretations of the Charter to align themselves with those of the ECHR where they concern rights laid down in the ECHR.

> **Charter, article 52(3)**
>
> Insofar as this Charter contains rights which correspond to rights guaranteed by the Convention for the Protection of Human Rights and Fundamental Freedoms, the meaning and scope of those rights shall be the same as those laid down by the said Convention. This provision shall not prevent Union law providing more extensive protection.

This statement reflects the recent practice of the Court of Justice. It has stated that the ECHR has a special status in EU law. The consequence has been a reticence in judgments involving rights covered by the ECHR: it does not articulate new principles or values, but, instead, exercises a 'cut-out and paste' reliance on the case law of the European Court on Human Rights.[66] The most significant example was the *Family Reunification* judgment, where the Court considered the Charter's place in EU law for the first time. The European Parliament challenged three elements of the Directive on family reunification, which set out the conditions under which family members of non-EU nationals resident in the Union could join those nationals. The first provided that the unification with their family of a child aged 12 years or above arriving independently from their parents could be subject to an integration test.[67] The second was an exception to the general provision that children 16 years old or younger have a right to family

---

[65] This is now found in the Explanations relating to the Charter of Fundamental Rights [2007] OJ C303/17.

[66] The most extreme example of this is Case C-109/01 *Secretary of State for the Home Department* v *Akrich* [2003] ECR I-9607. The case law of the European Court of Human Rights is cited but not its reasoning, so the judgment makes no sense unless one refers back to the judgments of the latter. For an argument that there has been a shift recently, see B. Kunoy and A. Dawes, 'Plate Tectonics in Luxembourg: The *Ménage à Trois* between EC Law, International Law and the European Convention on Human Rights following the UN Sanctions Cases' (2009) 46 *CMLRev.* 73.

[67] These tests typically require knowledge of the language and history of the host state as well as demonstration of commitment to its values.

reunification. The exception provided that this rule did not apply to children who were already 15 years old at the time of the submission of the application. The third concerned a provision which stipulated that Member States could provide that non-EU nationals be lawfully resident for two years in their territories before their families join them. The Directive provided in its Preamble that it complied with the right to respect for family life as set out in the ECHR and the Charter.

Case C-540/03 *Parliament* v *Council (family reunification)* [2006] ECR I-5769

38. The Charter was solemnly proclaimed by the Parliament, the Council and the Commission in Nice on 7 December 2000. While the Charter is not a legally binding instrument, the Community legislature did, however, acknowledge its importance by stating, in the second recital in the preamble to the Directive, that the Directive observes the principles recognised not only by Article 8 of the ECHR but also in the Charter. Furthermore, the principal aim of the Charter, as is apparent from its preamble, is to reaffirm 'rights as they result, in particular, from the constitutional traditions and international obligations common to the Member States, the Treaty on European Union, the Community Treaties, the [ECHR], the Social Charters adopted by the Community and by the Council of Europe and the case law of the Court ... and of the European Court of Human Rights'...

52. The right to respect for family life within the meaning of Article 8 of the ECHR is among the fundamental rights which, according to the Court's settled case law, are protected in Community law... This right to live with one's close family results in obligations for the Member States which may be negative, when a Member State is required not to deport a person, or positive, when it is required to let a person enter and reside in its territory.

53. Thus, the Court has held that, even though the ECHR does not guarantee as a fundamental right the right of an alien to enter or to reside in a particular country, the removal of a person from a country where close members of his family are living may amount to an infringement of the right to respect for family life as guaranteed by Article 8(1) of the ECHR...

54. In addition, as the European Court of Human Rights held in *Sen* v *The Netherlands*, no. 31465/96, § 31, 21 December 2001, 'Article 8 [of the ECHR] may create positive obligations inherent in effective "respect" for family life. The principles applicable to such obligations are comparable to those which govern negative obligations. In both contexts regard must be had to the fair balance that has to be struck between the competing interests of the individual and of the community as a whole; and in both contexts the State enjoys a margin of appreciation' ...

55. In paragraph 36 of *Sen* v. *The Netherlands*, the European Court of Human Rights set out in the following manner the principles applicable to family reunification:
    (a) The extent of a State's obligation to admit to its territory relatives of settled immigrants will vary according to the particular circumstances of the persons involved and the general interest.
    (b) As a matter of well-established international law and subject to its treaty obligations, a State has the right to control the entry of non-nationals into its territory.
    (c) Where immigration is concerned, Article 8 cannot be considered to impose on a State a general obligation to respect the choice by married couples of the country of their matrimonial residence and to authorise family reunion in its territory.

56. The European Court of Human Rights has stated that, in its analysis, it takes account of the age of the children concerned, their circumstances in the country of origin and the extent to which they are dependent on relatives...

57. The Convention on the Rights of the Child also recognises the principle of respect for family life. The Convention is founded on the recognition, expressed in the sixth recital in its preamble, that children, for the full and harmonious development of their personality, should grow up in a family environment. Article 9(1) of the Convention thus provides that States Parties are to ensure that a child shall not be separated from his or her parents against their will and, in accordance with Article 10(1), it follows from that obligation that applications by a child or his or her parents to enter or leave a State Party for the purpose of family reunification are to be dealt with by States Parties in a positive, humane and expeditious manner.

58. The Charter likewise recognises, in Article 7, the right to respect for private or family life. This provision must be read in conjunction with the obligation to have regard to the child's best interests, which are recognised in Article 24(2) of the Charter, and taking account of the need, expressed in Article 24(3), for a child to maintain on a regular basis a personal relationship with both his or her parents.

59. These various instruments stress the importance to a child of family life and recommend that States have regard to the child's interests but they do not create for the members of a family an individual right to be allowed to enter the territory of a State and cannot be interpreted as denying States a certain margin of appreciation when they examine applications for family reunification.

This unflinching deference to the case law of the ECHR raises a concern that it is being used as cover for highly illiberal judgments or a failure to engage properly with the issues raised. In *Family Reunification*, the measures challenged were highly illiberal. The Court nevertheless held that they did not restrict the right to respect for family life. The restrictions on the entry of children under the age of 16 years were justified on the grounds that Member States were required to have regard, inter alia, to the interest of the child in the exercise of their discretion. Yet it is difficult to think of any circumstance, other than that of parental abuse, in which it is right to separate 12-year-old children from their parents. The other requirement of lawful residence was justified on the grounds that Member States were entitled to ensure that family reunification will take place on favourable conditions, after the sponsor has been residing in the host state for a period sufficiently long for it to be assumed that the family members will settle down well and display a certain level of integration. This is specious. It is unclear how separating a family for two years makes conditions easier for their settling down. It is rather likely to lead to family disintegration. Similarly, deferring entry for two years simply defers the time it takes the family to integrate. If the question was whether there was an issue about the seriousness of intent on the part of the family, this could be assessed by other means.

The other concern in the judgment is the undue faith placed in the ECHR's decision-making processes and judgment.[68] The ECHR covers forty-six states. It is committed to a less intense form of political integration and governs a more diverse array of situations than the European Union. It is not clear that the judgments of a court such as the European Court of Human Rights, operating in that context, should be accepted almost unquestioningly. A more preferable arrangement would be one of mutual justification: the EU Courts treat any judgment

---

[68] For a withering but highly persuasive critique see S. Greer and A. Williams, 'Human Rights in the Council of Europe and the EU: Towards "Individual", "Constitutional" or "Institutional" Justice?' (2009) 15 *ELJ* 462, 466–70.

given by the European Court of Human Rights as a persuasive suggestion. If the latter's judgment is not considered to protect adequately either the individual freedom or collective interest in question, then they can depart from it, but must give reasons for their choice.[69]

The fourth and final principle of interpretation is that EU fundamental rights law be interpreted in harmony with national constitutional traditions.

Charter, article 52(4)

Insofar as this Charter recognises fundamental rights as they result from the constitutional traditions common to the Member States, those rights shall be interpreted in harmony with those traditions.

National constitutional traditions are not, however, codified into a single legal instrument. Whilst one finds certain types of right (e.g. freedom of expression) recurring in different constitutions, it is difficult to synthesise an overall level of protection from this or to make statements about one level of protection being higher than the other.[70] Individual constitutional settlements reflect choices between conflicting value claims: freedom of expression versus privacy in libel cases; freedom of expression versus respect for religion in blasphemy cases, etc. One cannot talk of a baseline of protection or overall EU picture without having a hierarchy of values, so that, for example, freedom of expression will trump freedom of religion, etc.[71] Whilst national constitutional traditions have been used as the basis for identifying the presence of a particular right,[72] such use is not prevalent with regard to interpreting the substance of that right. Instead, EU law defers to the national constitution being challenged. The logic is one of ethical surrender rather than that of tracing a common constitutional reasoning.

An example is *Omega*. Omega ran a game under a franchise from a British company, Pulsar, whereby competitors attempted to shoot each other with laser guns. Sensory tags worn by competitors picked up whether they had been shot and 'killed' under the rules of the game. The Bonn police authority issued a prohibition order against Omega, on the grounds that the game simulated murder, and therefore constituted an affront to human dignity under paragraph 1(1) of the German Basic Law. Omega argued before the German court that the prohibition violated Article 56 TFEU, the provision on the freedom to provide services. The view of the German court was that the order would not violate Article 56 TEU if it protected the right to human dignity. It therefore asked the Court of Justice as to the meaning of this right in EU law. It also asked whether there had to be a common conception across the Union that games such as these violated human dignity before it could be invoked in the case in hand.

---

[69] N. Krisch, 'The Open Architecture of European Human Rights Law' (2008) 71 *MLR* 183; D. Halberstam and E. Stein, 'The United Nations, The European Union, and the King of Sweden: Economic Sanctions and Individual Rights in a Plural World Order' (2009) 46 *CMLRev.* 13.

[70] See p. 241.

[71] R. García, 'The General Provisions of the Charter of Fundamental Rights of the European Union' (2002) 8 *ELJ* 492, 508.

[72] See e.g. Joined Cases 374/87 and 27/88 *Orkem & Solvay* v *Commission* [1989] ECR 3283.

Case C–36/02 *Omega Spielhallen –und Automatenaufstellungs* v *Oberbürgermeisterin der Bundesstadt Bonn* **[2004] ECR I-9609**

33. ...fundamental rights form an integral part of the general principles of law the observance of which the Court ensures, and..., for that purpose, the Court draws inspiration from the constitutional traditions common to the Member States and from the guidelines supplied by international treaties for the protection of human rights on which the Member States have collaborated or to which they are signatories. The ECHR has special significance in that respect...

34. ... the Community legal order undeniably strives to ensure respect for human dignity as a general principle of law. There can therefore be no doubt that the objective of protecting human dignity is compatible with Community law, it being immaterial in that respect that, in Germany, the principle of respect for human dignity has a particular status as an independent fundamental right.

35. Since both the Community and its Member States are required to respect fundamental rights, the protection of those rights is a legitimate interest which, in principle, justifies a restriction of the obligations imposed by Community law, even under a fundamental freedom guaranteed by the Treaty such as the freedom to provide services...

37. It is not indispensable in that respect for the restrictive measure issued by the authorities of a Member State to correspond to a conception shared by all Member States as regards the precise way in which the fundamental right or legitimate interest in question is to be protected ...

38. On the contrary...the need for, and proportionality of, the provisions adopted are not excluded merely because one Member State has chosen a system of protection different from that adopted by another State...

39. In this case, it should be noted, first, that, according to the referring court, the prohibition on the commercial exploitation of games involving the simulation of acts of violence against persons, in particular the representation of acts of homicide, corresponds to the level of protection of human dignity which the national constitution seeks to guarantee in the territory of the Federal Republic of Germany. It should also be noted that, by prohibiting only the variant of the laser game the object of which is to fire on human targets and thus 'play at killing' people, the contested order did not go beyond what is necessary in order to attain the objective pursued by the competent national authorities.

40. In those circumstances, the order...cannot be regarded as a measure unjustifiably undermining the freedom to provide services.

Omega can, of course, be applauded for its respect for national constitutional identities, in this instance the German one. Yet, this judgment is not simply about respecting the German constitutional autonomy, it also purports to set out a common EU fundamental rights law. In this regard, the substance of its vision on human dignity is completely empty, and the Court, by unquestioningly accepting the values of one state, may be accepting values as fundamental which other states find egregious.

Some authors have argued that reference to a multiplicity of sources for fundamental values and different courts (be it national constitutional courts, the Court of Justice or the European Court of Human Rights) having to justify their positions to one another leads to a marketplace of ideas in which fundamental rights can flourish.[73] This may be the case, but it has to be

---

[73] S. Douglas Scott, 'A Tale of Two Courts: Luxembourg, Strasbourg and the Growing European Human Rights Acquis' (2006) 43 *CMLRev.* 619; G. Harpaz, 'The European Court of Justice and its Relations with the European Court of Human Rights: The Quest for Enhanced Reliance, Coherence and Legitimacy' (2009) 46 *CMLRev.* 105.

questioned whether this is happening here.[74] It looks more like the Court of Justice is delegating the job of determining the content of EU fundamental rights law to other courts. Insofar as these judgments then resonate through EU law, there is an absence of safeguards where these courts make a mistake or hold values that are not widely shared. There is also a threat to the autonomy of EU law. The substance of article 52(3) and (4) of the Charter suggests that the content of the Charter must defer, in a dispute, to the ECHR provision or national constitutional provision governing that dispute. The latter should take precedence. In such circumstances, the threat to the supremacy of EU law looks compelling.[75]

5 FUNDAMENTAL RIGHTS AND THE INSTITUTIONAL SCHEME OF THE EUROPEAN UNION

A central concern of Article 6 TEU is that the Charter should not extend in any way the competences of the Union. This concern is also expressed in the Charter.

Charter, article 51(2)

This Charter does not extend the field of application of Union law beyond the powers of the Union or establish any new power or task for the Union, or modify powers and tasks in the other Parts of the Constitution.

One has to be clear, however, about how such an extension could be threatened. It is not possible for the EU legislative institutions to use Charter provisions as a legal base for legislation. The only possible route for this to happen is through judicial activity. The most obvious concern is that the Court of Justice might use the Charter to found new powers of judicial review for itself over activities that were thought to fall outside the Treaties. Another way would be if it were to interpret competences in the light of the Charter in such a way that they were to become 'stretched'. All these concerns go to the extent of review by the Court and its relationship with the other EU institutions and the Member States.

(i) Fundamental rights and the EU institutions

It is commonplace that fundamental rights are used as a basis for review whereby courts can strike down legislation or administrative acts that do not observe them. They are also used as an interpretive tool to shape the content of legislation and the scope of administrative discretion. In that regard, the Court of Justice has hitherto only been willing to grant social rights an interpretive function and has not been willing to strike down legislation for non-compliance with these. This interpretive role is not insignificant as it can be used to enlarge the scope and shape the ideological direction of legislation.

---

[74] This was astutely first spotted in M. Bronckers, 'The Relationship of the EC Courts with Other International Tribunals: Non Committal, Respectful or Submissive?' (2007) 44 *CMLRev.* 601.

[75] J. Liisberg, 'Does the EU Charter of Fundamental Rights Threaten the Supremacy of Community Law' (2001) 38 *CMLRev.* 1171, 1191. This article also provides an excellent summary of a parallel debate that took place at the time of the adoption of the Charter.

A good example is *Jaeger*. Directive 93/104/EC on the organisation of working time required amongst other things a minimum daily rest period of eleven consecutive hours per twenty-four-hour period. Jaeger was a doctor who worked in a hospital in the German town of Kiel. For about three-quarters of his working time, he was on-call. This required him to be present in the hospital to be available when needed. It was agreed that he performed services about 49 per cent of the time he was on call. The hospital considered that the time on call counted as a rest period for the purposes of the Directive. Jaeger believed it was work. The Court agreed with him.

Case C–151/02 *Landeshauptstadt Kiel* v *Jaeger* [2003] ECR I–8389

45. …it should be stated at the outset that it is clear both from Article 118a of the EC Treaty… which is the legal basis of Directive 93/104, and from the first, fourth, seventh and eighth recitals in its preamble as well as the wording of Article 1(1) itself, that the purpose of the directive is to lay down minimum requirements intended to improve the living and working conditions of workers through approximation of national provisions concerning, in particular, the duration of working time…

46. According to those same provisions, such harmonisation at Community level in relation to the organisation of working time is intended to guarantee better protection of the safety and health of workers by ensuring that they are entitled to minimum rest periods—particularly daily and weekly—and adequate breaks and by providing for a ceiling on the duration of the working week…

47. In that context it is clear from the Community Charter of the Fundamental Social Rights of Workers, adopted at the meeting of the European Council held at Strasbourg on 9 December 1989, and in particular points 8 and 19, first subparagraph, thereof, which are referred to in the fourth recital in the preamble to Directive 93/104, that every worker in the European Community must enjoy satisfactory health and safety conditions in his working environment and must have a right, inter alia, to a weekly rest period, the duration of which in the Member States must be progressively harmonised in accordance with national practices.

48. With regard more specifically to the concept of 'working time' for the purposes of Directive 93/104, it is important to point out that at paragraph 47 of the judgment in *Simap*,[76] the Court noted that the directive defines that concept as any period during which the worker is working, at the employer's disposal and carrying out his activity or duties, in accordance with national laws and/or practices, and that that concept is placed in opposition to rest periods, the two being mutually exclusive.

49. At paragraph 48 of the judgment in *Simap* the Court held that the characteristic features of working time are present in the case of time spent on call by doctors in primary care teams in Valencia (Spain) where their presence at the health centre is required. The Court found, in the case which resulted in that judgment, that it was not disputed that during periods of duty on call under those rules, the first two conditions set out in the definition of the concept of working time were fulfilled and, further, that, even if the activity actually performed varied according to the circumstances, the fact that such doctors were obliged to be present and available at the workplace with a view to providing their professional services had to be regarded as coming within the ambit of the performance of their duties.

[76] Case C-303/98 *Simap* [2000] ECR I-7963.

The Court used the Community Charter of Fundamental Social Rights in this instance to give a wide interpretation of what constitutes work. Whilst it did not broaden Treaty competences, it did enlarge the meaning of the legislation and extend the duties upon Member States. It also recalibrated the balance between employer interests and employee needs in favour of the latter.

The use of fundamental rights to interpret EU legislation is also used to limit the circumstances in which EU legislation is struck down, as the Court will seek to secure a benign interpretation wherever possible, and only if that is not possible will it strike down the measure.

In *Osterreichischer Rundfunk*, the Austrian Court of Auditors required from all local authorities and public bodies details of the salaries and pensions of senior officials for the annual report that it submitted to the Austrian Parliament. It argued this was necessary to keep state finances in check. A number of these refused to submit the information, arguing that it violated Directive 95/46/EC on the protection of individuals with regard to the processing of personal data. In interpreting the obligations set out by the Directive, the Court was eager to interpret them in the light of Article 8 ECHR, upholding the right to respect for private life.

Joined Cases C–465/00, C–138/01 and C–139/01 *Österreichischer Rundfunk* [2003] ECR I–4989

68. It should also be noted that the provisions of Directive 95/46, insofar as they govern the processing of personal data liable to infringe fundamental freedoms, in particular the right to privacy, must necessarily be interpreted in the light of fundamental rights, which, according to settled case law, form an integral part of the general principles of law whose observance the Court ensures...

70. Directive 95/46 itself, while having as its principal aim to ensure the free movement of personal data, provides in Article 1(1) that Member States shall protect the fundamental rights and freedoms of natural persons, and in particular their right to privacy with respect to the processing of personal data. Several recitals in its preamble...also express that requirement.

71. In this respect, it is to be noted that Article 8 of the Convention, while stating in paragraph 1 the principle that the public authorities must not interfere with the right to respect for private life, accepts in paragraph 2 that such an interference is possible where it is in accordance with the law and is necessary in a democratic society in the interests of national security, public safety or the economic well-being of the country, for the prevention of disorder or crime, for the protection of health or morals, or for the protection of the rights and freedoms of others.

72. So, for the purpose of applying Directive 95/46...it must be ascertained, first, whether legislation such as that at issue in the main proceedings provides for an interference with private life, and if so, whether that interference is justified from the point of view of Article 8 of the Convention...

91. If the national courts conclude that the national legislation at issue is incompatible with Article 8 of the Convention, that legislation is also incapable of satisfying the requirement of proportionality in... Directive 95/46. Nor could it be covered by any of the exceptions referred to in article 13 of that Directive, which likewise requires compliance with the requirement of proportionality with respect to the public interest objective being pursued. In any event, that provision cannot be interpreted as conferring legitimacy on an interference with the right to respect for private life contrary to Article 8 of the Convention.

The Data Protection Directive is thus to be interpreted in the light of the ECHR. On the one hand, this allows a more liberal application of the legislation. However, there is a danger that courts will look for mutual compatibility.[77] They will not merely interpret EU secondary legislation in the light of fundamental rights norms, but will also interpret fundamental rights norms in the light of the legislation being challenged, with the possibility of the safeguards offered by the latter being adjusted downwards to protect the legislation in question.

The principle also serves to reallocate risks between EU institutions and Member States. In adjusting their legislation to comply with EU measures, Member States must adopt interpretations of those measures which comply with EU fundamental rights norms. If they fail to do this, as *Österreichischer Rundfunk* shows, it is the Member State which is held accountable, not the EU legislature. This has the advantage that national administrations become guarantors of fundamental rights norms. To avoid being the targets of litigation, they will need to ensure that the legislation is not applied in any way that violates their understandings of fundamental rights. The judgment does, however, leave them between a rock and a hard place, as they have to choose between the apparent textual intent of a particular provision and compliance with an EU fundamental right. Adoption of either path is likely to leave them susceptible to legal challenge by individuals.

It is another matter when it comes to review of behaviour by the EU institutions. Whilst the General Court and Court of Justice are quite willing to strike down administrative acts by the Commission for not complying with EU fundamental rights law,[78] it is another matter when it comes to EU legislative acts. The Courts are pusillanimous here.[79] There is no instance of a Directive being struck down for failure to comply with fundamental rights. In recent times, there is only one instance of a Council Regulation being struck down and that was in *Kadi*. This, it will be remembered, was more of an administrative act as it listed individuals alleged to be associated with terrorist activities and froze their property. It was found to violate due process, in that the individuals never had the opportunity to make a case as to why they should not be listed, and the duty of judicial protection, as the listing could not be challenged before a court. Yet even there, the Court allowed the measure to be maintained for three months during the period in which Kadi could put his case before a court.

The lack of constraint is perhaps illustrated by the treatment of a commitment by the Commission to assess all proposals for their compatibility with the Charter.[80]

European Commission, *Application of the Charter of Fundamental Rights of the European Union*, SEC(2001)380/3

Any proposal for legislation and any draft instrument to be adopted by the Commission will ... as part of the normal decision-making procedures, first be scrutinised for compatibility with the Charter. Moreover, legislative proposals or draft instruments which have a specific link with fundamental rights will incorporate the following recital as a formal statement of compatibility...

---

[77] See Case C-101/01 *Lindqvist* [2003] ECR I-12971; Case C-553/07 *Rijkeboer*, Judgment of 7 May 2009.

[78] For a relatively recent example see T-185/05 *Italy* v *Commission* [2008] ECR II-3207.

[79] Particularly noteworthy examples of judicial feebleness are Case C-540/03 *Parliament* v *Council (family reunification)* [2006] ECR I-5769 (see pp. 243–5); Case C-303/05 *Advocaten voor de Wereld* v *Leden van de Ministerraad* [2007] ECR I-3633 (see pp. 601–2).

[80] H. Toner, 'Impact Assessments and Fundamental Rights Protection in EU Law' (2006) 31 *ELRev.* 316.

It would be easy for the Court to grant legal bite to such a procedural requirement. It necessitates less a direct involvement with the substance of the legislation but rather merely a
requirement that legislators direct their attention to fundamental rights. Measures could therefore be struck down not merely where they violate a fundamental right but also where the EU
institutions have failed to give due consideration to whether a measure potentially violates a
fundamental right. Yet, in the eight years since this commitment, the Court has been silent.
Consequently, commentators have suggested that the Commission's statement is no more than
a paper requirement used to legitimise dubious practices, rather than improve fundamental
rights compliance.[81]

(ii) Fundamental rights and the Member States

In the early years, fundamental rights were not used to review national action. In *Cinéthèque*,
a judgment involving a challenge to French legislation prohibiting the marketing of any film
shown in a cinema for a period between six and eighteen months after release, the Court stated
that it had no jurisdiction to assess the compatibility of national law with the ECHR.[82] This position posed difficulties. Most administration regulated by EU law was carried out by national
authorities. The coherence and unity of the EU legal order would be compromised if the EU
institutions were subject to a regime in which they were bound by fundamental rights but these
same rights did not bind implementing national authorities.[83]

In *Wachauf*, a German tenant farmer, upon expiry of his tenancy, requested compensation
for the discontinuance of the production of milk for sale. German legislation, implementing an
EU Regulation, provided that a milk producer could apply for compensation if he undertook to
discontinue milk production definitively within a period of six months from the grant of the
compensation. However, tenants were required to have the lessor's written consent to apply for
compensation. Since Wachauf's landlord had withdrawn this consent, Wachauf was unable to
receive the compensation. Wachauf argued that the German law violated his right to property,
as the compensation was for something he had built up through working the land during his
lease.

Case 5/88 *Wachauf* v *Germany* [1989] ECR 2609

18. The fundamental rights recognized by the Court are not absolute, however, but must be considered
in relation to their social function. Consequently, restrictions may be imposed on the exercise of
those rights, in particular in the context of a common organization of a market, provided that those
restrictions in fact correspond to objectives of general interest pursued by the Community and do not
constitute, with regard to the aim pursued, a disproportionate and intolerable interference, impairing
the very substance of those rights.

---

[81] G. de Búrca and J. Aschenbrenner, 'The Development of European Constitutionalism and the Role of the EU Charter of Fundamental Rights' (2003) 9 *CJEL* 355, 366–8.

[82] Joined Cases 60/84 and 61/84, *Cinéthèque* v *Fédération Nationale des Cinémas Français* [1985] ECR 2605. See
also Case 12/86 *Demirel* v *Stadt Schwäbisch Gmünd* [1987] ECR 3719.

[83] K. Lenaerts, 'Fundamental Rights to be Included in a Community Catalogue' (1991) 16 *ELRev.* 367, 368; J. Temple
Lang, 'The Sphere in which Member States are Obliged to Comply with the General Principles of Law and Community Fundamental Rights Principles' (1991/2) *LIEI* 23, 28–9.

19. Having regard to those criteria, it must be observed that Community rules which, upon the expiry of the lease, had the effect of depriving the lessee, without compensation, of the fruits of his labour and of his investments in the tenanted holding would be incompatible with the requirements of the protection of fundamental rights in the Community legal order. Since those requirements are also binding on the Member States when they implement Community rules, the Member States must, as far as possible, apply those rules in accordance with those requirements...

22. The Community regulations in question...leave the competent national authorities a sufficiently wide margin of appreciation to enable them to apply those rules in a manner consistent with the requirements of the protection of fundamental rights, either by giving the lessee the opportunity of keeping all or part of the reference quantity if he intends to continue milk production, or by compensating him if he undertakes to abandon such production definitively.

Although the Court did not rule directly, there was a strong implication that the German legislation, insofar as it deprived tenants of compensation, violated their fundamental rights. It was also made clear that the German authorities were responsible as they had not exercised the discretion available to them in a manner that complied with EU fundamental rights norms. This last nuance allowed the Court to expand the reach of EU fundamental rights law. National compliance with fundamental rights was no longer merely about the coherence of the EU legal order and making sure the formulation and implementation of a legislative act were bound by the same norms. Rather, it was now about ensuring that national authorities exercised the discretion available to them in accordance with fundamental rights.

In *ERT*, ERT, a Greek radio and television company enjoying exclusive broadcasting rights under Greek law, sought an injunction against an information company and Mr Kouvelas, the Mayor of Thessaloniki, who had set up a rival television station. The respondents argued that ERT's exclusive rights infringed, inter alia, the right to free provision of services. The Greek government invoked what are now Articles 52 and 62 TFEU, which allow it to impose restrictions for reasons of public policy. ERT counter-argued that these could not be invoked, as the conduct violated Article 10 ECHR relating to freedom of expression.

Case C–260/89 *Elliniki Radiophonia Tiléorassi AE and Others* v *Dimotiki Etairia Pliroforissis* [1991] ECR I-2925

42. As the Court has held..., it has no power to examine the compatibility with the ECHR of national rules which do not fall within the scope of Community law. On the other hand, where such rules do fall within the scope of Community law, and reference is made to the Court for a preliminary ruling, it must provide all the criteria of interpretation needed by the national court to determine whether those rules are compatible with the fundamental rights the observance of which the Court ensures and which derive in particular from the ECHR.

43. In particular, where a Member State relies on the combined provisions of [Articles 52 and 62 TFEU] in order to justify rules which are likely to obstruct the exercise of the freedom to provide services, such justification, provided for by Community law, must be interpreted in the light of the general principles of law and in particular of fundamental rights. Thus the national rules in question can fall under

the exceptions provided for by the combined provisions of [Articles 52 and 62 TFEU] only if they are compatible with the fundamental rights the observance of which is ensured by the Court.

44. It follows that in such a case it is for the national court, and if necessary, the Court of Justice to appraise the application of those provisions having regard to all the rules of Community law, including freedom of expression, as embodied in Article 10 ECHR, as a general principle of law the observance of which is ensured by the Court.

ERT expands the reach of EU fundamental rights law significantly. It provides that wherever a national measure, whatever its intent, restricts free movement it will be governed by EU fundamental rights norms, whether this free movement be of goods, services, capital or persons. Broadcasting laws, pornography laws, banning orders on hooligans or laws restricting individuals going abroad for assisted suicide – all would fall for assessment for their compliance with fundamental rights, insofar as they have the potential to restrict free movement between EU states.

However, the test is not a general one. In 2007, the Court stated that Member States were bound by fundamental rights norms when acting within the remit of the third pillar, but only when implementing EU law.[84] Prior to the coming into force of the Lisbon Treaty, two tests therefore existed. For measures falling within the first pillar, the test was whether the measure fell within the field of EC law, whilst for the third pillar it was whether it implemented an EU measure. The Lisbon Treaty now contains a single test, set out by the Charter.

Charter, article 51(1)

The provisions of this Charter are addressed to the institutions, bodies, offices and agencies of the Union with due regard for the principle of subsidiarity and to the Member States only when they are implementing Union law. They shall therefore respect the rights, observe the principles and promote the application thereof in accordance with their respective powers and respecting the limits of the powers of the Union as conferred on it in the Treaties.

The provision would seem to suggest a narrower test than *ERT*, as it suggests that only national implementing measures (not measures falling within the field of EU law) are to be reviewed. Yet ambiguity is provided by the Declaration of the Secretariat.[85] This draws a link between this provision and the existing case law of the Court of Justice, and suggests the latter can be incorporated within a wide notion of implementing measure.

---

[84] Case C-355/04 P *Segi* v *Council* [2007] ECR I-1657; Case C-354/04 P *Gestoras Pro Amnistía and Others* v *Council* [2007] ECR I-1579. See S. Peers, 'Salvation Outside the Church: Judicial Protection in the Third Pillar after the *Pupino* and *Segi* Judgments' (2007) 44 *CMLRev.* 883. A. Egger, 'EU Fundamental Rights in the National Legal Order: The Obligations of Member States Revisited' (2007) 25 *YBEL* 515.

[85] For a discussion see G. de Búrca, 'The Drafting of the EU Charter of Fundamental Rights' (2001) 26 *ELRev.* 126, 136–7.

Explanations (Charter, article 51)

As regards the Member States, it follows unambiguously from the case law of the Court of Justice that the requirement to respect fundamental rights defined in a Union context is only binding on the Member States when they act in the context of Community law (judgment of 13 July 1989, Case 5/88 *Wachauf* [1989] ECR 2609; judgment of 18 June 1991, *ERT* [1991] ECR I-2925…). The Court of Justice confirmed this case law in the following terms: 'In addition, it should be remembered that the requirements flowing from the protection of fundamental rights in the Community legal order are also binding on Member States when they implement Community rules…' (judgment of 13 April 2000, Case C-292/97 [2000] ECR I-2737, paragraph 37). Of course this principle, as enshrined in this Charter, applies to the central authorities as well as to regional or local bodies, and to public organisations, when they are implementing Union law.

It is stretching credulity to suggest that the two tests are the same and there is no difference between a measure that implements EU law and one that falls within the scope of EU law. This will have to be determined by the Court of Justice, but the matter was further muddied by the Czech Republic at the Lisbon Treaty.[86] It appended a Declaration emphasising its understanding that the Charter only applies to Member States when they are implementing EU law, but not when they are adopting and implementing national law independently from EU law.

Legal uncertainty is generated not simply by the nature of the test, which determines whether national measures are subject to EU fundamental rights law or not. It is also generated by the presence of a double test and the possibilities for arbitrage presented by this.[87] For, whether a measure is assessed for its legality for compliance with EU fundamental rights depends on whether the individuals choose to bring their activities within the reach of EU law or not.

The most celebrated instance of this is *SPUC* v *Grogan*. In 1986, the Irish Supreme Court ruled that it was against the Irish Constitution to help Irish women to have abortions by informing them of the identity and location of abortion clinics abroad. A number of Irish student unions provided the details of abortion clinics in the United Kingdom. This information was provided free. The Society for the Protection of the Unborn Child (SPUC) sought an undertaking that the student unions would cease to do this. The students invoked EU law, arguing their right to freedom of expression had been violated. SPUC countered, arguing that the measure fell outside the field of EU law, as it did not constitute a restriction on the freedom to provide services under what is now Article 56 TFEU.

Case C-159/90 *Society for the Protection of the Unborn Child (SPUC)* v *Grogan* [1991] ECR I-4685

22. …the national court seeks essentially to establish whether it is contrary to Community law for a Member State in which medical termination of pregnancy is forbidden to prohibit students associations from distributing information about the identity and location of clinics in another Member State where

---

[86] Declaration 53 by the Czech Republic on the Charter of Fundamental Rights of the European Union.
[87] For strong criticism see P. Huber, 'The Unitary Effect of the Community's Fundamental Rights: The *ERT* Doctrine Needs to be Reviewed' (2008) 14 *EPL* 323.

medical termination of pregnancy is lawfully carried out and the means of communicating with those clinics, where the clinics in question have no involvement in the distribution of the said information...

24. As regards, first, the provisions of [Article 56 TFEU], which prohibit any restriction on the freedom to supply services, it is apparent from the facts of the case that the link between the activity of the students associations of which Mr Grogan and the other defendants are officers and medical terminations of pregnancies carried out in clinics in another Member State is too tenuous for the prohibition on the distribution of information to be capable of being regarded as a restriction within the meaning of [Article 56 TFEU]...

26. The information to which the national court's questions refer is not distributed on behalf of an economic operator established in another Member State. On the contrary, the information constitutes a manifestation of freedom of expression and of the freedom to impart and receive information which is independent of the economic activity carried on by clinics established in another Member State.

27. It follows that, in any event, a prohibition on the distribution of information in circumstances such as those which are the subject of the main proceedings cannot be regarded as a restriction within the meaning of [Article 56 TFEU]...

30. It was important to bear in mind that when national legislation fell within the field of application of Community law the Court, when requested to give a preliminary ruling, must provide the national court with all the elements of interpretation necessary in order to enable it to assess the compatibility of that legislation with the fundamental rights – as laid down in particular in the ECHR – the observance of which the Court ensures. However, the Court had no such jurisdiction with regard to national legislation lying outside the scope of Community law.

Fundamental rights are treated in a paradoxical manner.[88] On the one hand, EU law stresses the indivisibility of fundamental rights. On the other, it does not protect their indefeasibility. Fundamental rights are only to be protected if they fall within the field of EU law but not if they fall outside it. This leads to inequality before the law, with individuals in analogous situations being differently protected. It also provides incentives to cheat. The clear message in *Grogan*, for example, was that the students should offer to advertise, for a nominal fee, on behalf of the British abortion clinics, in order to bring themselves within the field of EU law.

(iii) National contestation of EU fundamental rights

The application of EU fundamental rights norms to national laws is one of the most sensitive fields in EU law. On the one hand, it has been argued it is central to the European Union's mission. If the nation-state gives individuals a sense of community, identification and cultural differentiation, the task of the Union is to tame and discipline the less attractive pathologies generated by these features: those of xenophobia, exclusionary practices and introspection. This would be done through:

a commitment to the shared values of the Union as expressed in its constituent documents, a commitment, inter alia, to the duties and rights of a civil society covering discrete areas of public life, a commitment to membership in a polity which privileges exactly the opposites of nationalism – those human features which transcend the differences of organic ethno-culturalism.[89]

---

[88] P. Eeckhout, 'The EU Charter of Fundamental Rights and the Federal Question' (2002) 39 *CMLRev.* 945, 957–8; G. de Búrca, 'Fundamental Rights and the Reach of EC Law' (1993) 13 *OJLS* 283.

[89] J. Weiler, 'The Reformation of European Constitutionalism' (1997) 35 *JCMS* 97, 119.

If this assertion is very valuable, it is necessarily something very contentious. In all cases, upholding an EU fundamental right against a national law is stating that the national authorities have done something fundamentally wrong. Why else would we call it a fundamental right? It is invariably a condemnation of the character of the national polity. In some cases, the national authorities may be committing this sin by error but as often as not this Union judgment is setting out an assertion about a nation-state's firmly held beliefs. These might be egregious but they are generated by the same ties of community and of 'Them' and 'Us' as those that generate national senses of belonging.

The debate about the application of EU fundamental rights has therefore been characterised by two forms of national counter-reaction.

The first is resistance. There are cases of national protection of individual laws. Both Ireland and Malta have insisted, therefore, that their abortion laws are not to be touched by EU law.[90] Poland secured a Declaration at the Lisbon Treaty that the Charter does not affect in any way the right of Member States to legislate in the spheres of public morality, family law, protection of human dignity or respect for human physical and moral integrity.[91] The most wide-ranging challenge was made by the British and Polish governments. Concerned about judicial creativity and its effect on national choices, they secured a Protocol on the Application of the Charter to Poland and the United Kingdom. There was, furthermore, agreement at the European Council in October 2009 that the entitlements of this Protocol will extend to the Czech Republic at the conclusion of the next Accession Treaty with the next new Member State. The first provision of this Protocol states:

Protocol on the Application of the Charter to Poland and the United Kingdom, Article 1(1)

The Charter does not extend the ability of the Court of Justice of the European Union, or any court or tribunal of Poland or of the United Kingdom, to find that the laws, regulations or administrative provisions, practices or actions of Poland or of the United Kingdom are inconsistent with the fundamental rights, freedoms and principles that it reaffirms.

The Protocol does not give these two states an 'opt-out' from the Charter, as it allows both the courts of those states and the Court of Justice to rule on disputes occurring in those states. In those instances, the Charter can only be 'interpreted'. It cannot be extended. There were two particular areas of concern for those states. The first area was the 'solidarity' rights in Title IV of the Charter. These rights are largely concerned with labour protection, but also include wider social rights such as the right to health care and social assistance, as well as Union policies committing states to a high level of environmental and consumer protection. The states insisted on a provision that the Charter could not transform these into justiciable rights, if they were not already.

---

[90] Protocol on Article 40.3.3 of the Constitution of Ireland. A similar protection has been given for Malta, Protocol No. 7 Act of Accession 2003.
[91] Declaration 61 to the Treaty of Lisbon by the Republic of Poland on the Charter of Fundamental Rights of the European Union.

> **Protocol on the Application of the Charter to Poland and the United Kingdom, Article 1(2)**
>
> In particular, and for the avoidance of doubt, nothing in Title IV of the Charter creates justiciable rights applicable to Poland or the United Kingdom except insofar as Poland or the United Kingdom has provided for such rights in its national law.

The other area was the large number of provisions in the Charter which state that they are only to be recognised in accordance with the rules laid down by national laws.[92] There was a concern that 'national laws' would be understood as the general situation across the Union rather than the law in Poland or the United Kingdom, respectively. This would create problems for these states where their choices or level of protection differ markedly from the mean across the Union.

> **Protocol on the Application of the Charter to Poland and the United Kingdom, Article 2**
>
> To the extent that a provision of the Charter refers to national laws and practices, it shall only apply to Poland or the United Kingdom to the extent that the rights or principles that it contains are recognised in the law or practices of Poland or of the United Kingdom.

The Protocol is extremely clumsily worded. It makes a distinction between courts interpreting provisions and courts extending provisions that very few would recognise; a distinction which is likely to be inoperable. It is particularly inappropriate for the Charter, which describes itself as codifying human rights obligations present in other documents. There is nothing to stop the court in question 'extending' the right by having regard to these other instruments rather than the Charter. There is also a danger of interpretive chaos if the Court is being invited to provide a minimalist interpretation in references from Poland and the United Kingdom, but a different interpretation in references from other Member States. The situation in which the Court rules on the validity of Union measures forming the basis of national implementing measures is particularly murky. Is a Union measure to be struck down for twenty-five Member States but not for Poland and the United Kingdom on the basis that to do so would 'extend' the right being violated?

Notwithstanding these issues and contradictions, the chilling effect of the Protocol should not be underestimated. It is a clear indication to the Court of Justice, British and Polish courts to interpret the Charter restrictively. Insofar as it is unlikely that the Court of Justice will either accept that it 'extends' provisions in its judgments or that the same provision will be given two interpretations across the Union, a probable scenario is that it will just give very cautious interpretations. Indeed, when one looks at its interpretations of the substance of EU fundamental rights law, this seems already to be taking place.

The other strategy of opposition by national decision-makers to situations where national laws seem to be governed by EU fundamental rights law is avoidance. A tragic example is the case of *X* in Ireland.[93] X was a teenager who conceived after being raped. Her parents arranged

---

[92] See p. 240.
[93] *Attorney General* v *X* [1992] 2 CMLR 277.

for a termination at a British clinic but, as she was under 16 years old, notified the authorities of the reason for her trip abroad. The authorities refused to allow her to travel on the grounds that the Irish Constitution required them not to facilitate abortions. The matter was taken to the Irish Supreme Court. The case was legally similar to *Grogan*. It was covered by a point of EU law, namely the freedom to receive services in another Member State, and the Supreme Court should both have considered that and referred the matter to the Court of Justice for decision, as it was a court against whose decisions there was no judicial remedy under Article 267(3) TFEU. Instead, aware of both the terrible human tragedy of the case and of its considerable political implications for Ireland, the court chose to decide the case itself on the basis of Irish law. It held that, in the circumstances, abortion was compatible with the Irish Constitution, as the danger to the mother's life (X was suicidal) outweighed the case for protecting the foetus.

6 THE EUROPEAN UNION WITHIN THE EUROPEAN CONVENTION ON HUMAN RIGHTS

(i) The politics of Union accession to the ECHR

Article 6(2) TEU provides for European Union accession to the ECHR. A number of justifications can be found for this.

First, as the Union's activities have expanded, it has increasingly moved into fields where human rights concerns are frequently invoked. Examples include broadcasting, immigration, asylum, policing and judicial cooperation in criminal justice. In all fields, if an organisation setting norms applying across most of Europe were to be exempt from the safeguards of the ECHR, there would be a significant weakening of the latter.

Secondly, as the Union develops its own fundamental rights system, there is a concern that it might get things wrong. The ECHR acts as a safeguard on this. It acts as a check where the internal checks have failed or where a judgment has been reached that does not seem right.

The third reason is more contentious. It has more to do with the constitutionalisation of the Union. Union accession to the ECHR was first really pushed prior to the Treaty of Amsterdam. It was pushed by a number of Member States, who also proposed (unsuccessfully) the full incorporation of a European Bill of Rights into the TEU.[94] The debate was partly about strengthening fundamental rights protection within the Union. However, it was also about making protection of fundamental rights a central mission of the Union and, consequently, making the Union a central player in the development of fundamental rights in Europe. This posed questions about whether the Union was trying to oust the Council of Europe, the international organisation which had traditionally enjoyed that role. It also raised questions of competence creep, with the Union becoming the central locus for questions about fundamental rights rather than national settlements.

These last concerns have been carried forward in the Lisbon Treaty. Article 6(2) TEU makes clear that accession must not affect Union competences. A Protocol was also attached to the Treaties providing that special arrangements be made for participation by the Union in the Convention's control bodies and to ensure that proceedings by non-Member States and

---

[94] This was the position of Belgium, Finland, Italy, Spain and the German Länder. European Parliament, White Paper on the 1996 Intergovernmental Conference, vol. II (Brussels, European Parliament, 1997).

individual applications are correctly addressed to Member States and/or the Union.[95] The Protocol also emphasised that accession to the ECHR would not affect the situation of the Member States, particularly in relation to individual derogations from the Convention or choices of accession to particular Protocols of the ECHR.[96]

(ii) Obligations of the Union under the ECHR

The obligations of the Union under the ECHR are governed by the *Bosphorus* judgment. Bosphorus had leased two aircraft from Yugoslav National Airlines (JAT) and arranged for these to be subject to maintenance work in Ireland in 1993. At that time there were UN sanctions against the governments of Serbia and Montenegro. Acting under an EU Regulation, the Irish government impounded both aircraft. Bosphorus argued this contravened EU law as the Regulation violated the fundamental right of freedom to pursue a business. Following a reference by the Irish High Court, the Court of Justice ruled that it did not.[97] Bosphorus then took the Irish Government to the European Court of Human Rights, arguing that it had violated the right to property in Article 1 of Protocol 1.

No. 45036/98 *Bosphorus v Ireland*, Judgment of 30 June 2005

151. The question is therefore whether, and if so to what extent, that important general interest of compliance with Community obligations can justify the impugned interference by the Irish State with the applicant company's property rights.

152. The Convention does not, on the one hand, prohibit Contracting Parties from transferring sovereign power to an international (including a supranational) organisation in order to pursue cooperation in certain fields of activity... Moreover, even as the holder of such transferred sovereign power, that organisation is not itself held responsible under the Convention for proceedings before, or decisions of, its organs as long as it is not a Contracting Party...

153. On the other hand, it has also been accepted that a Contracting Party is responsible under Article 1 of the Convention for all acts and omissions of its organs regardless of whether the act or omission in question was a consequence of domestic law or of the necessity to comply with international legal obligations. Article 1 makes no distinction as to the type of rule or measure concerned and does not exclude any part of a Contracting Party's 'jurisdiction' from scrutiny under the Convention...

154. In reconciling both these positions and thereby establishing the extent to which a State's action can be justified by its compliance with obligations flowing from its membership of an international organisation to which it has transferred part of its sovereignty, the Court has recognised that absolving Contracting States completely from their Convention responsibility in the areas covered by such a transfer would be incompatible with the purpose and object of the Convention; the guarantees of the Convention could be limited or excluded at will, thereby depriving it of its peremptory character and undermining the practical and effective nature of its safeguards...

155. In the Court's view, State action taken in compliance with such legal obligations is justified as long as the relevant organisation is considered to protect fundamental rights, as regards both the substantive

---

[95] Protocol relating to Article 6(2) TEU on the Accession of the Union to the ECHR.

[96] The ECHR has five Protocols but not all are signed by all the Member States. Article 15(1) ECHR also allows states to make derogations from particular provisions in times of war or public emergency.

[97] Case C-84/95 *Bosphorus* [1996] ECR I-3953.

guarantees offered and the mechanisms controlling their observance, in a manner which can be considered at least equivalent to that for which the Convention provides... By 'equivalent' the Court means 'comparable'; any requirement that the organisation's protection be 'identical' could run counter to the interest of international cooperation pursued ... However, any such finding of equivalence could not be final and would be susceptible to review in the light of any relevant change in fundamental rights protection.

156. If such equivalent protection is considered to be provided by the organisation, the presumption will be that a State has not departed from the requirements of the Convention when it does no more than implement legal obligations flowing from its membership of the organisation.

   However, any such presumption can be rebutted if, in the circumstances of a particular case, it is considered that the protection of Convention rights was manifestly deficient. In such cases, the interest of international cooperation would be outweighed by the Convention's role as a 'constitutional instrument of European public order' in the field of human rights...

158. Since the impugned measure constituted solely compliance by Ireland with its legal obligations flowing from membership of the European Community ..., the Court will now examine whether a presumption arises that Ireland complied with the requirements of the Convention in fulfilling such obligations and whether any such presumption has been rebutted in the circumstances of the present case ...

165. ... the Court finds that the protection of fundamental rights by Community law can be considered to be, and to have been at the relevant time, 'equivalent' (within the meaning of paragraph 155 above) to that of the Convention system. Consequently, the presumption arises that Ireland did not depart from the requirements of the Convention when it implemented legal obligations flowing from its membership of the European Community (see paragraph 156 above).

166. The Court has had regard to the nature of the interference, to the general interest pursued by the impoundment and by the sanctions regime and to the ruling of the ECJ (in the light of the opinion of the Advocate General), a ruling with which the Supreme Court was obliged to and did comply. It considers it clear that there was no dysfunction of the mechanisms of control of the observance of Convention rights.

   In the Court's view, therefore, it cannot be said that the protection of the applicant company's Convention rights was manifestly deficient, with the consequence that the relevant presumption of Convention compliance by the respondent state has not been rebutted.

Having checked that the Union system of protection of fundamental rights is equivalent to that in the ECHR, the European Court of Human Rights held that actions against national measures governed by EU law would be upheld not if the measure breaches the ECHR, but only if it is 'manifestly deficient'.[98] This is a much weaker test than that applied to individual states under the ECHR. It appears that attention is paid to whether the judicial procedures worked within the Union rather than the substance of the breach. One has the feeling almost of a 'non-aggression pact' between the two European courts, whereby the Court of Justice will slavishly follow the case law of the European Court of Human Rights, whereas the latter will intervene only in cases of the most grotesque dysfunction. It may be that Union accession to the ECHR will change the reasoning of the European Court of Human Rights. It will no longer see itself as

[98] For criticism see C. Costello, 'The *Bosphorus* Ruling of the European Court of Human Rights: Fundamental Rights and Blurred Boundaries in Europe' (2006) 6 *Human Rights Law Review* 87; C. Eckes, 'Does the European Court of Human Rights Provide Protection from the European Community? The Case of *Bosphorus Airways*' (2007) 13 *EPL* 47.

having to mediate between two sets of international commitments, the ECHR and the TEU, but will rather say that this reasoning no longer applies now the Union is a member of the ECHR. It has to be treated like any other member and states cannot hide behind its obligations.

7 EU FUNDAMENTAL RIGHTS POLICY

Fundamental rights have not just been taken forward by the Court of Justice. In 1977, the Parliament, Commission and Council adopted a Joint Declaration on Fundamental Rights, in which they undertook to respect the ECHR in the exercise of their powers.[99] The commitment was one of constraint, however. The EU institutions were not to violate fundamental rights but, at the same time, these were not to become a central mission of the Union, pivotal to fashioning its political identity or orienting its activities. The Court of Justice confirmed the lack of a positive agenda for fundamental rights in Opinion 2/94, where it ruled there could be no accession to the ECHR, as there was no general human rights competence.[100] Alston and Weiler have characterised the approach of non-violation as negative integration, in that it indicates only a bald commitment not to breach fundamental rights rather than a commitment to realise them.[101] They argued that this led to a gap between rhetoric and reality, whereby the Union affirms the importance of many rights but did little to secure any of them. Concern with non-violation was marked by two further features: an inadequate information base, so that there was no real knowledge of what rights were being violated, and excessive reliance on judicial remedies.[102] Certainly by the early 1990s onwards, it was felt necessary to develop a human rights policy in two fields: external relations and accession.

(i) Fundamental rights and the external relations of the Union[103]

From the early 1990s, the European Union had begun to include human rights references in its trade and aid policies.[104] By the mid-1990s onwards, all trade and cooperation agreements had clauses committing both parties to respect human rights.[105] For example, the General Scheme of Preferences, which allows for certain goods from less developed countries to be imported free from customs duties or at lower tariffs, could also be suspended where beneficiary states failed to respect fundamental rights or basic labour standards.[106] Provision was also made for EU development projects to contribute to the promotion of human rights.[107] The Union has

---

[99] [1977] OJ C103/1.

[100] Opinion 2/94 *Re Accession of the Community to the ECHR* [1996] ECR I-1759.

[101] P. Alston and J. Weiler, '"An Ever Closer Union" in Need of a Human Rights Policy' (1998) 9 *EJIL* 658.

[102] Cf. A. v. Bogdandy, 'The European Union as a Human Rights Organization? Human Rights and the Core of the European Union' (2000) 27 *CMLRev.* 1307, 1319–20.

[103] For a fine overview see P. Leino, 'European Universalism? The EU and Human Rights Conditionality' (2005) 24 *YEL* 330.

[104] A. Brandtner and A. Rosas, 'Human Rights and the External Relations of the European Community: An Analysis of Doctrine and Practice' (1998) 9 *EJIL* 468.

[105] E. Riedel and M. Will, 'Human Rights Clauses in External Agreements' in P. Alston (ed.), *The EU and Human Rights* (Oxford, Oxford University Press, 1999).

[106] Regulation 980/2005/EC applying a scheme of generalised tariff preferences [2005] OJ L169/1, article 20(4). Preferences have been suspended to two states under this provision, Belarus and Myanmar.

[107] Regulation 975/1999/EC laying down the requirements for the implementation of development cooperation operations which contribute to the general objective of developing and consolidating democracy and the rule of law and to that of respecting human rights and fundamental freedoms [1999] OJ 1999 L120/1.

further applied these norms in fields closer to home. Its neighbourhood policy, which grants access to the EU market to neighbouring states in North Africa, the Middle East and Eastern Europe on the basis they engage in political and economic reforms, requires these states to respect human rights.[108] The arena in which the Union has sought most leverage for these is the enlargement process. The Copenhagen Criteria setting out the basis on which states can apply for membership include so-called political criteria, which require states to have, inter alia, stable institutions guaranteeing democracy, the rule of law, human rights and respect for and protection of minorities.[109] These criteria become the basis for Commission reports evaluating the state of human rights in all the applicant countries.[110] These reports have proved wide-ranging in their criticism of applicant state practices.[111]

This collage has been brought together by the Lisbon Treaty. Article 49 TEU provides that only states which respect the values set out in Article 2 TEU (which include respect for fundamental rights) may apply for membership of the Union. More generally, the formulation and application of fundamental rights norms in external relations policies have been brought together by a new provision in the Treaty of Lisbon.

Article 21 TEU

1. The Union's action on the international scene shall be guided by the principles which have inspired its own creation, development and enlargement, and which it seeks to advance in the wider world: democracy, the rule of law, the universality and indivisibility of human rights and fundamental freedoms, respect for human dignity, the principles of equality and solidarity, and respect for the principles of the United Nations Charter and international law.

2. The Union shall define and pursue common policies and actions, and shall work for a high degree of cooperation in all fields of international relations, in order to:
   (a) safeguard its values, fundamental interests, security, independence and integrity;
   (b) consolidate and support democracy, the rule of law, human rights and the principles of international law...

---

[108] European Commission, *Wider Europe – Neighbourhood: A New Framework for Relations with our Eastern and Southern Neighbours*, COM(2003)104 final. On this see P. Leino and R. Petrov, 'Between "Common Values" and Competing Universals: The Promotion of the EU's Common Values through the European Neighbourhood Policy' (2009) 15 *ELJ* 654.

[109] *EU Bulletin* 6–1993, 1.13.

[110] M. Nowak, 'Human Rights "Conditionality" in relation to Entry to, and Full Participation in the European Union' in P. Alston (ed.), *The EU and Human Rights* (Oxford, Oxford University Press, 1999); A. Williams, 'Enlargement and Human Rights Conditionality: A Policy of Distinction?' (2000) 25 *ELRev.* 601; C. Pinelli, 'Conditionality and Enlargement in Light of EU Constitutional Developments' (2004) 10 *ELJ* 354.

[111] Slovakia was initially denied pre-accession status in 1997 on the grounds of the quality of its political regime, and was then subject to sustained monitoring and criticism by the Commission. European Commission, *2002 Regular Report on Slovakia's Progress Towards Accession*, COM(2002)700. The 2008 reports on protection of human rights in the Former Yugoslav Republic of Macedonia and Turkey were damning: European Commission, *Progress Report on the Former Yugoslav Republic of Macedonia*, COM(2008)674, 15–21; European Commission, *Progress Report on Turkey*, COM(2008)674, 11–28. They were also wide-ranging. The one on Turkey condemned disproportionate use of force by police at public gatherings, honour killings, informal militias ('village guards'), the lack of resources and independence of human rights institutions, treatment of people with disabilities, and insufficient respect for cultural diversity and for the protection of minorities in accordance with European standards.

This codifies and brings together general practice in external relations. It does not, however, counter the dissatisfaction with the Union's practice in this area. It has been argued that it has been hypocritical for the Union to apply standards of scrutiny to other states that it does not apply to its own Member States.[112] It has also been argued that fundamental rights in external relations policy have been applied in a highly selective and uneven manner, and that negative opinions have often had counter-productive consequences.[113]

(ii) A domestic fundamental rights policy

A domestic human rights policy has proved less attainable. Beyond the injunction to EU institutions and Member States when implementing EU law not to violate fundamental rights, there is only one competence explicitly relating to fundamental rights.

Article 7 TEU

1. On a reasoned proposal by one-third of the Member States, by the European Parliament or by the European Commission, the Council, acting by a majority of four-fifths of its members after obtaining the consent of the European Parliament, may determine that there is a clear risk of a serious breach by a Member State of the values referred to in Article 2. Before making such a determination, the Council shall hear the Member State in question and may address recommendations to it, acting in accordance with the same procedure. The Council shall regularly verify that the grounds on which such a determination was made continue to apply.

2. The European Council, acting by unanimity on a proposal by one-third of the Member States or by the Commission and after obtaining the consent of the European Parliament, may determine the existence of a serious and persistent breach by a Member State of the values referred to in Article 2, after inviting the Member State in question to submit its observations.

3. Where a determination under paragraph 2 has been made, the Council, acting by a qualified majority, may decide to suspend certain of the rights deriving from the application of the Treaties to the Member State in question, including the voting rights of the representative of the government of that Member State in the Council. In doing so, the Council shall take into account the possible consequences of such a suspension on the rights and obligations of natural and legal persons. The obligations of the Member State in question under this Treaty shall in any case continue to be binding on that State.

4. The Council, acting by a qualified majority, may decide subsequently to vary or revoke measures taken under paragraph 3 in response to changes in the situation which led to their being imposed.

The voting thresholds for use of this provision are extremely high. Its use is likely to be highly restricted, if at all. In the one instance where they could have been used, Member States also preferred to go outside the formal procedures. In 2000, when the explicitly racist Freedom party joined the Austrian government, the other Member States entered into an extra-legal

---

[112] This is the central thesis of A. Williams, *European Union Human Rights Policy* (Oxford, Oxford University Press, 2004).

[113] For example, the treatment of Turkey during the 1990s, which led it to suspend relations with the European Union. See K. Smith, 'The Evolution and Application of EU Member State Conditionality' in M. Cremona (ed.), *The Enlargement of the European Union* (Oxford, Oxford University Press, 2003).

agreement in which they would have no bilateral contacts with the Austrian government. The matter was only resolved six months later, when a 'Committee of Wise Men' found both that the sanctions had inflamed nationalist feelings in Austria and that the Austrian government had a relatively good human rights record.[114]

The significance of the provision lies in the powers it bestows on the Union to monitor the Member States for compliance with fundamental rights. In this regard, a significant distinction exists between Article 7(1) and (2) TEU. The latter provision concerns the circumstances where a serious violation is found to exist and the ground is prepared for sanctions. The former concerns findings of a serious risk of a serious violation. It is an early warning system that is concerned with monitoring how the Member State is doing. This entails the Union acquiring an independent evidence-gathering and reporting capacity.

This capacity has been institutionalised with the establishment of the European Union Agency for Fundamental Rights.[115] The Agency has four central tasks:

- it has to collect, record, disseminate and compare data and research on fundamental rights and develop methods and standards to improve the comparability, objectivity and reliability of that data;
- at the request of EU institutions it can publish opinions for EU institutions and Member States implementing EU law;
- it is to publish both an annual report and thematic reports on fundamental rights issues in the areas of its activity, highlighting examples of good practice; and
- it is to mobilise public awareness of fundamental rights through promoting dialogue with civil society.[116]

The most powerful task of the Agency is the power to give opinions, notably on legislative proposals. The potential normative force of these opinions is unclear. In other fields, the Commission can only derogate from the opinions of the Agency, where it can provide a contrary opinion by a body of equal weight and can provide reasons for choosing one over the other.[117] The Commission, as a consequence, invariably follows the Agency's opinions. With fundamental rights teaching on all areas of EU law, the Fundamental Rights Agency is potentially a very powerful body. Yet the Regulation provides that the Agency can only provide opinions on the legality of proposals at the request of the Commission and cannot address the legality of the measure for the purposes of judicial review, or make an assessment as to whether a Member State has met its obligations within the context of an enforcement action.[118] Even though one of its tasks is to consider questions of fundamental rights in assessing the impact of any legislative proposal, there is presently little evidence of the Commission having consulted the Agency.

---

[114] M. Merlingen, M. Mudde and U. Sedelmeider, 'The Right and the Righteous? European Norms, Domestic Politics and the Sanctions Against Austria' (2001) 39 *JCMS* 59.

[115] Regulation 168/2007/EC establishing a European Union Agency for Fundamental Rights [2007] OJ L53/1. On the Agency see G. Toggenburg, 'The Role of the New EU Fundamental Rights Agency: Debating the "Sex of Angels" or Improving Europe's Human Rights Performance?' (2008) 33 *ELRev*. 385; A. v. Bogdandy and J. von Bernstoff, 'The EU Fundamental Rights Agency within the European and International Human Rights Architecture: The Legal Framework and Some Unsettled Issues in a New Field of Administrative Law' (2009) 46 *CMLRev*. 1035.

[116] Regulation 168/2007/EC article 4(1).

[117] In relation to the European Food Safety Authority, see Case T-13/99 *Pfizer Animal Health* v *Council* [2002] ECR II-3305.

[118] Regulation 168/2007/EC, article 4(2).

The Agency also has to work within the aegis of a Multi-annual Framework established by the EU political institutions, which sets out the thematic areas within which it is to function. Its work is confined either by institutional requests, in the case of opinions, or, more generally, by the political agenda of the EU institutions. This inevitably confines not only the Agency activities, but also the type of rights examined by the Agency. The Framework for 2007–2012 is a case in point. It takes a reasonably broad remit, but has excluded analysis of social rights, bioethical rights and the war on terror, all of which are touched upon significantly by Union activities.[119]

The Agency, therefore, is very much a reflection of the debate on the establishment of an EU fundamental rights policy. Its remit, as with the policy, is partial, unsteady and makes distinctions which are hard to justify. Yet, for those who advocate a fundamental rights policy, the establishment of an Agency with the legal power to police all EU legislation for compliance with fundamental rights, and with the power to act as a hub for European civil society and awareness of these matters, is indeed a powerful step forward.

FURTHER READING

P. Alston *et al.* (eds.), *The EU and Human Rights* (Oxford, Oxford University Press, 1999)

P. Alston and J. Weiler, '"An Ever Closer Union" in Need of a Human Rights Policy' (1998) 9 *European Journal of International Law* 658

M. Avbelj, *The European Court of Justice and the Question of Value Choices*, Jean Monnet Working Paper 6/04

F. Bignami, 'Creating European Rights: National Values and Supranational Interests' (2005) 11 *Columbia Journal of European Law* 241

A. v. Bogdandy, 'The European Union as a Human Rights Organization? Human Rights and the Core of the European Union' (2000) 27 *Common Market Law Review* 1307

S. Greer and A. Williams, 'Human Rights in the Council of Europe and the EU: Towards "Individual", "Constitutional" or "Institutional" Justice?' (2009) 15 *European Law Journal* 462

T. Hervey and J. Kenner (eds.), *Economic and Social Rights under the EU Charter of Fundamental Rights* (Oxford, Hart, 2003)

N. Krisch, 'The Open Architecture of European Human Rights Law' (2008) 71 *Modern Law Review* 183

B. Kunoy and A. Dawes, 'Plate Tectonics in Luxembourg: The *Ménage à Trois* between EC Law, International Law and the European Convention on Human Rights following the UN Sanctions Cases' (2009) 46 *Common Market Law Review* 73

K. Lenaerts and E. de Smijter, 'A "Bill of Rights" for the European Union' (2001) 38 *Common Market Law Review* 273

J. Liisberg, 'Does the EU Charter of Fundamental Rights Threaten the Supremacy of Community Law' (2001) 38 *Common Market Law Review* 1171

S. Peers and A. Ward (eds.), *The EU Charter of Fundamental Rights* (Oxford, Hart, 2004)

A. Williams, *EU Human Rights Policies: A Study in Irony* (Oxford, Oxford University Press, 2004)

---

[119] Decision 2008/203/EC implementing Regulation 168/2007/EC as regards the adoption of a Multi-annual Framework for the European Union Agency for Fundamental Rights for 2007–2012 [2008] OJ L63/14, article 2.

7

Rights and Remedies in National Courts

CONTENTS

1 INTRODUCTION

This chapter considers the rights and remedies that EU law allows to be invoked in national courts. It is organised as follows.

Section 2 looks at the origins of direct effect. Direct effect is the doctrine which provides for EU law to be invoked in national courts. Initially, direct effect was a 'defensive' right directed at administrations, which required them not to violate entitlements granted clearly and unconditionally to private parties by Treaty provisions.

Section 3 looks at how, over time, direct effect was reconceptualised as providing rights which generate a full set of entitlements against all parties and impose a duty on administrations and courts to protect and realise these entitlements for individuals. This led to EU Treaty provisions being capable of being invoked both against the state (vertical direct effect) and against private parties (horizontal direct effect).

Section 4 considers what remedies and procedures are available to individuals where an EU provision is invoked in a domestic court. As a general rule, these are a matter for domestic law. This autonomy is subject to two constraints. The remedies and procedures for infringement of EU law rights should be, first, no less favourable than those for similar domestic claims, and secondly, should not make it practically impossible to exercise EU rights. However, there is a right to EU remedies in four circumstances: a right to restitution for illegally levied taxes; a right to interim relief pending a preliminary reference to the Court of Justice; a right to claim damages or force repayment of illegal subsidies in the field of EU competition law; and, finally, a right to sue the state for damages where a serious breach of EU law by it has led to loss for the individual.

Section 5 considers the granting of direct effect to secondary legislation. Direct effect is granted to all binding instruments of EU law: Treaty provisions, Regulations, international agreements, Directives and Decisions. The first three sets of instruments are capable of both vertical and horizontal direct effect. Directives and Decisions are only capable of being invoked against the state. Whilst Directives are not capable of horizontal effect, like other binding instruments of EU law they can generate incidental effects for third parties. This occurs, first, where an individual invokes a Directive against the state and this imposes burdens on private parties. It occurs, secondly, where a private party challenges another under national law, and the latter invokes the Directive as a shield requiring the state to protect it from the private action under national law.

Section 6 considers the doctrine of indirect effect. As significant as direct effect, this requires national courts to interpret all national law, insofar as this is possible, in the light of all EU law. This duty encompasses non-binding instruments, such as Recommendations, as well as binding instruments. It has generated concerns about legal certainty, both as to when the duty first arises and as to the strength of the duty of interpretation.

Section 7 considers the doctrine of state liability. This requires states to compensate individuals where a breach of EU law by the state has led to loss for the individual and the provision breached creates rights for the individual. State liability covers all governmental institutions, including acts of the judiciary. If EU law allows Member States some discretion, there is a further condition to attract liability: the breach must be sufficiently serious. Typically, there are four circumstances which attract liability: failure to transpose a Directive; breach of a clear provision of EU law; failure to comply with settled case law; and failure to comply with a judgment of the Court of Justice.

Section 8 considers how the Lisbon Treaty might reshape the field through the introduction of a new provision, Article 19(1) TEU, which requires Member States to provide remedies sufficient to ensure effective legal protection in the fields covered by EU law. This might simply be a codifying provision. Alternately, it might impose a stronger duty on Member States to give effect to EU rights and to protect EU entitlements more fully.

2 DIRECT EFFECT AND THE IDEA OF A UNION RIGHT

We first considered *Van Gend en Loos* in Chapter 5. There are two central elements to that judgment.

The first concerns claims made about the quality of EU law. The Court of Justice claimed that EU law did not fall within traditional categories of international law but rather formed a new sovereign legal order with a new powerful authority. The consequences of this were addressed in Chapter 5.

The second element is the establishment of a new system of individual rights through the doctrine of direct effect. This element has different dynamics. The language of rights calls for us to rethink EU law in terms of the maximum benefits it can grant individuals, both collectively and individually. It therefore pushes for interpretations which maximise individual entitlements and autonomy. It also requires consistency in the interpretation of the Treaty. Provisions appearing on their face to grant individuals direct benefits cannot be interpreted differently, simply because the consequences for the reorganisation of legal authority between EU law and national law are too extravagant. Equally, interpretive techniques used to develop one provision cannot be denied without reason to the interpretation of another provision.

If these elements have distinct rationales, in *Van Gend en Loos* they inform one another. If the justification for the establishment of these rights is the presence of a sovereign legal order, the vehicle for the expression of this order is the development of a system of judicially protected rights.

The facts of the case have been discussed earlier.[1] At its heart, however, was the question whether the provision that is now Article 28 TFEU, prohibiting the imposition of customs duties or charges having equivalent effect on imports from other Member States, could be invoked as a matter of EU law in the Dutch court where it had been asserted.

Case 26/62 *Van Gend en Loos v Nederlandse Administratie der Belastingen* [1963] ECR 1

The first question ... is whether Article [28 TFEU] has direct application in national law in the sense that nationals of Member States may on the basis of this article lay claim to rights which the national court must protect.

To ascertain whether the provisions of an international treaty extend so far in their effects it is necessary to consider the spirit, the general scheme and the wording of those provisions ...

... The Community constitutes a new legal order of international law for the benefit of which the States have limited their sovereign rights, albeit within limited fields, and the subjects of which comprise not only Member States but also their nationals. Independently of the legislation of Member States, Community law therefore not only imposes obligations on individuals but is also intended to confer upon them rights which become part of their legal heritage. These rights arise not only where they are expressly granted by the Treaty, but also by reason of obligations which the Treaty imposes in a clearly defined way upon individuals as well as upon the Member States and the Institutions of the Community.

With regard to the general scheme of the Treaty as it relates to customs duties and charges having equivalent effect it must be emphasized that... [basing] the Community upon a customs union, includes as an essential provision the prohibition of these customs duties and charges. This provision is found at the beginning of the part of the Treaty which defines the foundations of the Community. It is applied and explained by Article [28 TFEU].

---

[1] See p. 14.

The wording of Article [28 TFEU] contains a clear and unconditional prohibition which is not a positive but a negative obligation. This obligation, moreover, is not qualified by any reservation on the part of states which would make its implementation conditional upon a positive legislative measure enacted under national law. The very nature of this prohibition makes it ideally adapted to produce direct effects in the legal relationship between Member States and their subjects.

The implementation of Article [28 TFEU] does not require any legislative intervention on the part of the States. The fact that under this article it is the Member States who are made the subject of the negative obligation does not imply that their nationals cannot benefit from this obligation.

It follows from the foregoing considerations that according to the spirit, the general scheme and the wording of the Treaty, Article [28 TFEU] must be interpreted as producing direct effects and creating individual rights which national courts must protect.

If ground-breaking in its development of a sovereign legal order, the judgment is narrow in two respects.

First, its ambit is circumscribed. The judgment does not state that all Treaty provisions can be invoked by individuals in national courts. It only holds that some provisions, which meet certain criteria – namely that they are clear, unconditional, negatively phrased and require no legislative intervention – can be invoked by individuals. Moreover, the judgment only indicated with certainty that one provision met this: the arcane Article 28 TFEU prohibiting customs duties and charges having equivalent effect. A sovereign legal order composed solely of the individual right to import or exports goods free of customs duties is a very limited creature, indeed. This is undoubtedly why the judgment did not provoke more controversy at the time. Yet, the judgment also created instability. For *Van Gend en Loos* offered an almost endless possibility for more provisions to be found to generate individual rights. In every case where this occurs, however, there will be a renewed debate about the reorganisation of legal power entailed by this. Does it grant too much power to the Union, to judges or to particular litigants? The open-ended nature of *Van Gend en Loos* entails this will be a recurring debate that erupts whenever a provision is held to generate individual rights for the first time.

Secondly, the judgment is narrow in its understanding of what is meant by a right. To be sure, the judgment talks about the Treaty imposing obligations on others, be these national courts, administrations or private parties,[2] but it is very vague about the extent and nature of the obligations that are owed to the right-holder by others. At its narrowest, EU law may only grant certain rights vis-à-vis the state: a duty for it not to violate certain interests. Such rights are little more than an immunity from national law in which the holder can do things that others cannot (e.g. withhold taxes). A broader conception of rights involves the holder being able to call on all parties to respect, protect and make good the interests that lie at the heart of the right. Such a right can be asserted against anybody and it calls for full redress of the interests if they are infringed.

The wording of *Van Gend en Loos* suggested that it was concerned with the former type of right.[3] The stipulation that provisions be negatively phrased meant that national administrations

---

[2] For a useful discussion see T. Downes and C. Hilsom, 'Making Sense of Rights: Community Rights in EC Law' (1999) 24 *ELRev.* 121.

[3] On this early period see T. Eilmansberger, 'The Relationship Between Rights and Remedies in EC Law: In Search of the Missing Link' (2004) 41 *CMLRev.* 1199, 1202–6.

could only be called upon to refrain from doing things but not be called upon to take positive action to protect individuals. It is a duty not to violate addressed only to the national administration. Equally, the requirement of textual clarity suggested that courts could not be called upon to exercise interpretive discretion on behalf of the right-holder, as 'unclear' provisions necessitating the exercise of such discretion would simply not be directly effective. Finally, the proviso that provisions be unconditional suggested courts could not be called upon to weigh individual entitlements against other public interests if these were recognised by EU law.

Alongside this, the judgment was silent on the types of procedure, sanction or enforcement mechanism that should be deployed to protect the right. If the language of rights pushes for full protection of an individual's entitlements by all parties, it looked in *Van Gend en Loos* as if its use was somewhat rhetorical, for the Court has been much more reserved in terms of the duties it imposes on other parties. As we shall see in the rest of this chapter, the case law of the Court is marked by a push and pull between these two elements.

3 EXPLOITATION OF DIRECT EFFECT

In the 1960s, the Court applied the doctrine of direct effect to a limited number of provisions, which met the criteria set out in *Van Gend en Loos*.[4] It also did not elaborate on the implications for parties when they benefited from a directly effective provision. Most Treaty provisions only entered fully into force, however, with the end of the transitional period in 1970. In the early 1970s, the Court sought to expand direct effect in a number of directions.

(i) Relaxing the criteria: towards a test of justiciability

First, the Court began to relax the criteria for when a provision may be directly effective. In *Van Duyn*, it stated that even if the provision did not set out an absolute entitlement, it could still be invoked in national courts if any qualification or condition was subject to judicial control. As no provision or condition in the Treaty has ever been held to be outside judicial control, this effectively discarded the requirement that a provision be unconditional.[5] In *Reyners*, the Court held that what is now Article 48 TFEU, which imposes positive obligations on Member States to enable freedom of establishment, was directly effective, thereby sweeping away the insistence that only negatively phrased provisions could be invoked in national courts.[6]

If EC Treaty provisions no longer needed to be negative or unconditional to be directly effective, this begged the question which criteria they did need to meet. This issue came up most acutely in the case of *Defrenne (No. 2)*. Under Belgian law, female air stewards were required to retire at the age of 40, unlike their male counterparts. Gabrielle Defrenne had been forced to retire from the Belgian national carrier, Sabena, on this ground in 1968. She brought an action claiming that the lower pension payments this entailed breached the principle now in Article

---

[4] Case 57/65 *Lütticke v HZA Sarrelouis* [1966] ECR 205; Case 27/67 *Firma Fink-Frucht GmbH v Hauptzollamt München-Landsbergerstrasse* [1968] ECR 327; Case 13/68 *Salgoil v Italian Ministry of Foreign Trade* [1968] ECR 453. On the early developments see A. Dashwood, 'The Principle of Direct Effect in European Community Law' (1978) 16 *JCMS* 229; P. Craig, 'Once upon a Time in the West: Direct Effect and the Federalization of EEC Law' (1992) 12 *OJLS* 453, 460–70.
[5] Case 41/74 *Van Duyn v Home Office* [1974] ECR 1337.
[6] Case 2/74 *Reyners v Belgium* [1974] ECR 631.

157(1) TFEU that 'each Member State shall ensure and maintain the principle that men and women should receive equal pay for work of equal value'. Yet, on the face of it, there appeared to be a number of obstacles to the provision being directly effective. It was argued, first, that the provision set out general principles about the broad treatment of men and women in the workforce rather than conferring individual rights and, secondly, that it was programmatic in nature, requiring further measures for its implementation.

Case 43/75 Defrenne v Sabena (No. 2) [1976] ECR 455

16. Under the terms of the first paragraph of Article [157 TFEU], the Member States are bound to ensure and maintain 'the application of the principle that men and women should receive equal pay for equal work'...

18. For the purposes of the implementation of these provisions a distinction must be drawn within the whole area of application of Article [157 TFEU] between, first, direct and overt discrimination which may be identified solely with the aid of the criteria based on equal work and equal pay referred to by the Article in question and, secondly, indirect and disguised discrimination which can only be identified by reference to more explicit implementing provisions of a Community or national character.

19. It is impossible not to recognise that the complete implementation of the aim pursued by Article [157 TFEU], by means of the elimination of all discrimination, direct or indirect, between men and women workers, not only as regards individual undertakings but also entire branches of industry and even of the economic system as a whole, may in certain cases involve the elaboration of criteria whose implementation necessitates the taking of appropriate measures at Community and national level ...

21. Among the forms of direct discrimination which may be identified solely by reference to the criteria laid down by Article [157 TFEU] must be included in particular those which have their origin in legislative provisions or in collective labour agreements and which may be detected on the basis of a purely legal analysis of the situation.

22. This applies even more in cases where men and women receive unequal pay for equal work carried out in the same establishment or service, whether public or private.

23. As is shown by the very findings of the judgment making the reference, in such a situation the court is in a position to establish all the facts which enable it to decide whether a woman worker is receiving lower pay than a male worker performing the same tasks.

24. In such situation, at least, Article [157 TFEU] is directly [effective] and may thus give rise to individual rights which the courts must protect.

The Court gave the provision a double meaning to enable the finding of direct effect. On the one hand, it acquired a programmatic, wide-ranging, ambitious purpose, namely to secure equality between men and women within the economic system as a whole. On the other hand, the Court gave the provision a second interpretation within this, namely to prohibit pay discrimination between men and women in individual workplaces. This was considered sufficiently precise to be invoked in national courts. However one looks at it, the Court had significantly relaxed the requirement for legal clarity. To acknowledge that a provision has too uncertain an ambit to be invoked, per se, in national courts and to suggest that it has a double meaning is to indicate that it is not clear.

Since *Defrenne (No. 2)*, the Court has moved away from using the criteria set out in *Van Gend en Loos*. Instead, the test has become whether the substance of the provision is sufficiently precise and unconditional.[7] In the eyes of one judge, the invocability of Treaty provisions has now been reduced to a simple question of justiciability.[8] Yet what does this mean? The Court will not look at whether the provision is qualified by other provisions or constraints, but simply at whether the provision is 'unequivocal'.[9] This suggests that it is not important simply that a provision sets out some entitlements that are clearly for the benefit of individuals but that it also sets out direct duties on national administrations to protect these entitlements. That these may have some discretion about how to protect the entitlements is not important.[10]

(ii) The state's duty to protect individual rights and the emergence of horizontal direct effect

If *DeFrenne (No. 2)* signalled a willingness on the part of the Court to allow a wider array of Treaty provisions to be directly effective, it was also important for a second reason. It was stated earlier that if only provisions which were negatively phrased were directly effective, that doctrine only imposed a duty on Member States not to violate individual entitlements set out in the Treaty. Any positively phrased obligation, such as a duty to protect or secure, would be held not to be directly effective. While *DeFrenne (No. 2)* was not the first case to hold a positively phrased obligation to be directly effective,[11] it was the first to address the institutional implications of this for the Member States. The Belgian government argued that the discrimination was not perpetrated by it but by Sabena, a commercial operator. It therefore could not be held liable for this. By contrast, it argued that Sabena could not be liable for obligations under Article 157 TFEU, as the latter explicitly addressed these to the Member States, and only the administration was therefore bound.

Case 43/75 *Defrenne v Sabena (No. 2)* [1976] ECR 455

30. It is … impossible to put forward arguments based on the fact that Article [157 TFEU] only refers expressly to 'Member States'.

31. Indeed, as the Court has already found in other contexts, the fact that certain provisions of the Treaty are formally addressed to the Member States does not prevent rights from being conferred at the same time on any individual who has an interest in the performance of the duties thus laid down.

32. The very wording of Article [157 TFEU] shows that it imposes on States a duty to bring about a specific result to be mandatorily achieved within a fixed period.

33. The effectiveness of this provision cannot be affected by the fact that the duty imposed by the Treaty has not been discharged by certain Member States and that the joint institutions have not reacted sufficiently energetically against this failure to act.

---

[7] See the early Case 148/78 *Ministero Pubblico v Ratti* [1979] ECR 1629. In more recent times, examples include Joined Cases C-397/01–C-403/01 *Pfeiffer and Others v Deutsches Rotes Kreuz* [2004] ECR I-8835; Joined Cases C-152/07–154/07 *Arcor v Bundesrepublik Deutschland* [2008] ECR I-5959.

[8] P. Pescatore, 'The Doctrine of "Direct Effect": An Infant Disease of Community Law' (1983) 8 *ELRev.* 155, 176–7.

[9] Case C-138/07 *Belgische Staat v Cobelfret*, Judgment of 12 February 2009, para. 64.

[10] Case C-226/07 *Flughafen Köln/Bonn*, Judgment of 17 July 2008; Case C-138/07 *Belgische Staat v Cobelfret*, Judgment of 12 February 2009.

[11] Case 2/74 *Reyners v Belgium* [1974] ECR 631.

34. To accept the contrary view would be to risk raising the violation of the right to the status of a principle of interpretation, a position the adoption of which would not be consistent with the task assigned to the Court by Article [19(1) TEU].

35. Finally, in its reference to 'Member States', Article [157 TFEU] is alluding to those States in the exercise of all those of their functions which may usefully contribute to the implementation of the principle of equal pay.

36. Thus, contrary to the statements made in the course of the proceedings this provision is far from merely referring the matter to the powers of the national legislative authorities.

37. Therefore, the reference to 'Member States' in Article [157 TFEU] cannot be interpreted as excluding the intervention of the courts in direct application of the Treaty.

38. Furthermore it is not possible to sustain any objection that the application by national courts of the principle of equal pay would amount to modifying independent agreements concluded privately or in the sphere of industrial relations such as individual contracts and collective labour agreements.

39. In fact, since Article [157 TFEU] is mandatory in nature, the prohibition on discrimination between men and women applies not only to the action of public authorities, but also extends to all agreements which are intended to regulate paid labour collectively, as well as to contracts between individuals.

Direct effect is not therefore just about protecting individuals from states violating their rights. The doctrine also imposes duties upon the state to secure the protection of these rights. In this regard, *Defrenne (No. 2)* makes two particularly important findings. First, it reminds national courts that they are part of the state and that this duty to protect falls particularly strongly on them. Secondly, it notes from this that courts may find that Treaty provisions can be invoked against other private parties, who therefore have a duty to respect EU law. It therefore established two forms of direct effect, which have been referred to in the academic literature in the following manner:

(a) vertical direct effect: this is where a party invokes a provision of EU law in a national court against a Member State;

(b) horizontal direct effect: this is where a party invokes a provision of EU law in a national court against a private party. A corollary of this right is that private parties have responsibilities in EU law for which they can be held liable in national courts if they fail to discharge them.

From a perspective of developing individual rights, this judgment can be viewed very positively. Discrimination on grounds of gender is both egregious and a long-standing problem in the workplace. The grant to the victims of this new legal instrument to protect themselves can only be viewed positively. Moreover, in a market economy, where most employment is in the private sector, it clearly makes sense for it to be available against private employers.

At the beginning of this chapter, we also noted that the story of direct effect was one of an ongoing reorganisation of legal power. Here, the judgment in *Defrenne (No. 2)* was far more disorientating. The grant of horizontal direct effect opens the possibility for Treaty provisions to be invoked not only in the relatively limited setting of litigation of illegal behaviour by the state, but also in the much more unconfined world of private litigation. EU law would not only be deployed to govern a much wider array of disputes, but it would also provide more opportunities to challenge national law, as individuals would no longer need to seek judicial review. They could simply say that it did not govern the legal dispute between them and another private party. This was all too much for the British and Irish governments. They argued, shamefully, that to allow the principle of equal pay for men and women for work of equal value to be invoked in national courts would lead to an unmanageable disruption of economic life. The Irish government argued that the costs of compliance would exceed Irish receipts from the European Regional Development Fund for the period 1975–77 and the British government argued that it would add 3.5 per cent to labour costs – a considerable admission, it might be thought, on the part of those two governments as to the degree of exploitation of women in their respective jurisdictions!

Case 43/75 *Defrenne v Sabena (No. 2)* [1976] ECR 455

69. The Governments of Ireland and the United Kingdom have drawn the Court's attention to the possible economic consequences of attributing direct effect to the provisions of Article [157 TFEU], on the ground that such a decision might, in many branches of economic life, result in the introduction of claims dating back to the time at which such effect came into existence.

70. In view of the large number of people concerned such claims, which undertakings could not have foreseen, might seriously affect the financial situation of such undertakings and even drive some of them to bankruptcy.

71. Although the practical consequences of any judicial decision must be carefully taken into account, it would be impossible to go so far as to diminish the objectivity of the law and compromise its future application on the ground of the possible repercussions which might result, as regards the past, from such a judicial decision.

72. However, in the light of the conduct of several of the Member States ... it is appropriate to take exceptionally into account the fact that, over a prolonged period, the parties concerned have been led to continue with practices which were contrary to Article [157 TFEU], although not yet prohibited under their national law ...

74. In these circumstances, it is appropriate to determine that, as the general level at which pay would have been fixed cannot be known, important considerations of legal certainty affecting all the interests involved, both public and private, make it impossible in principle to reopen the question as regards the past.

75. Therefore, the direct effect of Article [157 TFEU] cannot be relied on in order to support claims concerning pay periods prior to the date of this judgment, except as regards those workers who have already brought legal proceedings or made an equivalent claim.

The Court gave here what is known as a prospective ruling. To manage the consequences of departing so far from Member State expectations, it said, in effect, that what is now Article 157 TFEU was subject to two interpretations. For discrimination occurring prior to the date of the judgment, the provision was interpreted as not being directly effective. The opposite was true for discrimination which occurs after the date of the judgment. The symbolism of this is considerable, however. As Rasmussen has observed, these two interpretations destroy the illusion that the Court is engaging in a neutral exercise of merely giving life to the text. It is impossible 'to maintain this myth while ruling that Article [157] was deprived of direct effects until the day of pronouncement of the Court's decision; only to produce such effects from that day onwards'.[12]

---

[12] H. Rasmussen, *On Law and Policy in the European Court of Justice* (Dordrecht, Martinus Nijhoff, 1986) 441.

4 DIRECT EFFECT AND THE DEVELOPMENT OF EU REMEDIES AND PROCEDURES

Although direct effect refers only to the right to invoke a provision in a national court, this has little substance if no remedies follow. After all, individuals go to courts for redress; thus, to be meaningful, it would seem that remedies should follow from the successful invocation of direct effect. This begs the question whether direct effect also requires national courts to put in place particular procedures and remedies. This was first broached in *Rewe*. The German authorities had unlawfully levied charges for health inspections on fruit and vegetables in this instance. Rewe, a trader, claimed a refund of these before the German Administrative Court. The German authorities argued that the limitation period for claiming a refund had passed and Rewe would not have been able to claim a refund if the measure had breached an exclusively domestic law. Rewe saw this as a denial of its rights.

Case 33/76 *Rewe-Zentralfinanz and Others* v *Landwirtschaftskammer für das Saarland* [1976] ECR 1989

5. The prohibition(s) laid down ... have a direct effect and confer on citizens rights which the national courts are required to protect.

Applying the principle of cooperation laid down in Article [4(3) TEU], it is the national courts which are entrusted with ensuring the legal protection which citizens derive from the direct effect of the provisions of Community law.

Accordingly, in the absence of Community rules on this subject, it is for the domestic legal system of each Member State to designate the courts having jurisdiction and to determine the procedural conditions governing actions at law intended to ensure the protection of the rights which citizens have from the direct effect of Community law, it being understood that such conditions cannot be less favourable than those relating to similar actions of a domestic nature.

Where necessary ... the Treaty enable[s] appropriate measures to be taken to remedy differences between the provisions laid down by law, regulation or administrative action in Member States if they are likely to distort or harm the functioning of the common market.

In the absence of such measures of harmonization the right conferred by Community law must be exercised before the national courts in accordance with the conditions laid down by national rules.

The position would be different only if the conditions and time-limits made it impossible in practice to exercise the rights which the national courts are obliged to protect. This is not the case where reasonable periods of limitation of actions are fixed. The laying down of such time-limits with regard to actions of a fiscal nature is an application of the fundamental principle of legal certainty protecting both the tax-payer and the administration concerned.

The test set out in *Rewe* is beset by contradiction. On the one hand, it argues for national procedural autonomy by saying that the question of remedies is for the national legal system to decide, subject to those for breach of directly effective provisions being no less favourable than those relating to similar domestic claims.[13] On the other hand, the requirement that national

---

[13] This constraint is known as the equivalence principle. The question of deciding whether a domestic measure is comparable to an EU measure is one for the national court but the Court of Justice has stated that they must look to the purpose and essential characteristics of the legislation to see if they are similar. Case C-261/95 *Palmisani* v *INPS* [1997] ECR I-4025; Case C-326/96 *Levez* v *Jennings* [1998] ECR I-7835. M. Dougan, *National Remedies Before the Court of Justice* (Oxford and Portland, Hart, 2004) 25–6.

procedures and remedies should not make it practically impossible to exercise EU rights pushes for the development of a Union system of remedies. This is particularly the case if we think of direct effect as enabling individuals to require courts to protect their entitlements. This is nothing if it is not a remedy! If we say that these obligations are a matter for national courts themselves to decide, then the right becomes hollow.

This tension has led to considerable complexity in the case law. Yet it is possible to discern two trends. The first trend concerns those instances where the Court of Justice will require the national court to provide, as a matter of course, a particular remedy. In such circumstances, the failure to provide this remedy is seen as a failure to secure the right provided by the directly effective provision.

The second trend concerns those instances where EU law leaves it almost entirely for national law to determine the remedies and procedures for the protection of directly effective provisions, subject to some loose EU constraints. This is less prescriptive, but it also entails that the level of protection offered and, indeed, the substance of these rights, will vary from Member State to Member State.

(i) Pan-European remedies in national courts

There are four circumstances where EU law requires particular remedies to be provided in national courts. The first of these is the principle of state liability which allows for individuals, under certain circumstances, to sue the state for damages where they have suffered loss as a result of the state's illegal behaviour. This is dealt with later in the chapter,[14] and is a self-standing procedure that is conceptually distinct from direct effect. There are, however, three circumstances where directly effective rights lead to particular remedies. These are repayment of charges or taxes levied for breach of EU law; damages and repayment for breaches of EU competition law; and the granting of interim relief where a national court wishes to make a preliminary reference to the Court of Justice.[15] Each is constrained by a particular justification. The first two types of remedy are restitutionary in nature. At their heart lies the idea that an individual or state should not be enriched as a result of its behaviour, and that to allow this would be a denial of other parties' directly effective rights. The third remedy, as we shall see, is concerned to secure the effective operation of a procedure before the Court of Justice rather than a national court, namely the preliminary reference procedure.

Repayment of charges or taxes levied contrary to EU law was considered in *San Giorgio*, the facts in which were remarkably similar to *Rewe*.[16] The Italian state had levied charges for health inspections contrary to EU law. Under Italian law, however, there was no repayment of any illegal tax where the Italian state believed that the sums involved had been passed onto other persons, typically through higher pricing. San Giorgio challenged this. The structure of the Court's reasoning in this case was different from that in *Rewe*. In *San Giorgio*, the Court held that entitlement to the repayment of charges levied contrary to EU law was 'a consequence of, and an adjunct to, the rights' conferred by EU law. Whilst the Court created some

---

[14] See pp. 301–12.

[15] There is also, of course, the remedy of state liability described above where individuals can sue states in national courts for loss suffered as a result of a state's failure to comply with EU law.

[16] Case 199/82 *Amministrazione delle Finanze dello Stato* v *San Giorgio* [1983] ECR 3595.

leeway for the national system by providing that it was for it to determine when taxes have been passed on and therefore could not be recovered, the balance drawn was very different from *Rewe*. A concrete remedy, namely the right to restitution of illegally levied taxes, was put in place.

In subsequent years, the Court has extended this remedy.[17] It applies not just to taxes levied by the state, but to taxes and charges levied by public bodies,[18] illegal requirements to pay tax in advance[19] and the levying of guarantees in breach of EU law.[20] The conditions for non-repayment have also become highly circumscribed. If charges or taxes have only partially been passed on to other persons, the Court has ruled that the national authority can only refuse to pay that part which had been passed on by the person claiming repayment.[21] To determine the amount, the Court has held that national courts must engage in economic analysis, as the degree of enrichment will be affected not just by the increase in price but also by possible decline in volume of sales as a result of that increase.[22] Finally, the Court has touched on the level of compensation that may be recovered. It has ruled that complainants are entitled not only to repayment of the tax, but also compensation for any losses that accrued as a result of not having this revenue available to them.[23]

The second type of remedy is in the field of competition. The Court has ruled that contracts which breach Article 101 TFEU, the provision prohibiting cartels and anti-competitive conduct by two or more parties, are not only void, but allow individuals to claim damages where they can show that there is a direct causal link between the harm suffered and the illegal conduct or contract.[24] Similar reasoning operates in the field of state aids. The Court has ruled that if a national court finds that an unlawful aid has been paid to an undertaking by a national authority, it must order repayment of that aid, as it is under a duty to provide protection to individuals against illegal state aids.[25] We can draw parallels with the reasoning in these cases and the reasoning deployed in cases concerning illegally levied taxes because, in addition to wishing to secure the full effect of the provisions, the Court does not wish to see the unjust enrichment of those who have benefited from illegal conduct.[26] It is thus the recipient of the illegal aid whom the national authorities must recover the money from and the Court is silent about which third party may recover compensation for loss suffered from anti-competitive practices, focusing instead on the duty of the party engaging in the illegal practice to make good.

---

[17] On this remedy see P. Wattel, 'National Procedural Autonomy and the Effectiveness of EC Law: Challenge the Charge, File For Restitution, Sue For Damages?' (2008) 35(2) *LIEI* 109.

[18] Case C-242/95 *GT-Link* v *DSB* [1997] ECR I-4449.

[19] Joined Cases C-397/98 and C-410/98 *Metallgesellschaft* v *IRC* [2001] ECR I-1727; Case C-446/04 *Test Claimants in the FII Group Litigation* v *Commissioners of Inland Revenue* [2006] ECR I-11753, para. 203.

[20] Case C-470/04 *N* v *Inspecteur van de Belastingdienst Oostkantoor Almelo* [2006] ECR I-7409.

[21] Joined Cases C-192/95–C-218/95 *Comateb and Others* [1997] ECR I-165, paras. 27 and 28.

[22] Case C-147/01 *Weber's Wine World and Others* [2003] ECR I-11365; Case C-309/06 *Marks & Spencer* v *CCE* [2008] ECR I-2283.

[23] Joined Cases C-397/98 and C-410/98 *Metallgesellschaft* v *IRC* [2001] ECR I-1727; Case C-446/04 *Test Claimants in the FII Group Litigation* v *Commissioners of Inland Revenue* [2006] ECR I-11753.

[24] Case C-453/99 *Courage Ltd* v *Crehan* [2001] ECR I-6297; Joined Cases C-295/04–C-298/04 *Vincenzo Manfredi and Others* v *Lloyd Adriatico Assicurazioni SpA and Others* [2006] ECR I-6619. For discussion see S. Drake, 'Scope of *Courage* and the Principle of "Individual Liability" for Damages: Further Development of the Principle of Effective Judicial Protection by the Court of Justice' (2006) 31 *ELRev.* 841.

[25] Case C-39/94 *SFEI* [1996] ECR I-3547; Case C-71/04 *Xunta de Galicia* [2005] ECR I-7419.

[26] Case C-453/99 *Courage Ltd* v *Crehan* [2001] ECR I-6297 (on what was then Article 81 EC); Case C-354/90 *FNCE* [1991] ECR I-5505.

The third remedy is that of interim relief sought before national courts pending a reference to the Court of Justice. In *Factortame*, a challenge was made by a number of Spanish fishermen to the United Kingdom's Merchant Shipping Act 1988. This Act made it very difficult for non-British boats to fish in British waters by imposing, most notably, a series of residence requirements as a precondition. It was argued that this violated what is now Article 49 TFEU, the provision on freedom of establishment. The national court referred the matter to the Court of Justice. In the meantime, the House of Lords found that the applicants would suffer irreparable damage if interim relief was not granted. However, the House of Lords ruled that, notwithstanding this finding, English courts had no jurisdiction to suspend the Act as the remedy was at that time barred by statute. It referred the question of whether this rule of national law should be set aside in circumstances where its application would deprive a party of the enjoyment of rights derived from EU law. The Court of Justice had little difficulty in answering in the affirmative.

Case C–213/89 *R v Secretary of State for Transport, ex parte Factortame Ltd* [1990] ECR I-2433

19. In accordance with the case law of the Court, it is for the national courts, in application of the principle of cooperation laid down in Article [4(3) TFEU], to ensure the legal protection which persons derive from the direct effect of provisions of Community law …

20. The Court has also held that any provision of a national legal system and any legislative, administrative or judicial practice which might impair the effectiveness of Community law by withholding from the national court having jurisdiction to apply such law the power to do everything necessary at the moment of its application to set aside national legislative provisions which might prevent, even temporarily, Community rules from having full force and effect are incompatible with those requirements, which are the very essence of Community law …

21. It must be added that the full effectiveness of Community law would be just as much impaired if a rule of national law could prevent a court seised of a dispute governed by Community law from granting interim relief in order to ensure the full effectiveness of the judgment to be given on the existence of the rights claimed under Community law. It follows that a court which in those circumstances would grant interim relief, if it were not for a rule of national law, is obliged to set aside that rule.

22. That interpretation is reinforced by the system established by Article [267 TFEU] whose effectiveness would be impaired if a national court, having stayed proceedings pending the reply by the Court of Justice to the question referred to it for a preliminary ruling, were not able to grant interim relief until it delivered its judgment following the reply given by the Court of Justice.

23. Consequently, the reply to the question raised should be that Community law must be interpreted as meaning that a national court which, in a case before it concerning Community law, considers that the sole obstacle which precludes it from granting interim relief is a rule of national law must set aside that rule.

There are two features of note to *Factortame*.

The first is that the particular remedy sought is drawn (in paragraph 21) from a new line of reasoning: that of securing the full effectiveness of EU law. It is the strongest assertion made for pan-European remedies, as it suggests that wherever there is an EU right there should be a corresponding EU remedy. After *Factortame*, it looked for a while as if the Court might be moving to develop a fully fledged system of EU remedies[27] and a number of authors argued for this on the basis of the effectiveness of EU law alone, independent of any other doctrine, requiring the development of a system of substitute remedies applicable in national courts.[28]

The second issue is a corollary of this and questions, if this is so, what principles should govern the type of remedy provided. This goes above all to the law of remedies and not the uniformity of EU law. Its difficulties were illustrated in *Factortame*. The judgment is vague about when a national law should be suspended, suggesting that it should happen whenever the effectiveness of EU law is being undermined. By contrast, the Court has operated a different set of principles when relief is sought against a national law implementing an EU measure.[29] In such circumstances, the challenge is seen as being, in reality, against the EU measure. Relief will only be granted if there is serious and irreparable damage to the applicant, and this must be weighed against other considerations such as the damage to the Union legal order and its financial interests. From the perspective of two applicants, whose interests have been damaged equally, this difference seems perverse.[30] It also illustrates the challenges for EU law in developing a system of remedies that is both uniform and sensitive to different circumstances.

There has, thus, been a firm move away from developing pan-European remedies in recent years. With the exception of the limited instances described above, EU law accepts that the development of remedies to secure direct effect is overwhelmingly a role for the national legal system. The Union will intervene only if there has been a severe failure of protection by the domestic system.

This was most strongly set out in *Unibet*. Unibet, a British gambling company, sought to advertise its Internet gambling services in the Swedish media. These gambling activities contravened Swedish law. The Swedish authorities therefore obtained injunctions and initiated criminal proceedings against those who had provided advertising space to Unibet. No action was brought against Unibet itself. However, Unibet brought an action for a declaration that the Swedish law violated what is now Article 56 TFEU, which provides for the right to provide services in another Member State. In Swedish law, no possibility existed for an individual to bring a self-standing action for a declaration that a Swedish statute was illegal in the absence of a specific legal relationship. The Swedish court asked whether effective protection of an individual's rights in EU law required the creation of a new independent remedy permitting an action for a declaration that a national law is illegal.

[27] D. Curtin and K. Mortelmans, 'Application and Enforcement of Community Law by the Member States: Actors in Search of a Third Generation Script' in D. Curtin and T. Heukels (eds.), *Institutional Dynamics of European Integration* (The Hague, Martinus Nijhoff, 1994).

[28] See paras. 21–2. See also Case C-208/90 *Emmott v Minister for Social Welfare* [1991] ECR I-4269. For an excellent discussion of the debates see T. Tridimas, 'Black, White and Shades of Grey: Horizontality of Directives Revisited' (2002) 21 *YBEL* 327; K. Lenaerts and T. Corthaut, 'Of Birds and Hedges: The Role of Primacy in Invoking Norms of EU Law' (2006) 31 *ELRev.* 287; M. Dougan, 'When Worlds Collide: Competing Visions of the Relationship Between Direct Effect and Supremacy' (2007) 44 *CMLRev.* 931.

[29] Joined Cases C-143/88 and C-92/89 *Zuckerfabrik Süderdithmarschen and Zuckerfabrik Soest* [1991] ECR I-415; Case C-465/93 *Atlanta Fruchthandelsgesellschaft and Others (No. 1)* [1995] ECR I-3761; Case C-68/95 *T. Port* [1996] ECR I-6065; Joined Cases C-453/03, C-11/04, C-12/04 and C-194/04 *Martini v Ministero delle Politiche Agricole e Forestali* [2005] ECR I-10423.

[30] This has already been considered in some detail at pp. 172–3.

Case C–432/05 *Unibet* v *Justitiekanslern* [2007] ECR I–2271

37. It is to be noted at the outset that, according to settled case law, the principle of effective judicial protection is a general principle of Community law stemming from the constitutional traditions common to the Member States, which has been enshrined in Articles 6 and 13 of the European Convention for the Protection of Human Rights and Fundamental Freedoms ... and which has also been reaffirmed by Article 47 of the Charter of Fundamental Rights of the European Union ...

38. Under the principle of cooperation laid down in Article [4(3) TEU], it is for the Member States to ensure judicial protection of an individual's rights under Community law ...

39. It is also to be noted that, in the absence of Community rules governing the matter, it is for the domestic legal system of each Member State to designate the courts and tribunals having jurisdiction and to lay down the detailed procedural rules governing actions for safeguarding rights which individuals derive from Community law ...

40. Although the EC Treaty has made it possible in a number of instances for private persons to bring a direct action, where appropriate, before the Community Court, it was not intended to create new remedies in the national courts to ensure the observance of Community law other than those already laid down by national law ...

41. It would be otherwise only if it were apparent from the overall scheme of the national legal system in question that no legal remedy existed which made it possible to ensure, even indirectly, respect for an individual's rights under Community law ...

42. Thus, while it is, in principle, for national law to determine an individual's standing and legal interest in bringing proceedings, Community law nevertheless requires that the national legislation does not undermine the right to effective judicial protection ...

43. In that regard, the detailed procedural rules governing actions for safeguarding an individual's rights under Community law must be no less favourable than those governing similar domestic actions (principle of equivalence) and must not render practically impossible or excessively difficult the exercise of rights conferred by Community law (principle of effectiveness) ...

44. Moreover, it is for the national courts to interpret the procedural rules governing actions brought before them, such as the requirement for there to be a specific legal relationship between the applicant and the State, in such a way as to enable those rules, wherever possible, to be implemented in such a manner as to contribute to the attainment of the objective ... of ensuring effective judicial protection of an individual's rights under Community law ...

47. In that regard, it is to be noted ... that the principle of effective judicial protection does not require it to be possible, as such, to bring a free-standing action which seeks primarily to dispute the compatibility of national provisions with Community law, provided that the principles of equivalence and effectiveness are observed in the domestic system of judicial remedies.

48. Firstly, it is apparent from the order for reference that Swedish law does not provide for such a free-standing action, regardless of whether the higher-ranking legal rule to be complied with is a national rule or a Community rule ...

53. It is necessary ... to establish whether the effect of the indirect legal remedies provided for by Swedish law for disputing the compatibility of a national provision with Community law is to render practically impossible or excessively difficult the exercise of rights conferred by Community law.

54. In that regard, each case which raises the question whether a national procedural provision renders the application of Community law impossible or excessively difficult must be analysed by reference to the role of that provision in the procedure, its progress and its special features, viewed as a whole, before the various national instances ...

55. It is apparent from the order for reference that Swedish law does not prevent a person, such as Unibet, from disputing the compatibility of national legislation, such as the Law on Lotteries, with Community law but that, on the contrary, there exist various indirect legal remedies for that purpose.

56. Thus, firstly, the Högsta domstolen states that Unibet may obtain an examination of whether the Law on Lotteries is compatible with Community law in the context of a claim for damages before the ordinary courts.

57. It is also clear from the order for reference that Unibet brought such a claim and that the Högsta domstolen found it to be admissible.

58. Consequently, where an examination of the compatibility of the Law on Lotteries with Community law takes place in the context of the determination of a claim for damages, that action constitutes a remedy which enables Unibet to ensure effective protection of the rights conferred on it by Community law.

59. It is for the Högsta domstolen to ensure that the examination of the compatibility of that law with Community law takes place irrespective of the assessment of the merits of the case with regard to the requirements for damage and a causal link in the claim for damages.

60. Secondly, the Högsta domstolen adds that, if Unibet applied to the Swedish Government for an exception to the prohibition on the promotion of its services in Sweden, any decision rejecting that application could be the subject of judicial review proceedings before the Regeringsrätten, in which Unibet would be able to argue that the provisions of the Law on Lotteries are incompatible with Community law. Where appropriate, the competent court would be required to disapply the provisions of that law that were considered to be in conflict with Community law.

61. It is to be noted that such judicial review proceedings, which would enable Unibet to obtain a judicial decision that those provisions are incompatible with Community law, constitute a legal remedy securing effective judicial protection of its rights under Community law …

62. Moreover, the Högsta domstolen states that if Unibet disregarded the provisions of the Law on Lotteries and administrative action or criminal proceedings were brought against it by the competent national authorities, it would have the opportunity, in proceedings brought before the administrative court or an ordinary court, to dispute the compatibility of those provisions with Community law. Where appropriate, the competent court would be required to disapply the provisions of that law that were considered to be in conflict with Community law.

63. In addition to the remedies referred to at paragraphs 56 and 60 above, it would therefore be possible for Unibet to claim in court proceedings against the administration or in criminal proceedings that measures taken or required to be taken against it were incompatible with Community law on account of the fact that it had not been permitted by the competent national authorities to promote its services in Sweden.

64. In any event, it is clear from paragraphs 56 to 61 above that Unibet must be regarded as having available to it legal remedies which ensure effective judicial protection of its rights under Community law. If, on the contrary, as mentioned at paragraph 62 above, it was forced to be subject to administrative or criminal proceedings and to any penalties that may result as the sole form of legal remedy for disputing the compatibility of the national provision at issue with Community law, that would not be sufficient to secure for it such effective judicial protection.

65. Accordingly, the answer to the first question must be that the principle of effective judicial protection of an individual's rights under Community law must be interpreted as meaning that it does not require the national legal order of a Member State to provide for a free-standing action for an examination of whether national provisions are compatible with Article [56 TFEU], provided that other effective legal remedies, which are no less favourable than those governing similar domestic actions, make it possible for such a question of compatibility to be determined as a preliminary issue, which is a matter for the national court to establish.

The message of the judgment is twofold. First, there will only be Union review if there has been a very strong failure of protection of the applicant or she has not been given the same level of protection as that available in a comparable domestic action. There is a presumption of trust in the national system, which involves a presumption of good faith (the equivalence principle) and a presumption of capacity (the rules that redress not be impossible or excessively difficult to obtain). Secondly, the Court will look to the local legal context to decide whether these requirements have been fulfilled. This focus on local context emphasises the reluctance of the Court to develop an autonomous system of remedies to be applied in domestic courts. For the absence of a particular remedy or procedure may indicate inadequate protection in one national legal context but not in another. In such circumstances, it is difficult to develop general rules that all Member States must provide certain forms of redress.

(ii) Union oversight of local remedies in domestic courts

Notwithstanding that remedies are predominantly for the domestic system to decide, there must still be some standard which indicates when these remedies make the exercise of EU rights 'excessively difficult'. The Court's case law is quite intricate here. It is worth looking at its approach to substantive remedies, domestic procedural rules and limitations periods separately. For its degree of intervention has been different in each of these fields.

On remedies, the Court has said very little except where a Member State limits the level or type of compensation in an *a priori* way. National measures which try to cap levels of compensation at very low levels are thus illegal,[31] as are those which provide for only nominal compensation with no regard to the damage sustained.[32] Similarly, Member States are not allowed to prevent compensation for certain types of damage, notably economic loss.[33]

The Court's case law has been more extensive on procedures. The central thread here in recent times has been that judicial protection involves certain minimum fundamental rights guarantees. In *Unibet*, the Court thus roots its reasoning in the judicial guarantees provided by the European Convention on Human Rights and the EU Charter of Fundamental Rights and Freedoms. First mooted by the Court in the 1980s,[34] this reasoning has come to mean a number of things.

First, there is a requirement of judicial control so that national courts cannot be barred from considering directly effective provisions. A national requirement stating that certain forms of activities clearly falling within a Directive were not subject to judicial control was therefore found to be illegal.[35] The principle of effective judicial control also means that any decision of a professional or administrative body restricting an EU right must be subject to judicial review and, to enable that review to be meaningful, must state the reasons for the decision.[36]

---

[31] Case C-271/91 *Marshall v Southampton and South West Hampshire AHA* [1993] ECR I-4367.

[32] Case 14/83 *Von Colson and Kamann v Land Nordrhein-Westfalen* [1984] ECR 1891.

[33] Joined Cases C-46/93 and 48/93 *Brasserie du Pêcheur v Germany* and *R v Secretary of State for Transport, ex parte Factortame (No. 3)* [1996] ECR I-1029.

[34] For discussion, see A. Arnull, *The European Union and its Court of Justice* (2nd edn, Oxford, Oxford University Press, 2006) ch. 6.

[35] Case 222/84 *Johnston v Chief Constable of the Royal Ulster Constabulary* [1986] ECR 1651.

[36] Case 222/86 *UNECTEF v Heylens* [1987] ECR 4097.

Secondly, national courts must secure the proper conduct of the proceedings.[37] To that end, parties must be given a genuine opportunity to raise pleas based on EU law before them.[38] In addition to this, if parties are entitled to submit to the court observations on a piece of evidence, they must be afforded a real opportunity to comment effectively on it.[39] Parties must also be given sufficient time to prepare their defence and must be protected from abusive use of the litigation process by their adversaries.[40] Alongside this, in *Impact* v *MAFF*, although the Court did not refer to this line of reasoning, it stated that individuals should be able to bring their action before a single court for a single claim, and cannot be required to bring different elements of it before different courts.[41] The reasoning was that the procedural complications and cost thus imposed on parties made it excessively difficult for them to pursue their claims. Yet, this could be related to courts' duties to secure proper conduct of the proceedings.

There is a final category of cases, where the claimant has not pursued a claim within the limitation period set by national law or has not taken action to avert loss. In both instances, the Court of Justice has indicated that the Member State has to take action here provided it is reasonable. Reasonable limitation periods may be set[42] and Member States may impose requirements on claimants to mitigate the loss or exercise due diligence to avoid the loss.[43] Yet, as both limitation periods and due diligence preconditions can be used to bar access to courts, the Court has been willing to scrutinise the 'reasonableness' of national measures here in quite some depth.

With regard to limitation periods, the Court will look therefore at whether individuals did not bring a claim within the required time because of unconscionable behaviour by the defendant,[44] or the state,[45] which induced them to defer their action. In the field of consumer law, this has been taken a step further and also applied to failures to act, so that it is unreasonable for national limitation periods to apply if, in breach of EU legislation, vendors fail to tell consumers of their right to terminate contracts.[46] Dougan has thus talked of an estoppel principle where defendants guilty of some form of unconscionable conduct cannot benefit from national limitation periods. Yet, as he has noted, the doctrine is extremely vague as to the level of unconscionability required and the issue of when it is reasonable for the claimant to rely on it.[47] The Court of Justice will also look at the date from when the limitation period runs to ascertain that it does not start too early. It has thus held that limitation periods which begin from the day on which an anti-competitive practice is adopted might be unreasonable.[48] Similarly, it

---

[37] Case C-312/93 *Peterbroeck* v *Belgium* [1995] ECR I-4599.

[38] Joined Cases C-222/05–C-225/05 *Van der Weerd* v *Minister van Landbouw, Natuur en Voedselkwaliteit* [2007] ECR I-4233.

[39] Case C-276/01 *Steffenson* [2003] ECR I-3735.

[40] Case C-443/03 *Leffler* v *Berlin Chemie* [2005] ECR I-9611.

[41] Case C-268/06 *Impact* v *MAFF* [2008] ECR I-2483.

[42] Case C-261/95 *Palmisani* v *INPS* [1997] ECR I-4025.

[43] Joined Cases C-46/93 and C-48/93 *Brasserie du Pêcheur* v *Germany* [1996] ECR I-1029; Joined Cases C-95/07 and C-96/07 *Ecotrade* v *Agenzia delle Entrate – Ufficio di Genova*, Judgment of 21 June 2008.

[44] In *Levez*, an employer led a female employee to believe the disparity in pay between her and a male counterpart was less than it was, leading her to abstain from action until she discovered the full disparity: Case C-326/96 *Levez* v *Jennings* [1998] ECR I-7835.

[45] Case C-327/00 *Santex* v *Unità Socio Sanitaria Locale n. 42 di Pavia* [2003] ECR I-1877; Case C-241/06 *Lämmerzahl* [2007] ECR I-8415.

[46] Case C-481/99 *Heininger* [2001] ECR I-9945.

[47] Dougan, above n. 13, 280–2.

[48] Joined Cases C-295/04–C-298/04 *Vincenzo Manfredi and Others* v *Lloyd Adriatico Assicurazioni SpA and Others* [2006] ECR I-6619. Much will depend on when the harm and identity was identifiable. In *Dansk Slagterier*, the Court indicated that what will be crucial is when the injured party became aware of the loss: Case C-445/06 *Danske Slagterier* v *Germany*, Judgment of 24 March 2009.

has held that in the case of people employed on a series of short-term contracts, the limitation period begins from the end of the relationship, not the end of each of the contracts.[49]

The Court of Justice's central concern about national conditions requiring an applicant to exercise due diligence to avert loss revolves around national stipulations that an individual cannot claim for loss which would not have arisen if she had sued earlier. Initially, the Court suggested that a national requirement of due diligence could legitimately demand that parties show that they had used all legal remedies available to them before claiming for loss.[50] However, in *Metallgesellschaft*, the Court considered a British requirement that a firm could not claim for interest suffered from a tax advantage illegally denied to it on the grounds that it should have claimed and then sued. It considered that the requirement of prior litigation made the exercise of the applicant's rights excessively difficult and was therefore illegal. The Court reconciled these approaches in *Danske Slagterier*, a case concerning a German ban on uncastrated male pigs from Denmark which had lasted six years before it was challenged.[51] The Court considered that national courts could impose a duty of due diligence and this could include a requirement for the applicant to show that she had availed herself in time of all the legal remedies available. However, this requirement would not be available if use of these remedies would give rise to excessive difficulties or could not reasonably be required.

5 DIRECT EFFECT AND SECONDARY LEGISLATION

The vast bulk of EU law is contained not in the Treaties, but in secondary legislation.[52] It was not surprising, therefore, that early on after the end of the transitional period, the question arose as to whether the different types of secondary legislation were capable of direct effect.

The most straightforward case was that of Regulations. Deemed to have general application, be binding and directly applicable in all Member States, Regulations are the closest thing the Union has to domestic statutes.[53] They were therefore held to be capable of direct effect in the same way as Treaty provisions in *Leonesio*.[54]

International agreements made by the Union with non-EU states have also been held to be capable of direct effect. This will not be the case with all international agreements, however. The test is a two-tier one.[55] First, the wording, nature and purpose of the agreement is compared with some international agreements considered incapable of generating direct effect simply by virtue of their overall framework being too flexible and open-ended. Secondly, the specific provision is considered in the light of this. Only if it is sufficiently precise and unconditional will it be directly effective.

---

[49] Case C-78/98 *Preston* v *Wolverhampton Health Care Trust* [2000] ECR I-3201.

[50] Joined Cases C-46/93 and C-48/93 *Brasserie du Pêcheur* v *Germany* [1996] ECR I-1029.

[51] Case C-445/06 *Danske Slagterier* v *Germany*, Judgment of 24 March 2009.

[52] The different types of secondary legislation have been considered in Chapter 3. See pp. 98–100.

[53] Their replacements were therefore known as European laws in the failed Constitutional Treaty, Article I-33(1) CT. See also J. Winter, 'Direct Effect and Direct Applicability: Two Distinct and Different Concepts in Community Law' (1972) 9 *CMLRev*. 425.

[54] Case 93/71 *Leonesio* v *Italian Ministry of Agriculture* [1972] ECR 293. See also Case 39/72 *Commission* v *Italy (premiums for slaughtering cows)* [1973] ECR 101.

[55] The standard formulation is Case 104/81 *Hauptzollamt Mainz* v *Kupferberg* [1982] ECR 3641; Case 12/86 *Demirel* v *Stadt Schwäbisch Gmünd* [1987] ECR 2719. This test leads, in practice, to international agreements being given a wide variety of legal effects within EU law. P. Eeckhout, *External Relations of the European Union: Legal Constitutional Foundations* (Oxford, Oxford University Press, 2004) ch. 9.

(i) Establishment of the direct effect of Directives and national resistance

The position of Directives is more complicated. Directives are binding upon Member States as to the result to be achieved but leave discretion to the national authorities over how to realise this. This could lead to a number of objections being made against Directives being capable of direct effect:

- The discretion given to Member States to implement Directives should result in individuals being able to derive rights only from the acts of national authorities themselves, and not from the Directives themselves.
- To grant direct effect to Directives would blur the distinction between Directives and Regulations, a distinction clearly spelt out in Article 288 TFEU, as both would have similar legal effect.
- In numerous fields, the Union enjoys a competence to adopt Directives but not Regulations, so that according to Directives full direct effect would amount to a blurring of the distinction between the two legal forms, allowing the Union in effect to legislate through the backdoor in areas that the Treaty had not permitted through the front.[56]

Notwithstanding these arguments, the Court of Justice ruled in *Van Duyn* that Directives could generate direct effect.[57] Van Duyn was refused leave to enter the United Kingdom in order to take up an offer of a secretarial post at the Church of Scientology, as the UK government had imposed a ban on foreign scientologists entering the United Kingdom. She challenged the ban on the grounds, inter alia, that it breached Directive 64/221/EEC, which required that any ban be based upon the personal conduct of the individual. The Court considered that her association with the Church of Scientology met the requirements of the Directive. It considered, first, whether the Directive was capable of direct effect.

> **Case 41/74 Van Duyn v Home Office [1974] ECR 1337**
>
> 12. ... It would be incompatible with the binding effect attributed to a Directive by Article [288 TFEU] to exclude, in principle, the possibility that the obligation which it imposes may be invoked by those concerned. In particular, where the Community authorities have, by Directive, imposed on Member States the obligation to pursue a particular course of conduct, the useful effect of such an act would be weakened if individuals were prevented from relying on it before their national courts and if the latter were prevented from taking it into consideration as an element of Community law. Article [267 TFEU], which empowers national courts to refer to the Court questions concerning the validity and interpretation of all acts of the Community institutions, without distinction, implies furthermore that these acts may be invoked by individuals in the national courts. It is necessary to examine, in every case, whether the nature, general scheme and wording of the provisions in question are capable of having direct effects on the relations between Member States and individuals.

---

[56] On this debate see S. Prechal, *Directives in European Community Law: A Study of Directives and their Enforcement in National Courts* (2nd edn, Oxford, Oxford University Press, 2005) 216–20.

[57] Decisions have also been held, on similar grounds, to be capable of bearing direct effect: see Case 9/70 *Grad v Finanzamt Traustein* [1970] ECR 838.

This reasoning is remarkably weak. It starts from an *a contrario* position of whether there is any good reason why Directives should not have direct effect. The arguments that their binding nature and their effectiveness require that they be invoked in national courts are simply *non sequiturs*. For, put simply, neither of these qualities prescribes the types of effects a Directive should have in a domestic legal system. Indeed, no less a figure than Federico Mancini, a former judge at the Court, has admitted that 'this judgment goes beyond the letter of Article [288 TFEU]', the provision that sets out the central characteristics of Regulations and Directives.[58] More significantly, the ruling provoked a strong counter-reaction from both French and German courts. The view of the French Conseil d'Etat, the highest court of administrative law in France, can be seen in its judgment in the *Cohn-Bendit* case.[59] Cohn-Bendit was a German national who had been a leader of student disturbances in 1968. He was offered a job as a broadcaster in France. The French Minister of the Interior sought to deport him. Cohn-Bendit invoked Directive 64/221/EEC stating that it required that any decision be both formally reasoned and that the grounds for the decision be made known to the immigrant. As this had not happened, the decision was illegal, he argued.

Minister of the Interior v Cohn–Bendit [1980] 1 CMLR 543

... it appears clearly from the provisions of Article [288 TFEU] that if Directives bind Member States 'with regard to the result to be achieved' and if, in order to achieve the results which they define, the national authorities of Member States are under an obligation to adapt their legislative and regulatory provisions to the directives which are addressed to them, these authorities remain the only competent authorities to determine the form to give to the implementation of these directives and to determine themselves, under the control of the national judicial authorities, their own method for producing their effect in internal national law ...

... Directives cannot be invoked by persons within the jurisdiction of those Member States in order to support a legal action undertaken against any administrative action with regard to an individual ...

... It follows from the foregoing that M. Cohn-Bendit cannot hope to succeed in his argument ... to annul the decision of the Minister of the Interior ...

The Court of Justice tried to bolster its position by resorting to a new justification in *Ratti*:[60] the estoppel argument. This states that, as Directives impose a duty upon Member States to adopt the appropriate implementing measures by a certain date, it would be wrong for Member States to be able to rely upon and gain advantage through their failure to carry out this obligation. They are thus 'estopped' or prevented from denying the direct effect of Directives once the time limit for their implementation into national law has expired. Thus, in *Ratti*, a trader was prosecuted for not labelling his solvents in accordance with Italian law. He sought to rely upon two Directives. While the transitional period for one of these had expired, it had not for the other. The Court held that he could rely only upon the first Directive. The Member State was estopped by its failure to take the necessary implementing measures from denying this

---

[58] G. Mancini and D. Keeling, 'Language, Culture and Politics in the Life of the European Court of Justice' (1995) 1 *CJEL* 397, 401.

[59] Similar reasoning by the German Bundesfinanzhof can be found in *Re Value Added Tax Directives* [1982] 1 CMLR 527.

[60] Case 148/78 *Ministero Pubblico v Ratti* [1979] ECR 1629. See also Case 8/81 *Becker v Finanzamt Münster-Innenstadt* [1982] ECR 53.

Directive's direct effect. The other Directive was not directly effective, however, as the Member State was still within its period of grace. Directives will be directly effective, therefore, only from the end of the transposition period and, even then, will be capable of direct effect only if the Member State has failed to implement them or has not implemented them correctly. Where Directives are correctly implemented, individual rights flow from the national implementing provisions and not from the Directives themselves.

(ii) Vertical direct effect of Directives

The estoppel argument has one important implication. As the direct effect of Directives is predicated on the 'fault' of the Member State, parties may invoke Directives against the state. But it does not follow from the estoppel argument that parties may invoke Directives in national legal proceedings against other private parties. In other words, the estoppel argument may be used to justify the vertical direct effect of Directives, but not their horizontal direct effect. This limitation was set out in *Marshall*. Marshall, a dietician employed by a British health authority, was dismissed at the age of 62 on the ground that she had passed the pensionable age, which was, at that time, 60 years for women. A man would not have been dismissed at that age, but Marshall had no redress under the Sex Discrimination Act 1975 because of a blanket exclusion in that Act relating to terms and conditions relating to death and retirement. She claimed that there had been a breach of article 5 of the Equal Treatment Directive 76/207/EEC, which provides for equal treatment for men and women concerning the terms and conditions of dismissal.

Case 152/84 *Marshall* v *Southampton and SW Hampshire Area Health Authority* [1986] ECR 723

48. With regard to the argument that a Directive may not be relied upon against an individual, it must be emphasised that according to Article [288 TFEU], the binding nature of a Directive, which constitutes the basis for the possibility of relying on the Directive before a national court, exists only in relation to 'each Member State to which it is addressed'. It follows that a Directive may not of itself impose obligations on an individual and that a provision of a Directive may not be relied upon as such against such a person.

49. In that respect it must be pointed out that where a person involved in legal proceedings is able to rely on a Directive as against the State he may do so regardless of the capacity in which the latter is acting, whether employer or public authority. In either case it is necessary to prevent the State from taking advantage of its own failure to comply with Community law …

51. The argument submitted by the United Kingdom that the possibility of relying on provisions of the Directive against the respondent *qua* organ of the State would give rise to an arbitrary and unfair distinction between the rights of State employees and those of private employees does not justify any other conclusion. Such a distinction may easily be avoided if the Member State concerned has correctly implemented the Directive in national law.

Marshall created a distinction between Regulations and Directives by holding that only the former were capable of horizontal direct effect. This addressed some of the initial concerns about the direct effect of Directives but created problems of its own. For one thing, it generated uncertainty by begging the question as to which bodies formed part of the state and could consequently be sued. Defining the state can, to be sure, be something of a endless task. The multiple legal structures that form part of the state are frequently a consequence of historical happenstance, on the one hand, and recurring reinvention of the place of public intervention, on the other.[61]

The question was addressed most clearly in *Foster* v *British Gas*, which indicated that the test for when a body would form part of the state was one of EU law not national law. Like Marshall, Foster was forced to retire at 60 years, whereas men could continue working until aged 65. She and four other women invoked the Equal Treatment Directive against her former employer, British Gas. The latter was at the time a nationalised industry. Its board members were appointed by a British minister who could also issue to the board various directions and instruments. In addition, the board was required to submit periodic reports to the Secretary of State.

Case C-188/89 *Foster* v *British Gas* [1990] ECR I-3313

17. The Court further held in ... *Marshall* that where a person is able to rely on a Directive as against the State he may do so regardless of the capacity in which the latter is acting, whether as employer or as public authority. In either case it is necessary to prevent the State from taking advantage of its own failure to comply with Community law.

18. On the basis of those considerations, the Court has held in a series of cases that unconditional and sufficiently precise provisions of a Directive could be relied on against organisations or bodies which were subject to the authority or control of the State or had special powers beyond those which result from the normal rules applicable to relations between individuals.

19. The Court has accordingly held that provisions of a directive could be relied on against tax authorities ..., local or regional authorities ..., constitutionally independent authorities responsible for the maintenance of public order and safety ..., and public authorities providing public health services ...

20. It follows... that a body, whatever its legal form, which has been made responsible, pursuant to a measure adopted by the State, for providing a public service under the control of the State and has for that purpose special powers beyond those which result from the normal rules applicable in relations between individuals, is included ... among the bodies against which the provisions of a Directive capable of having direct effect may be relied upon.

The test of whether a body is part of the state is a dual one. A body may be deemed to be part of the state on functional grounds. In subsequent cases, the Court has made clear that it is sufficient that an entity is carrying out a public service and, for that reason, has special powers. Its legal form and the presence of state control is not determinative. In *Vassallo*, the Court held, therefore, that a Directive could be invoked against an Italian hospital which, although it received public funding, was not run by the Italian state but was an autonomous establishment with its own directors. In that instance, it was crucial for the Court of Justice that the hospital, notwithstanding this, was still seen by the national court as part of the public sector and performing a public service.[62]

---

[61] On this see D. Curtin, 'The Province of Government: Delimiting the Direct Effect of Directives in the Common Law Context' (1990) 15 *ELRev.* 195, 198–9.

[62] Case C-180/04 *Vassallo v Azienda Ospedaliera Ospedale San Martino di Genova e Cliniche Universitarie Convenzionate* [2006] ECR I-7251.

In other cases, the Court will look at the degree of state control. It has thus held that any entity which forms part of, or is subject to the authority of, public authority forms part of the state, and can be sued. In *Rohrbach*, two Austrian companies that were owned by a public authority and carried out launderette and gardening activities were held to be part of the state.[63] This was not done on the grounds that they carried out a social function (their mission was to employ people with disabilities) but purely by virtue of the local authority ownership.

The difficulties of definition were not the only problems generated by *Marshall*. Its style of analysis sits uncomfortably with *Defrenne* v *Sabena*.[64] The latter holds that obligations addressed to Member States lead, by virtue of their binding nature, to horizontal direct effect, as they require courts to apply EU law in cases before them, whereas in *Marshall* the opposite is stated. More practically, the rule in *Marshall* creates illogical outcomes: Marshall could rely on the Directive because she was employed by a public authority, a part of the state. Had she been employed by a private hospital she would not have been able to rely on the Directive. Thus, a somewhat arbitrary, two-tier legal system has been created, in which parties have greater protection against public bodies than against private ones, notwithstanding the fact that their functional relationship with the two may be the same. Finally, *Marshall* rests on a false assumption. It is difficult to see how the estoppel argument can justify reliance on a Directive against a public health authority. For, certainly, the state is responsible for implementing Directives and public health authorities are a part of the state, but there is no sense in which public health authorities are responsible for transposing the terms of equal pay Directives into national law – yet here, the Directive was held to be enforceable as against the authority.

(iii) Debate about horizontal direct effect and incidental direct effect

For the reasons outlined above, *Marshall* came under withering attack from academic commentators[65] and Advocates General[66] alike. Undoubtedly, this provided the context for some of the doctrines subsequently developed, notably indirect effect and state liability. Yet, notwithstanding this, the Court has resolutely stated that Directives are not capable of horizontal direct effect as they cannot impose obligations on individuals.[67] However, the full force of this has been overshadowed by the phenomenon of 'triangular situations' or 'incidental direct effects'. The idea of a triangular situation is that a dispute between two parties may affect the legal rights of a third party or impose a financial burden on them. This creates a dilemma: *Marshall* holds, on the one hand, that an individual can sue the state and, on the other, that it shall not impose obligations on a private party. What happens when both are present?

---

[63] Case C-297/03 *Sozialhilfeverband Rohrbach* v *Arbeiterkammer Oberösterreich* [2005] ECR I-4305.

[64] Case 43/75 *Defrenne* v *Sabena* [1976] ECR 455.

[65] D. Curtin, 'The Effectiveness of Judicial Protection of Individual Rights' (1990) 27 *CMLRev.* 709; S. Prechal, 'Remedies After Marshall' (1990) 27 *CMLRev.* 451; J. Coppell, 'Rights, Duties and the End of Marshall' (1994) 57 *MLR* 859; T. Tridimas, 'Horizontal Effect of Directives: A Missed Opportunity?' (1994) 19 *ELRev.* 621.

[66] Advocate General Van Gerven in Case C-271/91 *Marshall* v *Southampton and South-West Hampshire AHA* [1993] ECR I-4367; Advocate General Jacobs in Case C-316/93 *Vaneetveld* v *Le Foyer* [1994] ECR I-763; and Advocate General Lenz in Case C-91/92 *Faccini Dori* v *Recreb* [1994] ECR I-3325.

[67] The moment of truth is often seen as *Dori* where six governments intervened to argue against horizontal direct effect. Case C-91/92 *Faccini Dori* v *Recreb* [1994] ECR I-3325. For more recent examples see Case C-356/05 *Farrell* v *Whitty* [2007] ECR I-3067; Case C-80/06 *Carp* [2007] ECR I-4473; Joined Cases C-37/06 and C-58/06 *Viamex Agrar Handels and Others* v *Hauptzollamt Hamburg-Jonas* [2008] ECR I-69.

This was first addressed head on by the Court in *Wells*.[68] The case concerned a challenge to a British government decision authorising a quarry in Wales to carry out mining operations opposite the claimant's house without its having carried out an environmental impact assessment as required by Directive 85/337/EC.[69] The British government argued that to allow the challenge would have the effect of the Directive denying the quarry its rights under English and Welsh law. The Court was dismissive of this, stating that a Directive's having adverse repercussions on a third party could not prevent its being invoked against the state.

The Court extrapolated on this in *Arcor*. A telephone service provider challenged a decision by the German regulatory authority to allow Deutsche Telekom, the owner of the telephone network in Germany, to charge for use of that network. It was argued that two Directives precluded this charge where the network was run by a market dominant business, as was the case here, and the fees were unrelated to the costs of connection. Whilst the case was brought against the German regulators, its central target was, of course, Deutsche Telekom and the fees it was charging.

Joined Cases C-152/07–C-154/07 *Arcor v Bundesrepublic Deutschland* [2008] ECR I-5959

35. It should be recalled that, according to settled case-law, a directive cannot of itself impose obligations on an individual, but can only confer rights. Consequently, an individual may not rely on a directive against a Member State where it is a matter of a State obligation directly linked to the performance of another obligation falling, pursuant to that directive, on a third party ...

36. On the other hand, mere adverse repercussions on the rights of third parties, even if the repercussions are certain, do not justify preventing an individual from relying on the provisions of a directive against the Member State concerned ...

37. In the main proceedings ... the actions before the referring court have been brought by private persons against the Member State concerned, represented by the national regulatory authority which made the contested decision and has sole competence to set the rates of both the connection charge at issue in the main proceedings and the interconnection charge to which the former is added.

38. It is clear that Deutsche Telekom is a third party in relation to the dispute before the referring court and is only capable of suffering adverse repercussions because it levied the connection charge at issue in the main proceedings and because, if that charge were removed, it would have to increase its own subscribers' rates. Such a removal of benefits cannot be regarded as an obligation falling on a third party pursuant to the directives relied on before the referring court by the appellants in the main proceedings.

If *Arcor* held that additional costs or removal of benefits for a third party were not a reason to prevent an individual invoking a Directive in national courts, it was still opaque about when Directives can be invoked in national courts.[70] Nyssens and Lackhoff suggest that there are three circumstances. The first is when a Directive entitles an individual to require the Member State to do something but this places a burden on another party. This is uncontroversial. It happens when individuals invoke Directives requiring local authorities to set things out properly

---

[68] It had been touched on but not addressed in a number of cases, with the first being Case C-431/91 *Commission v Germany* [1995] ECR I-2189. For a review of these see H. Nyssens and K. Lackhoff, 'Direct Effect of Directives in Triangular Situations' (1998) 23 *ELRev.* 397; D. Colgan, 'Triangular Situations: The Coup de Grâce for the Denial of Horizontal Direct Effect of Community Directives' (2002) 8 *EPL* 545; F. Becker and A. Campbell, 'The Direct Effect of European Directives: Towards the Final Act?' (2007) 13 *CJEL* 401.

[69] Case C-201/02 *R* v *Secretary of State for Transport, Local Government and the Regions, ex parte Wells* [2004] ECR I-723.

[70] On this see Advocate General Mazák in Case C-411/05 *Félix Palacios de la Villa* v *Cortefiel Servicios SA* [2007] ECR I-8531, paras. 123–7.

for public tender. Such tenders require significant information from other companies and are costly.[71] The second is where Directives require states to impose a burden on third parties 'whilst not allowing any third party the symmetrical right to require that they do so. Nevertheless, any such third party might be able to invoke the provisions of a Directive in a national administrative court.'[72] This was the situation in *Wells* and *Arcor*. Neither of the applicants had an ex ante right to compel a decision to be taken, but once one was taken in breach of the Directive which affected their interests they were able to challenge it. The third situation is the most controversial. It occurs where a Directive grants a party a legal right to shield itself from certain activities by the Member State. In defiance of this, the Member State engages in these activities in such a way that they create rights in national law for third parties. Can the Directive be invoked by the individual in litigation with these third parties?

This happened in *CIA*. Signalson and Securitel sought to restrain CIA Security from marketing an alarm system on the grounds that it had not received authorisation as required by Belgian law. This requirement of prior authorisation breached EU law, however, as, under Directive 83/189/EC, it should have been notified to the Commission. This had not happened and CIA therefore argued that the national law was inapplicable.

Case C-194/94 *CIA Security International* v *Signalson & Securitel* [1996] ECR I-2201

44. That view cannot be adopted. Articles 8 and 9 of Directive 83/189 lay down a precise obligation on Member States to notify draft technical regulations to the Commission before they are adopted. Being, accordingly, unconditional and sufficiently precise in terms of their content, those articles may be relied on by individuals before national courts.

45. It remains to examine the legal consequences to be drawn from a breach by Member States of their obligation to notify and, more precisely, whether Directive 83/189 is to be interpreted as meaning that a breach of the obligation to notify, constituting a procedural defect in the adoption of the technical regulations concerned, renders such technical regulations inapplicable so that they may not be enforced against individuals.

46. The German and Netherlands Governments and the United Kingdom consider that Directive 83/189 is solely concerned with relations between the Member States and the Commission, that it merely creates procedural obligations which the Member States must observe when adopting technical regulations, their competence to adopt the regulations in question after expiry of the suspension period being, however, unaffected, and, finally, that it contains no express provision relating to any effects attaching to non-compliance with those procedural obligations.

47. The Court observes first of all in this context that none of those factors prevents non-compliance with Directive 83/189 from rendering the technical regulations in question inapplicable.

48. For such a consequence to arise from a breach of the obligations laid down by Directive 83/189, an express provision to this effect is not required. As pointed out above, it is undisputed that the aim of the directive is to protect freedom of movement for goods by means of preventive control and that the obligation to notify is essential for achieving such Community control. The effectiveness of Community control will be that much greater if the directive is interpreted as meaning that breach of the obligation to notify constitutes a substantial procedural defect such as to render the technical regulations in question inapplicable to individuals.

---

[71] Case 103/88 *Fratelli Costanzo* v *Milano* [1989] ECR 1839.
[72] Nyssens and Lackhoff, above n. 68, 402.

Whilst *CIA* was decided prior to *Arcor*, the latter reinforces it conceptually. If a Directive grants directly effective rights, no enforcement actions can be taken using state apparatus, be it through the courts, the administration or the police, to rob the individual of the benefit of these rights. It does not matter whether it is another private party asking the state to take this action or whether the administration does it at its own behest. Turned around, this means that whilst an individual cannot lodge a claim against another party invoking a Directive, by virtue of the lack of horizontal direct effect, she can always use the Directive as a shield to protect herself from actions brought against her by other parties.

If this does not result in Directives placing obligations on private parties, it does result in their affecting the latter's entitlements and rights significantly, and the question has to be asked how this is consistent with the ethos of *Marshall*, which is that states should bear the burden of unimplemented Directives as these are addressed to them.[73]

The other challenge is a substantive one. It is that of 'regulatory gaps'. If a Directive can be invoked to prevent a national law being applied but cannot be fully applied itself, this leaves a 'lawless' situation, where the public good at the heart of the dispute is unprotected. This arose in *Lemmens*. Lemmens was breathalysed by Dutch police, who used a breathalyser conforming to Dutch regulations, which had not been notified to the Commission as required by Directive 83/189/EC.[74] He challenged his ensuing conviction on the basis that a lawful test had not taken place, as the regulations authorising use of this breathalyser were illegal. The Court found that the Dutch regulations could be enforced against Lemmens. It observed that the purpose of the Directive was to facilitate free movement of goods. Whilst this required that an unnotified technical regulation would be unenforceable wherever it hindered the use or marketing of a product, it did not render regulations inapplicable where this was not the case. *Unilever* elaborated on this.[75] Unilever had delivered some Italian olive oil to Central Food. A condition of the contract was that the oil should be labelled in accordance with Italian law. Central Food refused to accept the oil as it did not comply with a 1998 Decree stating that olive oil could not be termed 'Italian' unless the entire cycle of harvesting, production, processing and packaging had taken place in Italy. This Decree had been notified to the Commission, but had been too quickly implemented. The Court stated that this illegal implementation meant that the law in question would be unenforceable against individuals if it hindered the marketing or use of a product. This was the case here. Marketing was hindered not merely where a good was directly prevented from being sold by a technical regulation but could also occur indirectly, where a regulation was used to allow a party in civil proceedings to revoke a contract and thereby prevent a good from being marketed.

These two cases limit but do not resolve the problem of the regulatory gap. To be sure, claims must be brought with the purpose of marketing goods. Yet, even where this is the motivation for the litigation, there is still the problem that public goods, such as protection of the consumer or the environment, will be unprotected once the national measure is declared invalid. In *Unilever*, for example, it is possible to argue that an effect of the judgment was to weaken consumer protection by leaving the consumers of this oil uninformed as to its origin.

---

[73] S. Weatherill, 'Breach of Directives and Breach of Contract' (2001) 26 *ELRev.* 177, 182–3.

[74] Case C-226/97 *Lemmens* [1998] ECR I-3711.

[75] Case C-443/98 *Unilever SpA v Central Food SpA* [2000] ECR I-7535.

6 INDIRECT EFFECT

Direct effect has, in the last twenty years, become merely one route amongst others through which individuals may invoke EU law in national courts. It is arguable, indeed, that it is no longer even the predominant doctrine in that regard – this may be the doctrine of indirect effect. As the development of direct effect has faltered, the doctrine of indirect effect has expanded. Back in 1998, an empirical study found that it was deployed more widely in British courts than direct effect.[76] Despite the greater academic attention that is generally given to direct effect, it has therefore been argued persuasively that indirect effect 'is currently the main form of ensuring effect of Directives whether correctly, incorrectly or not transposed at all'.[77]

(i) Arrival of indirect effect

Indirect effect began inauspiciously in *Von Colson*.[78] Two female social workers were refused employment in a German prison by virtue of their sex. They sued in the German labour court relying on the German law implementing Directive 76/207/EEC, the Equal Treatment Directive. Under that, the German court could only order that they be compensated for such losses as they had suffered as a result of applying for the positions which had been denied them, in this case the travel expenses to the interviews. The national court referred the question of whether such a restriction in the availability of compensation was compatible with EU law, in particular article 6 of the Directive, which required persons who considered themselves wronged to be able to pursue their claims by judicial process. The relevant provision was insufficiently clear and unconditional to satisfy the test for direct effect. However, the Court of Justice ruled that this did not necessarily mean that the Directive could be of no assistance to the claimants.

Case 14/83 Von Colson & Kamann v Land Nordrhein-Westfalen [1984] ECR 1891

22. It is impossible to establish real equality of opportunity without an appropriate system of sanctions. That follows not only from the actual purpose of the Directive but more specifically from Article 6 thereof which, by granting applicants for a post who have been discriminated against recourse to the courts, acknowledges that those candidates have rights of which they may avail themselves before the courts.

23. Although ... full implementation of the Directive does not require any specific form of sanction for unlawful discrimination, it does entail that that sanction be such as to guarantee real and effective judicial protection. Moreover it must also have a real deterrent effect on the employer. It follows that where a Member State chooses to penalize the breach of the prohibition of discrimination by the award of compensation, that compensation must in any event be adequate in relation to the damage sustained.

24. In consequence it appears that national provisions limiting the right to compensation of persons who have been discriminated against as regards access to employment to a purely nominal amount, such as, for example, the reimbursement of expenses incurred by them in submitting their application, would not satisfy the requirements of an effective transposition of the Directive ...

[76] D. Chalmers, 'The Positioning of EU Judicial Politics within the United Kingdom' (2000) 23 *WEP* 169, 190.
[77] G. Betlem, 'The Doctrine of Consistent Interpretation: Managing Legal Uncertainty' (2002) 22 *OJLS* 397, 399.
[78] See also Case 79/83 *Harz* v *Deutsche Tradax* [1984] ECR 192.

> 26. ... The Member States' obligation arising from a Directive to achieve the result envisaged by the Directive and their duty under Article [4(3) TEU] to take all appropriate measures, whether general or particular, to ensure the fulfilment of that obligation, is binding on all the authorities of Member States including, for matters within their jurisdiction, the courts. It follows that, in applying the national law and in particular the provisions of national law specifically introduced in order to implement Directive 76/207, national courts are required to interpret their national law in the light of the wording and purpose of the Directive ...

For many years, it seemed the application of the doctrine of indirect effect – the duty to interpret national law in accordance with EU law – was quite limited. Following *Von Colson*, the doctrine only applied where national laws were implementing Directives and a provision was highly ambiguous. However, such an interpretation was scotched by the Court in its ruling in *Marleasing*. Marleasing brought an action against La Comercial in order to have the latter's articles of association declared void as having been created for the sole purpose of defrauding and evading creditors. The Spanish Civil Code stated that contracts made with 'lack of cause' were void. Directive 68/151/EEC contained an exhaustive list of reasons under which companies could be declared void. Avoidance of creditors was not on that list.

> ### Case C–106/89 *Marleasing SA v La Comercial Internacionale de Alimentación SA* [1990] ECR I–4135
>
> 8. ... as the Court pointed out in its judgment in *Von Colson* ..., the Member States' obligation arising from a Directive to achieve the result envisaged by the Directive and their duty under Article [4(3) TEU] to take all appropriate measures, whether general or particular, to ensure the fulfilment of that obligation, is binding on all the authorities of Member States including, for matters within their jurisdiction, the courts. It follows that, in applying national law, whether the provisions in question were adopted before or after the Directive, the national court called upon to interpret it is required to do so, as far as possible, in the light of the wording and the purpose of the Directive in order to achieve the result pursued by the latter and thereby comply with the third paragraph of Article [288 TFEU].

Marleasing expanded the law of indirect effect in two ways. First, it required *all* national legislation to be interpreted in the light of EU law, irrespective of whether it is implementing legislation or not, and irrespective of whether it was enacted prior or subsequent to the provision of EU law in question. In this instance, the Spanish Civil Code, which concerned civil/contract law, had to be interpreted in the light of a subsequent piece of EU company legislation. Secondly, it strengthened the national courts' interpretive duty. As Docksey and Fitzpatrick observed 'it is no longer sufficient for a national court to turn to Community law only if the national provision is "ambiguous". Its priority must be to establish the meaning of the Union obligation and only then to conclude whether it is possible to achieve the necessary reconciliation with the national law.'[79]

The *Marleasing* judgment narrowed the gap that the Court of Justice had created in *Marshall*, where it held that Directives only had vertical direct effect. For the expansion of the duty of

---

[79] C. Docksey and B. Fitzpatrick, 'The Duty of National Courts to Interpret Provisions of National Law in Accordance with Community Law' (1991) 20 *ILJ* 113, 119.

consistent interpretation allowed Directives to govern the substance of disputes between private parties. As long as there was a national law which allowed some room for interpretation, it could be manoeuvred to comply with the Directive, thereby allowing it to determine the dispute 'indirectly' via the medium of the national law. It is to be emphasised, therefore, that *Marleasing* concerned a dispute between two private parties. While *Marleasing* allows for Directives to be involved in the adjudication of relations between private parties, the judgment does not go so far as to insist that Directives should govern such relations in an exclusive manner. Instead, it creates a new form of what might be termed 'inter-legality', in which a mix of national and EU law regulates a dispute, with the EU element opening up adjudication to wider norms and concerns, whilst the national law element ensures that the local traditions and trajectories surrounding the dispute are not overlooked.

M. Amstutz, 'In-Between Worlds: *Marleasing* and the Emergence of Interlegality in Legal Reasoning' (2005) 11 *European Law Journal* 766, 781–2

The internal culture-specific 'constraints' on national adjudication remain unaffected by the requirement for interpretation in conformity with Directives; local specificities of the various legal discourses are not pushed aside, say, by rational arguments that in the end are always weaker than the constraints of organically grown legal cultures. For ultimately it is the legal policies present in the private law of the individual Member States that act as 'regulators' in the process of incorporating Community private-law positions into the national legal discourses. They are ensuring that two separate sets of norms do not emerge in Member States' civil legal systems – one deriving from the historical trajectory of the State concerned, the other dictated by the Community. They alone can offer guarantees for a Community private law integrated into the national legal culture, and this fact immediately makes it clear how they ensure the evolutionary capacity of national law in the biotope of the European Community: by on the one hand – as artful combinations of 'flexible' and 'fixed' control parameters – blocking the propagation of the 'perturbations' from European law throughout the national private law, without on the other losing the national law's responsiveness to EC law.

Although some have argued that *Marleasing* created a skilful new balance between EU and national law, others have criticised the judgment for generating considerable uncertainty.[80] The sources of this uncertainty are twofold. The first stems from the strength of the duty of interpretation. It is clearly strong but the extent of that strength is uncertain. It is something stronger than giving effect to EU law-compliant interpretations when there are two equally plausible interpretations. It is something less than requiring national law to be overridden. Between these poles, however, it is very unclear whether the national judge is to give more weight to the national law or EU law provisions in question. The second derives from the duty to interpret the national law in the light of all EU law. Put simply, there is so much of the latter and it is so wide-ranging that it is very difficult for national lawyers or judges to consider any Union provision that might cut across some national dispute in an incidental manner.

The risks posed to legal certainty have been partially recognised by the Court of Justice. It has held that indirect effect does not require *contra legem* interpretations of national law. That is to say, the strength of the interpretive obligation is not so strong as to require a provision of

---

[80] G. de Búrca, 'Giving Effect to European Community Directives' (1992) 55 *MLR* 215.

national law to be given a meaning that contradicts its 'ordinary' meaning.[81] Furthermore, the Court has been particularly wary of using the doctrine in the field of criminal law, where the liberties of the individual are at stake, or where it seems that the effect will be to impose strong obligations on individuals. In *Arcaro*, the Court stated:

> The obligation of the national court to refer to the content of the Directive when interpreting the relevant rules of its own national law reaches a limit where such an interpretation leads to the imposition on an individual of an obligation laid down by a Directive which has not been transposed or, more especially, where it has the effect of determining or aggravating, on the basis of the Directive and in the absence of a law enacted for its implementation, the liability in criminal law of persons who act in contravention of that Directive's provisions.[82]

Notwithstanding this, the Court has continued to regard indirect effect as being as important as ever and, in recent years, as illustrated below, it has sought to expand it.[83]

(ii) When does the duty of indirect effect arise?

The date from when direct effect takes effect varies. For Regulations, it is stated in the Regulation or, failing that, twenty days after publication.[84] In the case of Directives, we saw that a Directive may have direct effect only after the date has passed by which Member States are required to transpose it into national law, and only if they have failed to do so.[85] However, the basis for indirect effect is different from direct effect. In the case of Directives it derives not from the state's failure to comply with EU law but rather from the duty in what is now Article 4(3) TEU to take all measures to ensure compliance with EU law.[86] This begs the question as to whether there is a different starting date for indirect effect.

This became an issue in *Mangold*.[87] In 2003, Mangold, who was 56 years old, entered into an eight month fixed-term employment contract with Helm, a German lawyer. He subsequently challenged the fixed term nature of this contract on the grounds that it contravened Directive 2000/78/EC which, inter alia, prohibited discrimination on grounds of age. The basis was that Germany introduced a 2002 law which only allowed fixed term contracts for workers younger than 52 years old in exceptional circumstances, whereas this restriction did not apply for older workers. Although adopted in 2000, the Directive was not due to be transposed until December 2003, and Member States could even request (provided they made annual reports to the Commission) that transposition not occur until December 2006. The German government argued that it had a freedom, and that the Directive could not generate legal effects, prior to that date. The Court disagreed. It stated that it was the duty of the national court to set aside

---

[81] Most notably, Case C-334/92 *Wagner-Miret* v *Fondo de Garantia Salarial* [1993] ECR I-6911.

[82] Case C-168/95 *Arcaro* [1996] ECR I-4705, para. 42. See also Case C-321/05 *Kofeod v Skatteministeriet* [2007] ECR I-5795. On this see P. Craig, 'The Legal Effects of Directives: Policy, Rules and Exceptions' (2009) 34 *ELRev.* 349, 360–4.

[83] Affirmations have included Joined Cases C-397/01–C-403/01 *Pfeiffer and Others* v *Deutsches Rotes Kreuz* [2004] ECR I-8835; Case C-212/04 *Adeneler and Others* v *ELOG (Ellinikos Organismos Galaktos)* [2006] ECR I-6057; Joined Cases C-378/07–C-380/07 *Angelidaki* v *ONAR*, Judgment of 23 April 2009. For analysis, see S. Drake, 'Twenty Years after *Von Colson*: The Impact of "Indirect Effect" on the Protection of the Individual's Community Rights' (2005) 30 *ELRev.* 329.

[84] Article 297 TFEU.

[85] See pp. 287–8.

[86] On this see Advocate General Kokott in Case C-212/04 *Adeneler and Others* v *ELOG (Ellinikos Organismos Galaktos)* [2006] ECR I-6057, paras. 47–50.

[87] Case C-144/04 *Mangold v Helm* [2005] ECR I-9981.

any provision of national law which conflicted with the Directive even if the time limit for transposition had not passed. Its reasoning was twofold. First, it argued that Member States were under a duty to refrain from taking any measures liable seriously to compromise the attainment of the result prescribed by the Directive. This was reinforced by the terms of the Directive, which provided for an exceptional period for transposition to enable progressive realisation of the measures necessary to meet its objectives. The 2002 law, insofar as it exacerbated age discrimination, violated this duty. Secondly, the Directive gave effect to a fundamental principle of EU law, that of non-discrimination. Observance of this principle could not be conditional simply upon expiry of a transposition period. The judgment was heavily criticised both within the Court and by academics for its opaque reasoning.[88] It was unclear whether the judgment's reasoning was confined to the particular Directive in question or what the underlying basis was for this new obligation.

The position was clarified in *Adeneler*. Eighteen employers were on a variety of fixed term contracts with the Greek milk board which came to an end between June and September 2003. Greece was due to have implemented Directive 1999/70/EC on fixed term work by July 2002, which provided that fixed term contracts would only be allowed if there were objective reasons. This had been interpreted to mean that there had to be precise and concrete circumstances which provided a need for a fixed term contract. The Greek court asked from what moment a national court was required to interpret the Directive.

Case C–212/04 *Adeneler and Others* v *ELOG (Ellinikos Organismos Galaktos)* [2006] ECR I-6057

113. With a view, more specifically, to determining the date from which national courts are to apply the principle that national law must be interpreted in conformity with Community law, it should be noted that that obligation, arising from the second paragraph of Article [4(3) TEU], the third paragraph of Article [288 TFEU] and the directive in question itself, has been imposed in particular where a provision of a directive lacks direct effect, be it that the relevant provision is not sufficiently clear, precise and unconditional to produce direct effect or that the dispute is exclusively between individuals.

114. Also, before the period for transposition of a directive has expired, Member States cannot be reproached for not having yet adopted measures implementing it in national law...

115. Accordingly, where a directive is transposed belatedly, the general obligation owed by national courts to interpret domestic law in conformity with the directive exists only once the period for its transposition has expired.

116. It necessarily follows from the foregoing that, where a directive is transposed belatedly, the date... on which the national implementing measures actually enter into force in the Member State concerned does not constitute the relevant point in time. Such a solution would be liable seriously to jeopardise the full effectiveness of Community law and its uniform application by means, in particular, of directives.

117. In addition, ... it should be pointed out that it is already clear from the Court's case law that the obligation on Member States, under the second paragraph of Article [4(3) TEU], the third paragraph of Article [288 TFEU] and the directive in question itself, to take all the measures necessary to achieve the

---

[88] For different views see A. Dashwood, 'From *Van Duyn* to *Mangold* via *Marshall*: Reducing Direct Effect to Absurdity?' (2006–07) 9 *CYELS* 81; C. Tobler, 'Putting *Mangold* in Perspective: In Response to *Editorial Comments*, Horizontal Direct Effect – A Law of Diminishing Coherence?' (2007) 44 *CMLRev.* 1177.

result prescribed by the directive is binding on all national authorities, including, for matters within their jurisdiction, the courts...

118. Also, directives are either (i) published in the *Official Journal of the European Communities* in accordance with Article [297 TFEU] and, in that case, enter into force on the date specified in them or, in the absence thereof, on the 20th day following that of their publication, or (ii) notified to those to whom they are addressed, in which case they take effect upon such notification, in accordance with Article [297(2) TFEU].

119. It follows that a directive produces legal effects for a Member State to which it is addressed – and, therefore, for all the national authorities – following its publication or from the date of its notification, as the case may be.

120. In the present instance, Directive 1999/70 states, in Article 3, that it was to enter into force on the day of its publication in the *Official Journal of the European Communities*, namely 10 July 1999.

121. In accordance with the Court's settled case law, it follows from [Article 4(3) TEU] in conjunction with the third paragraph of Article [288 TFEU] and the directive in question itself that, during the period prescribed for transposition of a directive, the Member States to which it is addressed must refrain from taking any measures liable seriously to compromise the attainment of the result prescribed by it... In this connection it is immaterial whether or not the provision of national law at issue which has been adopted after the directive in question entered into force is concerned with the transposition of the directive...

122. Given that all the authorities of the Member States are subject to the obligation to ensure that provisions of Community law take full effect... the obligation to refrain from taking measures, as set out in the previous paragraph, applies just as much to national courts.

123. It follows that, from the date upon which a directive has entered into force, the courts of the Member States must refrain as far as possible from interpreting domestic law in a manner which might seriously compromise, after the period for transposition has expired, attainment of the objective pursued by that directive.

There is, thus, a tiered obligation on national courts. The full force of the duty to interpret only takes effect from the date of transposition. Prior to that, there is a more limited duty. National courts must interpret national law in such a manner that it does not compromise realisation of a directive's objective from the end of the transposition period. The meaning of this obligation is very unclear. In *VTB-VAB* Advocate General Trstenjak stated:

> If ... the national court cannot avoid the suspicion that a piece of national legislation is liable to prevent the achievement of the result prescribed by a directive which is imminently due to be implemented once the period for transposition has expired, it is obliged to take the necessary measures even before the transposition phase has ended. Such measures also include, in principle, the possibility of disapplying the offending national law if an interpretation of the current law in conformity with the directive is out of the question.[89]

Asking, however, a national court to engage with a particular form of interpretation on the basis of a suspicion is a real threat to legal certainty. The concrete circumstances in which this will occur will invariably always be difficult to ascertain and the strength of interpretive obligation is extremely hazy. It is difficult to reconcile this with the Court's repeated concern that

---

[89] Joined Cases C-261/07 and C-299/07 *VTB-VAB* v *Total*, Judgment of 29 April 2009, para. 62.

Directives should not place obligations on individuals. For the latter now live under a shadow where they do not know what obligations Directives impose, and this can only have a chilling effect on their behaviour.

(iii) Range of measures that national courts must take into account

A final issue to be addressed is the question of which instruments national courts are required to consider. It might have been thought, in the wake of *Von Colson*, that national courts would be required to consider only such instruments as may be directly enforceable in national courts (i.e. Treaty provisions, Regulations, Decisions and Directives). As early as 1989, however, the Court established that the duty of consistent interpretation was a free-standing principle in its own right. It may have been *developed* in the context of seeking ways to make Directives effective before national courts, but from as early as 1989 that has not been its sole purpose. In *Grimaldi*,[90] the Court held that national courts were to take account not just of 'hard law' but also of legally non-binding recommendations.

More dramatic was the Court's ruling in *Pupino*, which controversially extended indirect effect to the third pillar of the European Union.[91] *Pupino* arose out of a dispute relating to the interpretation by an Italian criminal court of Council Framework Decision 2001/220/JHA, concerning the safeguards afforded to vulnerable victims when they appear as witnesses in criminal proceedings. Framework Decisions were pieces of legislation that existed under the third pillar of the original TEU. They were to be 'binding upon the Member States as to the result to be achieved but shall leave to the national authorities the choice of form and methods. They shall not entail direct effect.'[92] The Court noted, notwithstanding this, that the language of this provision is similar to that used by what is now Article 288(3) TFEU for Directives. The British and Italian governments argued, however, that this could not be the case as there was no third pillar equivalent of the duty of cooperation which was then set out in Article 10 EC, and is now contained in Article 4(3) TEU. The Court rejected this. It noted that what is now Article 1(2) TEU stated that the Treaty marked a new stage in the process of ever closer union and that the task of the Union was to organise, in a manner demonstrating consistency and solidarity, relations between the Member States and between their peoples. It stated this would be difficult if the principle of loyal cooperation did not apply to the third pillar. National courts were therefore under an obligation to interpret national law in the light of Framework Decisions.

With the coming into force of Lisbon, *Pupino* must be seen in a new light. Framework Decisions no longer exist, and there is no pillar structure in the previously understood sense. The decision's significance lies in the reasoning used. It provides an alternate basis for indirect effect: the general obligation residing in the objective of ever closer union set out in Article 1(2) TEU. This is intriguing and concerning. The language is vague and open-ended. It suggests that the duties of indirect effect might simply be part of a parcel of duties on Member States which is continually evolving and thus never fully known.

---

[90] Case 322/88 *Grimaldi* v *Fonds des Maladies Professionelles* [1989] ECR 4407.

[91] Case C-105/03 *Pupino* [2005] ECR I-5285. For analysis see M. Fletcher, 'Extending "Indirect Effect" to the Third Pillar: The Significance of Pupino' (2005) 30 *ELRev*. 862; S. Peers, 'Salvation Outside the Church: Judicial Protection in the Third Pillar After the *Pupino* and *Segi* Judgments' (2007) 44 *CMLRev*. 885; E. Spaventa, 'Opening Pandora's Box: Some Reflections on the Constitutional Effects of the Ruling in Pupino' (2007) 3 *European Constitutional Law Review* 5.

[92] Article 34(2)(b) TEU(M). On this see A. Hinarejos, 'On the Legal Effects of Framework Decisions and Decisions: Directly Applicable, Directly Effective, Self Executing, Supreme?' (2008) 14 *ELJ* 620.

7 STATE LIABILITY

(i) Arrival and challenges of state liability

The doctrine of indirect effect only partially addresses the 'gap' left by Directives only having vertical direct effect. There are two circumstances where it will not come to the rescue of individuals granted entitlements by Directives. One is where there is no national measure to interpret, and the other is where the national legislation contradicts the Directive. In each instance there is a problem, as there is nothing to interpret – so the individual cannot be helped – but these cases represent the most flagrant violations of EU law by Member States.

This scenario arose in *Francovich*. Italy had persistently failed to implement the terms of Directive 80/987/EC, a measure that was intended to guarantee to employees a minimum level of protection under Community law in the event of the insolvency of their employer. The Directive provided in particular for specific guarantees of payment of unpaid wage claims. It should have been implemented by October 1983, and in 1987 the Commission brought a successful enforcement action against the Italian government for its failure to transpose the Directive.[93] Even after the judgment, there was still no transposition. *Francovich* concerned an action by thirty-four employees, who were owed back-pay by employers that had now gone bankrupt, against the Italian state for the losses they had suffered as a consequence of its failure to transpose the Directive.

Joined Cases C–6/90 and C–9/90 *Francovich and Bonifaci v Italy* [1991] ECR I–5357

31. It should be borne in mind at the outset that the EEC Treaty has created its own legal system, which is integrated into the legal systems of the Member States and which their courts are bound to apply. The subjects of that legal system are not only the Member States but also their nationals. Just as it imposes burdens on individuals, Community law is also intended to give rise to rights which become part of their legal patrimony. Those rights arise not only where they are expressly granted by the Treaty but also by virtue of obligations which the Treaty imposes in a clearly defined manner both on individuals and on the Member States and the Community institutions ...

32. Furthermore, it has been consistently held that the national courts whose task it is to apply the provisions of Community law in areas within their jurisdiction must ensure that those rules take full effect and must protect the rights which they confer on individuals ...

33. The full effectiveness of Community rules would be impaired and the protection of the rights which they grant would be weakened if individuals were unable to obtain redress when their rights are infringed by a breach of Community law for which a Member State can be held responsible.

34. The possibility of obtaining redress from the Member State is particularly indispensable where, as in this case, the full effectiveness of Community rules is subject to prior action on the part of the State and where, consequently, in the absence of such action, individuals cannot enforce before the national courts the rights conferred upon them by Community law.

35. It follows that the principle whereby a State must be liable for loss and damage caused to individuals as a result of breaches of Community law for which the State can be held responsible is inherent in the system of the Treaty.

---

[93] Case 22/87 *Commission v Italy* [1989] ECR 143.

36. A further basis for the obligation of Member States to make good such loss and damage is to be found in Article [4(3) TEU], under which the Member States are required to take all appropriate measures, whether general or particular, to ensure fulfilment of their obligations under Community law. Among these is the obligation to nullify the unlawful consequences of a breach of Community law ...

37. It follows from all the foregoing that it is a principle of Community law that the Member States are obliged to make good loss and damage caused to individuals by breaches of Community law for which they can be held responsible.

38. Although State liability is thus required by Community law, the conditions under which that liability gives rise to a right to reparation depend on the nature of the breach of Community law giving rise to the loss and damage.

39. Where, as in this case, a Member State fails to fulfil its obligation under the third paragraph of Article [288 TFEU] to take all the measures necessary to achieve the result prescribed by a Directive, the full effectiveness of that rule of Community law requires that there should be a right to reparation provided that three conditions are fulfilled.

40. The first of those conditions is that the result prescribed by the Directive should entail the grant of rights to individuals. The second condition is that it should be possible to identify the content of those rights on the basis of the provisions of the Directive. Finally, the third condition is the existence of a causal link between the breach of the State's obligation and the loss and damage suffered by the injured parties.

41. Those conditions are sufficient to give rise to a right on the part of individuals to obtain reparation, a right founded directly on Community law.

42. Subject to that reservation, it is on the basis of the rules of national law on liability that the State must make reparation for the consequences of the loss and damage caused. In the absence of Community legislation, it is for the internal legal order of each Member State to designate the competent courts and lay down the detailed procedural rules for legal proceedings intended fully to safeguard the rights which individuals derive from Community law ...

43. Further, the substantive and procedural conditions for reparation of loss and damage laid down by the national law of the Member States must not be less favourable than those relating to similar domestic claims and must not be so framed as to make it virtually impossible or excessively difficult to obtain reparation ...

Francovich was seen as a seminal judgment.[94] At that time, most states did not provide a system of governmental liability for equivalent breaches of national law, and, in the negotiations leading up to Maastricht, drew the line at the notion that national courts should be able to award damages against the state for breach of Community law.[95] Notwithstanding this, most academic commentators welcomed the decision on the grounds that it would lead to better enforcement of EU law[96] and greater citizen empowerment.[97] Yet individual litigation has rarely

---

[94] The academic literature is voluminous. P. Craig, '*Francovich*, Remedies and the Scope of Damages Liability' (1993) 109 *LQR* 595; R. Caranta, 'Governmental Liability After *Francovich*' (1993) *CLJ* 272 and M. Ross, 'Beyond *Francovich*' (1993) 56 *MLR* 55; E. Szyszczak, 'Making Europe More Relevant to its Citizens' (1996) 21 *ELRev.* 35; J. Steiner, 'From Direct Effects to *Francovich*: More Effective Means of Enforcement of Community Law' (1993) 18 *ELRev.* 3; R. Caranta, 'Judicial Protection Against Member States: A New *jus commune* Takes Shape' (1995) 32 *CMLRev.* 703.

[95] J. Tallberg, 'Supranational Influence in EU Enforcement: The ECJ and the Principle of State Liability' (2000) 7 *JEPP* 104, 114–16.

[96] Caranta, above n. 94, 710.

[97] See e.g. E. Szyszczak, 'Making Europe More Relevant to its Citizens' (1996) 21 *ELRev.* 35; Steiner, above n. 94.

been seen as the most effective route to regulatory enforcement, and there was scepticism, particularly as Member States were being asked, for the most part, to establish a new form of remedy and this might lead to national resistance.[98]

The most wide-ranging study, by Marie-Pierre Granger, found this to be unfounded.[99] All Member States had adopted the principle, normally in adopting their tort laws, and national courts had not been hesitant to award substantial damages.[100] The only qualification to this picture was in cases of legislative liability, where a parliament has passed a law contradicting EU law. In such circumstances, there was widespread evasion, with decisions by courts in Belgium, Greece, France and Italy all giving cause for concern.[101]

Many of the actions cited by Granger involved group actions or actions by large undertakings and this begged the question of who is empowered by *Francovich*. One of the most powerful critiques of *Francovich* was offered by Harlow. She argued that no thought had been given to the question of who would actually benefit from the imposition of state liability and who would lose from it.

> ### C. Harlow, '*Francovich* and the Problem of the Disobedient State' (1996) 2 *European Law Journal* 199, 204
>
> At the outset we should dismiss the vision of a squad of citizen policemen engaged in law enforcement. There are, of course, actions fought by individuals or groups of individuals. *Marshall* falls into this category; *Francovich* ... and *Faccini Dori* may. In the field of environmental law, we find a developing pattern derived from human rights law, where a number of specialist organisations (NGOs) dedicated to the enforcement of human rights through courts operate; in Article [288] cases, their place has largely been assumed by State-funded agencies. Whether or not these groups and agencies can be said to represent 'citizens' is a moot point but they do embody the private enforcement machinery to which the ECJ apparently aspires. This is not to imply, however, that the model of 'politics through law' espoused by the ECJ is best pursued through the medium of the action for damages; ... there is much to be said in favour of judicial review as the standard procedure, with annulment or declaratory orders as the standard remedy, in this type of citizen enforcement. In other areas, citizen enforcement is in any event a fantasy ... [A]n overwhelming majority of actions against the Community are brought by corporations ... [in litigation that] typically involves licences and other economic interests ...

This was particularly apposite, she argued, because systems of government liability locked courts into tragic choices. Awarding compensation was never simply granting compensation to a plaintiff from some limitless budget. Instead, as states invariably never increased taxes to pay for liability claims, claims awarded to plaintiffs were awarded at the expense of other public goods – typically, as welfare spending is the highest proportion of national budgets, money intended for the old, the sick and the poor. She wondered whether a distributive exercise was best achieved through the happenstance of individual litigation.[102]

---

[98] Tallberg, above n. 95, 110–11.

[99] M.-P. Granger, 'Francovich and the Construction of a European Administrative *ius commune*' (2007) 32 *ELRev*. 157.

[100] The most widely reported was a fine of 26.4 million euros imposed by the Spanish Supreme Court in 2003 for failure to comply with EU broadcasting law: Tribunal Supremo, 12 June 2003, *CanalSatelite Digital* v *State Attorney* [2005] 5 *EuroCL* 33. S. Lage and H. Brokelmann, 'The Liability of the Spanish State for Breach of EC law: The Landmark Ruling of the Spanish Tribunal Supremo in the *Canal Satelite Digital* Case' (2004) 24 *ELRev*. 530.

[101] Granger, above n. 99, 163–7.

[102] *Ibid*. 210–12.

Both Granger's and Harlow's work assumes that formal legal structures lead to particular forms of enforcement. More recent work challenges this and argues that even when these are in place, widespread variation takes place. A series of case studies carried out by Slepcevic of public interest litigation in relation to nature protection Directives in the Netherlands, France and Germany found widespread variation.[103] He concluded that decentralised enforcement relied on a series of features, which were rarely all in place at the same time. These included organisational capacity of groups to litigate, effective access to courts unimpeded by standing rulings or financial restrictions, willingness by courts to give full interpretations, and preparedness of the administration to implement court rulings fully and quickly. In very few states can all these matters be taken for granted.

(ii) Conditions of liability

Francovich only considered the narrow circumstances of when a Member State had failed to transpose a Directive. Its language was wider than that, and this left open the question of when a Member State would be held liable for breaching EU law: a question that exercised all the national governments in the run up to the Treaty of Amsterdam.[104] This was addressed in *Brasserie du Pêcheur* and *Factortame III*. These joined cases were referred in 1993 but, aware of their sensitivity, the Court did not decide them until 1996. Brasserie du Pêcheur, a French firm, had been forced to discontinue exports of beer to Germany in 1981 by virtue of a German 'purity law' which prohibited beers being marketed as beer if they contained additives. This law was declared illegal in 1987 on the ground that it contravened Article 34 TFEU, the provision outlawing quantitative restrictions or measures having equivalent effect on the free movement of goods.[105] Brasserie du Pêcheur sought compensation of DM1,800,000 for the loss of sales between 1981 and 1987. The facts of *Factortame* were given above.[106] After the system of registration contained in the Merchant Shipping Act 1988 had been declared illegal, the applicants claimed for damages against the British government.

> **Joined Cases C‑46/93 and C‑48/93 *Brasserie du Pêcheur v Germany* and *R v Secretary of State for Transport, ex parte Factortame (No. 3)* [1996] ECR I‑1029**
>
> 38. Although Community law imposes State liability, the conditions under which that liability gives rise to a right to reparation depend on the nature of the breach of Community law giving rise to the loss and damage ...
> 39. In order to determine those conditions, account should first be taken of the principles inherent in the Community legal order which form the basis for State liability, namely first, the full effectiveness of Community rules and the effective protection of the rights which they confer and, second, the obligation to cooperate imposed on Member States by Article [4(3) TEU] ...
> 40. In addition ... it is pertinent to refer to the Court's case law on non‑contractual liability on the part of the Community.

[103] R. Slepcevic, 'The Judicial Enforcement of EU Law through National Courts: Possibilities and Limits' (2009) 16 *JEPP* 378.

[104] See, in particular, the Memorandum to the 1996 Intergovernmental Conference by the United Kingdom on the Court of Justice (London, FCO, 1996) 2.

[105] Case 178/84 *Commission v Germany (German beer)* [1987] ECR 1227.

[106] See p. 279.

41. First, ... Article [340 TFEU] refers as regards the non-contractual liability of the Community, to the general principles common to the laws of the Member States, from which, in the absence of written rules, the Court also draws inspiration in other areas of Community law.

42. Second, the conditions under which the State may incur liability for damage caused to individuals by a breach of Community law cannot, in the absence of particular justification, differ from those governing the liability of the Community in like circumstances. The protection of the rights which individuals derive from Community law cannot vary depending on whether a national authority or a Community authority is responsible for the damage.

43. The system of rules which the Court has worked out with regard to Article [340 TFEU], particularly in relation to liability for legislative measures, takes into account, inter alia, the complexity of the situations to be regulated, difficulties in the application or interpretation of the texts and, more particularly, the margin of discretion available to the author of the act in question.

44. Thus, in developing its case law on the non-contractual liability of the Community, in particular as regards legislative measures involving choices of economic policy, the Court has had regard to the wide discretion available to the institutions in implementing Community policies.

45. The strict approach taken towards the liability of the Community in the exercise of its legislative activities is due to two considerations. First, even where the legality of measures is subject to judicial review, exercise of the legislative function must not be hindered by the prospect of actions for damages whenever the general interest of the Community requires legislative measures to be adopted which may adversely affect individual interests. Second, in a legislative context characterised by the exercise of a wide discretion, which is essential for implementing a Community policy, the Community cannot incur liability unless the institution concerned has manifestly and gravely disregarded the limits on the exercise of its powers ...

46. That said, the national legislature – like the Community institutions – does not systematically have a wide discretion when it acts in a field governed by Community law. Community law may impose upon it obligations to achieve a particular result or obligations to act or refrain from acting which reduce its margin of discretion, sometimes to a considerable degree. This is so, for instance, where, as in the circumstances to which the judgment in *Francovich* relates, Article [288 TFEU] places the Member State under an obligation to take, within a given period, all the measures needed in order to achieve the result required by a directive. In such a case, the fact that it is for the national legislature to take the necessary measures has no bearing on the member State's liability for failing to transpose the directive.

47. In contrast, where a Member State acts in a field where it has a wide discretion, comparable to that of the Community institutions in implementing Community policies, the conditions under which it may incur liability must, in principle, be the same as those under which the Community institutions incur liability in a comparable situation.

48. In the case which gave rise to the reference in Case C-46/93, the German legislature had legislated in the field of foodstuffs, specifically beer. In the absence of Community harmonization, the national legislature had a wide discretion in that sphere in laying down rules on the quality of beer put on the market.

49. As regards the facts of Case C-48/93, the United Kingdom legislature also had a wide discretion. The legislation at issue was concerned, first, with the registration of vessels, a field which, in view of the state of development of Community law, falls within the jurisdiction of the Member States and, secondly, with regulating fishing, a sector in which implementation of the common fisheries policy leaves a margin of discretion to the Member States.

50. Consequently, in each case the German and United Kingdom legislatures were faced with situations involving choices comparable to those made by the Community institutions when they adopt legislative measures pursuant to a Community policy.

51. In such circumstances, Community law confers a right to reparation where three conditions are met: the rule of law infringed must be intended to confer rights on individuals; the breach must be sufficiently serious; and there must be a direct causal link between the breach of the obligation resting on the State and the damage sustained by the injured parties...

54. The first condition is manifestly satisfied in the case of Article [34 TFEU], the relevant provision in Case C-46/93, and in the case of Article [49 TFEU], the relevant provision in Case C-48/93 ...

55. As to the second condition, as regards both Community liability under Article [340 TFEU] and Member State liability for breaches of Community law, the decisive test for finding that a breach of Community law is sufficiently serious is whether the Member State or the Community institution concerned manifestly and gravely disregarded the limits of its discretion.

56. The factors which the competent court may take into consideration include the clarity and precision of the rule breached, the measure of discretion left by that rule to the national or Community authorities, whether the infringement and the damage caused was intentional or involuntary, whether any error of law was excusable or inexcusable, the fact that the position taken by a Community institution may have contributed towards the omission, and the adoption or retention of national measures or practices contrary to Community law.

57. On any view, a breach of Community law will clearly be sufficiently serious if it has persisted despite a judgment finding the infringement in question to be established, or a preliminary ruling or settled case law of the Court on the matter from which it is clear that the conduct in question constituted an infringement...

65. As for the third condition, it is for the national courts to determine whether there is a direct causal link between the breach of the obligation borne by the State and the damage sustained by the injured parties.

67. As appears from ... *Francovich*, subject to the right to reparation which flows directly from Community law where the conditions referred to in the preceding paragraph are satisfied, the State must make reparation for the consequences of the loss and damage caused in accordance with the domestic rules on liability, provided that the conditions for reparation of loss and damage laid down by national law must not be less favourable than those relating to similar domestic claims and must not be such as in practice to make it impossible or excessively difficult to obtain reparation ...

82. Reparation for loss or damage caused to individuals as a result of breaches of Community law must be commensurate with the loss or damage sustained so as to ensure the effective protection for their rights.

83. In the absence of relevant Community provisions, it is for the domestic legal system of each Member State to set the criteria for determining the extent of reparation. However, those criteria must not be less favourable than those applying to similar claims based on domestic law and must not be such as in practice to make it impossible or excessively difficult to obtain reparation.

The Court's judgment suggests a distinction between contexts where Member States have some discretion and contexts where they do not. In the latter contexts, three criteria must be met for liability:

- the provision must be intended to confer rights on individuals;
- the breach must be sufficiently serious; and
- there must be a direct causal link between the breach of the obligation resting on the state and the damage sustained by the injured parties. In the former contexts, there is no

requirement for the breach to be sufficiently serious. It suffices that the provision be intended to confer rights and that there be a causal link between the breach of EU law and the individual damage sustained.

Yet, in determining whether a breach is sufficiently serious to justify liability, the Court will look at the degree of discretion afforded by EU law. If there is little or no discretion, the Court will treat the breach as sufficiently serious to incur liability. This has led to the categories being fluid in recent years. It appears Member States will be deemed to have no discretion where they fail to transpose a Directive in any way at all.[107] In recent years, the Court has indicated these are not the only circumstances. In *AGM-COS.MET*, the Court held that a failure by the Finnish government to let machines, which complied with EU law, onto its market, led to liability without the need to consider the question of the seriousness of the breach. This was because the relevant EU Directive contained a market access clause requiring the machines to be allowed to be marketed, and this gave the Member States no discretion.[108] By contrast, in *Synthon*, the British government was held liable for refusing to recognise the marketing authorisation of a drug certified by the Dutch authorities on the ground that the breach was a sufficiently serious one.[109] It was held that it was sufficiently serious as the provision allowed states no discretion to refuse mutual recognition unless they followed a special procedure which had not been invoked by the British government in that case.

In such circumstances, it makes more sense to consider the precise circumstances when liability will be found. *Francovich* and *Brasserie du Pêcheur* suggest three circumstances where liability will be easily found. These are:

- a complete failure to transpose a Directive;
- breach of an order of the Court of Justice;
- breach of settled case law.

There are a whole host of other circumstances where liability might be incurred.[110] These include breach of an EU legal norm; breach of case law that is not completely settled; and inadequate transposition of or compliance with a Directive. In all these circumstances, the Court looks at the clarity of the provision or law. If it was reasonably capable of bearing the meaning understood by the Member State[111] or if there is no consensus as to the meaning of the provision, then no liability will be found.[112] In short, liability occurs only when Member States are breaching EU law in a manner that must be obvious to them and one which leaves little room for doubt. State liability is thus a backstop measure. It is there to penalise the very wayward state rather than to be concerned with redress for litigants. For, if it were the latter, there would be little justification for such a restrictive test. This, in turn, raises an important question: is it really for the Court of Justice to decide whether punitive measures should be attached to the Treaty?

---

[107] Joined Cases C-6/90 and C-9/90 *Francovich and Bonifaci v Italy* [1991] ECR I-5357.
[108] Case C-470/03 *AGM-COS.MET Srl v Suomen valtio and Tarmo Lehtinen* [2007] ECR I-2749.
[109] Case C-452/06 *R v Licensing Authority of the Department of Health, ex parte Synthon* [2008] ECR I-7681.
[110] For a discussion of the cases following *Brasserie du Pêcheur* see T. Tridimas, 'Liability for Breach of Community Law: Growing Up and Mellowing Down?' (2001) 38 *CMLRev.* 301, 310.
[111] Case C-392/93 *R v HM Treasury, ex parte British Telecommunications* [1996] ECR I-1631.
[112] Case C-278/05 *Robins v Secretary of State for Work and Pensions* [2007] ECR I-1053.

(iii) Liability of judicial institutions

Brasserie du Pêcheur indicated that states were liable for acts of all public institutions. This has led to arguably the most interesting and certainly the most challenging dimension to state liability, liability for rulings by national courts. This arose in *Köbler* v *Austria*.[113] Köbler was a professor employed in an Austrian university. Part of his salary was based on length of service, but periods of employment in universities in Member States other than Austria did not count towards this aspect of his salary. The Austrian Administrative Court initially decided to refer the matter to the Court of Justice, but then withdrew the reference on the grounds that the matter had already been decided by the Court, which had ruled it lawful.[114] Köbler brought an action in damages, arguing that the state was liable in respect of the court's ruling on the grounds that it failed to refer the matter when obliged to do so and had given an erroneous ruling. The Court of Justice agreed that the measure violated Article 45 TFEU on freedom of movement of workers. It considered whether this gave grounds for liability.

Case C-224/01 *Köbler* v *Austria* [2003] ECR I-239

33. In the light of the essential role played by the judiciary in the protection of the rights derived by individuals from Community rules, the full effectiveness of those rules would be called in question and the protection of those rights would be weakened if individuals were precluded from being able, under certain conditions, to obtain reparation when their rights are affected by an infringement of Community law attributable to a decision of a court of a Member State adjudicating at last instance.

34. It must be stressed, in that context, that a court adjudicating at last instance is by definition the last judicial body before which individuals may assert the rights conferred on them by Community law. Since an infringement of those rights by a final decision of such a court cannot thereafter normally be corrected, individuals cannot be deprived of the possibility of rendering the State liable in order in that way to obtain legal protection of their rights.

35. Moreover, it is, in particular, in order to prevent rights conferred on individuals by Community law from being infringed that under the third paragraph of Article [267 TFEU] a court against whose decisions there is no judicial remedy under national law is required to make a reference to the Court of Justice.

36. Consequently, it follows from the requirements inherent in the protection of the rights of individuals relying on Community law that they must have the possibility of obtaining redress in the national courts for the damage caused by the infringement of those rights owing to a decision of a court adjudicating at last instance ...

37. Certain of the governments which submitted observations in these proceedings claimed that the principle of State liability for damage caused to individuals by infringements of Community law could not be applied to decisions of a national court adjudicating at last instance. In that connection arguments were put forward based, in particular, on the principle of legal certainty and, more specifically, the principle of *res judicata*, the independence and authority of the judiciary and the absence of a court competent to determine disputes relating to State liability for such decisions.

38. In that regard the importance of the principle of *res judicata* cannot be disputed ... In order to ensure both stability of the law and legal relations and the sound administration of justice, it is important that

---

[113] P. Wattel, '*Köbler, CILFIT* and *Welthgrove*: We Can't Go on Meeting Like This' (2004) 41 *CMLRev.* 177.

[114] The Austrian court sought to rely on the Court of Justice's ruling in Case C-15/96 *Schöning-Kougebetopoulou* [1998] ECR I-47.

judicial decisions which have become definitive after all rights of appeal have been exhausted or after expiry of the time-limits provided for in that connection can no longer be called in question.

39. However, it should be borne in mind that recognition of the principle of State liability for a decision of a court adjudicating at last instance does not in itself have the consequence of calling in question that decision as *res judicata*. Proceedings seeking to render the State liable do not have the same purpose and do not necessarily involve the same parties as the proceedings resulting in the decision which has acquired the status of *res judicata*. The applicant in an action to establish the liability of the State will, if successful, secure an order against it for reparation of the damage incurred but not necessarily a declaration invalidating the status of *res judicata* of the judicial decision which was responsible for the damage. In any event, the principle of State liability inherent in the Community legal order requires such reparation, but not revision of the judicial decision which was responsible for the damage.

40. It follows that the principle of *res judicata* does not preclude recognition of the principle of State liability for the decision of a court adjudicating at last instance.

41. Nor can the arguments based on the independence and authority of the judiciary be upheld.

42. As to the independence of the judiciary, the principle of liability in question concerns not the personal liability of the judge but that of the State. The possibility that under certain conditions the State may be rendered liable for judicial decisions contrary to Community law does not appear to entail any particular risk that the independence of a court adjudicating at last instance will be called in question.

43. As to the argument based on the risk of a diminution of the authority of a court adjudicating at last instance owing to the fact that its final decisions could by implication be called in question in proceedings in which the State may be rendered liable for such decisions, the existence of a right of action that affords, under certain conditions, reparation of the injurious effects of an erroneous judicial decision could also be regarded as enhancing the quality of a legal system and thus in the long run the authority of the judiciary.

44. Several governments also argued that application of the principle of State liability to decisions of a national court adjudicating at last instance was precluded by the difficulty of designating a court competent to determine disputes concerning the reparation of damage resulting from such decisions.

45. In that connection, given that, for reasons essentially connected with the need to secure for individuals protection of the rights conferred on them by Community rules, the principle of State liability inherent in the Community legal order must apply in regard to decisions of a national court adjudicating at last instance, it is for the Member States to enable those affected to rely on that principle by affording them an appropriate right of action. Application of that principle cannot be compromised by the absence of a competent court ...

51. As to the conditions to be satisfied for a Member State to be required to make reparation for loss and damage caused to individuals as a result of breaches of Community law for which the State is responsible, the Court has held that these are threefold: the rule of law infringed must be intended to confer rights on individuals; the breach must be sufficiently serious; and there must be a direct causal link between the breach of the obligation incumbent on the State and the loss or damage sustained by the injured parties ...

52. State liability for loss or damage caused by a decision of a national court adjudicating at last instance which infringes a rule of Community law is governed by the same conditions.

53. With regard more particularly to the second of those conditions and its application with a view to establishing possible State liability owing to a decision of a national court adjudicating at last instance, regard must be had to the specific nature of the judicial function and to the legitimate requirements of legal certainty, as the Member States which submitted observations in this case have also contended. State liability for an infringement of Community law by a decision of a national court adjudicating at

last instance can be incurred only in the exceptional case where the court has manifestly infringed the applicable law.

54. In order to determine whether that condition is satisfied, the national court hearing a claim for reparation must take account of all the factors which characterise the situation put before it.

55. Those factors include, in particular, the degree of clarity and precision of the rule infringed, whether the infringement was intentional, whether the error of law was excusable or inexcusable, the position taken, where applicable, by a Community institution and non-compliance by the court in question with its obligation to make a reference for a preliminary ruling under [Article 267(3) TFEU].

56. In any event, an infringement of Community law will be sufficiently serious where the decision concerned was made in manifest breach of the case law of the Court in the matter ...

122. Community law does not expressly cover the point whether a measure for rewarding an employee's loyalty to his employer, such as a loyalty bonus, which entails an obstacle to freedom of movement for workers, can be justified and thus be in conformity with Community law. No reply was to be found to that question in the Court's case law. Nor, moreover, was that reply obvious.

123. In the second place, the fact that the national court in question ought to have maintained its request for a preliminary ruling ... is not of such a nature as to invalidate that conclusion. In the present case the Verwaltungsgerichtshof had decided to withdraw the request for a preliminary ruling, on the view that the reply to the question of Community law to be resolved had already been given in the judgment in *Schöning-Kougebetopoulou* ...Thus, it was owing to its incorrect reading of that judgment that the Verwaltungsgerichtshof no longer considered it necessary to refer that question of interpretation to the Court.

124. In those circumstances and in the light of the circumstances of the case, the infringement ... cannot be regarded as being manifest in nature and thus as sufficiently serious.

At the time, only Spain and Austria has systems of liability for judicial decisions in place. As illustrated below, the judgment raised questions about legal certainty and traditional judicial hierarchies.

H. Scott and N. Barber, 'State Liability under *Francovich* for Decisions of National Courts' (2004) 120 *Law Quarterly Review* 403, 404–5

The extension of *Francovich* liability to courts of final decision has profound implications for the domestic legal hierarchy. After *Köbler* the English High Court could find itself compelled to pass judgment on a decision of the English House of Lords. A litigant disappointed by the House of Lords' decision could start a fresh action against the United Kingdom. The High Court, a few months later, would then be called on to assess whether the House of Lords had made an error of law that was sufficiently serious to warrant damages. The High Court would, almost certainly, refer the question to the ECJ under Article [267 TFEU] if it thought there was any doubt as to the correctness of the Lords' ruling. In response to such a reference the ECJ would give a ruling on the content of European law ...

This prospect raises a number of problems for domestic legal systems. First, and most superficially, it reduces legal certainty. This is not, as some in *Köbler* tried to argue, because it allows the reopening of concluded cases. Once the State's highest court has ruled, the judgment is definitive between the parties and cannot be challenged; the principle of *res judicata* is not affected. The *Francovich* action is a separate legal right and is directed against the State; a body which, ordinarily, would not have been a party to the original action. However, *Köbler* does have the effect of allowing litigants a second chance to raise the legal question apparently resolved in the primary action: frustrated in the House of Lords, the litigant could re-start the process through *Francovich* in the High Court. Secondly, the decision upsets the domestic legal hierarchy. The High Court would be obliged to question the correctness of a decision of the House of Lords made a few months earlier: it would have to decide whether there was a sufficient chance of error to warrant a reference to the ECJ, and, when this ruling was returned, how severe the error had been. Further problems might arise as this secondary action progressed up the legal order, perhaps ending with one group of Law Lords ruling on the judgment of their colleagues. Thirdly, the decision has the potential to create serious constitutional conflict within the domestic legal order. The German Constitutional Court has ruled that in exceptional cases it might refuse to accept rulings of the ECJ (see *Brunner* [1994] 1 CMLR 57). If such a decision was then challenged under *Francovich*, a first instance judge might be forced to choose between loyalty to the final court of appeal and to the ECJ.

Köbler was challenged in *Traghetti*.[115] The Italian Court of Cassation, the top civil court, had ruled in a dispute between ferry operators that a subsidy granted to a ferry operation did not violate EU law on state aids as it followed the Court of Justice's settled case law. Traghetti, the ferry operator bringing the proceedings, had meanwhile gone into liquidation. Its administrator considered that the Court of Cassation had misapplied the law and brought an action for damages. However, Italian law excluded liability for damage where any infringement was the result of a court of last instance's interpretation of the law or assessment of the facts and evidence. The Court of Justice reiterated that the *Köbler* judgment applied to all courts, including courts of last instance, and that it applied not just to refusals to apply EU law but also to poor interpretations of EU law. This raised the question of what was the basis of such liability: was there a requirement for intentional fault and serious misconduct on the part of the court or was it sufficient that it was incompetent?

Case C-173/03 *Traghetti del Mediterraneo* v *Italy* [2006] ECR I-5177

42. With regard, finally, to the limitation of State liability to cases of intentional fault and serious misconduct on the part of the court, it should be recalled ... that the Court held, in the *Köbler* judgment, that State liability for damage caused to individuals by reason of an infringement of Community law attributable to a national court adjudicating at last instance could be incurred in the exceptional case where that court manifestly infringed the applicable law.

43. Such manifest infringement is to be assessed, inter alia, in the light of a number of criteria, such as the degree of clarity and precision of the rule infringed, whether the infringement was intentional, whether the error of law was excusable or inexcusable, and the non-compliance by the court in question with its obligation to make a reference for a preliminary ruling under the third paragraph of Article [267 TFEU]; it is in any event presumed where the decision involved is made in manifest disregard of the case law of the Court on the subject ...

44. Accordingly, although it remains possible for national law to define the criteria relating to the nature or degree of the infringement which must be met before State liability can be incurred for an infringement of Community law attributable to a national court adjudicating at last instance, under no circumstances may such criteria impose requirements stricter than that of a manifest infringement of the applicable law ...

[115] D. Nassimpian, ' ... And We Keep on Meeting: (De)fragmenting State Liability' (2007) 32 *ELRev.* 819.

Aside from reaffirming *Köbler, Traghetti* indicates liability is to be determined on the basis of a competence-based rather than fault-based test. It will be incurred not merely where a national court of last resort deliberately flouts EU law, but also where it fails to interpret EU law in the manner that one would expect of a reasonable court. To be sure, it is too simplistic to argue the test is merely one of whether a court could reasonably have come to the interpretation it did, and if not then the state is liable for damages. Yet, the test, namely whether the interpretation was manifestly inappropriate, is not so different from the standard applied to the notionally competent court. The relevant question would then be how far the national court must fall below that standard in order to attract state liability.[116] On this basis, an action for state liability may involve an action before a court of first instance attacking the most senior court in the land for behaving not just incompetently but very incompetently! This raises all kinds of questions about conflict of interest and about the actual competence of the junior court to hear the action. More structurally, there is the question of whether fining states is the best way to go about improving weak, often poorly funded judiciaries.

8 DRAWING THE THREADS TOGETHER

As mentioned at the beginning of this chapter, this field sits atop two tectonic plates. On the one hand, there is the logic of competing legal orders. This pushes for the primacy of EU law but acknowledges the autonomy of local legal orders, the sensitivities involved, and the difficulties of imposing uniform and centralised solutions. On the other, there is the logic of individual rights which pushes for the full protection of individual entitlements. If, at any moment, most notably over Directives but also over the question of remedies, one of these logics prevails, the other re-emerges through the establishment of a new doctrine.

Further uncertainty has been added by the Lisbon Treaty, which questions whether the balance needs to be readdressed with the introduction of the following provision.

Article 19(1) TEU

Member States shall provide remedies sufficient to ensure effective legal protection in the fields covered by Union law.

On the one hand, the appearance of this provision is that of a codifying provision. It seems to ask no more of Member States than the current case law, namely that they give effective protection to EU rights. In that sense, you might expect it to be no more than a rearticulation of existing case law. On the other hand, it might be thought that if a new provision is added, there has to be a reason for this. This reason might be to emphasise a stronger idea of effectiveness, in which the need for remedies is made more salient as a position of EU law, and in which a tighter, more overarching link is made between the grant of rights and the provision of remedies. It might be (and we cannot yet know) that it effects a revolution in which the logic of rights is made to prevail over that of the balance of legal orders.

---

[116] The general view is that the standard is quite low and that liability will be found only in exceptional cases.
B. Beutler, 'State Liability for Breaches of Community Law by National Courts: Is the Requirement of a Manifest Infringement of the Applicable Law an Insurmountable Obstacle?' (2009) 46 *CMLRev.* 773.

T. Eilmansberger, 'The Relationship Between Rights and Remedies in EC Law: In Search of the Missing Link' (2004) 41 *Common Market Law Review* 1199, 1238–9

The characteristic feature of an *absolute* subjective right is the imposition of an obligation on everybody to abstain from any acts considered to interfere with that right. The types of rights primarily of interest in the Community law context are more '*relative*' in nature, meaning that they create specific obligations between certain persons. These obligations, and corresponding rights, notably comprise (i) obligations to perform in a certain way (e.g. obligations to provide certain services, grant specific benefits, or effect equal treatment), furthermore (ii) (secondary) obligations to make good damage or restitute assets received without valid title, and, finally, (iii) obligations to abstain from certain conduct including the commitment of delicts.

With regard to remedies, the decisive point now is this: if the legal obligation making up the right is established in a clear and unequivocal manner, the necessary remedy for the protection of this right is equally apparent. This is so because this obligation can be directly translated into (or actually constitutes) a concrete claim. Such 'claim rights', in other words, automatically imply the appropriate remedy and cause of action required for its enforcement. Thus, once it is established that a private actor or the State is under an obligation towards certain persons to make good harm caused by illegal conduct, to repay money collected though not being due, or to abstain from or to commit certain acts, it follows that the beneficiaries have according rights, or to be more precise, claims. These claims to compensation, repayment or abstainment also constitute the respective components of these remedies. These remedies have a procedural component as well in that they represent the claims in a legally enforceable form, i.e. in a form which allows its enforcement by a (national) court. If the claim-right and resulting remedy is established by Community law, the division of labour between Community law and national law in the enforcement of individual rights becomes, in principle, clear. Exclusively Community law determines the existence of the remedy. National law would have a merely auxiliary function. It would designate the competent courts to adjudicate the substantive claims in question and provide the appropriate procedural framework.

FURTHER READING

G. Betlem, 'The Doctrine of Consistent Interpretation: Managing Legal Uncertainty' (2002) 22 *Oxford Journal of Legal Studies* 397

B. Beutler, 'State Liability for Breaches of Community Law by National Courts: Is the Requirement of a Manifest Infringement of the Applicable Law an Insurmountable Obstacle?' (2009) 46 *Common Market Law Review* 773

P. Craig, 'The Legal Effects of Directives: Policy Rules and Exceptions' (2009) 34 *European Law Review* 349

A. Dashwood, 'From *Van Duyn* to *Mangold* via *Marshall*: Reducing Direct Effect to Absurdity?' (2006–07) 9 *Cambridge Yearbook of European Legal Studies* 81

M. Dougan, *National Remedies Before the Court of Justice* (Oxford, Hart, 2005)
'When Worlds Collide: Competing Visions of the Relationship Between Direct Effect and Supremacy' (2007) 44 *Common Market Law Review* 931

S. Drake, 'Twenty Years After *Von Colson*: The Impact of "Indirect Effect" on the Protection of the Individual's Community Rights' (2005) 30 *European Law Review* 329

W. van Gerven, 'Bridging the Unbridgeable: Community and National Tort Laws After *Francovich* and *Brasserie*' (1996) 45 *International and Comparative Law Quarterly* 507

M.-P. Granger, '*Francovich* and the Construction of a European Administrative *ius commune*' (2007) 32 *European Law Review* 157

K. Lenaerts and T. Corthaut, 'Of Birds and Hedges: The Role of Primacy in Invoking Norms of EU Law' (2006) 31 *European Law Review* 287

S. Prechal, *Directives in EC Law* (2nd edn, Oxford, Oxford University Press, 2005)

J. Tallberg, 'Supranational Influence in EU Enforcement: the ECJ and the Principle of State Liability' (2000) 7 *Journal of European Public Policy* 104

8

Infringement Proceedings

CONTENTS

1 INTRODUCTION

This chapter considers the infringement proceedings that the Commission may bring against Member States for failure by the latter to comply with EU law. It is organised as follows.

Section 2 considers the main features of the infringement proceedings set out in Articles 258 to 260 TFEU. The central provision is Article 258 TFEU and it allows the Commission to take the Member State to the Court of Justice and to obtain a ruling that it has failed to comply with EU law. The roles of such proceedings are threefold: to secure the rule of EU law; as a public policy instrument to contribute to the effective functioning of EU policies; and as a public law arena, in which the different interests of the EU institutions, Member States, complainants and

EU citizens can be mediated. All three roles are important and there is a danger in overemphasising any one.

Section 3 considers the scope of Member States' responsibilities under Article 258 TFEU. Actions can be brought only against the state, but they can be brought for the failure of any state agency, including courts and local and regional government, even if it is constitutionally independent of the central government which is, in practice, the body against whom the action is taken. The state is also responsible not just for legal instruments that conflict with EU law but also administrative practices that conflict with EU law. These usually have to be general and consistent in nature to attract liability. The state is finally under a duty to secure and police the effective functioning of EU law, and will be held liable for a failure to do so.

Section 4 considers the stages of the Article 258 TFEU procedure. This will be begun following either a Commission investigation or, more often, a complaint by a third party. The procedure is a seven stage one, designed to give the Member State plenty of time to comply and plenty of scope for submitting observations on the Commission's complaint. Typically, it takes close to two years to complete. However, the overwhelming majority of cases are settled at the first stage where the Commission sends an informal letter to the Member State concerned. In addition, there are now moves to ascertain, where the procedure derives from a complaint, whether the complaint can be mediated between the complainant and the Member State without the Commission needing to be involved.

Section 5 considers the responsibilities and discretion of the Commission in the process. The Commission has complete freedom to decide whether to start the proceedings or to cease them. This has raised concerns about transparency, insufficiently rigorous prosecution by the Commission of EU law and, above all, exclusion of the complainant from the process. Following repeated criticism by the European Ombudsman, the Commission adopted a Communication in 2002, which grants the complainant some modest procedural guarantees. Centrally, there is a commitment to keep the complainant informed about the process and to reach a decision about whether to close a file or to instigate proceedings within twelve months.

Section 6 considers the sanctions that may be imposed. Following the Lisbon Treaty, the Court of Justice may impose a fine on the Member State under Article 258 TFEU where the proceedings concern a failure by the Member State to communicate national transposition of a Directive. For all other infringements, a second proceeding under Article 260 TFEU must be instigated. The Court may impose two types of fine. The lump sum penalises the state for non-compliance with the original judgment given under Article 258 TFEU. The penalty payment is calculated at a daily rate and is to induce the state to comply with the subsequent judgment given under Article 260 TFEU. The size of the fine is determined by the duration of the infringement, its seriousness and the capacity of the state to pay. Important guidelines were set out in a 2005 Commission Communication, although this does not bind the Court. In all cases, both the Commission and the Court will additionally look at what is needed to secure compliance and the overall proportionality of the sanction.

2 THE DIFFERENT ROLES OF INFRINGEMENT PROCEEDINGS

The enforcement of EU law through the assertion of individual rights before national courts discussed in the previous chapter is an important and distinctive feature of EU law. However, the enforcement of the EU legal order here is only seen as a byproduct of the assertion of individual rights. The primary focus is to secure individual redress and the question of enforcement is tailored around this. The judgment might thus address only some features of the illegality. The status of the Court of Justice might mean that its rulings are not binding or even persuasive for other courts in that state, and they will certainly not bind courts in other Member States. Most importantly, the EU law in question must give rise to rights and somebody must be willing to litigate those rights. If it does not, there can be no enforcement. As we saw, only a very small proportion of EU law is litigated regularly in national courts.[1]

With that in mind, it is worth turning our attention to the centralised procedures that exist for the enforcement of EU law against the Member States: the bodies that have the most extensive responsibilities for the administration of EU law in the Union. The principal procedures are set out in Article 258 TFEU.

Article 258 TFEU

If the Commission considers that a Member State has failed to fulfil an obligation under the Treaties, it shall deliver a reasoned opinion on the matter after giving the State concerned the opportunity to submit its observations.

If the State concerned does not comply with the opinion within the period laid down by the Commission, the latter may bring the matter before the Court of Justice of the European Union.

There are a number of other provisions which allow legal proceedings to be brought against Member States for breaches of EU law. Article 259 TFEU allows Member States to take other Member States before the Court of Justice for failure to comply with EU law. Its use has been rare, Member States preferring to leave it to the Commission to take action rather than to institute legal proceedings themselves.[2] Article 108(2) TFEU allows legal proceedings to be brought against Member States for breach of the EU law provisions on state aids. However, it is Article 258 TFEU which plays the central role. At the end of 2007, the Commission was looking at 3,400 cases under it.[3] In 2008 alone, the Commission filed 207 cases. Except for Bulgaria and Romania, actions were brought in that year against all states other than Denmark and Latvia.[4] The actions also cover all sectors of EU law. In its 2008 report, the Commission reported that it had to police the Treaties, 10,000 Regulations and over 1,700 Directives under the procedure. It was active in most sectors of EU activity:

> There continues to be a significant complaints and infringements case-load in environment, internal market, taxation and customs union, energy, transport and employment, social affairs and equal opportunities as well as health and consumer affairs and justice, freedom and security, with a rapidly increasing body of legislation of high interest to citizens.[5]

---

[1] See p. 157.

[2] Examples are rare. See Case 141/78 *France* v *United Kingdom* [1979] ECR 2923; Case C-388/95 *Belgium* v *Spain* [2000] ECR I-3123; Case C-145/04 *Spain* v *United Kingdom* [2006] ECR I-7917.

[3] European Commission, *25th Annual Report from the Commission on the Monitoring of Community Law*, COM (2008)777, 3.

[4] Court of Justice, *Annual Report for 2008* (Luxembourg, Court of Justice, 2009) 85–6. Bulgaria and Romania having only just acceded to the Union, there had not yet been time to consider whether there had been any infringements by them.

[5] See above n. 3, 2–3.

The use of Article 258 TFEU is wide-ranging and significant but its place within the architecture of EU law is far from settled. There are a number of different perspectives on the role it serves within the EU institutional settlement. Before going on to consider its legal dynamics, it is worth considering these perspectives not only for their own sake but because they shape analysis of the minutiae of the procedures themselves.

(i) Article 258 TFEU and the rule of law

The first view of Article 258 TFEU is that it is the procedure through which the Commission exercises its role as guardian of the Treaties. It is a policing procedure to secure the rule of EU law within the European Union. This is the view expressed in much legal scholarship.[6] As we shall see in the judgment below, it is also the view of the Court of Justice. In *Commission v Germany*, the government of Lower Saxony concluded a contract for the collection of waste water which broke EU law on public procurement. The German government admitted it violated EU law but stated that the contract could not be terminated without payment of substantial compensation to the contractor. The Commission brought the infringement before the Court. The German government argued that it was inadmissible as there was no good reason for the Commission's action. It had admitted its guilt and the payment of compensation was disproportionately large when put next to the benefits of securing the EU law in question.[7]

Joined Cases C-20/01 and C-28/01 *Commission v Germany* [2003] ECR I-3609

29. ... in exercising its powers under Article [258 TFEU] the Commission does not have to show that there is a specific interest in bringing an action. The provision is not intended to protect the Commission's own rights. The Commission's function, in the general interest of the Community, is to ensure that the Member States give effect to the Treaty and the provisions adopted by the institutions thereunder and to obtain a declaration of any failure to fulfil the obligations deriving therefrom with a view to bringing it to an end.

30. Given its role as guardian of the Treaty, the Commission alone is therefore competent to decide whether it is appropriate to bring proceedings against a Member State for failure to fulfil its obligations and to determine the conduct or omission attributable to the Member State concerned on the basis of which those proceedings should be brought. It may therefore ask the Court to find that, in not having achieved, in a specific case, the result intended by the directive, a Member State has failed to fulfil its obligations ...

41. The Court has already held that it is responsible for determining whether or not the alleged breach of obligations exists, even if the State concerned no longer denies the breach and recognises that any individuals who have suffered damage because of it have a right to compensation ...

42. Since the finding of failure by a Member State to fulfil its obligations is not bound up with a finding as to the damage flowing therefrom ... the Federal Republic of Germany may not rely on the fact that no third party has suffered damage ...

44. In the light of the foregoing, the actions brought by the Commission must be held to be admissible.

---

[6] A. Evans, 'The Enforcement Procedure of Article 169 EEC: Commission Discretion' (1979) 4 *ELRev.* 442; A. Dashwood and R. White, 'Enforcement Actions under Article 169 and 170 EEC' (1989) 14 *ELRev.* 388. For a differentiated account that still falls within this school see A. Gil Ibañez, *The Administrative Supervision and Enforcement of EC Law, Powers, Procedures and Limits* (Oxford and Portland, Hart, 1999) especially 26–35.

[7] For similar reasoning see Case C-76/08 *Commission v Malta*, Judgment of 10 September 2009.

The securing of the rule of law is an important function. As was stated above, Article 258 TFEU is the only institutional mechanism that gives practical legal support to many fields of EU law. It also has the advantage that it is, potentially at least, quite an egalitarian mechanism. The Commission, not private parties, bears the cost of litigation. It can therefore act for those who do not have resources or do not have standing, and also in cases where particularly large numbers of legal interests are adversely affected. There are, however, reservations to adopting such a view wholeheartedly.

First, conceiving the procedure in these terms is overly dogmatic. It can be excessively doctrinaire in individual cases. *Commission* v *Germany* is a case in point. The German government argued that there was no practical way for them to rescind the contract: it would violate individuals' property rights; it would disrupt construction of the waste water system as everything would have to be restarted; it would lead to the public authorities having to pay large amounts of compensation. The German government did not implement the judgment. It was then successfully prosecuted by the Commission under Article 260 TFEU and, finally, rescinded the contract.[8] The problems still remained, however.

There is a second danger. Protecting the rule of law is valuable. It is not, however, an exclusive value. There are other values that may sometimes have to be weighed against it, particularly as in most cases we are not talking here about 'law' or 'no law' but rather 'EU law' or 'national law'. This is not just an ethical question but also a problem of mischaracterising the procedure. As *Commission* v *Germany* indicates, the Commission has a discretion whether or not to prosecute. The presence of that discretion indicates that other values and considerations can be taken into account by the Commission. As Börzel has noted, the mission of Article 258 TFEU is to consider whether 'the observed level of non-compliance is considered as a serious problem for a community'.[9] The rule of law analysis treats this process as a black box, and this is questionable given its centrality in the process.

Thirdly, the analysis misdescribes the law. Article 258 TFEU does not permit the Commission to seek to secure 100 per cent compliance with EU law 100 per cent of the time. There seems to be a threshold of illegality where the breach must be of a certain gravity before proceedings can be launched. The Court of Justice has been far from clear on the level of this threshold. In a number of cases, it has intimated that the Commission may initiate proceedings against a Member State for violation of EU law even in a specific case.[10] The cases in which this has happened have all concerned residence or expulsion of non-nationals,[11] or public procurement. [12] The former often have particular civil liberties concerns, while the latter involve significant purchases whose tenders are necessarily very specific and in which it is difficult to look for a general practice. More often, the Court will find that the Commission may only bring an action if either the national law conflicts with EU law or there is a general and consistent administrative practice breaching EU law.

---

[8] Case C-503/04 *Commission* v *Germany* [2007] ECR I-6153.

[9] T. Börzel, 'Non Compliance in the European Union: Pathology or Statistical Artefact?' (2001) 8 *JEPP* 803, 818.

[10] Case C-441/02 *Commission* v *Germany* [2006] ECR I-3449; Case C-157/03 *Commission* v *Spain* [2005] ECR I-2911.

[11] See, in addition to the cases cited above n. 10, Case C-503/03 *Commission* v *Spain* [2006] ECR I-1097.

[12] Joined Cases C-20/01 and C-28/01 *Commission* v *Germany* [2003] ECR I-3609 is an example of the latter category.

In *Commission* v *Greece*, the Commission brought an action against Greece on the ground that its hospitals, in their tendering procedures for medical devices, were excluding devices that met EU law and standards. The Greek government claimed that it had transposed the relevant Directives into EU law and that it had sent a circular to Greek hospitals reminding them of their obligations under EU law. The Court nevertheless found a breach of EU law.

Case C–489/06 *Commission* v *Greece*, Judgment of 19 March 2009

46. ... even if the applicable national legislation itself complies with Community law, a failure to fulfil obligations may arise due to the existence of an administrative practice which infringes that law ...

48. In order for a failure to fulfil obligations to be found on the basis of the administrative practice followed in a Member State, the Court has held that the failure to fulfil obligations can be established only by means of sufficiently documented and detailed proof of the alleged practice; that administrative practice must be, to some degree, of a consistent and general nature; and, in order to find that there has been a general and consistent practice, the Commission may not rely on any presumption ...

49. It must be pointed out that, according to the information in the file before the Court, the products in question are products fulfilling the requirements of the European Pharmacopoeia technical standard and must, by their very nature, be purchased repeatedly and regularly by hospitals and, consequently, with an established degree of regularity.

50. None the less, at least 16 hospital contracting authorities rejected the medical devices in question, during tendering procedures, including the hospitals of Komotiní, Messolonghi, Agios Nikolaos of Crete, Venizeleio-Pananeio of Heraklion, Attica, Agios Savvas, Elpis, Argos, Korgialenio-Benakio, Geniko Nosokomio of Kalamata, Nauplie, P. & A. Kyriakou, Sparta, Panakardiko of Tripoli, Elena Venizelou and Asklipiio Voula.

51. The list of the hospitals mentioned by the Commission shows a variety in the size of the establishments, since some of the largest Greek hospitals such as Agios Savvas, Kyriakou and Asklipiio Voula are referred to, as well as medium-sized hospitals such as Argos, Agios Nikolaos of Crete or Sparta.

52. Moreover, that list refers to establishments with a geographical coverage encompassing the entire country with, in particular, hospitals in Athens, in the Peloponnese and on Crete, but concerns also a wide field of competence, including general hospitals, a children's hospital, a hospital treating cancer-related illnesses and a maternity hospital.

53. Therefore, it can be deduced that the administrative practice of the contracting authorities in question, ... demonstrates a certain degree of consistency and generality.

(ii) Article 258 TFEU as a public policy instrument

It has been suggested that in determining whether an infringement can be pursued, regard will have to be had to the duration, geographical spread and number of infringements.[13] As an overall statement, this might be right. Looking at the case law in the round, there seems to be policy sensitivity to whether a case can be pursued. It is not simply that within certain

---

[13] P. Wennerås, 'A New Dawn for Commission Enforcement under Articles 226 and 228: General and Persistent (GAP) Infringements, Lump Sums and Penalty Payments' (2006) 43 *CMLRev.* 31, 38. This article provides an excellent analysis of the development of this line of reasoning.

sectors a single breach will be sufficient whilst in others it will not. Different approaches are taken within individual sectors. Both *Commission* v *Germany* and *Commission* v *Greece* concerned public procurement but the latter looked for a general and consistent practice whereas the former did not. It is possible that this had to do with the size and scale of the tender in the first instance.

This suggests a second function to Article 258 TFEU: that of being a public policy tool. Such a conception sees its dominant role as being to secure the effective functioning of EU policies. To be sure, realising the rule of law is part of this but only insofar as it is instrumental to bringing about a successful policy.[14]

On such a view, there would be a gradated view to enforcement. If a Member State's laws fail to comply formally with EU law, then there is no hope of realising the policy. There must always be the possibility of prosecution, as no policy can be realised if not even the formal norms are in place. In other fields such as human rights, prosecution may be desirable for individual breaches as these are not measured simply in terms of general compliance but individual violations are seen as, per se, egregious, by virtue of the importance of these for the human condition. For other matters, prosecution only takes place where the alleged illegal behaviour seriously impedes the functioning of the policy. The Commission set out such a prioritisation in 2002.

European Commission, *Better Monitoring of the Application of Community Law*, COM(2002)725 final/4, 11–12

The Commission, in its White Paper on Governance,[15] announced that it would conduct surveillance and bring proceedings against infringements effectively and fairly by applying priority criteria reflecting the seriousness of the potential or known failure to comply with the legislation. Filling in the framework sketched out by the White Paper, the criteria are based on accumulated experience. They rank the following infringements as serious:

(a) Infringements that undermine the foundations of the rule of law
- Breaches of the principles of the primacy and uniform application of Community law (systemic infringements that impede the procedure for preliminary rulings by the Court of Justice or prevent the national courts from acknowledging the primacy of Community law, or provide for no redress procedures in national law: examples include the failure to apply the redress procedures in a Member State and national court rulings that conflict with Community law as interpreted by the Court of Justice).
- Violations of the human rights or fundamental freedoms enshrined in substantive Community law (e.g. interference with the exercise by European citizens of their right to vote, refusal of access to employment or social welfare rights conferred by Community law, threats to human health and damage to the environment with implications for human health).
- Serious damage to the Community's financial interests (fraud with implications for the Community budget, or violation of Community law in relation to a project receiving financial support from the Community budget).

---

[14] On this dimension see M. Mendrinou, 'Non-compliance and the Commission's Role in Integration' (1996) 3 *JEPP* 1; M. Smith, *Centralised Enforcement, Legitimacy and Good Governance in the EU* (Abingdon, Routledge, 2009) 10–15, 114–17.

[15] On this see pp. 352–61.

(b) Infringements that undermine the smooth functioning of the Community legal system
- Action in violation of an exclusive European Union power in an area such as the common commercial policy; serious obstruction of the implementation of a common policy.
- Repetition of an infringement in the same Member State within a given period or in relation to the same piece of Community legislation; these are mainly cases of systematic incorrect application detected by a series of separate complaints by individuals.
- Cross-border infringements, where this aspect makes it more complicated for European citizens to assert their rights.
- Failure to comply with a judgment given by the Court of Justice against a Member State on an application from the Commission for failure to comply with Community law.

(c) Infringements consisting in the failure to transpose or the incorrect transposal of directives which can in reality deprive large segments of the public of access to Community law and actually are a common source of infringements.

The above criteria will help the Commission to make the best use of the various mechanisms designed to restore a situation in line with the Treaties as rapidly as possible, bearing in mind that the Commission's purpose in monitoring the application of Community law and bringing proceedings against infringements is not to 'punish' a Member State, but to ensure that Community law is applied correctly.

In practice, where it is found that an infringement meets these priority criteria, infringement proceedings will be commenced immediately unless the situation can be remedied more rapidly by some other means. Other cases – of lower priority – will be handled on the basis of complementary mechanisms[16] ... which does not rule out the possibility of bringing proceedings for failure to fulfil an obligation. This approach will meet a concern for efficiency – more rapid and effective intervention including where proceedings for failure to fulfil an obligation would not be the most appropriate mechanism – while ensuring equal treatment for the Member States and for the different channels for identifying presumed infringements (complaints, cases identified by the Commission itself, cases referred by the European Parliament or the European Ombudsman).

These criteria indicate a willingness to prioritise cases according to policy needs but they have not been interpreted too strictly. Protection of the environment and public health are mentioned as top priorities in the communication. However, this was not strictly followed. In the years following the communication, environment was the sector in which the Commission examined most cases, followed by internal market, energy, tax and employment.[17]

If Article 258 TFEU is used as a policy tool, however, that means that it cannot just be deployed strategically across sectors or against states, but it also has to be receptive to national capacities to realise a policy. Pragmatism is the order of the day, as its role is that of a regulatory tool deployed as part of the policy to secure the best possible results for the policy. Its use takes place against a context where it is not possible in any Member State to realise perfect application of EU law on the ground on a day-to-day basis.[18] This derives from many

---

[16] See pp. 333–4.
[17] Smith, above n.14, 123–31.
[18] For a case study of British, German, Spanish and Dutch application (or non-application!) of Directive 91/155/EC, the Safety Data Sheets Directive, see E. Versluis, 'Even Rules, Uneven Practices: Opening the "Black Box" of EU Law in Action' (2007) 30 *WEP* 50.

things, not least administrative resources and the general law-abidingness of the society. Public policy specialists have therefore noted in detailed and wide-ranging case studies that the capacity of states to implement EU law falls into a number of categories.[19]

G. Falkner and O. Treib, 'Three Worlds of Compliance or Four? The EU–15 Compared to New Member States' (2008) 46 *Journal of Common Market Studies* 293, 296–7, 308–9

In the *world of law observance*, the compliance goal typically overrides domestic concerns. Even if there are conflicting national policy styles, interests or ideologies, transposition of EU Directives is usually both in time and correct. This is supported by a 'compliance culture' in the sense of an issue-specific 'shared interpretive scheme' …, a 'set of cognitive rules and recipes' … Application and enforcement of the national implementation laws is also characteristically successful, as the transposition laws tend to be well considered and well adapted to the specific circumstances and enforcement agencies as well as court systems are generally well-organized and equipped with sufficient resources to fulfil their tasks. Non-compliance, by contrast, typically occurs only rarely and not without fundamental domestic traditions or basic regulatory philosophies being at stake. In addition, instances of non-compliance tend to be remedied rather quickly …

Obeying EU rules is at best one goal among many in the *world of domestic politics*. Domestic concerns frequently prevail if there is a conflict of interests, and each single act of transposing an EU Directive tends to happen on the basis of a fresh cost-benefit analysis. Transposition is likely to be timely and correct where no domestic concerns dominate over the fragile aspiration to comply. In cases of a manifest clash between EU requirements and domestic interest politics, non-compliance is the likely outcome. While in the countries belonging to the world of law observance breaking EU law would not be a socially acceptable state of affairs, it is much less of a problem in one of the countries in this second category. At times, their politicians or major interest groups even openly call for disobedience with European duties – an appeal that is not met with much serious condemnation in these countries. Since administrations and judiciaries generally work effectively, application and enforcement of transposition laws are not a major problem in this world – the main obstacle to compliance is political resistance at the transposition stage …

In the countries forming the *world of transposition neglect*, compliance with EU law is not a goal in itself. Those domestic actors who call for more obedience thus have even less of a sound cultural basis for doing so than in the world of domestic politics. At least as long as there is no powerful action by supranational actors, transposition obligations are often not recognized at all in these 'neglecting' countries. A posture of 'national arrogance' (in the sense that indigenous standards are typically expected to be superior) may support this, as may administrative inefficiency. In these cases, the typical reaction to an EU-related implementation duty is inactivity. After an intervention by the European Commission, the transposition process may finally be initiated and may even proceed rather swiftly. The result, however, is often correct only on the surface. Where literal translation of EU Directives takes place at the expense of careful adaptation to domestic conditions, for example, shortcomings in enforcement and application are a frequent phenomenon. Potential deficiencies of this type, however, do not belong to the defining characteristics of the world of transposition neglect …

---

[19] Most extensively see G. Falkner *et al.*, *Complying with Europe: EU Harmonisation and Soft Law in the Member States* (Cambridge, Cambridge University Press, 2005).

... we suggest a fourth category: the 'world of dead letters'. Countries belonging to this cluster of our typology may transpose EU Directives in a compliant manner, depending on the prevalent political constellation among domestic actors, but then there is non-compliance at the later stage of monitoring and enforcement. In this group of countries, what is written on the statute books simply does not become effective in practice. Shortcomings in the court systems, the labour inspections and finally also in civil society systems are among the detrimental factors accounting for this.

Public policy analyses of Article 258 TFEU would have it be sensitive to the domestic environment with its deployment, mindful that it can only stimulate limited change and that use in the wrong circumstances could be counter-productive, leading to domestic counter-reactions or impoverishment of resources.[20] There is much in such approaches but there are difficulties with overemphasising this dimension. First, it is not clear whether an overcharacterisation of Article 258 TFEU is not taking place here. This is a relatively crude instrument in regulatory terms which ends up (as we shall see later) with the national government being fined under Article 260 TFEU if there is no compliance. To argue for its regulatory sensitivity is perhaps to argue for something that it is not. Secondly, as with all public policy instruments, there are concerns about things getting lost along the way. Regard to overarching Commission priorities can lead to local concerns which rely on Article 258 TFEU for protection getting lost. Finally, there is the law of perverse consequences. If one looks at the models of compliance suggested by Falkner and Treib, the lesson would be to punish the law-abiding states more harshly through Article 258 TFEU as they are the ones who will respond best to it. By contrast, the fourth class should be left alone, as no amount of judgments will remedy the structural flaws of poor court systems or weak labour inspections. Yet, it is not clear that Article 258 TFEU is there to reinforce a world in which states are categorised into those seeking perfection, on the one hand, and those damned by their lack of resources, on the other.

(iii) Article 258 TFEU as a public law arena

Concerns about the dogmatism of the rule of law approach and the instrumentalism of the public policy approach have led to a third conception of the Article 258 TFEU procedure. In this, Article 258 TFEU is characterised not 'simply as single-faceted legal provision, but also a unique space of interaction for a multitude of actors'.[21] The procedure is a legal procedure involving national governments and the Commission. As we shall see, it involves other EU institutions, notably the Ombudsman, and EU subjects, be they complainants or those affected by national compliance or non-compliance with EU law. It is thus both a forum for interaction between the institutions and a forum for interaction between institutions and citizens. It is also

---

[20] A study of environmental and social policy case studies in Germany found that enforcement proceedings could stimulate compliance by shaming the national administration and mobilising social groups in favour of change. It was not always effective and could stimulate a backlash, however. D. Panke, 'The European Court of Justice as an Agent of Europeanization? Restoring Compliance with EU Law' (2007) 14 *JEPP* 847.

[21] Smith, above n. 14, 17.

a procedure that involves the exercise of considerable administrative power. Successful Commission proceedings can change the quality of people's lives significantly.[22]

All these dimensions mean that there is a politics to Article 258 TFEU that must be regulated and constrained through public law, and that the need for public law constraints is as pressing as with any powerful administrative process.

Such constraints would focus, first, on public participation in the process itself and the public accountability of the Commission for its action or inaction.[23] This is discussed in more detail when we examine the responsibilities of the Commission under the procedures themselves. As we shall see, whilst there are some constraints to enable some participation and accountability, there is a consensus amongst analysts that these are weak.

The constraints would focus, secondly, on the constraint of administrative power. US scholars have suggested that, if the American experience is anything to go by, a central constraint on competence creep and the misuse of powers are what they describe as techniques of process. In the United States, the key ingredient in the protection of the various states against the legislative powers of the national government is the extreme difficulty of the process of passing federal law. Obtaining the agreement of the President and of sufficient numbers of Senators and Congressmen is, most of the time, far from straightforward. In the European Union, they suggest, the most effective check on excessive law-making may well lie in the fact that the vast bulk of EU law is administered, not by a pan-European executive, but by national and regional authorities within Member States.[24]

On such a view, the Article 258 TFEU procedure is Janus-faced. It can be conceived as a threat to local autonomy and democracy by being the remorseless, insensitive instrument that enforces unjust, intrusive or unnecessary EU laws. Alternatively, it can be conceived as a political arena, where the implications of an EU law for a Member State are considered in the light of the local, regional or national implications that have come to the fore. It is one of the few places where national democracy can meet Union democracy, namely that German or Slovenian citizens can discuss how an EU measure affects Germany or Slovenia, respectively. To be sure, it may be argued that this also takes place when a state transposes a Directive. In the latter case, however, the norms are already set. There is a debate about how to manoeuvre around within them. The type of debate is different in the former context. It is the discussion about how to mitigate the rigour of the norms, possibly the case for selective non-enforcement of some of them, which cause most difficulties. The other feature of such a debate at this stage is that it is a debate ex post facto, where the implications of an EU law on the ground are now more imminent and local concerns more focused.

This role for Article 258 TFEU is not yet formalised. However, the question of whether the rigour of EU law could be mitigated for non-legal reasons was addressed in *Commission v Poland*. The Commission brought an action against a Polish law, the Law on Seeds, which, in effect, prohibited the marketing of genetically modified seeds in Poland. This violated Directive 2001/18/EC on the deliberate release into the environment of genetically modified organisms,

---

[22] *Ibid.* 15–20 and ch. 7. Smith's book is unrivalled as a study of the process and the context to the process.

[23] The starting point for such an analysis is R. Rawlings, 'Engaged Elites: Citizen Action and Institutional Attitudes in Commission Enforcement' (2000) 6 *ELJ* 4.

[24] E. Young, 'Protecting Member State Autonomy in the European Union: Some Cautionary Tales from American Federalism' (2002) 77 *New York University Law Review* 1612, 1736; G. Bermann, 'Taking Subsidiarity Seriously: Federalism in the European Community and the United States' (1994) 94 *Colum. L Rev.* 331, 399.

which allowed the marketing of these where they had been authorised by EU authorities. The Polish government justified its non-compliance by challenging both the ethics of genetically modified food and by arguing that their release violated important tenets of Catholic thought.

Case C-165/08 Commission v Poland, Judgment of 16 July 2009

49. In its defence and its rejoinder, the Republic of Poland concentrated its arguments wholly on the ethical or religious considerations on which the contested national provisions are based ...

56. However, a Member State cannot rely in that manner on the views of a section of public opinion in order unilaterally to challenge a harmonising measure adopted by the Community institutions ... As the Court observed in a case specifically concerning Directive 2001/18, a Member State may not plead difficulties of implementation which emerge at the stage when a Community measure is put into effect, such as difficulties relating to opposition on the part of certain individuals, to justify a failure to comply with obligations and time-limits laid down by Community law ...

57. Secondly, and as regards the more specifically religious or ethical arguments put forward by the Republic of Poland for the first time in the defence and rejoinder submitted to the Court, it must be held that that Member State has failed to establish that the contested national provisions were in fact adopted on the basis of such considerations.

58. The Republic of Poland essentially referred to a sort of general presumption according to which it can come as no surprise that such provisions were adopted in the present case. First, the Republic of Poland relies on the fact that it is well known that Polish society attaches great importance to Christian and Roman Catholic values. Secondly, it states that the political parties with a majority in the Polish Parliament at the time when the contested national provisions were adopted specifically called for adherence to such values. In those circumstances, according to that Member State, it is reasonable to take the view that the Members of Parliament, who do not, as a general rule, have scientific training, are more likely to be influenced by the religious or ethical ideas which inspire their political actions, rather than by other considerations, in particular, those linked to the complex scientific assessments relating to the protection of the environment or of human health.

59. However, such considerations are not sufficient to establish that the adoption of the contested national provisions was in fact inspired by the ethical and religious considerations described in the defence and the rejoinder, especially since the Republic of Poland had, in the pre-litigation procedure, based its defence mainly on the shortcomings allegedly affecting Directive 2001/18, regard being had to the precautionary principle and to the risks posed by that directive to both the environment and human health.

The reasoning is finely textured. It holds that Poland has failed to meet its obligations in EU law. However, whilst it holds that a state cannot defy EU law for populist reasons, it leaves open the question whether a state can do so for ethical or religious reasons. It does suggest that if such a defence does exist, it must be argued from the start and that the law or administrative practice in question must be justified on those grounds. Leaving open the possibility of such a defence is not the same thing as suggesting that there is such a defence. We will have to await further clarification. At the moment, however, an opening is suggested for public deliberation at a local level where, if a state or locality comes to a view that an EU law poses insurmountable ethical or religious difficulties for it, and it wishes to protect a domestic provision on these grounds, this might not be incompatible with EU law.

Like the other two dimensions to Article 258 TFEU, there is a danger of focusing exclusively on it as 'public law' process. To do so would fail to distinguish Article 258 TFEU from other administrative processes. It clearly has distinctive functions of its own: namely, upholding the rule of EU law and contributing to the effective functioning of EU policies. There is also an internal tension in this vision of Article 258 TFEU. In some circumstances, it may seek to compel enforcement, namely where citizens adversely affected by illegal national behaviour press for enforcement action. In other circumstances, there is an idea that there should be constraints on enforcement action to allow local democracy to flourish. It is a challenge to know how to mediate between these tensions other than to suggest somewhat vaguely and unsatisfactorily that the procedure should be sensitive to both.

3 SCOPE OF MEMBER STATE RESPONSIBILITIES

One feature of the Article 258 TFEU process is that it may be used only against Member States. Although, formally, actions are brought against the state, in practice it is the central government which is proceeded against. This prompts two questions: first what is considered to be state action for the purposes of Article 258 TFEU; and secondly, what capacities and responsibilities are assumed of the state, in particular whether it should be accountable for everything that happens within its territory.

(i) Acts and omissions of all state agencies

The consistent position of the Court is that it is the state, not the government, which is responsible. From this it has derived two related doctrines.[25] First, it is the acts and omissions of state agencies, and only these acts and omissions, which attract liability. Secondly, the state is responsible for these agencies even if these are constitutionally independent.

The conception of a state agency is considered to comprise institutions from all tiers of government, be they national, regional or local.[26] It also comprises certain bodies that are not formally part of the state but which are subject to public authority.[27] Regulatory agencies, even if set up as independent private bodies, have therefore been held on this basis to be part of the state.[28] Private companies will be held to be a state agency if the government exercises considerable influence over them. In *CMA*, a public body financed by a levy on the German food and agriculture sector, the Fund, was set up to promote German agriculture. A private company, the CMA, was further established to realise the objectives of the Fund. It had to observe the latter's guidelines and was financed by it. The CMA adopted a quality label certifying the qualities of produce from Germany. The Commission argued this label violated the EU provisions on free movement, as it was only available to German produce. The German government argued, to no avail, that the CMA was a private body and, it, therefore, was not responsible.

---

[25] Case 77/69 *Commission v Belgium* [1970] ECR 237.
[26] Case 199/85 *Commission v Italy* [1987] ECR 1039.
[27] Case 249/81 *Commission v Ireland* [1982] ECR 4005; Case 222/82 *Apple & Pear Development Council* [1983] ECR 4083.
[28] Case T-187/06 *Netherlands v Commission* [2008] ECR II-3151.

Case C-325/00 *Commission v Germany (CMA)* **[2002] ECR I-9977**

17. In that regard, it must be recalled that the CMA, although set up as a private company, is
    - established on the basis of a law...is characterised by that law as a central economic body and has, among the objects assigned to it by that law, the promotion, at central level, of the marketing and exploitation of German agricultural and food products;
    - is bound, according to its Articles of Association, originally approved by the competent federal minister, to observe the rules of the Fund, itself a public body, and additionally to be guided, in particular in relation to the commitment of its financial resources, by the general interest of the German agricultural and food sector;
    - is financed, according to the rules laid down by the AFG, by a compulsory contribution by all the undertakings in the sectors concerned.

18. Such a body, which is set up by a national law of a Member State and which is financed by a contribution imposed on producers, cannot, under Community law, enjoy the same freedom as regards the promotion of national production as that enjoyed by producers themselves or producers' associations of a voluntary character ... Thus it is obliged to respect the basic rules of the Treaty on the free movement of goods when it sets up a scheme, open to all undertakings of the sectors concerned, which can have effects on intra-Community trade similar to those arising under the scheme adopted by the public authorities.

19. Furthermore, it must be observed that:
    - the Fund is a public law body;
    - the CMA is required to respect the Fund's guidelines;
    - the financing of the CMA's activities, under legislation, comes from resources which are granted to it through the Fund, and
    - the Fund supervises the CMA's activities and the proper management of the finances which are granted to it by the Fund.

20. In those circumstances, it must be held that the Commission could rightly take the view that the contested scheme is ascribable to the State.

21. Thus it follows that the contested scheme must be considered to be a public measure ... ascribable to the State.

Although it has never been raised in infringement proceedings under Article 258 TFEU, it seems that a body will be considered a state agency even if it is not subject to public authority but is performing a public service and, for that reason, has special powers.[29]

This wide definition of the state to include private bodies subject to state influence or performing a public service and enjoying special powers makes sense from all three perspectives set out above. For the purposes of securing the 'rule of law', the state should not be able to evade its responsibilities by contracting-out tasks. In terms of realising the public policy objectives of the Union, it is important, on the one hand, that States be able to organise themselves in the most efficient and effective manner possible, and this may involve privatisation. It is important, however, that their responsibility to secure a policy is not lost in this and their

---

[29] Case C-180/04 *Vassallo* v *Azienda Ospedaliera Ospedale San Martino di Genova e Cliniche Universitarie Convenzionate* [2006] ECR I-7251. This is dealt with in more detail in Chapter 7 at pp. 288–9.

responsibility to coordinate different organisations is not fragmented. Finally, in terms of public and democratic control, exposing the actions of private entities to public law procedures holds them accountable and subject to scrutiny.

The second dimension of the doctrine of state responsibility, that the government be responsible for the actions of constitutionally independent units, is more controversial. It has led to governments being accountable when they were unable, despite their best intentions, to get legislation through parliament.[30] It also has led to central governments being responsible for the actions of regional authorities even when the former do not have the power under their constitutions to compel action by the latter.[31] The most controversial application of this doctrine is holding states accountable for the actions of national courts. In *Commission* v *Italy*, infringement proceedings were brought against a series of decisions by the Italian Court of Cassation, the highest Italian civil court, in which the latter had consistently interpreted Italian law on customs duties in a way that conflicted with EU law.

Case C–129/00 *Commission* v *Italy* [2003] ECR I–14637

29. A Member State's failure to fulfil obligations may, in principle, be established under Article [258 TFEU] whatever the agency of that State whose action or inaction is the cause of the failure to fulfil its obligations, even in the case of a constitutionally independent institution ...

30. The scope of national laws, regulations or administrative provisions must be assessed in the light of the interpretation given to them by national courts ...

31. In this case what is at issue is Article 29(2) of Law No. 428/1990 which provides that duties and charges levied under national provisions incompatible with Community legislation are to be repaid, unless the amount thereof has been passed on to others. Such a provision is in itself neutral in respect of Community law in relation both to the burden of proof that the charge has been passed on to other persons and to the evidence which is admissible to prove it. Its effect must be determined in the light of the construction which the national courts give it.

32. In that regard, isolated or numerically insignificant judicial decisions in the context of case law taking a different direction, or still more a construction disowned by the national supreme court, cannot be taken into account. That is not true of a widely-held judicial construction which has not been disowned by the supreme court, but rather confirmed by it.

33. Where national legislation has been the subject of different relevant judicial constructions, some leading to the application of that legislation in compliance with Community law, others leading to the opposite application, it must be held that, at the very least, such legislation is not sufficiently clear to ensure its application in compliance with Community law.

There is an element of disingenuousness to the judgment. The problem is framed as one of poor Italian legislation rather than as one of judicial practice which fails to comply with EU law. It was the Italian Court of Cassation's interpretation of these laws which generated the problem, however. The disingenuousness was in order to avoid directly confronting national

---

[30] Case 77/69 *Commission* v *Belgium* [1970] ECR 237.
[31] Case 1/86 *Commission* v *Belgium* [1987] ECR 2797.

courts. A holding that national courts were in breach of EU law would have posed difficulties for the principle of judicial independence and *res judicata*, as it would have required the national government to intervene to suspend the judgments and would have thrown into doubt the binding effects of the judgment.[32]

If the challenge is most intense for breaches by the judiciary, it exists in relation to all constitutionally independent arms of government. The central authorities are being enjoined to trespass beyond their domestic constitutional limits to secure compliance with EU law. The problem arises from the fiction of the unitary state. In domestic law, individuals rarely sue the state but rather the agency which they allege is harming their interests. Litigation against the state in these instances causes many problems. Whilst it places duties on central authorities to uphold the rule of law, the constitutional independence of other actors may prevent effective measures by central government. They can only uphold the rule of law by violating domestic constitutional arrangements, thereby creating difficulties for the domestic rule of law. In public policy terms, a system of perverse incentives is established. As other governmental actors will not be litigated against, there is simply no reason for them to take measures to comply with EU law, as they know that central government (with whom they are often in competition) will be held accountable.[33] Finally, this can hardly be good for local democracy. Powers of enforcement are used to justify central intervention at the domestic level to secure compliance, thereby curbing local self-government.

(ii) Accountability of state actors

State agencies are clearly responsible for actions that violate EU law. The state will be responsible for any measure that formally conflicts with EU law, be it a law, statutory instrument or judgment. This is not completely clear-cut. It is for the Commission to prove that the national law conflicts with EU law. It is insufficient that it is ambiguous. The Court of Justice will therefore often insist that there be interpretations by national courts of the measure which conflict with EU law before holding that there is a violation.[34]

The state is also responsible for administrative practices conflicting with EU law. As we have seen, in some cases, a specific act may be sufficient whilst, in others, the Court will look for a generalised practice.[35] These practices can also consist of omissions and failures to act, for state agencies are under positive duties to secure the effective functioning of EU law. These duties have been developed through the interpretation of the fidelity principle, Article 4(3) TEU, and they have been explored in more detail in Chapter 5.[36] To recap, briefly, however, the central duties for which states can be subject to infringement proceedings are:

---

[32] Compare Case C-224/01 *Köbler* v *Austria* [2003] ECR I-239, discussed at pp. 308–11.

[33] In Belgium, for example, administrative coordination was so difficult and there was so much mistrust that the Wallonian regional government actually took the Flemish regional government to the Court of Justice through the preliminary reference procedure for its failure to observe the free movement provisions. Case C-212/06 *Government of the French Community and Walloon Government* v *Flemish Government (Flemish Insurance Case)* [2008] ECR I-1683.

[34] Case C-300/95 *Commission* v *United Kingdom* [1997] ECR I-2649; Case C-418/04 *Commission* v *Ireland* [2007] ECR I-10947.

[35] See pp. 319–20.

[36] See pp. 223–7.

- the duty to secure legal certainty for EU law;[37]
- the duty actively to police EU law;[38]
- the duty to penalise infringements of EU law under analogous conditions applicable to infringements of national law of a similar nature and importance[39] and to ensure that penalties for breach of EU law are effective, proportionate and dissuasive;[40]
- the duty to notify the Commission of any problems applying or enforcing EU law.[41]

These are general duties reflecting assumptions about state capacity and good faith in EU law. They apply with particular force in the case of enforcement proceedings, as it is here, in the context of an alleged failure by the state, that they are explored at most length. There is, however, one particular duty which is specific to the Article 258 TFEU procedure itself and relates to the question of the burden of proof. If the Commission notifies the state of a possible breach of EU law and provides sufficient evidence of that breach, the duty is on the state to investigate that breach in order to prove otherwise.

In *Commission* v *Ireland*, the Commission received twelve complaints of illegal dumping of waste or operating unlicensed waste dumps across Ireland in breach of EU environmental law. It wrote to the Irish government but received only limited replies. The Irish government argued that the Commission had failed to provide sufficient proof of its infringements.

Case C-494/01 *Commission v Ireland* [2005] ECR I-3331

41. ... in proceedings under Article [258 TFEU] for failure to fulfil obligations it is incumbent upon the Commission to prove the allegation that the obligation has not been fulfilled. It is the Commission's responsibility to place before the Court the information needed to enable the Court to establish that the obligation has not been fulfilled, and in so doing the Commission may not rely on any presumption ...

42. However, the Member States are required, under Article [4(3) TEU], to facilitate the achievement of the Commission's tasks, which consist in particular, pursuant to Article [17(1) TEU], in ensuring that the provisions of the Treaty and the measures taken by the institutions pursuant thereto are applied ...

43. In this context, account should be taken of the fact that, where it is a question of checking that the national provisions intended to ensure effective implementation of the directive are applied correctly in practice, the Commission which ... does not have investigative powers of its own in the matter, is largely reliant on the information provided by any complainants and by the Member State concerned ...

44. It follows in particular that, where the Commission has adduced sufficient evidence of certain matters in the territory of the defendant Member State, it is incumbent on the latter to challenge in substance and in detail the information produced and the consequences flowing therefrom ...

45. In such circumstances, it is indeed primarily for the national authorities to conduct the necessary on-the-spot investigations, in a spirit of genuine cooperation and mindful of each Member State's duty, recalled in paragraph 42 of the present judgment, to facilitate the general task of the Commission ...

---

[37] Case C-159/99 *Commission* v *Italy (conservation of wild birds)* [2001] ECR I-4007.
[38] Case C-265/95 *Commission* v *France (Spanish strawberries)* [1997] ECR I-6959.
[39] Case C-180/95 *Draehmpaehl* v *Urania Immobilienservice* [1997] ECR I-2195.
[40] Case 68/88 *Commission* v *Greece* [1989] ECR 2965.
[41] Case C-105/02 *Commission* v *Germany* [2006] ECR I-9659.

46. Thus, where the Commission relies on detailed complaints revealing repeated failures to comply with the provisions of the directive, it is incumbent on the Member State to contest specifically the facts alleged in those complaints ...

47. Likewise, where the Commission has adduced sufficient evidence to show that a Member State's authorities have developed a repeated and persistent practice which is contrary to the provisions of a directive, it is incumbent on that Member State to challenge in substance and in detail the information produced and the consequences flowing therefrom.

The onus on the Commission, in the case of administrative failure to comply with EU law, is to make no more than a prima facie case. It must provide sufficient evidence for it to be plausible that there has been non-compliance. Whilst this question appears just to be an evidentiary one, its consequence is to impose some investigatory duties on the Member States, which stem from the duty of cooperation in Article 4(3) TEU.[42] They must know what is going on in their own backyard. If they do not, they are responsible for the consequences. A lower threshold of proof will be adduced to show non-compliance.

4 THE DIFFERENT STAGES OF INFRINGEMENT PROCEEDINGS

The infringement proceedings are best seen as a series of stages which, extrapolated out, comprise:

- an informal letter to the Member State;
- a letter of formal notice to the Member State that it is in breach of EU law;
- the submission of observations by the Member State;
- the issuing of a reasoned opinion by the Commission setting out the breach of EU law;
- a period for the Member State to comply with the reasoned opinion and submit observations;
- referral to the Court by the Commission;
- judgment by the Court.

The process is arduous and time-consuming. In 2007, the average time taken was twenty-three months.[43] There are three central points in the process. These are the initial informal contacts between the Commission and the Member State; the letter of formal notice setting out the breach and the Member State's observations on this (sometimes known as the administrative stage); and the issue of a reasoned Opinion by the Commission with possible referral to the Court if the Member State does not comply with that Opinion.

(i) Informal letter

There are two procedures for detecting a complaint. The Commission may discover something problematic through its own investigations ('own initiative'), or it may receive a complaint of an infringement from a third party. Although this varies from year to year, in 2006, a not untypical

---

[42] See also Case C-135/05 *Commission v Italy* [2007] ECR I-3475.
[43] European Commission, *25th Annual Report on Monitoring the Application of Community Law*, COM(2008)777, 2.

year, the latter accounted for 35.9 per cent of detections of infringements.[44] This figure understates the role of complainants, however. Many infringement proceedings are begun because Member States have not communicated information that they have transposed an EU law to the Commission, as is required of them. When these are taken into account, complaints are the main way for the Commission of finding out what is happening on the ground.

Historically, whether on the basis of its own investigation or on the basis of receiving a complaint, the Commission then sets out the reasons why it suspects an infringement has taken place to the Member State concerned. The Member State government is invited to reply and to supply further information. Around 70 per cent of proceedings are closed at this stage.[45] In 2007, concerned that it was letting its enforcement strategy be determined by which complaints arrived at its door, the Commission changed tack. Own initiative proceedings would continue to be resolved in the traditional way. Complaints by third parties were to be treated, in the first place, as a matter of dispute settlement with the State concerned. The State would commit itself to resolve the dispute, with the Commission only stepping in and commencing proceedings if resolution was not possible. The approach is set out below.

European Commission, *A Europe of Results: Applying Community Law*, COM(2007)502, 7–8

As is the case now, enquiries and complaints raising a question of the correct application of Community law sent to the Commission would continue to be registered and acknowledged and the Commission would provide explanations of Community law. Where an issue requires clarification of the factual or legal position in the Member State, it would be transmitted to the Member State concerned. Unless urgency requires immediate action and when the Commission considers that the contact with the Member State can contribute to an efficient solution, the Member States would be given a short deadline to provide the necessary clarifications, information and solutions directly to the citizens or business concerned and inform the Commission. When the issue amounts to a breach of Community law, Member States would be expected to remedy, or offer a remedy, within set deadlines. When no solution is proposed, the Commission would follow-up, taking any further action, including through infringement proceedings, in accordance with existing practice.

In this way, Member States would have the opportunity to resolve issues arising within this agreed framework, operating at the point closest to the citizen within its national legal and institutional context, in conformity with the requirements of Community law. With the necessary commitment, there would be a greater possibility for enquiries and complaints to be seen through to an early conclusion.

Transmission mechanisms would be established between the Commission and Member States. A central contact point within the Member State would have to process incoming enquiries and outgoing responses. This contact point would encourage the appropriate authority in the Member State to respond constructively, providing information, solving the problem or at least explaining its position.

The outcome of cases would be recorded to enable reporting on performance and any follow up, including the registration and initiation of infringement proceedings. This reporting would identify the volume, nature and seriousness of problems remaining unresolved, indicating if additional specific problem-solving mechanisms or more tailored sector initiatives are needed.

---

[44] *Ibid.* 3.
[45] *Ibid.* 2.

These procedures are currently being tested in fifteen states but they move the Article 258 TFEU procedure away from the traditional paradigm of securing the rule of EU law. For, in instances where individuals settle with the Member State, that settlement may not address the wider legal issues that extend beyond the dispute. Enforcement would be privatised to the extent that complainant satisfaction would be the primary benchmark of whether the state had done enough legally. It is also to be wondered what this form of alternate dispute resolution will do in terms of securing the effective functioning of EU policies. These are something to be assessed in the round from a panoramic perspective, rather than from the point of view of tailoring them around the circumstances of individual disputes, which pull policy this way and that. This is particularly significant in the light of the large proportion of proceedings both instigated by complainants and resolved at this stage. It might be considered that Article 258 TFEU is here moving towards a role of facilitating local democracy and national accountability, whereby pressure groups and citizens can wave the sword of EU law against abusive state action that is harming their interests. Yet, the procedure is flawed even from this perspective, as the extract below suggests.

M. Smith, 'Enforcement, Monitoring, Verification, Outsourcing: The Decline and Decline of the Infringement Process' (2008) 33 *European Law Review* 777, 798

There are several worrying implications that flow from the adoption of the new 'pilot scheme'. The most obvious is that the already protracted 'normal' Article 226 procedure will be prolonged even further because if the Member State does not resolve the complaint to the Commission's satisfaction, the regular Article 226 process may be initiated (i.e. investigation, negotiation, formal letter, etc). Even if the complaint has already been through the pilot system it will not bypass any of the existing steps in the process. Another consequence of this elongated process is that complainants will no doubt suffer 'complaint fatigue' and simply give up pursuing the alleged infraction. This undermines the Commission's statements that the legitimacy of the Union depends on the continued participation of the citizen.

Despite this the Commission contends that 'with the necessary commitment' from the Member States, the pilot scheme will lead to a faster resolution of infractions. It is difficult to see how. If the Commission itself, with all its political and institutional weight, cannot easily obtain the information it requires from offending Member States, it is difficult to see how the citizen will manage this in its place. It is also possible that this will lead to a disparate enforcement of EC law across the Union depending on the administrative sophistication and the internal (political) characteristics of each Member State. It is unlikely that this new initiative will increase either the efficiency or effectiveness of the enforcement mechanism: it simply draws out the administrative phase even further, presenting the Member States with a greater opportunity to avoid their legal responsibilities.

The second major implication is that the Commission's new pilot scheme has the result of outsourcing its responsibility to deal with complainants *to the very entity committing the alleged infraction*. Whilst the Commission wishes to preserve its status as initial contact and registration point (to retain the 'information fodder' aspect of the complainant which is vital to the Commission's ability to detect infringements), the complainant will thereafter have been referred to the Member State and the Commission will play no further part.

(ii) Letter of formal notice and Member State observations

The process begins with the Commission issuing a letter of formal notice. The reason for this is that Article 258 TFEU only allows the Commission to issue a reasoned Opinion once the Member State concerned has had the opportunity to submit observations. For the latter to be able to do this, there must be a letter of formal notice upon which it can submit observations. As the letter of formal notice is seen as central to safeguarding the rights of defence, it is also seen as framing the dispute. The Commission can only take complaints to a Member State that are specifically set out in the letter of formal notice. A sense of the role of the letter of formal notice is provided in *Commission* v *Denmark*. The Commission brought an action against the Danish government for failing to transpose Directive 76/891/EC on electrical energy meters into Danish law. The Danish government claimed that the letter of formal notice was insufficient as it had merely noted Denmark's failure to act and not set out what positive steps the Danish government needed to take to remedy the breach.

Case 211/81 *Commission* v *Denmark* [1982] ECR 4547

8. It follows from the purpose assigned to the pre-contentious stage of the proceedings for failure of a state to fulfil its obligations that a letter giving formal notice is intended to delimit the subject matter of the dispute and to indicate to the Member State which is invited to submit its observations the factors enabling it to prepare its defence.

9. … the opportunity for the Member State concerned to submit its observations constitutes an essential guarantee required by the Treaty and, even if the Member State does not consider it necessary to avail itself thereof, observance of that guarantee is an essential formal requirement of the procedure under Article [258 TFEU].

10. It appears from the documents before the Court that by a letter dated 23 May 1979 giving formal notice the Commission merely asserted that in its view the Danish Government had not put into force the measures necessary to transpose Directive 76/891 into national law but refrained from specifying the obligations which, in its view, were imposed on that State by virtue of the directive and which had been disregarded.

11. In the present case, however, that fact did not have the effect of depriving the Danish Government of the opportunity of submitting its observations to good effect. On 7 June 1978 the Commission had addressed to the Danish Government a letter setting out the precise reasons which led it to conclude that the Kingdom of Denmark had failed to fulfil one of the obligations imposed on it by Directive 76/891. It was by reference to the position adopted by the Commission in that letter of 7 June 1978 that the Danish Government submitted its observations on 22 August 1979.

Whilst the Commission does not have to set out what Member States need to do to comply with EU law, it must set out all legal complaints in the letter of formal notice. Anything not mentioned there will be deemed inadmissible.[46] However, the Commission can subsequently bring in new evidence to clarify the grounds on which it is making the complaint on condition that this does not alter the subject-matter of the dispute.[47]

---

[46] Case C-371/04 *Commission* v *Italy* [2006] ECR I-10257.
[47] Case C-494/01 *Commission* v *Ireland* [2005] ECR I-3331.

(iii) Reasoned Opinion and the period for national compliance

If, after the Member State has submitted its observations on the letter of formal notice, agreement is still not reached, the Commission will issue a reasoned Opinion. As the subject-matter of the dispute is delimited by the formal letter of notice, the reasoned Opinion cannot modify the subject-matter of the dispute by introducing new claims.[48] It should therefore not amend conclusions contained in the letter of notice. However, account can be taken of changes in circumstances. In *Commission* v *Belgium*, the Commission challenged, in its letter of formal notice, a 1987 broadcasting law passed by the Flemish Communities.[49] The 1987 law was then replaced by a 1994 law. This latter law was challenged in the reasoned Opinion. The Court rejected a Belgian claim that this amendment compromised the latter's rights of defence, noting that the national provisions mentioned need not be identical if the change in legislation resulted in the system as a whole not being altered.

The Commission has less room for manoeuvre in the reasoned Opinion than in the letter of formal notice. Whilst the latter need do no more than give a summary of the complaints, the reasoned Opinion must give a coherent and detailed statement of reasons that led the Commission to believe that the Member State has breached EU law. This should include a detailed statement of the legal and factual context to the dispute and take account of any resolutions submitted by the Member State.[50] Finally, and importantly, the reasoned Opinion must also set out a reasonable period for compliance by the Member State. The following extract summarises the current position.

Case C-350/02 *Commission v Netherlands* [2004] ECR I-6213

18. In ... an action for failure to fulfil obligations the purpose of the pre-litigation procedure is to give the Member State concerned an opportunity, on the one hand, to comply with its obligations under Community law and, on the other, to avail itself of its right to defend itself against the charges formulated by the Commission ...

19. The proper conduct of that procedure constitutes an essential guarantee required by the Treaty not only in order to protect the rights of the Member State concerned, but also so as to ensure that any contentious procedure will have a clearly defined dispute as its subject-matter ...

20. It follows that the subject-matter of proceedings under Article [258 TFEU] is delimited by the pre-litigation procedure governed by that provision. The Commission's reasoned opinion and the application must be based on the same grounds and pleas, with the result that the Court cannot examine a ground of complaint which was not formulated in the reasoned opinion ... which for its part must contain a cogent and detailed exposition of the reasons which led the Commission to the conclusion that the Member State concerned had failed to fulfil one of its obligations under the Treaty ...

21. It should also be emphasised that, whilst the formal letter of notice, which comprises an initial succinct résumé of the alleged infringement, may be useful in construing the reasoned opinion, the Commission

---

[48] Case 278/85 *Commission* v *Denmark* [1987] ECR 4065.
[49] Case C-11/95 *Commission* v *Belgium* [1996] ECR I-4115.
[50] Case C-266/94 *Commission* v *Spain* [1995] ECR I-1975.

is none the less obliged to specify precisely in that opinion the grounds of complaint which it already raised more generally in the letter of formal notice and alleges against the Member State concerned, after taking cognizance of any observations submitted by it under the first paragraph of Article [258 TFEU]. That requirement is essential in order to delimit the subject-matter of the dispute prior to any initiation of the contentious procedure provided for in the second paragraph of Article [258 TFEU] and in order to ensure that the Member State in question is accurately apprised of the grounds of complaint maintained against it by the Commission and can thus bring an end to the alleged infringements or put forward its arguments in defence prior to any application to the Court by the Commission.

Once the reasoned Opinion has been issued, the Commission must afford Member States sufficient time both to respond to the views it sets out and to comply with the Opinion.[51] The minimum time limit laid down will depend upon a number of factors. These include the urgency of the matter and when the matter was first brought to the attention of the Member State by the Commission.[52]

Perhaps the most stark example of what circumstances might be taken into account is *Commission* v *Belgium*. Under a 1985 law, Belgian universities were authorised to charge a supplementary fee (a 'minerval') on nationals from other Member States who enrolled with them. The Commission considered such action to be illegal following the *Gravier* judgment, given on 13 February 1985.[53] It had an informal meeting with Belgian officials on 25 June 1985, where it expressed that view but also stated that it was still considering the effects of the judgment. On 17 July 1985, it issued a letter of formal notice stating that, in view of the onset of the new academic year, the Belgian government should submit its observations within eight days. The Belgian authorities asked for more time. On 23 August 1985, the Commission issued a reasoned Opinion, with the Belgian government being given fifteen days to comply. The Belgian government claimed that the action was inadmissible given the limited time periods allowed for compliance.

Case 293/85 *Commission v Belgium (Gravier)* [1988] ECR 305

13. It should be pointed out first that the purpose of the pre litigation procedure is to give the Member State concerned an opportunity, on the one hand, to comply with its obligations under Community law and, on the other, to avail itself of its right to defend itself against the complaints made by the Commission.

14. In view of that dual purpose the Commission must allow Member States a reasonable period to reply to the letter of formal notice and to comply with a reasoned opinion, or, where appropriate, to prepare their defence. In order to determine whether the period allowed is reasonable, account must be taken of all the circumstances of the case. Thus, very short periods may be justified in particular circumstances, especially where there is an urgent need to remedy a breach or where the Member State concerned is fully aware of the Commission's views long before the procedure starts.

---

[51] See e.g. Case 211/81 *Commission v Denmark* [1982] ECR 4547.

[52] In determining this, account is taken not of when the letter of formal notice was sent but when informal contacts were first made. Case C-56/90 *Commission v United Kingdom* [1993] ECR I-4109; Case C-473/93 *Commission v Luxembourg* [1996] ECR I-3207.

[53] Case 293/83 *Gravier v City of Liège* [1985] ECR 593.

15. It is therefore necessary to examine whether the shortness of the periods set by the Commission was justified in view of the particular circumstances of this case ...

16. ... the imminent start of the 1985 academic year may indeed be regarded as a special circumstance justifying a short time limit. However, the Commission could have taken action long before the start of the academic year because the major part of the Belgian provisions were already part of its legislation before the law of 21 June 1985. They were therefore known to the Commission at the latest when the judgment of 13 February 1985 was delivered, which was six months before the start of the 1985 academic year. Furthermore, it should be noted that at the time the Commission had not made any criticism of the minerval and had even given the impression, prior to the entry into force of the law in question, that it accepted that the minerval was compatible with Community law. In those circumstances the Commission cannot rely on urgency which it itself created by failing to take action earlier.

17. As for the Commission's alternative argument that the time limits laid down were not absolute and that consequently replies given after their expiry would have been accepted, it should be remarked that that factor is not relevant. A Member State to which a measure subject to a time limit is addressed cannot know in advance whether, and to what extent, the Commission will if necessary grant it an extension of that time limit. In this case, moreover, the Commission did not reply to the Kingdom of Belgium's request for an extension of time.

18. As regards the question whether the Kingdom of Belgium was aware sufficiently in advance of the Commission's views, it is common ground that although the commission had expressed its views to the competent officials of the Belgian ministries of national education on 25 June 1985, at a meeting of the education committee of 27 and 28 June 1985 it stated that it was still considering the effects of the judgments of the Court in the field of university education. It follows that the Kingdom of Belgium was not fully informed of the definitive views of the Commission before these proceedings were brought against it.

It is only if compliance with the reasoned Opinion does not occur that the matter may be brought before the Court. Indeed, once the period set out in the reasoned Opinion has elapsed there is nothing a Member State can do to prevent the matter being heard by the Court. The latter has repeatedly stated that it will consider the position at the end of the period laid down in the reasoned Opinion, and will not take account of subsequent changes.[54] Compliance by the Member State with the reasoned Opinion after the deadline set out in the latter but before judgment will not therefore prevent the Court's declaring that the Member State has acted illegally.[55] The reasons are, first, that the unwieldy nature of the procedure would, otherwise, be unable to capture breaches of a relatively short duration,[56] and, secondly, that Member States could, otherwise, manipulate the procedures by simply bringing their conduct to an end shortly before judgment was given.[57]

---

[54] See e.g. Case C-200/88 *Commission v Greece* [1990] ECR I-4299; Case C-133/94 *Commission v Belgium* [1996] ECR I-2323.

[55] See e.g. Case C-446/01 *Commission v Spain* [2003] ECR I-6053.

[56] Advocate General Lenz in Case 240/86 *Commission v Greece* [1988] ECR 1835.

[57] Advocate General Lagrange in Case 7/61 *Commission v Italy* [1961] ECR 317.

5 ADMINISTRATION OF INFRINGEMENT PROCEEDINGS

(i) The Commission's discretion

There are a number of remarkable features about the Article 258 TFEU process. The first is how few actions reach the Court of Justice. According to Commission figures, in 2007, only 7 per cent of proceedings reached the Court.[58] The heart of the infringement procedure is thus an administrative process, with judicial proceedings predominantly acting as a backdrop to structure the negotiations between the Commission and the Member States. Secondly, the Commission wins the overwhelming majority of cases that reach the Court. In 2008, for example, ninety-four Commission actions were successful and nine dismissed.[59] This is not atypical, with the Commission typically winning over 90 per cent of the cases arriving before the Court: a staggeringly high proportion when it is remembered that the case can be dismissed not just on substantive but also on procedural grounds.[60] The third feature is that the instigation and cessation of proceedings is entirely a matter of Commission discretion.[61] Its motives for starting or stopping proceedings cannot be challenged[62] and neither can protracted administrative delays in instigating proceedings unless they are so extreme that they would infringe the Member State's procedural rights by making it more difficult for the state concerned to refute the Commission's arguments.[63]

These three features have raised a number of concerns.[64] From the perspective of securing the rule of EU law, there is simply a concern about Commission leniency. It might not take up proceedings where there is a serious infraction of EU law and the statistics suggest that it may well cease proceedings when national compliance is still far from perfect. Indeed, in 2006, the European Parliament deployed strong words in its assessment of the Commission's exercise of its discretion. In its report on the Commission's 2004 and 2005 Annual Reports, the European Parliament stated that it:

> Calls on the Commission to place the principle of the rule of law and citizens' experience above purely economic criteria and evaluations; urges the Commission to monitor carefully the respect of the fundamental freedoms and general principles of the Treaty as well as the respect of regulations and framework directives; invites the Commission to use secondary legislation as a criterion for determining whether there has been an infringement of fundamental freedoms; [and]

> Calls on the Commission seriously to reassess its indulgence of Member States when it comes to the deadlines for submitting requested information to the Commission, adopting and communicating national implementing measures and correctly applying Community legislation at national, regional and local levels.[65]

---

[58] European Commission, *25th Annual Report*, above n. 3, 2.

[59] *Annual Report of the Court of Justice 2008* (Luxembourg, Office for Official Publications of the European Communities, 2009) 93.

[60] D. Chalmers, 'Judicial Authority and the Constitutional Treaty' (2005) 4 *ICON* 448, 452–3.

[61] Case 48/65 *Lütticke* v *Commission* [1965] ECR 19. More recently see Case C-205/98 *Commission* v *Austria* [2000] ECR I-7367.

[62] Case 416/84 *Commission* v *United Kingdom* [1988] ECR 3127.

[63] Case C-96/89 *Commission* v *Netherlands (own resources: manioc from Thailand)* [1991] ECR I-2461.

[64] For academic commentary see R. Mastroianni, 'The Enforcement Procedure under Article 169 of the EC Treaty and the Powers of the European Commission: *Quis Custodiet Custodes?*' (1995) 1 *EPL* 535; I. Harden, 'What Future for the Centralised Enforcement of Community Law?' (2002) 55 *CLP* 495.

[65] European Parliament, *Report on the Commission's 21st and 22nd Annual Reports on Monitoring the Application of Community Law (2003 and 2004)*, A6-0089/2006, paras, 13, 15.

Whilst this is something of an isolated condemnation, subsequent reports repeatedly focus on the lack of transparency of the process.[66] This is also of concern as it has led to abuse, with one celebrated instance of condemnation of the Commission by the Ombudsman in a case where a Greek official publicly involved with a Greek political party chose not to take action against the Greek government. The Ombudsman noted that it would be difficult for anybody not to doubt the impartiality of the Commission in this instance and to question whether it was acting in the Union interest.[67]

There is also a concern from a public policy perspective about what checks and balances are in place to ensure that the Commission acts in a coherent and systematic manner in this field. In principle, the Commission investigates and prosecutes proceedings on the basis of the priority criteria set out in its 2002 Communication on better monitoring of the application of Community law described above. Yet, as Smith has observed, enforcement policy owes as much to the structures and politics of the organisation as anything else.

M. Smith, *Centralised Enforcement, Legitimacy and Good Governance in the EU* (Abingdon, Routledge, 2009) 136–7

When assessing the statistical information produced by the Commission, it must be acknowledged that there does seem to be a coherent output of the enforcement policy, although not one that necessarily matches the stated policy criteria. Whatever the stated approach to the enforcement policy, the result appears to guarantee that the environment sector always produces the greatest number of investigations and referrals to the ECJ. This sector is followed by cases on the internal market and/ or energy and transport, although neither of these sectors are mentioned in the priority criteria at all. This of course may not be a result of the policy on enforcement, but rather the particular organisation of the Commission and the way in which each DG mobilises its resources to combat infringements. For instance, DG Environment is one of the few DGs that contain a unit specifically responsible for dealing with infringements, as opposed to (say) DG Justice, Freedom and Security, which has no such department and generates very few infringement cases. It may be that the type of legislation produced by DG Environment (predominantly directives) is particularly prone to generating infractions (which appears to be confirmed by the Commission's Annual Reports), or it may be that the subject matter is particularly unpopular with Member States. It could be that DG Environment is particularly focused upon enforcement more than other DGs.

The final concern is that this is an administrative process seemingly unconstrained by the usual public law disciplines of participation, accountability and transparency. The process has traditionally been an executive to executive one in which the only players were the central governments and the Commission. The Commission, as we shall see, was until recently not really publicly accountable for any of its actions. Finally, the process is secret. The General Court has held that Member States are entitled to expect that all documents relating to the investigative procedure as well as the reasoned Opinion remain confidential. They can therefore oppose

---

[66] See e.g. European Parliament, *Report on the 25th Annual Report from the Commission on Monitoring the Application of Community Law (2007)*, A6–0245/2009, para. 13.
[67] EO Decision on Complaint 1288/99/OV. For analysis of this see Smith, above n. 14, 175–83.

any publication by the Commission or dissemination to third parties. The reason, according to the General Court, is that such confidentiality facilitates amicable resolution of the dispute.[68] Nevertheless, it also creates a climate of public suspicion, as outsiders have no idea of what is being discussed or agreed, or even what conduct, however egregious, the Commission has discovered.

In recent years, there have been attempts to put some constraints on the exercise of Commission discretion in this area. These are, however, quite limited.

(ii) Complainants and Article 258 TFEU

Notwithstanding the key role which they play, complainants are frozen out of the procedure. They have no right to require the Commission to commence proceedings or to be involved in the dispute. In *Star Fruit*, a Belgian banana trader alleged that it had been prejudiced by the organisation of the French banana market, which it believed was contrary to EU law. The trader complained to the Commission but the latter did not commence proceedings against France. Star Fruit sought to take the Commission to court for failure to act. The Court of Justice ruled that the action was inadmissible.

Case 247/87 *Star Fruit* v *Commission* [1989] ECR 291

11. … it is clear from the scheme of Article [258 TFEU] that the Commission is not bound to commence the proceedings provided for in that provision but in this regard has a discretion which excludes the right for individuals to require that institution to adopt a specific position.

12. It is only if it considers that the Member State in question has failed to fulfil one of its obligations that the Commission delivers a reasoned opinion. Furthermore, in the event that the State does not comply with the opinion within the period allowed, the institution has in any event the right, but not the duty, to apply to the Court of Justice for a declaration that the alleged breach of obligations has occurred.

13. It must also be observed that in requesting the Commission to commence proceedings pursuant to Article [258 TFEU] the applicant is in fact seeking the adoption of acts which are not of direct and individual concern to it within the meaning of the second paragraph of Article [263(4) TFEU] and which it could not therefore challenge by means of an action for annulment in any event.[69]

14. Consequently, the applicant cannot be entitled to raise the objection that the Commission failed to commence proceedings against the French Republic pursuant to Article [258 TFEU].

This freezing out is controversial even within the EU judiciary. It excludes parties who are not merely at the centre of proceedings in that they are the impetus for them, but who are also often suffering significant adversity because of illegal acts by national governments. In *max. mobil* the General Court held that the 'principle of sound administration' required complainants to be able to seek judicial review of Commission decisions not to take action against Member States under Article 106(3) TFEU, the provision that allows the Commission to require Member

---

[68] Case T-191/99 *Petrie* v *Commission* [2001] ECR II-3677.
[69] These are the *locus standi* requirements for challenging EU acts. They are discussed at pp. 414–24.

States to bring public undertakings into line with EU law.[70] Even though the General Court distinguished this provision from Article 258 TFEU by suggesting (possibly for the moment) that this duty does not apply to the latter, the General Court was clearly laying the way for it to do so. It was the first time that it had been suggested that an individual could compel the Commission to take an action against a Member State and that the principle of sound administration is a general principle of EU law. The Court of Justice was, however, having none of it and, on appeal, overturned the judgments. It held that the Commission was not required to bring proceedings and that individuals could not require the Commission to take a position on a specific issue.[71]

This lack of success before the Union courts led complainants during the 1990s to turn to the European Ombudsman.[72] Sufficiently concerned by the complaints it was receiving, the Ombudsman launched in 1997 an 'own initiative' enquiry into the Commission's handling of individual complaints of a breach of EU law by a national government. In its report it observed:

> [T]he Ombudsman has received many complaints concerning the administrative procedures used by the Commission in dealing with complaints lodged by private citizens concerning Member States' failure to fulfil their Community law obligations. The object of these complaints was ... the administrative process which takes place before judicial proceedings may begin. The allegations ... concerned, in particular, excessive time taken to process complaints, lack of information about the ongoing treatment of the complaints and not receiving any reasoning as to how the Commission had reached a conclusion that there was no infringement.[73]

Matters reached a nadir in 2001 with the *Macedonian Metro* Decision. This concerned a complaint that the Greek authorities had violated EU public procurement law in a tender they had put out for construction of a metro in Thessaloniki. The Ombudsman found that there had been acts of maladministration, first, because the Commission had indicated to the complainant that it was closing the file because there was no breach of EU law. In fact, it had not told the truth. It closed the file as an act of political discretion rather than because of any finding as to the law.[74] Secondly, it found that the Commission had violated the complainant's right to be heard as it had sent its provisional views to the complainant eight days before closing the file and at the beginning of the summer holidays. This clearly gave the latter insufficient time.[75] As a consequence, in 2002, the Commission adopted a Communication setting out certain procedural entitlements for complainants.[76] This Communication includes the following central principles:

- Anybody may bring a complaint free of charge without having to prove an interest.
- All correspondence must be recorded. It will not be investigable if it is anonymous; fails to refer to a Member State; denounces private parties unless public authorities are involved or

---

[70] Case T-54/99 *max.mobil* v *Commission* [2002] ECR II-313.

[71] Case C-141/02 P *Commission* v *max.mobil* [2005] ECR I-1283.

[72] On these early years see Rawlings, above n. 23.

[73] European Ombudsman, *Own-Initiative Inquiry into the Commission's Administrative Procedures for Dealing with Complaints under Article 226 [now Article 258 TFEU]*, EO Annual Report 1997, 270.

[74] Decision of the European Ombudsman on Complaint 995/98/OV against the European Commission, 31 January 2001, 3.1–3.7, www.ombudsman.europa.eu/cases/decision.faces/en/1088/html.bookmark (accessed 1 September 2009).

[75] *Ibid.* paras. 4.1–4.6.

[76] European Commission, *On Relations with the Complainant in respect of Infringements of Community Law*, COM(2002)141.

fail to act; fails to set out a grievance or sets out a grievance on which the Commission has adopted a clear, public, consistent position or which falls outside EU law.

- The Commission Departments will communicate with the complainant and inform them after each Commission Decision of the steps taken in response to the complaint.
- The Commission will endeavour to close the case or issue a formal notice within one year from registering the complaint.
- If the Commission closes the case, unless there are exceptional circumstances, the Commission will give the complainant four weeks to submit comments having set out the reasons for its Decision.

Whilst all this brings some transparency to the processes, the Commission makes it clear that it still has complete discretion as to whether to initiate proceedings, and that any infringement action is a bilateral matter between it and the Member State concerned. It also leaves a number of procedural matters unaddressed. Rawlings has noted, for example, that citizen participation is left until very late in the day – four weeks before the closing of the file – and this rarely allows for effective input. He also noted that the commitment to close a file within a reasonable period of time tells us nothing about how the file is handled subsequent to a letter of formal notice being issued.[77] Smith has likewise noted that there is no commitment to fairness and non-discrimination in the investigation of the complaint and subsequent follow-up. She also wonders whether, significant though they are, these organisational changes are bringing any attitudinal change in the Commission.[78]

6 SANCTIONS

(i) Article 260 TFEU and the Lisbon reforms

The procedure in Article 258 TFEU is long and cumbersome. At the end of it there is a simple declaration by the Court of Justice that the Member State has breached EU law. Member States are given plenty of time before having to comply and plenty of time to negotiate a good deal. Furthermore, the effect of a Court ruling is uncertain. Research by Chalmers found that in 2002, Member States had failed to comply with 37.33 per cent of the judgments given against them within twelve months.[79] Legal commentators have claimed that this is because of the absence of sanctions in the procedure.[80] At Maastricht, a procedure was therefore introduced whereby the Commission could take non-compliant states back to the Court to have them fined. The procedure prior to Lisbon was a repeat of that in Article 258 TFEU. There would be a new informal letter, a letter of formal notice, Member State observations, etc.[81] This entailed a total of fourteen stages from the first registration by the Commission of the breach before a sanction was introduced. The procedure was amended by the Lisbon Treaty and is now contained in Article 260 TFEU.

---

[77] Rawlings, above n. 23, 18.
[78] Smith, above n. 14, 191–4.
[79] Chalmers, above n. 60, 453.
[80] E. Szyszczak, 'EC Law: New Remedies, New Directions?' (1992) 55 *MLR* 690, 691; J. Steiner, 'From Direct Effects to *Francovich*: Shifting Means of Enforcement of Community Law' (1993) 18 *ELRev.* 3.
[81] This was formerly Article 228 EC.

Article 260 TFEU

1. If the Court of Justice of the European Union finds that a Member State has failed to fulfil an obligation under the Treaties, the State shall be required to take the necessary measures to comply with the judgment of the Court.

2. If the Commission considers that the Member State concerned has not taken the necessary measures to comply with the judgment of the Court, it may bring the case before the Court after giving that State the opportunity to submit its observations. It shall specify the amount of the lump sum or penalty payment to be paid by the Member State concerned which it considers appropriate in the circumstances.

   If the Court finds that the Member State concerned has not complied with its judgment it may impose a lump sum or penalty payment on it.

   This procedure shall be without prejudice to Article 259.

3. When the Commission brings a case before the Court pursuant to Article 258 on the grounds that the Member State concerned has failed to fulfil its obligation to notify measures transposing a directive adopted under a legislative procedure, it may, when it deems appropriate, specify the amount of the lump sum or penalty payment to be paid by the Member State concerned which it considers appropriate in the circumstances.

   If the Court finds that there is an infringement it may impose a lump sum or penalty payment on the Member State concerned not exceeding the amount specified by the Commission. The payment obligation shall take effect on the date set by the Court in its judgment.

The new provision introduces two significant procedural amendments to the previous position.

The first is in Article 260(3) TFEU. When an infringement proceeding is brought for failure to notify measures transposing a Directive, it is unnecessary to go through the procedures set out in Article 260(2) TFEU. Instead, the Court can impose a sanction at the same time that it rules against the Member State under Article 258 TFEU.

The second concerns the procedure in Article 260(2) TFEU for other forms of breach of EU law. This has been truncated. There is no need for the Commission to issue a reasoned Opinion. It will still have to issue a Member State a letter of formal notice on which the latter can submit observations, but after that it can refer the matter to the Court. This does raise the question whether the letter of formal notice here is subject to the same legal constraints as the reasoned Opinion (but not the letter of formal notice) in Article 258 TFEU, namely whether it must give a statement of the reasons why there is still non-compliance and whether it must set out a reasonable period for compliance before the matter can be referred back to the Court. In *Commission v Portugal*, the Court stated that the opportunity for Member States to submit observations was an essential guarantee of both procedures.[82] It would appear from this, therefore, that the Commission could not subsequently include complaints that were not in the original letter of formal notice and is under a duty both to consider national observations submitted in response

---

[82] Case C-457/07 *Commission* v *Portugal*, Judgment of 10 September 2009.

to it and to give Member States a date for compliance. Otherwise, it would seem to prejudice these essential rights of defence. In short, therefore, the letter of formal notice would have to adopt the same features as the reasoned opinion in Article 258 TFEU.

Whilst these amendments speed up the procedure, there is the question of the distinction between breaches for non-notification of Directives and other breaches of EU law. For the latter, the requirement to go, first, through Article 258 TFEU and then through Article 260 TFEU renders prosecution of breaches still extremely cumbersome. The reason lies in national government opposition; this issue was discussed at the Future of Europe Convention, with national governments opposing the simultaneous imposition of sanctions for anything other than non-communication of measures transposing Directives.[83] Yet, given the length of the Article 258 TFEU procedure, it might be questioned where exactly their worries lie, and whether, at heart, they simply do not want EU law to be policed too vigorously. The length of the procedure limits the capacity of the proceedings both to uphold the rule of EU law and to be an effective and responsive public policy tool.

Finally, the effectiveness of the penalty payment should not be assumed. In the following extract, Harlow and Rawlings examined the impact of the first Article 260 TFEU case to reach the Court of Justice.[84]

C. Harlow and R. Rawlings, 'Accountability and Law Enforcement: The Centralised EU Infringement Procedure' (2006) 31 *European Law Review* **447, 462–3**

The first case to reach the Court involved Greece and concerned a toxic waste dump at Kouroupitos (Chania) in Crete. On the basis of five years' non-compliance with an ECJ ruling, it ended in the imposition of a daily penalty payment of €20,000 coupled with an order to close the dump. Yet the penalty itself proved to be only a first step towards compliance. Six months later, when Greece began payment under threat that the Commission would otherwise withhold its aid payments, nothing had been done to remove the offending dump that was the subject of the proceedings. Six months later again, when the European Parliament's Environment Committee met in Brussels, it heard that Greece, which by now owed €4.20 million, had paid off €2.98 million, though otherwise the position had not changed; the fines were now remitted with a promise of rehabilitation. By keeping the matter as a constant agenda item, the Committee helped to secure closure of the dump. But the Committee had to return to Kouroupitos in 2005, when it learned from the Commission that the new site was not functioning properly and that a formal notice had been served on the Greek authorities. These dismal facts underscore the difficulties associated with forcing governments into 'remedial action'.

This case appears to be a healthy reminder to lawyers that a problem is not cured just because there is a court ruling. Court judgments are not self-executing and the judicial enforce*ability* of the law can sometimes be a quite different thing from its judicial enforce*ment*.

---

[83] See *Final Report of the Discussion Circle on the Court of Justice*, CONV 636/03.

[84] Case C-387/97 *Commission v Greece (waste disposal: Kouroupitos)* [2000] ECR I-5047. For further analysis, see M. Theodossiou, 'An Analysis of the Recent Response of the Community to Non-compliance with Court of Justice Judgments: Article 228(2) EC' (2002) 27 *ELRev.* 25.

(ii) Types of sanction levied under Article 260 TFEU

Two types of financial sanction are mentioned in Article 260(3) TFEU: the lump sum and the penalty payment. The Commission has characterised these in the following way. The lump sum is a single one-off sanction that penalises the state for its non-compliance between the date of the original judgment given under Article 258 TFEU and the subsequent judgment given under Article 260 TFEU. The penalty payment is a sanction which applies to each day of delay in compliance after the judgment given under Article 260 TFEU. It is thus calculated at a daily rate. It applies from the date of the second judgment under Article 260 TFEU and goes on in-definitely (in theory at least) or until state compliance.[85]

The wording of Article 260(3) TFEU states that a lump sum *or* a penalty payment can be imposed. This would seem to suggest quite clearly that the Court cannot impose both in the same judgment. It must be one or the other. This assumption was overturned in *Commission* v *France*.[86] In 1991, the Court upheld a Commission complaint that France had failed to comply with EU fisheries law between 1984 and 1987 by not sufficiently carrying out inspections or monitoring the mesh sizes of nets and by allowing undersized fish to be sold. Following a series of inspections of French ports during the 1990s, the Commission considered that very little was being done to comply with the judgment. It instigated Article 260 TFEU proceedings. The Commission asked for both a lump sum sanction and penalty payment to be imposed. The reason, it argued, was that they pursued different functions: the former was to punish the Member State for its behaviour prior to the Article 260 TFEU judgment; the latter was to induce the Member State to comply with that judgment as quickly as possible following its pronouncement.

Case C-304/02 Commission v France (non-compliance with Judgment) [2005] ECR I-6263

80. The procedure laid down in Article [260 TFEU] has the objective of inducing a defaulting Member State to comply with a judgment establishing a breach of obligations and thereby of ensuring that Community law is in fact applied. The measures provided for by that provision, namely a lump sum and a penalty payment, are both intended to achieve this objective.

81. Application of each of those measures depends on their respective ability to meet the objective pursued according to the circumstances of the case. While the imposition of a penalty payment seems particularly suited to inducing a Member State to put an end as soon as possible to a breach of obligations which, in the absence of such a measure, would tend to persist, the imposition of a lump sum is based more on assessment of the effects on public and private interests of the failure of the Member State concerned to comply with its obligations, in particular where the breach has persisted for a long period since the judgment which initially established it.

82. That being so, recourse to both types of penalty provided for in Article [260(2) TFEU] is not precluded, in particular where the breach of obligations both has continued for a long period and is inclined to persist.

---

[85] European Commission, Application of Article 228 EC, SEC(2005)1658, para. 10.3.
[86] Case C-64/88 *Commission* v *France* [1991] ECR I-2727.

83. This interpretation cannot be countered by reference to the use in Article [260(2) TFEU] of the conjunction 'or' to link the financial penalties capable of being imposed. As the Commission and the Danish, Netherlands, Finnish and United Kingdom Governments have submitted, that conjunction may, linguistically, have an alternative or a cumulative sense and must therefore be read in the context in which it is used. In light of the objective pursued by Article [260 TFEU], the conjunction 'or' in Article [260(2) TFEU] must be understood as being used in a cumulative sense ...

91. ...The procedure provided for in Article [260(2) TFEU] is a special judicial procedure, peculiar to Community law, which cannot be equated with a civil procedure. The order imposing a penalty payment and/or a lump sum is not intended to compensate for damage caused by the Member State concerned, but to place it under economic pressure which induces it to put an end to the breach established. The financial penalties imposed must therefore be decided upon according to the degree of persuasion needed in order for the Member State in question to alter its conduct ...

103. As to those submissions, while it is clear that a penalty payment is likely to encourage the defaulting Member State to put an end as soon as possible to the breach that has been established...it should be remembered that the Commission's suggestions cannot bind the Court and are only a useful point of reference ... In exercising its discretion, it is for the Court to set the penalty payment so that it is appropriate to the circumstances and proportionate both to the breach that has been established and to the ability to pay of the Member State concerned ...

104. In that light, and as the Commission has suggested in its communication of 28 February 1997, the basic criteria which must be taken into account in order to ensure that penalty payments have coercive force and Community law is applied uniformly and effectively are, in principle, the duration of the infringement, its degree of seriousness and the ability of the Member State to pay. In applying those criteria, regard should be had in particular to the effects of failure to comply on private and public interests and to the urgency of getting the Member State concerned to fulfil its obligations...

113. ... the French Republic should be ordered to pay to the Commission, into the account 'European Community own resources', a penalty payment of 182.5 x EUR 316 500, that is to say of EUR 57 761 250, for each period of six months from delivery of the present judgment at the end of which the judgment in Case C-64/88 *Commission* v *France* has not yet been fully complied with.

114. In a situation such as that which is the subject of the present judgment, in light of the fact that the breach of obligations has persisted for a long period since the judgment which initially established it and of the public and private interests at issue, it is essential to order payment of a lump sum (see paragraph 81 of the present judgment).

115. The specific circumstances of the case are fairly assessed by setting the amount of the lump sum which the French Republic will have to pay at EUR 20 000 000.

The reference point for determining when there has been a failure to fulfil obligations under Article 260 TFEU and for prescribing sanctions is the date of expiry given in the letter of formal notice.[87] From that point on, there is discretion to impose both a lump sum payment and a penalty payment. The Commission indicated in a Communication following the judgment that, as a general rule, it will press for both.[88] Yet, the two have different functions, and this limits

---

[87] It used to be the date in the reasoned Opinion: Case C-304/02 *Commission* v *France* [2005] ECR I-6263, para. 30.
[88] European Commission Communication, n. 85 above, paras. 10.3, 10.4.

when this can be done. The lump sum punishes the earlier non-compliance whilst the periodic payment is intended to secure compliance with the final ruling under Article 260 TFEU. The Court has therefore indicated that it will not impose a penalty payment where the state concerned did not comply by the date set out in the letter of formal notice but has complied by the time of its ruling.[89] It may, however, impose a lump sum in such circumstances.

There is a discretion not to apply a sanction at all. The Court has indicated that the question of whether to impose a sanction is a matter for its decision. In deciding whether to impose a fine it will look at what is appropriate in the circumstances and proportionate both to the breach and the state's capacity to pay.[90] With respect to the lump sum, it will look at how long the breach persisted since the original judgment and its effect on public and private interests.

(iii) Level of fines imposed

The final amendment introduced by the Lisbon Treaty is set out in the final paragraph of Article 260(3) TFEU. This states that the Court cannot impose a fine in excess of that suggested by the Commission.[91] This amendment reinforces the importance of the guidelines announced by the Commission on 13 December 2005.[92]

On the penalty payment, the Communication sets out a two stage formula. The first stage is a daily flat rate of €600 per day multiplied by a coefficient for seriousness (on a scale 1–20) and a coefficient for duration (on a scale 1–3). The coefficient for duration will be 0.10 for each month of continued infringement after the Article 260 TFEU judgment. The coefficient for seriousness is determined by the importance of the provision breached[93] and the impact on particular and general interests. The second stage will apply a multiplier, n, to the amount reached in the first stage. This multiplier is based on the capacity of a state to pay and its votes in the Council, and ranges from 0.36 for Malta to 25.40 for Germany.

As regards the lump sum, the Communication suggests a minimum sum for each Member State based on the fault of the state in not complying with the initial judgment. These range from €180,000 for Malta to €12,700,000 for Germany. In addition, to calculate the lump sum a daily rate will be applied if its amount exceeds that of the minimum sum. This rate, which starts from the date of the Article 258 TFEU judgment, is €200 per day multiplied by the same coefficient for seriousness and by the same n multiplier as that described above.

The Commission acknowledges these formulae must operate in light of the proportionality principle. There may be times, therefore, when it has to depart from them. It may ask only for a lump sum penalty where the Member State has taken all the necessary measures but some time is needed for the results to be realised. Similarly, it acknowledges that more lenient treatment may be appropriate where a Member State has made 'best efforts': it has taken all

---

[89] Case C-177/04 *Commission v France* [2006] ECR I-2461. This is also acknowledged in the European Commission Communication, above n. 85, para. 10.5.

[90] Case C-121/07 *Commission v France*, Judgment of 9 December 2008.

[91] Previously, the Court considered it could impose a greater penalty than in the Commission's guidelines: Case C-177/04 *Commission v France* [2006] ECR I-2461.

[92] European Commission Communication, above n. 85.

[93] Importance is determined not by whether it is a Treaty provision or secondary legislation but by the perceived nature of the rules, so violations of fundamental rights or economic rights are always treated as very serious breaches. *Ibid.* para. 16.1.

practical steps but is still not yet fully compliant. There may also be times where the Commission has to suspend penalties to verify whether compliance has taken place or where it may only be practicable to award periodic penalties based on monthly intervals. The proportionality principle cuts both ways, however, and can be used to increase penalties. The Communication, therefore, indicates that where there are several heads of infringement, the Commission will ask for penalties, both the lump sum and daily penalty, to be applied to each one separately.

Whilst the Lisbon Treaty indicates that the Court cannot impose more severe penalties than those requested by the Commission, it can impose more lenient ones. The Court uses the same methodology as the Commission Communication but does not see it as binding. In cases brought before it, it reserves the right to apply the criteria in a manner independent from the Commission. This has resulted in its imposing alternative levels of fine from that proposed by the Commission where it sees issues such as the duration of the breach or its seriousness differently.[94]

FURTHER READING

G. Falkner *et al.*, *Complying with Europe: EU Harmonisation and Soft Law in the Member States* (Cambridge, Cambridge University Press, 2005)

A. Gil Ibañez, *The Administrative Supervision and Enforcement of EC Law, Powers, Procedures and Limits* (Oxford and Portland, Hart, 1999)

I. Harden, 'What Future for the Centralised Enforcement of Community Law?' (2002) 55 *Current Legal Problems* 495

C. Harlow and R. Rawlings, 'Accountability and Law Enforcement: The Centralised EU Infringement Procedure' (2006) 31 *European Law Review* 447

M. Mendrinou, 'Non-compliance and the Commission's Role in Integration' (1996) 3 *Journal of European Public Policy* 1

R. Rawlings, 'Engaged Elites: Citizen Action and Institutional Attitudes in Commission Enforcement' (2000) 6 *European Law Journal* 4

M. Smith, *Centralised Enforcement, Legitimacy and Good Governance in the EU* (Abingdon, Routledge, 2009)

E. Versluis, 'Even Rules, Uneven Practices: Opening the "Black Box" of EU Law in Action' (2007) 30 *West European Politics* 50

R. White and A. Dashwood, 'Enforcement Actions under Article 169 and 170 EEC' (1989) 14 *European Law Review* 388

---

[94] Most recently see Case C-70/06 *Commission v Portugal* [2008] ECR I-1.

9

Governance

CONTENTS

1 INTRODUCTION

This chapter considers EU governance. It is organised as follows.

Section 2 considers the nature of EU governance. Governance was set out at greatest length in the 2001 Commission White Paper. It comprises, in the first place, a series of norms guiding the exercise of Union power. These norms are openness, participation, accountability, effectiveness, coherence, subsidiarity and proportionality. The governance agenda in the White Paper also sets out an ethos as to how the European Union is to govern and when it is to govern. It suggests that the central mission of the Union is to solve problems that cannot be resolved by the Member States unilaterally. There is flexibility about the legal instruments to be deployed, as what matters is that the problem be resolved. The concern that the problem be resolved effectively and coherently also leads to a priority being given to expert knowledge, on the one hand, as this is seen as central to knowing the problem and the solution, and to impact assessment, on the other, as this requires policy-makers to anticipate the effects of the policy on others. Finally, the commitment to openness and participation has led to an engagement by the Union with the idea of a pan-European civil society.

Section 3 examines the principles of subsidiarity and proportionality. Subsidiarity sets out when, acting within its powers, the Union should intervene. It is based around two logics. One is concerned with protecting national identities from Union intrusion and is concerned with the loss of tradition and self-government. The other looks at whether a measure can, by reason of its scale and effects, be better realised at EU rather than national level. The two logics are difficult to combine and the Court of Justice has yet to strike down an EU measure for violating the principle of subsidiarity. The proportionality principle guides the quality of Union intervention. It states that EU measures shall not exceed what is necessary to realise the objectives of the Treaties. In practice, the Union courts will only intervene when the Union measure is manifestly inappropriate. This has resulted in the central importance of the proportionality principle being its reshaping of the EU legislative culture. The 2003 InterInstitutional Agreement on Better Law-Making led to a commitment to consider non-legislative instruments wherever these would be equally effective, and these have become pervasive in recent years.

Section 4 considers the principle that EU institutions should consult widely before taking any legislative action. Set out in Article 11 TEU and a 2002 Commission Communication, there is a commitment that the consultation should involve dialogue, be transparent and be plural. Whilst there is a duty to give reasons for any measure, this duty is a weak one, which allows EU institutions to give reasons in very general terms and does not require them to respond to particular observations. This has limited the requirement on them to engage in active dialogue rather than merely take views. The commitment to transparent consultation is expressed in a Register of lobbyists, all of whom must observe a Code of Conduct specifying certain standards. Whilst the EU institutions commit themselves to inclusive consultation, a central challenge is that most of the lobbyists in Brussels represent either corporate groups or are pan-European associations, often heavily funded by the Commission.

Section 5 considers the role of knowledge in the decision-making processes. EU institutions are neither free to adopt measures without taking scientific advice nor free to ignore it. They must take it from an independent body that is regarded as excellent and transparent, usually an EU agency, and can only not adopt it if it shows different advice from a body of equal scientific standing. The other role of knowledge in the process is the commitment to use impact assessments prior to developing proposals on significant legislative measures. These seek to anticipate the economic, social and environmental impacts of a measure.

Section 6 considers the transparency principle. Central to securing the accountability of EU institutions, its central expression is Regulation 1049/2001/EC. This secures transparency through an electronic register or through allowing individuals to seek access from EU bodies to documents in their possession. The central justifications for refusing access are the exceptions set out in article 4 of the Regulation. These fall into three categories. First, there are exceptions where the institution must refuse access to a document. Here, Union courts will look merely to see whether there has been a manifest error of assessment and whether accurate reasons have been given. Secondly, there are exceptions where EU institutions have a discretion and can grant access where disclosure is in the overriding public interest. Courts will engage in much stronger review here, starting from a presumption that there is always a public interest in disclosure and that institutions must explain quite specifically how disclosure would undermine a particular interest. Finally, there are documents originating from Member States. Member States can refuse to consent to a document being released if it falls within one of the categories justifying non-release of EU documents but they must also provide reasons.

2 THE GOVERNANCE AGENDA

The term 'governance' came to the fore in the Union as a consequence of the biggest administrative scandal to hit the European Union. In 1998, a series of allegations about fraud and financial mismanagement by the Santer Commission were made to the European Parliament. It established a Committee of Independent Experts to examine fraud, mismanagement and nepotism.[1] The report was damning. On its publication in March 1999, the entire College of Commissioners resigned.[2] To counter the damage, the incoming Prodi Commission published a series of Codes of Conduct and consultation papers on Commission reform and accountability which culminated in the White Paper on European Governance.[3] The document is an attempt to regain the high ground and recapture popular legitimacy through a commitment to exercise power in a particular way in the future:[4]

> The White Paper on European Governance concerns the way in which the Union uses the powers given by its citizens. Reform must be started now, so that people see changes well before further modification of the EU Treaties.
>
> The White Paper proposes opening up the policy-making process to get more people and organisations involved in shaping and delivering EU policy. It promotes greater openness, accountability and responsibility for all those involved. This should help people to see how Member States, by acting together within the Union, are able to tackle their concerns more effectively.[5]

To this end, the *White Paper* understands governance as:

> the rules, processes and behaviour that affect the way in which powers are exercised at European level, particularly as regards openness, participation, accountability, effectiveness and coherence.

Although terse, this definition hints at two dimensions to the governance agenda. First, it is about setting norms that justify and guide EU decision-making. Criteria are set for acceptable

---

[1] Committee of Independent Experts, *First Report on Allegations regarding Fraud, Mismanagement and Nepotism in the European Commission* (15 March 1999) para. 9.4.25. Both this report and the committee's second report (see below) are available at www.europarl.eu.int/experts/.

[2] For commentary, see A. Tomkins, 'Responsibility and Resignation in the European Commission' (1999) 62 *MLR* 744; P. Craig, 'The Fall and Renewal of the Commission: Accountability, Contract and Administrative Organisation' (2000) 6 *ELJ* 98; V. Mehde, 'Responsibility and Accountability in the European Commission' (2003) 40 *CMLRev.* 423.

[3] European Commission, *European Governance: A White Paper*, COM(2001)428.

[4] For criticism, see L. Metcalfe, 'Reforming the European Governance: Old Problems or New Principles?' (2001) 67 *International Review of Administrative Sciences* 415; F. Scharpf, 'European Governance: Common Concerns vs. the Challenge of Diversity' in C. Joerges *et al.* (eds.), *Mountain or Molehill: Critical Appraisal of the Commission White Paper on Governance*, Jean Monnet Working Paper 6/01 (New York, New York University, 2001).

[5] Above n. 3, 3.

behaviour and legal standards and procedures established on the basis of them. Secondly, governance is also a description of how the Union is to go about its decision-making. To that end, it sets out a mode of governing which prescribes a number of features that EU decision-making should incorporate. We shall now consider each of these in further detail.

(i) The norms of governance

The White Paper sets out seven principles of governance. In addition to the ones above, it sets out those of subsidiarity and proportionality. It then elaborates on these.

European Commission, *European Governance: A White Paper* COM(2001)428, 10–11

Openness. The Institutions should work in a more open manner. Together with the Member States, they should actively communicate about what the EU does and the decisions it takes. They should use language that is accessible and understandable for the general public. This is of particular importance in order to improve the confidence in complex institutions.

Participation. The quality, relevance and effectiveness of EU policies depend on ensuring wide participation throughout the policy chain – from conception to implementation. Improved participation is likely to create more confidence in the end result and in the Institutions which deliver policies. Participation crucially depends on central governments following an inclusive approach when developing and implementing EU policies.

Accountability. Roles in the legislative and executive processes need to be clearer. Each of the EU Institutions must explain and take responsibility for what it does in Europe. But there is also a need for greater clarity and responsibility from Member States and all those involved in developing and implementing EU policy at whatever level.

Effectiveness. Policies must be effective and timely, delivering what is needed on the basis of clear objectives, an evaluation of future impact and, where available, of past experience. Effectiveness also depends on implementing EU policies in a proportionate manner and on taking decisions at the most appropriate level.

Coherence. Policies and action must be coherent and easily understood. The need for coherence in the Union is increasing: the range of tasks has grown; enlargement will increase diversity; challenges such as climate and demographic change cross the boundaries of the sectoral policies on which the Union has been built; regional and local authorities are increasingly involved in EU policies. Coherence requires political leadership and a strong responsibility on the part of the Institutions to ensure a consistent approach within a complex system.

The application of these five principles reinforces those of *proportionality and subsidiarity.* From the conception of policy to its implementation, the choice of the level at which action is taken (from EU to local) and the selection of the instruments used must be in proportion to the objectives pursued. This means that before launching an initiative, it is essential to check systematically (a) if public action is really necessary, (b) if the European level is the most appropriate one, and (c) if the measures chosen are proportionate to those objectives.

These principles constrain Union decision-making in that it must respect them. It is important to note that they formulate a vision of Union decision-making, in that the principles also prescribe goals it must realise. That is to say, it must be as accountable, open, coherent, etc. as possible. A further feature of the governance agenda is its informality. It does not set out these principles as legally binding norms but rather as general principles to be realised in a number of ways. Care has to be taken in analysing them, as the devil lies in the detail and how they are institutionalised: be it through legal norms, new procedures or new institutions. Only through consideration of these will it be possible to see if these principles are met and also to observe whether there are any other consequences as a result.

(ii) The traits of governance

A feature of the White Paper is that it also describes how the Union is to govern. Union decision-making is to be marked by a number of traits.

First, Union decision-making is characterised as being about problem-solving. The question becomes how to solve the identified problem in a way that meets the governance criteria. It is a test that conceives the measure of Union performance as whether it is fit for purpose. Joseph Weiler has described this in the following way:

> The refocusing of the Commission's tasks proposed here takes on board the vision of a Union concentrating on the realisation of a few major projects with widespread appeal. It is by rallying support for such projects rather than seeking to replace national allegiances by a wider collective identity that we will encourage the people of the Union – in existing Member States and applicant countries alike – to see themselves as Europeans. Taking this line of thinking a step further, the political purpose of the Union is not to supplant the existing States with a new super-State, but to establish a system of shared legislative powers in order to carry through common projects.[6]

Weiler has lambasted this approach.

J. Weiler, 'The Commission as Euro-Skeptic: A Task Oriented Commission for a Project-Based Union, a Comment on the First Version of the White Paper' in C. Joerges *et al.* (eds.), *Symposium: Mountain or Molehill? A Critical Appraisal of the Commission White Paper on Governance*, Jean Monnet Working Paper 6/01 (EUI and NYU, 2002)

6. The thinking is clear: Concentration on 'a few major projects' will bring clarity – the lack of which is identified as one key to public confusion and disenchantment. The major projects the Union selects must have 'widespread appeal' which in turn will 'rally support' and such support, in its turn, will encourage people to see themselves as Europeans rather than by seeking to replace national allegiances by a wider European collective identity. Not a new super-State but a system to carry through common projects.

7. In similar manner, the principal strategy of restoring Commission legitimacy hearkens to its glorious past. It would consist of a '... a return to the original notion of a task oriented administration...' which evidently had been lost along the way. A Commission which is selective about that which it does is what is wanted. The implicit model being rejected is a Commission with plenary governance functions: a Commission-government. The Commission is about governance, not government.

---

[6] European Commission, Draft Memorandum to the Commission: Approaches to European Governance for Democratic European Governance, 10 March 2001, para. 2.4. This can be found at www.jeanmonnetprogram.org/papers/01/firstdraftwhitepaper.rtf (accessed 25 September 2009).

8. The Union is not a state and the Commission is not a government — it is instead a mere functional 'system of sharing or legislative powers to carry through common projects'. It is hard to recall, even in the most Euro-skeptic British or Danish literature, a more functionalist and impoverished conception and self-understanding of Europe.

9. The nostalgic harping back to the past which is evident in the rhetoric of the Draft is also the source of the biggest flaw in its legitimacy strategy: The false dichotomy which is set up in the understanding of Europe. The early functionalist and neo-functionalist theories also suggested a project based Community with an efficient task oriented Community. They predicted and hoped that it would result in a shift of allegiance and a replacement of national identity (the famous 'spillover'). The 'modernized' version presented by the Draft *rightly* abandons the notions of allegiance and all that. But then, amazingly, the alternative presented is the same old functionalism simply stripped of the early fanciful 'spillover' notions. The European construct is presented as a two-way choice between *either* a statal vision in which European legitimacy has to rest on a nation-like collective identity which would replace Member State national identities and allegiances *or* a rather bare pragmatic functionalism.

   In its opening paragraphs the Draft calls for a clarification and '[u]nderstanding what Europe is all about'. When you strip away the verbiage what is the answer given? Europe is about (appealing) projects. And what is the Commission about? An efficient and task oriented instrument for realizing these projects.

10. One should reject this 'either or' picture. It is possible to reject as undesirable and unfeasible a statal conception of Europe and a national conception of European identity and allegiance without going to the other extreme functionalist and reductionist approach presented here.

11. I can understand the temptation of packaging Europe as consisting of some well defined 'appealing' projects and the Commission as simply a friendly, attentive and responsive body concerned with the task of effectively realizing these projects. It can produce some important and immediate political capital. Who can, after all, object to appealing projects and such a minimalist conception of the Commission?

12. But it comes with some notable longer term dangers and costs. And in part it also leads to some naïve positions which will not be taken seriously by large constituencies. Let me explain.

13. There have always been two principal strands in the European debate which has taken place from time to time (and in some national quarters endlessly). In some Member States the debate has mostly followed functionalist premises: Whether or not Europe serves the national interest. 'What's-in-it-for-us?' Where that has been the premise of the debate (and it is not necessary to mention Member States by name) the legitimacy of the very European construct has remained contingent, subject to a continuous assessment and re-assessment of the 'appeal' of Europe and the extent that it continued to serve interests. Under this conception a failure of the Commission, like the Santer Commission, calls into question the very legitimacy of Europe itself. Europe under this form of discourse is analogous to a politician in power whose policies and efficiency in implementing these policies are subject to contingent acceptance and rejection. Europe becomes a continuous experiment not fully integrated into the political culture in the same way that some German historians claimed that in Post War Germany, democracy itself was treated as a contingent proposition, the approval of which was dependent on its success.

   This position is the hall mark of classical Euro-Skepticism.

14. The other strand, and this is the one that (inadvertently) has been sacrificed in the Draft, does not regard Europe only in functionalist terms. Under this strand Europe is not, for sure, considered as a proto-state or a would-be state nor is European identity conceived with a vocabulary associated with national identity and allegiance. But Europe is much more than project oriented. It is process oriented and above all it is a Community of Values the principal one of which is an historical commitment to a different, more civil, process of inter-statal intercourse, to a different, more civil, method of drawing boundaries

between states and nations, to a different, more civil, way of managing certain domains of the public sphere. To be European, under this conception, is a commitment to 'doing things' (hence process) in a different, European, way – *whatever the current major appealing project happens to be*. To be European is essentially about the way we do things, rather than what we do.

Secondly, the success of governance is measured by whether an external observer would consider that the Union measure in question meets the various criteria set out.[7] The assumption is that an observer can know what is good policy. This is expressed in the commitment to 'Better Policies, Regulation and Delivery', suggesting there is a verifiable good, better, best out there. It leads to faith being placed in what are perceived as external sources of truth: expertise and feedback.

European Commission, *European Governance: A White Paper* **COM(2001)428, 18–22**

..., the Union needs to boost confidence in the expert advice that informs its policy. It needs to improve the quality of its legislation, including better implementation and enforcement.

Confidence in expert advice...

Scientific and other experts play an increasingly significant role in preparing and monitoring decisions. From human and animal health to social legislation, the Institutions rely on specialist expertise to anticipate and identify the nature of the problems and uncertainties that the Union faces, to take decisions and to ensure that risks can be explained clearly and simply to the public ...

In many other areas, networking at European and even global level shows clear benefits. Expertise, however, is usually organised at a national level. It is essential that resources be put together and work better in the common interest of EU citizens. Such structured and open networks should form a scientific reference system to support EU policy-making. ...

At the same time, the Union must be able to react more rapidly to changing market conditions and new problems by reducing the long delays associated with the adoption and implementation of Community rules. In many cases these may run to three years or more. A tension between faster decisions and better, but time consuming consultation is not necessarily a problem: investment in good consultation 'upstream' may produce better legislation which is adopted more rapidly and easier to apply and enforce. ...

... proposals must be prepared on the basis of *an effective analysis* of whether it is appropriate to intervene at EU level and whether regulatory intervention is needed. If so, the analysis must also assess the potential economic, social and environmental impact, as well as the costs and benefits of that particular approach. A key element in such an assessment is ensuring that the objectives of any proposal are clearly identified. ...

...a stronger culture of *evaluation and feedback* is needed in order to learn from the successes and mistakes of the past. This will help to ensure that proposals do not over-regulate and that decisions are taken and implemented at the appropriate level.

Thirdly, governance is blind to the institutions or forms of norm deployed to realise its goals. These can be public institutions, private ones, binding instruments or soft law or a mix of all these.

[7] C. Möllers, 'European Governance: Meaning and Value of a Concept' (2006) 43 *CMLRev.* 313, 315–18.

European Commission, *European Governance: A White Paper* COM(2001)428, 20–22

The European Union will rightly continue to be judged by the impact of its regulation on the ground. It must pay constant attention to *improving the quality, effectiveness and simplicity of regulatory acts.* Effective decision-making also requires the combination of different policy instruments (various forms of legislation, programmes, guidelines, use of structural funding, etc.) to meet Treaty objectives …

… *legislation is often only part of a broader solution* combining formal rules with other non-binding tools such as recommendations, guidelines, or even self-regulation within a commonly agreed framework. This highlights the need for close coherence between the use of different policy instruments and for more thought to be given to their selection.

… the *right type of instrument* must be used whenever legislation is needed to achieve the Union's objectives:

- The *use of regulations* should be considered in cases with a need for uniform application and legal certainty across the Union. This can be particularly important for the completion of the internal market and has the advantage of avoiding the delays associated with transposition of directives into national legislation.

- So-called '*framework directives*' should be used more often. Such texts are less heavy-handed, offer greater flexibility as to their implementation, and tend to be agreed more quickly by the Council and the European Parliament.

Whichever form of legislative instrument is chosen, *more use should be made of 'primary' legislation* limited to essential elements (basic rights and obligations, conditions to implement them), leaving the executive to fill in the technical detail via implementing 'secondary' rules.

… under certain conditions, implementing measures may be prepared within the *framework of co-regulation.* Co-regulation combines binding legislative and regulatory action with actions taken by the actors most concerned, drawing on their practical expertise. The result is wider ownership of the policies in question by involving those most affected by implementing rules in their preparation and enforcement. This often achieves better compliance, even where the detailed rules are non-binding.

- It has already been used, for example, in areas such as the internal market (agreeing product standards under the so-called 'New Approach' directives)[8] and the environment sector (reducing car emissions).

- The exact shape of co-regulation, the way in which legal and non-legal instruments are combined and who launches the initiative — stakeholders or the Commission — will vary from sector to sector…

… in other areas, Community action may be complemented or reinforced by the use of the so-called '*open method of co-ordination*', which can already involve the applicant countries in some cases.

- The open method of co-ordination is used on a case by case basis. It is a way of encouraging co-operation, the exchange of best practice and agreeing common targets and guidelines for Member States, sometimes backed up by national action plans as in the case of employment and social exclusion. It relies on regular monitoring of progress to meet those targets, allowing Member States to compare their efforts and learn from the experience of others.

In some areas, such as employment and social policy or immigration policy, it sits alongside the programme-based and legislative approach; in others, it adds value at a European level where there is little scope for legislative solutions. This is the case, for example, with work at a European level defining future objectives for national education systems.

---

[8] See pp. 696–700.

A perusal of any field of EU policy therefore finds that, typically, an Action Plan or programme has been agreed which sets out the legal instruments needed to realise a policy and range of goals.[9] These instruments will usually include Regulations and Directives, but also soft law instruments, such as Recommendations, benchmarks or Codes of Conduct[10] and standards set up by private or professional bodies.[11] To many, this adaptability, flexibility and responsiveness is highly desirable. EU law is no longer simply about telling people what they do. Instead, it acquires a more enabling role. The formal norms provide a backdrop against which informal, collective arrangements are put in place, be it through soft law or other informal instruments, bringing actors together both to maximise their resources and to develop shared commitments to resolving common problems on the basis of shared criteria.[12]

C. Sabel and J. Zeitlin, 'Learning from Difference: The New Architecture of Experimentalist Governance in the EU' (2008) 14 *European Law Journal* 271, 307–8

This 'shadow of hierarchy' view extends to EU governance a trope originally developed to explain collective bargaining and neo-corporatist concertation between the state, labour and capital. The core idea is that the state or public hierarchy more generally is limited – perhaps because of the volatility of the situation in which it acts – in its ability to secure the outcomes that it prefers, or would prefer if it could identify them in advance. Given this limitation, the state enlists non-state actors who do command the necessary capacities in its problem solving by proposing an exchange: in return for their promise to bargain with one another fairly and in a public-regarding way, the relevant parties are endowed with a semi-constitutional authority to speak on behalf of their members and the assurance that their agreements will be backed by the authority of the state, provided only that they respect the conditions of the founding bargain itself. Parties to such agreements are thus reasonably said to be 'bargaining in the shadow of the state' and acting in some sense as its authorised agents or deputies in reaching solutions not directly available to the authorities themselves. Seen this way, the new architecture that we describe might be thought to be simply a capacity-increasing extension of the EU's formal hierarchical decision-making apparatus rather than a networked, deliberative alternative to it. At the limit, this argument simply applies to governance an idea familiar from organisational sociology, in which the capacities of a rigid formal organisation are rendered flexible by connecting it to an informal network over which the official hierarchy maintains control.

This view, however, is not uncontroversial and others have pointed to the dangers of too much informality.[13]

---

[9] On the single market, see European Commission, *A Single Market for 21st Century Europe*, COM(2007)724; on the Area of Freedom, Security and Justice, see European Commission, *An Area of Freedom, Security and Justice Serving the Citizen*, COM(2009)262. On the environment, see Decision 1600/2002/EC of the European Parliament and of the Council of 22 July 2002 laying down the Sixth Community Environment Action Programme [2002] OJ L242/1.

[10] See pp. 101–3.

[11] On the variety of these, see D. Chalmers, 'Private Power and Public Authority in European Union Law' (2005–06) 8 *CYELS* 59; D. Schiek, 'Private Rule-making and European Governance: Issues of Legitimacy' (2007) 32 *ELRev.* 443.

[12] The work of Chuck Sabel and Jonathan Zeitlin has been particularly pioneering and influential here. In addition, see J. Scott and D. Trubek, 'Mind the Gap: Law and New Approaches to Governance in the European Union' (2002) 8 *ELJ* 1; G. de Búrca and J. Scott (eds.), *Law and New Governance in the EU and the US* (Oxford and Portland, Hart, 2006).

[13] See also I. Chiu, 'On the Identification of an EU Legal Norm' (2007) 26 *YBEL* 193.

> **C. Joerges, 'Integration Through De-legalisation?' (2008) 33 *European Law Review* 291, 310**
>
> Iterative benchmarking of national practices, the management of national states to agree upon guidelines and the mutual learning thereby stimulated are seen as genuinely democratic processes through which a problem-related *demos* articulates itself. These are fascinating and highly conditioned perspectives which provoke sceptical questions: How can transnational criteria that enable and legitimate a benchmarking of national experience, national history and national expectations be found? Why can we reliably expect that confrontation with the experience of others will change national perceptions and practices so as to lead to coordinated policies? And if indeed learning occurs in some quarters, how is its successful implementation conceivable if we are confronted not only with extremely complex fields of social policy but also with vested interests? There are no valid reasons which could be put forward against transnational exchanges of ideas among bureaucracies and expert communities. What seems risky, however, is the delegation of quasi-regulatory tasks to such networks. This sort of governance would be considered 'soft' to the extent that it is no longer dependent on binding law. But it might be considered 'strong' because its informality permits its evasion of risks of being tied down and controlled by the regular political process including the constraints of the rule of law.

How to reconcile such different views? It is best to see each as characterisations which point to the potential advantages and risks of governance. In practice, many regimes will be set up in such a way that they are a little bit more prescriptive and a little less facilitative than their advocates would have it. By contrast, many will have checks and balances that will limit some of the risks.

The final feature of governance is a commitment to what the White Paper calls better involvement. This includes, inter alia, greater consultation, transparency and a stronger mobilisation of civil society.[14]

> **European Commission, *European Governance: A White Paper* COM(2001)428, 14–16**
>
> Democracy depends on people being able to take part in public debate. To do this, they must have access to reliable information on European issues and be able to scrutinise the policy process in its various stages ...
>
> Providing more information and more effective communication are a pre-condition for generating a sense of belonging to Europe. The aim should be to create a trans-national 'space' where citizens from different countries can discuss what they perceive as being the important challenges for the Union. This should help policy makers to stay in touch with European public opinion, and could guide them in identifying European projects which mobilise public support ...
>
> Involving civil society ...
> Civil society plays an important role in giving voice to the concerns of citizens and delivering services that meet people's needs. Churches and religious communities have a particular contribution to make.

---

[14] On civil society and the European Union more generally, see M. Wilkinson, 'Civil Society and the Re-imagination of European Constitutionalism' (2003) 9 *ELJ* 451; C. Ruzza, *Europe and Civil Society* (Manchester, Manchester University Press, 2004).

The organisations which make up civil society mobilise people and support, for instance, those suffering from exclusion or discrimination ...

Trade unions and employers' organisations have a particular role and influence. The EC Treaty requires the Commission to consult management and labour in preparing proposals, in particular in the social policy field. Under certain conditions, they can reach binding agreements that are subsequently turned into Community law (within the social dialogue). The social partners should be further encouraged to use the powers given under the Treaty to conclude voluntary agreements.

Civil society increasingly sees Europe as offering a good platform to change policy orientations and society. This offers a real potential to broaden the debate on Europe's role. It is a chance to get citizens more actively involved in achieving the Union's objectives and to offer them a structured channel for feedback, criticism and protest.

With better involvement comes greater responsibility. Civil society must itself follow the principles of good governance, which include accountability and openness. The Commission intends to establish, before the end of this year, a comprehensive on-line database with details of civil society organisations active at European level, which should act as a catalyst to improve their internal organisation.

What is needed is a *reinforced culture of consultation and dialogue*; a culture which is adopted by all European Institutions and which associates particularly the European Parliament in the consultative process, given its role in representing the citizen. The European Parliament should play a prominent role, for instance, by reinforcing its use of public hearings. European political parties are an important factor in European integration and contribute to European awareness and voicing the concerns of citizens.

Once again, this seems all highly desirable but it begs the question as to whom one is involving and who constitutes this civil society. As Armstrong suggests below, this is, itself, an uneasy question.[15]

K. Armstrong, 'Rediscovering Civil Society: The European Union and the White Paper on Governance' (2002) 8 *European Law Journal* 102, 114–15

It is one thing to seek to bridge the gap between society and transnational governance through a differentiated civic demos rooted in the structures and traditions of national civil society actors (even if they choose to cooperate transnationally). It is another to seek to bridge that gap through transnational structures that owe their legitimacy to their transnational functionality and authority. This latter position is less about European civil society's bridging the gap between society and governance, and more its jumping the gap to support the legitimation of transnational governance through transnational structures. The normative case for transnational civil society ... lies in the inclusion of a new constituency of voices, interests and expertise within transnational governance.

The difficulty is that in seeking to build a transnational civil society in its normative variant, civil society is subject to three processes, which, while contributing to the inclusion of the voice of civil society within governance, nonetheless sit uneasily with the democratic turn to civil society in the

---

[15] See also S. Smismans, 'European Civil Society: Shaped by Discourses and Institutional Interests' (2003) 9 *ELJ* 473.

first place. These processes are the 'Europeanisation' of civil society; its 'automatisation', and its 'governmentalisation'. By Europeanisation, I refer to processes by which civil society actors organise in larger, transnational structures not merely to act as a vehicle for national members, but in order to give an authoritatively, representative European voice. Plural voices are replaced by authoritative European voices. 'Autonomisation' is the process by which transnational structures develop their strategies autonomously from the direct control of constituency members. Governmentalisation refers not only to external pressures from government for changes to the organisational structures and strategies of civil society, but also the internal self-organisation of civil society as it takes on tasks of policy – influencing, decision-making and service-delivery.

Each of these processes is relative and each can positively contribute towards enhancing something that we might call the voice of European civil society. But in jumping rather than bridging the gap between society and transnational structures of governance, there is the danger that a transnationalised civil society suffers from the same sort of democratic defects as transnational governance itself. First, there is a *static* problem that the voices of national civil society actors may be lost or excluded as civil society becomes Europeanised and autonomised. Second, there is a more dynamic problem that legitimation through transnational civil society cannot make up on the transnational swings what is lost on the national roundabouts of the erosion of national structures of representative and participative democracy.

3 SUBSIDIARITY AND PROPORTIONALITY

Having looked at the general norms and traits of governance, it is now time to turn our attention to the individual principles and their interpretation and application. We shall look, first, at subsidiarity and proportionality as these go to when and how the Union intervenes.

(i) An outline of the subsidiarity and proportionality principles

The central elements of the subsidiarity and proportionality principles are set out in Article 5 TEU.

Article 5(3), (4) TEU

3. Under the principle of subsidiarity, in areas which do not fall within its exclusive competence, the Union shall act only if and insofar as the objectives of the proposed action cannot be sufficiently achieved by the Member States, either at central level or at regional and local level, but can rather, by reason of the scale or effects of the proposed action, be better achieved at Union level.

   The institutions of the Union shall apply the principle of subsidiarity as laid down in the Protocol on the application of the principles of subsidiarity and proportionality. National Parliaments ensure compliance with the principle of subsidiarity in accordance with the procedure set out in that Protocol.
4. Under the principle of proportionality, the content and form of Union action shall not exceed what is necessary to achieve the objectives of the Treaties.

On their face, the principles do two very different things.

The subsidiarity principle goes to when the Union should intervene. It expresses the political philosophy of self-government. The Preamble to the Treaty captures this by stating that the Member States are 'resolved to continue the process of creating an ever closer union among the peoples of Europe, in which decisions are taken as closely as possible to the citizen in accordance with the principle of subsidiarity'. Local decisions are, in principle, better than regional ones and national decisions are, likewise, better than international ones:[16] the closer to the people decisions are made, the more the people will be able to participate and the more responsive to the people's concerns the decisions will be.[17]

The proportionality principle goes, by contrast, not to when to intervene, but to the quality of that intervention. It is concerned with the density and intrusiveness of EU law. Originating in Prussia in the late nineteenth century, its philosophy is a presumption in favour of private autonomy and that state intrusion into that should always be justified.[18] This has led to three tenets within it. First, the measure must be suitable for realising the objectives set by the administration. This will only be the case if it is necessary for achieving the objectives in question. Secondly, of several equally suitable measures, the one chosen should be that which imposes the fewest constraints on individuals. Thirdly, the means should not be out of proportion to the ends sought.

As they seek different goals, the subsidiarity and proportionality principles have to be treated separately. Yet, as we shall see, they have been conflated in recent years by the governance agenda, and this also has to be considered. This conflation is even present in the central provision in the Protocol on the application of the principles of subsidiarity and proportionality.

Protocol on the application of the principles of subsidiarity and proportionality, Article 5

Draft legislative acts shall be justified with regard to the principles of subsidiarity and proportionality. Any draft legislative act should contain a detailed statement making it possible to appraise compliance with the principles of subsidiarity and proportionality. This statement should contain some assessment of the proposal's financial impact and, in the case of a directive, of its implications for the rules to be put in place by Member States, including, where necessary, the regional legislation. The reasons for concluding that an objective of the Union can be better achieved at the level of the Union shall be substantiated by qualitative and, wherever possible, quantitative indicators. Draft legislative acts shall take account of the need for any burden, whether financial or administrative, falling upon the Union, national governments, regional or local authorities, economic operators and citizens, to be minimised and commensurate with the objective to be achieved.

There are thus two strands in the provision. On the one hand, the Union has to justify the relative efficacy of EU legislation vis-à-vis its national or regional alternatives. On the other, there is a concern with the regulatory weight of EU legislation. Its financial and administrative impacts should be minimised and attention should be addressed to the legislative disturbance that it will cause.

---

[16] In its consultations on any legislative proposal, the Commission is required (where appropriate) to take into account the regional and local dimension of the action envisaged: Protocol on the application of the principles of subsidiarity and proportionality, Article 2.

[17] A. Follesdal, 'Subsidiarity' (1998) 6 *Journal of Political Philosophy* 190; Y. Soudan, 'Subsidiarity and Community in Europe' (1998) 5 *Ethical Perspectives* 177; N. Barber, 'The Limited Modesty of Subsidiarity' (2005) 11 *ELJ* 308.

[18] J. Schwarze, *European Administrative Law* (London, Sweet & Maxwell, 1992) 685.

(ii) Subsidiarity

Two logics sit at the heart of the subsidiarity principle.

The first logic expresses a concern that the Union should not intrude on national, regional and local political and cultural identities. It is directed at policing and limiting the reach and levels of EU legislation. Although the idea goes back to the mid-1970s,[19] it was first made a Treaty provision at Maastricht. This was in response to the perceived explosive growth in the quantity of EU legislation from 1984 onwards, which trebled between 1984 and 1992. Fligstein and McNichol estimated that just under 400 binding acts were adopted in 1984, while nearly 2,500 were adopted in 1992.[20] Estella, more conservatively, estimates that 254 binding acts were adopted in 1984 and 752 in 1992.[21] There has been a concern ever since that time with the amount of legislation produced by the Union.[22]

This logic is reflected in the first part of the test in Article 5(3) TEU: namely that the Union should only act if objectives of the proposed action cannot be sufficiently achieved by the Member States. This test is one of local self-government. It is not based on the efficiency of the measure but relates more to how the measure forms part of the national cultural identity. The British decision to drive on the left-hand side of the road is thus an expression of quirky Britishness. Left is chosen rather than right not because one is safer than the other but because that is the tradition within the United Kingdom and this tradition asserts British distinctiveness. There is no feeling that one has to justify why left is better than right, or vice versa. It is nevertheless felt to go to what it means to live in the United Kingdom.

The second logic emanates from that of comparative federalism. All federal systems have a principle mediating the relationship between federal and local government, and when it is appropriate for the central federal authorities to intervene and when it is not. A good example is that provided in article 72(2) of the German Basic Law.

Article 72(2)

In this field the [federal authorities] will have the right to legislate if federal legal regulation is needed:

(1) because a matter could not be settled effectively by the legislation of the various *Länder* [regions], or

(2) because the regulation of a matter by the law of a *Land* [region] could affect the interests of other or all *Länder*, or

(3) to safeguard the legal or economic unity, and in particular, to safeguard the homogeneity of the living conditions beyond the territory of a *Land*.

[19] *Tindemans Report on European Union, EC Bulletin* Supplement 1/76.

[20] N. Fligstein and J. McNichol, 'The Institutional Terrain of the European Union' in W. Sandholtz and A. Stone Sweet (eds.), *European Integration and Supranational Governance* (Oxford, Oxford University Press, 1998) 76.

[21] A. Estella, *The EU Principle of Subsidiarity and its Critique* (Oxford, Oxford University Press, 2002) 20.

[22] The British House of Commons noted that in 2006, 3,255 legal instruments were adopted by the Union. It quoted estimates suggesting that about half of all legislation affecting business and the voluntary sector stemmed from EU legislation and about 9 per cent of all statutory instruments. House of Commons Library, *EU Legislation*, Standard Note SN/IA/2888, 23 April 2007, 9–11.

The logic of comparative federalism is different. Everybody is part of a unitary legal and political order. Both the federal and regional authorities in Germany are thus assumed to be German! The test is therefore one of comparative efficiency, namely could the measure be more effectively resolved by central rather than local legislation. Article 72(2) therefore sets out three types of circumstance where that is the case. No regional authority in Germany would claim therefore to require drivers to drive on the left when in the rest of Germany they drive on the right. It would prevent an integrated road system and a national car industry, and concerns would be expressed about the effect on road safety if drivers suddenly had to swap from one side to the other.

This logic of comparative federalism is adopted in the second part of the test in Article 5(3) TEU and the indicators set out in article 5 of the Protocol on the application of the principles of subsidiarity and proportionality. This is that the objects of a measure can, by reason of its scale or effects, be better achieved at EU level. The test is essentially one of comparative efficiency: would one central measure be better than twenty-seven different ones? In this, it is highly centralising. For it is always possible to argue that one standard will generate economies of scale in that operators need only have one standard for their workplaces and that twenty-seven standards lead to problems of alignment and coordination. On this test, for example, it is very difficult to argue that the Union should not harmonise the side of the road on which people drive, for example.

The logic of each test slides past the other. One is about expression of cultural identity; the other is about realisation of economies of scale and minimising disruptions caused by different laws. Scharpf has talked, therefore, of the subsidiarity principle putting in place a bipolar constitutional logic.[23] The aim of the subsidiarity principle can never be for things to be decided according to one style of reasoning or the other. Instead, it must be to secure mutual accommodation and balance between the two logics.

This is a very difficult task for a court. The test is a struggle to apply in any one instance, and the Court of Justice must do so in a context where it may have to come to a different conclusion on the need for a measure after all three political institutions had indicated their support for a measure. It would be difficult for the Court to tell them that they were all wrong.[24] Although the principle of subsidiarity has regularly been invoked before the Court of Justice, the Court has yet to annul a measure for breach of the principle. An illustration of the lightness of touch is the judgment in *Netherlands* v *European Parliament and Council*, which concerns a Directive requiring Member States to protect biotechnological inventions by patents.[25] The Dutch government challenged this on the grounds that the Directive provided few reasons why its objectives were better realised at EU level and in the light of what is now Article 345 TFEU, which stipulates that nothing in the Treaties should prejudice national rules governing the system of property ownership.[26]

[23] F. Scharpf, 'Community and Autonomy: Multi-level Policy Making in the European Union' (1994) 1 *JEPP* 219, 225–6.

[24] It has thus been argued that subsidiarity is necessarily a centralising notion. G. Davies, 'Subsidiarity: The Wrong Idea, in the Wrong Place, at the Wrong Time' (2006) 43 *CMLRev.* 63.

[25] See to similar effect Case C-84/94 *United Kingdom* v *Council* [1996] ECR I-5755; Case C-491/01 *British American Tobacco* [2002] ECR I-11453; Joined Cases C-154/04 and C-155/04 *R* v *Secretary of State for Health, ex parte Alliance for Natural Health* [2005] ECR I-6451.

[26] The situation has been changed in this regard by the Lisbon Treaty which explicitly provides for the first time for some harmonisation of intellectual property rights: Article 118 TFEU.

Case C–377/98 *Netherlands v European Parliament and Council (Biotechnology Directive)* [2001] ECR I–7079

2. The Directive was adopted on the basis of Article [114 TFEU], and its purpose is to require the Member States, through their patent laws, to protect biotechnological inventions, whilst complying with their international obligations.

3. To that end the Directive determines inter alia which inventions involving plants, animals or the human body may or may not be patented ...

30. The applicant submits that the Directive breaches the principle of subsidiarity ... and, in the alternative, that it does not state sufficient reasons to establish that this requirement was taken into account ...

32. The objective pursued by the Directive, to ensure smooth operation of the internal market by preventing or eliminating differences between the legislation and practice of the various Member States in the area of the protection of biotechnological inventions, could not be achieved by action taken by the Member States alone. As the scope of that protection has immediate effects on trade, and, accordingly, on intra-Community trade, it is clear that, given the scale and effects of the proposed action, the objective in question could be better achieved by the Community.

33. Compliance with the principle of subsidiarity is necessarily implicit in the fifth, sixth and seventh recitals of the preamble to the Directive, which state that, in the absence of action at Community level, the development of the laws and practices of the different Member States impedes the proper functioning of the internal market. It thus appears that the Directive states sufficient reasons on that point.

Commentators have, therefore, suggested a variety of institutional innovations to compensate for this. Weiler has argued for the creation of a European Constitutional Court, presided over by the President of the European Court of Justice and comprising judges drawn from the constitutional courts or their equivalents in the various Member States.[27] He considers that only a body comprising the most senior judges in the European Union would have the authority and confidence to police the limits of Community powers. Others think the task should not be in the hands of judges. In 1994, the then British Commissioner, Leon Brittan, proposed the creation of a chamber of national parliamentarians who would vet the Union's legislative proposals on grounds of subsidiarity before they became law.[28] It is this latter suggestion which has been taken up in the Treaty of Lisbon. As was seen earlier,[29] a central function of national parliaments is now to patrol Commission drafts for verification with the principle of subsidiarity. This process is, of course, untested, and we will have wait and see whether the parliaments do it more effectively than the Court of Justice.

If it is difficult for the Court to engage in a substantive view in this field, it should be possible for it to verify that the legislative institutions address the question meaningfully. Article 5 of the Protocol on the application of the principles of subsidiarity and proportionality requires that any proposal be 'justified' (contain reasons) with regard to those principles.[30] The quality of the justification – whether the reasons given are consistent, properly considered and accurately

---

[27] J. Weiler, 'The European Union Belongs to its Citizens: Three Immodest Proposals' (1997) 22 *ELRev.* 150, 155–6.

[28] L. Brittan, *The Europe We Need* (London, Hamilton, 1994).

[29] See pp. 129–32.

[30] On this see G. Bermann, 'Taking Subsidiarity Seriously: Federalism in the EC and in the USA' (1994) 94 *Columbia Law Review* 331, 391–5; G. de Búrca, *Reappraising Subsidiarity's Significance after Amsterdam*, Jean Monnet Working Paper 7/99, http://centers.law.nyu.edu/jeanmonnet (accessed 21 November 2009).

reflected the legal text – is something that the Court ought to be able to monitor relatively easily. Crucial, however, is the extent to which the Court has the will to examine the detail of the reasons offered by the political institutions. In *Germany* v *European Parliament and Council*, Germany challenged Directive 94/19/EC, the Deposit Guarantee Directive. This required all credit institutions to have guarantee schemes for depositors which would provide the latter with some coverage if the institution ran into trouble. The German government argued that the compulsory nature of the scheme had insufficient regard to established national practices. It was forcing Germany to scrap an effective voluntary scheme. The German government argued that insufficient reasons were provided in the Directive why a binding EU scheme was necessary. The Court did not accept Germany's arguments and the Directive survived.

Case C-233/94 *Germany* v *European Parliament and Council* ('Deposit Guarantee Directive')* [1997] ECR I-2405

22. The German Government claims that the Directive must be annulled because it fails to state the reasons on which it is based ... It does not explain how it is compatible with the principle of subsidiarity ...

23. As to the precise terms of the obligation to state reasons in the light of the principle of subsidiarity, the German Government states that the Community institutions must give detailed reasons to explain why only the Community, to the exclusion of the Member States, is empowered to act in the area in question. In the present case, the Directive does not indicate in what respect its objectives could not have been sufficiently attained by action at Member State level or the grounds which militated in favour of Community action ...

26. In the present case, the Parliament and the Council stated in the second recital in the preamble to the Directive that 'consideration should be given to the situation which might arise if deposits in a credit institution that has branches in other Member States became unavailable' and that it was 'indispensable to ensure a harmonized minimum level of deposit protection wherever deposits are located in the Community'. This shows that, in the Community legislature's view, the aim of its action could, because of the dimensions of the intended action, be best achieved at Community level. The same reasoning appears in the third recital, from which it is clear that the decision regarding the guarantee scheme which is competent in the event of the insolvency of a branch situated in a Member State other than that in which the credit institution has its head office has repercussions which are felt outside the borders of each Member State.

27. Furthermore, in the fifth recital the Parliament and the Council stated that the action taken by the Member States in response to [a] Commission Recommendation has not fully achieved the desired result. The Community legislature therefore found that the objective of its action could not be achieved sufficiently by the Member States.

28. Consequently, it is apparent that, on any view, the Parliament and the Council did explain why they considered that their action was in conformity with the principle of subsidiarity and, accordingly, that they complied with the obligation to give reasons ... An express reference to that principle cannot be required.

The Court's failure to take seriously Germany's arguments in this case is worrying. The judgment suggests that the procedural requirements will be held to have been complied with even where there is no evidence to suppose that the institutions actually considered whether the measure satisfied the principle of subsidiarity and notwithstanding the fact that no part of the measure in question specifically refers to it. As Dashwood has concluded, the Court has shown that 'while the justiciability of the principle cannot any longer be doubted, the case law indicates equally clearly that annulment of a measure on the ground that it offends against subsidiarity is likely to occur only in extreme circumstances'.[31]

(iii) Proportionality

As set out in Article 5(4) TEU, the proportionality principle requires that the content and form of Union action shall not exceed what is necessary to achieve the objectives of the Treaties.[32] There is a long lineage of Court of Justice case law on the proportionality principle, however.[33] The modern formulation of the doctrine is set out in *Fedesa*, which concerned a challenge to a Directive that prohibited the use of certain hormonal substances in livestock farming.

Case C–331/88 *R* v *Minister of Agriculture, Fisheries and Food, ex parte Fedesa* [1990] ECR I–4023

12. It was argued that the directive at issue infringes the principle of proportionality in three respects. In the first place, the outright prohibition on the administration of the five hormones in question is inappropriate in order to attain the declared objectives, since it is impossible to apply in practice and leads to the creation of a dangerous black market. In the second place, outright prohibition is not necessary because consumer anxieties can be allayed simply by the dissemination of information and advice. Finally, the prohibition in question entails excessive disadvantages, in particular considerable financial losses on the part of the traders concerned, in relation to the alleged benefits accruing to the general interest.

13. The Court has consistently held that the principle of proportionality is one of the general principles of Community law. By virtue of that principle, the lawfulness of the prohibition of an economic activity is subject to the condition that the prohibitory measures are appropriate and necessary in order to achieve the objectives legitimately pursued by the legislation in question; when there is a choice between several appropriate measures recourse must be had to the least onerous, and the disadvantages caused must not be disproportionate to the aims pursued.

From this formulation it has been argued that the doctrine of proportionality entails a three-part test: (1) Is the measure suitable to achieve a legitimate aim? (2) Is the measure necessary to achieve that aim? (3) Does the measure have an excessive effect on the applicant's interests?[34]

---

[31] A. Dashwood, 'The Relationship between the Member States and the European Union/European Community' (2004) 41 *CMLRev.* 355, 368.

[32] For detailed analysis and commentary, see N. Emiliou, *The Principle of Proportionality in European Law* (Deventer, Kluwer, 1996); E. Ellis (ed.), *The Principle of Proportionality in the Laws of Europe* (Oxford, Oxford University Press, 1999); G. de Búrca, 'The Principle of Proportionality and its Application in EC Law' (1993) 13 *YEL* 105; P. Craig, *EU Administrative Law* (Oxford, Oxford University Press, 2006) chs. 17 and 18.

[33] The principle was stated to be a general principle of law in Case 11/70 *Internationale Handelsgesellschaft v Einfuhr- und Vorratstelle für Getreide und Futtermittel* [1970] ECR 1125.

[34] See de Búrca, above n. 32, 113; Emiliou, above n. 32, 24.

Tridimas has argued, by contrast, that the courts do not really distinguish between the second and third tests.[35]

T. Tridimas, *The General Principles of EU Law* **(2nd edn, Oxford, Oxford University Press, 2006) 139**

... proportionality requires that a measure must be appropriate and necessary to achieve its objectives. According to the standard formula used by the Court, in order to establish whether a provision of Community law is consonant with the principle of proportionality, it is necessary to establish whether the means it employs to achieve the aim correspond to the importance of the aim and whether they are necessary for its achievement. Thus, the principle comprises two tests: a test of suitability and a test of necessity. The first refers to the relationship between the means and the end ... The second is one of weighing competing interests.

Considerably more important than determining whether the doctrine of proportionality consists of two, three, or more tests is understanding what the doctrine actually enables the courts to do in judicial review cases.

T. Tridimas, *The General Principles of EU Law* **(2nd edn, Oxford, Oxford University Press, 2006) 140**

The application of the tests of suitability and necessity enable the Court to review not only the legality but also, to some extent, the merits of legislative and administrative measures. Because of that distinct characteristic, proportionality is often perceived to be the most far-reaching ground of review, the most potent weapon in the arsenal of the public law judge. It will be noted, however, that much depends on how strictly a court applies the tests of suitability and necessity and how far it is prepared to defer to the choices of the authority which has adopted the measure in issue ... [I]n Community law, far from dictating a uniform test, proportionality is a flexible principle which is used in different contexts to protect different interests and entails varying degrees of judicial scrutiny.

There is a marked contrast in the case law of the courts between the application of proportionality with regard to the Member States and its application with regard to the EU institutions. A strict test is applied to Member States' actions. If a party considers that a national authority has restricted its access to a market and argues that the restriction is disproportionate, the Court of Justice will hold that the national measure is unlawful unless the Member State can establish that it is necessary to achieve a legitimate aim and that no less restrictive alternative exists.[36] The application of the proportionality principle to the EU institutions is, by contrast, much more lenient.

---

[35] T. Tridimas, *The General Principles of EU Law* (2nd edn, Oxford, Oxford University Press, 2006) 139.
[36] See pp. 879 *et seq.*

Case C–331/88 R v Minister of Agriculture, Fisheries and Food, ex parte Fedesa [1990] ECR I-4023

14. ... with regard to judicial review ... it must be stated that in matters concerning the common agricultural policy the Community legislature has a discretionary power which corresponds to the political responsibilities given to it by ... the Treaty. Consequently, the legality of a measure adopted in that sphere can be affected only if the measure is manifestly inappropriate having regard to the objective which the competent institution is seeking to pursue ...

15. On the question whether or not the prohibition is appropriate in the present case, it should first be stated that even if the presence of natural hormones in all meat prevents detection of the presence of prohibited hormones by tests on animals or on meat, other control methods may be used and indeed were imposed on the Member States by [other legislation]. It is not obvious that the authorization of only those hormones described as 'natural' would be likely to prevent the emergence of a black market for dangerous but less expensive substances. Moreover, according to the Council, which was not contradicted on that point, any system of partial authorization would require costly control measures whose effectiveness would not be guaranteed. It follows that the prohibition at issue cannot be regarded as a manifestly inappropriate measure.

16. As regards the arguments which have been advanced in support of the claim that the prohibition in question is not necessary, those arguments are in fact based on the premise that the contested measure is inappropriate for attaining objectives other than that of allaying consumer anxieties which are said to be unfounded. Since the Council committed no manifest error in that respect, it was also entitled to take the view that, regard being had to the requirements of health protection, the removal of barriers to trade and distortions of competition could not be achieved by means of less onerous measures such as the dissemination of information to consumers and the labelling of meat.

17. Finally, it must be stated that the importance of the objectives pursued is such as to justify even substantial negative financial consequences for certain traders.

18. Consequently, the principle of proportionality has not been infringed.

The test that Union measures will only be illegal if the action is 'manifestly inappropriate' seems a weak one.[37] However, the impact of the proportionality principle may be felt not so much for the possibility of judicial review provided by it, but, instead, for its contribution to a change in legislative culture. In 2003, in an Inter-institutional Agreement on Better Law-Making, the EU institutions committed themselves to move away from a process of law-making to a process of regulation.[38] The latter process involves considering which is the best type of regulatory instrument to realise a task. This may be legislation or it may be

---

[37] The test is a standard one. See e.g. Case C-84/94 *United Kingdom v Council* [1996] ECR I-5755; Case C-233/94 *Germany v European Parliament and Council ('Deposit Guarantee Directive')* [1997] ECR I-2405; Case C-157/96 *National Farmers' Union and Others* [1998] ECR I-2211; Case C-491/01 *British American Tobacco (Investments) and Imperial Tobacco* [2002] ECR I-11453; Case C-210/03 *R v Secretary of State for Health, ex parte Swedish Match* [2004] ECR I-11893; Case C-380/03 *Germany v Parliament and Council (Tobacco Advertising II)* [2006] ECR I-11573. For detailed discussion see Craig, above n. 32, 658–72.

[38] On the shift to this, see A. Héritier, 'New Modes of Governance in Europe: Policy-Making Without Legislating' in A. Héritier (ed.), *Common Goods: Reinventing European and International Governance* (Lanham, Rowman & Littlefield, 2002); J. Caporaso and J. Wittenbrink, 'The New Modes of Governance and Political Authority in Europe' (2006) 13 *JEPP* 471.

co-regulation (the delegation to private parties to agree norms according to EU set criteria) or self-regulation (the possibility for any area to be regulated entirely by private operators).

Inter-institutional Agreement on Better Law-Making [2003] OJ C321/01

16. The three Institutions recall the Community's obligation to legislate only where it is necessary, in accordance with the Protocol on the application of the principles of subsidiarity and proportionality. They recognise the need to use, in suitable cases or where the Treaty does not specifically require the use of a legal instrument, alternative regulation mechanisms.

17. The Commission will ensure that any use of co-regulation or self-regulation is always consistent with Community law and that it meets the criteria of transparency (in particular the publicising of agreements) and representativeness of the parties involved. It must also represent added value for the general interest. These mechanisms will not be applicable where fundamental rights or important political options are at stake or in situations where the rules must be applied in a uniform fashion in all Member States. They must ensure swift and flexible regulation which does not affect the principles of competition or the unity of the internal market.

Co-regulation

18. Co-regulation means the mechanism whereby a Community legislative act entrusts the attainment of the objectives defined by the legislative authority to parties which are recognised in the field (such as economic operators, the social partners, non-governmental organisations, or associations). This mechanism may be used on the basis of criteria defined in the legislative act so as to enable the legislation to be adapted to the problems and sectors concerned, to reduce the legislative burden by concentrating on essential aspects and to draw on the experience of the parties concerned ...

20. In the context defined by the basic legislative act, the parties affected by that act may conclude voluntary agreements for the purpose of determining practical arrangements. The draft agreements will be forwarded by the Commission to the legislative authority. In accordance with its responsibilities, the Commission will verify whether or not those draft agreements comply with Community law (and, in particular, with the basic legislative act).

   At the request of inter alia the European Parliament or of the Council, on a case-by-case basis and depending on the subject, the basic legislative act may include a provision for a two-month period of grace following notification of a draft agreement to the European Parliament and the Council. During that period, each Institution may either suggest amendments, if it is considered that the draft agreement does not meet the objectives laid down by the legislative authority, or object to the entry into force of that agreement and, possibly, ask the Commission to submit a proposal for a legislative act.

21. A legislative act which serves as the basis for a co-regulation mechanism will indicate the possible extent of co-regulation in the area concerned. The competent legislative authority will define in the act the relevant measures to be taken in order to follow up its application, in the event of non-compliance by one or more parties or if the agreement fails. These measures may provide, for example, for the regular supply of information by the Commission to the legislative authority on follow-up to application or for a revision clause under which the Commission will report at the end of a specific period and, where necessary, propose an amendment to the legislative act or any other appropriate legislative measure.

Self-regulation

22. Self-regulation is defined as the possibility for economic operators, the social partners, non-governmental organisations or associations to adopt amongst themselves and for themselves common guidelines at European level (particularly codes of practice or sectoral agreements). As a general rule, this type of voluntary initiative does not imply that the Institutions have adopted any particular stance, in particular where such initiatives are undertaken in areas which are not covered by the Treaties or in which the Union has not hitherto legislated. As one of its responsibilities, the Commission will scrutinise self-regulation practices in order to verify that they comply with the provisions of the EC Treaty.

The use of co-regulation, in particular, is widespread with private standards deployed as a substitute for legislation across wide swathes of Union activity. They are prevalent in the fields of the internal market, employment and social policy, protection of the environment, financial services, information and communications technology, fighting crime and consumer protection.[39] The justification is that they enable market participants to decide the level and form of regulation in a manner suitable for them and in a way that minimises adjustment and financial costs. Yet such arrangements bring a host of unanswered questions: in particular there is a concern that by contracting out law-making, many of its checks and balances are being lost.[40]

D. Chalmers, 'Private Power and Public Authority in European Union Law' (2005–06) 8 *Cambridge Yearbook of European Legal Studies* 59, 79

[These] regimes consequently generate a number of possible difficulties. The first is with the protection of public goods, such as protection of the environment, administration of justice or an effective financial system. They are set up to protect these public goods, but, invariably, the questions arise as to how effectively they do it and whether they are ambitious enough in their reach. The second is the protection of so called 'credential goods'. Credential goods deal with problems of asymmetries of information. Professional regimes are, for example, typically justified on the ground that consumers will know little about the quality of services provided by professionals, and it is, therefore, important to have a professional regime to regulate them. Yet all problem-solving regimes surround the individual with a bewildering array of semi-formal structures, which open up some possibilities, whilst closing off others. The forms of advertising she sees; her Internet provision; the quality and price of the goods and services she buys; access to professional help; and much of her natural environment: all are governed by this twilight zone of EU private law making. An individual goes to replace a part in her car, but can no longer obtain it because a manufacturer has discontinued it to meet its CO_2 obligations under the Union agreements, and she is, therefore, unable to drive any more. She has no redress, no sense

---

[39] For a survey see Chalmers, above n. 11, 64–73.

[40] See also L. Senden, 'Soft Law, Self-regulation and Co-regulation in European Law: Where do They Meet?' (2005) 9 *Electronic Journal of Comparative Law* No. 1; P. Verbruggen, 'Does Co-Regulation Strengthen EU Legitimacy?' (2009) 15 *ELJ* 425.

of transparency, and no sense of identifying who is responsible for this significant change in her life. Moreover, in contrast to parliamentary statutes or case law, the opacity of her entitlements undermines her ability to feel comfortable about and trust her surrounding environment, and her sense of social status, self-esteem and confidence to make choices. The final difficulty is distributive asymmetries. Problem–solving regimes may benefit some participants at the expense of others, and the entitlements they provide for third parties may benefit some more than others or actually disadvantage some parties by withdrawing entitlements they might otherwise have had.

(iv) Subsidiarity, proportionality and 'better regulation'

The subsidiarity and proportionality principles were brought together in a 2005 Commission initiative. Concern with the impact of EU legislation on the competitiveness of enterprises in the Union led the Commission to identify 'simplification' of EU legislation as a priority action for the Union.[41] There was, in particular, a concern that, if not properly formulated, EU legislation could generate unnecessary costs, restrict business activities and limit efficiency and innovation. A Communication was therefore adopted whose objective was to establish a 'European regulatory framework that fulfils the highest standards of law making respecting the principles of subsidiarity and proportionality'.[42]

European Commission, *Implementing the Community Lisbon Programme: A Strategy for the Simplification of the Regulatory Environment*, COM(2005)535, 2–3

Following these principles, the EU should only regulate if a proposed action can be better achieved at EU level. Any such action should not go beyond what is necessary to achieve the policy objectives pursued. It needs to be cost efficient and take the lightest form of regulation called for. In this respect simplification intends to make legislation at both Community and national level less burdensome, easier to apply and thereby more effective in achieving their goals.

The development of the European Union over the last half century has produced a large body of Community legislation, the Community 'acquis', which has often replaced 25 sets of rules with one and thereby offered business a more certain legal environment and a level playing field in which to operate. This stock of legislation has been essential, for example, in establishing the single market, developing EU environmental policy and in setting EU wide levels for the protection of workers and consumers. At the same time, legislation can also entail costs, hamper business, channel resources away from more efficient uses and in some cases act as a constraint to innovation, productivity and growth. The challenge is to get the balance right so as to ensure that the regulatory environment is necessary, simple and effective ...

Better regulation is however not de-regulation. Simplification at Community and national level means making things easier for citizens and operators. In turn, this should lead to a more effective legislative framework which is better suited to delivering the policy objectives of the Community.

---

[41] European Commission, *Better Regulation for Growth and Jobs*, COM(2005)97.

[42] European Commission, *Implementing the Community Lisbon Programme: A Strategy for the Simplification of the Regulatory Environment*, COM(2005)535.

The commitment to EU regulation only where it is necessary, simple and effective led the Commission to propose a simplification strategy whose five central points were the following:

- repeal of all legislative acts that are irrelevant or obsolete. The Commission will introduce review clauses to all legislation to ensure that new legislation is reviewed within a particular time-frame (typically three to five years);
- codification of existing EU legislation into more readable, coherent texts;
- recasting of legislation; this is different from codification as it involves the merging of legal texts so as to increase consistency and minimise overlaps;
- modification of the regulatory approach to make more use of co-regulation;
- greater use of Regulations rather than Directives as the former are seen as having immediate application, guaranteeing that all actors are subject to the same rules at the same time, and focusing attention on the concrete enforcement of EU rules.[43]

The impact of this in quantitative terms has been significant. By January 2009, about 600 legal acts amounting to about 6,500 pages of the Official Journal had been repealed. Codification had led to 729 previous acts being replaced by 229 pieces of legislation. The Commission estimated that this reduced the acquis, the amount of EU law, by about 10 per cent.[44] In addition, many proposals were withdrawn: 108 between 2005 and the end of 2008.[45]

To be sure, the dismantling of unnecessary legislation is not to be decried. It runs the risk, however, of deregulatory bias. In this, there is a worrying lack of transparency about the process. It is not clear how measures are deemed obsolete. The American author Wiener has observed that the criteria for determining this will be central, and that in the case of the Union the simple idea of disuse for a long time as a criterion is too vague and invites selective enforcement. He observes, for example, that whilst some laws may be obsolete it may be the case with others that they are 'dormant' because they are widely accepted and rarely violated.[46] In short, as one would not accept a process for law enactment whose criteria and procedures are so opaque, it is unclear why it is deemed sufficient for the repeal of legislation.

4 CONSULTATION

(i) General standards and minimum principles for consultation

A central concern of governance is that EU institutions should consult widely before taking any legislative action.[47] This is contained in Article 11 TEU which also sets out three underlying principles – dialogue, transparency and pluralism – that must inform such consultations.

---

[43] *Ibid.* 6–9.

[44] European Commission, *Third Progress Report on the Strategy for Simplifying the Regulatory Environment*, COM(2009)19, 2–3.

[45] European Commission, *Third Strategic Review of Better Regulation in the European Union*, COM(2009)15, 3.

[46] J. Wiener, 'Better Regulation in Europe' (2006) 59 *CLP* 447, 503.

[47] On the evolution of the Commission's and Court's approaches to consultation, see F. Bignami, 'Three Generations of Participation Rights Before the Commission' (2004) 68 *Law and Contemporary Problems* 61.

Article 11 TEU

1. The institutions shall, by appropriate means, give citizens and representative associations the opportunity to make known and publicly exchange their views in all areas of Union action.
2. The institutions shall maintain an open, transparent and regular dialogue with representative associations and civil society.
3. The European Commission shall carry out broad consultations with parties concerned in order to ensure that the Union's actions are coherent and transparent.

These principles are detailed in the 2002 Commission Communication on general principles and minimum standards for consultation.[48] This sets out the following responsibilities for the Commission.

Content of consultation is to be clear   The Commission should set out a summary of the context, scope and objectives of consultation, including a description of the specific issues open for discussion or questions with particular importance for the Commission. It should make available details of any hearings, meetings or conferences, as well as contact details and information on deadlines. It should provide explanation of the Commission processes for dealing with contributions, what feedback to expect and details of the next stages involved in the development of the policy.

Relevant parties should have an opportunity to express their opinions   In its consultations, the Commission should ensure adequate coverage of those affected by the policy, those who will be involved in implementation of the policy, or bodies that have stated objectives giving them a direct interest in the policy. In determining the relevant parties for consultation, it should take into account the impact of the policy on other policy areas, the need for specific experience, expertise or technical knowledge and the need to involve non-organised interests. It should consider the track record of participants in previous consultations as well as the need for a proper balance between representatives of social and economic bodies, large and small organisations or companies, wider constituencies (such as churches and religious communities) and specific target groups (for example women, the elderly, the unemployed, or ethnic minorities).

The Commission should publish consultations widely   This is via the web portal, 'Your Voice in Europe',[49] which is the Commission's single access point for consultation.

Participants are to be given sufficient time to respond   The Commission should allow at least eight weeks for reception of responses to written public consultations and twenty working days' notice for meetings.

---

[48] European Commission, *General Principles and Minimum Standards for Consultation of Interested Parties by the Commission*, COM(2002)704. See D. Obradovic and J. Alonso, 'Good Governance Requirements Concerning the Participation of Interest Groups in EU Consultations' (2006) 43 *CMLRev.* 1049.

[49] See http://ec.europa.eu/yourvoice/consultations/index_en.htm (accessed 1 September 2009).

Acknowledgement and adequate feedback is to be provided   Receipt of contributions should be acknowledged and the results displayed on websites. Explanatory memoranda accompanying legislative proposals following a consultation process must include the results of these consultations, an explanation as to how these were conducted and how the results were taken into account in the proposal.

Like any procedures, there is a danger that these criteria are just paper obligations and are no more than hoops to climb through. To assess their bite, it is necessary to consider the surrounding legal context to see whether it gives rise to the dialogue, transparency and pluralism alluded to in Article 11 TEU.

(ii) Dialogue within the consultation process

Dialogue, to be meaningful, has to be a commitment to do more than merely talk; for one can talk forever without its necessarily having any bearing on the subsequent legislation. To be significant, dialogue has therefore to be similar to the notion of accountability used by Bovens in which he describes it as 'a relationship between an actor and a forum in which the actor has an obligation to explain and justify his or her conduct, the forum can pose questions and pass judgment and the actor may face consequences'.[50] The duty on EU institutions to give reasons is central to such a dialogue. It imposes duties on them to justify themselves, to be questioned and to be held to account for the reasons they present. There is, indeed, a duty to provide reasons which is set out in Article 296 TFEU.

Article 296(2) TFEU

Legal acts shall state the reasons on which they are based and shall refer to any proposals, initiatives, recommendations, requests or opinions required by the Treaties.

The duty is not a strong one, however. The reasons given can be quite general and they do not have to respond to points made by those who have been consulted. A good example is *Commission* v *Spain*.[51] Aid had been granted to farmers in Extremadura, one of the poorest areas of Spain. The aid to each farmer was for relatively small amounts and applied to just nine products, with the aid paid in the case of most of the vegetables only if they were to be used for processing. The Commission argued that, in the light of the significant trade in vegetables between Spain and the other states, the aid could distort competition and affect trade between Member States by virtue of the subsidy to production costs for Spanish undertakings. It declared the aid illegal. The Spanish government stated that the reasons were inadequate on a number of grounds. First, the decision looked at the market for all green vegetables rather than the nine vegetables in question. Secondly, it did not look at the share of Extremaduran produce in the national market and its contribution to trade within the Union. Finally, there was no explanation of the relationship between the total volume of trade between Spain and the other Member States and the quantity of aid in question, in particular it was not shown how

---

[50] M. Bovens, 'Analysing and Assessing Accountability: A Conceptual Framework' (2007) 13 *ELJ* 447, 450.

[51] In like vein, see Joined Cases C-346/03 and C-529/03 *Atzeni and Others* v *Regione autonoma della Sardegna* [2006] ECR I-1875; Case T-271/03 *Deutsche Telekom* v *Commission* [2008] ECR II-477.

the latter affected the former. These points had previously been made to the Commission by the Spanish government, and the latter's failure to address them was quite an indictment. The Court of Justice nevertheless held that the Commission's reasoning was sufficient.

Case C-113/00 *Spain v Commission* [2002] ECR I-7601

47. It should first of all be observed that the obligation to provide a statement of reasons laid down in Article [296(2) TFEU] is an essential procedural requirement, as distinct from the question whether the reasons given are correct, which goes to the substantive legality of the contested measure. Accordingly, the statement of reasons required by Article [296(2) TFEU] must be appropriate to the act at issue and must disclose in a clear and unequivocal fashion the reasoning followed by the institution which adopted the measure in question in such a way as to enable the persons concerned to ascertain the reasons for the measure and to enable the competent court to exercise its power of review.

48. Furthermore, that requirement must be appraised by reference to the circumstances of each case, in particular the content of the measure, the nature of the reasons given and the interest which the addressees of the measure, or other parties to whom it is of direct and individual concern, may have in obtaining explanations. It is not necessary for the reasoning to go into all the relevant facts and points of law, since the question whether the statement of reasons meets the requirements of Article [296(2) TFEU] must be assessed with regard not only to its wording but also to its context and to all the legal rules governing the matter in question.

49. In the light of that case law, it does not appear that the Commission failed in this case to fulfil its obligation to provide an adequate statement of reasons in the contested decision for the finding that the aid in question affects trade between Member States.

50. First of all ... the Commission provides figures on the total quantity of vegetables produced in Spain and on the volume of trade in vegetables between Spain and the other Member States in 1998. It is clear from this information that a sizeable portion of Spanish horticultural goods is exported to other Member States. Whilst the Commission did not provide detailed figures on exports of those vegetables to which the aid scheme in question applies, it none the less noted that the overall context in which the scheme operates is one of a high level of trade between Member States of products in the horticultural sector.

51. Next ... the Commission refers to the direct and immediate effect of the aid measures on the production costs of undertakings producing and processing fruit and vegetables in Spain, and to the economic advantage that they confer on such undertakings over those that do not have access to comparable aid in other Member States.

52. ... the Commission also refers explicitly to Regulation No. 2200/96 which established a common organisation of the market in the fruit and vegetable sector. The Spanish Government could therefore not be unaware that the Commission's assessment of the aid scheme in question, including its finding that trade between Member States was affected by it, necessarily had to be viewed in the context of the rules on the common organisation of the markets.

53. In that connection it must be pointed out that the regime under Regulation No. 2200/96, which contains a set of uniform rules on production, marketing and competition between the economic operators concerned, benefits both trade in the fruit and vegetable sector and the development and maintenance of effective competition at Community level.

54. Finally, whilst it is common ground that in the statement of reasons for its decision the Commission is bound to refer at least to the circumstances in which aid has been granted where those circumstances show that the aid is such as to affect trade between Member States ... it is not bound to demonstrate the real effect of aid already granted ...

The Commission is let off with very thin reasoning and with providing little engagement with the issues raised by the Spanish government. This derives from the functions that are ascribed to the duty to give reasons. It is not there to require EU institutions to enter into dialogue with and justify themselves to interested parties. Instead, as paragraph 47 sets out, it is merely there to enable the Court of Justice to orient the Decision. The duty to state reasons is therefore stated to be important to discover the rationale for the measure and to enable judicial review. The reasons do little more than serve as a context for understanding the Decision.

The consequence is that there is a very light onus on EU institutions to be responsive to the consultation. This is reflected in how the Commission treats the results of its consultations. Typically, a synthesis is brought together of all the central views. This synthesis will set out the views but will rarely express a Commission opinion. It is entirely descriptive in nature. The question of how these views inform any Commission proposal or how the Commission will respond to any of them is left completely opaque.[52] The Commission is also of the view that it is under no legal obligation to consult an individual party or to respond or give individual feedback to a particular view.[53]

(iii) Transparency of the consultation process

A central concern within the consultation process is knowing who the lobbyists are and who they represent. The 2002 Communication, thus, imposes some responsibilities on lobbyists. Representative institutions must set out which interests they represent and how inclusive that representation is.[54] If they fail to do so, their submission, though not disqualified, will be treated as an individual submission and given less weight. In a review of the procedure, the Commission identified the thinness of these responsibilities as the central weakness in the lobbying system.[55] It has therefore established a voluntary register for lobbyists.[56] Membership is only available to those who observe a Code of Conduct set out in the Register. This requires the lobbyist:

- to identify themselves by name and the entity they work for or represent;
- not to misrepresent themselves so as to mislead third parties and/or EU staff;
- to declare the interests, and where applicable the clients or the members, which they represent;
- to ensure that, to the best of their knowledge, information which they provide is unbiased, complete, up-to-date and not misleading;
- not to obtain or try to obtain information, or any decision, dishonestly;
- not to induce EU staff to contravene rules and standards of behaviour applicable to them;
- if employing former EU staff, to respect their obligation to abide by the rules and confidentiality requirements which apply to them.

---

[52] A good example is the Commission Consultation on the European Commission, *Green Paper on Agricultural Product Quality: Product Standards, Farming Requirements and Quality Schemes*, COM(2008)641. This elicited 560 responses. The Commission Conclusions on them are available at http://ec.europa.eu/agriculture/quality/policy/privstat_en.pdf (accessed 1 October 2009).

[53] For a description of the evolution of Commission views, see Obradovic and Alonso, above n. 48, 1059–61.

[54] European Commission, above n. 48, 17.

[55] European Commission, *Follow-up to the Green Paper: European Transparency Initiative*, COM(2007)127, 3–4.

[56] European Commission, *European Transparency Initiative: A Framework for Relations with Interest Representatives (Register and Code of Conduct)*, COM(2008)323.

Whilst membership is voluntary, the Register had more than 1,000 members after one year.[57] That said, it is not clear how some of the more wide-ranging transparency concerns will be policed. These include the presentation of distorted information by lobbyists to the EU institutions and the manufacture of organising campaigns exaggerating popular support for an initiative.[58]

(iv) Inclusiveness of EU consultation

The final question is the pluralism of the processes: to whom do the EU institutions talk and to whom do they listen? Clearly, it is undesirable that they only listen to a limited number of groups and that they listen to these groups exclusively and recurrently. There is a danger of 'capture', with the EU institutions possibly promoting policies that are too closely aligned to the interests of a particular constituency, and a problem of credibility with their not being perceived to act in the wider public interest. In its 2002 Communication, the Commission stated that it wished to be as inclusive as possible, but there were practical limits.

European Commission, *General Principles and Minimum Standards for Consultation of Interested Parties by the Commission*, COM(2002)704, 11–12

The Commission wishes to stress that it will maintain an inclusive approach in line with the principle of open governance: Every individual citizen, enterprise or association will continue to be able to provide the Commission with input. In other words, the Commission does not intend to create new bureaucratic hurdles in order to restrict the number of those that can participate in consultation processes.

However, two additional considerations must be taken into account in this context. First, best practice requires that the target group should be clearly defined prior to the launch of a consultation process. In other words, the Commission should actively seek input from relevant interested parties, so these will have to be targeted on the basis of sound criteria. Second, clear selection criteria are also necessary where access to consultation is limited for practical reasons. This is especially the case for the participation of interested parties in advisory bodies or at hearings.

The Commission would like to underline the importance it attaches to input from representative European organisations. However, the issue of representativeness at European level should not be used as the only criterion when assessing the relevance or quality of comments. The Commission will avoid consultation processes which could give the impression that 'Brussels is only talking to Brussels', as one person put it. In many cases, national and regional viewpoints can be equally important in taking into account the diversity of situations in the Member States. Moreover, minority views can also form an essential dimension of open discourse on policies. On the other hand, it is important for the Commission to consider how representative views are when taking a political decision following a consultation process.

---

[57] See http://ec.europa.eu/transparency/index_en.htm (accessed 6 October 2009).
[58] European Commission, *Green Paper: European Transparency Initiative*, COM(2006)194, 6.

EU institutions face two challenges to this ethos of inclusiveness. The first is the heavy predominance of corporate lobbyists. Economic interests are seen as having resources not available to other groups and a particularly strong presence in Brussels.[59] The second concerns the role of pan-European organisations. There is the issue of how representative these are. In the 2002 Communication, the Commission stated that they must have a permanent pan-European interest, represent general interests and have a presence in most Member States. Yet doubts have been raised about the representative nature of even the most well-known of these. In 1998, UEAPME, the pan-European organisation representing small and medium-sized enterprises, challenged an agreement on parental leave between UNICE, the main pan-European industrial association, and ETUC, the pan-European association representing the trade unions, on the grounds that it excluded them. Whilst the application before the General Court was unsuccessful, it indicated the difficulties involved, as it is hard to argue that small and medium-sized enterprises might not have a particular view on the particular issue that should be heard.[60] The other problem is that, as Greenwood has noted, 'extended partnership arrangements have become established as de facto practice' between the Commission and these pan-European groups.[61] In other words, particular attention is paid to their views. This is problematic not simply because they are best at representing concerns of a more universal nature, rather than particular local ones, but because many are funded by the Commission. In his 2007 article, Greenwood noted that the Commission spends around €1 billion annually in funding interest-group activities. Almost all the 300 pan-European citizen interest groups received funding, with this being 80–90 per cent of the income for prominent groups such as the European Network Against Racism and the European Social Platform.[62]

5 THE PRIORITY OF KNOWLEDGE

Central principles of the White Paper are that Union decision-making be effective and coherent. In part, this relates to regulatory responsiveness and the 'better regulation' strategy. Attention must be paid to the choice of regulatory instrument, the level of intervention and regular review of the measure. It also relates, however, to the use of knowledge to inform the policy-making process.

Knowledge is used here in two ways. First, expert knowledge is used to inform the policy-making process so the policy is based on the best we know. Secondly, knowledge is used to assess the impacts of the policy: what do we know about how this will affect us? This latter process, impact assessment, relies, of course, on expertise but is a slightly wider process as it is not simply looking at whether a policy will work but what its wider effects will be.

---

[59] This is acknowledged in European Commission, *ibid.* 6. See also for an overview S. Sarugger, 'Interest Groups and Democracy in the European Union' (2008) 31 *WEP* 1274, 1280–5.

[60] Case T-135/96 *UEAPME* v *Commission* [1998] ECR II-2335. For comment see N. Bernard, 'UEAPME and the Social Dialogue' in J. Shaw (ed.), *Social Law and Policy in an Evolving European Union* (Oxford and Portland, Hart, 2000); S. Smismans, 'The European Social Dialogue in the Shadow of Hierarchy' (2008) 28 *Journal of Public Policy* 161, 167–70.

[61] J. Greenwood, 'Organised Civil Society and Democratic Legitimacy in the European Union' (2007) 37 *BJPS* 333, 346.

[62] *Ibid.* 343.

(i) Expertise and the policy-making process

EU institutions are neither free to take measures without taking scientific advice nor free to ignore it. Any measure failing to give weight to scientific evidence is likely to be regarded as a breach of the proportionality principle insofar as it will be argued that it imposes an unnecessary constraint on an operator without a sound reason. The institutional implications of this were explored at greatest length in *Pfizer*. A ban was placed on virginiamycin, an antibiotic used in animal feeding stuffs, which had been lawfully marketed in the European Union for a number of years. The ban followed a conference in Copenhagen, which concluded that it could lead to new viruses which were resistant to antibiotics. The Danish government, therefore, asked for virginiamycin to be banned. The Commission consulted the Standing Committee on Animal Nutrition (SCAN), which considered that the scientific evidence did not justify a ban. The Council nevertheless decided to ban the antibiotic. Pfizer, the sole producer of the antibiotic, argued that such a measure was illegal as it lacked any scientific basis.

T–13/99 *Pfizer Animal Health* v *Council* [2002] ECR II–3305

149. ... risk assessment includes for the competent public authority, in this instance the Community institutions, a two-fold task, whose components are complementary and may overlap but, by reason of their different roles, must not be confused. Risk assessment involves, first, determining what level of risk is deemed unacceptable and, second, conducting a scientific assessment of the risks. ...

151. In that regard, it is for the Community institutions to determine the level of protection which they deem appropriate for society. It is by reference to that level of protection that they must then, while dealing with the first component of the risk assessment, determine the level of risk – i.e. the critical probability threshold for adverse effects on human health and for the seriousness of those possible effects – which in their judgment is no longer acceptable for society and above which it is necessary, in the interests of protecting human health, to take preventive measures in spite of any existing scientific uncertainty ... Therefore, determining the level of risk deemed unacceptable involves the Community institutions in defining the political objectives to be pursued under the powers conferred on them by the Treaty.

152. Although they may not take a purely hypothetical approach to risk and may not base their decisions on a zero-risk ... the Community institutions must nevertheless take account of their obligation under the first subparagraph of Article [168 TFEU] to ensure a high level of human health protection, which, to be compatible with that provision, does not necessarily have to be the highest that is technically possible ...

153. The level of risk deemed unacceptable will depend on the assessment made by the competent public authority of the particular circumstances of each individual case. In that regard, the authority may take account, inter alia, of the severity of the impact on human health were the risk to occur, including the extent of possible adverse effects, the persistency or reversibility of those effects and the possibility of delayed effects as well as of the more or less concrete perception of the risk based on available scientific knowledge.

154. As regards the second component of risk assessment, the Court of Justice has already had occasion to note that in matters relating to additives in feeding stuffs the Community institutions are responsible for carrying out complex technical and scientific assessments (see Case 14/78 *Denkavit* v *Commission* [1978] ECR 2497, paragraph 20). The Council itself has drawn attention in its arguments to the fact that the decision to withdraw the authorisation of virginiamycin was based on extremely complex scientific and technical assessments over which scientists have widely diverging views ...

155. In such circumstances a scientific risk assessment must be carried out before any preventive measures are taken.

156. A scientific risk assessment is commonly defined, at both international level … and Community level … as a scientific process consisting in the identification and characterisation of a hazard, the assessment of exposure to the hazard and the characterisation of the risk.

157. In that regard, it is appropriate to point out, first, that, when a scientific process is at issue, the competent public authority must, in compliance with the relevant provisions, entrust a scientific risk assessment to experts who, once the scientific process is completed, will provide it with scientific advice.

158. As the Commission pointed out in its Communication on Consumer Health and Food Safety … scientific advice is of the utmost importance at all stages of the drawing up of new legislation and for the execution and management of existing legislation… Furthermore, the Commission stated there that it will use this advice for the benefit of the consumer in order to ensure a high level of protection of health (*ibid*). The duty imposed on the Community institutions by the first subparagraph of Article [168 TFEU] to ensure a high level of human health protection means that they must ensure that their decisions are taken in the light of the best scientific information available and that they are based on the most recent results of international research, as the Commission has itself emphasised in the Communication on Consumer Health and Food Safety.

159. Thus, in order to fulfil its function, scientific advice on matters relating to consumer health must, in the interests of consumers and industry, be based on the principles of excellence, independence and transparency …

169. … in this case, in which the Community institutions were required to undertake a scientific risk assessment and to evaluate highly complex scientific and technical facts, judicial review of the way in which they did so must be limited. The Community judicature is not entitled to substitute its assessment of the facts for that of the Community institutions, on which the Treaty confers sole responsibility for that duty. Instead, it must confine itself to ascertaining whether the exercise by the institutions of their discretion in that regard is vitiated by a manifest error or a misuse of powers or whether the institutions clearly exceeded the bounds of their discretion.

170. In particular, under the precautionary principle the Community institutions are entitled, in the interests of human health, to adopt, on the basis of as yet incomplete scientific knowledge, protective measures which may seriously harm legally protected positions, and they enjoy a broad discretion in that regard.

171. However, according to … settled case law… in such circumstances, the guarantees conferred by the Community legal order in administrative proceedings are of even more fundamental importance. Those guarantees include, in particular, the duty of the competent institution to examine carefully and impartially all the relevant aspects of the individual case …

172. It follows that a scientific risk assessment carried out as thoroughly as possible on the basis of scientific advice founded on the principles of excellence, transparency and independence is an important procedural guarantee whose purpose is to ensure the scientific objectivity of the measures adopted and preclude any arbitrary measures …

197. … the role played by a committee of experts, such as SCAN, in a procedure designed to culminate in a decision or a legislative measure, is restricted, as regards the answer to the questions which the competent institution has asked it, to providing a reasoned analysis of the relevant facts of the case in the light of current knowledge about the subject, in order to provide the institution with the factual knowledge which will enable it to take an informed decision.

198. However, the competent Community institution must, first, prepare for the committee of experts the factual questions which need to be answered before it can adopt a decision and, second, assess the probative value of the opinion delivered by the committee. In that regard, the Community institution must ensure that the reasoning in the opinion is full, consistent and relevant.

199. To the extent to which the Community institution opts to disregard the opinion, it must provide specific reasons for its findings by comparison with those made in the opinion and its statement of reasons must explain why it is disregarding the latter. The statement of reasons must be of a scientific level at least commensurate with that of the opinion in question. In such a case, the institution may take as its basis either a supplementary opinion from the same committee of experts or other evidence, whose probative value is at least commensurate with that of the opinion concerned. In the event that the Community institution disregards only part of the opinion, it may also avail itself of those parts of the scientific reasoning which it does not dispute.

On the one hand, the judgment pays lip-service to the discretion enjoyed by policy-makers in how they treat scientific expertise.[63] A division is made between risk assessment and risk management. The former identifies and characterises the hazard (paragraph 156) while the latter determines how much exposure there should be to the risk. This is a matter for EU decision-makers (paragraph 151). Yet this discretion is more apparent than real. In areas characterised by scientific complexity, they must consult scientific bodies, which are marked by 'excellence, independence and transparency' (paragraph 172). This advice is not neutral in that it will characterise the hazard in terms of its danger (e.g. dangerous, not dangerous, high or low level of risk). Whilst the legislature is free not to follow the advice, it can only depart from it if it provides scientific evidence of equivalent authority as a justification for doing so (paragraph 199). In practice, it invariably follows it. This makes the scientific bodies very powerful as, in effect, they determine the body of the law in such cases.

Historically, as was the case in *Pfizer*, this process was carried out through the establishment of Scientific Committees which, whilst embedded within the institutional structures of the Commission, were often composed of outside experts. The governance agenda changed this. It proposed that the place of these be taken by new regulatory agencies which will be responsible for the carrying out of risk assessment.[64] The establishment of these has been discussed in Chapter 2.[65] There, an extract from Shapiro was considered about how this leads to government by technocracy and integration by stealth with deeply contentious issues reduced to questions of scientific expertise. Joerges has raised another issue, which is the ideological neutrality of these agencies. Frequently, the safety standards considered by these are industry standards based on industry research. He points out that they provide a venue for private interests free from traditional political scrutiny.

---

[63] For some of the wider implications of the judgment, see J. Scott and S. Sturm, 'Courts as Catalysts: Rethinking the Judicial Role in New Governance' (2007) 13 *CJEL* 565.

[64] European Commission White Paper, above n. 3, 23–4.

[65] See pp. 66–7.

C. Joerges, 'The Law's Problems with the Governance of the Single European Market' in C. Joerges and R. Dehousse (eds.) *Good Governance in Europe's Integrated Market* (Oxford, Oxford University Press, 2002) 1, 17

Charged with market entry/exit regulation and more general, informal, information-gathering and policy-informing duties, the new European agencies apparently meet a purely technical demand for market-corrective and sector-specific regulation. This seemingly technocratic and semi-autonomous status implicitly provides private market interests with a voice, and this gives credence to the lingering notion that internal market regulation has more to do with 'neutral' sustenance of individual economic enterprise than with the imposition of (collective) political/social direction. Notwithstanding their placement under the Commission's institutional structure and the presence of national representatives within their management structures, their founding statutes (Council Directives and Regulations), permanent staff, organizational independence, varying degrees of budgetary autonomy and direct networking with national administrators largely shield these agencies from explicitly political processes.

(ii) Impact assessment

In the White Paper, the Commission stated that the quality of EU policy proposals would be improved not only by reliance on expert advice but also through impact assessment.[66] This has been described by the Commission in the following terms:

> the process of systematic analysis of the likely impacts of intervention by public authorities. It is as such an integral part of the process of designing policy proposals and making decision-makers and the public aware of the likely impacts.[67]

It is a process whereby the EU institutions try to anticipate the social, economic and environmental impacts of different policy options, and model their choices accordingly. There is a tension here, as this suggests that impact assessment is about finding the best choice economically, ecologically and socially. The Commission, however, indicates that it is not to be so prescriptive and that it is an aid to, rather than a substitute for, policy planning.[68] As the procedure is time-consuming, it is not applied to all Commission proposals. Instead, the Commission will only use it if the proposal results in substantial economic, environmental and/or social impacts on a specific sector or sectors, has a significant impact on major interested parties, or represents a major policy reform.[69] That said, the number of assessments carried out is still significant, with 135 being formulated in 2008.[70] The procedure is a six stage one that takes place before the Commission makes its proposal. It is carried out in the first instance by the unit in the Commission developing the proposal and involves the following steps:

- identification of the problem: this will include the nature and extent of the procedure and the key players;
- defining the objectives of any action: this must consider in particular whether they are coherent, comply with other EU policies, and respect the European Union Charter of Fundamental Rights;

[66] European Commission White Paper, above n. 3, 30.
[67] European Commission, *Impact Assessment*, COM(2002)276, 3.
[68] *Ibid.* 9–10.
[69] *Ibid.* 7.
[70] European Commission, *Impact Assessment Board Report for 2008*, SEC(2009)55, 2.

- development of the main policy options: the development of these options must consider whether regulatory or non-regulatory choices should be adopted and compliance with the proportionality principle;
- analysis of the social, economic and environmental impacts of the options: this should be done in qualitative and, where possible, quantitative and monetary terms;
- comparison of the options: this involves looking at the impacts of the different options and selecting, if possible, a preferred one;
- outlining of policy monitoring and evaluation: this will look at the arrangements and the indicators used to inform the assessment.[71]

There should be consultation with stakeholders throughout the process.[72] In 2006, an external evaluation was carried out of the process. It found consultation was good but there was little evidence that impact assessment had much influence on policy proposals; strong resistance within the Commission to it; and the reports were of variable quality.[73] An Impact Assessment Board was therefore established to monitor the quality of the assessments done by the different parts of the Commission and to provide support. The effect of this Board is difficult to gauge. It reported in 2009 that many assessments it saw were sub-standard. It also stated that whilst in about 40 per cent of cases the Commission unit substantially revised its communication after the opinion of the Board, there were only minor or no changes in about 25 per cent of cases.[74]

The question of the effect of impact assessment on EU decision-making is thus still open. Yet, it can also be questioned as a policy tool. Radaelli has pointed to a number of concerns that are present in the regulation literature about impact assessment.[75] First, it can lead to an overly empirical analysis. In fields such as the environment, there is a real question as to how quality of life or ecological perspectives can be measured. Secondly, there is a danger of overstatement. Often, advocacy papers can be put forward as impact assessments. A position will be put forward as a truth that one option has less negative impacts than another, but the biases that lead to this view can be hidden. Finally, it is problematic for measuring or subsequently evaluating fast-changing regulatory regimes that involve a range of instruments and have to adapt continually to changing circumstances. For impact assessments are quite static processes that rely above all on an anticipation of what will happen, and this anticipation will invariably involve a number of assumptions.

6 TRANSPARENCY

The final virtue set out in the White Paper is that of accountability. Views on the meaning of accountability vary considerably. Earlier, a definition by Bovens was set out in which accountability was described as a relationship in which actors have to explain and justify their conduct, be questioned on it and face the consequences for it.[76] As important as the definition is

---

[71] European Commission, *Impact Assessment Guidelines*, SEC(2009)92, 4–5.
[72] *Ibid.* 19.
[73] The Evaluation Partnership, *Evaluation of the Commission's Impact Assessment System: Final Report* (April 2007), available at http://ec.europa.eu/governance/impact/key_docs/docs/tep_eias_final_report.pdf (accessed 5 October 2009).
[74] European Commission, *Impact Assessment Board Report*, above n. 70, 8–11.
[75] C. Radaelli, 'Whither Better Regulation for the Lisbon Agenda?' (2007) 14 *JEPP* 190.
[76] See p. 375.

the medium through which this accountability takes place. Harlow talks therefore of financial, legal and political accountability with different mechanisms (audit procedures, the courts, the political and administrative process) for securing institutional behaviour.[77] The White Paper is much blander. It sets out two ideas of accountability.[78]

First, it states that the institutional roles in the legislative and executive processes need to be clearer. This relates to the institutional checks and balances and the accountability institutions owe to each other. This is set out in Chapters 2 and 3 on institutional relations and the legislative procedures. In Chapter 10 we shall also consider the processes of institutional review, be it through the Ombudsman or the General Court. Secondly, each of the EU institutions must explain and take responsibility for what they do. In part, this is done through the duty to give reasons, which was discussed earlier.[79] More generally, this is secured through providing information on what they do. The principle of transparency is set out in Article 15(3) TFEU.[80]

Article 15(3) TFEU

Any citizen of the Union, and any natural or legal person residing or having its registered office in a Member State, shall have a right of access to documents of the Union institutions, bodies, offices and agencies, whatever their medium, subject to the principles and the conditions to be defined in accordance with this paragraph.

General principles and limits on grounds of public or private interest governing this right of access to documents shall be determined by the European Parliament and the Council, acting by means of regulations in accordance with the ordinary legislative procedure.

Each institution, body, office or agency shall ensure that its proceedings are transparent and shall elaborate in its own Rules of Procedure specific provisions regarding access to its documents, in accordance with the regulations referred to in the second subparagraph.

Article 15(3) TFEU is a framework provision. It sets out a principle of a right of access to EU documents and of transparency of procedures. However, the modalities are to be set out in secondary legislation. The central instrument is Regulation 1049/2001/EC.[81] However, there is currently a Commission proposal to amend this Regulation, and the two documents, the Regulation and the proposed amendment, should be read side by side.[82]

---

[77] C. Harlow, *Accountability in the European Union* (Oxford, Oxford University Press, 2002) ch. 1.

[78] European Commission White Paper, above n. 3, 10.

[79] See pp. 375–7.

[80] On the development of the principle in EU law, see A. Tomkins, 'Transparency and the Emergence of a European Administrative Law' (1999) 19 *YBEL* 217. The principle is also contained in Article 42 of the European Charter on Fundamental Rights and Freedoms.

[81] Regulation 1049/2001/EC regarding public access to European Parliament, Council and Commission documents [2001] OJ L145/43. See M. De Leeuw, 'The Regulation on Public Access to European Parliament, Council and Commission Documents in the European Union: Are Citizens Better Off?' (2003) 28 *ELRev.* 324.

[82] The latest Commission amended proposal is European Commission, Proposal for a Regulation regarding public access to European Parliament, Council and Commission documents, COM(2008)229. For discussion, see I. Harden, 'The Revision of Regulation 1049/2001 on Public Access to Documents' (2009) 15 *EPL* 239.

(i) Scope of the right to access to documents

The central entitlement is set out in article 2 of the Regulation.

Article 2

1. Any citizen of the Union, and any natural or legal person residing or having its registered office in a Member State, has a right of access to documents of the institutions, subject to the principles, conditions and limits defined in this Regulation.
2. The institutions may, subject to the same principles, conditions and limits, grant access to documents to any natural or legal person not residing or not having its registered office in a Member State.
3. This Regulation shall apply to all documents held by an institution, that is to say, documents drawn up or received by it and in its possession, in all areas of activity of the European Union.

This access is provided in two ways. First, all EU institutions are required to keep up-to-date electronic registers of documents to which the public should have access.[83] In debates surrounding amendment of the Regulation, this register was not seen as particularly user-friendly and was seen as incomplete, excluding many preparatory documents in particular. There is a commitment, therefore, that these should be placed on the register and where possible in an electronic form. If a document is not on the register, the latter should, if possible, indicate where it is located.[84]

Secondly, parties can request access to particular information. The number of requests have risen from year to year, with 3,841 requests in 2006, 4,196 in 2007 and 5,197 in 2008.[85] If this is about increasing popular engagement with the European Union, its impact appears extremely limited. It is not simply that the overall numbers are very small for a polity of close to half a billion people. The composition of those requesting is very skewed. 31 per cent of requests were from academics and 17.5 per cent from public institutions. Only 16.75 per cent were from members of the public and 18.26 per cent from civil society.[86] It is the latter two groups that would be particularly important in the context of public engagement, and it is concerning that they make up only around one-third of all requests for information.

Any request must be made in writing and must be sufficiently precise to enable the institution to identify the document.[87] If the application is not sufficiently precise, the institution must ask the applicant to clarify the application and should provide assistance to enable her to do so.[88] There is a more general duty on the EU institutions to provide information and assistance on how and where applications are to be made.[89] Institutions must acknowledge receipt of any application and, within fifteen days, provide either access to the documents or reasons for refusing access.[90] If the application is for a very long document or a very large number

---

[83] Regulation 1049/2001, art. 11.
[84] European Commission Proposal, above n. 82, art. 12.
[85] European Commission, *Report on the Application in 2008 of Regulation 1049/2001*, COM(2009)331, 10.
[86] *Ibid.* 13.
[87] Regulation 1049/2001, art. 6(1).
[88] *Ibid.* art. 6(2).
[89] *Ibid.* art. 6(4).
[90] *Ibid.* art. 7.

of documents, the institution may confer with the applicant informally to find a fair solution about what should be supplied.[91]

This raises the question about what happens when the institution feels unable to supply the documents. This was explored at most length in *Williams*. The applicant was writing a doctorate at the Free University of Brussels. She asked for all internal documentation within the Commission on six pieces of legislation that constituted the heart of the Union's regime on genetically modified organisms. The Commission stated that the request was very wide-ranging. Williams met with the Commission and agreed to her request being split into six, with a priority being made between the six. In relation to the first request, the Commission refused access to twenty-three documents. Before the General Court, one of the arguments raised by the Commission was that the request was too imprecise and wide-ranging.[92] This was rejected by the Court.

Case T–42/05 *Williams* v *Commission* [2008] ECR II–156

85. It must be observed that the Court has already had occasion (Case T-2/03 *Verein für Konsumenteninformation* v *Commission* [2005] ECR II-1121) to note that it is necessary to bear in mind that an applicant may make a request for access, under Regulation No. 1049/2001, relating to a manifestly unreasonable number of documents, perhaps for trivial reasons, thus imposing a volume of work for processing of his request which could very substantially paralyse the proper working of the institution. The Court also noted in the same judgment that, in such a case, the institution's right to seek a 'fair solution' together with the applicant, pursuant to Article 6(3) of Regulation No. 1049/2001, reflects the possibility of account being taken, albeit in a particularly limited way, of the need to reconcile the interests of the applicant with those of good administration. The Court concluded from this that an institution therefore had to retain the right, in particular cases where concrete, individual examination of the documents would entail an unreasonable amount of administrative work, to balance the interest in public access to the documents against the burden of work so caused, in order to safeguard, in those particular cases, the interests of good administration.

86. The Court stated, however, that that possibility was applicable only in exceptional cases, in view, in particular, of the fact that it is not, in principle, appropriate that account should be taken of the amount of work entailed by the exercise of the applicant's right of access and its interest in order to vary the scope of that right... In addition, in so far as the right of access to documents held by the institutions constitutes an approach to be adopted in principle, the institution relying on the unreasonableness of the task entailed by the request bears the burden of proof of the scale of that task...

87. In the present case, first of all, it must be noted that the Commission availed itself of the possibility provided by Article 6(3) of Regulation No. 1049/2001, which enabled it to divide the applicant's initial request into six. Accordingly, in the contested decision, the Commission replied only to the first of the applicant's requests — whereby the applicant sought access to preparatory documents relating to Directive 2001/18 — which means that the request cannot be regarded as very wide-ranging. Furthermore, there is nothing in the contested decision to suggest that the handling of that request

---

[91] *Ibid.* art. 6(3).

[92] For debate, see J. Helikoski and P. Leino, 'Darkness at the Break of Noon: The Case Law on Regulation No.1049/2001 on Access to Documents' (2006) 43 *CMLRev.* 735, 756–60; H. Kraneborg, 'Is it Time to Revise the European Regulation on Public Access to Documents?' (2006) 12 *EPL* 251, 267–71.

would entail an unreasonable amount of work, likely to be detrimental to the principle of good administration.

88. ... the fact that neither the initial request nor the confirmatory application mentions specific documents cannot be regarded as having prevented the Commission from understanding that the applicant wished to have access to all preparatory documents relating to the legislation on GMOs ... Nor can the Commission reasonably rely on that fact in support of its contention that the burden of work imposed by the handling of the first request was unreasonable and that, in those circumstances, if it was to observe the principle of good administration, it could not – due to its limited resources – be required, under the principle of transparency, to consider the disclosure of each and every document held by it that could be relevant to such a request.

89. In that regard, it is sufficient to note that the Commission confined itself in its written pleadings to maintaining that the first request amounted to an exceptional situation because it was actually not possible, on account of its imprecise and undefined nature, to calculate the number of files and documents liable to fall within its scope. Such an argument cannot be upheld, since the request was clear in referring to access to all preparatory documents relating to Directive 2001/18 and therefore the absence of a list of specific documents could have an impact only on the time-limits for reply – an issue which was resolved by the fair solution – but not on the scope of the request for access.

It would seem, therefore, that whilst the institution may refuse unreasonable requests for absurd levels of documentation for trivial reasons, this will be highly unusual. There has to be a consideration whether the request can be broken down, and provided it seems (according to paragraph 89) the documents are identifiable, it is not sufficient for the institution to refuse a request because it cannot calculate the number of files.

The duties on the other side are less. There is no duty on the party to state the reason for the application, to provide any justification or to declare its interest in any way at all. It is therefore possible for those who are subject to disciplinary investigations by the Commission to ask for documents. The current reasoning is that if this will undermine an investigation, then justification must be sought in one of the exceptions rather than an exclusion that will prevent the party from having information about the nature of the proceedings against them.[93] Yet the proposed amendments suggest this will be reversed. Access to information is to be excluded on investigations or proceedings concerning an act of individual scope until the proceedings are closed or a definitive act taken.[94]

There are a number of further things to note about what can be sought, who can seek it and from whom.

First, Article 2(3) of the Regulation makes clear that applicants can ask not just for documents drawn up by the EU institutions but also those that fall into their possession. This widens the scope of available information considerably, as the Commission, in particular, acts very much as a clearing house, receiving documentation from private parties, other institutions and, above all, national governments. All these can be requested. Alongside this, the right of access to documents is a right of access to the information in the document itself. As a consequence,

---

[93] Joined Cases T-391/03 and T-70/04 *Franchet and Byk v Commission* [2006] ECR II-2023.
[94] European Commission Proposal, above n. 82, art. 2(6). See also p. 7 of the proposal for an explanation.

the institution has to consider whether to give partial access to a document, that is it must give access to all information that does not fall within an exception.[95]

Secondly, at the moment, Article 2(1) allows only EU residents or EU citizens to make a request for information. This is seen as too narrow, and the amendments propose that any natural or legal person should be able to seek access to EU institutions' documents, irrespective of nationality or residence.[96]

Thirdly, prior to the Lisbon Treaty, the right of access to documents could only be invoked against EU institutions themselves. Whilst Article 2(1) and the proposed amendments still hold that to be the case, this has to be read in the light of Article 15(3) TFEU, which extends this right to be applied against EU bodies, offices and agencies. The Union courts are not mentioned in Article 15(3) TFEU, however. The proposed amendments suggest that it should not apply to documents submitted to them by parties other than the institutions.[97] It is difficult to see the rationale for this. If there is a concern about the administration of justice, then this applies to all parties involved, including the institutions. Otherwise, it is not clear why judicial proceedings are treated differently from any other context.

(ii) Exceptions to the right to access to information

Most litigation has not focused on the extent of the right of access to information but rather the exceptions to this right, which allow access to be refused. These are set out in article 4 of Regulation 1049/2001/EC. On its face, it may seem an arcane business, to ponder over and again the meaning of this provision. Yet, it has proved central as these exceptions are formulated in such a way as to cover whole fields of Union governmental or legislative activity. Debates about the remit of article 4 raise questions as to whether we can be denied access to knowledge about the way in which an entire field of EU law or politics is being conducted. In this regard, the rate of refusal is quite high, with 13.99 per cent of requests for information being refused in 2008, with a further 3.33 per cent only being given partial access.[98]

Article 4

1. The institutions shall refuse access to a document where disclosure would undermine the protection of:
   (a) the public interest as regards:
      - public security,
      - defence and military matters,
      - international relations,
      - the financial, monetary or economic policy of the Community or a Member State;
   (b) privacy and the integrity of the individual, in particular in accordance with Community legislation regarding the protection of personal data.
2. The institutions shall refuse access to a document where disclosure would undermine the protection of:
   - commercial interests of a natural or legal person, including intellectual property,

---

[95] Case C-353/99 P *Council v Hautala* [2001] ECR I-9565.
[96] European Commission Proposal, above n. 82, art. 2(1).
[97] *Ibid.* art. 2(5).
[98] European Commission, above n. 85, 10.

- court proceedings and legal advice,
- the purpose of inspections, investigations and audits, unless there is an overriding public interest in disclosure.

3. Access to a document, drawn up by an institution for internal use or received by an institution, which relates to a matter where the decision has not been taken by the institution, shall be refused if disclosure of the document would seriously undermine the institution's decision-making process, unless there is an overriding public interest in disclosure.

Access to a document containing opinions for internal use as part of deliberations and preliminary consultations within the institution concerned shall be refused even after the decision has been taken if disclosure of the document would seriously undermine the institution's decision-making process, unless there is an overriding public interest in disclosure.

4. As regards third-party documents, the institution shall consult the third party with a view to assessing whether an exception in paragraph 1 or 2 is applicable, unless it is clear that the document shall or shall not be disclosed.

5. A Member State may request the institution not to disclose a document originating from that Member State without its prior agreement.

6. If only parts of the requested document are covered by any of the exceptions, the remaining parts of the document shall be released.

There has been extensive case law on these exceptions, and only some of the more salient issues will be addressed here.[99] The starting point of the Union courts is that, as the public right of access to the documents is connected with the democratic nature of the EU institutions, the Regulation intends to give the public the widest access. The exceptions must therefore be interpreted and applied strictly.[100] This statement is, however, little more than rhetorical, particularly as the exceptions are grouped into three categories.

- The first category set out in article 4(1) of the Regulation is mandatory. It requires the institution to refuse access to the document if it falls within that category. The proposed amendments to the Regulation would create one further exception here relating to the public interest as regards the 'the environment, such as breeding sites of rare species'.[101] It deletes the privacy exception set out in the current Regulation, replacing it with a new exception which requires EU institutions only to disclose personal data in accordance with EU legislation on data protection.[102]
- The second exception set out in article 4(2) and (3) gives the EU institutions a discretion to grant access to a document if, notwithstanding that it falls within one of the categories, there is an overriding public interest. This category has been extended by the proposed amendments to include arbitration and dispute settlement proceedings and the objectivity and impartiality of selection procedures.

---

[99] For more extensive treatment, see D. Adamski, 'How Wide is the "Widest Possible"? Judicial Interpretation of the Exceptions to the Right of Access to Official Documents' (2009) 46 *CMLRev.* 521.

[100] See e.g. Case C-266/05 P *Sison* v *Council* [2007] ECR I-1233.

[101] European Commission Proposal, above n. 82, art. 4(1)(e).

[102] *Ibid.* art. 4(5).

- The third exception, in article 4(5), relates to documents originating from a Member State. In such instances, there is a requirement of prior agreement.

The Regulation, thus, sets out three tests of review. This is not uncontroversial, as it is hard to see why an overriding public interest can never exist in relation to the first or the third category. There may, for example, be 'security' documents or national documents whose disclosure makes the decision-maker uncomfortable, but which are nevertheless essential for public debate.

With regard to the mandatory exceptions, the courts apply a test of marginal review. That is to say that they accept that the issue will often be sensitive and the institution in question must have discretion over the matter. The courts will thus not substitute their judgement for that of the institution but confine themselves to seeing whether accurate reasons have been given for the refusal and whether there has been a manifest error of assessment. A recent example is *WWF European Policy Programme*. The WWF, an environmental NGO, asked for documents concerning international trade negotiations taking place within the World Trade Organization. These documents set out other states' positions as well as that of the Union in the negotiations, and also the minutes of the meetings. The Council refused to disclose under article 4(1)(a), arguing that this undermined the Union's commercial interests and would be prejudicial to its relations with other states.

Case T–264/04 *WWF European Policy Programme* v Council [2007] ECR II–911

39. ... the rule is that the public is to have access to the documents of the institutions and refusal of access is the exception to that rule. Consequently, the provisions sanctioning a refusal must be construed and applied strictly so as not to defeat the application of the rule. Moreover, an institution is obliged to consider in respect of each document to which access is sought whether, in the light of the information available to that institution, disclosure of the document is in fact likely to undermine one of the public interests protected by the exceptions which permit refusal of access. In order for those exceptions to be applicable, the risk of the public interest being undermined must therefore be reasonably foreseeable and not purely hypothetical ...

40. It is also apparent from the case law that the institutions enjoy a wide discretion when considering whether access to a document may undermine the public interest and, consequently, that the Court's review of the legality of the institutions' decisions refusing access to documents on the basis of the mandatory exceptions relating to the public interest must be limited to verifying whether the procedural rules and the duty to state reasons have been complied with, the facts have been accurately stated, and whether there has been a manifest error of assessment of the facts or a misuse of powers ...

41. As to whether there was a manifest error of assessment of the facts, as the applicant essentially submits is the case, it must be noted that the Council refused to grant access to the note so as not to risk upsetting the negotiations that were taking place at that time in a sensitive context, which was characterised by resistance on the part of both the developing and the developed countries and the difficulty in reaching an agreement, as illustrated by the breakdown of negotiations at the WTO Ministerial Conference in Cancun in September 2003. Thus, in considering that disclosure of that note could have undermined relations with the third countries which are referred to in the note and the room for negotiation needed by the Community and its Member States to bring those negotiations to a conclusion, the Council did not commit a manifest error of assessment and was right to consider that disclosure of the note would have entailed the risk of undermining the public interest as regards international relations and the Community's financial, monetary and economic policy, which was reasonably foreseeable and not purely hypothetical.

In this instance, the review was quite thin. The General Court defers to the Council's assessment in paragraph 41 that providing the information will upset negotiation. However, it has not been consistent and, in some instances, the review of whether there has been a manifest error of assessment will be quite exacting. In *Kuijer,* a university lecturer challenged a decision by the Council to refuse him access to human rights reports on a number of countries that had been prepared for CIREA, an EU body that compiled documentation and exchanged information on asylum.[103] As some of these were quite damning, the Council refused on the grounds that this would damage relations with these countries. The General Court did not agree with this characterisation and overturned the Council's decision. It held that refusal had to be made by reference to the specific content and context of each human rights report. These reports contained general information on the protection of human rights which had already been made public and did not involve any politically sensitive appraisal of the state by the Council itself. The Court held, therefore, that neither the content nor the nature of the reports justified a refusal to grant access.

In the case of the discretionary category in article 4(2) and (3) of the Regulation, EU institutions must allow access to a document if, notwithstanding that it falls within one of these categories, there is an overriding public interest which justifies disclosure. The strongest example of judicial review of this is *Turco.* Turco, an MEP, sought access to legal advice the Council had received from its legal services on the proposed Directive laying down minimum standards for the reception of applicants for asylum in Member States. This was refused under the legal advice exception in article 4(2). The Council stated that greater transparency alone was not an overriding public interest, and this view was upheld by the General Court. Turco and the Swedish government appealed to the Court of Justice, who upheld his appeal. Having found that the advice constituted legal advice for the purposes of article 4(2), the Court went on to assess whether there was an overriding public interest justifying disclosure.

Joined Cases C–39/05 and C–52/05 *Sweden and Turco* v *Council* [2008] ECR I-4723

44. ... if the Council takes the view that disclosure of a document would undermine the protection of legal advice as defined above, it is incumbent on the Council to ascertain whether there is any overriding public interest justifying disclosure despite the fact that its ability to seek legal advice and receive frank, objective and comprehensive advice would thereby be undermined.

45. In that respect, it is for the Council to balance the particular interest to be protected by non-disclosure of the document concerned against, inter alia, the public interest in the document being made accessible in the light of the advantages stemming, as noted in recital 2 of the preamble to Regulation No. 1049/2001, from increased openness, in that this enables citizens to participate more closely in the decision-making process and guarantees that the administration enjoys greater legitimacy and is more effective and more accountable to the citizen in a democratic system.

46. Those considerations are clearly of particular relevance where the Council is acting in its legislative capacity, as is apparent from recital 6 of the preamble to Regulation No. 1049/2001, according to which wider access must be granted to documents in precisely such cases. Openness in that respect contributes to strengthening democracy by allowing citizens to scrutinize all the information which

---

[103] Case T-211/00 *Kuijer* v *Council* [2002] ECR II-485.

has formed the basis of a legislative act. The possibility for citizens to find out the considerations underpinning legislative action is a precondition for the effective exercise of their democratic rights.

47. It is also worth noting that, under [Article 16(8) TEU], the Council is required to define the cases in which it is to be regarded as acting in its legislative capacity, with a view to allowing greater access to documents in such cases. Similarly, Article 12(2) of Regulation No. 1049/2001 acknowledges the specific nature of the legislative process by providing that documents drawn up or received in the course of procedures for the adoption of acts which are legally binding in or for the Member States should be made directly accessible.

The requirements to be satisfied by the statement of reasons

48. The reasons for any decision of the Council in respect of the exceptions set out in Article 4 of Regulation No. 1049/2001 must be stated.

49. If the Council decides to refuse access to a document which it has been asked to disclose, it must explain, first, how access to that document could specifically and effectively undermine the interest protected by an exception laid down in Article 4 of Regulation No. 1049/2001 relied on by that institution and, secondly, in the situations referred to in Article 4(2) and (3) of that Regulation, whether or not there is an overriding public interest that might nevertheless justify disclosure of the document concerned.

50. It is, in principle, open to the Council to base its decisions in that regard on general presumptions which apply to certain categories of documents, as considerations of a generally similar kind are likely to apply to requests for disclosure relating to documents of the same nature. However, it is incumbent on the Council to establish in each case whether the general considerations normally applicable to a particular type of document are in fact applicable to a specific document which it has been asked to disclose.

The judgment has been described as 'spectacularly progressive' by Adamski.[104] Certainly, it must be seen in its context which is that of an elected representative, an MEP, asking about an instrument which raised strong human rights concerns. Yet, the reasoning of the Court is general in nature and imposes significant constraints, both substantively and procedurally. It suggests that where disclosure enables increased participation in decision-making or greater accountability, then there is already the makings of a case of an overriding public interest (paragraph 45). Yet, disclosure will in many cases enable this. The procedural constraints are also quite precise. It is not enough simply to mention a category and leave it at that. The institution must explain specifically how the interest is undermined and whether or not there is a public interest.

The final exception is set out in article 4(5) and concerns documents originating from a Member State. The traditional view is that the state concerned can veto any disclosure.[105] This changed in *Sweden* v *Commission*,[106] where Sweden appealed against the *IFAW* decision of the General Court to the Court of Justice.[107] IFAW, a German NGO concerned with nature conservation, sought disclosure of certain documents relating to the reclaiming of part of an estuary for the construction of a runway that originated in Germany. The General Court held that if

---

[104] Adamski, above n. 99, 536.
[105] Case T-76/02 *Messina* v *Commission* [2003] ECR II-3203.
[106] Case C-64/05 P *Sweden* v *Commission* [2007] ECR I-11389.
[107] Case T-168/02 *IFAW Internationaler Tierschutz-Fonds* v *Commission* [2004] ECR II-4135.

a Member State requested, as Germany did here, that the document not be disclosed, then it should not be disclosed. The Member State need not give reasons and the question would be decided exclusively by the national law of that state. The Swedish government appealed. The Court of Justice upheld the appeal. It held that to give a national veto over documents originating from a Member State would be incompatible with the purpose of the Regulation, which was to grant the widest possible access to documents by allowing that right to be frustrated without any objective reason. It would also introduce arbitrary distinctions whereby documents of a similar kind held by the EU institutions would have different rules applying to them depending on the origin of the document. The national veto applied, therefore, only if the document fell within one of the categories set out in article 4(1)–(3) of the Regulation. If an EU institution received a request for a national document, it was required to open a dialogue with the Member State, which could only refuse disclosure if it provided reasons why the document fell within one of the exceptions set out in article 4(1)–(3).

The judgment indicates that the same substantive principles concerning grounds for disclosure will apply whatever the provenance of the document. In this way, it significantly expands the remit of the principle in that whole fields of activity, in which the predominant players are Member States, will now be subject to far greater scrutiny. It has led to a reaction, however. The proposed amendments suggest a new article 5(2).

Article 5(2)

Where an application concerns a document originating from a Member State, other than documents transmitted in the framework of procedures leading to a legislative act or a non-legislative act of general application, the authorities of that Member State shall be consulted. The institution holding the document shall disclose it unless the Member State gives reasons for withholding it, based on the exceptions referred to in Article 4 or on specific provisions in its own legislation preventing disclosure of the document concerned. The institution shall appreciate the adequacy of reasons given by the Member State insofar as they are based on exceptions laid down in this Regulation.

Two qualifications to the *Sweden* v *Commission* judgment are thus added, both of which narrow the scope of access. First, the substance of the national reasons cannot be second-guessed by the EU institution. Even if it disagrees with them, it must respect them and not disclose the document if that is what is requested. It may be open to the applicant to challenge the Member State's refusal but it can only do this before a national court, as it does not have standing to challenge Member States before the Court of Justice. Secondly, a further exception is added, namely exceptions allowed under national legislation. In this way, Member States can, if they so wish, restrict the access considerably by simply passing very draconian legislation.

FURTHER READING

D. Adamski, 'How Wide is the "Widest Possible"? Judicial Interpretation of the Exceptions to the Right of Access to Official Documents' (2009) 46 *Common Market Law Review* 521

G. Davies, 'Subsidiarity: The Wrong Idea, in the Wrong Place, at the Wrong Time' (2006) 43 *Common Market Law Review* 63

C. Joerges, 'Integration Through De-legalisation?' (2008) 33 *European Law Review* 291

C. Joerges, Y. Mény and J. Weiler (eds.), *Mountain or Molehill? A Critical Appraisal of the Commission White Paper on Governance* (EUI and NYU, 2002), available at www.jeanmonnetprogram.org/papers/01/010601.html

C. Möllers, 'European Governance: Meaning and Value of a Concept' (2006) 43 *Common Market Law Review* 313

D. Obradovic and J. Alonso, 'Good Governance Requirements Concerning the Participation of Interest Groups in EU Consultations' (2006) 43 *Common Market Law Review* 1049

C. Radaelli, 'Whither Better Regulation for the Lisbon Agenda?' (2007) 14 *Journal of European Public Policy* 190

J. Scott and D. Trubek, 'Mind the Gap: Law and New Approaches to Governance in the European Union' (2002) 8 *European Law Journal* 1

S. Smismans, 'New Governance: The Solution for Active European Citizenship, or the End of Citizenship?' (2007) 13 *Columbia Journal of European Law* 595

J. Wiener, 'Better Regulation in Europe' (2006) 59 *Current Legal Problems* 447

10 Judicial Review

CONTENTS

1 INTRODUCTION

This chapter considers judicial review by the European Court of Justice. It is organised as follows.

Section 2 considers the scope of Article 263 TFEU, the central provision governing direct actions for judicial review of Union measures before the General Court and the Court of Justice. It has been amended by the Lisbon Treaty to allow not just the traditional institutions to be reviewed but also the European Council and EU agencies, offices and bodies. The measures susceptible to review include not just formal legal acts but any measure intended to produce legal effects. This will be any measure which is clear, definitive and produces a change in the applicant's legal situation.

Section 3 considers the grounds for review. A measure will be annulled, first, if the institution does not have the formal competence to adopt it. Review is possible, secondly, if the institution has misused its power. This may be an abuse of power where a power is used for purposes other than that for which it was granted. More common is a manifest error of assessment. This requires Union measures to be substantiated by the evidence provided, and for that evidence to be accurate, reliable, consistent and sufficiently complete. The third heading of review is 'rights of process'. These include the right to know the reasons for a legal measure, the rights to a hearing where one's interests are restricted, protection of one's rights of defence in the case of possible sanction, and, finally, the right to administration of one's affairs with due care by the EU institutions. The final heading of review is infringement of the Treaties or any rule of law relating to its application. This includes breach of any substantive provision of EU law and violation of fundamental rights. It also encompasses EU legal principles developed by the Court of Justice, namely non-discrimination, proportionality, legal certainty and protection of legitimate expectations.

Section 4 considers the standing requirements for bringing an action under Article 263 TFEU. Privileged applicants – the Member States, Parliament, the Commission and Council – have unlimited standing to challenge a measure subject to their observance of the time limits. Semi-privileged applicants – the Court of Auditors, European Central Bank and Committee of the Regions – may bring an action to protect their institutional prerogatives. All other parties have standing to bring an action against a regulatory act if it is of direct concern to them and against other measures if these are of direct and individual concern to them. This distinction between regulatory and other acts is new. The best interpretation is to see regulatory acts as any non-legislative act. Direct concern will be established where the Union measure directly affects a legal entitlement of the applicant without any significant intermediation by another party. Individual concern is governed by the *Plaumann* formula. This requires the interest affected to belong to a fixed, ascertainable and limited group of interests which is not capable, even hypothetically, of being added to. This is a highly restrictive test and has been criticised for making economically arbitrary distinctions and for favouring private interests over public ones.

Section 5 considers Article 265 TFEU and the failure to act. This complements Article 263 TFEU and allows parties to challenge omissions by EU institutions where these are under a duty to act. The standing requirements are similar in the two provisions. However, an action under Article 265 TFEU can only be commenced against an EU institution if it is under a duty to perform a task. If there is only a discretion, no remedy exists. Secondly, an institution, if called upon to act, avoids any further action if it defines its position within two months. Finally, the institution must be called upon to act by the applicant before any action can be commenced.

Section 6 considers the plea of illegality set out in Article 277 TFEU. This is not an independent action, but in an action against a measure brought under another provision (e.g. Article 263 TFEU) it allows challenge of a parent measure. It is subject to two constraints. It cannot be brought where the measure is being challenged before a court elsewhere by the parties, and it cannot be brought by parties who have already had the opportunity to challenge the measure but did not take up that opportunity.

Section 7 considers the action for non-contractual liability under Article 340(2) TFEU. Parties can sue EU institutions for damages where three conditions are met: first, that the institution has infringed a rule of law intended to confer rights on individuals; secondly, that the breach is sufficiently serious; and finally, that there is a direct causal link between the breach and the damage sustained by the applicant. In fields where EU institutions enjoy no discretion, a simple breach of EU law or failure to exercise reasonable care will be sufficient to establish liability. In fields where they enjoy some discretion, liability will only exist if they manifestly and gravely disregard the limits of their discretion.

Section 8 considers the consequences of a finding of annulment. Such a ruling is binding on all institutional actors in the Union. A measure found to be illegal continues to have legal effects until it is withdrawn by the EU institution, albeit the latter is under a duty to withdraw the measure following a Court judgment. However, if the measure is so tainted with irregularity, the Court has the power to declare it void and without legal effects.

2 SCOPE OF JUDICIAL REVIEW AND ARTICLE 263 TFEU

There are four sets of issues that must be addressed with judicial review. These are: (i) who may be reviewed; (ii) the range of acts subject to review; (iii) the grounds of review; and (iv) the standing of various parties to seek judicial review. The starting point for consideration of all of these is Article 263 TFEU.

Article 263 TFEU

The Court of Justice of the European Union shall review the legality of legislative acts, of acts of the Council, of the Commission and of the European Central Bank, other than recommendations and opinions, and of acts of the European Parliament and of the European Council intended to produce legal effects vis-à-vis third parties. It shall also review the legality of acts of bodies, offices or agencies of the Union intended to produce legal effects vis-à-vis third parties.

It shall for this purpose have jurisdiction in actions brought by a Member State, the European Parliament, the Council or the Commission on grounds of lack of competence, infringement of an essential procedural requirement, infringement of the Treaties or of any rule of law relating to their application, or misuse of powers.

The Court shall have jurisdiction under the same conditions in actions brought by the Court of Auditors, by the European Central Bank and by the Committee of the Regions for the purpose of protecting their prerogatives.

Any natural or legal person may, under the conditions referred to in the first and second subparagraphs, institute proceedings against an act addressed to that person or which is of direct and individual concern to them, and against a regulatory act which is of direct concern to them and does not entail implementing measures.

Acts setting up bodies, offices and agencies of the Union may lay down specific conditions and arrangements concerning actions brought by natural or legal persons against acts of these bodies, offices or agencies intended to produce legal effects in relation to them.

The new provision widens the range of the bodies and institutions susceptible to judicial review by including not just the long-standing EU institutions but also the European Council and EU agencies as bodies whose acts can be challenged. As stated in Chapter 1, the inclusion of the European Council is potentially significant as the decision to subject the agreements of twenty-seven Heads of Government to judicial challenge is unprecedented and illustrates the symbolic importance attached to the rule of law in the European Union.[1] In a different way, the clarification as to the accountability of EU agencies is of equal significance. In recent years, agencies have proliferated.[2] Though their powers vary considerably, most dominate their fields through establishing technical norms or patterns of coordination between national agencies. There has been particular concern over their accountability, most notably in the field of policing and judicial cooperation in criminal matters.[3]

The wider range of actors subject to review raises new questions about the range of acts subject to review. The European Council cannot adopt legislative measures and very few agencies have the power to adopt legally binding decisions.[4] If the Court adopts a narrow view in which 'acts' capable of being reviewed must bring about a change in a party's legal position, then most of the activity of these bodies would fall outside the radar. This would be a pity, as European Council guidelines are intended to inform legal changes, while EU institutions invariably not only follow the expert opinions of agencies in setting out legal norms, but are also obliged to do so unless they can find a substitute expert body and provide reasons for following the opinion of the latter.[5] There are, therefore, strong arguments for the accountability of these activities.

Article 263(1) TFEU uses a formula that was first used in the *ERTA* judgment for determining when a measure is subject to review.[6] A measure will be reviewable not merely when it is a formal legal act but, notwithstanding its form, when it is intended to produce legal effects. When will this be the case? In *IBM*, the company IBM challenged a Commission Decision indicating that it had initiated proceedings against it to determine whether IBM was in breach of EU competition law. The Commission argued that the Decision to open proceedings was not a formal act in any way and was not therefore reviewable.

Case 60/81 *IBM* v *Commission* [1981] ECR 2639

8. According to Article[263 TFEU] proceedings may be brought for a declaration that acts of the council and the commission other than recommendations or opinions are void. That remedy is available in order to ensure, as required by Article [19(1) TEU], that in the interpretation and application of the Treaty the law is observed, and it would be inconsistent with that objective to interpret restrictively the conditions under which the action is admissible by limiting its scope merely to the categories of measures referred to in Article [288 TFEU].

9. In order to ascertain whether the measures in question are acts within the meaning of Article [263] it is necessary, therefore, to look to their substance … any measure the legal effects of which are binding on, and capable of affecting the interests of, the applicant by bringing about a distinct change in his legal position is an act or decision which may be the subject of an action under Article [263] for a declaration that it is void. However, the form in which such acts or decisions are cast is, in principle, immaterial as regards the question whether they are open to challenge under that Article.

---

[1] On the organisation of the European Council see pp. 78–81.
[2] See pp. 66–7.
[3] Case C-160/03 *Spain* v *Eurojust* [2005] ECR I-2077; Case T-411/06 *Sogelma* v *EAR* [2008] ECR II-2771.
[4] Article 15(1) TEU.
[5] Case T-13/99 *Pfizer Animal Health* v *Council* [2002] ECR II-3305.
[6] Case 22/70 *Commission* v *Council (ERTA)* [1971] ECR 263.

10. In the case of acts or decisions adopted by a procedure involving several stages, in particular where they are the culmination of an internal procedure, it is clear from the case law that in principle an act is open to review only if it is a measure definitively laying down the position of the Commission or the Council on the conclusion of that procedure, and not a provisional measure intended to pave the way for the final decision.

11. It would be otherwise only if acts or decisions adopted in the course of the preparatory proceedings not only bore all the legal characteristics referred to above but in addition were themselves the culmination of a special procedure distinct from that intended to permit the Commission or the Council to take a decision on the substance of the case.

12. Furthermore, it must be noted that whilst measures of a purely preparatory character may not themselves be the subject of an application for a declaration that they are void, any legal defects therein may be relied upon in an action directed against the definitive act for which they represent a preparatory step.

The measure will therefore be reviewable if it brings about a change in the applicant's legal position. However, in *IBM*, the Court found that the decision to initiate proceedings was just a preparatory measure. It did not compromise IBM's rights of defence which were safeguarded later in the procedure. Central to the Court's reasoning was that the Commission had not yet taken a 'definitive position' (paragraph 12). What does this mean?

First, there will be no 'definitive position' and no reviewable act if the institution does not have the competence to adopt the act. In *Sunzest*, the Commission instructed the Belgian authorities at Antwerp that they should not recognise certificates issued by the 'Turkish Federated State of Cyprus' certifying the fitness of citrus fruit from Northern Cyprus.[7] Whilst the language of the Commission's letter was mandatory in nature, the Court did not recognise it as producing legal effects. It noted that the national authorities had exclusive responsibility under the Directive to apply protective measures against fruit from third countries. The Commission, in the Court's view, could only have been expressing an opinion. Such opinions were not reviewable.[8] The challenge with this is that it will often be difficult to know if the institution has some competence or not, and everything will hang on fine-grained interpretations of whether it has the power to do something or not.[9]

Secondly, the act is likely only to be considered definitive if the language is both reasonably imperative and alters the institution's position. Thus, restating an existing position is not reviewable.[10] Conversely, indicating no more than an intention to follow a particular line of conduct will not be reviewable.[11] There must be some stronger reorientation. This is often difficult to predict. In *Commission* v *Netherlands*, the Court held that the Code of Conduct on Public Access to Documents was not a reviewable act.[12] It considered it to be no more than a voluntary coordination between the Council and the Commission to ensure their approaches did not diverge, which did no more than set out general principles. This was notwithstanding

---

[7] Case C-50/90 *Sunzest* v *Commission* [1991] ECR I-2917.

[8] More recently Case T-212/06 *Bowland Dairy Products* v *Commission*, Judgment of 29 October 2009.

[9] For different views of the same measure by the General Court and Court of Justice see Case T-185/94 *Geotronics* v *Commission* [1995] ECR II-2795; Case C-395/95 *Geotronics* v *Commission* [1997] ECR I-2271.

[10] Case T-351/02 *Deutsche Bahn* v *Commission* [2006] ECR II-1047.

[11] Case T-185/05 *Italy* v *Commission* [2008] ECR II-3207.

[12] Case C-58/94 *Netherlands* v *Council* [1996] ECR I-2169.

that the Code was actually a detailed document which is not much further elaborated in either the Council or Commission Decisions implementing it.

Thirdly, the Court is more likely to find an act reviewable if it brings to an end or suspends some decision-making procedure. Whilst in *IBM*, therefore, the Decision to initiate competition proceedings was not reviewable, the position is different if the Commission decides *not* to initiate proceedings.[13] In *Air France*, the Commission issued an oral statement that it had no jurisdiction to consider a takeover of Dan Air by British Airways.[14] There was no text nor was the oral statement addressed to anyone. Furthermore, the statement did not follow any notification of the takeover by British Airways to the Commission, as required by the then Merger Regulation 4064/89/EC. The Court considered the statement to be reviewable, claiming that the measure had legal effects by reaffirming national jurisdiction over the merger and absolving the parties of their duty to notify the takeover under the Merger Regulation.

A similar approach was shown in *Commission v Council (Stability and Growth Pact)*.[15] This case concerned the stability and growth pact which requires those states who have the euro as their currency to maintain fiscal discipline and avoid excessive government deficits. The Commission reported both France and Germany to the Council for running excessive budgetary deficits. The Council did two things. First, it decided not to follow the Commission's recommendations to impose sanctions on France and Germany. Secondly, it stated that the procedure would be held in abeyance. Germany and France had made certain commitments. The Council stated that if these were not met, the procedure could be continued. The Commission sought judicial review of the Council's two measures.

On the first measure, the Court of Justice ruled that there had simply been no decision. In its view, there was not the majority to act on the Commission's recommendations, and therefore nothing had taken place. There was thus nothing to review. It came to a different view on the second measure. It noted that this was not merely confirming the existing position but making it conditional on Germany and France meeting certain commitments. It was altering a defined position, and it was intended to change the legal responsibilities of those two states. The measure was therefore reviewable.

Whilst it is possible to rationalise the decisions of the Court, the case law is confusing and arbitrary. The two measures in *Commission v Council* were, in practice, part and package of the same thing, and it makes no sense to look at one but not the other. Similarly, the distinction between decisions to start and not to start competition investigations is economic nonsense. This confusion also holds out little prospect that the new actors, the European Council and the agencies, will be held to account.

3 GROUNDS OF REVIEW

Four grounds of review are formally listed in Article 263 TFEU: lack of competence; infringement of an essential procedural requirement; infringement of the Treaty or of any rule of law relating to its application; and misuse of power. These have been subject to significant case law and, over time, the grounds have been reconfigured around four headings:

---

[13] Case C-39/93 P *SFEI v Commission* [1994] ECR I-2681.
[14] Case T-3/93 *Air France v Commission* [1994] ECR II-121. R. Greaves, 'The Nature and Binding Effect of Decisions under Article 189 EC' (1996) 21 *ELRev.* 3, 9–10.
[15] Case C-27/04 *Commission v Council (Stability and Growth Pact)* [2004] ECR I-6649.

in its review of legality ... the Community judicature conducts a full review as to whether the Commission applied properly the relevant rules of law. On the other hand, the [General Court] cannot take the place of the Commission on issues where the latter must carry out complex economic and ecological assessments ... In this respect, the Court is obliged to confine itself to verifying that the measure in question is not vitiated by a manifest error or a misuse of powers, that the competent authority did not clearly exceed the bounds of its discretion and that the procedural guarantees, which are of particularly fundamental importance in this context, have been fully observed.[16]

Rearranging the order of these groupings, they can be categorised in the following way:

(i) the institution in question must not exceed the power granted to it;

(ii) it must not abuse the discretion granted to it by a manifest error of assessment or an abuse of power;

(iii) there must not be a breach of process; this will involve all cases of a failure to give reasons but it will also involve violation of the rights of defence of parties that are subject to administrative proceedings;

(iv) there must be no breach of the substantive obligations imposed by EU law. This comprises not just explicit provisions of EU law, but also fundamental rights[17] and certain principles on which there has been extensive case law: those of legal certainty, non-discrimination and proportionality.[18]

(i) Lack of competence

An EU institution will be found to have acted illegally if it has exceeded the legal powers granted to it. This is relatively rare. The Union has very broad powers, most notably in Article 352 TFEU, the flexibility provision, which allows it to take action necessary to realise the objectives of the Union where no other legislative procedure is available.[19] An EU institution will, therefore, rarely be found to have taken action which is not available to the Union.[20] Instead, there tend to be two circumstances where an EU institution is found to have exceeded its powers: first, if it has taken action that should have been taken by other EU institutions and, secondly, if it has exceeded delegated powers granted to it by a piece of EU legislation.

The first goes to institutional balance, preserving both the institutional checks and balances within the Treaties and protecting the prerogatives of the different institutions. This is addressed in part through the case law on whether legislation has been adopted under the appropriate legal base.[21] In institutional terms, this case law is above all about whether the legislative powers of the different institutions have been respected.

---

[16] Case T-263/07 *Estonia* v *Commission*, Judgment of 23 September 2009.

[17] See Chapter 6.

[18] These have traditionally been known as general principles of law. This will not be possible after the Lisbon Treaty as this term is now used for all the case law of the Court on fundamental rights which is inspired by the ECHR and the constitutional traditions of Member States, Article 6(3) TEU.

[19] See pp. 214–19.

[20] The only example is Opinion 2/94 *Re Accession of the Community to the ECHR* [1996] ECR I-1759.

[21] See pp. 95–8.

Occasionally, however, an institution adopts a unilateral measure which should have been adopted by another. In *Safe Countries of Origin*,[22] under the legal regime at the time, EU legislation on the granting or withdrawal of refugee status had to be based on the ordinary legislative procedure if there were already common rules in force. In 2005, a Directive was adopted setting out principles for the grant and withdrawal of refugee status. Provision was made in it for the idea of safe country of origin. Persons coming from such countries were presumed not to be entitled to refugee status. The Directive stated that the Council would draw up a list of safe countries of origin having consulted the Parliament. The Parliament challenged this procedure. It argued that as EU legislation was now in force, further rules on what was a safe country of origin could only be drawn up through the ordinary legislative procedure. The Council did not have competence to agree them unilaterally. The Court agreed. It held the rules regarding the manner in which EU institutions made decisions were set by the Treaty alone and were not at the disposal of the institutions or Member States. To allow the Council to set new procedures would undermine the institutional balance in the Treaty and the Council did not have the competence to do this.

The second context in which institutions are found to have formally exceeded their powers is where the Commission is delegated certain powers and acts outside these powers. *Boyle* concerned the common fisheries policies.[23] Funding was received from the Union but a number of conditions were attached to it, notably a concern not to increase the overall national fishing capacities. To this end, the Council delegated to the Commission powers to determine when modernisation of fishing vessels was appropriate. This was allowed, above all, for modernisation and safety reasons. The applicants, a group of Irish fishermen, successfully challenged a Commission Decision which introduced new criteria that were not in the parent instrument, namely that the boat be registered, be at least five years old and the works concern a particular part of the boat. It was argued successfully that nothing in the original legislation gave the Commission the power to introduce additional criteria, and these were therefore illegal.

(ii) Manifest error of assessment and abuse of power

More common than a lack of competence is an abuse of discretion. This will happen in two circumstances: where there has been a manifest error of assessment and where there has been an abuse of power.

The central judgment on manifest error of assessment is *Tetra Laval*. The case concerned a conglomerate merger between Tetra Laval, the world-leader for carton packaging, and Sidel, a company specialising in PET packaging.[24] This was a form of packaging composed of a resin through which oxygen and light can pass. The Commission disallowed the merger on the grounds that Tetra Laval would leverage its dominant position on the market for cartons to persuade its customers on that market switching to PET to use Sidel's goods, thereby eliminating competition in that market. The General Court found that the Commission had committed a manifest error of assessment in that it had used reports which overestimated the possibility for leveraging and the possibility for growth in the PET market. The Commission appealed to the Court of Justice.

---

[22] Case C-133/06 *Parliament* v *Council (safe countries of origin)*, Judgment of 6 May 2008.

[23] Joined Cases T-218/03–T-240/03 *Boyle* v *Commission* [2006] ECR II-1699. For another instance see also Case T-263/07 *Estonia* v *Commission*, Judgment of 23 September 2009.

[24] A conglomerate merger is a merger between firms engaged in unrelated business activities: here cartons and PET.

Case C-12/03 P *Commission* v *Tetra Laval* [2005] ECR I-987

39. Whilst the Court recognises that the Commission has a margin of discretion with regard to economic matters, that does not mean that the Community Courts must refrain from reviewing the Commission's interpretation of information of an economic nature. Not only must the Community Courts, inter alia, establish whether the evidence relied on is factually accurate, reliable and consistent but also whether that evidence contains all the information which must be taken into account in order to assess a complex situation and whether it is capable of substantiating the conclusions drawn from it ...

41. Although the [General Court] stated ... that proof of anti-competitive conglomerate effects of a merger of the kind notified calls for a precise examination, supported by convincing evidence, of the circumstances which allegedly produce those effects, it by no means added a condition relating to the requisite standard of proof but merely drew attention to the essential function of evidence, which is to establish convincingly the merits of an argument or, as in the present case, of a decision on a merger...

44. The analysis of a 'conglomerate-type' concentration is a prospective analysis in which, first, the consideration of a lengthy period of time in the future and, secondly, the leveraging necessary to give rise to a significant impediment to effective competition mean that the chains of cause and effect are dimly discernible, uncertain and difficult to establish. That being so, the quality of the evidence produced by the Commission in order to establish that it is necessary to adopt a decision declaring the concentration incompatible with the common market is particularly important, since that evidence must support the Commission's conclusion that, if such a decision were not adopted, the economic development envisaged by it would be plausible.

45. It follows from those various factors that the [General Court] did not err in law when it set out the tests to be applied in the exercise of its power of judicial review or when it specified the quality of the evidence which the Commission is required to produce in order to demonstrate that the requirements ... of the Regulation are satisfied.

46. With respect to the particular case of judicial review exercised by the [General Court] in the judgment under appeal, it is not apparent from the example given by the Commission, which relates to the growth in the use of PET packaging for sensitive products, that [General Court] exceeded the limits applicable to the review of an administrative decision by the Community Courts. Contrary to what the Commission claims, paragraph 211 of the judgment under appeal merely restates more concisely, in the form of a finding by the [General Court], the admission made by the Commission at the hearing ... that its forecast in the contested decision with regard to the increase in the use of PET for packaging UHT milk was exaggerated. In paragraph 212 of the judgment under appeal, the [General Court] gave the reasons for its finding that the evidence produced by the Commission was unfounded by stating that, of the three independent reports cited by the Commission, only the PCI report contained information on the use of PET for milk packaging. It went on, in that paragraph, to show that the evidence produced by the Commission was unconvincing by pointing out that the increase forecast in the PCI report was of little significance and that the Commission's forecast was inconsistent with the undisputed figures ... contained in the other reports. In paragraph 213 of the judgment under appeal, the [General Court] merely stated that the Commission's analysis was incomplete, which made it impossible to confirm its forecasts, given the differences between those forecasts and the forecasts made in the other reports ...

48. It follows from these examples that the [General Court] carried out its review in the manner required of it, as set out in paragraph 39 of this judgment. It explained and set out the reasons why the Commission's conclusions seemed to it to be inaccurate in that they were based on insufficient, incomplete, insignificant and inconsistent evidence.

The Court went on to dismiss the Commission's appeal. The Court was here stating that it will not substitute its assessment for that of the institutions but will check that any measure is sufficiently substantiated by the evidence provided, and the evidence deployed must be accurate, reliable, consistent and sufficiently complete. A distinction is therefore drawn between the assessment of the institution (not reviewable) and the grounds for the assessment (reviewable). Yet, the demanding level of evidence that must be presented leads, as Craig suggests, to the distinction being eroded.

P. Craig, *EU Administrative Law* (Oxford, Oxford University Press, 2006) 470

The determination of whether the evidence is factually accurate, reliable and consistent requires evaluation, not simply observation. This is *a fortiori* so in relation to issues such as whether the evidence contains all the information that must be taken into account in order to assess a complex situation and whether the evidence is capable of sustaining the conclusions drawn from it. The need for complex assessment is equally present when deciding on the 'various chains of cause with a view to ascertaining which of them are most likely'.[25] It is, however, precisely in relation to these more complex findings, where the facts are multifaceted and difficult, requiring a greater degree of evaluative judgment, that there can be real differences of view as to the facts and possible consequences flowing from them.

If, as Craig persuasively argues, the Union courts are constraining the discretion of the institutions here, this raises the question of what is really taking place. It is probably overstating the argument to say unconditionally that they intervene to replace the view of the latter with their own view. In *Tetra Laval*, neither Union court, for example, sets out a positive thesis on the anti-competitive effects of conglomerate mergers. Instead, they look at whether the argument of the EU institution is more plausible than that of the applicant. Whilst there may be a presumption that it is, it would appear from *Tetra Laval* that this is fairly easy to rebut. Furthermore, the difficulty with a test of comparative plausibility is its inherent instability. Every applicant will believe its arguments are better than those of the EU institution, and every EU institution will be wary about how Union courts measure this.[26]

In contrast to the doctrine of manifest error of assessment, that of misuse of powers can be mentioned almost as a postscript. It arises if it appears:

> on the basis of objective, relevant and consistent indications to have been adopted to achieve purposes other than those for which it was intended.[27]

However, the principle has rarely brought joy to applicants. First, as the test is essentially a subjective one it has proved difficult for applicants to prove the necessary bad faith on the part of the institution. Secondly, the threshold is further raised by the requirement that the decision

---

[25] Case C-12/03 P *Commission v Tetra Laval* [2005] ECR I-987, para. 43.

[26] An indication of the challenges can be found in the field of cartels. A study of challenges to Commission Decisions between 1995 and 2004 found that they were only fully successful in 6 per cent of cases. There were partially successful in securing a reduction of the fine in 122 cases (61 per cent). The predominant ground was insufficient evidence (manifest error of assessment) provided by the Commission. The Union courts were, thus, finding in these cases that it erred in some of its reasoning but not in all of it – a very woolly scenario. C. Harding and A. Gibbs, 'Why Go to Court in Europe? An Analysis of Cartel Appeals 1995–2004' (2005) 30 *ELRev.* 349, 365–7.

[27] Case C-323/88 *Sermes v Directeur de Service des Douanes de Strasbourg* [1990] ECR I-3027.

challenged must have been guided exclusively or predominantly by the motivation to use the power for purposes other than those for which they were conferred.[28] This is difficult to prove and, outside two staff cases,[29] the principle has only been successfully invoked once.[30]

(iii) Rights of process

There are, to be sure, procedures set out throughout the Treaties and also through secondary legislation. These are to secure institutional balance and to enable particular actors to have a voice. Breach of these is a violation of rights of process but is also a breach of substantial provisions of EU law. There are, however, more general rights of process in EU law which exist in the absence of specific guarantees. These include the right to know the reasons for a legal measure, the rights to a hearing where one's interests are restricted, and particular rights of defence. It is this latter group that is being considered here. Such rights of process are seen as having a dual function in EU law. Process is seen, first, as important for understanding the basis for the decision and whether this is lawful, and secondly, to enable parties to defend entitlements granted to them.

The rationale for both functions lies in that of securing effective judicial review of the acts of other EU institutions. This was set out most explicitly in *Kadi*. The judgment, addressed in Chapter 5,[31] concerned a challenge to an EU Regulation implementing UN sanctions restricting financial and material resources to individuals who were on a list of people suspected of associating with Usama Bin Laden and Al Qaeda. Kadi was on this list, which was contained in Annex I to the Regulation. He challenged the Regulation, claiming that due process had been ignored, in that he had been given no opportunity to make a case as to why he should not be on that list, nor to challenge the grounds for placing him on the list.

Joined Cases C–402/05 P and C–415/05 P *Kadi and Al Barakaat International Foundation v Council*, Judgment of 8 November 2008

335. According to settled case law, the principle of effective judicial protection is a general principle of Community law stemming from the constitutional traditions common to the Member States, which has been enshrined in Articles 6 and 13 ECHR, this principle having furthermore been reaffirmed by Article 47 EUCFR …

336. In addition, having regard to the Court's case law in other fields … it must be held in this instance that the effectiveness of judicial review, which it must be possible to apply to the lawfulness of the grounds on which, in these cases, the name of a person or entity is included in the list forming Annex I to the contested Regulation and leading to the imposition on those persons or entities of a body of restrictive measures, means that the Community authority in question is bound to communicate those grounds to the person or entity concerned, so far as possible, either when that inclusion is decided on or, at

---

[28] Case C–48/96 P *Windpark Groothusen* v *Commission* [1998] ECR I-2873; Case C–407/04 P *Dalmine SpA* v *Commission* [2007] ECR I-829.

[29] Joined Cases 18/65 and 35/65 *Gutmann* v *Commission* [1966] ECR 103; Case 105/75 *Giuffrida* v *Council* [1976] ECR 1395.

[30] Joined Cases 351/85 and 360/85 *Fabrique de Fer de Charleroi* v *Commission* [1987] ECR 3639.

[31] See pp. 217–19.

the very least, as swiftly as possible after that decision in order to enable those persons or entities to exercise, within the periods prescribed, their right to bring an action.

337. Observance of that obligation to communicate the grounds is necessary both to enable the persons to whom restrictive measures are addressed to defend their rights in the best possible conditions and to decide, with full knowledge of the relevant facts, whether there is any point in their applying to the Community judicature ... and to put the latter fully in a position in which it may carry out the review of the lawfulness of the Community measure in question which is its duty under the EC Treaty.

The Court went on to find a breach of Kadi's rights of defence. According to *Kadi*, the requirement of judicial control is satisfied, first, through the duty, set out in Article 296(2) TFEU, for all EU legal acts to provide the reasons on which they are based. As we have seen in Chapter 9, this relationship is not unproblematic. As the duty to give reasons is simply about enabling parties to know their rights and courts to know the basis for the measure, the reasons need be no more detailed than required for that purpose.[32]

It is satisfied, secondly, through parties being able to 'defend their rights in the best possible fashion, with full knowledge of the relevant facts' (paragraph 337). However, if the duty to provide reasons is a general duty in EU law, there is not an equivalent right for all actors to have a hearing in all circumstances. *Kadi* refers to it being present whenever restrictive measures are taken against the actors in question. The meaning of this is uncertain. The fact that a measure adversely affects a party's interests is insufficient to grant them a hearing.[33] However, if a party is named or addressed in a Union measure and their interests are significantly affected, they are entitled to a hearing.[34]

There is an intermediate category where a party is not named in a measure but nevertheless has standing under Article 263(4) TFEU. In *Al Jubail*, the Court stated that if a measure directly and individually concerned an undertaking, that undertaking would be entitled to a hearing.[35] By contrast, parties will not necessarily have a right to a hearing where they complain to the Commission about a state aid or anti-competitive practice. In such circumstances, the Court has ruled they are doing no more than provide information, and this is insufficient to justify a hearing.[36] They will have no right to a hearing unless secondary legislation requires it.[37]

Turning to the substance of the right, the right to be heard encompasses an obligation on the institution to make its case known to the party concerned, and the right of that party to reply.[38] There is a right to be heard on all matters of fact and law which form the basis for the

---

[32] Case C-113/00 *Spain* v *Commission* [2002] ECR I-7601.

[33] Case T-37/92 *BEUC and NCC* v *Commission* [1994] ECR II-285.

[34] Case C-32/95 P *Commission* v *Lisrestal and Others* [1996] ECR I-5373. See also recently Case C-141/08 P *Foshan Shunde Yongjian Housewares and Hardware Co.* v *Commission*, Judgment of 1 October 2009.

[35] Case C-49/88 *Al-Jubail* v *Council* [1991] ECR I-3187. It may be that this formulation will be changed for regulatory acts following the Lisbon Treaty. As these only have to be of direct concern to undertakings for the latter to have standing, it would make sense that undertakings need only be directly concerned by a measure to have a right to a hearing.

[36] Case T-198/01 *Technische Glaswerke Ilmenau* v *Commission* [2004] ECR II-2717.

[37] There is limited provision for this in the case of competition under Regulation 1/2003/EC on the implementation of the rules on competition [2003] OJ L1/1, article 27(3) and in the case of mergers under Regulation 139/2004/EC on the control of concentrations by undertakings [2004] OJ L24/22, article 18(4).

[38] Joined Cases 56/64 and 58/64 *Consten and Grundig* v *Commission* [1966] ECR 299.

measure but not on the final position which the administration intends to adopt.[39] The institution is thus not obliged to hear an applicant with regard to a factual assessment which forms part of its final decision.[40]

The rights of defence are distinct from the right to be heard as it applies where EU institutions are to impose some sanction on a party.[41] The rights of defence include the opportunity for the applicant to make known their views on the truth and relevance of the facts alleged;[42] a duty to set out to the applicant the presumed facts justifying the investigation;[43] prosecution only for criminal or administrative penalties that are clearly and unambiguously defined (*nullum crimen, nulla poena sine lege*);[44] the presumption of innocence;[45] the right not to be tried twice for the same facts (*ne bis in idem*);[46] the right to judicial review of any sanction;[47] the right to legal assistance and the right for all lawyer-client communications prepared for the purpose of defence to be privileged;[48] the right to be heard in one's own defence before any administrative sanction is imposed;[49] protection from self-incrimination,[50] and access to the file setting out the allegations.[51]

These rights of process have in recent years increasingly been subsumed within a new right, which is that of observance of the principle of sound administration.[52] There is a dual element to this principle. First, as set out by the General Court recently in *Holland Malt*:

> observance of that principle requires a diligent and impartial investigation by the Commission of the measure at issue. The Commission is therefore under an obligation to obtain all the necessary points of view, in particular by requesting information... in order to make a finding in full knowledge of all the facts relevant at the time of adoption of its decision.[53]

This imposes a duty of care on the institutions, which has both a substantive and procedural element. Substantively, the Commission must act in good faith[54] and give due consideration and attention both to all the arguments presented[55] and to the task in hand.[56] At the very least,

---

[39] Case T-16/02 *Audi v OHIM (TDI)* [2003] ECR II-5167.

[40] Case T-458/05 *Tegometall International v OHIM – Wuppermann (TEK)* [2007] ECR II-4721.

[41] They cover all proceedings leading up to this sanction, no matter how preparatory: Case 46/87 *Hoechst AG v Commission* [1989] ECR 2859.

[42] Joined Cases C-204/00 P, C-205/00 P, C-211/00 P, C-213/00 P, C-217/00 P and C-219/00 P *Aalborg Portland A/S and Others v Commission* [2004] ECR I-123.

[43] Joined Cases 46/87 and 227/88 *Hoechst AG v Commission* [1989] ECR 2859; Case T-99/04 *Treuhand v Commission*, Judgment of 8 July 2008.

[44] Case C-303/05 *Advocaten voor de Wereld v Leden van de Ministerraad* [2007] ECR I-3633.

[45] Case C-344/08 *Rubach*, Judgment of 16 July 2009.

[46] Case C-469/03 *Miraglia* [2005] ECR I-2009.

[47] Case 222/86 *UNECTEF v Heylens* [1987] ECR 4097.

[48] Case 155/79 *AM & S Europe Ltd v Commission* [1982] ECR 1575; Joined Cases T-125/03 and T-253/03 *Akzo Nobel Chemicals Ltd and Akcros Chemicals Ltd v Commission* [2007] ECR II-3523.

[49] Case 17/74 *Transocean Marine Paint v Commission* [1974] ECR 1063.

[50] Case 374/87 *Orkem v Commission* [1989] ECR 3283.

[51] This is not an unqualified right. It is subject to the principle that confidential information supplied by third parties be respected. Furthermore, only failure to disclose inculpatory information will render a measure automatically illegal. Failure to disclose exculpatory information will only render any measure illegal if it effectively hinders the applicant's rights of defence: Case T-30/91 *Solvay SA v Commission* [1995] ECR II-1775.

[52] On the evolution of this right, see H.-P. Nehl, *Principles of Administrative Procedure in EC Law* (Oxford and Portland, Hart, 1999) 127–49; P. Craig, *EU Administrative Law* (Oxford, Oxford University Press, 2006) 373–81.

[53] Case T-369/06 *Holland Malt v Commission*, Judgment of 9 September 2009, para. 195. See also Case T-198/01 *Technische Glaswerke Ilmenau v Commission* [2004] ECR II-2717.

[54] For a failure here see Case T-410/03 *Hoechst v Commission* [2008] ECR II-881.

[55] Case 210/81 *Demo-Studio Schmidt v Commission* [1983] ECR 3045.

[56] Case C-16/90 *Nölle v Hauptzollamt Bremen-Freihafen* [1991] ECR I-5163.

it must be able to show the basis for its decision and how this relates to the information provided to it. This extends beyond merely providing reasons for the measure. Those reasons must be coherent, take account of the evidence provided and form the basis for the measure itself.[57] Procedurally, the principle of sound administration requires EU institutions to be proactive in gathering information. There is, in particular, a duty to fill in gaps in information through seeking it from parties who have a right to a hearing.[58] However, it does not appear to give new rights to new parties, and goes more to the type of information that EU institutions can request of parties who are being offered a hearing.[59]

The second dimension to the principle of sound administration is that EU institutions must exercise their powers within a reasonable period of time.[60] The delay must not be such as to compromise the rights of defence.[61] The reasonableness of the time taken will, however, be assessed in relation to the particular circumstances of each case: its background, complexity, the procedural stages followed and its importance for the various parties involved.[62] These conditions can be read separately, so the complexity of a case may justify a lengthy investigation.[63] This has resulted in the Union courts taking a very relaxed view of what is an unreasonable period of time. Whilst, where the case seems uncomplicated, they have ruled that twenty-six months is excessive,[64] in other cases where the applicant has contributed to the delay or the matter has had to go through the domestic courts, they have not found seven or twelve years unduly long.[65]

(iv) Infringement of the Treaties or of any rule of law relating to their application

The final set of grounds for review relate to infringement of the Treaties or any rule relating to their application. This can be a breach of a substantive piece of EU law, be it a provision of the Treaties or a piece of secondary legislation that binds the institution in question.[66] It can also be a breach of a number of other types of norm:

- fundamental rights: the substance of these were set out in more detail in Chapter 6;[67]
- proportionality: this is also discussed in more detail elsewhere in Chapter 9. Insofar as it governs the behaviour of EU institutions, in fields where these enjoy discretion, measures will only be unlawful if the courts consider these to be manifestly inappropriate with regard to the objective in hand;[68]

---

[57] Case T-263/07 *Estonia* v *Commission*, Judgment of 23 September 2009.

[58] Case T-420/05 *Vischim* v *Commission*, Judgment of 7 October 2009.

[59] Case C-367/95 P *Commission* v *Sytraval* [1998] ECR I-1719.

[60] Joined Cases C-74/00 P and C-75/00 P *Falck and Acciaierie di Bolzano* v *Commission* [2002] ECR I-7869; Joined Cases C-346/03 and C-529/03 *Atzeni and Others* v *Regione autonoma della Sardegna* [2006] ECR I-1875.

[61] Joined Cases C-238/99 P, C-244/99 P, C-245/99 P, C-247/99 P, C-250/99 P–C-252/99 P and C-254/99 P *Limburgse Vinyl Maatschappij NV and Others* v *Commission* [2003] ECR I-8375.

[62] Case T-73/95 *Oliveira* v *Commission* [1997] ECR II-381.

[63] Joined Cases C-322/07 P, C-327/07 P and C-338/07 P *Papierfabrik August Koehler* v *Commission*, Judgment of 3 September 2009.

[64] Case 223/85 *RSV* v *Commission* [1987] ECR 4617.

[65] Joined Cases T-30/01–T-32/01 and T-86/02–T-88/02 *Diputación Foral de Álava* v *Commission*, Judgment of 9 September 2009; Case T-347/03 *Branco* v *Commission* [2005] ECR II-2555.

[66] There is one exception to this. The Court of Justice will not allow judicial review of a Union measure for non-compliance with the WTO agreement on the grounds that the agreement is not such as to generate rights for individuals. Case C-377/02 *Van Parys* v *BIRB* [2005] ECR I-1465.

[67] See pp. 248–52 in particular.

[68] Case C-331/88 *R* v *MAFF, ex parte Fedesa* [1990] ECR I-4023.

- non-discrimination;
- legal certainty;
- legitimate expectations.

As the first two of these have been addressed in detail elsewhere, this section will focus on the latter three norms: non-discrimination, legal certainty and legitimate expectations. Readers are asked, however, to refer to the other sections of the book for discussion of fundamental rights and proportionality.

(a) Non-discrimination

EU law protects against certain status harms, where parties are disadvantaged on grounds of their enjoying a particular status, be it gender, ethnicity, race, age, disability, religion, belief or sexual orientation. These are set out in Articles 10 and 19 TFEU, and are discussed in Chapter 13. Beyond these, there is a general principle that like cases be treated alike. The seminal case is *Ruckdeschel*. It concerned identical subsidies that were historically granted to starch and quellmehl producers by the EU institutions. The reason was that the two products were seen as economically substitutable. The quellmehl subsidy was withdrawn. Ruckdeschel, a producer, challenged this, arguing that there was a discrimination between it and starch producers. The Court of Justice agreed.

Joined Cases 117/76 and 16/77 *Ruckdeschel v Council* [1977] ECR 1753

7. The second subparagraph of [Article 40(2) TFEU] provides that the common organization of agricultural markets 'shall exclude any discrimination between producers or consumers within the [Union]'.

   Whilst this wording undoubtedly prohibits any discrimination between producers of the same product it does not refer in such clear terms to the relationship between different industrial or trade sectors in the sphere of processed agricultural products. This does not alter the fact that the prohibition of discrimination laid down in the aforesaid provision is merely a specific enunciation of the general principle of equality which is one of the fundamental principles of Community law.

   This principle requires that similar situations shall not be treated differently unless differentiation is objectively justified.

8. It must therefore be ascertained whether quellmehl and starch are in a comparable situation, in particular in the sense that starch can be substituted for quellmehl in the specific use to which the latter product is traditionally put.

   In this connexion it must first be noted that the Community Regulations were, until 1974, based on the assertion that such substitution was possible …

   While the Council and the Commission have given detailed information on the manufacture and sale of the products in question, they have produced no new technical or economic data which appreciably change the previous assessment of the position. It has not therefore been established that, so far as the Community system of production refunds is concerned, quellmehl and starch are no longer in comparable situations.

   Consequently, these products must be treated in the same manner unless differentiation is objectively justified.

The prohibition on discrimination will prohibit not just like cases being treated differently but also different cases being treated in a like manner.[69] In practice, however, it is rare that there will be a finding of discrimination. Often, where there is differential treatment the Court will simply state that the cases are not alike. This will always be the case where the EU institution can justify the differential treatment (e.g. there is a different basis for the treatment of each). In *Melli Bank*, for example, an Iranian bank pleaded discrimination on the grounds that Union sanctions had targeted it but not other British subsidiaries of Iranian banks.[70] The General Court had little difficulty in finding that there was no discrimination. It noted that the Regulation in question implemented a UN Security Council Resolution which targeted financial institutions engaged in assisting nuclear proliferation. For the Court this rationale provided a basis for the differential treatment.

The Court is thus engaged here in looking at the reasonableness of the Union measure. There is, correspondingly, less intense review where EU institutions enjoy a margin of discretion. Discrimination will only be found if the conduct borders on the 'arbitrary'.[71] In these circumstances the non-discrimination principle seems to add little to the proportionality principle.[72]

(b) Legal certainty

The principle of legal certainty has been protected within EU law for some time.[73] In *Heinrich*, it was stated as requiring that:

> Community rules enable those concerned to know precisely the extent of the obligations which are imposed on them. Individuals must be able to ascertain unequivocally what their rights and obligations are and take steps accordingly.[74]

The first dimension to this is a temporal one. There is a prohibition against retroactivity. A measure must not take effect prior to its publication.[75] It will thus not be retroactive if it regulates the future effects of situations which arose prior to publication. It will only be retroactive if it applies to events which have already been concluded.[76]

The principle is absolute in relation to penal measures.[77] The Court has also indicated that it should be observed strictly where the rules are liable to have financial consequences.[78] Other measures may exceptionally take effect before publication where the purpose to be achieved so demands and where the legitimate concerns of those concerned are respected. In *Fedesa*, following the annulment of a Directive outlawing the use of certain hormones, the subsequent Directive, which was published on 7 March 1988, stipulated that it was to take effect from the beginning of that year.[79] The reason was to prevent the market being unregulated for the period prior to March as a consequence of the annulment of an earlier Directive. The Court

---

[69] Joined Cases T-222/99, T-327/99 and T-329/99 *Martinez and Others* v *Parliament* [2001] ECR II-2823.
[70] Joined Cases T-246/08 and T-332/08 *Melli Bank* v *Council*, Judgment of 9 July 2009.
[71] Case 245/81 *Edeka* v *Commission* [1982] ECR 2745; Case C-479/93 *Francovich* v *Italian Republic (Francovich II)* [1995] ECR I-3843.
[72] M. Herdegen, 'The Equation Between the Principles of Equality and Proportionality' (1985) 22 *CMLRev.* 683.
[73] It was first set out in Joined Cases 42/59 and 49/59 *SNUPAT* v *High Authority* [1961] ECR 109.
[74] Case C-345/06 *Heinrich*, Judgment of 10 March 2009, para. 44.
[75] Case 84/78 *Tomadini* v *Amministrazione delle Finanze dello Stato* [1979] ECR 1801.
[76] Case 63/83 *R* v *Kent Kirk* [1984] ECR 2689.
[77] Case C-331/88 *R* v *MAFF, ex parte Fedesa* [1990] ECR I-4023.
[78] Case C-94/05 *Emsland-Stärke* [2006] ECR I-2619.
[79] Case C-331/88 *R* v *MAFF, ex parte Fedesa* [1990] ECR I-4023.

considered there to be no breach of the principle of the legal certainty in light of the short time-span between the annulment of the first Directive and the publication of the second.

The second dimension to legal certainty is that of clarity: enabling the subjects of EU law to know their rights and obligations. At the very least, this means that the EU law in question must be published. In *Heinrich*, an unpublished Annex to a Regulation which prohibited tennis rackets from being taken on civil air aircraft was found to be void because it had not been published.[80] Alongside this, the Court has repeatedly stated that EU legislation must be clear and its application foreseeable.[81] This would suggest that if a Union measure is obscure it could be struck down. However, this has yet to happen.

(c) Legitimate expectations

The principle of legitimate expectations is often linked to that of legal certainty. However, its roots lie in the concept of good faith and require that, having induced an operator to take one course of action, the administration should not then renege on that, so that the individual suffers loss.[82]

An example of how this might be claimed arose in *Branco*. Branco was awarded funding under the European Social Fund for the training of young adults. The training was certified by the Portuguese ministry who sent a request to the Commission for payment. The ministry subsequently found irregularities in the performance of Branco's duties under the contract. The Commission refused to make the final payment and sought repayment of the funds already granted. Branco claimed a violation of the principle of legitimate expectations in that the work had been certified by the Portuguese ministry in question. The General Court made the following observation:

> Three conditions must be satisfied in order to claim entitlement to the protection of legitimate expectations. First, precise, unconditional and consistent assurances originating from authorised and reliable sources must have been given to the person concerned by the Community authorities. Second, those assurances must be such as to give rise to a legitimate expectation on the part of the person to whom they are addressed. Third, the assurances given must comply with the applicable rules.[83]

In *Branco*, the General Court found that the action failed on the first condition. It noted that the decision to authorise payment was one for the Commission and not the Portuguese authorities, and it had given no assurances here. Even if assurances are made, they must create an expectation on the part of the applicant. This is not simply a subjective test. The expectation must be legitimate and Court will look to whether an ordinary, prudent trader would have relied on it on the basis of the institution's representation.[84] Finally, the Union measure in question must not be illegal. If it is, it will not generate any protected expectation.[85]

Although *Branco* refers to a precise, unconditional and consistent assurance, this assurance does not have to be individualised in the sense that the applicant must be named. It can be a

---

[80] Case C-345/06 *Heinrich*, Judgment of 10 March 2009. See also Case T-115/94 *Opel Austria v Council* [1997] ECR II-39.

[81] Case 325/85 *Ireland v Commission* [1987] ECR 5041; Case C-301/97 *Netherlands v Council* [2001] ECR I-8853.

[82] See generally S. Schonberg, *Legitimate Expectations in Administrative Law* (Oxford, Oxford University Press, 2000).

[83] Case T-347/03 *Branco v Commission* [2005] ECR II-255, para. 102.

[84] Case 265/85 *Van den Bergh en Jurgens v Commission* [1987] ECR 1155. On this see E. Sharpston, 'Legitimate Expectations and Economic Reality' (1990) 15 *ELRev.* 103, 108–15.

[85] Case T-336/94 *Efisol v Commission* [1996] ECR II-1343.

general statement or even a particular course of conduct which encourages certain expectations. In *Mulder*, farmers were paid by the Union to take land out of milk production to reduce milk surpluses. Mulder took his land out of production under the scheme but when he sought to resume milk production without paying a levy, he was refused on the ground that this possibility was only available to those who had produced milk in the preceding year. He argued that he had been encouraged to take his land out of production by the Union offering him premiums. This had led him to believe that there would be no penalties for his action. The Court of Justice agreed, ruling that:

> where a producer ... has been encouraged by a Community measure to suspend marketing for a limited period in the general interest ... he may legitimately expect not to be subject, upon the expiry of his undertaking, to restrictions which specifically affect him precisely because he availed himself of the possibilities offered by the Community provisions.[86]

In *Mulder*, the penalty was simply inconsistent with the existing policy framework. The question does arise, however, as to whether a reversal of policy could violate legitimate expectations.[87] The steady view of the Court is that it will not. Instead, there is a presumption of a freedom to legislate, as the Court considers that prudent traders ought to be able to take into account the possibility that the law might change.[88] In only one case has a reversal in policy given rise to a successful claim in legitimate expectations. In *CNTA*, the Commission suddenly stopped granting monetary compensation amounts (MCAs) in the colza and rape seed sectors.[89] MCAs are subsidies granted to traders designed to protect them against loss from currency fluctuations. This was a clear reversal of policy, which was unusual in that it was a sudden withdrawal of a subsidy. The financial effects were therefore immediate and unexpected. The Court found that there had been a breach of legitimate expectations in this case. Whilst MCAs could not be considered a guarantee against risks on the exchange rate, nevertheless, they meant, in practice, that a prudent trader might not insure himself against the risk. In the absence of an overriding public interest, the Court considered that the immediate withdrawal of MCAs with no provision for transitional measures breached EU law.

4 STANDING UNDER ARTICLE 263 TFEU

(i) Privileged and semi-privileged applicants

By virtue of Article 263(1) TFEU, the so-called privileged applicants – the Member States, the Commission, the Council and the European Parliament – have a general power to seek judicial review against acts of the EU institutions. This grants them general, unrestrained policing powers against the EU institutions, subject to the observance of the time limits set out in the final paragraph of Article 263 TFEU. The justification for this power to monitor and constrain is that each of these represents an important public interest that must be legally protected: the Member States represent individual national interests, the Council collective national interests,

---

[86] Case 120/86 *Mulder v Minister van Landbouw en Visserij* [1988] ECR 2321.
[87] For an argument that occasionally it should, see P. Craig, 'Substantive Legitimate Expectations in Domestic and Community Law' (1996) 55 *CLJ* 289, 299.
[88] Case 52/81 *Faust v Commission* [1982] ECR 3745.
[89] Case 74/74 *CNTA v Commission* [1975] ECR 533.

the European Parliament a pan-European democratic voice and the Commission a pan-European non-governmental public interest.

The actors in Article 263(2) TFEU – the European Central Bank, the Court of Auditors and the Committee of the Regions – are semi-privileged applicants. The justification for their interest in litigation is different. It is not to police generally but rather to protect their institutional prerogatives. It is a defensive power to ensure that other institutions do not trespass on their legal entitlements.

Infringement of these prerogatives can occur in three ways. First, an institution may fail to observe a procedure at the expense of another institution.[90] Secondly, an institution may use one procedure when it should have used another procedure which gives another institution greater entitlements:[91] so, for example, use of the consultation procedure rather than the ordinary legislative procedure. The final circumstance is when the institutional balance is shifted through the delegation of broad powers to the Commission at the expense of the primary legislative procedures. As this pre-empts other institutions' entitlements, they can challenge the delegation.

(ii) Non-privileged applicants

(a) Regulatory acts and legislative acts

Historically, most debate has centred around the circumstances under which private parties, so-called non-privileged applicants, can seek judicial review of acts of EU institutions. This is set out in Article 263(4) TFEU which introduces two amendments to the prior Treaty Article governing the same.

First, Article 263(4) TFEU provides that any natural or legal person may institute proceedings against an *act* which is either addressed to them or of direct and individual concern to them. This replaces an unhappy formulation which allowed individuals to challenge decisions addressed to them or decisions, which although in the form of regulation, were of direct and individual concern.[92] Over time, the Court focused attention away from the form of the act and more to the test of direct and individual concern. The procedure could therefore be used to challenge not only Decisions but also Regulations and Directives.[93] Yet the amendment represents a welcome and overdue clarification. It may also herald a slightly more expansive approach for, on its face, it allows instruments such as the Conclusions of the European Council or international agreements to be challenged by individuals, something that has not happened hitherto.

The second amendment concerns the establishment of a distinction between regulatory and other acts. To challenge regulatory acts individuals need only establish direct concern.[94] For other acts they must establish direct and individual concern. The distinction is therefore an

---

[90] Case C-65/90 *Parliament v Council* [1992] ECR I-4593.

[91] Case 70/88 *European Parliament v Council ('Chernobyl')* [1990] ECR 2041.

[92] On this see R. Greaves, 'Locus Standi under Article 173 EEC when Seeking Annulment of Regulation' (1986) 11 *ELRev.* 119.

[93] Case C-309/89 *Cordorníu v Council* [1994] ECR I-1853; Case C-10/95 P *Asocarne v Council and Commission* [1995] ECR I-4149; Case T-420/05 *Vischim v Commission*, Judgment of 7 October 2009.

[94] Prior to the Lisbon Treaty, the Court of Justice had already introduced more relaxed standing requirements in fields characterised by wide Commission regulatory powers (e.g. competition, state aids and anti-dumping). The change is part of a progression, therefore. On the earlier regime see A. Arnull, 'Challenging EC Anti-Dumping Regulations: The Problem of Admissibility' (1992) 13 *ECLR* 73.

axiomatic one. Unfortunately, whilst a distinction is made between legislative acts and non-legislative acts, with the latter comprising delegated acts and implementing acts,[95] no definition is provided of regulatory acts.

Some help can be found in the Future of Europe Convention that preceded the Constitutional Treaty. A Discussion Circle there considered the situation of the Court of Justice. In its Final Report, the *locus standi* requirements for non-privileged applicants were addressed:

> 22. A majority of those members who wanted the [provision] to be amended would prefer the option mentioning 'an act of general application'. However, some members felt that it would be more appropriate to choose the words 'a regulatory act', enabling a distinction to be established between legislative acts and regulatory acts, adopting, as the President of the Court had suggested, a restrictive approach to proceedings by private individuals against legislative acts (where the condition 'of direct and individual concern' still applies) and a more open approach as regards proceedings against regulatory acts.[96]

It seems that regulatory acts are intended to be non-legislative acts. Indeed, a strong case can be made for subjecting non-legislative acts to greater judicial scrutiny than legislative acts. The latter involve representative institutions. This is not the case with non-legislative acts taken by non-majoritarian institutions, such as the Commission or agencies. Judicial review can provide an opportunity for popular scrutiny and constraints that is lacking in non-legislative processes.

Yet, this begs the question as to what counts as a legislative act. Article 289(3) TFEU defines a legal act as anything adopted by one of the EU legislative procedures. This would leave all delegated and implementing acts as regulatory acts. This definition would make a lot of sense, as it suggests that any act not adopted by one of the legislative procedures should be subject to greater scrutiny precisely because it has not come through those procedures with their greater checks and balances and arguably greater legitimacy. However, historically, the Court of Justice has adopted a different definition of a legislative act: it is any measure that is couched in general and abstract terms.[97] In this regard, it is the phraseology that is important, as all that matters is the level of abstraction of the text rather than the number of interests affected or the procedure used.[98] It would be regrettable if such a test was adopted. It would allow EU institutions to escape judicial review through the formulation of the wording they deploy. More importantly, it would not address the justifications for increased judicial review. This is that processes have been used that do not involve representative institutions, and, in such circumstances, courts have to be particularly vigilant against executive abuse and more willing to consider the arguments of citizens who have not had the chance to press their arguments through their representatives.

(b) Direct concern

Historically, the case law on direct concern has been limited. This is because the greater impediment to standing for non-privileged applicants has been that of individual concern. This may change following the Lisbon Treaty. As we shall see, going through the case law, a high

---

[95] Articles 289–91 TFEU.

[96] The European Convention Secretariat, *Final Report of the Discussion Circle on the Court of Justice*, CONV 636/03.

[97] Joined Cases 16/62 and 17/62 *Confédération Nationale des Producteurs de Fruits et Légumes and Others* v *Council* [1962] ECR 471.

[98] Case C-10/95 P *Asocarne* v *Council and Commission* [1995] ECR I-4149.

proportion of the measures challenged may now be classified as regulatory acts. If that is so, direct concern will be the sole test for determining standing to challenge these measures. One would therefore expect considerably more litigation on its meaning and remit.

There are two dimensions to direct concern. The first involves causation. There must be a direct link between the act of the EU institution and the damage inflicted on the applicant. The second involves the nature of the interest affected by the Union measure. It must be a legal entitlement rather than any other form of interest.

Turning to the first of these, direct concern means that the measure which the applicant wishes to challenge must affect her legal position directly. It must be the Union measure that caused the change in her position:

> The contested measure must directly produce effects on the legal situation of the person concerned and its implementation must be purely automatic and follow solely from the [Union] rules, without the application of other intermediate measures.[99]

If the measure leaves the national authorities of a Member State a degree of discretion as to its implementation, this may be sufficient to break the chain of causation as it will be argued that it is the national measure not the Union one that inflicts the damage. In determining whether there is discretion, the Court will look, however, not merely to the leeway afforded by the Union measure but whether in practice the national authorities will exercise that discretion.

In *Piraiki-Pitraiki*, some Greek cotton exporters challenged a restriction on exporting to other parts of the Union that was applied to them after Greek accession to the European Union but during the transitional period when some restrictions were allowed.[100] The background was that the French government applied a pre-existing regime restricting cotton imports from Greece. It came to the Commission, as required by EU law, to ask for an authorisation to continue it. This was granted. When the exporters challenged this authorisation, the Commission argued that as the authorisation did not compel the French authorities to do anything, the applicants were not directly concerned by it. The Court of Justice rejected this argument. It noted the pre-existing French regime, and stated that there was no more than a theoretical possibility that the French would not continue it. The Commission authorisation, therefore, directly concerned the applicants by legalising a national regime.[101]

This stance is not uncontroversial, as the issue is about allocation of responsibilities. The test for direct concern is that actions should be brought against the EU institutions only if they have exclusive responsibility for the measure as the national authorities had no discretion over the matter. This is a high threshold, indeed. It could be argued that in many cases where the latter had some discretion, there is a shared responsibility in that national authorities would not have taken the action but for the Union measure. In such circumstances, it would seem more appropriate that if both parties are responsible, any action should lie against both of them.

---

[99] Case T-29/03 *BUPA and Others v Commission* [2008] ECR II-81. For an early ruling on this see Case 69/69 *Alcan v Commission* [1970] ECR 385.

[100] Case 11/82 *Piraiki-Pitraiki v Commission* [1985] ECR 207.

[101] That said, it will only be in exceptional circumstances that the Court will be willing to make inferences about behaviour by national authorities. It will normally therefore assume that if they have been granted a discretion, they will exercise it. Joined Cases C-445/07 P and C-455/07 P *Commission v Ente per le Ville Vesuviane*, Judgment of 10 September 2009.

The second dimension to direct concern is that the measure must adversely affect the applicant's legal position. If it affects an interest not recognised by the Court of Justice as being legally protected, the applicant will not be directly concerned. This is neatly illustrated in *Front National*. Most MEPs are members of a political group, for example the Socialist group, or the Green group. A few independent MEPs, including a number of far-right Front National MEPs, belonged to no group, meaning that they suffered some disadvantages in the European Parliament, particularly with regard to secretarial support. Accordingly, they sought to establish a *groupe mixte*, known as the TDI group. Other political groups objected and the European Parliament chose not to grant it group status. The decision was challenged by a number of MEPs individually and by the Front National. The General Court held that both sets of applicants were directly concerned, but that the applicants' substantive arguments were not made out.[102] The Front National appealed to the Court of Justice who overturned the decision of the General Court and ruled that it was not directly concerned by the European Parliament decision.

Case C–486/01 P *Front National v European Parliament* [2004] ECR I-6289

34. … the condition that the decision forming the subject-matter of [annulment] proceedings must be of 'direct concern' … requires the Community measure complained of to affect directly the legal situation of the individual and leave no discretion to the addressees of that measure, who are entrusted with the task of implementing it, such implementation being purely automatic and resulting from Community rules without the application of other intermediate rules …

35. In this instance there is no question that the contested act – to the extent to which it deprived the Members having declared the formation of the TDI Group, and in particular the Members from the Front National's list, of the opportunity of forming … a political group … – affected those Members directly. As the [General Court] rightly pointed out … those Members were in fact prevented, solely because of the contested act, from forming themselves into a political group and were henceforth deemed to be non-attached Members …; as a result, they were afforded more limited parliamentary rights and lesser material and financial advantages than those they would have enjoyed had they been members of a political group …

36. Such a conclusion cannot be drawn, however, in relation to a national political party such as the Front National. … [A]lthough it is natural for a national political party which puts up candidates in the European elections to want its candidates, once elected, to exercise their mandate under the same conditions as the other Members of the Parliament, that aspiration does not confer on it any right for its elected representatives to form their own group or to become members of one of the groups being formed within the Parliament. …

39. … the [General Court] admittedly found that, since the contested act deprived the Members concerned, particularly those elected from the Front National's list, of the opportunity to organise themselves into a political group, it directly impinged on the promotion of the ideas and projects of the party which they represented in the European Parliament and, hence, on the attainment of that political party's stipulated object at European level, the reason why the Front National was directly affected by the act.

40. Such effects, however, cannot be regarded as directly caused by the contested act.

---

[102] See Joined Cases T-222/99, T-327/99 and T-329/99 *Martinez and Others v Parliament* [2001] ECR II-2823.

The Front National was held not to be directly concerned because there was, according to the Court, no legal right directly infringed by the measure. This was because the former had no right to form its own grouping or to join another grouping (paragraph 38). The requirement that the measure must directly affect the legal situation of the applicant is, however, a very uncertain test. It has proved difficult to apply, as the presence of a legal entitlement is not always clear. In *Regione Siciliana*, the General Court and the Court of Justice disagreed about when this would be so. The Commission had cancelled regional assistance for the construction of a dam in Sicily. The Region of Sicily, named in the document as the authority to administer the assistance, challenged this. The General Court stated that the measure directly concerned the region by depriving it of assistance it would have otherwise received and requiring it to repay money already received.[103] The sums combined came to over €48 million. The Court of Justice overturned this. It stated that the region had no right in EU law to the assistance as, although it was noted as the administering authority, it was the Italian Republic which had made the application.[104] As the region had no legal entitlement to the assistance, in the Court of Justice's view, notwithstanding the financial impact, it could not be said to be directly concerned.

(c) Individual concern and the *Plaumann* formula

The other part of the test is that of individual concern. The seminal ruling is *Plaumann*. The German authorities wished to suspend customs duty, an import tax, on importation of clementines. They needed, under EU law, authorisation from the Commission. It refused them this. The applicant, an importer of clementines, sought judicial review of the Commission Decision. He had to show individual concern as the Decision had been addressed to the German authorities and not to him. The Court of Justice ruled that the applicant lacked standing.

Case 25/62 *Plaumann & Co.* v *Commission* [1963] ECR 95

Persons other than those to whom a decision is addressed may only claim to be individually concerned if that decision affects them by reason of certain attributes which are peculiar to them or by reason of circumstances in which they are differentiated from all other persons and by virtue of these factors distinguishes them individually just as in the case of the person addressed. In the present case the applicant is affected by the disputed Decision as an importer of clementines, that is to say, by reason of a commercial activity which may at any time be practised by any person and is not therefore such as to distinguish the applicant in relation to the contested Decision as in the case of the addressee.

The test is both restrictive and cryptic. It needs dissecting. *Plaumann* states that private parties will be able to seek judicial review of Decisions not expressly addressed to them only if they can distinguish themselves by virtue of certain attributes or circumstances from all other persons. Although not explicitly stated, these attributes/circumstances must be fixed and determinate and distinguish members from the rest of the world. Craig has observed that the test could have chosen three dates for deciding when this was the case. The first is the date of the measure. This would involve simply looking at the number of traders importing clementines

---

[103] Case T-60/03 *Regione Siciliana* v *Commission* [2005] ECR II-4139.
[104] Case C-15/06 P *Regione Siciliana* v *Commission* [2007] ECR I-2591.

into Germany at the date of the Commission Decision. This would be fixed. The simple question would be whether the number was sufficiently limited. The second would be the date of the challenge. This would involve an identical calculation but at the date when the application was made before the Court. The third date is any date in the future. The test becomes therefore whether there is a possibility that the group may cease to be fixed and determinate at some future, undefined date.

Plaumann adopted this last position.[105] The test was whether, even though not many of us are in fact engaged in the business of importing clementines, any of us could, in theory become clementine importers. As a consequence, Plaumann was part of a group that anybody could join and did not have attributes or circumstances that distinguished him from others. Hartley has therefore talked of *Plaumann* drawing a distinction between open categories and fixed categories.[106] An open category is one where the membership is not fixed and determined when the measure comes into force. A closed one is one where the membership is fixed and determined in such a way that it cannot be added to. Applicants can only claim individual concern if they fall into a closed category.

An example of the difference between the two is provided in *Koninklijke Friesland Campina*. A 1996 Dutch law created a scheme to give tax benefits to Dutch companies providing international financing activities (the GFA scheme). In 2000, Koninklijke Friesland Campina (KFC) applied for authorisation to join the scheme. In 2001, the Commission announced it was investigating the scheme to see if it was illegal state aid. Following this, the Dutch government announced it would not admit any more undertakings to the scheme, and would not, therefore, admit KFC to the scheme. In 2003, the Commission declared the scheme illegal but stated that all undertakings who were currently members of the scheme could continue to enjoy its benefits. KFC successfully challenged the Commission Decision before the General Court. The Commission successfully appealed this before the Court of Justice. One of the Commission's arguments, which was unsuccessful, was that KFC was not individually concerned.

Case C–519/07 P *Commission v Koninklijke Friesland Campina*, Judgment of 17 September 2009

52. ... natural or legal persons may claim that a contested provision is of individual concern to them only if it affects them by reason of certain attributes which are peculiar to them or by reason of circumstances in which they are differentiated from all other persons ...

53. An undertaking cannot, in principle, contest a Commission decision prohibiting a sectoral aid scheme if it is concerned by that decision solely by virtue of belonging to the sector in question and being a potential beneficiary of the scheme. Such a decision is, vis-à-vis that undertaking, a measure of general application covering situations which are determined objectively and entails legal effects for a class of persons envisaged in a general and abstract manner ...

54. By contrast, the Court has held that, where a contested measure affects a group of persons who were identified or identifiable when that measure was adopted by reason of criteria specific to the members

---

[105] P. Craig, 'Legality, Standing and Substantive Review in Community Law' (1994) 14 *OJLS* 507, 509–10.

[106] T. Hartley, *The Foundations of European Community Law: An Introduction to the Constitutional and Administrative Law of the European Community* (6th edn, Oxford, Oxford University Press, 2007) 348.

of the group, those persons might be individually concerned by that measure inasmuch as they form part of a limited class of traders ...

55. It is not in dispute, first, that the contested decision had the effect that requests for first GFA authorisation, which were pending on the date of notification of the contested decision, were rejected without being examined and, second, that the undertakings concerned were easily identifiable, owing to the very existence of such a request, at the time when that decision was adopted. In that regard, it should be recalled that KFC was part of a group of, at most, 14 applicants for first GFA authorisation, whose requests were pending at the time of the 11 July 2001 decision, that those requests were suspended following that decision, and that the Netherlands authorities announced on 5 December 2002 that they would be ceasing, with immediate effect, to consider any new requests for the application of the GFA scheme.

56. Thus, ... KFC formed part of a closed group of undertakings – and not of an indefinite number of undertakings belonging to the sector concerned – specifically affected by the contested decision.

57. It should be borne in mind that, in order to benefit from the GFA scheme, an undertaking which had made a request for first GFA authorisation must have already taken the necessary measures in order to fulfil the criteria required for that scheme. Furthermore, as the Netherlands authorities did not have any discretion in that regard, they were obliged to grant such an authorisation if those criteria were fulfilled. Thus, the undertakings whose requests for first GFA authorisation were pending must be regarded as being concerned by the contested decision, by reason of attributes which are peculiar to them and by reason of circumstances in which they are differentiated from every other undertaking in that sector which had not lodged a request for first GFA authorisation.

58. It follows that those undertakings have standing to bring an individual action against the contested decision.

A distinction is thus made between an open category and a closed category. The open category is that of companies engaging in international financial activities. In principle, anybody could engage in this category (hence its openness) and it is not enough to sustain individual concern. The closed category is composed of undertakings who have already made an application to join the GFA scheme at the time of the Commission Decision. This is closed in that nobody can join that category of pending applications prior to the Commission Decision, as once the Decision is taken the category closes definitively.

In practice, this means that closed categories comprise parties who are limited in number and have some special pre-existing legal relationship disrupted by the Union measure. In *KFC*, it was a formal application for tax exemption. Possibly crucial here was the fact that if a trader met the criteria they had an automatic right to join the scheme, so the application carried with it a certain legal entitlement. In other instances, the Court has found traders who had pre-existing contracts which could not be carried out because of a Commission Decision to be individually concerned.[107] It has also found traders to be concerned where they were part of a small group given a tax exemption in a particular year for a limited period by a Member State which was then subsequently withdrawn because of a Commission Decision.[108]

The applicant will also be individually concerned if, notwithstanding that they would otherwise be in an open category, they are part of a fixed group granted certain procedural safeguards. In

---

[107] Case 11/82 *Piraiki-Patraiki and Others* v *Commission* [1985] ECR 207; Case C-152/88 *Sofrimport* v *Commission* [1990] ECR I-2477.

[108] Joined Cases C-182/03 and C-217/03 *Belgium and Forum 187* v *Commission* [2006] ECR I-5479.

Vischim, EU legislation provided for the phasing out of certain plant protection products.[109] During a transitional period, manufacturers were invited to present dossiers setting out the qualities of these products. Vischim was one of sixteen who presented dossiers in relation to a product, chlorothalonil. A Directive was duly introduced prohibiting it. The General Court held that as Vischim was provided procedural safeguards by the original legislation it was individually concerned.

How to explain this standing rule? Two justifications are deployed. The first is that allowing too many challenges by private parties will unduly disrupt Union decision-making processes. A reason why this argument might have particular force in the EU setting is that Union decisions necessarily involve a delicate balance between many actors, which involve all the Member States and the central EU institutions. Exposing them to wide-ranging and incessant legal challenges ignores the precarious nature of this process and would make the job of realising this balance even harder..[110]

The second justification provided for such limited standing requirements is to protect the status of the Court of Justice. It has been argued that restrictive *locus standi* requirements have been used to channel applicants to challenge Union measures before national courts in the first resort. These then act as a filter for the Court of Justice.[111] This view re-emerged in the Discussion Circle on the Court of Justice at the Future of Europe Convention, with one group within the discussion arguing against reform on this basis.

The European Convention Secretariat, *Final Report of the Discussion Circle on the Court of Justice*, CONV 636/03 (2003)

18. It emerged from the discussion that the circle was clearly divided into two groups. For the first group, the current wording of the provision satisfied the essential requirements of providing effective judicial protection of the rights of litigants, taking account of the fact that, in the present decentralised system based on the subsidiarity principle, it was mainly national courts which were called upon to defend the rights of individuals and which might (or should, if at last instance) refer questions to the Court for a preliminary ruling on the validity of a Union act; it would therefore not be necessary to make any substantive changes to [Article 263(4) TFEU]. These members felt, on the other hand, that it would be appropriate for the Constitution to mention explicitly that, in accordance with the principle of loyal cooperation as interpreted by the Court of Justice, national courts are required, so far as possible, to interpret and apply national procedural rules governing the exercise of rights of action in a way that enables natural and legal persons to challenge before the courts the legality of any decision or other national measure relative to the application to them of a Community act of general application, by pleading the invalidity of such an act. It is in fact for the Member States to establish a system of legal remedies and procedures which ensures respect for the right of individuals to effective judicial protection as regards rights resulting from Union law …

---

[109] Case T-420/05 *Vischim v Commission*, Judgment of 7 October 2009. See also Case T-13/99 *Pfizer Animal Health v Council* [2002] ECR II-3305.

[110] On this see A. Arnull, 'Private Applicants and the Action for Annulment under Article 173 of the EC Treaty' (1995) 32 *CMLRev.* 7, 46; C. Harding, 'The Private Interest in Challenging Community Action' (1980) 5 *ELRev.* 354. Arnull is very critical of this argument. For excellent coverage of the different arguments, see A. Arnull, *The European Union and its Court of Justice* (2nd edn, Oxford, Oxford University Press, 2006) 91–4.

[111] This was first deployed by Rasmussen who argued that it was a strategy to transform the Court of Justice into a European Court of Appeal. H. Rasmussen, 'Why is Article 173 Interpreted Against Private Plaintiffs?' (1980) 5 *ELRev.* 112. For a defence of this argument, see J. Usher, 'Direct and Individual Concern: An Effective Remedy or a Conventional Solution?' (2003) 28 *ELRev.* 575.

Even on their own terms, both these arguments are highly problematic.

Taking first the argument about not disrupting EU decision-making processes: this may be an argument for restrictive rules of standing but it does not explain the arbitrariness of the current test and the obscure world of the difference between open and closed categories. The Court has ruled that a party is not individually concerned by a Union measure where it is the only party affected by it on the grounds that it belongs to an open category which others could potentially join.[112] If the rules on standing are concerned solely with restricting applicants, they could look at those actually affected by a measure, and confine standing to a very limited group and not those affected speculatively.

Turning to the argument about the preliminary reference procedure as the central route for judicial review, this begs the question whether national courts would be effective filters.[113] In principle, following the *Fotofrost* doctrine, they should refer everything to the Court as they are not allowed to declare a Union measure invalid themselves.[114] It could therefore become a free-for-all with the only question being whether the applicant has standing domestically. In some instances, this may be very liberal, whereas conversely, there may not even be a domestic measure that can be the subject of a challenge. There is, moreover, an institutional contradiction in this argument, as the procedures send the applicant to different courts. An action under Article 263(4) TFEU is brought before the General Court whilst a reference goes to the Court of Justice.[115] It would be absurd if the clear Treaty preference for individual administrative challenges to be the main concern of the General Court was undermined in this way. Viewed more broadly, there are further disadvantages to this vision. Legal proceedings would be highly protracted with all the disadvantages for legal certainty and costs.

The bulk of the academic literature has thus been highly critical of the *Plaumann* formula. It is viewed, in the first place, as highly restrictive, preventing applicants adversely affected by Union measures from any effective judicial redress. There is also a sense that it is textually unjustified.[116] The text of Article 263 TFEU clearly does not *require* it. Nor does it justify it. There is nothing in the Treaty to imply that the phrase 'direct and individual concern' should be interpreted as narrowly as the Court chose to in *Plaumann*.

The most robust critique of the *Plaumann* formula is that of Advocate General Jacobs in *UPA*. UPA, a Spanish trade association representing the interests of Spanish farmers, sought judicial review of a 1998 Council Regulation which abolished many forms of financial aid to olive oil farmers and producers. It was impossible to challenge this Regulation before the Spanish courts. The General Court dismissed the application for the reason that UPA lacked standing. UPA appealed to the Court of Justice. In his Opinion, Advocate General Jacobs set out a series of reasons why, in his view, the current law was in need of reform. Underlying the Advocate General's analysis was the idea that judicial review must be informed by the 'principle of effective judicial protection'.

---

[112] Case 231/82 *Spijker v Commission* [1983] ECR 2559.

[113] For a particularly thorough critique of the undesirability of this route, see the Opinion of Advocate General Jacobs in Case C-50/00 P *Unión de Pequeños Agricultores v Council* [2002] ECR I-6677, paras. 41–9.

[114] Case 314/85 *Firma Fotofrost v Hauptzollamt Lübeck-Ost* [1987] ECR 4199.

[115] Article 256(1) TFEU.

[116] A. Barav, 'Direct and Individual Concern: An Almost Insurmountable Barrier to the Admissibility of Individual Appeal to the EEC Court' (1974) 11 *CMLRev.* 191; A. Arnull, 'Private Applicants and the Action for Annulment since *Codorníu*' (2001) 38 *CML Rev.* 7; K. Lenaerts and T. Corthaut, 'Judicial Review as a Contribution to the Development of European Constitutionalism' (2003) 22 *YBEL* 1; P. Craig, *EU Administrative Law* (Oxford, Oxford University Press, 2006) 340–4.

Case C-50/00 P *Unión de Pequeños Agricultores* v Council **[2002] ECR I-6677, Opinion of Advocate General Jacobs**

38. As is common ground in the present case, the case law of the Court of Justice acknowledges the principle that an individual who considers himself wronged by a measure which deprives him of a right or advantage under Community law must have access to a remedy against that measure and be able to obtain complete judicial protection.

39. That principle is, as the Court has repeatedly stated, grounded in the constitutional traditions common to the Member States and in Articles 6 and 13 of the European Convention on Human Rights. Moreover, the Charter of Fundamental Rights of the European Union, while itself not legally binding, proclaims a generally recognised principle in stating in Article 47 that '[e]veryone whose rights and freedoms guaranteed by the law of the Union are violated has the right to an effective remedy before a tribunal'...

Suggested solution: a new interpretation of the notion of individual concern

59. The key to the problem of judicial protection against unlawful Community acts lies therefore, in my view, in the notion of individual concern laid down in the fourth paragraph of Article [263 TFEU]. There are no compelling reasons to read into that notion a requirement that an individual applicant seeking to challenge a general measure must be differentiated from all others affected by it in the same way as an addressee. On that reading, the greater the number of persons affected by a measure the less likely it is that judicial review under the fourth paragraph of Article [263 TFEU] will be made available. The fact that a measure adversely affects a large number of individuals, causing wide-spread rather than limited harm, provides however to my mind a positive reason for accepting a direct challenge by one or more of those individuals.

60. In my opinion, it should therefore be accepted that a person is to be regarded as individually concerned by a Community measure where, by reason of his particular circumstances, the measure has, or is liable to have, a substantial adverse effect on his interests.

61. A development along those lines of the case law on the interpretation of Article [263 TFEU] would have several very substantial advantages.

62. First ... [it avoids] what may in some cases be a total lack of judicial protection – a *déni de justice*.

63. Second, the suggested interpretation of the notion of individual concern would considerably improve judicial protection. By laying down a more generous test for standing for individual applicants than that adopted by the Court in the existing case law, it would not only ensure that individual applicants who are directly and adversely affected by Community measures are never left without a judicial remedy; it would also allow issues of validity of general measures to be addressed in the context of the procedure which is best suited to resolving them, and in which effective interim relief is available.

64. Third, it would also have the great advantage of providing clarity to a body of case law which has often, and rightly in my view, been criticised for its complexity and lack of coherence, and which may make it difficult for practitioners to advise in what court to take proceedings, or even lead them to take parallel proceedings in the national courts and the [General Court].

65. Fourth, by ruling that individual applicants are individually concerned by general measures which affect them adversely, the Court of Justice would encourage the use of direct actions to resolve issues of validity, thus limiting the number of challenges raised via Article [267 TFEU]. That would, as explained above, be beneficial for legal certainty and the uniform application of Community law ...

66. A point of equal, or even greater, importance is that the interpretation of Article [263 TFEU] which I propose would shift the emphasis of judicial review from questions of admissibility to questions of substance. While it may be accepted that the Community legislative process should be protected against undue judicial intervention, such protection can be more properly achieved by the application of substantive standards of judicial review which allow the institutions an appropriate margin of appreciation in the exercise of their powers than by the application of strict rules on admissibility which have the effect of blindly excluding applicants without consideration of the merits of the arguments they put forward.

Shortly after this Opinion was handed down, the General Court applied its reasoning in *Jégo Quéré*.[117] But when *UPA* was considered by the Court of Justice, it chose not to follow the advice of its Advocate General. The Court insisted on the continuing force of the *Plaumann* formula, stating that any reform to the law of standing must come not from the Court, but from the Member States. It has since then insisted resolutely on the *Plaumann* formula.[118] The Opinion of Advocate General Jacobs must be seen, therefore, as a critique of the existing law rather than anything more.

The debate about widening standing rules is monolithic and too black and white. It revolves around general statements about having either relaxed rules or restrictive rules. If standing requirements are relaxed they may, of course, address the concerns surrounding restrictive requirements. However, they open the door to other concerns. These involve disruption of the legislative process and government by courts. Significant numbers of Union measures will go up before the courts, with a danger of the latter substituting their views for those of the legislature. There is also the concern about capture of courts by minority interests. Groups unable to secure agreement for their view elsewhere may simply bombard the courts with actions as a way of undermining the legislative procedures and as a strategy for securing what they could not achieve elsewhere.

The strength of these arguments will vary according to the context. In some instances, the argument for efficient judicial protection might seem strong, whilst in others the case for restrictive standing is apparent. In this regard, the amendments introduced by Lisbon between regulatory and legislative acts in Article 263(4) TFEU are pertinent. In instances where there is EU legislation, there is restricted standing. In the case of administrative acts, individual concern is abolished and there is liberalised standing. This ethos is reinforced by Article 263(5) TFEU which provides that the acts setting up EU agencies and bodies may lay down specific arrangements allowing acts of these bodies to be challenged. The philosophy is clear. Non-legislative acts are taken by non-representative institutions and therefore there are less strong concerns about democratic process being disrupted by judicial challenge. Furthermore, there are strong reasons why questions of due process and the reach of executive power should be more actively policed. These institutions are not subject to the same levels of public debate and scrutiny as the legislative process, and, therefore, judicial review intervenes to substitute for that.

---

[117] Case T-177/01 *Jégo Quéré v Commission* [2002] ECR II-2365.
[118] See e.g. Joined Cases C-373/06 P, C-379/06 P and C-382/06 P *Flaherty and Others v Commission* [2008] ECR I-2649; Case C-362/06 P *Sahlstedt v Commission*, Judgment of 23 April 2009.

(d) Standing and interest groups

A further criticism of *Plaumann* is that the test of 'individual concern' is easier to meet for those who can point to some individual financial or material interest that has been prejudiced. It thus benefits trading interests over groups representing public interests such as the environment, the regions or the consumer. This is particularly problematic if judicial review is seen as also having a function of allowing different social groups to challenge legislative or administrative abuse. It cannot be right if this is only available to some interests or traders and not to others.

Interest groups will be granted standing if they are seen as having been granted certain procedural entitlements. This will be where they have been given certain procedural rights or privileges either by EU law or through the practice of the EU institutions. The argument is that this recognition by the political process confers a parallel entitlement to protection of this before the courts. The position was set out most cogently in *Associazione Nazionale Bieticoltori*. In this instance, Associazione Nazionale Bieticoltori (ANB), a trade association representing Italian sugar beet producers, brought an action against a Regulation that granted aid to their Portuguese counterparts whilst reducing aid for the Italian growers. It was found to lack standing.

Case T–38/98 *Associazione Nazionale Bieticoltori* v *Council* [1998] ECR II–4191

25. It should be pointed out, second, that an application for annulment lodged by an association may be admissible in three types of situation, namely:
    (a) where a legislative provision expressly confers a range of procedural powers on trade associations ...
    (b) where the association represents the interests of undertakings having *locus standi* to seek the annulment of the provision in question ...
    (c) where the association is distinguished because its own interests as an association are affected, in particular because its position as a negotiator has been affected by the measure whose annulment is sought ...
26. In those three types of situation the Court of Justice and the [General Court] have also taken into account the participation of the associations in question in the procedure ...
27. As regards the first type of situation, mentioned above, it is sufficient to point out that the regulations on the common organisation of the markets in the sugar sector do not recognise that associations have any right of a procedural nature.
28. As regards the second of the abovementioned types of situation, it should be observed that the fact that the contested provision will affect sugar beet producers whose interests are represented by the Associazione Nazionale Bieticoltori is not such as to differentiate those producers from all other persons, since they are in a situation which is comparable to that of any other operator who may enter the same market ...
29. As regards, last, the third type of situation referred to above, it should be pointed out that, according to a consistent line of decisions, an association formed to promote the collective interests of a category of persons cannot be regarded as individually concerned by a measure affecting the general interests of that category, and is therefore not entitled to bring an action for annulment where its members may not do so individually ... None the less, the existence of particular circumstances, such as the role played by an association in a procedure leading to the adoption of an act within the meaning of Article [263 TFEU], may justify admitting an action brought by an association whose members are not directly and individually concerned by the act at issue, particularly when its position as negotiator is affected by it ...

Such procedural entitlements will be rare, and they will only be given to 'insider' groups who have good relationships with the EU institutions. These are likely to be the last people who wish to challenge a measure as their privileged position in negotiations or consultations is likely to have already secured some influence for them.

More interesting, therefore, is whether other interest groups with a strong stake in a measure can challenge it. In *Greenpeace*, three environmental campaigning groups and several individuals resident on the Canary Islands challenged the legality of a series of Commission Decisions granting aid from the European Regional Development Fund (ERDF) to assist with the construction of two power stations, one on Gran Canaria and the other on Tenerife. The General Court ruled that neither the associations nor the individuals had standing.[119]

Case T-585/93 *Greenpeace and Others v Commission* [1995] ECR II-2205

32. The applicants ask the Court to adopt a liberal approach on this issue and recognize that, in the present case, their *locus standi* can depend not on a purely economic interest but on their interest in the protection of the environment ...

39. In the alternative, the applicants submit that the representative environmental organizations should be considered to be individually concerned by reason of the particularly important role they have to play in the process of legal control by representing the general interests shared by a number of individuals in a focused and coordinated manner. ...

56. Nor can the fact that [certain of the] applicants have submitted a complaint to the Commission constitute a special circumstance distinguishing them individually from all other persons and thereby giving them *locus standi* to bring an action under Article [263]. No specific procedures are provided for whereby individuals may be associated with the adoption, implementation and monitoring of decisions taken in the field of financial assistance granted by the ERDF. Merely submitting a complaint and subsequently exchanging correspondence with the Commission cannot therefore give a complainant *locus standi* to bring an action under Article [263] ...

59. ... [S]pecial circumstances such as the role played by an association in a procedure which led to the adoption of an act within the meaning of Article [263] may justify holding admissible an action brought by an association whose members are not directly and individually concerned by the contested measure ...

60. The three applicant associations ... claim that they represent the general interest, in the matter of environmental protection, of people residing on Gran Canaria and Tenerife and that their members are affected by the contested decision; they do not, however, adduce any special circumstances to demonstrate the individual interest of their members as opposed to any other person residing in those areas. The possible effect on the legal position of the members of the applicant associations cannot, therefore, be any different from that alleged here by the applicants who are private individuals. Consequently, in so far as the applicants in the present case who are private individuals cannot, as the Court has held, be considered to be individually concerned by the contested decision, nor can the members of the applicant associations, as local residents of Gran Canaria and Tenerife ...

62. In the present case ... the Commission did not, prior to the adoption of the contested decision, initiate any procedure in which Greenpeace participated; nor was Greenpeace in any way the interlocutor of the Commission with regard to the adoption of the ... decision. Greenpeace cannot, therefore, claim to have any specific interest distinct from that of its members to justify its *locus standi*.

---

[119] The judgment was affirmed on appeal. Case C-321/95 P *Greenpeace and Others v Commission* [1998] ECR I-1651.

Public interest associations will therefore only be able to seek judicial review of measures not addressed to them if they are granted specific procedural privileges or safeguards; their members are individually concerned; or in negotiations they are recognised by the EU institutions as the central interlocutor of particular interests. It will be rare that any of these conditions will be met. Since *Greenpeace*, the Court has consistently refused to relax standing requirements for public interest litigation.[120] EU law has therefore been criticised as resulting in diffuse public interests being less well protected than private interests.[121]

Whilst apparently attractive, this argument must be treated cautiously. There are dangers in substituting judicial review for political accountability. Take the *Greenpeace* case, for example: why should it be characterised as being a *legal* concern to decide whether European funds should be allocated to the environmentally controversial construction of a new power station? Is this not precisely the sort of question which is best resolved politically?

C. Harlow, 'Public Law and Popular Justice' (2002) 65 *Modern Law Review* 1, 13

In public interest litigation, campaigning groups can be treated as experts provided their hidden agenda is overtly recognised. Alternatively, they can be treated as single issue political parties, in which case their presence as advocates in the legal process needs a different justification. Otherwise ... the triumph of pressure groups or factions or special interests will mark a corruption of the legal process. To put this important point differently, too close a relationship between courts and campaigning groups may result in a dilution of the neutrality and objectivity of law.

Harlow suggests, therefore, that a middle way might be to give public interest groups wider rights of intervention in proceedings. As she makes clear, this has not yet happened.

C. Harlow, 'Towards a Theory of Access for the European Court of Justice' (1992) 12 *Yearbook of European Law* 213, 247–8

The most economical way to increase interest representation without overloading the Court is, however, undoubtedly through intervention procedure. Many modern courts feel able to allow intervention freely and interventions by interest groups are particularly a feature of constitutional courts. In the Court of Justice, in sharp contrast, group interventions are rare and Articles 37 and 20[122] of the Statute are largely the preserve of the privileged applicants.

---

[120] Case T-461/93 *An Taisce* v *Commission* [1994] ECR II-733; Case T-219/95 R *Danielsson and Others* v *Commission* [1995] ECR II-3051.

[121] M. Führ *et al.*, 'Access to Justice: Legal Standing for Environmental Associations in the European Union' in D. Robinson and J. Dunkley (eds.), *Public Interest Perspectives in Environmental Law* (Chichester, Chancery, 1995); L. Krämer, 'Public Interest Litigation in Environmental Matters before European Courts' (1996) 8 *JEL* 1; N. Gerard, 'Access to Justice on Environmental Matters: A Case of Double Standards?' (1996) 8 *JEL* 139.

[122] The right to intervene is now set out in article 40 of the current Statute of the Court of Justice which gives that right to all Member States and EU institutions. Others may intervene if they can show an interest and the dispute is not between Member States, EU institutions or between a Member State and an EU institution.

The Court's distinctive inquisitorial procedures could be used to design an appropriate intervention procedure without adding to burdens on applicants in the shape of greater expense or delay. Strict time-limits can already be imposed for interventions with limited rights of contradiction and oral observations already require the Court's permission. Submissions could be limited as to length. Increased use could be made of the *juge rapporteur* if orality were thought necessary; alternatively, they could be collected and evaluated by the Advocate General, forming part of his Opinion.

5 ARTICLE 265 TFEU AND THE FAILURE TO ACT

In certain circumstances positive duties are placed by EU law upon the EU institutions to act. They are under a duty to realise some Treaty objectives[123] and secondary legislation often places duties upon the institutions.[124] The conditions for bringing an action if an institution fails to act in such circumstances are set out in Article 265 TFEU.

Article 265 TFEU

Should the European Parliament, the European Council, the Council, the Commission or the European Central Bank, in infringement of the Treaties, fail to act, the Member States and the other institutions of the Union may bring an action before the Court of Justice to have the infringement established. This Article shall apply, under the same conditions, to bodies, offices and agencies of the Union which fail to act.

The action shall be admissible only if the institution, body, office or agency concerned has first been called upon to act. If, within two months of being so called upon, the institution, body, office or agency concerned has not defined its position, the action may be brought within a further period of two months.

Any natural or legal person may, under the conditions laid down in the preceding paragraphs, complain to the Court that an institution, body, office or agency of the Union has failed to address to that person any act other than a recommendation or an opinion.

There is a similar distinction between privileged and non-privileged applicants as in Article 263 TFEU, with the former laid out in Article 265(1) TFEU and the latter in 265(3). Privileged applicants comprise a wider group under Article 265 TFEU than under Article 263 TFEU, as all EU institutions and Member States are granted that status, whilst under the latter provision it is available just to Member States, the Commission, the Parliament and the Council. The European Council, the European Central Bank and (hypothetically) the Court of Justice all have a wider standing, therefore, under Article 265 TFEU.[125]

---

[123] On the common transport policy, see Case 13/83 *Parliament v Council* [1985] ECR 1513.

[124] For example, the Commission is required to examine the factual and legal particulars of any complaint about a breach of EU competition law which is made by a person with a legitimate interest: Case T-24/90 *Automec Srl v Commission (Automec II)* [1992] ECR II-2223.

[125] The list of institutions is set out in Article 13 TEU.

Quirks are also added to the provision by the Lisbon Treaty. Prior to the Treaty, only the Parliament, Council and Commission were institutions against whom an action could be brought. Two further institutions have been added to this: the European Council and the European Central Bank. The second paragraph, however, refers to an action only being available if the 'institution, body or agency' has been called upon to act. This suggests that, in principle, the action should be available against EU agencies, bodies and offices as well in the same way as Article 263 TFEU is available against acts taken by these. This is the preferable interpretation. It not only secures consistency between the provisions but also ensures that there is no lacuna in the rule whereby an EU body or agency can escape judicial scrutiny by simply doing nothing.[126]

Articles 263 and 265 TFEU were described in an early judgment as prescribing 'one and the same method of recourse'.[127] This means, as one author put it, that:

> the system of remedies … would be incomplete if Community institutions were subject to judicial control only in respect of their positive actions while they could evade the obligations imposed upon them by simply failing to act.[128]

It also means that the provisions should be interpreted in a parallel manner. There is thus a similar distinction between privileged and non-privileged applicants. Non-privileged applicants can only invoke Article 265 TFEU if they would be directly concerned by the regulatory act or directly and individually concerned by the non-regulatory act which has not been adopted.[129]

However, there are some lacunae in this coverage.

First, an action under Article 265 TFEU can only be commenced against an EU institution if it is under a duty to perform a task. If there is only a discretion, no remedy exists. The decision of the Court to rule in some circumstances that the matter is one of discretion rather than obligation has been controversial as it creates a gap in protection. We saw in Chapter 8 how the decision to hold that the Commission had complete discretion whether to launch enforcement proceedings against a Member State under Article 258 TFEU for infringement of EU law has led to private parties being largely excluded from this important process.[130]

Secondly, an institution, if called upon to act,[131] avoids any further action if it defines its position within two months. The principle of complementarity would require that this position be an act capable of being reviewed under Article 263 TFEU. However, an institution can define its position without adopting an act that is reviewable under that provision.[132] It can also act in a different way from that in which it was called upon to act.[133]

Finally, the institution must be called upon to act by the applicant. If this does not happen, there will be no action.[134] Whilst the Article sets no time limit within which an action must

---

[126] Case T-411/06 *Sogelma* v *EAR* [2008] ECR II-2771.

[127] Case 15/70 *Chevalley* v *Commission* [1970] ECR 979.

[128] A. Toth, 'The Law as it Stands on the Appeal for Failure to Act' (1975) 2 *LIEI* 65.

[129] Case T-395/04 *Air One* v *Commission* [2006] ECR II-1343; Case T-167/04 *Asklepios Kliniken* v *Commission* [2007] ECR II-2379.

[130] Case 247/87 *Star Fruit* v *Commission* [1989] ECR 291. See pp. 341–3.

[131] Joined Cases T-30/01–T-32/01 and T-86/02–T-88/02 *Diputación Foral de Álava* v *Commission*, Judgment of 9 September 2009.

[132] Case 377/87 *Parliament* v *Council* [1988] ECR 4017; Case 302/87 *European Parliament* v *Council* [1988] ECR 561; Case T-186/94 *Guérin Automobiles* v *Commission* [1995] ECR II-1753.

[133] Case C-25/91 *Pesqueras Echebastar* v *Commission* [1993] ECR I-1719; Case T-420/05 *Vischim* v *Commission*, Judgment of 7 October 2009.

[134] Joined Cases T-30/01–T-32/01 and T-86/02–T-88/02 *Diputación Foral de Álava* v *Commission*, Judgment of 9 September 2009.

be brought, if the institution's position on the matter is clear to the applicant, it must bring the request for action within a reasonable period. In *Netherlands* v *Commission*, a case which involved Article 35 ECSC, the parallel provision to Article 265 TFEU in the ECSC Treaty, the Commission informed the Dutch government that a French restructuring plan did not violate the Treaty provisions on state aids.[135] The Dutch government waited a further eighteen months before requesting the Commission to act. The Court, reasoning from the principle of legal certainty, stated that an applicant did not have a right to raise the matter with the Commission indefinitely and had delayed too long in this instance.

6 THE PLEA OF ILLEGALITY

Particularly in areas where the Commission enjoys delegated powers, parties face a problem if they want to challenge an act. The Commission measure may be addressed to them or be of direct and individual concern to them, but they may want to challenge the act on the basis that the parent measure is illegal. They may face difficulties here because the time limits have passed, or because they may not satisfy the *locus standi* requirements in relation to the parent instrument. The plea of illegality addresses this by allowing a party in proceedings against a measure to plead the inapplicability of its parent measure.

Article 277 TFEU

Notwithstanding the expiry of the period laid down in Article 263, fifth paragraph, any party may, in proceedings in which an act of general application adopted by an institution, body, office or agency of the Union is at issue, plead the grounds specified in Article 263, second paragraph, in order to invoke before the Court of Justice of the European Union the inapplicability of that act.

The plea of illegality is a parasitic procedure. It cannot be brought as an independent action but can only be invoked in the context of proceedings brought under some other provisions of the Treaties. To that end, the party must secure *locus standi* under the other procedure and observe the time limits set out in that procedure, albeit that the time limits for challenging the parent measure may have lapsed.[136] To give an example, a party might want to challenge a Decision on the grounds that the enabling Regulation was illegal. It would have to show that it had *locus standi* under Article 263 TFEU to challenge the Decision, and that it observed the time limits set out there for challenging the Decision within two months of its publication. It does not matter that it is more than two months since the Regulation was adopted.

The concern with the plea of illegality is that it should not lead to an abuse of process where it is used to subvert other procedures. This has led to two refinements.

First, a plea of illegality may not be invoked where a matter is pending before another court or in another action before the same court.[137] For this to be the case, it must be considered to be *lis pendens*. This will only happen if three conditions are met. The action must be between the same parties, must seek the same object and must do so on the basis of the same

---

[135] Case 59/70 *Netherlands* v *Commission* [1971] ECR 639.
[136] Joined Cases 31/62 and 33/62 *Wöhrmann* v *Commission* [1962] ECR 506.
[137] Joined Cases T-246/08 and T-332/08 *Melli Bank* v *Council*, Judgment of 9 July 2009.

submissions. This will very rarely be the case. Even if the substance of the dispute is similar, the litigation before the courts may look at slightly different dimensions, and parties will, in any case, often use different arguments.

Secondly, a party who had an earlier opportunity to challenge the parent measure cannot subsequently raise the plea of illegality.[138] The most obvious example is privileged parties under Article 263 TFEU who had unlimited standing to challenge the parent measure at the time of adoption. If they could subsequently raise a plea of illegality, this would allow them to evade the time limits in that procedure and generate uncertainty. In *Spain v Commission*, the Court refused to allow a Spanish challenge to a 1992 Commission Decision extending the regime on subsidies to the motor vehicle industry.[139] For the basis of the Spanish challenge was that the initial 1990 regime on which the 1993 Decision was based was illegal. The Court ruled that as Spain had not challenged the 1990 regime at the time, it could not subsequently raise a plea of illegality.

However, the principle applies not just to privileged parties but to any party who had an earlier opportunity to bring the matter directly to the Court of Justice. In *TWD (No. 2)*, a 1986 Commission Decision that a subsidy from the German *Land* of Bavaria to the applicant, a textile company, was illegal was not challenged.[140] A new subsidy was authorised by a second Commission Decision on condition that the initial subsidy granted to the applicant be repaid. The applicant challenged the 1986 Decision, under a plea of illegality, claiming that its economic effects only became apparent following the second Decision. The General Court deemed this inadmissible, noting that, as the applicant could have challenged the first Decision using Article 263 TFEU, it was debarred now from bringing a challenge under Article 277 TFEU.

7 NON-CONTRACTUAL LIABILITY

The final head of action under which Union measures can be reviewed is that of non-contractual liability. In such circumstances, the applicant will not be seeking merely annulment of the measure but also damages from the EU institutions. This is governed by Article 340(2) TFEU.

Article 340(2) TFEU

In the case of non-contractual liability, the Union shall, in accordance with the general principles common to the laws of the Member States, make good any damage caused by its institutions or by its servants in the performance of their duties.

Although an equivalent Treaty provision has been present since the Treaty of Rome in the 1950s, the law on the non-contractual liability of EU institutions was reshaped by the *Brasserie du Pêcheur* judgment.[141] This judgment, it will be remembered, set out the circumstances in

---

[138] On the early debate surrounding this, see G. Bebr, 'Judicial Remedy of Private Parties Against Normative Acts of the European Communities: The Role of the Exception of Illegality' (1966) 4 *CMLRev.* 7; A. Barav, 'The Exception of Illegality in Community Law: A Critical Analysis' (1974) 11 *CMLRev.* 366.

[139] Case C-135/93 *Spain v Commission* [1995] ECR I-1651.

[140] Joined Cases T-244 and T-486/93 *TWD Textilwerke Deggendorf v Commission* [1995] ECR I-2265.

[141] Joined Cases C-24/93 and C-48/93 *Brasserie du Pêcheur v Germany* [1996] ECR I-1029. See pp. 304–7. See also T. Tridimas, 'Liability for Breach of Community Law: Growing Up and Mellowing Down?' (2001) 38 *CMLRev.* 301.

which Member States could be liable for individual loss that arose from their failure to comply with EU law. Aware of the inconsistencies that might otherwise arise, the Court stated that the same criteria set out in that case delimiting Member State liability should also govern the liability of EU institutions under Article 340(2) TFEU.[142] To be sure, it has proved difficult for the Court of Justice to apply these parallels too formulaically but it has tried to reason from similar principles for both.

(i) Nature of the liability

The leading case following *Brasserie du Pêcheur* in which the Court considered the liability of the EU institutions was *Bergaderm*. A Commission Decision banned the use of a chemical, bergapten, in sun oil on the ground that it was carcinogenic. Bergaderm was the only company that produced sun oil using this chemical. Following the Decision, it went into liquidation. It sued the Commission, claiming that the latter had misinterpreted the scientific evidence. The application failed, but the Court set out new parameters for Article 340(2) TFEU.

Case C-352/98 P *Laboratoires Pharmaceutiques Bergaderm* v *Commission* [2000] ECR I-5291

39. [Article 340(2) TFEU] provides that, in the case of non-contractual liability, the Community is, in accordance with the general principles common to the laws of the Member States, to make good any damage caused by its institutions or by its servants in the performance of their duties.

40. The system of rules which the Court has worked out with regard to that provision takes into account, inter alia, the complexity of the situations to be regulated, difficulties in the application or interpretation of the texts and, more particularly, the margin of discretion available to the author of the act in question ...

41. The Court has stated that the conditions under which the State may incur liability for damage caused to individuals by a breach of Community law cannot, in the absence of particular justification, differ from those governing the liability of the Community in like circumstances. The protection of the rights which individuals derive from Community law cannot vary depending on whether a national authority or a Community authority is responsible for the damage ...

42. As regards Member State liability for damage caused to individuals, the Court has held that Community law confers a right to reparation where three conditions are met: the rule of law infringed must be intended to confer rights on individuals; the breach must be sufficiently serious; and there must be a direct causal link between the breach of the obligation resting on the State and the damage sustained by the injured parties ...

43. As to the second condition, as regards both Community liability under Article [288(2), the predecessor to 340(2) TFEU] and Member State liability for breaches of Community law, the decisive test for finding that a breach of Community law is sufficiently serious is whether the Member State or the Community institution concerned manifestly and gravely disregarded the limits on its discretion ...

44. Where the Member State or the institution in question has only considerably reduced, or even no, discretion, the mere infringement of Community law may be sufficient to establish the existence of a sufficiently serious breach ...

46. In that regard, the Court finds that the general or individual nature of a measure taken by an institution is not a decisive criterion for identifying the limits of the discretion enjoyed by the institution in question.

---

[142] *Brasserie du Pêcheur*, paras. 40–7.

The judgment sets out three conditions which must be met for the institutions to incur liability (paragraph 42). These are:

- the conduct of the institution must infringe a rule of law intended to confer rights on individuals;
- the breach of EU law must be sufficiently serious;
- there must be a direct causal link between the breach by the EU institution and the damage sustained by the applicant.

As there was no liability in *Bergaderm*, the Court did not address in detail the third condition but only the first two. In this, it recast a distinction that it had previously made between legislative acts involving economic policy choices and other acts, with a far higher degree of fault required for liability for the former.[143] In *Bergaderm*, the Court indicated that it will operate a single test which makes no distinction between the types of act being challenged. Within this single test, there will be a spectrum of cases. These will range from situations where the EU institutions are faced with complex choices and where they enjoy a fair degree of discretion, to more straightforward scenarios where they have little or no discretion. Questions of complexity and discretion will be central to determining the standard of liability in each case.

On relatively straightforward matters or where the EU institution has little or no discretion, the Court has stated, in regard to the first test that a superior rule must be breached, that the norm must grant rights for individuals. Breach of an instrument, such as the WTO agreement, that does not do this will not lead to liability.[144] Beyond that, any breach of any EU legal obligation, be it substantive or procedural, will be sufficient.[145] A failure to exercise due diligence will also incur liability.[146] With regard to the second head of the test, in such circumstances mere illegality or failure to exercise due diligence will be sufficient.

The situation is different where the EU institutions enjoy a measure of discretion. With regard to the first part of the test, general principles of EU law, fundamental rights and the doctrine of misuse of powers have been held to be norms that will lead to liability.[147] The duty to give reasons, on the other hand, is not regarded as having that status, so a failure to give reasons cannot give rise to an action under Article 340(2) TFEU.[148] Similarly a failure of due diligence, be it in the form of an error of assessment or a failure to consider evidence that should have been considered, will not be sufficient to incur liability.[149]

With regard to the second heading, *Bergaderm* indicated that a simple breach of EU law by an EU institution would not be sufficient for it to incur liability. The breach must be sufficiently serious and that would involve the EU institution 'manifestly and gravely' exceeding the limits on its discretion (paragraph 43). The meaning of this was addressed in most detail in *Schneider*. Schneider and Legrand were two companies specialising in electrical distribution and low voltage installations who merged into a single company. The Commission declared

---

[143] Case 5/71 *Aktien-Zuckerfabrik Schöppenstedt* v *Council* [1971] ECR 975. For an excellent discussion of the position since *Bergaderm*, see C. Hilson, 'The Role of Discretion in EC Law on Non-contractual Liability' (2005) 42 *CMLRev.* 677.

[144] Joined Cases C-120/06 and C-121/06 *FIAMM and Others* v *Council and Commission*, Judgment of 9 September 2008.

[145] Case T-351/03 *Schneider* v *Commission* [2007] ECR II-2237. The most extensive list of grounds can be found in Case T-48/05 *Franchet and Byk* v *Commission* [2008] ECR II-1585.

[146] Case T-178/98 *Fresh Marine* v *Commission* [2000] ECR II-3331.

[147] For a summary of the position, see Joined Cases T-481/93 and T-484/93 *Vereniging van Exporteurs in Levende Varkens* v *Commission* [1995] ECR II-2941.

[148] See e.g. Case C-76/01 P *Eurocoton* v *Council* [2003] ECR I-10091, para. 98 and the case law cited therein.

[149] Case T-212/03 *MyTravel* v *Commission*, Judgment of 9 September 2008.

the merger incompatible with the common market and ordered a break-up of the company. In 2002, the General Court found the Commission decision to be illegal on two grounds.[150] First, there were errors in its economic analysis of all the national markets other than the French market. Notwithstanding this, the General Court held that the competition effects on the French market were sufficient for the merger to be declared incompatible with the single market. In addition, in its initial statement of objections, the Commission had failed to tell Schneider in sufficiently clear terms what measures it needed to take to avoid the merger being declared illegal. Schneider then brought an action under Article 340(2) TFEU.

Case T–351/03 *Schneider v Commission* [2007] ECR II–2237

116. The system of rules which the Court of Justice has worked out in relation to the non-contractual liability of the Community takes into account, inter alia, the complexity of the situations to be regulated, difficulties in the application or interpretation of the legislation and, more particularly, the margin of discretion available to the author of the act in question …

121. In that context, the Commission contends that, if it were to incur financial liability in circumstances such as those of this case, its capacity fully to function as a regulator of competition, a task entrusted to it by the EC Treaty, would be compromised as a result of the possible inhibiting effect that the risk of having to bear damages alleged by the undertakings concerned might have on the control of concentrations.

122. It must be conceded that such an effect, contrary to the general Community interest, might arise if the concept of a serious breach of Community law were construed as comprising all errors or mistakes which, even if of some gravity, are not by their nature or extent alien to the normal conduct of an institution entrusted with the task of overseeing the application of competition rules, which are complex, delicate and subject to a considerable degree of discretion.

123. Therefore, a sufficiently serious breach of Community law, for the purposes of establishing the non-contractual liability of the Community, cannot be constituted by failure to fulfil a legal obligation, which, regrettable though it may be, can be explained by the objective constraints to which the institution and its officials are subject as a result of the provisions governing the control of concentrations.

124. On the other hand, the right to compensation for damage resulting from the conduct of the institution becomes available where such conduct takes the form of action manifestly contrary to the rule of law and seriously detrimental to the interests of persons outside the institution and cannot be justified or accounted for by the particular constraints to which the staff of the institution, operating normally, is objectively subject.

125. Such a definition of the threshold for the establishment of non-contractual liability of the Community is conducive to protection of the room for manoeuvre and freedom of assessment which must, in the general interest, be enjoyed by the Community regulator of competition, both in its discretionary decisions and in its interpretation and application of the relevant provisions of primary and secondary Community law, without thereby leaving third parties to bear the consequences of flagrant and inexcusable misconduct …

129. In principle, the possibility cannot be ruled out that manifest and serious defects affecting the economic analysis underlying competition policy decisions may constitute sufficiently serious breaches of a rule of law to cause the Community to incur non-contractual liability.

---

[150] Case T-310/01 *Schneider Electric SA* v *Commission* [2002] ECR II-4071.

130. However, for such a finding to be made it is first necessary to verify that the rule infringed by the incorrect analysis is intended to confer rights on individuals. Whilst certain principles and certain rules which must be observed in any competitive analysis are indeed rules intended to confer rights on individuals, not all norms, whether of primary or secondary law or deriving from case law, which the Commission must observe in its economic assessments can be automatically held to be rules of that kind.

131. Next, it must be noted that the economic analyses necessary for the classification, under competition law, of a given situation or transaction are generally, as regards both the facts and the reasoning based on the account of the facts, complex and difficult intellectual formulas, which may inadvertently contain certain inadequacies, such as approximations, inconsistencies, or indeed certain omissions, in view of the time constraints to which the institution is subject. That is even more so where, as in the case of the control of concentrations, the analysis has a prospective element. The gravity of a documentary or logical inadequacy, in such circumstances, may not always constitute a sufficient circumstance to cause the Community to incur liability.

132. Last, it must be borne in mind that the Commission enjoys discretion in maintaining control over Community competition policy, which means that rigorously consistent and invariable practice in implementing the relevant rules cannot be expected of it, and, as a corollary, that it enjoys a degree of latitude regarding the choice of the econometric instruments available to it and the choice of the appropriate approach to the study of any matter (see, for example, regarding the definition of the relevant market, …) provided that those choices are not manifestly contrary to the accepted rules of economic discipline and are applied consistently.

In *Schneider*, the General Court went on to find that there was liability because the Commission had violated Schneider's rights of defence by not telling it what corrective action it needed to take. It saw this question as unrelated to the complexity of the assessment, and therefore simple breach was sufficient to justify liability.[151]

The Court could have used a risk-based test. This would have involved the Court deciding, in conditions of uncertainty, whether EU institutions or private parties would be better equipped to bear responsibility for the costs of things going wrong. Misbehaviour by EU institutions would have been irrelevant to this test. Instead, the Court chose to apply a fault-based test. The virtues of such a test are that it carries with it a duty of care on the part of EU institutions to those affected by their actions. This test is not, however, without its own challenges. In this regard, EU law suggests a paradoxical standard. With regard to substantive obligations, only the most flagrant violations of clear obligations or arbitrary conduct will incur liability – a very narrow fault test indeed. As regards matters of process, the situation is reversed, with relatively small failures to observe due process or rights of defence being likely to lead to liability. The difficulty with this is that it provides incentives for EU institutions to focus on process in their activities at the expense of substance.

---

[151] The decision of the General Court on these points was upheld on appeal. Case C-440/07 P *Commission v Schneider Electric*, Judgment of 16 July 2009.

(ii) Presence of loss caused by the Union

The final condition for liability is the presence of a direct causal link between the breach of EU law and the damage. The range of types of loss that may be covered is, in principle, considerable. The position on the types of loss which may be recovered was most clearly set out by Advocate General Capotorti in *Ireks-Arkady*:

> It is well known that the legal concept of 'damage' covers both a material loss *stricto sensu*, that is to say, a reduction in the person's assets and also the loss of an increase in those assets which would have occurred if the harmful act had not taken place (these two alternatives are known respectively as *damnum emergens* and *lucrum cessans*)... The object of compensation is to restore the assets of the victim to the condition in which they would have been apart from the unlawful act, or at least to the condition closest to that which would have been produced if the unlawful act had not taken place: the hypothetical nature of that restoration often entails a certain degree of approximation.[152]

The Court has thus taken a broad view of which loss may be recovered. It will include any incidental loss, such as penalties the applicant had to pay as a result of having to repudiate a contract,[153] or bank interest as a result of loans taken out to pay money wrongfully levied.[154] The Court has also been ready to award compensation for non-pecuniary loss such as anxiety, hurt feelings[155] and slurs on professional reputation.[156] The 'expectation interest' will also be protected. Compensation will be awarded, therefore, for loss of profits.[157]

However, the establishment of loss is often a significant hurdle, in practice, for applicants.

The first problem is that of joint or concurrent liability: situations where both an EU institution and a Member State may be liable.[158] There are two situations where this may occur.[159] The first is where a national authority implements or administers an unlawful Union measure, such as the transposition of a Directive or the collection of agricultural levies. The second is where a decision is taken jointly by a Member State and an institution, such as in the field of external trade, where Member States are permitted to restrict imports of third country goods once they have received the permission of the Commission. The most equitable solution would be to establish a system of joint and several liability. The applicant could choose whom to sue, with unsuccessful defendants recovering contributions from each other afterwards. Such a scheme, however, has not been established in EU law. Instead, the Court presumes that parties should first exhaust remedies in domestic courts,[160] although the presumption is rebuttable where it would be impossible for an applicant to obtain a remedy in a national court.[161]

---

[152] Case 238/78 *Ireks-Arkady* v *Council and Commission* [1979] ECR 2955, 2998–9.

[153] Case 74/74 *CNTA* v *Commission* [1975] ECR 533.

[154] Case T-167/94 *Nölle* v *Council and Commission* [1995] ECR II-2589.

[155] Case 110/63 *Willame* v *Commission* [1965] ECR 649.

[156] Case T-48/05 *Franchet and Byk* v *Commission* [2008] ECR II-1585.

[157] Joined Cases 56/74–60/74 *Kampffmeyer* v *Commission and Council* [1976] ECR 711; Joined Cases C-104/89 and C-37/90 *Mulder* v *Council and Commission* [1992] ECR I-3061.

[158] For detailed critique see A. Ward, *Judicial Review and the Rights of Private Parties in EU Law* (2nd edn, Oxford, Oxford University Press, 2007) 375–90.

[159] W. Wils, 'Concurrent Liability of the Community and a Member State' (1992) 17 *ELRev.* 191, 194–8.

[160] Case 96/71 *Haegeman* v *Commission* [1972] ECR 1005.

[161] Case 281/82 *Unifrex* v *Commission and Council* [1984] ECR 1969.

This has resulted in unsatisfactory and needless complexity, requiring, in some instances, that applicants simultaneously commence actions in both the domestic courts and the Court of Justice.[162]

Secondly, the burden of proof is upon applicants to show a direct causal link between the loss and the illegal act.[163] The chain of causation can thus be severed by third parties, such as by an independent act of a Member State.[164] It is not sufficient to prove that the loss would not have occurred but for the illegal act.[165] There must a sufficient proximity between the illegal act and the loss suffered.[166] In practice, this has made it very difficult for applicants to claim for loss of profits as these will often be too remote or speculative. For the Court has stated that it will only compensate damage that is actual and certain.[167] Even where a causal link is established between the loss suffered and the illegal act, the applicant might still not recover full compensation. This may be, first, as a result of the doctrine of contributory negligence, where the applicant is considered to have contributed to the damage as a result of a failure to take due care.[168] Secondly, the applicant is under a duty to mitigate any loss suffered. A failure to do so will result in compensation being reduced.[169] Finally, compensation will be reduced if there is evidence that the applicant has, or could have, passed the loss on to somebody else.[170]

8 CONSEQUENCES OF ANNULMENT

The consequences of a finding of illegality are set out in Article 264 TFEU.

Article 264 TFEU

If the action is well founded, the Court of Justice shall declare the act concerned to be void.

In the case of a regulation, however, the Court of Justice shall, if it considers this necessary, state which of the effects of the regulation which it has declared void shall be considered as definitive.

A finding of invalidity can be made not just on the basis of Article 263 TFEU and under the plea of illegality, but also under a claim brought for damages.[171] This has *erga omnes* effect by binding all national courts in the European Union.[172] In *BASF*, the Court ruled that 'acts of the Community institutions are in principle presumed to be lawful and accordingly produce

---

[162] Case T-167/94 *Nölle v Council and Commission* [1995] ECR II-2589.

[163] Case T-168/94 *Blackspur DIY v Council and Commission* [1995] ECR II-2627. On this see A. Toth, 'The Concepts of Damage and Causality as Elements of Non-Contractual Liability' in H. Schermers *et al.* (eds.), *Non-Contractual Liability of the European Communities* (Dordrecht, Martinus Nijhoff, 1988).

[164] Case 132/77 *Société pour l'Exportation des Sucres SA v Commission* [1978] ECR 1061.

[165] This is, however, a *sine qua non*: Case T-478/93 *Wafer Zoo v Commission* [1995] ECR II-1479.

[166] Joined Cases 64/76, 113/76, 167/78, 239/78, 27/79, 28/79 and 45/79 *Dumortier Frères v Council* [1979] ECR 3091.

[167] Joined Cases T-3/00 and T-337/04 *Pitsiorlas v Council and ECB* [2007] ECR II-4779.

[168] Case 145/83 *Adams v Commission* [1985] ECR 3539.

[169] Joined Cases C-104/89 and C-37/90 *Mulder v Council and Commission* [1992] ECR I-3061.

[170] Case 238/78 *Ireks-Arkady v Council and Commission* [1979] ECR 2955.

[171] Joined Cases 5/66, 7/66, 13/66–24/66 *Kampfmeyer v Commission* [1967] ECR 245.

[172] See Case 66/80 *International Chemical Corporation v Amministrazione delle Finanze* [1981] ECR 1191.

legal effects, even if they are tainted by irregularities, until such time as they are annulled or withdrawn'.[173] The Court went on to add the following rider:

> by way of exception to that principle, acts tainted by an irregularity whose gravity is so obvious that it cannot be tolerated by the Community legal order must be treated as having no legal effect, even provisional, that is to say that they must be regarded as legally non-existent. The purpose of this exception is to maintain a balance between two fundamental, but sometimes conflicting, requirements with which a legal order must comply, namely stability of legal relations and respect for legality.[174]

A ruling to that effect will have the consequence of releasing all parties from any obligation to which they might have thought themselves subject under the measure. Otherwise, the effects will vary according to the measure declared invalid. A Regulation declared invalid is void not just between the parties to the dispute, but also in respect of third parties. While the presumption in the first paragraph of Article 264 TFEU is that it is void *ab initio*, considerable discretion is given to the Court under the second paragraph of Article 264 TFEU, enabling it to determine the effects of its ruling. Accordingly, the Court may declare that only part of a measure is void, maintaining in place other aspects of it. Temporal limitations may also be placed upon an annulment, meaning that the legislation will remain in force until new legislation is passed to replace it.[175]

FURTHER READING

A. Arnull, 'Private Applicants and the Action for Annulment Since *Codorníu*' (2001) 38 *Common Market Law Review* 7

The European Union and its Court of Justice (2nd edn, Oxford, Oxford University Press, 2006) ch. 3

P. Craig, *EU Administrative Law* (Oxford, Oxford University Press, 2006) chs. 10, 13, 20

C. Harlow, 'Towards a Theory of Access for the European Court of Justice' (1992) 12 *Yearbook of European Law* 213

C. Hilson, 'The Role of Discretion in EC Law on Non-contractual Liability' (2005) 42 *Common Market Law Review* 677

H. Nehl, *Principles of Administrative Procedure in EC Law* (Oxford, Oxford University Press, 1999)

E. Sharpston, 'Legitimate Expectations and Economic Reality' (1990) 15 *European Law Review* 103

T. Tridimas, 'Liability for Breach of Community Law: Growing Up and Mellowing Down?' (2001) 38 *Common Market Law Review* 301

The General Principles of EU Law (2nd edn, Oxford, Oxford University Press, 2006)

M. Vogt, 'Indirect Judicial Protection in EC Law: The Case of the Plea of Illegality' (2006) 31 *European Law Review* 364

A. Ward, *Judicial Review and the Rights of Private Parties in EU Law* (2nd edn, Oxford, Oxford University Press, 2007) chs. 6, 8

W. Wils, 'Concurrent Liability of the Community and a Member State' (1992) 17 *European Law Review* 191

---

[173] See Case C-137/92 P *Commission v BASF* [1994] ECR I-2555.
[174] *Ibid.* para. 49.
[175] See e.g. Case C-392/95 *Parliament v Council* [1997] ECR I-3213.

11

EU Citizenship

CONTENTS

1 INTRODUCTION

This chapter considers the ideas and rights associated with European Union citizenship. This is granted by the Treaty to all those who are citizens of one of the Member States of the European Union. It is organised as follows.

Sections 2 and 3 discuss ideas of citizenship.

(a) Modern citizenship evolved in the period of the industrial revolution, following the American and French revolutions. Society became less feudal and more democratic and individuals acquired more rights and possibilities. The core elements of the resulting notion of citizenship were legally enforceable rights, loyalty, a sense of belonging to the national community and participation in political decision-making.

(b) One view of European Union citizenship is that it follows this tradition. On this view, citizenship is a limited success. Rights are only for those who migrate and who are economically active or independent. The sense of a community of Europeans is thus but a pale shadow of that found in nation-states and citizens do not have political rights to participate in some of the most important elections.

(c) Others would like to see EU citizenship break with nationality and include all those living within the European Union, even if they have the nationality of a non-EU state. This would make EU citizenship more open, accessible and a true challenge to nationalism, arguably in the original spirit of the Union.

(d) An alternative view of EU citizenship is that its value is not as a free-standing institution at all, but as a mechanism for changing what national citizenship means. It works to transform national societies and should be judged against this measure.

Section 4 considers the right of EU citizens to move and reside throughout the Union.

(a) This right is found in Article 21 TFEU. It is complemented by Article 18 TFEU, the prohibition on nationality discrimination. The rights in these Articles are expressed in more detail in Directive 2004/38/EC ('Citizenship Directive').

(b) The right to free movement and residence is subject to conditions: citizens must either be economically active, or they must be economically independent of the state in which they live. Those who are not economically active must also show that they have sickness insurance covering their costs in the host state, which may be difficult for some to obtain. This exclusion of the poor and the sick from migration rights inspires the criticism that EU citizenship is still a quasi-economic policy as opposed to a proper constitutional citizenship embodying solidarity, equality and universality.

(c) Lawfully present migrant citizens and their families enjoy a right to equal treatment with nationals in their host state. A particularly sensitive issue concerns equal access to public benefits and support. States sometimes make these conditional upon a period of prior residence, or some degree of integration into society. Such requirements can come close to nationality discrimination, but the Court of Justice finds that they are acceptable if they are justified and proportionate in the particular circumstances.

(d) As a corollary of their own free movement rights, EU citizens who migrate may bring their family to live with them, even if these family members are not EU citizens. The Court has extended this right to citizens returning home from a period living abroad. This sometimes enables non-EU family members to avoid national immigration restrictions. It has been argued by some Member States, without much success so far, that this should be seen as 'abuse' of rights.

(e) EU citizens and their family members can only be excluded from a state under very serious circumstances. Mere criminality is not enough. They must represent a current and serious threat to one of the fundamental interests of society. In general, if a migrant citizen misbehaves, the host state should punish or prosecute him just as they would their own citizens. Expulsion is the exception.

Section 5 is about the political rights of citizens. The most important of these is that EU citizens may vote for the European Parliament in whichever state they live and may vote in local elections in the state where they live. However, if they are in a host state EU law gives them no right to vote in national elections.

2 EVOLUTION OF MODERN CITIZENSHIP

Contemporary national citizenship is the product of modernity. Economic, social and political change in the eighteenth and nineteenth centuries transformed the state, the national community and the position of the individual in that community.[1]

R. Bellamy, "Introduction: The Making of Modern Citizenship" in R. Bellamy et al. (eds.), *Lineages of European Citizenship: Rights, Belonging and Participation in Eleven Nation States* (Basingstoke, Palgrave Macmillan, 2004) 1, 6–7

[The American and French Revolutions] provided the basis for a distinctly modern conception of citizenship. First, it gave rise to the new political context of the nation-state. Rather than being the fiefdoms of monarchs, these new political units found legitimacy through being the territorial expression of a given culture and people. The political apparatus no longer referred simply to the administration of the monarch's domain and subjects, but likewise had a popular justification. Second, this development was linked in its turn to the emergence of commercial and increasingly industrial market economies. These required regular forms of government and justice that, in various ways facilitated the free movement and exchange of goods, capital, labour and services. Thus, states had to uphold the rule of law, particularly freedom of contract and the protection of property rights. Nation-building and a state education system that promoted a common language and guaranteed standards of numeracy and literacy helped create a mobile workforce capable of acquiring the generic skills needed for industry. Nation-states could also provide the infrastructural public goods required by market economies, such as a unified transport system, a single currency and a standardized system of weights and measures. Third, markets broke down traditional social hierarchies and systems of ascribed status, thereby fostering equality of opportunity. This feature was also associated with demands for equal political as well as legal rights by hitherto politically excluded sections of the nation. The national people gradually transformed into a demos, who sought to ensure that the state governed in their interest.

These three interrelated developments associated with the rise of national industrial states promoted the three key components of modern citizenship. First, they fostered an emphasis on individual rights. Lack of ascribed status led individuals to being treated as equals possessing certain rights simply by virtue of their humanity – including the right to be treated equally before the law. Their involvement as actors in markets also gave them equal rights to pursue their interests by buying and selling goods, services and labour. Meanwhile, they looked to the state to provide social and economic rights, as part of its regulatory function and demanded political rights to secure equal access and recognition within its policies, decision-making and organizational structures. Second, citizenship became closely associated with belonging to the national community. National identity shaped a common civic consciousness and allegiance to the state and one's fellow citizens. It encouraged reciprocity and solidarity in both politics and economics. National systems of education created a public political language and inducted citizens into a certain civic culture and set of values. Third, as a mark of citizenship was the capacity and right to participate as a full and equal member within the economy

---

[1] On the broader evolution of the term citizenship, see R. Bendix, *Nation-Building and Citizenship* (New York, Wiley, 1964); W. Brubaker, *Citizenship and Nationhood in France and Germany* (Cambridge, MA, Harvard University Press, 1992); P. Riesenberg, *Citizenship in the Western Tradition: Plato to Rousseau* (Chapel Hill, University of North Carolina Press, 1992).

and the polity, the right to vote was often obligatory and in any case tied to the payment of taxes, military service, and the undertaking of such public duties as sitting on juries. Similarly, social and economic rights were linked to the duty and ability to work and to contribute to national schemes of social insurance. Those deemed socially irresponsible, a label that at various times and places has been applied to lunatics, children, criminals, women, the propertyless and the indigent, either forfeited or were ineligible for most citizenship rights.

As the state was transformed from a personal fiefdom into a rational and efficient socio-economic machine, the subject was transformed into a citizen. The marks of this citizenship were rights, a sense of belonging and political participation. All three enhanced the position of the individual, protecting them from arbitrariness and extending their influence over the society around them. Yet, they also served the national interest, helping to create a cohesive and loyal population, better able to work and live together and act responsibly. Citizenship was part of a pragmatic and multifaceted social contract.

The specific content of citizenship has varied from state to state and over time. The Cambridge historian T. H. Marshall observed that the growth of the welfare state and its importance in contemporary understandings of justice following the Second World War led to a greater emphasis on social rights, as increasingly it was felt that equal membership of the political community entailed a right to participate in the wealth and welfare provided by that community.[2] More recently, the sociologist Bryn Turner has observed that politics has concerned itself with the protection of the individual against risk.[3] These risks might be environmental risks, such as that posed by floods or pollution, uncertainty generated by terrorism, or risks associated with financial markets, such as losing one's savings or pension. In such a world, he has argued, equal membership within a political community entails equal protection against risk. He speaks of the emergence of a new citizenship right, a 'right to security', which would give all citizens minimum assurances against certain types of risks.

Another event to transform understandings of citizenship was the migration into Western Europe since the Second World War. From being less than or around 1 per cent in most Western European states in 1960, the foreign population grew, by 1990, to between 3 and 9 per cent of the general population.[4] An important feature of this foreign population is its permanence. Many migrants who came to Europe did not return to their home states, something for which the states hosting them were ill-prepared.

This non-native population challenged the existing notion of citizenship. Although Shaw has argued that the decoupling of rights and identity is an important post-war phenomenon, as long as citizenship remained a significant vehicle for rights its link to nationality was problematic.[5] This tie turned citizenship into an exclusionary device. When citizens are just a sub-set

---

[2] This division was first made, most famously, in T. Marshall, *Citizenship and Social Class* (T. Bottomore (ed.), London, Pluto, 1992). This model was first applied to the European Union in J. Shaw, 'The Interpretation of Union Citizenship' (1998) 61 *MLR* 293.

[3] B. Turner, 'The Erosion of Citizenship' (2001) 52 *British Journal of Sociology* 189.

[4] Y. Soysal, *Limits of Citizenship: Migrants and Postnational Membership in Europe* (Chicago, University of Chicago Press, 1994) 23. These figures do not include migrants who subsequently became naturalised and thereby citizens of the nation-states in which they were resident.

[5] J. Shaw *Citizenship of the Union: Towards Post-national Membership*, Jean Monnet Working Paper 97/6, www.jeanmonnetprogram.org

of those living and participating in the nation, then citizenship takes on a less universalistic and idealistic flavour and tribal and ethnic undertones emerge. Is it about recognition of the dignity and rights of the individual or about closure against the outsider?

Scholars have sought to resolve the resulting tensions in different ways, with many arguing that citizenship should become more open and accessible. This can either occur by making nationality more accessible (it has traditionally been very hard to acquire the nationality of some EU Member States, even after decades of residence), or by decoupling citizenship from nationality. Balibar is the leading proponent of a citizenship based on factual presence rather than the accident of birth, although he is more concerned to expose the contradictions of national citizenship – to deconstruct it – than to lobby for concrete change.[6] His view of citizenship seems less exclusionary, as it opens up membership of a community to anyone who chooses to participate and to all those who do participate. Yet concerns have been raised that mere practical participation may not suffice to generate commitment of citizens to each other and to society, without which shared projects may not be achievable.[7] Participation may also not provide a shared identity, without which the community may not be a satisfying or enriching context for individuals to live in. This commitment and identity may be more likely to materialise in communities of fate – those where membership is not a choice, but is ascribed on the basis of factors outside individual control such as family origin or place of birth.[8] Commitment to such communities is arguably more profound because the individual enjoys unconditional membership. This also gives the community a certain tolerance, as people of opposing political views can seek to impose their own interpretation of the community without calling membership as such into question. An identity is maintained despite such political diversity through the use of myths and symbols, such as those surrounding the nation-state.

Habermas is the best known of those who seek a middle way between these extremes. He has suggested that a commitment to the values of a community, such as democracy and human rights, should be a condition for citizenship. This requirement, combined with participatory political practices, would offer a foundation for a citizenship lying between the mystical and closed, but tough, community of fate and the possibly shallow and unstable community of participation.[9] His view of citizenship has been particularly prominent in the debate on EU citizenship and he places his arguments in the context of Europe.

Like many other contemporary and recent scholars, Habermas is trying to reconcile closure with humanity. As Bosniak puts it, citizenship is inherently about membership and can never be fully open; a 'purely inclusionary inside' is a fantasy.[10] The task, in their view, is not to eliminate the bounded community, but to keep trying to make it more decent and fair. This is, rather like Kostakopoulou in the next section, citizenship at least partly as process.

---

[6] E. Balibar, *We the Peoples of Europe: Reflections on Transnational Citizenship* (Princeton, Princeton University Press, 2004). See also D. Schnapper, 'The European Debate on Citizenship' (1997) 126 *Daedalus* 199; L. Bosniak, 'Citizenship Denationalised' (2000) 7 *Indiana Journal of Global Law Studies* 447.

[7] D. Miller, *Citizenship and National Identity* (Oxford, Polity, 2000) ch. 2. See also R. Bellamy, 'Evaluating Union Citizenship: Belonging, Rights and Participation within the EU' (2008) 12 *Citizenship Studies* 597.

[8] *Ibid.*

[9] J. Habermas, 'Citizenship and National Identity: Some Reflections on the Future of Europe' (1992) 12 *Praxis International* 1. See also the thinking of Hannah Arendt on citizenship, presented in P. Hansen, *Hannah Arendt: Politics, History and Citizenship* (Stanford, Stanford University Press, 1993).

[10] L. Bosniak *The Citizen and the Alien* (Princeton, Princeton University Press, 2006) 139.

3 NATURE OF EU CITIZENSHIP

There was no mention of citizenship in the initial EC Treaty. Indeed, there was no discussion of the term until the 1970s. First use of the term was made in the Tindemans Report in 1975, which contained a chapter entitled 'Towards a Europe for Citizens'. The thrust of this was a number of proposals aimed at integrating Member State nationals resident in other Member States more fully into their host states. It was, therefore, proposed that they should be given a bundle of civil, political and social rights, which would place them on an equal footing with that state's own nationals. Throughout the 1970s and 1980s, the Commission and Parliament brought forward a series of proposals to try and flesh out and implement the ideas in this Report, but to little avail.[11] The breakthrough moment was the Intergovernmental Conference on Political Union that preceded the adoption of the Treaty on European Union at Maastricht. In September 1990, the Spanish government submitted a proposal entitled 'The Road to European Citizenship'. The Spanish government indicated in this paper that the move to political and economic union meant that it was no longer sufficient for EU nationals to be treated as 'privileged aliens' in other Member States. A European Union citizenship should be established. This was defined as:

> The personal and indivisible status of nationals of the Member States, whose membership of the Union means that they have special rights and duties that are specific to the nature of the Union and are exercised and safeguarded specifically within its boundaries.[12]

This proposal attracted support from both the Commission and the Parliament and from a number of Member States. The resulting citizenship provisions are now found in Part 2 of the TFEU. The rights of citizens are stated in full detail in Articles 21–4 of this Part. However, Article 20 is the central article. It establishes EU citizenship and summarises the associated rights.

Article 20 TFEU

1. Citizenship of the Union is hereby established. Every person holding the nationality of a Member State shall be a citizen of the Union. Citizenship of the Union shall be additional to and not replace national citizenship.
2. Citizens of the Union shall enjoy the rights and be subject to the duties provided for in the Treaties. They shall have, inter alia:
   (a) the right to move and reside freely within the territory of the Member States;
   (b) the right to vote and to stand as candidates in elections to the European Parliament and in municipal election in their Member State of residence, under the same conditions as nationals of that State;
   (c) the right to enjoy, in the territory of a third country in which the Member State of which they are nationals is not represented, the protection of the diplomatic and consular authorities of any Member State on the same conditions as the nationals of that State;

---

[11] On the history of European Union citizenship, see A. Wiener, *'European' Citizenship Practice: Building Institutions of a Non-state* (Boulder, Westview, 1998); S. O'Leary, *The Evolving Concept of Community Citizenship: from the Free Movement of Persons to Union Citizenship* (The Hague, Kluwer, 1996) 18–30.

[12] C. Dc SN/3940, 24 September 1990 in F. Laursen and S. van Hoonacker (eds.), *The Intergovernmental Conference on Political Union: Institutional Reforms, New Policies and International Identity of the European Community* (Dordrecht, Martinus Nijhoff, 1992).

(d) the right to petition the European Parliament, to apply to the European Ombudsman, and to address the institutions and advisory bodies of the Union in any of the Treaty languages and to obtain a reply in the same language.

These rights shall be exercised in accordance with the conditions and limits defined by the Treaties and by the measures adopted hereunder.

Article 20(1) TFEU creates a derivative or dependent citizenship. A person is a citizen of the Union if and only if she is a citizen of a Member State. The idea of replacing national citizenship is explicitly rejected. This has conceptual and practical consequences. Martiniello has said of EU citizenship:

> It stimulates a European political identity which is largely linked to a prior communitarian belonging: one can be a European citizen only if one is previously a French, a Belgian or a German citizen, for example. In its present shape, the citizenship of the European Union is thus a complementary set of rights which confirms the existence of the cultural and political identities corresponding to the Member States.[13]

As a result of Article 20(1), Member States also control access to EU citizenship, since it is they who determine who is a national citizen. The Court has been consistent in rejecting calls for it to interfere in this determination: 'Under international law, it is for each Member State, having due regard to Community law, to lay down the conditions for the acquisition and loss of nationality.'[14] While this phrase suggests EU law does impose some constraints on Member State nationality law, these constraints have not been apparent in practice.[15] It is nevertheless possible that, for example, national laws making naturalisation easier for citizens of some EU Member States than for others might violate the Article 18 TFEU ban on nationality discrimination.

The autonomy of Member States is, however, limited where the recognition of other nationalities is concerned. Spanish law at issue in *Micheletti* provided that, where foreign nationals had dual nationality, the nationality corresponding to the place of habitual residence prior to the residence in Spain took precedence and the other nationality was ignored.[16] Micheletti was Argentinian and Italian, but his previous habitual residence had been in Argentina. As a result, Spain refused to treat him as an Italian – as an EU citizen – recognising only his Argentinian nationality. The Court ruled that once a citizen has established his EU citizenship, by showing his citizenship of a Member State, it is not open to another Member State to challenge that status or refuse to recognise it. To do so would not only undermine the rights and freedoms associated with EU citizenship, but would also mean that whether dual nationals could benefit from such citizenship would vary from state to state.[17]

---

[13] M. Martiniello, 'The Development of European Union Citizenship' in M. Roche and R. van Berkel (eds.), *European Citizenship and Social Exclusion* (Aldershot, Ashgate, 1998) 35, 37–8.

[14] Case C-369/90 *Micheletti v Delegación del Gobierno Cantabria* [1992] ECR I-4239. But see now Case C-135/08 *Rottman v Freistaat Bayern*, Judgment of 2 March 2010.

[15] Although see *Rottman*, above n.14; G. Davies and K. Rostek, 'The Impact of Union Citizenship on National Citizenship Policies' (2006) 10 *European Integration Online Papers* no. 5.

[16] *Micheletti*, above n. 14.

[17] See also Case C-192/99 *Kaur* [2001] ECR I-1237 and Case C-200/02 *Zhu and Chen* [2004] ECR I-9925.

As a result of this hard-wiring to national citizenship, EU citizenship sometimes seems to fall between two stools. It has not escaped the nation-state to become a truly new, open and voluntary form of community, as the more cosmopolitan and anti-nationalist theorists would like. Yet, by the standards of traditional modern citizenship it is weak and shallow. It has created nothing close to the loyalty or sense of belonging that attach to nation-states.

Kostakopoulou has argued that this is an incomplete analysis of what EU citizenship is and what it does. It should not be judged just on its contents, but also on its effects. She argues that the value of EU citizenship is partly that it transforms national communities. These are vulnerable to insularity, but the imposition of EU citizenship on top of its national peers inserts a globalising element into the nation. That fact that to be French is also to be an EU citizen changes what it means to be French, and that change is in the direction of the more open and cosmopolitan perspective that is necessary for states to thrive in the contemporary world. Thus, EU citizenship is not to be understood as a free-standing entity, but as something that penetrates national citizenship and changes it.[18]

D. Kostakopoulou, 'European Union Citizenship: Writing the Future' (2007) 13(5) *European Law Journal* 623

But the reduction of European citizenship to a transnational citizenship downplays both the resourcefulness of Union citizenship and the supranational character of EU law … Above all, it conceals the extent to which European citizenship penetrates and subverts national citizenship, thereby triggering off tensions, institutional displacement and the incremental transformation of domestic structures and practices in ways that had not been anticipated. …

I would suggest that the novelty, and in many respects the challenge, of the European citizenship design does not lie simply in the emergence of 'nested' citizenships (supranational, national, sub-national citizenships) and institutional pluralism. More significant is the interaction between 'old' (national) and 'new' (European) citizenships and the ensuing process of incremental, transformative change. European legal and political dynamics subvert the fundamental premises of the nationality model of citizenship and change the organisational logic and practices of national citizenship.

This transformative view of EU citizenship resonates upon reading the case law, upon which Kostakopoulou carefully builds her argument in the article above. The theme in the cases in this chapter is the way in which the institution of EU citizenship requires Member States to re-define and reconstitute their own structures of membership. Despite the fact that EU citizenship is expressed to complement rather than replace national citizenship, and despite the fact that most EU citizenship rights only apply to those who migrate, there are several ways in which the relationship between citizens and their home states is nevertheless regulated by EU law.

First, national communities are no longer free to exclude others. The power to discriminate and exclude is an important part of group definition, but is now confined to very limited spheres such as national elections and certain very sensitive occupations.[19] National citizenship may still exist, but it confers very few special rights. It is, therefore, diminished and constrained.

---

[18] Bellamy, n. 7 above; P. Magnette, 'How Can One be European? Reflections on the Pillars of European Civic Identity' (2007) 13(5) *European Law Journal* 664.

[19] See pp. 481–2.

Secondly, Article 21 TFEU, the right to move and reside throughout the European Union, applies to national measures which discourage exit from a state as well as those limiting entry. A citizen can enforce this against her own state where national measures make it harder for her to emigrate.[20]

Thirdly, the risk of a loss of rights upon returning home is considered by the Court to be a deterrent to migrating in the first place. Rights acquired upon migration therefore become vested and the returning migrant can enforce them against her own state, as if she were entering a state not her own. This fact is of particular importance where family rights are concerned and is discussed further below.[21]

4 RIGHT TO MOVE AND RESIDE WITHIN THE UNION

The most useful right for EU citizens, and the one demanding most adaptation from national authorities, is the right to move and reside throughout the Union. This right is conceptually very similar to the free movement rights relating to goods, economically active persons, services and capital, discussed in later chapters in this book.[22] Many of the abstract themes, such as the notions of discrimination, of the proportionality of national measures and of wholly internal situations, will recur in those chapters, which provide a useful complement to this one. However, the citizenship right also has its own unique nuances and flavour. The constitutional tone of citizenship, and the fact that citizens must be considered as human beings, with broad needs and concerns, has generated a diverse and purposive body of law that is increasingly self-contained.

This right to move and reside within the Union is first stated in Article 20(2)(a) TFEU and then repeated in Article 21.

Article 21(1) TFEU

Every citizen of the Union shall have the right to move and reside freely within the territory of the Member States, subject to the limitations and conditions laid down in the Treaties and by the measures adopted to give them effect.

This is elaborated in the Citizenship Directive.[23] This Directive consolidates previous Directives applying to different categories of persons and now provides the framework for almost all legal issues concerning the free movement of persons. It sets out the rights of citizens to move and reside in other Member States, bring their families to live with them and participate in socio-economic life without experiencing discrimination.

Its provisions on movement and residence fall naturally into three categories.

Right to movement and short-term residence   Articles 4 to 6 of the Directive provide that citizens may move throughout the territory of the Union and live in any state for up to three months, without any formalities other than the possession of a valid identity card or passport.

---

[20] See pp. 460–2.
[21] See pp. 462–4.
[22] See Chapters 16–21.
[23] Directive 2004/38/EC on the right of citizens of the Union and their family members to move and reside freely within the territory of the Member States [2004] OJ L158/77 ('Citizenship Directive').

The only condition imposed is that the citizen not be an unreasonable burden on the social assistance system of the host state.[24] Citizens who are employed or self-employed, or looking for work and able to show that they have a genuine chance of finding it, may not, however, be expelled.[25] They are in substance exempt from the 'unreasonable burden' condition.[26]

Residence in another Member State for periods of more than three months   For periods greater than three months, the conditions are more restrictive.

Citizenship Directive, article 7(1)

All Union citizens shall have the right of residence on the territory of another Member State for a period of longer than three months if they:
(a) are workers or self-employed persons in the host Member State; or
(b) have sufficient resources for themselves and their family members not to become a burden on the social assistance system of the host Member State during their period of residence and have comprehensive sickness insurance cover in the host Member State;
(c) are enrolled at a private or public establishment, accredited or financed by the host Member State on the basis of its legislation or administrative practice, for the principal purpose of following a course of study, including vocational training; and have comprehensive sickness insurance cover in the host Member State and assure the relevant national authority, by means of a declaration or by such equivalent means as they may choose, that they have sufficient resources for themselves and their family members not to become a burden on the social assistance system of the host Member State during their period of residence ...

To fall into the first category, the citizen must be employed or self-employed within the definitions in the Court of Justice's case law on Articles 45 and 49 TFEU respectively.[27] They can retain this status and its associated residence rights if they subsequently cease to fulfil these definitions. The general position is that the person who loses their job involuntarily, is temporarily unable to work because of ill health, or makes a choice to stop working in order to do further training, continues to enjoy the status of worker or self-employed person for the purposes of residence.[28]

Permanent residence   Citizens who have resided legally in another Member State for five years acquire the right of permanent residence.[29] This brings certain benefits, notably exemption from conditions concerning sufficient resources.[30] Once acquired, the status is only lost after two consecutive years of absence.[31]

Some people can acquire permanent residence status in less than five years. In general, this applies to persons who move to another state, work there and then, as a result of retirement

---

[24] *Ibid.* article 14(1).
[25] *Ibid.* article 14(4).
[26] See p. 449.
[27] See Chapter 20.
[28] Citizenship Directive, article 7(3).
[29] *Ibid.* article 16.
[30] *Ibid.* article 16(1).
[31] *Ibid.* article 16(4).

or permanent ill health, stop working before five years is up. For these persons, shorter time limits are provided in article 17 of the Citizenship Directive. The purpose of this is to prevent these citizens, who are no longer economically active but cannot reasonably be expected to be, from having their rights of residence threatened by the article 7(1)(b) condition of 'sufficient resources'.

(i) Conditions of residence

The fear of Member States has traditionally been that citizens would use their free movement rights to move to states with high levels of public assistance, where they would live as parasites, enjoying benefits without contributing to society. In order to ease this fear, EU law has always imposed conditions of self-sufficiency on free movement, requiring certain categories of migrants to have sickness insurance and sufficient resources to live from. On the one hand, these conditions make free movement viable: Member States do not yet feel enough mutual solidarity to accept a free movement regime which permits migration purely for the purposes of claiming benefits. More practically, national communities are the primary locus of taxation and spending. In the absence of mechanisms for redistribution between states (as for example exist in a federal state such as Germany or the United States), benefit tourism is easily portrayed as inequitable.

Yet the practical effect of these conditions is that 'expensive' members of society do not enjoy free movement rights. Those dependent upon state support or suffering medical conditions which are expensive or difficult to insure are excluded from the Europe without borders. EU citizenship is a citizenship for all Europeans who are not poor or sick. This goes to the justice of citizenship, but also to the question of whether it deserves its name.[32] Are not equality and solidarity a part of what citizenship entails? The cases below suggest that the Court's answer is 'to some extent'.

A caveat is that these conditions do not apply to economically active persons. It may be the case, therefore, that a worker or self-employed citizen earns little from their activity and so is entitled to social assistance, perhaps even significant social assistance. Yet, this has no consequences for their residence rights.[33] This softens the conditions a little in practice, since the threshold for economic activity is relatively low and may often be met by just one day of work per week.[34] Yet, it also highlights the economic roots of free movement and suggests that despite its constitutional tone, citizenship has not fully transformed the law on free movement of persons from an economic policy tool to a dignified and socially cohesive institution.

For the non-economically active citizen, however, the conditions apply, in terms varying according to the period of residence. Short-term residence, up to three months, is conditional upon not being an 'unreasonable burden' on the host state.[35] This is probably of limited impact, since the Directive provides later that migrants in this first period of residence have no right to social assistance anyway.[36] It is therefore unlikely that they will be an unreasonable

---

[32] D. Kochenov, 'Ius Tractum of Many Faces: European Citizenship and the Difficult Relationship between Status and Rights' (2009) 15 *CJEL* 169.

[33] Citizenship Directive, article 7; see also Case 139/85 *Kempf* [1986] ECR 1741.

[34] Case 53/81 *Levin* v *Staatssecretaris van Justitie* [1982] ECR 1035.

[35] Citizenship Directive, article 14.

[36] *Ibid.* article 24(2).

burden. The condition may, however, bite on those who have large families with, for example, children of school age, or are medically expensive and so do cost the state money without the migrant receiving direct financial assistance as such.

After the three-month period, residence for the non-economically active is conditional upon possessing 'sufficient resources ... not to become a burden' as well as 'comprehensive sickness insurance'.[37] This sounds strict. However, as with the concept of an 'unreasonable burden', national interpretations of these conditions are subject to the principle of proportionality. In *Baumbast*, the UK government objected to the fact that a German citizen and his family had sickness insurance which did not cover all of the costs which they might incur (although had not incurred) in the United Kingdom.[38] This looked like a fairly straightforward breach of the Directive then in force, which was similarly worded to the Citizenship Directive. However, the family had been in the United Kingdom for some time, had never been a burden on the state in the past and it seemed harsh to deny them further residence for a breach which had not actually cost the United Kingdom any money and was, it seemed, fairly minor.

Case C-413/99 *Baumbast v Secretary of State for the Home Department* [2002] ECR I-7091

90. In any event, the limitations and conditions which are referred to in Article [21 TFEU] and laid down by Directive 90/364 are based on the idea that the exercise of the right of residence of citizens of the Union can be subordinated to the legitimate interests of the Member States. In that regard, according to the fourth recital in the preamble to Directive 90/364 beneficiaries of the right of residence must not become an 'unreasonable' burden on the public finances of the host Member State.

91. However, those limitations and conditions must be applied in compliance with the limits imposed by Community law and in accordance with the general principles of that law, in particular the principle of proportionality. That means that national measures adopted on that subject must be necessary and appropriate to attain the objective pursued. ...

93. Under those circumstances, to refuse to allow Mr Baumbast to exercise the right of residence which is conferred on him by Article [21(1) TFEU] by virtue of the application of the provisions of Directive 90/364 on the ground that his sickness insurance does not cover the emergency treatment given in the host Member State would amount to a disproportionate interference with the exercise of that right.

Proportionality is an open-textured concept and it will often be open to dispute whether a denial of residence rights on the basis of an application for social assistance or a defect in sickness insurance is proportionate or not.[39] It is important to bear in mind that the aim of preventing migrants from draining public resources needs to be balanced against the openness and solidarity inherent in the idea of EU citizenship. In *Grzelczyk*, the Court pointed out that EU law 'accepts a certain degree of financial solidarity between nationals of a host Member State and nationals of other Member States, particularly if the difficulties which a beneficiary

---

[37] *Ibid.* article 7(1)(b).

[38] Case C-413/99 *Baumbast v Secretary of State for the Home Department* [2002] ECR I-7091.

[39] G. De Búrca, 'The Principle of Proportionality and its Application in EC Law' (1993) 13 *YBEL* 105; G. Davies, 'Abstractness and Concreteness in the Preliminary Reference Procedure' in N. Nic Shuibhne (ed.), *Regulating the Internal Market* (Cheltenham, Edward Elgar Publishing, 2006); E. Spaventa, 'Seeing the Wood Despite the Trees? On the Scope of Union Citizenship and its Constitutional Effects' (2008) 45 *CMLRev.* 13.

of the right of residence encounters are temporary'.[40] It is unreasonable for a migrant to ask too much, but equally unreasonable for a state to accept only those who need nothing at all.

Moreover, the determination of a sufficient level of resources is to be decided with reference to the particular circumstances of the individual. A state may use rules of thumb, but inflexible rules are prohibited.

Citizenship Directive, article 8(4)

Member States may not lay down a fixed amount which they regard as 'sufficient resources' but they must take into account the personal situation of the person concerned. In all cases this amount shall not be higher than the threshold below which nationals of the host Member State become eligible for social assistance, or where this criterion is not applicable, higher than the minimum social security pension paid by the host Member State.

Some interpretation of 'the personal situation of the person concerned' is provided by recital 16 to the Directive, which refers to the length of time which the citizen has already been resident and the amount of public assistance they have needed, as well as other 'personal circumstances'. Where a denial of residence would have consequences for family life, Article 8 ECHR may also be relevant.[41]

This citizen-centred approach to resources makes it difficult to know exactly what a Member State may demand. In *Commission v Netherlands*, the Court found that a state could not require demonstrable resources sufficient for a year of residence before recognising the residence right.[42] This was, again, disproportionate. Furthermore, the citizen does not need to personally possess any resources at all provided there is someone covering their costs. In *Chen*, a baby was able to establish residence because her non-EU mother had sufficient resources to care for her,[43] while in *Commission v Belgium*, the Court found that there was no need for the provider of resources to be either a family member or someone with a legal relationship with the citizen.[44]

Moreover, the sufficient resources condition will be, for most citizens, a one-time test. Once they have received their residence document they should not generally be subject to continuing checks on their resources, as long as they do not in fact behave in a way raising a legitimate doubt about their self-sufficiency. If they get by without public assistance there is no reason why the state should revisit the issue.

Citizenship Directive, article 14(2)

Union citizens and their family members shall have the right of residence provided for in Articles 7, 12 and 13, as long as they meet the conditions set out therein. In specific cases where there is a reasonable doubt as to whether a Union citizen or his/her family member satisfies the conditions set out in Articles 7, 12 and 13, Member States may verify if these conditions are fulfilled. This verification shall not be carried out systematically.

---

[40] Case C-184/99 *Grzelczyk* [2001] ECR I-6193; see also recital 16 to the Citizenship Directive.
[41] See p. 469.
[42] Case C-398/06 *Commission v Netherlands* [2008] ECR I-56.
[43] Case C-200/02 *Zhu and Chen* [2004] ECR I-9925.
[44] Case C-408/03 *Commission v Belgium* [2006] ECR I-2647.

Even if a citizen does subsequently make an application for public assistance this does not necessarily lead to a loss of residence rights. Article 14(3) provides that 'An expulsion measure shall not be the automatic consequence of a Union citizen's or his or her family member's recourse to the social assistance system of the host Member State.' By contrast, expulsion can only follow a decision-making process in which the citizen enjoys the protection of strict procedural safeguards.[45]

(ii) Right to equal treatment

For the migrant who has gained entry to a host state, the most useful additional legal tool is usually the prohibition on nationality discrimination. This enables her to participate in work and society on equal terms with nationals. The primary rule is found in Article 18 TFEU.

Article 18 TFEU

Within the scope of application of the Treaties, and without prejudice to any special provisions contained therein, any discrimination on grounds of nationality shall be prohibited.

Article 24(1) of the Citizenship Directive extends and refines this slightly.

Citizenship Directive, article 24(1)

Subject to such specific provisions as are expressly provided for in the Treaty and secondary law, all Union citizens residing on the basis of this Directive in the territory of the host Member State shall enjoy equal treatment with the nationals of that Member State within the scope of the Treaty. The benefit of this right shall be extended to family members who are not nationals of a Member State and who have the right of residence or permanent residence.

The Directive chooses to speak of equal treatment rather than discrimination, and extends the right to non-EU family members. This extension is important and not yet fully reflected in the practices of national institutions and national laws. One often sees job vacancies, for example, that are 'open to EU citizens', which should, correctly, be 'open to EU citizens and their family members'.

(a) Meaning of discrimination

Discrimination is often defined by the Court in these classical words: 'the principle of non-discrimination requires that comparable situations must not be treated differently and that different situations must not be treated in the same way'.[46] This elegant formulation is not always the most transparent or practical. It does not reveal how to determine what is comparable and what is different, which is really the essence of the matter. A less compressed approach, which amounts to the same in substance and is also reflected in case law, is to ask two questions. First, does a measure tend to advantage or disadvantage one group or another? Secondly, if so,

[45] See Citizenship Directive, articles 15, 30, 31; see pp. 476–9.
[46] Case C-148/02 *Garcia Avello* [2003] ECR I-11613 at para. 31.

is it sufficiently justified: does it serve a legitimate goal, is it based on objective and legitimate criteria and is it proportionate? This approach originated in older cases on free movement of workers, *Sotgiu* and *O'Flynn*, but is still relied on by the Court, as will be seen in some of the extracts below.[47] It reflects the understanding of discrimination that is also used in other areas of EU law, such as employment regulation.[48] The more explicit the distinction between nationalities – the greater the discriminatory effect – the harder it will usually be to justify it. A rule providing free museum entry only to national citizens would have to have truly exceptional justifications to survive, but a municipal rule providing free entry to local school-children, while it might tend to relatively disadvantage foreign tourists, would probably be easier to justify.[49]

(b) Scope of the prohibition

The prohibition applies 'within the scope of the Treaty'. In the context of citizenship, the Court has repeatedly found that where a national measure affects a migrant citizen exercising her Treaty rights to move and reside, this is in itself enough to bring the measure within the Treaty. As a result, the non-discrimination rule may affect all areas of national law. Even if these are primarily national and not EU competences, if they discriminate against migrants the rule will bite. Thus, Article 18 has been applied to compensation for victims of crime in France and criminal procedure in Italy, motorway toll reductions for disabled people, as well as to national laws implementing the European Arrest Warrant, among other matters.[50] Some of the cases involve discrimination against mere movers, those transiting a state or on holiday there.[51] However, the majority involve discrimination against migrant residents.

In *Garcia Avello*, it was the Belgian law on surnames that was in issue.[52] A Spanish citizen resident in Belgium was unable to persuade the Belgian authorities to register his children with a Spanish style surname, consisting of the father's surname followed by the mother's surname. The children were Spanish/Belgian dual nationals.

Case C-148/02 *Garcia Avello* [2003] ECR I-11613

20. It is first of all necessary to examine whether, contrary to the view expressed by the Belgian State and by the Danish and Netherlands Governments, the situation in issue in the main proceedings comes within the scope of Community law and, in particular, of the Treaty provisions on citizenship of the Union.

---

[47] Case 152/73 *Sotgiu v Deutsche Bundespost* [1974] ECR 153; Case C-237/94 *O'Flynn v Adjudication Officer* [1996] ECR I-2617. See G. Davies, *Nationality Discrimination in the European Internal Market* (The Hague, Kluwer Law International, 2003).

[48] See generally C. Costello and E. Barry (eds.), *Equality in Diversity. The New Equality Directives* (Dublin, Irish Centre for European Law, 2003).

[49] See Case C-388/01 *Commission v Italy* [2001] ECR I-721; Case C-45/93 *Commission v Spain* [1994] ECR I-911.

[50] Case C-164/07 *Wood* [2008] ECR I-4143; Case C-274/96 *Bickel and Franz* [1998] ECR I-7637; see also Case 186/87 *Cowan v Trésor Public* [1989] ECR 195; Case C-103/08 *Gottwald v Bezirkshauptmannschaft Bregenz*, Judgment of 1 October 2009; Case C-123/08 *Wolzenburg v London Borough of Ealing and Secretary of State for Education and Skills*, Judgment of 6 October 2009.

[51] See e.g. C-103/08 *Gottwald v Bezirkshauptmannschaft Bregenz*, Judgment of 1 October 2009; Case C-388/01 *Commission v Italy* [2001] ECR I-721.

[52] See also C-96/04 *Standesamt Stadt Niebüll* [2006] ECR I-3561.

21. Article [20 TFEU] confers the status of citizen of the Union on every person holding the nationality of a Member State. Since Mr Garcia Avello's children possess the nationality of two Member States, they also enjoy that status.

22. As the Court has ruled on several occasions, citizenship of the Union is destined to be the fundamental status of nationals of the Member States.

23. That status enables nationals of the Member States who find themselves in the same situation to enjoy within the scope *ratione materiae* of the EC Treaty the same treatment in law irrespective of their nationality, subject to such exceptions as are expressly provided for.

24. The situations falling within the scope *ratione materiae* of Community law include those involving the exercise of the fundamental freedoms guaranteed by the Treaty, in particular those involving the freedom to move and reside within the territory of the Member States, as conferred by Article [21 TFEU].

25. Although, as Community law stands at present, the rules governing a person's surname are matters coming within the competence of the Member States, the latter must none the less, when exercising that competence, comply with Community law, in particular the Treaty provisions on the freedom of every citizen of the Union to move and reside in the territory of the Member States.

This is the reply to national authorities who claim that a certain matter is 'a Member State competence outside EU law'.

Perhaps the broadest use of Article 18 TFEU to date was in *Huber*.[53] The German government kept a central database with information about all resident EU citizens, but did not gather and process equivalent information concerning German citizens. They claimed that the information system was necessary to fight crime, but the Court could not think of a reason why this required different treatment of foreigners. It found the system to violate Article 18.

Although Mr Huber, an Austrian resident in Germany, no doubt felt that his privacy rights were violated by the database, it is not obvious that it directly impeded his movement or residence as an EU citizen in any functional sense. *Huber* suggests that there is no need to show a concrete hindrance resulting from discrimination against migrants in order to bring it within the scope of the Treaty.

(c) Equal treatment and social assistance

European states provide financial assistance to individuals in many ways, including direct payment of benefits of many different kinds, but also including indirect support via subsidies, which enable services and facilities such as housing, education and some kinds of care to be provided to individuals at below cost. It is inevitable that access to this support is restricted in some ways: no single state can or wants to support the needy of the world. Every state therefore uses a battery of measures to confine its generosity to those that it considers to be members of its society. However, within the European Union, some of the restrictions used can come very close to discrimination on grounds of nationality. This has generated a complex body of case law.

The general principle is that EU citizens are entitled to equal treatment with nationals where benefits are concerned. This first clearly emerged in *Martinez Sala*.[54] In that case, a Spanish

---

[53] Case C-524/06 *Huber v Bundesrepublik Deutschland* [2008] ECR I-9705.
[54] Case C-85/96 *Martinez Sala v Freistaat Bayern* [1998] ECR I-2691. See annotation by S. O'Leary, 'Flesh on the Bones of European Citizenship' (1999) 24 *ELRev.* 68.

woman living in Germany was denied a child benefit because she could not produce a particular residence document. She could show that she had applied for the document and even that she was entitled to receive it, but she did not have it yet; the authorities were slow. The Court took a strict, almost formal approach to the situation. The German authorities were not entitled to ask for this residence document from Ms Sala because they would not have asked for it, or any equivalent permit, from a German citizen. *Sala* has since been confirmed in numerous cases, including *Trojani*.[55]

In *Trojani*, as in *Sala*, the Court emphasised that equal access to benefits was conditional upon lawful residence, although that lawfulness may derive from either EU or national law. However, this was in the context of benefits that were legitimately restricted to residents, a child-raising allowance and a minimum income benefit. This will not necessarily be the case. In *Gottwald*, the Court seriously considered whether a German disabled person who regularly drove through Austria was entitled to the same reduced motorway tolls as an Austrian resident, although it finally concluded that this subsidy could legitimately be confined to those who lived in Austria.[56] The Court has also ruled that subsidised access to museums may not always be restricted to residents.[57]

Nevertheless, where a benefit is legitimately restricted to residents the unlawfully present migrant will have no claim. This is hardly surprising, but interacts in a complex way with the sufficient resources condition in the Directive. An application for benefits is most likely to be made because of a lack of resources, which may well indicate that there is no right of residence. This will tempt states to reply automatically to every unemployed migrant who applies for benefits with the statement that they are refused because they have no resources, and therefore have no right of residence and no right to benefits. It should be remembered, however, that a simple application for benefits does not in itself show the condition is violated, and so benefits cannot be refused without further evidence or investigation.[58]

In any case, direct discrimination as in *Sala* is not the main issue in the subsequent case law. Nor are rules which restrict benefits to those living in the state. While an important restriction, it is not enough to prevent benefit migration, given the relative ease with which initial lawful residence can be established. The cases instead focus on a new generation of benefit restrictions which states have introduced in recent decades to protect their budgets. These restrictions apply to both nationals and foreigners alike and typically they restrict benefits to those who are in some sense 'integrated' or 'linked' to that state.[59] The most common type is usually referred to as a residence condition: a condition that a benefit will only be granted to a person who has been resident for a certain period in that state. However, there are also more complex requirements, such as rules which give priority to applicants for subsidised housing who can show 'a link with the employment market in that area'.[60] This allows those who have got a job, or are seriously looking, to get such housing quickly, but not those who come to the area for the housing alone.

The important characteristic of rules of these integration-oriented restrictions is that although they do not distinguish between nationals and foreigners as such, in practice they

---

[55] Case C-456/02 *Trojani* [2004] ECR I-7573.

[56] Case C-103/08 *Gottwald* v *Bezirkshauptmannschaft Bregenz*, Judgment of 1 October 2009.

[57] Case C-388/01 *Commission* v *Italy* [2001] ECR I-721.

[58] See p. 452.

[59] See C. O'Brien, 'Real Links, Abstract Rights and False Alarms: The Relationship Between the ECJ's "Real Link" Case Law and National Solidarity' (2008) 33 *EL Rev*. 643.

[60] The approach used in Amsterdam and some other Dutch cities.

obviously tend to have a greater impact on migrants. They will therefore amount to indirect discrimination unless they are sufficiently justified. The case law is largely concerned with the circumstances in which this occurs.

In general, the Court accepts the principle of such restrictions. It has conceded that financial and social realism make it unavoidable that some benefits are only available to society's 'members'; i.e. to those with 'a certain degree of integration' in that society.[61] However, the Court takes a fairly strict view of proportionality and whether the particular restriction is genuinely suited to the particular benefit. Early cases on this issue concerned benefits specifically available for job-seekers. Member States accept migrants coming to look for work, but do not wish to provide them financial support to do so. The Court first considered these in *Collins*, where it accepted the principle that such benefits could be restricted to those with a link to the job market, as long as the specific rules were proportionate.[62] In *Ioannidis* they were not. The case concerned a Belgian 'tideover allowance', which was only available to those who had completed their secondary schooling in Belgium. Mr Ioannidis, a Greek citizen, had been to school in Greece, but was now looking for work in Belgium.

Case C-258/04 *Ioannidis* [2005] ECR I-8275

26. According to settled case law, the principle of equal treatment prohibits not only overt discrimination based on nationality but also all covert forms of discrimination which, by applying other distinguishing criteria, lead in fact to the same result.

27. The national legislation at issue in the main proceedings introduces a difference in treatment between citizens who have completed their secondary education in Belgium and those who have completed it in another Member State with only the former having a right to a tideover allowance.

28. That condition could place, above all, nationals of other Member States at a disadvantage. Inasmuch as it links the grant of that allowance to the requirement that the applicant has obtained the required diploma in Belgium, that condition can be met more easily by Belgian nationals.

29. Such a difference in treatment can be justified only if it is based on objective considerations which are independent of the nationality of the persons concerned and proportionate to the aim legitimately pursued by the national law.

30. As the Court has already held, it is legitimate for the national legislature to wish to ensure that there is a real link between the applicant for that allowance and the geographic employment market concerned.

31. However, a single condition concerning the place where the diploma of completion of secondary education was obtained is too general and exclusive in nature. It unduly favours an element which is not necessarily representative of the real and effective degree of connection between the applicant for the tideover allowance and the geographic employment market, to the exclusion of all other representative elements. It therefore goes beyond what is necessary to attain the objective pursued.

The requirement in this case was to have been schooled in Belgium. The most common form of benefit restriction that migrants experience is one based on length of residence. The Court's view on this form of benefit restriction was developed in *Bidar*. A French student in London was denied a (subsidised) student loan because she had not been resident in the United Kingdom for long enough

---

[61] See e.g. Case C-209/03 *Bidar* [2005] ECR I-2119; Case C-103/08 *Gottwald* v *Bezirkshauptmannschaft Bregenz*, Judgment of 1 October 2009. See generally O'Brien, above n. 59.

[62] C-138/02 *Collins* [2004] ECR I-2703.

prior to starting her studies. She had been there for several years, but did not meet the complex UK requirements which included a three-year residence period and being 'settled' in the United Kingdom. The case is now redundant on the specific issue of student finance, as the Citizenship Directive now regulates this. However, on the logic and acceptability of integration requirements, it remains helpful. The three-year residence period applied to both UK and foreign nationals, but the requirement to be 'settled', which entailed its own residence period, only applied to foreigners.

Case C-209/03 *Bidar* [2005] ECR I-2119

56. On this point, it must be observed that, although the Member States must, in the organisation and application of their social assistance systems, show a certain degree of financial solidarity with nationals of other Member States, it is permissible for a Member State to ensure that the grant of assistance to cover the maintenance costs of students from other Member States does not become an unreasonable burden which could have consequences for the overall level of assistance which may be granted by that State.

57. In the case of assistance covering the maintenance costs of students, it is thus legitimate for a Member State to grant such assistance only to students who have demonstrated a certain degree of integration into the society of that State.

58. In this context, a Member State cannot, however, require the students concerned to establish a link with its employment market. Since the knowledge acquired by a student in the course of his higher education does not in general assign him to a particular geographical employment market, the situation of a student who applies for assistance to cover his maintenance costs is not comparable to that of an applicant for a tideover allowance granted to young persons seeking their first job or for a jobseeker's allowance.

59. On the other hand, the existence of a certain degree of integration may be regarded as established by a finding that the student in question has resided in the host Member State for a certain length of time.

The Court went on to find that although the principle of a prior residence period was acceptable, the fact that the 'settled' requirement applied unequally to UK nationals and foreign nationals was contrary to the Treaty's non-discrimination rule. The Court, therefore, accepts the idea that benefits may be restricted by reference to integration-type requirements, so long as they are proportionate and equally applicable to foreign citizens and nationals.

However, this equal treatment rule is now called into question by article 24(2) of the Directive and by the ruling in *Förster*.[63]

Citizenship Directive, article 24(2)

By way of derogation from paragraph 1, the host Member State shall not be obliged to confer entitlement to social assistance during the first three months of residence or, where appropriate, the longer period provided for in Article 14(4)(b), nor shall it be obliged, prior to acquisition of the right of permanent residence, to grant maintenance aid for studies, including vocational training, consisting in student grants or student loans to persons other than workers, self-employed persons, persons who retain such status and members of their families.

---

[63] Case C-158/07 *Förster v Hoofddirectie van de Informatie Beheer Groep* [2008] ECR I-8507.

Article 24(1), quoted earlier, states the requirement that migrant citizens be granted equal treatment to nationals. Paragraph 2 now provides in derogation from this rule that short-term residents, or those seeking employment (the group referred to in article 14(4)(b)), shall not be entitled to social assistance. Moreover, non-economically active migrants shall not be entitled to study finance until they have been resident for five years. The first of these exclusions may be of limited importance in the light of *Vatsouras*.[64] Here, the Court limited the notion of 'social assistance' in article 24(2) quite importantly, by excluding from that term benefits which are 'intended to facilitate access to the labour market'. Since the benefit that Mr Vatsouras was seeking was of such a type, he was entitled to rely on the equal treatment principle to obtain it, even though he was in fact a job-seeker. However, while the benefit was called a 'job-seekers' benefit, it was in substance a financial benefit granted to all those above a certain age 'capable of earning a living'. If a simple phrase of this type is enough to transform a benefit from 'social assistance' to 'labour market facilitation' in the eyes of the Court, then the scope of article 24(2) is very severely limited.

The restriction on study finance, by contrast, continues to be of great practical and political importance. It sketches the limits of the assimilation of migrants to national citizens and shows where states are entitled to favour their own. Article 24(2) suggests that if a UK citizen lives in Italy and then returns to the United Kingdom, the United Kingdom is entitled to grant her study finance even if this would not be granted to the Italian coming over on the same aeroplane. This is entirely at odds with the normal approach of EU law, yet *Förster* confirms it is correct. Although the facts of the case occurred before the Citizenship Directive came into force, the Court nevertheless used the Directive to frame its judgment.

In *Förster* a German woman in the Netherlands was denied study finance because she was not economically active and had not been resident for five years, as the Dutch rules required. However, these conditions did not apply to Dutch nationals. One of the questions that the national court referred was whether this was compatible with what is now Article 18 TFEU. The Court began by reaffirming that the principle of non-discrimination applied to the case and by approving the discussion of integration requirements in *Bidar*. It then continued:

Case C-158/07 *Förster* [2008] ECR I-8507

55. ... [the Citizenship Directive], although not applicable to the facts in the main proceedings, provides in Article 24(2) that, in the case of persons other than workers, self-employed persons, persons who retain such status and members of their families, the host Member State is not obliged to grant maintenance assistance for studies, including vocational training, consisting in student grants or student loans, to students who have not acquired the right of permanent residence, while also providing, in Article 16(1), that Union citizens will have a right of permanent residence in the territory of a host Member State where they have resided legally for a continuous period of five years.

56. The Court has also stated that, in order to be proportionate, a residence requirement must be applied by the national authorities on the basis of clear criteria known in advance. ...

58. It must therefore be stated that a residence requirement of five years, such as that laid down in the national legislation at issue in the main proceedings, does not go beyond what is necessary to attain the

---

[64] Case C-22/08 *Vatsouras* v *Arbeitsgemeinschaft Nürnberg*, Judgment of 4 June 2009.

objective of ensuring that students from other Member States are to a certain degree integrated into the society of the host Member State.

59. That finding is without prejudice to the option for Member States to award maintenance grants to students from other Member States who do not fulfil the five year residence requirement should they wish to do so.

60. In the light of the foregoing, the response to the second to fourth questions must be that a student who is a national of a Member State and travels to another Member State to study there can rely on the first paragraph of Article [18 TFEU] in order to obtain a maintenance grant where he or she has resided for a certain duration in the host Member State. The first paragraph of Article [18 TFEU] does not preclude the application to nationals of other Member States of a requirement of five years' prior residence.

The unusual aspect of *Förster* is that the Court does not see the Dutch rule as violating the principle of non-discrimination. Its conclusion is that Article 18 TFEU is not violated because the rule is justified. While it is clear that Dutch citizens are treated differently from those of other Member States, this is not discrimination because it corresponds to a genuine difference between them. This is an example of a justified distinction.[65] The question *Förster* leaves open is whether the different treatment was justified only because of article 24(2) and its specific reference to a waiting period for study finance, or whether distinctions between nationals and foreigners could be justified in the context of some other benefits, not mentioned in article 24.

What *Förster* embodies is the idea that there remains a special bond between a citizen and their home state, not just in the realm of security and high politics, but also in the socio-economic arena.[66] In this respect, nationals and foreigners *are* different and thus may be treated differently without this being discrimination. For a foreigner, it takes time or work to integrate, but for a national, it does not.

This reflects cultural reality to some extent, but is nevertheless odd because it is precisely such reality that one might think EU citizenship aims to overcome. *Förster* seems to attack the very idea of EU citizenship and flies in the face of other recent cases on residence conditions, such as *Bidar* and *Collins*, where the Court made a point of emphasising that the rules in question, insofar as they were acceptable, were equally applicable to nationals.[67] Moreover, it does not cost a state anything to make its residence requirements equally applicable, and in fact some states, such as the United Kingdom, tend to do so. *Förster* cannot be seen as a reaction to urgent policy imperatives.

Yet, if nationals are subject to such restrictions, it creates the risk that individuals will find themselves without any state to which they can turn for support. The migrant may find that she has not yet reached the stage of integration in her host state which entitles her to all public benefits, but on the other hand, by emigrating, she has lost the right to immediate support if she returns home. Should she want to study, or enrol for social housing, or certain other kinds of

---

[65] See also Case C-22/08 *Vatsouras*, Judgment of 4 June 2009; Case C-123/08 *Wolzenburg* v *London Borough of Ealing and Secretary of State for Education and Skills*, Judgment of 6 October 2009.

[66] Case 186/87 *Cowan* v *Trésor Public* [1989] ECR 195.

[67] Case C-209/03 *Bidar* [2005] ECR I-2119; Case C-138/02 *Collins* [2004] ECR I-2703. See S. O'Leary, 'Equal Treatment and EU Citizens: A New Chapter on Cross-Border Educational Mobility and Access to Student Financial Assistance' (2009) 34 *ELRev.* 612; G. Davies 'Any Place I Hang my Hat? Or: Residence is the New Nationality' (2005) 11 *ELJ* 43.

benefits, she may find that there is nowhere where she is treated as a full member. This may not seem shocking: first, travel is a choice and secondly, the kinds of benefits made subject to integration requirements and residence periods are usually at the 'luxury' end of the scale. It is, in general, unlikely that the European citizen will be left hungry or homeless as a result of migration. Yet, most EU Member States have made a point of creating a generous and encompassing support system, in which things like access to affordable education and good housing are basic rights. It would be ironic, to say the least, if EU citizenship combined with the non-discrimination requirement in EU law led to some individuals falling through this welfare net. Thus, perhaps paradoxically, the welfare of migrants may be a reason for permitting occasional distinctions between nationals and foreigners. The European Union is not yet so integrated that the idea of a 'home' state, where one's membership does not lapse through absence, has become superfluous.[68]

(d) Restrictions on movement

As well as the right to equal treatment, or non-discrimination, the Treaty also provides a directly effective right to free movement. In *D'Hoop*, *Pusa*, *Tas-Hagen*, *Schwarz* and *Ruffler*, the Court has found that national measures deterred movement of EU citizens and were not sufficiently justified. The measures therefore violated Article 21 TFEU, without needing to rely on nationality discrimination at all.[69] The particular importance of this free movement approach is that it enables citizens to rely on the right to move and reside against their own state, in circumstances where an analysis in terms of nationality discrimination would often be artificial or even impossible.[70]

D'Hoop, like *Ioannidis*, which it preceded, concerned the Belgian tideover allowance, available to job-seeking school-leavers if they have been to school in Belgium. The facts are essentially the same, except that Ms D'Hoop, who had been to school in France, was in fact a Belgian citizen. It was therefore difficult for her to say that she was being discriminated against on grounds of her nationality, as Mr Ioannidis had claimed.

Case C-224/98 *D'Hoop* [2002] ECR I-6191

27. Article 8 of the Treaty confers the status of citizen of the Union on every person holding the nationality of a Member State. Since she possesses the nationality of a Member State, Ms D'Hoop enjoys that status.

28. Union citizenship is destined to be the fundamental status of nationals of the Member States, enabling those who find themselves in the same situation to enjoy within the scope *ratione materiae* of the Treaty the same treatment in law irrespective of their nationality, subject to such exceptions as are expressly provided for.

29. The situations falling within the scope of Community law include those involving the exercise of the fundamental freedoms guaranteed by the Treaty, in particular those involving the freedom to move and reside within the territory of the Member States, as conferred by Article [21 TFEU].

---

[68] See Case C-123/08 *Wolzenburg* v *London Borough of Ealing and Secretary of State for Education and Skills*, Judgment of 6 October 2009.

[69] Case C-224/98 *D'Hoop* [2002] ECR I-6191; Case C-224/02 *Pusa* [2004] ECR I-5763; Case C-76/05 *Schwarz and Gootjes-Schwarz* v *Finanzamt Bergisch Gladbach* [2007] ECR I-6849; Case C-192/05 *Tas-Hagen and Tas* v *Raadskamer WUBO van de Pensioen- en Uitkeringsraad* [2006] ECR I-10451; Case C-11/06 *Morgan* v *Bezirksregierung Köln* [2007] ECR I-9161; Case C-221/07 *Zablocka*, Judgment of 4 December 2008; Case C-499/06 *Nerkowska* [2008] ECR I-3993; Case C-403/03 *Schempp* [2005] ECR I-6421.

[70] M. Cousins, 'Citizenship, Residence and Social Security' (2007) 32 *ELRev.* 386.

30. In that a citizen of the Union must be granted in all Member States the same treatment in law as that accorded to the nationals of those Member States who find themselves in the same situation, it would be incompatible with the right of freedom of movement were a citizen, in the Member State of which he is a national, to receive treatment less favourable than he would enjoy if he had not availed himself of the opportunities offered by the Treaty in relation to freedom of movement.

31. Those opportunities could not be fully effective if a national of a Member State could be deterred from availing himself of them by obstacles raised on his return to his country of origin by legislation penalising the fact that he has used them.

32. That consideration is particularly important in the field of education. The objectives set for the activities of the Community include [in the light of Articles 9 and 165(2) TFEU] mobility of students and teachers.

33. In situations such as that in the main proceedings, national legislation introduces a difference in treatment between Belgian nationals who have had all their secondary education in Belgium and those who, having availed themselves of their freedom to move, have obtained their diploma of completion of secondary education in another Member State.

34. By linking the grant of tideover allowances to the condition of having obtained the required diploma in Belgium, the national legislation thus places at a disadvantage certain of its nationals simply because they have exercised their freedom to move in order to pursue education in another Member State.

35. Such inequality of treatment is contrary to the principles which underpin the status of citizen of the Union, that is, the guarantee of the same treatment in law in the exercise of the citizen's freedom to move.

36. The condition at issue could be justified only if it were based on objective considerations independent of the nationality of the persons concerned and were proportionate to the legitimate aim of the national provisions.

The same approach has now been applied to a host state in *Ruffler*.[71] Mr Ruffler, a German citizen, lived in Poland but received a pension from Germany, where he had worked. Polish tax calculations did not take account of insurance premiums deducted from that pension in Germany before it was paid to Mr Ruffler, but they would have taken account of equivalent deductions made in Poland. The judgment is similarly reasoned to *D'Hoop*, but by contrast to paragraph 31 above, the Court in *Ruffler* said:

> it would be incompatible with the right to freedom of movement were a citizen to receive, *in the host Member State*, treatment less favourable than that which he would enjoy if he had not availed himself of the opportunities offered by the Treaty in relation to freedom of movement. (Emphasis added)

A recent example of this reasoning, which is of some practical importance, is *Morgan*.[72] In this case a German citizen, Ms Morgan, wanted to go and study in the United Kingdom and applied for her German study finance to be paid to her there. This was refused because the German rules only permitted export of study finance when the course to be followed was a continuation of a course already followed for at least a year in Germany. In practice, this meant that German study finance could be used for foreign exchange years or foreign master's courses, but not for foreign bachelor's degrees.

The Court found that the German rules discouraged students in Germany from going abroad and therefore comprised a restriction on movement in the Article 21 sense and could not be

---

[71] Case C-544/07 *Ruffler*, Judgment of 23 April 2009.
[72] Case C-11/06 *Morgan* v *Bezirksregierung Köln* [2007] ECR I-9161.

adequately justified. They were therefore contrary to the Treaty. One of the German government's arguments was that the so-called 'first stage rule' prevented foreign students coming to Germany in order to receive study finance which they would then use to go and study in their home states. The Court accepted the need for financial control and the use of integration requirements to limit study finance, but found that a requirement to have spent one year studying in Germany was too much of a blunt instrument:

> it unduly favours an element which is not necessarily representative of the degree of integration into the society of that Member State at the time the application for assistance is made. It thus goes beyond what is necessary to attain the objective pursued and cannot therefore be regarded as proportionate.

Morgan is important because it seems to establish a right to export student grants and loans, probably enhancing student mobility considerably, but possibly raising the risk that students depart *en masse* if national educational institutions fail to perform, with consequences for those institutions and the Member State that may be both financially and socially significant.[73]

What these cases create is a new kind of non-discrimination rule, not between citizens of different nationalities, but between citizens who exercise their EU rights and those who do not.[74] Where cross-border activities are treated less advantageously than domestic ones, or where migration is made more difficult than staying at home or leads to disadvantages under national rules, Article 21 TFEU applies.

(e) The internal situation and reverse discrimination

In *Uecker and Jacquet*, two German citizens attempted to rely on EU family rights to bring their partners to Germany.[75] They failed to establish a case because '[i]t has consistently been held that the Treaty rules governing freedom of movement and regulations adopted to implement them cannot be applied to cases which have no factor linking them with any of the situations governed by Community law and all elements of which are purely internal to a single Member State'. Since Uecker and Jacquet had not exercised EU movement rights, there was no such linking factor and the Treaty simply did not apply. The situation would be no different today.[76] As non-migrants they would not fall within the scope of the Citizenship Directive.

The core objection of the parties in *Uecker* was that they were worse off than a foreign EU citizen in Germany would have been. They experienced so-called reverse discrimination: discrimination against home nationals, in favour of EU migrants. It has been argued that this is just as objectionable as discrimination against foreigners; it is still nationality discrimination and therefore the Court should not have allowed it.[77] However, the Court's response was that the non-discrimination rule only applies within the scope of the Treaty and the whole point is that situations with no cross-border aspect are not within that scope. It could be argued that

---

[73] M. Dougan, 'Cross-border Educational Mobility and the Exportation of Student Financial Assistance' (2008) 33 *ELRev.* 723.

[74] N. Bernard 'Discrimination and Free Movement' (1996) 45 *ICLQ* 82, 85–6.

[75] Joined Cases C-64/96 and C-65/96 *Uecker and Jacquet* [1997] ECR I-3171; see also Joined Cases 35/82 and 36/82 *Morson and Jhanjan* v *Netherlands* [1982] ECR 3723.

[76] See A. Tryfonidou, 'Reverse Discrimination in Purely Internal Situations: An Incongruity in a Citizens' Europe' (2008) 35 *IEI* 43; N. Nic Shuibhne 'Free Movement of Persons and the Wholly Internal Rule: Time to Move On?' (2002) 39 *CMLRev.* 731.

[77] *Ibid.*

citizenship supports a broad and constitutional approach to equality, which can balance these technical legal arguments,[78] but the Court disagreed: 'citizenship of the Union is not intended to extend the material scope of the Treaty to internal situations which have no link with Community law'. Jurisdiction is prior to substance.

Since the matter was not within the Treaty, any discrimination was the result of German law, not EU law and so not the Court's concern. If Germany wanted to solve the problem by granting its nationals the same rights as migrants, it was free to do so. Some states do in fact take this approach, granting their own nationals rights equivalent to migrant citizens.[79]

The Court's answer is not fully satisfying. It remains the case that EU law played a central role in creating the inequality and that within a state, EU law does distinguish between nationals and foreigners, which is prima facie at odds with Article 18 TFEU. Nevertheless, for the Court to take a different approach and extend free movement rights to internal situations would extend the scope of the Treaty significantly, which was certainly not the intention of the Treaty writers. For this reason it has maintained with complete consistency that wholly internal situations are outside the scope of EU law.

Nevertheless, the law has developed through refinements of what an internal situation actually is. A number of cases have extended the ways in which a connection can be made to cross-border movement, so that EU law can be engaged. The most important single case is *Singh*.[80] This concerned a British woman who went to work in Germany, where she lived with her Indian husband on the basis of EU law. After a few years she wanted to return to the United Kingdom, but was told that her husband would not be granted a right of residence. The United Kingdom considered that if she was in the United Kingdom, then as a British citizen she would be in an internal situation, outside the scope of EU law and so only national immigration rules would apply, to the disadvantage of Mr Singh.

The Court of Justice took a different view. It argued that to take away Ms Singh's EU rights upon her return would be a deterrent to movement: had she known this would happen it would have made it less attractive for her to go to Germany in the first place. This is quite difficult to understand. In reality, the Court was probably motivated by a human rights perspective, that it was simply wrong to split a couple under these circumstances. However, it laid down a rule which has also been applied in other contexts and is now well established: when an individual returns to their home state after exercising EU rights, they do not return to an internal situation. On the contrary, the status of migrant 'sticks' and they can rely on EU rights against their home state to challenge any measures making their return more difficult, or 'punishing' them for having been away. *Singh* is thus the forerunner of the cases in the previous section, although these cases do not even consider the internal situation explicitly, the rule in *Singh* being now so well internalised and usually only controversial in the context of family rights.

The returnee principle has been most recently applied in the *Flemish Insurance* case, which concerned a type of long-term care insurance in Flanders, the Dutch speaking part of Belgium.[81] This insurance was available to those who worked in Flanders, but only if they also lived

---

[78] *Ibid.*
[79] See e.g. Case C-448/98 *Guimont* [2000] ECR I-10663.
[80] Case C-370/90 *Singh* [1992] ECR I-4265.
[81] Case C-212/06 *Government of the French Community, and Walloon Government v Flemish Government (Flemish Insurance Case)*, Judgment of 1 April 2008. See C. Dautricourt and S. Thomas, 'Reverse Discrimination and the Free Movement of Persons under Community Law: All for Ulysses, Nothing for Penelope?' (2009) 34 *ELRev.* 433.

there. If they lived in the French-speaking areas of Belgium, they were not eligible. The facts were therefore internal to one state and in fact the intention was to exclude French-speaking Belgians rather than other nationals. Nevertheless, the Court found that the situation was not internal. Both foreign nationals and Belgians living abroad might be deterred from moving to Belgium by a rule which penalised them for living in one part of the country. Their freedom of movement and residence within Belgium was hindered, which was sufficient to say that their free movement to Belgium was deterred. The specific inclusion by the Court of Belgians who had gone abroad and might be put off from coming home puts this case in the *Singh* tradition, although the reasoning in *Flemish Insurance* is somewhat easier to follow.

A case that caused some surprise is *Carpenter*.[82] Here, the Court found that EU law on the free movement of services could be applied by a British citizen resident in the United Kingdom, against the UK government, simply because he often travelled on the continent to provide services and therefore was engaged in cross-border service provision. There is nothing un-orthodox about the reasoning as such, but it does show a willingness to find even a relatively marginal cross-border connection sufficient to invoke EU law. This is also evident in *Garcia Avello*, discussed above.[83] The children in that case were born in Belgium, of a Spanish and a Belgian parent. They obtained both nationalities. When they challenged Belgian rules on family names, the Belgian state claimed that the situation was internal: these were Belgians who had never been abroad, let alone exercised EU cross-border rights. On the contrary, the mere fact that they had Spanish nationality was sufficient to engage EU law. They were lawfully resident citizens of another Member State.

These cases, in combination with *D'Hoop*, *Ruffler* and the other cases in that line, highlight that the important distinction within EU citizenship is less and less between different nationalities and more between migrants and stay-at-homes. This distinction can be more precisely drawn out as between those whose life is connected to more than one state and those whose life is encompassed by one state. The former can draw on EU citizenship rights, whether against their own state or another state to which they move, while the latter remain exclusively subject to domestic law. EU law has created a privileged and cosmopolitan client group to whom it affords protection wherever they are in the European Union. Given that EU citizenship was introduced to connect the European Union with the national citizen, it is perhaps an irony that it becomes most real precisely when it liberates the citizen from national law.

(iii) Family rights

Family members of the EU citizen, whether or not they are themselves EU citizens, have a series of parallel rights to those of the EU citizen:

- the same right of entry and exit between Member States as the citizen;[84]
- the right to reside up to three months in the host state provided that they are accompanying or joining the citizen;[85]

---

[82] Case C-60/00 *Carpenter* v *Secretary of State for the Home Department* [2002] ECR I-6279.
[83] Case C-148/02 *Garcia Avello* [2003] ECR I-11613. See p. 453.
[84] Citizenship Directive, articles 4(1) and 5(2).
[85] *Ibid.* article 6(2).

- the right to reside for longer than three months provided the EU citizen to whom they are related satisfies the conditions for residence and the family members are accompanying or joining the citizen;[86]
- family members enjoying the right of residence or permanent residence have the right to take up employment or self-employment in the host state,[87] and the right to equal treatment with nationals of that state;[88]
- the right to permanent residence when they have legally resided in the host state with the EU citizen for a continuous period of five years.[89]

(a) The EU idea of the family

The family members acquiring these rights are set out in article 2(2) of the Citizenship Directive:

(a) the spouse;

(b) the partner with whom the EU citizen has contracted a registered partnership, on the basis of the legislation of a Member State, if the legislation of the host Member State treats registered partnerships as equivalent to marriage and in accordance with the conditions laid down in the relevant legislation of the host Member State;

(c) the direct descendants who are under the age of 21 or are dependants and those of the spouse or partner as defined in point (b);

(d) the dependent direct relatives in the ascending line and those of the spouse or partner as defined in point (b).

In addition, a second group of family members enjoy more conditional rights.

> ### Citizenship Directive, article 3(2)
>
> Without prejudice to any right to free movement and residence the persons concerned may have in their own right, the host Member State shall, in accordance with its national legislation, facilitate entry and residence for the following persons:
> (a) any other family members, irrespective of their nationality, not falling under the definition in point 2 of Article 2 who, in the country from which they have come, are dependants or members of the household of the Union citizen having the primary right of residence, or where serious health grounds strictly require the personal care of the family member by the Union citizen;
> (b) the partner with whom the Union citizen has a durable relationship, duly attested.
>   The host Member State shall undertake an extensive examination of the personal circumstances and shall justify any denial of entry or residence to these people.

The notion of a 'dependant' was defined in *Jia*, a case in which the mother-in-law of a German resident in Sweden sought entry to Sweden from China on the basis of the legislation then in force that was equivalent to article 2(2)(d). A family member qualifies as a dependant, the Court found, when 'having regard to their financial and social conditions they are not

[86] *Ibid.* article 7(1) and (2).
[87] *Ibid.* article 23.
[88] *Ibid.* article 24(1).
[89] *Ibid.* article 16(2).

in a position to support themselves. The need for material support must exist in the State of origin of those relatives or the state whence they came at the time when they apply to join the Community national.'[90] The Court went on to consider how dependency could be proved and rejected the Swedish government's claim that only an official document from the Chinese authorities could suffice. The Court found that 'evidence could be adduced by any appropriate means', in line with its generally pragmatic and flexible approach to questions of evidence, discussed below.[91]

An important element of this definition is that a dependant is a relative who depends upon the EU citizen in the country where she (the dependant) is coming from. Dependency must exist prior to reunification: it is a reason for reunification, not a result of it. This is particularly important for parents from relatively poor countries, who may be able to support themselves in their home state, but would become dependent if living in an expensive EU country where they do not speak the language. They would not, following *Jia*, be dependants within the sense of the Directive.

It seems likely that in the light of article 3 as a whole, states should in principle admit family members falling within its scope, unless they are able to provide a particularly convincing justification. However, the article seems to envisage that the family members may be asked to comply with national immigration requirements (such as visas or language tests) to a greater extent than may be required of the core family members in article 2. If article 3 family members are admitted, it seems probable that they then fall within the scope of 'family members' as used elsewhere in the Directive and as such enjoy the same rights to employment and equality as article 2 family members.

An issue which the Directive does not resolve clearly and is therefore likely to engage the Court soon is same-sex marriage.[92] At the time the Directive was adopted, no states had instituted this, but now several have. The right to bring a spouse is unconditional in article 2(2)(a), and it remains to be seen whether the Court will permit conservative states to refuse recognition to same-sex spouses by reliance on a public policy derogation.

(b) Separation, death and divorce

If family members lose their link with the migrant citizen, either through his or her death or the break-up of the relationship, their own rights of residence may become threatened. The Directive provides a degree of protection.

For EU family members, their right of residence continues after divorce or the death of the partner.[93] For non-EU family members, it continues under a number of conditions: that they had lived together in the state for at least a year before the death or divorce, and in the case of divorce had also been married for at least three years.[94] The stricter approach partly reflects a fear of marriages of convenience, and partly a view that non-EU family members who have only been present for a short period have less right to remain. Non-EU family members

---

[90] Case C-1/05 *Jia* v *Migrationsverket* [2007] ECR I-1.
[91] See pp. 474–5.
[92] See generally H. Toner, *Partnership Rights, Free Movement and EU Law* (Oxford and Portland, Hart, 2004); M. Bell, 'Holding Back the Tide? Cross-border Recognition of Same Sex Partnerships within the European Union' (2004) 5 *ERPL* 613.
[93] Citizenship Directive, articles 12–13.
[94] *Ibid.*

also maintain their right of residence after a divorce if they have custody of the EU citizen's children or a right of access to them, or if particular circumstances such as domestic violence warrant more generosity.[95]

For both EU and non-EU partners, the post-relationship right of residence is subject to conditions. EU family members are subject to the same article 7 conditions as any other citizen, while non-EU family members must be either economically active or have resources and sickness insurance.[96] However, these conditions do not apply to the children of the dead or departed EU citizen if they are in school in the host state, nor to the parent who has custody of them.[97] Irrespective of nationality or resources, these retain their right of residence until school-leaving age has been reached.

In reality, family life may encompass more options than married cohabitation and divorce. For various reasons, partners may live apart while still having a legal bond to each other. In *Diatta* and *Baumbast*, the Court maintained that (i) until a marriage was finally dissolved, it was to be considered as existing,[98] thus a divorce in progress did not affect residence rights; and (ii) cohabitation was not as such a condition for residence rights for a family member. However, these were decided under older Directives and the Citizenship Directive grants the right of residence only to family members 'accompanying or joining' the citizen. It is possible that this will lead to a stricter approach to non-cohabiting families. However, it is suggested that the Court is unlikely to depart from its generally realistic approach to the law in this area and demand cohabitation at all times and circumstances. A spirit of proportionality will prevail.

(c) Rights of children and carers

As mentioned above, children of school age enjoy protection of their residence rights in the event of family breakdown, as does the parent with custody of them. Children who are EU citizens also enjoy an independent right of free movement and residence; they are citizens just as much as adults are.[99] Baby Catherine Zhu had Irish nationality and to the dismay of the Irish and UK governments, her mother, Mrs Chen, who was Chinese, asserted a right for them both to live in the United Kingdom. They had sufficient resources and sickness insurance.

Case C-200/02 *Zhu and Chen* [2004] ECR I-9925

20. Moreover, contrary to the Irish Government's contention, a young child can take advantage of the rights of free movement and residence guaranteed by Community law. The capacity of a national of a Member State to be the holder of rights guaranteed by the Treaty and by secondary law on the free movement of persons cannot be made conditional upon the attainment by the person concerned of the age prescribed for the acquisition of legal capacity to exercise those rights personally …

---

[95] *Ibid.* article 13(2).

[96] *Ibid.* articles 12(1) and 13(1), on EU family members after death or divorce, provide 'Before acquiring the right of permanent residence, the persons concerned must meet the conditions laid down in point (a),(b),(c) or (d) of Article 7(1)'.

[97] Citizenship Directive, articles 12(3), 13(2). See now Case C-310/08 *Ibrahim*, Judgment of 23 February 2010; Case C-480/08 *Teixeira*, Judgment of 23 February 2010.

[98] See Case C-267/83 *Diatta v Land Berlin* [1985] ECR 567; Case C-413/99 *Baumbast v Secretary of State for the Home Department* [2002] ECR I-7091.

[99] See H. Stalford and E. Drywood, 'Coming of Age: Children's Rights in the EU' (2009) 46 *CMLRev.* 143.

45. On the other hand, a refusal to allow the parent, whether a national of a Member State or a national of a non-member country, who is the carer of a child to whom Article [21 TFEU] and Directive 90/364 grant a right of residence, to reside with that child in the host Member State would deprive the child's right of residence of any useful effect. It is clear that enjoyment by a young child of a right of residence necessarily implies that the child is entitled to be accompanied by the person who is his or her primary carer and accordingly that the carer must be in a position to reside with the child in the host Member State for the duration of such residence.

46. For that reason alone, where, as in the main proceedings, Article [21 TFEU] and Directive 90/364 grant a right to reside for an indefinite period in the host Member State to a young minor who is a national of another Member State, those same provisions allow a parent who is that minor's primary carer to reside with the child in the host Member State.

The Court here adds a new category of family member to those in the Directive. Where EU children exercise their EU movement and residence rights, the person primarily responsible for their care is granted parallel rights of movement and residence, irrespective of the carer's nationality. It does not even appear from the judgment that the carer must necessarily be a parent or even a family member, simply 'the person who is his or her primary carer'. Carers have also been discussed in *Baumbast*, where the Court confirmed that the dependent right of residence continues as long as the child is of school age. Since, in most cases, by the time the child leaves school the family will have been present in the state for a number of years, it is then very unlikely that it will be possible to remove the carer, for reasons of human rights. It is also arguable that as family members assimilated to those covered by the Directive, carers should have a parallel right to acquire permanent resident status after five years.

A speculative, but not entirely academic, question is how far such carer's rights extend. It seems clear following *Chen* that a parent arriving from outside the Union with a baby in their arms which they can demonstrate to be an EU citizen will consequently have a right to remain, providing they can meet the resources conditions. Would they be entitled to claim residence by claiming the intention to find work? Logic would suggest they can, since family members covered by the Directive are entitled to work without discrimination in the host state and once working they would have sufficient resources (although note that they would not be exempted from the sufficient resources condition because the EU citizen himself would continue to be economically inactive, being a baby). Suppose that they cannot prove that the baby is an EU citizen, but they have a plausible claim that he has a right to such citizenship – perhaps it is the fruit of a holiday romance with an EU tourist? Arguably, the Member State where they are present should grant them a period, for example, to make contact with the father and take legal steps to establish paternity. This may seem far-fetched but the alternative is that a Member State risks deporting an EU citizen from the Union, possibly to deeply disadvantageous socio-economic circumstances, which is entirely at odds with the perspective expressed in *Chen* and *Baumbast*. One might even extrapolate to the position of a pregnant woman arriving at Heathrow airport from a non-EU state and claiming she carries a baby which will be entitled to citizenship of a Member State upon its birth, say a few months away. Would it be in the spirit of the law to turn her away and let the little proto-European be born in possibly dangerous conditions outside the European Union?

(d) The family and human rights

The Directive does not operate in a legal vacuum. Like all EU law, it is subject to the fundamental rights case law of the Court of Justice.[100] Where families are concerned and their rights to be together or not, both the right to respect for family life (as set out in Article 8 ECHR and Article 7 of the European Union Charter of Fundamental Rights) and the right to marry and found a family (as set out in Article 12 ECHR and Article 9 EUCFR) become particularly relevant. These rights may even prevent Member States from excluding a family member who does not otherwise comply with the residence conditions of the Directive. This first became clear in *Akrich*, where, having found that the spouse of a migrant citizen in fact had no right of residence deriving from the Directive,[101] the Court went on to consider whether Article 8 ECHR might nevertheless prevent their deportation by the United Kingdom.

Case C-109/01 *Secretary of State for the Home Department* v *Akrich* [2003] ECR I-9607

58. … That right is among the fundamental rights which, according to the Court's settled case law, restated by the Preamble to the Single European Act and by Article [6 TEU], are protected in the Community legal order.

59. Even though the Convention does not as such guarantee the right of an alien to enter or to reside in a particular country, the removal of a person from a country where close members of his family are living may amount to an infringement of the right to respect for family life as guaranteed by Article 8(1) of the Convention. Such an interference will infringe the Convention if it does not meet the requirements of paragraph 2 of that article, that is unless it is in accordance with the law, motivated by one or more of the legitimate aims under that paragraph and necessary in a democratic society, that is to say justified by a pressing social need and, in particular, proportionate to the legitimate aim pursued.

60. The limits of what is necessary in a democratic society where the spouse has committed an offence have been highlighted by the European Court of Human Rights in *Boultif* v *Switzerland*, judgment of 2 August 2001, Reports of Judgments and Decisions 2001-IX §§ 46 to 56, and *Amrollahi* v *Denmark*, judgment of 11 July 2002, not yet published in the Reports of Judgments and Decisions, §§ 33 to 44.

In *Boultif*, the case referred to in the judgment, the Swiss authorities wished to deport an Algerian national who had been convicted of a particularly brutal robbery. His wife, a Swiss national, stated that it would be impossible for her to live in Algeria and the effect of the deportation would be to break the marriage. The European Court of Human Rights stated that in determining what restrictions could be imposed on the right to respect for a family life it would:

> consider the nature and seriousness of the offence committed by the applicant; the duration of the applicant's stay in the country from which he is going to be expelled; the time which has elapsed since the commission of the offence and the applicant's conduct during that period; the nationalities of the various persons concerned; the applicant's family situation, such as the length of the marriage; other factors revealing whether the couple lead a real and genuine family life; whether the spouse knew about the offence at the time when he or she entered into a family relationship; and whether there are children in the marriage and, if so,

---

[100] See Chapter 6.
[101] On this point the case has been overruled by Case C-127/08 *Metock*, [2008] ECR I-6241. This does not affect the use of Article 8 ECHR.

their age. Not least, the Court will also consider the seriousness of the difficulties which the spouse would be likely to encounter in the applicant's country of origin, although the mere fact that a person might face certain difficulties in accompanying her or his spouse cannot in itself preclude expulsion.[102]

In this instance, it found that it would be impossible for Mr Boultif's wife to live in Algeria, a place in which she had never lived. Notwithstanding the severity of the crimes, deportation in such circumstances would violate the right to respect for family life.

It would appear, therefore, that the deportation of a family member who is already resident can only take place after an examination of their personal circumstances and the consequences for them of the deportation. In practice, the deportation must overcome a high legal threshold to be justified. On the other hand, denying first entry to a family member, particularly a more peripheral one than a spouse, in circumstances where the family were not living together previously, may be less likely to violate Article 8 ECHR.

Article 12 ECHR may also be relevant. This provides for the right to marry, which may be helpful where national law has hindered marriage, for example of transsexuals, with consequent effects on residence rights.[103]

(e) Family members coming from outside the Union

That migrant citizens can take their family from one Member State to another is a logical corollary of their own right of free movement. In practice, if people cannot take their family they will not move. However, it is less obvious that the migrant should have the right to bring family members into the Union for the first time. It is certainly true that the quality of migration will be enhanced if it is possible to bring distant family members to the host state. However, if this is not the case the migrant will be no worse off in the host state than at home, so it is not clear that there is any deterrent to free movement. It may perhaps be argued that the position of a migrant in a host state is particularly lonely and difficult and therefore the presence of family members is a necessary accompaniment, whether or not they were with the EU citizen prior to her migration. The Directive seems to reflect this latter view, simply providing for a right of residence for family members 'joining' the citizen, without any condition that they join from within the European Union.

In *Akrich*, the Court wrote such a condition into the Directive, saying that it only applied to family members already lawfully present in an EU Member State.[104] However, this innovation was short-lived and has been reversed in *Metock*.[105] The latter case concerned asylum seekers in Ireland, who had married UK citizens resident in Ireland and thereby become the spouses of migrant citizens. The judgment was complex, but set out a number of important points:

- The right of a family member to live with the EU citizen is simply dependent upon compliance with the definitions and conditions in the Directive. A state may impose no other conditions (such as previous lawful residence in another Member State).

---

[102] *Boultif* v *Switzerland*, Judgment of 2 August 2001, Reports of Judgments and Decisions 2001-IX §§ 46.

[103] Case C-117/01 *KB* v *National Health Service Pensions Agency* [2004] ECR I-541.

[104] Case C-109/01 *Secretary of State for the Home Department* v *Akrich* [2003] ECR I-9607.

[105] Case C-127/08 *Metock* [2008] ECR I-6241. See C. Costello, '*Metock*: Free Movement and "Normal Family Life" in the Union' (2009) 46 *CMLRev.* 587; S. Currie, 'Accelerated Justice or a Step Too Far? Residence Rights of Non-EU Family Members and the Court's Ruling in Metock' (2009) 34 *ELRev.* 310.

- It does not matter that the citizen met and married their partner in the host state, as in *Metock*. This still counts as family 'joining' the citizen.[106]
- It does not matter if the partner previously entered the country illegally, or prior to the marriage was illegally present.
- Becoming a family member in the Directive sense has the effect of wiping the slate almost clean. The slate is only wiped 'almost' clean because the state may still impose proportionate sanctions upon the family member for any previous violations of immigration law, but these must not go so far as to deter free movement – one should think of a fine, but not of a denial of residence.[107]

The policy reasons for the *Metock* decision are diverse. An important one put forward by the Court is that Directives concerning non-EU nationals who are long-term residents in an EU Member State give them the right to bring their family into the European Union.[108] It would be odd if migrant EU citizens then had lesser rights. This is not entirely logical. Such a comparison would suggest that EU citizens should be able to bring their family members into the Union if they were previously resident together in the non-EU country (avoiding family break-up) but not necessarily otherwise, where migration does not change the family circumstances. However, this approach would have entailed a rather complex judicial rewriting of the Directive, which is perhaps one reason why the Court chose to simply accept the wording of the Directive at face value, over the protests of several Member States about the effect on immigration.

The judgment has huge implications. In a time where many Member States make it difficult for their own nationals to bring family members in from outside the Union, EU migrants have a significant legal advantage. The Danish citizen struggling to bring his Angolan wife to Denmark because of Danish immigration law may move to Sweden, whereupon both he and she can rely on the Directive rights. A small but growing number of EU citizens now engage in such migration for the purposes of family reunification, to the concern of some national authorities.

The effect of *Metock* is greatly enhanced by *Singh*:[109] where a citizen returns to her home state after spending a period exercising EU rights in another Member State, she continues to fall within the scope of EU law and continues to enjoy the EU rights that she had while she was abroad.

This has since been clarified and confirmed in *Eind*.[110] In this case, a Dutch citizen working in the United Kingdom brought his daughter to live with him in Britain from outside the Union. When he returned to the Netherlands, the Dutch authorities claimed that the situation was internal and governed by Dutch immigration law, which did not permit the daughter's residence. Mr Eind, by contrast, claimed that he could continue to rely on EU rights as a returning migrant. The Court agreed with him.

---

[106] See also Case C-551/07 *Sahin* [2008] ECR I-1043.

[107] See p. 475.

[108] *Metock*, above n. 105, para. 69; see Directive 2003/86/EC.

[109] Case C-370/90 *Singh* [1992] ECR I-4265. See A. Tryfonidou, 'Family Reunification Right of (Migrant) Union Citizens: Towards a More Liberal Approach' (2009) 15 *ELJ* 634.

[110] Case C-291/05 *Minister voor Vreemdelingenzaken en Integratie* v *Eind* [2004] ECR I-10719. See also the cases at pp. 462–4.

Case C-291/05 *Minister voor Vreemdelingenzaken en Integratie v Eind* [2004] ECR I-10719

35. A national of a Member State could be deterred from leaving that Member State in order to pursue gainful employment in the territory of another Member State if he does not have the certainty of being able to return to his Member State of origin, irrespective of whether he is going to engage in economic activity in the latter State.

36. That deterrent effect would also derive simply from the prospect, for that same national, of not being able, on returning to his Member State of origin, to continue living together with close relatives, a way of life which may have come into being in the host Member State as a result of marriage or family reunification.

37. Barriers to family reunification are therefore liable to undermine the right to free movement which the nationals of the Member States have under Community law, as the right of a Community worker to return to the Member State of which he is a national cannot be considered to be a purely internal matter.

38. It follows that, in circumstances such as those in the case before the referring court, Miss Eind has the right to install herself with her father, Mr Eind, in the Netherlands, even if the latter is not economically active.

There seem to be two ways of understanding *Singh* and *Eind*. One is that people often have vested rights, for example residence permits for their non-EU spouses. They will only give these up to migrate if they are guaranteed they can reclaim residence rights in the future. An inability to bring rights home would then be a deterrent to initial migration. The other explanation is that if a citizen migrates, but cannot take their rights home, then their further freedom of movement from their host state is limited: there is one state they are put off migrating to because it would entail loss of rights. Article 21 TFEU, and the idea that a citizen can migrate to the state of her choice is not realised.

Returning migrants therefore continue to enjoy the family rights that they had while abroad. The Dane who has brought his Angolan wife to Sweden and lived there for a while may then return to Denmark and rely on EU law against his own state to enforce her right to live with him. This U-turn construction is becoming increasingly popular and while states have claimed in the past that it amounts to an 'abuse' of free movement, the Court has never shown much enthusiasm for this idea.[111] It is likely that in egregious circumstances an 'abuse' claim might stick (if the migrant just spends a few weeks abroad, perhaps), but the mere fact that the migrant went to another state for the purposes of acquiring EU family rights does not in itself amount to abuse.[112]

The effect of these cases is that migrants' rights become vested and can be applied against their home state. This raises a number of difficult questions, notably whether there are financial conditions or limits to the time that such rights continue at home. In *Eind*, the Dutch government argued that any such returnee rights should only continue as long the returnee was

---

[111] See K. Engsig Sorensen, 'Abuse of Rights in Community Law: A Principle of Substance or Merely Rhetoric?' (2006) 43 *CMLRev.* 423. See Case C-330/07 *Jobra Vermögensverwaltungs-Gesellschaft mbH v Finanzamt Amstetten Melk Scheibbs*, Judgment of 4 December 2008; Case C-109/01 *Secretary of State for the Home Department v Akrich* [2003] ECR I-9607; Case C-110/99 *Emsland-Stärke* [2000] ECR I-11569.

[112] *Secretary of State for the Home Department v Akrich, above n.111.*

economically active in his home state. It may be noted that in *Singh*, the Court referred to a worker who returns to take up economic activity in their home state. However, the introduction of citizenship and of broader residence rights changes the position and the Court rejected the Dutch government's argument. It pointed out that citizens have an unconditional right of residence in their home state, so reference to conditions for residence, which might be applied to non-nationals, was not appropriate. This suggests that not only do returnees not need to work to maintain their EU rights, but they do not need to comply with the conditions on resources and sickness insurance.

In practice this is likely to be a moot point. Given the Court's view on the role of Article 8 ECHR, it will be difficult for a home state to expel the family of a returning migrant if they have previously been together in another Member State, whatever their economic situation. Family rights brought home may well be permanent and unconditional in practice.

These cases may be read alongside *Carpenter*.[113] In that case, the Court found that it was not necessary to live abroad to fall within the scope of EU law; a UK citizen based in the United Kingdom but often travelling to the continent to provide services could rely on Article 56 TFEU, the free movement of services, to prevent the United Kingdom obstructing his activities. This much is relatively orthodox, but the Court then went on to find that a refusal to permit his Filipina wife to reside in the United Kingdom amounted to such an obstruction:

> 39. It is clear that the separation of Mr and Mrs Carpenter would be detrimental to their family life and, therefore, to the conditions under which Mr Carpenter exercises a fundamental freedom. That freedom could not be fully effective if Mr Carpenter were to be deterred from exercising it by obstacles raised in his country of origin to the entry and residence of his spouse.

Mr Carpenter had argued that if his wife was deported to the Philippines he would have to move there too, or break up his family, so his economic activities in the Union would clearly be threatened. Moreover, his wife cared for his children while he was away for work so her deportation would hinder his business travel. The Court appears, in a somewhat untransparent way, to be accepting these arguments. Family rights therefore now extend not just to returnees but also to those who stay at home, provided that they engage in cross-border economic activity. It remains open to argument whether the result would have been different had there been no children and so a less direct link between the wife's presence and the economic activity would have been present. However, the text of the judgment does not confirm this and distinguishing between family members who enhance the exercise of an economic activity and those who do not could be difficult, not to say tasteless.

National immigration law is made increasingly untenable by these developments, with all those having the initiative and capacity to find some kind of work abroad now able to bring themselves within the more family-friendly EU legal regime and opt out of national immigration law. The judgment in *Metock* contained an extensive discussion of the relative competences of the Member States and the Union and it is most likely that future years will see increasing harmonisation in this area.

---

[113] Case C-60/00 *Carpenter v Secretary of State for the Home Department* [2002] ECR I-6279.

(iv) Administrative formalities

Member States are entitled to ask EU migrants and their families to comply with a number of administrative formalities. For entry to a state, a valid passport or identity card may be demanded from EU citizens, whereas non-EU family members may also have to have a visa under certain circumstances, at least until they have obtained a residence card, whereupon this and their passport are sufficient for travel.[114]

For short-term residence, up to three months, no conditions or formalities may be imposed other than the requirement that the citizen and family members report their presence to the police within a reasonable and non-discriminatory time.[115]

For longer residence, states may require that citizens and their families register with the authorities.[116] To do so they may be required to present valid identity documents and evidence that they comply with the substantive conditions for residence. Thus, citizens may be required to show that they are economically active, or that they have resources and sickness insurance. Students do not have to show evidence of resources, but can simply sign a declaration that they have them.[117] Family members have to show evidence of their relationship with the migrant citizen. Those falling within the 'extra' family members whose entry is to be facilitated under article 3 of the Citizenship Directive are required to produce evidence that they are indeed dependants or family members.[118]

Despite the sometimes forbidding sound of all these requirements, a number of factors mitigate them so that they should (in principle) rarely be a cause of problems for migrants.

First, it has long been established that the residence documents issued by states upon registration are merely evidentiary and not constitutive of the rights of the citizen, and *Oulane* confirms that this remains the case after the Directive. In this case, a French citizen had neither a residence card, nor even a valid passport. The Dutch authorities claimed he was therefore illegally present in the Netherlands. On the contrary, the Court took the view that he had a Treaty right as a result of being an EU citizen and such documents (including the residence card) were simply evidence of this, but not necessary evidence.

Case C-215/03 *Oulane* v *Minister voor Vreemdelingenzaken en Integratie* [2005] ECR I-1215

17. ... the right of nationals of a Member State to enter the territory of another Member State and reside there for the purposes intended by the Treaty is a right conferred directly by the Treaty or, as the case may be, by the provisions adopted for its implementation ....

18. It follows that issuance of a residence permit to a national of a Member State is to be regarded not as a measure giving rise to rights but as a measure by a Member State serving to prove the individual position of a national of another Member State with regard to provisions of Community law ...

The citizen or family member who fails to comply is therefore not in any sense illegally present in the host state and cannot be expelled. In fact the Directive goes further than this.

---

[114] Citizenship Directive, article 5(2).
[115] *Ibid.* article 5(5).
[116] *Ibid.* article 8(1).
[117] *Ibid.* article 8(3); C-424/98 *Commission* v *Italy* [2000] ECR I-4001.
[118] *Ibid.* article 8(5).

> **Citizenship Directive, article 25(1)**
>
> Possession of a residence certificate as referred to in Article 8, of a document certifying permanent residence, of a certificate attesting submission of an application for a family member residence card, of a residence card or of a permanent residence card, may under no circumstances be made a precondition for the exercise of a right or the completion of an administrative formality, as entitlement to rights may be attested by any other means of proof.

A failure to register should therefore have no consequences for functioning in the host state. Work, education, access to benefits and other aspects of life should be unaffected. The registration procedure and documents are not to be conditions for access to host state life, but merely a mechanism for states to gather information and establish those present on their territory. In practice, obtaining the registration documents tends to make life in the host state much easier, as they comprise evidence that the state has recognised the right of residence. Despite article 25, it is common for public authorities to want to see these documents before granting access to other rights and benefits.

Since article 25 prohibits registration being a condition for the exercise of other rights, states who wish to enforce the registration requirement have to hunt for and punish non-registered migrants and their families. However, the Directive limits any sanctions to those that are proportionate and non-discriminatory.[119] Sanctions of such a severity that they seriously impair the very right of residence are disproportionate.[120] A proper approach to determining appropriate sanctions is to consider how comparable infringements by nationals are punished; for example, violations of an obligation to inform the authorities of a new address when moving house.

The importance of formalities and documentary requirements is further diminished by the Court's approach to evidence, which is highly pragmatic and non-formalistic. In *Oulane*, it went so far as to find that possession of a valid passport or identity card is not a condition for lawful residence, since nationality may be proved in other ways:

> If the person concerned is able to provide unequivocal proof of his nationality by means other than a valid identity card or passport, the host Member State may not refuse to recognise his right of residence on the sole ground that he has not presented one of those documents.[121]

This approach was continued in *MRAX*, where the Court considered Belgian practice on third country partners of EU citizens.[122] The Belgian state took the view that if these were not in possession of a valid identity document and visa, as the Directives in force required, they were not entitled to a residence card and could be deported. In a long but important judgment, the Court affirmed that just as with EU citizens, the right of the third country partner stems directly from the Treaty and a failure to comply with formalities does not remove it. If they have no documents, they may have difficulty proving their identity and family relationship, but if they can somehow do this (the Court noted that an expired passport may still be evidence of identity), then the responsibility of the state is to assist them in obtaining the necessary documents

---

[119] See also Case C-230/97 *Awoyemi* [1998] ECR I-6781.
[120] Case 118/75 *Watson and Belmann* [1976] ECR 1185.
[121] Case C-215/03 *Oulane* v *Minister voor Vreemdelingenzaken en Integratie* [2005] ECR I-1215.
[122] Case C-459/99 *MRAX* [2002] ECR I-6591.

in the host state, as quickly as possible, while any sanctions imposed must be no more than are proportionate.

(v) Grounds for exclusion

A feature of nationality is protection against statelessness. No matter how egregious her behaviour, the national has a right to remain on the territory of her state of nationality. EU citizenship does not give its citizens an equivalent right in their host states. In tandem with other provisions on movement of EU nationals, the Citizenship Directive sets out certain circumstances in which EU citizens can be expelled from or refused entry to another Member State, even though they would otherwise meet the requirements for residence. The rules in article 27 also apply to national measures restricting a migrant to a particular part of the national territory, or excluding him from one part of it.[123]

Citizenship Directive, article 27

1. Subject to the provisions of this Chapter, Member States may restrict the freedom of movement and residence of Union citizens and their family members, irrespective of nationality, on grounds of public policy, public security or public health. These grounds shall not be invoked to serve economic ends.
2. Measures taken on grounds of public policy or public security shall comply with the principle of proportionality and shall be based exclusively on the personal conduct of the individual concerned. Previous criminal convictions shall not in themselves constitute grounds for taking such measures. The personal conduct of the individual concerned must represent a genuine, present and sufficiently serious threat affecting one of the fundamental interests of society. Justifications that are isolated from the particulars of the case or that rely on considerations of general prevention shall not be accepted.

In any case where a decision is made to deport an individual, the person must be notified in writing of the decision. They must be told the reasons for exclusion, precisely and in full, unless this is contrary to the interests of state security.[124] All persons must have access to judicial and administrative redress procedures to appeal against or seek review of any decision taken against them.[125] These procedures will consider the legality and proportionality of the decision, as well as the facts and circumstances on which the decision was based.[126] Individuals must be told in the initial decision by the relevant court or administrative authority where they may lodge an appeal, the time limits for the appeal and the time allowed to leave the territory.[127]

These procedural guarantees apply to all migrant citizens, not just those lawfully present in the Member State.[128] To impose a condition of lawfulness on the procedural protections would be to some extent to pre-empt precisely the issue that the procedures in question are to determine.

The most commonly used grounds for exclusion are public policy and public security. Although these are two separate criteria, article 27(2) provides that they both turn on the

---

[123] Case C-100/01 *Ministre de l'Intérieur* v *Olazabal* [2002] ECR I-10981.
[124] Citizenship Directive, article 30(1) and (2).
[125] *Ibid.* article 31(1).
[126] *Ibid.* article 31(3).
[127] *Ibid.* article 30(3).
[128] Case C-459/99 *MRAX* [2002] ECR I-6591; Case C-50/06 *Commission* v *Netherlands* [2007] ECR I-4383; Case C-136/03 *Dörr and Ünal* [2005] ECR 1-4759.

question whether the individual's conduct poses a genuine, present and sufficiently serious threat to the fundamental interests of society. States have some discretion in determining the threshold here, since norms may vary. However, the derogations are EU law concepts, subject to the jurisdiction of the Court, which interprets them restrictively, since they are derogations from the fundamental freedom to move. The Court is particularly vigilant in asking whether a consistent approach is being taken to nationals and foreigners.[129] In *Adoui*,[130] Belgium wished to deport some French women who worked in a brothel.

Joined Cases 115/81 and 116/81 *Adoui and Cornuaille* v *Belgian State and City of Liège* [1982] ECR 1665

8. Although Community law does not impose upon the Member States a uniform scale of values as regards the assessment of conduct which may be considered as contrary to public policy, it should nevertheless be stated that conduct may not be considered as being of a sufficiently serious nature to justify restrictions on the admission to or residence within the territory of a Member State of a national of another Member State in a case where the former Member State does not adopt, with respect to the same conduct on the part of its own nationals, repressive measures or other genuine and effective measures intended to combat such conduct.

The deportation of foreign prostitutes was conditional upon adequately harsh repression of national ones.

The threat to society which the individual represents must, moreover, be a present one. However bad their behaviour has been in the past, if there is no reason to believe that they will reoffend, then there are no grounds for deportation. This demands that each case be looked at on its facts and rules which provide for automatic deportation after committal of certain offences will inevitably contravene the Directive. In *Orfanopoulos*, a Greek and an Italian drug addict had each been convicted of multiple drugs-related offences, as well as for violent offences and for theft. Germany had a law that any foreigner sentenced to a custodial sentence of two years or more for drugs-related offences would be automatically deported. The German court asked whether the automatic nature of the deportation was disproportionate.

Joined Cases C-482/01 and C-493/01 *Orfanopoulos* v *Land Baden-Württemberg* [2004] ECR I-5257

65. ... a particularly restrictive interpretation of the derogations from that freedom is required by virtue of a person's status as a citizen of the Union ...

67. While it is true that a Member State may consider that the use of drugs constitutes a danger for society such as to justify special measures against foreign nationals who contravene its laws on drugs, the public policy exception must, however, be interpreted restrictively, with the result that the existence of

---

[129] Case 41/74 *Van Duyn* v *Home Office* [1974] ECR 1337; Joined Cases C-65/95 and C-111/95 *R* v *Secretary of State for the Home Department, ex parte Shingara and ex parte Radiom* [1997] ECR I-03343; Case 121/85 *Conegate* v *Customs and Excise Commissioners* [1986] ECR 1007; Case 34/79 *R* v *Henn and Darby* [1979] ECR 3795.

[130] Joined Cases 115/81 and 116/81 *Adoui and Cornuaille* v *Belgian State and City of Liège* [1982] ECR 1665.

a previous criminal conviction can justify an expulsion only insofar as the circumstances which gave rise to that conviction are evidence of personal conduct constituting a present threat to the requirements of public policy.

68. … Community law precludes the deportation of a national of a Member State based on reasons of a general preventive nature, that is one which has been ordered for the purpose of deterring other aliens, in particular where such measure automatically follows a criminal conviction, without any account being taken of the personal conduct of the offender or of the danger which that person represents for the requirements of public policy.

69. The question asked by the national court refers to national legislation which requires the expulsion of nationals of other Member States who have received certain sentences for specific offences.

70. It must be held that, in such circumstances, the expulsion automatically follows a criminal conviction, without any account being taken of the personal conduct of the offender or of the danger which that person represents for the requirements of public policy.

71. In the light of the foregoing, the answer to the first question must be that [EU law] preclude[s] national legislation which requires national authorities to expel nationals of other Member States who have been finally sentenced to a term of youth custody of at least two years or to a custodial sentence for an intentional offence against the Law on narcotics, where the sentence has not been suspended.

A similar automatism was present in *Commission* v *Spain*, which addressed a Spanish practice of denying entry to those against whose name an alert had been entered in the Schengen Information System.[131] This is a database shared by a number of Member States for the purposes of communicating information about those who may be a threat, in order to prevent their entry to and movement within the European Union. It has now been incorporated within EU law, so the Spanish government argued that it was simply following its EU legal obligations. These obligations, it said, required it to react to an alert that had been entered by another state precisely for the purposes of ensuring an individual was denied entry to Member States. The Court conceded that the Spanish government could give 'due consideration' to the alert, but it was not entitled to deny entry purely on this basis without making its own independent assessment of 'whether their presence constituted a genuine, present and sufficiently serious threat affecting one of the fundamental interests of society'.

The requirement that the citizen pose a present threat to public policy has further consequences. If an expulsion order is enforced more than two years after it was issued (as will often be the case where the citizen has to serve a lengthy prison sentence before deportation), the Member State must consider whether, at the moment of enforcement, the individual is still a current and genuine threat to public policy or security.[132] In addition, if a citizen has been deported, she can submit an application for a lifting of the exclusion order after a reasonable period and, in any event, after three years, arguing that there has been a material change to circumstances justifying a lifting of the order.[133]

There is, additionally, a scale of seriousness, which determines whether exclusion can take place. Residents, or those applying for residency, can be excluded for conduct which would not

---

[131] Case C-503/03 *Commission v Spain* [2006] ECR I-1097. See also Case C-348/96 *Calfa* [1999] ECR I-11.

[132] Citizenship Directive, article 33(2). See also Joined Cases C-482/01 and C-493/01 *Orfanopoulos v Land Baden-Württemberg* [2004] ECR I-5257.

[133] Citizenship Directive, article 32(1).

justify exclusion if they were permanent residents, for the latter may only be expelled on 'serious grounds' of public policy or security.[134] Moreover, if a citizen has been resident in another state for the previous ten years or is a minor, she may not be expelled except for imperative grounds of public security or, in the case of the minor, if it is in the best interests of the child.[135]

The exceptions also apply to restrictions on exit. In *Jipa*, the Romanian government imposed an order on one of its own citizens that he not travel to Belgium for three years.[136] This was because he had earlier been expelled from Belgium, and had as background a cooperation agreement between these states relating to 'illegal' Romanians in Belgium. The Court accepted that such an order could, in principle, be legitimate. It seems reasonable that if one state legitimately expels an EU citizen, there should be little objection to other states helping to make this expulsion effective. However, the judgment shows suspicion of whether the measure was actually disproportionate, with the Court emphasising that such measures, given their fundamental conflict with free movement, should not go beyond what was strictly necessary. A part of the doubt was whether the Belgian order had in fact been legitimate. This was something the national judge should examine. It may be noted that although *Jipa* concerned the Member State of origin of the EU citizen, its logic should be applicable to any state imposing exit restrictions.

There is one further feature, which complicates the debate on exclusion. Even if the citizen's conduct poses a sufficient threat to public policy or public security, it will still not automatically follow that she can be excluded. Account must be taken of whether the exclusion might violate the fundamental rights of the citizen or her family. The discussion on the family and human rights, above, is relevant here. Also, article 28(1) of the Citizenship Directive lists a whole host of factors which must be taken into account before making an exclusion order.

Citizenship Directive, article 28(1)

Before taking an expulsion decision on grounds of public policy or public security, the host Member State shall take account of considerations such as how long the individual concerned has resided on its territory, his/her age, state of health, family and economic situation, social and cultural integration into the host Member State and the extent of his/her links with the country of origin.

Public policy and public security are not trump cards, but rather factors to be weighed in the balance against the interests and circumstances of the individual in question and those close to them.

5 POLITICAL RIGHTS OF EU CITIZENS

At the heart of modern citizenship is the right to engage fully and equally in the common affairs of the political community. This is usually translated into a series of political rights: the right to vote, to hold office and to hold office holders accountable.[137]

---

[134] *Ibid.* article 28(2).
[135] *Ibid.* article 28(3).
[136] Case C-33/07 *Jipa* [2008] ECR I-5157.
[137] See J. Shaw, *The Transformation of Citizenship in the European Union* (Cambridge, Cambridge University Press, 2007); H. Lardy, 'The Political Rights of Union Citizenship' (1997) *EPL* 611; T. Kostakopoulou, 'Ideas, Norms and European Citizenship: Explaining Institutional Change' (2005) 68 *MLR* 233, 239–40.

(i) Rights to vote and hold office

Where EU citizens reside in a Member State not their own, Article 22 TFEU (and Article 20(2)(b) TFEU) grant them the right to vote and stand in municipal and European elections on the same conditions as nationals of that state. The procedure is regulated by two Directives, which also provide for limited exceptions and conditions in municipalities where there are particularly high levels of non-national EU citizens. Only Luxembourg and Belgium have made use of these.[138]

Spain v *United Kingdom* raised the question whether only EU citizens can vote for the European Parliament.[139] Spain challenged the United Kingdom's grant of voting rights to some commonwealth citizens resident in Gibraltar. Qualified commonwealth citizens are also entitled to vote in elections, including European Parliament elections, in mainland United Kingdom, although Spain was less upset about this. The Spanish government made both textual and purposive arguments that the right to vote for the European Parliament was an essential privilege of EU citizens, that it was regulated by EU law and therefore a matter within the sphere of EU law. Hence, Spain argued, a single Member State could not unilaterally extend the franchise to others. The Commission, by contrast, argued that '[a] link does not exist, in all Member States, between the legitimacy of public power and nationality. It is appropriate to take account of different approaches, such as that resulting from the constitutional tradition of the United Kingdom.' The Court appeared to adopt this latter view, finding that the Treaty simply required that citizens could vote on equal terms with nationals, but did not anywhere suggest that only EU citizens could vote. Indeed, it noted that '[n]o clear conclusion can be drawn in that regard from Article [14 TFEU] relating to the European Parliament, which state[s] that it is to consist of representatives of the peoples of the Member States, since the term "peoples", which is not defined, may have different meanings in the Member States and languages of the Union'. The Court also made repeated references to the ways in which EU law grants and acknowledges rights for non-EU citizens within the Union. The judgment is symbolically important for setting out a vision in which non-EU citizens are still part of the community of Europe.[140] Citizens may be the first clients of the Union, but they are not the only ones. It remains to be seen whether this judgment still stands in the light of Article 14(2) TEU, which now provides that 'The European Parliament shall be comprised of representatives of the Union's citizens.' While this undermines the textual argument in *Spain* v *United Kingdom*, it is suggested that the underlying policy approach may still prevail.

The Court intervened in national electoral procedure for the European Parliament in a more critical way in *Eman and Sevinger*, a judgment delivered on the same day as *Spain* v *United Kingdom*.[141] These two Dutch citizens complained that they were not allowed to vote in European elections because they lived in Aruba, an overseas territory of the Netherlands to which EU law, in general, does not apply. Moreover, to rub salt in the wound, Dutch citizens

---

[138] Directive 94/80/EC [1994] OJ L368/38, article 12; Directive 93/109/EC [1993] OJ L329/34, article 14; European Commission, *Report on the Right to Vote and to Stand as a Candidate in Elections to the European Parliament*, COM(2007)846 final; European Commission, *Report on the Right to Vote and Stand as a Candidate in Municipal Elections*, COM(2005)382 final.

[139] Case C-145/04 *Spain* v *United Kingdom* [2006] ECR I-7917.

[140] Cf. M. Bell, 'Civic Citizenship and Migrant Integration' (2007) 13 *EPL* 311; D. Kochenov, 'Ius Tractum of Many Faces: European Citizenship and the Difficult Relationship Between Status and Rights' (2009) 15 *CJEL* 169.

[141] Case C-300/04 *Eman and Sevinger* [2006] ECR I-8055.

resident in a third country (the United States, or Australia, for example) could vote for the European Parliament. It was only those in the overseas territories that were excluded.

The Court did not object to states having territorial requirements for voting 'best adapted to their constitutional structure'. However, it found that any such rules had to comply with the principle of equality, which is a general principle of EU law and therefore applied to European Parliament elections. This prevented arbitrary distinctions of any kind and the Court was not convinced that the distinction between Dutch citizens in Aruba and those in third countries had any coherent reasoning behind it. In fact it does, but that reasoning is of a highly political and historical nature and reflects the complex ex-colonial relationship between the Netherlands and Aruba. The Dutch government was, however, unable to explain the distinction in a way that made it seem constitutionally rational.[142]

Despite this fairly high-powered litigation, EU citizenship has not been a great success as a political citizenship. Turn-out in European Parliament elections is generally low, presenting a challenge to the idea of a European political community and to the idea that by stimulating public participation in the political process, EU citizenship can add to Union legitimacy.[143] Similarly, the rate of participation by migrant citizens in local elections in their host states has also been low.[144] Clearly, many non-national citizens do not feel sufficient attachment to their place of residence to wish to participate in the management of its affairs. This may be because their political horizons hark back to their state of origin, because there are no transnational political parties reflecting their interests, or because they conceive of themselves only as temporary residents of their host state.[145]

A factor limiting the impact of EU political rights is that they do not extend to participation in core national political decision-making processes. First, migrant citizens do not acquire a right to participate in national elections, either as voters or candidates. Even in federal states such as Spain, Belgium and Germany, these remain the most high-profile and most significant elections in every state in the European Union. Secondly, EU citizenship also does not give citizens any right to hold high office or exercise any duties which require them regularly to safeguard the interests of the state. Two provisions of EU law set out these latter exclusions, Article 45(4) and Article 51 TFEU. The first provides that the free movement of workers shall not apply to 'employment in the public service', while the second provides that the free movement of services gives no right to provide services connected 'even occasionally, with the exercise of official authority'. While these articles are not formally part of the provisions on citizenship,[146] the idea that they embody is very much a limit on what EU citizenship is.

The Articles, which are interpreted in parallel, suggest that while foreigners may participate in economic life, that participation may justifiably be limited to matters outside the heart of the

---

[142] See annotations of *Spain* v *United Kingdom* and *Eman and Sevinger* by J. Shaw (2008) 4 *ECLRev.* 162; L. Besselink (2008) 45 *CMLRev.* 787.

[143] Bellamy, above n. 7.

[144] European Commission, *Report to the European Parliament and Council on the Application of Directive 94/80/ EC on the Right to Vote and Stand as a Candidate in Municipal Elections*, COM(2002)260 final. See also Bellamy, above n. 7.

[145] H. Schmitt, 'The European Parliament Elections of June 2004: Still Second-Order?' (2005) 28 *West European Politics* 650; S. Hix and M. Marsh, 'Punishment or Protest? Understanding European Parliament Elections' (2007) 69 *Journal of Politics* 495.

[146] They are discussed in more detail in Chapter 21.

state and of public authority. They have been interpreted strictly. 'Public service' does not mean, in the eyes of the Court, any state employment, but only the more sensitive public positions. The Court has said that citizens of other states may legitimately be excluded only from functions which 'presume on the part of those occupying them the existence of a special relationship of allegiance to the state and reciprocity of rights and duties which form the foundation of the bond of nationality'.[147] Advocate General Mancini referred to those who 'don full battle dress' in the service of the state.[148] Jobs as postal workers,[149] teachers,[150] nurses, railway drivers, cleaners and canteen staff working in the public sector,[151] may therefore not be reserved for nationals, even if these are public posts. On the other hand, most functions in the armed forces or police, the higher parts of the civil service or the judiciary, probably do fall within the exception.[152] While the scope of the exception may therefore be limited, it does reveal starkly the limits of EU citizenship. There is an inner core of national membership to which the migrant is not admitted. Fundamentally, she cannot be trusted, because she is foreign.

(ii) Right to petition and hold the administration accountable

The right to representative government includes not only the right to choose one's representative or, even, to put oneself forward as a representative. The idea of representation also suggests an enduring relationship beyond the elections in which the government is to act on behalf of its constituents. This entitles individual citizens to hold government to account and to ask how government is attempting to realise their interests.

Article 24 TFEU

The European Parliament and the Council, acting by means of regulations in accordance with the ordinary legislative procedure, shall adopt the provisions for the procedures and conditions required for a citizens' initiative within the meaning of Article 11 of the Treaty on European Union, including the minimum number of Member States from which such citizens must come.

Every citizen of the Union shall have the right to petition the European Parliament in accordance with Article 227.

Every citizen of the Union may apply to the Ombudsman established in accordance with Article 228.

Every citizen of the Union may write to any of the institutions, bodies, offices or agencies referred to in this Article or in Article 13 of the Treaty on European Union in one of the languages mentioned in Article 55(1) of the Treaty on European Union and have an answer in the same language.

---

[147] Case C-405/01 *Colegio de Oficiales de la Marina Mercante Española* v *Administración del Estado* [2003] ECR I-10391.

[148] Case 307/84 *Commission* v *France* [1986] ECR 1725, para. 5 of the Opinion.

[149] Case 152/73 *Sotgiu* v *Deutsche Bundespost* [1974] ECR 153.

[150] Case 33/88 *Allue* v *Università degli Studi di Venezia* [1989] ECR 1591; Case 4/91 *Bleis* v *Ministère de l'Education Nationale* [1991] ECR I-5627.

[151] Case 149/79 *Commission* v *Belgium (No. 2)* [1982] ECR 1845.

[152] European Commission, *Free Movement of Workers: Achieving the Full Benefits and Potential*, COM(2002)694, 18–19. See also J. Handoll, 'Article 48(4) EEC and Non-national Access to Public Employment' (1988) 13 *ELRev.* 223; D. O'Keeffe, 'Judicial Interpretation of the Public Service Exception to the Free Movement of Workers' in D. Curtin and D. O'Keeffe (eds.), *Constitutional Adjudication in European Community and National Law: Essays for the Hon. Mr. Justice O'Higgins* (Dublin, Butterworths, 1992).

The first paragraph of this Article refers to Article 11 TEU, which provides, inter alia, that a million or more citizens may, presumably by petition, invite the Commission to initiate a proposal for law. This is innovative and potentially engaging of the public, although the fact that the Commission is not compelled to follow the citizens' initiative, but merely invited to, is a significant weakness.

The other parts of Article 24 TFEU seem rather limited, but there are two other significant related legal provisions. The first is Article 15 TFEU, which entitles any EU citizen or natural or legal person, residing or having its registered office in a Member State, to a right of access to European Parliament, Council and Commission documents, subject to certain limitations. The second is contained in Article 41 EUCFR, which codifies existing case law of the Court of Justice on the right to administrative due process. These two provisions are not explicitly confined to EU citizens. However, in their determination of the accountability of the Union they inevitably help define the power and status that EU citizens have. The issues that they raise are dealt with in detail elsewhere in this book.[153]

(iii) Right to diplomatic protection

Traditionally, it is states, through their consular offices, which make representations about the civil liberties and interests of their nationals abroad and assist those who have fallen into trouble. EU law provides that where there is no representation of a Member State in a non-EU state, citizens of that state are entitled to the diplomatic protection of other Member States.

> **Article 23 TFEU**
>
> Every citizen of the Union shall, in the territory of a third country in which the Member State of which he is a national is not represented, be entitled to protection by the diplomatic or consular authorities of any Member State, on the same conditions as the nationals of that State. Member States shall adopt the necessary provisions and start the international negotiations required to secure this protection.
>
> The Council, acting in accordance with a special legislative procedure and after consulting with the European Parliament, may adopt Directives establishing the coordination and cooperation measures necessary to facilitate such protection.

The provision only bites where the citizen's state has no diplomatic presence on the territory of the third state in question. A citizen in trouble in Vladivostok in Russia has no right to assistance from other states with consular authorities if her state has one diplomat in Moscow several thousand kilometres away. The practical arrangements for implementing Article 23 are spelt out in Decision 95/553/EC.[154] Assistance is to be offered in cases of death, serious accident, illness, arrest, detention or where the victim is subject to violent crime. It is also to include relief and repatriation of 'distressed citizens' of the Union.[155] Financial aid can only be provided with the permission of the state of the citizen in question, who will reimburse the assisting state.[156]

---

[153] See Chapter 9.
[154] Decision 95/553/EC [1995] OJ L314/73.
[155] *Ibid.* article 5.
[156] *Ibid.* article 6.

FURTHER READING

N. Barber, 'Citizenship, Nationalism and the European Union' (2002) 27 *European Law Review* 241

L. Bosniak, *The Citizen and the Alien* (Princeton, NJ, Princeton University Press, 2006)

M. Everson, 'The Legacy of the Market Citizen' in J. Shaw and G. More (eds.), *New Legal Dynamics of the European Union* (Oxford, Oxford University Press, 1995)

F. Jacobs, 'Citizenship of the European Union: A Legal Analysis' (2007) 13(5) *European Law Journal* 591

D. Kochenov, 'Ius Tractum of Many Faces: European Citizenship and the Difficult Relationship between Status and Rights' (2009) 15 *Columbia Journal of European Law* 169

D. Kostakopoulou, *Citizenship, Identity and Immigration in the European Union: Between Past and Future* (Manchester, Manchester University Press, 2001)

'European Union Citizenship: Writing the Future' (2007) 13(5) *European Law Journal* 623

P. Magnette, 'How Can One be European? Reflections on the Pillars of European Civic Identity' (2007) 13(5) *European Law Journal* 664

N. Nic Shuibhne, 'Derogating from the Free Movement of Persons: When Can Union Citizens be Deported?' (2006) 8 *Cambridge Yearbook of European Legal Studies* 187

J. Shaw, *The Transformation of Citizenship in the European Union* (Cambridge, Cambridge University Press, 2007)

Citizenship of the Union: Towards Post-national Membership, Jean Monnet Working Paper 97/6, www.jeanmonnetprogram.org

A. Somek, 'Solidarity Decomposed: Being and Time in European Citizenship' (2007) 32(6) *European Law Review* 818

E. Spaventa, 'Seeing the Wood Despite the Trees? On the Scope of Union Citizenship and its Constitutional Effects' (2008) 45(1) *Common Market Law Review* 13

12

EU Law and Non-EU Nationals

CONTENTS

1 INTRODUCTION

This chapter considers the treatment of non-EU nationals by EU law.[1] It is organised as follows.

Section 2 looks at the central Union competences, Articles 77–9 TFEU, which provide for EU law to be adopted in the fields of border checks, asylum and immigration respectively. These provisions are subject to the Protocol on the Schengen Acquis. The Schengen Acquis is composed of the measures adopted to implement the 1985 and 1990 Schengen Conventions, which provide for common external frontiers and visa, immigration and asylum policies. Ireland and the United Kingdom are not signatories to these Conventions. Measures developing the acquis should be adopted under the Protocol, with Ireland and the United Kingdom only participating with the agreement of all the other Member States. If the measure is not governed by the Protocol on the Schengen Acquis, those two states have a further Protocol, the Protocol on United Kingdom and Ireland, which gives them the right to decide whether to participate in the legislation. There is a further Protocol on Denmark which provides that any measure adopted in this field will only bind it as a matter of international law.

Section 3 considers the central themes governing this field. EU law on non-EU nationals forms part of the Area of Freedom, Security and Justice. This Area is seen as contributing to a wider European way of life, with the Union measures on non-EU nationals regulating the latter's perceived contribution and threat to this way of life. This has led to a number of competing themes. The first is economic mercantilism which treats non-EU nationals as a human resource and considers their impact on labour markets, welfare systems and EU competitiveness. The second is the protection of national sovereignty and security. Non-EU nationals are considered in terms of their perceived cultural, political and social risks. This has led to a strong emphasis on policing of non-EU nationals and territorial and visa control. The third is humanitarianism and the idea that the Union should shelter those in need. This is the basis for its humanitarian policies, notably asylum, subsidiary protection and refugee policies. EU law is also subject to significant human rights constraints in this field. The final theme is that of European solidarity. Member States should share the costs of policy in this field.

Section 4 considers Directive 2008/115/EC ('Returns Directive'). This requires Member States to return non-EU nationals who have irregularly entered or remained on their territory, unless there are strong compassionate reasons. In principle, the return should be voluntary. This will not be the case if the non-EU national does not leave within the term set or, inter alia, there is a risk of her absconding. In such circumstances, there will be a forced return. There is also provision for a ban on her re-entering the Union and there is the possibility of detention.

Section 5 considers the grant of long-term resident status to non-EU nationals. This is provided to those who can show lawful residence in a Member State for five years and sufficient resources to support themselves and their families. It grants the right to permanent residence in the Member State concerned and the right to the same socio-economic entitlements as a state's own nationals. These rights can be limited. The right to permanent residence can be lost if the non-EU national is absent for twelve months, and Member States can restrict social benefits to core benefits. There is also a right to family reunification where a non-EU national has been lawfully resident in a Member State for more than one year and has reasonable prospects of

[1] It does not consider the situation where non-EU nationals acquire rights by virtue of a relationship with an EU citizen. This is addressed in Chapter 11. See pp. 464–73.

permanent residence. Family members 12 years or older can be required, however, to undergo integration tests before reunification and Member States can require that the non-EU national be lawfully resident for two years before her family is able to join her.

Section 6 considers the entitlements granted to asylum seekers. There is an entitlement to remain on the territory of the Member State pending consideration of their case unless the applicant comes from a safe country of origin or there is a safe state to which it is reasonable for them to go. The other central benefit is that the Member States must provide material reception conditions. These include housing, food, health care and education for minors. All these benefits are contingent on, inter alia, asylum seekers complying with the reporting and accommodation requirements set by Member States. They can also be withdrawn if the asylum claim is not made as soon as reasonably practicable on entering the Member State.

Section 7 considers EU law on refugees and those seeking subsidiary protection. Refugee status is granted to those who have a well-founded fear of being persecuted for reasons of race, religion, nationality, political opinion or membership of a particular social group. The acts of persecution must be sufficiently serious to constitute a severe violation of human rights. Subsidiary protection is granted to those who are at risk of serious harm. This consists of death, torture or a serious and individual threat to a civilian's life from indiscriminate violence. Both groups are granted family, education and housing rights as well as the right to free movement. Refugees are also given full socio-economic rights whilst those acquiring subsidiary protection status are not given the right to work and are only granted core benefits.

2 UNION COMPETENCES ON BORDER CHECKS, ASYLUM AND IMMIGRATION

(i) Central competences

The history of Union competences on immigration and asylum is convoluted. Introduced at Maastricht, the issue was governed on a largely intergovernmental basis under the third pillar of the TEU and under separate international treaties. The Treaty of Amsterdam inserted it into the EC Treaty but subjected it to a number of very restrictive rules, with unanimity voting being the rule and very limited possibilities for national courts to refer matters to the Court of Justice. Voting requirements were gradually liberalised, first by the Treaty of Nice and then by a 2004 Council Decision.[2]

The Treaty of Lisbon has made things a lot easier. The policies on border checks, asylum and immigration, as they are now known, are subject to the same judicial procedures and legal norms as the rest of the TFEU. They are all (with two limited exceptions)[3] to be governed by the ordinary legislative procedure. They are clustered around three pillars. The first is a common policy on border checks.

---

[2] Decision 2004/927/EC providing for certain areas covered by Title IV of the EC Treaty to be governed by the procedure laid down in Article 251 EC [2004] OJ L396/45.

[3] These are the rights of non-EU national family members derived from EU citizens moving and residing in another Member State and emergency measures to deal with a sudden inflow of non-EU nationals into one Member State. These are both governed by the consultation procedure: Articles 77(3) and 78(3) TFEU respectively.

Article 77(1) TFEU

The Union shall develop a policy with a view to:

(a) ensuring the absence of any controls on persons, whatever their nationality, when crossing internal borders;

(b) carrying out checks on persons and efficient monitoring of the crossing of external borders;

(c) the gradual introduction of an integrated management system for external borders.

The second is a common policy on asylum and other forms of humanitarian protection.

Article 78(1) TFEU

The Union shall develop a common policy on asylum, subsidiary protection and temporary protection with a view to offering appropriate status to any third-country national requiring international protection and ensuring compliance with the principle of *non-refoulement*. This policy must be in accordance with the Geneva Convention of 28 July 1951 and the Protocol of 31 January 1967 relating to the status of refugees, and other relevant treaties.

The third policy is a common immigration policy.

Article 79(1) TFEU

The Union shall develop a common immigration policy aimed at ensuring, at all stages, the efficient management of migration flows, fair treatment of third-country nationals residing legally in Member States, and the prevention of, and enhanced measures to combat, illegal immigration and trafficking in human beings.

On their face, the catalogue of these three competences looks clear-cut, particularly as they are governed predominantly by the same legislative procedure. However, they have not been established against a blank canvas. Their operation must be seen alongside that of the Protocol on the Schengen Acquis.

(ii) Protocol on the Schengen Acquis

The Schengen Conventions of 1985 and 1990 were international agreements concluded between thirteen of the EU-15 Member States, Norway and Iceland.[4] All Member States are currently signatory to them except Ireland, the United Kingdom, Cyprus, Bulgaria and Romania. Provision is, however, made for the latter three to join. The Conventions provide for the

---

[4] They were mentioned briefly in Chapter 1 and Chapter 3. See p. 24 and pp. 115–16. The central Convention is the Implementing Convention agreed in 1990. The text is at [2000] OJ L239/19. For critical comment see J. Schutte, 'Schengen: Its Meaning for the Free Movement of Persons in Europe' (1991) 28 *CMLRev.* 549; H. Meijers *et al.* (eds.), *Schengen: Internationalisation of Central Chapters of the Law of Aliens, Refugees, Privacy, Security and Police* (2nd rev. edn, Leiden, Stichting NJM-Boekerij, 1992); D. O' Keeffe, 'The Schengen Convention: A Suitable Model for European Integration?' (1992) 12 *YBEL* 185.

abolition of internal frontier checks[5] and a common external frontier.[6] There is provision for a common visa,[7] asylum[8] and immigration policy.[9] To this end, a number of implementing measures, known as the Schengen Acquis, were adopted by an Executive Committee set up by those states to further those policies. As they were adopted prior to the Union having a competence in these fields, at the Treaty of Amsterdam, it was agreed to incorporate them into the TEU framework. In 1999, a Decision was taken granting EU legal status to all individual measures comprising the Schengen Acquis. [10]

The matter is, however, not closed. The Protocol on the Schengen Acquis allows the Schengen states to continue to take measures to build on the Schengen Acquis, albeit that these are now measures of EU law.

Protocol on the Schengen Acquis Integrated into the Framework of the European Union

Article 1
[All Member States other than Ireland and the United Kingdom] shall be authorised to implement closer cooperation among themselves in areas covered by provisions defined by the Council which constitute the Schengen acquis. This cooperation shall be conducted within the institutional and legal framework of the European Union and with respect for the relevant provisions of the Treaties.

Article 5(1)
Proposals and initiatives to build upon the Schengen *acquis* shall be subject to the relevant provisions of the Treaties.

The non-participating states, Ireland and the United Kingdom, can request to participate in any measure that is already part of the acquis or builds upon it. They will only be allowed to participate if the other Member States agree to the request by unanimity.[11]

The consequence is that there are two parallel sets of decision-making procedures governing this field: those set out in Articles 77–9 TFEU and those set out in the Protocol on the Schengen Acquis. The latter will base the measure on Article 77, 78 or 79 TFEU, but then will restrict who can participate as a Schengen participant, thereby excluding the right of the British or Irish to be automatically involved.

These two procedures overlap and raise the question which should prevail in the case of such overlap. The latter question was addressed in the British challenge to the establishment of the European Frontiers Agency (Frontex) under the Protocol. In the judgment, the Court stated

---

[5] Schengen Implementing Convention, Article 2.
[6] *Ibid.* Articles 3–8.
[7] *Ibid.* Articles 9–18.
[8] *Ibid.* Articles 28–39.
[9] *Ibid.* Articles 19–27.
[10] Decision 1999/436/EC determining the legal basis for each of the provisions or decisions which constitute the Schengen acquis [1999] OJ L176/19. On these measures, see P. Kuijper, 'Some Legal Problems Associated with the Communitarization of Policy on Visas, Asylum and Immigration under the Amsterdam Treaty and Incorporation of the Schengen Acquis' (2000) 37 *CMLRev.* 345; D. Thym, 'The Schengen Law: A Challenge for Legal Accountability in the European Union' (2002) 8 *ELJ* 218, 235.
[11] Protocol on the Schengen Acquis integrated into the framework of the European Union, Article 4.

that if a measure is built upon the Schengen Acquis, it should be governed by the procedures set out in the Protocol.[12] The procedures in the Protocol should prevail over the more general ones in Articles 77–9 TFEU.

This leads onto the next question of what is covered by the Protocol on the Schengen Acquis. Article 5 refers to anything which builds upon the Schengen Acquis. The meaning of this was addressed in a British challenge to Regulation 2252/2004/EC, which set standards for security features in passports. This was adopted under the Protocol. The United Kingdom notified the other Member States of its request to participate. However, the request was refused. The United Kingdom argued that measures building upon the acquis were only measures that were integral to it and amended existing measures of the acquis. It did not include related measures which complemented existing measures and pursued similar objectives. The Court, following on from its reasoning in the *Frontex* case, rejected this argument.

Case C-137/05 *United Kingdom* v *Council* [2007] ECR I-11593

56. Consequently, and by analogy with what applies in relation to the choice of the legal basis of a Community act, it must be concluded that in a situation such as that at issue in the present case the classification of a Community act as a proposal or initiative to build upon the Schengen acquis within the meaning of the first subparagraph of Article 5(1) of the Schengen Protocol must rest on objective factors which are amenable to judicial review, including in particular the aim and the content of the act …

57. It is in the light of those considerations that it must be examined whether, as the United Kingdom submits, the Council was wrong to classify Regulation No. 2252/2004 as a measure developing provisions of the Schengen acquis.

58. As to the purpose of Regulation No. 2252/2004, it is apparent from recitals 2 and 3 in the preamble and from Article 4(3) that it was intended to combat falsification and fraudulent use of passports and other travel documents issued by the Member States.

59. To achieve that objective, Regulation No. 2252/2004, as is apparent from Articles 1 and 2, harmonises and improves the minimum security standards with which passports and travel documents issued by the Member States must comply, and provides for a number of biometric features relating to the holders of such documents to be inserted in those documents.

60. In that connection, it should be recalled that, as the Court held in paragraph 84 of its judgment of today's date in Case C-77/05 *United Kingdom* v *Council*, checks on persons at the external borders of the Member States and consequently the effective implementation of the common rules on standards and procedures for those checks must be regarded as constituting elements of the Schengen acquis.

65. Insofar as the verification of the authenticity of passports and other travel documents thus constitutes the main element of checks on persons at external borders, measures which make it possible to establish that authenticity and the identity of the holder of the document in question more easily and more reliably must be regarded as capable of guaranteeing and improving the effectiveness of those checks and thereby of the integrated management of external borders established by the Schengen acquis.

---

[12] Case C-77/05 *United Kingdom* v *Council* [2007] ECR I-11459. The full reasoning of the judgment is set out in Chapter 3 at pp. 115–16.

The Court will look therefore to the principal objectives of the Schengen Agreements to see what is governed by the Protocol. External checks on borders constitute one of these objectives (paragraph 60), and measures on these are therefore to be adopted under the Protocol. Institutional practice has led to all measures on border checks that fall within Article 77 TFEU being governed by the Protocol. This covers not just Frontex and passports, but also external borders management[13] and visa policy.[14] However, the test is uncertain. The Directive leading to the return of irregular migrants (part of immigration policy) has been seen as developing the Schengen acquis.[15] The United Kingdom is currently challenging whether visa measures can be adopted under the Protocol.[16] More generally, we have seen that the Schengen Conventions also provide for common rules on asylum. Although current measures have not been adopted under the Protocol, the *United Kingdom* v *Council* judgments open the question as to whether they could be.

(iii) Protocols on the United Kingdom and Ireland and on Denmark

The position is further complicated by three additional Protocols: two relate to the United Kingdom and Ireland and one to Denmark.

The first Protocol provides that nothing in EU law affects the rights of the United Kingdom and Ireland to exercise frontier controls on persons entering from other parts of the European Union or elsewhere.[17] As a quid pro quo, the other Member States may impose border checks on persons coming from the United Kingdom and Ireland.[18]

The second Protocol on the position of the United Kingdom and Ireland in respect of the Area of Freedom, Security and Justice provides that these states will not participate in Title V of Part 3 of the TFEU and that no measures adopted under the Title or any Court judgment interpreting it shall bind them.[19] This title includes Articles 77–9 TFEU: the competences on border checks, asylum and immigration.[20] There is, however, provision for them to participate, should they so desire, in individual measures. Article 3(1) of the Protocol allows them, within three months of the Commission's publication of a proposal, to 'opt in' and participate in the adoption and application of any proposed measures. Yet, the bargaining strength of each is reduced by Article 3(2) as the Council may adopt the measure without either participating if 'after a reasonable period of time a measure... cannot be adopted with the United Kingdom or Ireland taking part'. Each may also subsequently adopt a measure by notifying the Council and Commission of its intention to do so.[21] The Commission must, within three months, give its opinion to the Council on such a notification and on what arrangements it deems necessary.

---

[13] Regulation 562/2006/EC establishing a Community Code on the rules governing the movement of persons across borders [2006] OJ L105/1.

[14] For example, Regulation 810/2009/EC on the Community Code on Visas [2009] OJ L243/1.

[15] Directive 2008/115/EC on common standards and procedures in Member States for returning illegally staying third-country nationals [2008] OJ L348/98.

[16] Case C-482/08 *United Kingdom* v *Council* [2009] OJ C32/15.

[17] Protocol on the application of certain aspects of Article 26 TFEU, Article 1. The position is a little complicated with regard to Ireland. This entitlement exists only for so long as it forms a common travel area allowing for free movement between it and the United Kingdom: Article 2.

[18] *Ibid.* Article 3.

[19] Protocol on the position of the United Kingdom and Ireland in respect of the Area of Freedom, Security and Justice, Articles 1 and 2.

[20] It also includes judicial cooperation in civil and criminal matters and police cooperation and some anti-terrorism measures. In relation to EU criminal law, see pp. 593–4.

[21] Protocol on the position of the United Kingdom and Ireland, Article 4.

Although Denmark did not want its immigration and asylum policies to be governed by EU law, it is bound by international law commitments to the other Member States, as it is a signatory to the Schengen Conventions. A Protocol was agreed, therefore, which provides that Denmark will not be bound by or participate in the adoption of any measures under Title V of Part 3 of the TFEU.[22] Nor is there any possibility for it to opt in should it so desire, unlike Ireland or the United Kingdom. Denmark's obligations under the Schengen Conventions mean, however, that if the Council decides to build upon the Schengen acquis, Denmark has six months to decide whether it will implement the decision.[23] If it chooses to do so, the decision will create an obligation under international law between Denmark and those Member States who participated in the measure. If Denmark decides against implementation, the other Member States and Denmark are to consider what appropriate measures should be taken.[24]

3 NON-EU NATIONALS AND THE AREA OF FREEDOM, SECURITY AND JUSTICE

The Union competences on border checks, asylum and immigration form part of the Area of Freedom, Security and Justice (AFSJ). They are consequently bound by its general principles and procedures.[25] But what is this AFSJ? The AFSJ is conceived, on the one hand, as a series of policies. These are summarised in Article 67 TFEU.

Article 67 TFEU

1. The Union shall constitute an area of freedom, security and justice with respect for fundamental rights and the different legal systems and traditions of the Member States.
2. It shall ensure the absence of internal border controls for persons and shall frame a common policy on asylum, immigration and external border control, based on solidarity between Member States, which is fair towards third-country nationals. For the purpose of this Title, stateless persons shall be treated as third-country nationals.
3. The Union shall endeavour to ensure a high level of security through measures to prevent and combat crime, racism and xenophobia, and through measures for coordination and cooperation between police and judicial authorities and other competent authorities, as well as through the mutual recognition of judgments in criminal matters and, if necessary, through the approximation of criminal laws.
4. The Union shall facilitate access to justice, in particular through the principle of mutual recognition of judicial and extrajudicial decisions in civil matters.

The policies comprising the AFSJ are not, therefore, just external border controls, asylum and immigration. They also include removal of internal border controls; access to justice; judicial cooperation in civil and criminal matters; police cooperation; and combating racism and xenophobia. Bringing these policies together subjects them not merely to certain common norms and procedures but suggests that they should be developed in a complementary manner and inform one another.

---

[22] Protocol on the position of Denmark, Articles 1 and 2.
[23] *Ibid.* Article 4(1).
[24] *Ibid.* Article 4(2).
[25] These principles perform a similar role for EU criminal law, which also forms part of this Title. See pp. 583–4.

But what are the norms that are to inform and align these policies? Whilst Article 67(1) TFEU refers to respect for fundamental rights, other documents use rather broader terms. The Commission has talked of freedom, security and justice as 'an integral part of the European model of society'.[26] The Working Group on Freedom, Security and Justice in the Future of Europe Convention used similar language. It argued that the AFSJ should lead to citizens feeling that a 'proper sense of "European public order" has taken shape and is actually visible in their daily lives'.[27] These views see the policies set out in Article 67 TFEU as contributing to a wider European way of life. Within such a vision, the AFSJ comprises not just EU policies but also all the institutions, procedures and norms, be they EU, national, regional or local, which contribute to a particular European way of life.

This chapter argues that this is a better way to understand EU law on non-EU nationals. It is conceived both formally and substantively as central to the establishment of a European Area of Freedom, Security and Justice and this field is not simply a formal array of policies but rather a Union contribution to sustaining a particular way of life for its citizens. EU border control, immigration and asylum law can only be understood through consideration of how immigration and asylum is identified as affecting this way of life.

Analysis of EU protection of this way of life starts with a paradox in that migration is seen as both contributing to and sustaining it, and as threatening it. In 2006, 18.5 million non-EU nationals lawfully resided in the European Union, about 3.8 per cent of its total population. Since 2002, levels have increased by between 1.5 and 2 million a year, so that it is now the main element in EU population growth.[28] However, alongside this, the official rhetoric and the policing measures taken against non-EU nationals have arguably never been harsher. Many are subject to deprivation and abuse, and enter and live in the Union under the most precarious of circumstances.

To understand the tensions within this paradox and how the Union's legal norms have been shaped by it, it is necessary to consider four central pressures which underpin this regime and which have each left an institutional imprint. The first, economic mercantilism, is concerned to manage migration in a way that advantages national economies and does not impose burdens on welfare states. It conceives migrants in terms of the economic benefits and costs they bring to European societies. The second theme concerns the perceived security risk posed by non-EU nationals, be it as potential sources of crime, political threats or threats to local public services or labour markets. In all cases, they are conceived, often in highly racist terms, as a threat to *national* security, and this has led to corollary concerns with protecting national territory and national sovereignty. The third theme embodies concerns of a humanitarian nature. It is the idea that the European way of life requires hospitality to be offered to the stranger, particularly those in most need. This has led to EU law treating some categories, such as family members and asylum seekers, more favourably than others, and to a commitment to respect a whole series of fundamental rights in this field. The final theme is that of solidarity towards protecting a shared European way of life. There is a responsibility to manage migration but a wish to share that responsibility and the costs amongst the Member States of the Union.

---

[26] European Commission, *An Area of Freedom, Security and Justice Serving the Citizen*, COM(2009)262, 2.

[27] European Convention, *Final Report of Working Group X 'Freedom, Security and Justice'*, CONV 426/02, 2.

[28] European Commission, *Third Annual Report on Migration and Integration*, COM(2007)512, 3.

(i) Economic mercantilism

Policy towards non-EU nationals has been framed to a large extent by the economic benefits or costs these are perceived to entail. Attitudes depend as much on the economic circumstances of the time as on the skills of the individual. The 1950s was a period of labour market shortages across Europe, with workers being actively recruited from outside Europe to fill posts. This was reflected in the EU law of the time. Whilst only EU nationals enjoyed the right to freedom of establishment, it was initially envisaged that the right to move freely to work within the Union was available to all.[29] In similar vein, a significant Association Agreement with Turkey was signed in 1963.[30] It grants Turkish nationals the rights to renewal of their employment contract with their employer after one year's legal employment in the Union and the right to free access to the labour market after four years' legal employment. It also grants them a right to permanent residence after five years lawful residence in the Union. Finally, the Agreement grants rights to family reunion and, to those lawfully resident in the Union, the right to equal access to a number of social security benefits, most notably retirement pensions, invalidity benefits and unemployment benefits.[31] This Agreement, coupled with a number of implementing decisions, is still the central instrument governing the rights of the large number of Turkish nationals lawfully resident in the Union.

By the end of the 1960s, the European Union was moving from a period of labour shortages to one of unemployment. In 1968, legislation confining the right to work within the Union to EU nationals was enacted.[32] Increasingly, non-EU nationals were seen as threats to national labour markets and Member States developed restrictive immigration laws throughout the 1980s and 1990s to foreclose economic migration by non-EU nationals.[33] By the beginning of the millennium, there were signs that the pendulum was swinging back towards the opening of labour markets. A Commission Communication in 2000 suggested that economic migration could be a means of coping with falling populations within the Union, skills shortages and the lack of a sufficient workforce to pay for the increased cost of pensions.[34] The consequence has been a shift away from *restricting* economic migration to *managing* it, with the Union trying to cherry-pick those non-EU nationals who will benefit its economy, whilst preventing others from entering its markets.[35]

Treatment of non-EU nationals has thus become, in part, a human resource strategy. In case of asylum law where the law has to accommodate other concerns, most notably humanitarian ones, this is done through asylum legislation finding ways to manage the welfare and reception costs of asylum seekers.[36] In the case of economic migration, there is a tiered response.

---

[29] See Articles 52 and 48 of the EEC Treaty, respectively.

[30] [1973] OJ C113/2 and 1970 Protocol [1972] OJ L293/1.

[31] S. Peers, 'Towards Equality: Actual and Potential Rights of Third-Country Nationals in the European Union' (1996) 33 *CMLRev.* 7; E. Guild, *Immigration Law in the European Community* (The Hague, Kluwer, 2001) ch. 5.

[32] Directive 68/360/EEC [1968] OJ Spec. Ed. L257/13, Article 1. See the debates in W. Böhning, *The Migration of Workers in Britain and the EC* (Oxford, Oxford University Press/Institute for Race Relations, 1972); P. Oliver, 'Non-Community Nationals and the Treaty of Rome' (1985) 5 *YBEL* 57.

[33] On the evolution of immigration policies within the Member States, see C. Joppke, *The Challenge to the Nation State: Immigration in Western Europe and the United States* (Oxford, Oxford University Press, 1998); A. Geddes, *The Politics of Migration and Immigration in Europe* (London, Sage, 2003); A. Messina, *The Logics and Politics of Post-WW II Migration to Western Europe* (Cambridge, Cambridge University Press, Cambridge).

[34] European Commission, *On a Community Immigration Policy*, COM(2000)757.

[35] European Commission, *On an EU Approach to Managing Economic Migration*, COM(2004)811.

[36] This is examined more closely in section 6.

The question is treated in the first place as one of national political economy. That is to say, Member States have the entitlement to do what is generally right for their labour markets, economies and welfare costs. Responsibility for overall levels of migration is treated as a matter, therefore, of exclusive domestic concern.

Article 79(5) TFEU

This Article shall not affect the right of Member States to determine volumes of admission of third-country nationals coming from third countries to their territory in order to seek work, whether employed or self-employed.

In line with this the Commission withdrew a proposal for a Directive governing conditions of entry and residence of non-EU nationals for the purpose of paid employment and self-employment.[37] So-called reception capacities of labour markets and public services are treated as a matter for Member States.

However, this does not mean that there is no EU interest. Whilst overall levels of migration are seen as a national matter, the skills-set of the migrant labour force is seen as an EU matter. There is perhaps a concern that Member States do not secure cheap labour or highly sought after skills in a way that undercuts each other. With regard to the former, a 1996 Council Resolution was agreed setting out the 'Community preference' principle whereby:

Member States will consider requests for admission to their territories for the purpose of employment only where vacancies in a Member State cannot be filled by national and Community manpower or by non-Community manpower lawfully resident on a permanent basis in that Member State and already forming part of the Member State's regular labour market.[38]

With regard to highly qualified workers, the Commission proposed a Directive facilitating entrance to the Union for highly qualified workers. These will be people who hold higher education qualifications or at least three years of equivalent professional experience and have been offered a job by an EU employer. For such individuals, the doctrine of Community preference is not applied, and entry is to be facilitated. The rationale is that the Union does not attract as many high-skills migrants as the United States or Canada. The numbers are substantial. In 2003, for the EU-15 there were about 74,000 individuals entering the Union every year.[39]

There is thus a dual track system. For so-called low-skills workers, a policy of Fortress Europe is adopted. It is all but impossible to secure economic migration. The opposite is the case for those seen as high-skills. For these the intention is to make the Union as attractive a place as possible.[40]

---

[37] The original proposal is COM(2001)386. The withdrawal is to be found at [2006] OJ C64/8.

[38] Council Resolution on limitation on admission of third-country nationals to the territory of the Member States for employment [1996] OJ C274/3.

[39] The proposal and rationale is set out in European Commission, Proposal for a Directive on the conditions of entry and residence of third-country nationals for the purposes of highly qualified employment, COM(2007)637. It was agreed by the Council in March 2009 but is not yet adopted as a Directive: EU Council, Council Directive on the conditions of entry and residence of third-country nationals for the purposes of highly qualified employment, Council Doc. 17426/08, 18 March 2009.

[40] It is summarised in EU Council, *European Pact on Immigration and Asylum*, Council Doc. 13440/08, 5–7.

(ii) National security and national sovereignty

Migration by non-EU nationals has come to be seen as threatening at two levels. At a bureaucratic level, there has been a concern with 'dangerous foreigners', most notably those engaged in crime and terrorism. At a more elemental, ethno-cultural level, the 'securitisation' of migration has been concerned with the threat it is perceived to pose to established ideas of societal identity and integrity.[41] The perceived threat, in both cases, is to an idea of security that is national in nature and which has to be regulated by the Member States. Article 4(2) TEU therefore states that national security is to be the sole responsibility of the Member States. This is reaffirmed, more specifically, by Article 72 TFEU, with regard to the competences set out in the AFSJ.

> **Article 72 TFEU**
>
> This Title shall not affect the exercise of the responsibilities incumbent upon Member States with regard to the maintenance of law and order and the safeguarding of internal security.

Yet, other than as a claim to non-interference by the Union, how does this Article shape Union competences in respect of non-EU nationals?

(a) Frontiers as national markers

There is a concern that Member States retain control over national frontiers when it comes to policing security. Borders are seen as important cultural markets of sovereignty, so there is provision that the geographical demarcation of their borders not be affected by EU immigration policy.[42] They are also seen as important policing points. This concern is most explicit in the case of the United Kingdom and Ireland for whom a Protocol has been adopted allowing them a general power to retain frontier controls.[43] Yet, even for the other states who claim to have abolished internal frontier controls an exception is made in the case of security. This is now set out in the Community Borders Code.[44]

> **Article 21**
>
> The abolition of border control at internal borders shall not affect:
>
> (a) the exercise of police powers by the competent authorities of the Member States under national law, insofar as the exercise of those powers does not have an effect equivalent to border checks; that shall also apply in border areas. Within the meaning of the first sentence, the exercise of police powers may not, in particular, be considered equivalent to the exercise of border checks when the police measures:

---

[41] M. Heisler and Z. Layton-Henry, 'Migration and the Links Between Social and Societal Security' in O. Waever (ed.), *Identity, Migration and the New Security Agenda* (London, Pinter, 1993); J. Huysmans, 'The European Union and the Securitization of Migration' (2000) 38 *JCMS* 751; A. Triandafyllidou, *Immigrants and National Identity in Europe* (London, Routledge, 2001).

[42] Article 77(4) TFEU.

[43] See above n. 19.

[44] Regulation 562/2006/EC establishing a Community Code on the rules governing the movement of persons across borders (Community Borders Code) [2006] OJ L105/1.

(i) do not have border control as an objective,

(ii) are based on general police information and experience regarding possible threats to public security and aim, in particular, to combat cross-border crime,

(iii) are devised and executed in a manner clearly distinct from systematic checks on persons at the external borders,

(iv) are carried out on the basis of spot-checks;

(b) security checks on persons carried out at ports and airports by the competent authorities under the law of each Member State, by port or airport officials or carriers, provided that such checks are also carried out on persons travelling within a Member State;

(c) the possibility for a Member State to provide by law for an obligation to hold or carry papers and documents.

Thus, even internal frontier points within the Schengen zone are to remain as important points of policing. Frontier policing is allowed, in other words, provided it does not call itself a border check.

(b) The criminalisation of migration

The second dimension to this theme of national security is the establishment of links between the policing of migration and the policing of crime. As Anderson has indicated, this has a number of elements. There is an ideological dimension in which migration is placed alongside crime and terrorism as part of an 'internal security' continuum. There is also an institutional dimension in which cooperation between law-enforcement and migration agencies is strengthened, and, in some instances, merged. There is finally the pseudo-criminalisation of the migrant. She is to be policed in similar ways to criminal suspects and, although not herself a criminal, to be subject to similar types of measures as criminals.

M. Anderson et al., Policing the European Union (Oxford, Clarendon Press, 1995) 165–6

There are three modes in which internal security concerns have become amalgamated with immigration and asylum. The first of these is ideological merging: law enforcement agencies in Europe started to redefine internal security threats. The old external threat of communism was replaced by an external threat established by mass immigration, organized crime, and imported terrorism, the penetration of which would, like the old threat, lead to the destabilization of 'well-balanced' western societies. The second component – instrumental merging – is to be found in the range of instruments which are employed against illegal immigration. There is an increase in the use of intelligence, of 'high tec' detection equipment, and of concerted proactive investigation generally by all agencies involved in immigration control. The EU Ministers of Justice and Interior have negotiated the introduction of joint compensatory measures and instruments of control. Striking examples are international information systems (such as the SIS, and in the future, the EIS), fingerprint systems, carrier sanctions and visa requirements. Law enforcement officials will have on-line access to these international information systems. These instruments used for migration and asylum controls will simultaneously be used for crime control. The third component is institutional merging: institutions engaged in international police co-operation and immigration, such as Trevi and the Ad Hoc Group on Immigration are – as a consequence of the Treaty on European Union – reconstituted and merged into the K4 Co-ordinating Committee.

Indeed, the third pillar of TEU may be seen as the culmination of the integration between international law enforcement concerns and concerns about migratory movements and asylum seekers.

The creation of the security continuum is also apparent in a narrower organisational sense. The association between organised crime and ethnic groups encourages a linking of law enforcement agencies: co-operation between ordinary police forces, immigration services, customs and intelligence agencies, therefore, is based on and reinforces the continuum which runs from terrorism to immigration, and from ordinary crime to political and subversive crime. In most European countries, immigration control is a shared responsibility of a variety of law enforcement agencies. Although this does not result in a merging of institutions, close relationships must be maintained on a daily basis. Immigration services, customs services and border control agencies, and regular police forces are all involved in certain stages of immigration control. Police services have assumed an expanding role in this field. In addition to enforcing the criminal law against illegal and clandestine immigrants, police officers also tend to perform the administrative function of registration, and to play a co-operative role alongside the immigration service in the enforcement of immigration law in areas such as housing and employment. But even where the police are entrusted with administrative functions, they often retain a level of discretion normally associated with the policing function.

Of the different dimensions mentioned by Anderson, the ideological dimension takes place through the establishment of the AFSJ which places migration and asylum alongside policing and criminal justice, and insists they be developed in complementary manners. The institutional dimension is well-established. In 1986, the TREVI group, a group of national civil servants set up in 1975 initially to discuss terrorism and organised crime, established an ad hoc group to consider migration.[45] When the Maastricht Treaty brought policing and immigration and asylum within the Union framework, it was a single Committee, the K3 Committee, that considered both. This is perpetuated and reinforced by Lisbon with the establishment of an internal security committee that is to consider, inter alia, immigration and asylum.

Article 71 TFEU

A standing committee shall be set up within the Council in order to ensure that operational cooperation on internal security is promoted and strengthened within the Union. Without prejudice to Article 240, it shall facilitate coordination of the action of Member States' competent authorities. Representatives of the bodies, offices and agencies of the Union concerned may be involved in the proceedings of this committee. The European Parliament and national parliaments shall be kept informed of the proceedings.[46]

Finally, the pseudo-criminalisation of the migrant takes many forms. It is particularly acute in the field of asylum and illegally staying non-EU nationals.[47] The central machinery is the development of large information databases on non-EU nationals. The longest

---

[45] J. Benyon *et al.*, *Police Cooperation in Europe: An Investigation* (Leicester, Centre for Study of Public Order, 1993) 162.

[46] Article 240 TFEU is the provision which provides for the establishment of COREPER. See pp. 74–5.

[47] On the detention of asylum seekers see pp. 524–5.

established in EU law is the EURODAC Regulation. This was established following concerns about asylum seekers subverting the regime by illegally crossing from one Member State to another and making multiple applications under different identities. It provides a central database which stores the identities of all individuals seeking asylum within the Union. Member States must fingerprint all asylum seekers of 14 years or over entering the Union.[48] They must transfer this data to a Central Unit with the asylum seeker's Member State of origin, the place and date of the application, and the reference number used by the Member State of entry. Although the Regulation provides for the storage of the same data for those irregularly staying or crossing into the Union,[49] its use is mainly for asylum. In 2008, 357,421 'successful transactions' submitting data were made. Of these, 211,552 related to asylum seekers and the remainder related to individuals trying to enter the Union irregularly and/or staying there irregularly.[50]

More wide-ranging is the 'Schengen Information System' (SIS). This is a databank established under the Schengen Convention of people and objects who may pose a threat to security.[51] It includes details of all non-EU nationals who have been refused entry to or deported from the Union or are considered to be a security risk.[52] For such persons an 'alert' is entered on the system notifying other Member States. Individuals for whom an alert has been issued will normally be refused a visa or entry to the Union. On 30 January 2008, 81 per cent of the individuals were non-EU nationals.[53] In 2006, legislative provision was made for a second generation database (Schengen Information System II).[54] This is not yet operational but will be a more powerful system that allows for the inclusion of biometric data with respect to individuals (e.g. data identifying the physical features of individuals, such as photographs, fingerprints, DNA profiles or retina scans).

The move to generalised databases with considerable information on all non-EU nationals was taken a step further forward with the establishment of the Visa Information System. Not yet operational, it will contain the fingerprints, travel document details and photographs of all persons who have applied for a short-term visa to enter the Union. It will also include any details of refusal or revocation of a visa.[55] This database will dwarf the other two. It is estimated by the Commission that about 13 million short-term visas are issued annually by the Schengen zone.[56]

---

[48] Regulation 2725/2000/EC concerning the establishment of 'EURODAC' for the comparison of fingerprints for the effective application of the Dublin Convention [2000] OJ L316/1, article 4. See also Regulation 407/2002/EC laying down certain rules to implement Regulation 2725/2000 concerning the establishment of 'Eurodac' [2002] OJ L62/1. Both the United Kingdom and Ireland have opted in to this Regulation.

[49] Regulation 2725/2000/EC, Articles 8 and 11.

[50] European Commission, *Annual Report on the Activities of the EURODAC Central Unit*, COM(2009)494.

[51] Schengen Implementing Convention, Articles 92–119. The United Kingdom and Ireland participate in the system. Decision 2000/365/EC concerning the request of the United Kingdom to take part in some of the provisions of the Schengen acquis [2000] OJ L131/43; Decision 2002/192/EC concerning Ireland's request to take part in some of the provisions of the Schengen acquis [2002] OJ L64/20.

[52] Schengen Implementing Convention, Article 96.

[53] EU Council, SIS Database Statistics at 1 January 2008, Council Doc. 30 January 2008.

[54] Regulation 1987/2006/EC on the establishment, operation and use of the second generation Schengen Information System (SIS II) [2006] OJ L381/4.

[55] Regulation 767/2008/EC concerning the Visa Information System (VIS) and the exchange of data between Member States on short-stay visas ('VIS Regulation') [2008] OJ 2008 L218/60. Ireland and the United Kingdom cannot participate in it.

[56] See http://ec.europa.eu/justice_home/fsj/freetravel/visa/fsj_freetravel_visa_en.htm (accessed 10 November 2009).

It is a measure of how things have developed that the EURODAC model is increasingly one that is being generalised for non-EU nationals. At the time, however, EURODAC was criticised for criminalising the asylum seeker.[57] It was also criticised on data protection grounds. Typically, data can only be stored with respect to an individual if it is for specified, explicit and legitimate purposes and the data retained is not excessive in relation to the purposes for which it is collected.[58] Neither of these concerns were addressed in EURODAC.[59]

Commission proposals to amend the EURODAC Regulation are perhaps an indication of future developments. In the Visa Information System, law-enforcement agencies may have access to individual data if there reasonable grounds to consider that this will substantially contribute to the prevention, detection or investigation of terrorist offences and of other serious criminal offences.[60] The Commission has taken this further with EURODAC. It wishes to make the data available on EURODAC to all law-enforcement and policing agencies within the Union irrespective of any link with crime.[61] If there is a presumption in favour of privacy for EU citizens, the reverse seems to be increasingly true with regard to non-EU nationals. Their privacy is seen as something threatening and dangerous, with surveillance increasingly the name of the game with them.

(c) The external frontier

The third dimension to this concern with protection of national sovereignty and national security is the concern that the relaxing of internal frontier controls must be compensated through the strengthening of the external Union frontier. The central legal instrument regulating this is the Community Borders Code.[62] This imposes duties on states only to let entry into their territories through designated external border points,[63] to carry out border checks at those points,[64] and to stamp systematically the entry and exit of non-EU nationals from their territories.[65] They are also under duties to carry out border surveillance and to put aside appropriate resources for this.[66] To this end, a Union agency, Frontex, was established in 2004 to assist and coordinate operational cooperation between Member States in the field of border control.[67]

In some ways, the most important provision is article 5 of the Community Borders Code. Although nominally for short-stay visitors, it acts as the residual category for non-EU nationals who do not otherwise have a recognised status. In principle, anybody not meeting the conditions below should be refused entry.[68]

---

[57] E. Brouwer, 'Eurodac: Its Limitations and Temptations' (2002) 4 *EJML* 231.

[58] Directive 95/46/EC on the protection of individuals with regard to the processing of personal data and on the free movement of such data [1995] OJ L281/31, Article 6(1).

[59] E. Guild, 'Seeking Asylum: Storm Clouds Between International Commitments and EU Legislative Measures' (2004) 29 *ELRev.* 198, 209–10.

[60] Regulation 767/2008/EC, Article 3(1).

[61] European Commission, Proposal for a Council Decision on requesting comparisons with Eurodac data by Member States' law enforcement authorities and Europol for law enforcement purposes, COM(2009)344 final.

[62] Community Borders Code, above n. 44. Ireland and the United Kingdom do not participate.

[63] *Ibid.* Article 4.

[64] *Ibid.* Article 7.

[65] *Ibid.* Article 10.

[66] *Ibid.* Articles 12 and 14.

[67] Regulation 2007/2004/EC establishing a European Agency for the management of operational cooperation at the external borders of the Member States of the European Union [2004] OJ 2004 L349/1 as amended by Regulation 863/2007 establishing a mechanism for the creation of Rapid Border Intervention Teams [2007] OJ L199/30.

[68] Community Borders Code, article 13. There are a few limited exceptions in article 5(4) for transit, humanitarian reasons or where visas may be issued at a border.

Community Borders Code, article 5(1)

For stays not exceeding three months per six-month period, the entry conditions for third-country nationals shall be the following:

(a) they are in possession of a valid travel document or documents authorising them to cross the border;

(b) they are in possession of a valid visa, if required ... except where they hold a valid residence permit;

(c) they justify the purpose and conditions of the intended stay, and they have sufficient means of subsistence, both for the duration of the intended stay and for the return to their country of origin or transit to a third country into which they are certain to be admitted, or are in a position to acquire such means lawfully;

(d) they are not persons for whom an alert has been issued in the SIS for the purposes of refusing entry;

(e) they are not considered to be a threat to public policy, internal security, public health or the international relations of any of the Member States, in particular where no alert has been issued in Member States' national databases for the purposes of refusing entry on the same grounds.

There are two points of immediate note. First, in article 5(1)(d) is the legal power of the alert in the Schengen Information System. It requires that the person in question not be admitted. There is at the moment no way of challenging whether the alert has been fairly issued. The second is the discretion granted to the border guard. By virtue of article 5(1)(c), they can test the veracity of the non-EU national's tale and whether they have sufficient means. Article 5(1)(e) gives them a series of further grounds for refusing entry even where the non-EU national meets the formal conditions.[69]

Arguably, the most significant feature is the seemingly arcane point in article 5(1)(b) that the non-EU national have a valid visa. The Union has a list of states whose nationals require short-term visas to enter the Union and the list is considerable.[70] It includes all states who are seen as a significant source of economic migration, irregular migration, political radicalism and asylum seekers.[71] For all non-EU nationals falling within this category, article 5(1)(b) transfers decision-making over entry away from the physical Union frontier to two other points, both usually within the non-EU national's state of origin.

The first is the EU Member State's consular office in the state where the non-EU national applies for the visa. It is there that her case for entering the Union is considered in most depth at the time of deciding whether to grant her a visa. The test is set out in article 21 of Regulation 810/2009/EC.[72]

---

[69] On this discretion see S. Peers, *Justice and Home Affairs Law* (2nd edn, Oxford, Oxford University Press, 2006) 149–50.

[70] Regulation 539/2001/EC listing the third countries whose nationals must be in possession of visas when crossing the external borders and those whose nationals are exempt from that requirement, [2001] OJ L81/1.

[71] The Regulation refers to criteria including 'illegal immigration, public policy and security, and to the European Union's external relations with third countries'. *Ibid.* Preamble, para. 5. For discussion see Peers, above n. 69, 156–60. More broadly on this, see A. Meloni, 'The Community Code on Visas: Harmonisation at Last?' (2009) 34 *ELRev.* 671.

[72] Regulation 810/2009/EC establishing a Community Code on Visas [2009] OJ L243/1.

> **Regulation 810/2009/EC, article 21(1)**
>
> In the examination of an application for a uniform visa, it shall be ascertained whether the applicant fulfils the entry conditions set out in Article 5(1)(a), (c), (d) and (e) of the Schengen Borders Code, and particular consideration shall be given to assessing whether the applicant presents a risk of illegal immigration or a risk to the security of the Member States and whether the applicant intends to leave the territory of the Member States before the expiry of the visa applied for.

This test is significantly different from that in article 5 of the Community Borders Code. It thereby sets out the function of the visa regime extremely clearly, which is to apply more severe criteria away from the frontiers to states whose nationals are seen as a particular threat. The criteria additional to those in the Community Borders Code are those of illegal migration and overstaying. It also applies a different threshold. Whilst the border officer must consider that the migrant threatens security, the consular officer must only consider whether she presents a risk to security or of irregular migration. This is an extremely nebulous test. The risk does not need to be quantified and can only be marginal. Notwithstanding that there is a right to appeal,[73] the matter appears to be still entirely one of official discretion.

If the central decision for entry for visa holders is applied away from the frontiers using different parameters, it is also policed away from the frontiers. This is because of the Carriers Sanctions Directive.[74] This imposes sanctions on carriers (whether transporting people by air, land or sea) for bringing people to Union frontiers without proper travel documents. Penalties are a minimum of €3,000 for each case.[75] There is also an obligation on the carrier to take responsibility for the migrant if they are refused entry, notwithstanding that they may have the right travel documents. In such circumstances, the carrier is responsible for the costs of return and for returning the migrant as soon as possible, if necessary with another carrier.[76] This leads to carriers engaging in two tasks before they will admit a migrant on board their vessel. They will, first, check that they have the necessary travel documents and visas. Secondly, they will carry out their own assessment as to the risk of refusal of entry. The policing role of the carrier as a long arm of the immigration authorities is completed by its having to communicate information about passengers, the names, travel documents and dates of birth, to the latter before the end of check-in in the State of departure.[77]

The carrier's decision on whether to admit a migrant to their vessel is likely to be highly cautious, as the carrier will not want to risk having to bear the costs of return. There is, of course, no accountability for it in EU law as the terms of the contract between the carrier and migrant are that of a private transaction between two parties in a non-EU state. This outsourcing of immigration has been criticised, particularly in fields where the Union has humanitarian responsibilities. Visa requirements are imposed on states which act as sources of large numbers of asylum seekers. The nature of asylum is that it will often be impossible for the asylum seeker

---

[73] *Ibid.* article 32(3).
[74] Directive 2001/51/EC supplementing the provisions of Article 26 of the Convention implementing the Schengen Agreement of 14 June 1985 [2001] OJ L187/45. Ireland and the United Kingdom do participate in this Directive.
[75] *Ibid.* Article 4.
[76] *Ibid.* Articles 2 and 3.
[77] Directive 2004/82/EC on the obligation of carriers to communicate passenger data [2004] OJ L261/24, article 3.

to obtain a visa and therefore lawfully gain access to the carrier. Incentives are thereby reduced for asylum seekers to find ways around these provisions, with the consequence that those arriving at the Union's external frontiers are likely to be the more resourceful and better financed rather than necessarily the most needy.[78]

(iii) Humanitarianism

Competing against the attitudes above is a powerful discourse of fundamental rights. This emphasises the universalism of the human condition and the arbitrariness of distinguishing between individuals on grounds of nationality.[79] It presses for lenient immigration policies and the granting of more extensive rights to non-EU nationals once they are on the territory of the Union. Despite its being reported in a less strident manner than opposing views, this perspective has surprising force with policy-makers, possibly because its advocates, NGOs and big business, tend to be forces capable of organising themselves well within the political decision-making and judicial processes.[80]

This humanitarian impulse is set out most strongly in Article 67(1) TFEU which states that the AFSJ must respect fundamental rights. There are three rights, in particular, that are particularly pertinent in this field.

The first is that of non-refoulement. Article 78(1) TFEU states that the Union's asylum and refugee policy must comply with this principle. It is set out in Article 33(1) of the 1951 Geneva Convention on Refugees:

> No Contracting State shall expel or return ('refouler') a refugee in any manner whatsoever to the frontiers of territories where his life or freedom would be threatened on account of his race, religion, nationality, membership of a particular social group or political opinion.

Although the provision only refers to refugees, it also applies to asylum seekers who, until a decision has been taken on their status, are to be regarded as potential refugees.[81]

The right is assumed to have, at least, three elements.[82] First, as it applies to anybody claiming to have a well-founded fear that they will be subject to persecution in their country of origin, Member States are not permitted to turn people away from their territory without assessing the veracity of the claim. Secondly, Member States must carry out an individual assessment of each case, observing requirements of due process.[83] Finally, the individual may neither be transferred to unsafe territories nor be transferred to any state which may subsequently return her to a territory in which she may be at risk. This last principle applies not just to transfers to

---

[78] N. El-Enany, 'Who is the New European Refugee?' (2008) 33 *ELRev.* 313.

[79] A fine survey of the arguments is provided in V. Bader, 'The Ethics of Immigration' (2005) 12 *Constellations* 331.

[80] G. Freeman, 'Modes of Immigration Politics in Liberal States' (1995) 29 *International Migration Review* 881. On this logic becoming more predominant within the European Union, see G. Sasse, 'Securitization or Securing Rights? Exploring the Conceptual Foundations of Policies towards Minorities and Migrants in Europe' (2005) 43 *JCMS* 673.

[81] It is thus set out as a right to asylum in Article 18 EUCFR. It is also acknowledged in Directive 2005/85/EC on minimum standards on procedures in Member States for granting and withdrawing refugee status [2005] OJ L326/13, article 20(2).

[82] E. Lauterpacht and D. Bethlehem, 'The Scope and Content of the Principle of Non-Refoulement' in E. Feller *et al.* (eds.), *Refugee Protection in International Law: UNHCR's Global Consultations on International Protection* (Cambridge, Cambridge University Press, 2003) 78–177.

[83] Although see Directive 2005/85/EC on minimum standards on procedures in Member States for granting and withdrawing refugee status, articles 25–7 [2005] OJ L326/13.

territories outside the European Union, but also to transfers to other Member States within the European Union. In *Adan*,[84] Adan, a Somali, and Aitseguer, an Algerian, both sought asylum in the United Kingdom. In both cases, the threat to their lives came not from a government, but from private parties. In the case of Adan, he had been threatened by a rival clan. The threat to Aitseguer was from the Groupe Islamique Armé, a radical Muslim group. The Home Office argued that they should be deported to Germany and France respectively. These were the states of entry into the European Union and were thus, in principle, responsible for considering the applications. Neither France nor Germany, however, recognised persecution by private parties as justifying a claim to refugee status, whereas the United Kingdom did. The House of Lords considered that deportation to Germany or France would be in violation of the principle of non-refoulement, as the Convention protected those persecuted by private parties, and thus individuals should not be returned to Member States where it was known that these might send individuals back to their country of origin to face such persecution.

The second fundamental right of note is the right to respect for family life. This is set out in Article 8 ECHR.[85]

Article 8 ECHR

1. Everyone has the right to respect for his private and family life, his home and his correspondence.
2. There shall be no interference by a public authority with the exercise of this right except such as is in accordance with the law and is necessary in a democratic society in the interests of national security, public safety or the economic well-being of the country, for the prevention of disorder or crime, for the protection of health or morals, or for the protection of the rights and freedoms of others.

Activities compromising this right are those leading to the break-up of an existing family by preventing members having regular contacts with each other.[86] This could either be because some members of the family are allowed into the Member State whilst others are not, or because, in cases of asylum, families are detained in different parts of the country. The European Court of Human Rights has said that the right to respect for family life does not necessarily give one family member the right to join others living in a Member State. The key question is whether that state is the only place in which the family could be united.[87] Even where this is the case, Member States might still be able to invoke the exception in Article 8(2) ECHR, which allows for a restriction on the right to be justified in the case of a pressing social need. This can be economic wellbeing, prevention of crime or national security. However, any restriction must be proportionate. This requires a number of factors to be weighed against the social need in question. These include the difficulties likely to be encountered by the family in returning to the state of origin, the time spent in the Member State in question, the family situation and matters such as the length of marriage and the position of any children involved.[88]

---

[84] *R v Secretary of State for the Home Department, ex parte Adan* [2001] 2 AC 477.
[85] See also Article 7 EUCFR, which reiterates this.
[86] *Berrehab v The Netherlands* (10730/84) [1988] ECHR 14.
[87] *Gül v Switzerland* (23218/94) [1996] ECHR 5.
[88] *Amrollahi v Denmark* (56811/00), Judgment of 11 July 2002.

The final right to crop up frequently in immigration and asylum cases is the right not to be subjected to inhuman and degrading treatment, set out in Article 3 ECHR:[89]

No one shall be subjected to torture or to inhuman or degrading treatment or punishment.

This restricts the type of treatment that Member States can inflict on non-EU nationals in their care. It also limits expulsions to third states. The European Court of Human Rights has held that Member States who expel an individual to be tortured in a third state are as responsible for that torture as the perpetrating state.[90] It also prohibits any expulsion to a state where an individual will not be tortured but will undergo considerable suffering. A decision by the British government to deport a patient who was terminally ill with AIDS back to St Kitts, which had no facilities to treat him in the last stages of his life, was held, therefore, to violate Article 3, as it both hastened his death and heightened his suffering.[91]

These humanitarian norms inform EU legislation in three fields, in particular. First, they form the basis for Article 78 TFEU, and for granting protection to those suffering human rights abuses in their country of origin. EU law has thus developed a gamut of different types of law to address these needs. These include legislation on asylum, refugee protection, temporary protection and subsidiary protection. To be sure, these laws can be subject to much criticism but their very presence can only be explained by a concern about human need. Secondly, there is a concern with family rights. Certain non-EU relatives of EU citizens are given rights to reside, work and enjoy social benefits in other Member States with the latter.[92] Provision is also made for the families of Turkish nationals exercising their rights under the EC–Turkey Association Agreement to join the latter and for their children to have the same access to schools as a state's own nationals.[93] Finally, in 2004 a Directive was adopted granting the right for certain family members of non-EU nationals lawfully resident in the Union to join them.[94] The third group is non-EU nationals who have been lawfully resident in the Union for some period of time. EU policy is to seek to integrate these into EU society as much as possible and approximate their rights to those of EU citizens.

Humanitarian norms have also informed the progressive liberalisation of a number of Member State practices. Dual nationality is permitted in many states with the result that many individuals with only limited connections with the European Union have the right to EU nationality and the benefits of EU citizenship. Even more strikingly, Member States increasingly give similar civil, social, economic and, sometimes, political rights to non-EU nationals lawfully resident on their territories as they give to their own citizens.[95]

The influence of humanitarian norms will probably be felt most keenly within the judiciary. They grant individual entitlements that will allow Union and national measures to be struck

---

[89] This is repeated verbatim in Article 4 EUCFR.

[90] *Soering* v *United Kingdom* (14038/88) [1989] ECHR 14. This responsibility is also spelt out in Article 3(1) of the 1984 UN Convention Against Torture or other Cruel, Inhuman or Degrading Treatment, 1465 UNTS 113.

[91] *D* v *United Kingdom* (30240/96) [1997] ECHR 25.

[92] Directive 2004/38/EC on the right of citizens of the Union and their family members to move and reside freely within the territory of the Member States [2004] OJ L158/77. This is discussed at pp. …

[93] Articles 7 and 9 of Decision 1/80 of the EC-Turkey Association Council. This can be found at EC Council, *EEC-Turkey Association Agreement and Protocols and Other Basic Texts* (Luxembourg, Office for Official Publications of the European Communities, 1992).

[94] See pp. 464–5.

[95] Y. Soysal, *Limits of Citizenship: Migrants and Postnational Membership in Europe* (Chicago, Chicago University Press, 1994) 22–8 and ch. 7.

down if they are violated. Much will depend, therefore, on how the Court of Justice and national courts interpret them.[96] In this regard, there may be a pressure on the courts to give relatively passive interpretations. In Chapter 6, we saw how in the *Family Reunification* judgment, the Court of Justice was willing to sanction three highly illiberal requirements which appeared to compromise the right to respect for family life.[97] Where the Court gives liberal judgments, there is also a strong danger of powerful political reactions. In *Metock*, the Court held that EU citizens residing in another Member State had a right to marry non-EU nationals granted asylum there.[98] The Danish government responded by asking for an amendment to the EU legislation in question and by seeking to impose a new criterion before non-Danish EU citizens could marry non-EU nationals in Denmark: namely that the former had to show genuine and effective residence in Denmark.[99] These measures were intended not just to counter the judgment but also as a shot across the bows of the Court of Justice not to develop that case law.

(iv) European solidarity

The final theme in this field is that of burden-sharing. Member States should share the costs for managing this policy and support should be offered to those states who struggle to find the resources to meet their obligations in this field.

Article 80(1) TFEU

The policies of the Union set out in this Chapter and their implementation shall be governed by the principle of solidarity and fair sharing of responsibility, including its financial implications, between the Member States. Whenever necessary, the acts of the Union adopted pursuant to this Chapter shall contain appropriate measures to give effect to this principle.

This principle has led to the establishment of a number of common funds to help states manage the costs of receiving refugees, returning non-EU nationals and policing their external frontiers.[100] Beyond this, EU law has been more concerned with administrative managerialism and efficient management of migration flows than distribution between the states, with a concern above all to channel and limit the number of applications and attempts a non-EU national can make to enter the Union. This policy is particularly apparent in two fields: visas and asylum.

---

[96] On the scope of national and EU institutions' fundamental rights responsibilities, see pp. 248–56.

[97] These were that a child aged 12 years or above arriving independently could be subject to an integration test before joining her family; the waiving of a right to family reunification for children aged 15 years old; and a requirement that non-EU nationals be lawfully resident for two years in their territories before their families join them. Case C-540/03 *Parliament* v *Council (family reunification)* [2006] ECR I-5769.

[98] Case C-127/08 *Metock* [2008] ECR I-6241.

[99] For a summary, see www.nyidanmark.dk/en-us/news/news/integrationsministeriet/2008/september (accessed 10 November 2009).

[100] Decision 573/2007/EC establishing the European Refugee Fund [2007] OJ L144/1; Decision 574/2007/EC establishing the External Borders Fund [2007] OJ L144/22; Decision 575/2007/EC establishing a European Return Fund [2007] OJ L144/45.

In the field of visas, the Community Code for Visas establishes the idea of a uniform visa. If a non-EU national is granted a visa, the presumption is that this does not just enable her to present herself at the frontiers of the state that issued it but that it is valid for all the Schengen states.[101] The attractiveness of this for the non-EU national is offset by an entitlement, in principle, only to a single state considering her application. The state competent for considering her application is determined by article 5 of the Community Borders Code.

Article 5(1)

The Member State competent for examining and deciding on an application for a uniform visa shall be:
(a) the Member State whose territory constitutes the sole destination of the visit(s);
(b) if the visit includes more than one destination, the Member State whose territory constitutes the main destination of the visit(s) in terms of the length or purpose of stay; or
(c) if no main destination can be determined, the Member State whose external border the applicant intends to cross in order to enter the territory of the Member States.

The principle – that of destination or entry – for allocating which state should consider the application is uncontroversial. More arguable is the implicit principle of negative mutual recognition in the Code. Any refusal is entered on the Visa Information System.[102] The implication is that other authorities may look at it and use it as a basis for refusal of subsequent applications. Given the lack of effective controls on consideration of visa applications, there is thus a danger of a snowball effect whereby a non-EU national's subsequent application is refused on the basis of a (possibly mistaken) earlier assessment. A further application is then refused on the grounds that she has been refused twice, and so on.

The system set up for visas merely follows the trajectory established for asylum, which is governed by Regulation 343/2003/EC (the so-called 'Dublin Regulation').[103] Under this, the European Union has set up a one-stop-shop whereby any asylum seeker may make one single application for asylum.

Regulation 343/2003/EC, article 3

1. Member States shall examine the application of any third country national who applies at the border or in their territory to any one of them for asylum. The application shall be examined by a single Member State, which shall be the one which the criteria set out in Chapter III indicate is responsible.
2. By way of derogation from paragraph 1, each Member State may examine an application for asylum lodged with it by a third-country national, even if such examination is not its responsibility under the criteria laid down in this Regulation. In such an event, that Member State shall become the Member State responsible within the meaning of this Regulation and shall assume the obligations associated with that responsibility...

---

[101] Regulation 810/2009/EC, articles 2(2), (3), 25.
[102] *Ibid.*, article 32(5).
[103] Regulation 343/20003/EC establishing the criteria and mechanisms for determining the Member State responsible for examining an asylum application lodged in one of the Member States by a third-country national [2003] OJ L50/1. Both the United Kingdom and Ireland have opted in to this Regulation.

Chapter III of the Regulation sets out the hierarchy of criteria for the allocation of responsibilities. The criteria are bedevilled by exceptions but, broadly speaking, the criteria for allocating the state which considers the asylum seeker are that any Member State in which a family member is resident will take priority; then, any state that has issued a residence permit or visa to the applicant or failing that has waived the visa requirement for the applicant; thirdly, any state that the applicant has irregularly entered. Only if all these are exhausted will it be the state where the asylum seeker lodged the application.[104]

If the criteria are intended to establish some sort of equity between Member States by sharing the burden of asylum applications between them, they have failed. The number of transfers from one Member State to another under these criteria is, as a proportion of the total number of applications to the Union, trivial.[105] The overwhelming majority of the cases are heard, therefore, in the state in which the asylum seeker makes the application. Sweden has had over 100 times the number of cases per capita of population than Denmark or Portugal, and in the case of Malta it is over 300 times more cases per capita than those states.[106] As the choice of the asylum seeker is the paramount factor governing where the case is heard, Neumayer has suggested that the elements influencing this choice (the presence of ethnic or national communities, geographical proximity, common language, hostility towards foreigners and generosity of welfare provisions) should have been the central determinants in shaping asylum flows into the Union.[107]

The Regulation has been more successful in institutionalising the principle of negative mutual recognition.[108] Whilst Member States are not bound to recognise positive decisions by other Member State authorities granting refugee status under the 'one-stop-shop' principle, they are required to recognise decisions by other national authorities denying that status to asylum seekers. In doing this, they recognise the capacity of other Member States to consider the claims of asylum seekers in an equivalent manner, notwithstanding that these may have used different tests and procedures. This has, thus, been heavily criticised by a number of commentators, who observe that there is a breach of the principle of non-refoulement if a Member State sends an asylum seeker to another state which has a narrower interpretation of refugee status than its own, and which it knows is likely to return the asylum seeker to her country of origin.[109]

---

[104] *Ibid.*, articles 6–13.

[105] The Commission found that by mid-2006, only 16,842 transfers had been made out of just over 657,000 asylum applications. European Commission, *Report on the Evaluation of the Dublin System*, COM(2007)299, 4.

[106] Eurostat, *Asylum Applicants and Decisions on Asylum Applications in Q1 2009* (Luxembourg, Office for Official Publications of the European Communities, 2009) 2.

[107] E. Neumayer, 'Asylum Destination Choice: What Makes Some West European Countries More Attractive than Others' (2004) 5 *EUP* 155.

[108] There is a proposal to extend the principles to those seeking subsidiary protection. European Commission, Proposal for a Regulation establishing the criteria and mechanisms for determining the Member State responsible for examining an application for international protection lodged in one of the Member States by a third-country national or a stateless person, COM(2008)820, article 2(b).

[109] A. Hurwitz, 'The 1990 Dublin Convention: A Comprehensive Assessment' (1999) 11 *IJRL* 646; R. Marx, 'Adjusting the Dublin Convention: New Approaches to Member State Responsibility for Asylum Applications' (2001) 3 *EJML* 7; G. Noll, 'Formalism v Empiricism. Some Reflections on the Dublin Convention on the Occasion of Recent European Case Law' (2001) 70 *NJIL* 161.

4 UNWELCOME NON-EU NATIONALS: THE RETURNS DIRECTIVE

Non-EU nationals may enjoy a right to enter or reside in the European Union by virtue of having acquired a particular status. They may be long-term residents, benefiting from humanitarian protection or family members of an EU citizen. These categories are quite limited. For other non-EU nationals, the conditions of entry into the Union continue to bind them during their stay in the Union. The basis for this lies in article 6 of Directive 2008/115/EC ('Returns Directive').[110]

Returns Directive, article 6(1)

Member States shall issue a return decision to any third-country national staying illegally on their territory, without prejudice to the exceptions referred to in paragraphs 2 to 5.

The obligation on the Member States to issue a return decision is new, as previously they enjoyed a discretion over whether to allow return.[111] It was intended, above all, to stop Member States from granting large-scale amnesties to irregular migrants as a way of integrating them into the host society.[112] There is only one significant exception. Member States may offer authorisation to stay for 'compassionate, humanitarian or other reasons'.[113] However, there is no requirement to be compassionate. The Directive still allows for states to split up families and to send back very sick people to poor medical facilities.[114] The only obligation is to respect the principle of non-refoulement and to 'take due account' of the best interests of any children, family life or the state of health of the non-EU national.[115]

The second feature of note is the idea of 'illegal stay' set out in article 6(1). It does not mean that the non-EU national need have broken the law. It is rather that she has breached the terms of her entry.

Returns Directive, article 3(2)

'Illegal stay' means the presence on the territory of a Member State, of a third-country national who does not fulfil, or no longer fulfils the conditions of entry as set out in Article 5 of the Schengen Borders Code or other conditions for entry, stay or residence in that Member State...

---

[110] Directive 2008/115/EC on common standards and procedures in Member States for returning illegally staying third-country nationals [2008] OJ L348/98 ('Returns Directive'). Ireland and the United Kingdom are not participating in this Directive. The Directive does not apply to the categories mentioned in this paragraph and other non-EU nationals who enjoy more favourable status by virtue of rights given to them in some other EU law: article 4.

[111] Joined Cases C-261/08 and C-348/08 *Zurita García* v *Delegado del Gobierno en la Región de Murcia*, Judgment of 22 October 2009.

[112] The most wide-ranging in recent times was given by Spain who regularised an estimated 700,000 to 800,000 non-EU nationals in 2005.

[113] Returns Directive, article 6(4). Other exceptions are limited. These include where the non-EU national has a right to reside in another Member State, in which case she should go to the latter state unless there is a security risk, *ibid.*, article 6(2); or where she is the subject of a pending decision renewing her authorisation to stay, in which case there is a discretion not to refer, *ibid.*, article 6(5).

[114] It is highly likely that this will be challenged under Articles 3 and 8 ECHR. See p. 238.

[115] Returns Directive, article 5.

A stay can be illegal because the non-EU national has breached the conditions of entry. Alternatively, it can be for the reasons in article 5 of the Community Borders Code.[116] The central ones are no longer having a valid travel document or visa or sufficient means; and being a threat to public policy, public health or public security. Falling ill, being robbed or civil disobedience could, thus, all be reasons for return.[117]

If a return decision is issued, it should provide for the possibility of voluntary departure, typically between seven and thirty days.[118] This is, in principle, to make the issue as consensual as possible. There are thus possibilities for extension because of schooling issues or family reasons.[119] There are also certain procedural guarantees. The non-EU national is granted the right of appeal and review against the decision before an independent judicial or administrative body.[120] She must also be provided with legal advice and linguistic help.[121]

The strongest criticisms of the Directive are in response to the situations where voluntary return is not provided. This will occur where the non-EU national does not return within the period granted.[122] It can also happen as a matter of first resort where there is a risk of the non-EU national absconding; she poses a risk to public policy or national security; or her application to stay is manifestly fraudulent or unfounded.[123] Baldaccini has noted that these stipulations are wide.[124] As risk of absconding is a very general and subjective category, it will be very easy for states to assert, with the consequence that forced return may become an instrument of first rather than last resort.

In the case of forced removal, two sanctions kick in.

The first is an automatic ban on re-entry into the Union.[125] Provision is made for this to be up to five years, and longer where there is a risk to public policy or public security.[126] It is doubtful whether this is a powerful incentive for voluntary return. Member States still have discretion to impose a re-entry ban even in cases of voluntary return.[127] If this discretion is habitually exercised, the consequences will, in practice, be the same for the non-EU national. More generally, a re-entry ban will simply provide incentives for determined non-EU nationals to seek irregular entry, possibly through being trafficked and possibly through hazardous means.[128]

The bigger sanction, however, is the possibility for detention.

---

[116] See pp. 500–1.
[117] There are three groups excluded from the Directive. These are those refused entry; those subject to a criminal sanction; and family members of EU citizens or those covered by an agreement between the EU and a non-Member State, Returns Directive, article 2(2).
[118] *Ibid.*, article 7(1).
[119] *Ibid.*, article 7(2).
[120] *Ibid.*, article 13(1).
[121] *Ibid*, article 13(3).
[122] *Ibid.*, article 8(1).
[123] *Ibid.*, article 7(4).
[124] A. Baldaccini, 'The Return and Removal of Irregular Migrants under EU Law: An Analysis of the Returns Directive' (2009) 11 *EJML* 1, 8.
[125] Returns Directive, article 11(1).
[126] *Ibid.*, article 11(2).
[127] *Ibid.*, article 11(1).
[128] Baldaccini, above n. 124, 9–10.

> **Returns Directive, article 15(1)**
>
> Unless other sufficient but less coercive measures can be applied effectively in a specific case, Member States may only keep in detention a third-country national who is the subject of return procedures in order to prepare the return and/or carry out the removal process, in particular when:
> (a) there is a risk of absconding or
> (b) the third-country national concerned avoids or hampers the preparation of return or the removal process.
>
> Any detention shall be for as short a period as possible and only maintained as long as removal arrangements are in progress and executed with due diligence.

The provision is watered down from the initial Council draft which provided for mandatory detention for up to eighteen months.[129] The provision is now framed so that detention is a last resort and a matter of discretion. In particular, detention may only be used to prepare the return. In principle, it should be reviewed regularly and should not be for an initial period of more than six months, although it can be extended by a further twelve months.[130] Notwithstanding these limits, it marks the ultimate criminalisation of the migrant in that she may still be detained up to eighteen months for doing no more than breaching a condition of entry and posing a risk of absconding.

5 'DESIRABLE' NON-EU NATIONALS: THE LONG-TERM RESIDENTS DIRECTIVE

If irregular migrants sit at one end of the spectrum, long-term residents occupy the other end. They enjoy favourable rights under Directive 2003/109/EC ('Long-term Residents Directive').[131] The Directive was adopted against a backdrop of pre-existing rights. In the overwhelming majority of Member States, individuals had a right to secure residence status in law after five years, which was permanent in nature. They also had the right to free access to employment and the right to social assistance and social security on the same basis as the state's own nationals. All states granted such residents the right to family reunion, and seven states granted them voting rights at the local level.[132]

Whilst the Directive allows Member States to retain more favourable conditions for long-term residents on their own territories,[133] it takes, as we shall see, a lowest common denominator

---

[129] On the history, see D. Acosta, 'The Good, the Bad and the Ugly in EU Migration Law: Is the European Parliament Becoming Bad and Ugly? (The Adoption of Directive 2008/15: The Returns Directive)' (2009) 11 *EJML* 19.

[130] Returns Directive, article 15(3), (5).

[131] Directive 2003/109/EC concerning the status of third-country nationals who are long-term residents [2003] OJ L16/44 ('Long-term Residents Directive'). The United Kingdom and Ireland are not participating in the Directive. See E. Guild, *The Legal Elements of European Identity* (Dordrecht, Kluwer, 2004) ch. 12; S. Peers, 'Implementing Equality? The Directive on Long-term Resident Third Country Nationals' (2004) 29 *ELRev.* 437; L. Halleskov, 'The Long-Term Residents Directive: A Fulfilment of the Tampere Objective of Near Equality' (2005) 7 *EJML* 181; S. Buolart-Suominen, 'Non-EU Nationals and Council Directive 2003/109/EC on the Status of Third Country Nationals who are Long-Term Residents: Five Paces Forward and Possibly Three Paces Back' (2005) 42 *CMLRev.* 1011.

[132] K. Groenendijk and E. Guild, 'Converging Criteria: Creating an Area of Security of Residence for Europe's Third Country Nationals' (2001) 3 *EJML* 37.

[133] Long-term Residents Directive, article 13.

approach whereby the rights it bequeaths to long-term residents are lower than those found in most Member States. Beyond this, its central philosophy is one of 'managed migration'. This holds that there are certain thresholds which must not be exceeded if national economies, welfare states and cultural traditions are not to be endangered. These thresholds are highly notional but are frequently used in invidious ways to deny long-term residents key membership rights in the societies of their home Member States.

(i) Acquisition of long-term residence status

Individuals must apply for long-term resident status, providing documentary evidence showing that they satisfy two conditions.[134] They must first demonstrate that they have lawfully resided for a period of five years in the Member State in question.

> **Long-term Residents Directive, article 4(1)**
>
> Member States shall grant long-term resident status to third-country nationals who have resided legally and continuously within its territory for five years immediately prior to the submission of the relevant application.

However, there are many forms of lawful residence which will not be considered sufficient to entitle the non-EU national to acquire long-term residence status. These include students; those applying for humanitarian protection whose final status has not been determined; seasonal workers; and au pairs and diplomats.[135] If an individual falls into any of these categories, she cannot claim long-term resident status. Neither can she claim for periods where she has lived in one Member State, but then moves to another.

The second condition to be met to acquire long-term resident status is set out in article 5 of the Long-term Residents Directive.

> **Long-term Residents Directive, article 5**
>
> 1. Member States shall require third-country nationals to provide evidence that they have, for themselves and for dependent family members:
>   (a) stable and regular resources which are sufficient to maintain himself/herself and the members of his/her family, without recourse to the social assistance system of the Member State concerned. Member States shall evaluate these resources by reference to their nature and regularity and may take into account the level of minimum wages and pensions prior to the application for long-term resident status;
>   (b) sickness insurance in respect of all risks normally covered for his/her own nationals in the Member State concerned.
> 2. Member States may require third-country nationals to comply with integration conditions, in accordance with national law.

---

[134] *Ibid.*, article 7(1).
[135] *Ibid.*, article 3(2).

From a civil liberties perspective, there is something deeply pernicious about asking individuals to provide sufficient resources after they have already lawfully resided for five years in a society. Of equal concern is the stipulation in article 5(2) that Member States can require individuals to comply with integration conditions: typically tests to show their knowledge of local culture, language or history. Whatever the value of such tests, they are normally reserved for the granting of citizenship status, where the individual is being asked to commit herself to and show knowledge of the civic values of a society from which she wishes to claim equal membership rights. Kofman has observed, in this, a shift to a limited cultural tolerance of migrants into which these have to show that they fit before they be granted important entitlements.

E. Kofman, 'Citizenship, Migration and the Reassertion of National Identity' (2005) 9 *Citizenship Studies* **453, 461–2**

Though the values to which migrants are increasingly required to subscribe are in fact general liberal values such as human rights, the rule of law, tolerance for others, and so on, they are also presented with a certain view of national identity re-inscribing these liberal values within a national framework. Amongst these values, tolerance by the majority is seen to have been stretched to a breaking point, and…tolerance is clearly showing its limits. In critiquing the acceptance of tolerance as a quality of European societies, Essed suggests that the dominated is dependent on the goodwill of the dominant who have the power to be tolerant and what, in effect, is a form of cultural control.[136] The identity of the dominant group or 'us' is formulated around its tolerance and adherence to human rights compared to the intolerant other. In the latest Dutch integration measures, it is stipulated that people must integrate into and understand the norms and values of a broadly tolerant Dutch community.

In the UK, David Blunkett, the Home Secretary, was to announce on the eve of the publication of the Cantle Report on the disturbances, 'We have norms of acceptability and those who come into our home – for that is what it is – should accept these norms'. As he had already stated in the White Paper, newcomers would have to 'develop a sense of belonging, an identity and shared mutual understanding which can be passed from one generation to another'. The White Paper also noted problematic practices, such as arranged marriages, especially where these involved bringing in partners from countries of origin.

Demands for conformity to an unchanging and homogeneous cultural norm have advanced furthest in Denmark. We hear echoes of the earlier British rhetoric of the 1970s of the swamping of the settled population by newcomers. A conservative Danish politician expounded the view that: Denmark is a country that is built around one people… Danish Christianity, history, culture, view on democracy and our thoughts about freedom must continue to be the foundation that Denmark rests on… We don't want a Denmark where the Danish become a temporary ethnic minority and where our freedom is pulled away.

This impression is reinforced by Member States still being able to refuse long-term resident status to those who meet these conditions if an individual poses a threat to public policy or public security.[137] This stipulation is puzzling here. The acquisition of long-term residence does not protect a non-EU national from deportation on these grounds.[138] It is frankly bizarre, therefore, that an individual whose lawful residence has not been interrupted for five years

---

[136] P. Essed, *Understanding Everyday Racism: An Interdisciplinary Theory* (London, Sage, 1991) 210.
[137] Long-term Residents Directive, article 6(1).
[138] *Ibid.*, article 12. See below.

should, at the end of that period, be told that she poses a sufficient threat to public policy or security so as not to be granted long-term resident status. If that were the case, one would wonder why deportation or exclusion proceedings had not been instigated earlier. The provision can only make sense if a lower standard is to apply here than for regular deportation proceedings, and the individual may be refused long-term resident status for some more generic public policy reason. If that were so, the effect of this provision would be to turn the status of long-term resident, which had been bestowed on a rights basis in most national legal systems prior to the adoption of the Directive, into something which is largely a question of administrative discretion, whereby it can be refused for general reasons of 'public policy'.

Once acquired, long-term resident status may be lost in certain circumstances. It will be lost if there is subsequent evidence that it was fraudulently acquired or the non-EU national poses a threat to public policy and is expelled as a consequence.[139] Perhaps more draconian, however, is the possibility for loss if a non-EU national spends more than twelve consecutive months outside the Union.[140] Whilst this is a matter of discretion for the Member States, it is difficult to believe that such a short period indicates any kind of loss of attachment. Indeed, given the period of residence required for a person to acquire the status of long-term resident, it seems draconian to insist that if she spends more than twelve months away she may be stripped of that status. It is possible that a person who has lived for thirty years in the Union may be stripped of that status because of this.

(ii) Rights acquired against the host state

Long-term resident status secures three rights: some security of residence, the right to equal treatment and the right to family reunion.

First, the right to long-term residence gives the non-EU national the right, in principle, to reside permanently in the Member State in which they are resident.[141] The only circumstance in which she may be expelled is, in article 12, where she constitutes an actual and sufficiently serious threat to public policy or security.[142] This is a slightly different test from that which may be used to expel EU citizens. In the latter case, the individual must pose a genuine, present and sufficiently serious threat affecting one of the fundamental interests of society. In addition, the reasons for expulsion of an EU citizen must be based exclusively on her personal conduct, whereas no explicit proviso is made for this with regard to long-term residents.[143] However, there is some protection for long-term residents even where it is determined that they do pose such a threat. Before expulsion, Member States must have regard to the duration of residence on the territory, the individual's age, the consequences for her and her family and the relative links she has with both her country of residence and country of origin.[144]

Secondly, long-term residents have the right to equal treatment.

---

[139] *Ibid.*, article 9(1)(a), (b).
[140] *Ibid.*, article 9(1)(c).
[141] *Ibid.* article 8. On national practice, see E. Guild and P. Minderhood (eds.), *Security of Residence and Expulsion: Protection of Aliens in Europe* (The Hague, London and Boston, Kluwer, 2001).
[142] Long-term Residents Directive, article 12(1).
[143] Directive 2004/38/EC, article 27(2).
[144] Regulation 810/2009/EC, article 12(3). Once again, they are treated less generously than EU citizens, for whom a wider range of considerations must be balanced. Directive 2004/38/EC, article 28(1).

Long-term Residents Directive, article 11(1)

Long-term residents shall enjoy equal treatment with nationals as regards:

(a) access to employment and self-employed activity, provided such activities do not entail even occasional involvement in the exercise of public authority, and conditions of employment and working conditions, including conditions regarding dismissal and remuneration;

(b) education and vocational training, including study grants in accordance with national law;

(c) recognition of professional diplomas, certificates and other qualifications, in accordance with the relevant national procedures;

(d) social security, social assistance and social protection as defined by national law;

(e) tax benefits;

(f) access to goods and services and the supply of goods and services made available to the public and to procedures for obtaining housing;

(g) freedom of association and affiliation and membership of an organisation representing workers or employers or of any organisation whose members are engaged in a specific occupation, including the benefits conferred by such organisations, without prejudice to the national provisions on public policy and public security;

(h) free access to the entire territory of the Member State concerned, within the limits provided for by the national legislation for reasons of security.

Member States may choose to grant additional benefits.[145] Notwithstanding this, the provision is less generous than it might appear due to a series of limitations. These include public sector activities that are also excluded for EU citizens.[146] The most significant exclusion is in article 11(4):

Member States may limit equal treatment in respect of social assistance and social protection to core benefits.

The Preamble to the Directive states that the notion of 'core benefits' is one for national law, but must cover at least minimum income support, assistance in case of illness, pregnancy, parental assistance and long-term care.[147] Kofmann suggests that national practice here has considerably restricted the right to equal treatment.

E. Kofmann, 'Contemporary European Migrations: Civic Stratification and Citizenship' (2002) 21 *Political Geography* 1035, 1046

The postnational thesis is based on the idea that the only major difference between the citizen and the denizen is the absence of political rights for the latter. In fact there are other rights that migrants do not fully enjoy, such as civil rights, which are often violated in practice, and economic rights. There is a tendency to focus on broad categories of rights, for example economic or social rights, rather than specific rights, and on formal rights to the detriment of substantive rights. Even in relation to formal

---

[145] Long-term Residents Directive, article 11(5).
[146] *Ibid.*, article 11(2), (3).
[147] *Ibid.* Preamble, recital 12.

rights, large-scale official discrimination often prevails in employment. For example, about a third of French employment in the public sector and a wide range of liberal professions, such as doctors, lawyers, vets, is barred to non-EU citizens. These laws were introduced as part of the xenophobic sentiment sweeping through Europe in the inter-war years and have never been repealed (but see section on European harmonisation for recent measures in this field). In Italy, too, large sectors of municipal and public employment are closed to non-EU citizens but there has so far been little public discussion of this issue. Many other countries also include the situation of the labour market as grounds to exclude foreigners from all kinds of employment. Informal discrimination can also be effective in preventing migrants from entering particular occupations or to progress within them... In relation to the family, third country nationals do not enjoy the same rights as citizens in most European states. Though based on normative principles, regulations and conditions (income, housing standards, family members who qualify) of family reunion and visits have been constantly modified in the 1990s to such an extent that the scope of the right may be severely constrained. In France, the Pasqua laws of 1993/4 imposed more restrictive conditions on family reunion, which led to a substantial reduction in the number entering. Housing has been the most difficult criterion to satisfy in France and Italy, especially in the large cities.

The third right granted to long-term residents is the right to family reunion. This right is unusual in that it is granted not by virtue of the acquisition of long-term residence, but when long-term residence looks imminent. It is governed by Directive 2003/86/EC on the right to family reunification.[148]

Directive 2003/86/EC, article 3(1)

This Directive shall apply where the sponsor is holding a residence permit issued by a Member State for a period of validity of one year or more and has reasonable prospects of obtaining the right of permanent residence, if the members of his or her family are third country nationals of whatever status.[149]

The right to family reunion is set out in article 4(1) of the Directive. However, the Directive has a narrow conception of the family. Member States are only required to admit the spouse of the sponsor and minor children (including those adopted) over which the sponsor or spouse has exclusive custody.[150] The age of minority is governed by national law and is typically up to eighteen years old. Although the Directive provided, controversially, that Member States have the right to treat children as young as 15 as not being minors,[151] no Member State has implemented this.[152]

---

[148] Directive 2003/86/EC [2003] OJ L251/12. Ireland and the United Kingdom are not participating in this Directive.

[149] The Directive also applies where national measures grant a right to permanent residence independently of the Directive. Refugees benefit from the Directive (*ibid.* articles 9–12). Whilst those benefiting from humanitarian protection are excluded from the scope of the Directive (*ibid.* article 3(2)), nine Member States still choose to let them benefit from the rights in the Directive nonetheless. European Commission, *On the Application of Directive 2003/86/EC on the Right to Family Reunification*, COM(2008)610/3, 4–5.

[150] Directive 2003/86/EC, article 4(2).

[151] *Ibid.* article 4(6). This was challenged unsuccessfully in Case C-540/03 *Parliament v Council (family reunification)* [2006] ECR I-5769.

[152] European Commission, above n. 149, 5.

In the case of polygamous marriages, only one spouse may join the sponsor.[153] In cases where custody is shared, Member States are required to allow minors to join the long-term resident where the party sharing custody agrees.[154] The Directive grants Member States discretion as to whether or not to admit other family members.[155] Over half of Member States admit parents of the non-EU national. Regrettably, only seven allow unmarried partners to enter even where there is a registered partnership or evidence of a stable long-term relationship.[156] The bias against same sex relationships is still very present in this area of the law.

The right to family reunification is a contingent one. Some of the conditions have proved relatively uncontroversial. Any family member may be refused entry for reasons of public policy, public health or public security.[157] Member States may require that the sponsor demonstrate she has sufficient resources to support herself and her family without recourse to social assistance. There is also a requirement to have sickness insurance for all the family and to provide family accommodation that is regarded as normal for the region and complies with health and safety requirements.[158]

There are two more controversial requirements. First, Member States are permitted to require the sponsor to have lawfully resided for two years in the territory before her family can join her.[159] It seems draconian that a non-EU national can be separated from her spouse and children for two years. It was challenged by the Parliament on the grounds that it violates Article 8 ECHR, which grants the right to respect for family life. The Court of Justice rejected this argument. It observed that Member States were granted a margin of appreciation here which requires them to have due regard to the interests of the child and allows them to ensure that:

> family reunification will take place in favourable conditions, after the sponsor has been
> residing in the host State for a period sufficiently long for it to be assumed that the family
> members will settle down well and display a certain level of integration.[160]

This is quite simply nonsense. It cannot be seen how a period of family separation allows family members to settle down when they arrive. The reverse is likely to be true because of the strains it will put on the relationship.

The other contentious condition is that Member States can require family members to comply with 'integration' measures, such as language assessments and tests on the culture, politics and history of the host state.[161] Particularly contentious is the possibility for these tests to be applied to children as young as 12 years old where they arrive independently of the rest of the family.[162] This was also challenged by the Parliament as violating Article 8 ECHR. Once again, the Court's reasoning was unconvincing. It noted that the Directive requires Member States to have due

---

[153] Directive 2003/86/EC, article 4(4).
[154] *Ibid.* article 4(1).
[155] *Ibid.* article 4(2) and (3).
[156] European Commission, above n. 149, 6.
[157] *Ibid.* article 6.
[158] *Ibid.* article 7(1).
[159] *Ibid* article 8(1). Austria had legislation in place in 2003, which determines the number of family members who can enter its territory by reference to its 'reception capacity'. The provision provides that Member States with such legislation can insist upon a period of lawful residence of three years. Austria now requires a three year wait but it is no longer contingent on reception capacity.
[160] Case C-540/03 *Parliament* v *Council (family reunification)* [2006] ECR I-5769, para. 98.
[161] Directive 2003/86/EC, article 7(2).
[162] *Ibid.* article 4(1).

regard to the interests of the child. Moreover, the Directive only granted a discretion here. In exercising that discretion, Member States would have to observe the right to respect for family life.[163] However, there is an air of disingenuousness in this. The Union cannot wash its hands of this, as it has authorised the possibility of children as young as 12 years old being separated from their parents because they do not pass an 'integration test'. It is difficult to think of any circumstance where such a monstrous state of affairs secures the right to respect for family life.

Family members are granted a limited number of rights once they have entered the European Union.

Directive 2003/86/EC, article 13

1. The sponsor's family members shall be entitled, in the same way as the sponsor, to:
   (a) access to education;
   (b) access to employment and self-employed activity;
   (c) access to vocational guidance, initial and further training and retraining.
2. Member States may decide according to national law the conditions under which family members shall exercise an employed or self-employed activity. These conditions shall set a time limit which shall in no case exceed 12 months, during which Member States may examine the situation of their labour market before authorising family members to exercise an employed or self-employed activity.
3. Member States may restrict access to employment or self-employed activity by first-degree relatives in the direct ascending line or adult unmarried children...

Whilst this provision suggests that family members acquire a right to employment or to self-employment after twelve months, significant entitlements are lacking, namely social assistance and social security. The implication is that the long-term resident must not only have sufficient resources to support her family on first arriving in the Member State. She is also required to have the necessary resources to support them for the first twelve months of residence and to assume any risks to their health or economic self-sufficiency thereafter.

6 'SUSPICIOUS FOREIGNERS': THE EU REGIME ON ASYLUM SEEKERS

Until the mid-1980s, the legacy of the Second World War had resulted in Member States being content to offer quite liberal regimes to asylum seekers, and this was aided by the fact that flows of asylum seekers vis-à-vis other forms of migrants were quite limited. This began to change in the mid-1980s. Asylum applications to the Union tripled from 200,000 in 1980 to 700,000 per year in 1990.[164] The cost of administering asylum increased in major industrialised states from US$500 million per annum to US$7 billion per annum.[165] This led to increasingly draconian measures being taken to deny asylum seekers many welfare benefits.[166] In 1986, Denmark introduced a law whereby it would not hear an asylum seeker's claim if she could have applied for protection in a safe third country, i.e. one she had passed through en

---

[163] *Parliament* v *Council*, above n. 160, paras. 52–76.
[164] For trends, see ECRE, *Asylum Trends in 35 Industrialised Countries 1982–2002* (Brussels, ECRE, 2004).
[165] UNHCR, *The State of the World's Refugees: In Search of Solutions* (Oxford, Oxford University Press, 1995) 199.
[166] See L. Schuster, *The Use and Abuse of Political Asylum in Britain and Germany* (London, Frank Cass, 2003) ch. 3.

route to its territory. This law marked the beginning of a swathe of restrictive national legislation being enacted across the Union, with the most high-profile being the German amendment to the unconditional right to asylum in its Constitution in 1993.[167] These measures have led to a fall-off in the number of asylum applications since 2002, with numbers in the EU-15 back down close to the 1980 figures by 2007.[168]

Tensions have materialised most acutely over the entitlements offered to asylum seekers once they arrive in the Union. Until an applicant's need of protection has been established as bona fide, it remains unclear whether she is in fact a refugee or merely engaged in economic migration or welfare tourism. There is thus a strong institutional suspicion about offering her too generous economic or social benefits. At the same time, however, many arrive destitute and traumatised by their prior experiences.

(i) Right to remain pending consideration of the application

The asylum seeker acquires a number of rights not granted to many other types of migrants: economic migrants or migrants fleeing from starvation.[169] However, the rights granted are so full of caveats and exceptions that, from a civil liberties perspective, many are deeply problematic. As we shall see, almost all are conditional on meeting certain obligations, which enables the asylum seeker to be heavily policed during their time on the territory of the Member States. Almost all allow for the possibility for the asylum seeker to be segregated from the society of their host state.

The central entitlement, set out in article 7 of Directive 2005/85/EC, is a right to remain whilst the application for protection is being considered.[170]

> **Directive 2005/85/EC, article 7(1)**
>
> Applicants shall be allowed to remain in the Member State, for the sole purpose of the procedure, until the determining authority has made a decision in accordance with the procedures [set out]. This right to remain shall not constitute an entitlement to a residence permit.

The right is a qualified one, however. It grants no resident rights in the sense that it cannot contribute to the asylum seeker claiming long-term residence. It is also subject to one big exception. It will not apply where the asylum seeker is deemed to come from a 'safe third

---

[167] On the recent history of asylum law in 1980s and 1990s Europe, see I. Boccardi, *Europe and Refugees: Towards an EU Asylum Policy* (The Hague, Kluwer, 2002); R. Byrne *et al.*, 'Understanding Refugee Law in an Enlarged European Union' (2004) 15 *EJIL* 355. On the relationship between the practice of states and the wider ethical issues, see M. Gibney, *The Ethics and Politics of Asylum: Liberal Democracy and the Response to Refugees* (Cambridge, Cambridge University Press, 2004).

[168] The number of asylum seekers entering these states in 2008 was 216,000, with 238,100 entering the Union as a whole. UNHCR, *Asylum Trends in Industrialized Countries: Statistical Overview of Asylum Applications Lodged in European and Non European Countries*, available at www.unhcr.org/statistics/STATISTICS/49c796572.pdf (accessed 10 November 2009).

[169] J. Hathaway, 'A Reconsideration of the Underlying Premises of Refugee Law' (1990) 31 *Harvard International Law Journal* 129.

[170] Directive 2005/85/EC on minimum standards on procedures in Member States for granting and withdrawing refugee status, [2005] OJ L326/13. The United Kingdom and Ireland participate in this Directive. We do not consider the detailed procedural rules in the Directive. For comment see C. Costello, 'The Asylum Procedures Directive and the Proliferation of Safe Country Practices: Deterrence, Deflection and the Dismantling of International Protection' (2005) 7 *EJML* 35.

country'.[171] This is highly controversial as it indicates that there are some states from which the Member States will not accept asylum seekers.

There are two types of safe state: safe countries of origin and other safe states. Any asylum application from a safe state of origin will be considered inadmissible.[172] There was provision for the Union to draw up a list of safe countries of origin.[173] This was annulled by the Court of Justice.[174] Member States will therefore draw up their own lists.[175] These must be based on the following criteria:

> A country is considered as a safe country of origin where, on the basis of the legal situation, the application of the law within a democratic system and the general political circumstances, it can be shown that there is generally and consistently no persecution as defined in Article 9 of Directive 2004/83/EC,[176] no torture or inhuman or degrading treatment or punishment and no threat by reason of indiscriminate violence in situations of international or internal armed conflict. [177]

The safe state principle also applies if there is a safe state where it would be 'reasonable' for the asylum seeker to go.[178] Typically, these may be neighbouring states to the state of origin or states through which the asylum seeker has transited. The consequence is that it will only be where the asylum seeker can make a case that there was no safe state that is more accessible for her than the European Union that she will be provided asylum. Each Member State can draw up its own list of these states. However, it must base its decision on a methodology set out in national law for determining whether particular countries are safe.[179] The conditions for these are set out in article 27 of the Directive.

Directive 2005/85/EC, article 27(1)

Member States may apply the safe third country concept only where the competent authorities are satisfied that a person seeking asylum will be treated in accordance with the following principles in the third country concerned:

(a) life and liberty are not threatened on account of race, religion, nationality, membership of a particular social group or political opinion;

(b) the principle of non-refoulement in accordance with the Geneva Convention is respected;

(c) the prohibition of removal, in violation of the right to freedom from torture and cruel, inhuman or degrading treatment as laid down in international law, is respected; and

(d) the possibility exists to request refugee status and, if found to be a refugee, to receive protection in accordance with the Geneva Convention.

---

[171] *Ibid.* article 25(2)(c). All EU states are considered safe states: Protocol on asylum for nationals of Member States of the European Union.

[172] Directive 2005/85/EC, article 31(2).

[173] *Ibid.* article 29.

[174] Case C-133/06 *Parliament v Council (safe countries of origin)*, Judgment of 6 May 2008.

[175] Directive 2005/85/EC, article 30(1).

[176] These are acts of persecution that are sufficiently serious by their nature or repetition as to constitute a severe violation of basic human rights. See below n. 211.

[177] Directive 2005/85/EC, Annex II.

[178] *Ibid.* article 27(2)(a).

[179] *Ibid.* article 27(2)(b).

The criteria for both types of safe state are troublingly vague. The civil liberties organisation, Statewatch, noted that when the issue was discussed in the Council, there was substantial disagreement about at least nine states. It also noted that the criteria seemed to be applied in ways that gave misgivings. Senegal had, in 2001, about 10,000 refugees living in neighbouring states but was considered safe in thirteen out of seventeen responses.[180] Equally troubling in the case of asylum seekers being sent back to states other than their state or origin is the absence of safeguards for the asylum seeker. For the real risk is not that she will be mistreated there but that she will be sent back to a place of danger. Member States can only be sure this will not happen if they can check the robustness of the asylum procedures in these non-EU states – something that may be very difficult for them to do.

(ii) Provision of material reception conditions

Directive 2003/9/EC sets out the material benefits provided to the asylum seeker.[181] It sets out a series of civil rights and social and economic benefits to be granted to asylum seekers. However, these are granted contingently and are used to police the asylum seeker and impose obligations on her. This is reflected in the rights of due process available to asylum seekers here. Thus, asylum seekers have the right to appeal against negative decisions relating to the grant of benefits or the imposition of detention.[182] They must also be informed in writing within a reasonable period of time not exceeding fifteen days of any benefits granted to them. Yet, this latter entitlement comes with a twist. They must also have been told at the same time of any obligations with which they must comply.[183]

The central duty here is for Member States to provide material reception conditions adequate for the health and subsistence of the asylum seeker.[184] These are set out in article 13(2) of Directive 2003/9/EC.

Directive 2003/9/EC, article 13(2)

Member States shall make provisions on material reception conditions to ensure a standard of living adequate for the health of applicants and capable of ensuring their subsistence.

Material reception conditions include housing, food and clothing. However, these can be provided in a doubled-edged way that separates out and identifies the asylum seeker. In the case of food and clothing, provision may take the form of vouchers or a daily expense allowance.[185] Housing 'in kind' can include housing used specifically for asylum seekers (e.g. accommodation centres).[186] In such cases, Member States must ensure that the housing protects

---

[180] See www.statewatch.org/analyses/no-38-safe-countries.pdf (accessed 10 November 2009).
[181] Directive 2003/9/EC [2003] OJ L31/18. The United Kingdom is participating in this Directive, whereas Ireland is not.
[182] *Ibid.* article 21.
[183] *Ibid.* article 5.
[184] *Ibid.* article 13(1).
[185] *Ibid.* article 2(j).
[186] *Ibid.* article 14(1).

the family life of the applicants, that they are not subject to assault within the premises, and that they have the possibility of communicating with relatives, legal advisers and United Nations High Commission for Refugees (UNHCR) representatives.[187] Persons working in the accommodation centres must be trained and bound by the confidentiality principle as defined in national law.[188]

Alongside these material reception conditions, Member States must ensure that applicants receive necessary health care which, at the least, shall include emergency care and essential treatment of illness.[189] Provision is also made here for persons with special needs. Member States are to take account of the specific situation of vulnerable persons in its provision of material reception conditions and health care.[190]

However, Member States are permitted to grant benefits on the basis of a means test. They may require the asylum seeker to cover the cost of material reception conditions and health care if she is determined to have sufficient resources.[191] In addition, Member States may set exceptional reception conditions which cover only 'basic needs' where resources in a certain geographical area have been temporarily exhausted, or where the asylum seeker is in detention, or confined to border posts.[192]

In addition to the entitlements above, there are a number of family, education and economic rights granted to asylum seekers.

Asylum seekers do not have a right to respect for their family life. The Directive only provides that Member States must take appropriate measures as far as possible to secure family unity.[193] The Directive also provides that the best interests of the child are to be a primary consideration for Member States.[194] These are weak provisions which allow for families to be split up for administrative or economic reasons. Although the Directive makes clear that this must be done with the asylum seeker's agreement,[195] it will be difficult for an individual who is aware that the decision to award her refugee status is a matter of discretion to refuse to cooperate with the authorities.

Member States should grant access to the education system to minor asylum seekers under *similar* conditions as for their own nationals. These are not the same conditions, however. Member States can therefore provide for the ghettoisation of these children by requiring them to be educated in accommodation centres.[196]

Finally, asylum seekers have certain employment rights. Member States must assign a period during which asylum seekers will not be permitted access to the labour market.[197] If a first instance decision on the asylum seeker's status has not been taken within one year of the

---

[187] *Ibid.* article 14(2). The protection of family life requires that, where appropriate, minors are lodged with their parents or adults responsible for them. *Ibid.* article 14(3).
[188] *Ibid.* article 14(5).
[189] *Ibid.* article 15.
[190] For example, pregnant women, the disabled, the elderly, minors, single parents and torture victims.
[191] Directive 2003/9/EC, article 13(3) and (4).
[192] *Ibid.* article 14(8).
[193] *Ibid.* article 8.
[194] *Ibid.* article 18.
[195] *Ibid.* article 8.
[196] *Ibid.* article 10.
[197] *Ibid.* article 11(1).

application and this delay cannot be attributed to the applicant, the Member State must grant access to its labour market. It is not required, however, to grant equal access to the labour market and may give priority to EU citizens and EEA nationals.[198]

(iii) Policing of asylum seekers through welfare

The asylum seeker must meet a series of conditions and behave in a particular way if almost all the benefits on offer are not to be subject to withdrawal.

Directive 2003/9/EC, article 16

1. Member States may reduce or withdraw reception conditions in the following cases:
   (a) where an asylum seeker:
     – abandons the place of residence determined by the competent authority without informing it or, if requested, without permission, or
     – does not comply with reporting duties or with requests to provide information or to appear for personal interviews concerning the asylum procedure during a reasonable period laid down in national law, or
     – has already lodged an application in the same Member State.
   When the applicant is traced or voluntarily reports to the competent authority, a duly motivated decision, based on the reasons for the disappearance, shall be taken on the reinstallation of the grant of some or all of the reception conditions;
   (b) where an applicant has concealed financial resources and has therefore unduly benefited from material reception conditions.
   If it transpires that an applicant had sufficient means to cover material reception conditions and health care at the time when these basic needs were being covered, Member States may ask the asylum seeker for a refund.
2. Member States may refuse conditions in cases where an asylum seeker has failed to demonstrate that the asylum claim was made as soon as reasonably practicable after arrival in that Member State.
3. Member States may determine sanctions applicable to serious breaching of the rules of the accommodation centres as well as to seriously violent behaviour.

The sanctions are there to ensure that the asylum seeker can be policed and is traceable (the reporting and residence requirements); is not disruptive (violent behaviour and breach of rules of the accommodation centre) and is frank about her financial circumstances. They are sweeping in the conduct that they cover, but perhaps the most draconian is the possibility for their withdrawal if the asylum claim is not made as soon as reasonably practical after arrival. These measures have been criticised in particular by the UNHCR.[199]

---

[198] *Ibid.* article 11(4).
[199] *R v Secretary of State for the Home Department, ex parte Adam* [2006] 1 AC 396.

E. Guild, 'Seeking Asylum: Storm Clouds Between International Commitments and Legislative Measures' (2004) 29 *European Law Review* 198, 216–17

By the draft of April 2002, agreement had been reached in the Council that withdrawal of reception conditions would apply where: the asylum applicant abandons the place of residence allocated without permission; fails to comply with report duties; has already lodged an application in the same Member State; where the individual has sufficient resources of his or her own; or for serious breaches of the rules on places of accommodation or violent behaviour. The ground proposed by the Commission of withdrawal for war crimes and national security had been removed.[200] It was believed that political agreement on the Directive had been reached in April 2002, indeed UNHCR prepared a press release regarding the proposal, referring to the achievement of political agreement. However, this was not the case.

By September 2002 new demands for changes to the text were put forward by the UK Government which had decided to introduce draconian national legislation to exclude asylum seekers who failed to apply for asylum at the port of entry from any benefits. Apparently the Council could not agree the new insertion at the Justice and Home Affairs Council meeting of October 2002. It is believed that the Swedish delegation refused to accede to the UK demand. However, by the December 2002 JHA meeting the issue was resolved in favour of the UK. A change to the 'almost' agreed text was made to Article 16(2) that 'a Member State may refuse conditions in cases where an asylum seeker has failed to demonstrate that the asylum claim was made as soon as reasonably practicable after arrival in that Member State'. UNHCR reserved its strongest criticism of the Directive for this provision in general and Article 16(2) in particular. It considered that if Member States identify real abuse in their asylum systems these should be dealt with in the procedures themselves not be used as an excuse to starve asylum seekers or leave them homeless. It noted that 'the core content of human rights applies to everyone in all situations'. As regards Article 16(2) UNHCR stated 'this provision may constitute an obstacle for asylum-seekers to have access to fair asylum procedures. Asylum-seekers may lack basic information on the asylum procedure and be unable to state their claims formally or intelligibly without adequate guidance … These difficulties would be exacerbated where asylum-seekers arrive with insufficient means and are denied assistance through the rigid application of the "reasonably practicable" criteria.'

Alongside the withdrawal of benefits, the other possibility available to Member States is to detain asylum seekers.

Directive 2003/9/EC, article 7(2), (3)

2. Member States may decide on the residence of the asylum seeker for reasons of public interest, public order or, when necessary, for the swift processing and effective monitoring of his or her application.
3. When it proves necessary, for example for legal reasons or reasons of public order, Member States may confine an applicant to a particular place in accordance with their national law.

The provision does not require the asylum seeker to have broken the law in order to warrant detention. Its breadth has caused concern.

---

[200] Outcome of Proceedings of Council on 25 April 2002, Council Doc. 8351/02 of 29 April 2002.

E. Guild, 'Seeking Asylum: Storm Clouds Between International Commitments and Legislative Measures' (2004) 29 *European Law Review* 198, 214

...detention is not prescribed, however, it is set out to be the exception to the norm and it must be justified on the grounds permitted in the Directive. In the original proposal of the Commission, this provision was much stronger in favour of the asylum applicant. Specifically Article 7(2) required that 'Member States shall not hold applicants for asylum in detention for the sole reason that their applications for asylum need to be examined'. This part of the provision was removed completely. UNHCR, concerned about the width of the detention powers recommended that national legislation take into account a number of factors for determining the area of location where applicants could be required to reside:

the presence of NGOs, legal aid providers, language training facilities and, where possible, an established community of the asylum-seekers' national or ethnic group; the possibilities for harmonious relations between asylum-seekers and the surrounding communities; the need for supplementary financial support to cover the cost which the asylum-seekers will incur when they have to travel to the assigned area.[201]

7 'POOR FOREIGNERS': REFUGEES AND SUBSIDIARY PROTECTION

Whilst there are no pan-Union statistics, in 2007, in the whole of Europe, 44,500 people were granted refugee status and 49,400 were granted alternative forms of international protection status.[202] Whilst refugee law and asylum law are intimately connected, and there has been strong criticism on humanitarian grounds of both, EU refugee law is more informed by humanitarian norms and less concerned with policing than EU asylum law. The central ethos is one of humanitarianism and the criticisms arise where the regime is alleged to have deviated from this path.

EU refugee law grants protection to two groups of individuals: refugees and persons eligible for subsidiary protection.

The notion of the refugee is derived directly from the 1951 Geneva Convention relating to the status of refugees, and is set out in article 2(c) of Directive 2004/83/EC.[203] Its central elements are that there must be a well-founded fear of persecution, and that persecution must rest on specific grounds:

'refugee' means a third country national who, owing to a well-founded fear of being persecuted for reasons of race, religion, nationality, political opinion or membership of a particular social group, is outside the country of nationality and is unable or, owing to such fear, is unwilling to avail himself or herself of the protection of that country, or a stateless person, who, being outside of the country of former habitual residence for the same reasons as mentioned above, is unable or, owing to such fear, unwilling to return to it...

---

[201] UNHCR annotated comments on Council Directive 2003/9/EC of 27 January 2003.

[202] UNHCR, *Statistical Yearbook for 2007* (Geneva, UNHCR, 2008) 48–9.

[203] Directive 2004/83/EC on minimum standards for the qualification and status of third-country nationals or stateless persons as refugees or as persons who otherwise need international protection and the content of the protection granted [2004] OJ L304/12. Both Ireland and the United Kingdom are participating in this Directive.

In many ways, this definition is too narrow to protect everybody who might suffer harm, and so an alternative concept, subsidiary protection, has emerged and is set out in article 2(e) of the same Directive:

> 'person eligible for subsidiary protection' means a third country national or a stateless person who does not qualify as a refugee but in respect of whom substantial grounds have been shown for believing that the person concerned, if returned to his or her country of origin, or in the case of a stateless person, to his or her country of former habitual residence, would face a real risk of suffering serious harm...[204]

Much of the Directive is concerned with setting out in more detail the core elements needed for acquiring either refugee or subsidiary protection status. In both cases the onus is on the applicant to furnish proof of all the elements necessary to substantiate her case.[205] She satisfies this requirement if she makes a genuine effort to substantiate the application, has submitted all the elements at her disposal and applied at the earliest possible time, and her general credibility has been established.[206] Member States are then required to assess each case individually, taking account of all the relevant circumstances.[207]

There are a number of features common to both refugee status and subsidiary protection. First, the fear of harm or persecution may stem from events occurring after the applicant has left the country of origin or from acts committed outside the country of origin.[208] Secondly, a liberal interpretation has been taken of which actors may be considered perpetrators of harm or persecution. In some Member States, notably France and Germany, international protection could formerly only be sought if a state had committed the persecutory acts. The test has been widened.

Directive 2004/83/EC, article 6

Actors of persecution or serious harm include:

(a) the State;
(b) parties or organisations controlling the State or a substantial part of the territory of the State;
(c) non-State actors, if it can be demonstrated that the actors mentioned in (a) and (b), including international organisations, are unable or unwilling to provide protection against persecution or serious harm...

Protection in the country of origin is considered sufficient if the actors in article 6(a) or (b) have taken reasonable steps to prevent the persecution or harm by operating an effective legal system for the detection and punishment of the acts causing harm or persecution.[209] In this regard, it is a little disturbing that international protection may be refused where, although the government in the country of origin cannot offer protection, the parties or organisations controlling a substantial part of the territory of the state are capable of doing so. For it suggests

---

[204] On this dimension of the Directive, see J. McAdam, 'The European Union Qualifications Directive: The Creation of a Subsidiary Protection Regime' (2005) 17 *IJRL* 461.
[205] Directive 2004/83/EC, article 4(1).
[206] *Ibid.* article 4(5).
[207] *Ibid.* article 4(3).
[208] *Ibid.* article 5.
[209] *Ibid.* article 7(2).

deportation may take place to territories in which there is no stable government in place and government is instead by party whim. International protection is also not available if there is a part of the country of origin within which the applicant may be protected and she could reasonably be expected to stay there.[210]

(i) Acquisition and loss of refugee status

For an individual to acquire refugee status she must have a well-founded fear of an act or acts of persecution and the persecution must be for reasons of race, religion, nationality, political opinion or membership of a particular social group. There is also a threshold to be met for the level of persecution. The acts of persecution must be sufficiently serious to constitute a severe violation of human rights or, alternately, be sufficiently serious to 'affect an individual in a similar manner'.[211] Article 10 of the Directive sets out in more detail the reasons for persecution.

Directive 2004/83/EC, article 10

1. Member States shall take the following elements into account when assessing the reasons for persecution:
   (a) the concept of race shall in particular include considerations of colour, descent, or membership of a particular ethnic group;
   (b) the concept of religion shall in particular include the holding of theistic, non-theistic and atheistic beliefs, the participation in, or abstention from, formal worship in private or in public, either alone or in community with others, other religious acts or expressions of view, or forms of personal or communal conduct based on or mandated by any religious belief;
   (c) the concept of nationality shall not be confined to citizenship or lack thereof but shall in particular include membership of a group determined by its cultural, ethnic, or linguistic identity, common geographical or political origins or its relationship with the population of another State;
   (d) a group shall be considered to form a particular social group where in particular:
      – members of that group share an innate characteristic, or a common background that cannot be changed, or share a characteristic or belief that is so fundamental to identity or conscience that a person should not be forced to renounce it, and
      – that group has a distinct identity in the relevant country, because it is perceived as being different by the surrounding society; depending on the circumstances in the country of origin, a particular social group might include a group based on a common characteristic of sexual orientation. Sexual orientation cannot be understood to include acts considered to be criminal in accordance with national law of the Member States: Gender related aspects might be considered, without by themselves alone creating a presumption for the applicability of this Article;
   (e) the concept of political opinion shall in particular include the holding of an opinion, thought or belief on a matter related to the potential actors of persecution mentioned in Article 6 and to their policies or methods, whether or not that opinion, thought or belief has been acted upon by the applicant.
2. When assessing if an applicant has a well-founded fear of being persecuted it is immaterial whether the applicant actually possesses the racial, religious, national, social or political characteristic which attracts the persecution, provided that such a characteristic is attributed to the applicant by the actor of persecution.

---

[210] *Ibid.* article 8.
[211] *Ibid.* article 9.

The concepts of race, religion, nationality, political opinion or membership of a particular social group have been interpreted reasonably generously to include elements which go beyond typical forms of state oppression. Criteria such as sexual orientation, atheism and gender are mentioned, although not anticipated in the 1951 Geneva Convention. Combined with the fact that persecution perpetrated by non-state actors is considered relevant, the scope for attaining refugee status has been considerably widened. Relevant grounds for claiming refugee status have now been held to include forced female circumcision, child slavery or where one's freedom to express one's sexual orientation is not protected by the courts. In all this, there is a move towards the central concern being the dignity of the individual rather than the nature of the oppression. From a humanitarian perspective this is to be welcomed, but it has been argued that this dynamism has both generated uncertainty and, by increasing the number of individuals entitled to refugee status, led to an increased reluctance on the part of Member States to accept refugees, including those who have been subject to traditional protection.[212]

A Member State may revoke or refuse to renew refugee status if the applicant has misrepresented decisive facts in her application;[213] there are serious reasons to believe that she has committed crimes against humanity or serious non-political crimes; she is guilty of acts contrary to the purposes and principles of the United Nations;[214] or there are reasonable grounds for regarding her as a danger to the security of the Member State.[215] She will also cease to have refugee status if the circumstances that gave rise to the persecution have ceased or the refugee has availed herself of the protection of her state of nationality.[216]

(ii) Subsidiary protection

Subsidiary protection is a complementary category, which applies only when the individual is not eligible for refugee status, but is still in need of international protection. The test is whether there are substantial grounds for believing that the individual runs a real risk of serious harm if she returns to her state of origin. The content of 'serious harm' is set out in article 15.

Directive 2004/83/EC, article 15

Serious harm consists of:

(a) death penalty or execution; or

(b) torture or inhuman or degrading treatment or punishment of an applicant in the country of origin; or

(c) serious and individual threat to a civilian's life or person by reason of indiscriminate violence in situations of international or internal armed conflict.

The first two headings are self-explanatory and relate to threats that relate individually to the applicant. It is the category in article 15(c) which is most wide-ranging. This was considered by the Court of Justice in *Elgafaji*, one of its most liberal judgments of recent time.

---

[212] A. Fabbricotti, 'The Concept of Inhuman and Degrading Treatment in Asylum Cases' (1998) 10 *IJRL* 637.
[213] Directive 2004/83/EC, article 14(3)(b).
[214] *Ibid.* article 12(2).
[215] *Ibid.* articles 14(4)(a) and (5).
[216] *Ibid.* article 11(a) and (e).

Elgafaji, an Iraqi, was a Shiite Muslim who had worked for a British security firm there and was married to a Sunni Muslim. His uncle, employed by the same firm, had been killed by militia and a letter had been pinned on Elgefaji's home door threatening 'death to collaborators'. He sought temporary residence in the Netherlands but this was refused by the Dutch authorities who thought that there was no serious risk of his being executed or tortured. He invoked article 15(c), claiming that there was a risk of his being killed. The Dutch with a number of other Member States, to their shame, argued that article 15(c) did not establish a separate category of protection but only related to where people were to be executed under article 15(a).

Case C-465/07 *Elgefaji v Staatssecretaris van Justitie*, Judgment of 17 February 2009

32. ...it must be noted that the terms 'death penalty', 'execution' and 'torture or inhuman or degrading treatment or punishment of an applicant in the country of origin', used in Article 15(a) and (b) of the Directive, cover situations in which the applicant for subsidiary protection is specifically exposed to the risk of a particular type of harm.

33. By contrast, the harm defined in Article 15(c) of the Directive as consisting of a 'serious and individual threat to [the applicant's] life or person' covers a more general risk of harm.

34. Reference is made, more generally, to a 'threat ... to a civilian's life or person' rather than to specific acts of violence. Furthermore, that threat is inherent in a general situation of 'international or internal armed conflict'. Lastly, the violence in question which gives rise to that threat is described as 'indiscriminate', a term which implies that it may extend to people irrespective of their personal circumstances.

35. In that context, the word 'individual' must be understood as covering harm to civilians irrespective of their identity, where the degree of indiscriminate violence characterising the armed conflict taking place – assessed by the competent national authorities before which an application for subsidiary protection is made, or by the courts of a Member State to which a decision refusing such an application is referred – reaches such a high level that substantial grounds are shown for believing that a civilian, returned to the relevant country or, as the case may be, to the relevant region, would, solely on account of his presence on the territory of that country or region, face a real risk of being subject to the serious threat referred in Article 15(c) of the Directive.

36. That interpretation, which is likely to ensure that Article 15(c) of the Directive has its own field of application, is not invalidated by the wording of recital 26 in the preamble to the Directive, according to which '[r]isks to which a population of a country or a section of the population is generally exposed normally do not create in themselves an individual threat which would qualify as serious harm'.

37. While that recital implies that the objective finding alone of a risk linked to the general situation in a country is not, as a rule, sufficient to establish that the conditions set out in Article 15(c) of the Directive have been met in respect of a specific person, its wording nevertheless allows – by the use of the word 'normally' – for the possibility of an exceptional situation which would be characterised by such a high degree of risk that substantial grounds would be shown for believing that that person would be subject individually to the risk in question.

38. The exceptional nature of that situation is also confirmed by the fact that the relevant protection is subsidiary, and by the broad logic of Article 15 of the Directive, as the harm defined in paragraphs (a) and (b) of that article requires a clear degree of individualisation. While it is admittedly true that collective factors play a significant role in the application of Article 15(c) of the Directive, in that the

person concerned belongs, like other people, to a circle of potential victims of indiscriminate violence in situations of international or internal armed conflict, it is nevertheless the case that that provision must be subject to a coherent interpretation in relation to the other two situations referred to in Article 15 of the Directive and must, therefore, be interpreted by close reference to that individualisation.

39. In that regard, the more the applicant is able to show that he is specifically affected by reason of factors particular to his personal circumstances, the lower the level of indiscriminate violence required for him to be eligible for subsidiary protection.

The central feature of the judgment, which widens the scope of protection considerably, is the test in paragraph 35 that a region becomes so dangerous that simple presence there places an individual at risk of death. This opens the way for protection being sought by individuals wherever there is a conflict zone, without their having to show that they have some trait that places them at risk. The Court makes clear in the last four paragraphs that a sliding scale operates here. If the violence in a region is intense, that will be sufficient. If it is of a lesser scale, the Court will look to the level of individual threat in the case of the applicant.

Subsidiary protection was welcomed by non-governmental organisations, as it was not a legally protected category in some Member States. However, as article 2(e) of the Directive indicated, the probative threshold is much higher for subsidiary protection than for refugees, with individuals having to show that there are substantial grounds for believing that they run a real risk of serious harm, rather than simply a well-founded fear of serious harm. There are also a number of exceptions. Some are similar to those for refugees. The individual may be excluded from protection where she has committed a war crime or other serious crime, is guilty of acts contrary to the purposes and principles of the United Nations, or constitutes a danger to the community or to the security of the Member State in which he or she is present.[217] Most problematically, a Member State may exclude an individual because she has committed criminal acts that are subject to imprisonment in her country of origin.[218] This provision reduces the scope of subsidiary protection drastically, as many individuals are fleeing their country of origin with such charges, often trumped up, hanging over their heads. It is also not clear why torture or the death penalty is any less egregious simply because an individual has been imprisoned beforehand.

(iii) Varying benefits of international protection

The benefits granted by Directive 2004/83/EC can be divided into three. There are those benefits which are granted on equal terms to both refugees and those entitled to subsidiary protection; those granted only to refugees; and those to which only those granted subsidiary protection are entitled. The common rights are the following.

Right to family unity   Member States are to ensure that family unity can be maintained.[219] Family members include spouses or unmarried partners in a stable relationship where these are treated by national law as equivalent to spouses. It also includes minor children who

---

[217] *Ibid.* article 17(1).
[218] *Ibid.* article 17(3).
[219] *Ibid.* article 23(1).

are unmarried and dependent. In all cases, these are only granted rights if they are present in the same Member State where the application is made.[220] There is, therefore, no Community right to family reunion requiring states to accept family members from other Member States. These are entitled to the same rights and benefits as the refugee, unless there are public order or national security reasons why these cannot be given.[221]

Education   Access to the education system must be granted on the same terms as to a Member State's nationals and is to be given to all minors.[222] Adults must also be granted access to a Member State's education system on the same basis as other non-EU nationals lawfully resident there.[223]

Access to accommodation   Access to accommodation must be granted under equivalent conditions as for other non-EU nationals legally resident in the Member State.[224]

Free movement   Member States must grant freedom of movement within their territories on the same basis as for other non-EU nationals legally resident there.[225]

Repatriation assistance   Assistance may be given to those who wish to repatriate.[226]

Individuals with special needs   Member States must take into account the specific situation of vulnerable persons such as minors, unaccompanied minors, disabled people, the elderly, pregnant women, single parents and persons who have been subjected to torture, rape or other serious forms of psychological, physical or sexual violence.[227] These individuals are, in all cases, to be given adequate health care on the same basis as a Member State's own nationals.[228]
    Refugees are given a number of further rights.

Right to non-refoulement   A Member State must respect the principle of non-refoulement unless there are reasonable grounds for considering the refugee a danger to that Member State's national security or she has been convicted of a particularly serious offence and constitutes a danger to the community of that Member State.[229]

Documentation securing residence and travel   Unless there are compelling reasons of public order and national security, refugees should be given a residence permit for at least three years,[230] and travel documents which allow them to travel outside the territory.[231]

---

[220] *Ibid.* article 2(h).
[221] *Ibid.* article 23(2) and (4).
[222] *Ibid.* article 27(1).
[223] *Ibid.* article 27(2).
[224] *Ibid.* article 31.
[225] *Ibid.* article 32.
[226] *Ibid.* article 34.
[227] *Ibid.* article 20(3).
[228] *Ibid.* article 29(3).
[229] *Ibid.* article 21.
[230] *Ibid.* article 24(1).
[231] *Ibid.* article 25(1).

Socio-economic rights   Refugees should be allowed to work and enter into vocational training or self-employment on the same terms as a state's own nationals.[232] They must be granted social assistance and health care on the same terms as a state's own nationals.[233] Finally, Member States must make provision for programmes which enable the refugee to integrate into their societies.[234]

Combined, the rights granted to refugees are similar to those granted to EU citizens and provide refugees with nearly complete membership rights in their new societies. The clear intention is to provide them with the support to start and plan a new life in the Member State on the assumption that this may well be a permanent move.

The philosophy behind subsidiary protection is very different. The rights granted are more limited and transient, with the idea being that sufficient dignity for the beneficiary is secured pending her return to her country of origin. No right of non-refoulement is granted to her explicitly. In addition, it is only required that she be given residence documents for the duration of one year,[235] and need only be given travel documents if serious humanitarian reasons arise requiring her presence in another Member State.[236] She is also given more limited socio-economic rights. In the fields of social assistance and health care, she is only to be given access to 'core benefits' on the same terms as a state's own nationals.[237] These are to be defined by national law but are to include, at the least, minimum income support, assistance in case of illness, pregnancy and parental assistance.[238] There is no right to enter employment or self-employment, with the Directive stipulating only that beneficiaries should have access to employment-related or vocational training under conditions to be determined by the Member States,[239] and integration facilities should only be provided by Member States where they consider this appropriate.[240]

This discrimination may be heavily criticised. There is something very invidious in differentiating between two groups of people, both of whom are in dire humanitarian need. Against this, it can be argued that the Directive is only setting out minimum rights.[241] There is nothing to stop Member States treating both equally. At the very least, the Directive secures the protection of a category, subsidiary protection, which was not formerly protected in all Member States. The discrimination only becomes a wider problem if Member States, ignoring the principle that subsidiary protection occupies a complementary position to refugee status and is only triggered where the latter is unavailable, deny refugee status to many deserving cases and give them the less generous offerings of subsidiary protection.

---

[232] *Ibid.* article 26(1).
[233] *Ibid.* articles 28(1) and 29(1).
[234] *Ibid.* article 33(1).
[235] *Ibid.* article 24(2).
[236] *Ibid.* article 25(2).
[237] *Ibid.* articles 28 and 29(2).
[238] *Ibid.* Preamble, para. 34.
[239] *Ibid.* article 26(4).
[240] *Ibid.* article 33(2).
[241] *Ibid.* articles 1 and 3.

FURTHER READING

A. Baldaccini, 'The Return and Removal of Irregular Migrants under EU Law: An Analysis of the Returns Directive' (2009) 11 *European Journal of Migration and Law* 1

I. Boccardi, *Europe and Refugees: Towards an EU Asylum Policy* (The Hague, London and Boston, Kluwer, 2002)

R. Byrne *et al.*, 'Understanding Refugee Law in an Enlarged European Union' (2004) 15 *European Journal of International Law* 355

C. Costello, 'The Asylum Procedures Directive and the Proliferation of Safe Country Practices: Deterrence, Deflection and the Dismantling of International Protection' (2005) 7 *European Journal of Migration and Law* 35

K. Groenendijk *et al.* (eds.), *In Search of Europe's Borders* (The Hague, Kluwer, 2003)

E. Guild and P. Minderhood (eds.), *Security of Residence and Expulsion: Protection of Aliens in Europe* (The Hague, London and Boston, Kluwer, 2001)

L. Halleskov, 'The Long-Term Residents Directive: A Fulfilment of the Tampere Objective of Near Equality' (2005) 7 *European Journal of Migration and Law* 181

D. Kostakopoulou, *Citizenship, Identity and Immigration in the European Union: Between Past and Future* (Manchester, Manchester University Press, 2001)

J. McAdam, 'The European Union Qualification Directive: The Creation of a Subsidiary Protection Regime' (2005) 17 *International Journal of Refugee Law* 461

A. Meloni, 'The Community Code on Visas: Harmonisation at Last?' (2009) 34 *European Law Review* 671

S. Peers, *EU Justice and Home Affairs Law* (2nd edn, Oxford, Oxford University Press, 2006)

N. Walker (ed.), *Europe's Area of Freedom, Security and Justice* (Oxford, Oxford University Press, 2004)

13

Equal Opportunities Law and Policy

CONTENTS

1 INTRODUCTION

The EEC Treaty of 1957 provided limited grounds for developing European equal opportunities law, but there has been a dramatic increase since then, in particular as a result of judicial activism and the incorporation of Article 19 TFEU (ex Article 13 EC) by the Amsterdam

Treaty.[1] EU law now regulates discrimination on grounds of sex, gender, race, ethnic origin, religion or belief, sexual orientation, age and disability. In this chapter we examine the key legislative provisions, the motivation for the European Union to intervene, and the evolution of the Union's equal opportunities policy.

Section 2 explores three issues to place the law in a wider context. First we ask why the Union needs an equal opportunities policy. On the one hand, banning discrimination is a necessary complement to the economic project of creating an internal market: discrimination reduces economic welfare and so must be prohibited. On the other hand, the tasks of the Union are wider: to enhance the rights of its citizens, irrespective of economic considerations.[2] The Court of Justice has indicated a preference for the second view, most controversially in its *Mangold* judgment.[3] Secondly, we consider what kind of anti-discrimination policy the European Union is developing. One model sees discrimination law as promoting equality of opportunities, and the other suggests that discrimination laws can be successful only if they yield equality of results. Thirdly, we outline the common core of EU equal opportunities law, which is found in the field of labour law, where a rights-based model operates and has been utilised successfully in the past forty years by victims of sex discrimination.[4]

Section 3 considers the grounds upon which discrimination is forbidden. In tracing the way the Union has come to protect certain groups, a number of common themes emerge. First, the claims of each group have been supported by non-governmental organisations (NGOs) which have 'framed' discrimination in an economic manner, noting how discrimination against that group (e.g. homosexuals or ethnic minorities) hampers the achievement of the internal market. Secondly, NGOs have used test cases as a means of asserting the rights of protected groups. Thirdly, EU institutions have responded in different ways: the European Parliament has for a long time been most receptive to demands to develop EU-wide discrimination laws, but its legislative powers are limited.[5] Recently, the Commission has also supported the development of equal opportunities law but its scope for activity is limited to drafting soft law measures in the form of recommendations or codes of practice. Yet, these have proven to be effective in anticipating future legislation.[6] The Council's legislative intervention has been hampered by the resistance of Member States, thus legislation tends to follow a pattern of lobbying, cajoling by the Parliament and Commission, rulings of the Court of Justice, and external political events that precipitate action, as in the case of race discrimination.

In Section 4 we examine the common core of EU equal opportunities law more fully by considering the three main grounds upon which an employee may assert her rights (direct discrimination, indirect discrimination and harassment); what justifications might be offered by employers to escape liability; and the remedies available to the employee.

---

[1] On the background, see M. Bell and L. Waddington, 'The 1996 Intergovernmental Conference and the Prospects of a Non-Discrimination Treaty Article' (1996) 25 *ILJ* 320.

[2] M. Bell, *Anti-Discrimination Law and the European Union* (Oxford, Oxford University Press, 2002).

[3] Case C-144/04 *Mangold* v *Helm* [2005] ECR I-9981.

[4] It is beyond the scope of this chapter to examine this field exhaustively. See C. Barnard, *EC Employment Law* (3rd edn, Oxford, Oxford University Press, 2006); A. McColgan, *Discrimination Law: Text, Cases and Materials* (2nd edn, Oxford, Hart, 2005).

[5] See further Chapter 2.

[6] S. Sciarra, 'European Social Policy and Labour Law: Challenges and Perspectives' (1995) IV *Collected Courses of the Academy of European Law* 301, 340.

In Section 5 we consider the limitations of the policy discussed in section 4 and analyse four novel ways through which EU equal opportunities law is evolving. First, the policy is extended to areas beyond the workplace, protecting victims who suffer discrimination in education or the provision of services, for example; secondly, inviting Member States to experiment with affirmative action programmes; thirdly, promoting various forms of dialogue to entrench existing rights; finally, embracing 'mainstreaming' as a means of integrating equality rights within the framework of EU law.

2 DEVELOPMENT OF EU EQUAL OPPORTUNITIES LAW

(i) Economic versus non-economic visions of EU law

EU discrimination policy is largely based upon Article 19 TFEU, first included in the Treaty of Amsterdam.[7]

Article 19 TFEU (ex Article 13 EC)

1. Without prejudice to the other provisions of the Treaties and within the limits of the powers conferred by them upon the Union, the Council, acting unanimously in accordance with a special legislative procedure and after obtaining the consent of the European Parliament, may take appropriate action to combat discrimination based on sex, racial or ethnic origin, religion or belief, disability, age or sexual orientation.
2. By way of derogation from paragraph 1, the European Parliament and the Council, acting in accordance with the ordinary legislative procedure, may adopt the basic principles of Union incentive measures, excluding any harmonisation of the laws and regulations of the Member States, to support action taken by the Member States in order to contribute to the achievement of the objectives referred to in paragraph 1.

Article 19(1) grants the EU legislative competence to safeguard the rights of a range of groups, and it is not confined to prohibiting discrimination in the workplace. This breadth was achieved with certain limitations: the Article does not have direct effect, the European Parliament (the institution which had most assiduously pursued the cause of discrimination law) is given a relatively limited role in the law-making process,[8] and the requirement for unanimity creates a risk that the legislation imposes only low standards, or results in tests that are so ambiguous that they can be watered down by national implementation measures. During the negotiations leading to the Treaty of Nice there were attempts to make it easier for the Union to legislate. The result was Article 19(2), but this only applies for measures designed to help Member States in giving effect to the legislation enacted under Article 19(1).[9]

While the Union has expanded the scope of EU equal opportunities law only recently, Member States had, independently, already moved to combat discrimination, albeit with differing vigour. If national law already combats discrimination, why is EU law needed? One answer to

---

[7] L. Waddington, 'Article 13 EC: Mere Rhetoric or a Harbinger of Change?' (1998) 1 *CYELS* 175, 187.
[8] But Article 19 TFEU enhances it. Under Article 13 EC it merely had the right to be consulted.
[9] An alternative (but more limited) legal basis would be Article 153 TFEU (ex Article 137 EC).

this can be discovered by looking back at the reason why discrimination law found its way into the 1957 EEC Treaty. Its beginnings were humble, limited to guaranteeing equal pay between men and women, and only a more limited version of the first two paragraphs of what is now Article 157 TFEU was in place.

Article 157 TFEU (ex Article 141 EC)

1. Each Member State shall ensure that the principle of equal pay for male and female workers for equal work or work of equal value is applied.
2. For the purpose of this Article, 'pay' means the ordinary basic or minimum wage or salary and any other consideration, whether in cash or in kind, which the worker receives directly or indirectly, in respect of his employment, from his employer.

    Equal pay without discrimination based on sex means:
    (a) that pay for the same work at piece rates shall be calculated on the basis of the same unit of measurement;
    (b) that pay for work at time rates shall be the same for the same job.
3. The European Parliament and the Council, acting in accordance with the ordinary legislative procedure, and after consulting the Economic and Social Committee, shall adopt measures to ensure the application of the principle of equal opportunities and equal treatment of men and women in matters of employment and occupation, including the principle of equal pay for equal work or work of equal value.
4. With a view to ensuring full equality in practice between men and women in working life, the principle of equal treatment shall not prevent any Member State from maintaining or adopting measures providing for specific advantages in order to make it easier for the underrepresented sex to pursue a vocational activity or to prevent or compensate for disadvantages in professional careers.

The reason for including this provision was a concern of the French government that it would be at a competitive disadvantage because its laws guaranteed equal pay for men and women while the laws of other states did not.[10] This suggests that one rationale for EU discrimination law is economic: it prevents Member States who do not safeguard equality at work from exploiting lower labour costs, thereby gaining an advantage. Discrimination is thus harmful because it means that human resources are not used to their full capacity: if an employer has a policy of not hiring women, he may lose out by not hiring the best candidate for the job. This can stifle economic progress and undermine the EU's desire to develop a competitive single market.[11] From an economic perspective then, harmonised discrimination legislation complements the internal market rules and enhances competitiveness.[12]

An alternative justification for equal opportunities is that the EU is gradually recognising the political aspect to European integration whereby discrimination law forms a fundamental plank in the protection of EU citizens. Those who support this argument draw upon the

---

[10] B. Ohlin, 'Social Aspects of European Economic Co-operation: Report by a Group of Experts' (1956) 102 *International Labour Review* 99; C. Barnard, 'The Economic Objectives of Article 119' in T. Hervey and D. O'Keefe, *Sex Equality Law of the European Union* (Chichester, Wiley, 1996).

[11] See recital 9 of Directive 2000/43/EC implementing the principle of equal treatment between persons irrespective of racial or ethnic origin [2000] OJ L180/22.

[12] Green Paper, *Equality and Non-Discrimination in an Enlarged European Union*, COM(04)379 final, 15–16.

underlying intentions of the Treaties, the development, especially since the late 1980s by the then President of the Commission, Jacques Delors, of a 'social' dimension to accompany economic integration, resulting in the Community Charter of Basic Social Rights for Workers,[13] and the Court of Justice's recognition that the principle of equal treatment set out in Article 157 TFEU enshrines a fundamental right:[14]

> the economic aim pursued by Article [157 TFEU], namely the elimination of distortions of competition between undertakings established in different Member States, is secondary to the social aim pursued by the same provision, which constitutes the expression of a fundamental human right.[15]

This judicial pronouncement is reflected in the enlargement of Community competence in the field of social policy in the Amsterdam Treaty,[16] the evolution of the concept of citizenship (noted in Chapter 11), and the increased role of fundamental rights in the European Union (discussed in Chapter 6).[17] The Preambles to the discrimination Directives based on Article 19 TFEU lend support to the non-economic vision by their reference to the importance of creating an ever closer Union among the peoples of Europe, the principles of liberty, democracy, human rights and fundamental freedoms that underpin the European Union, and the universality of the right to equality recognised in several international instruments.[18]

The Court of Justice has recently taken the above further, with its controversial ruling in *Mangold* v *Helm*.[19] In 2003, Mr Mangold (at the time 56 years old) entered into a fixed-term employment contract with Helm. The terms specified that the duration was fixed in accordance with German law at the time, which was designed to make it easier to enter into fixed-term contracts with older workers (recently defined as workers aged 52 and above), while restricting the freedom to enter into fixed-term contracts with younger workers. Mangold argued that his contract was in breach of Directive 2000/78/EC ('Framework Directive') and constituted discrimination based on age. At that time the Directive had not yet been transposed into German law; it appears that the parties to the litigation had designed the employment contract as a means of launching a challenge to test the legality of the German legislation against the forthcoming EU standards. The Court found that the Framework Directive applied even though it had not yet been transposed into German law, even if Germany had secured an extension of time to implement the Directive. This was based on the Court discovering a general principle in EU law prohibiting age discrimination.

---

[13] Declaration by Council of the Community Charter of Basic Social Rights for Workers, COM(89)568 final.

[14] Case 43/75 *Defrenne* v *Sabena* [1976] ECR 455; Case C-13/94 *P* v *S and Cornwall County Council* [1996] ECR I-2143, para. 18. See C. Barnard, '*P* v *S*: Kite Flying or a New Constitutional Approach' in A. Dashwood and S. O'Leary (eds.), *The Principle of Equal Treatment in European Community Law* (London, Sweet & Maxwell, 1997).

[15] Case C-50/96 *Deutsche Telekom AG* v *Lilli Schröder* [2000] ECR I-743, para. 57.

[16] Article 153 TFEU (ex Article 137 EC). See C. Barnard, 'The United Kingdom, the "Social Chapter" and the Amsterdam Treaty' (1997) 26 *ILJ* 275.

[17] See e.g. E. Spaventa, 'From *Gebhard* to *Carpenter*: Towards a (Non) Economic Constitution' (2004) 41 *CMLRev.* 743.

[18] Directive 2000/43/EC, recitals 1–3; Directive 2000/78/EC establishing a general framework for equal treatment in employment and occupation, recitals 1, 3 and 4 [2000] OJ L303/16; Directive 2006/54/EC on the implementation of the principle of equal opportunities and equal treatment of men and women in matters of employment and occupation (recast), recitals 2 and 4 [2006] OJ L204/23 ('Equal Treatment Directive').

[19] Case C-144/04 *Werner Mangold* v *Rüdiger Helm* [2005] ECR I-9981.

Case C–144/04 *Werner Mangold* v *Rüdiger Helm* [2005] ECR I–9981

75. The principle of non-discrimination on grounds of age must thus be regarded as a general principle of Community law. Where national rules fall within the scope of Community law, which is the case with [the German law in question], as being a measure implementing Directive 1999/70, and reference is made to the Court for a preliminary ruling, the Court must provide all the criteria of interpretation needed by the national court to determine whether those rules are compatible with such a principle.

76. Consequently, observance of the general principle of equal treatment, in particular in respect of age, cannot as such be conditional upon the expiry of the period allowed the Member States for the transposition of a Directive intended to lay down a general framework for combating discrimination on the grounds of age, in particular so far as the organisation of appropriate legal remedies, the burden of proof, protection against victimisation, social dialogue, affirmative action and other specific measures to implement such a Directive are concerned.

77. In those circumstances it is the responsibility of the national court, hearing a dispute involving the principle of non-discrimination in respect of age, to provide, in a case within its jurisdiction, the legal protection which individuals derive from the rules of Community law and to ensure that those rules are fully effective, setting aside any provision of national law which may conflict with that law.

The possible implications of this finding are significant.[20] From a constitutional law perspective it means that the obligations in the Directive become enforceable before it is to be transposed. More seriously, the judgment confuses the supremacy of EU law with its direct effect. From the narrower perspective of equal opportunities law, the ruling means that, irrespective of the specific obligations in the Framework Directive, Member States have a general obligation not to discriminate on grounds of age; for example, legislation that offers discriminatory access to health services based on age may be challenged as contrary to EU law even if the Directive only applies to employment relations. Moreover, the door is open for this general principle to have horizontal effect and regulate private parties (as in this case),[21] or even to apply as a ground to review Community legislation should it fall foul of this general principle. The Court's approach has been criticised vigorously.[22] A particularly influential attack was co-authored by the former President of the German Supreme Court who issued a call to 'Stop the European Court of Justice'.[23] A case is pending before that court testing the legality of the approach in *Mangold*. More optimistically, Professor Schiek thought the judgment constituted 'a first step in what will hopefully lead towards judicial development of a coherent framework for equal treatment of persons from a less than satisfactory legislative package'.[24] It seems as though the critics have won the day as the Court has retreated from *Mangold*. In a number of cases,

---

[20] For further discussion see Chapter 7 at pp. 297–8.

[21] See the critical reflections in E. Muir, 'Enhancing the Effects of Community Law on National Employment Policies: The *Mangold* Case' (2006) 31 *ELRev.* 879.

[22] Editorial, 'Out with the Old...' (2006) 31 *ELRev.* 1; A. Masson and C. Micheau, 'The *Werner Mangold* Case: An Example of Legal Militancy' (2007) *EPL* 587; Editorial Comments, (2006) 43 *CMLRev.* 1.

[23] R. Herzog and L. Gerken, 'Stop the European Court of Justice', *Frankfurter Allgemeine Zeitung*, 8 September 2008 (available in English at www.cep.eu/fileadmin/user_upload/Pressemappe/CEP_in_den_Medien/Herzog-EuGH-Webseite_eng.pdf).

[24] D. Schieck, 'The ECJ Decision in *Mangold*: A Further Twist on Effects of Directives and Constitutional Relevance of Community Equality Legislation' (2006) 35 *ILJ* 329.

the Court declined to apply the general principle it set out and ruled in a more restrictive manner.[25] Advocates General have also criticised the approach taken by the Court, and Advocate General Geelhoed has rightly noted the economic repercussions of *Mangold* in a disability discrimination case.

Case C-13/05 *Sonia Chacón Navas* v *Eurest Colectividades SA* [2006] ECR I-6467, Opinion of Advocate General Geelhoed

50. The object of some of the prohibitions of discrimination listed in Article [19 TFEU], such as that based on age and disability, means that the identification of prohibited formal inequality of treatment will always entail a substantive claim to equal access to or continued employment in an occupation or business, equal conditions of employment, the availability of special training or of facilities which compensate for or alleviate the limitations due to age or disability. In view of the potentially far-reaching consequences, economic and financial, which such prohibitions of discrimination may have in horizontal relationships among citizens and in vertical relationships between public authorities and interested citizens, national legislatures tend to provide precise definitions of such prohibitions of discrimination in terms of their scope — including justified exceptions and limitations and the provision reasonably to be made for compensatory facilities.

51. ... the Community legislature, too, was aware of those potentially far-reaching economic and financial consequences.

52. The definitions and delineations set out in Directive 2000/78 should be taken seriously, since the economic and financial effects of the prohibition of discrimination on grounds of disability are felt primarily in areas which are indeed covered by the Treaty, but where the Community has at best shared, but for the most part complementary powers. This is true of employment policy, ... and of social policy ... In the areas of education and vocational training, and public health, which are also relevant in the present context, the Community's powers are similarly of a complementary nature.

53. I infer from this that the Court must respect the choices made by the Community legislature in the rules on the application of Article [19 TFEU] with regard to the definition of the prohibition of discrimination and the substantive and personal delineation of that prohibition and must not stretch them by relying on the general qualification reflected in that article by the words 'Within the limits of the powers conferred by [the Treaty] upon the Community'. There is even less room, in my view, for widening the scope of Article [19 TFEU] by relying on the general policy of equality.

54. So broad an interpretation of Article [19 TFEU] and of the rules adopted by the Community legislature on the implementation of that article results, as it were, in the creation of an Archimedean position, from which the prohibitions of discrimination defined in Article [19 TFEU] can be used as a lever to correct, without the intervention of the authors of the Treaty or the Community legislature, the decisions made by the Member States in the exercise of the powers which they – still – retain. Given that, according to the EC Treaty, the core of those powers continues to rest with the Member States, even if the Community competence in that respect is activated by the Community legislature, this is an undesirable outcome from the viewpoint of both the system underlying the Treaty and institutional balance.

---

[25] For example, in three cases on age discrimination. In Case C-427/06 *Birgit Bartsch* v *Bosch und Siemens Hausgeräte* [2008] ECR I-7245, the Court found that the national rules did not fall within the scope of EU law; in Case C-411/05 *Félix Palacios de la Villa* v *Cortefiel Servicios SA* [2007] ECR I-8531, the Court applied the relevant Directive; in C-227/04 P *Lindorfer* [2007] ECR I-6767 (a mixed age and sex discrimination case) the Court decided on grounds of sex discrimination.

55. I would also point out, for the sake of completeness, that the implementation of the prohibitions of discrimination of relevance here always requires that the legislature make painful, if not tragic, choices when weighing up the interests in question, such as the rights of disabled or older workers versus the flexible operation of the labour market or an increase in the level of participation of older workers. Not infrequently the application of these prohibitions of discrimination necessitates financial compensation, the reasonableness of which partly depends on available public resources or the general level of prosperity in the Member States concerned. Within the national sphere such considerations do not take place in a legal vacuum. As a rule, they are examined for their compatibility with fundamental national constitutional rights and the relevant provisions of international human rights treaties. That being the case, the Court must surely, as the Community's judicial authority, have an indisputable and superior basis of competence if it wishes to correct decisions taken by a national legislature within the limits set by the national constitution and international law, and in accordance with its retained powers.

Prohibiting certain forms of discrimination (especially age and disability) can be very expensive for employers and society as a whole. Appreciating this dimension of the controversy raised by *Mangold* serves to explain the observation that when new equality measures are proposed, an attempt is made to emphasise the economic dimension so as to persuade recalcitrant Member States that the measure in question contributes to the traditional economic aims of the Treaties.[26] Furthermore, the policy considerations underpinning legislation in this field also explain the haphazard (and unequal) nature of equal opportunities legislation. EU law addresses sex discrimination in one set of instruments (e.g. a Directive that consolidates previous disparate Directives on equal pay and equal treatment,[27] a Directive relating to equal treatment in the access to and supply of goods and services,[28] and a Directive extending non-discrimination in the field of social security);[29] race and ethnic origin discrimination is covered by Directive 2000/43/EC ('Race Directive'); while religion, belief, disability, age and sexual orientation discrimination are regulated by a single Directive (the Framework Directive).[30] There are small and not so small divergences between the scope of protection offered to different victims of discrimination, depending on which Directive applies.[31] For instance, the Framework Directive only applies to discrimination in the workplace, while the Race Directive also applies to prohibit discrimination outside of the workplace. This contradicts the Council's position that the 'different forms of discrimination cannot be ranked: all are equally intolerable'.[32] The lack of consolidated protection for discriminated groups is not a problem that besets EU law exclusively: differentiated political willingness to address all forms of discrimination equally is deeply embedded in national politics.

[26] M. A. Pollack and E. Hafner-Burton, 'Mainstreaming Gender in the European Union' (2000) 7 *JEPP* 432, 441–2.

[27] Equal Treatment Directive, above n. 18. N. Burrows and M. Robison, 'An Assessment of the Recast of Community Equality Laws' (2006) 13 *ELJ* 186.

[28] Council Directive 2004/113/EC of 13 December 2004 implementing the principle of equal treatment between men and women in the access to and supply of goods and services.

[29] Council Directive 79/7/EC [1979] OJ L6/24 ('Social Security Directive').

[30] See above n. 18.

[31] L. Waddington and M. Bell, 'More Equal than Others: Distinguishing European Union Equality Directives' (2001) 38 *CMLRev.* 587.

[32] Council Decision 2000/750/EC establishing a Community Action Programme to combat discrimination [2000] OJ L303/23, recital 5.

(ii) Equal opportunities versus substantive equality

It is beyond the scope of this chapter to explore all the theories that have been deployed to justify discrimination legislation.[33] However, it is important to have a feel for what discrimination law might be used to achieve as a means of evaluating the efforts of the European Union. We therefore sketch two contrasting approaches: one focusing on equality of opportunity, the other on equality of results. The first view provides that like should be treated alike. When an employer hires someone, race, religion, sex, sexual orientation or age must not play a part in selecting the successful candidates. This approach guarantees 'formal' equality among persons. The competing model favours the use of discrimination law to generate substantive equality. From this perspective, discrimination laws are successful if the result is that more underrepresented groups have access to employment, education and other opportunities. This may entail discriminating in favour of an excluded group, for example by determining that a certain percentage of the workforce should consist of women or ethnic minorities. This can discriminate against men or those who are not from ethnic minorities. Therefore this model provides equality of results by sacrificing equality of opportunities. This vision is incompatible with the liberal, formal equality model.[34]

There are three main differences between the formal and the substantive approach to equality. First, formal equality does not guarantee equality of results and does not address the causes of inequality. Secondly, the formal equality model is concerned with individual rights (and therefore its primary means of enforcement is litigation by the person who is wronged), while the substantive equality model is concerned to promote the rights of persons who have been systemically discriminated against, and models of enforcement which support group rights are preferred. Thus, regulatory means of achieving equality are seen as superior to private litigation. A third and wider difference between the two models is that the formal equality model requires the disadvantaged to act like the privileged group, thus it does not recognise the legitimacy of differences between groups; whereas supporters of substantive equality argue that merely promoting the participation of women or blacks is meaningless if we demand that they comply with a white, male culture.[35] Substantive equality models entail a respect for differences and the integration of differences within society, allowing the previously excluded group to bring their values into the mainstream.

(iii) The core framework of EU equality law: the labour market

As we will see, there are differences in the level of protection offered to different underrepresented groups, with the majority opinion being that those discriminated against because of sex, race and ethnic origin are best protected, and those suffering from age discrimination have the least rights. However, there is a floor of protection that EU law guarantees to each group, and in this section we set out what this comprises. The legislation provides the plaintiff with a right she can exercise against private or public bodies when she faces discrimination in the following fields.

---

[33] See S. Fredman, *Discrimination Law* (Oxford, Oxford University Press, 2002) ch. 1; N. Bamforth, 'Conceptions of Anti-discrimination Law' (2004) 24 *OJLS* 693.

[34] For an attempted justification of reverse discrimination, see M. Rosenfeld, *Affirmative Action and Justice: A Philosophical and Constitutional Inquiry* (New Haven, CT, Yale University Press, 1991); L. Jacobs, *Pursuing Equal Opportunities* (Cambridge, Cambridge University Press, 2004) ch. 5.

[35] For this critique, see S. Fredman, *Women and the Law* (Oxford, Oxford University Press, 1997) chs. 1 and 4.

Framework Directive, article 3

1. Within the limits of the areas of competence conferred on the Community, this Directive shall apply to all persons, as regards both the public and private sectors, including public bodies, in relation to:
   (a) conditions for access to employment, to self-employment or to occupation, including selection criteria and recruitment conditions, whatever the branch of activity and at all levels of the professional hierarchy, including promotion;
   (b) access to all types and to all levels of vocational guidance, vocational training, advanced vocational training and retraining, including practical work experience;
   (c) employment and working conditions, including dismissals and pay;
   (d) membership of, and involvement in, an organisation of workers or employers, or any organisation whose members carry on a particular profession, including the benefits provided for by such organisations

The rights listed above are also available for victims of discrimination on grounds of race and sex, but are based on different Directives.[36] The right is to be free from four forms of discrimination: direct discrimination (which is aimed at an individual because of, for example, her race or religion); indirect discrimination (when an apparently neutral job requirement is more easily satisfied by one sex or racial group than another; for example if a job is only available to people who are clean-shaven this indirectly excludes Sikhs); harassment; and victimisation (i.e. adverse treatment directed at a person who has made a discrimination claim against an employer). Direct and indirect discrimination are justified in certain circumstances; for example all Directives provide for the defendant to claim that discrimination was on the basis of a genuine occupational requirement (thus, e.g., a Buddhist cannot be eligible to work as a priest in a Roman Catholic church).[37] If discrimination is unjustified, the plaintiff has a right to a remedy, and Member States have an obligation to provide an enforcement mechanism, as well as to grant effective remedies to the plaintiff (including financial compensation).

Supplementing this common core of rights have been the decisions of the Court of Justice. It will be recalled that the Court's early case law established that EU law had supremacy over national law, and that certain provisions of EU law (including Article 157 TFEU) have direct effect.[38] In the sphere of sex discrimination, these principles have had a profound impact because they have allowed the Court to challenge national sex equality law. Supremacy meant that a national court would be required to disapply national law which conflicts with EU law. For example, in *Macarthys Ltd* v *Smith*, a woman made a claim for equal pay based on the fact that her predecessor (a man) had been paid more for doing the same work as her. At that time it was not clear whether her claim was admissible under the UK Equal Pay Act 1970, but the Court of Justice held that Article 157 TFEU did cover this dispute,[39] therefore the national court was required to disapply national law in order to afford the plaintiff her EU law rights.[40] In the 1980s, the UK's Equal Opportunities Commission devised a highly successful litigation

---

[36] Race Directive, article 3(1)(a)–(d); Article 157 TFEU and Equal Treatment Directive for sex discrimination.
[37] Equal Treatment Directive, article 14(2); Race Directive, article 4; Framework Directive, article 4.
[38] See Chapter 7 and note that many of the key cases on direct effect are based upon sex discrimination.
[39] Case 129/79 *Macarthys Ltd* v *Smith* [1980] ECR 1275.
[40] *Macarthys Ltd* v *Smith* [1980] ICR 672, 693–4.

strategy bringing test cases like this one to challenge national sex equality laws based on their infringement of EU equality law.[41]

The limitations of the Court of Justice's contribution to EU equal opportunities policy can be explored with a recent judgment which challenged the lack of protection afforded by UK sex discrimination law when employers contract out work. The plaintiff, Ms Allonby, had been employed part-time by a teaching college. The college found that part-time employees were too expensive because the law required that they be entitled to statutory benefits equal to those of full-time teachers and she, along with other part-timers, was made redundant. She was then engaged by a new company, ELS, who supplied her as a self-employed teacher to the same college that had made her redundant. This arrangement was cheaper for the college because they had no obligations to provide her with the same benefits as when she was a part-time employee, and Ms Allonby received less pay than before. Moreover, because she was classified as self-employed, she lost her right to be a member of the teachers' pension scheme. Her claim for unequal pay against ELS was based on the fact that men employed directly by the college were paid more. This was not successful because she could only compare her rate of pay with people that had the same employer as herself (and she was engaged by ELS, not the college).[42] The policy consideration that led the Court to refuse comparing Ms Allonby's pay to that of men doing the same work for other employers is practical, as it is near to impossible for employers to monitor what the pay is in other institutions.[43]

Her second claim was against the state (represented by the Department for Education and Employment), in which she claimed that she suffered discrimination because the law made it impossible for her to join the pension scheme merely because she was classified as self-employed. As a preliminary matter, the Court had no hesitation in finding the denial of access to an occupational pension scheme to be an unequal pay claim. This reflects the breadth of the meaning of the concept of 'pay' developed by the Court of Justice.[44] Throughout the 1980s and early 1990s, the Court expanded the concept of pay to include a range of benefits, e.g. occupational pension schemes,[45] travel concessions,[46] redundancy pay,[47] maternity leave pay,[48] unfair dismissal compensation[49] and statutory sick pay.[50] The test set out by the Court is that any consideration that the worker receives directly or indirectly in respect of employment from her employer is to be considered pay.[51] The Court held that the fact that she was not an 'employee' under national law did not mean that she was not a worker for the purposes of Article 157 TFEU, and went on to explore the meaning of the term 'worker'.

---

[41] K. J. Alter and J. Vargas, 'Explaining Variation in the Use of European Litigation Strategies: European Community Law and British Gender Equality Policy' (2000) 33 *Comparative Political Studies* 452; C. Kilpatrick, 'Gender Equality: A Fundamental Dialogue' in S. Sciarra (ed.), *Labour Law in the Courts* (Oxford, Hart, 2001).

[42] The Court of Justice followed Case C-320/00 *Lawrence and Others* v *Regent Office Care Ltd and Others* [2002] ECR I-7325.

[43] *Macarthys Ltd* v *Smith* [1980] ICR 672.

[44] It is beyond the scope of this chapter to examine in detail the meaning of 'pay'. See E. Ellis, *EU Anti-Discrimination Law* (Oxford, Oxford University Press, 2005) ch. 4.

[45] Case 170/84 *Bilka-Kaufhaus GmbH* v *Karin Weber von Hartz* [1986] ECR 1607.

[46] Case 12/81 *Garland* v *British Rail Engineering* [1982] ECR 359.

[47] Case 262/88 *Barber* v *Guardian Royal Exchange Assurance Group* [1990] ECR I-1889.

[48] Case C-342/93 *Gillespie* v *Northern Health and Social Services Board* [1996] ECR I-457.

[49] Case C-167/97 *R* v *Secretary of State for Employment, ex parte Seymour-Smith and Perez* [1999] ECR I-623.

[50] Case 171/88 *Rinner-Kühn* v *FWW Spezial-Gebäudereinigung GmbH & Co. KG* [1989] ECR 2743.

[51] Case C-167/97 *R* v *Secretary of State for Employment, ex parte Seymour-Smith and Perez* [1999] ECR I-623, para. 23.

Case C–256/01 *Allonby* v *Accrington and Rossendale College* [2004] ECR I–873

66. ... the term 'worker' used in Article [157(1) TFEU] cannot be defined by reference to the legislation of the Member States but has a Community meaning. Moreover, it cannot be interpreted restrictively.

67. For the purposes of that provision, there must be considered as a worker a person who, for a certain period of time, performs services for and under the direction of another person in return for which he receives remuneration.

68. Pursuant to the first paragraph of Article [157(2) TFEU], for the purpose of that article, 'pay' means the ordinary basic or minimum wage or salary and any other consideration, whether in cash or in kind, which the worker receives directly or indirectly, in respect of his employment, from his employer. It is clear from that definition that the authors of the Treaty did not intend that the term 'worker', within the meaning of Article [157(1) TFEU], should include independent providers of services who are not in a relationship of subordination with the person who receives the services.

69. The question whether such a relationship exists must be answered in each particular case having regard to all the factors and circumstances by which the relationship between the parties is characterised.

70. Provided that a person is a worker within the meaning of Article [157(1) TFEU], the nature of his legal relationship with the other party to the employment relationship is of no consequence in regard to the application of that article.

71. The formal classification of a self-employed person under national law does not exclude the possibility that a person must be classified as a worker within the meaning of Article [157(1) TFEU] if his independence is merely notional, thereby disguising an employment relationship within the meaning of that article.

72. In the case of teachers who are, vis-à-vis an intermediary undertaking, under an obligation to undertake an assignment at a college, it is necessary in particular to consider the extent of any limitation on their freedom to choose their timetable, and the place and content of their work. The fact that no obligation is imposed on them to accept an assignment is of no consequence in that context.

The effect of this ruling is to widen the meaning of 'workers' so that Member States are unable to reclassify persons as 'self-employed' merely to avoid obligations under Article 157 TFEU. For Ms Allonby this meant that the national court might now classify her as a worker by considering the nature of her work. Assuming she was a worker, she would have a remedy if it was proven that the exclusion of self-employed teachers from the scheme adversely affected more women than men.[52]

Thus, the judgment was good news for the plaintiff in that she may be entitled to join the relevant pension scheme, but bad news for her in that her complaint about her lower salary was not accepted.[53] It is interesting to note that the reason why Ms Allonby was in the predicament she was in was, paradoxically, because of Article 157 TFEU. In earlier cases, the Court had moved to protect part-time workers (who are predominantly female) using sex discrimination rules, thus guaranteeing that their remuneration was comparable to full-time workers.[54] The employer in this dispute was responding to the implications of one such ruling, which

---

[52] Thus, it is a claim for indirect discrimination, a concept explored in detail at pp. 559–60.
[53] S. Fredman, 'Marginalising Equal Pay Laws' (2004) 33 *ILJ* 281.
[54] See now Directive 97/81/EC on part-time work [1998] OJ L14/9, which broadly codifies the case law.

compelled employers to grant equivalent rights to part-time workers.[55] It sought to evade the costs placed upon it by contracting Ms Allonby's services out so she was no longer their part-time worker. The irony was not lost on Advocate General Geelhoed:

> [a] legal device has been used precisely … in order to evade the consequences of the principle of equal treatment laid down in Article [157 TFEU]. A change in the legal form of the relationship between Ms Allonby and her original employer, the College, thus results in the loss of the protection conferred by Article [157 TFEU] on Ms Allonby as a female employee.[56]

However, he felt that a solution to this loophole required legislative action rather than judicial creativity. In recasting the equality Directives in 2006, the Commission wished to overrule the first ground in *Allonby* but was persuaded to drop this, because the process of recasting only allows for legislation to be consolidated and clarified.[57]

3 EQUALITY GROUNDS

Discrimination is wrong when we treat a person differently because of a 'morally irrelevant' characteristic,[58] or where we treat her with unwarranted contempt,[59] for example, refusing to hire a person because she is black or has blonde hair. However, refusing to hire a person as a doctor because she has no qualifications for the job is a legitimate basis for discrimination. More blurred is the refusal to hire a Sikh who wears a turban because he is unable to wear a protective helmet, or preventing a female pupil from wearing her traditional religious dress at school on the basis that this may lead to her being bullied. Moreover, it is not clear why law prohibits discrimination on the basis of religion but not on the basis of political opinion, given that both are by and large freely chosen. These trite examples hide a difficult question, which we consider in this part: what grounds of discrimination are morally irrelevant? As we will see in the sections that follow, the European Union has identified certain personal attributes that make discrimination unlawful, but has excluded others. Furthermore, one important omission in the discrimination Directives is any definition of the protected group. This gives Member States discretion on setting out a definition, but it also means that the Court of Justice will have a determinative role in shaping the meaning of concepts like race, ethnicity and religion. The disadvantages of legal uncertainty and diversity among the Member States can be balanced by the potential for the definitions to evolve organically in response to changing social conditions.

As we have seen, the discrimination Directives protect workers who belong to one protected group. Moreover, the Directives are also designed to safeguard the rights of a person who does not belong to a protected group but suffers discrimination 'on the grounds' of, for example, sex or race.[60] This means that if a person is discriminated against because he is caring for an

---

[55] Employment Protection (Part-time Employees) Regulations 1995, SI 1995/31, which were the result of *R v Secretary of State for Employment, ex parte EOC* [1994] 1 All ER 910, where the House of Lords held that inferior rights for part-time workers were contrary to EU law.

[56] Case C-256/01 *Allonby v Accrington and Rossendale College* [2004] ECR I-873, para. 43.

[57] J. Shaw, J. Hunt and C. Wallace, *Economic and Social Law of the European Union* (Basingstoke, Palgrave MacMillan, 2007) 372–3.

[58] D. Feldman, *Civil Liberties and Human Rights in England and Wales* (2nd edn, Oxford, Oxford University Press, 2002) 135–6.

[59] M. Cavanagh, *Against Equality of Opportunity* (Oxford, Clarendon Press, 2002) ch. 4.

[60] Equal Treatment Directive, article 2(1); Race Directive, article 1; Framework Directive, article 2(1).

elderly relative, or because he has homosexual friends, he is discriminated against 'on grounds' of age or sexual orientation.[61] The Court confirmed this in *Coleman*, where the plaintiff was the primary carer of a disabled child and claimed she was harassed and discriminated against on the grounds of her child's disability when she sought flexible working arrangements to care for him.

Case C–303/06 *S. Coleman* v *Attridge Law and Steve Law* [2008] ECR I–5603

38. ... the purpose of the Directive, as regards employment and occupation, is to combat all forms of discrimination on grounds of disability. The principle of equal treatment enshrined in the Directive in that area applies not to a particular category of person but by reference to the grounds mentioned in Article 1. That interpretation is supported by the wording of Article [19 TFEU], which constitutes the legal basis of Directive 2000/78, and which confers on the Community the competence to take appropriate action to combat discrimination based, inter alia, on disability ....

50. Although, in a situation such as that in the present case, the person who is subject to direct discrimination on grounds of disability is not herself disabled, the fact remains that it is the disability which, according to Ms Coleman, is the ground for the less favourable treatment which she claims to have suffered. As is apparent from paragraph 38 of this judgment, Directive 2000/78, which seeks to combat all forms of discrimination on grounds of disability in the field of employment and occupation, applies not to a particular category of person but by reference to the grounds mentioned in Article 1.

51. Where it is established that an employee in a situation such as that in the present case suffers direct discrimination on grounds of disability, an interpretation of Directive 2000/78 limiting its application only to people who are themselves disabled is liable to deprive that Directive of an important element of its effectiveness and to reduce the protection which it is intended to guarantee.

It remains to be seen how close the bond between the victim of discrimination and the person with whom she is associated must be. Here the plaintiff was the primary carer, but what if the bond was looser, say a white person is discriminated against because he has friends of other ethnicities?

(i) Sex/gender

The early development of sex discrimination laws owes much to a French civil servant, Jacqueline Nonon, who pressed for the adoption of feminist policies in the 1970s.[62] There are now several bodies that coordinate and promote gender equality, including the Advisory Committee on Equal Opportunities for Women and Men,[63] and in 2007 the European Institute for Gender Equality was established, with a budget of €52.5 million for 2007–2013.[64] The Court

---

[61] R. Whittle, 'The Framework Directive for Equal Treatment in Employment and Occupation: An Analysis from a Disability Rights Perspective' (2002) 27 *ELRev.* 303, 321–2.

[62] C. Harlow and R. Rawlings, *Pressure Through Law* (London, Routledge, 1992) 282.

[63] Decision 82/43/EEC relating to the setting up of an Advisory Committee on Equal Opportunities for Women and Men [1982] OJ L20/35.

[64] Regulation 1922/2006/EC of the European Parliament and of the Council of 20 December 2006 on establishing a European Institute for Gender Equality [2006] OJ L403/9.

of Justice's heavy involvement in sex discrimination is the result of a concerted effort by one Belgian lawyer, Eliane Vogel-Polsky, who in the 1970s tested the legality of Belgian law with Article 157 TFEU by taking up a complaint from Gabrielle Defrenne, an air hostess who had been awarded a pension inferior to that of her male colleagues. In *Defrenne* v *Sabena*, the Court held that the equal pay provision, Article 157 TFEU, had direct effect,[65] and this led to increased litigation testing the compatibility of national law with EU law, especially emanating from the United Kingdom and the Netherlands.[66] The pace of sex equality legislation stalled in the 1980s and 1990s, in part because of the reluctance of Member States to take equality further. The Commission responded to this hiatus by drafting a range of soft law measures to encourage Member State action.[67] It has been suggested that the increased legislative output in the mid-1990s was in part motivated by the need for the Union to show that it was not merely about achieving economic goals (at the time the establishment of a single currency).[68]

As we have indicated, the Court of Justice has played a significant role in shaping and extending the scope of sex equality legislation, and some of the principles established in the judgments were later translated into legislation.[69] Moreover, the Court extended the scope of sex equality to discrimination against transsexuals. In *P* v *S and Cornwall County Council*, P was dismissed after her decision to undergo male-to-female gender reassignment, a medical procedure designed to allow her to have a more integrated identity. The Court found that this constituted discrimination on the basis of sex in breach of Directive 2006/54/EC ('Equal Treatment Directive').

Case C-13/94 *P v S and Cornwall County Council* [1996] ECR I-2143

20. ... [t]he scope of the Directive cannot be confined simply to discrimination based on the fact that a person is of one or other sex. In view of its purpose and the nature of the rights which it seeks to safeguard, the scope of the Directive is also such as to apply to discrimination arising, as in this case, from the gender reassignment of the person concerned.

21. Such discrimination is based, essentially if not exclusively, on the sex of the person concerned. Where a person is dismissed on the ground that he or she intends to undergo, or has undergone, gender reassignment, he or she is treated unfavourably by comparison with persons of the sex to which he or she was deemed to belong before undergoing gender reassignment.

22. To tolerate such discrimination would be tantamount, as regards such a person, to a failure to respect the dignity and freedom to which he or she is entitled, and which the Court has a duty to safeguard.

---

[65] Case 43/75 *Defrenne* v *Sabena* [1976] ECR 455.

[66] Harlow and Rawlings, above n. 62, 283–4; C. Kilpatrick, 'Community or Communities of Courts in European Integration? Sex Equality Dialogues between UK Courts and the ECJ' (1998) 4 *ELJ* 121.

[67] See e.g. Recommendation 84/635 on the promotion of positive action for women [1984] OJ L331/34; Directive 92/85/EC of 19 October 1992 on the introduction of measures to encourage improvements in the safety and health at work of pregnant workers and workers who have recently given birth or are breastfeeding [1992] OJ L348/1.

[68] Bell, above n. 2, 47–8.

[69] See e.g. Case 109/88 *Handels- og Kontorfunktionærernes Forbund I Danmark* v *Dansk Arbejdsgiverforening, acting on behalf of Danforss* [1989] ECR 3199 and Case C-127/92 *Enderby* v *Frenchay Health Authority and Secretary of State for Health* [1993] ECR I-5535, leading to Directive 97/80/EC on the burden of proof in cases of discrimination based on sex [1998] OJ L14/6.

This was widely welcomed because the Court moved away from a narrow emphasis on sex discrimination towards an appreciation of gender identities.[70] It was affirmed in *KB* v *National Health Service Pensions Agency*, where a female employee wished to assign her survivor's pension rights to R, a female-to-male transsexual, but was unable to do so because at the time UK law did not allow R's sex change to be legally recognised, and so KB and R were unable to marry.[71] As a result KB was unable to nominate R as the person entitled to receive KB's pension should she die before R. The Court held that while there was no discrimination in the law restricting the right to the survivor's pensions to married spouses,[72] UK law de facto prevented R from qualifying by denying her the right to marry. Having noted that the European Court of Human Rights (ECtHR) had earlier ruled that UK law was incompatible with the European Convention on Human Rights' right to marry,[73] the fact that R was unable to qualify to obtain the survivor's pension was in breach of Article 157.[74] However, the Court of Justice left it to the national court to determine whether KB could rely on Article 157 to gain recognition of her right to nominate R as beneficiary.[75] It is not clear why the national court has any discretion in the matter, given the Court's firm stance that R's inability to qualify constituted a breach of EU law. One answer is that the Court implicitly refuses to challenge the Member State's choices about which persons can marry, and fails to engage in resolving more complex disputes, e.g. in relation to those who choose not to undergo gender reassignment and yet consider themselves as belonging to the other sex (transgender).[76] Judicial reluctance to engage with the complexities of gender identity is matched by the legislature's timid revision of the Equal Treatment Directive.[77]

(ii) Racial or ethnic origin

The need for EU legislation in this field has been discussed since the 1980s. However, there was little action, in part because there was no certain legal basis for legislation.[78] Increased immigration brought racism to the attention of legislators in the 1990s and was accompanied by more effective lobbying, in particular the 'Starting Line Group' (a coalition of 200 non-governmental organisations established in 1989).[79] It proposed a Race Directive in 1992, and

---

[70] It was applied to retirement pensions for transsexuals in Case C-423/04 *Richards* v *Secretary of State for Work and Pensions* [2006] ECR I-3585.

[71] Case C-117/01 *KB* v *National Health Service Pensions Agency* [2004] ECR I-541. For a critique, see M. Bell, 'A Hazy Concept of Equality' (2004) 12 *Feminist Legal Studies* 223.

[72] Case C-117/01 *KB* v *National Health Service Pensions Agency* [2004] ECR I-541, paras. 28–9.

[73] *Goodwin* v *United Kingdom* (2002) 35 EHRR 18 and *I* v *United Kingdom* [2002] ECHR 592. See now the Gender Recognition Act 2004.

[74] Case C-117/01 *KB* v *National Health Service Pensions Agency* [2004] ECR I-541, para. 34.

[75] *Ibid.* para. 35.

[76] Bell, above n. 66, 223. But see Case C-423/04 *Richards* v *Secretary of State for Work and Pensions*, Opinion of Advocate General Jacobs, 15 December 2005, para. 45.

[77] Equal Treatment Directive, recital 3, merely provides that it also applies to discrimination arising from the gender reassignment of a person.

[78] See e.g. Joint Declaration of the Institutions against Racism and Xenophobia [1986] OJ C158/1; European Parliament, Resolution on racism and xenophobia and anti-semitism and further steps to combat further racial discrimination [1999] OJ C98/488.

[79] On the origins of this group, see P. Iganski, 'Legislating Morality and Competing Rights: Legal Instruments against Racism and Anti-semitism in the European Union' (1999) 25 *Journal of Ethnic and Migration Studies* 509; I. Chopin, 'The Starting Line Group: A Harmonised Approach to Fighting Racism and to Promote Equal Treatment' (1999) 1 *European Journal of Migration and Law* 111.

this gained wide support.[80] At the same time, the EU institutions were becoming increasingly concerned about racism, although there were differences among Member States preventing legislative action.[81] The European Year Against Racism in 1997 was designed to raise awareness, and the European Monitoring Centre on Racism and Xenophobia was established that year to gather further information on these social problems and aid in the formulation of policy.[82] Once Article 19 TFEU was introduced, however, it only took six months for the Commission's proposed Race Directive to be adopted by the Council.[83] The main reason for this urgency was the election of an extreme right-wing government in Austria in 2000 and the wish of the European Union to assert a set of values to underscore its commitment to racial equality.[84] A second factor was the forthcoming enlargement of the Union and incorporating non-discrimination in the Community acquis was a means of sending a strong message against racial intolerance to new Member States, but also a means of addressing concerns expressed about manifestations of racism in the older Member States, e.g. France and the United Kingdom.[85]

The central difficulty in applying the Race Directive in practice is that there is no definition of race or ethnic origin, and there is no uniform practice in this context that can be drawn upon.[86] The Preamble to the Race Directive states that the European Union 'rejects theories which attempt to determine the existence of separate human races'.[87] This reflects the practice in the United States, where the Supreme Court has taken a wide, purposive approach to identifying race.[88] It recognises that a person's race is a social construct based upon certain attributes, e.g. skin colour, language, culture or religion. One criticism of the Directive is its failure to suggest that 'observable characteristics' like skin colour can be the basis for defining race, as this would have facilitated the implementation of effective laws.[89] Ethnicity is an even more complex term to define. In UK law, the House of Lords identified two essential conditions for the existence of an ethnic group: first, a long shared history as a separate group and, secondly, a cultural tradition, including family and social customs.[90] Other features indicative of ethnicity are a common geographical origin, common language, literature or religion, and being a separate group within a larger community. On this basis, Sikhs, Jews and gypsies form distinct ethnic groups, while Rastafarians do not because they lack a sufficiently long shared history.[91] This creates a complex borderline between discrimination on the grounds of race and religion.

---

[80] A. Dummett, 'The Starting Line: A Proposal for a Draft Community Directive concerning the Elimination of Racial Discrimination' (1994) 20 *New Community* 530. On their impact on the Directive, see A. Tyson, 'The Negotiation of the European Community Directive on Racial Discrimination' (2001) 3 *European Journal of Migration and Law* 199.

[81] Bell, above n. 2, 70–1.

[82] Regulation 1035/97/EC [1997] OJ L151/1.

[83] European Commission, Proposal for a Council Directive implementing the principle of equal treatment between persons irrespective of racial or ethnic origin, COM(1999)566.

[84] See G. de Búrca, 'The Drafting of the European Union Charter of Fundamental Rights' (2001) 26 *ELRev.* 126, 136.

[85] For background, see C. Brown, 'The Race Directive: Towards Equality for *All* Peoples of Europe?' (2002) *YEL* 195, 196–204.

[86] E. Guild, 'The EC Directive on Race Discrimination: Surprises, Possibilities and Limitations' (2000) 24 *ILJ* 416.

[87] Race Directive, recital 6.

[88] *St Francis College* v *Al-Khazraji* 481 US 604 (1987).

[89] F. Brennan, 'The Race Directive: Recycling Racial Inequality' (2002–03) 5 *CYELS* 311, 320–1.

[90] *Mandla* v *Lee* [1983] 2 AC 548.

[91] See, respectively, *Deide* v *Gillette* [1980] IRLR 427 (Jews); *CRE* v *Dutton* [1989] QB 783 (gypsies); *Dawkins* v *Department of the Environment* [1993] ICR 517 (Rastafarians).

Difficulties in providing definitions of race and ethnic origin might be surmounted by eschewing a literal approach in favour of a purposive interpretation which explores the social and historical context of racism. If this might lead to divergent definitions of race and ethnicity among the Member States, this should be welcomed, for it allows each state to develop the law in a manner consistent with the origins of racism within each state.[92]

(iii) Religion or belief

Forbidding discrimination on grounds of religion is particularly significant because while some religious groups would be able to secure protection on the basis of the Race Directive, others might fall outside it. In the context of the United Kingdom, for example, Muslims found it difficult to make a claim for race discrimination.[93] The Directive is likely to cover Buddhists as 'believers' in a specific way of life,[94] but it is uncertain whether pacifists or vegetarians are protected, even though they hold a set of beliefs that informs their life choices.[95] In implementing the Framework Directive, the United Kingdom has taken the view that the Directive only prohibits discrimination on the grounds of 'any religion, religious belief or *similar* philosophical belief'.[96] Following the approach taken by the ECtHR, it means the belief in question must be coherent and serious, and must be one which merits respect in a democratic society.[97] Atheism and humanism fall within this definition, but the support of a political party or a football team do not. Absence of belief is also protected, so a religious employer may not refuse a job to a non-believer.[98]

(iv) Disability

Before the Framework Directive, the European Union had devoted some energies to addressing the difficulties faced by disabled persons via action programmes. The first was designed to exchange information and notes on good practice in education and employment of disabled persons.[99] But the Union was unsuccessful in implementing legislation conferring rights on disabled persons; for example, it failed to obtain agreement on legislation obliging employers to adopt quotas to promote employment of disabled people.[100] Nevertheless, as of the

---

[92] See J. Rex, 'Multiculturalism in Europe and America' (1995) 1 *Nations and Nationalism* 243, who notes that it would be difficult to transplant the United Kingdom's race relations laws to France.

[93] B. Hepple and T. Choudhury, *Tackling Religious Discrimination: Practical Implications for Policy-Makers and Legislators*, Home Office Research Study 221 (London, Home Office, 2001) 12; S. Poulter, 'Muslim Headscarves in School: Contrasting Approaches in England and France' (1997) *OJLS* 43.

[94] Ellis, above n. 44, 33.

[95] Under Article 9 of the ECHR (which safeguards 'freedom of thought, conscience and religion'), the ECtHR extended its scope to atheism and agnosticism (*Kokkinakis v Greece* (1994) 17 EHRR 397), and the European Commission on Human Rights had included pacifism (*Arrowsmith v United Kingdom* (1978) 19 DR 5) and veganism (*H v United Kingdom* (1993) 16 EHRR CD 44).

[96] Employment Equality (Religion or Belief) Regulations 2003, SI 2003/1660, reg. 2(1).

[97] *Campbell and Cosans v United Kingdom* (1982) 4 EHRR 293, 304.

[98] *Kokkinakis v Greece* (1994) 17 EHRR 397, 418.

[99] Community Social Action Programme on the Social Integration of Handicapped People, 1983–88 [1981] OJ C347/1.

[100] D. Mabbett, 'The Development of Rights-based Social Policy in the European Union: The Example of Disability Rights' (2005) 43 *JCMS* 97, 107.

mid-1990s, the Council was resolved to legislate to provide equality of opportunity for disabled people,[101] and the European Parliament's Disability Intergroup pressed for the inclusion of disability discrimination in Article 19 TFEU.[102]

The Court was asked to interpret the concept of disability in *Chacón Navas* where the employee was certified as unfit for work on grounds of sickness and while she was on leave from work the employer terminated her contract because of this. The question arose whether sickness was a kind of disability so that the employee's termination was discriminatory. The Court's view was that disability for the purposes of the Directive meant 'a limitation which results in particular from physical, mental or psychological impairments and which hinders the participation of the person concerned in professional life'.[103] The legislature specifically chose to focus on disability, not sickness, so the two terms were not equivalent and a dismissal based on sickness did not give the employee protection under EU law. The most disappointing feature of the judgment is that the Court was given insufficient detail about the nature of the employee's illness. It must surely be the case that certain forms of sickness would contribute to disability (e.g. chronic fatigue syndrome), while some forms of disability might perhaps not count (e.g. an employee who suffers injury on holiday and is on crutches for six months), so the Court cannot be taken to mean that all forms of 'sickness' are not forms of disability.[104] Secondly, it has been argued that the Court narrowed the scope of the concept of disability by giving a 'medical' as opposed to a 'social' definition of the term that focuses on discrimination based on stereotypes; the latter would give protection to a wider range of persons (e.g. those who have had a mental illness, those who have a condition that shows no symptoms).[105] That said, it may be argued that certain aspects of the Directive do embrace a social model of discrimination, recognising that disability is also the result of barriers in the workplace;[106] and that it is socially constructed.[107]

Framework Directive, article 5

In order to guarantee compliance with the principle of equal treatment in relation to persons with disabilities, reasonable accommodation shall be provided. This means that employers shall take appropriate measures, where needed in a particular case, to enable a person with a disability to have access to, participate in, or advance in employment, or to undergo training, unless such measures would impose a disproportionate burden on the employer. This burden shall not be disproportionate when it is sufficiently remedied by measures existing within the framework of the disability policy of the Member State concerned.

---

[101] Draft Resolution of the Council and of Representatives of the governments of the Member States on equality of opportunity for people with disabilities, COM(96)406.

[102] See www.disabilityintergroup.eu

[103] Case C-13/05 *Sonia Chacón Navas* v *Eurest Colectividades SA* [2006] ECR I-6467, para. 43.

[104] To a degree this is recognised in the Advocate General's Opinion, *ibid.*, paras. 77–80.

[105] D. L. Hosking, 'A High Bar for EU Disability Rights' (2007) 36 *ILJ* 228. See further M. Oliver and C. Barnes, *Disabled People and Social Policy: from Exclusion to Inclusion* (Harlow, Longman, 1998).

[106] K. Wells, 'The Impact of the Framework Employment Directive on UK Disability Discrimination Law' (2003) 32 *ILJ* 253.

[107] See generally C. Barnes, 'A Working Social Model? Disability, Work and Disability Politics in the 21st Century' (2000) 20 *Critical Social Policy* 441.

The practical significance of this policy can be illustrated with an example. Say an employer wishes to hire a new IT technician and the offices are located in the basement. Refusing to employ a person who because of his disability is confined to a wheelchair would constitute discrimination if reasonable accommodation can be made, e.g. moving the IT department to a more accessible part of the building or installing a lift. It has been argued that article 5 does not impose an obligation to discriminate positively in favour of the disabled, rather it is merely an appropriate manner of recognising the implications of a duty not to discriminate against disabled persons.[108] The obligation is not unlimited, however. The employer need not make adjustments when these would cause a disproportionate burden. Therefore, if moving a large IT department would entail considerable costs or security risks, then the employer would be justified in not hiring a disabled person unable to access the workspace.

(v) Age

Before Article 19 TFEU, the major legal step that had an impact on older workers was the *Barber* ruling, where the Court of Justice held that it was unlawful to have different retirement ages for men and women insofar as occupational pension schemes were concerned.[109] The effect is that most Member States have implemented a common retirement age of 65, increasing the participation of women in the marketplace.[110] On a legislative plane, by contrast, there was reluctance amongst Member States to give the European Union competence in developing policy towards the aged.[111] The inclusion of age discrimination in the Framework Directive is probably the result of Europe's large ageing population.[112] Having encouraged early retirement for some decades, states find themselves with a pensions crisis whereby it is unlikely that sufficient funds are available for retired persons. Moreover, people are living longer. These patterns have stimulated the demand for legislation aimed at lengthening the time people are able to work, and promoting the continued employment of older workers. As Sandra Fredman notes, '[t]he new emphasis on combating age discrimination is not ... a result of a sudden appreciation of the need for fairness, but gains its chief impetus from business and macro-economic imperatives'.[113]

However, the Directive is not limited to discrimination against the elderly, so that discrimination against young employees is also forbidden.[114] This is in contrast to US law where comparable legislation is directed at persons aged 40 or over.[115] Given that workers of all ages require protection, it may be suggested that the aim of age discrimination law should be to promote age diversity among the working population. This aspiration is reflected in the Commission's Green Paper on demographic change, which suggests that EU policy should

---

[108] R. Whittle, 'The Framework Directive for Equal Treatment in Employment and Occupation: An Analysis from a Disability Rights Perspective' (2002) 27 *ELRev*. 303.

[109] Case C-262/88 *Barber* v *Guardian Royal Exchange Assurance Group* [1990] ECR I-1889.

[110] F. McDonald and M. Potton, 'The Nascent European Policy towards Older Workers: Can the European Union Help the Older Worker?' (1997) 26 *Personnel Review* 293, 299–300.

[111] *Ibid.* 302.

[112] Framework Directive, recital 6.

[113] Fredman, above n. 33, 62.

[114] Young workers are also protected by Directive 94/33/EC of 22 June 1994 on the protection of young people at work [1994] OJ L216/12, establishing a minimum age for work and several protective measures for young workers.

[115] Age Discrimination in Employment Act 1967, 29 USC 621–34.

develop to ensure solidarity across generations by granting opportunities and benefits to all age groups.[116] However, there are two limits to what the Framework Directive can achieve in this context: first, discrimination is not the sole cause of the current social problems, and it must be seen as part of a wider range of social policy measures. Secondly, an empirical study of the US statute outlawing discrimination of older workers suggests that it has mainly benefited white men.[117] Taken together, these observations indicate the inherent limitations of a legal framework premised upon a formal equality model.

(vi) Sexual orientation

In common with other protected groups, a combination of factors led to the progressive incorporation of sexual orientation in the EU's discourse.[118] In the 1990s, NGOs, in particular one UK-based organisation (Stonewall) and the International Lesbian and Gay Association, began to lobby, focusing upon the barriers to the internal market resulting from national laws. The AIDS crisis led to the EU policy which intimated the need to combat discrimination against HIV-positive workers. Then in the 1990s, Member States began to draw up legislation to protect persons from discrimination on the grounds of sexual orientation, which facilitated the development of soft law at EU level,[119] and led to increased support from the European Parliament.[120]

Discrimination on grounds of sexual orientation operates at two levels: first, there is discrimination against those who are open about their sexuality, but secondly (and distinct from other grounds of discrimination) some choose to keep their sexual orientation a secret for fear of discrimination. The Framework Directive addresses the first type of discrimination, but there seems little which may be done to address the second, which requires a societal shift in attitudes. Nevertheless, a potentially helpful dimension for those who wish to keep their sexuality hidden is that the plaintiff does not have to disclose his or her sexual orientation, because discrimination arises if an assumption is made about the plaintiff's sexual orientation. This seems to be the position in the Directive.[121] According to some, this can help to encourage litigation as gays and lesbians may be reluctant to disclose their sexual orientation in the workplace precisely for fear of discrimination.[122]

While the Directive might be seen to provide an effective means for guaranteeing the rights of the homosexual employee, it excludes any interference with the design of national law insofar as family rights are concerned. Recital 22 of the Framework Directive provides that '[t]his Directive is without prejudice to national laws on marital status and the benefits dependent thereon'. However, this recital was read narrowly by the Court in *Tadao Maruko*. The claimant was in a same sex registered partnership (a 'life partnership' under German law) and was denied a widower's pension on his partner's death because the rules of the association

---

[116] Green Paper, *Confronting Demographic Change: A New Solidarity between the Generations*, COM(2005)94 final.

[117] G. Rutherglen, 'From Race to Age: The Expanding Scope of Employment Discrimination Law' (1995) 24 *Journal of Legal Studies* 491.

[118] This paragraph draws on Bell, above n. 2, 91–7.

[119] See e.g. the reference to sexual orientation in para. 5 of the Code of Practice on Harassment [1992] OJ L49/1.

[120] Resolution on equal rights for homosexuals and lesbians in the EC [1994] OJ C61/40.

[121] But some have expressed caution: Bell, above n. 2, 115.

[122] H. Oliver, 'Sexual Orientation Discrimination: Perceptions, Definitions and Genuine Occupational Requirements' (2004) 33 *ILJ* 1.

managing that pension made no provision for same sex partners. After finding that the pension constituted 'pay' so that the dispute fell within the Framework Directive, the Court noted that the conditions for life partnerships were increasingly aligned with those of marriage. It followed that if the national court should decide that surviving spouses and surviving life partners are in a comparable situation, then the denial of a widower's pension to the latter would constitute direct discrimination.[123] This leaves national courts with the task of determining if married couples and registered partners are in a comparable situation having regard to the issue at stake. On the facts, the German law gave life partners increasingly similar rights to married couples, allowing a successful claim. However, in Member States where the rights of registered partners are not similar to those of married couples, claimants will have to rest their arguments on indirect discrimination, which may prove more arduous.

(vii) Excluded groups

In view of the universality of the right to equality, and the recognition that discrimination against foreigners was likely in the face of increased migration into the Union, the Council's expert committee on racism (the Kahn Commission) had recommended that Article 19 TFEU should prohibit discrimination against EU and non-EU citizens. However, there is no reference to citizenship in Article 19,[124] and the Directives expressly exclude from their coverage discrimination on the basis of nationality.

Framework Directive and Race Directive, article 3(2)

This Directive does not cover differences of treatment based on nationality and is without prejudice to provisions and conditions relating to the entry into and residence of third-country nationals and stateless persons in the territory of Member States, and to any treatment which arises from the legal status of the third-country nationals and stateless persons concerned.

While EU nationals have little to worry about, since they remain protected by Article 18 TFEU (which we discussed in Chapter 11), third country nationals are open to discrimination on the basis of nationality. From a practical perspective, the exclusion of nationality can cause problems when the defendant discriminates against a black Kenyan national. Does he have a defence if he claims the discrimination is based on nationality and not race? In some Member States, discrimination on the grounds of nationality is covered by race discrimination legislation,[125] but in other Member States the exclusion of nationality can lead to the risk that nationality discrimination is used as a way of concealing race discrimination. Moreover, article 3(2) of the Directives means that discrimination against nationalities like the Welsh or the Catalans is not covered, thus a sign excluding Scots from a bar would not fall foul of the Directive. The text of article 3(2) was heavily influenced by Member States

---

[123] Case C-267/06 *Tadao Maruko* v *Versorgungsanstalt der deutschen Bühnen* [2008] ECR I-1757, para. 72.

[124] European Council Consultative Commission on Racism and Xenophobia, *Final Report*, 6906/1/95 Rev. 1 Limite RAXEN 24 (General Secretariat of the Council of the European Union, 1995).

[125] Race Relations Act 1976, s. 3(1).

who were keen to keep immigration controls outside the scope of the Race Directive, thus third country nationals who are discriminated against because of their race or ethnicity by immigration officials where their entry into the country is concerned gain no protection from the Directive.

The major criticism to be levelled at this provision is that it threatens to undermine the European Union's equality policy, and in particular its race equality policy, by maintaining discrimination against immigrants.[126]

B. Hepple, 'Race and Law in Fortress Europe' (2004) 67 *Modern Law Review* 1, 7

The effects of this exclusion are felt disproportionately by ethnic minorities, who make up the majority of third country nationals (TCNs). Their inferior legal status has serious repercussions on the perception of ethnic minorities generally, and on their integration. Any policy that aims to promote integration needs to take account of the interrelationship between human rights, citizenship and the labour market. The recent history of European immigration shows that migrants are often seen simply as a means of filling temporary needs in the labour market. This means that little attention is paid to citizenship or human rights. It is an illusion to believe that the forces of the labour market, generated by globalisation, can be halted by limiting the rights of TCNs to those of temporary 'guest workers' or by withholding citizenship rights. The political rhetoric of 'Fortress Europe' and restrictions on migrant workers and other legal residents undermine the civil and social rights which belong to all human beings. Inhumane restrictions on welfare benefits, harsh policies against family reunification, and marginalisation in the labour market prevent the realisation of the principle of equality which must be the foundation of all integration policies.

This undermines the commitment to race equality, although of course a third country national living in the European Union has every right to claim on the basis of race, sex or other forms of discrimination.[127] In addition, there are other grounds of discrimination which have been omitted. Article 21 of the European Union Charter of Fundamental Rights and Freedoms ('Charter'), for example, has a wider list of discrimination grounds.

Charter, article 21

1. Any discrimination based on any ground such as sex, race, colour, ethnic or social origin, genetic features, language, religion or belief, political or any other opinion, membership of a national minority, property, birth, disability, age or sexual orientation shall be prohibited.
2. Within the scope of application of the Treaty establishing the European Community and of the Treaty on European Union, and without prejudice to the special provisions of those Treaties, any discrimination on grounds of nationality shall be prohibited.

---

[126] See also J. Weiler, 'Thou Shalt Not Oppress a Stranger: On the Judicial Protection of the Human Rights of Non-EC Nationals – A Critique' (1992) 3 *EJIL* 65; Lord Lester, 'New European Equality Measures' (2000) *PL* 562; Brown, above n. 85, 212.

[127] Race Directive, recital 13; Framework Directive, recital 12.

As we have seen, the grounds provided in the European Union are the result of political compromise and lobbying, but the incomplete coverage of EU law calls into question the idealism displayed in the Preambles to the Directives, which hail the Union's wish to safeguard human rights.

The Directives also fail to take into consideration the phenomenon of 'intersectional discrimination', first raised by US scholars.

> **Kimberle Crenshaw, 'Demarginalizing the Intersection of Race and Sex: A Black Feminist Critique of Antidiscrimination Doctrine, Feminist Theory and Antiracist Politics' (1989) *University of Chicago Legal Forum* 139, 149–50**
>
> Black women can experience discrimination in ways that are both similar to and different from those experienced by white women and Black men. Black women sometimes experience discrimination in ways similar to white women's experiences; sometimes they share very similar experiences with Black men. Yet often they experience double-discrimination – the combined effects of practices which discriminate on the basis of race, and on the basis of sex. And sometimes, they experience discrimination as Black women – not the sum of race and sex discrimination, but as Black women. Black women's experiences are much broader than the general categories that discrimination discourse provides. Yet the continued insistence that Black women's demands and needs be filtered through categorical analyses that completely obscure their experiences guarantees that their needs will seldom be addressed.

For example, a black woman may be passed over for promotion but fail in a claim for sex discrimination if there is evidence that the employer promotes white women, and may fail on grounds of racial discrimination because the employer promotes black men. The employer discriminates against 'black women' but there is no such legal category. There are examples of this in the UK and US case law where the plaintiff is reduced to making a claim under only one ground, which fails to reflect the real reason for her experience.[128] The Framework and Race Directives allude to this problem by exhorting Member States, when implementing the principle of equal treatment, to 'promote equality between men and women, especially since women are often victims of multiple discrimination' but provide no concrete means for addressing the issue.[129]

4 DISCRIMINATION: MEANING, DEFENCES AND REMEDIES

(i) Direct discrimination

The discrimination Directives use a common formula in defining direct discrimination:

> direct discrimination shall be taken to occur where one person is treated less favourably than another is, has been or would be treated in a comparable situation on grounds of [sex, race, ethnic origin, religion, belief, age, disability, sexual orientation].[130]

---

[128] S. Hannett, 'Equality at the Intersections: The Legislative and Judicial Failure to Tackle Multiple Discrimination' (2003) 23 *OJLS* 65.

[129] Framework Directive, recital 3; Race Directive, recital 14. S. Fredman, 'Equality: A New Generation?' (2001) 30 *ILJ* 145, 159.

[130] Race Directive, article 2(1); Framework Directive, article 2(2)(a); Equal Treatment Directive, article 2(1)(a).

There is no need to show that the employer intended to discriminate, nor that he was negligent. Direct discrimination is found when 'but for' the relevant 'ground' (e.g. sex or race), the employer would not have discriminated. To show the causal link between the relevant ground and the less favourable treatment, the plaintiff must compare her treatment with that of others. The Directive allows her to show less favourable treatment in three ways: that there *is* a difference between her treatment and that of others, that there *has been* a difference (by reference to former employees), or that other employees *would be* treated differently. The ability to rely on a hypothetical comparison is likely to be helpful where, because of certain stereotypes, all actual comparators are of the same group as the plaintiff. For example, if all cleaners are black women, they may be unable to compare their less favourable treatment with a white, male cleaner but they may be able to show that such a person would be treated differently because of a general practice to discriminate against black women.

Normally claims of direct discrimination are brought by an individual who suffers a disadvantage, but a recent judgment indicates the possibilities of using direct discrimination in a wider context. The Centre for Equal Opportunities and Opposition to Racism, a body charged with the promotion of equal treatment in Belgium, took action against an employer who had stated publicly that he was not going to recruit persons of certain races, seeking a declaration that these statements breached the Belgian laws implementing the Race Directive. Significantly, there was no evidence that the employer had in fact rejected a job applicant on the basis of race or ethnicity, so the question arose whether on the facts the defendant had acted illegally.

Case C–54/07 *Centrum voor Gelijkheid van Kansen en voor Racismebestrijding* v *Firma Feryn NV* [2008] ECR I–5187

22. It is true that ... Article 2(2) of Directive 2000/43 defines direct discrimination as a situation in which one person 'is treated' less favourably than another is, has been or would be treated in a comparable situation on grounds of racial or ethnic origin. Likewise, Article 7 of that Directive requires Member States to ensure that judicial procedures are available to 'all persons who consider themselves wronged by failure to apply the principle of equal treatment to them' and to public interest bodies bringing judicial proceedings 'on behalf or in support of the complainant'.

23. Nevertheless, it cannot be inferred from this that the lack of an identifiable complainant leads to the conclusion that there is no direct discrimination within the meaning of Directive 2000/43. The aim of that Directive, as stated in recital 8 of its preamble, is 'to foster conditions for a socially inclusive labour market'. For that purpose, Article 3(1)(a) states that the Directive covers, inter alia, selection criteria and recruitment conditions.

24. The objective of fostering conditions for a socially inclusive labour market would be hard to achieve if the scope of Directive 2000/43 were to be limited to only those cases in which an unsuccessful candidate for a post, considering himself to be the victim of direct discrimination, brought legal proceedings against the employer.

25. The fact that an employer declares publicly that it will not recruit employees of a certain ethnic or racial origin, something which is clearly likely to strongly dissuade certain candidates from submitting their candidature and, accordingly, to hinder their access to the labour market, constitutes direct discrimination in respect of recruitment within the meaning of Directive 2000/43. The existence of such direct discrimination is not dependent on the identification of a complainant who claims to have been the victim.

While the ruling might be criticised for not explaining that the rights of those discriminated against trump the defendant's freedom of expression, this ruling serves to emphasise the role that national equality bodies can play in promoting the rights of victims of discrimination.

(ii) Indirect discrimination

(a) Concept of indirect discrimination

Indirect discrimination takes place where, even though the conditions for access to employment seem non-discriminatory, in fact they exclude a particular group; for example, a rule that employees must work all of Friday indirectly discriminates against Muslims who require time off for prayers. Note that by prohibiting indirect discrimination, the law safeguards the interests of an entire group, not just those of the individual plaintiff, because a finding that one person is indirectly discriminated against requires that the employer change the unlawful working practice, which benefits everyone in the underrepresented group. The discrimination Directives provide a uniform definition:

> indirect discrimination shall be taken to occur where an apparently neutral provision, criterion or practice would put persons of [the protected group] at a particular disadvantage compared with other persons, unless that provision, criterion or practice is objectively justified by a legitimate aim and the means of achieving that aim are appropriate and necessary.[131]

The Court of Justice, in the sex discrimination case law, requires that the plaintiff demonstrate indirect discrimination by way of statistics indicating that a considerably smaller percentage of women than men are able to satisfy the condition.[132] This has raised some questions about what 'considerably smaller' means. The new legislation removes this stumbling block because there is no requirement to show that a practice affects a significantly higher proportion of persons of a particular group. Instead, it is enough to show a disadvantage for the protected group in a statistically significant way. Moreover, it is also sufficient to demonstrate that an apparently neutral provision *would* put a person at a particular disadvantage. This can be particularly valuable in cases where the ethnic minority population is small and there is little statistical information on ethnic minorities. Proof of a particular disadvantage creates a prima facie case of discrimination, and it is for the employer to justify his practices.

(b) Legitimate aim defence

A specific defence applies in indirect discrimination cases. The Directives codify the case law: first, there must be a legitimate aim; secondly, the means to achieve the aim must be appropriate; and thirdly, the means to achieve that end must be necessary.[133] This means that if there is a less discriminatory alternative practice that achieves the same goal, the defence is defeated.[134]

---

[131] Equal Treatment Directive, article 2(1)(b); Race Directive, article 2(2)(b); Framework Directive, article 2(2)(b) (although note special provisos for disability discrimination, discussed further below).

[132] Case C-167/97 *R v Secretary of State for Employment, ex parte Seymour-Smith and Perez* [1999] ECR I-623, para. 60.

[133] Case 170/84 *Bilka-Kaufhaus GmbH v Karin Weber von Hartz* [1986] ECR 1607.

[134] M. Connolly, 'Discrimination Law: Justification, Alternative Measures and Defences Based on Sex' (2001) 30 *ILJ* 311, 318.

Two questions remain: first, what reasons can be put forward to justify discrimination? And secondly, how much discretion is afforded to the defendant? Many of the cases in which the Court of Justice has had to confront these questions concern provisions which give lesser benefits to part-time workers. These constitute indirect sex discrimination because women are more likely to be part-time workers. It seems that lesser benefits may be justified if they are an incentive for persons to take up full-time employment,[135] or if the employer wishes to ensure that there are staff working at all times and part-time workers tend not to want to work at weekends or evenings.[136] The Court has also insisted that there must be convincing evidence that indirect discrimination is necessary to obtain the results sought and generalisations about certain types of worker are insufficient.[137] The defence may also be invoked by the Member State to defend indirectly discriminatory legislation, but here the Court has given Member States greater room to apply the defence, holding that there is a justification when the law meets a necessary aim of a state's social policy and the measures are 'suitable' (not necessary, as in the case of businesses trying to rely on the defence) for attaining the aim.[138] For example, the Court suggested that legislation which exempts small businesses from giving part-time workers certain employment rights could be justified given the economic importance of small firms.[139] Given that the Directives codify the stricter standard set out in the case law, Member States may in future find it more difficult to benefit from the defence.

(iii) Harassment

There is a broad consensus that harassment is a harmful workplace practice, which can range from unpleasant remarks directed at a person to physical violence, or the creation of a work environment that is intimidating or humiliating for a group, e.g. displaying pornography in the workplace.[140] The Commission recommended that Member States promote awareness of sexual harassment and implement a code of practice.[141] However, the Commission was dissatisfied with the progress made by Member States,[142] and harassment is now covered in the discrimination Directives. It is not clear why harassment constitutes discrimination, however.[143] In the context of US and UK law, the lack of a specific statute prohibiting harassment led the courts to extend the meaning of discrimination to encompass sexual harassment.[144] In contrast, in some Member

---

[135] Case 96/80 *Jenkins v Kingsgate (Clothing Productions) Ltd* [1981] ECR 911.

[136] Case 170/84 *Bilka-Kaufhaus GmbH v Karin Weber von Hartz* [1986] ECR 1607.

[137] See e.g. Case 171/88 *Rinner-Kühn v FWW Spezial-Gebaudereingung GmbH & Co. KG* [1989] ECR 2743; Case C-184/89 *Nimz v Freie und Hansestadt Hamburg* [1991] ECR I-297; Case C-167/97 *R v Secretary of State for Employment, ex parte Seymour-Smith and Perez* [1999] ECR I-623, paras. 75–6.

[138] Case 171/88 *Rinner-Kühn v FWW Spezial-Gebaudereingung GmbH & Co. KG* [1989] ECR 2743. See also Case C-322/98 *Kachelmann v Bankhaus Hermann Lampe KG* [2000] ECR I-7505.

[139] Case C-189/91 *Kirsammer-Hack v Sidal* [1993] ECR I-6185. See T. Hervey, 'Small Business Exclusion in German Dismissal Law' (1994) 23 *ILJ* 267.

[140] European Commission, *Sexual Harassment at the Workplace in the European Union* (1998).

[141] Commission Recommendation 92/131/EEC of 27 November 1991 on the protection of the dignity of women and men at work [1992] OJ L49/1.

[142] Communication initiating the second-stage consultation of management and labour on the prevention of sexual harassment at work, SEC(97)568 final.

[143] J. Dine and B. Watt, 'Sexual Harassment: Moving Away from Discrimination' (1995) 58 *MLR* 343.

[144] *Porcelli v Strathclyde Regional Council* [1986] ICR 564; *Meritor Savings Bank v Vinston*, 477 US 57 (1986). See generally, Fredman, above n. 33, 320–30.

States (e.g. Ireland, France, Germany and Sweden) harassment is a discrete wrong.[145] The European Union follows the US and UK approach and locates harassment in discrimination legislation, and there are differences between the approach taken by the Framework and Race Directives, on the one hand, and the Equal Treatment Directive, on the other. The former provide:

> Harassment shall be deemed to be a form of discrimination … when unwanted conduct related [to any of the protected grounds except sex] takes place with the purpose or effect of violating the dignity of a person and of creating an intimidating, hostile, degrading, humiliating or offensive environment. In this context, the concept of harassment may be defined in accordance with the national laws and practice of the Member States.[146]

The final sentence is problematic. If it were not there, then we would be able to say that the Directive defines harassment in a way that excludes the need to show discrimination. The second sentence, however, adds a complication because it may be read to suggest that the definition of harassment is a matter for Member States, which allows each to water down the meaning of harassment. In practical terms, then, a Member State might be able to implement the Directive by legislating that the plaintiff prove that the harassment was because of the plaintiff's attribute (e.g. race or religion), allowing an employer to escape liability if he shows that he harassed others of a different race or religion. Under this approach, a wide range of forms of discrimination may not be caught; for example, if an employer displays a poster degrading blacks, this would not constitute discriminatory harassment because all persons would be offended by it. In contrast, article 2 of the recast Equal Treatment Directive avoids this by providing that harassment is wrongful per se.

Harriet Samuels, 'A Defining Moment: A Feminist Perspective on the Law of Sexual Harassment in the Workplace in the Light of the Equal Treatment Amendment Directive' (2004) 12 *Feminist Legal Studies* 181, 203–4

One of the most important changes that the [recast Equal Treatment Directive] makes is to deem sexual harassment as discrimination, which eliminates the need for a comparator of the opposite sex … It also resonates with the approach taken with regard to pregnancy by the European Court of Justice in *Webb* where dismissal of a woman on the grounds of pregnancy was deemed to be discrimination. This is an important development that denies a defence to the 'equal opportunity harasser' who is accused of harassing men and women equally … Despite the fact that the comparator has been removed in sexual harassment cases, the male standard may still prevail if women have to establish that the conduct complained of was not reasonable. The complete elimination of the male comparator will also depend on the way in which the courts are likely to interpret concepts such as reasonableness and unwelcomeness. If men can argue that behaviour that is offensive to women is reasonable then the law on sexual harassment will be ineffective in tackling harassment. These imprecise concepts may well provide opportunities for courts and tribunals to reintroduce sexist ideas on acceptable behaviour in the workplace and women's response to such conduct.

---

[145] Irish Employment Act 1998, s. 26; French Labour Code, art. L.122–46; German Act for the Protection of Employees Against Sexual Harassment 1994. For comment, see A. C. Saguy, 'French and American Lawyers Define Sexual Harassment' in C. A. MacKinnon and R. B. Siegal (eds.), *Directions in Sexual Harassment Law* (New Haven, CT, Yale University Press, 2004); S. Baer, 'Dignity or Equality? Responses to Workplace Harassment in European, German, and US Law' in C. A. MacKinnon and R. B. Siegal (eds.), *Directions in Sexual Harassment Law* (New Haven, CT, Yale University Press, 2004).

[146] Race Directive, article 2(3); Framework Directive, article 2(3).

The notion of sexual harassment in the Directive is drawn from the US case law, which identified as harassment conduct that creates a 'hostile environment'. Unfortunately, the Directives do not follow the US approach to harassment completely because omitted is a second method of harassment which the US courts have called 'quid pro quo' sexual harassment, where the employer demands sexual favours in exchange for granting the victim a better position or other working conditions. Moreover, the Directives leave it for each Member State to determine the question of whether the employer is liable for harassment carried out by an employee or a client against the victim. Reducing the scope for vicarious liability can have a detrimental impact on the victim's right to meaningful compensation.

(iv) Defences

(a) Genuine occupational requirements

It has been argued that there should be no basis for the defendant to justify directly discriminatory practices.[147] However, outside of the equal pay context, the discrimination Directives provide that differences in treatment on the basis of sex, race or ethnic origin, age, sexual orientation, religion or belief or disability may be justified:

> where, by reason of the nature of the particular occupational activities concerned or of the context in which they are carried out, such a characteristic constitutes a genuine and determining occupational requirement.[148]

Examples include hiring a male actor for a man's role, or banning men from the profession of midwifery.[149] The Preamble to the recast Equal Treatment Directive cites the case law of the Court of Justice, which provides that in applying this defence it must be shown that the objective sought was legitimate, and that the discrimination was proportionate to the objective being sought.[150] Arguably, those principles also apply to the other discrimination Directives.

The application of this provision can be explored by considering the Court's approach to laws restricting women's access to employment in the army. In *Kreil*, German law forbade women from serving in military positions involving the use of arms. It meant women could only be engaged in the medical and military music services. An attempt was made to justify the exclusion on the basis that it was necessary to guarantee public security, but this was rejected on two grounds. First, the Court held that discrimination on the basis of a genuine occupational requirement applied to specific activities and could not exclude women from almost all military positions.[151] Secondly, the Court found that arms training was provided to all army personnel, including for those services to which women had access, thus the restriction was disproportionate.[152] In contrast, the exclusion of women from a segment of the armed forces was upheld in *Sirdar*.[153] The plaintiff wished to work as a chef in the Royal Marines but this regiment had a policy that every member should be able to fight in a commando unit whatever

---

[147] Ellis, above n. 44, 111–13.
[148] Equal Treatment Directive, article 14(2); Race Directive, article 4; Framework Directive, article 4(1).
[149] Case 165/82 *Commission* v *United Kingdom* [1983] ECR 3431.
[150] Equal Treatment Directive, recital 19.
[151] C-285/98 *Kreil* v *Germany* [2000] ECR I-69, para. 27.
[152] *Ibid.* para. 28.
[153] Case C-273/97 *Sirdar* v *Army Board and Secretary of State for Defence* [1999] ECR I-7403.

their rank, and used this to justify not hiring women for any position. The Court of Justice held that because of the specific role played by the Royal Marines in the United Kingdom's armed forces (inter alia, that they are a small force and intended to be the first line of attack) meant that it was legitimate to exclude women if this was seen as necessary to maintain the effectiveness of this military unit. The Court in these cases sought to balance the application of EU law with the rights of the Member States to protect their security interests, and while some have considered that the Court has drawn an appropriate balance by banning blanket exclusions of women,[154] it has been criticised because the Court accepted without analysis the claim that women would not be able to join men in commando units.[155] There is a risk, therefore, that the 'genuine occupational requirements' exception can be used to retain gender and other stereotyped roles in employment practices.[156] On the other hand, these two cases addressed a highly sensitive field where national policy clashed with sex equality rights, and the Court may adopt a more demanding stance where a private employer wishes to justify a discriminatory practice, e.g. if the owner of a Chinese restaurant tries to defend a policy of only hiring Oriental waiters in his restaurant to maintain an authentic atmosphere, especially as the Preambles indicate that this defence applies in 'very limited circumstances'.[157]

Applying this defence in the disability context means that an employer does not have to hire a person when the disability prevents the person from carrying out an essential part of the job, and where the employer is unable to make any modifications to the workplace to accommodate the disabled person. Sexual orientation may be a genuine occupational requirement that allows an employer to select a person or choose not to select a person on the basis of her sexual orientation. It is likely that this will be invoked only rarely, e.g. a centre that offers counselling to gays and lesbians might consider it necessary to have as its chair someone who is homosexual.[158] In most other instances (e.g. banning gays from the army), it seems likely that the ban would be disproportionate.[159] Nevertheless, the possibility of establishing a genuine occupational requirement in the context of sexual orientation discrimination raises two difficult issues. The first is that some argue that one's sexuality is not fixed but fluid, as persons may experiment with their sexuality over time. On this view, it may be asked whether a requirement of homosexuality for a position in a centre advising gays and lesbians would not be met by a candidate who in the past has had heterosexual relationships.[160] The second problem is that the genuine occupational requirement defence means that the prospective employee has to disclose his sexuality. There is a tension between this and the point noted earlier that a person may be reluctant to disclose her sexuality.

---

[154] P. Koutrakos, 'EC Law and Equal Treatment in the Armed Forces' (2000) 25 *ELRev.* 433.

[155] E. Ellis, 'The Recent Jurisprudence of the Court of Justice in the Field of Sex Equality' (2000) 37 *CMLRev.* 1403, 1414–15.

[156] See also Case 222/84 *Johnston* v *Chief Constable of the Royal Ulster Constabulary* [1986] ECR 1651.

[157] Race Directive, recital 18; Framework Directive, recital 23.

[158] A view taken by the United Kingdom's Advisory, Conciliation and Arbitration Service, 'Sexual Orientation and the Workplace: Putting the Employment Equality (Sexual Orientation) Regulations 2003 into Practice: for Employers and their Staff' available at www.acas.org.uk/publications/pdf/guide_sexualO.pdf.

[159] In *Smith and Grady* v *United Kingdom* [1999] IRLR 734, the ECtHR held that banning gays from the armed forces was disproportionate and infringed the individuals' right to private life. Arguably, the interpretation of the Directive by national courts and the Court of Justice has to have regard to safeguarding fundamental rights, so a similar conclusion is likely in the EU context.

[160] H. Oliver, 'Sexual Orientation Discrimination: Perceptions, Definitions and Genuine Occupational Requirements' (2004) 33 *ILJ* 1, 18–20.

(b) Other defences

The Framework Directive contains an additional set of defences: one of general application and some that are limited to one specific ground.

> ### Framework Directive, article 2(5)
>
> This Directive shall be without prejudice to measures laid down by national law which, in a democratic society, are necessary for public security, for the maintenance of public order and the prevention of criminal offences, for the protection of health and for the protection of the rights and freedoms of others.

Tolerance of others is the norm in liberal society but the rationale for this defence is that acts which undermine the moral and political values of the state must be suppressed.[161] Seen in this light, the defence is necessary and it may be surprising that a similar provision is not present in other Directives. The defence seems to have been inserted at the insistence of the United Kingdom, which wished to make it clear that measures to 'protect the public from the activities of religious cults or individuals with a disabling illness such as paranoid schizophrenia which could make them a danger to others would not be prohibited under the Directive'.[162] However, the defence might have a bigger impact and may be applied to justify a ban on Muslim women wearing the veil at work.[163]

The first specific defence applies to religious organisations and was inserted at the request of some Member States, in particular the Irish government, concerned that the Directive might hamper the employment practices of religious institutions.[164]

> ### Framework Directive, article 4(2)
>
> Member States may maintain national legislation in force at the date of adoption of this Directive or provide for future legislation incorporating national practices existing at the date of adoption of this Directive pursuant to which, in the case of occupational activities within churches and other public or private organisations the ethos of which is based on religion or belief, a difference of treatment based on a person's religion or belief shall not constitute discrimination where, by reason of the nature of these activities or of the context in which they are carried out, a person's religion or belief constitute a genuine, legitimate and justified occupational requirement, having regard to the organisation's ethos. This difference of treatment shall be implemented taking account of Member States' constitutional provisions and principles, as well as the general principles of Community law, and should not justify discrimination on another ground.
>
> Provided that its provisions are otherwise complied with, this Directive shall thus not prejudice the right of churches and other public or private organisations, the ethos of which is based on religion or belief, acting in conformity with national constitutions and laws, to require individuals working for them to act in good faith and with loyalty to the organisation's ethos.

---

[161] S. Mendus, *Toleration and the Limits of Liberalism* (London, Macmillan, 1989) 8–9.

[162] House of Lords Select Committee on the EU, 'The EU Framework Directive on Discrimination', Session 2000–01, 4th Report, HL Paper 13, para. 37.

[163] An issue discussed under Article 9 ECHR: see *Leyla Shain* v *Turkey* [2004] ECHR 299.

[164] Bell, above n. 2, 154–5.

The exception conforms with the autonomy that states tend to grant to religious organisations, although it may be argued that such organisations could be protected by the genuine occupational requirement defence so that article 4 is unnecessary. It has been noted that the article is the result of lobbying by religious groups who wished to have a wider exclusion for religious organisations,[165] but it remains to be seen how far-reaching this provision is. The first paragraph seems intended to justify not hiring a Buddhist as a Catholic priest, but the second paragraph seems to allow Member States considerable flexibility to discriminate against the entire workforce. The US Supreme Court, for example, has shown considerable deference to religious organisations under comparable legislation. In *Amos*, a Mormon church terminated the employment of a gymnasium building engineer who was not a Mormon and who had failed to obtain a 'Temple recommend' which is issued only to individuals who observe the Church's standards in such matters as regular church attendance, tithing, and abstinence from coffee, tea, alcohol and tobacco. While it might be argued that his job was unrelated to the religious activities of his employer, the court declined to interfere with the decision of the church, because:

> it is a significant burden on a religious organization to require it, on pain of substantial liability, to predict which of its activities a secular court will consider religious. The line is hardly a bright one, and an organization might understandably be concerned that a judge would not understand its religious tenets and sense of mission. Fear of potential liability might affect the way an organization carried out what it understood to be its religious mission.[166]

Such judicial deference on the part of the Court of Justice would risk excluding religious organisations from their obligations under the Framework Directive altogether.[167]

A second exception provides that the Framework Directive does not apply to discrimination on the grounds of age and disability in the armed forces.[168] This blanket exception contrasts with the approach taken by the Court when reviewing sex discrimination in the armed forces, where disproportionate sex discrimination was prohibited.

Lastly, the Framework Directive has a special defence in cases of age discrimination designed to reflect the link between discrimination law and national employment policies.

Framework Directive, article 6(1)

Notwithstanding Article 2(2), Member States may provide that differences of treatment on grounds of age shall not constitute discrimination, if, within the context of national law, they are objectively and reasonably justified by a legitimate aim, including legitimate employment policy, labour market and vocational training objectives, and if the means of achieving that aim are appropriate and necessary.

Such differences of treatment may include, among others:

(a) the setting of special conditions on access to employment and vocational training, employment and occupation, including dismissal and remuneration conditions, for young people, older workers and persons with caring responsibilities in order to promote their vocational integration or ensure their protection;

---

[165] *Ibid.* 117.

[166] *Corporation of the Presiding Bishop of the Church of Jesus Christ of Latter-Day Saints* v *Amos*, 483 US 327, 337 (1987).

[167] For a wide-ranging analysis of the difficulties in reconciling the demands of liberal society with religious doctrine, see B. Barry, *Culture and Equality* (London, Polity Press, 2001) ch. 5.

[168] Framework Directive, article 3(4).

(b) the fixing of minimum conditions of age, professional experience or seniority in service for access to employment or to certain advantages linked to employment;

(c) the fixing of a maximum age for recruitment which is based on the training requirements of the post in question or the need for a reasonable period of employment before retirement.

This defence is necessary when states provide for certain advantages to encourage the recruitment of younger or older workers. Professor Ellis found that the article 'explicitly sacrifices the principle of non-discrimination to commercial interests' and that it risks legalising age discrimination.[169] The Court has already had the opportunity to explore this defence three times, but with inconsistent outcomes.[170] In *Mangold*, the Court found that legislation making the conclusion of fixed-term contracts with older workers easier was based on a legitimate objective: 'to promote the vocational integration of unemployed older workers, insofar as they encounter considerable difficulties in finding work'.[171] But the Court ruled that the law went beyond what was necessary to achieve that aim by taking into consideration only age and not the personal circumstances of the individual or the conditions in the labour market.[172] This suggested a strict standard of review when Member States seek to depart from the general obligation not to discriminate. But in *Palacios de la Villa*, the Court was more willing to defer to national policy.[173] The employer terminated the employee's contract pursuant to a collective agreement which governed the relationship between the parties which established a compulsory retirement age of 65 unless an employee had not worked enough years to qualify for a pension. The Court found that the Spanish law which facilitated this agreement pursued a legitimate objective (i.e. promoting employment), and that the measure was proportionate.

Case C–411/05 *Félix Palacios de la Villa* v *Cortefiel Servicios SA* [2007] ECR I-8531

72. It does not appear unreasonable for the authorities of a Member State to take the view that a measure such as that at issue in the main proceedings may be appropriate and necessary in order to achieve a legitimate aim in the context of national employment policy, consisting in the promotion of full employment by facilitating access to the labour market.

73. Furthermore, the measure cannot be regarded as unduly prejudicing the legitimate claims of workers subject to compulsory retirement because they have reached the age-limit provided for; the relevant legislation is not based only on a specific age, but also takes account of the fact that the persons concerned are entitled to financial compensation by way of a retirement pension at the end of their working life, such as that provided for by the national legislation at issue in the main proceedings, the level of which cannot be regarded as unreasonable.

74. Moreover, the relevant national legislation allows the social partners to opt, by way of collective agreements – and therefore with considerable flexibility – for application of the compulsory retirement mechanism so that due account may be taken not only of the overall situation in the labour market concerned, but also of the specific features of the jobs in question.

---

[169] Ellis, above n. 44, 296.

[170] The third case is C-227/04 P *Lindorfer* [2007] ECR I-6767.

[171] Case C-144/04 *Werner Mangold* v *Rüdiger Helm* [2005] ECR I-9981, para. 59. P. Skidmore, 'The European Employment Strategy and Labour Law: A German Case Study' (2004) 29 *ELRev.* 52.

[172] Case C-144/04 *Werner Mangold* v *Rüdiger Helm* [2005] ECR I-9981, paras. 64–5.

[173] Case C-411/05 *Félix Palacios de la Villa* v *Cortefiel Servicios SA* [2007] ECR I-8531.

It is likely that the procedural safeguards inherent in the scheme are a significant factor, but one can also see this ruling as one where the Court reverses its earlier position, acknowledging that addressing the social problems of an ageing population at national level should not be hampered unduly by EU discrimination laws.

(v) Remedies

(a) Procedures

Rights are meaningless without remedies, and the new Directives seek to enhance the plaintiffs' prospects for success, especially in the light of evidence that litigation under the sex equality legislation has proved difficult.[174] A common procedure is prescribed in the Directives.[175]

Framework Directive, article 9

1. Member States shall ensure that judicial and/or administrative procedures, including where they deem it appropriate conciliation procedures, for the enforcement of obligations under this Directive are available to all persons who consider themselves wronged by failure to apply the principle of equal treatment to them, even after the relationship in which the discrimination is alleged to have occurred has ended.
2. Member States shall ensure that associations, organisations or other legal entities which have, in accordance with the criteria laid down by their national law, a legitimate interest in ensuring that the provisions of this Directive are complied with, may engage, either on behalf or in support of the complainant, with his or her approval, in any judicial and/or administrative procedure provided for the enforcement of obligations under this Directive.
3. Paragraphs 1 and 2 are without prejudice to national rules relating to time limits for bringing actions as regards the principle of equality of treatment.

The Directives do not interfere with national procedures regarding the appropriate forum to hear claims (thus the procedure may be judicial and/or administrative) and time limits remain to be set according to national law. The major innovation is article 9(2), which empowers organisations to offer support and advice to the victim, which can be decisive for the success of a claim. These organisations are also able to select and support cases likely to set significant precedents and have repercussions for all employers, benefiting future victims of discrimination.[176] However, these organisations have limited budgets and evidence from the United Kingdom suggests that little of it is spent assisting claimants.[177] Moreover, the Directives do not require that these organisations should be empowered to bring a claim directly. Finally, Member States may determine which groups have a legitimate interest, which can lead to the exclusion of certain influential groups.

---

[174] See J. Blom, B. Fitzpatrick, J. Gregory, R. Knegt and U. O'Hare, *The Utilisation of Sex Equality Litigation in the Member States of the European Community*, V/782/96-EN (Report to the Equal Opportunities Unit of D-G V, 1995).
[175] Race Directive, article 7; Equal Treatment Directive, articles 17, 20.
[176] On the use of test cases to advance EU law, see Harlow and Rawlings, above n. 62, 282–5.
[177] H. Collins, K. Ewing and E. McColgan, *Labour Law: Text and Materials* (Oxford, Hart, 2005) 332.

An additional procedural advantage is that first provided by the Burden of Proof Directive,[178] and which is now available for all grounds of discrimination.[179]

> ### Framework Directive, article 10
>
> 1. Member States shall take such measures as are necessary, in accordance with their national judicial systems, to ensure that, when persons who consider themselves wronged because the principle of equal treatment has not been applied to them establish, before a court or other competent authority, facts from which it may be presumed that there has been direct or indirect discrimination, it shall be for the respondent to prove that there has been no breach of the principle of equal treatment.
> 2. Paragraph 1 shall not prevent Member States from introducing rules of evidence which are more favourable to plaintiffs.

If the plaintiff establishes a presumption that there has been direct or indirect discrimination, it is for the defendant to prove that there has been no discrimination. This aids the plaintiff considerably because while the presumption may be rebutted, it is very difficult to prove the non-existence of something. Moreover, it has been suggested that the best way for an employer to prevent claims, given the reversal of the burden of proof, is to ensure that there is no discrimination in the workplace so that the plaintiff is unable to raise the presumption of discrimination in the first place.[180] The Directives also extend the scope of protection in two ways: first, the employer's duties extend beyond the period of employment (for example, the employer refusing to provide a past employee a reference).[181] Secondly, the Directives protect plaintiffs from reprisals once they initiate a claim, a significant provision in that many who are successful in discrimination cases experience difficulties in finding employment.[182] The Directives codify the Court of Justice's case law on victimisation.[183]

> ### Framework Directive, article 11[184]
>
> Member States shall introduce into their national legal systems such measures as are necessary to protect employees against dismissal or other adverse treatment by the employer as a reaction to a complaint within the undertaking or to any legal proceedings aimed at enforcing compliance with the principle of equal treatment.

---

[178] Directive 97/80/EC on the burden of proof in the cases of discrimination based on sex [1998] OJ L14/6, article 4 as amended by Directive 98/52/EC [1998] OJ L205/66.

[179] Race Directive, article 8(1); Equal Treatment Directive, article 19.

[180] D. Chalmers, 'The Mistakes of the Good European?' in S. Fredman (ed.), *Discrimination and Human Rights: The Case of Racism* (Oxford, Oxford University Press, 2001) 216–17.

[181] Race Directive, article 7(1); Framework Directive, article 9(1); Equal Treatment Directive, article 17(1).

[182] A. Leonard, *Pyrrhic Victories: Winning Sex Discrimination and Equal Pay Cases in the Industrial Tribunals 1980–1984* (London, HMSO, 1987).

[183] Case C-185/97 *Coote* v *Granada Hospitality* [1998] ECR I-5199; M. Dougan, 'The Equal Treatment Directive: Retaliation, Remedies and Direct Effect' (1999) 24 *ELRev.* 664.

[184] Race Directive, article 9; Equal Treatment Directive, article 24.

(b) Compensation

The victim of sex discrimination normally has a right to damages, and in its case law the Court of Justice has exercised some control over the quantum by indicating that no upper limit may be imposed, except in cases where even without sex discrimination the applicant would not have obtained employment because she is less well qualified than the successful applicant,[185] and that the award must be adequate in relation to the damage suffered.[186] These principles have now been codified in the context of sex discrimination claims.

Recast Equal Treatment Directive, article 18

Member States shall introduce into their national legal systems such measures as are necessary to ensure real and effective compensation or reparation as the Member States so determine for the loss and damage sustained by a person injured as a result of discrimination on grounds of sex, in a way which is dissuasive and proportionate to the damage suffered. Such compensation or reparation may not be restricted by the fixing of a prior upper limit, except in cases where the employer can prove that the only damage suffered by an applicant as a result of discrimination within the meaning of this Directive is the refusal to take his/her job application into consideration.

In contrast, the Race and Framework Directives are less prescriptive.

Race Directive, article 15; Framework Directive, article 17

Member States shall lay down the rules on sanctions applicable to infringements of the national provisions adopted pursuant to this Directive and shall take all measures necessary to ensure that they are applied. The sanctions, which may comprise the payment of compensation to the victim, must be effective, proportionate and dissuasive.

However, it may well be that, as in the case of sex discrimination, the Court of Justice will bolster the remedies available by removing national limits like caps on remedies. Moreover, it must not be forgotten that the Article 19 Directives were implemented by unanimity and the weaker remedial structure may have been necessary to gain agreement. Thus, looking at individual Member States reveals some with more progressive remedies. For instance, in Italy a finding of discrimination may lead to a bar on public tenders, in Italy, Spain and Hungary the findings are published in the press; and in some states like France criminal law applies.[187]

5 WIDENING THE SCOPE OF EU EQUAL OPPORTUNITIES POLICY

For most commentators, the common core of EU equality law reviewed above is disappointing because it rests on an antiquated approach to discrimination.[188] As Professor Hepple has

---

[185] Case C-180/95 *Draehmpaehl* v *Urania Immobilienservice* [1997] ECR I-2195.
[186] Case C-271/91 *Marshall* v *Southampton and South-West Hampshire AHA* [1993] ECR I-4367.
[187] V. Guiraudon, 'Equality in the Making: Implementing European Non-discrimination Law' (2009) 13 *Citizenship Studies* 527, 536–7.
[188] A. Masselot, 'The New Equal Treatment Directive: Plus ça Change…' (2004) 12 *Feminist Legal Studies* 93, 103.

put it in discussing the Race Directive, the EU's approach borrows from the UK Race Relations Act 1976 and reproduces a model for combating racism which is out of date with modern conceptions about how to address discrimination and integrate excluded groups more fully in society.[189] However, this criticism may be countered by noting that the discrimination Directives have to be implemented across twenty-seven diverse jurisdictions, not all of which have engaged seriously with discrimination in the workplace.[190] Thus, as the Commission notes, for some states the Directives 'involved the introduction of an entirely new rights-based approach to anti-discrimination legislation and policy'.[191] In this light, they constitute a necessary starting point, equalising the scope of protection across the European Union.

In this section we consider some of the more innovative means by which EU equality law moves beyond protecting rights in the labour market, and towards a model that might secure the fulfilment of the right to equality in a more effective manner.

(i) Beyond the labour market

In addition to safeguarding rights in the labour market, the Race Directive was the first to forbid discrimination in other fields as well. It has been suggested that this indicates a move to a broader conception of European social law.[192] This seems necessary because confining discrimination law to the labour market disenfranchises many by assuming that the central form of citizenship is manifested by participation in the labour market.

Race Directive, article 3(1)

Within the limits of the powers conferred upon the Community, this Directive shall apply to all persons, as regards both the public and private sectors, including public bodies, in relation to: ...

(e) social protection, including social security and health care;

(f) social advantages;

(g) education;

(h) access to and supply of goods and services which are available to the public, including housing.

Thus, EU norms regulate matters like university fees, restrictions on the preparation of Halal meat, the allocation of housing by municipal authorities, employer bans on the playing of rap music because of its misogynistic content and bans on wearing the veil at school.[193] However, there is some uncertainty over the scope of these four categories. In article 3(1)(e), it is not clear whether social security embraces the rules set out in Directive 79/7/EC ('Social Security Directive'), which applies to sex discrimination. It is not clear to what 'social protection' extends, and how far non-discrimination in healthcare can be regulated given that the Treaty indicates that the delivery of health care is a matter for the Member States.[194] The reference to 'social advantages'

---

[189] B. Hepple, 'Race and Law in Fortress Europe' (2004) 67 *MLR* 1.

[190] For a critique of French discrimination law, see K. Berthou, 'New Hopes for French Anti-Discrimination Law' (2003) 19 *International Journal of Comparative Labour Law and Industrial Relations* 109.

[191] Green Paper, *Equality and Non-Discrimination in an Enlarged European Union* (May 2004) 11.

[192] M. Bell, 'Beyond European Labour Law? Reflections on the EU Racial Equality Directive' (2002) 8 *ELJ* 384, 387.

[193] Chalmers, above n. 178, 215.

[194] Article 168(7) TFEU.

in article 3(1)(f) is drawn from the law on free movement of persons.[195] It includes subsidised public transport, free school meals, unemployment benefits and assistance with funeral costs. On the other hand, some have suggested that because the Race Directive is premised upon equality and not merely encouraging the free movement of workers, the phrase 'social advantages' might be read more widely.[196] In the context of education it is not clear whether the Directive is only about access to school for persons of a given race or whether it can also forbid the teaching of subjects that may be discriminatory, e.g. a law requiring schools to teach the virtues of colonisation. Services for the public may include the provision of housing, although it is unclear if this also applies to the provision of private services, e.g. banking, hotels and shops. Moreover, it has been argued that the provision of general public services (e.g. policing) should also be included, especially in the light of evidence that the police may discriminate by providing less effective investigations in cases involving racial minorities,[197] as graphically illustrated by the findings of 'institutional racism' in the Stephen Lawrence Inquiry.[198] In sum, the potential for the Race Directive to integrate racial and ethnic minorities by preventing such a potentially wide range of discriminatory practices is undermined by the uncertainty as to the scope of the obligations imposed by the Directive and as to the 'constitutional validity' of the Directive when it comes to health care and housing, which seem to fall outside the Union's competences.[199]

The Race Directive pioneered these measures. In the context of sex discrimination, the Council later agreed a Directive establishing the right of equal treatment in the access to and supply of goods and services.

Directive 2004/113/ EC of 13 December 2004 implementing the principle of equal treatment between men and women in the access to and supply of goods and services [2004] OJ L373/37

Article 3

1. Within the limits of the powers conferred upon the Community, this Directive shall apply to all persons who provide goods and services, which are available to the public irrespective of the person concerned as regards both the public and private sectors, including public bodies, and which are offered outside the area of private and family life and the transactions carried out in this context.

2. This Directive does not prejudice the individual's freedom to choose a contractual partner as long as an individual's choice of contractual partner is not based on that person's sex.

3. This Directive shall not apply to the content of media and advertising nor to education.

The scope of this Directive is narrower than the Race Directive because it does not apply to education, but it is potentially wider because it applies to both public and private services, although the Commission insisted that in this respect the scope of the two Directives is the same.[200] Article 3 also shows how thinking in the European Union in this sphere has evolved:

---

[195] Regulation 1612/68/EEC [1968] OJ Spec. edn L257/2, article 7(2).
[196] E. Ellis, 'Social Advantages: a New Lease of Life?' (2003) 40 *CMLRev.* 639.
[197] C. Brown, 'The Race Directive: Towards Equality for All the Peoples of Europe?' (2002) 21 *YEL* 195, 215
[198] W. MacPherson, *Stephen Lawrence Inquiry Report* (Cm 4262-I, 1999). Race Relations (Amendment) Act 2000, s. 1.
[199] Brown, above n. 197, 214–15; M. Bell, 'The New Article 13 EC Treaty: A Sound Basis for European Anti-Discrimination Law?' (1999) 6 *MJ* 5.
[200] COM(2003)657, 13.

the Race Directive was criticised in some quarters for infringing the freedom of contract, thus this Directive is careful to stipulate that the obligation not to discriminate in the provision of services affects freedom of contract only insofar as this is necessary to prevent discrimination.

One of the criticisms of the 2004 Race Directive was that the evidence base on which the legislation had been implemented was weak, and insufficient attention had been paid to the needs of certain industries.[201] In proposing a similar Directive for other protected groups, the Commission has consulted more broadly.[202]

(ii) Positive action

Equality of opportunities does not guarantee equality of results because the problem of discrimination is more deeply rooted in society, which has historically denied rights to certain groups, known as 'systematic' discrimination.[203] One solution to this gap are measures of positive discrimination that tackle the causes of inequality by encouraging the underrepresented group to participate or by going as far as to discriminate in favour of an underrepresented group, for instance by giving a job to a woman in favour of a man because women are underrepresented.[204] EU law does not compel Member States to deploy positive action; rather the Commission has encouraged Member States to take positive action to promote women in employment as far back as 1984, on the one hand,[205] while the Court of Justice has limited the scope of such programmes when these are incompatible with EU law, on the other.

Before 1997, positive discrimination measures were regulated only in the field of sex discrimination by article 2(4) of the 1976 Equal Treatment Directive, whereby the principle of equal treatment was 'without prejudice to promote equal opportunities for men and women, in particular by removing existing inequalities which affect women's opportunities'.[206] However, the Court of Justice limited the scope of positive discrimination: a measure providing that a percentage of jobs should go to women is unlawful because it does not grant equality of opportunity as between men and women, but prescribes equality of results. Similarly, a scheme whereby if a man and a woman are equally well qualified, the job should go to the woman, infringes the equality principle.[207] The Court of Justice tolerated positive action schemes only when these were consistent with the principle of equal opportunities. To achieve this, national measures may be designed in the following way: first, a presumption that the female should be employed arises when her qualifications are equal to the man, and secondly, the man may

---

[201] In particular there was criticism from the insurance market. See Paul MacDonnell, 'Equal Treatment Directive Misunderstands Risk and Threatens Insurance Markets' (2005) 25 *Economic Affairs* 48; House of Lords European Union Committee, *Sexual Equality in Access to Goods and Services* (27th Report of Session 2003–04, HL Paper 165-I) ch. 9. The main concern was that prohibiting discrimination would actually harm women, who are charged lower insurance premiums than men because they present less risk statistically.

[202] Proposal for a Council Directive on implementing the principle of equal treatment between persons irrespective of religion or belief, disability, age or sexual orientation, COM(2008)426 final.

[203] S. Joseph, J. Schultz and M. Castan, *The International Covenant on Civil and Political Rights: Cases, Materials and Commentary* (Oxford, Oxford University Press, 2000) 563–4.

[204] See generally S. Fredman, 'Reversing Discrimination' (1997) 113 *LQR* 575.

[205] Council Recommendation 84/635/EEC of 13 December 1984 on the promotion of positive action for women [1984] OJ L331/34.

[206] Directive 76/207/EEC on the principle of equal treatment for men and women, article 2(4) [1976] OJ L39/40.

[207] Case C-450/93 *Kalanke v Freie Hansestadt Bremen* [1995] ECR I-3051.

rebut the presumption by pointing out certain characteristics that entitle him to the post (so-called 'secondary selection criteria'). For example, he could point out that his seniority, or certain family responsibilities, made him a worthier candidate.[208] These schemes satisfy two conditions: they do not give automatic priority to women and they allow for an objective evaluation that takes into account the personal situation of each candidate.

Several criticisms were levelled at the Court of Justice's approach.[209] First, the Court narrowed down considerably the ability of Member States to engage in positive discrimination and undermined the potential of such measures. Moreover, positive discrimination policies that are lawful under EU law are easy to evade. For instance, it has been said that it is easy to indicate that the woman is not equally qualified, and the 'secondary selection criteria' cannot be subjected to strict judicial scrutiny, therefore leaving the employer free to favour men instead of women.[210] The upshot is that states find it very difficult to implement meaningful positive discrimination measures.

The new generation of discrimination legislation seeks to give Member States greater freedom to design positive action measures. The principle in Article 157(4) TFEU is replicated in the Race Directive and in the Framework Directive:[211]

> With a view to ensuring full equality in practice, the principle of equal treatment shall not prevent any Member State from maintaining or adopting specific measures to prevent or compensate for disadvantages linked to [race, ethnic origin, sexual orientation, age, religion, or disability].

The potential scope of Article 157(4) TFEU was considered briefly in *Abrahamsson*. The relevant Swedish law provided that a candidate belonging to an underrepresented sex and possessing sufficient qualifications for the post may be chosen in preference to a candidate belonging to the opposite sex who would otherwise have been chosen, provided that the difference in their respective qualifications is not so great. The Court of Justice was quick to quash this scheme on the basis of the 1976 Equal Treatment Directive but then moved to consider whether the scheme could be justified under Article 157(4) and set out a brief comment that suggests a potentially more helpful basis for considering the legality of positive action measures.[212]

Case C-407/98 *Abrahamsson and Anderson* v *Fogelqvist* [2000] ECR I-5539

55. ... even though Article [157(4) TFEU] allows the Member States to maintain or adopt measures providing for special advantages intended to prevent or compensate for disadvantages in professional careers in order to ensure full equality between men and women in professional life, it cannot be inferred from this that it allows a selection method of the kind at issue in the main proceedings which appears, on any view, to be disproportionate to the aim pursued.

---

[208] Case C-409/95 *Hellmut Marschall* v *Land Nordrhein-Westfalen* [1997] ECR I-6363.

[209] See generally S. Fredman, 'After *Kalanke* and *Marschall*: Affirming Affirmative Action' (1998) 1 *CYELS* 199.

[210] D. Caruso, 'Limits of the Classic Method: Positive Action in the European Union after the New Equality Directives' (2003) 44 *Harvard International Law Journal* 331, 342.

[211] Directive 2000/78/EC, article 7 and Directive 2000/43/EC, article 5.

[212] Likewise in Case C-319/03 *Serge Brihenche* v *Ministre de l'Intérieur* [2004] ECR I-8807, the Court noted that Article 157 TFEU warrants a different interpretation from article 2(4).

The Court suggests that Article 157(4) may be read as allowing a departure from the principle of equal treatment, subject to the principle of proportionality. The language of the Framework and Race Directives can also be read as permitting discrimination as a way of promoting an underrepresented group, because all the texts begin with the same prefatory words: 'with a view to achieving full equality in practice'. This suggests that equality of results is now an EU objective, which may open the way for more aggressive positive discrimination schemes, perhaps even allowing for a quota system whereby a given proportion of persons from an underrepresented group must be employed provided this is the least restrictive way of achieving equal participation of women. Support for this may be drawn from the use of the language in article 19 (combating discrimination, not merely preventing it),[213] and from the fact that the Framework Directive tolerates a fairly aggressive form of positive discrimination in one region of the European Union.

Framework Directive, article 15

1. In order to tackle the under-representation of one of the major religious communities in the police service of Northern Ireland, differences in treatment regarding recruitment into that service, including its support staff, shall not constitute discrimination insofar as those differences in treatment are expressly authorised by national legislation.
2. In order to maintain a balance of opportunity in employment for teachers in Northern Ireland while furthering the reconciliation of historical divisions between the major religious communities there, the provisions on religion or belief in this Directive shall not apply to the recruitment of teachers in schools in Northern Ireland insofar as this is expressly authorised by national legislation.

While this provision was included to safeguard a policy of specific interest to a politically troubled region, it represents a sign of increased support for positive discrimination more generally. However, even if this interpretation is accepted, the Court of Justice in *Abrahamsson* applied a very strict proportionality standard, ruling that the scheme was clearly disproportionate even when faced with evidence that the Swedish government considered the low number of women professors to be a significant problem requiring extraordinary measures.[214] Furthermore, that EU law leaves positive discrimination measures to the Member States does not imply that these measures will be put in place. In contrast, the transposition of the Race Directive in the Netherlands led to a limited positive action measure being rescinded; and in Germany and Hungary, where the law was amended to take into account the Court's case law, there has been no use of positive action measures.[215]

Perhaps the way forward here is to supplement an attempt to enhance the rights of disadvantaged groups with the imposition of positive duties on those best placed to eliminate discrimination. This model has been advocated by Professor Sandra Fredman, making reference to legislation that places statutory duties on public bodies (and sometimes on private actors)

---

[213] Z. Apostolopoulou, *Equal Treatment of People with Disabilities in the EC: What Does "Equal" Mean?*, Jean Monnet Working Paper 09/04, 10–11.
[214] *Abrahamsson and Anderson* v *Fogelqvist* [2000] ECR I-5539, para. 13
[215] Guiraudon, above n. 187, 538.

to promote equality, which do not give rise to individual rights. In her view this kind of legislation has the following advantages: it spreads the obligation to remedy inequality to those who have the power and capacity to change it; reform is systematic and not dependent upon individual lawsuits; finally the causes of discrimination are addressed collectively, harnessing local actors who know where the barriers lie and are best placed to propose measures to resolve them. By increasing participation among stakeholders the system gains more legitimacy and is also flexible to adjust as needs change.[216]

(iii) Dialogue

To a limited extent, the discrimination Directives introduce some methods for promoting equality suggested by Fredman by establishing three types of dialogue. First, the Member State has an obligation to inform those concerned of their rights and obligations under the Directive.[217] This is a relatively inexpensive way of bringing employers and other potential defendants up to date on their obligations.

Secondly, Member States are to promote social dialogue between employers and employees. All three Directives impose the following obligations.[218]

Race Directive, article 11

1. Member States shall, in accordance with national traditions and practice, take adequate measures to promote the social dialogue between the two sides of industry with a view to fostering equal treatment, including through the monitoring of workplace practices, collective agreements, codes of conduct, research or exchange of experiences and good practices.
2. Where consistent with national traditions and practice, Member States shall encourage the two sides of the industry without prejudice to their autonomy to conclude, at the appropriate level, agreements laying down anti-discrimination rules ... which fall within the scope of collective bargaining. These agreements shall respect the minimum requirements laid down by this Directive and the relevant national implementing measures.

In addition, the Equal Treatment Directive obliges Member States to encourage employers to promote equal treatment and to provide employees with information on equal treatment, e.g. statistics on the promotion of men and women.[219] Moreover, all the Directives call upon Member States to encourage dialogue with non-governmental organisations with a legitimate interest in discrimination.[220]

These forms of dialogue encourage 'reflexive regulation', i.e. a kind of self-regulation which encourages the employer to be self-reflective and self-critical about his practices. One potential use of these forms of dialogue is to address the problem of 'intersectional

---

[216] Sandra Fredman, *Human Rights Transformed: Positive Rights and Positive Duties* (Oxford, Oxford University Press, 2008) 190.
[217] Race Directive, article 10; Framework Directive, article 12; Equal Treatment Directive, article 30.
[218] Equal Treatment Directive, article 21; Framework Directive, article 13.
[219] Equal Treatment Directive, article 8b(3) and (4).
[220] Race Directive, article 12; Framework Directive, article 14; Equal Treatment Directive, article 8c.

discrimination', which as we noted earlier is not covered by the Directives. An employer with several Asian women might use social dialogue as a means of understanding and remedying the specific concerns of this group, which would remain invisible if he merely sought to avoid sex and race discrimination separately. Given that the Race Directive extends beyond the labour market, it is unfortunate that the provisions for dialogue are restricted to the labour market and are not extended to other points of authority (e.g. schools or hospitals).[221]

Thirdly, and perhaps most significantly, Member States must set up a regulatory body under the Race and Equal Treatment Directives.[222]

Race Directive, article 13

1. Member States shall designate a body or bodies for the promotion of equal treatment of all persons without discrimination on the grounds of racial or ethnic origin. These bodies may form part of agencies charged at national level with the defence of human rights or the safeguard of individuals' rights.
2. Member States shall ensure that the competences of these bodies include:
   - without prejudice to the right of victims and of associations, organisations or other legal entities … providing independent assistance to victims of discrimination in pursuing their complaints about discrimination,
   - conducting independent surveys concerning discrimination,
   - publishing independent reports and making recommendations on any issue relating to such discrimination.

These organisations can be indispensable in Member States for whom the implementation of discrimination legislation is a novelty, although their success will depend upon the agencies being well funded and politically independent. Their success will depend on how much power and how many resources Member States commit, and some have appeared to do as little as necessary.[223] One inherent limitation is that none of these organisations have any independent powers to enforce the law. This has been criticised because many entrenched forms of discrimination cannot easily be resolved through individuals litigating to assert individual rights.[224] However, as suggested above, the litigation model should not be seen as the exclusive means to bring about equality.

(iv) Mainstreaming

Perhaps the most significant commitment to promoting equality outside the framework of the rights-based model is found in the Lisbon Treaty's commitment to 'mainstreaming' equality.

---

[221] Chalmers, above n. 180, 238.
[222] Equal Treatment Directive, article 8a.
[223] Guiraudon above n. 187, singling out Italy and Spain as having weak agencies to address racial discrimination.
[224] M. Bell, 'Beyond European Labour Law? Reflections on the EU Racial Equality Directive' (2002) 8 *ELJ* 384, 397–8.

Article 8 TFEU (ex Article 3(2) TEC)

In all its activities, the Union shall aim to eliminate inequalities, and to promote equality, between men and women.

Article 10 TFEU

In defining and implementing its policies and activities, the Union shall aim to combat discrimination based on sex, racial or ethnic origin, religion or belief, disability, age or sexual orientation.

The separate reference to gender policy probably has to do with lobbying by the European Women's Group for a separate provision on gender equality.[225] According to the Commission, 'mainstreaming' means:

> The systematic integration of the respective situations, priorities and needs of women and men in all policies and with a view to promoting equality between women and men and mobilizing all general policies and measures specifically for the purpose of achieving equality by actively and openly taking into account, at the planning stage, their effects on the respective situation of women and men in implementation, monitoring and evaluation.[226]

The aim is to ensure gender (or race, disability, etc.) issues are considered and integrated in all Union actions. Potentially, this is an imaginative way of addressing the systemic causes of inequality between men and women. We begin by exploring how this policy emerged in the context of sex equality, then we look into how it has been implemented to tackle discrimination against all protected groups.

A range of factors brought gender mainstreaming onto the European Union's agenda in the mid-1990s.[227] First, political opportunities for greater action in the sex equality field emerged: the accession of Sweden and Finland (Member States with a strong tradition of gender equality policies), the appointment by Jacques Santer of an unprecedented five women Commissioners, the Commission's establishment of a high level group on gender equality, and the increased powers given to the European Parliament by the Maastricht Treaty. Secondly, these political changes strengthened the ability of the Commission's Equal Opportunity Unit and the Parliament's Women's Rights Committee to insist on new policy initiatives. For example, the Parliament had the power to approve the new Commission and expressed concerns that the person nominated as Commissioner for equal opportunities was not sufficiently committed to gender equality. This led Jacques Santer to a commitment that the Commission would devote itself as a group to gender equality. The European Women's Lobby was also instrumental in the adoption of gender

---

[225] M. Bell, 'Equality and the European Constitution' (2004) 33 *ILJ* 242, 257–8. A declaration attached to Article 8 TFEU also provides that 'the Union will aim in its different policies to combat all kinds of domestic violence. The Member States should take all necessary measures to prevent and punish these criminal acts and to support and protect the victims.' This may impact the measures adopted under Title V TFEU (Area of Freedom, Security and Justice).

[226] Communication from the Commission, Incorporating equal opportunities for women and men into all Community policies and activities, COM(96)67 final, 2.

[227] This section draws from M. A. Pollack and E. Hafner-Burton, 'Mainstreaming Gender in the European Union' (2000) 7 *JEPP* 432.

mainstreaming in the Treaty.[228] Thirdly, the reason why mainstreaming was selected as the keystone of the new equality policy was because it fitted with international political events (it gained prominence during the United Nations' Fourth World Conference in Beijing in 1995) and it was a policy with which the Union was familiar because a similar approach had been taken in the context of developing the European Union's environmental policy.

The effect of mainstreaming on EU institutions is mixed. On the one hand, the Commission undertook to increase the participation of women (the number of women in committees and expert groups has increased somewhat as a result),[229] establishing a Commissioner's Group on Equal Opportunities chaired by the President, and training Commission staff on the impact of Community policies on gender equality.[230] However, women remained underrepresented, and mainstreaming was also marginalised in the White Paper on Governance,[231] and has had less of an impact on the Council and the Court of Justice.[232]

In terms of Union policies, a test case for implementing mainstreaming is in the field of the EU's Structural Funds. In brief, the Union has four funds (the Regional Fund, the Social Fund, the Fisheries Fund and the Guidance and Guarantee Fund) from which it provides financial support to reduce the gap in living standards across the European Union and to promote economic and social cohesion. The Commission's efforts in this field were to insert gender equality as one criterion to allocate the relevant funds. Thus, in all Regulations setting out the operation of the structural funds we find reference to the promotion of gender equality as a condition for releasing funds.[233] In practical terms, the funds have financed a range of programmes designed to facilitate women's access to jobs that were traditionally reserved for men, or to facilitate working opportunities for women in poor European regions.[234] In addition to supporting programmes directly linked to improving the economic position of women, the release of funds for any other purpose is conditional on applicants indicating how their proposal promotes gender equality, which allows the Union to force Member States to embed gender equality as a condition for Community assistance.[235] But the results are modest: between 2000 and 2006, only 6 per cent of the European Social Fund went to gender-specific actions.[236] A similar approach could be attempted in the field of public procurement.[237]

Thus, mainstreaming in this field is not premised upon legislative measures that Member States must implement, rather it is designed to create incentives for the Union and Member States to embed gender considerations in their policies. To this end, the Union's role is to facilitate increased action at national level. This role was enhanced by the EU employment and social

---

[228] S. Mazey, 'Gender Mainstreaming Strategies in the EU: Delivering on an Agenda?' (2002) 10 *Feminist Legal Studies* 227.

[229] For example, Decision 2000/407/EC of 19 June 2000 relating to gender balance within the committees and expert groups established by it [2000] OJ L154/34. See European Commission, Work Programme for 2002 for the Implementation of the Framework Strategy on Gender Equality, SEC(2001)773 final, 5, noting an increase in women from 13 to 29 per cent from 2000 to 2001.

[230] European Commission, Work Programme for 2005 for the Implementation of the Framework Strategy on Gender Equality, SEC(2005)1044, 7.

[231] J. Shaw, 'The European Union and Gender Mainstreaming: Constitutionally Embedded or Comprehensively Marginalised?' (2002) 10 *Feminist Legal Studies* 213, 224–6.

[232] Mazey, above n. 228.

[233] For example, Regulation 1784/1999/EC on the European Social Fund [1999] OJ L213/5, article 2.

[234] See http://europa.eu.int/comm/employment_social/esf2000/index-en.htm for an overview.

[235] Mazey, above n. 228, 230.

[236] Assessment document SEC(2006)275.

[237] C. Tobler, 'Encore: Women's Clauses in Public Procurement under Community Law' (2000) 25 *ELRev.* 618.

solidarity programme, PROGRESS, launched in 2007. It is designed to promote mainstreaming of the principle of non-discrimination and to promote gender equality by commissioning studies on the effect of current legislation, supporting the implementation of EU discrimination law and raising awareness of the key policy issues.[238] Mainstreaming also occurs in the context of the European Employment Strategy.[239] In brief, the strategy provides for the Council to review national employment policies and make recommendations to Member States on, inter alia, the success of national policies in improving the work prospects of women.[240] However, the effectiveness of gender mainstreaming on national employment policies is uneven and one study concludes that, aside from Sweden, there is little sustained effort in mainstreaming in employment policy.[241]

Mainstreaming also occurs beyond the sphere of gender.[242] For example, disability-related issues have affected a number of legislative initiatives: a Directive on special provisions for certain vehicles requires that they should be accessible to disabled persons,[243] and the Directive on Universal Services in the field of electronic communication, which is designed to ensure that all citizens have affordable access to telecommunication services, guarantees access to disabled persons by requiring Member States to ensure that disabled users have access 'equivalent to that enjoyed by other end-users'.[244] These measures are supported by the European Parliament's Disability Intergroup and as their work programme makes clear, the effect of provisions like these is to remove barriers faced by disabled people.[245] This takes us very far away from the traditional vision of discrimination law, which is about granting individuals the right to sue. Rather, the political philosophy that motivates mainstreaming is that of ensuring social inclusion.[246] That said, mainstreaming has yet to achieve significant results.[247] Perhaps one of the reasons for the failure of mainstreaming to live up to its promise is that it remains focused on looking at and resolving an issue merely from the perspective of the disadvantage suffered by a group (e.g. flexible hours to facilitate women's employment) rather than insisting on transforming employers' practices, the real cause of disadvantage.[248]

---

[238] Decision 1672/2006 establishing a Community Programme for Employment and Social Solidarity, articles 2, 7 and 8 [2006] OJ L315/1.

[239] F. Beveridge and S. Velluti (eds.), *Gender and the Open Method of Coordination* (Aldershot, Ashgate, 2008).

[240] For example, see Council Recommendation on the implementation of Member States' employment policies [2004] OJ L326/47 where each Member State's employment policy towards women is assessed.

[241] C. Fagan, J. Rubery, D. Grimshaw, M. Smith, G. Hebson and H. Figueiredo, 'Gender Mainstreaming in the Enlarged European Union: Recent Developments in the European Employment Strategy and Social Inclusion Process' (2005) 36 *Industrial Relations Journal* 568, 587. See also L. Mósesdóttir and R. Gerlingsdóttir, 'Spreading the Word Across Europe: Gender Mainstreaming as a Political and Policy Project' (2005) 7 *International Feminist Journal of Politics* 513.

[242] In the sphere of race, see M. Bell, *Racism and Equality in the European Union* (Oxford, Oxford University Press, 2008).

[243] Directive 2001/85/EC of the European Parliament and of the Council of 20 November 2001 relating to special provisions for vehicles used for the carriage of passengers comprising more than eight seats in addition to the driver's seat, and amending Directives 70/156/EEC and 97/27/EC [2002] OJ L42/1, article 3.

[244] Directive 2002/22/EC, article 7 [2002] OJ L108/51('Universal Service Directive'),

[245] European Parliament Disability Intergroup, *Annual Report 2007–2008*, 12, available at www.disabilityintergroup.eu/.

[246] H. Collins, 'Discrimination, Equality and Social Inclusion' (2003) 66 *MLR* 16.

[247] F. Beveridge, 'Bulding Against the Past: The Impact of Mainstreaming on EU Gender Law and Policy' (2007) 32 *European Law Review* 193; Bell, above n. 2, 185–8.

[248] J. Rubery, 'Gender Mainstreaming and Gender Equality in the EU: The Impact of the EU Employment Strategy' (2002) 33 *Industrial Relations Journal* 500, 503.

FURTHER READING

K. J. Alter and J. Vargas, 'Explaining Variation in the Use of European Litigation Strategies: European Community Law and British Gender Equality Policy' (2000) 33 *Comparative Political Studies* 452

C. Barnard, 'The Changing Scope of the Fundamental Principle of Equality?' (2001) 46 *McGill Law Journal* 955

M. Bell, *Anti-Discrimination Law and the European Union* (Oxford, Oxford University Press, 2002)

C. Brown, 'The Race Directive: Towards Equality for *All* Peoples of Europe?' (2002) *Yearbook of European Law* 195

D. Caruso, 'Limits of the Classic Method: Positive Action in the European Union after the New Equality Directives' (2003) 44 *Harvard International Law Journal* 331

D. Chalmers, 'The Mistakes of the Good European?' in S. Fredman (ed.), *Discrimination and Human Rights: The Case of Racism* (Oxford, Oxford University Press, 2001)

E. Ellis, *EU Anti-Discrimination Law* (Oxford, Oxford University Press, 2005)

S. Fredman, *Discrimination Law* (Oxford, Oxford University Press, 2002)

S. Fredman and S. Spencer, *Age as an Equality Issue* (Oxford, Hart, 2003)

V. Guiraudon, 'Equality in the Making: Implementing European Non-discrimination Law' (2009) 13 *Citizenship Studies* 527

C. Hoskins, *Integrating Gender: Women, Law and Politics in the European Union* (London, Verso, 1996)

E. Howard, 'The European Year of Equal Opportunities for All 2007: Is the EU Moving Away from a Formal Idea of Equality?' (2008) 14 *European Law Journal* 168

A. Lawson and C. Gooding (eds.), *Disability Rights in Europe* (Oxford, Hart, 2005)

S. Mazey, 'Gender Mainstreaming Strategies in the EU: Delivering on an Agenda?' (2002) 10 *Feminist Legal Studies* 227

H. Oliver, 'Sexual Orientation Discrimination: Perceptions, Definitions and Genuine Occupational Requirements' (2004) 33 *Industrial Law Journal* 1

M. A. Pollack and E. Hafner-Burton, 'Mainstreaming Gender in the European Union' (2000) 7 *Journal of European Public Policy* 432

D. Schieck, 'A New Framework on Equal Treatment of Persons in EC Law?' (2002) 8 *European Law Review* 290

J. Shaw, 'Mainstreaming Equality and Diversity in European Union Law and Policy' (2005) 58 *CLP* 255

R. Whittle, 'The Framework Directive for Equal Treatment in Employment and Occupation: An Analysis from a Disability Rights Perspective' (2002) 27 *European Law Review* 303

14

EU Criminal Law

CONTENTS

1 INTRODUCTION

This chapter considers EU criminal law and police cooperation. It is organised as follows.

(i) Section 2 considers the relationship between EU criminal law and internal security. EU criminal law is part of the area of freedom, security and justice and comprises three central competences. These are judicial cooperation in criminal matters; the establishment of minimum rules concerning the definition of criminal offences and sanctions; and police cooperation. However, these are all subject to Article 4(2) TEU, which states that protection of national security is the sole responsibility of each Member State. Furthermore, the German Constitutional Court has ruled that as the central elements of criminal law are pivotal to German constitutional identity, these must be decided nationally. This limits both the scope and the development of EU criminal law and has influenced its position within the Lisbon Treaty. Previously, it was governed by the largely intergovernmental arrangements of the third pillar. This has been abolished and, for the first time, full supranational disciplines now extend to cover EU criminal law. However, qualifications have been made. First, instruments adopted prior to the Lisbon Treaty retain their earlier status. The usual procedures concerning Commission enforcement actions and the preliminary reference procedure shall not apply to these for five years or until the instruments are amended. Secondly, 'emergency brake procedures' have put in place in relation to the law-making procedures in this field so that sensitive matters can be referred to the European Council. Thirdly, there is differentiated integration. As with other parts of the area of freedom, security and justice, the United Kingdom and Ireland can choose whether to participate in legislation adopted after Lisbon, and Denmark is only bound by virtue of its commitments in international law under the Schengen Convention.

Section 3 considers judicial cooperation in criminal matters. This is built around the principle of the mutual recognition of judicial decisions. Mutual recognition requires strong trust in the judicial, investigative and prosecutorial systems of other Member States. Its most prominent instrument is the European Arrest Warrant which requires surrender of a person sought for prosecution or detention where this is requested by the judicial authority of another Member State. For thirty-two offences this will be the case even if the act is not an offence in the surrendering Member State (abolition of double criminality). This has raised constitutional challenges in the Cypriot, Czech, German and Polish Constitutional Courts. Concerns have been raised about checks over due process in the requesting state; the surrender of a citizen by a state for detention for acts it does not consider illegal; and the violation of national citizenship provisions in which states surrender their own citizens for trial abroad. Mutual recognition is also expressed in the *ne bis in idem* principle. This provides that a person may not be tried in another Member State for materially identical acts which have either been subject to judicial decision in another Member State or of which the prosecution has definitely disposed.

Section 4 considers the harmonisation of criminal offences and sanctions in EU law. There are two types of offence that can be subject to harmonisation. The first are serious offences with a cross-border dimension. Both these two constraints have been weakened over time so that many offences have now been subject to some harmonisation. The common feature of most of these offences is that they fit some loose definition of organised crime, involve more than one perpetrator and have some prior infrastructure. Harmonising measures are often vague in such instances and are used to require Member States to criminalise activities that were not previously illegal. The second type of offence is where EU criminal law is used as a regulatory tool to ensure the effective implementation of an EU policy. In such circumstances, there must be prior EU measures and the use of criminal sanctions must be considered essential to securing the effectiveness of the policy.

Section 5 considers police cooperation. EU law has centred around three activities here. The first is the development of the principle of availability of information so that law enforcement authorities in one Member State which need information to carry out their duties can obtain it from the authorities of another Member State. This raises data protection concerns and has been used to require Member States to strengthen surveillance capacities over their own citizens. The second is the development of private policing regimes. Most notably in the field of money laundering and electronic communications, Member States must require operators to hold and make available information on their customers. The third is the development of pan-European intelligence capacities. This has been done partly through the establishment of pan-European databases, most notably the Schengen Information System and the Europol Information System. It has also been done through the establishment of Europol and granting it a competence to analyse and build work files on serious crime with a transnational dimension.

2 EU CRIMINAL LAW AND THE PROBLEM OF INTERNAL SECURITY

The most significant deepening of the integration process by the Lisbon Treaty occurred in the fields of criminal law and policing. Prior to the Maastricht Treaty, the Union had no formal competences in these fields.[1] At Maastricht, it was placed in the third pillar on Justice and Home Affairs. It remained there through both the Amsterdam and Nice Treaties under the heading of 'Title VI TEU Provisions on Police and Judicial Cooperation in Criminal Matters'. However, the supranational reach of EU law only applied in an attenuated manner. Decision-making in the Council was by unanimity.[2] The Commission had to share its power of initiative with the Member States.[3] The Parliament only had limited consultative powers.[4] The Court of Justice only had very limited powers with Member States having the possibility to choose whether to grant their national courts the powers to refer to it.[5] Finally, the Union had no power to adopt directly effective legislation in the field.[6]

This all changed at Lisbon with, in principle, the same disciplines of EU law being applied to criminal law and policing as all other fields.[7]

Article 67 TFEU

1. The Union shall constitute an area of freedom, security and justice with respect for fundamental rights and the different legal systems and traditions of the Member States. ...
3. The Union shall endeavour to ensure a high level of security through measures to prevent and combat crime, racism and xenophobia, and through measures for coordination and cooperation between police and judicial authorities and other competent authorities, as well as through the mutual recognition of judgments in criminal matters and, if necessary, through the approximation of criminal laws.

EU criminal law has become in many ways a field like any other. It forms part of the area of freedom, security and justice, and comprises three central competences: judicial cooperation in criminal matters based on the mutual recognition of judgments;[8] the establishment of minimum rules concerning the definition of criminal offences and sanctions;[9] and police

---

[1] See E. Baker and C. Harding, 'From Past Imperfect to Future Perfect? A Longitudinal Study of the Third Pillar' (2009) 34 *ELRev.* 25.
[2] Article 34(2) TEU(M).
[3] *Ibid.*
[4] Article 39 TEU(M).
[5] Article 35(2) TEU(M).
[6] Article 34(2) TEU(M).
[7] S. Peers, 'Finally "Fit for Purposes"? The Treaty of Lisbon and the End of the Third Pillar Legal Order' (2008) 27 *YBEL* 47.
[8] Article 82 TFEU.
[9] Article 83 TFEU.

cooperation.[10] There is provision for qualified majority voting (QMV) in the Council in almost all competences.[11] Parliament acquires rights by virtue of the wide application of the assent[12] and ordinary legislative procedures here.[13] The Court of Justice has full jurisdiction. Regulations and Directives are to be adopted in this field as in any other.

(i) The Member States and internal security

A significant caveat has to be placed on treating EU criminal law and policing like other fields of EU law. Criminal law and policing set out the monopoly of lawful violence enjoyed by a state over its territory. It has powers of detention, coercion and surveillance not granted to private citizens to allow it to secure order and to enforce binding decisions. Criminal law and policing, thus, go to the very heart of the sovereignty and the identity of the nation-state. These considerations of sovereignty and identity correspondingly exercise a more powerful influence on EU law in this field than possibly in any other. This is reflected in Article 4(2) TEU.[14]

Article 4(2) TEU

[The Union] shall respect their essential State functions, including ensuring the territorial integrity of the State, maintaining law and order and safeguarding national security. In particular, national security remains the sole responsibility of each Member State.

The provision has a double dimension. On the one hand, it imposes injunctions on the EI institutions. Their laws and activities must respect Member States' right to maintain law and order on their territory. On the other, it creates a monopoly for the Member States. The protection of national security is for them alone. As this is a matter of such sensitivity, it cannot be seen as a matter for the Treaties alone. National constitutional courts, in particular, will become involved shaping the limits and features of EU criminal law. In its judgment on the Lisbon Treaty, the German Constitutional Court stated that it would strike down EU law if it transgressed on a matter central to Germany's constitutional identity.[15] As criminal law and policing are fields central to this identity, any EU intervention has to be limited and leave substantial scope for national action.

[10] Article 87 TFEU.
[11] The only competences where unanimity is required involve operational cooperation (Articles 86(3) and 89 TFEU), the establishment of the European Public Prosecutor's Office (Article 86(1) TFEU) and the establishment of new crimes for which there should be harmonisation in addition to those mentioned in Article 83 TFEU (Article 83(1) TFEU).
[12] This applies to the rules on specific aspects of criminal procedure (Article 82(2)(d) TFEU); the establishment of new crimes for which there should be harmonisation (Article 83(1) TFEU) and the establishment of the European Public Prosecutor's Office and extension of its powers (Article 86(1), (4) TFEU).
[13] This applies in all areas other than those specified above n.12, and measures concerning operational cooperation (Articles 87(3) and 89 TFEU).
[14] A corresponding provision stating that the area of freedom, security and justice shall not affect the exercise of the responsibilities incumbent upon Member States with regard to the maintenance of law and order and the safeguarding of internal security is set out in Article 72 TFEU.
[15] See pp. 194–7 for further analysis.

2 BvE 2/08 *Gauweiler v Treaty of Lisbon,* Judgment of 30 June 2009

252. What has always been deemed especially sensitive for the ability of a constitutional state to democratically shape itself are decisions on substantive and formal criminal law, on the disposition of the police monopoly on the use of force towards the interior…

253. As regards the preconditions of criminal liability as well as the concepts of a fair and appropriate trial, the administration of criminal law depends on cultural processes of previous understanding that are historically grown and also determined by language, and on the alternatives which emerge in the process of deliberation and which move the respective public opinion… The common characteristics in this regard, but also the differences, between the European nations is shown by the relevant case law of the European Court of Human Rights concerning the procedural guarantees in criminal proceedings… The penalisation of social behaviour can, however, only to a limited extent be normatively derived from values and moral premises that are shared Europe-wide. Instead, the decision on punishable behaviour, on the rank of legal interests and the sense and the measure of the threat of punishment, is to a particular extent left to the democratic decision-making process… In this context, which is of importance as regards fundamental rights, a transfer of sovereign powers beyond intergovernmental cooperation may only under restrictive preconditions lead to harmonisation for certain cross-border circumstances; the Member States must, in principle, retain substantial space of action in this context…

351. …Particularly the newly conferred competences in the areas of judicial cooperation in criminal… matters… can, and must, be exercised by the institutions of the European Union in such a way that on the level of the Member States, tasks of sufficient weight as to their extent as well as their substance remain which legally and practically are the precondition of a living democracy. The newly established competences are – at any rate with the required interpretation – not 'elements that establish a state', which also in an overall perspective do not infringe the sovereign statehood of the Federal Republic of Germany in a constitutionally relevant manner. For the assessment of the challenge of an unconstitutional depletion of the competences of the German Bundestag, it can remain undecided how many legislative acts in the Member States are already influenced, pre-formed or determined by the European Union … What is decisive for the constitutional assessment of the challenge is not the quantitative relations but whether the Federal Republic of Germany retains substantial national scope of action for central areas of statutory regulation and areas of life….

355. Securing legal peace by the administration of criminal law has always been a central duty of state authority. As regards the task of creating, securing and enforcing a well-ordered social existence by protecting the elementary values of community life on the basis of a legal order, criminal law is an indispensable element to secure the unswervingness of this legal order… Every provision in criminal law contains a social and ethical verdict of unworthiness on the action which it penalises. The specific content of this verdict of unworthiness results from the constituent elements of the criminal offence and the sanction… To what extent and in what areas a polity uses exactly the means of criminal law as an instrument of social control is a fundamental decision. By criminal law, a legal community gives itself a code of conduct that is anchored in its values, whose violation is, according to the shared convictions on law, regarded as so grievous and unacceptable for social existence in the community that it requires punishment…

356. With the decision on punishable conduct, the legislature takes the democratically legitimised responsibility for a form of sovereign action that counts among the most intensive encroachments on individual freedom in a modern constitutional state. The legislature is in principle free concerning the decision of whether it wants to defend a specific legal interest whose protection it regards as essential exactly with the means of criminal law how it wants to do this… Within the boundaries of the

commitment to the constitution, it can additionally decide which sanction it will impose on culpable conduct. The investigation of crimes, the detection of the perpetrator, the establishment of his guilt and his punishment are incumbent on the bodies of administration of criminal law, which for this purpose and under the conditions determined by the law, have to institute and to conduct criminal proceedings and have to execute imposed sanctions …

357. Due to the integration of the German constitutional state into the order of international law of the community of states, the legislature's freedom of action may be constitutionally restricted by the obligation to enforce supranational law in its own area of responsibility. It can for instance be required to impose sanctions on certain actions with the purpose of enforcing essential provisions of the general international law vis-à-vis the individual … This applies above all to the process of the formation of an international criminal justice for genocide, crimes against humanity and war crimes … As a Member State of the European Union, Germany has made other commitments. With the construction and further development of the area of freedom, security and justice, which has taken place essentially according to the provisions relating to the intergovernmental 'Third Pillar' of the law of the European Union, the European Union follows the objective of combining the process of growing together and the opening of the borders for persons, goods, services and capital with an improved cooperation of the prosecution authorities. The Member States have agreed on creating provisions of criminal law and law of criminal procedure in specific areas which do justice to the conditions of European circumstances with a cross-border dimension.

358. Due to the fact that democratic self-determination is affected in an especially sensitive manner by provisions of criminal law and law of criminal procedure, the corresponding foundations of competence in the Treaties must be interpreted strictly – on no account extensively – and their use requires particular justification. The core content of criminal law does not serve as a technical instrument for effectuating international cooperation but stands for the particularly sensitive democratic decision on the minimum standard according to legal ethics.

Two grounds are suggested as to why criminal law is central to Germany's constitutional identity. First, it anchors a state's social values (paragraphs 253 and 355). Secondly, it is where the state encroaches most strongly on individual freedom. It is axiomatic that these are subject to democratic processes (paragraphs 356 and 358): processes that exist only at a national level. This being so, any EU measure impinging on either of these rationales would run the risk of being subject to constitutional review. The Constitutional Court suggests (in paragraph 356) this is most likely to be the case in relation to 'the decision on punishable behaviour, on the rank of legal interests (protected) and the sense and the measure of the threat of punishment'. This is wide-ranging indeed, and seems to embrace most of criminal law and policing.

(ii) Towards an EU idea of collective security

On its face, the highly restrictive terms of Article 4(2) TEU and the tight controls imposed by the German Constitutional Court leave little scope for the development of EU criminal and policing law. Yet, in paragraph 357, the German Constitutional Court leaves some undefined room for international cooperation, and ultimately finds the terms of the Lisbon Treaty provisions on judicial cooperation in criminal matters and police cooperation unproblematic. This begs the question as to what the basis is for their presence and their operation, given the constraints placed on them. There are two narratives: augmentation of a state's own national security and protection of a pan-European public order.

By cooperating with other states, a state can augment protection of its own internal security. Other states may have information or resources unavailable to it in the fight against crime or might be able to take action against threats to it which are located outside its borders or track down persons or evidence wanted by it that are on their territories. Viewed in this light, EU law is not about creating a pan-European criminal law or policing capacity but about augmenting individual state security capacity.[16] Undoubtedly, some of the provisions in the Lisbon Treaty can only be understood in this way. A committee is established to augment operational capacity precisely for these purposes.

Article 71 TFEU

A standing committee shall be set up within the Council in order to ensure that operational cooperation on internal security is promoted and strengthened within the Union. Without prejudice to Article 240,[[17]] it shall facilitate coordination of the action of Member States' competent authorities. Representatives of the bodies, offices and agencies of the Union concerned may be involved in the proceedings of this committee. The European Parliament and national Parliaments shall be kept informed of the proceedings.

Furthermore, as the ethos is about augmenting individual domestic security, Member States are free to organise other arrangements between themselves as they see fit.

Article 73 TFEU

It shall be open to Member States to organise between themselves and under their responsibility such forms of cooperation and coordination as they deem appropriate between the competent departments of their administrations responsible for safeguarding national security.

This narrative is present in EU law but there is something deeply unattractive about it. It carries with it the vision of law-enforcement agencies increasing each other's powers and resources through European integration unfettered from domestic constraints and checks and balances.

S. Lavenex and W. Wagner, 'Which European Public Order? Sources of Imbalance in the European Area of Freedom, Security and Justice' (2007) 16 *European Security* 225, 239–40

Reminiscent of the 'new raison d'état' thesis, we argued that European integration opens up a transgovernmental venue which allows national justice and home affairs officials to pool their respective 'monopolies over the use of violence' while shielding them from the established liberal norms and procedures that limit this monopoly in national constitutions. As Elspeth Guild has put it, this

---

[16] B. Bowling, 'Transnational Policing: The Globalization Thesis, a Typology and Research Agenda' (2009) 3 *Policing* 1, 6–7.

[17] This is the provision that sets out the powers of COREPER. See pp. 74–5.

system is incomplete, because 'it is only criminal judgements that have this power to cross the border without risk of further control. The individual's rights in respect of a criminal charge, trial, and sentence remain bound within the territory of each member state'.[18] There are strong parallels with the Single Market, in which goods, services, capital and EU citizens move freely, but where production standards, social policies or pension systems remain nationally bound. As we have argued, these parallels result from the diffusion of market-based mechanisms of integration from the economic to the political field, that is, an emphasis on negative integration and mutual recognition.

The mutual recognition of asylum procedures, criminal laws or warrants, however, presupposes a high level of mutual trust in the member states' judicial systems. As our cases show, even among near neighbours who have a long history of cooperation, this trust cannot be taken for granted. As long as doubts remain about the proper respect for individual rights in other Member States, courts are unlikely to accept other states' decisions without further scrutiny and citizens are unlikely to welcome such a Europeanisation of internal security cooperation as an advancement. Thus, there is a strong case for the neofunctionalist notion that European cooperation in criminal law necessitates a common approach to defendants' rights, that European police-cooperation 'spills over' into European level controls of data protection and asylum cooperation needs an integrated asylum system. Legal approximation, as an alternative or complement to mutual recognition, would have the advantage of replicating the fundamental rights and guarantees found in national legal systems at the European level, enforceable through supranational judicial control.

This critique illustrates also why the narrative of augmenting domestic security tells only part of the story about what is taking place in EU law. Security is treated as a public good like any other – protection of the environment, public health – which simply has to be expanded. As its qualities are not discussed, no explanation can be provided of why security is so jealously protected by nation-states or why EU law in this field should extend beyond arrangements of mutual advantage for national law enforcement agencies. To answer these questions, it is worth considering the notion of security that underpins both criminal law and policing. Loader and Walker have argued it has three dimensions. First, security is seen as a safe environment that can be externally measured as a safe environment. This is the security referred to in crime statistics. Secondly, security is a sense of secure belonging to and trust in a community. This is important as people only feel safe, notwithstanding statistics, if they live in a world of stable relations and stable identities. Thirdly, the realisation of security is central to the creation of political community and to a collective feeling of 'We'.[19] The nation-state's ability to bring security brings not only faith in its institutions but contributes to our feeling British, Czech, Polish, etc. These different dimensions are why security is vested so heavily in the nation-state. Only it has the symbolic authority and resources to provide the environment and social relations upon which ideas of security depend.[20] Any EU criminal law or policing arrangements must engage with all three dimensions. Security arrangements are increasing the

---

[18] E. Guild, 'Crime and the EU's Constitutional Future in an Area of Freedom, Security and Justice' (2004) 10 *ELJ* 218, 220.

[19] I. Loader and N. Walker, *Civilizing Security* (Cambridge University Press, Cambridge University Press, 2007) 146–66.

[20] A. Crawford, 'Networked Governance and the Post-regulatory State? Steering, Rowing and Anchoring the Provision of Policing and Security' (2006) 10 *Theoretical Criminology* 449, 459.

resources available to governments but they will rarely be seen as legitimate, as the extract from Lavenex and Wagner illustrates, if they do not set out the social order that they wish to protect or if they lead to people being policed by bodies or processes they do not recognise or are subject to offences whose pedigree is unclear.

Loader and Walker have therefore suggested a possible second justification for EU criminal law and policing. It is about the establishment and protection of a common *European public order*, which is not there just to contribute to a safe environment but also to embed its own certain social relations and develop an autonomous sense of community.

I. Loader and N. Walker, *Civilizing Security* (Cambridge, Cambridge University Press, 2007) 260–1

[F]irst… the fact that states have a strong self-interest in security means that they are, and will always remain, willing participants in collaborative strategies, notwithstanding the difficulties in stabilizing these strategies in institutional terms. Indeed, the problems of stabilization do not arise from a lack of awareness of their interdependence, but, rather, from an *acute and constant* awareness of interdependence coupled with a sometimes unbridled determination to assert one's own national interest in the light of the factors of interdependence. Secondly, as the content of the internal security imperative of states is in all cases strikingly similar, states may be encouraged nevertheless to think of the global public good as something more than the optimal convergence of presumptively diverse individual state interests… perhaps more so than in any other policy domain all states adhere to the same broad conception of general order – the same appreciation of (and appreciation of their need to respond to) their populations' desire to live in a state of tranquillity and in a context of predictable social relations. Thirdly, and relatedly, states may find common cause in their very understanding of the social quality of the public good of security… For all that their particular interests may differ, states also have a common understanding of the social and public quality of that which they seek to defend, which in turn allows, however unevenly and intermittently, for a greater imaginative openness to the possibility of *other* sites and levels of social and public 'added value' in the accomplishment of security.

In the Commission's early documents on the area of freedom, justice and security, it thus talked of the mission of EU law in this field to establish a European public order.[21] Protection of this European public order would exist independently of protection of national security. Similarly, the Member States have just established an action programme in this field, the Stockholm Action Programme, which is to focus 'on the interests and needs of citizens'.[22] Most importantly, however, insofar as many of the competences here concern provision for mutual recognition of judgments and harmonisation of laws, this suggests some underlying values and interests in common. All this suggests some pan-European agenda, which exists independently of individual domestic security concerns and which has public and social qualities of its own. This idea of the pan-European agenda is also consistent with the supranationalisation

---

[21] European Commission, *Towards an Area of Freedom, Security and Justice*, COM(98)459, 9. On the need to see this field as part of the area of freedom, security and justice, see V. Mitsilegas, 'The Transformation of Criminal Law in the "Area of Freedom, Security and Justice"' (2007) 26 *YBEL* 1.

[22] EU Council, *The Stockholm Programme: An Open and Secure Europe Serving and Protecting the Citizens*, Council Doc. 17024/09, 3.

of EU law in this field. If a European public order is to be protected through pan-European policing and criminal measures, then a corollary is that these measures should be subject to pan-European democratic controls: both in the enactment of laws and in the establishment of systems of accountability.

Walker has noted that, in the absence of the state, it is difficult to find robust frameworks of common understanding and attachment that will structure debate. He observes that a supranational security community offers the possibility of a participatory political culture but is more likely to offer a lowest common denominator where common marginalised groups are demonised. Indeed, the substance of this European public order is undefined, as are the needs and interests of the EU citizens that the area of freedom, security and justice is to protect.[23] This leaves open this possibility of drift. Above all, the relationship of the European public order to ideas of national security is still unclear. This is important normatively. Is the European public order just to bring together common anxieties? It is also important institutionally. If something is seen as only a matter of national internal security, EU law should not intervene. If it is seen as something augmenting national security through cooperation rather than securing a European public order, then one might expect to see more intergovernmental elements to the law in the field, whereas more supranational elements would be present if it is about securing the latter.

(iii) Mediation of national and collective security concerns

(a) Retention of the pre-Lisbon normative order

All is not as it appears with the Lisbon Treaty. Measures adopted prior to the Lisbon Treaty are not transformed automatically into Regulations and Directives. Moreover, for the first five years post ratification of the Lisbon Treaty, unless they are amended, the institutional arrangements concerning the enforcement and application of individual legislative acts will remain the same as those prior to Lisbon.

Protocol on Transitional Provisions, Article 10

1. As a transitional measure, and with respect to acts of the Union in the field of police cooperation and judicial cooperation in criminal matters which have been adopted before the entry into force of the Treaty of Lisbon, the powers of the institutions shall be the following at the date of entry into force of that Treaty: the powers of the Commission under Article 258 TFEU shall not be applicable and the powers of the Court of Justice of the European Union under Title VI TEU, in the version in force before the entry into force of the Treaty of Lisbon, shall remain the same, including where they have been accepted under Article 35(2) TEU(M).

2. The amendment of an act referred to in paragraph 1 shall entail the applicability of the powers of the institutions referred to in that paragraph as set out in the Treaties with respect to the amended act for those Member States to which that amended act shall apply.

3. In any case, the transitional measure mentioned in paragraph 1 shall cease to have effect five years after the date of entry into force of the Treaty of Lisbon.

---

[23] N. Walker, 'Policing and the Supranational' (2002) 12 *Policing and Society* 307, 317–18.

In practical terms, as there is already a significant body of EU law in this field the traditional, largely intergovernmental way of enforcing and applying EU law will be the norm for some time to come even if law-making will be done largely through the ordinary legislative procedure. In addition, Article 10 indicates uncertainties about deepening integration in this field. For the next five years the decision to grant supranational qualities to an EU legal instrument will be taken on a case-by-case basis. In each instance, reflection will be had on whether the measure should have direct effect, be susceptible to unfettered referral by national courts and enforcement action by the Commission. The Lisbon Treaty does not therefore establish a general change from a largely intergovernmental arrangement to a largely supranational legal order. Instead, the change is to be managed on a case-by-case basis.

This being so, it is necessary to consider the legal arrangements prior to Lisbon. Article 34(2) TEU(M) set out three forms of legislative measure.[24] Instruments will retain these qualities until they are amended or replaced.[25]

Framework Decisions These are used for harmonisation of legislation, and are the central instrument. They are binding upon the Member States as to the result to be achieved, but leave the form and method of implementation to national authorities. They are analogous to Directives, although they are not capable of direct effect. However, they are capable of indirect effect. National courts are required to interpret national law so far as possible in the light of the wording and purpose of any relevant Framework Decision.[26]

Decisions These are to be adopted for all purposes other than harmonisation of legislation. A good example of this is Decision 98/701/JHA on common standards for filling in the residence permit for non-EU nationals.[27] These would appear to be harmonising procedures for administrative officials on how to fill in residence permits. A Framework Decision was not chosen, however, as the measure was intended to be purely administrative, and was not intended to affect the competence of Member States relating either to the recognition of states or to passports from these states. Decisions are binding, but, like Framework Decisions, they cannot generate direct effect.

Conventions These are similar to international agreements. They generate commitments between the Member States and the European Union, but their effects upon the internal legal order of Member States is unclear. For the Union can only recommend to the Member States that they be adopted within a time limit in accordance with national constitutional requirements. They tend to be adopted in areas of particular national sensitivity, a good example being the Convention on Jurisdiction and the Recognition and Enforcement of Judgments in

---

[24] Article 34(2) TEU lists 'common positions' as a measure that can be adopted. These define the approach of the Union to a particular matter, but cannot be considered legislation as it is not clear what legislative effects these have.

[25] For more on these instruments, see A. Hinarejos, 'On the Legal Effects of Framework Decisions and Decisions: Directly Applicable, Directly Effective, Self-Executing, Supreme?' (2008) 14 *ELJ* 620.

[26] Case C-105/03 *Pupino* [2005] ECR I-5285. On the judgment see M. Fletcher, 'Extending "Indirect Effect" to the Third Pillar: The Significance of Pupino' (2005) 30 *ELRev.* 862; B. Kuracz and A. Lazowski, 'Two Sides of the Same Coin? Framework Decisions and Directives' (2006) 25 *YBEL* 177; S. Peers, 'Salvation Outside the Church: Judicial Protection in the Third Pillar after the *Pupino* and *Segi* Judgments' (2007) 44 *CMLRev.* 883.

[27] [1998] OJ L333/8.

Matrimonial Matters.[28] This allowed mutual recognition of divorce arrangements and marriages, but addresses highly charged matters such as judicial procedure and the nature of the family in modern societies. A Convention was, therefore, seen as the best way to proceed.

The institutional arrangements for these measures limit the extent to which these may be enforced by EI institutions against the Member States. Article 10(2) indicates that Member States cannot be subject to infringement proceedings brought by the Commission for non-compliance with their obligations under these measures. The possibility of preliminary references is also more limited as the Protocol indicates that this is to be governed by Article 35 TEU(M). Whilst this allows the Court to make preliminary rulings on the interpretation and validity of the measures, individual Member States only accept the Court's jurisdiction to entertain references from their courts if they have given a Declaration to that effect.[29] Furthermore, states can choose whether to allow only courts against whose decision there is no judicial remedy to make a reference.[30] As of 1 December 2009, sixteen Member States allow all courts to make a reference in the field.[31] States can also choose whether to oblige a court against whose decisions there is no judicial remedy to make a reference. At the moment, ten Member States have chosen that option.[32] Ten states have chosen not to allow their courts to refer at all. The latter is something of a counter-productive option as rulings of the Court of Justice bind all national courts and not simply the referring court. A choice not to opt into the reference procedure is a choice to exclude oneself from a procedure that nevertheless creates legal effects for one's territory and this explains why the procedure has expanded over the years.

(b) National controls over the law-making process

Whilst the law-making process is 'supranationalised' from the date of entry into force of the Lisbon Treaty, a number of national controls are placed on legislation here that distinguish it from other fields of EU law.

The first is that the Commission does not have the monopoly of initiative. Instead, it is shared with the Member States, so that, besides the Commission, one-quarter of Member States can make a proposal for a measure in this field.[33] However, it is not the control of agenda-setting that most pre-occupies Member States. It is rather the enactment of EU laws that intrude too much on their monopoly over the provision of internal security or criminal justice.

The second, and most high profile, constraint is the emergency brake procedure. This applies to measures on judicial cooperation in criminal matters,[34] measures harmonising minimum rules on the definition of criminal offences and criminal sanctions, and operational cooperation in policing.[35] In the first two instances, if a Member State considers that a measure affects fundamental aspects of its criminal justice system it may ask for the matter to be referred to the European Council. With operational cooperation in policing, it is assumed all aspects are

---

[28] [1998] OJ C221/1.
[29] Article 35(2) TEU(M).
[30] Article 35(2)(a) TEU. Only Spain has chosen this option.
[31] These are Belgium, Czech Republic, Germany, Greece, France, Italy, Latvia, Lithuania, Luxembourg, Hungary, Netherlands, Austria, Portugal, Slovenia, Finland and Sweden. Notice from the Council [2008] OJ C69/1.
[32] These are Belgium, Czech Republic, Germany, Spain, France, Italy, Luxembourg, Netherlands, Austria and Slovenia.
[33] Article 76 TFEU.
[34] Article 82(3) TFEU.
[35] *Ibid.*

sensitive. If it is not possible to secure unanimity within the Council, the matter is automatically referred to the European Council.

> ### Article 83(3) TFEU
>
> Where a member of the Council considers that a draft directive … would affect fundamental aspects of its criminal justice system, it may request that the draft directive be referred to the European Council. In that case, the ordinary legislative procedure shall be suspended. After discussion, and in case of a consensus, the European Council shall, within four months of this suspension, refer the draft back to the Council, which shall terminate the suspension of the ordinary legislative procedure.

Although the European Council has a time limit of four months to reach a decision, a reference is likely in most cases to lead to the measure not being generally adopted. Decisions there are reached by unanimity and it would need the Head of State to agree to an EU measure which his own government has already stated affects fundamental aspects of the national criminal justice system. This would be politically very difficult to concede. For the German Constitutional Court in *Gauweiler*, even this constraint was not sufficient. For it, if the emergency brake procedure is invoked, agreement in the European Council can only be granted with the assent of the German parliament.[36]

There is acknowledgment that Member States' perceptions of what will be fundamental in their criminal justice systems is likely to be highly individual. In all instances, therefore, if there is no agreement and nine or more Member States still want to proceed they will be deemed to have authorisation for the purposes of engaging in enhanced cooperation and adopting an EU law that binds them.[37] This proviso would seem to be an implicit admission that agreement in such circumstances will be impossible but that it should not impede others proceeding if they so wish.

The other constraint in this field is provision for more intense patrolling by national parliaments. They have powers to monitor and evaluate the supranational policing and investigative institutions in this field,[38] and there is explicit provision that national parliaments must ensure that proposals and legislative initiatives comply with the subsidiarity principle here.[39] The thresholds for their intervention are correspondingly different. In all other fields, if one-third of legislative chambers raise concerns over subsidiarity the Commission is required to review the legislative proposal. In this field, it is only one-quarter of legislative chambers, thereby suggesting a lower tolerance for Union intervention here than in other fields.[40]

(c) Differentiated integration

As part of the area of freedom, security and justice, a similar regime applies to judicial cooperation in criminal matters and policing as applies for immigration, asylum and border controls. The United Kingdom and Ireland do not participate in legislative procedures and are not bound

---

[36] 2 BvE 2/08 *Gauweiler* v *Treaty of Lisbon*, Judgment of 30 June 2009, para. 365.
[37] On enhanced cooperation, see pp. 113–16.
[38] Article 12(c) TEU provides for their monitoring of Europol and evaluation of Eurojust. See also Articles 88(2) and 85(1) TFEU correspondingly.
[39] Article 69 TFEU.
[40] Protocol on Subsidiarity and Proportionality, Article 7(2). On the procedure see pp. 130–1.

by EU measures adopted under the competences here unless either notifies the Council of its intention to participate in the adoption of a measure.[41] Denmark neither takes part in nor is bound by measures adopted here.[42] If the measure builds upon the Schengen acquis, as Denmark is party to the Schengen Convention, it must decide within six months whether to implement the measure. In such a case, Denmark has a commitment in international law to the other Member States to comply with the measure.[43] If it is not willing to adopt the measure, it must notify the other states and all parties should consider what appropriate measures should be taken.[44]

There is a particular twist in this field, however. The Protocol on the Position of Denmark makes clear that, whatever the position post Lisbon, it is bound by all measures adopted in these fields prior to the Lisbon Treaty.[45] The position for the United Kingdom and Ireland differs. Pre-existing acts will continue to bind both. If they are amended, both states will have to decide whether to participate in and be bound by the amended act. If they do not, insofar as the original measure is repealed it will not bind them. Insofar as it remains in force, it will continue to bind them. For the United Kingdom, however, existing measures have a time horizon. Up to six months before the end of the transitional period (by 1 June 2014) it must notify the other Member States if it wishes to continue to be bound by acts adopted prior to the Lisbon Treaty. If it does not, all these acts will cease to apply to it.[46] However, following this, the United Kingdom can still subsequently notify the Member States that it wishes to participate in a measure which has ceased to apply to it. In such an instance, it can 'opt in' if the other Member States agree unanimously.[47] No such procedures exist for Ireland which will continue to be bound by the measures even after the expiry of the transitional period.

3 JUDICIAL COOPERATION IN CRIMINAL MATTERS

(i) Principle of mutual recognition

One of the central principles of EU criminal law is mutual recognition of judicial decisions. The principle was set out in a Commission Communication:

> once... a decision taken by a judge in exercising his or her official powers has been taken, that measure – in so far as it has extranational implications – would automatically be accepted in all other Member States, and have the same or at least similar effects there.[48]

It has been given effect in the Treaties by Article 82(1) TFEU.

---

[41] Protocol on the Position of the United Kingdom and Ireland, Articles 1–4.
[42] Protocol on the Position of Denmark, Article 2.
[43] *Ibid.* Article 4(1).
[44] *Ibid.* Article 4(2).
[45] *Ibid.* Article 2.
[46] Protocol on Transitional Provisions, Article 10(4).
[47] *Ibid.* Article 10(5). For criticism see M. Fletcher *et al.*, *EU Criminal Law and Justice* (Cheltenham, Edward Elgar, 2008) 225–6, who argue this will allow the United Kingdom to cherry-pick measures by opting out and then selectively choosing individual measures. The requirement of unanimity in the Council to do this will, however, reduce the possibilities for opportunism.
[48] European Commission, *Mutual Recognition of Final Decisions in Criminal Matters*, COM(2000)495, 2.

Article 82 TFEU

1. Judicial cooperation in criminal matters in the Union shall be based on the principle of mutual recognition of judgments and judicial decisions and shall include the approximation of the laws and regulations of the Member States in the areas referred to in paragraph 2 and in Article 83.

   The European Parliament and the Council, acting in accordance with the ordinary legislative procedure, shall adopt measures to:

   (a) lay down rules and procedures for ensuring recognition throughout the Union of all forms of judgments and judicial decisions;

   (b) prevent and settle conflicts of jurisdiction between Member States;

   (c) support the training of the judiciary and judicial staff;

   (d) facilitate cooperation between judicial or equivalent authorities of the Member States in relation to proceedings in criminal matters and the enforcement of decisions.

2. To the extent necessary to facilitate mutual recognition of judgments and judicial decisions and police and judicial cooperation in criminal matters having a cross-border dimension, the European Parliament and the Council may, by means of Directives adopted in accordance with the ordinary legislative procedure, establish minimum rules. Such rules shall take into account the differences between the legal traditions and systems of the Member States.

   They shall concern:

   (a) mutual admissibility of evidence between Member States;

   (b) the rights of individuals in criminal procedure;

   (c) the rights of victims of crime;

   (d) any other specific aspects of criminal procedure which the Council has identified in advance by a decision; for the adoption of such a decision, the Council shall act unanimously after obtaining the consent of the European Parliament.

   Adoption of the minimum rules referred to in this paragraph shall not prevent Member States from maintaining or introducing a higher level of protection for individuals.

Mutual recognition can operate in two diametrically opposed ways. There can, first, be mutual recognition of national decisions which inculpate or punish the defendant. In such circumstances, the Member State is seeking to strengthen its capacity to punish. It is doing this by granting it an extra-territorial reach. Persons wanted or convicted of offences in its territory can now be sought in other Member States. There can be, secondly, however, mutual recognition of decisions which exculpate the defendant. Known under its Latin title of *ne bis in idem*, a court finding of innocence or no case to answer in one Member State would mean that an individual could not be tried in another Member State for a similar offence.

The structure of the principle is such that it is predominantly about enhancing the Member States' capacities to punish. The circumstances when two or more states are claiming jurisdiction to try the same offence are rare. By contrast, it is quite common for persons that the state wishes to punish, question or prosecute to leave the territory if only to seek refuge elsewhere. This might, in itself, be something to ponder. More questionable, as Mitsilegas has observed, is deploying a principle borrowed from single market law for this purpose.

V. Mitsilegas, *EU Criminal Law* (Oxford and Portland, Hart, 2009) 118–19

Mutual recognition in the internal market involves the recognition of national regulatory standards and controls, is geared to national administrators and legislators. And results in facilitating the free movement of products and persons, thus enabling the enjoyment of fundamental Community law rights. Mutual recognition in criminal matters on the other hand involves the recognition and execution of court decisions by judges, in order to primarily facilitate the movement of enforcement rulings. Moreover, the intensity of intervention of the requested authority is greater in criminal matters, as further action may be needed to execute the judgment/order (such as arrest and surrender to the requesting state). While the logic behind recognition in the internal market and criminal law may be similar (there should be no obstacles to movement in a borderless Europe) – which, in criminal matters leads to calls for compensatory measures (criminals should not benefit from the abolition of borders in the EU) – there is a different rationale between facilitating the exercise of a right to free movement of an individual and facilitating a decision that may ultimately limit this and other rights.

These differences notwithstanding, the founding principle of mutual recognition in both internal market and criminal law is similar: the recognition of national standards by other EU Member States. In that sense, as Nicolaidis and Shaffer have noted, 'recognition creates extra-territoriality'.[49] National standards must be recognised 'extra-territorially', in the sense that they must be applied and/or enforced by another Member State. The central element of the mechanism is that it is an individual *national* standard, judgment or order that must be recognised by other Member States, and not a Union-wide negotiated standard. In recognising these standards in specific cases, national authorities implicitly accept as legitimate the national/regulatory/legal/justice system which has produced them in the first place. In that sense, mutual recognition represents a 'journey into the unknown', where national authorities are in principle obliged to recognise standards emanating from the national system of any EU Member State on the basis of mutual trust, with a minimum of formality.

The leap of faith required by mutual recognition to trust another authority unconditionally has led to its being applied absolutely only infrequently in the field of the single market. In cases of criminal law which involve the deprivation of liberty, there might be even more need to seek further safeguards to bolster this idea of mutual trust.[50] This is alluded to in Article 82(1) TFEU which provides for some harmonisation. However, this is to provide no more than minimum safeguards. Furthermore, to date, action on mutual recognition has progressed faster than action on common safeguards. As we shall see, this has led to this area generating more concern amongst national constitutional courts than any other.

---

[49] K. Nicolaidis and G. Shaffer, 'Transnational Mutual Recognition Regimes: Governance Without Global Government' (2005) 68 *Law and Contemporary Problems* 263, 267.

[50] For more criticism see S. Alegre and M. Leaf, 'Mutual Recognition and Judicial Co-operation: A Step Too Far Too Soon? Case Study, The European Arrest Warrant' (2004) 10 *ELJ* 200; S. Peers, 'Mutual Recognition and Criminal Law in the European Union: Has the Council Got It Wrong?' (2004) 41 *CMLRev.* 5; V. Mitsilegas, 'The Constitutional Implications of Mutual Recognition in Criminal Matters in the EU' (2006) 43 *CMLRev.* 1277.

(ii) The European Arrest Warrant

The most controversial application of mutual recognition is the European Arrest Warrant (EAW) set out in Framework Decision 2002/584/JHA.[51] The EAW is:

> a judicial decision issued by a Member State with a view to the arrest and surrender by another Member State of a requested person, for the purposes of conducting a criminal prosecution or executing a custodial sentence or detention order.[52]

It is different, first, from traditional extradition procedures as the authority requesting it is a judicial authority and it is made to the judicial authorities in the executing state where the person is being sought. The second noteworthy feature of the process is its speed. In principle, in cases where the person being sought consents to his surrender to the requesting state, the surrender should take place within ten days of consent.[53] If there is no consent, surrender should take place within sixty days of arrest.[54] In all cases, there must be a judicial hearing in the executing state before a decision is made to surrender the person being sought.[55] The third noteworthy feature, its most controversial, is the abolition of double criminality for a number of offences (article 2(2)). For thirty-two offences, the state is required to surrender the requested person even though the acts alleged do not constitute an offence within the executing state. For offences where the period of detention is of at least twelve months or a detention order has been given of at least four months, the judicial authority in the executing state can choose to waive the requirement of double criminality (article 2(4)).

Framework Decision 2002/584/JHA, article 2

1. A European arrest warrant may be issued for acts punishable by the law of the issuing Member State by a custodial sentence or a detention order for a maximum period of at least 12 months or, where a sentence has been passed or a detention order has been made, for sentences of at least four months.

2. The following offences, if they are punishable in the issuing Member State by a custodial sentence or a detention order for a maximum period of at least three years and as they are defined by the law of the issuing Member State, shall, under the terms of this Framework Decision and without verification of the double criminality of the act, give rise to surrender pursuant to a European arrest warrant:[56] ...

---

[51] Framework Decision 2002/584/JHA on the European Arrest Warrant and the surrender procedures between Member States [2002] OJ L190/1. The literature is significant: see R. Blextoon *et al.* (eds.), *Handbook on the European Arrest Warrant* (TMC Asser, The Hague, 2004); J. Spencer, 'The European Arrest Warrant' (2003) 6 *CYELS* 201; J. Wouters and F. Naert, 'Of Arrest Warrants, Terrorist Offences and Extradition Deals: An Appraisal of the EU's Main Criminal Law Measures against Terrorism after "11 September"' (2004) 41 *CMLRev.* 911.

[52] Framework Decision 2002/584/JHA, article 1(1).

[53] *Ibid.* article 17(2).

[54] *Ibid.* article 17(3). The time limits may be extended by thirty days where it is impossible for the surrendering state to meet the deadlines. In such cases, it must notify the judicial authorities in the requesting state and give reasons for its failure to meet the deadlines. *Ibid.* article 17(4).

[55] *Ibid.* article 19.

[56] The Framework Decision then lists the thirty-two offences. They are participation in a criminal organisation, terrorism, trafficking in human beings, sexual exploitation of children and child pornography, illicit trafficking in narcotics and weapons, corruption, fraud, money laundering, counterfeiting and piracy, environmental crime, facilitation of unauthorised entry and residence, murder, grievous bodily injury, illicit trade in hormonal substances, human organs, kidnapping, hostage-taking, racism and xenophobia, organised or armed robbery, illicit trafficking in cultural goods, swindling, racketeering and extortion, forgery, illicit trafficking in radioactive materials, trafficking in stolen vehicles, rape, arson, crimes within the jurisdiction of the International Criminal Court, unlawful seizure of aircraft/ships and sabotage.

4. For offences other than those covered by paragraph 2, surrender may be subject to the condition that the acts for which the European arrest warrant has been issued constitute an offence under the law of the executing Member State, whatever the constituent elements or however it is described.

The duty to surrender is subject to some exceptions. The executing state is not to surrender the person if the offence is covered by an amnesty in that state; the person sought is below the age of criminal responsibility in that state; or where the person has already been judged and sentenced by another Member State in respect of the same acts.[57] There are a number of exceptions, furthermore, where it may choose not to surrender the person:

- the executing state is prosecuting,[58] has chosen not to prosecute or has passed judgment on the requested person for the same act;[59]
- the prosecution of the requested person falls within the executing state's jurisdiction and is statute barred;[60]
- the requested person has been judged by a third state in respect of the same acts, and, where there has been sentence, the sentence has been or is being served, or may no longer be executed in the sentencing state;[61]
- if the EAW is served for purposes of a detention order, and (a) the requested person is staying in, or is a national or resident of, the executing state and (b) that state undertakes to execute the detention in accordance with its own law;[62]
- the offence was committed in whole or in part in the territory of the executing state or was committed outside the territory of the issuing state and the law of the executing state does not allow for prosecution of the offence;[63] and
- the person was not present at their trial.[64]

These exceptions, although numerous, are limited. The duty of mutual recognition, moreover, covers not only the duty to arrest and surrender the person in connection with the offences laid out in Framework Decision 2002/584/JHA. It also provides for the recognition of

---

[57] *Ibid.* article 3.
[58] *Ibid.* article 4(2).
[59] *Ibid.* article 4(3).
[60] *Ibid.* article 4(4).
[61] *Ibid.* article 4(5).
[62] *Ibid.* article 4(6). Residence is not simply presence. It involves a stable period of presence in which the person has acquired connections with the state: Case C-66/08 *Kozlowski* [2008] ECR I-6041. The executing state can, furthermore, impose conditions before granting residence if these are proportionate. A Dutch requirement of five years' residence before residence was granted was held to be lawful on the grounds that it was a proportionate method to secure the social integration of a person. Only if the person had been five years in the Netherlands could their link be sufficient for it to be seen as one of primary attachment: Case C-123/08 *Wolzenburg* v *London Borough of Ealing and Secretary of State for Education and Skills*, Judgment of 6 October 2009.
[63] *Ibid.* article 4(7).
[64] Framework Decision 2009/299/JHA amending Decision 2002/584//JHA enhancing the procedural rights of persons and fostering the application of the principle of mutual recognition to decisions rendered in the absence of the person concerned at the trial [2009] OJ L81/24, article 4a(1). This is subject to a number of exceptions such as where the person was summoned and informed in due time, or where the person will be served the decision within a reasonable period and informed of the time frame within which he can request a retrial or appeal.

financial penalties[65] and confiscation of property orders made by the judicial authorities in the issuing state.[66] For these, as with the EAW, in respect of the thirty-two offences listed in article 2(2) there is no requirement of double criminality. In respect of other offences, states may make execution subject to a condition that the conduct would constitute an offence under the law of the executing state.

The EAW has prompted more challenges before constitutional courts than any other EU law.[67] It has provoked concerns on three grounds: first, that there are insufficient guarantees that the surrendered person will receive a fair trial back in the issuing state; secondly, the abolition of double criminality in article 2(2) requires states to expose individuals to criminal processes and sanctions for activities which are not illegal within their territories; thirdly, many states have traditionally provided that they cannot surrender their citizens for punishment to other states, as a key part of the compact between state and citizen is that the basis for state punishment is that the citizen had the opportunity to participate in the making of the laws enforced against him, which is not true of states where he is not a national.

The first concern questions the notion of trust in the prosecutorial and judicial process of the issuing state, and requires the judicial authorities in the executing state not to scrutinise the procedures of the former. They have no way, therefore, of knowing whether they are being complicit in exposing individuals to sanctions where due process has not been observed and where the individual has not had a fair trial.[68] This issue was raised before the German Constitutional Court concerning an arrest warrant issued by the Spanish judiciary for a dual German and Syrian national who was accused of membership of Al Qaeda. He challenged the German law implementing Framework Decision 2002/ 584/JHA. Part of the law was held to be illegal on the grounds that it allowed extradition of German nationals who had committed acts that were on German territory.[69] The more wide-ranging thrust of the judgment concerned article 16(2) of the German Basic Law, the German constitutional document. This prohibits extradition of a German national to a foreign state unless it is to an EU Member State or an international court, provided in such circumstances that 'the rule of law is observed'. The question was whether no real scrutiny of the procedures in the requesting state met this test of observance of the rule of law. The Constitutional Court held that this test would not be met unless there was judicial scrutiny in each individual case by a German court to see whether the individual's fundamental rights would be respected in the state to which he was surrendered.

---

[65] Framework Decision 2005/214/JHA on the application of the principle of mutual recognition to financial penalties [2005] OJ L76/16, article 5.

[66] Framework Decision 2006/783/JHA on the application of the principle of mutual recognition to confiscation orders [2006] OJ L328/59, articles 4–6.

[67] The literature is enormous. See the outstanding V. Mitsilegas, *EU Criminal Law* (Oxford and Portland, Hart, 2009) 133–8 which refers to most of the literature. Also helpful is the Special Issue (2008) 6(1) *I-CON*. Not all national courts have seen the matter as problematic. Fundamental rights concerns have been regularly raised before Irish courts without success: E. Fahey, 'How to be a Third Pillar Guardian of Fundamental Rights? The Irish Supreme Court and the European Arrest Warrant' (2008) 33 *ELRev.* 563.

[68] This issue is also likely to come up in relation to the European Evidence Warrant which allows judicial authorities to obtain evidence from authorities in other Member States for proceedings before them. Framework Decision 2008/978/JHA on the European Evidence Warrant for the purpose of obtaining objects, documents and data for use in proceedings in criminal matters [2008] OJ L350/72.

[69] This was an over-implementation of the Framework Decision and therefore posed no challenge to EU law.

Re Constitutionality of German Law Implementing the Framework Decision on a European Arrest Warrant [2006] 1 CMLR 16

77. Article 16(2), second sentence, of the Basic Law, as a qualified proviso of legality, permits the extradition of a German national only 'if the rule of law is observed'. This condition for extradition is not just a repetition of the applicability of the rule of law, and in particular the principle of proportionality, which is indispensable for restriction of fundamental rights. Rather, it concerns an expectation in relation to the requesting Member State and the International Court, in the sense that there should be a correspondence in legal structures... The legislator permitting the extradition of German nationals must therefore verify whether these rules of law requirements are fulfilled by the issuing State.

78. The legislator restricting a fundamental right must be convinced that observance of the rule of law is ensured by those claiming criminal jurisdiction over a German national. In the process, account must be taken of the fact that each Member State of the European Union also has to observe the principles listed in Art. 6(1) EU, and thus the rule of law, and therefore a basis for mutual trust exists. Nevertheless, that does not liberate the legislator from the need to react to later grounds to doubt whether the general procedural rules of a Member State are in conformity with the rule of law, independently of any procedure under Art. 7 EU.

79. The specific limits mentioned in the wording of Art.16(2), second sentence, of the Basic Law do not, therefore, replace the constitutional limits already existing in relation to any legislation restricting fundamental rights. A law restricting a fundamental right must comply with all constitutional requirements, should not create conflict with other provisions of the constitution and must formulate the encroachment considerately with respect to the principle of proportionality. ...

97. If the German legislator on the basis of Art.16(2)... seeks to set a constitutional limit on the protection of German nationals from extradition, he must at least put the executing authorities in a position, by means of considerations determined by the rule of law, where they can determine the weight to be accorded to the confidence of nationals in the German legal system in the individual case in accordance with these constitutional principles. Placing a general obligation on the judge to respect fundamental rights in combination with the principle of proportionality... does not satisfy these requirements, which must be met by any law restricting fundamental rights...

118. The legislator will have to reformulate the grounds on which the extradition of Germans is considered impermissible, and structure the decision-making process for individual extradition requests as an exercise in interest analysis. Primary European Union law has homogeneity of the legal structures of the Member States as a central theme in Art. 6 EU. However, the mere existence of this provision, of a supporting sanction mechanism (Art. 7 EU) and of a set of standards for human rights protection which extends throughout Europe in the form of the ECHR does not justify the assumption that the structures for the rule of law are substantively harmonised throughout the EU Member States and that therefore national checks on the situation in an individual case, of the kind under consideration, are unnecessary. The entry into force of a strict principle of mutual recognition and the considerable mutual trust between the States expressed therein cannot restrict the guarantee of fundamental rights provided by the constitution.

The judgment set out the issues quite starkly. Protection of fundamental rights requires a court not to take the action of any other public authority on trust. It met a strong reaction, however. Spain suspended its arrangements under the EAW with Germany. Komárek has observed, moreover, that the judgment has a parochial flavour.[70] For him, although there is talk of mutual trust, it has an empty meaning. In particular, it does not look sufficiently carefully at whether adequate protection is provided in the other Member States. It may be that there are sufficient guarantees here. Mutual trust is treated in absolute terms as something that is either absolutely present (Framework Decision 2002/584/JHA) or completely absent (the German Constitutional Court). This is possibly a little too dogmatic and a little too black and white.

The second controversial aspect is the abolition of double criminality in article 2(2). This is a significant issue as the majority of offences in that provision are not harmonised in any way at EU level, and some are not even crimes in every Member State.[71] The consequence is that in many cases, a state may have to arrest and surrender a person, confiscate their property or fine them for activities that the state itself does not consider illegal. This was challenged in *Advocaten voor de Wereld*. The latter was a Belgian non-profit organisation which challenged the EAW before the Belgian courts. One of the grounds of challenge was that the Framework Decision violated the principle of legality of criminal offences.

Case C-303/05 *Advocaten voor de Wereld* v *Leden van de Ministerraad* [2007] ECR I-3633

48. According to Advocaten voor de Wereld, the list of more than 30 offences in respect of which the traditional condition of double criminality is henceforth abandoned if those offences are punishable in the issuing Member State by a custodial sentence or detention order for a maximum period of at last three years is so vague and imprecise that it breaches, or at the very least is capable of breaching, the principle of legality in criminal matters. The offences set out in that list are not accompanied by their legal definition but constitute very vaguely defined categories of undesirable conduct. A person deprived of his liberty on foot of a European arrest warrant without verification of double criminality does not benefit from the guarantee that criminal legislation must satisfy conditions as to precision, clarity and predictability allowing each person to know, at the time when an act is committed, whether that act does or does not constitute an offence, by contrast to those who are deprived of their liberty otherwise than pursuant to a European arrest warrant.

49. The principle of the legality of criminal offences and penalties (*nullum crimen, nulla poena sine lege*), which is one of the general legal principles underlying the constitutional traditions common to the Member States, has also been enshrined in various international treaties, in particular in Article 7(1) ECHR ...

50. This principle implies that legislation must define clearly offences and the penalties which they attract. That condition is met in the case where the individual concerned is in a position, on the basis of the wording of the relevant provision and with the help of the interpretative assistance given by the courts, to know which acts or omissions will make him criminally liable ...

51. In accordance with Article 2(2) of the Framework Decision, the offences listed in that provision give rise to surrender pursuant to a European arrest warrant, without verification of the double criminality of the act, 'if they are punishable in the issuing Member State by a custodial sentence or a detention order for a maximum period of at least three years and as they are defined by the law of the issuing Member State'.

---

[70] J. Komárek, *European Constitutionalism and the European Arrest Warrant: Contrapunctual Principles in Disharmony*, Jean Monnet Working Paper 10/05, 16–18.

[71] M. Fichera, 'The European Arrest Warrant and the Sovereign State: A Marriage of Convenience' (2009) 15 *ELJ* 70, 79.

52. Consequently, even if the Member States reproduce word-for-word the list of the categories of offences set out in Article 2(2) of the Framework Decision for the purposes of its implementation, the actual definition of those offences and the penalties applicable are those which follow from the law of 'the issuing Member State'. The Framework Decision does not seek to harmonise the criminal offences in question in respect of their constituent elements or of the penalties which they attract.

53. Accordingly, while Article 2(2) of the Framework Decision dispenses with verification of double criminality for the categories of offences mentioned therein, the definition of those offences and of the penalties applicable continue to be matters determined by the law of the issuing Member State, which, as is, moreover, stated in Article 1(3) of the Framework Decision, must respect fundamental rights and fundamental legal principles as enshrined in Article 6 TEU, and, consequently, the principle of the legality of criminal offences and penalties.

54. It follows that, insofar as it dispenses with verification of the requirement of double criminality in respect of the offences listed in that provision, Article 2(2) of the Framework Decision is not invalid on the ground that it infringes the principle of the legality of criminal offences and penalties.

The Court of Justice argues that it does not matter if the individual is exposed to sanctions for activities which are not illegal in the executing state if they are illegal in the issuing state. Yet, this side-steps the challenge, as the question was *why* somebody should be exposed to criminal sanctions for activities that are not illegal in the state where they are present and whether illegality in the issuing state is sufficient to justify this exposure. The Court did not engage with this question of sufficiency. It simply repeated the structure of the Framework Decision. There is a lack of candour about this reasoning and the sense that it may not be enough is present in the statement by the Court of Justice – which was not called for by the referring court – that the issuing state must respect fundamental rights.[72] It is not clear how far this extends. Are all the evidence-gathering, inquisitorial, prosecutorial, adjudicatory and penal processes of the issuing state to be subject to EU fundamental rights law? If so, this would extend the reach of EU fundamental rights law, which is considered only to bind Member States when they are implementing EU law.[73] If the latter were true, EU fundamental rights law would only seem to bind national authorities from the moment of issue of the warrant onwards and last until the moment of surrender, as only these activities are covered by the Framework Decision. Yet, the judgment hints in a vague way at something broader.

However, most opposition from national constitutional courts has come on the basis of a third ground. A number of national constitutions, notably the Cypriot, Czech, German and Polish, provide for a ban on extradition on the grounds that this amounts to a de facto stripping of citizenship. For such Member States, citizenship means above all the state giving the individual a secure place and a sure status that cannot be stripped away. If citizens can be expelled from their own state, there is a danger of this not happening. This ethos was expressed most strongly in the judgment of the German Constitutional Court.

---

[72] Mitsilegas, n. 67 above, 141–2.
[73] See pp. 254–5.

> **Re Constitutionality of German Law Implementing the Framework Decision on a European Arrest Warrant [2006] 1 CMLR 16**
>
> 66. ... Nationality is the legal requirement for a shared status as citizens, which gives rise to shared duties on the one hand and, most fundamentally, gives rise to rights the guaranteeing of which legitimates state power in a democracy on the other hand. Citizens' rights and duties, which are linked to the individual possession of citizenship, at the same time create the basis for the whole of community existence. It is commensurate with the relationship of the citizen to a free democratic polity, that the citizen may not, in principle, be excluded from this association. The trust placed by citizens in the security of their residence in the territory of the State to which they have a constitutionally guaranteed relationship in the form of nationality is also recognised by international law. States have the obligation under international law to accept their own citizens, and thus to allow them entry into the territory of the State and residence there... This right of entry correlates to the rights of States to deport foreigners from their territory.
>
> 67. The fundamental right to nationality and the right to remain in one's own legal domain is of high priority. Its formulation is also based on the experiences in recent German history, where directly after the coup d'état in 1933 the national socialist dictatorship increasingly excluded those Germans of Jewish faith or Jewish origin in particular from the formal protection conferred by law on the basis of German nationality, and created a situation in which nationality as an institution was made worthless, establishing a new 'volkischen status' in its place for nationals who enjoyed the rights of citizenship... The conviction, shared throughout Europe since the French Revolution, that citizens could only enjoy their political and civil legal status if that status was secure also formed a background to the guarantee provided by Article 16 of the Basic Law...
>
> 68. So that the ban on extradition does not become an open invitation to criminal conduct by our own nationals abroad, and in order to meet the responsibility for their conduct which goes together with the promise of protection, the criminal jurisdiction of Germany in principle extends to crimes committed abroad... so that it is usually possible to prosecute Germans for crimes committed abroad.

The issue was side-stepped in the German Basic Law by an amendment being made for extradition to other EU Member States. In the case of the Czech Republic, it was also circumvented. Article 14(4) of the Charter of Rights prevented a Czech citizen from being expelled from his homeland. Expulsion is slightly different from extradition, and this was used by the majority in the Court, who argued that there was no violation if the Czech citizen was entitled to return to the Czech Republic after serving his sentence as the possibility of return remained and the absence was a temporary one.[74] In Poland and Cyprus, there were, however, absolute prohibitions on extradition. The Cypriot Supreme Court reacted to this by arguing that, as Framework Decision 2002/584/JHA was a third pillar measure, it enjoyed no direct effects and could not be invoked over Cypriot law.[75]

The Polish Constitutional Tribunal was more direct. As noted earlier, in Poland the Constitution takes primacy over EU law.[76] Article 55 of the Polish Constitution prohibits the extradition

---

[74] *Re Constitutionality of Framework Decision on the European Arrest Warrant* [2007] 3 CMLR 24.

[75] *Attorney General of the Republic of Cyprus* v *Konstantinou* [2007] 3 CMLR 42.

[76] *Polish Membership of the European Union (Accession Treaty)* (Polish Constitutional Court), Judgment K18/04, 11 May 2005. See pp. 191–4.

of Polish nationals. The Polish Constitutional Tribunal found that the Polish law implementing the Framework Decision 2002/584/JHA was unconstitutional.

Case P1/05 *Re Enforcement of a European Arrest Warrant (Polish Constitutional Tribunal)* [2006] 1 CMLR 36

4.2. ... one has to assume that the prohibition of extradition formulated in article 55(1) of the Constitution expresses the right of the citizen of the Republic of Poland to penal liability to a Polish court of law. His surrender on the basis of the EAW to another EU Member State, however, would be an infringement of such substance. From this point of view it should be recognised that the prohibition of extradition of a Polish citizen, formulated in art. 55, para.1 of the Constitution, is of the absolute kind, and the subjective personal right of the citizens stemming from it cannot be subject to any limitations, as their introduction would make it impossible to exercise that right.

  The Constitutional Tribunal shares the view that the right of the individual anchored in art. 55(1) is an absolute one and it cannot be limited by any ordinary legislative acts. This is substantiated both by the categorical wording of that constitutional provision and by the very nature of the institution regulated therein...

4.3. ... It should be stressed, above all, that even if citizenship of the Union is connected with the gaining of certain rights, it cannot result in the diminishment of the guarantee functions of the provisions of the Constitution concerning the rights and freedoms of the individual. Moreover, as long as the Constitution attaches a certain set of rights and obligations with the fact of possession of Polish citizenship (regardless of the rights and obligations pertaining to 'anyone', who is subject to the jurisdiction of the Republic of Poland), such citizenship must constitute an essential criterion for the assessment of the legal status of the individual. The weakening of the juridical significance of citizenship when reconstructing the significance and scope of obligations of the state stemming from the provisions of the Constitution – especially those formulated as categorically as it is done in art. 55, para.1 – would have to lead, in consequence, to the undermining of the obligations of the citizens linked with them... It should be recognised, therefore, that regardless of the observable universal phenomenon of limitation of the role of state citizenship in determining the legal status of individuals (both in systems of national law and on the international plane), without an appropriate change of the provisions of the Constitution, which attaches certain legal consequences to Polish citizenship, it is not possible to modify the latter only by means of interpretation ...

4.4. In conclusion it should be stated that art. 607t, s.1 of the Code of Penal Procedure, within the scope allowing the surrender of a Polish citizen to an EU Member State on the basis of the European Arrest Warrant, is incompatible with art. 55, para.1 of the Constitution.

To avoid the possibility of the dispute escalating, the Polish Constitutional Tribunal deferred annulment of the measure for eighteen months to give the Polish legislature time to make amendments to the Polish Constitution. It might also be added that many of these last disputes can be handled in a similarly pragmatic manner. The EAW does not require surrender of a state's own national for a custodial or detention order if the state is willing to execute the detention in accordance with its own law.[77] There is, moreover, an EU policy, for the purposes

---

[77] See above n. 62. This is the policy pursued by Greece, for example: *Re Enforcement of a European Arrest Warrant against Tzoannos* (Greek Court of Appeal) [2008] 2 *CMLR* 38.

of social rehabilitation, of allowing the convicted person to serve their sentence, where they consent, in their state of nationality.[78]

These pragmatic resolutions, however, just cloud the point of principle further. Intuitively, of course, it does not seem right that a national, for example, who committed a heinous murder in one state should be able to escape justice by fleeing back to their home state and pleading the ban on extradition. Typically, to counter this, states refusing to extradite their own nationals have claimed a jurisdiction to try their nationals for offences committed abroad (see paragraph 68 of the judgment of the German Constitutional Court above). The justification is that there is a notional social contract between the national and their state where the former has had the opportunity to participate in the national legislative definition of what constitutes a criminal offence. Once this happens, it is irrelevant where they commit the offence. This argument does not work, however, where the act is not an offence in the state of nationality, as there is no possibility of even notional participation in the formulation of the offence. If a citizen is imprisoned within their own state for an offence that was not committed within their state and may not even be a crime within that state, this begs the question of what is the justification for that punishment.

One explanation is that states have engaged in a crude quid pro quo. They have extended their power to punish people extra-territorially but this has been done at the expense of a particular idea of political community, whereby political communities may have to acquiesce in the punishment of one of their members for an activity they do not consider a crime and would not wish to see as a crime. Another explanation was put forward by the Czech Constitutional Court based on the idea of European citizenship when it considered the constitutionality of the EAW.

Re Constitutionality of Framework Decision on the European Arrest Warrant (Czech Constitutional Court) [2007] 3 CMLR 24

92. The currently existing rules for extradition in the majority of European states trace their origin to the model formed in the nineteenth century. On the one hand, that model did not allow for judicial decisions in criminal matters, including arrest warrants, to operate directly in other states ... on the other hand, the state arrogated to itself total control and full criminal jurisdiction over its own citizens (in the original conception, its subjects), which no third state whatsoever was permitted to exercise. Initially, the traditional canon that a state does not extradite its own citizens for criminal proceedings abroad, thus, did not by a long way reflect a citizen's fundamental right not to be extradited, rather it was the manifestation of a state's sovereign control over its own citizens, in the conception then current. The canon that a state does not extradite its own citizens for criminal prosecution abroad had at that time a strong justification in the widely prevailing distrust among the competing European powers.

93. Only later, after the tragic events which occurred, primarily in Europe, in the first half of the twentieth century, did the basis for the canon against the extradition of one's own citizens transform, from

---

[78] Framework Decision 2008/909/JHA on the application of the principle of mutual recognition to judgments in criminal matters imposing custodial sentences or measures involving deprivation of liberty for the purpose of their enforcement in the European Union [2008] OJ L327/27.

state-claimed responsibility for their own citizens into the principle of the protection of one's own citizens from extradition abroad. The practice remained the same; only the justification therefor changed. On the basis of their own historical experiences, certain states even went so far as to incorporate this prohibition on extradition into their constitutions (e.g. as regards neighbouring states, art. 55 para. 1 of the Constitution of Poland or art. 16 para. 2 of the Basic Law of Germany). The prohibition on extradition thus gradually shifted into the area of fundamental rights, which is quite understandable in circumstances where the world still contained a large number of non-democratic regimes which did not guarantee the right to fair process measuring up to one's own standards, e.g. those of EU Member States.

94. It cannot be overlooked that the current period is characterised by an extraordinarily high mobility of people, ever-increasing international co-operation and growing confidence among the democratic states of the European Union, a fact which places new demands on the arrangements for extradition within the framework of the Union. A qualitatively new situation exists in the European Union. Citizens of the Member States enjoy, in addition to the rights arising from citizenship in their own state, also rights arising from EU citizenship, which guarantee, among other things, free movement within the province of the entire Union. The European Union is an area of freedom, security and justice, which facilitates the free movement of citizens while guaranteeing their safety and security (see the Preamble to the Treaty on the European Union). The European Arrest Warrant proceeds from this reality and renders more effective the co-operation of organs taking part in criminal proceedings. Co-operation between central state authorities of Member States has been replaced by the direct co-operation of bodies of the justice system and an exception is made to the principle prohibiting the extradition of one's own citizens for criminal proceedings abroad.

95. If Czech citizens enjoy certain advantages connected with the status of EU citizenship, then, in this context, they naturally must accept, along with these advantages, also a certain degree of responsibility. The investigation and suppression of criminality which takes place in the European area cannot be successfully accomplished within the framework of individual Member States, but requires extensive international co-operation. The consequence of this co-operation is the replacement of the previous procedures for the extradition of persons suspected of criminal offences by new and more effective mechanisms, reflecting the life and institutions of the twenty-first century. In the Constitutional Court's view, the contemporary standard within the European Union for the protection of fundamental rights does not give rise to any presumption that this standard for the protection of fundamental rights, through the assertion of the principles arising therefrom, is of a lesser quality than the level of protection provided in the Czech Republic.

According to the reasoning here, EU citizenship and the area of freedom, security and justice create a new reality at whose hub are mobile actors who have moved between Member States. Such actors have many entitlements because of this new reality but they also have to accept multiple legal responsibilities which extend not just to their own state but to other states. If the basis for a state's traditional monopoly of punishment over its own nationals was some sort of notional social contract between the two, by exercising EU citizenship rights mobile actors are creating notional social contracts between themselves and the Member States they have moved to or through.

There is, however, something unpersuasive about this. To be sure, the idea of a notional social contract based on political participation whereby the citizen is deemed to acquiesce to the sanctioning of criminal offences because of the possibility of contributing to criminal law-making is unrealistic. Yet, EU citizenship substitutes this political participation with an idea of movement, which has no idea of political enfranchisement within it. The only idea of social contract within it is that of the guest. By spending time in another Member State, the EU citizen agrees to all its rules. Guest arrangements are, however, temporary, and only apply when one is in somebody else's space. It is not clear why they should extend beyond that, and this has the paradoxical effect of criminalising the mobile. The more Member States one visits, the more types of criminal liability one attracts and the more exposure one incurs to the risk of prosecution.

(iii) Principle of *ne bis in idem*

As mentioned earlier, the principle of mutual recognition can be applied in an exculpatory manner so that national courts recognise the decisions of authorities elsewhere in the European Union which deal with a particular set of allegations of criminal activity. The principle, that of *ne bis in idem*, is set out in Article 54 of the 1990 Schengen Implementing Convention (often referred to by its French acronym CISA).

CISA, Article 54

A person whose trial has been finally disposed of in one Contracting Party may not be prosecuted in another Contracting Party for the same acts provided that, if a penalty has been imposed, it has been enforced, is actually in the process of being enforced or can no longer be enforced under the laws of the sentencing Contracting Party.

On an initial reading, the provision seems narrow. It seems only to cover where a person had already been subject to a judicial trial, and appears only to be a prohibition on a double trial, which is furthermore not absolute in that a person could still be tried if the penalty had been waived. This interpretation was rejected and the provision was given an unanticipated reach in *Gözütok and Brügge*.[79] Gözütok owned a coffee shop in the Netherlands. He was charged with possession of large amounts of marijuana. He did a plea bargain with the Dutch prosecution authorities under which, in return for making a financial settlement, charges were dropped. A similar sequence of events occurred with Brügge. He was charged with assault and wounding by the Belgian authorities. The charges were dropped in return for him paying an out-of-court settlement. Both Gözütok and Brügge subsequently went to Germany where they were charged with the offences. The German authorities argued that they were not bound by Article 54 as the case had not been disposed of by a court but merely dropped by the prosecuting authorities.

---

[79] M. Fletcher, 'Some Developments to the *ne bis in idem* Principle in the European Union' (2003) 66 *MLR* 769.

Joined Cases C–187/01 and C–385/01 *Gözütok and Brügge* [2003] ECR I–1345

26. It is clear from the wording of Article 54 of the CISA that a person may not be prosecuted in a Member State for the same acts as those in respect of which his case has been 'finally disposed of' in another Member State.

27. A procedure whereby further prosecution is barred, such as those at issue in the main actions, is a procedure by which the prosecuting authority, on which national law confers power for that purpose, decides to discontinue criminal proceedings against an accused once he has fulfilled certain obligations and, in particular, has paid a certain sum of money determined by the prosecuting authority.

28. Therefore, it should be noted, first, that in such procedures, the prosecution is discontinued by the decision of an authority required to play a part in the administration of criminal justice in the national legal system concerned.

29. Second, a procedure of this kind, whose effects as laid down by the applicable national law are dependent upon the accused's undertaking to perform certain obligations prescribed by the Public Prosecutor, penalises the unlawful conduct which the accused is alleged to have committed.

30. In those circumstances, the conclusion must be that, where, following such a procedure, further prosecution is definitively barred, the person concerned must be regarded as someone whose case has been 'finally disposed of' for the purposes of Article 54 of the CISA in relation to the acts which he is alleged to have committed. In addition, once the accused has complied with his obligations, the penalty entailed in the procedure whereby further prosecution is barred must be regarded as having been 'enforced' for the purposes of Article 54.

31. The fact that no court is involved in such a procedure and that the decision in which the procedure culminates does not take the form of a judicial decision does not cast doubt on that interpretation, since such matters of procedure and form do not impinge on the effects of the procedure, as described at paragraphs 28 and 29 of this judgment, which, in the absence of an express indication to the contrary in Article 54 of the CISA, must be regarded as sufficient to allow the *ne bis in idem* principle laid down by that provision to apply.

32. Furthermore, it should be pointed out that nowhere … is the application of Article 54 of the CISA made conditional upon harmonisation, or at the least approximation, of the criminal laws of the Member States relating to procedures whereby further prosecution is barred.

33. In those circumstances, whether the *ne bis in idem* principle enshrined in Article 54 of the CISA is applied to procedures whereby further prosecution is barred (regardless of whether a court is involved) or to judicial decisions, there is a necessary implication that the Member States have mutual trust in their criminal justice systems and that each of them recognises the criminal law in force in the other Member States even when the outcome would be different if its own national law were applied.

34. For the same reasons, the application by one Member State of the *ne bis in idem* principle, as set out in Article 54 of the CISA, to procedures whereby further prosecution is barred, which have taken place in another Member State without a court being involved, cannot be made subject to a condition that the first State's legal system does not require such judicial involvement either.

35. The aptness of that interpretation of Article 54 of the CISA is borne out by the fact that it is the only interpretation to give precedence to the object and purpose of the provision rather than to procedural or purely formal matters, which, after all, vary as between the Member States concerned, and to ensure that the principle has proper effect.

36. First, … the European Union set itself the objective of maintaining and developing the Union as an area of freedom, security and justice in which the free movement of persons is assured.

37. Furthermore, as the first paragraph of the Preamble to the Protocol shows, the integration of the Schengen acquis (which includes Article 54 of the CISA) into the framework of the European Union is aimed at enhancing European integration and, in particular, at enabling the Union to become more rapidly the area of freedom, security and justice which it is its objective to maintain and develop.

38. Article 54 of the CISA, the objective of which is to ensure that no one is prosecuted on the same facts in several Member States on account of his having exercised his right to freedom of movement, cannot play a useful role in bringing about the full attainment of that objective unless it also applies to decisions definitively discontinuing prosecutions in a Member State, even where such decisions are adopted without the involvement of a court and do not take the form of a judicial decision.

39. Second, national legal systems which provide for procedures whereby further prosecution is barred do so only in certain circumstances or in respect of certain exhaustively listed or defined offences which, as a general rule, are not serious offences and are punishable only with relatively light penalties.

40. In those circumstances, if Article 54 of the CISA were to apply only to decisions discontinuing prosecutions which are taken by a court or take the form of a judicial decision, the consequence would be that the *ne bis in idem* principle laid down in that provision (and, thus, the freedom of movement which the latter seeks to facilitate) would be of benefit only to defendants who were guilty of offences which – on account of their seriousness or the penalties attaching to them – preclude use of a simplified method of disposing of certain criminal cases by a procedure whereby further prosecution is barred, such as the procedures at issue in the main actions.

The thrust of the judgment is an odd one for criminal justice, as it is centred around securing free movement of persons (paragraphs 36–9), which is not something that would feature in many criminal law textbooks on double jeopardy. Individuals should not be deterred from moving to another Member State for fear of being prosecuted again on the same facts. As this is about securing a central EU goal, free movement of persons, the Court has interpreted this to expand the protection granted to individuals by this principle considerably.

The *ne bis in idem* principle requires, first, that 'the trial be disposed of'. In *Gözütok and Brügge* this was interpreted as meaning that the *prosecution* be disposed of. The reasons for the disposal are not important. In *Gaspirini*, a Spanish prosecution of the defendant, who had illegally imported olive oil into the European Union, was found to violate the principle. This was because a prior prosecution in Portugal had failed as it had not been brought within sufficient time under Portuguese law.[80] In *Bourquain*, a German national had been found guilty in absentia by a French military tribunal of a murder committed during the Algerian war of independence, and was sentenced to death.[81] He fled to Eastern Germany. Under French law, penalties not enforced within twenty years lapse, and Bourquain's offence was also covered by an amnesty granted by the French government. In 2001, the German authorities discovered what happened and sought to prosecute him for the murder. It was held that *Bourquain* was protected by the *ne bis in idem* principle as the case had been disposed of both because of the twenty-year rule and because the penalty was unable to be enforced.

---

[80] Case C-467/04 *Gaspirini* [2006] ECR I-9199.
[81] Case C-297/07 *Bourquain*, Judgment of 11 December 2008.

There are, however, qualifications to the principle. First, there must be no possibility of further prosecution in the original Member State. In *Turansky*, a decision by the police in Slovakia to suspend prosecution against Turansky for robbery of an Austrian national did not under Slovak law stop them re-opening the prosecution if they judged fit.[82] This was held not to bar an Austrian court hearing the case, as it had not been finally disposed of in Slovakia, and it was this idea of final disposition that lay at the heart of *ne bis in idem*. Secondly, an authority will not be held to have disposed of the matter unless it has assessed the facts. In *Miraglia*, the defendant was charged with importing heroin into the European Union by both the Dutch and the Italian authorities.[83] The Dutch authorities brought charges one month before the Italian authorities but dropped them on the basis that Miraglia was in Italy and being tried in Italy. Miraglia argued that as the case had been dropped in the Netherlands, it had been disposed of there and should be dropped in Italy. This was rejected by the Court of Justice. It noted that there had been no assessment of the unlawful conduct by the Dutch authorities, and to consider the dropping of the case because the Italian authorities were prosecuting it as sufficient to dispose of the matter and thus forestall further investigation would run contrary to the ethos of the area of freedom, security and justice which was to prevent crime.

The *ne bis in idem* principle requires, secondly, that the 'same acts' be disposed of. In *Van Esbroeck*, the Court had to consider a Belgian who had been convicted in Norway of illegally importing narcotics into Norway.[84] On his return to Belgium, he was charged with illegally exporting narcotics from Belgium. The Court held that one should not look at how acts are classified in national law as national classifications would necessarily vary. Instead, an EU definition was set out of whether the acts were materially identical or not. This would be the case where a set of concrete circumstances 'are inextricably linked together', something that appeared to be the case here but which the Court of Justice left for the national court to decide. The test is necessarily dependent on the factual context, and has to be somewhat vague for that reason. It does seem, however, that it will cover a range of actions rather than just a single act or transaction.

In *Van Straaten*, the accused was convicted in the Netherlands with one co-accused of importing and possessing heroin on 26 March 1983. He was subsequently convicted in Italy with another co-accused of exporting a far larger amount of heroin to the Netherlands on 27 March 1983.[85] Van Straaten appealed against the Italian conviction, arguing that he was protected by the principle of *ne bis in idem* because of the earlier Dutch conviction notwithstanding that the drugs and the co-accused in each case were different. The Court stated that the activities could still be classified as the same acts if the national court considered them to be inextricably linked. This suggests that where prosecution or sentencing is brought against just a part of the activity of the defendant it will still be held to bar a subsequent prosecution or court decision against the activity as a whole. This is a very broad interpretation of what constitutes the 'same acts', and limits were placed on it in *Kraaijenbrink*.[86] Kraaijenbrink was sentenced in the Netherlands for several offences of drug trafficking committed over a seven month period.

---

[82] Case C-491/07 *Turansky*, Judgment of 22 December 2008.
[83] Case C-469/03 *Miraglia* [2005] ECR I-2009.
[84] Case C-436/04 *Van Esbroeck* [2006] ECR I-2333. Norway is party to the Schengen Convention if a disposal by it counts here in the same way as that by a Member State which is party to Schengen.
[85] Case C-150/05 *Van Straaten* [2006] ECR I-9327. For similar reasoning see Case C-288/05 *Kretzinger* [2007] ECR I-6441.
[86] Case C-367/05 *Kraaijenbrink* [2007] ECR I-6619.

She was subsequently tried for other drugs offences in Belgium that began at the same time but continued for another ten months. She claimed that these were all part of the same activity based on a common intention to deal in drugs. Neither the Dutch nor the Belgian court shared this view, with both believing that the offences were discrete. The Court of Justice agreed. It stated that the fact that there was a common intention behind the offences was insufficient to make them materially identical. For that to happen, the offences needed to be inextricably linked, something that did not appear to be the case in this instance.

The wide interpretation of the *ne bis in idem* principle has led to Member States being required to recognise not merely each other's judicial decisions but also each other's criminal procedure and prosecutorial policy. The principle of mutual recognition is also applied in a fairly absolute way, and this has led to many references, as Mitsilegas has noted, reflecting unease at authorities having to acquiesce to decisions by other authorities within the Union with which they do not agree.[87] In *Bourquain*, other states were being asked to recognise the procedures of a military tribunal that were widely seen by all states intervening in the case as esoteric. The judgment offended their sense of when murder cases should be prosecuted, and so struck a very deep moral chord. Arguing that these sentiments should be trumped to enable an interpretation that secures free movement seems perverse indeed. The system is also odd as a basis for allocating jurisdiction. It is a 'first come, first served' approach to jurisdiction which can allow criminals to play the system by inviting prosecution in the jurisdiction which treats them most leniently. Furthermore, if criminal activities extend across more than one state, it is unclear why prosecution and sentencing should be confined to a single state. It may be that it is better to allocate different dimensions of the criminality to different jurisdictions.[88]

4 HARMONISATION OF CRIMINAL LAW

The procedures for harmonisation of the constituent elements of particular criminal offences and the sanctions for these offences are set out in Article 83 TFEU. The provision does not establish a general power for the European Union to harmonise criminal law but rather sets out two classes of offences which may be subject to harmonising measures.

The first class comprises a limited number of crimes explicitly listed in the Treaty because they are deemed both to be serious and to have a transnational dimension. There is an internal tension to the provision. Historically, it has been these qualities of the gravity of the offence and its perceived transnational qualities that have been the motors for harmonisation, with the offences listed being illustrative of the types of offence that fall under this umbrella.[89] Article 83(1) TFEU has sought to address this by allowing offences to be added to those it explicitly mentioned through use of the assent procedure.

---

[87] Mitsilegas, above n. 67, 149–51.

[88] On the debate see M. Fletcher, 'The Problem of Multiple Criminal Prosecutions: Building an Effective EU Response' (2007) 26 *YBEL* 33; Mitsilegas, above n. 67, 153–5. In relation to serious crime, this is the role of Eurojust whose mission is to support and strengthen coordination and cooperation between national investigating and prosecuting authorities in relation to serious crime affecting two or more Member States. Eurojust is composed of prosecutors from each Member State, and was established under Framework Decision 2002/187/JHA setting up Eurojust with a view to reinforcing the fight against serious crime [2002] OJ L63/1 as amended by Decision 2009/426/JHA [2009] OJ L138/14. It is also acknowledged in Article 85 TFEU. It is not addressed in any detail here. See Mitsilegas, above n. 67, 187–209.

[89] Article 29 TEU(M).

Article 83(1) TFEU

The European Parliament and the Council may, by means of directives adopted in accordance with the ordinary legislative procedure, establish minimum rules concerning the definition of criminal offences and sanctions in the areas of particularly serious crime with a cross-border dimension resulting from the nature or impact of such offences or from a special need to combat them on a common basis. These areas of crime are the following: terrorism, trafficking in human beings and sexual exploitation of women and children, illicit drug trafficking, illicit arms trafficking, money laundering, corruption, counterfeiting of means of payment, computer crime and organised crime.

On the basis of developments in crime, the Council may adopt a decision identifying other areas of crime that meet the criteria specified in this paragraph. It shall act unanimously after obtaining the consent of the European Parliament.

With the second class of offences, criminal law is seen as a regulatory tool which is parasitic on a prior EU policy, be it protection of the Union budget, the common transport policy or environment policy, and is assessed in how it contributes to the realisation of that policy.

Article 83(2) TFEU

If the approximation of criminal laws and regulations of the Member States proves essential to ensure the effective implementation of a Union policy in an area which has been subject to harmonisation measures, directives may establish minimum rules with regard to the definition of criminal offences and sanctions in the area concerned. Such directives shall be adopted by the same ordinary or special legislative procedure as was followed for the adoption of the harmonisation measures in question, without prejudice to Article 76.[90]

The two classes are subject to similar constraints. The emergency brake, outlined earlier, applies to both.[91] The German Constitutional Court in *Gauweiler* implied that this is one of the fields it is likely to patrol most intensely. In particular, it suggests that the Union should leave the German legislature free to determine which legal interests should be legally protected and which sanctions should be imposed on culpable conduct.[92] The idea that harmonisation should be limited in this field was reaffirmed by the Stockholm Action Programme, which stated that 'criminal law provisions should be introduced when they are considered essential in order for the interests to be protected and, as a rule, be used only as a last resort'.[93] However, otherwise, these two procedures are subject to different dynamics.

---

[90] This provision, it will be remembered, allows a proposal to be made either by the Commission or one-quarter of Member States.

[91] Article 83(3) TFEU.

[92] 2 BvE 2/08 *Gauweiler* v *Treaty of Lisbon*, Judgment of 30 June 2009, para. 356. See pp. 585–6.

[93] EU Council, *The Stockholm Programme: An Open and Secure Europe Serving and Protecting the Citizens*, Council Doc. 17024/09, 29.

(i) Euro-crimes

The Union already has secondary legislation setting out the constituent elements and minimum penalties for a wide and diverse array of crimes. These include fraud and counterfeiting,[94] money laundering,[95] human trafficking,[96] terrorism,[97] corruption in the private sector,[98] drug trafficking,[99] sex exploitation of children,[100] cybercrime,[101] ship pollution,[102] organised crime[103] and racism and xenophobia.[104] These parallel but extend a little beyond those mentioned in Article 83(1) TFEU. There is the suspicion, indeed, that the provision was drafted to reflect the corpus of existing law rather than to set forth an agenda. This does beg the question: what is the rationale behind Union intervention in such diverse areas? Chaves has noted that, heinous though many of those crimes may be, there is little to suggest that these crimes have significant and transnational dimensions which distinguish them from other crimes. Instead, she suggests that the Union is moving towards establishing a new form of 'Euro-crime' centred around a loose idea of organised crime in which the common and distinguishing feature of these offences is that they rely for their realisation upon a sense of common enterprise and prior infrastructure.[105]

> ### M. Chaves, *European Criminal Law: Reshaping Criminal Justice Across the European Union?* (Mimeo, London, 2009)
>
> [The Treaty] made reference to concepts of transnationality or seriousness of the criminality at stake. However, these concepts not only are not systematically addressed in the measures adopted as they often collapse in the light of specific examples. Take for instance the examples of private corruption and trafficking in human beings. Corruption for example does not necessarily need to be transnational, although trafficking in human beings most likely is. As for the seriousness of the offences, in principle,

---

[94] Framework Decision 2001/413/JHA combating fraud and counterfeiting of non-cash means of payment [2001] OJL149/1; Framework Decision 2000/383/JHA on increasing protection by criminal penalties and other sanctions against counterfeiting in connection with the introduction of the euro [2000] OJ L140/1 as amended by Framework Decision 2001/888/JHA [2001] OJ L329/3.

[95] Framework Decision 2001/500/JHA on money laundering, the identification, tracing, freezing, seizing and confiscation of instrumentalities and the proceeds of crime [2001] OJ L182/1.

[96] Framework Decision 2002/629/JHA on combating trafficking in human beings [2002] OJL203/1.

[97] Framework Decision 2002/475/JHA on combating terrorism [2002] OJ L164/3 as amended by Framework Decision 2008/919/JHA [2008 OJ L330/21.

[98] Framework Decision 2003/568/JHA of 22 July 2003 on combating corruption in the private sector [2003] OJ L192/54.

[99] Framework Decision 2004/757/JHA laying down minimum provisions on the constituent elements of criminal acts and penalties in the field of illicit drug trafficking [2004] OJ L335/8.

[100] Framework Decision 2004/68/JHA on combating the sexual exploitation of children and child pornography [2004] OJ L13/44.

[101] Framework Decision 2005/222/JHA on attacks against information systems [2005] OJ L69/67.

[102] Framework Decision 2005/667/JHA to strengthen the criminal-law framework for the enforcement of the law against ship-source pollution [2005] OJ L255/164.

[103] Framework Decision 2008/841/JHA on the fight against organised crime [2008] OJ L300/42.

[104] Framework Decision 2008/913/JHA on combating certain forms and expressions of racism and xenophobia by means of criminal law [2008] OJ L328/55.

[105] It seems that this may be in part because the concept of organised crime is so malleable that it has become a convenient container for both further criminalisation and EU intervention, resulting in an over-extension of the concept. F. Calderoni, 'A Definition that Could Not Work: The EU Framework Decision on the Fight Against Organised Crime' (2008) 16 *European Journal of Crime, Criminal Law and Criminal Justice* 265.

they both are serious offences, but this is a vague criterion. Corruption wise, how much is enough to be considered serious? Trafficking wise, would an offence of transporting two passengers in a private vehicle by the price of £500 each into UK territory be considered serious? Would the evaluation change if the payment was of £5000 or if the number of people illegally inserted in the UK was of two hundred instead of two?

But, even if the Treaty appears not to have adopted clear criteria in choosing the types of crimes to intervene in, it will be argued that the majority of these offences endorsed by secondary legislation in this realm do share common traits, such as the use of infrastructure and an element of collective action. Indeed, the large majority of offences the Union legislates on require infrastructure in the sense of technology, means of transport, or telecommunications or a network which allows for the completion of the offence. Trafficking in human beings, for example, often requires the use of transport to move people or the setting up of physical structures to keep them in. Similarly, terrorist acts traditionally also involve the use of materials and the construction of chemical or other types of weaponry able to cause severe bodily harm to others, and perpetrators often use sites for assembly and to prepare for the crime. Likewise, the laundering of profits of crime involves necessary infrastructures such as particular businesses or the use of the financial system in general through which money can be moved and laundered. Furthermore, the large majority of examples given also require a certain degree of organisation, or at least a certain degree of collective action, at least, if they are to be effective. Organised crime, terrorism, trafficking in human being, drugs or theft of works of art or money laundering, for example, are all offences that usually require more than one perpetrator and a certain degree of coordination. These two ideas are close to what Levi calls a contemporary legal construction or form of organised crime which, accordingly, has a close relationship to 'tools of later modernity', such as 'transnational air travel and communications, internet and the spread of information about weapons construction, globalisation of financial services and commerce including the arms trade and covert networking'.[106] Hence, the European Union seems to have begun to focus on a very particular type of criminality, which could be serious, potentially transnational and which usually required the use of infrastructure and collective action. It is clear that crimes such as rape, murder or robbery per se, for example, were not the Union's target.

Some of the offences harmonised did not exist in all Member States. In others, they often existed in a much more restricted form. Article 83(1) TFEU is used above all, therefore, to extend criminalisation of activities that were previously not criminal in some Member States. Chaves, after finding similar patterns with regard to the Framework Decisions on cyber-crime, illicit drug trafficking and terrorism, provides the example of the Framework Decision on Human Trafficking. Some Member States did not have such an offence and others had narrower offences, because Framework Decision 2002/629/JHA included as trafficking the recruitment, transportation, transfer, harbouring, or subsequent reception of a person for the exploitation of labour or services: a very broad definition indeed.

[106] M. Levi, 'Organized Crime and Terrorism' in M. Maguire *et al.* (eds.), *The Oxford Handbook of Criminology* (4th edn, Oxford, Oxford University Press, 2007) 775.

M. Chaves, *European Criminal Law: Reshaping Criminal Justice Across the European Union?* (Mimeo, London, 2009)

Examples can be found with regard to trafficking in human beings, countries such as Estonia and Poland did not have criminal offences corresponding with the conducts described in the Framework Decision, while all other Member States already contained provisions relating to such acts.[107] Even in countries where such acts were already considered as offences, the definition of trafficking in the Framework Decision is broader than most pre-existing definitions in national laws and even in international instruments. This is because the EU introduced the additional general element of 'labour exploitation', while most legislation covered trafficking only for the purposes of sexual exploitation, prostitution or forced or slave labour.

Dutch law did not include in its definition of trafficking any other purpose beside sexual exploitation. However, with the Framework Decision, the provision was amended in order to include 'coerced or forced work or services, slavery and practices and bondage comparable to slavery'.[108] Likewise, Portuguese law, in the earlier versions of the Portuguese Penal Code, only considered trafficking of persons for the purpose of sexual exploitation.[109] However, in 2007 the crime was expanded in order to incorporate the purpose of labour exploitation and extraction of organs,[110] thus complying with the Framework Decision.

Consequently, the harmonisation here is of a different kind from other areas of EU law. It does not seek to create definitions that are sufficiently uniform to allow free movement of goods or services but rather to create those which act as a starting point for a Member State to take a criminal offence further.[111] An example is the new offence of 'conduct related to a criminal organisation' set out in Framework Decision 2008/841/JHA.

Framework Decision 2008/841/JHA on the fight against organised crime[112]

Article 1
For the purposes of this Framework Decision:
1. 'criminal organisation' means a structured association, established over a period of time, of more than two persons acting in concert with a view to committing offences which are punishable by deprivation of liberty or a detention order of a maximum of at least four years or a more serious penalty, to obtain, directly or indirectly, a financial or other material benefit;
2. 'structured association' means an association that is not randomly formed for the immediate commission of an offence, nor does it need to have formally defined roles for its members, continuity of its membership, or a developed structure.

---

[107] European Commission, *Report Based on Article 10 of Framework Decision on Combating Trafficking in Human Beings*, COM(2006)187, 6.

[108] Criminal Code, article 250a, after changes introduced by the Act of 13 July 2002.

[109] Article 169 of the version of Decreto Lei 48/95 of 15 March and following the alterations of Lei 99/2001 of 25 August.

[110] Lei 59/2007 of 4 September.

[111] Cf. the criticism that the Framework Decisions are too vague to act as a basis for common action: Calderoni, above n. 105, 271.

[112] [2008] OJ L300/42.

Article 2

Each Member State shall take the necessary measures to ensure that one or both of the following types of conduct related to a criminal organisation are regarded as offences:

(a) conduct by any person who, with intent and with knowledge of either the aim and general activity of the criminal organisation or its intention to commit the offences in question, actively takes part in the organisation's criminal activities, including the provision of information or material means, the recruitment of new members and all forms of financing of its activities, knowing that such participation will contribute to the achievement of the organisation's criminal activities;

(b) conduct by any person consisting in an agreement with one or more persons that an activity should be pursued, which if carried out, would amount to the commission of offences referred to in Article 1, even if that person does not take part in the actual execution of the activity.

Article 3

1. Each Member State shall take the necessary measures to ensure that:

   (a) the offence referred to in Article 2(a) is punishable by a maximum term of imprisonment of at least between two and five years; or

   (b) the offence referred to in Article 2(b) is punishable by the same maximum term of imprisonment as the offence at which the agreement is aimed, or by a maximum term of imprisonment of at least between two and five years.

2. Each Member State shall take the necessary measures to ensure that the fact that offences referred to in Article 2, as determined by this Member State, have been committed within the framework of a criminal organisation, may be regarded as an aggravating circumstance.

The definition is vague and general. It could include three teenagers who have got together over a month to commit a number of burglaries, but it could also encompass the largest scale of Mafia-like activity. Whilst in the former case, it is clear why they should be prosecuted for burglary it is not clear why they are to be subject to further criminal liability for offences, which, by virtue of article 3, are to be treated as serious offences with potentially long prison terms. There is a concern that harmonisation in this area is creating new forms of criminalisation and leading to an unnecessary and unconstrained extension of repressive measures.[113]

(ii) Criminal law and securing the effectiveness of other EU policies

The second class of offences has its roots in the EC pillar of the TEU prior to Lisbon. The Court of Justice imposed duties on Member States to secure the effective functioning of policies within that pillar and take appropriate criminal sanctions which were effective enough to meet that duty.[114] There was, prior to 2005, considerable doubt about whether, with

---

[113] For findings similar to those of Chaves see A. Weyembergh, 'Approximation of Criminal Laws, the Constitutional Treaty and the Hague Programme' (2005) 42 *CMLRev.* 1567, 1588–90; T. Elholm, 'Does EU Criminal Cooperation Necessarily Mean Increased Repression?' (2009) 17 *European Journal of Crime, Criminal Law and Criminal Justice* 191.

[114] Case 68/88 *Commission* v *Greece* [1989] ECR 2965.

one limited exception,[115] the Community, as it then was, could pass legislation setting out criminal sanctions to secure the more effective application of its policies.[116] Measures were therefore adopted requiring Member States to prohibit unauthorised use of firearms, insider dealing and money laundering, but in no instances did EU law explicitly require them to take criminal sanctions. Instead, it required them to provide appropriate penalties allowing them, notionally at least, discretion over whether to adopt criminal sanctions.[117] However, in 2005 the Court of Justice ruled that there was a competence to adopt criminal instruments where the legislature considered that effective, proportionate and dissuasive criminal penalties were essential to ensuring the full effectiveness of rules in a field of Community law.[118] However, it subsequently ruled that there was no competence to determine the level or type of criminal penalties within Community law.[119] Three measures were subsequently adopted requiring Member States to provide criminal sanctions,[120] but it did beg the question of how effective this could be as a regulatory tool if the nature and level of penalty could not be fixed.

The uncertainty surrounding this has been resolved by the new Article 83(2) TFEU in the Lisbon Treaty. It establishes that the Union may set minimum rules on both the definition of offences and on sanctions. Supranational disciplines have therefore been extended to the setting out of types and levels of criminal penalty that may be applied to implement an EU policy which did not exist previously. However, there are two constraints. First, criminal measures may only be adopted where these are essential to ensuring the effective implementation of an EU policy. This would suggest that they can only be used as a measure of last resort where other measures have not been effective. Otherwise, if there are substitute non-criminal measures available, it will be impossible to argue that criminal measures are essential. Secondly, the area must already have 'been subject to harmonisation measures'. The gist of this phrase is that criminal measures can only be deployed within a prior legislative framework which has already been set out by EU legislation. However, it could have been expressed much more clearly. A narrow interpretation would be that such measures can only be adopted in respect of activities that breach a norm set out in prior EU legislation. A broader interpretation would allow for the possibility that where an area has been subject to partial harmonisation, criminal measures can be adopted touching on activities that are not fully regulated by an EU measure but nevertheless operate within a context that is strongly informed by EU law. This

---

[115] This related to protection against defrauding of the Union's financial interests: Article 280(3) EC.

[116] See, in particular, C. Harding, 'Exploring the Intersection of European Law and National Criminal Law' (2000) 25 ELRev. 374; M. Wasmeier and N. Thwaites, 'The "Battle of the Pillars": Does the European Community have the Power to Approximate National Criminal Laws?' (2004) 29 ELRev. 613.

[117] Directive 91/477/EC on control of the acquisition and possession of firearms, article 16 [1991] OJ L256/51; Directive 2003/6/EC on insider dealing and market manipulation, article 14(1) [2003] OJ L96/16; Directive 2005/60/EC on the prevention of the use of the financial system for the purpose of money laundering and terrorist financing, article 39 [2005] OJ L309/15.

[118] Case C-176/03 Commission v Council (Environmental Crimes) [2005] ECR I-7879.

[119] Case C-440/05 Commission v Council (Ship-Source Pollution) [2007] ECR I-9097.

[120] Directive 2008/99/EC on the protection of the environment through criminal law, article 3 [2008] OJ L309/15,; Directive 2009/123/EC amending Directive 2005/35/EC on ship-source pollution and on the introduction of penalties for infringements, article 8a [2009] OJ L280/52; Directive 2009/52/EC providing for minimum sanctions and measures against employers of illegally staying third country nationals, article 9 [2009] OJ L168/20. Ireland and the United Kingdom are not participating in the last Directive.

would not require the breach of a prior EU law. It would be enough that EU law regulates the field generally.[121]

5 POLICE COOPERATION

The central provision on policing is Article 87 TFEU.

Article 87 TFEU

1. The Union shall establish police cooperation involving all the Member States' competent authorities, including police, customs and other specialised law enforcement services in relation to the prevention, detection and investigation of criminal offences.
2. For the purposes of paragraph 1, the European Parliament and the Council, acting in accordance with the ordinary legislative procedure, may establish measures concerning:
   (a) the collection, storage, processing, analysis and exchange of relevant information;
   (b) support for the training of staff, and cooperation on the exchange of staff, on equipment and on research into crime-detection;
   (c) common investigative techniques in relation to the detection of serious forms of organised crime.
3. The Council, acting in accordance with a special legislative procedure, may establish measures concerning operational cooperation between the authorities referred to in this Article. The Council shall act unanimously after consulting the European Parliament.

Although a number of tasks are set out in the provision, the central thrust of EU policing is the development and augmentation of surveillance capacities. The approach adopted has been multifaceted.[122] First, a large number of bodies – national and supranational, public and private – have data or information that might be valuable for policing. EU law is thus about setting up information networks that builds relationships between these bodies, which allow for a free flow of information to investigating authorities. Secondly, it is about improving the quality of information available. This might be asking private bodies to acquire new surveillance capacities by gathering and storing new information from customers, asking national authorities to build new kinds of databases holding new types of evidence, or the generation of pan-European databases or data analysis capacities. Finally, EU law must respond to the variety of relationships that exist within these networks. Some might be ad hoc and 'one off' where an investigating authority considers on a specific occasion that another authority might have valuable information. Others are more ongoing and systematised, such as those between EU and national authorities that involve the development of large databases covering organised crime.

---

[121] An example of the latter would be Directive 2009/52/EC on the application of criminal sanctions to those employing non-EU nationals illegally staying in the Union. The Union has a Borders Code, the Schengen Borders Code (Regulation 562/2006/EC [2006] OJ L105/1), which governs when states can admit a non-EU national onto the territory of the Union, and does provide obligations on Member States to return non-EU nationals who are illegally resident (Directive 2008/115/EC [2008] OJ L348/98). It is, however, the Member State which sets the condition of residence. The Directive requires criminal sanctions for employment which breaches the latter: *ibid.* article 2(b).

[122] On the privatisation and transnationalisation of policing as part of the same phenomenon, see J. Sheptycki, 'Policing, Postmodernism and Transnationalization' (1998) 38 *British Journal of Criminology* 485.

The civil liberties challenges with such networks are clear. They concern the amount and quality of information held about people; who holds that data and for what purposes; and the security of that data. It has led to data protection emerging as one of the central battlefields for fundamental rights in EU law in recent years.

(i) Principle of availability of information

A central goal of EU policing is the realisation of the principle of availability between national law-enforcement authorities. This principle entails that:

> a law enforcement officer in one Member State of the Union who needs information in order to carry out his duties can obtain it from another Member State and that the law enforcement authorities in the Member State that holds this information will make it available for the declared purpose, taking account of the needs of investigations pending in that Member State.[123]

The instrument which most clearly structures day-to-day relations between law-enforcement authorities around this principle is Framework Decision 2006/690/JHA.[124] This provides a system whereby a law-enforcement authority, be it police, customs or judicial, has on request all the information available to enforcement authorities within the Union. At the heart of the instrument is article 3.

Article 3

1. Member States shall ensure that information and intelligence can be provided to the competent law enforcement authorities of other Member States in accordance with this Framework Decision.
2. Information and intelligence shall be provided at the request of a competent law enforcement authority, acting in accordance with the powers conferred upon it by national law, conducting a criminal investigation or a criminal intelligence operation.
3. Member States shall ensure that conditions not stricter than those applicable at national level for providing and requesting information and intelligence are applied for providing information and intelligence to competent law enforcement authorities of other Member States. In particular, a Member State shall not subject the exchange, by its competent law enforcement authority with a competent law enforcement authority of another Member State, of information or intelligence which in an internal procedure may be accessed by the requested competent law enforcement authority without a judicial agreement or authorisation, to such an agreement or authorisation.

The information and intelligence in question is any information held by the law-enforcement authorities,[125] and should be provided, in principle, within eight hours of the request.[126] However, there are a number of safeguards.

---

[123] Framework Decision 2008/615/JHA, Preamble para. 4. For an extensive discussion see Mitsilegas, above n. 67, 250–63.

[124] Framework Decision 2006/960/JHA on simplifying the exchange of information and intelligence between law enforcement authorities of the Member States of the European Union [2006] OJ L386/89.

[125] *Ibid.* article 2(d).

[126] *Ibid.* article 4(1). If this is not possible, reasons must be given. In any case, the information must be given within fourteen days. *Ibid.* article 4(4).

The procedure is not to be used to provide evidence before a judicial authority and where the information is subsequently to be used for that purpose, the consent of the requested state authorities must be granted and it can only be granted if it is in accordance with their law.[127] As an information-gathering exercise,[128] the authority can only make the request if there are factual reasons to believe the information is available in the other Member State, so the former cannot engage in 'fishing' whereby it asks just on the off-chance that evidence might be there.

As set out above in article 3, both sets of authorities must act within the limits of their respective national laws. They cannot apply stricter conditions than for domestic requests, but if judicial authorisation is required in the requested state for the release of information then that must be sought before the information is passed over.[129] Whilst the national legal constraints are the central forms of protection, there are a number of further checks. One is procedural. The request must set out the factual reasons for believing the information is available in the requested state and explain the purpose for which the information is sought and the connection between that and the person who is the subject of the information.[130] The requested state authorities can, moreover, irrespective of their national law, refuse to pass over the information for a number of reasons. These are that it would harm essential national security interests; would jeopardise the success of a current investigation or a criminal intelligence operation or the safety of individuals; or is disproportionate or irrelevant with regard to the purposes for which it has been requested. This last check in particular allows the requested state authorities to act as guardians of the overall process.[131] If they believe it to be too heavy-handed, they do not need to cooperate.

Availability has not merely been extended to requests for information from law-enforcement authorities in other Member States. It is also to apply, albeit in a limited form, to mutual availability of national databases. Framework Decision 2008/615/JHA requires every Member State to establish databases on DNA analysis files, fingerprint identification systems and vehicle registration and to make available 'reference data' to other national law-enforcement authorities.[132] The latter is data which does not, by itself, allow an individual to be identified but allows the requesting authority to check its own data against it (e.g. a DNA match involving offences in two Member States). If, on the basis of this search, the national authority making the search requires further data which is personal data, that will be governed by the law of the requested state. There is a two-tier process: the first is a general one where authorities can compare reference data freely. A second more personalised process may follow, but there is no guarantee of access to the data in such cases. All will depend on the national law of the requested state in question.[133]

---

[127] *Ibid.* article 1(4).
[128] *Ibid.* article 5(1).
[129] *Ibid.* article 3(4).
[130] *Ibid.* article 5(1).
[131] *Ibid.* article 10(1).
[132] Framework Decision 2008/615/JHA on the stepping up of cross-border cooperation, particularly in combating terrorism and cross-border crime: articles 8, 9, 12 [2008] OJ L210/1. This Decision had an earlier incarnation as the Treaty of Prüm. On this see Chapter 3 at p. 116.
[133] *Ibid.* articles 5 and 10.

The first concern about these measures is that they may be used by law-enforcement authorities to develop surveillance tools that they did not have previously. Thus, a number of Member States do not currently have DNA databases but will be required to set them up by the Framework Decision.[134] The Decision requires states to have such databases but is non-specific about the nature or form.

The second goes to the quality of data protection in either of the states involved in the exchange of information. To that end, Framework Decision 2008/977/JHA was adopted. Its central provision is that data may only be collected for specified, explicit and lawful purposes.

Framework Decision 2008/977/JHA on the protection of personal data processed in the framework of police and judicial cooperation in criminal matters[135]

Article 1

1. Personal data may be collected by the competent authorities only for specified, explicit and legitimate purposes in the framework of their tasks and may be processed only for the same purpose for which data were collected. Processing of the data shall be lawful and adequate, relevant and not excessive in relation to the purposes for which they are collected.
2. Further processing for another purpose shall be permitted insofar as:
   (a) it is not incompatible with the purposes for which the data were collected;
   (b) the competent authorities are authorised to process such data for such other purpose in accordance with the applicable legal provisions; and
   (c) processing is necessary and proportionate to that other purpose.

Article 4

1. Personal data shall be rectified if inaccurate and, where this is possible and necessary, completed or updated.
2. Personal data shall be erased or made anonymous when they are no longer required for the purposes for which they were lawfully collected or are lawfully further processed. Archiving of those data in a separate data set for an appropriate period in accordance with national law shall not be affected by this provision.

Authorities are also under a duty to take all reasonable steps to ensure that the data is accurate, complete and up-to-date. To that end, they should verify the quality of it before transmitting it.[136] In principle, individuals also have a right to know whether data has been transmitted and whether the necessary verifications have taken place.[137] However, the right is heavily conditional. Information can be refused on grounds of security, to protect the rights and freedoms of others, and to prevent the obstruction of inquiries, investigations or prosecutions.[138]

---

[134] R. Bellanova, 'The Prüm Process: The Way Forward for EU Police Cooperation and Data Exchange' in E. Guild and F. Geyer (eds.), *Security versus Justice? Police and Judicial Cooperation in the European Union* (Aldershot, Ashgate, 2008) 201, 214–15.

[135] Framework Decision 2008/977/JHA [2008] OJ L350/60. A criticism of the Framework Decision has been its scope. It focuses on checks concerning the use of the data but not sufficiently on why the data should be held: H. Helkmans and A. Scirocco, 'Shortcomings in EU Data Protection in the Third and Second Pillars: Can the Lisbon Treaty be Expected to Help?' (2009) 46 *CMLRev.* 1485, 1494–6.

[136] *Ibid.* article 8. [137] *Ibid.* article 17(1). [138] *Ibid.* article 17(2).

(ii) Private policing regimes

EU law does not just establish information networks between peer law-enforcement authorities in which each passes information to their peer. It also provides for public-private policing networks within national territories in which law-enforcement authorities require particular businesses to report to them or to store information on their behalf. These policing regimes have emerged most strongly in fields identified with globalisation: the financial sector, electronic communications and international transport. However, if these processes are often classified as 'global' ones, then they are also very local, as every financial transaction, telephone call or logging on taps into them.

In the field of financial services, this has been done through money laundering legislation. Directive 2005/60/EC imposes a number of duties on a range of actors which include credit and finance institutions, auditors, lawyers, estate agents, casinos, notaries, anyone engaged in a cash transaction of €15,000 or more,[139] and professions likely to be exposed to money laundering.[140] The central duty is the reporting of any suspicious behaviour.

Directive 2005/60/EC on the prevention of the use of the financial system for the purpose of money laundering and terrorist financing[141]

Article 20
Member States shall require that the institutions and persons covered by this Directive pay special attention to any activity which they regard as particularly likely, by its nature, to be related to money laundering or terrorist financing and in particular complex or unusually large transactions and all unusual patterns of transactions which have no apparent economic or visible lawful purpose.

Article 21
1. Each Member State shall establish a Financial Intelligence Unit (FIU) in order effectively to combat money laundering and terrorist financing.
2. That FIU shall be established as a central national unit. It shall be responsible for receiving (and to the extent permitted, requesting), analysing and disseminating to the competent authorities, disclosures of information which concern potential money laundering, potential terrorist financing or are required by national legislation or regulation. It shall be provided with adequate resources in order to fulfil its tasks.
3. Member States shall ensure that the FIU has access, directly or indirectly, on a timely basis, to the financial, administrative and law enforcement information that it requires to properly fulfil its tasks.

Article 22
1. Member States shall require the institutions and persons covered by this Directive, and where applicable their directors and employees, to cooperate fully:
   (a) by promptly informing the FIU, on their own initiative, where the institution or person covered by this Directive knows, suspects or has reasonable grounds to suspect that money laundering or terrorist financing is being or has been committed or attempted;
   (b) by promptly furnishing the FIU, at its request, with all necessary information, in accordance with the procedures established by the applicable legislation.

---

[139] *Ibid.* article 2(1).
[140] *Ibid.* article 4(1).
[141] [2005] OJ L309/15.

The other field where the imposition of such duties is prevalent is electronic communications. Directive 2006/24/EC requires Internet service providers to store various bits of data of electronic communications.[142] These do not include the content but include the date, time and duration, and the identity of the source and destination of the communication.[143] They are required to store them for between six months and two years, and to make them available to law-enforcement authorities for the detection of serious crime.

Directive 2006/24/EC on the retention of data generated or processed in connection with the provision of publicly available electronic communications services or of public communications networks and amending Directive 2002/58/EC

Article 1
This Directive aims to harmonise Member States' provisions concerning the obligations of the providers of publicly available electronic communications services or of public communications networks with respect to the retention of certain data which are generated or processed by them, in order to ensure that the data are available for the purpose of the investigation, detection and prosecution of serious crime, as defined by each Member State in its national law.

Article 4
Member States shall adopt measures to ensure that data retained in accordance with this Directive are provided only to the competent national authorities in specific cases and in accordance with national law. The procedures to be followed and the conditions to be fulfilled in order to gain access to retained data in accordance with necessity and proportionality requirements shall be defined by each Member State in its national law, subject to the relevant provisions of European Union law or public international law, and in particular the ECHR as interpreted by the European Court of Human Rights ...

Article 6
Member States shall ensure that the categories of data specified... are retained for periods of not less than six months and not more than two years from the date of the communication.

The purpose of these arrangements is to augment the authorities' information-gathering and policing capacities. There are a number of common features. The relationship between the service provider and the national authority is always vaguely drawn with important parameters for intervention being left undefined or a matter for national law. Thus, in the case of electronic communications, the question of what constitutes 'serious crime' and therefore can justify a search is not defined (article 1(1)). In the case of money laundering, EU law leaves undefined when authorities can request information. Alongside this, a veil of suspicion is drawn over both the relationship between the service provider and customer and that between service provider and national authority.

---

[142] [2006] OJ L105/54. This was unsuccessfully challenged in Case C-301/06 *Ireland* v *Council and Parliament*, Judgment of 10 February 2009.
[143] *Ibid.* article 5.

D. Chalmers, *Constitutional Reason in an Age of Terror*, Global Law Working Paper 6/04, xlv–xlvi[144]

On the one hand, public security surveillance is essentially privatised as internet service providers become the providers of such large databases of information that the need for the administration to develop its own in-house specialised bases becomes less. Instead, it can exercise an *à la carte* approach of dipping in selectively to these archives. On the other, the industry becomes the guardian of individual privacy. It is responsible for ensuring no unauthorised access, with the consequence that real tensions emerge, as the problems of storage lead to increased risks that it cannot safeguard this.

These private policing regimes are not some autonomous private 'node of governance' free from State involvement. Instead, they form part of a politically constituted regime in which administrative interests are prevalent. The political nature of the powers granted to these institutions not only represents an administrative choice to empower them at the expense of other parties, but provides a justification for a double policing where they, the 'private police', are also intensely policed. This can take the form of heavy external constraints. The obligations of data retention on service providers are thus extremely constraining... These regimes also justify administrative intervention in the internal constitution of private relations. The Money Laundering Directive therefore requires all the institutions and persons covered by it to establish their own internal systems of control and monitoring for countering laundering, and to train their employees in how to recognise laundering.

(iii) An EU intelligence capacity

The final central feature of EU policing has been the development of a pan-European intelligence capacity. This has two dimensions: first, the development of pan-European databases and, secondly, the creation of central analytical capacities.

Three central databases have been established.

The Schengen Information System (SIS)[145]   This is the largest database, and applies only to the Schengen states. It is predominantly used for non-EU nationals who should be denied entry. With regard to EU citizens, it includes information on persons wanted for extradition to a Schengen state;[146] missing persons or persons to be placed under police protection;[147] persons wanted as witnesses, or for the purposes of prosecution or the enforcement of sentences;[148] persons or vehicles to be placed under surveillance or subjected to specific checks;[149] and objects sought for the purpose of seizure or use in criminal proceedings.[150] As of 1 January 2008, there were just under 23 million entries. However, of these, nearly 21 million related to suspect

---

[144] See www.law.nyu.edu/global/workingpapers/2004/index.htm (accessed 20 November 2009).

[145] This is to be replaced by a new more powerful system which will allow for the storage of biometric data. Framework Decision 2007/533/JHA on the establishment, operation and use of the second generation Schengen Information System [2007] OJ L205/63. See Chapter 12 at pp. 499–500 also in relation to non-EU nationals.

[146] Convention implementing the Schengen Agreement on the gradual abolition of checks at their common borders [2000] OJ L239/19, Article 95.

[147] *Ibid.*, Article 97.

[148] *Ibid.* Article 98.

[149] *Ibid.* Article 99.

[150] *Ibid.* Article 100.

vehicles or stolen or forged ID papers or passports, and nearly 700,000 of the remainder related to non-EU nationals. About 85,000 entries related to people wanted for arrest, extradition or prosecution.[151]

Europol Information System   This is a database of persons convicted of having committed or suspected of having committed one of the offences that fall within Europol's mandate.[152] It also includes persons for whom there are serious grounds to believe that they will commit such offences.[153] The offences that fall within the mandate are 'serious crime' with a transnational dimension. This is taken to comprise the thirty-two offences for which double criminality has been abolished under the European Arrest Warrant.[154] The number of entries has grown significantly from just over 25,000 in January 2006 to 88,419 in January 2009.[155] Unlike the other databases, it is not linked up to national automating systems so is not widely available to national law-enforcement officers. It is only available to the national units which are designated to liaise between Europol and the national authorities.[156]

Customs Information System   This is a database on sightings of customs offences which was established by a Convention in 1995.[157] It is widely regarded as having been used in only a very limited manner. No regular statistics are published, but at the end of 2006 only 409 cases were active.[158]

The development of these databases casts EU policing as a heavily informationalised activity that is 'experientially distant' from the everyday lives of most EU citizens and which they will know little about.[159] It has been criticised on a number of grounds. One is the presence of such databases at all. It is argued that they act as processes of categorisation which both generate anxiety in citizens over levels of intrusion and surveillance and create suspect populations who are subject to increased surveillance and restriction, allegedly because they are perceived as more likely to abuse their freedom, but in reality simply because they fall within a formal category.[160] The other concern is regarding abuse of their operation: that insufficient checks will be placed on whether correct data is entered or data will be used for wide-ranging purposes.[161] Whilst these concerns carry some weight with the Europol Information System, for reasons explained below, they have less weight in respect of the SIS. The Court of Justice has indicated that entry on it will not, by itself, justify EU citizens being barred from other Member States.[162] Furthermore, individuals have a right to access to data on them under the relevant

---

[151] EU Council, SIS Database Statistics dd. 1 January 2008, Council Doc. 5441/08.

[152] This is dealt with below. Framework Decision 2009/371/JHA establishing the European Police Office (Europol) [2009] OJ L121/37.

[153] *Ibid.* article 12.

[154] *Ibid.* article 4(1) and Annex.

[155] EU Council, *Europol Annual Report 2008*, Council Doc. 8131,09, 37.

[156] Framework Decision 2009/371/JHA, article 13(1).

[157] Convention on the Use of Information Technology for Customs Purposes [1995] OJ C316/34. For analysis see Mitsilegas, above n. 67, 243–4.

[158] On this see F. Geyer, *Taking Stock: Databases and Systems of Information Exchange in the Area of Freedom, Security and Justice* (CEPS, Brussels, 2008) 17.

[159] I. Loader, 'Governing European Policing: Some Problems and Prospects' (2002) 12 *Policing and Society* 291, 297.

[160] J. Huysmans, *The Politics of Insecurity: Fear, Migration and Asylum in the EU* (Routledge, Abingdon, 2006) 101.

[161] E. Brouwer, *The Other Side of the Moon, The Schengen Information System and Human Rights: A Task for National Courts*, CEPS Working Document 288 (Brussels, CEPS, 2008); T. Balzacq, 'The Policy Tools of Securitization: Information Exchange, EU Foreign and Interior Policies' (2008) 46 *JCMS* 75, 84–7.

[162] Case C-503/03 *Commission* v *Spain* [2006] ECR I-1097.

national law and to have incorrect data deleted.[163] At the moment, furthermore, in relation to EU citizens, the SIS has limited efficacy. National authorities have no general power of search and can only enter a name to see if there is a 'hit' or 'no hit'. The data provided is highly limited: the name, gender, nationality, date of birth, whether the person is armed or violent, the reason for the alert and any action to be taken.[164] Very often, this does not give the authorities the data they need.[165]

The development of a pan-European intelligence capacity involves not merely the establishment of databases but also pan-European analytical capacities. These are institutionalised in the establishment of Europol, which was set up by a Convention between the Member States in 1995, but whose position has now been formalised in Framework Decision 2009/371/JHA. It is also recognised in the TFEU.

Article 88 TFEU

1. Europol's mission shall be to support and strengthen action by the Member States' police authorities and other law enforcement services and their mutual cooperation in preventing and combating serious crime affecting two or more Member States, terrorism and forms of crime which affect a common interest covered by a Union policy.
2. The European Parliament and the Council, by means of regulations adopted in accordance with the ordinary legislative procedure, shall determine Europol's structure, operation, field of action and tasks. These tasks may include:
   (a) the collection, storage, processing, analysis and exchange of information, in particular that forwarded by the authorities of the Member States or third countries or bodies;
   (b) the coordination, organisation and implementation of investigative and operational action carried out jointly with the Member States' competent authorities or in the context of joint investigative teams, where appropriate in liaison with Eurojust.
   These regulations shall also lay down the procedures for scrutiny of Europol's activities by the European Parliament, together with national Parliaments.
3. Any operational action by Europol must be carried out in liaison and in agreement with the authorities of the Member State or States whose territory is concerned. The application of coercive measures shall be the exclusive responsibility of the competent national authorities.

Europol is based in The Hague and has its own legal personality.[166] It works exclusively with national units designated by Member States who supply Europol with information and require information and analysis from Europol whilst also responding to Europol's requests for information.[167] Each national unit must also second a liaison officer to Europol who is both to act as a bridge for information and facilitate cooperation between the two.[168] At the end of

---

[163] Convention implementing the Schengen Agreement, above n. 157, Articles 109–10.
[164] *Ibid.* Article 94(3).
[165] House of Lords European Union Committee, *The Schengen Information System II* (London, SO, 9th Report, 2007) para. 54.
[166] Framework Decision 2009/371/JHA, article 2. On its development see J. Occhipinti, *The Politics of EU Police Cooperation: Towards a European FBI?* (Boulder, Lynne Rieder, 2003).
[167] *Ibid.* article 8.
[168] *Ibid.* article 9.

2008, it had 461 staff and 124 liaison officers working for it.[169] Europol's initial mandate was to cover transnational organised crime. This mandate has now expanded, and now includes serious crime. As mentioned above, a liberal interpretation of this is taken and 'serious crime' is taken to comprise any of the thirty-two offences in the EAW for which double criminality is not required.[170] However, the criminal activities must have a transnational dimension so that they affect 'two or more Member States in such a way as to require a common approach by the Member States owing to the scale, significance and consequences of the offences'.[171]

Whilst both Article 88(2) TFEU and Framework Decision 2009/371/JHA provide for Europol to be involved in investigative and operational action, this is very much a supplementary task. Framework Decision 2009/371/JHA confines its role to participating in joint investigations in a supporting capacity[172] and to requesting states to initiate investigations.[173] Europol's central work is its analytic work. This is done in part through the maintenance of the Europol Information System. It is done more proactively through the establishment of Analysis Work Files. These are to be opened wherever it will assist criminal investigations[174] and national units are under an obligation to communicate all the information Europol may require for a particular file.[175] The data on Analysis Work Files is much more wide-ranging than any other data on EU databases. For persons on the Europol Information System, it can include DNA profiles and fingerprints, ID and social security numbers, criminal offences and means of committing these offences, and suspected membership of criminal organisations.[176] It can also include data on witnesses, victims, contacts and associates, and (most broadly) persons who can provide information on the criminal offences under consideration.[177] The only data that cannot be included is that on 'racial or ethnic origin, political opinions, religious or philosophical beliefs or trade-union membership and the processing of data concerning health or sex life shall not be permitted unless strictly necessary for the purposes of the file concerned and unless such data supplement other personal data already input in that file'.[178] The data available to Europol is extremely broad. Moreover, there are very broad exceptions which justify it refusing individuals access to data.

Framework Decision 2009/371/JHA establishing the European Police Office (Europol), article 30(5)

The provision of information in response to a request under paragraph 1 shall be refused to the extent that such refusal is necessary to:
(a) enable Europol to fulfil its tasks properly;
(b) protect security and public order in the Member States or to prevent crime;
(c) guarantee that any national investigation will not be jeopardised;
(d) protect the rights and freedoms of third parties.

---

[169] EU Council, *Europol Annual Report 2008*, above n. 155, 43.
[170] Framework Decision 2009/371/JHA, article 4 and Annex.
[171] *Ibid.* article 4(1).
[172] *Ibid.* article 6(1).
[173] *Ibid.* article 7(1).
[174] *Ibid.* article 14(2).
[175] *Ibid.* article 14(3).
[176] *Ibid.* article 12(2) and (3).
[177] *Ibid.* article 14(1).
[178] *Ibid.* article 14(1).

The first exception, in particular, gives Europol almost a complete *carte blanche* to refuse information. Even if Europol's remit remained confined to serious organised crime, this would be something upon which to reflect. As it has been widened to include any offence on which double criminality has been abolished, to include a wide array of data and anybody who could provide information on the offence, there are real causes for concern here. Given these dangers, this begs the question as to the value of Europol, namely: what analytic capacity does it enjoy which could not be enjoyed by national authorities? As Müller-Wille has shown, the answer is not immediately clear.

B. Müller-Wille, 'The Effect of International Terrorism on EU Intelligence Co-Operation' (2008) 46 *Journal of Common Market Studies* 49, 57–8

It is particularly important to note that national agencies are both the main providers of intelligence to Europol and its main customers. The work done by Europol does not therefore replace national assessment efforts or constitute a link of its own in the intelligence production chain. Rather it should be seen as an add-on, paralleling the work of national services.

Put simply, as good as the intelligence from The Hague may be, the primary responsibility for analysis remains with national agencies. Europol's centralized work does not replace, but merely complements a national service's own analysis and the decentralized direct bi- and multi-lateral co-operation it has established with other services. Hence, feeding Europol with information may be perceived as an extra burden added to an agency's own work with selected partners. This can start a vicious circle in that Europol's ability to add value is not exhausted for lack of information, which makes the expectations of its utility fall and allows the contributions to diminish. There is no obvious solution to this dilemma: national agencies will continue to be responsible for producing intelligence in support of counter-terrorist operations; and, even if authority was transferred, the public would continue to hold their national governments responsible for the provision of security in case of an attack, in effect enforcing a return of the responsibility to the national level.

FURTHER READING

E. Baker and C. Harding, 'From Past Imperfect to Future Perfect? A Longitudinal Study of the Third Pillar' (2009) 34 *European Law Review* 25

T. Elholm, 'Does EU Criminal Cooperation Necessarily Mean Increased Repression?' (2009) 17 *European Journal of Crime, Criminal Law and Criminal Justice* 191

M. Fletcher, R. Löof and W. Gilmore, *EU Criminal Law and Justice* (Cheltenham, Edward Elgar, 2008)

E. Guild and F Geyer (eds.), *Security versus Justice? Police and Judicial Cooperation in the European Union* (Aldershot, Ashgate, 2008)

V. Mitsilegas, 'The Constitutional Implications of Mutual Recognition in Criminal Matters in the EU' (2006) 43 *Common Market Law Review* 1277

   EU Criminal Law (Oxford and Portland, Hart, 2009)

S. Peers, *EU Justice and Home Affairs Law* (Oxford, Oxford University Press, 2006) chs. 8–10

   'Finally "Fit for Purposes"? The Treaty of Lisbon and the End of the Third Pillar Legal Order' (2008) 27 *Yearbook of European Law* 47

N. Walker, 'Policing and the Supranational' (2002) 12 *Policing and Society* 307

A. Weyembergh, 'Approximation of Criminal Laws, the Constitutional Treaty and the Hague Programme' (2005) 42 *Common Market Law Review* 1567

J. Wouters and F. Naert, 'Of Arrest Warrants, Terrorist Offences and Extradition Deals: An Appraisal of the EU's Main Criminal Law Measures against Terrorism after "11 September"' (2004) 41 *Common Market Law Review* 911

15

External Relations

CONTENTS

1 INTRODUCTION

This chapter considers the external relations of the European Union. It is organised as follows.

Section 2 examines the nature of the European Union's international legal presence. The Union is granted legal personality and so enjoys a status in international law, just as states do. To that end, the Union can adopt two types of measure: unilateral measures, which are targeted at other states or people and organisations resident in other states, and international agreements with other states. The European Council is the central agenda-setter in all this, setting the aims, duration and means for any external action. The mission of EU external action set out in Article 21 TEU is, however, to be centred less around crisis-management and more around a structural foreign policy, setting out long-term agendas, which are based on exporting EU values such as democracy, the rule of law and economic liberalism to its partner states in hopes that closer alignment of the former by the latter will promote peace, global security and political stability.

Section 3 looks at the competences of the Union. A hotchpotch of competences scattered across various EU instruments makes it difficult for the Union to achieve coherence in its external action. The TFEU includes competences which are overtly external, such as external trade or development, but also competences such as protection of the environment or sport and education whose centre of gravity is domestic but which allow for international agreements to be made in the field. The TEU contains the Common Foreign and Security Policy, which is subject to different procedures from the other external policies, and the European Neighbourhood Policy. Alongside these, the Union has implied powers in other competences to conclude international agreements wherever this is necessary to achieve, within the framework of the Union's policies, one of the objectives referred to in the Treaties, is provided for in a legally binding EU act, or the agreement is likely to affect or alter the scope of EU laws.

Section 4 looks at the allocation of powers between the Union and Member States. Agreements may be exclusive so that only the Union may conclude the agreement and is also exclusively responsible for its implementation. They may be mixed so that both the Union and Member States negotiate and conclude the agreement, and responsibility for implementation is divided on the basis of the internal allocation of powers. This question is a litmus test of EU legal identity, as a feature of federal states is that the central authorities have wide external powers which are exclusive in nature and that the central authorities are responsible for domestic implementation of international agreements even if they would not otherwise have the power. The European Union is not based on this model. In practice, most agreements are mixed and even when the Union has exclusive competences a variety of mechanisms are used to safeguard the national voice.

Section 5 considers how EU law meets its international legal obligations. Formally, the Union is bound by international law and the treaties concluded by it form part of its legal order. EU law, however, gives a variety of legal effects to international legal obligation. Some international treaties are granted direct effect by it. Others, most notably the WTO agreement which governs international trade, are considered too open-textured either to have direct effect or be a basis for review. They carry only a soft interpretive obligation. A similarly varied approach has been applied more generally to international law. In *Kadi*, the Court of Justice struck down a Regulation implementing a UN resolution because it infringed basic principles of EU law. These developments have led some to question the Union's commitment to international law.

Section 6 considers the Common Foreign and Security Policy. This is deployed when measures do not fall under the aegis of other forms of Union external action, and is consequently a policy concerned with securing international security and EU security. There is limited parliamentary and judicial influence and it is governed predominantly by the European Council and the Council of Ministers, with the former responsible for strategic matters and the latter for operational and thematic issues. There is no general power of legislation but the Union has the power to adopt guidelines and decisions. The policy is heavily intergovernmental but a central innovation of the Lisbon Treaty was the establishment of the High Representative. A member of the Commission and chairing the Council of Ministers, she is responsible for bringing the policy together and being the central external representative of the Union.

Section 7 considers the European Security and Defence Policy. An integral part of the Common Foreign and Security Policy, there is only provision for eventual movement to a common defence policy. In the meantime, there is a commitment to mutual assistance in the case of attack and two forms of Union action. The first is out-of-area action in arenas away from the EU territory involving the so-called 'Petersberg tasks': humanitarian intervention, conflict prevention and peace-keeping. The second field is joint improvement of military capabilities. This is to be facilitated by a European Defence Agency which will identify the necessary operational requirements. Progress has, however, been very slow as it relies on states being committed both to higher military spending and to stronger integration in this field. Very few subscribe to both these agendas.

2 NATURE OF THE UNION'S INTERNATIONAL PRESENCE

(i) Legal personality

The strongest statement of the European Union's external presence is found in Article 47 TEU.

Article 47 TEU

The Union shall have legal personality.

This is assumed to mean international legal personality.[1] The Campaign against Euro-Federalism thus saw the acquisition of this personality, which prior to Lisbon was enjoyed only by the Community and not by the Union, as granting the European Union a 'distinct corporate existence for the first time, something that all States possess. The new Union would be separate from and superior to its Member States.'[2] Whilst it is an overstatement to suggest that legal personality makes the Union superior to the Member States, it is right to say that traditionally only states have had international legal personality. Whilst the Union is not the only international organisation to enjoy legal personality,[3] the grant of that endows it with an external, independent presence that places it on a par with states. Like states, the Union can engage in two forms of external actions.

There are, first, autonomous actions that can be carried out unilaterally. Examples are sanctions against other states or individuals.[4] Alternatively, they can be trade measures. These might be Regulations imposing anti-dumping duties on goods that are being sold in the Union at a price

---

[1] Case 22/70 *Commission* v *Council (ERTA)* [1971] ECR 263.
[2] This is quoted in House of Lords European Union Committee, *The Treaty of Lisbon: An Impact Assessment* (London, SO, 10th Report 2007–8) vol. 1, para. 2.50.
[3] For example, the United Nations: see *Reparation for Injuries Suffered in the Service of the United Nations (Advisory Opinion)* [1949] ICJ Rep. 174.
[4] Regulation 423/2007/EC concerning restrictive measures against Iran [2007] OJ L103/1.

lower than that on the exporter's market;[5] the imposition of safeguard measures when imports threaten domestic industries;[6] or regulations banning the import of certain goods on environmental grounds.[7] Alternatively, they could be more general common foreign and security measures.[8]

The second type of measure is the conclusion of international agreements with third states. These are not just formal treaties but any undertaking which is binding in international law.[9] The procedure for concluding treaties is a three-stage one spelled out in detail in the TFEU.[10]

(1) The first stage is the opening of negotiations. This can only be done from an authorisation granted by the Council of Ministers.[11] This will usually be done on the basis of a recommendation from the Commission or, in the case of the Common Foreign and Security Policy (CFSP), the High Representative.[12]

(2) The second stage is the carrying out of the negotiations. Although not designated by the Treaties, it will usually be the Commission or the High Representative. The Council may set out directives to these on how to negotiate or designate a committee of national representatives with whom the negotiator must consult during negotiations.[13]

(3) The third stage is the signing of the agreement. The Council takes an initial decision authorising the signing of the agreement.[14] The conclusion of the agreement is for the Council, with some involvement from the European Parliament in certain circumstances. A second decision is then taken concluding the agreement. In some areas, notably where the internal policy field is governed by either the ordinary or the assent legislative procedure, the consent of the Parliament is required.[15] In all other fields bar the CFSP, the Council need only consult the Parliament.[16] In regard to the CFSP, there is no possibility even of consultation.[17]

---

[5] For example, Regulation 1202/2009/EC imposing a definitive anti-dumping duty on imports of furfuryl alcohol originating in the People's Republic of China [2009] OJ L323/48.

[6] Regulation 260/2009/EC on the common rules for imports [2009] OJ L84/1.

[7] Regulation 3254/91/EC prohibiting the use of leghold traps in the Community and the introduction into the Community of pelts and manufactured goods of certain wild animal species originating in countries which catch them by means of leghold traps or trapping methods which do not meet international humane trapping standards [1991] OJ L308/1.

[8] Joint Action 2009/854/CFSP amending Joint Action 2005/889/CFSP on establishing a European Union Border Assistance Mission for the Rafah Crossing Point (EU BAM Rafah) [2009] OJ L312/73.

[9] Opinion 1/75 *Draft Understanding on a Local Cost Standard drawn up under the auspices of the OECD* [1975] ECR 1355; Case C-327/91 *France v Commission* [1994] ECR I-3641.

[10] In the case of mixed agreements (see pp. 647–52) Member States participate in the negotiations and also sign the agreements separately, although in many cases the Commission acts as sole negotiator on behalf of the Union and Member States. See P. Koutrakos, *EU International Relations Law* (Oxford and Portland, Hart, 2006) 160–80.

[11] Article 218(2) TFEU. The Council acts by QMV throughout the procedure unless the domestic policy field is one where unanimity is required, for accession and association agreements and for accession to the ECHR. In these fields, it must act by unanimity: Article 218(8) TFEU.

[12] Article 218(3) TFEU. The role of the latter is spelt out later. See pp. 663–4.

[13] Article 218(4) TFEU.

[14] Article 218(5) TFEU.

[15] Article 218(6)(a)(v) TFEU. Other fields where consent is required include association agreements, accession to the ECHR, agreements setting up institutional frameworks for cooperation and agreements with important budgetary implications for the Union: Article 218(6)(a) TFEU.

[16] Article 218(6)(b) TFEU.

[17] Article 218(6)(a) TFEU.

These procedures are new and bolster the role of the European Parliament.[18] In addition to its powers in concluding the agreement, the European Parliament is now to be informed at all stages of the procedure.[19] It remains to be seen whether this assuages those concerned about the democratic deficit in this area.[20] Critics point to a lack of accountability and transparency, which is more pronounced now that non-governmental organisations play an important role, and that agreements touch on a much wider range of issues affecting citizens, indicating the need for greater political involvement.[21]

As a final note, there is a special jurisdiction for the Court of Justice in relation to international agreements. Any Member State, the Parliament, the Council of Ministers or the Commission can obtain the opinion of the Court of Justice as to the legality of the agreement envisaged. If the Court rules that the agreement conflicts with EU law, it may not enter into force unless it is amended or the Treaties are revised.[22] The purpose of the provision is to avoid any legal dispute that may arise once the agreement has been signed, which would damage not only the Union's international image but also the interests of the third countries who have signed the agreement. Consistent with this policy, the Court has held that it will not provide an Opinion when the agreement has been concluded.[23] However, challenges to the legality of an agreement after it has been entered into may be brought as actions for annulment under Article 263 TFEU.[24]

Finally, whilst the Union's legal personality grants it a power to enter into international agreements, this is not a general power akin to that held by states. The Union's powers exist only where the Union has been granted competences to act.

Declaration 24 concerning the legal personality of the European Union

The Conference confirms that the fact that the European Union has a legal personality will not in any way authorise the Union to legislate or to act beyond the competences conferred upon it by the Member States in the Treaties.

Before considering what the Union formally can do, it is worth pausing to consider the nature of the foreign policy in which it seeks to engage.

(ii) Direction of EU external action

Leadership in the direction of foreign policy rests with the European Council, whose task is to 'identify the strategic interests and objectives of the Union'.[25] The European Council acts on the basis of unanimity based on a recommendation by the Council of Ministers, who in turn

---

[18] However, the role of Parliament is more limited for international agreements entered into on the basis of the common commercial policy, for which a separate procedure is established: see Article 207 TFEU.

[19] Article 218(10) TFEU.

[20] R. Gosalbo Bono, 'The International Powers of the European Parliament, the Democratic Deficit and the Treaty of Maastricht' (1992) 12 *YBEL* 85.

[21] S. Vanhoonacker, 'The Institutional Framework' in C. Hill and M. Smith (eds.), *International Relations and the European Union* (2nd edn, Oxford, Oxford University Press, 2005) 74.

[22] Article 218(11) TFEU.

[23] Opinion 1/75, above n. 9.

[24] For example, Joined Cases C-317/04 and C-318/04 *Parliament v Council and Commission* [2006] ECR I-4721.

[25] Article 22(1) TEU.

may receive proposals from the High Representative of the Union (for matters relating to the CFSP) and from the Commission for other policy fields. The European Council acts by issuing Decisions.

Article 22 (1) TEU

Decisions of the European Council on the strategic interests and objectives of the Union shall relate to the common foreign and security policy and to other areas of the external action of the Union. Such decisions may concern the relations of the Union with a specific country or region or may be thematic in approach. They shall define their duration, and the means to be made available by the Union and the Member States.

The impact of these decisions will be to set out the policy framework for the European Union's external relations with various countries or regions. In so doing, the European Council will base its approach on the following general vision of the Union's foreign policy.

Article 21 TEU

1. The Union's action on the international scene shall be guided by the principles which have inspired its own creation, development and enlargement, and which it seeks to advance in the wider world: democracy, the rule of law, the universality and indivisibility of human rights and fundamental freedoms, respect for human dignity, the principles of equality and solidarity, and respect for the principles of the United Nations Charter and international law.

   The Union shall seek to develop relations and build partnerships with third countries, and international, regional or global organisations which share the principles referred to in the first subparagraph. It shall promote multilateral solutions to common problems, in particular in the framework of the United Nations.

2. The Union shall define and pursue common policies and actions, and shall work for a high degree of cooperation in all fields of international relations, in order to:
   (a) safeguard its values, fundamental interests, security, independence and integrity;
   (b) consolidate and support democracy, the rule of law, human rights and the principles of international law;
   (c) preserve peace, prevent conflicts and strengthen international security, in accordance with the purposes and principles of the United Nations Charter, with the principles of the Helsinki Final Act and with the aims of the Charter of Paris, including those relating to external borders;
   (d) foster the sustainable economic, social and environmental development of developing countries, with the primary aim of eradicating poverty;
   (e) encourage the integration of all countries into the world economy, including through the progressive abolition of restrictions on international trade;
   (f) help develop international measures to preserve and improve the quality of the environment and the sustainable management of global natural resources, in order to ensure sustainable development;
   (g) assist populations, countries and regions confronting natural or man-made disasters; and
   (h) promote an international system based on stronger multilateral cooperation and good global governance.

3. The Union shall respect the principles and pursue the objectives set out in paragraphs 1 and 2 in the development and implementation of the different areas of the Union's external action covered by this Title and by Part Five TFEU, and of the external aspects of its other policies.

The Union shall ensure consistency between the different areas of its external action and between these and its other policies. The Council and the Commission, assisted by the High Representative of the Union for Foreign Affairs and Security Policy, shall ensure that consistency and shall cooperate to that effect.

A helpful paradigm through which to think about foreign policy is to distinguish between conventional foreign policy (premised on military security and the management of crises and conflicts) and structural foreign policy, which is conducted over the long term and 'seeks to influence sustainable political, legal, socio-economic, security and mental structures'.[26] Article 21 evidences a mix of both of these aspects, but with a strong emphasis on structural foreign policy, reflecting the Union's greater institutional capacity in that regard. This policy is carried out mainly through association and cooperation agreements, which include provisions to liberalise trade and for economic cooperation. An illustrative example is the relationship with the Union's former colonies in the African, Caribbean and Pacific (ACP) states. Relations are currently governed by the Cotonou Convention, which has been signed by seventy-seven states.[27] Originally the relationship was mainly about giving ACP states access to the EU market and economic assistance, but the Cotonou agreement is wider in scope. It is based upon five themes: (1) political reform (promoting democracy and human rights); (2) the involvement of non-state actors; (3) the reduction of poverty; (4) promoting economic reform and trade liberalisation; (5) financial assistance, with greater flexibility for recipients in that aid is not earmarked for a given purpose.[28]

A second theme implicit in Article 21(1) is how the Union proposes to influence third countries' political development: there is to be close cooperation with them on the condition that they share the Union's political principles. This reflects the Union's practice since 1995 of concluding agreements with third countries that include a clause identifying 'essential elements' of an agreement, for example Article 9(2) of the Cotonou Agreement:

Respect for human rights, democratic principles and the rule of law, which underpin the ACP-EU Partnership, shall underpin the domestic and international policies of the Parties and constitute the essential elements of this Agreement.

Infringement of these essential principles allows for sanctions to be imposed against the state in breach.[29] These provisions are controversial and unwelcome for developing countries. Moreover, their effectiveness has been doubted and it is not clear that the pattern of assistance

---

[26] S. Keukeleire and J. MacNaughtan, *The Foreign Policy of the European Union* (Basingstoke, Palgrave Macmillan, 2008) 25.

[27] Partnership agreement between the Members of the African, Caribbean and Pacific Group of States and the European Community and its Member States signed in Cotonou on 23 June 2000 [2000] OJ L317/3, revised [2005] OJ L209/27.

[28] For an assessment, see S. Hurt, 'Cooperation or Coercion? The Co-operation Agreement Between the European Union and ACP States and the End of the Lomé Convention' (2003) 24 *Third World Quarterly* 161; A. Hadfield, 'Janus Advances? An Analysis of EC Development Policy and the 2005 Amended Cotonou Partnership Agreement' (2007) 12 *European Foreign Affairs Review* 39.

[29] Cotonou Agreement, Articles 96 and 97.

truly reflects political reform or whether it is more influenced by the interests of Member States, crises (coups, natural disasters) or geopolitical considerations (e.g. stability of the Union).[30] Finally, it is uncertain how far this strategy for exporting the Union's political and economic values will subsist as beneficiaries find other players (e.g. China) with the capacity to offer assistance and channels of trade while not insisting on political reforms.[31]

One should not consider the European Union's commitment to exporting values like democracy and human rights to be selfless. Rather, and this is a third theme in the Union's foreign policy strategy, reflected for example in the European Neighbourhood Policy (ENP) launched in 2004 (it applies to the Union's immediate neighbours by land or sea, Algeria, Armenia, Azerbaijan, Belarus, Egypt, Georgia, Israel, Jordan, Lebanon, Libya, Moldova, Morocco, Occupied Palestinian Territory, Syria, Tunisia and Ukraine): 'to develop a zone of prosperity and a friendly neighbourhood – a "ring of friends" – with whom the EU enjoys close, peaceful and co-operative relations'.[32] The Union thus hopes to develop markets for its exports, to be secure from mass migration, and to cooperate with its partners to fight terrorism. Again, a form of conditionality is at play here where the reward for economic reform and convergence with EU norms is closer relations with the European Union, with consequential economic benefits for the states, but without the prospect of membership.

The final theme which emerges from Article 21(3) is consistency. In the EU context this has three distinct dimensions: horizontal consistency (between EU policies, where one of the major inconsistencies is between its support of the Common Agricultural Policy and its development policy); institutional consistency (between different bureaucratic apparatuses within the Union, where the major inconsistencies are between measures taken within the TEU and those taken under the TFEU); and vertical consistency (between actions taken by the Union and Member States).[33] The aim of Articles 21 and 22 is to enhance horizontal and institutional consistency. Regarding the former, these Articles provide for joined-up policy-making; regarding the latter, giving the European Council a lead role in defining the Union's international strategy may help bridge the gap between matters of low politics (trade, development, addressed in the TFEU) and high politics (diplomacy, military intervention, addressed in the TEU). It remains to be seen whether institutional clashes like that in the *ECOWAS* case (discussed in section 7 below) can be avoided.

3 THE EXTERNAL COMPETENCES OF THE UNION

(i) Express powers

As with its internal powers, the Union's external powers are guided by the principle of conferred powers in Article 5 TEU under which the Union can only act within the limits set out by the Treaties. One scholar has explained that the implication of this is that '[u]nlike most nation

---

[30] S. Zanger, 'Good Governance and European Aid: The Impact of Political Conditionality' (2000) 1 *European Union Politics* 293.

[31] Keukeleire and MacNaughtan, above n. 26, 209.

[32] European Commission, *Wider Europe – Neighbourhood: A New Framework for Relations with our Eastern and Southern Neighbours*, COM(2003)104 final, 4. For an assessment, see M. Cremona, 'The European Neighbourhood Policy: More than a Partnership?' in M. Cremona (ed.), *Developments in EU External Relations Law* (Oxford, Oxford University Press, 2008).

[33] S. Nuttall, 'Coherence and Consistency' in Hill and Smith, above n. 21.

states, when considering a response to an international situation, the [Union] must always give precedence to considerations of competence over considerations of effectiveness in international action'.[34] The position is not made any easier as the Treaties contain a hotchpotch of provisions on the external relations of the European Union. The highest concentration of provisions is within Parts IV, V and VI of the TFEU, which provide for five types of external action.[35]

Common commercial policy This governs the Union's external trade relations with non-EU states. It comprises the customs union, which allows the Union to set a common external tariff (tax) for goods entering the Union from other states.[36] In many ways, it is traditionally the most salient of all the external policies, and covers not just trade in goods and services, but also trade-related aspects of intellectual property and investment.

Article 207(1) TFEU

The common commercial policy shall be based on uniform principles, particularly with regard to changes in tariff rates, the conclusion of tariff and trade agreements relating to trade in goods and services, and the commercial aspects of intellectual property, foreign direct investment, the achievement of uniformity in measures of liberalisation, export policy and measures to protect trade such as those to be taken in the event of dumping or subsidies. The common commercial policy shall be conducted in the context of the principles and objectives of the Union's external action.

Development cooperation and humanitarian aid This covers a wide array of policies with humanitarian objectives, including development cooperation;[37] economic, technical and financial cooperation;[38] and humanitarian aid.[39]

Restrictive measures This is a piece of jargon for sanctions. These may be targeted at states and/ or at private parties: be these companies, natural persons or 'non-state entities' such as Al Qaeda. These are unusual as they straddle the TEU and TFEU in that they require, first, a prior decision to be taken under the CFSP before formal measures can be adopted under the TFEU.[40]

Relations with international organisations This requires that the Union establish 'appropriate forms of cooperation' with international bodies like the United Nations and its agencies, the Council of Europe, the Organisation for Security and Cooperation in Europe and the OECD.[41]

---

[34] G. de Baere, *Constitutional Principles of EU External Relations* (Oxford, Oxford University Press, 2008) 10. Cf. the complaint of another scholar, B. De Witte, 'Too Much Constitutional Law?' in M. Cremona and B. De Witte (eds.), *EU Foreign Relations Law: Constitutional Fundamentals* (Oxford and Portland, Hart, 2008).

[35] Within the TFEU, the same principles for determining legal base apply to external measures as apply to internal ones, namely one looks at the predominant aim and content of the measure and determines the base with which it corresponds: Opinion 2/00 *Cartagena Protocol on Biosafety* [2001] ECR I-9713.

[36] Article 206 TFEU.

[37] Articles 208–211 TFEU.

[38] Articles 212, 213 TFEU.

[39] Article 214 TFEU.

[40] Article 215 TFEU.

[41] Article 220 TFEU.

However, the European Union is a member of only a few organisations: the WTO, the Food and Agriculture Organisation, the Codex Alimentarius Commission within the United Nations, and the European Bank for Reconstruction and Development. It is only a 'Full Participant' or 'Observer' in UN Bodies, and has no status in international financial institutions, like the IMF and World Bank. In large part this is explained by Member States wanting to keep their positions in these influential bodies, so that in the UN context the Union's energies are said to be devoted to reconciling the divergent interests of Member States, rather than using diplomacy to articulate an EU position.[42]

Associations of overseas countries and territories   This allows for association agreements with twenty 'non-European countries and territories which have special relations with Denmark, France, the Netherlands and the United Kingdom'.[43] The association agreements are designed to promote economic and social development and to establish close economic relations between those states and the European Union.[44]

In addition to this, there are a number of competences which, whilst their central thrust is not externally directed, allow for international agreements or cooperation. These include immigration;[45] asylum and temporary and subsidiary protection;[46] education and sport;[47] vocational training;[48] culture;[49] public health;[50] Trans European Networks;[51] Research and Development;[52] environment;[53] and the euro.[54]

However, in addition to these measures, the Union provides for two external policies in the TEU. The first is the Common Foreign and Security Policy.

Article 2(4) TEU

The Union shall have competence, in accordance with the provisions of the Treaty on European Union, to define and implement a common foreign and security policy, including the progressive framing of a common defence policy.

This policy is subject to its own set of procedures which sit outside those for other external policies, and is considered in section 7 below. The other policy in the TEU is a neighbourhood policy. This allows the Union to conclude agreements developing 'special relationships' with

---

[42] Keukeliere and MacNaughtan, above n. 26, 302–7.
[43] Article 198 TFEU. An exhaustive list is found in Annex II of the TFEU.
[44] Council Decision of 27 November 2001 on the association of the overseas countries and territories with the European Community [2001] OJ L314/1.
[45] Provision is made for readmission agreements with non-EU states: Article 78(2)(g) TFEU.
[46] Article 79(3) TFEU.
[47] Article 165(3) TFEU.
[48] Article 166(3) TFEU.
[49] Article 167(3) TFEU.
[50] Article 168(3) TFEU.
[51] Article 171(3) TFEU.
[52] Articles 180(b) and 186 TFEU.
[53] Article 191(4) TFEU.
[54] Article 219 TFEU; Protocol on the Statute of the ESCB, Article 23, first indent.

neighbouring countries (such as the ENP discussed above).[55] These agreements may take the form of preferential trade arrangements, commitments for cooperation across a wide array of policy fields, or arrangements preparing a country to make a formal accession application. Finally, it may be worth mentioning that insofar as there is provision for the Union to accede to the European Convention on Human Rights,[56] and other states to accede to the Union,[57] these have an external dimension as each relies on an international agreement by the Union.

(ii) Implied powers

Wide-ranging as these competences may be, they still allow the Union to do less externally than it can do within its territory.[58] This has created problems. How was the Union to regulate pollution of the Mediterranean if it could not enter into agreements with other countries in the region to abate pollution? How could it regulate the transport of goods if countries through which the goods might pass do not apply the same standards? In 1971, the Court of Justice began a line of case law which ruled that where the Treaty granted a competence, notwithstanding the absence of an explicit external dimension, a parallel treaty-making power would be implied in many circumstances.[59] Controversial as this case law was, it has now been crystallised in the TFEU by the Lisbon Treaty, reflecting political acceptance of the Court's approach.

Article 216(1) TFEU

The Union may conclude an agreement with one or more third countries or international organisations where the Treaties so provide or where the conclusion of an agreement is necessary in order to achieve, within the framework of the Union's policies, one of the objectives referred to in the Treaties, or is provided for in a legally binding Union act or is likely to affect common rules or alter their scope.

The provision changes the way we need to think about the European Union's external relations. The Union has external treaty-making powers not only where this is explicitly stated ('where the Treaties so provide') but also in a number of other circumstances. Because the provision codifies prior case law, this is not particularly happily phrased, and this has caused some consternation particularly in the light of national sensitivity about foreign policy. The Czech Constitutional Court considered it the most problematic of all the Treaty provisions as it seemed to allow the Union powers to act in very ill-defined circumstances.

---

[55] Article 8 TEU.
[56] Article 6(2) TEU.
[57] Article 49 TEU.
[58] For a comparison see T. Hartley, *European Union Law in a Global Context* (Cambridge, Cambridge University Press, 2004) ch.12.
[59] This was first developed in Case 22/70 *Commission* v *Council* (*ERTA*) [1971] ECR 263. For discussion of the development of the doctrine of implied powers see P. Eeckhout, *The External Relations of the European Union: Legal and Constitutional Foundations* (Oxford, Oxford University Press, 2004) ch. 3; Koutrakos, above n. 10, 77–132.

ÚS 19/08 *Treaty of Lisbon*, Judgment of 26 November 2008

186. ...we must emphasize that Article 216, because of its vagueness, is on the borderline of compatibility with the requirements for normative expression of a legal text that arise from the principles of a democratic, law-based state. The Constitutional Court itself ... concluded that this transfer must be delimited, recognizable, and sufficiently definite. It is precisely the 'definiteness' of a transfer of powers to an international organization that is quite problematic in Article 216 TFEU; it is obvious at first glance that its formulations are (... 'or' ... 'either' ... 'or' ... 'or' ... 'or' ...) 'vague', and difficult to predict. Here, for comparison, we can mention, for example, the generally known settled case law of the European Court of Human Rights, which – as regards the term 'law' – requires that it be accessible, precise, and with predictable consequences. Even though the Constitutional Court recognizes that the requirements for precision in an international treaty (obviously) cannot be interpreted as strictly as in the case of a statute, it nevertheless concludes that an international treaty must also meet the fundamental elements of precision, definiteness and predictability of a legal regulation. However, while Article 216 TFEU is quite disputable, nevertheless it does not go so far that the Constitutional Court could and should declare – only as regards the above-mentioned normative expression of the given text – that Article 216 is inconsistent with the constitutional order of the Czech Republic.

In spite of these uncertainties, it is possible to identify three circumstances where the Union has the power to reach international agreements even though it has no formal external competences. In each instance, reference must be had to the earlier case law.

The first is where an international agreement is 'necessary in order to achieve, within the framework of Union policies, one of the objectives of the Treaty'. The key word is 'necessary'. In its early case law the Court of Justice did not read anything into the word, and where there was a domestic competence a parallel external competence was implied.[60] This has been reversed in recent years, with the Court holding that an external competence can only be implied if it would be impossible to realise an EU policy through domestic measures alone. The seminal judgments are the *Open Skies* cases which involved a series of actions against Member States for concluding bilateral air transport agreements with the United States, facilitating air traffic. The Commission had been in the process of negotiating a collective agreement with the United States. It took action claiming that what is now Article 100(2) TFEU provided for legislation in the field of air transport. A European-wide agreement was necessary to realise EU objectives within this framework as individual agreements concluded by each Member State would distort competition in air transport between the Member States. The Court rejected this argument.[61]

---

[60] Opinion 1/76 *Draft Agreement establishing a European laying-up fund for inland waterway vessels* [1977] ECR 741; Opinion 2/91 *Convention No. 170 ILO on Safety in the Use of Chemicals at Work* [1993] ECR I-1061.

[61] See also Case C-467/98 *Commission v Denmark (Open Skies)* [2002] ECR I-9519; Case C-468/98 *Commission v Sweden (Open Skies)* [2002] ECR I-9575; Case C-469/98 *Commission v Finland (Open Skies)* [2002] ECR I-9627; Case C-471/98 *Commission v Belgium (Open Skies)* [2002] ECR I-9681; Case C-472/98 *Commission v Luxembourg (Open Skies)* [2002] ECR I-9741; Case C-475/98 *Commission v Austria (Open Skies)* [2002] ECR I-9797.

Case C–476/98 *Commission v Germany (Open Skies)* [2002] ECR I-9855

80. In relation to air transport, Article [100(2) TFEU] merely provides for a power for the Community to take action, a power which, however, it makes dependent on there being a prior decision of the Council.

81. Accordingly, although that provision may be used by the Council as a legal basis for conferring on the Community the power to conclude an international agreement in the field of air transport in a given case, it cannot be regarded as in itself establishing an external Community competence in that field.

82. It is true that the Court has held that the Community's competence to enter into international commitments may arise not only from express conferment by the Treaty but also by implication from provisions of the Treaty. Such implied external competence exists not only whenever the internal competence has already been used in order to adopt measures for implementing common policies, but also if the internal Community measures are adopted only on the occasion of the conclusion and implementation of the international agreement. Thus, the competence to bind the Community in relation to non-member countries may arise by implication from the Treaty provisions establishing internal competence, provided that participation of the Community in the international agreement is necessary for attaining one of the Community's objectives (see Opinion 1/76, paragraphs 3 and 4).

83. In a subsequent opinion, the Court stated that the hypothesis envisaged in Opinion 1/76 is that where the internal competence may be effectively exercised only at the same time as the external competence (Opinion 1/94, paragraph 89), the conclusion of the international agreement thus being necessary in order to attain objectives of the Treaty, that cannot be attained by establishing autonomous rules.

84. That is not the case here.

85. There is nothing in the Treaty to prevent the institutions arranging, in the common rules laid down by them, concerted action in relation to the United States of America, or to prevent them prescribing the approach to be taken by the Member States in their external dealings, so as to mitigate any discrimination or distortions of competition which might result from the implementation of the commitments entered into by certain Member States with the United States of America under 'open skies' agreements (see, to that effect, Opinion 1/94, paragraph 79).[62] It has therefore not been established that, by reason of such discrimination or distortions of competition, the aims of the Treaty in the area of air transport cannot be achieved by establishing autonomous rules.

86. In 1992, moreover, the Council was able to adopt the 'third package', which, according to the Commission, achieved the internal market in air transport based on the freedom to provide services, without its having appeared necessary at the time to have recourse, in order to do that, to the conclusion by the Community of an air transport agreement with the United States of America. On the contrary, the documents before the Court show that the Council, which the Treaty entrusts with the task of deciding whether it is appropriate to take action in the field of air transport and to define the extent of Community intervention in that area, did not consider it necessary to conduct negotiations with the United States of America at Community level ...

88. This case, therefore, does not disclose a situation in which internal competence could effectively be exercised only at the same time as external competence.

The circumstances when an international agreement will be 'necessary' to realise an EU objective will be rare. The test set out in paragraph 83 is that of the internal competence being exercised only at the same time as the external competence. An example might be a

---

[62] Opinion 1/94 *Re World Trade Organization Agreements* [1994] ECR I-5267.

sustainable fisheries policy over a marine area bordered by the Union and non-EU states. Yet, it is difficult to think of many examples where the Union could not realise some policy, albeit possibly less than effectively, through autonomous unilateral action. The *Open Skies* judgments have whittled down considerably what was previously the most wide-ranging implied external power.[63]

The reason for the first scenario being narrow is the presence of the second scenario which states that the Union shall have external legal competence 'wherever it is provided for in a legally binding Union act'. This requires a word of explanation as, on its face, it seems bizarre that the Union cannot have competence where it wishes to enter directly into an international agreement, but it can where the EU institutions first take a decision, mandating themselves to take the agreement, and then enter the agreement. The reason has to do with something we shall examine later: the exclusive competences of the Union in this field. Under the first scenario where the Union is considered to have treaty-making powers necessary to realise an EU objective, it is deemed, as the *Open Skies* judgments make clear, to have exclusive powers.[64] Only it can enter the agreement and the Treaty operates mechanistically to prevent Member States doing anything in this field. The scenario is controversial not just because the Union acquires a competence but also because Member States are prevented from acting.

The second scenario, by contrast, brings political choice back into the picture. It does not say that Member States have lost power by virtue of the legal logic of the Treaties but rather that they can choose to surrender treaty-making power to the Union in a binding instrument if they so wish. Whilst allowing more flexibility, there are a couple of things to note about this condition. First, it is narrower than the case law on which it builds, which referred to the Union acquiring competence wherever it was expressly conferred by a legislative act or the act referred to non-EU nationals.[65] The latter circumstance has gone and the act must now clearly be a binding instrument. Soft law will not count. Secondly, whilst there is the constraint that the instrument must fall within an internal field where the Union can adopt binding instruments, the flexibility in this instance is the very thing that causes concerns. It allows the political institutions to adopt international agreements, say under Article 352 TFEU, at the very limits of their internal powers. This is a very wide treaty-making power indeed, and it is not clear why the Union should have treaty-making powers in all areas where it can adopt binding instruments unless one assumes that there is no more sensitivity to a treaty than any other binding act.

The third scenario arises when the international agreement is 'likely to affect common rules or alter their scope'. This comes closest to the internal doctrine of pre-emption, which means that when EU measures have occupied a field, the Union is deemed to be the central actor in this field until the measures are repealed.[66] The matter was considered in most detail in Opinion 1/03 on a proposed new Lugano Convention. Regulation 44/2001/EC provided a general scheme for the recognition and enforcement of judgments in civil and commercial matters

---

[63] See L. Heffernan and C. McAuliffe, 'External Relations in the Air Transport Sector: The Court of Justice and the Open Skies Agreements' (2003) 28 *ELRev.* 601; R. Holdgaard, 'The European Community's Implied External Competence after the *Open Skies* Cases' (2003) 8 *EFARev.* 365; Koutrakos, above n. 10, 117–28.

[64] Case C-476/98 *Commission* v *Germany (Open Skies)* [2002] ECR I-9855, paras 103–4.

[65] Opinion 1/94, above n. 62, para. 95; Opinion 2/92 *Third Revised Decision of the OECD on National Treatment* [1995] ECR I-521, para. 33; Case C-476/98 *Commission* v *Germany (Open Skies)* [2002] ECR I-9855, para. 109.

[66] On pre-emption see pp. 206–7.

between Member States. The proposed Lugano Convention largely replicated this Regulation in an agreement between the Union and the EFTA states (Norway, Iceland and Switzerland). The Convention had a 'disconnection' clause whereby in any dispute between parties based in Member States, it stated that Regulation 44/2001/EC and not the Convetion would apply. The Commission argued that it was the Union which had competence as the Convention replicated the Regulation. A number of Member States argued that the disconnection clause prevented the Convention affecting the Regulation and therefore they could sign the Convention.

Opinion 1/03 *Lugano Convention* [2006] ECR I–1145

122. Ruling in much more general terms, the Court has found there to be exclusive Community competence in particular where the conclusion of an agreement by the Member States is incompatible with the unity of the common market and the uniform application of Community law ... where, given the nature of the existing Community provisions, such as legislative measures containing clauses relating to the treatment of nationals of non-member countries or to the complete harmonisation of a particular issue, any agreement in that area would necessarily affect the Community rules ...

123. On the other hand, the Court did not find that the Community had exclusive competence where, because both the Community provisions and those of an international convention laid down minimum standards, there was nothing to prevent the full application of Community law by the Member States ... Similarly, the Court did not recognise the need for exclusive Community competence where there was a chance that bilateral agreements would lead to distortions in the flow of services in the internal market, noting that there was nothing in the Treaty to prevent the institutions from arranging, in the common rules laid down by them, concerted action in relation to non-member countries or from prescribing the approach to be taken by the Member States in their external dealings ...

124. It should be noted in that context that the Community enjoys only conferred powers and that, accordingly, any competence, especially where it is exclusive and not expressly conferred by the Treaty, must have its basis in conclusions drawn from a specific analysis of the relationship between the agreement envisaged and the Community law in force and from which it is clear that the conclusion of such an agreement is capable of affecting the Community rules.

125. In certain cases, analysis and comparison of the areas covered both by the Community rules and by the agreement envisaged suffice to rule out any effect on the former ...

126. ... it is not necessary for the areas covered by the international agreement and the Community legislation to coincide fully. Where the test of 'an area which is already covered to a large extent by Community rules' is to be applied, the assessment must be based not only on the scope of the rules in question but also on their nature and content. It is also necessary to take into account not only the current state of Community law in the area in question but also its future development, insofar as that is foreseeable at the time of that analysis.

127. That that assessment must include not only the extent of the area covered but also the nature and content of the Community rules is also clear from the Court's case-law ... stating that the fact that both the Community rules and the international agreement lay down minimum standards may justify the conclusion that the Community rules are not affected, even if the Community rules and the provisions of the agreement cover the same area.

128. In short, it is essential to ensure a uniform and consistent application of the Community rules and the proper functioning of the system which they establish in order to preserve the full effectiveness of Community law.

129. Furthermore, any initiative seeking to avoid contradictions between Community law and the agreement envisaged does not remove the obligation to determine, prior to the conclusion of the agreement, whether it is capable of affecting the Community rules ...

130. In that regard, the existence in an agreement of a so-called 'disconnection clause' providing that the agreement does not affect the application by the Member States of the relevant provisions of Community law does not constitute a guarantee that the Community rules are not affected by the provisions of the agreement because their respective scopes are properly defined but, on the contrary, may provide an indication that those rules are affected. Such a mechanism seeking to prevent any conflict in the enforcement of the agreement is not in itself a decisive factor in resolving the question whether the Community has exclusive competence to conclude that agreement or whether competence belongs to the Member States; the answer to that question must be established before the agreement is concluded ...

133. It follows from all the foregoing that a comprehensive and detailed analysis must be carried out to determine whether the Community has the competence to conclude an international agreement and whether that competence is exclusive. In doing so, account must be taken not only of the area covered by the Community rules and by the provisions of the agreement envisaged, insofar as the latter are known, but also of the nature and content of those rules and those provisions, to ensure that the agreement is not capable of undermining the uniform and consistent application of the Community rules and the proper functioning of the system which they establish.

The Union will have competence, therefore, to enter into an international agreement if that agreement affects the uniformity and consistent application of current or imminent EU legislation. This is a complicated test to apply. First, the relationship is not always a simple one. International agreements setting out minimum standards may replicate EU law but, insofar as they only form a bed of rights, they may not prevent its application. By contrast, the Union may have competence to enter international agreements even where there is no domestic legislation yet, on the ground either that the matter is largely governed by EU law and there is some room for conflict or it is foreseeable that the Union will develop measures in the field governed by the agreement, and the agreement will therefore affect future developments. Secondly, even when the relationship is established much will depend on the fine print of the international agreement to determine its remit. Thus, the Court of Justice held the Union to have competence to sign the Lugano Convention on two main grounds that prevented complete coordination. First, if there were some circumstances where a Member State would have competence under Regulation 44/2001/EC, this would be transferred to the EFTA state under the proposed Convention. Secondly, there were some exceptions to the disconnection clause, most notably in consumer, employment and insurance contracts, and it could not be said that the provisions of the Convention would not apply here rather than those of the Regulation.

4 EU EXTERNAL RELATIONS AND THE AUTONOMY OF THE MEMBER STATES

(i) External relations and the federal question

In the previous section we saw the express and implied competences acquired by the Union. What does this mean? To be sure, it means, on the one hand, that the Union can enter into international agreements with non-EU states, apply measures targeted at or for people resident in those states, and develop corresponding policies. Yet, there remains the other question of how it affects relations between the Union and the Member States. External relations remains one of the most contested fields of EU law, for external relations is central to questions of legal identity and political community. Traditionally, states have been the only recognised actors in international law and external relations, and they still retain a dominant status there. To be granted the power to act on the international plane is to be placed in a highly select community. It is to be recognised as having 'state-like' qualities. As the extract from Weiler suggests, in federal states where power is shared between federal authorities and regional authorities, the former have always acquired more power externally than they have internally as a way of asserting the sense of their being a single political community.

J. Weiler, *The Constitution of Europe* (Cambridge, Cambridge University Press, 1999) 184

Our analysis so far has revealed two possible constructions for the application of the federal principle to the international legal relations of non-unitary actors. According to one view external relations in general and treaty-making in particular are *instruments* and as such must be subordinate to the internal division of competences between the central authority and the constituent members.

A second view is that external capacity and power have a *substantive* quality and are themselves not mere instruments to further other policies. In earlier times it could perhaps be maintained that the issues of foreign policy and external legal relations fell naturally within the central authority domain. But when it became clear that matters which were reserved to the constituent units rather than the central authority could have international implications, this second view was reconstructed. Now it is suggested that as regards any matter with an international dimension, even in non-unitary states, the exercise of international legal relations by the central authority maximizes in the international environment the power of the federal entity as a whole which is consequently also beneficial to the constituent member states. Under this view the concentration of external power and capacity in the central authority is in itself part of the federal allocation of competences within the non-unitary entity, and the interests of the constituent units could at best be vindicated by the internal processes of foreign policy formation

It is this second view which has characterized the constitutional doctrine and practice of federal states. The other instrumental view, if taken to its logical conclusion, seemed an unacceptable option to the federations. It raised the spectre not only of a multiplicity of different foreign policies but also of a multiplicity of international legal relations which would, because of their internal effects, over-accentuate diversity rather than unity within the body politic and call into question the very *raison d'être* of the federal state in which the one and the many, the uniform and the diverse, must find a workable equilibrium. In one sense the federal state experience might allay fears regarding respect for the internal autonomy of member states. All writers speak of a federal reluctance to exploit the wide external capacity, power and implementing competence to the detriment of the authority of constituent units. The respect for the member state is manifested either by refraining from treaty conclusion or by developing structures for co-operative federalism. It is clearly however a *centralist model* and one which historically has seen the effective elimination of member states as serious international actors.

Weiler measures the nature of external power in federal systems across three parameters:

(1) the external capacity granted to the federal authorities, in particular the remit of their powers to engage in external relations with third states and whether these extend beyond their internal powers;
(2) the loss of competence for local actors; this looks at whether action or the presence of a competence for the central actors pre-empts a local actor for entering into relations on the international scene;
(3) the allocation of responsibilities for the internal implementation of commitments made to third states, in particular whether the central authorities acquire full responsibility for these on the grounds that they made the commitment, notwithstanding that these commitments fall within a field that would otherwise be the responsibility of local actors.

Weiler observes that in federal systems one tends to see central actors having wider external powers and wider implementing powers than they would otherwise have internally, and that they usually granted exclusive powers of representation externally so that local actors have no significant external powers.[67] How the Treaties and the Court of Justice develop these parameters therefore goes very much to the Union's legal identity. We have seen how in recent times the Court has retrenched on the first parameter. The Union has the explicit power to enter into international agreements in a number of limited external competences and a limited number of fields where it has an internal competence. Beyond that, the doctrine of implied powers restricts quite considerably the circumstances where there is *a priori* competence in other fields for the Union to enter an international agreement. We now turn to how the Treaties address these parameters.

(ii) Exclusive competences and mixed agreements

The effect of Union treaty-making on the external powers of Member States and on the allocation of internal responsibilities for implementing the treaty is governed in EU law by the doctrine of exclusive competence. In a field where there is exclusive competence only the Union can, in principle, enter into agreements with non-states or take unilateral measures.[68] Even where it has not acted, Member States are not free to act. It is also exclusively responsible for the internal implementation of any agreement. This may be the case where the provision is found to be directly effective (that is, where the international agreement is not found to be too flexible and open-ended and the provision in question is sufficiently precise and unconditional to be considered to generate individual rights).[69] If provisions are not directly effective, implementation will be carried out through EU legislation (e.g. Regulations, Directives, etc.).

As mentioned in Chapter 5,[70] the Union is explicitly granted exclusive competence in a number of fields. These include the customs union, monetary policy for the Member States whose currency is the euro, the common commercial policy, the establishing of the competition rules necessary for the functioning of the internal market and the conservation of marine biological resources under the common fisheries policy.[71] Of these, it only has explicit treaty-making

---

[67] J. Weiler, *The Constitution of Europe* (Cambridge, Cambridge University Press, 1999) 136–58.
[68] Opinion 1/75, above n. 9.
[69] Case 104/81 *Hauptzollamt Mainz* v *Kupferberg* [1982] ECR 3641.
[70] See pp. 207–8.
[71] Article 3(1) TFEU.

competences in commercial policy and monetary policy.[72] In addition, although slightly different wording is used from Article 216(1) TFEU, the Union enjoys an exclusive competence in the three scenarios where it has an implied external competence.

Article 3(2) TFEU

The Union shall also have exclusive competence for the conclusion of an international agreement when its conclusion is provided for in a legislative act of the Union or is necessary to enable the Union to exercise its internal competence, or insofar as its conclusion may affect common rules or alter their scope.

In areas other than commercial and monetary policy and implied external competences, where the Union has explicit treaty-making competences, it does not enjoy exclusive competences. In all these other fields, the competence is a shared one and the Union enters into mixed agreements, which are negotiated and entered into by both the European Union and the Member States.[73] Mixed agreements will be entered into not only where the Treaty provides but also where the substance of the agreement falls partly within the competence of the Union and partly within the competence of the Member States.

Mixed agreements also differ from exclusive agreements in their implementation. Implementation depends on the allocation of internal competences. The central principles can be illustrated by a dispute between a pharmaceutical company (Merck) and a company manufacturing generic drugs. Merck had obtained a patent in Portugal with respect to a pharmaceutical compound in 1981 and used it to sell a pharmaceutical product. In 1996 the generics company used the same compound to make a cheaper version of the same product, on the basis that under Portuguese law Merck's patent expired after fifteen years. Merck counterclaimed relying on Article 33 of the TRIPS Agreement which provided that the patent should last for twenty years and so the generics drug company had infringed Merck's rights. Merck was successful in the Court of Appeal, which ruled that under Portuguese law, the TRIPS Agreement had direct effect and could be relied upon by Merck. On a further appeal the Portuguese Supreme Court asked whether it would be contrary to EU law for the national court to apply Article 33 of the TRIPS Agreement directly.

Case C-431/05 *Merck Genéricos – Produtos Farmacêuticos v Merck* [2007] ECR I-7001

31. The WTO Agreement, of which the TRIPs Agreement forms part, has been signed by the Community and subsequently approved by Decision 94/800. Therefore, according to settled case-law, the provisions of that convention now form an integral part of the Community legal order. Within the framework of that legal order the Court has jurisdiction to give preliminary rulings concerning the interpretation of that agreement.

---

[72] Although the customs union falls within the commercial policy for these purposes.
[73] Koutrakos, above n. 10, ch. 4; Eeckhout, above n. 59, ch. 7. See also P. Koutrakos and C. Hillion (eds.), *Mixed Agreements Revisited: The EU and Its Member States in the World* (Oxford and Portland, Hart, 2010).

32. The WTO Agreement was concluded by the Community and all its Member States on the basis of joint competence and ... without any allocation between them of their respective obligations towards the other contracting parties.

33. It follows that, the TRIPs Agreement having been concluded by the Community and its Member States by virtue of joint competence, the Court, hearing a case brought before it in accordance with the provisions of the EC Treaty ... has jurisdiction to define the obligations which the Community has thereby assumed and, for that purpose, to interpret the provisions of the TRIPs Agreement.

34. In addition, as the Court has previously held, when the field is one in which the Community has not yet legislated and which consequently falls within the competence of the Member States, the protection of intellectual property rights and measures taken for that purpose by the judicial authorities do not fall within the scope of Community law, so that the latter neither requires nor forbids the legal order of a Member State to accord to individuals the right to rely directly on a rule laid down in the TRIPs Agreement or to oblige the courts to apply that rule of their own motion.

35. On the other hand, if it should be found that there are Community rules in the sphere in question, Community law will apply, which will mean that it is necessary, as far as may be possible, to supply an interpretation in keeping with the TRIPs Agreement, although no direct effect may be given to the provision of that agreement at issue.

36. In order to answer the question which of the two hypotheses set out in the two paragraphs above is concerned, in relation to the relevant sphere covering the provision of the TRIPs Agreement at issue in the main proceedings, it is necessary to examine the matter of the sharing of competence between the Community and its Member States.

37. That last question calls for a uniform reply at Community level that the Court alone is capable of supplying.

38. There is, therefore, some Community interest in considering the Court as having jurisdiction to interpret Article 33 of the TRIPs Agreement in order to ascertain, as the national court has asked it to, whether it is contrary to Community law for that provision to be given direct effect.

39. Having regard to the principles noted in paragraphs 34 and 35 above, it is now appropriate to examine whether, in the particular sphere into which Article 33 of the TRIPs Agreement falls, that is to say, that of patents, there is any Community legislation.

40. As Community law now stands, there is none.

The crucial distinction drawn by the Court is between those parts of the TRIPS Agreement that have been implemented by EU law and those that have not. If there is no EU law implementation, the direct effect of the relevant provision is a question for the national courts. This makes sense because the plaintiff will be challenging the legality of national law against the standards set by the international agreement. In contrast, if the relevant part of the agreement in question fell within the framework of EU law, it would be possible for the Commission to challenge the Member State if it had failed to fulfil its obligations under the international agreement.[74]

(iii) Mixity and exclusivity: part of a continuum?

On paper, a mixed message emerges. In a significant number of fields, the Union has exclusive competence and present itself externally in the same way as federal states. In a large

---

[74] For example, Case C-239/03 *Commission* v *France* [2004] ECR I-9325.

number of other fields, the converse takes place. Nothing is done to recalibrate the balance of competences between the Union and Member States. Mixed agreements are signed involving both the EU institutions and the national governments, and the agreement is implemented according to the internal allocation of competences. In practice, however, the position is less dichotomous. Even in fields where the Union might appear to have exclusive competences, Member States have limited its capacity to undermine their ability to engage in international relations.

This has been done, first, by the use of mixed agreements even where the international agreement seems to be predominantly one for exclusive EU competence. This is justified on the ground that the subject matter of the agreement might touch, albeit slightly, either on matters of national competence or on EU legal fields which allow national involvement (e.g. environment, development).[75]

J. Weiler, *The Constitution of Europe* (Cambridge, Cambridge University Press, 1999) 177

Mixed agreements, especially when they do not specify the demarcation line between Community and Member States, defuse at a stroke the explosive issues of the scope of Community competences (and treaty making power) and the parameters of the preemptive effect. It may thus be employed, illegally. ... even in those cases where the Community should act alone. From the legal point of view this particular practice must be condemned since it is a breach of the principle of preemption-exclusivity ... But preemption does not operate in a legal vacuum. One purpose of the doctrine of preemption in general is to induce, even force, the Member States to act in a Community framework. Preemption is designed for situations where there is an objective necessity for action. By precluding unilateral Member State activity (or joint non-Community action) it is hoped that the objective necessity will force the Member States into joint *Community* action. In some cases the reluctance of Member States to allow exclusive Community action might be so great – especially if this could mean, say, a de facto confirmation of the ever-growing scope of the Common Commercial Policy – that they would prefer not to act at all. It may be that mixity is the best compromise between Community exclusivity and no action at all. Since most mixed agreements do not specify the demarcation between Community and Member State competences, this issue is left murky though it can surface again in the implementation of the mixed agreement, its amendment, termination and/ or breach. Mixity may also have advantages, even in this 'false' situation, from the international point of view in terms of voting or other rights in multilateral contexts. In conclusion, one can say that this type of mixity is a symptom of the cleavage between legal doctrine and political power which at present seems unavoidable.

Secondly, even in areas of exclusive competence, Member States can seek to control the negotiating and implementing processes. The central example is the common commercial policy, which, although a matter of exclusive competence, is dominated by the Member States.

---

[75] See the discussion in G. de Baere, *Constitutional Principles of EU External Relations* (Oxford, Oxford University Press, 2008) 235–7.

Article 207 TFEU

3. Where agreements with one or more third countries or international organizations need to be negotiated and concluded ... The Commission shall make recommendations to the Council, which shall authorise it to open the necessary negotiations. The Council and the Commission shall be responsible for ensuring that the agreements negotiated are compatible with internal Union policies and rules.

     The Commission shall conduct these negotiations in consultation with a special committee appointed by the Council to assist the Commission in this task and within the framework of such directives as the Council may issue to it. The Commission shall report regularly to the special committee and to the European Parliament on the progress of negotiations.

4. For the negotiation and conclusion of the agreements referred to in paragraph 3, the Council shall act by a qualified majority.

     For the negotiation and conclusion of agreements in the fields of trade in services and the commercial aspects of intellectual property, as well as foreign direct investment, the Council shall act unanimously where such agreements include provisions for which unanimity is required for the adoption of internal rules.

     The Council shall also act unanimously for the negotiation and conclusion of agreements:
     (a) in the field of trade in cultural and audiovisual services, where these agreements risk prejudicing the Union's cultural and linguistic diversity;
     (b) in the field of trade in social, education and health services, where these agreements risk seriously disturbing the national organisation of such services and prejudicing the responsibility of Member States to deliver them ...

6. The exercise of the competences conferred by this Article in the field of the common commercial policy shall not affect the delimitation of competences between the Union and the Member States, and shall not lead to harmonisation of legislative or regulatory provisions of the Member States insofar as the Treaties exclude such harmonisation.

National control is engaged at a number of moments. It is the Council of Ministers which grants the Commission the mandate to start negotiations. Negotiations are carried out by the Commission not unilaterally but with a committee of national representatives. In areas of sensitivity (set out in Article 207(4)(a) and (b) TFEU) unanimity is the rule in the Council, thus granting every government a veto over any international agreement. Finally, one can point to Article 207(6) TFEU which limits the capacity of the common commercial policy to rearrange the balance of powers by stating that it shall not lead to any new internal legislative competences.

All this suggests that the dichotomy between exclusive and mixed agreements is not rigid. In fields of exclusive competence, the institutional controls lead to a practice of cooperation between Member States and EU institutions in the opening and negotiation of agreements.[76] This is no different in the case of mixed agreements, where the Court has ruled that the Union and Member States must cooperate throughout the negotiation, conclusion and implementation of the mixed agreement.[77]

---

[76] A. Niemann, 'Between Communicative Action and Strategic Action: The 113 Committee and the Negotiations on the WTO Basic Telecommunications Services Agreement' (2004) 11 *JEPP* 379.
[77] Case C-25/94 *Commission* v *Council (FAO Fisheries Agreement)* [1996] ECR I-1469.

There are also similarities in the relationship between EU institutions and Member States in circumstances where there is no agreement and negotiations have not yet been opened. In the field of exclusive competences, Member States can, in principle, not engage in any external action. However, this has been qualified where the Union has not taken any action itself. The Court has ruled that, in the absence of EU measures, Member States may take measures of their own provided they have the authorisation of the EU institutions for doing so.[78] There is thus some scope for national action. By contrast, in the field of mixed agreements, by virtue of the fidelity principle in Article 4(3) TEU which requires Member States, inter alia, to refrain from any measure which could jeopardise the attainment of the Union's objectives, national autonomy is limited where the Commission has been authorised to conclude an international agreement. In such circumstances, Member States cannot enter independent agreements with the non-EU state concerned unless this is done with the cooperation of the EU institutions.[79]

5 EU LAW AND INTERNATIONAL LAW

(i) Legal effect of international agreements

The Union will be bound by treaty commitments in two circumstances. The first, and most evident, is where it has concluded the treaty.

Article 216(2) TFEU

Agreements concluded by the Union are binding upon the institutions of the Union and on its Member States.

Such agreements have therefore been ruled to be a central part of the EU legal order, which bind the institutions and the Member States.[80] The other circumstance where the Union will be considered to be bound by a treaty obligation is where, although it has not concluded the agreement itself, the Member States had previously concluded the treaty and it has now assumed the powers exercised by the Member States in that field.[81] For that to happen, the Union must have assumed *all* the powers exercised by Member States in that field. The Union will not be bound if it merely legislates on some of the activities covered by the Treaties.[82]

It is one thing to state that the Union is bound, but what does this mean in EU law? What entitlements and responsibilities does it engender? The binding effect of EU legal instruments has been held, for example, to generate direct effect so that they could be invoked in national

---

[78] Case 41/76 *Donckerwolcke* v *Procureur de la République* [1976] ECR 1934; Case 804/78 *Commission* v *United Kingdom* [1981] ECR 1072.

[79] Case C-266/03 *Commission* v *Luxembourg* [2005] ECR I-4805.

[80] Case 181/73 *Haegeman* [1974] ECR 449; Case 12/86 *Demirel* v *Stadt Schwäbisch Gmünd* [1987] ECR 3719; Case C-321/97 *Andersson and Wåkerås-Andersson* [1999] ECR I-3551.

[81] Joined Cases 21/72–24/72 *International Fruit Company and Others* v *Produktschap voor Groenten en Fruit* [1972] ECR 1219; Case C-379/92 *Peralta* [1994] ECR I-3453.

[82] Case C-301/08 *Bogiatzi* v *Deutscher Luftpool*, Judgment of 22 October 2009.

courts.[83] In some circumstances the Court has adopted such an approach. An example is *Kupferberg*, where the question arose whether a German tax on wine was applicable to imports from Portugal (at a time when Portugal had not joined the European Union), when this tax conflicted with a provision of the Free Trade Agreement between the Union and Portugal. It was held that the relevant provision in the Agreement could be relied upon to challenge the German tax.[84] The approach the Court took is analogous to that used to test for the direct effect of EU law. There is good reason for this approach: international agreements entered into by the Union will require implementation and support at national level; it would be damaging if Member States could undermine the international agreement by adopting national laws that are inconsistent with the agreement.

Yet, the Court has not been consistent. The most prominent example is the World Trade Organisation (WTO) Agreement, the central agreement governing international trade. Early on, the Court held that the Union was bound by its predecessor, the GATT, but that the nature of the Agreement – its reciprocity, flexibility and open-endedness – prevented it from being directly effective.[85] This position has been continually reiterated with the leading case restating this general approach involving a challenge by Portugal against a Decision by the Council establishing a memorandum of understanding between the European Union and India and Pakistan relating to trade in textiles. Portugal argued that the Decision was contrary to the WTO Agreement into which the Union had entered.

Case C–149/96 *Portugal* v *Council* [1999] ECR I–8395

42. As regards, more particularly, the application of the WTO agreements in the Community legal order, it must be noted that, according to its Preamble, the agreement establishing the WTO, including the annexes, is still founded, like GATT 1947, on the principle of negotiations with a view to 'entering into reciprocal and mutually advantageous arrangements' and is thus distinguished, from the viewpoint of the Community, from the agreements concluded between the Community and non-member countries which introduce a certain asymmetry of obligations, or create special relations of integration with the Community, such as the agreement which the Court was required to interpret in *Kupferberg*.

43. It is common ground, moreover, that some of the contracting parties, which are among the most important commercial partners of the Community, have concluded from the subject-matter and purpose of the WTO agreements that they are not among the rules applicable by their judicial organs when reviewing the legality of their rules of domestic law.

44. Admittedly, the fact that the courts of one of the parties consider that some of the provisions of the agreement concluded by the Community are of direct application whereas the courts of the other party do not recognise such direct application is not in itself such as to constitute a lack of reciprocity in the implementation of the agreement.

---

[83] Case 41/74 *Van Duyn* v *Home Office* [194] ECR 1337.
[84] Case 104/81 *Hauptzollamt Mainz* v *Kupferberg* [1982] ECR 3641.
[85] Joined Cases 21/72–24/72 *International Fruit Company NV and Others* v *Produktschap voor Groenten en Fruit* [1972] ECR 1219, paras 4–6. Similar principles apply if the legal basis for challenging EU action is Article 263 TFEU: Case C-280/93 *Germany* v *Council* [1994] ECR I-4973.

45. However, the lack of reciprocity in that regard on the part of the Community's trading partners, in relation to the WTO agreements which are based on 'reciprocal and mutually advantageous arrangements' and which must ipso facto be distinguished from agreements concluded by the Community, referred to in paragraph 42 of the present judgment, may lead to disuniform [sic] application of the WTO rules.

46. To accept that the role of ensuring that Community law complies with those rules devolves directly on the Community judicature would deprive the legislative or executive organs of the Community of the scope for manoeuvre enjoyed by their counterparts in the Community's trading partners.

47. It follows from all those considerations that, having regard to their nature and structure, the WTO agreements are not in principle among the rules in the light of which the Court is to review the legality of measures adopted by the Community institutions.

48. That interpretation corresponds, moreover, to what is stated in the final recital in the Preamble to Decision 94/800, according to which 'by its nature, the Agreement establishing the World Trade Organisation, including the Annexes thereto, is not susceptible to being directly invoked in Community or Member State courts'.

This reasoning of the Court is overtly policy-based. One further policy argument that has been said to motivate the Court is that given the breadth of coverage of the WTO Agreement, granting it direct effect would subsume EU regulation to WTO law, endangering the autonomy of EU law.[86] Furthermore, direct effect would risk exposing the Union to damages claims, as demonstrated when two Italian firms sought damages from the Union arising from these facts: the EU import regime for bananas was challenged by the United States in the WTO and as a result the United States was entitled to 'retaliate' by imposing trade restrictions on certain imports, including those of the two Italian firms. However, the Court maintained its position that even when the breach of WTO rules had been established, a claim for damages against the Union could not be sustained.[87]

An alternative policy perspective is that affording citizens the right to question the compatibility of EU law against the standards of the WTO Agreement would yield benefits to those that the free trade rules seek to protect.

E. Petersmann, 'National Constitutions, Foreign Trade Policy and European Community Law' (1992) 3 *European Journal of International Law* 1, 34

From the perspective of constitutionally limited democracies, such as those of the major trading countries, liberalism and internationalism must therefore begin at home. Problems in the implementation of international trade rules arise mostly at the level of domestic trade law and policy-making. International legal prohibitions of mutually harmful trade restrictions and trade discrimination

---

[86] P. Mengozzi, 'Private International Law and the WTO Law' (2002) *Academie de la Haye, Recueil des Cours* 292, 316–17.

[87] Joined Cases C-120/06 P and C-121/06 P *FIAMM and Others* v *Council and Commission* [2008] ECR I-6513.

are necessary not only for the external relations of states but even more so for protecting the equal liberties and property rights of domestic citizens participating in and benefitting from the international division of labour. The effectiveness of international GATT obligations depends upon the more effective incorporation of the international rules into a domestic 'trade policy constitution' so that the rules are binding and protected under domestic laws.

Such a 'constitutional' approach would require a number of important policy changes. Rather than leaving the domestic implementation of liberal international trade rules to the discretion of each government, international trade agreements should regulate their 'domestic law effects' in a manner enabling producers, traders and consumers to invoke and defend their 'freedoms of foreign trade' against government restrictions and against non-transparent interest group politics. International trade agreements should also provide for domestic judicial review, for it is the courts which ultimately have to protect the transnational exercise of individual rights by domestic citizens. Likewise, the effectiveness of individual rights and their judicial protection depend upon procedural guarantees of due process and access to justice as well as on the interpretation of international and domestic foreign trade law as mutually complementary rules designed to enhance the individual rights and welfare of domestic citizens.

It should be noted, however, that the Court has created two limited exceptions to the general approach discussed above. The Court will review the legality of EU measures having regard to WTO rules when: (i) the Union has intended to implement a particular obligation assumed in the context of the WTO;[88] or (ii) where the EU measure refers expressly to the WTO Agreement.[89] The Court has applied this approach in annulling an anti-dumping regulation on the grounds that it was incompatible with the WTO anti-dumping code.[90]

Furthermore, the Court has also sought to interpret EU law in the light of the provisions of the WTO Agreement.[91] In addition, it has been suggested that the Court of Justice is also influenced by the position taken by the WTO Appellate Body with respect to EU law: the Court renders judgments that are consistent with the positions taken by the WTO tribunals, without, however, referring to these, in an effort to avoid inconsistencies with the WTO decisions.[92] These approaches do not confer direct effect on the WTO Agreement but do give the Court some powers with which to ensure that EU measures are compatible with international agreements.

So far we have limited the discussion to the effects of the WTO Agreement, which has spawned significant litigation in the light of the economic significance of the agreement. From a legal perspective, the Court's approach to the WTO Agreement is significant because it differs from the position taken with respect to other international agreements, where direct effect has been established more readily.[93] Admittedly, this has happened mostly when testing national law against the international agreement in question. However, in a recent judgment the Court

---

[88] Case C-69/89 *Nakajima All Precision Co. Ltd* v *Council* [1991] ECR I-2069.

[89] Joined Cases C-120/06 P and C-121/06 P *FIAMM and Others*, above n. 87, para. 112.

[90] Case C-76/00 P *Petrotub and Others* v *Council and Commission* [2003] ECR I-79.

[91] Case C-83/94 *Leifer and Others* [1995] ECR I-3231, para. 24; Case C-53/96 *Hermès International* v *FHT Marketing Choice BV* [1998] ECR I-3603. See F. Snyder, 'The Gatekeepers: The European Courts and WTO Law' (2003) 40 *CMLRev.* 313.

[92] M. Bronckers, 'Private Appeals to WTO Law: An Update' (2008) 42(2) *J. World Trade* 245.

[93] For example, Case C-469/93 *Amministrazione delle Finanze dello Stato* v *Chiquita Italia SpA* [1995] ECR I-4533; Case 12/86 *Demirel* v *Stadt Schwäbisch Gmünd* [1987] ECR 3719.

has refused to test the legality of an EU Directive against the standards in the UN Convention on the Law of the Sea (UNCLOS) on the basis that the 'nature and broad logic' of the Convention (to which the Union was a party) prevented the Court from assessing EU law by reference to it.[94] Whether or not this case is the beginning of a trend away from finding that international agreements have direct effect, it raises the need to reflect whether testing the legality of EU legislation against international agreements is desirable.

M. Bronckers, 'From "Direct Effect" to Muted Dialogue: Recent Developments in the European Courts' Case Law on the WTO and Beyond' (2008) 11 *Journal of International Economic Law* 885, 895–6

Some scholarly practitioners have been arguing that the Court should abandon this older case law, and defer much more to the executive and legislative institutions of the EC in general, and not just where the WTO is concerned. They believe that the EC has become much more powerful on the international scene, and imply that the Court's threat of granting 'direct effect' to international agreements would circumscribe the EC's growing negotiating power too much.

Others have pointed out that the Court's methodology might differ depending on whether it is dealing with bilateral as opposed to multilateral agreements, such as the WTO and UNCLOS. This distinction could also reflect a different balance of negotiating power. It is more difficult for the EC to press its point of view in a multilateral than in a bilateral context, as in a bilateral context the EC by now will almost always be the stronger party...

But there are other reasons as well... Other EC institutions (Commission, Council, and Parliament) are not only charged with the negotiation but also with the implementation of international norms. In our era of globalization, with an ever denser network of international agreements, their implementation raises new issues for the traditional relations between the *trias politica*.

Furthermore, in EC law the notion of 'direct effect' is coupled with supremacy. In other words, to the extent the ECJ grants direct effect to a provision of an international agreement, this provision will invalidate inconsistent secondary legislation both from a prior and also a later date. Accordingly, the EC legislature will normally not be able to correct the Court's interpretation. In such a case, the only way for the EC institutions to overturn the Court's interpretation of the international provision at issue would conceivably be to amend the EC Treaty, or to persuade the other countries to amend the international agreement at issue. Neither alternative is practicable; the experiences with the WTO's Doha Round illustrate the difficulties international organizations have in amending or creating rules. Withdrawing from the international agreement will not be an obvious option either for the EC. Thus, once an international provision has been granted 'direct effect' it imposes an inflexible constraint on the democratic choices of the EC legislature.

From this perspective, the Court's more subtle mechanisms to ensure that EU law complies with WTO obligations appear preferable and might be applied to other international agreements.

---

[94] Case C-308/06 *R* v *Secretary of State for Transport, ex parte Intertanko* [2008] ECR I-4057, para. 65.

(ii) EU law and international law

As suggested in the discussion above, the Court of Justice respects the binding nature of international agreements. In a number of cases, the Court has also relied on rules of international law, for example stating that rules of customary international law are binding on the European Union.[95] This judicial attitude is matched by the TEU: Article 3(5) TEU provides that the Union shall contribute to, among other goals, 'the strict observance and the development of international law, including respect for the principles of the United Nations Charter'. This is in line with one of the strategic objectives of the European Security Strategy devised in 2003: contributing to well functioning international institutions and a rule-based international order, and upholding and developing international law.[96]

However, the relationship between international law and EU law has recently been addressed in a somewhat different manner in the *Kadi and Al Barakaat International Foundation* judgment. Kadi's and the foundation's financial assets in the Union had been frozen under a Regulation enacted to implement an EU common position, which in turn had been adopted to implement a UN Security Council Resolution which required all states to freeze the funds of individuals identified by the UN Sanctions Committee as supporters of terrorism. Two challenges were launched against the Council's Regulation: that it lacked an appropriate legal basis and that the measure in question infringed the applicants' fundamental right to defend themselves and their right to property.[97] The Court ruled that the Regulation did infringe these rights, but of significance is the reasoning deployed by the Court to identify the method by which it could check the legality of the Regulation, and on the relationship between the UN Security Resolution and EU fundamental rights law.

Joined Cases C-402/05 P and C-415/05 P *Kadi and Al Barakaat International Foundation v Council* [2008] ECR I-6351

282. It is also to be recalled that an international agreement cannot affect the allocation of powers fixed by the Treaties or, consequently, the autonomy of the Community legal system, observance of which is ensured by the Court by virtue of the exclusive jurisdiction conferred on it ... jurisdiction that the Court has, moreover, already held to form part of the very foundations of the Community.

283. In addition, according to settled case-law, fundamental rights form an integral part of the general principles of law whose observance the Court ensures. For that purpose, the Court draws inspiration from the constitutional traditions common to the Member States and from the guidelines supplied by international instruments for the protection of human rights on which the Member States have collaborated or to which they are signatories. In that regard, the ECHR has special significance.

284. It is also clear from the case-law that respect for human rights is a condition of the lawfulness of Community acts and that measures incompatible with respect for human rights are not acceptable in the Community.

285. It follows from all those considerations that the obligations imposed by an international agreement cannot have the effect of prejudicing the constitutional principles of the EC Treaty, which include

---

[95] For example, Case C-162/96 *Racke GmbH & Co. v Hauptzollamt Mainz* [1998] ECR I-3655, para. 46.

[96] European Council, *A Secure Europe in a Better World: European Security Strategy* (12 December 2003) 8.

[97] On these arguments, see the discussion in Chapters 5 and 6 at pp. 217–19 and pp. 231–2 respectively.

the principle that all Community acts must respect fundamental rights, that respect constituting a condition of their lawfulness which it is for the Court to review in the framework of the complete system of legal remedies established by the Treaty.

286. In this regard it must be emphasised that, in circumstances such as those of these cases, the review of lawfulness thus to be ensured by the Community judicature applies to the Community act intended to give effect to the international agreement at issue, and not to the latter as such.

287. With more particular regard to a Community act which, like the contested regulation, is intended to give effect to a resolution adopted by the Security Council under Chapter VII of the Charter of the United Nations, it is not, therefore, for the Community judicature, under the exclusive jurisdiction provided for by Article 220 EC, to review the lawfulness of such a resolution adopted by an international body, even if that review were to be limited to examination of the compatibility of that resolution with *jus cogens*.

288. However, any judgment given by the Community judicature deciding that a Community measure intended to give effect to such a resolution is contrary to a higher rule of law in the Community legal order would not entail any challenge to the primacy of that resolution in international law ...

316. ... [T]he review by the Court of the validity of any Community measure in the light of fundamental rights must be considered to be the expression, in a community based on the rule of law, of a constitutional guarantee stemming from the EC Treaty as an autonomous legal system which is not to be prejudiced by an international agreement.

317. The question of the Court's jurisdiction arises in the context of the internal and autonomous legal order of the Community, within whose ambit the contested regulation falls and in which the Court has jurisdiction to review the validity of Community measures in the light of fundamental rights.

On the one hand, the judgment should be welcomed in ensuring that suspects, whose innocence must be assumed, have adequate safeguards.[98] However it has been argued that the judgment is only good news 'to those for whom outcomes are more important than process and reasoning'.[99] In particular, a number of scholars have criticised the Court for failing to engage with international law more constructively and instead engaging in 'local constitutional resistance';[100] and have claimed that it marks a departure from the European Union's traditional engagement with international law, and its commitment to multilateralism.[101] The judgment could even be evaluated together with the case law denying direct effect to the WTO Agreement on the basis that both rulings exemplify a sort of 'selective multilateralism' whereby international obligations are respected when convenient. A further critique is that the Court of Justice did not understand its role on the global stage.

[98] For a positive assessment, see T. Tridimas and J. A. Gutierrez-Fons, 'EU Law, International Law and Economic Sanctions Against Terrorism: The Judiciary in Distress?' (2009) 32 *Fordham International Law Journal* 901.

[99] J. Weiler, 'Editorial: *Kadi* – Europe's Medellin?' (2008) 19 *EJIL* 895.

[100] D. Halberstam and E. Stein, 'The United Nations, the European Union, and the King of Sweden: Economic Sanctions and Individual Rights in a Plural World Order' (2009) 46 *CMLRev.* 13.

[101] G. de Búrca, *The EU, the European Court of Justice and the International Legal Order after Kadi*, Jean Monnet Working Paper 1/09.

J. Weiler, 'Editorial: *Kadi* – Europe's *Medellin*?' (2008) 19 *European Journal of International Law* 895, 895–6

Imagine two identical *Kadi*-like measures within the European Legal Space – one entirely autonomous (i.e., not a measure implementing a Community measure) originating in a Member State and one originating in, say, the form of a Regulation from the Council of Ministers. Imagine further that they came up for judicial review before a national court. As regards the first, we would expect the national jurisdiction to follow the domestic process, apply the domestic substantive tests for legality and constitutionality, in the course of which they would also be engaging in an inevitable 'balancing' of the values of, say, due process, natural justice, etc. against the security interests of the state. Both the factual, legal and, critically, the matrix of values at play would be, appropriately, those prevalent in the Member State (which may of course be influenced by international norms to the extent that those are received by the domestic legal order, directly or indirectly). All this would be '*normale amministrazione*'. It would not be at all '*normale amministrazione*' were the same court, in reviewing the Union measure (questions of preliminary references apart), to pursue the very same process and set of values as it applied to the purely domestic measure as if it made no difference that in one case it was dealing with an entirely domestic situation and in the other with a communitarized measure implicating the geographical, political, and value system of the entire Union. We would consider that an aberration. Both the factual and the 'valorial' matrices would be entirely different – not those of a single Member State but those of the Union as a whole, with a far more complex set of considerations which would have to go into the balancing hopper. In a domestic context, it may be considered a correct balance between individual liberty and the fight against crime that any search and seizure be accompanied by a judge-signed search warrant. In the European context, it may be considered sufficient that when searching commercial premises a warrant signed by the Commission will suffice. If so, we would expect a national judge to understand the different factual and 'valorial' contexts and be willing in principle to uphold the European measure even if an identical situation wholly within the state would be struck down.

However, one might ask why fundamental rights have a different value depending on the source of the competing interest. Surely, the basis of fundamental rights is such that they are not displaced more easily the more international the source of the restraint. It may be preferable to have multiple sources of vigilance to prevent the overly aggressive use of anti-terrorism legislation. As Advocate General Maduro opined, this is especially relevant in cases such as this one, where 'the political process is liable to become overly responsive to immediate popular concerns, leading the authorities to allay the anxieties of the many at the expense of the rights of a few'.[102]

6 COMMON FOREIGN AND SECURITY POLICY

(i) Norms and procedures of the Common Foreign and Security Policy

The Common Foreign and Security Policy (CFSP) is set out in Article 24(1) TEU.

---

[102] Joined Cases C-402/05 P and C-415/05 P *Kadi and Al Barakaat International Foundation* v *Council* [2008] ECR I-6351, para. 45.

Article 24 TEU

1. The Union's competence in matters of common foreign and security policy shall cover all areas of foreign policy and all questions relating to the Union's security, including the progressive framing of a common defence policy that might lead to a common defence...
2. Within the framework of the principles and objectives of its external action, the Union shall conduct, define and implement a common foreign and security policy, based on the development of mutual political solidarity among Member States, the identification of questions of general interest and the achievement of an ever increasing degree of convergence of Member States' actions.
3. The Member States shall support the Union's external and security policy actively and unreservedly in a spirit of loyalty and mutual solidarity and shall comply with the Union's action in this area.

    The Member States shall work together to enhance and develop their mutual political solidarity. They shall refrain from any action which is contrary to the interests of the Union or likely to impair its effectiveness as a cohesive force in international relations.

    The Council and the High Representative shall ensure compliance with these principles. ...

It is the only EU policy the detail of which is addressed within the TEU rather than the TFEU. This is, in large part, because of the uneasy relationship that this policy enjoys with other EU policies and the procedures and norms that exist more generally elsewhere within the Treaties. On the one hand, the relationship between the CFSP and these norms has been radically transformed by the Lisbon Treaty. Previously, the CFSP existed within its own pillar, the second pillar, having only a limited relationship to the activities carried out in the other two pillars. This is changed by Lisbon, which renders it part of the Union's 'External Action'. It is thus to be guided by the same set of principles, set out above in Article 21 TEU, as other EU external policies.[103] In this, it is not only to contribute to the goals of that Article but must also align itself with these other EU policies. On the other hand, CFSP is governed by a particular set of procedures and institutions, as the second paragraph of Article 24(1) TEU makes clear.

Article 24(1) TEU

...The common foreign and security policy is subject to specific rules and procedures. It shall be defined and implemented by the European Council and the Council acting unanimously, except where the Treaties provide otherwise. The adoption of legislative acts shall be excluded. The common foreign and security policy shall be put into effect by the High Representative of the Union for Foreign Affairs and Security Policy and by Member States, in accordance with the Treaties. The specific role of the European Parliament and of the Commission in this area is defined by the Treaties. The Court of Justice of the European Union shall not have jurisdiction with respect to these provisions, with the exception of its jurisdiction to monitor compliance with Article 40 of this Treaty and to review the legality of certain decisions as provided by Article 275(2) TFEU.[104]

---

[103] Article 23 TEU.
[104] Article 40 TEU relates to policing the borderline between CFSP and other EU policies. Article 275(2) TFEU relates to sanctions.

The instruments through which the CFSP is to be conducted are set out in Article 25 TEU.

Article 25 TEU

The Union shall conduct the common foreign and security policy by:

(a) defining the general guidelines,

(b) adopting decisions defining:

    (i)   actions to be undertaken by the Union;

    (ii) positions to be taken by the Union;

    (iii) arrangements for the implementation of the decisions referred to in points (i) and (ii); and by

(c) strengthening systematic cooperation between Member States in the conduct of policy.

The three mechanisms of general guidelines, decisions and systematic cooperation cannot be seen separately from their institutional context. The European Council is predominantly responsible for the first; the Council of Ministers predominantly for the second, and Member States for the third.

Article 26 TEU

1. The European Council shall identify the Union's strategic interests, determine the objectives of and define general guidelines for the common foreign and security policy, including for matters with defence implications. It shall adopt the necessary decisions.

   If international developments so require, the President of the European Council shall convene an extraordinary meeting of the European Council in order to define the strategic lines of the Union's policy in the face of such developments.

2. The Council shall frame the common foreign and security policy and take the decisions necessary for defining and implementing it on the basis of the general guidelines and strategic lines defined by the European Council.

   The Council and the High Representative of the Union for Foreign Affairs and Security Policy shall ensure the unity, consistency and effectiveness of action by the Union.

3. The common foreign and security policy shall be put into effect by the High Representative and by the Member States, using national and Union resources.

The central distinction in the CFSP is drawn between guidelines and decisions. The former steer the CFSP but have no binding effects. By contrast, decisions are binding on those to whom they are addressed just in the same way as a decision taken under one of the provisions in the TFEU.[105]

---

[105] M. Cremona, 'The Draft Constitutional Treaty: External Relations and External Action' (2003) 40 *CMLRev.* 1347, 1356.

Decisions give legal bite and substance to the CFSP in a number of ways. First, they can be used for implementing the guidelines.[106] They turn the latter into a legal reality through imposing specific duties, responsibilities and entitlements on particular actors and setting out the legal detail of a policy. Secondly, decisions are used to set out any operational action that may be required of the Union on the international scene.[107] This may include the objectives and duration of the actions, the means to be made available to the Union and the conditions for their implementation. Thirdly, decisions are used for defining the CFSP. In particular, whilst this must be done on the basis of guidelines set by the European Council,[108] the Council of Ministers can take decisions which define the Union's approach to a particular matter of a geographical or thematic nature.[109] As almost all foreign policy issues can be described either geographically or thematically, this would seem to give the Council the possibility to act as an agenda-setter in its own right.

The consequence of the wide array of matters on which decisions can be taken is that the Council of Ministers is the central actor in the CFSP. This allows the Council to define the CFSP, implement it and have control over operational matters. The impression of the Council as the central actor is reinforced by two further features.

First, a Political and Security Committee is established. Composed of top civil servants from national foreign ministries, it is, in many ways, the brain of the CFSP. It is to monitor the international situation, deliver opinions to the Council, monitor implementation of agreed policies and take strategic control of any joint defence and security operations.[110] The power of this Committee should not be understated and emphasises the control that national foreign ministries have over the CFSP.

Secondly, the voting rules create a particular relationship between the European Council and the Council of Ministers in which the former acts above all as a political brake dictating how fast the latter can go. The general voting rule is that both act by unanimity. However, there is an abstention rule whereby if a Member State abstains that will not prevent the decision being adopted unless one-third of the Member States representing one-third of the population abstain. If a state abstains and makes a declaration, it is not bound by the measure.[111] Differentiated integration is therefore the rule whereby the majority can go forward if they wish but they will carry those who have doubts. However, decisions can be taken by the Council by QMV in certain circumstances.

Article 31 TEU

2. ... the Council shall act by qualified majority:
   - when adopting a decision defining a Union action or position on the basis of a decision of the European Council relating to the Union's strategic interests and objectives, as referred to in Article 22(1),

---

[106] Article 26(1) TEU.
[107] Article 28(1) TEU.
[108] Article 26(2) TEU.
[109] Article 29 TEU.
[110] Article 38 TEU.
[111] Article 31(1) TEU.

– when adopting any decision defining a Union action or position, on a proposal which the High Representative of the Union for Foreign Affairs and Security Policy has presented following a specific request from the European Council, made on its own initiative or that of the High Representative,
– when adopting any decision implementing a decision defining a Union action or position,
– when appointing a special representative in accordance with Article 33.[112]

If a member of the Council declares that, for vital and stated reasons of national policy, it intends to oppose the adoption of a decision to be taken by qualified majority, a vote shall not be taken. The High Representative will, in close consultation with the Member State involved, search for a solution acceptable to it. If he does not succeed, the Council may, acting by a qualified majority, request that the matter be referred to the European Council for decision by unanimity.

3. The European Council may unanimously adopt a decision stipulating that the Council shall act by a qualified majority in cases other than those referred to in paragraph 2.
4. Paragraphs 2 and 3 shall not apply to decisions having military or defence implications.

The feature of all these is that a prior authorisation or prior policy has, first, been set out by the European Council. Once this is done, QMV in the Council of Ministers becomes the norm. The only checks for Member States on such QMV are that it cannot apply to military and defence matters and that a Member State for 'vital and stated reasons' can have the matter referred back to the European Council. There is a paradox here. The more decisions and policies are adopted by the European Council, the more it will empower the Council of Ministers to act by QMV relatively free from the European Council's constraints. It is possible to imagine, therefore, over time, many fields of CFSP being decided predominantly by the Council by QMV with the Political and Security Committee acting as the central agenda-setter.

(ii) The High Representative

The possibility for QMV in the Council is one supranational feature of CFSP. The other – the central innovation of the Lisbon Treaty in this field – is the High Representative. The High Representative is both a member of the Commission (one of its Vice Presidents)[113] and chairs the Council in this field,[114] albeit that she does not vote. This position whereby one person is a member of two EU institutions is unique in EU law. The reason is simple and is present in the initial description of her role 'to conduct the Union's common foreign and security policy'.[115] She is to enable a single, coherent foreign policy which brings the different actors together and which is seen by non-EU actors as a single policy. To help her in her work she is assisted with the establishment of what is in effect an EU diplomatic service. Known as the European External Action Service, it comprises Commission officials, members of the Council Secretariat, and staff seconded from national diplomatic services.[116] Whilst the High Representative is

---

[112] A special representative on a policy area can be appointed albeit under a specified mandate and under the authority of the High Representative.
[113] Article 18(1) TEU.
[114] Articles 18(2) and 27(1) TEU.
[115] Article 18(2) TEU.
[116] Article 27(3) TEU.

presented as a person, it can also be thought of as an organisation which competes with the Political and Security Committee as the brain of the CFSP. The High Representative's concrete tasks are numerous. In addition to chairing the Council, she is to:

- submit proposals on CFSP jointly with the Commission to the Council or European Council;[117]
- be the External Representative of the Union; in particular, she will conduct political dialogue with third parties on the European Union's behalf and express the Union's position in international organisations and at international conferences;[118]
- ensure the consistency of different EU policies in the field of external action;[119]
- ensure the implementation of CFSP decisions and the consistency of national positions with the CFSP;[120]
- organise the coordination of Member State action in international conferences and organisations;[121]
- preside over any special representative appointed by the Union;[122]
- act as a conduit for the supranational institutions. The High Representative does this for the Commission purely by being a member of the Commission. Whilst she has powers autonomous from the Commission, her membership would require her to listen to that institution's views. In relation to the European Parliament, she is to consult the European Parliament regularly and ensure that its views are taken into consideration.[123]

The powers are varied and wide-ranging but there are grounds to be sceptical. Put simply, can one person bring together so many different actors in such a sensitive policy field? First, it is not clear how much authority will be accorded to the High Representative by the Member States. Two Declarations were attached to the Treaty of Lisbon in which the Member States asserted that neither the High Representative nor the European External Action Service would affect their existing foreign policy powers and responsibilities, or their participation in international organisations or relations with third states.[124] If this is so, it is difficult to see how strong the High Representative's coordinating, representative or agenda-setting roles will be. Third states will continue to talk to individual states to find out their positions. Secondly, the High Representative will be in competition with other supranational actors. The President of the European Council is also to represent the Union externally.[125] In addition, various other Commissioners have portfolios with strong external dimensions (e.g. trade, development, neighbourhood, environment). Whilst these are to be without prejudice to the High Representative's role, it does suggest that a variety of actors will represent the Union internationally, and it remains to be seen whether their relationship is one based more on coordination than on competition.[126]

---

[117] Articles 22(2) and 30 TEU.
[118] Article 27(2) TEU.
[119] Articles 18(2) and 21(3) TEU.
[120] Articles 24(3) and 26(3) TEU.
[121] Article 34(1) TEU.
[122] Article 33 TEU.
[123] The European Parliament can also ask questions of the Council and hold biannual debates: Article 36 TEU.
[124] Declarations 30 and 31 on the Common Foreign and Security Policy.
[125] Article 15(6) TEU.
[126] P. Koutrakos, 'Primary Law and Policy in EU External Relations: Moving from the Big Picture' (2008) 33 *ELRev*. 666, 672–3.

(iii) National foreign policy cooperation and the autonomy of the CFSP

Although the CFSP puts in place its own institutional framework, these procedures are part of a broader regime of foreign and defence policy cooperation between Member States.

First, the Council and European Council act not just as institutions in their own right but also as forums for cooperation between the Member States. Member States are therefore to consult within both institutions to determine common approaches and before taking any action on the international scene which affects EU interests.[127] This suggests that these institutions do not just set the agenda for national foreign policies but also, conversely, are used instrumentally by Member States as settings to advance intergovernmental cooperation between themselves.

Secondly, the CFSP imposes duties of cooperation on national governments that extend beyond the aegis of the European Council and Council of Ministers. National governments are, thus, under a general duty to coordinate their actions in international organisations and conferences.[128] If certain Member States are not represented in an international organisation, other Member States must keep them and the High Representative informed of matters of common interest. Similarly, Member States sitting on the UN Security Council will keep other Member States and the High Representative fully informed.[129] Diplomatic missions of both the Member States and the Union are to cooperate ensuring that decisions defining EU positions are complied with and implemented. However, this cooperation extends not just to formal implementation, but also to exchange of information and joint assessments between the Member States.[130]

The extension of national cooperation to coordination of actions within multilateral settings, exchange of information and joint assessments widens the reach of the CFSP. However, it raises a 'chicken and egg' question. Are Member States doing this to implement an EU policy or is CFSP no more than an expression of combined national foreign policies? The case for the former is the high level of institutionalisation set out by CFSP with its particular procedures and norms, and the placing of CFSP squarely within the Treaties as an EU policy. The case for the latter is that national intergovernmental cooperation extends well beyond the institutional framework of the Council of Ministers and the European Council. Furthermore, it makes little sense therefore to talk of an EU foreign policy when the Union has no law-making power here and the roles of the traditional supranational institutions are limited. Many foreign policy measures are not adopted through the CFSP. Those adopted have no enforcement mechanisms, are subject to national vetoes and are dependent on national resources.

Larsen has argued that such an 'either/or' analysis is unhelpful. The CFSP is clearly an EU policy but it is also a highly distinctive one. Instead of trying to analyse the autonomy of the CFSP and its general effects on national policies, it is better to consider when national foreign policy is conducted within the EU context.[131] Most authors, he notes, observe that whilst this does not always happen, it does happen much of the time. In some instances, EU measures

---

[127] Article 32 TEU.
[128] Article 34(1) TEU.
[129] Article 34(2) TEU.
[130] Article 35 TEU.
[131] H. Larsen, 'A Distinct FPA for Europe? Towards a Comprehensive Framework for Analysing the Foreign Policy of EU Member States' (2009) 15 *European Journal of International Relations* 537, 543–9.

will supplement national policy here whilst in others they will supplant it. This may possibly happen because the Union brings resources that enhance an existing role, or because it allows states to have an international role or presence that they did not have previously. He observes that, in turn, participation in CFSP can shape perceptions of the collective interest that is being protected so that it is not always just a national interest but an EU one as well. However, as national traditions, perceptions and roles vary, this will not be an even process but will differ from Member State to Member State.

H. Larsen, 'A Distinct FPA for Europe? Towards a Comprehensive Framework for Analysing the Foreign Policy of EU Member States' (2009) 15 *European Journal of International Relations* 537, 551–2

The crucial question is who the 'we' is in particular policy areas and what the content, qualities and aims of this 'we' are. Countries' understandings of their own role in different functional and geographical areas of world politics vary greatly according to historical experiences and cultural background. Larger countries usually understand themselves as naturally engaged in many areas across the globe, and sometimes see themselves as natural leaders with a special responsibility for developments in these areas. Smaller countries are often more engaged in their own close surroundings and fewer policy areas. There is a huge difference between the British and French sense of natural engagement in many, if not most, international policy areas on the one hand and, for example, Luxembourg's understanding of its engagement with regard to international policy issues on the other ... But one cannot assume that being a major state always means a strong national sense of importance in a given policy area, or that smallness always means a lack of interest in a policy area. This is where a poststructuralist approach to analysing agency in foreign policy can be said to be particularly fruitful. By way of example, the relatively modest interest in Africa displayed by larger countries such as Poland or Hungary contrasts with the extensive interest and understanding of self-importance in many parts of Africa that can be found in countries such as Denmark or Sweden. In other words, it is an empirical question what the content of the presumed national 'we' is in particular areas, not one that can be derived *a priori* from size. Such understandings play a role for the different ways in which the EU policy frame is read and used. The EU policy frame may be read and used as a supplement to national efforts as is the case for Britain and France in many geographical areas, Spain with regard to Latin America and North Africa ..., Italy with regard to parts of the Mediterranean, Africa and Latin America ..., Belgium and the Netherlands with regard to their former colonies in Central Africa and Indonesia/Surinam, respectively ... or Denmark, Sweden and the Netherlands in the field of development.

Alternatively, the EU policy frame may be understood and treated as the main forum for conducting national foreign policy in the area as is the case for Denmark's policy towards Latin America or Finland and Sweden towards Russia ... Or it may be the only forum for national policy as, for example, in the case of the field of development for some of the new Member States or Greece, Belgium with regard to Albania, Cambodia or West Sahara ..., or the field of trade for all EU Member States.

Moreover, the analysis of the articulations of agency should not take for granted that the 'we' articulated is necessarily a narrow national 'we'. It is also possible that the national 'we' is articulated together with the EU, thus blurring the national character of the 'we' in particular areas.

(iv) Mission of the Common Foreign and Security Policy

The generality of the CFSP and its distinctive features raises the question of its relationship with the other EU external competences. In principle, it takes effect subject to them.

Article 40 TEU

The implementation of the common foreign and security policy shall not affect the application of the procedures and the extent of the powers of the institutions laid down by the Treaties for the exercise of the Union competences referred to in Articles 3 to 6 TFEU.

Whilst the CFSP takes subject to the exclusive and shared competences of the Union, its economic policies and supporting, supplementary and coordinating action, it does not take subject to the flexibility provision, which enables EU action where this is necessary to realise EU objectives and there is no other legislative procedure, as that provision cannot be deployed in the field of the CFSP.[132] Notwithstanding this hierarchy, there is still the question of what happens to measures which seem to be predominantly about foreign or security policy rather than environment, trade or development.

This was addressed in the *ECOWAS* judgment. In 2000, the Union signed its main development and cooperation agreement, the Cotonou Agreement, with a large number of African, Caribbean and Pacific States. The agreement provided for measures to stimulate peace-building and conflict resolution and an implementing Memorandum was signed between the Union and ECOWAS (Economic Community of West African States). This referred to the UN-sponsored moratorium on the import and export of small arms into West Africa. At the request of ECOWAS, the Union developed a technical assistance programme designed to help ECOWAS states eliminate surplus small arms and ammunition within their territories. The measure was adopted under the second pillar. The Commission challenged this, arguing it should have been adopted under the development cooperation competence of what is now Article 209 TFEU. The Commission relied, in particular, on Article 47 TEU(M), the predecessor of Article 40 TEU, which stated that nothing in the second pillar was to affect the EC Treaty. The Court of Justice found for the Commission.

Case C-91/05 *Commission v Council (ECOWAS)* [2008] ECR I-3651

60. Contrary to what is submitted by the United Kingdom Government, a measure ... affects the provisions of the EC Treaty within the meaning of Article 47 TEU whenever it could have been adopted on the basis of the EC Treaty, it being unnecessary to examine whether the measure prevents or limits the exercise by the Community of its competences. It is apparent from the case-law of the Court that, if it is established that the provisions of a measure adopted under Titles V or VI of the EU Treaty, on account of

---

[132] Article 352(4) TFEU.

both their aim and their content, have as their main purpose the implementation of a policy conferred by the EC Treaty on the Community, and if they could properly have been adopted on the basis of the EC Treaty, the Court must find that those provisions infringe Article 47 TEU ...

71. ... a concrete measure aiming to combat the proliferation of small arms and light weapons may be adopted by the Community under its development cooperation policy only if that measure, by virtue both of its aim and its content, falls within the scope of the competences conferred by the EC Treaty on the Community in that field.

72. That is not the case if such a measure, even if it contributes to the economic and social development of the developing country, has as its main purpose the implementation of the CFSP.

73. If examination of a measure reveals that it pursues a twofold aim or that it has a twofold component and if one of those is identifiable as the main one, whereas the other is merely incidental, the measure must be based on a single legal basis, namely that required by the main aim or component.

74. It follows that measures combating the proliferation of small arms and light weapons do not fall within the competences conferred on the Community in the field of development cooperation policy if, on account of their main aim or component, they are part of the pursuit of the CFSP.

75. With regard to a measure which simultaneously pursues a number of objectives or which has several components, without one being incidental to the other, the Court has held, where various legal bases of the EC Treaty are therefore applicable, that such a measure will have to be founded, exceptionally, on the various corresponding legal bases ...

76. However, under Article 47 TEU, such a solution is impossible with regard to a measure which pursues a number of objectives or which has several components falling, respectively, within development cooperation policy, as conferred by the EC Treaty on the Community, and within the CFSP, and where neither one of those components is incidental to the other.

77. Since Article 47 TEU precludes the Union from adopting, on the basis of the EU Treaty, a measure which could properly be adopted on the basis of the EC Treaty, the Union cannot have recourse to a legal basis falling within the CFSP in order to adopt provisions which also fall within a competence conferred by the EC Treaty on the Community.

The Court found that the measure pursued CFSP objectives insofar as it aimed to secure peace and stability and international security but it also pursued development cooperation objectives insofar as it sought to help a group of West African countries combat a phenomenon which hindered their path to sustainable development. As the latter was not incidental to the former, the Court ruled that the measure should have been adopted under the development cooperation provisions. A measure, following *ECOWAS*, can only be adopted under the CFSP provisions therefore if it does not relate to any of the other policies of the Treaties or these are only incidental to the aim and content of the measure.

Placing CFSP as a residual category affects evaluations of it. It cannot be about the securing of economic, ecological or social wellbeing for the citizens of the Union through cooperation with other states, as these are addressed by action under other EU law competences. Nor can it be about securing these goods for citizens of other states, as this is dealt with through Neighbourhood Policy and Development Policy. That being so, this raises the question as to the rationale of the CFSP. Looking at Article 21 TEU, there seem to be three main roles for it. These are (a) protecting the security of the Union; (b) promoting international law, democracy, human rights and good global governance; and (c) promoting international security. These roles have been reflected in the practice of the CFSP, and have led to two conceptions of it.

The first is a benign view of the CFSP as a source of normative power.[133] Such a view, rooted in the absence of an EU army and the Union being the most developed example of liberal international cooperation, characterises EU foreign policy as primarily being about the promotion of human rights, good governance and democracy. The difficulty with this argument, at least on a legal level, is that the main levers available to the Union are economic and financial, namely trade restrictions or financial aid. It is not clear, following *ECOWAS*, that such measures can be brought under CFSP. More generally, the legitimacy and effectiveness of such measures has been contested. It has opened the Union to charges of double standards and uneven implementation,[134] and, in some cases, it is not clear that EU injunctions to promote human rights have been anything more than rhetorical or, where they have been noticed, counter-productive.[135]

The second view takes an altogether different perspective. CFSP is above all seen as a security policy.[136] This policy emerges wherever the Union perceives its international environment as possessing anarchic and destabilising effects which threaten either EU interests directly or the Union's sense of its place in the world. Thus, much recent CFSP activity has focused on security threats, such as threats from perceived rogue states like Iraq under Saddam Hussein, nuclear proliferation, discontinuity of energy supplies, terrorism, the breakdown of the financial system, or violence hotspots such as Afghanistan that destabilise local regions. If this perspective is right, the predominant feature of the CFSP is not that it concerns external action but that it is about internal security. This has a number of implications.

Security is constructed in the Treaties above all as a matter of national rather than supranational concern.[137] This might explain the intergovernmentalism of the CFSP. It raises, however, more troubling issues. Those working in security studies have observed that labelling something as a threat or a security issue has powerful disenfranchising effects. Treating something as a security matter makes a distinction between somebody and something that has a right to survival and to flourish and a threat to it which does not necessarily have that right and has to be countered, or even nullified.[138] The interests behind the latter are not necessarily to be considered or debated with, but are to be confronted. In respect of countries subject to a neighbourhood policy or trade or development and cooperation agreement, the Union commits itself to a mutuality of shared interests. In the case of the CFSP, there is more often something or somebody to be combated. This may, of course, be necessary, but it begs the question when something should be considered under one heading of external action rather than the other. The other feature of treating something as a security issue is the implication that it should be subject to exceptional procedures or emergency procedures.[139] A feature of the CFSP is weak

---

[133] I. Manners, 'Normative Power Europe: A Contradiction in Terms?' (2002) 40 *JCMS* 235; H. Sjursen, 'The EU as a "Normative" Power: How Can This Be?' (2006) 13 *JEPP* 235.

[134] A. Williams, 'Enlargement and Human Rights Conditionality: A Policy of Distinction?' (2000) 25 *ELRev.* 601.

[135] The treatment of Turkey during the 1990s led it to suspend relations with the European Union. See K. Smith, 'The Evolution and Application of EU Member State Conditionality' in M. Cremona (ed.), *The Enlargement of the European Union* (Oxford, Oxford University Press, 2003).

[136] O. Wæver, 'The EU as a Security Actor: Reflections from a Pessimistic Constructivist on Post-Sovereign Security Orders' in M. Kelstrup and M. Williams (eds.), *International Relations Theory and the Politics of European Integration: Power, Security and Community* (London, Routledge, 2000).

[137] Article 4(2) TEU.

[138] B. Buzan, O, Wæver and J. de Wilde, *Security: A New Framework for Analysis* (Boulder, Lynne Riemer, 1998) 36.

[139] *Ibid.* 26.

parliamentary and judicial controls, not just at the Union level. It is not clear that there is any compensation for this at the national level, with weak controls also operating there.

7 EUROPEAN SECURITY AND DEFENCE POLICY

If a dominant part of the CFSP is about the provision of security, one would expect defence policy to be a central part of the CFSP. Indeed, the only part of the CFSP not formulated in general terms is the European Security and Defence Policy (ESDP). However, the ESDP is not a conventional defence policy whose immediate aim is protecting national territory. Instead, it is concerned with 'out-of-area' operations which take place away from the territories of the EU Member States.

Article 42(1) TEU

The common security and defence policy shall be an integral part of the common foreign and security policy. It shall provide the Union with an operational capacity drawing on civilian and military assets. The Union may use them on missions outside the Union for peace-keeping, conflict prevention and strengthening international security in accordance with the principles of the United Nations Charter. The performance of these tasks shall be undertaken using capabilities provided by the Member States.

There is provision for mutual assistance in case of attack.[140] This is not seen, however, as turning the Union into a military alliance, because the obligation is only to give aid and assistance, and not to join in collective armed struggle against the aggressor.[141] Most of the ESDP is about out-of-area action away from the territories of the Member States. As such, it is better to see it as an international security policy. This is reflected in the specific tasks that are granted to the Union for the purposes of realising the ESDP.

Article 43(1) TEU

The tasks referred to in Article 42(1), in the course of which the Union may use civilian and military means, shall include joint disarmament operations, humanitarian and rescue tasks, military advice and assistance tasks, conflict prevention and peacekeeping tasks, tasks of combat forces in crisis management, including peace-making and post-conflict stabilisation. All these tasks may contribute to the fight against terrorism, including by supporting third countries in combating terrorism in their territories.

The central tasks listed are the so-called 'Petersberg' tasks:[142] those of humanitarian intervention, conflict prevention and peace-keeping. They have little to do with defence in a narrow sense but rather (on paper at least) with securing a more liberal world order in which

---

[140] Article 42(7) TEU.

[141] See the views expressed by Council officials in House of Lords European Union Committee, *The Treaty of Lisbon: An Impact Assessment*, above n. 2, 7.113–7.117.

[142] These were first defined in 1992 by the Western European Union, a pan-European defence organisation established in 1948 to facilitate economic recovery and self-defence.

conflict is averted and human suffering mitigated.[143] However, over time, broader security dimensions have acquired a stronger emphasis. In 2003, the European Council approved a European Security Strategy which talks of the Union taking a bigger responsibility for the maintenance of global security.[144] The list of tasks in Article 43 TEU is therefore illustrative, holding out the possibility of wider types of military intervention. More concretely, the last sentence of Article 43 TEU allows for the possibility of the Union supporting non-EU states in the fight against terrorism. Reformulated, this suggests the possibility of military intervention in internal domestic conflicts between governments and their opponents.

All Member States are, in principle, to make civilian and military capabilities available for implementation of the ESDP.[145] Yet, much of it may be very controversial. Any out-of-area action smacks of neocolonialism, and suspicion increases as humanitarian justifications become less salient.[146] Some states have no modern tradition of such intervention. For others, it is best done through more established security structures such as NATO. This has led to strong differentiation within the field. Denmark has opted out of the ESDP.[147] More generally, the Treaties only talk of a progressive framing of a common security and defence policy. Such a common policy would only be realised, first, by a unanimous decision of the European Council. Even that would not be sufficient, as this would be a recommendation to the Member States which each could only adopt in accordance with its respective constitutional requirements.[148] With such high thresholds, a common defence policy is extremely unlikely in the short-medium term. This is particularly so in the light of the Declaration made by the European Council in December 2008, which enabled the second (successful) referendum on the Treaty of Lisbon in Ireland. Although adopted as a concession to Ireland, it was formulated in general terms:

> The Treaty of Lisbon does not prejudice the security and defence policy of Member States, including Ireland's traditional policy of neutrality, and the obligations of most other Member States.[149]

EU law is therefore to be understood as not prejudicing the policies of individual Member States, be it a commitment to NATO or to neutrality.

Article 42(2) TEU

The policy of the Union in accordance with this Section shall not prejudice the specific character of the security and defence policy of certain Member States and shall respect the obligations of certain Member States, which see their common defence realised in the North Atlantic Treaty Organisation (NATO), under the North Atlantic Treaty and be compatible with the common security and defence policy established within that framework.

---

[143] For an overview of EU practice up until the end of 2005 see Koutrakos, above n. 10, 463–70.

[144] EU Council, *A Secure Europe in a Better World: European Security Strategy* (Brussels, 12 December 2003) www.consilium.europa.eu/uedocs/cmsUpload/78367.pdf (accessed 20 November 2009). On the strategy see Koutrakos, above n. 10, 459–62; S. Duke, 'The European Security Strategy in a Comparative Framework: Does It Make for Secure Alliances in a Better World' (2004) 9 *EFARev.* 459.

[145] Article 42(3) TEU.

[146] W. Wagner, 'The Democratic Control of Military Power Europe' (2006) 13 *JEPP* 200.

[147] Protocol on the Position of Denmark, Article 5.

[148] Article 42(2) TEU.

[149] Conclusions of the Presidency of the European Council of 11 and 12 December 2008, Council Doc. 17271/1/08/REV1.

In many instances, therefore, not all Member States will be able to commit to EU measures. This may be for political reasons, but it may also be for operational ones, as, at any one time, only 10–15 per cent of the Union's armed forces are deemed to be deployable.[150]

In addition to providing a basis for the Petersberg tasks, a second role for the ESDP is to facilitate the development of military capabilities.

Article 42(3) TEU

Member States shall undertake progressively to improve their military capabilities. An Agency in the field of defence capabilities development, research, acquisition and armaments (hereinafter referred to as 'the European Defence Agency') shall identify operational requirements, shall promote measures to satisfy those requirements, shall contribute to identifying and, where appropriate, implementing any measure needed to strengthen the industrial and technological base of the defence sector, shall participate in defining a European capabilities and armaments policy, and shall assist the Council in evaluating the improvement of military capabilities.

The Agency was, in fact, established prior to the Lisbon Treaty.[151] Member States are free to participate within the Agency or with specific groups working on joint projects.[152] Whilst it has established a voluntary Code of Conduct on procurement, its early years were bedevilled by disputes about its budget which were, in reality, disputes about how much influence it should wield.[153] This does not augur well for realisation of the central goal of the establishment of permanent structured cooperation. This is a form of enhanced cooperation open to those states who have both a political will to engage in a stronger EU defence policy and a commitment to a higher level of military capability.[154] States wishing to participate in it must notify the Council, who will decide by QMV whether they meet a number of criteria.[155] The two central ones are that each Member State must agree (a) to develop its defence capabilities through contributions in multinational forces, the European Defence Agency and European equipment programmes; and (b) be ready by 2010 to supply targeted combat units for realisation of the Petersberg tasks.[156] The ethos behind this initiative is to enable Member States to have greater possibilities for intervention through pooling resources, and also to stimulate defence spending and interoperability between national units.

---

[150] S. Biscop, 'Permanent Structured Cooperation and the Future of the ESDP: Transformation and Integration' (2008) 13 *EFRARev.* 431.

[151] Joint Action 2004/551/CFSP [2004] OJ L245/17. For discussion see M. Trybus, 'The New European Defence Agency: A Contribution to a Common European Security and Defence Policy or a Challenge to the Community Acquis?' (2006) 43 *CMLRev.* 667.

[152] Article 45(2) TEU. Its tasks are identified in more detail in Article 45(1) TEU.

[153] P. Koutrakos, 'Primary Law and Policy in EU External Relations: Moving from the Big Picture' (2008) 33 *ELRev.* 666, 680–1.

[154] Article 42(6) TEU. See the article by Biscop, above n. 150.

[155] Article 46 TEU.

[156] Protocol on Permanent Structured Cooperation Established by Article 42(6) TEU, Article 1.

FURTHER READING

G. de Baere, *Constitutional Principles of EU External Relations* (Oxford, Oxford University Press, 2008)

G. de Búrca, *The EU, the European Court of Justice and the International Legal Order after Kadi*, Jean Monnet Working Paper 1/09

M. Cremona, 'The Draft Constitutional Treaty: External Relations and External Action' (2003) 40 *Common Market Law Review* 1347

M. Cremona and B. De Witte (eds.), *EU Foreign Relations Law: Constitutional Fundamentals* (Oxford and Portland, Hart, 2008)

P. Eeckhout, *The External Relations of the European Union: Legal and Constitutional Foundations* (Oxford, Oxford University Press, 2004)

S. Keukeleire and J. MacNaughtan, *The Foreign Policy of the European Union* (Palgrave Macmillan, Basingstoke, 2008)

P. Koutrakos, *EU International Relations Law* (Oxford and Portland, Hart, 2006)
'Primary Law and Policy in EU External Relations: Moving from the Big Picture' (2008) 33 *European Law Review* 666

P. Koutrakos and C. Hillion (eds.), *Mixed Agreements Revisited: The EU and Its Member States in the World* (Oxford and Portland, Hart, 2010)

S. Meunier and K. Nicolaïdis, 'The European Union as a Conflicted Trade Power' (2006) 13 *Journal of European Public Policy* 906

W. Wagner, 'The Democratic Control of Military Power Europe' (2006) 13 *Journal of European Public Policy* 200

16

The Internal Market

CONTENTS

1 INTRODUCTION

This chapter provides an overview of what the internal market is, and the current debates about what it should be. It provides background and context to the chapters on free movement which follow. The chapter is organised as follows.

Section 2 sets out the purposes of the internal market. Primarily, the internal market aims to integrate the national markets of the Member States into a single European market. It does this by removing regulatory barriers to trade between states. The reasons for pursing this project are partly economic, but also social and political: for some, the market entrenches a form of individualism (ordoliberalism) that has strong roots in continental European philosophy, while for others, its main benefit is that it sucks Member States into deeper integration in other areas. More recently, it has come to be seen by many as a regulatory project, balancing social and economic interests.

Section 3 considers the legal tools used to build the internal market and the concepts underlying them. As well as free trade, a central idea in the internal market is that of 'undistorted competition'. If states have different rules on matters relevant to industry (for example, environmental or labour law), then companies in states with low regulatory burdens will have an advantage. This may be economically problematic, but is also seen as unfair. Harmonisation often aims to remove such distortions.

Section 4 discusses competence to harmonise. Harmonisation is the replacement of national laws by a common Union-wide law. The most important legal basis for internal market harmonisation is Article 114 TFEU, which is controversial because it appears to be very broad. In *Tobacco Advertising I*, the Court of Justice set some limits: distortions of competition can only be harmonised away when they are 'appreciable'. However, this is not very precise. Moreover, recent cases show that, under certain conditions, Article 114 can be used to set up new agencies and regulatory bodies.

Sections 5 and 6 consider techniques of harmonisation and the problems they bring. Harmonisation is a difficult political and technical process. In recent years, the Union has been using the 'new approach', in which legislation concentrates on laying down general safety and health standards, while European standardisation agencies work these out in detail. This has been fairly successful, but attracts some democratic criticism: are these agencies accountable and do they take into account interests that are not scientific or economic? This last question is particularly important where EU law touches on matters that are politically sensitive, such as Genetically Modified Organisms (GMOs). Many scholars take the view that decentralising much market regulation away from the representative bodies – the Council and Parliament – to the Commission and agencies has made decisions so technocratic and science-based that there is a danger that ethical and social concerns are no longer heard. Others argue that this is precisely the point: Member States want the Union to be an objective regulator, beyond the reach of populist whims.

Section 7 discusses regulatory competition. Many internal market debates can be reduced to 'Should the Union regulate, or should the Member States?' Regulatory competition is an important part of this question. If states can choose their own rules, some fear that they will lower standards in order to attract business. Other states will be forced to follow and there will be a 'race to the bottom', in which social and environmental policies are sacrificed to business interests. This view supports widespread harmonisation. Others argue that the race to the bottom does not happen in practice: businesses do not just want low standards. There are reasons why they may even prefer states with high standards and well-functioning social welfare systems. Finding the right compromise means preventing destructive competition, while still allowing states enough autonomy to experiment, reflect local preferences and learn from each other.

2 PURPOSE OF THE INTERNAL MARKET

For most of the history of the Union, its central policy has been the creation of the internal market (or single market, or common market, as it has been called at various times).[1] The reasons for this are diverse. The classical economic perception that because nations do not do everything equally well or efficiently, trade between nations can be beneficial for all, has of

---

[1] See K. Mortelmans, 'The Common Market, the Internal Market and the Single Market: What's in a Market?' (1998) 35 *CMLRev.* 101; L. W. Gormley, 'Competition and Free Movement: Is the Internal Market the Same as a Common Market?' (2002) 13 *EBLRev.* 522.

course always been important.[2] However, the internal market has ambitions beyond interstate trade. It aims to merge the markets of the Member States into one larger market, something which entails a greater degree of uniformity of structure and conditions. This is partly at odds with the simple trade-maximisation approach: instead of only capitalising on difference, the Union aims to reduce it. While such homogeneity may bring economic benefits, notably via economies of scale as firms become European rather than purely national operators, the integrative goals of the market reveal that it is not, and never has been, just an economic policy.

On the contrary, a number of normative agendas were prominent in defining and shaping the Treaty rules. First, economic integration was seen as an essential step towards social and political integration. The neofunctionalist analysis of European integration, associated with Haas, argued that because of the interconnection of policy areas, integration in one would lead inevitably to integration in another.[3] This theory is no longer dominant, or even widely accepted in its pure form, but it played a significant role in early support for the internal market. Even today it resonates. Many of the cases in the following chapters show how an apparently simple desire to facilitate interstate transactions has led to involvement of the Union in matters of broader social concern, be it with the families and working conditions of workers, or with the quality of foodstuffs. The following extract portrays a recent theory of integration which maintains some of these ideas, while also emphasising the role of Member States in steering integration.

**A. Stone Sweet and W. Sandholtz, 'European Integration and Supranational Governance'
(1997) 4** *Journal of European Public Policy* **297, 299–300**

We claim that transnational activity has been the catalyst of European integration; but transnational exchange cannot, in and of itself, determine the specific details, or the precise timing, of Community rule-making. Instead it provokes, or activates, the Community's decision-making bodies, including the Council of Ministers. Member state governments often possess (but not always) the means to facilitate or to obstruct rule-making, and they use these powers frequently. Nevertheless, we argue, among other things, that as transnational exchange rises in any specific domain (or cluster of related domains), so do the costs, for governments, of maintaining disparate national rules. As these costs rise, so do incentives for governments to adjust their policy positions in ways that favor the expansion of supranational governance. Once fixed in a given domain, European rules – such as relevant treaty provisions, secondary legislation, and the European Court of Justice's (ECJ's) case law – generate a self-sustaining dynamic that leads to the gradual deepening of integration in that sector and, not uncommonly, to spillovers into other sectors. Thus, we view intergovernmental bargaining and decision-making as embedded in processes that are provoked and sustained by the expansion of transnational society, the pro-integrative activities of supranational organizations, and the growing density of supranational rules. And, we will argue, these processes gradually, but inevitably, reduce the capacity of the member states to control outcomes.

---

[2] See D. Ricardo, *On the Principles of Political Economy and Taxation* (London, John Murray, 1821), also available at www.econlib.org/library/Ricardo/ricP.html, and S. Suranovic, 'The Theory of Comparative Advantage' ch. 40 in *International Trade Theory and Policy* (Center for International Economic Policy, George Washington University), available at http://internationalecon.com/Trade/tradehome.php.

[3] See J. Ruggie, P. Katzenstein, R. Keohane and P. Schmitter, 'Transformations in World Politics: The Intellectual Contributions of Ernst B. Haas' (2005) 8 *Annual Review of Political Science* 271.

Secondly, many of the most ardent early supporters of the internal market were believers in ordoliberalism. This political view, with origins in early twentieth-century Germany, regards the regulation of economic activity as essentially about the regulation of public and private power.[4] On the one hand, competition law is necessary to prevent private power becoming dominant enough to challenge the state. But on the other hand, individual economic rights are a normative good in themselves and an important bulwark against tyranny.

M. Maduro, 'Reforming the Market or the State? Article 30 and the European Constitution:[5] Economic Freedom and Political Rights' (1997) 3 *European Law Journal* 55, 61–2

Neo-liberal or 'laissez-faire' interpretations of the free movement rules and of the European Economic Constitution owe much to traditional ordo-liberal theories and their contribution in both the initial debate on European integration and in the provision of a coherent theoretical framework for an understanding of integration. The ordo-liberal aim is the creation of a free-market, liberal economy, protected through constitutional principles... The main concern is a political one: the protection of a free and equal society. 'Within society itself no power groups should be formed which would make it possible for others, individually or as groups, to be subjugated and exploited.' Ordo-liberals and other neo-liberals have been active participants in the project of European integration; they entrusted to Community law the process of constitutionalising a free market economy with undistorted competition.

...It should be recalled that these neo-liberal ideas developed as a reaction to recent German and European history. For Röpke, there was an inevitable connection between the aims of individual freedom and the avoidance of nationalism, on the one hand, and free trade and the prevention of state control of the economy, on the other. According to ordo-liberals and other neo-liberals, the failure of the initial device of separation of powers to achieve its aim of controlling power and government meant that a new device had to be created. That device was a federation of States with an international authority to limit governments' economic powers and assure international order without taking over the power of the States. The division of powers inherent in this form of federalism 'would inevitably act at the same time also as a limitation of the power of the whole as well as of the individual state'. Hence, a federation is seen more as a source of individual rights than as a source of common policies.

Trade facilitation, empowerment of individuals, and the integration of Europe all continue to influence market-building decisions today.

3 LEGAL FRAMEWORK OF THE INTERNAL MARKET

The umbrella Treaty article is Article 26 TFEU.

---

[4] See D. Gerber, *Law and Competition in Twentieth Century Europe: Protecting Prometheus* (Oxford, Oxford University Press, 1998).

[5] Article 30 is now Article 34 TFEU.

> **Article 26 TFEU**
>
> 1. The Union shall adopt measures with the aim of establishing or ensuring the functioning of the internal market, in accordance with the relevant provisions of the Treaties.
> 2. The internal market shall comprise an area without internal frontiers in which the free movement of goods, persons, services and capital is ensured in accordance with the provisions of the Treaties...

One way of achieving the goals of Article 26 is by the development of Union-wide rules on matters which may affect interstate trade, such as product standards and consumer rights. Such harmonisation is discussed further in the next section. However, the requirement to abolish borders is also developed later in the Treaty in a number of specific Treaty Articles, which are the subject of the following chapters. These Articles prohibit restrictions on the free movement of goods, persons, services and capital. The essential question of all these Articles is what this prohibition means. What is free movement? What is a restriction on this? There are so many measures, public and private, which might tend to make us stay at home (trains still aren't free). Which should be caught and which not? There is an ongoing debate between two views. One is that only measures which make movement across borders harder than staying at home, or which discriminate against the foreign, should be caught: the idea of a restriction on movement between states entails some kind of comparison.[6] Advocate General Maduro considered in a recent case how the Court of Justice should interpret the provisions in the Treaty on the free movement of goods.

> **Joined Cases C-158/04 and C-159/04 *Alfa Vita Vassilopoulos AE v Elliniko Dimosio, Nomarkhiaki Aftodioikisi Ioanninon; Carrefour Marinopoulos AE v Elliniko Dimosio, Nomarkhiaki Aftodioikisi Ioanninon* [2006] ECR I-8135, Advocate General M. Poiares Maduro**
>
> 41. In such circumstances it is obvious that the task of the Court is not to call into question as a matter of course Member States' economic policies. It is instead responsible for satisfying itself that those States do not adopt measures which, in actual fact, lead to *cross-border situations being treated less favourably than purely national situations.*
> 42. In order to carry out such a review, it is necessary to rely on concrete criteria. Three principal criteria can be drawn from the relevant case-law.
> 43. Firstly, the Court maintains, in this respect, that any discrimination based on nationality, whether direct or indirect, is prohibited. For example, it is clear that a publicity campaign promoting the purchase of national products to the detriment of intra-Community trade constitutes a breach of Treaty rules.
> 44. Secondly, it is established that imposing supplementary costs on goods in circulation in the Community or on traders carrying out a cross-border activity creates a barrier to trade which needs to be duly justified...

[6] G. Marenco, 'Pour une interpretation traditionelle de la notion de mesure d'effet équivalent à une restriction quantitative' (1984) *Cahiers du Droit Européen* 291; J. Snell, *Free Movement of Goods and Services in EC Law* (Oxford, Oxford University Press, 2002); G. Davies, *Nationality Discrimination in the European Internal Market* (The Hague, Kluwer Law International, 2003).

45. Thirdly, any measure which impedes to a greater extent the access to the market and the putting into circulation of products from other Member States is considered to be a measure having equivalent effect within the meaning of Article [34 TFEU]...

46. It seems to me that a consistent approach emerges from this case-law. These three criteria, as they have been applied by the Court, amount in substance to identifying *discrimination against the exercise of freedom of movement.*

The Advocate General suggests that the Treaty internal market rules should aim to remove measures that have some specifically trade-negative effect, rather than those which just diminish economic activity generally.

The other view, put forcefully by Advocate General Jacobs and developed by several academic writers, is that comparison is irrelevant.[7] Any measure restricting cross-border movement is clearly caught, whether or not it has an equivalent domestic effect.

Case C–412/93 *Société d'Importation Edouard Leclerc-Siplec v TF1 Publicité SA and M6 Publicité SA* [1995] ECR I-179, Opinion of Advocate General Jacobs

39. Secondly, the exclusion from the scope of Article [34 TFEU] of measures which 'affect in the same manner, in law and in fact, the marketing of domestic products and those from other Member States' amounts to introducing, in relation to restrictions on selling arrangements, a test of discrimination. That test, however, seems inappropriate. The central concern of the Treaty provisions on the free movement of goods is to prevent unjustified obstacles to trade between Member States. If an obstacle to inter-State trade exists, it cannot cease to exist simply because an identical obstacle affects domestic trade. I have difficulty in accepting the proposition that a Member State may arbitrarily restrict the marketing of goods from another Member State, provided only that it imposes the same arbitrary restriction on the marketing of domestic goods. If a Member State imposes a substantial barrier on access to the market for certain products, for example, by providing that they may be sold only in a very limited number of establishments and a manufacturer of those products in another Member State suffers economic loss as a result, he will derive little consolation from the knowledge that a similar loss is sustained by his competitors in the Member State which imposes the restriction.

40. Equally, from the point of view of the Treaty's concern to establish a single market, discrimination is not a helpful criterion: from that point of view, the fact that a Member State imposes similar restrictions on the marketing of domestic goods is simply irrelevant. The adverse effect on the Community market is in no way alleviated; nor is the adverse effect on the economies of the other Member States, and so on the Community economy. Indeed the application of the discrimination test would lead to the fragmentation of the Community market, since traders would have to accept whatever restrictions on selling arrangements happened to exist in each Member State, and would have to adapt their own arrangements accordingly in each State. Restrictions on trade should not be tested against local conditions which happen to prevail in each Member State, but against the aim of access to the entire Community market. A discrimination test is therefore inconsistent as a matter of principle with the aims of the Treaty.

---

[7] S. Weatherill, 'After Keck: Some Thoughts on How to Clarify the Clarification' (1996) 33 *CMLRev.* 885; C. Barnard 'Fitting the Remaining Pieces into the Goods and Persons Jigsaw' (2001) 26 *ELRev.* 35.

> 41. The question then is what test should be applied in order to determine whether a measure falls within the scope of Article [34 TFEU]. There is one guiding principle which seems to provide an appropriate test: that principle is that all undertakings which engage in a legitimate economic activity in a Member State should have unfettered access to the whole of the Community market, unless there is a valid reason for denying them full access to a part of that market...
>
> 42. If the principle is that all undertakings should have unfettered access to the whole of the Community market, then the appropriate test in my view is whether there is a substantial restriction on that access...

This extract, like the preceding one, concerns the law on goods, but the analyses are equally relevant to the other freedoms. Advocate General Jacobs is presenting a vision of the Treaty as a tool for deregulation and trade-facilitation per se. If this is not to result in the abolition of huge amounts of law, it is because measures which seem to be reasonable may, he proposes, remain.[8] The Treaty rules on free movement would then amount to a general proportionality review of national law affecting economic activity.[9] This might have the effect of creating a more dynamic and integrated European marketplace, but would expand the scope of EU law at the expense of national autonomy.[10] The debate over the scope of free movement is essentially about this.

A number of other legal tools also contribute to free movement. Article 30 TFEU prohibits customs duties between Member States, while Article 110 TFEU prohibits discriminatory taxation on foreign goods. Customs duties, although now rarely an issue, were the primary obstacle to movement in the early days of the Union. Article 110 continues to be important. It provides as follows.

Article 110 TFEU

No Member State shall impose, directly or indirectly, on the products of other Member States any internal taxation of any kind in excess of that imposed directly or indirectly on similar domestic products.

Furthermore, no Member State shall impose on the products of other Member States any internal taxation of such a nature as to afford indirect protection to other products.

The Court has interpreted this globally as imposing a rationality requirement on the taxation of goods, to prevent covert protectionism.

---

[8] *Ibid.*

[9] E. Spaventa, 'From Gebhard to Carpenter. Towards a (Non)economic European Constitution' (2004) 41 *CMLRev.* 743; M. Dougan, 'The Constitutional Dimension to the Case Law on Union Citizenship' (2006) 31 *ELRev.* 613.

[10] Spaventa, above n. 9.

Case C-221/06 *Stadtgemeinde Frohnleiten* [2007] ECR I-9643

56. First of all, although it is settled case-law that, as it now stands, Community law does not restrict the freedom of each Member State to establish a tax system which differentiates between certain products, even products which are similar within the meaning of the first paragraph of Article [110 TFEU], on the basis of objective criteria, such differentiation is compatible with Community law, however, only if it pursues objectives which are themselves compatible with the requirements of the Treaty and its secondary legislation, and if the detailed rules are such as to avoid any form of discrimination, direct or indirect, against imports from other Member States or any form of protection of competing domestic products.

A particular issue is what kind of criteria may be used: do they have to be related to the physical product, or can they extend to the way it is made? This is of increasing importance as Member States seek to use tax policy to encourage respect for social interests and human rights, or environmentally friendly production of goods such as wood and electricity. They increasingly wish to impose taxes linked to sustainability, carbon dioxide emissions, or good labour practices, none of which are reflected directly in the finished product. The reason to permit this is that it allows tax to be used as a progressive tool of social engineering. The reason to be suspicious is that it results in different taxes being imposed on apparently identical products and may be a back-door to protectionism. In *Outokumpu Oy*,[11] the Court seemed to cautiously open the door to social- and environmental-impact taxation. It found that tax criteria might include factors 'such as the nature of the raw materials used or the production processes employed'. A tax benefit for green electricity was therefore permitted.

Analogous issues arise in the context of the Directives on public procurement, an important part of the free movement acquis.[12] Here, states increasingly try to use their purchasing power to influence the social and environmental behaviour of suppliers, by requiring them to comply with conditions if they wish to supply public bodies. There is a growing scholarship on the legality of this.[13] Such demands may also amount to closet protectionism, requiring foreign suppliers to conform to local norms, even when producing in their home jurisdiction.

The public procurement Directives require public bodies to tender openly and Europe-wide for purchases above a certain threshold. This has admirable goals: the state is by far the largest purchaser of goods and services and has tended traditionally to purchase from favoured suppliers, who were usually national. Yet, the attempt to break open public purchasing markets has been a challenge, with intensely complicated procedural requirements employed in order to minimise discretionary space which might be used for secret favouritism. Despite such efforts, and the transaction costs they bring for public bodies, public markets are not yet considered to have been opened to the extent that private ones have. The difficulties and ambitions are outlined by Bovis.

---

[11] Case C-213/96 *Outokumpu Oy* [1998] ECR I-1777.

[12] Directive 2004/18/EC on the coordination of procedures for the award of public works contracts, public supply contracts and public service contracts [2004] OJ L134/114; Directive 2004/17/EC coordinating the procurement procedures of entities operating in the water, energy, transport and postal services sectors [2004] OJ L134/1.

[13] C. McCrudden, *Purchasing Social Justice* (Oxford, Oxford University Press, 2007); C. Hilson, 'Going Local? EU Law, Localism and Climate Change' (2008) 33 *EL Rev.* 194; G. Davies, 'Process and Production Method-Based Trade Restrictions in the EU' (2007–08) 10 *CYELS* 69.

C. Bovis, 'The Regulation of Public Procurement as a Key Element of European Economic Law' (1998) 4 *European Law Journal* 220, 224–5, 229

After all the attempts of European institutions to stimulate the demand side of public procurement in the Member States, one could justifiably question the relative slow progress and the underlying reasons behind such a recalcitrant rejection of the envisaged competitive regime in public markets. The answer seems simple, although cynical in terms of reference to commitment to European integration and the completion and functioning of a genuinely common market in Europe. By perpetuating discriminatory and preferential public purchasing, Member States pay attention to immediate needs relating to domestic / national priorities such as balance of payments, sustainability of strategic industries, employment and, last but not least, national pride. This exercise, in terms of the envisaged integrated public markets of the EU, represents a sub-optimal allocation of resources (human and capital) throughout the common market at the expense of the public sector, which pays more than it should for equivalent or even better products or deliveries. It is tantamount to geographical market segmentation imposed by the demand side on the supply side, with a view to determining and controlling the latter as far as its activities vis-à-vis the public sector are concerned...

Combating discrimination on grounds of nationality in public procurement and eliminating domestic preferential purchasing schemes could result in efficiency gains at European and national levels through three major effects which would influence the supply side. These include a trade effect, a competition effect and a restructuring effect. The trade effect is associated with the actual and potential savings that the public sector will be able to achieve through lower cost purchasing. This effect appears to have a static dimension. On the other hand, the competition effect relates to the changes of price behaviour of national firms which have been protected from competition by means of discriminatory procurement practices. Finally, the third effect reflects the restructuring dimension in the supply side as a result of increased competition. The restructuring effect is dynamic and refers to the long-term...

Making interstate trade easier has consequences for competition. The removal of borders exposes national firms to foreign competition. This generates lobbying for two kinds of rules. First, there is a consensus that the behaviour of firms in the European market requires regulation both in the interests of economic wellbeing (preventing, for example, the exploitation of consumers by Europe-wide monopolists), and of interfirm fairness (say, larger firms in one state dominating or crushing smaller ones elsewhere).[14] Hence, a European-wide competition law, the subject of Chapters 22 to 24, has always been a part of Union market-building. Secondly, the creation of interstate competition draws attention to the fact that the conditions under which businesses operate vary significantly from Member State to Member State. Prices and taxes vary, but so do regulations. Variations in, particularly, labour law and environmental rules may provide a significant advantage for firms located in one state rather than another, as it is often expensive to comply with social and environmental requirements. Industrial lobbies are quick to cry that such disparities create unfair competition. The firm in a state which requires six weeks paid holiday, a minimum wage, and the recycling of waste may find itself unable to compete with a competitor located in a place where none of these things are required.

[14] R. Van der Laan and A. Nentjes, 'Competitive Distortions in EU Environmental Legislation: Inefficiency versus Inequity' (2001) 11 *EJL and E* 131.

This creates a political momentum for the replacement of diverse national rules by a common Union-wide one. Such political harmonisation has inevitably a somewhat ad hoc character. Some matters which are important to competitiveness lend themselves to harmonisation, notably environmental regulation of industry, on which a social and political consensus can often be reached, and where uniform standards are practically achievable. However, the creation of uniform tax rates has always been politically impossible (although a legal basis exists: see Articles 113 and 115 TFEU), while the creation of uniform wage levels is economically impossible. Thus, it seems that two of the most important factors affecting location-based competitiveness are largely outside the power of the Union to address.

The economics of harmonisation tends to regard cost differences between states as less problematic.[15] Considering welfare as a whole, the loss to country Y when its industry migrates to a low cost jurisdiction is often outweighed by the benefit of cheaper products combined with the benefit to country X, to where the industry has moved. Moreover, where a competitive edge is obtained by matters such as loose environmental or social standards, this may simply reflect different preferences. Perhaps people in country X don't care as much about holidays or clean rivers? In that case, it is better if dirty and labour-intensive industry moves to X. On this view, the major – some argue the only – reason to adopt obligatory harmonisation is where there are interstate externalities.[16] These occur where a part of the cost of an activity is not taken into account in its production because the producer is able to 'dump' that cost on someone else. Thus, if industry in country X emits air pollution which makes the population of that country less healthy, but they think the benefits of increased industrial profit, or increased economic dynamism, are worthwhile, there is an argument that this is their free choice, to be respected. However, if prevailing winds blow that air pollution over to another state and make people ill there, then in fact country X is not 'internalising' the costs of its industry, and the low price which products from X bear is not their 'real' price. Here, there is an interstate externality which justifies interstate rules.[17]

The question of when harmonisation is appropriate is one of the most bitterly contested in EU law.[18] The economic approach outlined above assumes democracy: that the local regulation genuinely reflects the preferences of the population. Yet, preferences are not static, and a more ambitious, political approach to the Union sees it partly as a mechanism to develop preferences and change the world views of its citizens. The economic approach also ignores the political sustainability of a Union of widely diverging preferences. An irony of a narrowly economic approach to harmonisation may be that it leads to political stresses which result in greater protectionism and a diminished market – and so, in fact, less of the benefits of interstate trade.

---

[15] A. Ogus, 'Competition Between National Legal Systems: A Contribution of Economic Analysis to Comparative Law' (1999) 48 *ICLQ* 405.

[16] *Ibid.*

[17] J. N. Bhagwati and R. Hudoc (eds.), *Fair Trade and Harmonization: An Economic Analysis* (Massachusetts, Massachusetts Institute of Technology Press, 1996).

[18] See for overviews e.g. S. Woolcock, 'Competition Among Rules in the Single European Market' in W. Bratton, J. McCahery, S. Picciotto and C. Scott (eds.), *International Regulatory Competition and Coordination: Perspectives on Economic Regulation in Europe and the United States* (Oxford, Oxford University Press, 1996); R. van den Bergh, 'Regulatory Competition or Harmonization of Laws? Guidelines for the European Regulator' in A. Marciano and J.-M. Josselin, *The Economics of Harmonizing European Law* (Cheltenham, Edward Elgar, 2002); Z. Drabak, 'Limits to the Harmonisation of Domestic Regulations' (2008) 2 *Journal of International Trade and Diplomacy* 47; G. Wagner, 'The Economics of Harmonisation: The Case of Contracts' (2002) 39 *CML Rev.* 995.

As a result, decisions to harmonise to remove what EU law calls 'distortions of competition' continue to be a complex intertwining of political, social and economic arguments.[19] As is discussed below,[20] the legal conditions for such harmonisation are open enough to allow considerable legislative discretion.

The final tool in the internal market toolbox is the law on state aid. Allowing a national champion to fail often brings a high political price and the instinct of governments is to reach for their wallet. In general, this is prohibited by the Treaty, in Article 107 TFEU, which provides only limited derogations for exceptional situations, such as situations following a natural disaster, or where a failure would have unacceptable social consequences, such as the failure of a bank.

State aid raises complex issues. It has been said that the proper response to state aid by a foreign government is 'thank you'.[21] If Germany subsidises Volkswagen, then insofar as the cars produced are bought in Germany this is just money going in circles. But if the cars are exported, then the German tax-payer is in fact subsidising foreign consumers. However, if the result is that foreign car producers are threatened, then the political perception will inevitably be different, and this may also make economic sense. First, while it may be good for us as consumers if the German state wishes to subsidise our cars, this requires our industry to adapt to making something else. That is not always easy, nor costless. Investment in such adaptation costs may be particularly problematic if it is not certain how long the German subsidies will exist. This leads to the second objection to state aid; it can be used as a tactical short-term measure. By ensuring that a national champion emerges stronger from a crisis, a state may enable that champion to take longer term European-wide profits in a market from which many of its competitors have disappeared. Both arguments are particularly forceful in markets where there are high barriers to entry and exit. Finally, there is a fear that state aid by one state will make it politically impossible for other states not to aid their local industries. Permitting government support of industry may therefore lead to a spiral of subsidy which will not result in a generally efficient economy. The state aid ban may be seen as a pact between states not to engage in a form of financial mutual-assured-destruction.

One of the difficulties surrounding state aid is distinguishing between public measures which help industry generally, and those which help specific industries. The internal market has no objection to states which invest in infrastructure or education and training, even though this is all public money which will benefit local industry. However, if that money is used in a way which only benefits specific firms, then it will be state aid. This distinction has as much political as economic basis, and just how political it can be was highlighted in the recent *Azores* case. The Azores is an island group in the Atlantic that belongs to Portugal. Because it is a relatively poor part of the country, the government provided support to the local economy by imposing a lower rate of tax on firms in the Azores than on firms elsewhere in Portugal. This clearly helped industry in the Azores, but was the measure sufficiently specific that it amounted to state aid?

---

[19] Van der Laan and Nentjes, above n. 14; S. Weatherill, 'Why Harmonise?' in T. Tridimas and P. Nebbia, *European Union Law for the Twenty-First Century* (Oxford and Portland, Hart, 2004) 11.

[20] See pp. 686–95.

[21] See Alan O. Sykes, 'Countervailing Duty Law: An Economic Perspective' (1989) *Colum. L Rev.* 199.

Case C-88/03 *Portugal* v *Commission (Azores)* [2006] ECR I-7115

63. In paragraph 50 *et seq* of his Opinion, the Advocate General specifically identified three situations in which the issue of the classification as State aid of a measure seeking to establish, in a limited geographical area, tax rates lower than the rates in force nationally may arise.

64. In the first situation, the central government unilaterally decides that the applicable national tax rate should be reduced within a defined geographic area. The second situation corresponds to a model for distribution of tax competences in which all the local authorities at the same level (regions, districts or others) have the autonomous power to decide, within the limit of the powers conferred on them, the tax rate applicable in the territory within their competence. The Commission has recognised, as have the Portuguese and United Kingdom Governments, that a measure taken by a local authority in the second situation is not selective because it is impossible to determine a normal tax rate capable of constituting the reference framework.

65. In the third situation described, a regional or local authority adopts, in the exercise of sufficiently autonomous powers in relation to the central power, a tax rate lower than the national rate and which is applicable only to undertakings present in the territory within its competence.

66. In the latter situation, the legal framework appropriate to determine the selectivity of a tax measure may be limited to the geographical area concerned where the infra-State body, in particular on account of its status and powers, occupies a fundamental role in the definition of the political and economic environment in which the undertakings present on the territory within its competence operate.

67. As the Advocate General pointed out in paragraph 54 of his Opinion, in order that a decision taken in such circumstances can be regarded as having been adopted in the exercise of sufficiently autonomous powers, that decision must, first of all, have been taken by a regional or local authority which has, from a constitutional point of view, a political and administrative status separate from that of the central government. Next, it must have been adopted without the central government being able to directly intervene as regards its content. Finally, the financial consequences of a reduction of the national tax rate for undertakings in the region must not be offset by aid or subsidies from other regions or central government.

68. It follows that political and fiscal independence of central government which is sufficient as regards the application of Community rules on State aid presupposes, as the United Kingdom Government submitted, that the infra-State body not only has powers in the territory within its competence to adopt measures reducing the tax rate, regardless of any considerations related to the conduct of the central State, but that in addition it assumes the political and financial consequences of such a measure.

The Court found that whether or not the tax rate was state aid depended on the degree of financial autonomy that the region enjoyed. If it could determine its own tax rates, and bore the consequences of them in lower tax receipts for the regional government, then there was no question of state aid. This was just general tax policy being carried out at the level of government provided for by the Portuguese constitutional system. However, if the central government in fact ensured that the Azorean government did not bear any consequences from the lower tax rate, by providing central funds to compensate for diminished receipts, then there was in fact a central subsidy to a selected group of firms – Azorean firms. This was the case, so the Azorean tax break was state aid.

This has constitutional implications.[22] Generality and specificity are to be judged by looking at constitutional structure. If a central government targets a specific area, this will be specific.

---

[22] See R. Greaves, 'Autonomous Regions, Taxation and EC State Aids Rules' (2009) 34 *ELRev.* 779; J. A. Winter, annotation at (2008) 45 *CMLRev.* 183.

If a local government takes measures for all of its area, this will be general. State aid law encourages fiscal decentralisation, a matter of great constitutional sensitivity. It is acceptable for a financially autonomous Basque country to support Basque industry, but not for Madrid to do the same. This was precisely the issue in *Unión General de Trabajadores de La Rioja*, which followed the *Azores* case.[23] Here, the Court of Justice found that the constitutional and legal relationship between the Basque country and the central government of Spain was deeply complex, and it was not clear whether tax cuts at the local level would in some way be compensated by national financing. Because of the many different financial linkages between local and national level, this required a full investigation, which was for the national judge to conduct.

Joined Cases C-428/06–C-434/06 *Unión General de Trabajadores de La Rioja* [2008] ECR I-6747

144. In the light of all of the foregoing, the answer to the question referred must be that Article [107(1) TFEU] is to be interpreted as meaning that, for the purpose of assessing whether a measure is selective, account is to be taken of the institutional, procedural and economic autonomy enjoyed by the authority adopting that measure. It is for the national court, which alone has jurisdiction to identify the national law applicable and to interpret it, as well as to apply Community law to the cases before it, to determine whether the Historical Territories and the Autonomous Community of the Basque Country have such autonomy, which, if so, would have the result that the laws adopted within the limits of the areas of competence granted to those infra-State bodies by the Constitution and the other provisions of Spanish law are not of a selective nature within the meaning of the concept of State aid as referred to in Article [107(1) TFEU].

No doubt the Spanish courts will have welcomed the chance to state their view on how much autonomy exactly the Basque country enjoys.

4 COMPETENCE TO LEGISLATE

There are a number of Treaty Articles which provide a legal basis for legislation relevant to the internal market. However, the most important is Article 114 TFEU.

Article 114 TFEU

1. Save where otherwise provided in the Treaties, the following provisions shall apply for the achievement of the objectives set out in Article 26. The European Parliament and the Council shall, acting in accordance with the ordinary legislative procedure and after consulting the Economic and Social Committee, adopt the measures for the approximation of the provisions laid down by law, regulation or administrative action in Member States which have as their object the establishment and functioning of the internal market.
2. Paragraph 1 shall not apply to fiscal provisions, to those relating to the free movement of persons nor to those relating to the rights and interests of employed persons.

---

[23] Joined Cases C-428/06–C-434/06 *Unión General de Trabajadores de La Rioja* [2008] ECR I-6747.

Article 115 provides analogous powers for harmonisation concerning persons and tax, but by unanimity in the Council.

The leading case interpreting Article 114 continues to be the first Tobacco Directive case, *Tobacco Advertising I*.[24] In this case, the Court of Justice annulled a Directive based on Article 114 for the first time, on the grounds that the Directive exceeded what the legal basis allowed.[25] The Directive amounted to a ban on all tobacco advertising in media other than television (which was addressed in an earlier Directive). This included sponsorship of sport by tobacco firms, tobacco advertising in magazines, and even tobacco advertising on ashtrays, parasols and posters in cafes. The argument put forward for the Directive was that the laws on tobacco advertising varied from state to state, which resulted in obstacles to free movement and distortions of competition. A magazine with tobacco advertisements could be printed and sold in one state, but not exported to another. Advertising firms based in states which permitted tobacco advertising had a source of revenue denied to firms in other states, giving them a competitive advantage, as did sports competitions and teams in those states. The development of pan-European advertising campaigns was prevented by the different rules in different states.

However, there were a number of forceful objections to the Directive. First, the distortions of competition were claimed to be marginal. Theoretically, there might be advantages for firms in one state or another but these did not reach the level of a serious market problem. Secondly, while there were certainly some obstacles to movement resulting from different advertising laws, notably where magazines were concerned, the Directive went beyond addressing these and banned advertising in contexts where it was not obvious that this made any contribution at all to interstate trade. For example, it was unclear in what way the banning of tobacco advertisements in cinemas or cigar shops would make any kind of movement easier. Thirdly, for some of the goods on which advertising was banned, such as ashtrays and parasols, the level of interstate trade was negligible. Finally, the Directive was claimed to be a covert health protection measure. Rather than being primarily aimed at improving the operation of the market, it was really aimed at improving public health. Not only was this outside the remit of Article 114, but it was in fact prohibited, it was claimed, elsewhere in the Treaty, in Article 168(5) TFEU. This Article permits the Union to take public health measures but 'excluding harmonisation'.

Case C-376/98 *Germany* v *Parliament & Council (Tobacco Advertising I)* [2000] ECR I-8419

80. In this case, the approximation of national laws on the advertising and sponsorship of tobacco products provided for by the Directive was based on Articles [114, 53 and 62 TFEU] of the Treaty....

83. Those provisions, read together, make it clear that the measures referred to in Article [114(1) TFEU] of the Treaty are intended to improve the conditions for the establishment and functioning of the internal market. To construe that article as meaning that it vests in the Community legislature a general power to regulate the internal market would not only be contrary to the express wording of the provisions cited above but would also be incompatible with the principle embodied in Article [5 TEU] that the powers of the Community are limited to those specifically conferred on it.

---

[24] Case C-376/98 *Germany* v *Parliament & Council (Tobacco Advertising I)* [2000] ECR I-8419.

[25] See generally J. Usher, annotation at (2001) 38 *CMLRev.* 1520; T. Hervey, 'Up in Smoke? Community (Anti)-Tobacco Law and Policy' (2001) 7 *ELRev.* 101.

84. Moreover, a measure adopted on the basis of Article [114 TFEU] of the Treaty must genuinely have as its object the improvement of the conditions for the establishment and functioning of the internal market. If a mere finding of disparities between national rules and of the abstract risk of obstacles to the exercise of fundamental freedoms or of distortions of competition liable to result therefrom were sufficient to justify the choice of Article [114 TFEU] as a legal basis, judicial review of compliance with the proper legal basis might be rendered nugatory. The Court would then be prevented from discharging the function entrusted to it by Article [19 TEU] of ensuring that the law is observed in the interpretation and application of the Treaty.

85. So, in considering whether Article [114 TFEU] was the proper legal basis, the Court must verify whether the measure whose validity is at issue in fact pursues the objectives stated by the Community legislature.

86. It is true, that recourse to Article [114 TFEU] as a legal basis is possible if the aim is to prevent the emergence of future obstacles to trade resulting from multifarious development of national laws. However, the emergence of such obstacles must be likely and the measure in question must be designed to prevent them....

88. Furthermore, provided that the conditions for recourse to Articles [114, 53 and 62 TFEU] as a legal basis are fulfilled, the Community legislature cannot be prevented from relying on that legal basis on the ground that public health protection is a decisive factor in the choices to be made. On the contrary, [Article 168 TFEU] provides that health requirements are to form a constituent part of the Community's other policies and Article [114(3) TFEU] expressly requires that, in the process of harmonisation, a high level of human health protection is to be ensured....

Elimination of obstacles to the free movement of goods and the freedom to provide services

96. It is clear that, as a result of disparities between national laws on the advertising of tobacco products, obstacles to the free movement of goods or the freedom to provide services exist or may well arise.

97. In the case, for example, of periodicals, magazines and newspapers which contain advertising for tobacco products, it is true, as the applicant has demonstrated, that no obstacle exists at present to their importation into Member States which prohibit such advertising. However, in view of the trend in national legislation towards ever greater restrictions on advertising of tobacco products, reflecting the belief that such advertising gives rise to an appreciable increase in tobacco consumption, it is probable that obstacles to the free movement of press products will arise in the future.

98. In principle, therefore, a Directive prohibiting the advertising of tobacco products in periodicals, magazines and newspapers could be adopted on the basis of Article [114 TFEU] with a view to ensuring the free movement of press products, on the lines of Directive 89/552, Article 13 of which prohibits television advertising of tobacco products in order to promote the free broadcasting of television programmes.

99. However, for numerous types of advertising of tobacco products, the prohibition under Article 3(1) of the Directive cannot be justified by the need to eliminate obstacles to the free movement of advertising media or the freedom to provide services in the field of advertising. That applies, in particular, to the prohibition of advertising on posters, parasols, ashtrays and other articles used in hotels, restaurants and cafés, and the prohibition of advertising spots in cinemas, prohibitions which in no way help to facilitate trade in the products concerned.

100. Admittedly, a measure adopted on the basis of Articles [114, 53 and 62 TFEU] of the Treaty may incorporate provisions which do not contribute to the elimination of obstacles to exercise of the

fundamental freedoms provided that they are necessary to ensure that certain prohibitions imposed in pursuit of that purpose are not circumvented. It is, however, quite clear that the prohibitions mentioned in the previous paragraph do not fall into that category.

101. Moreover, the Directive does not ensure free movement of products which are in conformity with its provisions....

103. Under Article 5 of the Directive, Member States retain the right to lay down, in accordance with the Treaty, such stricter requirements concerning the advertising or sponsorship of tobacco products as they deem necessary to guarantee the health protection of individuals.

104. Furthermore, the Directive contains no provision ensuring the free movement of products which conform to its provisions, in contrast to other directives allowing Member States to adopt stricter measures for the protection of a general interest.

105. In those circumstances, it must be held that the Community legislature cannot rely on the need to eliminate obstacles to the free movement of advertising media and the freedom to provide services in order to adopt the Directive on the basis of Articles [114, 53 and 62 TFEU]...

Elimination of distortion of competition

106. In examining the lawfulness of a directive adopted on the basis of Article [114 TFEU] of the Treaty, the Court is required to verify whether the distortion of competition which the measure purports to eliminate is appreciable (Case C-300/89 *Titanium Dioxide* [1991] ECR I-2867).

107. In the absence of such a requirement, the powers of the Community legislature would be practically unlimited. National laws often differ regarding the conditions under which the activities they regulate may be carried on, and this impacts directly or indirectly on the conditions of competition for the undertakings concerned. It follows that to interpret Articles [114, 53 and 62 TFEU] as meaning that the Community legislature may rely on those articles with a view to eliminating the smallest distortions of competition would be incompatible with the principle, already referred to in paragraph 83 of this judgment, that the powers of the Community are those specifically conferred on it.

108. It is therefore necessary to verify whether the Directive actually contributes to eliminating appreciable distortions of competition.

109. First, as regards advertising agencies and producers of advertising media, undertakings established in Member States which impose fewer restrictions on tobacco advertising are unquestionably at an advantage in terms of economies of scale and increase in profits. The effects of such advantages on competition are, however, remote and indirect and do not constitute distortions which could be described as appreciable. They are not comparable to the distortions of competition caused by differences in production costs...[such as those in Case C-300/89 *Titanium Dioxide*].

110. It is true that the differences between certain regulations on tobacco advertising may give rise to appreciable distortions of competition. As the Commission and the Finnish and United Kingdom Governments have submitted, the fact that sponsorship is prohibited in some Member States and authorised in others gives rise, in particular, to certain sports events being relocated, with considerable repercussions on the conditions of competition for undertakings associated with such events.

111. However, such distortions, which could be a basis for recourse to Article [114 TFEU] of the Treaty in order to prohibit certain forms of sponsorship, are not such as to justify the use of that legal basis for an outright prohibition of advertising of the kind imposed by the Directive.

The Court provides a framework of legal principle which continues to define the scope of Article 114:[26]

(1) Measures based on that article must contribute to removing obstacles to interstate trade, or to removing distortions of competition.

(2) While there is no *de minimis* for obstacles to movement (even minor ones may be harmonised away), harmonisation to remove distortions is only possible when those distortions are 'appreciable'. The reason for this is that almost any differences between national laws have some kind of effect on business, and so could be claimed to cause some degree of market distortion. Without a minimum threshold for harmonisation, Article 114 would amount to an open-ended harmonisation power, which would be contrary to the principle that the Union only has conferred powers.[27]

(3) It is acceptable to harmonise to prevent obstacles arising, rather than removing already existing problems, but those future problems must be likely. One cannot harmonise on the basis of a theoretical possibility.

(4) Provided that a measure does in fact contribute to free movement or undistorted competition, it is not rendered invalid because it also contributes to public health. On the contrary, the Union is required to take other interests into account when deciding how obstacles and distortions should be removed. Article 168(5) TFEU is only a ban on harmonising public health as such, not on integrating public health considerations into internal market rules.

The Court applied these thoughts to the Directive on the basis of several findings of fact. First, the claimed distortions of competition were not significant. Secondly, a number of provisions of the Directive did not in fact contribute to free movement. The Court was unable to see how, for example, banning tobacco advertising in cinemas, or cigar shops, or on ashtrays or parasols, facilitated interstate trade.

This second finding is not entirely convincing. The trade in new or second-hand ashtrays or parasols, or for that matter in posters, may be small, even non-existent, but there is no reason in principle why it should not exist, and there will clearly be obstructions caused if tobacco advertising is permitted in some states and not others. A ban on tobacco advertising would prevent this problem from arising. Ironically, in fact, interstate trade in these goods may barely exist if tobacco advertising is permitted because they will be given away free for promotional reasons. However, without such advertising cafés may have to buy their parasols and ashtrays, and an interstate trade may well come into being. In any case, the Court's finding that no obstacles were being removed should probably be seen in the context of the rule that future obstacles must be likely. Since it had not been demonstrated that there actually was any present or likely future trade that was being obstructed – it is simply an imaginable possibility – the ban on these forms of advertising could not be based on Article 114.

[26] See for commentary e.g. M. Kumm, 'Constitutionalising Subsidiarity in Integrated Markets: The Case of Tobacco Regulation in the European Union' (2006) 12 *ELJ* 503; F. Duina and P. Kurzer, 'Smoke in Your Eyes: The Struggle over Tobacco Control in the European Union' (2004) 11 *JEPP* 57; J. Snell, 'Who Has Got the Power: Free Movement and Allocation of Competences' (2003) 22 *YBEL* 323; A. Somek, *Individualism: An Essay on the Authority of EU Law* (Oxford, Oxford University Press, 2008) ch. 7; S. Weatherill, 'Competence Creep and Competence Control' (2004) 23 *YBEL* 1; T. Hervey, 'Up in Smoke? Community (Anti) Tobacco Law and Policy' (2001) 26 *ELRev.* 101.

[27] See Chapter 5.

A final objection to the Directive was that it permitted tobacco advertising in very limited circumstances (trade publications and third country publications not primarily aimed at the European market), but permitted states to derogate from this and ban advertising even in these. As a result, the Directive did not guarantee free movement for these products. This objection is rather facile. If the rest of the Directive had been legitimate there would be no particular reason why it could not contain a limited derogation permitting states to be stricter. This is quite common in legislation. The Court's view on the derogation should probably be seen in the context of its general irritation with a Directive that had a marginal impact on trade and looked like a disguised attempt to regulate public health.

Tobacco Advertising I has since been followed by two other cases addressing similar issues. While these do not in fact add any new law, they do confirm several points which the judgment in *Tobacco Advertising I* left slightly ambiguous. *Tobacco Advertising II* addressed the Directive adopted to replace the one annulled in *Tobacco Advertising I*.[28] The broad idea of the replacement Directive was the same, but it was more limited. It confined itself generally to printed media and radio, where it could be shown that there actually was cross-border trade in goods or cross-border provision of radio services, and to sponsorship of sports with some international aspect, and it moreover included a clause ensuring that products within its limited derogations (trade publications and third country publications) could be traded throughout the Union. It thus created a greater degree of uniformity than the previous Directive in the areas that mattered, while leaving other matters alone.

Nevertheless, objections were still raised, notably that all printed media and radio programmes were covered, while in fact many magazines and radio broadcasts were for an exclusively local market. Some radio transmissions were not even strong enough to reach a border.

The judgment applies the same principles as the previous one, but this time the Court found the Directive to be valid. This time it did confine itself to matters relevant to interstate trade. Local sports tournaments with no international aspect at all were excluded, as were the ashtrays and parasols for which apparently no market exists. The fact that the printed media and radio ban extended to local media was not seen by the Court as a problem. Cross-border radio and trade in magazines existed, and could be disturbed by variations in tobacco advertising rules. Harmonisation was therefore justified. However, to try and distinguish between what might be traded or heard across the border and what would not be was practically impossible and would distort the market in itself. Therefore a general approach was justified. An internal market Directive may regulate purely internal matters if this is an inseparable part of regulating cross-border ones.

The judgment also clarifies two further matters. First, a Directive does not have to pursue both the removal of obstacles to movement and undistorted competition. Either is enough. The first *Tobacco Advertising* judgment had been a little unclear on this. Secondly, it is possible to harmonise public health matters under Article 114 TFEU provided this is part of genuine internal market regulation. *Tobacco Advertising I* had made clear that a contribution to public health was not excluded, but it might have been argued that this could not go so far as harmonisation. However, tobacco advertising rules *are* intended to protect public

---

[28] C-380/03 *Germany v Parliament and Council (Tobacco Advertising II)* [2006] ECR I-11573.

health, and they *were* harmonised in the second Tobacco Directive, and the Court found this to be acceptable. The Article 168 ban on harmonisation prevents that Article being used for this purpose, but it does not prevent incidental harmonisation within the context of the internal market.

The second post-*Tobacco Advertising I* case is *Swedish Match*.[29] This concerned a Directive banning tobacco for chewing. Sweden enjoys an exemption from this ban, as a result of the particular popularity of chewing tobacco in that country. However, this was not enough for the complainants in this case who wished to market the chewing tobacco in the United Kingdom and, in a parallel case decided on the same day, Germany.[30] The Directive prevented this. They therefore challenged the validity of the Directive, saying a ban on a product did not contribute to the internal market. The Court disagreed, pointing out that without the Directive it was very likely that states would adopt different laws on the product, creating obstacles to trade. A pre-emptive approach, preventing these obstacles from arising, was appropriate.

It cannot, of course, be argued that trade in chewing tobacco is facilitated by the Directive: it is banned. It looks as if the Court is saying 'better not to permit the product at all than to allow a product which cannot be traded throughout the Union'. This is not so much facilitating interstate trade as sour grapes: if you can't sell them everywhere, you won't get to sell them at all. However, from a broader perspective the judgment makes sense. Chewing tobacco needs to be seen as a product that probably exists within a broader market, perhaps for tobacco products generally or perhaps for oral products generally (this would have to be investigated). This means that, to some extent, consumers are prepared to switch between these products. The Directive then helps regulate that product market as a whole so that all the products available to consumers are tradeable. This goal inevitably entails limiting the range of available products. That is what all product regulation does.

The other major question on Article 114, which has concerned Member States recently, is the meaning and scope of 'approximation'. Can this Article be used only for legislation which actually harmonises, or can it be used for measures which contribute to the process of harmonising, without engaging in it as such? The latter position appears to be correct, following the *Smoke Flavourings* case and the *ENISA* case.[31]

The first of these concerned the British passion for chemically flavoured potato crisps, some varieties of which used flavourings which were likely to be banned under EU food safety rules. Faced with this sacrifice of national culture at the altar of mere safety, the British claimed that the procedure which had been created to decide on such bans lacked a legal basis. This procedure was found in a Regulation, which enabled the Commission to regulate food additives according to a number of principles and processes, of which an important element was that they would receive advice from the European Food Safety Authority. The Regulation was based on Article 114. The British government argued that this article could only be used to actually approximate national rules directly, not to create a system leading to such approximation, as the Regulation did.

---

[29] C-210/03 *R v Secretary of State for Health, ex parte Swedish Match* [2004] ECR I-11893.
[30] Case C-434/02 *Arnold André GmBH & Co. KG v Landrat des Kreises Herford* [2004] ECR I-11825.
[31] Case C-217/04 *United Kingdom v Parliament and Council (ENISA)* [2006] ECR I-3771.

Case C-66/04 *United Kingdom* v *Parliament and Council (Smoke flavourings)* [2005] ECR I-10553

45. ...in Article [114 TFEU] the authors of the Treaty intended to confer on the Community legislature a discretion, depending on the general context and the specific circumstances of the matter to be harmonised, as regards the harmonisation technique most appropriate for achieving the desired result, in particular in fields which are characterised by complex technical features.

46. That discretion may be used in particular to choose the most appropriate harmonisation technique where the proposed approximation requires physical, chemical or biological analyses to be made and scientific developments in the field concerned to be taken into account. Such evaluations relating to the safety of products correspond to the objective imposed on the Community legislature by Article [114(3) TFEU] of ensuring a high level of protection of health.

47. Finally, it should be added that where the Community legislature provides for a harmonisation which comprises several stages, for instance the fixing of a number of essential criteria set out in a basic regulation followed by scientific evaluation of the substances concerned and the adoption of a positive list of substances authorised throughout the Community, two conditions must be satisfied.

48. First, the Community legislature must determine in the basic act the essential elements of the harmonising measure in question.

49. Second, the mechanism for implementing those elements must be designed in such a way that it leads to a harmonisation within the meaning of Article [114 TFEU]. That is the case where the Community legislature establishes the detailed rules for making decisions at each stage of such an authorisation procedure, and determines and circumscribes precisely the powers of the Commission as the body which has to take the final decision. That applies in particular where the harmonisation in question consists in drawing up a list of products authorised throughout the Community to the exclusion of all other products.

Article 114 can therefore be used to create mechanisms leading to harmonisation, as well as for immediate harmonisation.

This was taken a step further in *ENISA*. The European Network and Information Society Agency provided non-binding advice on technical matters concerning electronic communications, for example, on current threats, or techniques for using electronic signatures, and so on. It was created by secondary legislation based on Article 114 and again the British government argued that this went beyond approximation.

Case C-217/04 *United Kingdom* v *Parliament and Council* [2006] ECR I-3771

44. It must be added in that regard that nothing in the wording of Article [114 TFEU] implies that the addressees of the measures adopted by the Community legislature on the basis of that provision can only be the individual Member States. The legislature may deem it necessary to provide for the establishment of a Community body responsible for contributing to the implementation of a process of harmonisation in situations where, in order to facilitate the uniform implementation and application of acts based on that provision, the adoption of non-binding supporting and framework measures seems appropriate.

45. It must be emphasised, however, that the tasks conferred on such a body must be closely linked to the subject-matter of the acts approximating the laws, regulations and administrative provisions of the Member States. Such is the case in particular where the Community body thus established provides services to national authorities and/or operators which affect the homogeneous implementation of harmonising instruments and which are likely to facilitate their application.

The activities of ENISA took place in the context of a number of Directives on electronic communication and networks. These outlined the functions and goals which Member State agencies were to adopt and pursue for the objective of creating compatible and secure European information systems and networks. However, much detailed implementation was left to the national agencies. The Court therefore found that ENISA, by providing information on common approaches and problems, even in a non-binding way, helped states to develop standardised and compatible systems, and therefore made a contribution to a harmonisation process. Provided the activities of ENISA were closely linked to the matter being harmonised, this was sufficient to justify Article 114 as a legal base.

The scope of Article 114 is now reasonably clear. However, what is unaddressed is the ambiguity of the term 'appreciable' in *Tobacco Advertising I*. This is really the only word which prevents Article 114 from becoming a general power to harmonise national laws.[32] On the one hand, there seems no particular reason to fear that Article 114 will spiral out of control. Both the Council and Parliament must agree to legislation, and the Court of Justice is also likely to annul Directives which go too far.[33] Nevertheless, it is striking and, for many, problematic that the legal limit on harmonisation is so vague. One may still talk of limited Union powers, but hardly of well-defined ones.

Nor is 'appreciable' always an adequate limit. There are matters which cause very appreciable distortions of competition yet which we would not expect to see harmonised. The existence of different languages hinders trade and distorts competition in many and significant ways. It is beyond doubt that a common European language would contribute hugely to the internal market. Nothing in 'appreciable' provides an argument against a Directive legislating to make French the language of Europe.[34] Moreover, the appreciability threshold does not apply to the removal of obstacles to free movement. A fierce academic debate rages over whether the use of Article 114 to create a common European Contract Code would be appropriate.[35] There is much discussion over the extent to which differing laws on contracts hinder firms and individuals from doing business across borders, and whether a common code would make a significant difference. However, it seems likely that a common code would facilitate interstate contracts and business to at least some extent, and thus is prima facie possible under Article 114.

The objection to both these measures would be that they are disproportionate: the benefits to trade do not justify the cultural and social cost.[36] While the Court did not find the measures in *Tobacco Advertising II* or *Swedish Match* disproportionate, it is significant that it gave the matter explicit consideration. Proportionality is the other barrier to an open-ended Article 114.

---

[32] A. Dashwood, 'The Limits of European Community Powers' (1996) 21 *ELRev.* 113.

[33] *Ibid.*

[34] G. Davies, 'Subsidiarity: The Wrong Idea, in the Wrong Place, at the Wrong Time' (2006) 43 *CML Rev.* 63.

[35] S. Weatherill, 'Why Object to the Harmonisation of Private Law by the EC?' (2004) 12(5) *European Review of Private Law* 633; S. Weatherill and Stefan Vogenauer (eds.), *The Harmonisation of European Contract Law: Implications for European Private Laws, Business and Legal Practice* (Oxford, Hart, 2006); P. van den Bergh, 'Forced Harmonisation of Contract Law in Europe: Not to be Continued' in S. Grundmann and J. Stuyck (eds.), *An Academic Green Paper on European Contract Law* (Kluwer, The Hague, 2002) 245–64; M. van Hoecke and F. Ost (eds.), *The Harmonisation of European Private Law* (Oxford, Hart, 2000); A. Hartkamp and E. Hondius *et al.*, *Towards a European Civil Code* (3rd edn, The Hague, Kluwer Law International, 2004); P. Legrand, 'Against a European Civil Code' (1997) 60 *MLR* 44; M. Hesselink, *The Politics of a European Civil Code* (The Hague, Kluwer Law International, 2006).

[36] Davies, above n.34.

What this all shows is the problem of containing purposive powers. Article 114 is not defined in terms of a particular area of activity – health, education, foodstuffs – but in terms of the achievement of goals – free movement and undistorted competition. These cut across other areas of activity, because so many different kinds of law may impact upon them. Goal-oriented powers have thus an inherent tendency to spread.[37] As governments have always known, if the end justifies the means then much can be achieved.

Finally, a note must be made on the changes in the law since these judgments. They all took place in the context of the EC Treaty in which Article 3(g) provided that the Union would have 'a system ensuring that competition in the internal market is not distorted'. This provided the traditional intellectual background and support for the thesis that the 'establishment and functioning' of the internal market encompassed not only removing obstacles to movement, as explicitly mentioned in Article 26 TFEU, but also removing distortions of competition. However, in the new Treaties this clause has been cut out and moved to a Protocol.

Protocol No. 27 on the internal market and competition

THE HIGH CONTRACTING PARTIES,

CONSIDERING that the internal market as set out in Article 3 of the Treaty on European Union includes a system ensuring that competition is not distorted,

HAVE AGREED that:

To this end, the Union shall, if necessary, take action under the provisions of the Treaties, including under Article 352 of the Treaty on the Functioning of the European Union. This protocol shall be annexed to the Treaty on European Union and to the Treaty on the Functioning of the European Union.

It remains to be seen whether this will impact on the Court and Commission's interpretation of Article 114, which in itself is unchanged. On the one hand, a Protocol has the same legal status as a Treaty Article. Given the traditional interpretation of the words of Article 114, there is no doctrinal reason to take a new view now, and this would even be rather inconsistent. Nevertheless, the choice to move undistorted competition away from the headline Articles of the Treaty to a Protocol represents a political aversion to overemphasis on competition, and it is not unimaginable that the new mood will infect the institutions. There would, however, be some irony in this. The major objections to the clause were from the traditional left rather than the free-market right, those who felt that unmitigated competition was no good thing and was being pursued too enthusiastically. Yet, removing distortions prevents states from capitalising on low regulatory burdens to gain a competitive edge. Undistorted competition is a more fettered form of competition than competition without harmonisation would be. Were the Court to limit such harmonisation, while harmonisation to remove obstacles to movement continues, it would in fact be making the internal market an even more ruthlessly competitive place.

[37] *Ibid.*

5 TECHNIQUES OF REGULATION

(i) The old and new approaches

One of the fundamental obstacles to free trade between states is technical standards. These vary from state to state, with the result that a product made according to French law probably does not conform to the requirements of German or UK law. Manufacturers thus have a difficult time making products that they can freely trade throughout the European Union.

In the early days of the Union (when it was the European Economic Community), the approach to this problem was relatively straightforward. Wherever necessary, the Commission sought to propose legislation replacing national product standards with equivalent European ones. Common standards, combined with mutual recognition of inspections, removed the trade problem.[38] However, standards are a complex business, not only for complicated technical products, but even for apparently simple ones, such as toys, where one may have to think about paint types, strength, resistance to strain, and so on. Each piece of legislation was a time consuming business, and the Community was simply not able to produce enough legislation to create a single market, particularly given the pace of product development and the constant introduction of new product types.[39]

In the mid-1980s a new approach was introduced, still called 'the new approach' today.[40] This was based on a much more minimalist legislative approach. Instead of detailed and technical legislation for each product type, Directives would be adopted for broad product categories, toys, machinery, and so on. These would lay down, at a high level of abstraction, general demands concerning the essential health and safety requirements that such products should meet. A selection of the requirements from Directive 2009/48/EC on toy safety provides a flavour of the style of these requirements, abstract almost to the point of being banal.

Directive 2009/48/EC of the European Parliament and of the Council of 18 June 2009 on the safety of toys, Annex II, Particular Safety Requirements

I. Physical and Mechanical Properties

1. Toys and their parts and, in the case of fixed toys, their anchorages, must have the requisite mechanical strength and, where appropriate, stability to withstand the stresses to which they are subjected during use without breaking or becoming liable to distortion at the risk of causing physical injury.

2. Accessible edges, protrusions, cords, cables and fastenings on toys must be designed and manufactured in such a way that the risks of physical injury from contact with them are reduced as far as possible.

3. Toys must be designed and manufactured in such a way as not to present any risk or only the minimum risk inherent to their use which could be caused by the movement of their parts....

5. Aquatic toys must be designed and manufactured so as to reduce as far as possible, taking into account the recommended use of the toy, any risk of loss of buoyancy of the toy and loss of support afforded to the child.

6. Toys which it is possible to get inside and which thereby constitute an enclosed space for occupants must have a means of exit which the intended user can open easily from the inside...

---

[38] See General Programme on the Removal of Technical Obstacles to Trade [1969] OJ C76/1.

[39] Commission White Paper, *Completing the Single Market*, COM(85)310; *The Development of Standardisation: Action for Faster Technical Integration in Europe*, COM(90)456.

[40] For policy documents, details of legislation and background, see www.newapproach.eu and http://ec.europa.eu/enterprise/newapproach/index_en.htm.

The responsibility of the Member States under new approach Directives is to ensure that products placed onto their domestic markets conform to the essential requirements in the Directive.[41] How exactly they do this is up to them. There are two important differences from the old approach. First, the new approach gives states a considerable freedom to standardise in different ways. There is no uniform approach. Thus, the virtues of experiment and diversity are maintained. Essential health and safety requirements can be satisfied by different regulatory styles and methods according to the traditions and preferences of the state. Secondly, the legislation only deals with essential health and safety requirements. Matters that are purely concerned with quality are not harmonised. Thus, the Union may legislate to ensure that sausages are safe, but under the new approach will not be concerned with how much meat a sausage has to contain.

This decision not to harmonise quality standards was made possible by the decision in *Cassis de Dijon*, where the Court decided that pure quality issues are not a sufficient reason to exclude foreign products from the market.[42] Germany may decide that German-made sausages should have more than 50 per cent meat, but it cannot use this requirement to exclude British ones that may have much less. The EU approach to quality requirements is now no longer based on compulsory quality standards, but on informing the consumers, who then decide for themselves what they prefer: Germany may, for example, require sausages to indicate on the packaging how much meat they contain. Since quality standards therefore no longer create (in principle) obstacles to trade, there is no need to harmonise them. This is the core insight of the new approach.

(ii) Mechanics of the new approach

The new approach does not rest on the broad-spectrum Directives alone. There are two other aspects which are in practice essential to its success. First, European standardisation is not abandoned. Rather, it is moved away from the legislative process to specialist standardisation agencies.[43] These create technical standards of a more detailed and specific type, although often less specific and detailed than under the old approach, still leaving a certain discretion and freedom in how to meet substantive requirements. The advantage of this outsourcing is that it decouples the making of standards (which can be slow and difficult) from the legislative process, so that this latter is no longer seized up. The Council and Parliament can agree on a

---

[41] On the new approach, see J. Pelkmans, 'The New Approach to Technical Harmonization and Standardization' (1987) 25 *JCMS* 249; European Commission, *Enhancing the Implementation of New Approach Directives*, COM(2003)240; A. McGee and S. Weatherill, 'The Evolution of the Single Market: Harmonisation or Liberalisation?' (1990) 53 *MLR* 578. See further M. Egan, *Constructing a European Market* (Oxford, Oxford University Press, 2001) ch. 4; S. Weatherill, 'Pre-emption, Harmonisation and the Distribution of Competence to Regulate the Internal Market' in C. Barnard and J. Scott (eds.), *The Law of the Single European Market: Unpacking the Premises* (Oxford and Portland, Hart, 2002); K. Armstrong, 'Governance and the Single European Market' in P. Craig and G. de Búrca (eds.), *The Evolution of EU Law* (Oxford, Oxford University Press, 1998).

[42] Case 120/78 *Rewe-Zentral AG* v *Bundesmonopolverwaltung für Branntwein (Cassis de Dijon)* [1979] ECR 649. See pp. 760–73.

[43] For example European Committee for Standardisation (CEN), European Committee for Electrotechnical Standardisation (CENELEC) and European Telecommunication Standards Institute (ETSI). See European Commission Communication, *The Role of European Standardisation in the Framework of European Policies and Legislation*, COM(2004)674 final of 18 October 2004; H. Schepel, *The Constitution of Private Governance* (Oxford and Portland, Hart, 2005) ch. 2; C. Frankel and E. Højbjerg, 'The Constitution of a Transnational Policy Field: Negotiating the EU Internal Market for Products' (2007) 14 *JEPP* 96; M. Austin and H. Milner, 'Strategies of European Standardization' (2001) 8 *JEPP* 411.

general framework, and then let the experts deal with the details at their own pace. Moreover, the new European standards are voluntary: there is no obligation to adopt them. A state, or a manufacturer, may prefer to meet the requirements of the Directive in another way, and they are free to do so. However, they will then have to show that their products do in fact meet the health and safety requirements. It may be easier to simply follow the European standards, since if a producer does this it creates a strong presumption that the product conforms to the Directive. She should then be able to sell her goods throughout the Union without problem. The idea of a new European standard is therefore that it shows one way of manufacturing a product so that it is sufficiently safe and conforms to the relevant Directive, but it does not insist that this is the only way. Room for production-method innovation and deviation is allowed.

The second additional aspect of the new approach is its procedural requirements concerning certification. It is all very well to say that products conforming to the European standard, or complying with the Directive by another method, must be accepted by all Member States. This begs the question of who establishes that there actually is such conformity. The new approach comes with a certification system for products, but it is this system which has been at the root of its problems. The system is decentralised and Member States do not trust each other's implementation.

Commission Staff Working Document SEC(2007)173

1.2.2. What are the specificities of the New Approach?
As discussed above, instead of setting out detailed technical requirements in the legislation, New Approach directives limit themselves to defining essential requirements in relation to issues such as health, safety, consumer protection and the protection of the environment. The legislation fixes the level of safety which products must meet but does not pre-determine the technical solutions to achieve this level of safety. The choice of different solutions leading to the same result is therefore open to manufacturers.

Technical specifications, in the form of standards, coming under the framework of the New Approach directives, allow products to meet the essential requirements needed and are considered as an 'easy' way to meet compliance with the legislation (presumption of conformity). Use of standards guarantees the required level of safety of products, but use of harmonised standards is voluntary and a manufacturer may use any other technical solution which demonstrates that his product meets the essential requirements.

The directives also set out requirements for conformity assessment, which depending upon the product need to be done either by a third party testing, inspection or certification body or by the manufacturer himself. The different types of conformity assessment procedures were identified by Decision 93/465/EEC and are set out in the form of 'modules'. Each directive has chosen the modules which are considered to be appropriate for demonstrating conformity, taking into account the type of risk related to the particular product.

Certain modules require the intervention of third party conformity assessment bodies, known as notified bodies. These bodies are chosen ('designated') by Member States on the basis of certain minimum criteria (competence, impartiality, integrity, etc.) which are set out in the directives. They are then 'notified' to the Commission, after which they are authorised to carry out conformity assessment activities according to the procedures set out in the directives.

In addition to this, the Commission has also supported the development at European level of a new evolution at national level: Accreditation. In the past, Member States' public authorities approved products prior to them being placed on the market.

However, national testing and certification resources were not always sufficient and the national authorities began to use the services of private conformity assessment bodies. In order to ensure that these private bodies were able to provide the correct level of service, they were submitted to the control of a national public authority body: the national accreditation body. This was devised in all Member States as a means to ensure an appropriate level of credibility for test results and product certification or inspection.

Last but not least the New Approach introduced a common marking of conformity, which has become its most visible and well known element. The CE marking is in effect a declaration by the manufacturer that the product conforms to all the essential requirements of the relevant legislation and that it has been subject to the applicable conformity assessment procedures. Since products bearing the CE marking are presumed to be in compliance with the applicable directives and hence benefit from free circulation, the CE marking operates as a 'passport' to the whole EU market....

2.1. Performance of notified bodies and weaknesses in the notification process

Certain conformity assessment procedures require that a product is tested, inspected or certified by an independent third party, a 'notified body', before it is placed on the market. Notified bodies hence play an important role within the New Approach system to guarantee the safety of products on the market. Therefore, it is crucial to ensure that they have the necessary competence and capacity to carry out their tasks correctly. Furthermore, confidence in their competence is crucial to ensure EU wide recognition of certificates issued by these bodies.

Most notified bodies do a professional and complete job. However, sometimes certain notified bodies apply practices which can undermine the confidence of this type of work in the whole sector.

The 'modules' referred to above are different procedures by which a producer may show that her goods comply with the relevant Directive. These very often involve testing by an accredited 'notified body', a body authorised by the Member State of production to test and certify those products as complying with EU law. However, as the extract suggests, and goes on to explain in more detail, the major weakness of the new approach is a lack of trust between states on the performance and reliability of these bodies, leading to a reluctance to accept their results as proof of compliance.[44]

The core problem is that if standards leave room for variety, then it becomes a harder and less objective process to assess whether they are met. It is easier to objectively certify a teddy-bear if every detail of its manufacture is specified than if the rules say 'it must be able to resist normal use by a child'. Clearly, bodies will take different approaches to measuring compliance. The problems this creates are magnified by the fact that there is no uniform European approach to accreditation of notified bodies, and these vary greatly in character and quality. They may be private companies, public authorities or quasi-public agencies. There are repeated complaints that the bodies are not of consistent quality, that market pressures encourage them

---

[44] See G. Majone, *Mutual Trust, Credible Commitments and the Evolution of the Rules of the Single Market*, EUI Working Paper RSC No. 95/1 (Florence, European University Institute, 1995); Pelkmans, above n. 41.

to be over-easy with their certification, that not all Member States adequately supervise the notified bodies or are strict enough about accreditation.

Thus, the principle of the new approach is attractively easy: a producer contracts with a notified body to have her products tested and certified to show they comply with the Directive; the body does this, whereupon the producer attaches a CE mark to her product, and supplies the certification documents to the authorities of the state to which she is exporting and the goods are accepted onto their market. However, this relies on these authorities trusting the notified bodies of other states, which they often do not. Thus, despite a CE mark and evidence of certification, it is not at all uncommon for states to block market access on the grounds that the products are not in fact sufficiently safe. They may take the view that the way the producer has chosen to meet the Directive's requirements is not adequate, or that there is insufficient evidence of such compliance.

It may well be that if the producer litigates, then ultimately she will win.[45] National authorities are still often over-suspicious of foreign standards and notifying bodies and their refusals may be unjustified. However, litigation is slow and expensive. If producers have to use the courts regularly to gain market access, then the new approach has failed. In fact the picture is mixed; in many cases it works well, but too often it does not.[46]

As a result of these concerns, the new approach is being updated. While trying to maintain its light legislative touch and flexibility, new legislation has been adopted aiming to improve trust surrounding the certification process. Regulation 765/2008/EC creates a Union framework for the operation, accreditation and supervision of conformity assessment bodies (notified bodies) in the hope that this will create a more uniform quality and approach, and therefore more trust and more effective interstate mutual recognition of certification.[47] It is perhaps an irony that minimising the harmonisation of products is only possible by increasing the harmonisation of procedure.

Alongside this, the old approach is not dead. Technical legislation usually provided for updating by the comitology process, so that it survives product development.[48] A significant number of products are therefore still subject to 'old style' Directives. The following section, particularly the extract from Joerges, discusses some of the more political aspects of the difference between these two parallel approaches to regulation.[49]

(iii) Minimum harmonisation

The new and old approaches are both about technical product standards, but much internal market harmonisation concerns production processes and the ironing out of distortions of competition, or less urgent aspects of product regulation such as consumer protection. Here the Union has other techniques which it uses to try and reach the right balance between harmonisation and local autonomy.

---

[45] See e.g. Case C-254/05 *Commission v Belgium* [2007] ECR I-4269.

[46] See J. Pelkmans, *Mutual Recognition in Goods and Services: An Economic Perspective*, ENEPRI Working Paper No. 16/2003 (Brussels, ENEPRI, 2003).

[47] Regulation 765/2008/EC setting out the requirements for accreditation and market surveillance relating to the marketing of products [2008] OJ L218/30.

[48] See pp. 117–25.

[49] See pp. 703–4.

An approach often used is minimum harmonisation.[50] This lays down a minimum standard, but leaves Member States free to have stricter standards if they wish. Where this is applied to harmonisation of the conditions of competition it is relatively unproblematic in principle. The competitive impact of legal differences is not eliminated, but it is reduced. However, where minimum harmonisation is applied to matters related to tradable goods or services it raises legal problems. If a Member State chooses to maintain higher standards, is it entitled to apply these to imports or not? If so, then the Directive does not ensure free movement, and its purpose and validity may be questioned (if it is based on Article 114 TFEU at least; where it is based on other Treaty Articles such as those providing for environmental legislation, the matter becomes more complex).[51] Yet if not, then Member States are not in fact able to guarantee a higher level of protection on their territory, since they may only apply the higher standard to domestic producers, and not to imports. The minimum level may in practice become the actual level prevailing in the marketplace, rendering the option to maintain higher standards a little hollow.

The answer turns on the wording and context of each Directive. However, in general, the imperative that measures based on Article 114 facilitate free movement means that internal market Directives usually require states to admit products that meet the minimum standards. Thus, states may usually only apply stricter requirements to domestic production, and not to imports. One consequence of this is that domestic production may bear a heavier regulatory burden than imported goods. The Court confirmed in *Gallaher* that this is not to be seen as prohibited discrimination, but simply as an inevitable and acceptable result of the choice for minimum harmonisation.[52] *Gallaher* concerned the size of health warnings on cigarette packets. Directive 89/622/EC required these to cover at least 4 per cent of the packet, but allowed Member States to be stricter. The United Kingdom required 6 per cent but, as the Directive required, did not enforce this against imports. UK producers complained, without avail, that they were unfairly disadvantaged.

6 NON-ECONOMIC INTERESTS IN THE INTERNAL MARKET

Economic and non-economic interests cannot feasibly be separated. Economic activity inevitably impacts on the environment, society and individual safety and security. Nor does the Treaty intend that such matters should be considered in isolation. It explicitly demands an integrated approach. Article 7 TFEU provides that the Union shall ensure consistency between all its policies, and Articles 8 to 12 require anti-discrimination goals, social policy, the environment and consumer protection to be integrated into all other policies. Moreover, Article 114 enables both the Commission, in its proposals, and Member States, by means of derogations from harmonisation measures, to take into account and react to health, safety and environmental concerns.

---

[50] M. Dougan, 'Minimum Harmonization and the Internal Market' (2000) 37 *CMLRev.* 853.
[51] *Ibid*; J. Jans and H. H. B. Vedder, *European Environmental Law* (3rd edn, Groningen, Europa Law Publishing, 2008).
[52] Case C-11/92 *R* v *Secretary of State for Health, ex parte Gallaher Ltd* [1993] ECR I-3545.

Article 114 TFEU

3. The Commission, in its proposals envisaged in paragraph 1 concerning health, safety, environmental protection and consumer protection, will take as a base a high level of protection, taking account in particular of any new development based on scientific facts. Within their respective powers, the European Parliament and the Council will also seek to achieve this objective.

4. If, after the adoption of a harmonisation measure by the European Parliament and the Council, by the Council or by the Commission, a Member State deems it necessary to maintain national provisions on grounds of major needs referred to in Article 36, or relating to the protection of the environment or the working environment, it shall notify the Commission of these provisions as well as the grounds for maintaining them.

5. Moreover, without prejudice to paragraph 4, if, after the adoption of a harmonisation measure by the European Parliament and the Council, by the Council or by the Commission, a Member State deems it necessary to introduce national provisions based on new scientific evidence relating to the protection of the environment or the working environment on grounds of a problem specific to that Member State arising after the adoption of the harmonisation measure, it shall notify the Commission of the envisaged provisions as well as the grounds for introducing them.

The remainder of the Article provides for procedures to assess and police the derogations above.

The right balance between interests is of course always contested. This is the stuff of politics. However, an issue of current concern is the process of achieving that balance. An accusation levelled at the Union is that it is deaf to voices other than scientific ones, and presents scientific analyses of health and safety and environmental issues as more objective and less contested than they in fact are, and also as more important than they in fact are: scientific perspectives are only a part of a picture in which moral and social and democratic preferences are also relevant.

This issue arose in the *Austrian GMOs* case, in which the region of Upper Austria sought to ban the release of GMOs on its territory.[53] To do this it needed a derogation from Directive 2001/18/EC, which it sought on the basis of Article 114(5). This was refused by the Commission, and the Commission's view was upheld in both the General Court and Court of Justice. The Court emphasised that Article 114(5) TFEU could only be relied upon where there was new scientific evidence, problems specific to a Member State arising after the harmonisation measure had been adopted, and where those problems related to the working or natural environment. These were cumulative requirements: a failure on any ground made derogation impossible. The Austrian view was that its unique eco-systems, sizeable organic production and large number of small farms made it a special case. It was not so much that they had new evidence on the science, as that the consequences for an industry and society where naturalness and purity are especially important were particularly frightening. There was no room for this within Article 114(5). The Court's view is textually understandable – the Article is fairly clear – but it raises the question whether EU law is adapted to modern risk management, which has to face situations where threats to health and safety are bound up with ethics and social norms, or whether it is only suited for less controversial and more lumpen issues.

The same question may be asked about the EU legislative process. Chapter 9 goes into more detail on how this process deals with risk, and on the distinction between determining the acceptable

[53] Joined Cases C-439/05 P and C-454/05 P *Land Oberösterreich & Austria* v *Commission* [2007] ECR I-7141.

level of risk, which is a political task for the legislator, and determining what the actual level of risk is, which is outsourced to the scientists in specialist agencies.[54] Yet, while this distinction makes apparent sense, it glosses the complexity of the decision-making process. In practice, the centrality of the scientific risk-assessment process may have the effect of marginalising legitimate ethical concerns or public doubts about scientific reliability. One of the ways in which this occurs results from the decision-making framework and practices of the Commission. Kritikos argues that it tends not to actively engage with non-scientific concerns, and structures its processes in a way that excludes them.[55] Although it has the power to take into account many interests, in practice it chooses as quantitative and expert-based an approach as possible. In particular, adoption of the distinction between questions of fact (what is the risk?) and value (what should be done about this risk?) has led to the exclusion of the vast majority of public concerns from the most influential stage of the decision-making model: the process of risk-framing. The result is that 'it is less the case that those critics who are currently excluded from decision-making... do not "possess" the "necessary" knowledge to participate; rather, what counts as knowledge has been defined in such a way as to exclude their potential contributions and legitimacy'.[56]

An additional reason for concern about this alleged science bias arises from the role of technocratic agencies. Given that their views may in practice often be constitutive of legislative decisions, there is a fear of government by an undemocratic technocracy. Chapters 2 and 9 have more detail on this issue, and portray the fear that agencies may not be so much neutral as the embodiment of entrenched ideologies, isolated from alternative views.[57] Joerges has portrayed, by contrast, the advantages of the traditional comitology process. This is run by national experts who he suggests are more connected to the worlds of politics and democracy than their agency peers. As a result they are better able to take account of diverse political concerns.

C. Joerges, 'The Law's Problems with the Governance of the Single European Market' in C. Joerges and R. Dehousse (eds.), *Good Governance in Europe's Integrated Market* (Oxford, Oxford University Press, 2002) 1, 17–18

Committees were born of a strong national desire to retain control over the setting and consequences of European regulatory norms/standards. And they thus embody the functional and structural tensions that characterize internal market regulation. First, they hover between 'technical' and 'political' considerations, or between the functional needs and the ethical/social criteria that inform European regulation. Second, they often have very fluid compositions that reflect upon the regulatory goal of balancing rationalizing technical criteria against broader political concerns, and that also forcefully highlight schisms between the political interests of those engaged in the process of internal market regulation. Committees are deeply implicated in political processes, even when they have been established with the explicit role of supporting and overseeing the implementing powers delegated to the Commission. They are the fora for the balancing of a market integrationist logic against a Member State's interest in the substance and costs of consumer protection and cohesive economic development. As such, they often resemble mini-Councils.

[54] Case T-13/99 *Pfizer Animal Health* v *Council* [2002] ECR II-3305.

[55] M. Kritikos, 'Traditional Risk Analysis and Releases of GMOs into the European Union: Space for Non-Scientific Factors' (2009) 44 *ELRev.* 405.

[56] D. Smith and S. Tombs, 'Of Course It's Safe, Trust Me!' in E. Coles, D. Smith and S. Tombs, *Risk Management and Society* (Dordrecht, Kluwer Academic Publishers, 2000) 68. Cited in Kritikos, above, n. 55.

[57] See pp. 66–7 and pp. 380–3.

Yet, it is precisely in the context of the market that the wisdom of this call for democratic responsiveness is sometimes questioned. There is an argument that market regulation should not be politicised, because the scientific and economic issues involved are a matter of technical competence more than political choices.

Support for this view is most prominently and passionately provided by Giandomenico Majone, who has argued that the Union is not intended to be a place of political contestation, but a technocratic regulator in the service of the states. He fears that the more agencies depart from a narrowly technical approach to their task, the more they will undermine their own credibility.

G. Majone, 'The Credibility Crisis of Community Regulation' (2002) 38 *Journal of Common Market Studies* 273, 285

One of the core insights of functionalist theories is that integration is most likely to occur within a domain shielded from the direct clash of political interests. For several decades, law and economics – the discourse of legal and market integration – provided a sufficient buffer to achieve results that could not be directly obtained in the political realm. It was generally admitted that the credibility and coherence of European regulatory law depends crucially on the perception that the Commission is able and willing to enforce the common rules in an objective and even-handed way.

Follesdahl and Hix, disagreeing with him, summarise his view as follows.

A. Follesdal and S. Hix, 'Why there is a Democratic Deficit in the EU: A Response to Majone and Moravcsik' (2006) 44 *Journal of Common Market Studies* 533, 537–8

...The EU governments have delegated regulatory policy competences to the European level – such as the creation of the single market, the harmonization of product standards and health and safety rules and even the making of monetary policy by the European Central Bank – to deliberately isolate these policies from domestic majoritarian government. From this perspective, the EU is a glorified regulatory agency, a 'fourth branch of government', much like regulatory agencies at the domestic level in Europe, such as telecoms agencies, competition authorities, central banks, or even courts.

Following from this interpretation, Majone asserts that EU policy-making *should not* be 'democratic' in the usual meaning of the term...

Politicization would result in redistributive rather than Pareto-efficient outcomes, and so in fact undermine rather than increase the legitimacy of the EU...

It is questionable whether this discussion, which focuses on the legislator, can be translated to the Court of Justice. Its role is in the context of judicial review, where one should expect it to be reticent and cautious.[58] The argument that non-scientific concerns deserve a greater role in decision-making should be primarily addressed at the legislator.[59]

---

[58] See J. Corkin, 'Science, Legitimacy and the Law: Regulating Risk Regulation Judiciously in the European Community' (2008) 33 *ELRev.* 359; Case C-405/07 P *Netherlands* v *Commission* [2008] ECR I-8301.

[59] See Case T-13/99 *Pfizer Animal Health* v *Council* [2002] ECR II-3305, para. 169, extracted in Chapter 9 at pp. 380–2.

Nevertheless, this is not to say that the Commission's powers to supervise non-economic interventions in the internal market are beyond judicial control. While the Court may be unable to depart from the terms of Article 114, it is able to interpret them strictly and hold the Commission to relatively high scientific and procedural standards. In *Commission* v *Netherlands*, the Netherlands wanted to introduce stricter regulation of motor vehicles than was permitted by the harmonisation measures in force. Its justification was the exceptional air pollution problem in the Netherlands, and it sought to rely on Article 114(5). The Commission refused, but was defeated on appeal to the Court of Justice. It had failed to take into account all the data that had been submitted to it. The Court provides a useful overview of how Article 114(5) is to work.

Case C–405/07 P *Netherlands* v *Commission* [2008] ECR I-8301

51. Under Article [114(5) TFEU], after the adoption of harmonisation measures, Member States are obliged to submit to the Commission for approval all national derogating provisions which they deem necessary.

52. That provision requires that the introduction of such provisions be based on new scientific evidence relating to the protection of the environment or the working environment made necessary by reason of a problem specific to the Member State concerned arising after the adoption of the harmonisation measure, and that the proposed provisions as well as the grounds for introducing them be notified to the Commission.

53. Those conditions are cumulative in nature and must therefore all be satisfied if the derogating national provisions are not to be rejected by the Commission.

54. To determine whether those conditions are, in fact, satisfied, which can, depending on the circumstances, necessitate complex technical evaluations, the Commission has a wide discretion.

55. The exercise of that discretion is not, however, excluded from review by the Court. According to the case-law of the Court of Justice, not only must the Community judicature establish whether the evidence relied on is factually accurate, reliable and consistent but also whether that evidence contains all the information which must be taken into account in order to assess a complex situation and whether it is capable of substantiating the conclusions drawn from it.

56. Moreover, it must be recalled that, where a Community institution has a wide discretion, the review of observance of guarantees conferred by the Community legal order in administrative procedures is of fundamental importance. The Court of Justice has had occasion to specify that those guarantees include, in particular for the competent institution, the obligations to examine carefully and impartially all the relevant elements of the individual case and to give an adequate statement of the reasons for its decision.

57. The review of observance of those procedural guarantees is even more important in the procedure under Article [114(5) TFEU] since the right to be heard does not apply to it.

---

7 REGULATORY COMPETITION

Does the market actually need legislation? It is quite imaginable to build a market purely on the basis of a simple and directly effective rule of free movement. Member States would be required to accept onto their domestic markets any goods and services made according to the laws of other Member States. Such a rule is sometimes called a country of origin principle, or a principle of mutual recognition.[60] As will become evident from subsequent chapters, the case law on free movement embodies such a rule to a considerable extent.

The merits of this minimalist market would be that it apparently permits local regulatory diversity and autonomy. These should be valued as such. If populations are required to accept regulation that does not correspond to their preferences, then one gets what economists call a reduction in welfare. The population may not necessarily be less well off in narrowly financial terms, but they are less well off in terms of the things that they value, which are the things that matter, and which a competent economic policy aims to maximise. As was discussed earlier in the chapter, there is an argument that harmonisation should only be undertaken when local regulation is creating externalities; when the local population is getting what they want by imposing some of the costs on their neighbours.[61] The question of what comprises an externality is difficult: one could argue that getting wealthy creates externalities since research shows that other people become less happy when those near to them get richer, particularly if they do so by means that others feel to be unfair.[62] At this point, the economics of harmonisation collapses into little more than a consideration of what is fair and decent. However, there is a specific economic argument about a minimalist internal market which has attracted much commentary and continues to be central in policy debates. It is taken by different commentators to support different standpoints.

The argument is that a market based on mutual recognition and free movement alone, or to an excessive extent, creates what is called regulatory competition. Sun and Pelkmans were among the first to frame the debate in the European context.

J.-M. Sun and J. Pelkmans, 'Regulatory Competition in the Single Market' (1995) 33 *Journal of Common Market Studies* 67, 68

Once the EC-1992 process had begun to take shape, a fundamental debate on the optimal regulatory strategy for the single market emerged. Following the advocacy of 'competition among rules' in the Padoa-Schioppa Report (1987), [a report published in 1987 on, among other things, the internal market] this debate came to be focused on the merits of, and potential for, 'regulatory competition'. There is now an emerging literature on regulatory competition, which is inspired by the literature on economic regulation and the economics of federalism. Crucial in the former is that regulation can only be economically justified if it remedies a market failure, while minimizing its (regulatory) costs.

The latter provides the economic underpinning of subsidiarity, in seeking the optimal economic assignment of regulatory competencies in a multi-layer structure of government.

The essence of regulatory competition is that if firms are able to locate in the state of their choice, produce there, and market their products throughout the Union, then they will be

---

[60] See e.g. G. Davies, *Services, Citizenship and the Country of Origin Principle*, Mitchell Working Paper No. 2/2007 (Edinburgh, Europa Institute, 2007).

[61] Ogus, above n. 15.

[62] See B. Frey, *Happiness: A Revolution in Economics* (Massachusetts, Massachusetts Institute of Technology Press, 2008) 31, and generally ch. 3, 'How Income Affects Happiness' and ch. 5, 'How Inflation and Inequality Affect Happiness'.

inclined to locate in the states with the most attractive business environment.[63] Since states need businesses to provide tax revenue and employment, states will be forced to make their regulation business-friendly. This has both advantages and disadvantages. The advantages are claimed to be that regulation will improve in quality. There will be a form of competition between states, and as with competition between producers, this will result in better products for the consumer. In this case the 'product' will be law, and the consumer will be the mobile firm, or individual. In general, a diversity of different national approaches to law will result in a more creative and dynamic legal Union than central harmonisation, and not only will individual states produce better laws, but they will learn from each other.[64]

Yet, the claimed downside of regulatory competition is that it forces states to take account of only some of those who are affected by regulation: mobile economic actors. The citizen's voice is lost. Laws become tailored to those who are able to threaten exit, while others are ignored.[65] In practice, this may lead to what is called a 'race to the bottom' as states impose ever lighter regulatory standards to attract businesses.[66] As one state cuts environmental or social obligations, other states will be forced to do the same or lose their tax and employment base, leading to a general lowering of standards. Harmonisation of the conditions of competition is seen as an essential balance to prevent this happening. Deakin provides an overview of these issues.

S. Deakin, 'Legal Diversity and Regulatory Competition: Which Model for Europe?' (2006) 12 *European Law Journal* 440, 441–3

Regulatory competition can be defined as a process whereby legal rules are selected and de-selected through competition between decentralised, rule-making entities, which could be nation states, or other political units, such as regions or localities. A number of beneficial effects are expected to flow from this process. Insofar as it avoids the imposition of rules by a centralised, 'monopoly' regulator, it promotes diversity and experimentation in the search for effective laws. In addition, by providing mechanisms for the preferences of the different users of laws to be expressed and for alternative solutions to common problems to be compared, it enhances the flow of information on what works in practice. Above all, it allows the content of rules to be matched more effectively to the preferences or *wants* of those consumers, that is, the citizens of the polities concerned. In some versions of the theory, the first two of these goals are, in essence, simply the means by which the third is achieved.

The idea of regulatory competition is not new, but it was first formalised within the framework of modern welfare economics in the mid-1950s, in relation to the issue of the production of local public goods. The timing is significant: Tiebout's celebrated article, entitled 'A pure theory of public expenditure', was, essentially, an application of theories of general equilibrium that were prevalent at the time. The article constructs a model in which competition operates on the basis of mobility of persons and resources

---

[63] See generally in the European context C. Barnard and S. Deakin, 'Market Access and Regulatory Competition' in C. Barnard and S. Deakin (eds.), *The Law of the European Single Market* (Oxford and Portland, Hart, 2005); N. Reich, 'Competition Between Legal Orders: A New Paradigm of EC Law?' (1992) 29 *CMLRev.* 459; Ogus, above n. 15; S. Deakin, 'Legal Diversity and Regulatory Competition: Which Model for Europe?' (2006) 12 *ELJ* 440; H. Søndergaard Birkmose, 'Regulatory Competition and the European Harmonisation Process' (2006) *EBLRev.* 1075.

[64] See especially Deakin, above n. 63.

[65] See A. O. Hirschmann, *Exit, Voice and Loyalty: Responses to Decline in Firms, Organizations and States* (Harvard, Harvard University Press, 1970).

[66] See Barnard and Deakin, 'Market Access and Regulatory Competition', above n. 63.

across the boundaries of local government units within a sovereign state. In the model, local authorities compete to attract residents by offering packages of services in return for levying taxes at differential rates. Consumers with similar wants then 'cluster' in particular localities. The effect is to match local preferences to particular levels of service provision, thereby maximising the satisfaction of wants, while also maintaining diversity and promoting information flows between jurisdictions.

Tiebout's model is of wider interest because laws, like aspects of local public infrastructure, can be seen as indivisible public goods. By showing formally that they can be understood as products which jurisdictions *supply* in response to the *demands* of consumers of the laws, Tiebout demonstrated the relevance, even to public goods of this kind, of a market analogy. However, in Tiebout's 'pure theory', freedom of movement was *assumed* for the purpose of setting up the formal economic model. The model was aimed at showing that, *given* an effective threat of exit, spontaneous forces would operate in such a way as to discipline states against enacting laws that set an inappropriately high (or low) level of regulation. Tiebout's article did not set out the institutional conditions that would have to be met for the process of competition to occur in the 'real' world; in common with other applications of the general equilibrium model at this time, these conditions were simply assumed. However, the model could be, and was, used as a benchmark against which to judge institutional measures aimed at creating regulatory competition. Since the mid-1950s, the identification of these conditions has become the central question uniting various new-institutional movements in economics and law; it is no longer adequate simply to assume their existence. Sensitivity to the need to consider the institutional framework has not, however, avoided a tendency on the part of many analyses to present the 'pure model' of unfettered competition as the goal to which laws and institutions should be directed, and the debate over regulatory competition is no exception to this.

The most obvious institutional implication of the Tieboutian model is that regulatory competition, in its various forms, requires a particular division of labour between different levels of rule making. It cannot work unless effective regulatory authority is exercised by entities operating at a devolved or local level. Law-making powers should be conferred on lower-level units, subject only to the principle that there must be some level below which further decentralisation becomes unfeasible because of diseconomies of scale.

But even this gives rise to a need for a federal or transnational body that involves superintending the process of competition between the lower level units. Individual units could shut down competition unilaterally, either by placing barriers to the movement of the factors of production beyond their own territory, or by denying access to incoming capital, labour, and services, or both. Hence the central or federal authority has the task of guaranteeing effective freedom of movement. This task, in and of itself, may well require active interventions of various kinds.

Since, in the 'real' world, mobility of persons and of non-human economic resources is self-evidently more limited than it is in the world of pure theory, three prerequisites for making exit effective may be identified. One is the legal guarantee of freedom of movement – entry and exit – for persons and resources. The second is a requirement of non-discrimination, sometimes described in terms of 'mutual recognition' or the concept of 'most favoured nation' status in international economic law. The third is the acceptance of the presence of unwanted side effects of competition: 'externalities' or spill-over effects of various kinds. Even if there is in general a presumption against federal intervention and in favour of allowing rules to emerge through the competitive process, a space remains for harmonisation to protect standards against a 'race to the bottom'. Only the most Panglossian or willfully unobservant would deny that this problem exists; the controversy relates to how serious it is, and whether harmonisation at the federal level is the best way to deal with it.

The fear that regulatory competition makes it impossible for states to maintain high standards has been applied with particular force to welfare states. Fritz Scharpf is the most prominent scholar amongst those arguing that the disciplines of economic liberalism take away the capacity of states to maintain expensive welfare institutions. They are no longer able to impose the legal framework necessary to maintain these. Firms will migrate rather than pay for luxurious welfare systems via taxation or via worker-friendly social legislation. States are therefore forced to cut regulatory burdens.

F. Scharpf, 'The European Social Model: Coping with the Challenges of Diversity' (2002) 40 *Journal of Common Market Studies* 645, 648–9

[Having discussed the constraints on national policy resulting from the Euro rules, free movement, and state aid law]... compared to the repertoire of policy choices that was available two or three decades ago, European *legal* constraints have greatly reduced the capacity of national governments to influence growth and employment in the economies for whose performance they are politically accountable. In principle, the only national options which under European law remain freely available are supply-side strategies involving lower tax burdens, further deregulation and flexibilization of employment conditions, increasing wage differentiation and welfare cutbacks to reduce reservation wages. At the same time, governments face strong *economic* incentives to resort to just such strategies of competitive deregulation and tax cuts in order to attract or retain mobile firms and investments that might otherwise seek locations with lower production costs and higher post-tax incomes from capital. By the same token, unions find themselves compelled to accept lower wages or less attractive employment conditions in order to save existing jobs. Conversely, welfare states are tempted to reduce the generosity or tighten the eligibility rules of tax-financed social transfers and social services in order to discourage the immigration of potential welfare clients.

Scharpf goes on to argue that the only way to prevent economic freedom impacting destructively on welfare systems is to move welfare to a European level, but that this is not possible because of the diversity of different national systems. For him, if the European Union is to retain its social character, it faces a choice between a less demanding internal market or more social integration. He contrasts the situation with the United States, where the development of state welfare systems was initially prevented by regulatory competition considerations similar to those at work in Europe today.[67] However, after the New Deal in the 1930s, it became possible for the federal government to play a significant role in welfare, removing the local competitive element. It is that federal involvement which is neither existent, nor currently possible, in the Union today, he suggests.

Yet, many consider his fears exaggerated. The empirical evidence to date is ambiguous, and economists never tire of pointing out that there is very limited evidence that a race to the bottom often takes place. Whether or not it will is something depending on the specific circumstances.[68] It may well be that states consider it in their national interest to maintain

---

[67] F. Scharpf, 'Democratic Legitimacy under Conditions of Regulatory Competition: Why Europe Differs from the United States' in K. Nicolaidis and R. Howse, *The Federal Vision* (Oxford, Oxford University Press, 2001) 355.

[68] See e.g. Ogus, above n. 15; J.-M. Sun and J. Pelkmans, 'Regulatory Competition in the Single Market' (1995) 33 *Journal of Common Market Studies* 67.

high standards and that certain kinds of industry are even attracted by this. There is certainly plenty of evidence that a high-tax high-standard economic model can work. It may be easier to attract good employees to a state with high environmental and social standards, and a generous welfare net may not be a net burden on firms: otherwise they would perhaps be forced by the employment market to offer even more expensive private facilities and protection. On the whole, solidarity can be cost-effective.

In any case, we should beware of over-easy reliance on apparently 'social' arguments against regulatory diversity and for harmonisation. They are open to abuse.

G. Majone, 'The Common Sense of European Integration' (2006) 13 *Journal of European Public Policy* 607, 624

Moreover, as Revesz has pointed out, race-to-the-bottom arguments are incomplete because they fail to consider that there are more direct means of attracting foreign direct investments than lowering social standards. The advocates of harmonisation assume implicitly that states compete over only one variable, such as environmental quality. Given the assumption of a 'race', however, it is more reasonable to suppose that if harmonisation prevents competition on the environmental dimension, states would try to compete over other variables, such as worker safety, minimum wages or taxation of corporate profits. To avoid these alternative races, the central regulators would have to harmonise national rules so as to eliminate the possibility of any form of interstate competition altogether. This would amount to eliminating any trace of national autonomy, so that the race-to-the-bottom argument is, in the end, an argument against subsidiarity.

A number of writers have argued that there is a need to move beyond the simple opposition of a race to the bottom and regulatory diversity. The goal of policy should be to seek the ideal mix between these, summed up in a well known article by Esty and Gerardin as 'regulatory co-opetition'.[69] Deakin has emphasised that harmonisation which reduces diversity so much that states can no longer experiment would be destructive. He introduces the idea of 'reflexive harmonisation' in which states learn from each other, and develop their own laws in the light of their neighbours. He sees a role for EU harmonisation as framing this process, facilitating communication between states and preventing competition which would, in practice, reduce state autonomy and ultimately diversity.

S. Deakin, 'Legal Diversity and Regulatory Competition: Which Model for Europe?' (2006) 12 *European Law Journal* 440, 444–5

The model of reflexive harmonisation holds that the principal objectives of judicial intervention and legislative harmonisation alike are two-fold: first, to protect the autonomy and diversity of national or local rule-making systems, while, second, seeking to 'steer' or channel the process of adaptation of rules at state level away from 'spontaneous' solutions that would lock in sub-optimal outcomes, such

---

[69] D. Esty and D. Gerardin, 'Regulatory Co-opetition' (2000) 3 *JIEL* 235.

as a 'race to the bottom'. In this model, the process by which states may observe and emulate practices in jurisdictions to which they are closely related by trade and by institutional connections is more akin to the concept of 'co-evolution' than to convergence around the 'evolutionary peak' or end-state envisaged by Tiebout's general equilibrium model. The idea of co-evolution, borrowed from the modern evolutionary synthesis in the biological sciences, argues that a variety of diverse systems can coexist within an environment, with each one retaining its viability. It thereby combines diversity and autonomy of systems with their interdependence within a single, overarching set of environmental parameters.

Nevertheless, any legislative framework has to correspond to popular notions of fairness if it is to be legitimate and politically stable. There is only a limited tolerance for diverse conditions of competition within the Union, and harmonisation is often driven by a desire for uniformity that transcends nuanced policy thinking and comes from a much deeper constitutional and cultural place.[70]

FURTHER READING

C. Barnard and S. Deakin, 'Market Access and Regulatory Competition' in C. Barnard and J. Scott (eds.), *The Law of the European Single Market* (Oxford and Portland, Hart, 2005)

C. Barnard and J. Scott (eds.), *The Law of the European Single Market* (Oxford and Portland, Hart, 2005)

D. Chalmers, 'Risk, Anxiety and the European Mediation of the Politics of Life' (2005) 30 *ELRev.* 649

D. Gerber, *Law and Competition in Twentieth Century Europe: Protecting Prometheus* (Oxford, Oxford University Press, 1998)

A. O. Hirschmann, *Exit, Voice and Loyalty: Responses to Decline in Firms, Organizations and States* (Harvard, Harvard University Press, 1970)

C. Joerges and R. Dehousse (eds.), *Good Governance in Europe's Integrated Market* (Oxford, Oxford University Press, 2002)

G. Majone, *Europe as the Would-be World Power* (Cambridge, Cambridge University Press, 2009)

N. Nic Shuibhne (ed.), *Regulating the Internal Market* (Cheltenham, Edward Elgar, 2006)

K. Nicolaides and G. Schaffer, 'Transnational Mutual Recognition Regimes: Governance Without Global Government' (2005) 68 *Michigan Review of International Law* 267

M. Poiares Maduro, *We the Court* (Oxford and Portland, Hart, 1998)

F. Scharpf, 'Democratic Legitimacy under Conditions of Regulatory Competition: Why Europe Differs from the United States' in K. Nicolaidis and R. Howse, *The Federal Vision* (Oxford, Oxford University Press, 2001)

S. Weatherill, 'Why Harmonise?' in T. Tridimas and P. Nebbia (eds.), *European Union Law for the Twenty-First Century* (Oxford and Portland, Hart, 2004)

---

[70] See J. Weiler, *The State "Uber Alles": Demos, Telos and the German Maastricht Decision*, Jean Monnet Working Paper No. 95/6 (New York, Jean Monnet Center, 1995).

17

Economic and Monetary Union

CONTENTS

1 INTRODUCTION

This chapter considers economic and monetary union. It is organised in the following manner.

Section 2 considers the central four mechanisms of economic and monetary union. These are, first, free movement of capital between the Member States and between Member States and non-EU states; secondly, the adoption of a 'single' currency, the euro; thirdly, the commitment not to incur excessive deficits, a commitment policed by the Excessive Deficit Procedure where the Council of Ministers can sanction the Member State concerned for running an excessive deficit; and, fourthly, the issue by the Council of the Broad Economic Policy Guidelines (BEPG) on macro-economic, micro-economic and employment policy to Member States. Economic and Monetary Union is a field where differentiated integration applies. States have to meet certain criteria, the Convergence Criteria, before they can participate in the euro. Nine Member States, known as 'states with a derogation', have not met these criteria. In addition,

Denmark and the United Kingdom have Protocols which allow them not to participate in the euro. Together, these eleven states are not bound by the EU monetary or exchange rate arrangements. In addition, no sanctions can be applied against them for running an excessive deficit. They are also excluded from certain procedures. They can participate neither in the government of the European Central Bank nor in the Euro Group, a group of finance ministers who consider coordination of economic policy in relation to the euro.

Section 3 considers free movement of capital. Article 63 TFEU prohibits three types of measure: measures which discourage transnational investments by treating them less favourably than national investments; measures which restrict investment in a Member State, albeit in a non-discriminatory manner; and measures which limit in a non-transparent manner investors' control over their investment. In all cases, any restriction will be lawful if it is in the public interest, proportionate and does not arbitrarily discriminate against capital movements from another Member State. In addition, Article 65 TFEU sets out a number of formal exceptions, most notably those which allow tax laws to differentiate against non-residents and laws to protect public policy.

Section 4 considers the institutional arrangements governing monetary policy. The European Central Bank is exclusively responsible for authorising the issue of euros and setting short-term interest rates for the euro. It also has certain regulatory powers regarding minimum reserves for credit institutions and payment systems. It is the Council, however, which makes exchange rate arrangements with non-EU states. The decision-making bodies of the European Central Bank are the Governing Council, which sets guidelines and interest rates, and the Executive Board, which manages day-to-day relations with national central banks. The Governing Council comprises the Executive Board plus the Governors of the national central banks who participate in the euro. The Executive Board comprises its President, Vice-President and four other members all appointed for eight-year non-renewable terms. The European Central Bank and national central banks participating in the euro must all be independent.

Section 5 considers the Excessive Deficit Procedure. States were initially considered to be running an excessive deficit if either their annual budget deficit exceeded 3 per cent of GDP or their total debt exceeded 60 per cent of GDP. These figures have been relaxed so that the Commission will not consider a budget deficit of more than 3 per cent excessive if this results from a severe economic downturn. It can also look now to the Member State's wider economic position in determining whether the deficit is excessive. If the Commission considers the deficit excessive it must make a proposal to that effect to the Council, which must take a view on this. If the Council considers the deficit to be excessive, it must make recommendations to the Member State concerned to reduce the deficit. If the state does not comply, the Council has a discretion to make these recommendations public or to take a decision that the state is non-compliant, which will lead to sanctions.

Section 6 considers the broad economic policy guidelines. These guidelines are agreed every three years by the Council. States agree action plans committing themselves to observe these guidelines and have to report back and be assessed annually by the Council on their compliance with these. There are currently twenty-five guidelines ranging across all areas of economic and employment policy. Since 2005, the reporting obligations have become significant and this has led to substantial debate within the Council about national economic policies. It is unclear how far this has led individual states to change their policies.

2 THE ARCHITECTURE OF ECONOMIC AND MONETARY UNION

(i) Central pillars of Economic and Monetary Union

The creation of a single currency was first considered by the Heads of Government at the Hague in 1969. They established a working group under the chairmanship of the Prime Minister of Luxembourg, Pierre Werner, which produced a fully-fledged blueprint for the establishment of Economic and Monetary Union by 1980.[1] This would be achieved in three stages, involving the gradual coordination of the national economic policies of the Member States and the imposition of limits to the fluctuation of exchange rates, leading to a final and irrevocable fixing of the exchange rates and a common monetary policy. The subsequent years of economic crisis and currency instability meant that this came to nothing. Instead, efforts turned to managing exchange rates. An initial attempt to manage exchange rates in 1972 in the so-called 'Snake' failed as a result of currency turmoil in the 1970s.[2] It was replaced in 1979 by the European Monetary System (EMS) and its exchange rate mechanism (ERM).[3] The currency of each Member State was assigned fixed central exchange rates as against every other participating currency and a notional composite unit of account, the ECU (European Currency Unit). The actual market exchange rate could fluctuate around the central rate within strict bands (generally, of +/−2.5 per cent). The central banks of the Member States undertook to intervene collectively in the markets to ensure that the exchange rates would not move outside the set bands.

The seminal moment for the establishment of Economic and Monetary Union was the Hanover summit in June 1988. Flushed from the success of the Single European Act, the European Council decided to explore the precise means by which Economic and Monetary Union could be achieved. It entrusted the task of producing a report on this to a committee chaired by the then President of the Commission, Jacques Delors, and comprising the governors of the central banks of the Member States as well as three experts in monetary affairs. The report of the Delors Committee, adopted at the Madrid European Council in 1990, set out the blueprint for the Economic and Monetary Union we have today in the European Union.

Committee for the Study of Economic and Monetary Union, *Report on Economic and Monetary Union in the European Community* (Luxembourg, 1989)

22. A *monetary union* constitutes a currency area in which policies are managed jointly with a view to attaining common macroeconomic objectives. As already stated in the 1970 Werner Report, there are three necessary conditions for a monetary union:
    - the assurance of total and irreversible convertibility of currencies;
    - the complete liberalization of capital transactions and full integration of banking and other financial markets; and
    - the elimination of margins of fluctuation and the irrevocable locking of exchange rate parities.

---

[1] Supplement to *EC Bulletin* 11–1970.

[2] The Basel Agreement created a multilateral intervention mechanism in the foreign exchange market and the European Monetary Co-operation Fund the following year; Regulation 907/73/EC establishing a European Monetary Cooperation Fund [1973] OJ L89/2.

[3] *EC Bulletin* 6–1978, 1.5.2. See also J. van Ypersele and J.-C. Koeune, *The European Monetary System: Origins, Operation and Outlook* (Commission, Brussels, 1984).

The first two of these requirements have already been met, or will be with the completion of the internal market programme. The single most important condition for a monetary union would, however, be fulfilled only when the decisive step was taken to lock exchange rates irrevocably....

23. ... The adoption of *a single currency*, while not strictly necessary for the creation of a monetary union, might be seen — for economic as well as psychological and political reasons — as a natural and desirable further development of the monetary union. A single currency would clearly demonstrate the irreversibility of the move to monetary union, considerably facilitate the monetary management of the Community and avoid the transaction costs of converting currencies. A single currency, provided that its stability is ensured, would also have a much greater weight relative to other major currencies than any individual Community currency....

25. *Economic union* – in conjunction with a monetary union – combines the characteristics of an unrestricted common market with a set of rules which are indispensable to its proper working. In this sense economic union can be described in terms of four basic elements: the single market within which persons, goods, services and capital can move freely; competition policy and other measures aimed at strengthening market mechanisms; common policies aimed at structural change and regional development; and macroeconomic policy coordination, including binding rules for budgetary policies....

   ... A coherent set of economic policies at the Community and national levels would be necessary to maintain permanently fixed exchange rates between Community currencies and, conversely, a common monetary policy, in support of a single currency area, would be necessary for the Community to develop into an economic union....

29. *Community policies in the regional and structural field* would be necessary in order to promote an optimum allocation of resources and to spread welfare gains throughout the Community ...

30. *Macroeconomic policy* is the third area in which action would be necessary for a viable economic and monetary union. This would require an appropriate definition of the role of the Community in promoting price stability and economic growth through the coordination of economic policies. Many developments in macroeconomic conditions would continue to be determined by factors and decisions operating at the national or local level. This would include not only wage negotiations and other economic decisions in the fields of production, savings and investment, but also the action of public authorities in the economic and social spheres. Apart from the system of binding rules governing the size and the financing of national budget deficits, decisions on the main components of public policy in such areas as internal and external security, justice, social security, education, and hence on the level and composition of government spending, as well as many revenue measures, would remain the preserve of Member States even at the final stage of economic and monetary union.

   However, an economic and monetary union could only operate on the basis of mutually consistent and sound behaviour by governments and other economic agents in all member countries. In particular, uncoordinated and divergent national budgetary policies would undermine monetary stability and generate imbalances in the real and financial sectors of the Community....

31. ... Economic and monetary union would require the creation of a new monetary institution, placed in the constellation of Community institutions (European Parliament, European Council, Council of Ministers, Commission and Court of Justice). The formulation and implementation of common policies in non-monetary fields and the coordination of policies remaining within the competence of national authorities would not necessarily require a new institution; but a revision and, possibly, some restructuring of the existing Community bodies, including an appropriate delegation of authority, could be necessary.

32. A new monetary institution would be needed because a single monetary policy cannot result from independent decisions and actions by different central banks. Moreover, day-to-day monetary policy operations cannot respond quickly to changing market conditions unless they are decided centrally. Considering the political structure of the Community and the advantages of making existing central banks part of a new system, the domestic and international monetary policy-making of the Community should be organized in a federal form, in what might be called a *European System of Central Banks* (ESCB). This new System would have to be given the full status of an autonomous Community institution …

The Delors Report suggests a number of dimensions to Economic and Monetary Union which are, to a large extent, now replicated in Article 119 TFEU.

Article 3(4) TEU

The Union shall establish an economic and monetary union whose currency is the euro.

Article 119 TFEU

1. For the purposes set out in Article 3 of the TEU, the activities of the Member States and the Union shall include, as provided in the Treaties, the adoption of an economic policy which is based on the close coordination of Member States' economic policies, on the internal market and on the definition of common objectives, and conducted in accordance with the principle of an open market economy with free competition.
2. Concurrently with the foregoing, and as provided in the Treaties and in accordance with the procedures set out therein, these activities shall include a single currency, the euro, and the definition and conduct of a single monetary policy and exchange-rate policy the primary objective of both of which shall be to maintain price stability and, without prejudice to this objective, to support the general economic policies in the Union, in accordance with the principle of an open market economy with free competition.

It is worth unpacking the different elements as, combined, these form the architecture of Economic and Monetary Union (EMU) within the European Union.

Free movement of capital   It has to be possible for people in one part of the Union to make investments and payments for assets in other parts of the Union. National restrictions on payments and investments, which limit the movement of capital from one part of the Union to another, in principle, therefore have to be abolished. Alongside this, if there is not a single currency all currencies have to be fully convertible. That is to say there should be no limits on the amount of one legal tender that can be exchanged into another EU legal tender. Otherwise, it would be possible to limit the amount that could be invested in a state with another legal tender. To this end, Article 63 TFEU prohibits, subject to certain limited exceptions, restrictions on the free movement of capital and payments.

> **Article 63 TFEU**
>
> 1. Within the framework of the provisions set out in this Chapter, all restrictions on the movement of capital between Member States and between Member States and third countries shall be prohibited.
> 2. Within the framework of the provisions set out in this Chapter, all restrictions on payments between Member States and between Member States and third countries shall be prohibited.

A single currency whose issue is authorised by the European Central Bank   The model of EMU adopted by the Union requires a single currency issued by a central bank, the European Central Bank (ECB). Based in Frankfurt, this bank has a monopoly over the authorisation of the issue of the euro and over the setting of short-term interest rates as these set the terms at which it will lend money to financial institutions.

> **Article 128 TFEU**
>
> 1. The European Central Bank shall have the exclusive right to authorise the issue of euro banknotes within the Union. The European Central Bank and the national central banks may issue such notes. The banknotes issued by the European Central Bank and the national central banks shall be the only such notes to have the status of legal tender within the Union.
> 2. Member States may issue euro coins subject to approval by the European Central Bank of the volume of the issue …

Controls on national deficits[4]   The Delors Report talks of 'binding rules governing the size and the financing of national budget deficits' (paragraph 30). The philosophy behind this is that excessive borrowing (in other words the running of an excessive deficit) by one government creates costs for other governments. To finance the deficit the borrowing government will have to turn to the capital markets to borrow the money. These will insist on higher interest rates for the currency both to offset the risk of the greater size of the debt and as a price for payment.[5] This penalises other states who now have to borrow on less favourable terms. This can in turn lead them to pressurise the central bank to reduce short-term interest rates, which, as this affects the cost of borrowing for investors, will in turn lower long-term interest rates. Alternatively, to counter inflationary pressures generated by excessive borrowing, the central

---

[4] The controls on national budgets and the coordination of economic policy are known as the Stability and Growth Pact. It comprises the following instruments. Resolution of the European Council on the Stability and Growth Pact [1997] OJ C236/1; Regulation 1466/97/EC on the strengthening of the surveillance of budgetary positions and the surveillance and coordination of economic policies [1997] OJ L209/1; Regulation 1467/97/EC on speeding up and clarifying the implementation of the excessive deficit procedure [1997] OJ L209/6; Regulation 1055/2005/EC amending Regulation 1466/97 on the strengthening of the surveillance of budgetary positions and the surveillance and coordination of economic policies [2005] OJ L174/1; and Regulation 1056/2005/EC amending Regulation 1467/97/EC on speeding up and clarifying the implementation of the excessive deficit procedure [2005] OJ L174/5.

[5] If a government wishes to borrow euros from investors, this pushes up demand so they can sell their euros at a higher price (the long-term interest rate). They may also push for a risk premium as they will be unsure whether it can pay.

bank may increase short-term interest rates, thus penalising governments who have not borrowed in this way.[6] The TFEU therefore prohibits excessive government deficits.

Article 126(1) TFEU

Member States shall avoid excessive government deficits.

A simple injunction is not seen as sufficient. A procedure is put in place, therefore, the Excessive Deficit Procedure, which places the determination of whether there is an excessive deficit in the hands of the Commission and the Council.[7] If they find an excessive deficit, recommendations will be made to the Member State. It can then be warned and even strongly sanctioned if it does not reduce the deficit.

Coordination and surveillance of national economic policy   Other instruments, notably fiscal policy, can be as important as monetary policy in managing the economy. Thus, if the European Union is experiencing strong growth this can be reduced by high interest rates, but this is countered if Member States continue to engage in significant public spending. By contrast, if the Union is in recession, it may no longer be possible to lower interest rates, in which case government spending becomes important. Within a monetary union with a single interest rate, national policies have to be coordinated on this if they are to support each other and not cancel each other out. In addition, some states (notably France) argued for an EU dimension to fiscal policy by proposing European economic government in which fiscal policy would be coordinated at EU level.[8] There is therefore coordination of national economic policy within the Council.

Article 120 TFEU

Member States shall conduct their economic policies with a view to contributing to the achievement of the objectives of the Union, as defined in Article 3 TEU, and in the context of the broad guidelines referred to in Article 121(2). The Member States and the Union shall act in accordance with the principle of an open market economy with free competition, favouring an efficient allocation of resources, and in compliance with the principles set out in Article 119.

Article 121(1) TFEU

Member States shall regard their economic policies as a matter of common concern and shall coordinate them within the Council, in accordance with the provisions of Article 120.

---

[6] For an accessible explanation see W. Buiter, 'The "Sense and Nonsense of Maastricht" Revisited: What Have we Learnt about Stabilization in EMU?' (2006) 44 *JCMS* 687, 693–705.

[7] Article 126 TFEU.

[8] J. Pisani-Ferry, 'Only One Bed for Two Dreams: A Critical Retrospective on the Debate over the Economic Governance of the Euro Area' (2006) 44 *JCMS* 823. See also K. Dyson and K. Featherstone, *The Road to Maastricht: Negotiating Economic and Monetary Union* (Oxford, Oxford University Press, 1999) 221–5.

This coordination is not just about aligning national economic policies. It is also about guiding them. A commitment to coordination has been judged not to be sufficient. There must also be surveillance of whether national policies are actually coordinated both with each other and with the policies of the ECB.[9] This coordination and surveillance is known by the institutional levers that guide it: the broad economic policy guidelines.

EMU therefore has four dimensions: free movement of capital, a single monetary policy, constraints on excessive government deficits and broad economic policy guidelines. However, these arrangements cannot be seen in a vacuum. There is a mission underlying these institutional arrangements, which both provides a partial explanation for them and constrains the actors in the exercise of their powers under this regime. It is that of securing price stability.[10]

> ## Article 128(3) TFEU
>
> These activities of the Member States and the Union shall entail compliance with the following guiding principles: stable prices, sound public finances and monetary conditions and a sustainable balance of payments.

Herdegen has observed that it is highly unusual to entrench an economic objective in this way, so that it becomes a constitutional imperative. Although the Treaties borrowed heavily from the successful post-War German monetary model, he noted that traditionally the commitment to low inflation was not so constitutionally entrenched there.[11] The decision to control inflation is a political choice which invariably carries both benefits and costs. There is also a concern about fighting yesterday's wars. To be sure, concerns about high inflation dominated debates in the 1970s and 1980s leading up to the decision to establish the euro. It is, however, simply not possible to know what the most significant economic evil will be considered to be in the future. To tie the Union's objectives to one single issue, albeit a highly significant one, is thus both dogmatic and holding the Union's institutional arrangements open to fortune.

(ii) Differentiated obligations of Economic and Monetary Union

On 1 January 1999, eleven Member States adopted the euro as their currency. The group comprised Austria, Belgium, Finland, France, Germany, Ireland, Italy, Luxembourg, the Netherlands, Portugal and Spain. Since then a further five states — Greece, Slovenia, Cyprus, Malta and Slovakia — have followed suit and adopted the euro. To adopt the euro each of these Member States had, in principle, to meet a series of economic conditions known as the convergence criteria. These are currently:[12]

---

[9] See Articles 121 and 136 TFEU.

[10] See also Articles 119(2) and 219 TFEU which make it a norm of exchange rate and monetary policy, and Article 127 TFEU which makes it the central objective of the ESCB.

[11] M. Herdegen, 'Price Stability and Budgetary Restraints in the Economic and Monetary Union: The Law as Guardian of Economic Wisdom' (1998) 35 *CMLRev.* 9, 11–15.

[12] The need for observance of these criteria is set out in Article 140 TFEU. The reference values are in the two Protocols below nn. 13 and 14.

- the annual government deficit should not exceed 3 per cent of GDP and the total government debt should not exceed 60 per cent of GDP;[13]
- an annual rate of inflation not more than 1.5 percentage points above the three best performing Member States;
- participation within the exchange rate mechanism for at least two years, without devaluing against the euro;
- long-term nominal interest rates that are not more than 2 percentage points above the three best performing states in terms of price stability.[14]

States adjudged not yet to have met these criteria are not entitled to participate in the euro. They are known in the Treaties as states 'with a derogation'.[15] These currently include all the other states in the Union except Denmark and the United Kingdom. At least once every two years or at their own request, states 'with a derogation' are considered as to whether they meet the criteria and should be invited to join the euro.[16]

Denmark has notified the other states that it will not participate in the euro, and there is a Protocol acknowledging its position.[17] The position for the United Kingdom is slightly different. It has a Protocol granting it the right to decide at some future date whether it wishes to participate in the euro.[18] There is no sign that it will exercise that right in the near future. Although there are some slight differences, the obligations of Denmark,[19] the United Kingdom[20] and the states 'with a derogation'[21] are similar:

- the free movement of capital rules apply fully to them;
- the euro is not legal tender within their jurisdictions; they are not bound by measures concerning use of the euro and they do not take part in the tasks of the European System of Central Banks (the network of central banks that administers the euro);
- whilst a finding can be made that they have an excessive deficit, they cannot be required to take steps to remedy it or be sanctioned for failing to do so;
- they are guided by the broad economic policy guidelines unless these relate specifically to the euro area.

These states are also denied certain entitlements. They do not take part in the governing arrangements of the European Central Bank or the appointment of its members.[22] This is uncontroversial. As the euro states do not run their monetary policy, there is no reason why they should contribute to the running of the monetary policy of the euro states. More controversial is their exclusion from the Euro Group. Established as an informal group in 1999, this comprises the finance ministers of the euro states, the ECB and the Commission. This group

---

[13] Protocol on Excessive Deficit Procedure, Article 1.
[14] The last three criteria are set out in the Protocol on Convergence Criteria.
[15] Article 139(1) TFEU.
[16] Article 140 TFEU.
[17] Protocol on Certain Provisions relating to Denmark.
[18] Protocol on Certain Provisions relating to the United Kingdom.
[19] Protocol on Certain Provisions relating to Denmark, para. 1.
[20] Protocol on Certain Provisions relating to the United Kingdom, para. 4. The central difference relates to excessive deficits. The United Kingdom makes no commitment to avoid excessive deficits whereas all the other states are constrained by this commitment.
[21] Article 139(2) TFEU.
[22] They also do not take part in the formulation of the broad economic policy guidelines insofar as these relate specifically to the euro-zone: Article 136(2) TFEU.

discusses questions related to the specific responsibilities these all share in relation to the single currency. The Euro Group is seen as extremely powerful.[23] It meets before the Council meets, and is seen as an ante-chamber for discussing all questions of economy policy within the Union, pre-empting decisions that might subsequently be taken in the Council. It is also the place where most political feedback or pressure is placed on the European Central Bank by finance ministers over its interest rate policies. The first President of the Group, Jean-Claude Juncker, publicly stated in 2005 that in his view inflation was under control and warned the ECB that a rise in interest rates could hit growth in the euro-zone.[24] There is a dual concern, therefore. The Group could, first, decide matters over which other states are entitled to a voice under the Treaty arrangements, notably on coordination of economic policy. Secondly, it could erode institutional arrangements, most notably by putting pressure on the ECB, which might have negative effects for the whole Union and not just the euro-zone. It was initially accepted by the other states, notably the United Kingdom, on the condition that the Euro Group remain informal. It has, however, been, granted a formal status and recognised by the Lisbon Treaty.[25] It remains to be seen whether this affects its power.

3 FREE MOVEMENT OF CAPITAL

The prohibition in Article 63(1) TFEU on restrictions on the movement of capital between Member States and between Member States and third countries is directly effective.[26] The types of activity that could potentially restrict free movement of capital are any restrictions or regulation of profit-making activity. For free movement of capital is about the accessibility of a particular economic sector to market operators, namely whether they can invest in it and can buy and sell in it. It is, moreover, not just a question of access but also one about making profit out of that activity. If this is not possible, there will be no investment. Insofar as any measure might lower the possibility for profit, a question arises about a possible restriction on free movement of capital. On such a view, restrictions on the narcotics trade could breach Article 63(1) TFEU by preventing foreign investors investing and thereby preventing these investors moving their capital into narcotics or companies which traded narcotics.

Such an interpretation would lead the Court of Justice into intervening in almost everything. Article 63(1) TFEU raises three questions, therefore: first, what constitutes a capital movement for the purpose of the Treaty; secondly, as with other economic freedoms, what national measures are perceived as illegal restrictions; thirdly, what types of justification might be legally provided for such restrictions.

The Court has followed the lead of the legislature on the first question of the material remit of the provision and what constitutes a 'capital movement'. In the late 1980s, Member States liberalised capital movements in a phased manner. They adopted Directive 88/361/EEC which

---

[23] U. Puetter, 'Governing Informally: The Role of the Eurogroup in EMU and the Stability and Growth Pact' (2004) 11 *JEPP* 854. For a more extensive analysis of the powerful links between the ministers see U. Puetter, *The Eurogroup: How a Secretive Group of Finance Ministers Shapes European Economic Governance* (Manchester, Manchester University Press, 2006).

[24] G. Parker, R. Atkins and S. Daneshkhu, 'ECB Warned over Rate Rise', *Financial Times*, 30 November 2005, 1.

[25] Article 137 TFEU; Protocol on the Euro Group.

[26] This provision is directly effective. Joined Cases C-163/94, C-165/94 and C-250/94 *Sanz de Lera* [1995] ECR I-4821.

set out the different types of capital of movement that were to be liberalised.[27] The Court has consistently interpreted this document, in particular Annex I, as setting out what constitutes a capital movement for the purpose of Article 63(1) TFEU.[28] The Annex is too long to set out verbatim. Broadly speaking, it is non-exhaustive but sets out thirteen groups of transactions which are to be covered now by Article 63(1) TFEU. These include direct investments, such as investment in a company or finance provided to an entrepreneur; investments in real estate, such as a purchase of a house; operations in securities, such as trading in bonds, shares and any other money market instruments; financial loans and sureties; operations in current and deposit accounts with financial institutions; transfers relating to insurance contracts, and finally, personal capital movements, such as gifts, inheritances or personal loans. The Court has indicated that these will only not fall within Article 63(1) TFEU if the constituent elements all fall within a single Member State:[29] so a tax on an inheritance left by a national of that state to her children who are resident within that state will not fall within Article 63(1) TFEU as none of the constituent elements have a transnational dimension.

The second question is what sort of restriction is covered by this provision. Annex I to Directive 88/361/EEC indicates that Article 63(1) TFEU is not merely to cover restrictions on use of currency to purchase an asset, but must also cover restrictions that go to the heart of the transaction, and those which prevent an asset being sold. This is quite logical. A restriction on the sale or purchase of property in a Member State is as restrictive of investment as one that prevents one exchanging the currency necessary to purchase it. But does Article 63(1) TFEU only cover discriminatory restrictions which prevent foreigners investing or foreign capital investments in such schemes, or is it to be interpreted in a similar manner to the other economic freedoms as covering both discriminatory and non-discriminatory restrictions on movement of capital? The Court has, unsurprisingly, followed a similar line here as elsewhere, although its language has been vaguer than with the other economic freedoms.

The most prominent example of its reasoning is its famous 'golden shares' judgment in relation to the German authorities' involvement with the German car manufacturer, Volkswagen (VW).[30] The Commission brought an action against Germany for breach of Article 63(1) TFEU because of three provisions in its VW Law. Paragraph 4(3) provided many important decisions over Volkswagen could be blocked by a blocking minority of 20 per cent of shareholders. The Land of Lower Saxony, the regional authority, owned about 20 per cent of the shares. Paragraph 2(1) provided that no shareholder could have voting rights of more than 20 per cent, no matter how many shares they owned. Finally, paragraph 4(1) provided that the federal authorities and the authorities of the Land of Lower Saxony could each appoint two representatives to the supervisory board of the company. The German government observed that none of these measures stopped anybody buying and selling shares in Volkswagen. Indeed, these were amongst the most highly traded shares in Europe. The Court of Justice rejected these arguments

[27] Directive 88/361/EEC for the implementation of Article 67 EEC [1988] OJ L178/5.

[28] Case C-222/97 *Trummer and Mayer* [1999] ECR I-1661; Case C-452/01 *Ospelt v Schössle Weissenberg Familienstiftung* [2003] ECR I-9743; Case C-386/04 *Centro di Musicologia Walter Stauffer v Finanzamt München für Körperschaften* [2006] ECR I-8203.

[29] Case C-513/03 *van Hilten-van der Heijden v Inspecteur van de Belastingdienst* [2006] ECR I-1957; Case C-43/07 *Arens-Sikken v Staatssecretaris van Financiën* [2008] ECR I-6887.

[30] The wider context of the judgment is explored in P. Zumbansen and D. Saam, *The ECJ, Volkswagen and European Corporate Law: Reshaping the European Varieties of Capitalism*, CLPE Research Paper 30/2007, http://ssrn.com/abstractid=1030652 (accessed 30 November 2009).

on the basis that these provisions restricted the influence and value of what was being bought, and therefore constituted a restriction under Article 63(1) TFEU.

Case C-112/05 *Commission v Germany* [2007] ECR I-8995

18. In the absence of a Treaty definition of 'movement of capital' within the meaning of Article [63(1) TFEU], the Court has previously recognised the nomenclature set out in Annex I to Council Directive 88/361/EEC ... as having indicative value. Movements of capital within the meaning of Article [63(1) TFEU] therefore include direct investments, that is to say, as that nomenclature and the related explanatory notes show, investments of any kind undertaken by natural or legal persons and which serve to establish or maintain lasting and direct links between the persons providing the capital and the undertakings to which that capital is made available in order to carry out an economic activity ... As regards shareholdings in new or existing undertakings, as those explanatory notes confirm, the objective of establishing or maintaining lasting economic links presupposes that the shares held by the shareholder enable him, either pursuant to the provisions of the national laws relating to companies limited by shares or in some other way, to participate effectively in the management of that company or in its control.

19. Concerning this form of investment, the Court has stated that national measures must be regarded as 'restrictions' within the meaning of Article 63(1) TFEU if they are liable to prevent or limit the acquisition of shares in the undertakings concerned or to deter investors of other Member States from investing in their capital ...

50. Paragraph 4(3) of the VW Law thus creates an instrument enabling the Federal and State authorities to procure for themselves a blocking minority allowing them to oppose important resolutions, on the basis of a lower level of investment than would be required under general company law.

51. By capping voting rights at the same level of 20%, paragraph 2(1) of the VW Law supplements a legal framework which enables the Federal and State authorities to exercise considerable influence on the basis of such a reduced investment.

52. By limiting the possibility for other shareholders to participate in the company with a view to establishing or maintaining lasting and direct economic links with it which would make possible effective participation in the management of that company or in its control, this situation is liable to deter direct investors from other Member States.

53. This finding cannot be undermined by the argument advanced by the Federal Republic of Germany to the effect that Volkswagen's shares are among the most highly-traded in Europe and that a large number of them are in the hands of investors from other Member States.

54. As the Commission has argued, the restrictions on the free movement of capital which form the subject-matter of these proceedings relate to direct investments in the capital of Volkswagen, rather than portfolio investments made solely with the intention of making a financial investment ... and which are not relevant to the present action. As regards direct investors, it must be pointed out that, by creating an instrument liable to limit the ability of such investors to participate in a company with a view to establishing or maintaining lasting and direct economic links with it which would make possible effective participation in the management of that company or in its control, paragraphs 2(1) and 4(3) of the VW Law diminish the interest in acquiring a stake in the capital of Volkswagen.

55. This finding is not affected by the presence, among Volkswagen's shareholders, of a number of direct investors, which, according to the Federal Republic of Germany, is similar to such a presence among

the shareholders of other large undertakings. This circumstance is not such as to cast doubt on the fact that, because of the disputed provisions of the VW Law, direct investors from other Member States, whether actual or potential, may have been deterred from acquiring a stake in the capital of that company in order to participate in it with a view to establishing or maintaining lasting and direct economic links with it which would make possible effective participation in the management of that company or in its control, even though they were entitled to benefit from the principle of the free movement of capital and the protection which that principle affords them…

65. The fact that the supervisory board, as the Federal Republic of Germany submits, is not a decision-making body, but a simple monitoring body, is not such as to undermine the position and influence of the Federal and State authorities concerned. While German company law assigns to the supervisory board the task of monitoring the company's management and of providing reports on that management to the shareholders, it confers significant powers on that body, such as the appointment and dismissal of the members of the executive board, for the purpose of performing that task. Furthermore, as the Commission has pointed out, approval by the supervisory board is necessary for a number of transactions, including, in addition to the setting-up and transfer of production facilities, the establishment of branches, the sale and purchase of land, investments and the acquisition of other undertakings.

66. By restricting the possibility for other shareholders to participate in the company with a view to establishing or maintaining lasting and direct economic links with it such as to enable them to participate effectively in the management of that company or in its control, paragraph 4(1) of the VW Law is liable to deter direct investors from other Member States from investing in the company's capital.

67. For the same reasons as those set out in paragraphs 53 to 55 of this judgment, this finding cannot be undermined by the Federal Republic of Germany's argument that there is a keen investment interest in Volkswagen shares on the international financial markets.

68. In the light of the foregoing, it must be held that paragraph 4(1) of the VW Law constitutes a restriction on the movement of capital within the meaning of [Article 63(1) TFEU].

A measure will be found to be in breach of Article 63(1) TFEU if it is liable to prevent or limit investment (here the acquisition of shares) or deter investment, notably from other Member States (paragraph 19). By disproportionately limiting the influence of investors in the governance of the company, the Court found the German measures deterred investment (paragraphs 52 and 66) and therefore breached Article 63 TFEU. Yet, is this convincing? If this were the case, why was there such high trade in Volkswagen shares? Almost certainly, this was because these limited rights of participation were priced into the share price by the market. The slightly lower price compensated for the reduction of participation – something all those investing seemed to accept.

A more accurate rationale for the judgment would be that investors did not have effective participation in the control or management of the company.[31] In particular, the German authorities' rights within the company allowed them to take decisions as shareholders, which might

[31] This dimension to the judgment has been emphasised in subsequent, similar cases. Joined Cases C-463/04 and C-464/04 *Federconsumatori and Others* [2007] ECR I-10419; Case C-531/06 *Commission v Italy*, Judgment of 19 May 2009.

lower the value of the investors' shares. The argument is about the quality and transparency of public intervention in the market place and not restrictions on investment. Advocate General Poiares Maduro has therefore stated:

Case C–112/05 *Commission* v *Germany* [2007] ECR I–8995, Opinion of Advocate General Maduro

29. The Treaty entitles the Member States to maintain public ownership of certain companies. Nevertheless, it does not entitle them to curtail selectively the access of market operators to certain economic sectors once those sectors have been privatised. If the State were entitled to maintain special forms of market control over privatised companies, it could easily frustrate the application of the rules on free movement by granting only selective and potentially discriminatory access to substantial parts of the national market.

30. When the State privatises a company, therefore, the free movement of capital requires that the company's economic autonomy be protected, unless there is a need to safeguard fundamental public interests recognised by Community law. In this way, any State control, given that it is outside the normal market mechanism, of a privatised company must be linked to carrying out the activities of general economic interest associated with that company.

31. ... The Court has recognised that 'certain concerns may justify the retention by Member States of a degree of influence within undertakings that were initially public and subsequently privatised, where those undertakings are active in fields involving the provision of services in the public interest or strategic services'.[32] However, it is clear that such influence must be strictly limited to guaranteeing fundamental public interest obligations. Hence, the Court has emphasised the 'principle of respect for the decision-making autonomy of the undertaking concerned'. The State must thus identify the specific public interest which warrants protection. Moreover, the rules granting special rights to the State should be based on objective and precise criteria which do not go beyond what is necessary for the purpose of securing that public interest and guarantee the possibility of effective judicial review.[33]

This being so, we have currently three types of restriction that fall within Article 63(1) TFEU.

There are, first, those measures which discourage investment in another Member State. This may be by either deterring residents investing in other Member States or deterring non-residents investing in the Member State itself.[34] The key element is discrimination against transnational activities here. Thus, tax measures which result in the value of inheritances to non-residents being less than those to residents are illegal.[35] Equally illegal are laws granting tax exemption to charities registered in Germany but not to charities registered in other Member States as this allows a better return on investment for the former than the latter.[36] Secondly, there are measures which restrict investment in a Member State. Schemes requiring prior authorisation

---

[32] Case C-503/99 *Commission* v *Belgium* [2002] ECR I-4809.

[33] Joined Cases C-282/04 and C-283/04 *Commission* v *Netherlands (direct and portfolio investments)* [2006] ECR I-9141.

[34] Case C-370/05 *Festersen* [2007] ECR I-1129; Case C-101/05 *A* [2007] ECR I-11531.

[35] Case C-11/07 *Eckelkamp* [2008] ECR I-6845.

[36] Case C-386/04 *Centro di Musicologia Walter Stauffer* v *Finanzamt München für Körperschaften* [2006] ECR I-8203.

before one can invest in a sector or activity fall foul of Article 63(1) TFEU.[37] Equally, an Italian law that stated pharmacies could only be owned by people or companies who were exclusively pharmacists fell foul of the provision, as it restricted investors engaged in other activities from investing in the sector.[38]

The third type of measure is that which limits control over the investment. This has been set out in the 'golden shares' cases. This concerns the quality and predictability of public intervention in the marketplace.[39]

This is certainly multifaceted, but the language in all three tests is imprecise, and it has been observed that Article 63 TFEU runs the same danger of overreach as the other freedoms.[40] The Court has therefore held that if the effects of a measure on investment are too uncertain or indirect, they will not fall within Article 63 TFEU. In *ED*, a German company had supplied goods to Italo Fenocchio, an Italian company, for which it had not been paid.[41] It sought a summary order for payment against assets of Italo Fenocchio outside Italy. Italian law prevented a summary payment order being served on a defendant outside Italian territory. It was argued that this might violate Article 63(2) TFEU as, by making it more difficult to secure judicial protection, Italian law made it less attractive for foreigners to enter into contracts in Italy as it would be more difficult to enforce payment. The Court rejected this argument. It noted that Article 63(2) TFEU was there to allow individuals to discharge obligations on transnational payments without restriction. It was not there to challenge questions of civil procedure in national courts.

As with the other economic freedoms, national measures will be found to be lawful if they pursue a legitimate public interest.[42] In addition to this broad heading, Article 65(1) TFEU provides a series of explicit Treaty grounds on which Member States can derogate from Article 63(1) TFEU.

Article 65 TFEU

1. The provisions of Article 63 shall be without prejudice to the right of Member States:
   (a) to apply the relevant provisions of their tax law which distinguish between taxpayers who are not in the same situation with regard to their place of residence or with regard to the place where their capital is invested;
   (b) to take all requisite measures to prevent infringements of national law and regulations, in particular in the field of taxation and the prudential supervision of financial institutions, or to lay down procedures for the declaration of capital movements for purposes of administrative or statistical information, or to take measures which are justified on grounds of public policy or public security.
2. The provisions of this Chapter shall be without prejudice to the applicability of restrictions on the right of establishment which are compatible with the Treaties.

---

[37] Case C-302/97 *Konle* [1999] ECR I-3099; Case C-567/07 *Minister voor Wonen, Wijken en Integratie v Woningstichting Sint Servatius*, Judgment of 1 October 2009.

[38] Case C-531/06 *Commission v Italy*, Judgment of 19 May 2009.

[39] In addition to the cases cited above n. 31, see Joined Cases C-282/04 and C-283/04 *Commission v Netherlands (direct and portfolio investments)* [2006] ECR I-9141; Case C-326/07 *Commission v Italy*, Judgment of 26 March 2009.

[40] L. Flynn, 'Coming of Age: The Free Movement of Capital Case Law 1993–2002' (2002) 39 *CMLRev.* 773, 783–4.

[41] Case C-412/97 *ED v Italo Fenocchio* [1999] ECR I-3845.

[42] Case C-503/99 *Commission v Belgium* [2002] ECR I-4809; Case C-452/01 *Ospelt v Schlössle Weissenberg Familienstiftung* [2003] ECR I-9743.

3. The measures and procedures referred to in paragraphs 1 and 2 shall not constitute a means of arbitrary discrimination or a disguised restriction on the free movement of capital and payments as defined in Article 63.

The most significant exceptions are, first, that which allows differential fiscal treatment of non-residents, provided there is no arbitrary discrimination between residents and non-residents, and, secondly, public policy, which allows restrictions on investments that would otherwise finance illegal activities.

There is one distinctive feature of the provisions on free movement of capital. They apply not just to movements of capital between Member States, but also to movements of capital between Member States and third states. As a consequence, certain limited exceptions apply only to restrictions on movements of capital to and from third states. First, controls on the movement of funds in or out of the Community, which were already in place prior to 31 December 1993 and relate to direct investment, establishment, the provision of financial services or the admission of securities to capital markets, are allowed to be retained.[43] Secondly, it is possible to impose provisional restrictions on movements of capital to or from third countries in situations where these cause, or threaten to cause, serious difficulties for the operation of EMU: in this case, safeguard measures may be adopted by qualified majority voting (QMV) for a period of up to six months.[44]

4 THE INSTITUTIONS OF EMU: THE ECB AND THE ESCB

(i) The European System of Central Banks and its tasks

The TFEU places the responsibility for defining and implementing the monetary policy of the single currency in the hands of the European System of Central Banks (ESCB),[45] a composite organisation comprising the ECB and the national central banks (NCBs) of the twenty-seven Member States.[46] All central tasks of monetary policy within the euro-zone are to be carried out through the ESCB. These are set out in Article 127(2) TFEU.

Article 127(2) TFEU

The basic tasks to be carried out through the ESCB shall be:
- to define and implement the monetary policy of the Union,
- to conduct foreign-exchange operations consistent with the provisions of Article 219;[47]
- to hold and manage the official foreign reserves of the Member States,
- to promote the smooth operation of payment systems.

---

[43] Article 64(1) TFEU. The date is 31 December 1999 for Bulgaria, Estonia and Hungary.
[44] Article 66 TFEU. This is done by the Council on a proposal from the Commission after consulting the ECB.
[45] Article 127 TFEU.
[46] Article 282 TFEU; Protocol on the Statute of the ESCB, Article 1. On the legal arrangements see B. Krauskopf and C. Steven, 'The Institutional Framework of the European System of Central Banks: Legal Issues in the Practice of the First Ten Years of Its Existence' (2009) 46 *CMLRev.* 1143.
[47] This is the provision which governs exchange rate policy between the euro and other currencies. See pp. 736–7.

There is a *primus inter pares* principle, as, within the ESCB, the ECB has certain defined tasks:[48]

(a) the supply of money: we have already seen that it is exclusively responsible for authorising the issue of euros and setting short-term interest rates for the euro;[49]
(b) legislative powers: it has the power to make regulations, in particular, on minimum reserves for credit institutions,[50] clearing and payment systems, and, where the Council provides, on the prudential supervision of credit institutions;
(c) executive powers: it can take decisions necessary for the carrying out of the tasks entrusted to the ESCB; it can in particular instruct NCBs;
(d) regulatory powers: it can impose fines and periodic penalty payments on undertakings that do not comply with its Regulations;[51]
(e) provision of opinions: the ECB can make recommendations and deliver opinions. In particular, it is to be consulted on all proposed EU measures and national regulatory measures that fall in areas within its responsibilities.[52]

The ESCB is governed by the decision-making bodies of the ECB: the Governing Council and the Executive Board.[53] The membership of each is set out in Article 283 TFEU.

Article 283 TFEU

1. The Governing Council of the European Central Bank shall comprise the members of the Executive Board of the European Central Bank and the Governors of the national central banks of the Member States whose currency is the euro.

2. The Executive Board shall comprise the President, the Vice-President and four other members.

   The President, the Vice-President and the other members of the Executive Board shall be appointed by the European Council, acting by a qualified majority, from among persons of recognised standing and professional experience in monetary or banking matters, on a recommendation from the Council, after it has consulted the European Parliament and the Governing Council of the European Central Bank.

   Their term of office shall be eight years and shall not be renewable.

   Only nationals of Member States may be members of the Executive Board.

The respective tasks of the two bodies are set out in Article 12 of the Protocol on the Statute of the ESCB:

12.1. The Governing Council shall adopt the guidelines and take the decisions necessary to ensure the performance of the tasks entrusted to the ESCB under these Treaties and this

---

[48] Unless otherwise stated, these tasks are set out in Article 132 TFEU.
[49] Article 128 TFEU.
[50] See, in particular, Regulation 1745/2003/EC on the application of minimum reserves [2003] OJ L250/10.
[51] On the circumstances when these may be imposed, see Regulation 2157/1999/EC on the powers of the ECB to impose sanctions [1999] OJ L264/21.
[52] Articles 127(4) and 282(5) TFEU; Protocol on the Statute of the ESCB, Article 4.
[53] Article 129(1) TFEU. See also Article 282(2) TFEU.

Statute. The Governing Council shall formulate the monetary policy of the Union including, as appropriate, decisions relating to intermediate monetary objectives, key interest rates and the supply of reserves in the ESCB, and shall establish the necessary guidelines for their implementation.

The Executive Board shall implement monetary policy in accordance with the guidelines and decisions laid down by the Governing Council. In doing so the Executive Board shall give the necessary instructions to national central banks. In addition the Executive Board may have certain powers delegated to it where the Governing Council so decides.

To the extent deemed possible and appropriate and without prejudice to the provisions of this Article, the ECB shall have recourse to the national central banks to carry out operations which form part of the tasks of the ESCB.

The supreme decision-making body is therefore the Governing Council. It takes the decisions that we most readily associate with the ECB: the setting of interest rates and supply of reserves. The Executive Board, by contrast, is responsible for the preparation of the Governing Council meetings and the management of the daily business of the ESCB and the giving of instructions to the NCBs.

The position is a complicated one. To recap, monetary policy is run through an organisation, the ESCB. This organisation is governed by an institution, the ECB. The most powerful decision-making body of this institution, the Governing Council, comprises, however, almost all the banks that make up this organisation.[54] It is partly for this reason that the ECB's legal adviser suggests that it is better to see the ECB as an organisation rather than an institution.[55]

Yet, what are the organisational dynamics? It is probably best to see two sets of dynamics. First, there are those between the Executive Board and the NCBs which relate to the implementation of policy and daily business of the ESCB. Secondly, there are the internal decision-making dynamics of the Governing Council.

Turning to the first relationship, whilst the creation of a unitary central bank is unthinkable for political reasons, the Treaties create a streamlined central banking system. For this purpose, they erect a hierarchical structure behind a federal façade. NCBs retain their separate legal personality under their respective statutes, which are instruments of national law, and may perform, in addition to their functions as participants in the ESCB, other functions, wearing their hat as national authorities.[56] Yet, NCBs are superfluous as monetary authorities[57] and they are required to act in accordance with the guidelines and under the instructions of the ECB.[58] NCBs act, in this context, in a purely executory role, as the arms of the ECB, and exercise very little decisional autonomy.

---

[54] It will not include NCBs not participating in the euro.

[55] C. Zilioli and M. Selmayr, 'The Constitutional Status of the European Central Bank' (2007) 44 *CMLRev.* 355, 359–60.

[56] However, Article 14.4 of the Statute of the ESCB sets limits to the ability of NCBs to perform functions outside the ESCB's mandate, in their capacity as true national authorities. If the Governing Council considers, by a majority of two-thirds of the votes cast, that such national functions interfere with the objectives and tasks of the ESCB, it can prevent an NCB from undertaking them.

[57] C. Zilioli and M. Selmayr, 'The European Central Bank, Its System and Its Law' (1999) *Euredia* 187.

[58] Protocol on the Statute of the ESCB, Article 14.3.

The resulting arrangements are the price for soothing national sensibilities.[59] It has led to an increased reliance within the ESCB on formal legal techniques to implement monetary policy, in situations where a unitary central bank would treat similar issues informally as purely internal affairs. These are set out in Article 12(1) above. They may take the form of guidelines from the Governing Council or instructions from the Executive Board. This situation raises the possibility of formal legal disputes between the ECB and its national offshoots. The Treaties, consequently, empower the ECB to commence enforcement proceedings before the Court of Justice against NCBs that fail to fulfil their ESCB-related obligations.[60] Correspondingly, measures of the ECB may also be challenged by the NCBs, insofar as the relevant measures are addressed to them or are 'of direct and individual concern' to them.[61]

The position is different with regard to the second relationship, that of the decision-making dynamics of the Governing Council. The governors of the NCBs of the euro-zone form a large majority of the ECB Governing Council's membership. Currently, with sixteen states participating in the euro, they comprise sixteen out of twenty-two members. Whilst they act here as Union decision-makers there is a risk that their voting may still be determined by specifically national considerations. The governors are part of their respective national elites, are subject to national societal pressure and rely for their briefing primarily on their own staff.[62] Potentially, a coalition of NCB governors might be able to exercise a strong influence over the direction of the single monetary policy. The Treaties try to protect against this in two ways. First, it is the Executive Board which prepares and sets the agenda for the meetings, with the President of the Executive Board chairing those meetings.[63] Secondly, the voting membership of the Governing Council is capped at twenty-one, including the six members of the Executive Board. The roster of fifteen NCB governor votes is selected through a system of asymmetrical rotation, whereby in the future the governors of the NCBs of the large countries will exercise voting rights more frequently than those of smaller ones.[64]

The sufficiency of these safeguards depends on the stance of the members of the Governing Council. If NCB governors perceive themselves primarily as pan-European decision-makers, or as professionals whose primary responsibility is towards the financial markets and whose personal credibility is on the line, they are likely to act consistently with the objective of price stability. In such case, it would make no difference in terms of voting behaviour, whether one is the governor of the Banca d'Italia or a German member of the Executive Board. However, there is no guarantee that this will be the case. The additional domestic tasks performed by some NCBs, especially in the area of banking and financial regulation, may occasionally provide reasons for relaxation of the NCB governors' commitment to the monetary objectives of the ESCB.

---

[59] These included a need to preserve jobs in the NCBs and to retain some financial operations at the national level in order to avoid the concentration of financial activities in a single financial centre, such as London or Frankfurt. W. Buiter, 'Alice in Euroland' (1999) 37 *JCMS* 181, 202–4; N. Thygesen, *EMU, Britain and Other Outsiders* (London, LSE, FMG Paper No. 102, 1998) 16–17.

[60] Article 271 TFEU; Protocol on the Statute of the ESCB, Article 35.6.

[61] Article 263(1), (4) TFEU; Protocol on the Statute of the ESCB, Article 35(1). On judicial review in relation to the ECB, see R. Smits, *The European Central Bank: Institutional Aspects* (The Hague, Kluwer Law International, 1997) 106–10; and P. Craig, 'EMU, the European Central Bank, and Judicial Review' in P. Beaumont and N. Walker (eds.), *Legal Framework of the Single European Currency* (Oxford, Hart, 1999).

[62] Thygesen, above n. 59, 15.

[63] Protocol on the Statute of the ESCB, Articles 12(2), 13 respectively.

[64] Protocol on the Statute of the ESCB, Article 10(2).

(ii) Central bank independence and accountability

The institutional set-up of the ESCB was largely modelled on the German Bundesbank, with its federal structure and strong tradition of independence.[65] Germany's record of successful monetary management and its huge political leverage defined the terms of the debate on the ESCB's institutional design, making almost impossible the adoption of solutions that would mark a drastic departure from its own domestic practices. This, however, was not the only factor determining the institutional choices. The framers of the Treaties were persuaded by the significant academic literature which drew a link between strong price stability and independent central banks.[66] Full responsibility for monetary decision-making is vested in the ESCB, but only subject to a reasonably precise legal mandate, in which price stability is the overriding objective.[67] Alongside this, the ESCB's institutional design is aimed at ensuring, to the maximum degree practicable, its isolation or 'independence' from Europe's political arenas, whether national or supranational.[68]

> ### Article 130 TFEU
>
> When exercising the powers and carrying out the tasks and duties conferred upon them by the Treaties and the Statute of the ESCB and of the ECB, neither the ECB, nor a national central bank, nor any member of their decision-making bodies shall seek or take instructions from Union institutions, bodies, offices or agencies, from any government of a Member State or from any other body. The Union institutions, bodies, offices or agencies and the governments of the Member States undertake to respect this principle and not to seek to influence the members of the decision-making bodies of the ECB or of the national central banks in the performance of their tasks.

In a series of provisions, the Treaty sets out specific institutional guarantees.[69] These include the ECB's having separate legal personality[70] and organisational autonomy. It has financial and accounting independence.[71] The Treaty, thus, sets aside for the ECB the financial resources (capital and foreign-reserve assets) required for the effective conduct of monetary operations, thus ensuring its financial independence from the EU institutions and the Member States.[72] It is also not allowed to enter financial arrangements with them, such as the provision of overdraft

---

[65] On the institutional design of the ECB and the ESCB, see R. M. Lastra, 'European Monetary Union and Central Bank Independence' and J. de Haan and L. Gormley, 'Independence and Accountability of the European Central Bank' in M. Andenas, L. Gormley, C. Hadjiemmanuil and I. Harden (eds.), *European Economic and Monetary Union: The Institutional Framework* (London, Kluwer Law International, 1997); R. Smits, *The European Central Bank: Institutional Aspects* (The Hague, Kluwer Law International, 1997); and F. Amtenbrink, *The Democratic Accountability of Central Banks: A Comparative Study of the European Central Bank* (Oxford, Hart, 1999).

[66] A review of the arguments can be found in R. Burdekin *et al.*, 'A Monetary Constitution Case for an Independent European Central Bank' (1992) 15 *World Economy* 231.

[67] Article 127(1) TFEU; Protocol on the Statute of the ESCB, Article 2.

[68] The same text also appears in the Protocol on the Statute of the ESCB, Article 7.

[69] See Lastra, above n. 65; R. C. Effros, 'The Maastricht Treaty, Independence of the Central Bank, and Implementing Legislation' in T. J. T. Baliño and C. Cottarelli (eds.), *Frameworks for Monetary Stability: Policy Issues and Country Experiences* (Washington, DC, IMF, 1994); and Smits, above n. 65, 152–78.

[70] Article 282(3) TFEU; Protocol on the Statute of the ESCB, Article 9(1).

[71] See, generally, Protocol on the Statute of the ESCB, Articles 26–33.

[72] Protocol on Statute of the ESCB, Articles 28–30.

facilities, which might compromise that independence.[73] Finally, there are provisions to protect the personal independence of its decision-makers. The Board's conditions of employment are set by the Governing Council.[74] Members of the Board are to avoid conflicts of interest and to take the job on a full-time basis.[75] They are appointed for one eight-year non-renewable term.[76] This term is sufficiently long so that it exceeds the term of any single government. The government which is present at the appointment of a Board member will not necessarily be that when her term of office finishes. It is non-renewable so that the hope of reappointment will not be a factor that might lead the Board's members to heed political pressures in their decision-making.

The principle of central bank independence is applied not only to the ECB, but also to the NCBs of the euro-zone. A condition of participation in the euro is that Member States are required to take steps to achieve the independence of their central banks and the compatibility of their domestic legal rules with the relevant provisions of the Treaties and the Statute of the ESCB.[77]

In addition to this independence, the TFEU confines institutional contacts between the political institutions and the ESCB to what is considered strictly necessary in order to ensure that their respective policy stances are mutually understood. For this purpose, it gives the president of the Council and a member of the Commission the right to participate, without vote, in the meetings of the ECB's Governing Council.[78] Conversely, it requires that the President of the ECB be invited to meetings of the Euro Group[79] and to Council meetings whenever matters relating to the ESCB's field of competence are discussed.[80] These institutional contacts are intended to provide opportunities for policy-making coordination, however, rather than as any point of mutual accountability.

The flip-side of this regime is the ECB's exceptionally weak accountability in terms of its having to justify or explain its conduct or face the consequences for its mistakes.[81] This has not been helped by a resistance within the ECB to any sense of accountability on the grounds that this would compromise its independence.[82] Thus, whilst the Governing Council meetings are confidential, there was the possibility for the ECB to make its deliberations public.[83] It has refused to do so.[84] In like vein, one of its most senior legal officials claimed that the ECB

---

[73] Article 123(1) TFEU.

[74] Protocol on the Statute of the ESCB, Article 11(3). Their removal from their positions is possible only following a decision of the Court of Justice, if they no longer fulfil the conditions required for the performance of their duties or if they have been guilty of serious misconduct. *Ibid.* Article 11(4).

[75] Protocol on the Statute of the ESCB, Article 11(2).

[76] Article 283(2) TFEU; Protocol on the Statute of the ESCB, Article 11(1).

[77] Articles 130 and 131 TFEU; Protocol on the Statute of the ESCB, Article 14(1). The governors of the NCBs must be appointed for a term of office of at least five years. They may be relieved from their duties only on the same grounds as the members of the Executive Board: Protocol on the Statute of the ESCB, Article 14.2.

[78] Article 284(1) TFEU.

[79] Protocol on the Euro Group.

[80] Article 284(2) TFEU.

[81] On the nature of accountability within the Union see Chapter 9 at p. 375.

[82] For criticism, see Buiter above n. 59, 191–6. See also the reply of Otmar Issing, a member of the ECB's Executive Board, 'The Eurosystem: Transparent and Accountable or "Willem in Euroland"?' (1999) 37 *JCMS* 503.

[83] Protocol on the Statute of the ESCB, Article 10(4).

[84] Decision 2004/257/EC adopting the Rules of Procedure of the European Central Bank [2004] OJ L80/33, Article 23.1; Decision 2004/526/EC adopting the Rules of Procedure of the General Council of the European Central Bank [2004] OJ L230/61, Article 10(1).

constituted an independent supranational specialised organisation and even a 'new Community', sitting alongside the Union, with which it was legally associated only through the judicial supervision of its actions by the Court of Justice.[85]

These views had to be revised in the light of the *OLAF* judgment. The Commission sought the annulment of a decision of the ECB instituting its own internal system of anti-fraud investigations. The clear intention of the ECB was to exclude itself from the wide investigative powers conferred on the European Anti-Fraud Office (OLAF) in relation to fraud, corruption and other illegal activities adversely affecting the Union's financial interests.

Case C-11/00 *Commission v ECB ('OLAF')* [2003] ECR I-7147

92. As regards more specifically the ECB, it may be noted in that respect that it is clear from Article [13(1) TEU] and Article [282(3) TFEU] that the ECB was established and given legal personality by the [Treaties]. Furthermore, under Article [3(3) TEU] and Article [127(1) TFEU], the primary objective of the ESCB, at the heart of which is the ECB, is to maintain price stability and, without prejudice to this objective, to lend support to the general economic policies in the European Community... It follows that the ECB... falls squarely within the EC framework....

130. For the purposes of adjudicating on the ECB's plea, it is appropriate to state at the outset that the draftsmen of the EC Treaty clearly intended to ensure that the ECB should be in a position to carry out independently the tasks conferred upon it by the Treaty.

131. The most direct evidence of that intention is in Article [130 TFEU] which expressly prohibits the ECB and the members of its decision-making bodies, when exercising the powers and carrying out the tasks conferred on the ECB by the EC Treaty and the ESCB Statute, from seeking or taking instructions from Community institutions or bodies, from any government of a Member State or from any other body, and prohibits those Community institutions or bodies and those governments from seeking to influence the members of the ECB's decision-making bodies in the performance of their tasks....

133. However, EC institutions such as, notably, the Parliament, the Commission or the Court itself, enjoy independence and guarantees comparable in a number of respects to those thus afforded to the ECB....

134. As is clear from the wording of Article [130 TFEU], the outside influences from which that provision seeks to shield the ECB and its decision-making bodies are those likely to interfere with the performance of the 'tasks' which the EC Treaty and the ESCB Statute assign to the ECB. As the Advocate General has pointed out ... Article [130 TFEU] seeks, in essence, to shield the ECB from all political pressure in order to enable it effectively to pursue the objectives attributed to its tasks, through the independent exercise of the specific powers conferred on it for that purpose by the EC Treaty and the ESCB Statute.

135. By contrast, ... recognition that the ECB has such independence does not have the consequence of separating it entirely from the European Community and exempting it from every rule of Community law. First, it is evident from Article [127 TFEU] that the ECB is to contribute to the achievement of the objectives of the European Community, whilst Article [13 TEU] states that the ECB is to act within the limits of the powers conferred upon it by the EC Treaty and the ESCB Statute. Second, as the Commission has observed, the ECB is, on the conditions laid down by the EC Treaty and the ESCB Statute, subject to various kinds of Community controls, notably review by the Court of Justice

---

[85] C. Zilioli and M. Selmayr, 'The European Central Bank: An Independent Specialized Organization of Community Law' (2000) 37 *CMLRev.* 591, 642–3.

and control by the Court of Auditors. Finally, it is evident that it was not the intention of the Treaty draftsmen to shield the ECB from any kind of legislative action taken by the Community legislature…

137. Furthermore, … the ECB has not established how the fact that it is subject to measures adopted by the Community legislature in the area of fraud prevention and the prevention of any other unlawful activities detrimental to the European Community's financial interests … is such as to undermine its ability to perform independently the specific tasks conferred on it by the EC Treaty.

The Court of Justice thus held that the ECB can be held subject to certain legal constraints. Crucially, as OLAF was established by secondary legislation, these legal constraints were not just those imposed by the Treaties but also those imposed by secondary legislation. However, the Court indicates that only some secondary legislation will bind the ECB (paragraph 135). In particular, it will not be bound by any legislation which undermines its ability to perform its tasks independently.[86]

When this will be the case is not specified but it allows the possibility that EU legislation could provide for greater accountability and transparency. It has not chosen to do this. As such, the only constraints on the ECB are those in the Treaties. These are certain reporting duties. It must publish quarterly reports on the activities of the ECB and present an Annual Report to the Parliament, European Council, Commission and Council of Ministers.[87] The President and other members of the Executive Board can also at either their request or that of the European Parliament be heard by the competent committees of the European Parliament.[88]

These are weak constraints. In an extensive study, Amtenbrink analysed the accountability mechanisms of seven different central banking systems.[89] His comparisons focused on eight parameters: the legal basis of the central bank's operations, that is, whether this is constitutionally entrenched or subject to legislative amendment; the range and degree of precision of the monetary objectives; the relationship with the executive branch of government; the mechanisms for the appointment and dismissal of central bank officials; the availability of override mechanisms, under which the political branches of government can intervene in the conduct of monetary policy or suspend the legal objectives of the central bank; the arrangements regarding the central bank's accountability to parliament; the openness and transparency of its decision-making procedures; and its budgetary accountability.

He found that the accountability mechanisms in the institutional structure of the ESCB are uniquely feeble. Its legal mandate does not provide a clear yardstick against which the ECB's monetary performance may be judged. Institutionalised contacts with the EU institutions are scarce. There is no override mechanism. The openness of the decision-making process is limited as a result of weak reporting requirements. While the procedures for the appointment of Executive Board members and NCB governors provide ample opportunities for the exercise of political control, performance-based disciplining or dismissal is excluded, and only in cases of inability to perform their duties and serious misconduct can these officials be dismissed.

---

[86] C. Zilioli and M. Selmayr, 'The Constitutional Status of the European Central Bank' (2007) 44 *CMLRev.* 355, 370–2.

[87] Protocol on the Statute of the ESCB, Article 15(1), (3) respectively. On the latter see also Article 284(3) TFEU.

[88] Article 284(3) TFEU.

[89] Amtenbrink, above n. 65, in particular ch. 4.

The ECB enjoys financial independence, and only the accounting regularity of its operations is subject to review by the Court of Auditors.[90] As Amtenbrink correctly points out, however, in the case of the ESCB, the main limit to the exercise of democratic control relates to the legal basis of the ECB's operations. The system's legal objectives and guarantees of independence are entrenched to an exceptionally high degree through their inclusion in the Treaties.

F. Amtenbrink, *The Democratic Accountability of Central Banks: A Comparative Study of the European Central Bank* (Oxford, Hart, 1999) 362, 364

The unique position which the ECB holds even among the most independent of central banks is due to the fact that its entire legal basis has been enshrined in primary Community law. A change of the institutional structure requires a change of primary Community law itself. The restraining effect which the threat of an amendment of the legal basis can have on the behaviour of a central bank is virtually non-existent in the case of the ECB, as the probability of such a Treaty amendment is remote....

With regard to preconditions for democratic accountability, the legal basis of the ECB could be enhanced, introducing a clear yardstick for monetary policy and enhancing the arena in which the performance of the ECB is reviewed.... Contrary to what is sometimes suggested, it should not be left to the ECB to define its objective [through its own interpretations of the Treaty's rather abstract price stability objective]. One suggestion could be to put the ECOFIN Council, the members of which are democratically legitimised through the respective Member States, in charge of defining the monetary policy objective in the form of a point target or a target range for inflation.

Others have suggested, therefore, that a distinction be made between ends and means. If the ECB has independence over the means, it should be the responsibility of other political actors to set the overall goals of monetary policy, such as the inflation target.[91] For, ultimately, this is not a technical question but a deeply political one. The European Parliament has picked up on this in the questions it asks of the ECB. It has thus increasingly asked questions about the ECB's primary objectives, namely its inflation target, and its relationship to wider economic policy. Whilst this has allowed some public debate, Amtenbrink and van Duin have noted that it brings only limited accountability, as encounters look less at the performance of the ECB and turn more into wider debates about the state of the European economy.[92]

Finally, one should note that the ESCB's extraordinarily strong legal guarantees of independence and limited accountability are not necessarily sufficient to protect the central bank from de facto high-level political interventions. Europe's political leaders may come to see the principle of central bank independence only as a legal smokescreen, to which they must pay

---

[90] *Ibid.* 359–63. See also the numerical index of central bank accountability in J. de Haan, F. Amtenbrink and S. Eijffinger, *Accountability of Central Banks: Aspects and Quantifications*, Tilburg University, Center for Economic Research Discussion Paper No. 98–54, 1998, which produces a particularly low mark for the ECB.

[91] L. Gormley and J. De Haan, 'The Democratic Deficit of the European Central Bank' (1996) 21 *ELRev.* 95.

[92] F. Amtenbrink and K. van Duin, 'The European Central Bank Before the European Parliament: Theory and Practice after 10 Years of Monetary Dialogue' (2009) 34 *ELRev.* 561, 572–82.

lip-service, all the while violating it in practice. If so, the central bankers may prove unable or unwilling to resist the practical political pressures.[93]

(iii) The external relations of the euro-zone

In matters of monetary policy, there is an indissoluble link between the internal and external aspects. Especially in conditions where a currency's external value floats freely against other currencies, the internal decisions regarding the level of interest rates also affect the exchange rate. In this context, by defending price stability and the euro's purchasing power, the monetary policy of the ECB may also strengthen the external value of the euro. However, the Treaties do not include the management of the exchange rate as such within the objectives of the ESCB.

The management of exchange rates between the euro and the currencies of the other Member States, to the extent that it exists, takes place in the context of the revamped exchange rate mechanism (ERM II) of the EMS, which was introduced on 1 January 1999 to link other Member State currencies to the euro.[94] Participation in the ERM II is voluntary for the non-euro-zone Member States. As of December 2009, only four currencies (Danish krone, Estonian kroon, Latvian lats, Lithuanian litas) participate in ERM II. All other currencies are floating freely against the euro. For each participating currency, the system involves the establishment of a bilateral central rate of exchange against the euro. The exchange rate can then fluctuate within a band, normally set at +/−15 per cent, around the central rate.[95] An agreement between the ECB and the non-euro-zone NCBs demands intervention by the signatories in the foreign exchange markets as necessary for keeping the actual rates within the bands at all times.[96]

Notwithstanding the strong relationship between exchange rate policy and monetary policy, the legal regulation of the relations between the euro and non-ERM II currencies is dominated by the Council. Specifically, it can conclude formal agreements on an exchange rate system for the euro in relation to non-EU currencies[97] or, in the absence of an exchange rate agreement, general orientations for exchange rate policy with these currencies.[98] More generally, the Council can, on a proposal from the Commission, adopt decisions establishing common positions on matters of particular interest for EMU within the respective international financial institutions and conferences.[99] In addition, to the extent that EU level measures have not exhausted the

---

[93] Buiter observes that the 'collegiate' presentation of the Governing Council's decisions on interest rates shields its members from the need to defend publicly their individual voting record; but it cannot provide effective protection from pressures that may be exercised by the governments of their respective Member States, since the latter may still be able to find out what has gone on behind the curtains. Buiter, above n. 59, 191–3, 195–6.

[94] Resolution of the European Council on the establishment of an exchange rate mechanism in the third stage of economic and monetary union [1997] OJ C236/5. See K. Rohde Jensen, 'Inside EU, Outside EMU: Institutional and Legal Aspects of the Exchange Rate Mechanism II' in ECB, *Legal Aspects of the European System of Central Banks: Liber Amicorum Paolo Zamboni Garavelli* (Frankfurt, ECB, 2005).

[95] The Danish krone fluctuates within a +/−2.5 per cent band.

[96] This is now set out in the Agreement of 16 March 2006 between the ECB and the national central banks of the Member States outside the euro area laying down the operating procedures for an exchange rate mechanism in stage three of Economic and Monetary Union [2006] OJ C73/9.

[97] Article 219(1) TFEU. The Council acts unanimously and has also to consult the Parliament.

[98] Article 219(2) TFEU.

[99] Article 138(1) TFEU.

field, individual Member States may also retain an autonomous international presence in relation to EMU-relevant matters. For this purpose, they can participate in international organisations and conclude international agreements.[100] Finally, the ECB has its own explicit external competences, which allow it to establish 'relations with central banks and financial institutions in other countries and, where appropriate, with international organisations'.[101]

There is, thus, the possibility of inter-institutional conflict between the Council with its hegemony over exchange rate policy and the ECB with its hegemony over monetary policy.[102] There are attempts to avoid this. In all cases, the Council must observe the principle of price stability, and there is always provision for ECB involvement. International agreements or general orientations taken by the Council must be done either on the basis of an ECB Recommendation or on a Commission proposal after the Council has consulted the ECB. Similarly, the Council is required to consult the ECB before adopting a common position. Whilst this might create opportunities for reconciliation of objectives, it does not do away with the tension as, at the end of the day, the ECB cannot veto Council actions in the field of exchange rate policy. This creates a jurisdictional loop: the Council appears to be hierarchically superior to the ECB in the area of external monetary policy, since it may give orientations to the ECB; but, as external monetary policy is said to be subject to price stability, of which the ECB is the guarantor, the latter may insist on having the final say.

5 THE EXCESSIVE DEFICIT PROCEDURE

The loss of monetary sovereignty leads to fiscal policy acquiring additional importance as an economic level for the national governments of the euro-zone. Tax rises can be used to dampen down demand and spending when the economy is growing too strongly. By contrast, tax reductions, by liberating private spending, can boost the economy when it is depressed. Public expenditure can be used in the same way. Increased expenditure can boost the economy whilst reduced expenditure can lower economic activity. Insofar as either of these can lead to excessive borrowing, we have seen that this can impose costs for other national governments.[103]

Member States have therefore committed themselves to avoid excessive deficits.[104] Excessive deficits are stated in the Treaties to be either an annual government deficit of more than 3 per cent of GDP or a government debt of more than 60 per cent of GDP.[105] The running of an excessive deficit triggers legal consequences for a Member State as it is the precondition for the instigation of the excessive deficit procedure. These figures of 3 per cent and 60 per cent, particularly the former, have become increasingly contested. As early as 1997, the French government insisted that they not be treated too formulaically and a compromise was agreed where the figure of 3 per cent would not be applied in an exceptionally severe economic

---

[100] Article 219(4) TFEU.
[101] Protocol on the Statute of the ESCB, Article 23, first indent.
[102] For detailed commentary, see C. Zilioli and M. Selmayr, 'The External Relations of the Euro Area: Legal Aspects' (1999) 36 *CMLRev.* 273; also C. Zilioli and M. Selmayr, *The Law of the European Central Bank* (Oxford, Hart, 2001) ch. 5; and Smits, above n. 65, part III.
[103] See earlier, pp. 717–18.
[104] Article 126(1) TFEU.
[105] Article 126(2) TFEU; Protocol on the Excessive Deficit Procedure, Article 1.

downturn.[106] The matter came to a head in 2004. In 2002 and 2003, France and Germany, the two largest economies in the euro-zone, both ran government deficits of more than 3 per cent. The Commission opened the Excessive Deficit Procedure up against them but this was held in abeyance by the Council. This was found to be illegal by the Court of Justice which held that whilst the Council was not required to take a decision if there was not the necessary majority (QMV), it could not lawfully take a decision to hold the proceedings in abeyance.[107]

A number of reforms were adopted.[108] Crucially, two amendments were made to when an excessive deficit will be reported. First, an excessive deficit will not be found to exist, notwithstanding that a Member State has exceeded the thresholds, if this results from a severe economic downturn. This is interpreted to be wherever there is negative annual growth or an accumulated loss of output during a protracted period of low economic growth.[109] Secondly, the Commission is now required to make a 'balanced' overall assessment of when there is an excessive deficit. It can take account of a number of factors. These include the medium-term budgetary and economic position of the Member State, namely can this be seen as a blip in the longer perspective? It is also required to take account of qualitative factors that may be brought to its attention by the Member State. These can include a number of things but mentioned are obligations arising from European unification and contributions to fostering international solidarity.[110]

The first set of controls exempt a Member State from having an excessive deficit declared whenever it is in significant – but not savage – economic difficulties. The second grant considerable 'wiggle room' for not finding an excessive deficit. Buiter has described the criteria as having a 'kitchen sink quality' and fatally weakening the controls on Member States running excessive deficits.[111] To be sure, there is something a little bit cobbled together about the criteria. However, subsequent experience suggests that they have not stopped Member States being found to have an excessive deficit. As of 1 December 2009, twenty of the Member States have been found to have an excessive deficit by the Commission,[112] and of these eleven have also been found to have an excessive deficit by the Council.[113]

---

[106] This was the so-called 'Dublin compromise'. On the Pact see M. Weale, 'Monetary and Fiscal Policy in Euroland' (1999) 37 *JCMS* 153; see the chapters by I. Harden, J. von Hagen and R. Brookes, 'The European Constitutional Framework for Member States' Public Finances', C. T. Taylor, 'The Separation of Monetary and Fiscal Policy in Stage Three of EMU' and I. Italianer, 'The Excessive Deficit Procedure: A Legal Description' in M. Andenas, L. Gormley, C. Hadjiemmanuil and I. Harden (eds.), *European Economic and Monetary Union: The Institutional Framework* (London, Kluwer Law International, 1997); I. Harden, 'The Fiscal Constitution of EMU' in P. Beaumont and N. Walker (eds.), *Legal Framework of the Single European Currency* (Oxford, Hart, 1999); J.-V. Louis, 'The Review of the Stability and Growth Pact' (2006) 43 *CMLRev.* 85, 94–6.

[107] Case C-27/04 *Commission v Council (Stability and Growth Pact)* [2004] ECR I-4829. I. Maher, 'Economic Coordination and the European Court: Excessive Deficits and ECOFIN Discretion' (2004) 29 *ELRev.* 83; D. Doukas, 'The Frailty of the Stability and Growth Pact and the European Court of Justice: Much Ado About Nothing' (2005) 32 *LIEI* 293.

[108] These are set out in Regulation 1055/2005/EC amending Regulation 1466/97/EC on the strengthening of the surveillance of budgetary positions and the surveillance and coordination of economic policies [2005] OJ L174/1; and Regulation 1056/2005/EC amending Regulation 1467/97/EC on speeding up and clarifying the implementation of the excessive deficit procedure [1997] OJ L174/5.

[109] Regulation 1056/2005/EC, Article 1(2).

[110] *Ibid.* Article 1(3).

[111] W. Buiter, '"The Sense and Nonsense of Maastricht" Revisited: What Have We Learnt about Stabilization in EMU?' (2006) 44 *JCMS* 687, 690.

[112] See http://ec.europa.eu/economy_finance/sg_pact_fiscal_policy/excessive_deficit9109_en.htm (accessed 1 December 2009). It is easier to list those that do not have an excessive deficit. These are Bulgaria, Cyprus, Denmark, Estonia, Finland, Luxembourg and Sweden.

[113] These are France, Greece, Poland, Hungary, Ireland, Latvia, Lithuania, Malta, Romania, Spain and the United Kingdom.

The finding of an excessive deficit triggers the Excessive Deficit Procedure, a procedure that can lead (theoretically) to the levying of very heavy fines on the national government if it does not correct the excessive deficit.

The process starts with the Commission being obliged to write a report if there is an excessive deficit or a risk of an excessive deficit.[114] If it believes an excessive deficit exists or may occur, it must then address an opinion to the Member State concerned and inform the Council accordingly.[115] These elements are obligatory for the Commission. It then has a discretion whether to make a proposal to the Council to find an excessive deficit. From then on, events are determined by the Council.

Article 126 TFEU

6. The Council shall, on a proposal from the Commission, and having considered any observations which the Member State concerned may wish to make, decide after an overall assessment whether an excessive deficit exists.

7. Where the Council decides, in accordance with paragraph 6, that an excessive deficit exists, it shall adopt, without undue delay, on a recommendation from the Commission, recommendations addressed to the Member State concerned with a view to bringing that situation to an end within a given period. Subject to the provisions of paragraph 8, these recommendations shall not be made public.

8. Where it establishes that there has been no effective action in response to its recommendations within the period laid down, the Council may make its recommendations public.

9. If a Member State persists in failing to put into practice the recommendations of the Council, the Council may decide to give notice to the Member State to take, within a specified time limit, measures for the deficit reduction which is judged necessary by the Council in order to remedy the situation.

    In such a case, the Council may request the Member State concerned to submit reports in accordance with a specific timetable in order to examine the adjustment efforts of that Member State…

11. As long as a Member State fails to comply with a decision taken in accordance with paragraph 9, the Council may decide to apply or, as the case may be, reinforce one or more of the following measures:
    - to require the Member State concerned to publish additional information, to be specified by the Council, before issuing bonds and securities,
    - to invite the European Investment Bank to reconsider its lending policy towards the Member State concerned,
    - to require the Member State concerned to make a non-interest-bearing deposit of an appropriate size with the Union until the excessive deficit has, in the view of the Council, been corrected,
    - to impose fines of an appropriate size.

    The President of the Council shall inform the European Parliament of the decisions taken.

---

[114] Article 126(3) TFEU.
[115] Article 126(5) TFEU.

Over time, the discretion granted to the Council is limited in a number of ways.

First, it has been left with a largely 'take it or leave it' position in regard to the Commission proposal to find an excessive deficit. Following the Lisbon Treaty, it can only amend this proposal by unanimity. As this will be difficult to obtain, the Council will simply have to decide whether it agrees with the Commission's proposal or not. It cannot fine-tune it or bring in new interpretations of what constitutes an excessive deficit in the case in hand.

Secondly, Article 126(7) TFEU introduces a new obligation on the Council to make recommendations without undue delay. In short, it is not open to it to make a finding of an excessive deficit and do nothing more. It must suggest a positive plan of action for the Member State concerned.

The third type of constraint applies in relation to sanctions. If a Member State fails to comply with a Council Decision under Article 126(9) TFEU within the time limit provided, the Council must apply sanctions.[116] The sanctions are also predetermined. For the first two years of running a deficit, the Member State is required to leave a deposit with the Council. The size of the deposit is large, amounting to a sum which is 0.2 per cent of GDP and one-tenth of the size of the excessive deficit for each year the state runs an excessive deficit.[117] If the deficit is not brought under control within two years, this deposit is to be converted into a fine.[118]

However, there is a complete implausibility about all of this. The size of the fines are eye-watering, running into billions of euros. It is difficult to believe that national governments would dare to impose it on one another, and there is something paradoxical about fining a bankrupt state. If a state cannot manage its deficit, it is going to struggle to pay its debt. Furthermore, notwithstanding the constraints, there is still considerable 'wiggle room' for the Council. Most notably, the Council has a discretion both whether to make its recommendations public (Article 126(8) TFEU) and whether to take a decision requiring action (Article 126(9) TFEU). Leblond has thus noted that investors did not react negatively either to the French or German difficulties in 2002–2004 or the relaxation of the excessive deficit definition in 2005. He suggested that this was a sure sign that the markets did not believe the sanctions were credible and looked instead for other assurances of budgetary discipline.[119]

6 ECONOMIC SURVEILLANCE AND THE BROAD ECONOMIC POLICY GUIDELINES

In section 2, we mentioned that a central part of EMU was coordination of national economic policies, which Member States had to treat as a matter of common concern under Article 121(1) TFEU. The procedures, known as the broad economic policy guidelines (BEPG), for verifying this are set out in the rest of Article 121 TFEU.

---

[116] Regulation 1467/97/EC on speeding up and clarifying the implementation of the excessive deficit procedure, article 6 [1997] OJ L209/6.
[117] *Ibid.* article 12.
[118] *Ibid.* article 13.
[119] P. Leblond, 'The Political Stability and Growth Pact is Dead: Long Live the Economic Stability and Growth Pact' (2006) 44 *JCMS* 969, 976–82.

Article 121 TFEU

2. The Council shall, on a recommendation from the Commission, formulate a draft for the broad guidelines of the economic policies of the Member States and of the Union, and shall report its findings to the European Council.

   The European Council shall, acting on the basis of the report from the Council, discuss a conclusion on the broad guidelines of the economic policies of the Member States and of the Union. On the basis of this conclusion, the Council shall adopt a recommendation setting out these broad guidelines. The Council shall inform the European Parliament of its recommendation.

3. In order to ensure closer coordination of economic policies and sustained convergence of the economic performances of the Member States, the Council shall, on the basis of reports submitted by the Commission, monitor economic developments in each of the Member States and in the Union as well as the consistency of economic policies with the broad guidelines referred to in paragraph 2, and regularly carry out an overall assessment. For the purpose of this multilateral surveillance, Member States shall forward information to the Commission about important measures taken by them in the field of their economic policy and such other information as they deem necessary.

4. Where it is established, under the procedure referred to in paragraph 3, that the economic policies of a Member State are not consistent with the broad guidelines referred to in paragraph 2 or that they risk jeopardising the proper functioning of economic and monetary union, the Commission may address a warning to the Member State concerned. The Council, on a recommendation from the Commission, may address the necessary recommendations to the Member State concerned. The Council may, on a proposal from the Commission, decide to make its recommendations public.

   Within the scope of this paragraph, the Council shall act without taking into account the vote of the member of the Council representing the Member State concerned...

5. The President of the Council and the Commission shall report to the European Parliament on the results of multilateral surveillance. The President of the Council may be invited to appear before the competent committee of the European Parliament if the Council has made its recommendations public.

The procedure works therefore by guidelines being issued by the Council to the Union and individual Member States (Article 121(2) TFEU).[120] Member States must then report to the Council on how they are meeting these guidelines and their performance will be assessed by the Council (Article 121(3) TFEU). If a Member State does not comply with the overall guidelines or its performance is seen as jeopardising EMU, it can be formally warned by the Council and given public recommendations about its economic policy (Article 121(5) TFEU).

The BEPG are formulated once every three years. On the basis of this, each Member State produces an Action Plan which sets out how it will meet the guidelines. Its performance is assessed against this and against the guidelines. Their content has expanded considerably since their genesis in 1993.[121] Since 2002, they have focused not just on macro-economic policies, notably securing economic and fiscal sustainability, but also micro-economic policies and employment policies. The 2008–2010 BEPG contain twenty-five guidelines, therefore,

---

[120] There is also the possibility for guidelines and surveillance to be applied just to the euro-zone: Article 136 TFEU.

[121] On their history see S. Deroose *et al.*, 'The Broad Economic Policy Guidelines: Before and After the Re-launch of the Lisbon Strategy' (2008) 46 *JCMS* 827.

which include guidelines on wage development, research and development, information, communication and technology, sustainable development, competitiveness, small and medium-sized enterprises, the inclusiveness of labour markets and education and training cycles.[122]

The BEPG are, therefore, extremely wide-ranging and raise a number of questions. One set relate to legitimacy concerns. The Council considering the BEPG is the ECOFIN Council, comprising economic and finance ministries. They are bringing a lot of policy fields (education, environment, employment, social security) within their remit through this mechanism. There is a real question to be asked about whether discussions between finance ministers is an appropriate mechanism for the development of environment, education or social assistance policies. Typically, economic ministry involvement with these is for reasons of cost containment.[123] A similar concern is the lack of popular involvement with the drafting of National Action Plans. Deroose, Hodson and Kuhlmann quote data that suggests nine out of twenty-five national parliaments were not involved with the National Action Plans, whilst eighteen were not involved with any follow-up.[124]

The other type of concern relates to the effectiveness of this surveillance mechanism. It is, after all, only soft law with no strong sanctions and many of the guidelines express medium-term targets. One of the 2005 reforms was therefore to introduce stronger reporting requirements. National governments are now required to set out their objectives and projections but also certain of their assumptions and how changes to these would affect their economic position. They are also required to do this convincingly by providing a detailed and quantitative assessment of the budgetary and other economic policy measures being taken and detailed cost-benefit analysis of the main structural reforms being undertaken.[125] Schelkle has observed that this has transformed the process. Member States now have to fill out templates that require them to produce more than 100 figures. One of her interviewees described the process consequently as now more about reporting than explaining. Assessments were also subject to detailed discussions within the Council.[126] It is not clear that this reporting induces policy change. Schelkle notes that it is not clear how far this shifts government economic priorities. She notes that this is in part because the priorities of the BEPG are so wide-ranging and diverse.[127] As this book goes to press, another reason is apparent. For all the reporting and duties to converge, we have a situation where one of the states participating in the euro, Greece, has a debt of over 120 per cent of GDP and a deficit of 12.7 per cent of GDP, and there is talk of possible default by it.[128] There have been scant attempts to bring it into line with the excessive deficit criteria and, in this, both the stick of the Excessive Deficit Procedure and the persuasive effects of the BEPGs have been insufficient. It may simply be that it is too much to expect any form of EU law to have the authority to change something as fundamental and as embedded as a Member State's economic performance.

---

[122] Recommendation 2008/390/EC on the BEPG for the Community and the Member States [2008] OJ L137/13.

[123] D. Chalmers and M. Lodge, *The Open Method of Coordination and the European Welfare State* (London, LSE CARR Discussion Paper 11, 2003).

[124] Deroose *et al.*, above n. 121, 838–9.

[125] Regulation 1466/97/EC as amended by Regulation 1055/2005/EC, article 3(2)(c), 7(2)(c).

[126] W. Schelkle, 'EU Fiscal Governance: Hard Law in the Shadow of Soft Law?' (2007) 13 *CJEL* 705, 716–17.

[127] *Ibid.* 717–19.

[128] W. Münchau, 'Greece Can Expect No Gifts from Europe', *Financial Times*, 30 November 2009.

FURTHER READING

F. Amtenbrink, *The Democratic Accountability of Central Banks: A Comparative Study of the European Central Bank* (Oxford, Hart, 1999)

F. Amtenbrink and K. van Duin, 'The European Central Bank Before the European Parliament: Theory and Practice after 10 Years of Monetary Dialogue' (2009) 34 *European Law Review* 561

P. Beaumont and N. Walker (eds.), *Legal Framework of the Single European Currency* (Oxford, Hart, 1999)

W. Buiter, 'Alice in Euroland' (1999) 37 *Journal of Common Market Studies* 181

S. Deroose, D. Hodson and J. Kuhlmann, 'The Broad Economic Policy Guidelines: Before and After the Re-launch of the Lisbon Strategy' (2008) 46 *Journal of Common Market Studies* 827

J. de Haan, C. Eijffinger and S. Waller, *The European Central Bank: Credibility, Transparency, and Centralization* (Cambridge, MA, MIT Press, 2005)

J.-V. Louis, 'The Review of the Stability and Growth Pact' (2006) 43 *Common Market Law Review* 85

T. Padoa-Schioppa, *The Euro and Its Central Bank: Getting United after the Union* (Cambridge, MA, MIT Press, 2004)

W. Schelkle, 'EU Fiscal Governance: Hard Law in the Shadow of Soft Law?' (2007) 13 *Columbia Journal of European Law* 705

C. Zilioli and M. Selmayr, *The Law of the European Central Bank* (Oxford, Hart, 2001)
    'The Constitutional Status of the European Central Bank' (2007) 44 *Common Market Law Review* 355

18

The Free Movement of Goods

CONTENTS

1 INTRODUCTION

Article 34 TFEU prohibits restrictions on the import of goods from other Member States. Case law has divided measures which may be restrictions into three categories, governed by three important cases, *Dassonville*, *Cassis de Dijon* and *Keck*. The structure of the chapter reflects this.

Section 2 discusses the umbrella notion of a restriction on imports, which is provided in *Dassonville*. This case established a very broad scope to Article 34, applying to any measure which impedes imports, however that effect is achieved. A recent case, *Alfa Vita*, even suggests that if a measure results in reduced sales of certain goods this may be enough to bring it within Article 34.

Section 3 discusses the application of Article 34 to product rules. The basis for this application is provided in *Cassis de Dijon*. Product rules are rules which require producers to change some aspect of the physical product or its packaging before it may be sold. Examples are rules which only allow the sale of foodstuffs made in certain ways, or which limit the kinds of containers that can be used for soft drinks. The Court of Justice held in *Cassis de Dijon* that even if these rules apply equally to imports and domestic products, they are nevertheless restrictions on imports.

(a) The reason for the ruling was that in practice it is very difficult to export to other Member States if one has to amend products to adapt to the different rules in each state.

(b) The judgment created a principle of 'mutual recognition' of the adequacy of other Member State laws. It established that goods should only be subject to the regulation of their country of production. The principles of country of origin regulation and mutual recognition are now applied throughout free movement law.

(c) It is possible to derogate from mutual recognition for legitimate and proportionate reasons, but this is strictly policed. It is often argued, for example, that permitting foreign products to be sold when these do not conform to national rules and expectations undermines consumer protection. However, the Court usually finds that labelling provides the consumer with sufficient information and protection, and is a lesser hindrance to trade.

Section 4 discusses *Keck* and the idea of 'selling arrangements'. These are rules which regulate the way products are sold. Examples are advertising and rules on shop opening times. The Court held in *Keck* that these are generally not restrictions on imports, as long as they do not have a greater effect on imports than on domestic products. States may therefore regulate selling arrangements however they like, so long as the effect on imports and domestic products is the same. *Keck* is criticised by many because even if selling arrangements do not have an unequal effect, they may still have the effect of hindering trade, by making marketing more difficult.

Some principles are common to all categories of restrictions on imports.

(a) Restrictions on imports which discriminate directly between national and foreign goods may only be saved by Article 36 TFEU. This is discussed in Chapter 21.

(b) Restrictions on imports which are equally applicable (equal on their face, although they may have some unequal effect) will not be prohibited if they are necessary for some legitimate public interest objective (often called a 'mandatory requirement') and are proportionate.

(c) Article 34 only applies insofar as measures affect imports. If states wish to burden domestic producers with heavy regulation this is a matter of purely national law. However, in exceptional situations stricter regulation of domestic production may actually give it a reputational advantage, and so be a hindrance to imports.

(d) Article 34 also only applies to public measures, not private ones. However, the notion of public catches all bodies and measures in which the state is implicated or has control, even if the measure is apparently implemented by a private organisation. Moreover, the state has a positive obligation to prevent private parties from obstructing free movement, for example where demonstrators block roads. This may entail sensitive balancing between free movement and fundamental rights to free expression and to demonstrate.

Section 5 discusses Article 35 TFEU, which prohibits restrictions on exports. It has a different logic from Article 34. It only applies to measures which have some greater negative effect on export sales than on domestic sales. As with Article 34, if these measures are equally applicable they may be saved if they serve a legitimate aim in a proportionate way.

2 GENERAL DEFINITION OF A MEASURE EQUIVALENT TO A QUANTITATIVE RESTRICTION

Article 34 TFEU provides that:

> Quantitative restrictions on imports and all measures having equivalent effect shall be prohibited between Member States.

A quantitative restriction is a limit on the amount of imports.[1] That limit may be constructed in various ways, by reference to value, or physical quantity, or some other factor. Examples could be a rule permitting only so many cars to be imported per year or limiting imports of cheese to a percentage of total domestic sales. Quantitative restrictions do not arise often any more: their prohibition is too clear.

The second part of Article 34 is rather more important in practice. This prohibits measures which do not actually set a limit to imports, but have the same effect as such a limit. These 'measures of equivalent effect' (MEQRs), as they are often called, result in imports being reduced just as if there was in fact an explicit limit.

The case law on Article 34 consists of attempts to define and explain what constitutes an MEQR. The problems of such a definition are twofold. First, an MEQR, by definition, produces its import-reducing effects by a more or less indirect path. That can make causation difficult to establish. The first problem is therefore to know, as a matter of fact, which measures actually do result in imports being reduced or are likely to do so. In some cases it may be obvious, but other cases are difficult. The Court of Justice has dealt with this by drawing broad-brush distinctions of convenience, as will be seen below in the discussions of *Dassonville* and *Keck*.[2] The second problem is to decide whether Article 34 is about combating rules with a protectionist effect, or about deregulating economic activity.[3] Many measures restrict or reduce economic activity generally: tax rises, rules on transport and advertising, labour regulation. Such measures are likely, therefore, to reduce imports too. However, they do not *specifically* reduce imports. They do not have any effect on imports that they do not also have on domestic production. On the whole, as will be seen below, the Court excludes such measures from Article 34, although the position is far from entirely clear and recent cases suggest a rethinking may be under way.[4]

In the current state of the law, measures potentially within Article 34 can be divided into three groups, each falling within a distinct legal regime. The most recent group consists of measures which concern the way goods are marketed or sold. Whether or not this type of measure is prohibited is decided according to the principles laid down in *Keck*, discussed later in this chapter.[5] Perhaps the most important group in practice consists of measures concerning the way products are produced or packaged — their physical specifications. Whether or not these

---

[1] See Case 2/73 *Riseria Luigi Geddo* v *Ente Nazionale Risi* [1973] ECR 865.
[2] Case 8/74 *Procureur du Roi* v *Benoît and Gustave Dassonville* [1974] ECR 837; Joined Cases C-267/91 and C-268/91 *Keck and Mithouard* [1993] ECR I-6097.
[3] See Chapter 16; Advocate General Tesauro in Case C-292/02 *Hünermund* v *Landesapotheker Baden-Württemburg* [1994] ECR I-6787.
[4] See pp. 749–52.
[5] See pp. 773–80.

measures contravene Article 34 is decided according to the principles laid down in *Cassis de Dijon*, also discussed below.[6] The third group consists of measures which affect imports or trade in some way, but do not fall within the other groups. These are measures which cannot be easily captured by the *Cassis* definition of a product rule or the *Keck* definition of a selling arrangement. The legality of this third group of measures is decided according to the principles in *Dassonville*.[7] In fact, this is the oldest of the three central goods cases, and is the case which provides the general umbrella definition of an MEQR. In the years immediately after it was decided, it was the starting point for all questions of free movement of goods. However, now that the specialised sub-regimes of *Cassis* and *Keck* are well established, *Dassonville* has become residual in practice, if not unimportant.

(i) *Dassonville*

Mr Dassonville was a Belgian trader who bought Scotch whisky in France and imported it to Belgium for sale there. The reason why he did this was that whisky was much cheaper in France than in Belgium. The French, at the time of the case, did not have as high a disposable income as Belgians, and could not be persuaded to pay as much for whisky. Moreover, while whisky was a fairly well-established tipple in Belgium, it was less so in France, where it had to compete against domestic spirits and aperitifs. A common technique used to enter a new market is to sell the product at a low price initially, and whisky producers and retailers did precisely this. The hope was, of course, that eventually the French would come to love whisky and the price could be raised, and large profits finally made.

However, such market-specific pricing is made very difficult by Article 34, since what is called parallel trading quickly reduces the price differences. People like Mr Dassonville go and buy the goods in the cheap market and sell in the expensive one, until the prices converge. This is possible because, given Article 34, there should be no obstacles to the trading of goods between states.

Nevertheless, Mr Dassonville encountered a problem in the form of a Belgian law on 'designations of origin'. The law prohibited the import of products bearing such a 'designation of origin' without a certificate from the authorities of the state of production to prove that this designation was correct. Thus, whisky labelled as Scotch (from Scotland) could not be imported to Belgium without a certificate of origin from the British customs.

For retailers who imported their whisky directly from the United Kingdom this was not a problem, since the whisky would be delivered with the appropriate certificate if desired. However, such certificates were typically removed at the point of importation, and were no longer attached to the whisky by the time it was on sale within the country. Thus, when Mr Dassonville bought his whisky for a good price in France it came without a certificate. Moreover, it was difficult for him to obtain such a certificate since the goods had already left the United Kingdom. He was therefore in possession of Scotch whisky which could not be lawfully sold in Belgium according to Belgian law. He claimed that this law was an MEQR, and in the Court's judgment it gave what continues to be the standard description of what an MEQR is.

---

[6] Case 120/78 *Rewe-Zentral AG* v *Bundesmonopolverwaltung für Branntwein* (*Cassis de Dijon*) [1979] ECR 649, discussed at pp. 760 *et seq.*

[7] Case 2/73 *Riseria Luigi Geddo* v *Ente Nazionale Risi* [1973] ECR 865.

Case 8/74 *Procureur du Roi v Benoît and Gustave Dassonville* [1974] ECR 837

5. All trading rules enacted by Member States which are capable of hindering, directly or indirectly, actually or potentially, intra-community trade are to be considered as measures having an effect equivalent to quantitative restrictions.

6. In the absence of a community system guaranteeing for consumers the authenticity of a product's designation of origin, if a Member State takes measures to prevent unfair practices in this connection, it is however subject to the condition that these measures should be reasonable and that the means of proof required should not act as a hindrance to trade between Member States and should, in consequence, be accessible to all community nationals.

7. Even without having to examine whether or not such measures are covered by Article [34 TFEU], they must not, in any case, by virtue of the principle expressed in the second sentence of that article, constitute a means of arbitrary discrimination or a disguised restriction on trade between Member States.

8. That may be the case with formalities, required by a Member State for the purpose of proving the origin of a product, which only direct importers are really in a position to satisfy without facing serious difficulties.

9. Consequently, the requirement by a Member State of a certificate of authenticity which is less easily obtainable by importers of an authentic product which has been put into free circulation in a regular manner in another Member State than by importers of the same product coming directly from the country of origin constitutes a measure having an effect equivalent to a quantitative restriction as prohibited by the Treaty.

There are three elements of this judgment worth noting: first, the definition in paragraph 5, which continues to be cited in almost unchanged terms, although with the words 'all trading rules' replaced in some judgments by the words 'all rules' or 'all measures'.[8] This definition is very broad. It extends an MEQR to include measures which have not yet had any actual effect, but may potentially do so, as well as those whose effect on trade is indirect. Article 34 applies to any measure which may somehow hinder interstate trade. Yet, the second aspect of the judgment mitigates this. The Court appears to accept in paragraph 6 that even measures which might fall within its own definition may be permitted if they are 'reasonable'. This notion was later developed and brought to fruition in *Cassis de Dijon*. As a result, even though paragraph 5 of the judgment establishes a broad scope of supervision of Article 34, some of the measures caught may in fact ultimately escape its prohibition.

Secondly, the breadth of the definition can then be understood as an establishment of jurisdiction. By making Article 34 broad, the Court is granting itself equally broad powers to supervise national measures via the preliminary reference procedure, even if in some cases it will find those measures compatible with the Treaty. This was particularly important in a time where the internal market was in its infancy and national protectionist traditions were

---

[8] See e.g. Case C-88/07 *Commission v Spain*, Judgment of 5 March 2009; Case C-319/05 *Commission v Germany* [2007] ECR I-9811; Joined Cases C-158/04 and C-159/04 *Alfa Vita v Elliniko Dimosio and Nomarchiaki Aftodioikisi Ioanninon* [2006] ECR I-8135; Case C-383/97 *Van der Laan* [1999] ECR I-731.

well-entrenched, while national judges were still often unfamiliar with EU law. Thirdly, one may note the emphasis in paragraphs 7 to 9 on discrimination. There is no mention of this in the paragraph 5 definition, and yet the Belgian rule is finally ruled incompatible not because it makes all imports difficult, but because it makes imports from France harder than those from the United Kingdom (paragraph 9). The traditional view of free trade agreements, and of Article 34, that they are fundamentally about equal treatment of goods from different states,[9] is clearly influential here.

(ii) Limits of the notion of an MEQR

The situations to which *Dassonville* has been applied are diverse. Examples include government campaigns encouraging consumers to purchase domestic goods,[10] rules requiring electricity suppliers to purchase a percentage of their electricity from domestic wind farms,[11] obligations on petrol importers to maintain a reserve store,[12] requirements to obtain a licence to import certain goods,[13] even where the licence is a formality granted as of right,[14] public tenders requiring goods made according to national standards[15] and procedures whereby alcoholic drinks could only be imported via certain state-controlled channels.[16] The most important common factor which these measures share is simply that in practice they hinder imports, or are likely to do so.[17] *Dassonville* is usually applied in a very pragmatic and non-theoretical way.

An additional factor linking most measures which the Court has found to be MEQRs is that they have some unequal effect: either they discriminate against imported products directly, or they create some specific hindrance to cross-border trade which they do not create for internal trade.[18] Even measures which seem at first glance to have equal effects often turn out to have some specifically import-restricting effect upon closer examination. In *Commission* v *Austria*, an Austrian rule prohibiting heavy goods traffic from an alpine motorway, on environmental grounds, was found to contravene Article 34.[19] The rule applied without reference to nationality, but the Commission argued, without being contradicted, that most of the heavy trucks on that road were in fact transiting Austria, and were likely to be foreign or to be carrying foreign goods, while local freight traffic tended to use smaller vehicles.

Thus, although the definition in *Dassonville* does not make protectionism or discrimination part of the definition of an MEQR, in practice the Court has seemed reluctant to extend Article 34 to measures which have no specific cross-border impact, but just reduce trade or economic activity generally. However, several very recent cases call this into question, and suggest that

---

[9] See G. de Búrca, 'Unpacking the Concept of Discrimination in EC and International Trade Law' in C. Barnard and J. Scott (eds.), *The Law of the European Single Market* (Oxford, Hart, 2002) 181.

[10] Case 249/81 *Commission* v *Ireland* [1982] ECR 4005; Case 207/83 *Commission* v *United Kingdom (marks of origin)* [1985] ECR 1201.

[11] Case C-379/98 *PreussenElektra* [2001] ECR I-2099.

[12] Case C-398/98 *Commission* v *Greece* [2001] ECR I-7915.

[13] Case C-54/05 *Commission* v *Finland* [2007] ECR I-2473.

[14] Case C-434/04 *Ahokkainen* [2006] ECR I-9171.

[15] Case 45/87 *Commission* v *Ireland* [1988] ECR 4929.

[16] Case C-170/04 *Klas Rosengren and Others* v *Riksåklagaren* [2007] ECR I-4071.

[17] Tax measures are generally excluded from Article 34; see Case C-383/01 *De Danske Bilimportører* [2003] ECR I-6065; Case 47/88 *Commission* v *Denmark* [1990] ECR 4509.

[18] See G. Davies, *Nationality Discrimination in the European Internal Market* (The Hague, Kluwer Law International, 2003).

[19] Case C-320/03 *Commission* v *Austria* [2005] ECR I-9871.

the Court may be letting go of this implicit limit, applying Article 34 whenever access to a market is hindered.

One group of cases have involved rules concerning the use of goods. In *Mickelsson and Roos*, the Finnish government prohibited the use of jet-skis except on designated waterways, and then did not designate any waterways, so that in practice jet-skis could not be used in Finland.[20] In *Commission* v *Portugal*, a Portuguese measure was successfully challenged which prohibited sticking tinted plastic to car windows to turn them into tinted windows.[21] Then in *Commission* v *Italy*, a challenge was brought to Italian rules which prohibited the towing of a trailer behind a motorcycle.[22]

In these three cases there was no outright prohibition on the importation or sale of a product, but a measure which indirectly achieved more or less the same effect. If something cannot be used (jet-skis, tinted window stickers or motorcycle trailers), then in practice trying to import and sell that product will be a hopeless venture. It will not be illegal, but no one will want to buy it.

Case C-110/05 *Commission* v *Italy*, Judgment of 10 February 2009

33. It should be recalled that, according to settled case-law, all trading rules enacted by Member States which are capable of hindering, directly or indirectly, actually or potentially, intra-Community trade are to be considered as measures having an effect equivalent to quantitative restrictions and are, on that basis, prohibited by Article [34 TFEU].

34. It is also apparent from settled case-law that Article [34 TFEU] reflects the obligation to respect the principles of non-discrimination and of mutual recognition of products lawfully manufactured and marketed in other Member States, as well as the principle of ensuring free access of Community products to national markets ….

55. In its reply to the Court's written question, the Commission claimed, without being contradicted by the Italian Republic, that, in the case of trailers specially designed for motorcycles, the possibilities for their use other than with motorcycles are very limited. It considers that, although it is not inconceivable that they could, in certain circumstances, be towed by other vehicles, in particular, by automobiles, such use is inappropriate and remains at least insignificant, if not hypothetical.

56. It should be noted in that regard that a prohibition on the use of a product in the territory of a Member State has a considerable influence on the behaviour of consumers, which, in its turn, affects the access of that product to the market of that Member State.

57. Consumers, knowing that they are not permitted to use their motorcycle with a trailer specially designed for it, have practically no interest in buying such a trailer. Thus, Article 56 of the Highway Code prevents a demand from existing in the market at issue for such trailers and therefore hinders their importation.

58. It follows that the prohibition laid down in Article 56 of the Highway Code, to the extent that its effect is to hinder access to the Italian market for trailers which are specially designed for motorcycles and are lawfully produced and marketed in Member States other than the Italian Republic, constitutes a measure having equivalent effect to quantitative restrictions on imports within the meaning of Article [34 TFEU], unless it can be justified objectively.

---

[20] Case C-142/05 *Åklagaren* v *Mickelsson and Roos*, Judgment of 4 June 2009.

[21] Case C-265/06 *Commission* v *Portugal* [2008] ECR I-2245.

[22] Case C-110/05 *Commission* v *Italy*, Judgment of 10 February 2009.

It is possible to argue that rules on use do have an unequal effect. In practice, domestic producers are unlikely to manufacture goods which cannot be used in their state. They will be conditioned by their local legal environment. Thus, the producers whose goods are affected by the use ban will almost always be foreign: it will be the producer in state X, who makes something that the people of X enjoy using, and who wants to try and convert the people of state Y, but discovers that the rules of Y prevent him from doing so. This argument is particularly relevant because all the cases concerned an effective ban on the use of a product, not simply a restriction. It remains to be seen whether, for example, a restriction on the use of cars to those who possess a licence, which also limits sales of cars and therefore of imports, would be found to be an MEQR, and it is suggested that this is unlikely.

However, it is notable that in the extract above the Court finds that Article 34 requires equal treatment and market access, as if the latter is more than an interpretation of the former, but an extension of it. Whether or not the measure in fact has an unequal effect, there is no suggestion in the judgment that the Court considers this relevant. The Court's reasoning is simply that because these measures effectively prevent sale of the goods, they effectively prevent imports, and are therefore MEQRs.

Alfa Vita goes a step further, applying Article 34 to a measure which did not prevent sales, but merely diminished them. This case concerned Greek regulation of the operation of bakeries.[23] Greek law required all bakeries to have an operating licence, which was granted only if they complied with a number of physical requirements, such as having an area for kneading bread and a flour store. A number of supermarkets were prosecuted because they had bakery sections, but did not comply with these norms. Their defence was that they did not in fact make their own bread products, but bought frozen dough, or frozen part-cooked bread, which then simply had to be placed in the ovens for a while to complete its baking process. Thus, the bakery requirements were completely inappropriate to their activities, and imposed an unreasonable cost on their business. The sale of 'bake-off' bread products was burdened and therefore inhibited.

The Court agreed entirely, finding the rules to be an MEQR. They inhibited the sale of a product which might be imported. However, it did not address the question whether these bakery requirements had any import-specific effect, and there was no discussion of whether the 'bake-off' products were in fact imported or not. It is possible to argue that bread baked on the premises is inevitably a local product, whereas frozen bake-off products may be domestically produced but may equally be imported. Thus rules which favour the former at the expense of the latter will tend to support local products and discourage possible imports. However, the Court did not emphasise this possible inequality. By contrast, its reasoning was merely that by imposing an unreasonable cost on the sale of a product, the rules would inhibit or diminish its sale and therefore also its import.

The judgments in the usage cases and *Alfa Vita* therefore suggest that it is not necessary to show unequal effect to engage Article 34, although the fact that the rules in these cases probably did hit imports particularly hard must temper this conclusion somewhat. Moreover, while the usage cases concern measures which effectively prevent sales entirely, *Alfa Vita* concerns a measure which merely inhibited sales by imposing a cost burden. If the fact that a measure

---

[23] Case C-188/04 *Alfa Vita* v *Elliniko Dimosio and Nomarchiaki Aftodioikisi Ioanninon* [2006] ECR I-8135.

has a potential sales-reducing effect is enough to make it an MEQR, then Article 34 is indeed broad. It may also be noted that *Alfa Vita* is in tension with another pillar of the case law, *Keck*, a matter discussed further below.[24]

It remains to be seen where the Court will go. The extension of Article 34 to any measure reducing sales, even without unequal effect, would enable its application to a huge range of measures, and potentially raise constitutional problems.[25] It would require some new limit, for example a condition that a measure have a sufficiently 'direct' effect, or that its impact on sales be 'significant' or 'substantial'.[26] As yet the Court has not developed such concepts, and they are sufficiently vague that they might present problems of justiciability.[27] There are therefore good reasons to be sceptical that a true 'market access' approach to Article 34 will ever be implemented, or should be. However, *Commission* v *Italy* was a Grand Chamber judgment, and it is hard to believe that the way the judgment was phrased was not a deliberate choice, so perhaps a message is being sent that Article 34 is about to undergo another expansionary phase.

(iii) Form of an MEQR

The form of an MEQR has never been something of great significance. The Court looks at the effects, and does not limit Article 34 to any particular legal type of measure. National laws and regulations may be caught, but so may administrative practices without a formal legal basis.[28] Most notably, in the recent *AGM* case, the Court found a mere pronouncement by a public official to comprise an MEQR.[29] AGM, an Italian company, exported lifting machines to Finland. There was some doubt in Finland as to whether they complied with the safety requirements of Finnish law and of the relevant European standards. After negotiations with AGM, which agreed to make some alterations to the machines, the Finnish government decided that no further action was necessary. However, there were clearly differences of opinion within the safety authorities, because the safety official who had initially investigated the machines, Mr Lehtinen, went on television in an interview and declared that the machines were dangerous, and did not comply with the relevant Directive. A storm of media interest followed, with newspaper reports about 'treacherous vehicle lifts', concern from the Finnish metalworkers union, and so on. Inevitably, sales of AGM machines were badly affected.

The Court was asked to consider whether Mr Lehtinen's statements could be an MEQR. It took into account the fact that he had initially been authorised by his superiors to appear in the interview, but that he was later removed from the case and disciplined for making public

---

[24] See p. 775.

[25] See J. Snell, *Free Movement of Goods and Services in EC Law* (Oxford, Oxford University Press, 2002); G. Davies, 'Discrimination is Better than Market Access' in *Nationality Discrimination in the European Internal Market* (The Hague, Kluwer Law International, 2003) 93.

[26] See S. Weatherill, 'After *Keck*: Some Thoughts on How to Clarify the Clarification' (1996) 33 *CMLRev.* 885; C. Barnard, 'Fitting the Remaining Pieces into the Goods and Persons Jigsaw' (2001) 26 *ELRev.* 35; A. Tryfonidou, 'Was *Keck* a Half-baked Solution After All?' (2007) 34 *LIEI* 167.

[27] See Davies, above n. 25.

[28] Case 21/84 *Commission* v *France* [1985] ECR 1355; Case C-192/01 *Commission* v *Denmark* [2003] ECR I-9693; Case C-212/03 *Commission* v *France* [2005] ECR I-4213.

[29] Case C-470/03 *AGM-COS.MET Srl* v *Suomen valtio and Tarmo Lehtinen* [2007] ECR I-2749; see N. Reich, '*AGM-COS.MET* or Who is Protected by EC Safety Regulation?' (2008) 31 *ELRev.* 85; S. De Vries, 'Annotation of *AGM*' (2008) 45 *CMLRev.* 569.

statements which did not conform to the official position. The extent to which his statements should therefore be attributed to the state was therefore arguable.

The discussion in the case took place in the context of article 4(1) of the relevant harmonisation Directive. That article provided that machinery complying with the Directive should benefit from free movement. It essentially translates Article 34 TFEU to this particular context.

AGM–COS.MET Srl v Suomen Valtio and Tarmo Lehtinen [2007] ECR I–2749

55 ... the referring court's first question should be reformulated so that the court essentially asks whether it is possible to classify the opinions expressed publicly by Mr Lehtinen as obstacles to the free movement of goods for the purposes of Article 4(1) of the Directive, attributable to the Finnish State.

56. Whether the statements of an official are attributable to the State depends in particular on how those statements may have been perceived by the persons to whom they were addressed.

57. The decisive factor for attributing the statements of an official to the State is whether the persons to whom the statements are addressed can reasonably suppose, in the given context, that they are positions taken by the official with the authority of his office.

58. In this respect, it is for the national court to assess in particular whether:
   – the official has authority generally within the sector in question;
   – the official sends out his statements in writing under the official letterhead of the competent department;
   – the official gives television interviews on his department's premises;
   – the official does not indicate that his statements are personal or that they differ from the official position of the competent department; and
   – the competent State departments do not take the necessary steps as soon as possible to dispel the impression on the part of the persons to whom the official's statements are addressed that they are official positions taken by the State.

59. It remains to examine whether the statements at issue in the main proceedings, on the assumption that they are attributable to the Finnish State, infringe Article 4(1) of the Directive.

60. Any measure capable of hindering, directly or indirectly, actually or potentially, intra-Community trade is to be considered as an obstacle. That principle applies also where the interpretation of Article 4(1) of the Directive is concerned ... .

65. Since the statements at issue described the vehicle lifts, in various media and in widely circulated reports, as contrary to standard EN 1493:1998 and dangerous, they are capable of hindering, at least indirectly and potentially, the placing on the market of the machinery.

66. In the light of the above considerations, the answer to Question 1 must be that statements which, by reason of their form and circumstances, give the persons to whom they are addressed the impression that they are official positions taken by the State, not personal opinions of the official, are attributable to the State. The decisive factor for the statements of an official to be attributed to the State is whether the persons to whom those statements are addressed can reasonably suppose, in the given context, that they are positions taken by the official with the authority of his office. To the extent that they are attributable to the State, statements by an official describing machinery certified as conforming to the Directive as contrary to the relevant harmonised standard and dangerous thus constitute a breach of Article 4(1) of the Directive.

It is long established that if the state were to campaign in favour of national products, using appeals to patriotism or chauvinism, or criticising foreign products, this would contravene Article 34.[30] It seems, following *AGM*, that the same principles apply to statements by individual officials where these are reasonably attributed to the state by their addressees, something which will encourage official organs to keep an even stricter rein on their functionaries. The Court went on to find that the normal principles of state liability applied, so that it was open to the national court to find the state liable to compensate AGM. EU law also permitted, but did not require, that officials such as Mr Lehtinen attract personal liability for behaviour amounting to an MEQR.

Cases such as *AGM* beg the question whether Article 34 has a *de minimis* threshold. Not every comment by a civil servant causes as much excitement as Mr Lehtinen's did. One can imagine discriminatory statements or acts by individuals or authorities that are wrongful in principle, but simply too insignificant to merit much concern. Does Article 34 apply?

(iv) *De minimis*

The Court's formal position has always been that there is no *de minimis* for the application of Article 34.

Joined Cases 177/82 and 178/82 *Van de Haar* [1984] ECR 1797

13. It must be emphasized in that connection that Article [34 TFEU] does not distinguish between measures having an effect equivalent to quantitative restrictions according to the degree to which trade between Member States is affected. If a national measure is capable of hindering imports it must be regarded as a measure having an effect equivalent to a quantitative restriction, even though the hindrance is slight and even though it is possible for imported products to be marketed in other ways.

Thus, if a measure is an MEQR within the *Dassonville* definition, it is not important that its effect is in fact very small.

However, a quasi-*de minimis* rule is introduced by the doctrine, consistently present in the case law on goods and on the other freedoms, that measures whose effect is too 'uncertain and indirect' will not be caught by the Treaty.

Case C–379/92 *Peralta* [1994] ECR I–3453

23. The national court enquires about the compatibility of the Italian legislation with Article [34 TFEU] insofar as it requires Italian vessels to carry costly equipment. It asks itself whether this makes imports of chemical products into Italy more expensive and therefore creates an obstacle prohibited by that article.

24. On this point, it is sufficient to observe that legislation like the legislation in question makes no distinction according to the origin of the substances transported, its purpose is not to regulate trade in goods with other Member States and the restrictive effects which it might have on the free movement of goods are too uncertain and indirect for the obligation which it lays down to be regarded as being of a nature to hinder trade between Member States.

---

[30] Case 249/81 *Commission v Ireland* [1982] ECR 4005; Case 207/83 *Commission v United Kingdom (marks of origin)* [1985] ECR 1201.

This is potentially important in the light of the recent market access cases discussed above. In the event that Article 34 is increasingly applied in the future on the basis that a measure has the effect of reducing sales, the rule in *Peralta* could provide a useful counter-balance, preventing every tax rise or change to public transport becoming subject to Article 34.

(v) The internal situation

Article 34 TFEU only applies to measures hindering imports. If a measure does not apply to imports but only to domestic producers, then in general it will be outside Article 34.[31] Thus, in *Dassonville*, the Court found that applying the origin-certificates rule to imports was contrary to Article 34, but if the Belgian state had continued to apply that rule only to Belgian drinks brewed in Belgium and bearing origin marks from Belgian towns or regions, this would have been of no interest to EU law. It is true that this approach can lead to reverse discrimination, whereby EU law tolerates a situation in which domestic producers are more heavily burdened by law than importers. However, the Court is unconcerned by this: 'As regards the general principle of non-discrimination, it must be observed that community law does not apply to treatment which works to the detriment of national products as compared with imported products or to the detriment of retailers who sell national products.'[32]

In some, relatively unusual, circumstances even though a measure does not apply to imports it may nevertheless create a problem or disadvantage for them and so comprise an MEQR. *Pistre* concerned French law on product designations, and the particular designation 'mountain ham'.[33] Apparently ham from pigs who have lived in the mountains is often particularly good, and so in marketing such ham, specific reference is made to its high altitude origin. To protect the consumer, French law regulated the use of such references. Ham could only be called 'mountain ham' if its production complied with a number of rules. However, in practice it was only possible to comply with these rules if the ham was French. They were so formulated that ham even from very high places in other countries would not comply.

Realising that this amounted to discrimination against imported goods, the French government chose not to apply the rules to imports. It was therefore possible to sell Spanish or Scottish ham in France which bore the word 'mountain' on the package, or reference to a specific mountain area, without legal problems. In the case, therefore, it was not an importer, but a French producer who complained. He was being prosecuted for selling French ham bearing the word 'mountain' without complying with the rules associated with that name. In his defence he challenged the legality of the French rules. The French government claimed that since these rules did not apply to imports, Article 34 was not relevant. The Court disagreed.

---

[31] Case C-98/86 *Mathot* [1987] ECR 809.
[32] Case 355/85 *Driancourt* v *Cognet* [1986] ECR 3231, para. 11.
[33] Case C-321/94 *Pistre* [1997] ECR I-2343.

Case C–321/94 *Pistre* [1997] ECR I-2343

43. According to settled case-law, the prohibition laid down in Article [34 TFEU] covers all trading rules enacted by Member States which are capable of hindering, directly or indirectly, actually or potentially, intra-Community trade.

44. Accordingly, whilst the application of a national measure having no actual link to the importation of goods does not fall within the ambit of Article [34 TFEU], Article [34 TFEU] cannot be considered inapplicable simply because all the facts of the specific case before the national court are confined to a single Member State.

45. In such a situation, the application of the national measure may also have effects on the free movement of goods between Member States, in particular when the measure in question facilitates the marketing of goods of domestic origin to the detriment of imported goods. In such circumstances, the application of the measure, even if restricted to domestic producers, in itself creates and maintains a difference of treatment between those two categories of goods, hindering, at least potentially, intra-Community trade.

The Court found that the measure contravened Article 34 even though it only applied to domestic products – in fact precisely because it only applied to domestic products. By having a designation with which only domestic ham could comply, French law provided a marketing advantage to national ham over foreign ham. The mere creation of a distinction between national and foreign products may itself amount to a barrier to imports.[34] This was the case even though the importer was in fact subject to fewer requirements than the domestic producers, and thus at first glance was advantaged rather than disadvantaged.

EU law often also applies indirectly to internal situations, via national law. Sometimes national law prohibits reverse discrimination, meaning that a court faced with internal facts, as in *Pistre*, is required by national law to treat the litigant in the same way as they would were she an importer. This means that the court needs to know what EU law would say in the hypothetical situation that the measure is applied to imports. The Court answers such questions, because the answer is necessary for the national judge if she is to reach her decision. However, the actual situation in question, being internal, is not within the scope of EU law.[35]

A variation on the internal situation is the U-turn, whereby goods are exported and then reimported. This may simply be the result of several sales, from party to party. Sometimes goods are traded quite extensively before reaching the final consumer. However, it may be a deliberate construction, aimed at bringing the goods within Article 34 so that they can benefit from EU law and be exempted from burdensome national rules. In *Au Blé Vert*, the Court decided that reimports must be treated as imports, unless it could be shown that the goods were exported for the sole purpose of reimportation, in order to circumvent national legislation. This is doctrinally quite straightforward, but raises very difficult questions of evidence.[36] Where goods are sold to a trader abroad, and then resold to a new domestic trader, it is a considerable challenge to demonstrate that these were working together.[37]

---

[34] See G. Davies, 'Consumer Protection as an Obstacle to the Free Movement of Goods' (2007) 4 *ERA-Forum* 55.

[35] Case C-448/98 *Guimont* [2000] ECR I-10663; see C. Ritter, 'Purely Internal Situations, Reverse Discrimination, *Guimont, Dzodzi* and Article 234' (2006) 31 *ELRev.* 690.

[36] Case 229/83 *Association des Centres Distributeurs Leclerc v SARL 'Au Blé Vert'* [1985] ECR 1.

[37] Case C-322/01 *Deutscher Apothekerverband* v *DocMorris* [2003] ECR I-14887.

(vi) Article 34 TFEU and private actors

The Court has consistently held that Article 34 only applies to measures taken by public bodies: 'Articles [34 and 35 TFEU] concern only public measures and not the conduct of undertakings.'[38] This is in contrast with the law on free movement of workers and services, which in many cases also applies to private actors.[39] However, if companies or individuals act in a way that excludes foreign products, the Court sees this as a matter for competition law.[40]

This principled limit to Article 34 is mitigated somewhat by a broad conception of the public. For Article 34 to apply, a body does not have to be formally a part of the government. It is sufficient that it is carrying out a public duty on behalf of the state, or that it is controlled by the state. In *Apple and Pear Development Council*, a body representing fruit growers ran a 'buy English apples and pears' campaign. The council was not a public body, but it enjoyed public law privileges, such as the power to levy fruit growers.

Case 222/82 *Apple and Pear Development Council* [1983] ECR 4083

17. As the Court held in its judgment of 24 November 1982 in Case 249/81 *Commission v Ireland*, a publicity campaign to promote the sale and purchase of domestic products may, in certain circumstances, fall within the prohibition contained in Article [34 TFEU] ..., if the campaign is supported by the public authorities ... [I]n fact, a body such as the development council, which is set up by the government of a Member State and is financed by a charge imposed on growers, cannot under Community law enjoy the same freedom as regards the methods of advertising used as that enjoyed by producers themselves or producers' associations of a voluntary character.

The Court refers here to the *Buy Irish* case, in which the Irish government set up a marketing organisation to promote Irish goods.[41] This was clearly discrimination against foreign goods, but was it attributable to the Irish state? They argued that the body was incorporated as an independent company, acting on behalf of Irish producers, for whose actions the state could not be held accountable.

Case 249/81 *Commission v Ireland* [1982] ECR 4005

23. The first observation to be made is that the campaign cannot be likened to advertising by private or public undertakings ..., or by a group of undertakings, to encourage people to buy goods produced by those undertakings. Regardless of the means used to implement it, the campaign is a reflection of the Irish government's considered intention to substitute domestic products for imported products on the Irish market and thereby to check the flow of imports from other Member States.

---

[38] Case 311/85 *Vereniging van Vlaamse Reisbureaus v ASBL Sociale Dienst van de Plaatselijke en Gewestelijke Overheidsdiensten* [1987] ECR 3801.

[39] See Chapters 19 and 20; E. Lohse, 'Fundamental Freedoms and Private Actors' (2007) 13 *EPL* 159; S. Van den Bogaert, 'Horizontality' in C. Barnard and J. Scott (eds.), *The Law of the European Single Market* (Oxford, Hart, 2002) 123.

[40] See generally on the competition/free movement boundary W. Sauter and H. Schepel, *State and Market in EU Law* (Cambridge, Cambridge University Press, 2008) ch. 4; K. Mortelmans, 'Towards Convergence in the Application of the Rules on Free Movement and on Competition' (2001) 38 *CMLRev.* 613.

[41] Case 249/81 *Commission v Ireland* [1982] ECR 4005.

It is clear that the link between state and organisation does not need to be legally watertight, as long as it is demonstrably real. In this case it was the Irish state that was the object of the Commission's enforcement action, but given the way the Court in *Apples and Pears* draws a parallel between that case and the *Buy Irish* case, it seems likely that it would have been possible to apply Article 34 directly to the Buy Irish organisation itself. This is what happened in the *German Quality Products* case.[42] German producers complying with various quality rules were able to apply for the right to affix a mark to their goods, 'German Quality Product'. This was clearly not available to foreign goods, and so amounted to a discriminatory marketing scheme. It was found to violate Article 34 even though the scheme was operated by a non-governmental body, because that body was a product of statute, and so was essentially acting on behalf of and under the auspices of the state.

A more difficult situation is where the state does not actively support market-closing measures, but simply refrains from taking action against them. This first occurred in *Commission v France*, in which the Court found that France had violated a combination of Articles 34 and 4(3) TEU (the duty of loyalty) by failing to remove French farmers who were blocking border crossings to prevent imported agricultural goods from reaching the French market.[43] The leading case, however, is now *Schmidberger*, in which the relevant principles have been most clearly developed. In *Schmidberger*, a group of Austrian demonstrators blocked motorways coming into Austria from Italy, as a protest against the pollution caused by transit traffic in Alpine valleys. This clearly restricted the import of goods by blocking freight traffic, and the Austrian government therefore had an obligation as in *Commission v France* to clear the roads. However, this obligation had to be balanced against the fundamental right to association, which the protesters claimed would be violated by an unmitigated application of Article 34. The question, ultimately, was whether the Austrian government had behaved in a proportionate and reasonable way in the light of the balance which needed to be struck. The Court found that it had, and provided a very clear framework for the balancing of free movement and fundamental rights.

Case C–112/00 *Schmidberger v Republic of Austria* [2003] ECR I–5659

57. In this way the Court held in particular that, as an indispensable instrument for the realisation of a market without internal frontiers, Article [34 TFEU] does not prohibit only measures emanating from the State which, in themselves, create restrictions on trade between Member States. It also applies where a Member State abstains from adopting the measures required in order to deal with obstacles to the free movement of goods which are not caused by the State.

58. The fact that a Member State abstains from taking action or, as the case may be, fails to adopt adequate measures to prevent obstacles to the free movement of goods that are created, in particular, by actions by private individuals on its territory aimed at products originating in other Member States is just as likely to obstruct intra-Community trade as is a positive act.

59. Consequently, Articles [34 and 35 TFEU] require the Member States not merely themselves to refrain from adopting measures or engaging in conduct liable to constitute an obstacle to trade but also,

---

[42] Case C-325/00 *Commission v Germany (CMA)* [2002] ECR I-9977.
[43] Case C-265/95 *Commission v France (Spanish strawberries)* [1997] ECR I-6959.

when read with Article [4(3) TEU], to take all necessary and appropriate measures to ensure that that fundamental freedom is respected on their territory. Article [4(3) TEU] requires the Member States to take all appropriate measures, whether general or particular, to ensure fulfilment of the obligations arising out of the Treaty and to refrain from any measures which could jeopardise the attainment of the objectives of that Treaty.

60. Having regard to the fundamental role assigned to the free movement of goods in the Community system, in particular for the proper functioning of the internal market, that obligation upon each Member State to ensure the free movement of products in its territory by taking the measures necessary and appropriate for the purposes of preventing any restriction due to the acts of individuals applies without the need to distinguish between cases where such acts affect the flow of imports or exports and those affecting merely the transit of goods.

69. It is apparent from the file in the main case that the Austrian authorities were inspired by considerations linked to respect of the fundamental rights of the demonstrators to freedom of expression and freedom of assembly, which are enshrined in and guaranteed by the ECHR and the Austrian Constitution....

77. The case thus raises the question of the need to reconcile the requirements of the protection of fundamental rights in the Community with those arising from a fundamental freedom enshrined in the Treaty and, more particularly, the question of the respective scope of freedom of expression and freedom of assembly, guaranteed by Articles 10 and 11 of the ECHR, and of the free movement of goods, where the former are relied upon as justification for a restriction of the latter.

78. First, whilst the free movement of goods constitutes one of the fundamental principles in the scheme of the Treaty, it may, in certain circumstances, be subject to restrictions for the reasons laid down in Article [36 TFEU] or for overriding requirements relating to the public interest, in accordance with the Court's consistent case-law since the judgment in Case 120/78 *Rewe-Zentral* (*'Cassis de Dijon'*) [1979] ECR 649.

79. Second, whilst the fundamental rights at issue in the main proceedings are expressly recognised by the ECHR and constitute the fundamental pillars of a democratic society, it nevertheless follows from the express wording of paragraph 2 of Articles 10 and 11 of the Convention that freedom of expression and freedom of assembly are also subject to certain limitations justified by objectives in the public interest, insofar as those derogations are in accordance with the law, motivated by one or more of the legitimate aims under those provisions and necessary in a democratic society, that is to say justified by a pressing social need and, in particular, proportionate to the legitimate aim pursued.

80. Thus, unlike other fundamental rights enshrined in that Convention, such as the right to life or the prohibition of torture and inhuman or degrading treatment or punishment, which admit of no restriction, neither the freedom of expression nor the freedom of assembly guaranteed by the ECHR appears to be absolute but must be viewed in relation to its social purpose. Consequently, the exercise of those rights may be restricted, provided that the restrictions in fact correspond to objectives of general interest and do not, taking account of the aim of the restrictions, constitute disproportionate and unacceptable interference, impairing the very substance of the rights guaranteed.

81. In those circumstances, the interests involved must be weighed having regard to all the circumstances of the case in order to determine whether a fair balance was struck between those interests.

82. The competent authorities enjoy a wide margin of discretion in that regard. Nevertheless, it is necessary to determine whether the restrictions placed upon intra-Community trade are proportionate in the light of the legitimate objective pursued, namely, in the present case, the protection of fundamental rights.

The Court went on to find that the Austrian authorities had not violated Article 34. Their actions reflected a justified and proportionate approach to balancing free movement of goods and the right to demonstrate. The factors which influenced the Court in particular were that this was a lawful and peaceful demonstration, approved in advance, for a limited period of time (around thirty hours), and for the purpose of demonstrating a legitimate concern – the protection of the environment. Moreover, the authorities could show that they had considered whether limiting the place and time of the demonstration so that the effect on goods traffic was reduced was a realistic alternative, but had for reasonable grounds come to the conclusion that these would deprive the demonstration of its very purpose and so be an excessive restriction on the right to demonstrate. Finally, once the demonstration was approved the authorities tried to minimise disruption by diverting traffic to other possible routes. In short, the Austrian authorities were a model of good governance, balancing interests in a carefully reasoned way. *Schmidberger* can be contrasted with *Commission* v *France*, in which the demonstration was explicitly aimed at preventing imports as such yet the French authorities tolerated border closure for an extended and open-ended period, showed little concern about occasional violence by those involved, allowed a climate of fear and hostility to trade to develop and expressed complete passivity over the consequences.

Schmidberger has been criticised because the Court appears to put the 'fundamental freedom' embodied in Article 34, which is essentially about trade, on an equal level with the fundamental rights to free association and expression.[44] Despite the actual result, it has been argued that the case opens the door to a degradation of the status of fundamental rights. However, as the Court noted, the rights to free expression and assembly are not absolute, and neither is Article 34, so it is hard to see what the Court could have done other than look for an appropriate balance. However, whether the Court always takes such a rights-friendly stance needs to be considered in the light of recent cases in the field of services, *Laval* and *Viking*, discussed in Chapter 19.[45]

3 PRODUCT STANDARDS AND *CASSIS DE DIJON*

Germany, like a number of EU Member States, traditionally regulates products strictly, leading to a marketplace with a limited range of goods but high quality. This creates problems for importers located in less demanding states. Their goods, made according to different, or laxer, standards do not comply with local rules in many other states and so cannot gain access to the markets of these states. In the early days of European integration this was not seen as unfair. A 'when in Rome' approach was taken.[46] If importers wished to sell in state X they should comply with its rules. *Dassonville* was not generally considered to prohibit product standards if these were equally applicable to domestic and to foreign products.

However, this approach brings with it a number of problems. First, it requires producers to make their products according to a number of different standards, depending upon where

---

[44] J. Morijn, 'Balancing Fundamental Rights and Common Market Freedoms in Union Law' (2006) 12 *ELJ* 15.

[45] See N. Nic Shuibhne, 'Margins of Appreciation: National Values, Fundamental Rights and EC Free Movement Law' (2009) 34 *ELRev.* 230; C. Kombas, 'Fundamental Rights and Fundamental Freedoms: A Symbiosis on the Basis of Subsidiarity' (2006) 12 *EPL* 433.

[46] The use of the phrase in this context is borrowed from K. Nicolaidis and G. Shaffer, 'Managed Mutual Recognition Regimes: Governance Without Global Government' (2005) 68 *Law and Contemporary Problems* 263.

they wish to export to. The idea that the internal market will enable consolidation of industry and economies of scale is undermined if factories have to run numerous separate production lines for different markets. Moreover, in practice, producers will not always do this, so that the realisation of an undivided European market will be impeded. Markets will remain local, as producers decide that it is too difficult or expensive to rework their goods to comply with local rules. The markets in smaller states will be particularly isolated, as potential profits are less and may not justify adapting production.

Traditionally such issues were to be dealt with by harmonisation. However, this did not turn out to be the easy and effective market-building tool that some had hoped, as product development and national regulation outpaced the capacity of the European institutions to harmonise.[47] It was in this context, and during a period of European political stagnation, that the Court intervened with its judgment in *Cassis de Dijon*.

German law required fruit liqueurs to possess at least 25 per cent alcohol. Cassis de Dijon, a blackcurrant liqueur, was made in France and typically contained between 15 and 20 per cent alcohol. As a result it could not be sold in Germany. A German importer, refused authorisation to import and sell *Cassis*, challenged this decision on the basis that it contravened Article 34.

Case 120/78 *Rewe–Zentral AG v Bundesmonopolverwaltung für Branntwein (Cassis de Dijon)* [1979] ECR 649

8. In the absence of common rules relating to the production and marketing of alcohol … it is for the Member States to regulate all matters relating to the production and marketing of alcohol and alcoholic beverages on their own territory.

Obstacles to movement within the community resulting from disparities between the national laws relating to the marketing of the products in question must be accepted insofar as those provisions may be recognized as being necessary in order to satisfy mandatory requirements relating in particular to the effectiveness of fiscal supervision, the protection of public health, the fairness of commercial transactions and the defence of the consumer.

9. The government of the Federal Republic of Germany, intervening in the proceedings, put forward various arguments which, in its view, justify the application of provisions relating to the minimum alcohol content of alcoholic beverages, adducing considerations relating on the one hand to the protection of public health and on the other to the protection of the consumer against unfair commercial practices.

10. As regards the protection of public health the German government states that the purpose of the fixing of minimum alcohol contents by national legislation is to avoid the proliferation of alcoholic beverages on the national market, in particular alcoholic beverages with a low alcohol content, since, in its view, such products may more easily induce a tolerance towards alcohol than more highly alcoholic beverages.

11. Such considerations are not decisive since the consumer can obtain on the market an extremely wide range of weakly or moderately alcoholic products and furthermore a large proportion of alcoholic beverages with a high alcohol content freely sold on the German market is generally consumed in a diluted form.

12. The German government also claims that the fixing of a lower limit for the alcohol content of certain liqueurs is designed to protect the consumer against unfair practices on the part of producers and distributors of alcoholic beverages.

---

[47] See Chapter 16.

This argument is based on the consideration that the lowering of the alcohol content secures a competitive advantage in relation to beverages with a higher alcohol content, since alcohol constitutes by far the most expensive constituent of beverages by reason of the high rate of tax to which it is subject.

Furthermore, according to the German government, to allow alcoholic products into free circulation wherever, as regards their alcohol content, they comply with the rules laid down in the country of production would have the effect of imposing as a common standard within the community the lowest alcohol content permitted in any of the Member States, and even of rendering any requirements in this field inoperative since a lower limit of this nature is foreign to the rules of several Member States.

13. As the Commission rightly observed, the fixing of limits in relation to the alcohol content of beverages may lead to the standardization of products placed on the market and of their designations, in the interests of a greater transparency of commercial transactions and offers for sale to the public.

However, this line of argument cannot be taken so far as to regard the mandatory fixing of minimum alcohol contents as being an essential guarantee of the fairness of commercial transactions, since it is a simple matter to ensure that suitable information is conveyed to the purchaser by requiring the display of an indication of origin and of the alcohol content on the packaging of products.

14. It is clear from the foregoing that the requirements relating to the minimum alcohol content of alcoholic beverages do not serve a purpose which is in the general interest and such as to take precedence over the requirements of the free movement of goods, which constitutes one of the fundamental rules of the Community.

In practice, the principal effect of requirements of this nature is to promote alcoholic beverages having a high alcohol content by excluding from the national market products of other Member States which do not answer that description.

It therefore appears that the unilateral requirement imposed by the rules of a Member State of a minimum alcohol content for the purposes of the sale of alcoholic beverages constitutes an obstacle to trade which is incompatible with the provisions of Article [34 TFEU].

There is therefore no valid reason why, provided that they have been lawfully produced and marketed in one of the Member States, alcoholic beverages should not be introduced into any other Member State; the sale of such products may not be subject to a legal prohibition on the marketing of beverages with an alcohol content lower than the limit set by the national rules.

15. Consequently, the first question should be answered to the effect that the concept of 'measures having an effect equivalent to quantitative restrictions on imports' contained in Article [34 TFEU] is to be understood to mean that the fixing of a minimum alcohol content for alcoholic beverages intended for human consumption by the legislation of a Member State also falls within the prohibition laid down in that provision where the importation of alcoholic beverages lawfully produced and marketed in another Member State is concerned.

The Court finds that the application of product standards to imports hinders their importation, as is obviously correct. Therefore such rules, applied to imports, are MEQRs.

The solution, however, is not to prohibit product standards as such. This would result in an unregulated European product market, undesirable for many reasons. By contrast, the Court begins paragraph 8 by noting that since there is no EU legislation harmonising alcohol levels (there is now, there was not then), it is quite legitimate for Member States to regulate this matter. It is thus not the existence of product standards as such that is the problem, but just their application to products imported from other Member States.

The trade-restricting effects of such application are dealt with by developing two ideas, which are the major contribution of *Cassis de Dijon* to EU law, and which are both among the most important legal developments since the Union's foundation.

The first of these is mutual recognition. The Court finds in paragraph 14 that if products comply with the laws of the Member State where they are produced, then there is no reason why they should not be sold in all other Member States. Each Member State is required to accept products made according to the laws of other Member States. What is good enough for France is good enough for Germany. The name subsequently given to this idea is 'mutual recognition', because Member States recognise as adequate each other's laws and regulations, and therefore do not impose additional requirements on products complying with these. This idea is immensely powerful and has become a general principle of EU law, applied not only to the free movement of goods, but throughout the internal market.[48] It provides a conceptual basis for accepting not just foreign products, but foreign qualifications, tests and certificates, official documents, and so on.[49] As a general rule, the foreign (from another Member State) must be recognised as functionally equivalent, at least in all really important respects, to the domestic.

The second idea is that of mandatory requirements. While the Court states that in principle goods from one state should be marketable in all others, it also concedes in paragraph 8 that there may sometimes be a need for derogation from this general principle. Sometimes the application of standards to imports may be necessary to protect important interests such as consumer protection or public health. The name given to these, 'mandatory requirements', sounds somewhat odd in English, but has stuck and is still used, although the phrase 'public interest objectives' is now also used.

It is therefore the case that an equally applicable rule which would otherwise violate Article 34 may be saved if it can be shown that it is necessary to protect some public interest objective. There is therefore a balancing process involved, in which proportionality is the central concept. Cases subsequent to *Cassis* are in fact a litany of judicial attempts to decide whether a given general interest is, on the facts, sufficient to justify derogation from the mutual recognition rule. The following two sections go into more detail first on the general rule, and then the application of the mandatory requirement exceptions.

(i) Mutual recognition

It seems fairly intuitive that a factory located in a certain Member State should be subject to the rules and regulations of that state. It also seems fairly intuitive that a product on the supermarket shelves in a Member State should be subject to the rules and regulation in that state. Yet, if products are required to comply with the laws of both the state of production and the state of sale this can create impossible burdens. Imagine, for example, that France had a maximum alcohol limit of 20 per cent and Germany a minimum of 25 per cent; it would be impossible to manufacture in France for sale in Germany. Even without such extreme situations, the burden of complying with two sets of laws would impose cost and inconvenience on producers.

---

[48] See Chapter 16.
[49] See Chapters 19 and 20.

This is, of course, an import-specific problem. Goods sold domestically would face no problem because the state of production and state of sale would be the same. They would only have one set of laws to comply with. However, any goods traded between states would face at least two.[50] The application of product standards to imports would therefore not just make trade difficult, but it would often disadvantage imports relative to domestic production.

The solution is to construct a regime in which a given product (or service, the principle is generalised now) is only subject to one set of rules. If there has been harmonisation then this will provide that unique regulatory framework. However, in the absence of harmonisation the question is whether it is better to apply the rules of the state of sale or of production.

Given that product standards exist to protect the consumers of the products, and that the relevant consumers are in the state of sale, it might seem most logical to make these the relevant laws. On such a model, a factory located in France could gain exemption from local product regulations by declaring that it was manufacturing for export. However, this approach has great practical difficulties. First, it fragments the production process, by requiring producers to make different goods for different markets, as discussed above. Secondly, it is hard to supervise. On the whole, supervision of production facilities is easier than of the marketplace. A factory is fixed, hard to hide and easy to inspect. By contrast, if liqueurs have not been subject to any French laws or control because they were declared to be destined for the German market, then the German authorities will want to conduct very thorough controls before admitting them, creating new and significant barriers to movement, and sometimes, given the openness of borders, being hard to enforce. There is a real risk that a choice for state of destination regulation would result in products or services actually escaping any effective supervision.

The Court in *Cassis* therefore made a choice for regulation by the country of origin. It is now a general rule of free movement law that products or services are primarily subject to the laws of their origin state, and should not, except where mandatory requirements apply, be subjected to further requirements based on destination state law.[51] Joerges has described *Cassis de Dijon* as creating a meta-norm which both parties to a free movement conflict (France and Germany in this case) can accept, and which mediates between their different laws.[52]

This approach has great legal elegance. It has been described as a principle of tolerance, akin to multiculturalism in products, because it requires Member States to accept products that are different from those they are used to domestically.[53] It embodies an idea of 'different but equal'. Moreover, in a few lines it provides a framework for an entire internal market.[54] Using the ideas in *Cassis* it is possible to implement trade between states while still allowing Member States to maintain their own laws and avoiding the need for harmonisation.

---

[50] See Case C-470/93 *Verein gegen Unwesen in Handel und Gewerbe Köln v Mars GmbH* [1995] ECR I-1923.

[51] See Case C-288/89 *Gouda v Commissariat voor de Media* [1991] ECR I-4007; Directive 2006/123/EC on services in the internal market [2006] OJ L376/36; see Chapter 19.

[52] See C. Joerges and J. Neyer, *Deliberative Supranationalism Revisited*, EUI Working Paper No. 2006/20, 25 (Florence, European University Institute, 2006).

[53] See Nicolaidis and Shaffer, above n. 46, 317; G. Davies, 'Is Mutual Recognition an Alternative to Harmonisation: Lessons on Trade and Tolerance of Diversity from the EU' in F. Ortino and L. Bartels (eds.), *Regional Trade Agreements and the WTO* (Oxford, Oxford University Press, 2006) 265–80.

[54] For a very thorough discussion of the policy issues, see the special edition of the *Journal of European Public Policy* on mutual recognition: S. Schmidt (ed.), 'Mutual Recognition as a New Mode of Governance' (2007) 14(5) *JEPP*; K. Armstrong, 'Mutual Recognition' in C. Barnard and J. Scott (eds.), *The Law of the European Single Market* (Oxford, Hart, 2002) 225.

Yet, it is open to powerful criticism from various perspectives. It has been claimed that applying mutual recognition results in non-economic concerns being trumped by free trade; that it crushes diversity and replaces it by a deregulated and uniform marketplace;[55] and yet also that it is ineffective in creating free trade, that mutual recognition is too open-ended and abstract to be effectively applied by national courts and authorities.[56] It can even therefore be seen as a stalking horse for harmonisation, an approach to free movement that is apparently based on local diversity of regulation but by its very failure to create a market turns into a justification for centralised rules.[57]

The first criticism is that standards are not in fact equal in different states. While it may be true that all Member States generally ensure that their products are adequately safe, it is a fantasy to think that the quality guaranteed by different standards is the same. Some states have a *laissez-faire* approach to quality regulation, and are content to let the consumer decide what she is prepared to pay for. Others are strict, as will be seen in the subsequent section. Admitting goods made according to foreign laws therefore undermines the quality standards in force in strict states. The populations of those countries are no longer able to express their collective preference for a certain kind of strictly regulated market in which low quality goods are prohibited. Trade trumps both local democracy and product quality.[58]

Moreover, mutual recognition has potential economic effects. The Court is quite clear that it is not the product rule as such which is contrary to Article 34, but its application to imports. Thus, Germany is able to apply its 25 per cent rule to domestically made liqueurs, just not to foreign ones. But this puts German producers at a distinct disadvantage. Alcohol is a significant part of the cost of such liqueurs (one of the reasons for the conflict), so foreign liqueur will probably be cheaper. The German government is then faced with the choice between abandoning its rule for domestic producers, and moving to a *laissez-faire* marketplace, or continuing to enforce the rule and risking domestic producers being priced out of the market. Ultimately, as the German government argued in the case, there is a risk that the lowest standard state provides the de facto standard everywhere; their exports are the cheapest products in every shop in Europe. A regulatory race to the bottom is then feared as other states abandon their own rules. In fact, as discussed in Chapter 16, it is notable that this does not always, or even often, happen but the risk is real in some circumstances.

The discussion above may suggest that mutual recognition tends to sacrifice non-economic concerns in the cause of free trade. However, the principle is also criticised from a free trade perspective, with the claim being that in practice it is ineffective.[59] The problem is that applying *Cassis* entails balancing interests, since the possibility of derogations, the mandatory requirements, does exist. This balancing is so politically laden that it is seen as a heavy burden on national judges and authorities, who may well be inclined to defer to national laws and

---

[55] See K. Alter and S. Meunier-Aitsahalia, 'Judicial Politics in the European Community: European Integration and the Pathbreaking *Cassis de Dijon* Decision' (1994) 26 *Comparative Political Studies* 535.

[56] See J. Pelkmans, 'Mutual Recognition in Goods: On Promises and Disillusions' (2007) 14 *JEPP* 699; Commission Report to the Council, Parliament and ESC, *Second Biennial Report on the Application of the Principle of Mutual Recognition in the Single Market*, COM(2002)419 final, 23 July 2002.

[57] See Davies, above n. 53; W. Kerber and R. van den Bergh, 'Mutual Recognition Revisited: Misunderstandings, Inconsistencies, and a Suggested Reinterpretation' (2008) 61 *Kyklos* 447.

[58] Kerber and van den Bergh, above n. 57; H.-C. von Heydebrand u.d. Lasa, 'Free Movement of Foodstuffs, Consumer Protection and Food Standards in the European Community: Has the Court Got it Wrong?' (1991) 16 *ELRev.* 391.

[59] See Pelkmans, above n. 56.

quickly concede their necessity when faced with governmental arguments to that effect.[60] Expecting national bodies to set aside national law to an extent sufficient to really create a single market is perhaps unrealistic. Thus, it can be argued that mutual recognition has not turned out to be the legal panacea it may seem, and leaves many obstacles to movement in place. In practice, what often happens is that litigation over national product rules identifies a particular problem, at which point the Commission may begin the process of harmonisation. *Cassis de Dijon* itself did not lead to a European market in which alcohol products are freely traded on the basis of that mutual recognition. On the contrary, shortly afterwards harmonising legislation on alcohol levels was adopted.

Most of these abstract criticisms depend for their force upon the extent to which mandatory requirements actually limit the general rule of mutual recognition. It is thus these requirements, rather than the general principle, which have been the concrete subject matter of post-*Cassis* legal debate.

(ii) Mandatory requirements

In *Cassis de Dijon*, the Court provided a list of the sorts of reasons which might justify restricting the free movement of goods. It mentioned the 'effectiveness of fiscal supervision, the protection of public health, the fairness of commercial transactions and the defence of the consumer'. This list was broadened in subsequent cases, and the category of mandatory requirements is now considered to be open-ended. A formulation which is often cited by the Court was used in *Bellamy and English Shop*, where the Court had to consider whether Belgium was justified in applying its food labelling laws to imported English foodstuffs, which the Belgians claimed was necessary to protect the consumer.

Case C-123/00 *Criminal Proceedings Against Bellamy and English Shop Wholesale* [2001] ECR I-2795

18. In that regard, it should be borne in mind that, in the absence of harmonisation of legislation, obstacles to free movement of goods which are the consequence of applying, to goods coming from other Member States where they are lawfully manufactured and marketed, rules that lay down requirements to be met by such goods (such as those relating to designation, form, size, weight, composition, presentation, labelling, packaging) constitute measures having equivalent effect which are prohibited by Article [34 TFEU], even if those rules apply without distinction to all products, unless their application can be justified by a public-interest objective taking precedence over the free movement of goods ...

An equally applicable rule restricting movement may therefore be justified by any reason within the umbrella concept of the 'public interest'. The Court has set certain limits to this concept, such as the rule that purely economic reasons may not be relied upon,[61] and these limits

---

[60] See M. Jarvis, *The Application of EC Law by National Courts: The Free Movement of Goods* (Oxford, Oxford University Press, 1998) 220–1.

[61] Case 72/83 *Campus Oil* v *Minister for Industry and Energy* [1984] ECR 2727; J. Snell, 'Economic Aims as Justifications for Restrictions on Free Movement' in A. Schrauwen (ed.), *The Rule of Reason: Rethinking Another Classic of European Legal Doctrine* (Groningen, Europa Law Publishing, 2005).

are discussed further in Chapter 21. However, the class of legitimate justifications remains broad. Nevertheless, in practice the majority of cases have concerned consumer protection, while those concerning environmental protection also form an important group. These are looked at in the next two sections, to show how the Court determines what is justified and, in particular, what is proportionate.

The legal status of these judicially invented derogations is odd. Article 36 TFEU provides for exceptions to Article 34 where necessary to protect really important interests such as public health or security.[62] Yet when the Court referred to mandatory requirements in *Cassis*, it was not offering a broad interpretation of Article 36. On the contrary, it was creating a new class of exception to free movement, existing alongside and in addition to the exceptions in the Treaty.[63] These exceptions are in one sense broader than Article 36: they cover a wider range of interests. However, they are narrower than Article 36 in that they only apply to equally applicable measures.[64] Where a measure discriminates directly, an appeal to the doctrine of mandatory requirements may not be made.

(a) Consumer protection

The most common justification for applying national product rules to imports is the protection of the consumer. One of the most well-known examples is the *German Beer* case.[65] The Reinheitsgebot, a centuries-old German rule defining the ingredients permitted in beer, was challenged as contrary to Article 34. Many foreign beers used ingredients not on the list, varying from rice to various chemical additives, and so were denied access to the German market under the name beer – they could be sold under some other name, say 'rice-chemical alcoholic beverage', but this was clearly unattractive. The German government claimed that the rule was necessary to prevent consumers being deceived about what they were buying: the German consumer had certain expectations, which beers made from non-conforming ingredients did not fulfil. The impure brew was simply not, in German eyes, beer.

Case 178/84 *Commission v Germany (German beer)* [1987] ECR 1227

29. It is not contested that the application of article 10 of the Biersteuergesetz to beers from other Member States in whose manufacture raw materials other than malted barley have been lawfully used, in particular rice and maize, is liable to constitute an obstacle to their importation into the Federal Republic of Germany.

30. Accordingly, it must be established whether the application of that provision may be justified by imperative requirements relating to consumer protection.

31. The German government's argument that article 10 of the Biersteuergesetz is essential in order to protect German consumers because, in their minds, the designation 'Bier' is inseparably linked to the beverage manufactured solely from the ingredients laid down in article 9 of the Biersteuergesetz must be rejected.

---

[62] See Chapter 21.
[63] See P. Craig and G. de Búrca, *EU Law* (4th edn, Oxford, Oxford University Press, 2006) 706–7.
[64] Case 788/79 *Gilli and Andres* [1980] ECR 2071.
[65] Case 178/84 *Commission v Germany (German beer)* [1987] ECR 1227.

32. Firstly, consumers' conceptions which vary from one Member State to the other are also likely to evolve in the course of time within a Member State. The establishment of the common market is, it should be added, one of the factors that may play a major contributory role in that development. Whereas rules protecting consumers against misleading practices enable such a development to be taken into account, legislation of the kind contained in article 10 of the Biersteuergesetz prevents it from taking place. As the court has already held in another context (Case 170/78 *Commission* v *United Kingdom*), the legislation of a Member State must not 'crystallize given consumer habits so as to consolidate an advantage acquired by national industries concerned to comply with them'.

33. Secondly, in the other Member States of the Community the designations corresponding to the German designation 'Bier' are generic designations for a fermented beverage manufactured from malted barley, whether malted barley on its own or with the addition of rice or maize. The same approach is taken in Community law as can be seen from heading no. 22.03 of the common customs tariff. The German legislature itself utilizes the designation 'Bier' in that way in article 9(7) and (8) of the Biersteuergesetz in order to refer to beverages not complying with the manufacturing rules laid down in article 9(1) and (2).

34. The German designation 'Bier' and its equivalents in the languages of the other Member States of the Community may therefore not be restricted to beers manufactured in accordance with the rules in force in the Federal Republic of Germany.

35. It is admittedly legitimate to seek to enable consumers who attribute specific qualities to beers manufactured from particular raw materials to make their choice in the light of that consideration. However, as the court has already emphasized, that possibility may be ensured by means which do not prevent the importation of products which have been lawfully manufactured and marketed in other Member States and, in particular, 'by the compulsory affixing of suitable labels giving the nature of the product sold'. By indicating the raw materials utilized in the manufacture of beer 'such a course would enable the consumer to make his choice in full knowledge of the facts and would guarantee transparency in trading and in offers to the public'. It must be added that such a system of mandatory consumer information must not entail negative assessments for beers not complying with the requirements of article 9 of the Biersteuergesetz.

The Court accepts that consumers may have preferences, for example for pure beer, and that their ability to satisfy these preferences is important and deserves protection. However, it takes the view that prohibiting the sale as 'beer' of any non-conforming product is disproportionate. Consumers can be adequately protected by a labelling requirement: if it is clear from the label which ingredients the beer contains and whether it is made according to the purity rules then this is sufficient consumer protection, and is more proportionate because it has a far lesser effect on interstate trade. It is easier for foreign beer producers to amend their labels than their product.

This is the Court's consistent approach. It insists that matters of quality and preference, rather than safety or health, do not need to be dealt with by bans, but can be more proportionately addressed by rules on labels.[66] This is a coherent part of the Court's relatively liberal philosophy of consumer protection, which assumes that if adequate information is available to

---

[66] See e.g. Case 261/81 *Rau* v *De Schmedt* [1982] ECR 3961; Case 407/85 *Drei Glocken* [1988] ECR 4233; see also Case 788/79 *Gilli and Andres* [1980] ECR 2071. See also Joined Cases C-158/04 and C-159/04 *Alfa Vita* v *Elliniko Dimosio and Nomarchiaki Aftodioikisi Ioanninon* [2006] ECR I-8135, para. 23.

consumers they are then able to make their own decisions about quality.[67] This is by contrast with the more paternalistic approach reflected in the rules in *Cassis* and *German Beer*, where the state determined what consumers could buy and what they could not.

This information-based approach assumes that consumers read labels, and are reasonably circumspect.[68] It is vulnerable to the criticism that in fact these assumptions are not true, and consumers will simply seize a product without realising that it is not quite what they are used to. There is a considerable scholarship on whether the information approach is a sensible and proportionate approach to consumer protection, or rather its sacrifice on the altar of free trade.[69]

This debate can be kept in perspective by remembering that it is only quality that is in issue. Where there is a genuine health risk, the Court is much more deferential to national rules.[70] Moreover, there is an issue of principle involved, which is addressed in paragraph 32 of the judgment above: consumer behaviour and expectations are not fixed, but changing, and so the law should not try to entrench them as they are, but provide a framework within which they can develop. The European consumer may be unused to diversity, but the goals of the internal market are that she should become used to this, and this means she will need to become someone used to making decisions on the basis of information, rather than having products selected for her by the state. Whether this is necessarily an improvement in quality of life is another issue, but it is a persuasive corollary of the free trade agreement which Article 34 represents.

In the judgment, this question of consumer change was framed around the issue of naming. The German government had argued that impure beer was, in the eyes of the local consumer, not beer. The Court takes this as an example of the kind of expectation which must not be crystallised in law, precisely because it has a trade-hindering effect.[71] The Court further suggests that what is 'beer' should be understood in the context of other national definitions and the EU customs definition. National product definitions no longer stand in isolation.

This has recurred in several cases. Italy challenged the phrase 'apple vinegar' saying that it was a fraud on consumers because vinegar was inherently made from grapes, while France challenged foreign foie gras which did not entirely conform to French rules.[72]

---

[67] See S. Weatherill, *EU Consumer Law and Policy* (Northampton, Edward Elgar, 2005); M. Radeideh, *Fair Trading in EC Law: Information and Consumer Choice in the Internal Market* (Groningen, Europa Law Publishing, 2005).

[68] See Case C-210/96 *Gut Springenheide* [1998] ECR I-4657; Case C-51/94 *Commission v Germany* [1995] ECR I-3599; Case 27/80 *Fietje* [1980] ECR 3839.

[69] See L. W. Gormley, 'The Consumer Acquis and the Internal Market' (2009) 20 *EBLRev.* 409; von Heydebrand u.d. Lasa, above n. 58; C. Macmaolain, 'Waiter, There's a Fly in my Soup. Yes Sir, that's E120: Disparities Between Actual Individual Behaviour and Regulating Labelling for the Average Consumer in EU Law' (2008) 45 *CMLRev.* 1147; M. Radeideh, *Fair Trading in EC Law: Information and Consumer Choice in the Internal Market* (Groningen, Europa Law Publishing, 2005); H. Unberath and A. Johnston, 'The Double-headed Approach of the ECJ Concerning Consumer Protection' (2007) 44 *CMLRev.* 1237; S. Weatherill, 'Recent Case Law Concerning the Free Movement of Goods: Mapping the Frontiers of Market Deregulation' (1999) 36 *CMLRev.* 51; S. Weatherill, *EU Consumer Law and Policy* (Northampton, Edward Elgar, 2005).

[70] See Chapter 21.

[71] See also Case C-358/01 *Commission v Spain* [2003] ECR I-13145, para. 52.

[72] Case 788/79 *Gilli and Andres* [1980] ECR 2071; Case C-166/03 *Commission v France (Gold)* [2005] ECR I-6535; Case C-12/00 *Commission v Spain (Spanish chocolate)* [2003] ECR I-459; Case C-14/00 *Commission v Italy (Chocolate)* [2003] ECR I-513; Case C-358/01 *Commission v Spain* [2003] ECR I-13145; see also Case C-6/02 *Commission v France* [2003] ECR I-2389.

Case C–184/96 Commission v France [1998] ECR I–6197

23. So far as concerns the argument based on the necessity to prevent offences with respect to false descriptions, the Court, in its judgment in *Deserbais*, did not exclude the possibility that Member States could require those concerned to alter the denomination of a foodstuff where a product presented under a particular denomination is so different, as regards its composition or production, from the products generally known under that denomination in the Community that it cannot be regarded as falling within the same category (Case 286/86 *Ministère Public v Deserbais* [1988] ECR 4907).

24. Nonetheless, the mere fact that a product does not wholly conform to the requirements laid down in national legislation on the composition of certain foodstuffs with a particular denomination does not mean that its marketing can be prohibited.

If someone tried to market a generic paté as foie gras, it would be justifiable to prevent this on consumer protection grounds. However, the fact that foie gras is made in slightly different ways in other places is not enough to justify a prohibition on using the name.

The concept of the informed and circumspect consumer defines the Court's approach to consumer protection, but leaves open the question of what information the consumer can be expected to process and understand, and how much information she needs. While labelling requirements are in general the legislative approach that states should follow, even these may be disproportionate under some circumstances. Because the label is a physical part of the product, national labelling rules are themselves product rules in the *Cassis* sense, and so must still be justified. Labelling requirements impose relatively low costs on producers, and so are preferable to rules about the product itself, but they do impose some costs, so that if the labelling rules are in some sense unreasonable then these too will be contrary to Article 34.

There are two kinds of potential labelling problems. One is where the information to be displayed is in some sense discriminatory. The Court warned about this in *German Beer*. If, for example, non-conforming beer was required to bear a red stamp saying 'impure' then while this might not be very difficult to comply with, and while it might make matters clear to the consumer, it would nevertheless contravene Article 34 because it would have an unnecessarily negative effect on marketing of foreign beer, and so would be disproportionate. Something rather similar to this occurred in the *Irish Souvenirs* case, in which Ireland proposed that souvenirs not made in Ireland be stamped with their country of production or with the word 'foreign'.[73] A requirement to indicate the country of production, even if it applies to all goods, the Court has found, may have the effect of steering consumers towards national goods, while it is not in fact necessary information.[74]

The other kind of labelling problem is where the information to be displayed is pointless. When Belgium required medicinal labels to bear the 'notification number' which was associated with the application for approval to sell that medicine in Belgium, the Court found this to be disproportionate.[75] It imposed a small, but not trivial, burden on producers while realistically, what use was it to the consumer?

---

[73] Case 113/80 *Commission v Ireland (Irish souvenirs)* [1981] ECR 1625.

[74] *Ibid*; Case 207/83 *Commission v United Kingdom (marks of origin)* [1985] ECR 1201.

[75] Case C-217/99 *Commission v Belgium* [2000] ECR I-10251; Case C-55/99 *Commission v France* [2000] ECR I-11499.

The protective approach to product regulation which was traditionally applied to the substance of the goods can also be seen in national rules on packaging and information. In *Clinique*, for example, the German government objected to the marketing of cosmetics under that name, because it was too similar to *Klinik*, the German word for hospital.[76] Consumers might therefore think that the products were medically approved, and believe that they really would look younger or more beautiful if they used them.

The Court disagreed. In the circumstances (the products were sold not by pharmacists but in shops selling make-up), it felt the dangers did not justify the trade-hindering effects of the rule. The European consumer is expected to show a certain awareness and scepticism. If this is not yet always reality, that fact does not justify legislation entrenching passivity and naivety.

(b) Protection of the environment

Environmental issues are often dealt with under Article 36, and are discussed further in Chapter 21. However, the protection of the environment has also been recognised as a mandatory requirement, especially in the context of recycling schemes and their effect on trade.

These recycling cases have been about soft drinks containers. In each case a state has imposed obligations on producers related to the types of containers they used for their drinks. In *Commission* v *Denmark*, a system was successfully challenged in which only certain types of soft drinks containers were permitted in Denmark, the goal being to make recycling more efficient and practical.[77] Since this dramatically limited the possibilities for importing soft drinks from elsewhere in Europe where many different kinds of containers were in use, the rule was disproportionate. The reasoning of the Court was that it was not necessary to limit the types of containers, since the goal of promoting recycling could be met by other means.

The case was heavily criticised.[78] While it is, of course, true that many different kinds of containers can be recycled, the point is that this is expensive. A recycling scheme is most efficient if it only has to deal with a limited range of packaging types. In reality, recycling will be successful if it is not too expensive, and so the Danish considered that their strict limits on container types were in fact an essential part of increasing the amount of recycling. That the Court did not consider economic reality, but merely the theoretical fact that other kinds of containers were in principle also recyclable, suggested that environmental protection was not being taken seriously, and would be subordinated to trade.

In more recent cases, the environment has been more successful. In *Radlberger Getränkegesellschaft*, the German government amended its laws to require producers selling more than a certain proportion of soft drinks in non-reusable containers to set up a deposit-and-return scheme, whereby they would take back the waste packaging they generated, and deal with it themselves.[79] Since such a scheme costs money, producers using a large proportion of non-reusable packaging faced a cost burden which might hinder their access to the German market.

---

[76] Case C-315/92 *Verband Sozialer Wettbewerb* v *Clinique Laboratories* [1994] ECR I-317.

[77] Case 302/86 *Commission* v *Denmark* [1988] ECR 4607.

[78] See J. Scott, *EC Environmental Law* (London, Longman, 1998) 69–72, quoted in J. Holder and M. Lee, *Environmental Protection: Law and Policy* (Cambridge, Cambridge University Press, 2007) 179; H. Temmink, 'From Danish Bottles to Danish Bees: The Dynamics of Free Movement of Goods and Environmental Protection – A Case Law Analysis' (2000) 1 *YEEL* 61.

[79] Case C-309/02 *Radlberger Getränkegesellschaft* v *Land Baden-Württemberg* [2004] ECR I-11763; see also the almost identical Case C-463/01 *Commission* v *Germany* [2004] ECR I-11705, decided on the same day.

The Court was particularly concerned about the fact that non-German producers used more non-recyclable packaging than German ones, so that they would be relatively more affected. Moreover, a return system is clearly more expensive if the goods have to be returned to a distant production location in another state than if production is local. The scheme therefore imposed a greater burden on more distant producers. In the light of this, the Court considered whether the environmental benefits outweighed these trade concerns:

Case C-309/02 *Radlberger Getränkegesellschaft mbH & Co. v Land Baden-Württemberg* [2004] ECR I-11763

75. In accordance with settled case-law, national measures capable of hindering intra-Community trade may be justified by overriding requirements relating to protection of the environment provided that the measures in question are proportionate to the aim pursued.

76. The obligation to establish a deposit and return system for empty packaging is an indispensable element of a system intended to ensure that packaging is reused.

77. With regard to non-reusable packaging, as the defendant in the main proceedings and the German Government state, the establishment of a deposit and return system is liable to increase the proportion of empty packaging returned and results in more precise sorting of packaging waste, thus helping to improve its recovery. In addition, the charging of a deposit contributes to the reduction of waste in the natural environment since it encourages consumers to return empty packaging to the points of sale.

78. Furthermore, insofar as the rules at issue in the main proceedings make the entry into force of a new packaging-waste management system conditional on the proportion of reusable packaging on the German market, they create a situation where any increase in sales of drinks in non-reusable packaging on that market makes it more likely that there will be a change of system. Inasmuch as those rules thus encourage the producers and distributors concerned to have recourse to reusable packaging, they contribute towards reducing the amount of waste to be disposed of, which constitutes one of the general objectives of environmental protection policy.

79. However, in order for such rules to comply with the principle of proportionality, it must be ascertained not only whether the means which they employ are suitable for the purpose of attaining the desired objectives but also whether those means do not go beyond what is necessary for that purpose.

80. In order for national rules to satisfy the latter test, they must allow the producers and distributors concerned, before the deposit and return system enters into force, to adapt their production methods and the management of non-reusable packaging waste to the requirements of the new system. While it is true that a Member State may leave to those producers and distributors the task of setting up that system by organising the taking back of packaging, the refunding of sums paid by way of deposit and any balancing of those sums between distributors, the Member State in question must still ensure that, at the time when the packaging-waste management system changes, every producer or distributor concerned can actually participate in an operational system.

81. Legislation, such as the VerpackV, that makes the establishment of a deposit and return system dependent on a packaging reuse rate, which is certainly advantageous from an ecological point of view, complies with the principle of proportionality only if, while encouraging the reuse of packaging, it gives the producers and distributors concerned a reasonable transitional period to adapt thereto and ensures that, at the time when the packaging-waste management system changes, every producer or distributor concerned can actually participate in an operational system.

In principle, therefore, the Court was prepared to accept rules which would not only have a significant effect on trade, but probably impact on importers much more than on domestic producers, because those rules did serve an important environmental goal. The only requirements that it imposed, in the name of proportionality, was that producers be given a reasonable amount of time to adapt to the new rules and that the system be so constructed that producers were in practice able to participate and comply.

4 SELLING ARRANGEMENTS AND *KECK*

The acceptance in *Cassis* that equally applicable rules could be MEQRs led to cases testing the limits of this principle, applying it to any kind of measure which could be argued to have a negative effect on import quantities. Most well-known, the rules on Sunday trading in the United Kingdom were challenged as contrary to Article 34: if shops could open on Sundays they could sell more goods, and some of those goods would be imported.[80] *Ergo*, requiring shops to close on Sundays limited imports.

This turns a Treaty Article that is apparently about goods into a tool for policing wider socio-economic regulation, which brings with it risks of constitutional discontent among the Member States. Moreover, it is inefficient. In the Sunday trading cases, the Court unsurprisingly found that the measures were justified by legitimate social goals, and therefore not contrary to the Treaty. All that was happening was that many creative cases were being brought, but they were not being won. Such a broad reading of the Treaty was not therefore opening up the internal market or increasing trade. It was just increasing work for the Court.

In *Keck*, the Court finally set a limit to the kinds of equally applicable rules which could be MEQRs. It excluded one group, which it called *selling arrangements*. These, it said, were simply outside the scope of the Treaty, as long as they were in fact equal in impact on both domestic goods and imports.

Joined Cases 267/91–268/91 *Keck and Mithouard* [1993] ECR I-6097

11. By virtue of Article [34 TFEU], quantitative restrictions on imports and all measures having equivalent effect are prohibited between Member States. The Court has consistently held that any measure which is capable of directly or indirectly, actually or potentially, hindering intra-Community trade constitutes a measure having equivalent effect to a quantitative restriction.

12. National legislation imposing a general prohibition on resale at a loss is not designed to regulate trade in goods between Member States.

13. Such legislation may, admittedly, restrict the volume of sales, and hence the volume of sales of products from other Member States, insofar as it deprives traders of a method of sales promotion. But the question remains whether such a possibility is sufficient to characterize the legislation in question as a measure having equivalent effect to a quantitative restriction on imports.

14. In view of the increasing tendency of traders to invoke Article [34 TFEU] as a means of challenging any rules whose effect is to limit their commercial freedom even where such rules are not aimed at products from other Member States, the Court considers it necessary to re-examine and clarify its case-law on this matter.

---

[80] See e.g. Case C-145/88 *Torfaen Borough Council v B & Q* [1989] ECR 3851; Case C-169/91 *Stoke-on-Trent and Norwich City Council v B & Q* [1992] ECR I-6635; for full discussion see C. Barnard, *The Substantive Law of the EU* (2nd edn, Oxford, Oxford University Press, 2007) 137–43.

15. It is established by the case-law beginning with 'Cassis de Dijon' that, in the absence of harmonization of legislation, obstacles to free movement of goods which are the consequence of applying, to goods coming from other Member States where they are lawfully manufactured and marketed, rules that lay down requirements to be met by such goods (such as those relating to designation, form, size, weight, composition, presentation, labelling, packaging) constitute measures of equivalent effect prohibited by Article [34 TFEU]. This is so even if those rules apply without distinction to all products unless their application can be justified by a public-interest objective taking precedence over the free movement of goods.

16. By contrast, contrary to what has previously been decided, the application to products from other Member States of national provisions restricting or prohibiting certain selling arrangements is not such as to hinder directly or indirectly, actually or potentially, trade between Member States within the meaning of the *Dassonville* judgment, so long as those provisions apply to all relevant traders operating within the national territory and so long as they affect in the same manner, in law and in fact, the marketing of domestic products and of those from other Member States.

17. Provided that those conditions are fulfilled, the application of such rules to the sale of products from another Member State meeting the requirements laid down by that State is not by nature such as to prevent their access to the market or to impede access any more than it impedes the access of domestic products. Such rules therefore fall outside the scope of Article [34 TFEU].

18. Accordingly, the reply to be given to the national court is that Article [34 TFEU] of the EEC Treaty is to be interpreted as not applying to legislation of a Member State imposing a general prohibition on resale at a loss.

The rule that the Court lays down is that rules governing the way products are sold are not MEQRs within the meaning of *Dassonville* and Article 34. States may therefore legislate however they like on matters such as advertising, shop opening hours, sales techniques and prices.[81] However, this is subject to the proviso that the measures taken must not have a greater effect on imports than they do on domestic goods or producers. If this is the case, then even measures concerning selling arrangements will be MEQRs. It has been made clear in later cases that the usual approach then applies: such measures will be prohibited unless they are justified by a mandatory requirement or a Treaty exception.[82]

The reasoning provided by the Court for this position is that, it says, rules on selling arrangements do not generally have the effect of preventing access to the market for imports, nor of impeding it any more than is the case for domestic products. If a shop has to close on Sundays, or advertising of certain goods is prohibited, this does not actually prevent those goods being sold. It may have some effect on their sales, but in general this effect is the same for domestic and foreign goods. The implicit contrast is with product rules, which do tend to prevent non-conforming products reaching the market, and which also tend to impact on foreign goods more than domestic.

Keck therefore interprets Article 34 to prohibit two things: (i) measures which have a greater effect on imports than on domestic products, and (ii) measures which effectively prevent certain

---

[81] See below nn. 97–8 for examples of the range of selling arrangements.
[82] See e.g. Case C-20/03 *Burmanjer* [2005] ECR I-4133; Case C-441/04 *A-Punckt Schmuckhandels* [2006] ECR I-2093.

imports from being sold.[83] This second category does not appear to be dependent upon show-ing any unequal effect, although it may be argued that in practice the complete exclusion of a class of goods from the marketplace almost invariably has the effect of protecting established, usually national, alternatives.

Keck therefore broadly reflects an inequality-based understanding of Article 34. It is for this reason that *Alfa Vita*, discussed above,[84] is so surprising: the measure involved was argued neither to be unequal in effect, nor to prevent access completely, but merely to reduce sales. *Alfa Vita* and *Keck* apply to different categories of measures, so there is no hard conflict, but there is a conceptual inconsistency. It is as if the idea of an MEQR underlying the law on sell-ing arrangements is not the same as that underlying the law on other types of MEQR. This highlights the ongoing policy tensions surrounding Article 34, between those who would like to see it used to reduce all unjustified regulatory inhibition of economic activity (*Alfa Vita*), and those who remain attached to a non-discrimination rule (*Keck*).

Keck is, and has always been, a controversial case, largely because its business sense has been doubted.[85] In reality, it has been argued, rules on advertising may have a greater effect on sales of goods than some product rules do. Adapting a product is not always expensive or difficult, while there may be contexts where an inability to advertise, or to sell via certain channels, or to offer certain kinds of discounts (all of which are selling arrangements) might seriously undermine a marketing campaign and make market access impractical. *Keck* is of-ten considered to be a very formalist approach to Article 34. Instead of trying to distinguish between rules according to their actual effect on trade, it divides them into convenient, but somewhat arbitrary, groups which do not correspond to practical importance for the trader.

The advantage of *Keck* is that it is relatively clear. In most cases it is easy to distinguish be-tween a selling arrangement and a product rule, and both states and market actors are able to determine what their legal position is. An alternative interpretation of Article 34 which is some-times put forward is that it should prohibit all measures which substantially restrict market ac-cess. This interpretation is very close to the goals of the Article, and has an obvious integrationist appeal, but would result in a very open and vague rule. It is, moreover, open to question whether such an open norm would be effective in practice because it would be so difficult to apply in an apparently apolitical way, perhaps causing national judges to be shy of using it forcefully.[86]

There is also a principled defence of *Keck*. Unlike product rules, selling arrangements do not impose a double burden on imports, nor do selling arrangements require products to be adapt-ed at all, so there is no question of excluding non-conforming goods. There is a fundamental difference between the market effects of selling arrangements and the market effects of product rules, which does not make it entirely obvious that they should be treated in the same way.

Keck also needs to be seen in constitutional terms given the important limit it sets to the Union's capacity to second-guess state regulatory choices. Maduro's constitutional interpre-tation of *Keck* has been one of the most influential.[87] He notes that when states regulate

---

[83] *Keck and Mithouard*, above n. 2, paras. 16 and 17.
[84] See p. 751.
[85] L. Gormley, 'Two Years after *Keck*' (1996) 19 *Fordham International Law Journal* 866; Weatherill, above n. 26. Cf. L. Rossi, 'Economic Analysis of Article 28 after the *Keck* Judgment' (2006) 7(5) *German Law Journal* 479.
[86] See D. Wilsher, 'Does Keck Discrimination Make Any Sense? An Assessment of the Non-discrimination Principle within the European Single Market' (2008) 33 *ELRev*. 3.
[87] M. Poiares Maduro, *We the Court* (Oxford, Hart, 1998).

economic activity this does not only have an effect on domestic actors, but also on foreign ones who want to participate in the domestic market. Yet, while domestic actors are represented in the law-making process via national democratic institutions, foreign actors, in general, are not. States therefore impose costs on non-domestic actors without taking this into account. In the context of an integrating Union in which states accept a certain degree of responsibility towards each other, this should be seen as a democratic problem. The justification for the Court's intervention in national economic regulation is therefore that it safeguards the interests of the unrepresented foreign actor.

This logic explains *Cassis*, because when states regulate products they usually produce legislation reflecting local production norms – established tastes and products – and do not consider what is accepted or usual elsewhere, with the effect that their legislation tends to have a protectionist effect. However, where selling arrangements are concerned this is not the case. The legislator makes a trade-off between economic freedom and other interests, but in general the interests and concerns of the importer are exactly the same as those of the domestic producers. Both want, for example, freedom to advertise and set prices, and both want this for the same reasons. If the domestic producers are represented in the domestic democratic process then this serves as an adequate proxy for foreign producers, and there should usually be no need for a democratically-justified correction of national law by the Court of Justice.

In any case, *Keck* has resisted criticism from many commentators and is still a pillar of the Court's case law. Its apparent clarity and ease of use are among the major reasons for its resilience. Yet, while most of the time it is fairly easy to see whether a measure is a selling arrangement and whether it has an unequal effect, there are cases where this becomes very difficult. Recently the Court has seemed to take a slightly narrower approach to what a selling arrangement is, as if, having used *Keck* to limit Article 34, it now wishes to set limits to *Keck*.[88]

(i) The notion of a selling arrangement

The distinction between a selling arrangement and a product rule was laid down in *Familiapress*.[89] A product rule is a measure which requires some physical aspect of the product or its packaging or labelling to be changed, while a selling arrangement is concerned only with the way in which goods are sold or marketed. Measures conforming to neither definition are to be considered under *Dassonville*.

The boundary between categories becomes difficult when measures are concerned with the sale of particular types of products, for example a rule restricting sale of alcohol with a percentage above 25 per cent to licensed shops. Is that a product rule, because it is to do with the amount of alcohol in the drink, or a selling arrangement, because it regulates the place where the product is sold? The Court seems to find rules like this to be product rules, because the obligation or burden that they contain is specifically linked to the physical characteristics of the product. There is thus a pressure, if not an absolute requirement, on producers to amend their product to avoid the burdensome rule.

---

[88] See P. Pecho, 'Good-Bye *Keck*: A Comment on the Remarkable Judgment in *Commission v Italy*' (2009) 36 *LIEI* 257; A. Tryfonidou, 'Was *Keck* a Half-baked Solution After All?' (2007) 34 *LIEI* 167.

[89] Case C-368/95 *Familiapress v Heinrich Bauer Verlag* [1997] ECR I-3689. See also Case C-159/00 *Sapod Audic* [2002] ECR I-5031.

For example, in *Schwarz*, an Austrian rule was in issue which prohibited the sale of un-wrapped bubble gum from vending machines.[90] This was said to be unhygienic. The Court found that this was a product rule because those 'importers wishing to put those goods up for sale in Austria have to package them'. A producer who wanted to sell bubble gum to vending machine operators in Austria would have to make adjustments to her production process. Similarly, in *Dynamic Medien*, a rule prohibiting the sale by mail order of DVDs without an age-classification sticker was found to be a product rule, because the rule, while restricting the method of sale, was linked to a physical part of the packaging.[91]

By contrast, *Morellato* concerned an Italian law on semi-baked bread.[92] This is bread that is bought by shops as half-baked frozen dough. The shops then finish baking it in their own ovens. This enables them to sell warm fresh bread, without having all the facilities for making bread from scratch. The process is quite controversial in some countries, because it threatens the traditional artisanal baker, and enables all kinds of shops to apparently sell their own fresh-baked bread. It was in this context that Italy required shops selling bread made by this process to prepackage it in bags with labels clearly indicating its nature. The measures informed the consumer, but also distinguished the bread from bread made on the premises, which did not need to be packaged, allowing this latter to preserve some distinctive aura of naturalness.

The Court found that the measure was a selling arrangement.

Case C–416/00 *Morellato* [2003] ECR I-9343

32. The distinctive feature of the main proceedings is that the product put on sale by Mr Morellato was imported at a stage when its production process was not yet finished. In order to be able to market the product in Italy as bread ready for consumption, it was necessary to complete the baking of the pre-baked bread imported from France.

33. The fact that a product must, to a certain extent, be transformed after importation does not in itself preclude a requirement relating to its marketing from falling within the scope of application of Article [34 TFEU]. It is possible that, as in the main proceedings, the imported product is not simply a component or ingredient of another product but in reality constitutes the product that is intended for marketing as soon as a simple transformation process has been carried out.

34. In such a situation, the relevant question is whether the requirement for prior packaging laid down in the legislation of the Member State of import makes it necessary to alter the product in order to comply with that requirement.

35. In the present case, nothing in the file indicates that it was necessary for the pre-baked bread, as imported into Italy, to be altered in order to comply with that requirement.

36. In those circumstances, the requirement for prior packaging, since it relates only to the marketing of the bread which results from the final baking of pre-baked bread, is in principle such as to fall outside the scope of Article [34 TFEU], provided that it does not in reality constitute discrimination against imported products.

---

[90] Case C-366/04 *Georg Schwarz* v *Bürgermeister der Landeshauptstadt Salzburg* [2006] ECR I-10139.
[91] Case C-244/06 *Dynamic Medien Vertriebs GmbH* v *Avides Media AG* [2008] ECR I-1505.
[92] Case C-416/00 *Morellato* [2003] ECR I-9343.

As in *Schwarz* the product had to be packaged before it could be sold. There was thus a physical adjustment necessary. However, the difference was that in Schwarz the nature of the adjustment was such that it could only realistically be done by the producer. One could not expect vending machine operators to put balls of bubble gum in individual sealed plastic bags. *Schwarz* therefore imposed a production burden. However, in *Morellato*, there was no need for the producer of the semi-baked dough to change anything at all. While shops had to put the bread in bags, they had no need to get those bags from the dough producers, and the packaging had to be done by the shops, not by the producers, since, as the Court said, the production process was incomplete when the dough was delivered – it still had to be partly baked. Thus, although *Morellato* is superficially similar to *Schwarz* and *Dynamic Medien*, it is very different from the perspective of the producer of the imported product. These cases highlight that the question determining whether a measure is a selling arrangement or a product rule is whether that producer is required, or pressured, to change some physical aspect of the product that she ships.

A variation on *Morellato* was offered by *Alfa Vita*, in which 'bake-off' products were also considered.[93] Greek law required that vendors of these had to have all the facilities that were required of a normal bakery, which included areas for kneading bread and a flour store. Clearly such facilities were inappropriate in, for example, a supermarket, and the law was again an attempt to protect traditional bakeries. The Court, however, found that this could not be considered a selling arrangement because it aimed 'to specify the production conditions for bakery products'. It was not, unlike *Morellato*, about the circumstances of sale, but rather about the final stage of production.

On the other hand, the rule in *Alfa Vita* does not pressure the producer of the bake-off dough to change their product. This is probably why the case was decided without reference to *Cassis*, and not treated as a product rule. Nevertheless, the imposition of a cost imposed on vendors of bake-off bread (they had to maintain facilities) might tend to discourage them from selling it, so that it could have an effect on imports. Hence, it was treated as a general MEQR within *Dassonville*.

Finally, a number of recent cases have concerned use of goods, and whether usage rules should be seen as selling arrangements or not. Once again, the Court seems to be choosing to confine that category to its literal meaning. In *Commission* v *Italy*, *Åklagaren* v *Mickelsson and Roos*, and *Commission* v *Portugal*, which concerned rules prohibiting the use of motorcycle trailers, jet-skis and tinted plastic window stickers for cars respectively, the Court found *Keck* not to apply.[94] The reason why these rules were found to be MEQRs was discussed above.[95] However, the reason why they were not selling arrangements was not explained by the Court explicitly, and seems to be no more complicated than the fact that they did not in fact concern the circumstances of sale.[96]

(ii) Unequal effect of selling arrangements

Where a selling arrangement has a greater effect on imported products than on domestic ones, it will fall within Article 34, and will be prohibited unless justified. If it discriminates directly a justification must be sought in Article 36, while if it is equally applicable but tends as a matter of fact to burden imports more then it may be saved by proportionate reliance on a mandatory requirement.

---

[93] Case C-188/04 *Alfa Vita* v *Elliniko Dimosio and Nomarchiaki Aftodioikisi Ioanninon* [2006] ECR I-8135.
[94] See above nn. 20–2.
[95] See pp. 750–1.
[96] See also Case C-170/04 *Klas Rosengren and Others* v *Riksåklagaren* [2007] ECR I-4071.

For some years after *Keck* was decided, this proviso was largely theoretical, with the Court being reluctant to investigate whether a measure might have some unequal effect.[97] There are good reasons for this. Restrictions on selling arrangements tend to keep markets static, but this tends to be to the advantage of incumbents and the disadvantage of market newcomers. Since the former are often national it can be argued that most selling arrangements in fact hurt importers most. An over-realistic approach to the proviso might therefore bring most selling arrangements back within Article 34 and once again extend that Article beyond the judicial and constitutional comfort zone.

Nevertheless, in several cases, most importantly *De Agostini* and *Gourmet International*, the Court has recognised that the above logic could apply, particularly where advertising is concerned.[98] The former case concerned television advertising aimed at children, and the latter case concerned advertising of alcohol in Sweden. Bans on these, claimed the litigants, preserved domestic incumbents at the expense of foreign 'wannabe' market entrants. In *De Agostini*, the Court left it to the national court to decide whether the rule did, as a matter of fact, affect importers more. By contrast, in *Gourmet*, it felt able to take a view itself.

Case C–405/98 *Konsumentombudsmannen (KO)* v *Gourmet International Products AB* [2001] ECR I–1795

19. The Court has also held... that it cannot be excluded that an outright prohibition, applying in one Member State, of a type of promotion for a product which is lawfully sold there might have a greater impact on products from other Member States.

20. It is apparent that a prohibition on advertising such as that at issue in the main proceedings not only prohibits a form of marketing a product but in reality prohibits producers and importers from directing any advertising messages at consumers, with a few insignificant exceptions.

21. Even without its being necessary to carry out a precise analysis of the facts characteristic of the Swedish situation, which it is for the national court to do, the Court is able to conclude that, in the case of products like alcoholic beverages, the consumption of which is linked to traditional social practices and to local habits and customs, a prohibition of all advertising directed at consumers in the form of advertisements in the press, on the radio and on television, the direct mailing of unsolicited material or the placing of posters on the public highway is liable to impede access to the market by products from other Member States more than it impedes access by domestic products, with which consumers are instantly more familiar.

The key factor was the nature of the product. Alcoholic drinks are not usually bought only on price, but also on the basis of tradition, reputation, image and brand. Market entry is very difficult without the chance to speak directly to consumers via advertising.

Other recent examples of unequal selling arrangements include *DocMorris*, in which the Court found that a prohibition on Internet sales of pharmaceutical products had an unequal effect because it was inevitably pharmacies at a distance who would be most affected, and these

---

[97] See e.g. Case C-391/92 *Commission v Greece (Greek milk)* [1995] ECR I-1621; Joined Cases 69/93 and 258/93 *Punto Casa v Sindaco del Comune di Capena* [1994] ECR I-2355.

[98] See also Case C-254/98 *Schutzverband v TK-Heimdienst* [2000] ECR I-151; Case C-531/07 *Fachverband der Buch- und Medienwirtschaft*, Judgment of 30 April 2009; Case C-20/03 *Burmanjer* [2005] ECR I-4133; Case C-441/04 *A-Punckt Schmuckhandels* [2006] ECR I-2093; Case C-322/01 *Deutscher Apothekerverband v DocMorris* [2003] ECR I-14887; see also Case C-71/02 *Karner* [2004] ECR I-3025.

were most likely to be foreign.[99] The physical pharmacy, inevitably domestic, was protected from pharmacies abroad wishing to supply products from other states. Most recently, in *Fachverband*, the Court found that minimum book prices deprived imports, which might otherwise be cheaper than domestic goods, of an important competitive advantage.[100] Although the goal of the rule, protecting cultural diversity, was legitimate, a uniform price for domestic books and imports was disproportionate. The Court found that a minimum price could be set for imports, but it had to be one which reflected the possibility of cheaper production abroad.

5 ARTICLE 35 TFEU AND RESTRICTIONS ON EXPORTS

Article 35 is the equivalent of Article 34 for exports, and provides:

> Quantitative restrictions on exports, and all measures having equivalent effect, shall be prohibited between Member States.

The leading case until recently was *Groenveld*, which concerned a ban on the possession of horsemeat by sausage makers in the Netherlands.[101] This was to make Dutch sausages acceptable in states where horsemeat was prohibited, by removing any risk of contamination. The measure was therefore aimed at protecting exports. However, a sausage producer who wanted to branch out into horsemeat sausages attempted to overturn the rule by claiming that it contravened Article 35. Since he could not possess horsemeat, he could not export horsemeat sausages.

Although the Dutch rule could be conceived of as a product rule in the *Cassis* sense, limiting the way sausages are produced, the Court found that the measure fell outside Article 35, since it applied to all producers and products, whether aimed for the domestic market or for export:

> 7. That provision concerns national measures which have as their specific object or effect the restriction of patterns of exports and thereby the establishment of a difference in treatment between the domestic trade of a Member State and its export trade in such a way as to provide a particular advantage for national production or for the domestic market of the state in question at the expense of the production or of the trade of other Member States.

This made clear that Article 35 has its own logic, and Article 34 reasoning cannot simply be transposed. A measure within Article 35 must provide some specific disadvantage for exports, by comparison with goods sold domestically, thereby encouraging domestic sales at the expense of export sales.

An example is *Ravil*, which concerned Italian rules on the sale of grated cheese.[102] The specific cheese in question, 'Grana Padano', could only be sold under that name in grated form if it had been grated within the region of production. If it was exported whole, and grated abroad, the name could not be used. This rule was enforced by means of bilateral conventions with other states, and it was one such with France that was at the centre of the case. The Court found that this was an Article 35 MEQR because it treated cheese which had been transported across a border for grating differently from cheese which had been transported within the Grana

---

[99] Case C-322/01 *Deutscher Apothekerverband v DocMorris* [2003] ECR I-14887.
[100] Case C-531/07 *Fachverband der Buch- und Medienwirtschaft*, Judgment of 30 April 2009.
[101] Case 15/79 *Groenveld BV v Produktschap voor Vee en Vlees* [1979] ECR 3409.
[102] Case C-469/00 *Ravil v Bellon Import* [2003] ECR I-5053; see also Case C-388/95 *Belgium v Spain* [2000] ECR I-3123.

Padano region of Italy for grating, grating often being done not by the cheese producer but by the large retail firms who package and sell the grated cheese to consumers.

By contrast, *Gybrechts* concerned a rule which applied without distinction between domestic sale and exports yet which the Court nevertheless found to be within Article 35.[103] It had long been assumed that equally applicable rules were not within Article 35, as a result of comments in *Groenveld* and the result in that case. It is now clear that this assumption was mistaken. Even an equally applicable rule may, as a matter of fact, disadvantage exports relative to domestic sales, contrary to Article 35.[104]

The rule in *Gysbrechts* prohibited those selling goods at a distance, for example by Internet, from requiring buyers to pay in advance or even to provide details of their payment card. Buyers were only required to pay once they had received the goods. This, of course, created a significant risk of non-payment. However, it is far simpler and cheaper for a firm to pursue a domestic customer for payment than one abroad. Thus, this rule had a more discouraging effect on sales abroad than on domestic sales.

Case C–205/07 *Gysbrechts*, Judgment of 16 December 2008

40. In that regard, the Court has classified as measures having equivalent effect to quantitative restrictions on exports national measures which have as their specific object or effect the restriction of patterns of exports and thereby the establishment of a difference in treatment between the domestic trade of a Member State and its export trade in such a way as to provide a particular advantage for national production or for the domestic market of the State in question, at the expense of the production or of the trade of other Member States.

41. In the main proceedings, it is clear, as the Belgian Government has moreover noted in its written observations, that the prohibition on requiring an advance payment deprives the traders concerned of an efficient tool with which to guard against the risk of non-payment. That is even more the case when the national provision at issue is interpreted as prohibiting suppliers from requesting that consumers provide their payment card number even if they undertake not to use it to collect payment before expiry of the period for withdrawal.

42. As is clear from the order for reference, the consequences of such a prohibition are generally more significant in cross-border sales made directly to consumers, in particular, in sales made by means of the Internet, by reason, inter alia, of the obstacles to bringing any legal proceedings in another Member State against consumers who default, especially when the sales involve relatively small sums.

43. Consequently, even if a prohibition such as that at issue in the main proceedings is applicable to all traders active in the national territory, its actual effect is nonetheless greater on goods leaving the market of the exporting Member State than on the marketing of goods in the domestic market of that Member State.

44. It must therefore be held that a national measure, such as that at issue in the main proceedings, prohibiting a supplier in a distance sale from requiring an advance or any payment before expiry of the period for withdrawal constitutes a measure having equivalent effect to a quantitative restriction on exports. The same is true of a measure prohibiting a supplier from requiring that consumers provide their payment card number, even if the supplier undertakes not to use it to collect payment before expiry of the period for withdrawal.

---

[103] Case C-205/07 *Gysbrechts* [2008] ECR I-9947.
[104] A. Dawes, 'A Freedom Reborn? The New Yet Unclear Scope of Article 29' (2009) 34 *ELRev.* 639.

Article 35 therefore applies to all national measures which tend to make export sales more difficult or burdensome than domestic sales, whether or not this is by direct discrimination or simply as a matter of fact.[105] However, as with Article 34, equally applicable measures hindering exports may in principle be permitted if they are necessary to meet some mandatory requirement and are proportionate. In *Gysbrechts*, the Court found the prohibition on advance payment to be justified by consumer protection, while the prohibition on even asking for a payment card number was held to be disproportionate.

Finally, in *Jersey Potatoes*, the Court ruled that measures hindering the movement of potatoes from Jersey to the United Kingdom were contrary to Article 35.[106] The oddity of the case is that Jersey is not an independent Member State, and free movement of goods law only applies to it via a Protocol as a result of its special ties with the United Kingdom. For the purposes of EU law, UK–Jersey trade is not cross-border.[107] However, the Court's reasoning was that the potatoes sent to the United Kingdom might in some cases be exported on to other Member States. Extrapolating the reasoning it would seem that internal barriers to movement may fall within Article 35 where they may hinder export by, for example, making access to ports or roads more difficult.[108]

FURTHER READING

C. Barnard, 'Fitting the Remaining Pieces into the Goods and Persons Jigsaw' (2001) 26 *European Law Review* 35

S. Enchelmaier, 'The Awkward Selling of a Good Idea, or a Traditionalist Interpretation of Keck' (2003) 22 *Yearbook of European Law* 259

H.-C. von Heydebrand u.d. Lasa, 'Free Movement of Foodstuffs, Consumer Protection and Food Standards in the European Community: Has the Court got it Wrong?' (1991) 16 *European Law Review* 391

P. Oliver and S. Enchelmaier, 'Free Movement of Goods: Recent Developments in the Case Law' (2007) 44 *Common Market Law Review* 649

N. Reich, 'The "November Revolution" of the European Court of Justice: Keck, Meng and Audi Revisited' (1994) 31 *Common Market Law Review* 459

A. Tryfonidou, 'Was Keck a Half-baked Solution After All?' (2007) 34 *Legal Issues of Economic Integration* 167

S. Weatherill, 'After Keck: Some Thoughts on How to Clarify the Clarification' (1996) 33 *Common Market Law Review* 885

'Recent Case Law Concerning the Free Movement of Goods: Mapping the Frontiers of Market Deregulation' (1999) 36 *Common Market Law Review* 51

J. Weiler, 'The Constitution of the Common Market Place: The Free Movement of Goods' in P. Craig and G. de Búrca (eds.), *The Evolution of EU Law* (Oxford, Oxford University Press, 1999) 349

D. Wilsher, 'Does *Keck* Discrimination Make Any Sense? An Assessment of the Non-discrimination Principle within the European Single Market' (2008) 33 *European Law Review* 3

[105] See Case C-12/02 *Grilli* [2003] ECR I-11585.
[106] Case C-293/02 *Jersey Potatoes* [2005] ECR I-9543.
[107] See P. Oliver and S. Enchelmaier, 'Free Movement of Goods: Recent Developments in the Case Law' (2007) 44 *CMLRev.* 649.
[108] See similarly Joined Cases C-1/90 and C-176/90 *Aragonesa* [1991] ECR I-4151; Case C-72/03 *Carbonati Apuani* [2004] ECR I-8027. See I. Kvesko, 'Is There Anything Left Outside the Reach of the European Court of Justice?' (2006) 33 *LIEI* 405.

19

The Free Movement of Services

CONTENTS

1 INTRODUCTION

Article 56 TFEU prohibits restrictions on the provision of services between Member States. Trade in services comprises the largest part of a modern economy, yet interstate trade is hindered by the high level of regulation applying to many service activities. EU law has taken a threefold approach to breaking down these barriers: the direct application of Article 56 by courts is now complemented by Directive 2006/123/EC on services in the internal market ('Services Directive'), and by sector specific regulation for many complex services of particular social or economic importance. This chapter addresses Article 56 and the Services Directive. It is organised as follows.

Section 2 provides an overview of why services markets are hard to integrate. Because services involve people interacting, they raise issues of power and knowledge inequalities, requiring protective legislation. Also, services are often of great social importance and some services arouse strong moral feelings.

Section 3 is concerned with defining the services to which Article 56 applies. A core aspect is that the services must be provided for remuneration. Genuinely non-economic services, such as free public education, are excluded. Yet, where the service consumer, or an insurer acting on her behalf, does pay for services, Article 56 applies, however socially sensitive the services may be. Health care has been subjected to Article 56 on this basis.

Section 4 considers prohibited restrictions on the free movement of services. The range of these is broad. The Court of Justice applies Article 56 to any measure which makes access to the service market of a state more difficult. Since *Gebhard* and *Alpine Investments*, it does not appear to be necessary to show that the measure promotes either domestic service providers or domestic transactions. Yet in *Mobistar*, the Court said that measures which merely impose costs, but have no unequal impact, are outside Article 56. A certain ambiguity about the limits of Article 56 remains.

Section 4(ii) is devoted to the application of Article 56 to non-state actors. The powers of the bodies governing sport, and of trade unions, have both been subjected to the principle that they must not be exercised in a way that unjustifiably hinders the movement of services. This has been deeply controversial. In particular, the right of trade unions to both protect their members against low-cost competition from other Member States and preserve levels of worker protection in their home state are seen as threatened. Yet, the Court notes that if non-state bodies do not have to respect Article 56, this greatly reduces its effectiveness, and allows an opening for nationality discrimination and protectionism.

Section 5 is about justifying restrictions on the movement of services. This is possible where the restrictions are equally applicable, and the restrictive measure is necessary for a good public interest reason. However, service providers cannot be subjected to all host state legislation. First, account must be taken of whether the interest concerned is already protected by measures in the home state. Secondly, in deciding whether a regulatory burden is proportionate it is important to remember that a service provider may only have weak bonds with the host state market, perhaps just a few clients. Over-regulation of them would then be disproportionate, the Court has found.

Section 6 considers the way Article 56 impacts on society beyond business. In particular, the free movement of services requires that many sensitive and important activities be looked at through an economic lens. Abortion, gambling and prostitution are legally provided for remuneration in some states, enabling reliance on Article 56 to challenge restrictive measures. These challenges will not necessarily be successful, but the mere fact that courts must place non-economic concerns in the context of a right to trade in services has been offensive to some, and may rebalance public reasoning so that the non-economic interests are marginalised.

Section 6(iii) focuses in more detail on Article 56 and welfare states. The case law on health care has been the most significant here, and provides patients with a right to go abroad to receive medical treatment at the expense of their home state. States claim this may add to the cost of health care and threaten budgets, and in response the Court permits limited restrictions where hospital treatment is concerned. Nevertheless, both the general principle, and the procedural and transparency requirements which the Court has attached to it, are transformative, and are causing health care systems to rethink their financing and organisation. Some of the Court's reasoning has now been adopted in a proposal for a Directive on patients' rights to cross-border health care.

Section 7 is about the Services Directive. This is the most significant recent development in the law on services. The Directive applies a strict country of origin principle to services, so that providers need hardly concern themselves with the rules of their host state. The only exceptions are the narrowly interpreted public policy, public security, public health and the environment. Yet, the Directive, the product of a dramatically controversial legislative process, is full of exclusions and limitations, so that there will be just as many situations to which it does not apply as to which it does, and the direct application of Article 56 will remain important.

2 REGULATING THE SERVICES MARKET

Creating a single market for services is difficult.[1] Service providers are people, or companies, and when they are active in host states they interact with a wide range of regulations. These may be to do with the actual service, but may also be to do with the nature of the provider: their qualifications, or legal form, or financial position. A comparison with goods may be helpful: imagine if sale of goods were to be made conditional not just on aspects of the product, but on aspects of the company producing it, their factory and work methods. The creation of free movement would become even more of a challenge.

It is, of course, natural for a state to apply their laws to all on their territory. The EU law rejection of this is counter-intuitive from a national perspective. Yet, it is equally natural for a service provider to find it deeply frustrating when she is forced to demonstrate compliance with all kinds of professional and technical regulation which essentially duplicates similar demands in her state of establishment. Nor is such duplication the only problem. Other local rules may impose costs and make it harder for her to do business in the way she is used to – according to her business model, as the Court of Justice has recently put it.[2] Examples might be a prohibition on a particular marketing method, such as cold-calling, or a tax on the equipment necessary for the service, advertising rules, or rules about the legal form of the service provider. These rules might not discriminate, nor have any protectionist intent, but they might nevertheless have the effect that some service providers decide it is just not worth entering that market, or that market entry should be on a smaller scale. Trade is inhibited.

This makes Article 56 TFEU constitutionally dangerous. If all law affecting a service provider imposes costs on her somehow, then all law deters her activities to some extent, and Article 56 might just become a tool for a general review of national legislative proportionality. One of the central issues of the free movement of services is, as with the other freedoms, how to define its limits in a way reflecting the right balance between purposive market-creation, and practical, attribution-respecting, limits to EU law. The Court has not yet created a *Keck* for services, a case which is accepted to draw such lines, perhaps partly because the types of restrictions which impact on services are less easy to categorise than is the case for goods.[3]

---

[1] European Commission, *The State of the Internal Market in Services*, COM(2002)441 final.

[2] Case C-518/06 *Commission v Italy*, Judgment of 28 April 2009.

[3] Although see the parallels drawn in W.-H. Roth, 'The European Court of Justice's Case Law on Freedom to Provide Services: Is *Keck* Relevant' in M. Andenas and W.-H. Roth (eds.), *Services and Free Movement in EU Law* (Oxford, Oxford University Press, 2002) 1; V. Hatzopoulos, 'Annotation of *Alpine Investments*' (1995) 29 *CMLRev.* 1427; J. L. Da Cruz Vilaca, 'On the Application of *Keck* in the Field of Free Provision of Services' in M. Andenas and W.-H. Roth (eds.), *Services and Free Movement in EU Law* (Oxford, Oxford University Press, 2002) 25.

Rather, the Court uses a variety of formulas and phrases to sum up the scope of Article 56, not all of which are entirely consistent with each other. In particular, it is unclear whether regulation which has an entirely equal impact on domestic and cross-border services, and which merely imposes costs rather than actually preventing service provision, is caught by the Treaty.

The challenges for the Court and legislator are increased by the fact that services can be both economically and socially extremely sensitive. Partly this is a matter of scale. At one extreme, huge service industries like banking, telecoms and transport are of such importance to the wider economy that they demand intensive regulation and control. This makes transnational integration even harder, but it is difficult for a generalist court to tamper with complex national supervisory systems. In practice, free movement in this kind of industry is usually pursued via sector-specific legislation. Yet, services can equally be very local, very small-scale, and sometimes very traditional, which raises its own problems, often political. In France, the debate around the Services Directive focused on the image of a French plumber threatened by Polish competition. The ability to remain established in Poland, with associated low costs, while providing services in France, would enable the Polish plumbers to undercut the French, plunder the local market, and wipe out a class of small-scale artisanal service providers, it was claimed by opponents. This is globalisation brought down to a human scale, and all the more politically potent as a result.

Other services are hard to integrate, or adjudicate, because they are part of the structure of the state, or the fabric of national society. Health care, education and sport are examples. Breaking down national barriers to these affects the sense of national community and identity, and so free movement has to be balanced against factors which are hard to voice, hard to weigh, impossible to quantify, and sometimes not easy to distinguish from unacceptable nationalism.[4]

Finally, services are about people doing things to, or for, each other. Some of the things people do enrage others: abortion, gambling, prostitution.[5] Adjudicating the free movement of these is always controversial. Other things that people do involve risk for others: lay clients buying complex professional services are vulnerable to exploitation by their provider, while providers of sex services may be vulnerable to their clients; services tend to involve unequal relationships. In all these cases, the Court is faced with human, moral and social concerns and interests which complicate its decision-making but cannot be ignored.

The Court is not the primary regulator of such issues: it supervises Member State legislation, and acknowledges the national margin of appreciation where choices of social or moral policy are concerned.[6] It shows no enthusiasm to be a social or moral arbiter as such. However, since free movement and non-discrimination are also values within the European legal system, it is forced to balance national priorities against EU priorities. Where matters such as the opening of the welfare state or trade in morally controversial services are concerned, there is no safe neutral position, only value-laden choices to be made.

---

[4] See C. Hilson, 'The Unpatriotism of the Economic Constitution? Rights to Free Movement and the Impact on National and European Identity' (2008) 14 *ELJ* 156.

[5] See Case C-268/99 *Jany* v *Staatssecretaris van Justitie* [2001] ECR I-8615.

[6] See N. Nic Shuibhne, 'Margins of Appreciation: National Values, Fundamental Rights and EC Free Movement Law' (2009) 34 *ELRev.* 230.

3 CROSS-BORDER SERVICES

The free movement of services is regulated by Article 56 TFEU, which provides in its first paragraph:

> Within the framework of the provisions set out below, restrictions on freedom to provide services within the Union shall be prohibited in respect of nationals of Member States who are established in a Member State other than that of the person for whom the services are intended.

Article 57 TFEU then provides that:

> Services shall be considered to be 'services' within the meaning of the Treaties where they are normally provided for remuneration...

Subsequent Articles address aspects of certain specific services (transport, banking and insurance services) and aspects of the process of harmonisation and liberalisation.

A number of derogations are also provided. The free movement of services may be restricted on grounds of public policy, public security or public health, and it does not apply at all to the exercise of official authority. These derogations are found in the Treaty Chapter on freedom of establishment, and are applied to the services Chapter by Article 61 TFEU. They are discussed further in Chapter 21.

The free movement of services raises several issues of definition. What is a service? What is 'remuneration'? And, when does a service have a sufficient cross-border element to fall within Article 56? These questions are addressed below.

(i) What is a service?

The distinction between goods and services is relatively simple. Goods are things that one can feel. Hence, electricity is treated by the Court as goods. The sale of e-books, however, would fall within the provision of services, since there is no tactile object being traded. If the book were on a CD, by contrast, then this CD would be a good.[7]

Sometimes the provision of a service is attached to the provision of a physical thing. Most notably, in *Schindler*, the Court found that buying a lottery ticket fell within the free movement of services, not goods, because the physical ticket was purely ancillary to the real substance of the transaction, which was the chance of winning a prize.[8] The customer paid in order to participate in the lottery – a service – not in order to own a piece of paper.

The distinction between services and establishment is less precise. If a person or company has a number of customers in another Member State to which they provide services, this will fall within Article 56. However, if their position in that Member State reaches a sufficient level of permanence and solidity that one might speak of them being 'established' there, then any restrictions on their activities will be seen as restrictions on freedom of establishment, not of services.[9]

---

[7] Case 155/73 *Giuseppe Sacchi* [1974] ECR 409; L. Woods, *Free Movement of Goods and Services within the European Community* (Aldershot, Ashgate, 2004) 19.

[8] Case C-275/92 *HM Customs and Excise v Schindler* [1994] ECR I-1039. See also Case C-55/93 *Van Schaik* [1994] ECR I-4837; Case C-71/02 *Karner v Troostwijk* [2004] ECR I-3025; Case C-36/02 *Omega Spielhallen- und Automatenaufstellungs v Oberbürgermeisterin der Bundesstadt Bonn* [2004] ECR I-9609; Case C-97/98 *Jägerskiöld v Gustafsson* [1999] ECR I-7319; Case C-451/99 *Cura Anlagen v Auto Source Leasing* [2002] ECR I-3193.

[9] Case 2/74 *Reyners v Belgium* [1974] ECR 631; Case C-55/94 *Gebhard v Consiglio dell'ordine degli avvocati eprocuratori di Milano* [1995] ECR I-4165.

Deciding when a service provider is embedded enough that they become established entails looking at several factors.

Case C-215/01 *Schnitzer* [2003] ECR I-14847

27. The third paragraph of Article [57 TFEU] states that the person providing a service may, in order to do so, temporarily pursue his activity in the Member State where the service is provided, under the same conditions as are imposed by that State on its own nationals. Insofar as pursuit of the activity in that Member State remains temporary, such a person thus continues to come under the provisions of the chapter relating to services.

28. The Court has held that the temporary nature of the activity of the person providing the service in the host Member State has to be determined in the light not only of the duration of the provision of the service but also of its regularity, periodical nature or continuity. The fact that the activity is temporary does not mean that the provider of services within the meaning of the Treaty may not equip himself with some form of infrastructure in the host Member State (including an office, chambers or consulting rooms) insofar as such infrastructure is necessary for the purposes of performing the services in question.

(ii) The cross-border element

Article 56 says that it applies whenever the service provider and service recipient are established in different Member States.[10] This covers several situations.[11] The most obvious is where the service provider (who must be an EU company or an EU citizen established in a Member State)[12] travels to another state, as in *van Binsbergen*, where a Dutch lawyer established in Belgium travelled to the Netherlands to see and represent clients.[13] However, Article 56 also applies where it is the recipient who travels. This was established in *Luisi and Carbone*, where two Italians wanted to go to Germany to receive medical services. Italian laws which obstructed this fell within Article 56.[14] It may even be the case that recipient and provider both travel, and meet in a third Member State.[15]

Equally important today is the situation where the service itself moves. Services provided over the Internet, telesales and the cross-border provision of telecoms and television are all commercially important examples of cross-border service provision in which neither provider nor recipient has to physically move. Thus, measures which prevent companies from cold-calling customers abroad, or which impose restrictions on the supply or receipt of television

---

[10] Wholly internal situations are thus excluded: see Case C-108/98 *RI-SAN v Commune de Ischia* [1999] ECR I-5219; Case 52/79 *Procureur du Roi v Debauve* [1980] ECR 833. Cf. Case 15/78 *SG Alsacienne v Koestler* [1978] ECR 1971.

[11] See G. Sampson and R. Snape, 'Identifying the Issues in Trade in Services' (1985) 8 *World Economy* 171, 172–3; P. Eeckhout, *The European Internal Market and International Trade: A Legal Analysis* (Oxford, Clarendon Press, 1994) 10; J. Snell, *Goods and Services in EC Law: A Study of the Relationship Between the Freedoms* (Oxford, Oxford University Press, 2002) 16–17. The situation is very similar in Article I(2) of the central treaty regulating international trade in services, the General Agreement on Trade in Services (GATS).

[12] Case C-290/04 *FKP Scorpio* [2006] ECR I-9461; Case C-452/04 *Fidium Finanz v Bundesanstalt für Finanzdienstleistnugsaufsicht* [2006] ECR I-9521. As EU citizens, service providers and recipients enjoy the citizenship rights discussed in Chapter 11.

[13] Case 33/74 *Van Binsbergen v Bestuur van de Bedrijsvereniging voor de Metaalnijverheid* [1974] ECR 1299.

[14] Joined Cases 286/82 and 26/83 *Luisi and Carbone v Ministero del Tesoro* [1984] ECR 377. Also Case 186/87 *Cowan v Trésor Public* [1989] ECR 195.

[15] As is often the case with tour guides. See e.g. Case 180/89 *Commission v Italy* [1991] ECR 709; Case C-398/95 *Syndesmos ton en Elladi Touristikon kai Taxidiotikon Grafeion v Ypourgos Ergasias* [1997] ECR I-3091.

programmes from abroad, and many other examples of this type, have been found to fall within Article 56.[16]

The Court has also extended Article 56 beyond its literal wording. In *Vestergard*, a Danish company organised training courses for Danish workers on Greek islands. On the one hand, provider and recipients all travelled to another Member State, so there was clearly an international element to the service provision. However, both provider and recipient were established in Denmark, so the transaction was domestic.[17] Nevertheless, the Court applied Article 56.

Case C–55/98 *Skatteministeriet* v *Vestergard* [1999] ECR I–7641

18. Thirdly, it is important to point out that in order for services such as those in question in the main proceedings, namely the organisation of professional training courses, to fall within the scope of Article [56 TFEU], it is sufficient for them to be provided to nationals of a Member State on the territory of another Member State, irrespective of the place of establishment of the provider or recipient of the services.

19. Article [56 TFEU] applies not only where a person providing a service and the recipient are established in different Member States, but also whenever a provider of services offers those services in a Member State other than the one in which he is established, wherever the recipients of those services may be established.

This was taken a step further in *ITC*, where a German employment agency found a job in the Netherlands for its German client, who at that time lived in Germany. The Court found that Article 56 applied even though client, provider and payment all took place in Germany. The judgment does not indicate very clearly what reasoning was behind this, but the Advocate General, whose Opinion was followed, provides a useful analysis.

Case C–208/05 *ITC Innovative Technology Center GmbH* v *Bundesagentur für Arbeit* [2007] ECR I–181, Opinion of Advocate General Léger

118. Next, unlike the German Government, I am of the view that the situation at issue in the main proceedings does indeed involve a sufficient cross-border extraneous element.

119. I would point out in that regard that the Court of Justice has held that Article [56 TFEU] applies even where the provider and the recipient of the services are established in the same Member State, on condition that the services are being provided in another Member State.

120. In the case in the main proceedings, the cross-border dimension is made clear by the fact that the job searching, which forms an integral part of the activity of recruitment, was done by the private-sector

---

[16] See e.g. Case 352/85 *Bond van Adverteerders* v *Netherlands* [1988] ECR 2085; Case C–422/01 *Försäkringsaktiebolaget Skandia* v *Riksskatteverket* [2003] ECR I–6817; Case C–243/01 *Gambelli* [2003] ECR I–13031; Case C–70/99 *Commission* v *Portugal* ('Flight taxes') [2001] ECR I–4845. See also Case C–18/93 *Corsica Ferries France* [1994] ECR I–1783; Case C–381/93 *Commission* v *France* [1994] ECR I–5145; Case C–384/93 *Alpine Investments* v *Minister van Financiën* [1995] ECR I–1141.

[17] See also Case C–381/93 *Commission* v *France* [1994] ECR I–5145.

agency in another Member State. It is, moreover, to be expected that, as part of the performance of a recruitment contract the service provider will have contacts with potential employers based in other Member States, in order to increase the chances of a successful recruitment.

121. Thus, the fact that a recruitment contract was concluded between a person seeking employment and a private-sector recruitment agency each of which are located in the same Member State does not in my view preclude the applicability of Article [56 TFEU] since the job searching, which is the main purpose of the recruitment activity, was undertaken in another Member State.

The Advocate General takes the view that the actual service was the finding of a job, and this was done in the Netherlands – that was where the company went to look. It therefore appears, following *Vestergard* and *ITC*, that even a domestic service contract falls within Article 56 if an important part of the work for which the service provider is paid takes place abroad.

It is not necessary that the cross-border element be already realised. As is the case in goods, if a measure could restrict cross-border service provision, then the fact that no actual complainant can be found does not exclude a reference or an answer. Potential restrictions are also caught by Article 56.[18]

(iii) Remuneration

Services provided out of charity, or without any desire for payment, are not covered by Article 56. It is concerned with economic activity, and Article 57 provides that services must be 'normally provided for remuneration'. The word 'normally', although it has not been discussed by the Court, is probably intended to ensure that the occasional provision of a service for free in a generally commercial context (as part of a sales promotion, for example) does not result in essentially economic activities falling outside the Treaty.

Remuneration need not be money, as long as it can be valued in money.[19] Food and lodging has been found by the Court to be remuneration in the context of employment, and there is no reason why it should take a different stance on services.[20] Nor does remuneration need to be paid by the recipient of the service.[21] If an insurance company pays for medical care abroad this is remuneration just as much as if the patient had paid herself, and is sufficient to bring that care within Article 56.

However, not every payment to the service provider is remuneration. In *Humbel*, the Court had to consider whether university education was a Treaty service.[22] Universities receive most of their funding from the state, but students paid a small contribution.

---

[18] Case C-6/01 *Anomar v Estado Português* [2003] ECR I-8621; Case C-398/95 *Syndesmos ton en Elladi Touristikon kai Taxidiotikon Grafeion v Ypourgos Ergasias* [1997] ECR I-3091. In like vein, Case C-384/93 *Alpine Investments v Minister van Financiën* [1995] ECR I-1141. See annotation by Hatzopoulos, above n. 3.

[19] Case 154/80 *Staatsecretaris van Financieën v Coöperative Aardappelenbewaarplaats* [1981] ECR 445; Case 324/82 *Commission v Belgium* [1984] ECR 1861; Case C-288/94 *Argos Distributors Ltd v CCE* [1996] ECR I-5311; Case C-258/95 *Söhne v Finanzamt Neustadt* [1997] ECR I-5577.

[20] Case 196/87 *Steymann v Staatssecretaris van Justitie* [1988] ECR 6159.

[21] Joined Cases C-51/96 and C-191/97 *Deliège v Asbl Ligue Francophone de Judo* [2000] ECR I-2549.

[22] Case 263/86 *Humbel v Belgium* [1988] ECR 5365.

Case 263/86 *Humbel* v *Belgium* [1988] ECR 5365

17. The essential characteristic of remuneration thus lies in the fact that it constitutes consideration for the service in question, and is normally agreed upon between the provider and the recipient of the service.

18. That characteristic is, however, absent in the case of courses provided under the national education system... First of all, the State, in establishing and maintaining such a system, is not seeking to engage in gainful activity but is fulfilling its duties towards its own population in the social, cultural and educational fields... Secondly, the system in question is, as a general rule, funded from the public purse and not by pupils or their parents...

19. The nature of the activity is not affected by the fact that pupils or their parents must sometimes pay teaching or enrolment fees in order to make a certain contribution to the operating expenses of the system.

The Court makes an implicit contrast between payments which are essentially consideration for the services – where there is a transaction between payer and provider – and payments which are intended to fund or support the provider, for non-commercial motives.[23] One way of looking at this is to ask whether the service provider would consider the payer (here the state) to be her 'client', or to be acting on behalf of her client. In the case of free public education this would usually be a somewhat artificial perspective.

It is arguable that there must be some legal obligation to pay. In *Tolsma*, the Court had to consider whether busking on the highway fell within the ambit of article 2 of the Sixth VAT Directive.[24] This is similarly phrased to Article 57 TFEU, as it provides that services provided by a taxable person must, in principle, be taxed if they are made for payment or consideration.[25] The Court of Justice held that money given by passers-by could not be seen as value provided for a service. Donations were voluntary and the passers-by did not request the music. Thus, it was difficult to find any legal relationship that provided a context for remuneration.

It should also be noted that in *Humbel*, the Court suggested that very small payments will not amount to remuneration. The function of the essentially symbolic fees which many states require students to pay is not really to pay for the education they receive, but to encourage the students to take their education seriously.

In later cases, notably *Wirth*, the Court has suggested that as long as the state 'essentially' funds public education, this will fall outside Article 56.[26] This suggests that if private payments, from students or their parents, or from scholarship funds, for example, amount to more than half of the total funds received for the service provided, then these payments will be remuneration and Article 56 will apply.

An odd tension in the case law is that while the motivation of the payer appears to be important in characterising services, the motivation of the provider is not. The Court has ruled that there is no need for service providers to seek to make a profit, and the mere fact

---

[23] See also EFTA Case E-5/07 *Private Barnehagers Landsforbund* v *EFTA Surveillance Authority*, Judgment of 21 February 2008 (available at www.eftacourt.lu).

[24] See also Case C-16/93 *Tolsma* v *Inspecteur der Omzelbelastingen Leeuwarden* [1994] ECR I-743 on busking.

[25] Directive 77/388/EEC [1977] OJ L145/1.

[26] Case C-109/92 *Wirth* v *Landeshauptstadt Hannover* [1993] ECR I-6447; Case C-318/05 *Commission* v *Germany* [2007] ECR I-6957.

that they are providing very important public services, such as health or education, does not as such take them outside of Article 56.[27] Nor does it matter what legal or institutional form they have: they need not be a company or a business, but might be, for example, a school or a foundation.[28] They do not even have to be 'doing it for the money'. In *Jundt*, a university teacher received a fee for a guest lecture.[29] It was argued that his post was 'quasi-honorary'. The Court found this to be irrelevant, since he did in fact receive a payment in return for his teaching. The only question appears to be whether the service provider receives consideration for their activities.

One of the consequences of this case law is that the mechanism of funding public services becomes very important. In some Member States, health care is provided free on the basis of need, and is probably not therefore a Treaty service. In other Member States, the state guarantees universal health care by requiring residents to purchase medical insurance from private companies, in the context of a legislative framework in which insurance for the poor or sick is cross-subsidised by the richer and healthier. Because the actual medical care in such a system is paid for by insurers, Article 56 will apply. Similarly, if universities have high fees, but students can take out subsidised loans to pay them, then university education will probably be remunerated. If, on the other hand, the state funds universities directly, there will be no remuneration. In both cases the state ultimately pays, but the choice of mechanism determines the extent to which the Treaty applies.

This interaction of Article 56 and aspects of the welfare state is of great current importance, and has been the source of much case law. It is discussed further in section 6 below.

4 RESTRICTIONS ON THE MOVEMENT OF SERVICES

(i) The notion of a restriction on the provision of services

As with the other freedoms, the most complex and slippery aspect of the case law on services is the definition of a prohibited restriction. It has never been in doubt that direct and indirect nationality discrimination is prohibited within the sphere of Article 56,[30] but the extent to which the prohibition does and should extend beyond this is less clear. In *Arblade*, the Court said:

> 33. It is settled case law that Article [56] of the Treaty requires not only the elimination of all discrimination on grounds of nationality against providers of services who are established in another Member State, but also the abolition of any restriction, even if it applies without distinction to national providers of services and to those of other Member States, which is liable to prohibit, impede, or render less advantageous the activities of a provider of services established in another Member State where he lawfully provides similar services.

---

[27] Case C-157/99 *Geraets-Smits v Stichting Ziekenfonds; Peerbooms v Stichting CZ Groep Zorgverzekeringen* [2001] ECR I-5473; Case C-158/96 *Kohll v Union des Caisses de Maladie* [1998] ECR I-1931. See p. 811.

[28] Case C-109/92 *Wirth v Landeshauptstadt Hannover* [1993] ECR I-6447; Case C-318/05 *Commission v Germany* [2007] ECR I-6957; G. Davies, 'Welfare as a Service' (2002) 29 *LIEI* 27, 29–30.

[29] Case C-281/06 *Jundt and Jundt v Finanzamt Offenburg* [2007] ECR I-12231.

[30] Article 57 TFEU, last paragraph; see e.g. Case 33/74 *Van Binsbergen v Bestuur van de Bedrijsvereniging voor de Metaalnijverheid* [1974] ECR 1310; Case 39/75 *Coenen v Sociaal-Economische Raad* [1975] ECR 1547; Case C-288/89 *Gouda v Commissariat voor de Media* [1991] ECR I-4007; Case C-17/92 *FDC v Estado Español and UPCT* [1993] ECR I-2239; Case C-294/97 *Eurowings v Finanzamt Dortmund-Unna* [1999] ECR I-7447. For definitions of discrimination in EU law, see pp. 452–3.

Although this makes clear that equally applicable measures may be caught by Article 56, it does not tell us how we are to understand 'prohibit, impede or render less advantageous'.[31] Is it necessary to show that an equally applicable measure may have some unequal impact – that it has a greater effect on the foreign or the cross-border than on the domestic? Or is Article 56 engaged simply whenever a measure may affect cross-border services, without any kind of comparison being involved?

In *Gebhard*, the Court found that all national measures 'liable to hinder or make less attractive the exercise of fundamental freedoms' are to be seen as restrictions on movement.[32] The case was about establishment, but the formulation was general, and is very often cited for services too. It is even more open than *Arblade*, and suggests a broad scope to Article 56, in which comparison between the domestic or the foreign is irrelevant, the only question being whether some hindrance to service provision can be argued.

This view is also reflected in *Alpine Investments*.[33] A Dutch law prohibited Dutch companies from cold-calling customers, even those in other Member States where cold-calling was not prohibited. The aim was to prevent the Dutch financial services industry from getting a bad reputation, but frustrated Dutch providers who wanted to cold-call German clients claimed that the measure was a restriction on services. The Court agreed, for the very straightforward reason that:

> 28. ... such a prohibition deprives the operators concerned of a rapid and direct technique for marketing and for contacting potential clients in other Member States. It can therefore constitute a restriction on the freedom to provide cross-border services.

This suggests, as in *Gebhard*, a naive reading of Article 56 in which not discrimination, but factual barriers to trade are central: is there a service provider who finds doing business abroad is made more difficult by some national measure? Then, the measure is a restriction on services. This broad reading may be slightly tempered by the facts: it is arguable that a restriction on cold-calling has a greater effect on contact with distant clients than local ones, so that *Alpine* is really about a measure of unequal impact. However, the Court did not address this, and *Alpine* is usually cited as support for the view that Article 56 applies even to equal impact measures.

On the other hand, in *Mobistar*, the Court took a more precise and more limited approach to Article 56. *Mobistar* was about a tax on telecoms masts and pylons, necessary for the transmission of phone calls. It was argued that this hindered the provision of cross-border telecoms services, by imposing an additional cost on the necessary infrastructure. But the masts were just as necessary for domestic phone calls as for cross-border ones.

C-544/03 *Mobistar* v *Commune de Fléron* [2005] ECR I-7723

29. According to the Court's case-law, Article [56 TFEU] requires not only the elimination of all discrimination on grounds of nationality, against providers of services who are established in another Member State, but also the abolition of any restriction, even if it applies without distinction to national

---

[31] Joined Cases C-369/96 and C-376/96 *Arblade* [1999] ECR I-8453; Case C-165/98 *Mazzoleni and ISA* [2001] ECR I-2189; Case C-49/98 *Finalarte* [2001] ECR I-7831.

[32] Case C-55/94 *Gebhard v Consiglio dell'ordine degli avvocati eprocuratori di Milano* [1995] ECR I-4165.

[33] Case C-384/93 *Alpine Investments* v *Minister van Financiën* [1995] ECR I-1141.

providers of services and to those of other Member States, which is liable to prohibit or further impede the activities of a provider of services established in another Member State where he lawfully provides similar services.

30. Furthermore, the Court has already held that Article [56 TFEU] precludes the application of any national rules which have the effect of making the provision of services between Member States more difficult than the provision of services purely within one Member State.

31. By contrast, measures, the only effect of which is to create additional costs in respect of the service in question and which affect in the same way the provision of services between Member States and that within one Member State, do not fall within the scope of Article [56 TFEU].

The exclusion in paragraph 31 of the judgment contrasts with the broad concept of a restriction in *Gebhard* and *Alpine Investments*. However, there are other cases which take a similar approach to *Mobistar*, notably *Viacom Outdoor*.[34] This case concerned a tax on bill-posting in Genoa. The extra cost which this added to poster advertising in Genoa was argued to be a restriction on advertising services: it made it harder for agencies which arranged local advertising to attract foreign clients.

Case C-134/03 *Viacom Outdoor* v *Giotto Immobilier and Others* [2005] ECR I-1167

37. With regard to the question of whether the levying by municipal authorities of a tax such as the advertising tax constitutes an impediment incompatible with Article [56 TFEU], it must first of all be noted that such a tax is applicable without distinction to any provision of services entailing outdoor advertising and public bill-posting in the territory of the municipality concerned. The rules on the levying of this tax do not, therefore, draw any distinction based on the place of establishment of the provider or recipient of the bill-posting services or on the place of origin of the goods or services that form the subject-matter of the advertising messages disseminated.

38. Next, such a tax is applied only to outdoor advertising activities involving the use of public space administered by the municipal authorities and its amount is fixed at a level which may be considered modest in relation to the value of the services provided which are subject to it. In those circumstances, the levying of such a tax is not on any view liable to prohibit, impede or otherwise make less attractive the provision of advertising services to be carried out in the territory of the municipalities concerned, including the case in which the provision of services is of a cross-border nature on account of the place of establishment of either the provider or the recipient of the services.

As in *Mobistar*, the Court ruled that the mere imposition of an equally applicable cost is not a restriction on services,[35] but in *Viacom* it made clear that this is because such costs do not, in its view, impede or make less attractive the provision of services. Using the language of *Gebhard*, in paragraph 38, makes *Viacom* an interpretation of that case, rather than a rejection of it, in a way reminiscent of *Keck* and *Dassonville*.

A distinction may be made between *Mobistar* and *Viacom*, on the one hand, and *Alpine Investments*, on the other. *Alpine* concerned prohibition of a sales technique, which restricted

---

[34] See also Case C-177/94 *Perfili* [1996] ECR I-161.
[35] Cf. Case C-165/98 *Mazzoleni and ISA* [2001] ECR I-2189.

access to a foreign market. Merely imposing a cost, the Court says in *Mobistar* and *Viacom*, does not. However, this distinction is vulnerable to criticism. In practice, costs may deter market entry in just the same way as regulation does: for companies it is all about cost. Equally, the business objection to restriction of a marketing technique may often be that it raises the costs of contacting customers. Distinguishing between mere cost burdens and access restrictions is somewhat artificial.[36]

Yet a line has to be drawn somewhere, and the distinction above is at least reasonably adjudicable. More importantly, *Mobistar* has some very solid policy behind it. If a mere cost burden that has an equal impact on domestic and foreign trade is a restriction on services, then almost every tax or regulation relevant to a service industry will fall within Article 56. This is undesirable and unrealistic, and an unconvincing reading of the intention of Article 56. It is very reminiscent of the situation in goods pre-*Keck*. Thus, it is suggested that *Mobistar* is likely to be followed in similar situations, and should, like *Keck*, be treated as a specific exception to the general rule. Mere cost burdens, like mere selling arrangements, if they have an equal impact on national and foreign, domestic and cross-border, are not restrictions on trade.

Most recently, the Court has taken a new rhetorical path. In *Commission* v *Italy*, it had to address a national rule which prohibited motor insurers from rejecting a client.[37] Such rules are quite common where socially important insurance is concerned, as they ensure universal access, even for individuals who may be bad risks, and who would be refused cover in a free market. However, insurance companies are not always happy, since they are obliged to accept clients who are likely to cost them money. In *Commission* v *Italy*, it was argued that foreign insurance companies would be deterred from offering insurance services in Italy by the acceptance obligation, and that it therefore amounted to a restriction on the free movement of services. The judgment does not substantively change the law, but offers an interestingly clear and practical analysis of Article 56.

Case C-518/06 *Commission* v *Italy*, Judgment of 28 April 2009

62. It is settled case-law that the term 'restriction' within the meaning of Articles [49 TFEU] and [56 TFEU] covers all measures which prohibit, impede or render less attractive the freedom of establishment or the freedom to provide services.

63. As regards the question of the circumstances in which a measure applicable without distinction, such as the obligation to contract at issue in the present case, may come within that concept, it should be borne in mind that rules of a Member State do not constitute a restriction within the meaning of the EC Treaty solely by virtue of the fact that other Member States apply less strict, or more commercially favourable, rules to providers of similar services established in their territory.

64. By contrast, the concept of restriction covers measures taken by a Member State which, although applicable without distinction, affect access to the market for undertakings from other Member States and thereby hinder intra-Community trade.

65. In the present case, it is common ground that the obligation to contract does not have any repercussions for the acceptance by the Italian authorities of the administrative authorisation, referred to in paragraph 13 of this judgment, which insurance undertakings having their head office in a

---

[36] Cf. V. Hatzopoulos, 'Annotation of *Alpine Investments*' (1995) 29 *CMLRev.* 1427.
[37] Case C-518/06 *Commission* v *Italy*, Judgment of 28 April 2009.

Member State other than the Italian Republic obtain in the Member State in which they have their head office. It therefore leaves intact the right of access to the Italian market as regards third-party liability motor insurance resulting from that authorisation.

66. Nevertheless, the imposition by a Member State of an obligation to contract such as that at issue constitutes a substantial interference in the freedom to contract which economic operators, in principle, enjoy.

67. In a sector like that of insurance, such a measure affects the relevant operators' access to the market, in particular where it subjects insurance undertakings not only to an obligation to cover any risks which are proposed to them, but also to requirements to moderate premium rates.

68. Inasmuch as it obliges insurance undertakings which enter the Italian market to accept every potential customer, that obligation to contract is likely to lead, in terms of organisation and investment, to significant additional costs for such undertakings.

69. If they wish to enter the Italian market under conditions which comply with Italian legislation, such undertakings will be required to re-think their business policy and strategy, inter alia, by considerably expanding the range of insurance services offered.

70. Inasmuch as it involves changes and costs on such a scale for those undertakings, the obligation to contract renders access to the Italian market less attractive and, if they obtain access to that market, reduces the ability of the undertakings concerned to compete effectively, from the outset, against undertakings traditionally established in Italy.

71. Therefore, the obligation to contract restricts the freedom of establishment and the freedom to provide services.

The Court here explicitly notes, in paragraph 65, that foreign insurance companies are not excluded from the Italian market. They can receive authorisation to offer insurance services just as companies established in Italy can. The only effect on cross-border service provision of the 'obligation to contract' is that companies may incur extra costs, since they may have to rethink their business strategy. This, however, is enough to make the measure a restriction on the free movement of services. Access to the national market does not have to be prevented to engage Article 56. It is enough that it is 'affected' (paragraph 64) and this includes making such access more expensive.

This is not necessarily contrary to *Mobistar*. In *Commission* v *Italy*, the Court implies very strongly that the obligation to accept has an unequal impact. Companies based outside Italy will be disadvantaged relative to those established in Italy, whose business model already takes account of the Italian laws. The Court appears to be taking the approach that laws which are equally applicable, but in practice require foreign service providers to adapt their business models, will tend to be exclusionary, and therefore fall within Article 56.

Moreover, the Italian rule was not just to do with marketing or advertising, but required an amendment to the terms of the insurance contracts on sale. It was analogous to a product rule, in the *Cassis de Dijon* sense, and it is well-established that requiring service providers to adapt their product to domestic rules is a restriction on trade.[38] Yet, the judgment goes further

[38] See W.-H. Roth, 'The European Court of Justice's Case Law on Freedom to Provide Services: Is *Keck* Relevant' in M. Andenas and W.-H. Roth (eds.), *Services and Free Movement in EU Law* (Oxford, Oxford University Press, 2002) 1.

than this. A business model may include the way a service is advertised or sold. It appears that, consistently with *Alpine Investments*, a need to change these matters is also a restriction on trade. Implicit in *Commission* v *Italy* is that a service provider should be able to do business throughout the EU in the same way, and with the same products, as she provides in her home state, unless there is a very good reason justifying derogation from this rule.

A restriction on services therefore seems to comprise any measure which affects access to the national market for services. This includes measures which disadvantage the foreign or the cross-border by comparison with the national or the domestic,[39] and any measure which requires a service provider to amend their services or business model in order to provide those services in another state.[40] It does not, if *Mobistar* is correct, include rules which merely impose a cost burden that has no unequal effect. However, experience with *Keck* indicates that this exception may shrink with time. Serious factual investigation often reveals unequal effects even where rules are apparently neutral,[41] and the discussion of business models in *Commission* v *Italy* indicates a certain judicial preparedness to engage with this commercial reality.

(ii) Horizontal application of Article 56 TFEU

Article 56 is, like the other free movement Articles, apparently addressed primarily to Member States. However, unlike the case with goods, Article 56 may also be directly applied to private actors under certain circumstances.[42] The reason why the Court allows this is that the Article would be deprived of some of its effectiveness if private actors were permitted to act in ways obstructing service provision by others. This is even more so as the trend of recent decades has been for states to outsource ever more of their regulatory functions to non-governmental bodies of different types. Yet, many private organisations represent the views and interests of individuals and constraining their freedom of choice and action is also a constraint on the capacity of those individuals to collectively express and act on their views and preferences, raising issues of fundamental rights.

The most common situation to have occurred in practice is where a private organisation is involved in regulating some area of activity. In *Walrave and Koch*, the rules of the International Cycling Union (ICU) were involved.[43] This non-governmental body organised and regulated international bicycling competitions, and made certain demands concerning the nationality of members of the support team. Because these team members received payment for their work, the matter fell within free movement law, and it was decided that they were self-employed providers of services rather than employed people. The claim was therefore made that the ICU rules restricted the freedom to provide services in other states, by preventing team members with the wrong nationality from taking part in international competitions. However, it was disputed whether Article 56 could be applied to the ICU, since it was a private body.

---

[39] See e.g. Case C-375/92 *Commission* v *Spain* [1994] ECR I-923; Case C-224/97 *Ciola* v *Land Vorarlberg* [1999] ECR I-2517; Case C-70/99 *Commission* v *Portugal* ('Flight taxes') [2001] ECR I-4845.

[40] Case C-384/93 *Alpine Investments* v *Minister van Financiën* [1995] ECR I-1141; Case C-518/06 *Commission* v *Italy*, Judgment of 28 April 2009.

[41] See pp. 778–80.

[42] See generally J. Snell, 'Private Parties and Free Movement of Goods and Services' in M. Andenas and W.-H. Roth (eds.), *Services and Free Movement in EU Law* (Oxford, Oxford University Press, 2002) 211; S. Prechal and S. de Vries, 'Seamless Web of Judicial Protection in the Internal Market?' (2009) 34 *ELRev.* 5.

[43] Case 36/74 *Walrave and Koch* v *Association Union Cycliste Internationale* [1974] ECR 1405.

Case 36/74 *Walrave and Koch v Association Union Cycliste Internationale*
[1974] ECR 1405

19. Since, moreover, working conditions in the various Member States are governed sometimes by means of provisions laid down by law or regulation and sometimes by agreements and other acts concluded or adopted by private persons, to limit the prohibitions in question to acts of a public authority would risk creating inequality in their application.

20. Although the third paragraph of Article [57 TFEU], and Articles [59 and 61 TFEU], specifically relate, as regards the provision of services, to the abolition of measures by the state, this fact does not defeat the general nature of the terms of Article [56 TFEU], which makes no distinction between the source of the restrictions to be abolished...

21. It is established, moreover, that Article [45 TFEU], relating to the abolition of any discrimination based on nationality as regards gainful employment, extends likewise to agreements and rules which do not emanate from public authorities.

22. Article 7(4) of Regulation No. 1612/68 in consequence provides that the prohibition on discrimination shall apply to agreements and any other collective regulations concerning employment...

23. The activities referred to in Article [56] are not to be distinguished by their nature from those in Article [45 TFEU], but only by the fact that they are performed outside the ties of a contract of employment.

24. This single distinction cannot justify a more restrictive interpretation of the scope of the freedom to be ensured...

Several points emerge. First, Article 56 is applied to the rules of the ICU because these are part of the regulation of an area of economic activity. To exclude private agreements and rules, which are often an important part of the employment context, from the scope of Article 56 would allow private parties to create obstacles to movement, and create an arbitrary distinction between the rights of economic actors according to the particular mode of regulation prevailing in their industry and state. This view has particular force as states privatise ever more of their regulatory functions, and the distinction between public and private becomes ever less clear and principled.[44]

Secondly, the Court sees no reason to make a principled distinction between the free movement of workers and services. It is a technical matter whether an economic relationship is structured as one of employment or self-employed service provision, and this should not affect the scope of the freedom or the degree to which it may be restricted. Since the free movement of workers applies to all aspects of employment regulation and agreements, private or public, it would be arbitrary to exclude such matters from Article 56. This approach has continued in later cases, and the principles of horizontal application appear to be the same whether workers, services or establishment are concerned.[45]

[44] Case 90/76 *Van Ameyde v UCI* [1997] ECR 1091; J. Baquero Cruz, *Between Competition and Free Movement: The Economic Constitutional Law of the European Community* (Oxford and Portland, Hart, 2002) 123.

[45] Case C-281/98 *Roman Angonese v Cassa di Risparmio di Bolzano* [2000] ECR I-4139; Case C-415/93 *Union Royale Belge des Sociétés de Football Association and Others v Bosman and Others* [1995] ECR I-4921; Case C-176/96 *Jyri Lehtonen and Castors Canada Dry Namur-Braine Asbl v Fédération royale belge des sociétés de basket-ball Asbl (FRBSB)* [2000] ECR I-2681; Case C-438/05 *International Transport Workers' Federation and Finnish Seamen's Union v Viking Line ABP and OÜ Viking Line Eesti* [2007] ECR I-10779.

This application of Article 56 to sport has been very controversial. Sport is, for many people, a matter of social and cultural importance. It can be socially cohesive, and provides a relatively harmless outlet for national identity and the urge to sublimate oneself to a greater whole. To subject it to economic law is not just to miss the point, but to actively threaten the values it embodies and the positive role that it can play in society.[46] Yet, sport is also economic: modern sporting competitions involve large amounts of money, and sportspeople are often well paid for their services.

The case law shows the Court trying to maintain a distinction between rules which are an inherent part of the regulation of sport, and should not be seen as restrictions on free movement, and those that are to do with the economic aspects of sporting activity and may be assessed in the light of free movement law. In *Deliège*, a judoka who had not been selected by the Belgian judo association to represent Belgium in the Olympics claimed that this restricted her freedom to provide services in another Member State. The process of selection limited participation, she argued, and thereby restricted the provision of services.[47] Clearly, she could not win, as this would have created sporting chaos, but rather than finding that there was a restriction which was justified, the Court of Justice found there to be no restriction at all. Its reasoning was that restrictions on participation were inherent to the organisation of a sporting event, and as such did not fall within Article 56.

The General Court explained this idea in more detail in *Meca Medina*. A Spanish and a Slovenian long-distance swimmer both tested positive for nandrolone, a banned substance. They were suspended for four years by FINA, the International Swimming Federation, acting under the rules of the International Olympic Committee, reduced on appeal to two years. The swimmers appealed to the Commission that the ban breached EU competition law and what is now Article 56 TFEU. When the Commission took no action, they brought their case before the General Court.

Case T-313/02 *Meca Medina and Majcen v Commission* [2004] ECR II-3291

37. ... having regard to the objectives of the Community, sport is subject to Community law only insofar as it constitutes an economic activity within the meaning of Article 2 EC...

38. That is also borne out by Declaration on Sport No. 29, annexed to the final act of the Conference which adopted the text of the Amsterdam Treaty, which emphasises the social significance of sport and calls on the bodies of the European Union to give special consideration to the particular characteristics of amateur sport. In particular, that Declaration is consistent with the abovementioned case law insofar as it relates to situations in which sport constitutes an economic activity.

39. Where a sporting activity takes the form of paid employment or a provision of remunerated service, it falls, more particularly, within the scope of Article [45 TFEU] *et seq.* or of Article [56 TFEU] *et seq.*, respectively...

40. Therefore...the prohibitions laid down by those provisions of the Treaty apply to the rules adopted in the field of sport which concern the economic aspect which sporting activity can present. In

---

[46] The Declaration on Sport attached to the Treaty of Amsterdam. See also the 'Helsinki Report' by the Commission. European Commission, *Report to the European Council with a View to Safeguarding Current Sports Structures and Maintaining the Social Function of Sport within the Community Framework*, COM(1999)644. For discussion, see S. Weatherill, 'European Football Law' in *Collected Courses of the 7th Session of the Academy of European Law* (Florence, Kluwer and European Union Institute, 1999) 339–82; S. Weatherill, 'The Helsinki Report on Sport' (2000) 25 *ELRev.* 282.

[47] Joined Cases C-51/96 and C-191/97 *Deliège* v *Asbl Ligue Francophone de Judo* [2000] ECR I-2549.

that context, the Court has held that the rules providing for the payment of fees for the transfer of professional players between clubs (transfer clauses) or limiting the number of professional players who are nationals of other Member States which those clubs may field in matches (rules on the composition of club teams), or fixing, without objective reasons concerning only the sport or justified by differences in the circumstances between players, different transfer deadlines for players coming from other Member States (clauses on transfer deadlines) fall within the scope of those provisions of the Treaty and are subject to the prohibitions which they enact...

41. On the other hand, the prohibitions enacted by those provisions of the Treaty do not affect purely sporting rules, that is to say rules concerning questions of purely sporting interest and, as such, having nothing to do with economic activity... In fact, such regulations, which relate to the particular nature and context of sporting events, are inherent in the organisation and proper conduct of sporting competition and cannot be regarded as constituting a restriction on the Community rules on the freedom of movement of workers and the freedom to provide services. In that context, it has been held that the rules on the composition of national teams ... or the rules relating to the selection by sports federations of those of their members who may participate in high-level international competitions... constitute purely sporting rules which therefore, by their nature, fall outside the scope of Articles [45 TFEU] and [56 TFEU]. Also among such rules are 'the rules of the game' in the strict sense, such as, for example, the rules fixing the length of matches or the number of players on the field, given that sport can exist and be practised only in accordance with specific rules. That restriction on the scope of the above provisions of the Treaty must however remain limited to its proper objective...

44. It is appropriate to point out that, while it is true that high-level sport has become, to a great extent, an economic activity, the campaign against doping does not pursue any economic objective. It is intended to preserve, first, the spirit of fair play, without which sport, be it amateur or professional, is no longer sport. That purely social objective is sufficient to justify the campaign against doping. Secondly, since doping products are not without their negative physiological effects, that campaign is intended to safeguard the health of athletes. Thus, the prohibition of doping, as a particular expression of the requirement of fair play, forms part of the cardinal rule of sport.

45. It must also be made clear that sport is essentially a gratuitous and not an economic act, even when the athlete performs it in the course of professional sport. In other words, the prohibition of doping and the anti-doping legislation concern exclusively, even when the sporting action is performed by a professional, a non-economic aspect of that sporting action, which constitutes its very essence...

47. In view of the foregoing, it must be held that the prohibition of doping is based on purely sporting considerations and therefore has nothing to do with any economic consideration. That means, in the light of the case law and the considerations set out ... above, that the rules to combat doping cannot ... come within the scope of the Treaty provisions on the economic freedoms.

The General Court's judgment was later overturned by the Court of Justice, but not on grounds relevant to the extract above.

The other area where horizontal application of services law has been applied to significant effect, perhaps even more controversially, is labour regulation, in particular the activities of trade unions. This is the result of *Laval* and *Viking Line*, two recent judgments.[48]

Of the two, *Laval* was decided a week later, but is the more concerned with service provision, whereas *Viking* is primarily about establishment. In *Laval*, the Court applied Article 56

[48] Case C-341/05 *Laval un Partneri Ltd* v *Svenska Byggnadsarbetareförbundet, Svenska Byggnadsarbetareförbundets avdelning 1, Byggettan and Svenska Elektrikerförbundet* [2007] ECR I-11767; Case C-438/05 *International Transport Workers' Federation and Finnish Seamen's Union* v *Viking Line ABP and OÜ Viking Line Eesti* [2007] ECR I-10779.

to the law concerning trade unions. Swedish unions took industrial action against foreign employers using posted workers. The unions were trying to force the employers to sign Swedish collective agreements. The union fear was that otherwise the posted workers would receive lower pay and worse conditions, and would undercut local workers and undermine local standards. The employers, however, considered that their freedom to provide services was being restricted by the industrial action, which was effectively preventing them from carrying out their building projects. Citing cases on services, workers and establishment, the Court ruled:

> 98. Furthermore, compliance with Article [56 TFEU] is also required in the case of rules which are not public in nature but which are designed to regulate, collectively, the provision of services. The abolition, as between Member States, of obstacles to the freedom to provide services would be compromised if the abolition of State barriers could be neutralised by obstacles resulting from the exercise of their legal autonomy by associations or organisations not governed by public law...

This application of Article 56 to trade unions raised fears because of its implications for union autonomy and the freedom of workers to fight for their interests, but it was doctrinally hardly different from *Walrave*.[49] In the Swedish employment system, trade unions were an important part of the system of employment regulation, and via their role in collective bargaining, contributed to de facto regulation of labour terms and conditions.

However, in *Viking Line*, the Court appears to go further, and suggests that the application of free movement law to private bodies is not dependent upon them playing some quasi-regulatory role. In *Viking Line*, it was Finnish trade unions that were objecting to free movement, but in this case they took industrial action to try and prevent a Finnish shipping company from reflagging a ship under a Latvian flag. The company wanted to employ workers under cheaper Latvian terms and conditions. It was therefore the freedom of the shipping company to choose their state of establishment that was being restricted by the unions. The Court reaffirmed that Article 49 TFEU must be interpreted to apply to private bodies, in terms almost identical to those in the paragraph above from *Laval*, and then continued as follows.

Case C-438/05 *International Transport Workers' Federation and Finnish Seamen's Union v Viking Line ABP and OÜ Viking Line Eesti* [2007] ECR I-10779

64. It must be added that, contrary to the claims, in particular, of ITF, it does not follow from the case-law of the Court...that that interpretation applies only to quasi-public organisations or to associations exercising a regulatory task and having quasi-legislative powers.

---

[49] See C. Barnard, *Employment Rights, Free Movement under the EC Treaty and the Services Directive*, Mitchell Working Paper No. 5/08 (2008); N. Reich, 'Free Movement v Social Rights in an Enlarged Union: The *Laval* and *Viking* Cases before the ECJ' (2008) 9 *German Law Journal* 125; J. Malmberg and T. Sigeman, 'Industrial Actors and EU Economic Freedoms: The Autonomous Collective Bargaining Model Curtailed by the European Court of Justice' (2008) 43 *CMLRev.* 1115; C. Barnard, '*Viking* and *Laval*: An Introduction' in C. Barnard (ed.) (2007–08) 10 *CYELS* 463; A. Dashwood, '*Viking* and *Laval*: Issues of Horizontal Direct Effect' in C. Barnard (ed.) (2007–08) 10 *CYELS* 525; T. Novitz, 'A Human Rights Analysis of the *Viking* and *Laval* Judgments' in C. Barnard (ed.) (2007–08) 10 *CYELS* 541; S. Sciarra, '*Viking* and *Laval*: Collective Labour Rights and Market Freedoms in the Enlarged EU' in C. Barnard (ed.) (2007–08) 10 *CYELS* 563; S. Deakin, 'Regulatory Competition after *Laval*' in C. Barnard (ed.) (2007–08) 10 *CYELS* 581.

65. There is no indication in that case-law that could validly support the view that it applies only to associations or to organisations exercising a regulatory task or having quasi-legislative powers. Furthermore, it must be pointed out that, in exercising their autonomous power, pursuant to their trade union rights, to negotiate with employers or professional organisations the conditions of employment and pay of workers, trade unions participate in the drawing up of agreements seeking to regulate paid work collectively.

This is an important clarification of *Laval* and *Walrave*. Although there is a certain tension between paragraph 64, and the comment in the next paragraph that trade unions do in fact contribute to labour regulation, it appears that the Court is saying that Article 49 does not apply to private parties because they have some specific legally assigned role in economic activity, but merely because as a matter of fact they have the power to obstruct free movement. The application to unions is therefore not because of any particular legal status that they may enjoy, but because as a matter of fact the action they were undertaking was making establishment in Latvia harder. There seems no reason why the Court should take a different approach in the context of services.

This raises the question whether a private restriction on services or establishment will only be found when there is some general measure or action, or whether an individual decision may also be a restriction.[50] It is well established that if an individual employer decides not to employ someone because of their nationality, this is prohibited by the free movement of workers, which has general horizontal application. Is the same true if an individual decides not to engage a self-employed gardener for discriminatory reasons, or chooses their hairdresser on the basis of nationality? It is suggested that the reasoning used in all the cases above supports a positive answer: services and establishment should have general horizontal application because otherwise inequalities and arbitrary distinctions will be created, and private parties will be able to obstruct free movement. This is not to deny that in practice horizontal enforcement will often be very hard, as the examples given may indicate.

The situation where a provider discriminates is less clear. If the gardener charges foreign clients higher fees it may be said that this interferes with their freedom to receive services less, since they can usually find an alternative provider. Nevertheless, it is nationality discrimination within the sphere of EU law, so in principle one would expect this to be prohibited behaviour.

The implications of such individual application of Article 56 – and the other freedoms – are striking. The limitation on personal autonomy is significant. If we cannot choose an Italian hairdresser, does that mean that the time will come when we cannot choose French cheese without discriminating illegally? It is suggested that it is possible to draw a clear distinction: people are different, and a rejection of discrimination against them is not new to policy. It may be noted that recent Directives prohibit discrimination on grounds of sex and race in the supply of goods and services.[51] The application of normative constraints to individual choices is something EU law has already begun to embrace.

---

[50] See G. Marenco, 'Competition Between National Economies and Competition Between Businesses: A Reply to Judge Pescatore' (1987) 10 *Fordham International Law Journal* 424.

[51] Council Directive 2004/113/EC of 13 December 2004 implementing the principle of equal treatment between men and women in the access to and supply of goods and services [2004] OJ L373/37–43; Council Directive 2000/43/EC of 29 June 2000 implementing the principle of equal treatment between persons irrespective of racial or ethnic origin [2000] OJ L180/22–6.

5 JUSTIFYING RESTRICTIONS ON SERVICES

The analytical structure of the law on services is summarised in *Gebhard*:[52]

> 37. It follows, however, from the Court's case-law that national measures liable to hinder or make less attractive the exercise of fundamental freedoms guaranteed by the Treaty must fulfil four conditions: they must be applied in a non-discriminatory manner; they must be justified by imperative requirements in the general interest; they must be suitable for securing the attainment of the objective which they pursue; and they must not go beyond what is necessary in order to attain it.

Rephrasing this, it can be said that as with the law on the other freedoms, a restriction on services will be permitted if it is:

(i) equally applicable to the national and the foreign;
(ii) justified by some legitimate public interest objective; and
(iii) proportionate to that objective.

If a restriction on services is not equally applicable, but discriminates on its face, then it may only be saved by reliance on one of the Treaty exceptions.[53]

The justifications which may be put forward for equally applicable measures are diverse, and the list is not closed.[54] Any good policy reason that is not discriminatory or purely economic is acceptable. The need to regulate a profession in the public interest, consumer protection and the protection of workers are examples.[55] However, the imposition of national laws on service providers is not justified where the interest concerned is protected by legislation in the state of establishment.[56] In *Guiot*, employers were required to pay social security payments for workers in Belgium. However, this applied not only if the company and its workers were established in Belgium, but also if the company was established in another Member State and had temporarily posted workers to Belgium to supply services there. The Court found that compulsory social security payments could be justified in general by the protection of workers, but imposing them on companies that might be making similar contributions in their home states, without taking any account of this, was disproportionate.[57]

Case C-272/94 *Guiot* [1996] ECR I-1905

14. National legislation which requires an employer, as a person providing a service within the meaning of the Treaty, to pay employer's contributions to the social security fund of the host Member State in addition to the contributions already paid by him to the social security fund of the State where he

---

[52] Case C-55/94 *Gebhard v Consiglio dell'ordine degli avvocati eprocuratori di Milano* [1995] ECR I-4165.

[53] Case C-288/89 *Gouda v Commissariat voor de Media* [1991] ECR I-4007; see also pp. 877–8.

[54] S. O'Leary and J. Fernández-Mártin, 'Judicially Created Exceptions to Free Provision of Services' in M. Andenas and W.-H. Roth (eds.), *Services and Free Movement in EU Law* (Oxford, Oxford University Press, 2002); Snell, above n. 11, 169–219.

[55] See Case C-288/89 *Gouda v Commissariat voor de Media* [1991] ECR I-4007, para. 14 for a long list.

[56] Case C-288/89 *Gouda v Commissariat voor de Media* [1991] ECR I-4007; Case 205/84 *Commission v Germany (German insurance)* [1986] ECR 3755; Case C-439/99 *Commission v Italy ('trade fairs')* [2002] ECR I-305.

[57] Similarly, Joined Cases 62/81 and 63/81 *Seco v Etablissement d'assurance contre la vieillesse et l'invalidité* [1982] ECR 223; Case 3/88 *Commission v Italy* [1989] ECR 4035.

is established places an additional financial burden on him, so that he is not, so far as competition is concerned, on an equal footing with employers established in the host State.

15. Such legislation, even if it applies without distinction to national providers of services and to those of other Member States, is liable to restrict the freedom to provide services within the meaning of Article [56 TFEU].

16. The public interest relating to the social protection of workers in the construction industry may however, because of conditions specific to that sector, constitute an overriding requirement justifying such a restriction on the freedom to provide services.

17. However, that is not the case where the workers in question enjoy the same protection, or essentially similar protection, by virtue of employer's contributions already paid by the employer in the Member State of establishment.

Requiring a service provider to undergo police checks when similar ones have been performed in the home state is another example of an attempt to make a foreign provider jump through two sets of hoops, in violation of mutual recognition.[58]

It is also disproportionate to subject service providers to all the rules which would apply to them if they were established.[59] The logic of the internal market is that as far as possible each economic actor should be subject to the law of their home state, and mutual recognition should ensure that other states recognise the adequacy of this law and permit that actor to do business on their national markets without further ado. Thus, if a company chooses to establish in state X it is reasonable that in principle it should comply fully with the regulation of X. However, if it is merely providing temporary services in X, then full compliance with the laws of X will almost always be a disproportionate demand. This would take away the regulatory distinction between services and establishment, and undermine the capacity of service providers to choose where to establish. In *Säger*, the German government obstructed the provision of patent services in Germany by patent agents based in the United Kingdom.[60] They did not possess the qualifications required in Germany for the service they were providing. The Court did not object to the German rules as such: appropriate rules on qualifications are a way of protecting the consumer in a complex and technical field. However, it went on to hold as follows.

Case C-76/90 *Säger* v *Dennemeyer* [1991] ECR I-4221

...a Member State may not make the provision of services in its territory subject to compliance with all the conditions required for establishment and thereby deprive of all practical effectiveness the provisions of the Treaty whose object is, precisely, to guarantee the freedom to provide services. Such a restriction is all the less permissible where, as in the main proceedings, and unlike the situation governed by the third paragraph of Article [57 TFEU], the service is supplied without its being necessary for the person providing it to visit the territory of the Member State where it is provided.

---

[58] Case 279/80 *Webb* [1981] ECR 3305.
[59] Case 205/84 *Commission* v *Germany (German insurance)* [1986] ECR 3755.
[60] Case C-76/90 *Säger* v *Dennemeyer* [1991] ECR I-4221.

What is proportionate clearly depends partly on the closeness of the relationship between the service provider and the national market. The following sections provide examples which will illustrate this.

(i) Restrictions on marketing and prices

The way that a service is marketed and priced may be just as important to the commercial success of the service provider as the content or quality of the service. Moreover, where a market is dominated by established providers, an innovative marketing or pricing policy can help a new market player break in. The Court has therefore acknowledged that rules which limit price competition may restrict trade.[61] Most notably, in *Cipolla*, it considered regional rules in Italy which fixed legal fees at a set level, and prohibited lawyers from charging less.[62]

Joined Cases C-94/04 and C-202/04 *Federico Cipolla and Others* v *Rosaria Fazari, née Portolese and Roberto Meloni* [2006] ECR I-11421

59. That prohibition deprives lawyers established in a Member State other than the Italian Republic of the possibility, by requesting fees lower than those set by the scale, of competing more effectively with lawyers established on a stable basis in the Member State concerned and who therefore have greater opportunities for winning clients than lawyers established abroad...

60. Likewise, the prohibition thus laid down limits the choice of service recipients in Italy, because they cannot resort to the services of lawyers established in other Member States who would offer their services in Italy at a lower rate than the minimum fees set by the scale....

62. In order to justify the restriction on freedom to provide services which stems from the prohibition at issue, the Italian Government submits that excessive competition between lawyers might lead to price competition which would result in a deterioration in the quality of the services provided to the detriment of consumers, in particular as individuals in need of quality advice in court proceedings. ...

64. In that respect, it must be pointed out that, first, the protection of consumers, in particular recipients of the legal services provided by persons concerned in the administration of justice and, secondly, the safeguarding of the proper administration of justice, are objectives to be included among those which may be regarded as overriding requirements relating to the public interest capable of justifying a restriction on freedom to provide services, on condition, first, that the national measure at issue in the main proceedings is suitable for securing the attainment of the objective pursued and, secondly, it does not go beyond what is necessary in order to attain that objective.

65. It is a matter for the national court to decide whether, in the main proceedings, the restriction on freedom to provide services introduced by that national legislation fulfils those conditions. For that purpose, it is for that court to take account of the factors set out in the following paragraphs.

66. Thus, it must be determined, in particular, whether there is a correlation between the level of fees and the quality of the services provided by lawyers and whether, in particular, the setting of such minimum fees constitutes an appropriate measure for attaining the objectives pursued, namely the protection of consumers and the proper administration of justice.

---

[61] Case 82/77 *Van Tiggele* [1978] ECR 25; Case 231/83 *Cullet* [1985] ECR 305; Case C-442/02 *Caixabank France* [2004] ECR I-8961.
[62] See M. J. Frese and H. J. van Harten, 'How Extravagant the Fees of Counselors at Law Sometimes Appear: Competition Law and Internal Market Constraints to Fixed Remuneration Schemes' (2007) 34 *LIEI* 393.

67. Although it is true that a scale imposing minimum fees cannot prevent members of the profession from offering services of mediocre quality, it is conceivable that such a scale does serve to prevent lawyers, in a context such as that of the Italian market which, as indicated in the decision making the reference, is characterised by an extremely large number of lawyers who are enrolled and practising, from being encouraged to compete against each other by possibly offering services at a discount, with the risk of deterioration in the quality of the services provided.

68. Account must also be taken of the specific features both of the market in question, as noted in the preceding paragraph, and the services in question and, in particular, of the fact that, in the field of lawyers' services, there is usually an asymmetry of information between 'client-consumers' and lawyers. Lawyers display a high level of technical knowledge which consumers may not have and the latter therefore find it difficult to judge the quality of the services provided to them.

69. However, the national court will have to determine whether professional rules in respect of lawyers, in particular rules relating to organisation, qualifications, professional ethics, supervision and liability, suffice in themselves to attain the objectives of the protection of consumers and the proper administration of justice.

The argument that minimum prices prevent excessive competition leading to lower standards and thereby protect the consumer is a very common one, used in most professional contexts. What is striking about *Cipolla* is the extent to which the Court is prepared to critically examine this argument on the particular facts, and to question whether professional quality could be protected by less restrictive means. What is also interesting is that while it leaves the final answer to the national court to decide, the Court implies that facts specific to Italy or the local legal market may be relevant to that answer. It is therefore possible that a minimum price might be justified and proportionate in Italy, but not in another Member State, or even in one region of Italy but not in another, because of the different characteristics of the market for legal services in each area. Such a market-specific approach to proportionality is only politically sustainable because it is local judges who finally decide whether local rules are proportionate. Were the Court of Justice to rule that, for example, minimum prices were permissible in Italy but not in Germany, this would probably be seen as grossly unfair.

In *Alpine Investments*, discussed above, the Court found a restriction on services to be present because cold-calling (making unsolicited telephone calls to potential clients) can be an effective marketing technique.[63] It did not expand on its reasoning, but in reality it is a particularly good technique for a non-established market actor, and the judgment reflects an integrationist use of Article 56, as well as a very practical and business-oriented one.

Yet, the Court went on to find the restriction justified. It was argued that it was not for the Dutch government to protect German consumers, particularly since Germany did not in fact prohibit cold-calling. However, the Court accepted Dutch arguments that in the particular branch of the financial services industry involved, customers were relatively vulnerable and allowing cold-calling could easily result in the Dutch finance industry getting a bad name, which was a legitimate thing to want to prevent. Moreover, the Dutch authorities could not just rely on their German peers to prevent customers being exploited,

---

[63] Case C-384/93 *Alpine Investments* v *Minister van Financiën* [1995] ECR I-1141.

since it would be difficult for them to prevent or to regulate cold-calls coming from other states. The state of establishment was best placed to control the calls a company made, and therefore justified in taking a stance on this issue. *Alpine Investments* has an unusual fact-set, but establishes that restrictions on the export of services are no different from restrictions on import for the purposes of Article 56: they are equally prohibited but equally open to justification.[64]

(ii) Access to regulated industries and professions

The largest group of cases on services concern access to regulated professions and industries. Foreign service providers wishing to provide services in a highly regulated industry, such as the law, medicine, gambling, or private security, typically find that many measures stand in their way. One of the most common problems is obtaining recognition of foreign qualifications, which is dealt with in Chapter 20.[65] However, other aspects of authorisation and regulation have also been the subject of much case law.

Corsten is a relatively simple example. An architect working from the Netherlands contracted to arrange floor laying in Germany, but was fined when he did the work because he was not entered on the local German register of skilled traders. In order to go on this register, he had to submit various documents, pay a fee, and become a member of the local chamber of skilled trades, which entailed paying a subscription. The process also took some time, and he was not permitted to practise his trade in the area until it was completed.

Case C-58/98 *Corsten* [2000] ECR I-7919

45. Even if the requirement of entry on that Register, entailing compulsory membership of the Chamber of Skilled Trades for the undertakings concerned and therefore payment of the related subscription, could be justified in the case of establishment in the host Member State, which is not the situation in the main proceedings, the same is not true for undertakings which intend to provide services in the host Member State only on an occasional basis, indeed perhaps only once.

46. The latter are liable to be dissuaded from going ahead with their plans if, because of the compulsory requirement that they be entered on the Register, the authorisation procedure is made lengthier and more expensive, so that the profit anticipated, at least for small contracts, is no longer economically worthwhile. For those undertakings, therefore, the freedom to provide services, a fundamental principle of the Treaty, and likewise Directive 64/427 are liable to become ineffective.

47. In consequence, the authorisation procedure instituted by the host Member State should neither delay nor complicate exercise of the right of persons established in another Member State to provide their services on the territory of the first State where examination of the conditions governing access to the activities concerned has been carried out and it has been established that those conditions are satisfied.

48. Moreover, any requirement of entry on the trades Register of the host Member State, assuming it was justified, should neither give rise to additional administrative expense nor entail compulsory payment of subscriptions to the chamber of trades.

---

[64] See also Case C-18/93 *Corsica Ferries France* [1994] ECR I-1783; Case C-379/92 *Peralta* [1994] ECR I-3453.
[65] See pp. 846–52.

The Court highlights the importance of distinguishing between established persons and those providing services. Service providers may do very little business in their host state, and so even relatively light administrative burdens wipe out their profit and deter them from entering the market. The aim of the register was to ensure the quality of traders and protect consumers, which was legitimate, but proportionality demanded that where a service provider was concerned the procedure for register entry be as minimal and simple as possible. In particular, it must not add 'administrative expense' and nor must it delay the start of work – meaning that either a trader can begin work while the process of registration is underway, or registration must be available immediately.

Somewhat more burdensome demands have been involved in the considerable number of cases concerning private security firms.[66] These are highly regulated for understandable reasons, but the nature of the regulation is at times bizarre, and very often disproportionate. In *Commission* v *Italy*, security guards were required to swear an oath of allegiance to the Italian state, obviously disproportionate, and particularly irksome for the temporary service provider; while in *Commission* v *Belgium*, private security firms were required to be established in Belgium, and the managers and employees were required to live in Belgium.[67] Such territorial requirements have been the subject of many cases over the years, and are invariably disproportionate.[68] The proposed justification is that it enables better supervision of the firms and individuals by the national authorities, but the Court finds that this can be achieved by less restrictive means. It is possible to communicate with authorities in other states, and it is possible to carry out checks on firms and individuals wherever they live or are established.[69]

A number of recent gambling cases have concerned the right to offer gambling services, such as lotteries or betting on horse-races, at a distance, usually over the Internet.[70] The Court accepts that this kind of service requires strict controls in the cause of preventing crimes such as fraud and money-laundering and preventing addiction to gambling by the public. These issues are discussed more in Chapter 21.[71] However, even justifiably protective measures can be prohibited restrictions on free movement if they have some discriminatory or protectionist element in the way they are applied. This was the case with horse-betting licences in *Commission* v *Italy*. Italy permitted a fixed number of these, but they were awarded and renewed without any publicity so that there was little turnover of licence holders, and for a new entrant it was difficult to obtain a licence. The Court found an obligation of transparency to be imposed on public authorities by Article 56.

---

[66] Case C-355/98 *Commission v Belgium* [2000] ECR I-1221; Case C-171/02 *Commission v Portugal* [2004] ECR I-5645; Case C-514/03 *Commission v Spain* [2006] ECR I-963; Case C-465/05 *Commission v Italy* [2007] ECR I-11091.

[67] Case C-465/05 *Commission v Italy* [2007] ECR I-11091; Case C-355/98 *Commission v Belgium* [2000] ECR I-1221.

[68] Case 33/74 *Van Binsbergen v Bestuur van de Bedrijsvereniging voor de Metaalnijverheid* [1974] ECR 1310; Case 39/75 *Coenen v Sociaal-Economische Raad* [1975] ECR 1547; Case 205/84 *Commission v Germany (German insurance)* [1986] ECR 3755. Similarly Case C-299/02 *Commission v Netherlands* [2004] ECR I-9761.

[69] Case C393/05 *Commission v Austria* [2007] ECR I-10195; Case C-404/05 *Commission v Germany* [2007] ECR I-10239; Case C-383/05 *Talotta v Belgium* [2007] ECR I-2555; Case C-107/83 *Ordre des Avocats au Barreau de Paris v Klopp* [1984] ECR I-2971; Case 33/74 *Van Binsbergen v Bestuur van de Bedrijsvereniging voor de Metaalnijverheid* [1974] ECR 1310.

[70] Case C-67/98 *Questore di Verona v Zenatti* [1999] ECR I-7289; Case C42/02 *Lindman* [2003] ECR I-13519; Case C-6/01 *Anomar v Estado Português* [2003] ECR I-8621; Case C-243/01 *Gambelli* [2003] ECR I-13031; Joined Cases C-338/04, C-359/04 and C-360/04 *Placanica, Palazzese and Soricchio* [2007] ECR I-1891; Case C-42/07 *Liga Portuguesa de Futebol Profissional and Bwin International Ltd v Departamento de Jogos da Santa Casa da Misericórdia de Lisboa*, Judgment of 8 September 2009.

[71] See pp. 891–2.

Case C-260/04 *Commission v Italy* [2007] ECR I-7083

22. The Court has held that, notwithstanding the fact that public service concession contracts are, as Community law stands at present, excluded from the scope of Directive 92/50 [on public procurement] the public authorities concluding them are, nonetheless, bound to comply with the fundamental rules of the EC Treaty, in general, and the principle of non-discrimination on the grounds of nationality, in particular.

23. The Court then stated that the provisions of the Treaty applying to public service concessions, in particular Articles [49 and 56 TFEU], and the prohibition of discrimination on grounds of nationality are specific expressions of the principle of equal treatment.

24. In that regard, the principles of equal treatment and non-discrimination on grounds of nationality imply, in particular, a duty of transparency which enables the concession-granting public authority to ensure that those principles are complied with. That obligation of transparency which is imposed on the public authority consists in ensuring, for the benefit of any potential tenderer, a degree of advertising sufficient to enable the service concession to be opened up to competition and the impartiality of procurement procedures to be reviewed.

25. In the present case, it must be observed that the complete failure to invite competing bids for the purposes of granting licences for horse-race betting operations does not accord with Articles [49 and 56 TFEU] and, in particular, infringes the general principle of transparency and the obligation to ensure a sufficient degree of advertising. The renewal of the 329 old licences without a call for tenders precludes the opening up to competition of the licences and review of the impartiality of the procurement procedures.

(iii) Tax and investment issues

Tax is still a very national matter. In the current state of European integration, it can neither be levied nor spent in a way that takes no account of national boundaries, creating an unavoidable tension with free movement law, which pursues a Europe in which those boundaries are gone. What is simply practical and responsible tax policy, focused on those living and working in a given Member State, may look like nationality discrimination from another perspective. The necessary compromises have created a complex body of EU law which cannot be fully addressed here.

The underlying principles are no different from those applicable to other measures discussed above. It is just that in deciding what is justified, it is often necessary to have a detailed knowledge of how the tax system works. However, in some cases the facts are more accessible, and these provide a taste of how tax and the free movement of services interact.

Tax discrimination based on location is the most common problem.[72] The Spanish government exempted winnings from a number of lotteries from tax, but all the relevant lotteries were organised by Spanish organisations.[73] Lottery winnings from lotteries established abroad were not exempted. This placed lotteries established abroad at a disadvantage on the Spanish market and discouraged them from offering their services there. The case is also an example of the

---

[72] Case C-39/04 *Laboratoires Fournier SA* v *Direction des vérifications nationales et internationals* [2005] ECR I-2057; Case C-383/05 *Talotta* v *Belgium* [2007] ECR I-2555; Case C-330/07 *Jobra Vermögensverwaltungs-Gesellschaft mbH* v *Finanzamt Amstetten Melk Scheibbs*, Judgment of 4 December 2008.

[73] Case C-153/08 *Commission* v *Spain*, Judgment of 6 October 2009.

well-established principle that it is not necessary to advantage every national operator in order to discriminate: advantaging some national businesses at the expense of foreign ones will suffice.[74]

In *Jundt*, it was tax on the provider rather than the recipient that was in issue.[75] The German government exempted expense payments to part-time university teachers from tax, but only if the university in question was established in Germany. This was prohibited because it made the provision of services abroad less attractive than equivalent domestic provision and so amounted to a restriction on cross-border service provision.

Commission v *Belgium* is the mirror of *Jundt*.[76] Belgian laws required those employing building contractors not established in Belgium to withhold 15 per cent of any payment to them against possible tax liabilities of those contractors in Belgium. The contractors had to go through an administrative procedure to show they owed no tax before they could get this money. This deterred foreign contractors from working in Belgium. The justification of preventing tax fraud was not enough to convince the Court, which suggested, quite consistently with its case law, that a more proportionate approach would be for the authorities to exchange information with employers and contractors so that tax obligations could be enforced.

De Coster concerned indirect discrimination.[77] A tax was imposed on satellite dishes by the municipal authorities in a town in Belgium. This was claimed to be largely on aesthetic grounds: dishes are not pretty, and the tax was intended to discourage them. However, satellite dishes tend to be used to receive cross-border television transmissions, whereas most national programmes are transmitted by cable. Since there was no analogous tax on cable connections, the measure disadvantaged foreign television providers. The Court found that it could not be justified:

> 38. As the Commission observed, there are methods other than the tax in question in the main proceedings, less restrictive of the freedom to provide services, which could achieve an objective such as the protection of the urban environment, for instance the adoption of requirements concerning the size of the dishes, their position and the way in which they are fixed to the building or its surroundings or the use of communal dishes. Moreover, such requirements have been adopted by the municipality of Watermael-Boitsfort, as is apparent from the planning rules on outdoor aerials adopted by that municipality and approved by regulation of 27 February 1997 of the government of the Brussels-Capital region.

The odd thing here is that the municipality had already adopted the measures proposed by the Court, and clearly considered that they were not enough. Yet, the Court uses their adoption as an argument against the tax. This perhaps shows two things. One is that the Court is very strict where unequal effects are involved, particularly if there is the suspicion of deliberate discrimination against foreign service providers. The other is that the Court may have been aware of the considerable unspoken social background to taxes such as these: satellite dishes are most popular among immigrant groups, and this colours the aesthetic arguments against them, however real these may be.

Laws requiring or deterring investment are usually treated as restrictions on the free movement of capital. However, *UTECA* provides an example where the provision of services is also

---

[74] See also Case C-169/08 *Presidente del Consiglio dei Ministri* v *Regione Sardegna*, Judgment of 17 November 2009.
[75] Case C-281/06 *Jundt and Jundt* v *Finanzamt Offenburg* [2007] ECR I-12231.
[76] Case C-433/04 *Commission* v *Belgium* [2006] ECR I-10653.
[77] Case C-17/00 *De Coster* v *Collège des bourgmestre et échevins de Watermael-Boitsfort* [2001] ECR I-9445.

involved.[78] The Spanish government required television operators to use 5 per cent of their revenue to fund European films, and to use 60 per cent of that 5 per cent for films made in one of the official languages of Spain. The Court rather surprisingly found that the first requirement was not a restriction on any of the freedoms. It seems likely that many television companies would be deterred from establishing in Spain by this rule. The second requirement, by contrast, was a restriction on capital, services and establishment. Spanish television operators would be less likely to buy, or finance the making of, non-Spanish films. Foreign suppliers or makers of films would therefore find their position on the Spanish market weakened. Nevertheless, the measures were found to be justified by the need to defend Spanish multilingualism. As with other culture and language cases, the Court shows a greater deference to national concerns than is usually the case.[79]

6 SERVICES AND THE MARKET SOCIETY

(i) Right to trade and socially sensitive services

Article 56 embodies a right to trade services. This applies even to services which have not traditionally been seen as tradeable or as primarily economic. Health care, education, sport and ethically sensitive services like abortion or gambling have traditionally been regulated from a primarily non-economic perspective.

It has been put to the Court that such services should not fall within Article 56 because of their special social, cultural or ethical importance. The Court has consistently rejected this.[80] In *Kohll*, speaking of rules on social security and health care, it said: 'The Court has held that the special nature of certain services does not remove them from the ambit of the fundamental principle of freedom of movement.'[81] Similarly, when it was argued in *Schindler* that gambling could not be regarded as a service because in some states it was illegal, the Court refused to take a moral stance.

Case C-275/92 *HM Customs and Excise* v *Schindler* [1994] ECR I-1039

32. In these circumstances, lotteries cannot be regarded as activities whose harmful nature causes them to be prohibited in all the Member States and whose position under Community law may be likened to that of activities involving illegal products (see, in relation to drugs, the judgment in Case 294/82 *Einberger* v *Hauptzollamt Freiburg* [1984] ECR 1177) even though, as the Belgian and Luxembourg Governments point out, the law of certain Member States treats gaming contracts as void. Even if the morality of lotteries is at least questionable, it is not for the Court to substitute its assessment for that of the legislatures of the Member States where that activity is practised legally...

---

[78] Case C-222/07 *UTECA* v *Administración General del Estado*, Judgment of 5 March 2009.

[79] See also Case 379/87 *Groener* v *Minister for Education and the City of Dublin Vocational Educational Committee* [1989] ECR I-3967; Case C-424/97 *Salomone Haim* v *Kassenzahnärztliche Vereinigung Nordrhein* [2000] ECR I-5123; Case C-250/06 *United Pan-Europe Communications Belgium SA and Others* v *Belgian State* [2007] ECR I-11135. See also Case C-506/04 *Graham J. Wilson* v *Ordre des avocats du barreau de Luxembourg* [2006] ECR I-8613.

[80] By contrast, it has been more reluctant to apply competition law. See Joined Cases C-159/91 and C-160/91 *Poucet* v *Assurances Générales de France and Caisse Mutuelle Régionale du Languedoc-Roussillon* [1993] ECR I-637. See generally W. Sauter and H. Schepel, *State and Market in European Union Law* (Cambridge, Cambridge University Press, 2009).

[81] Case C-158/96 *Kohll* v *Union des Caisses de Maladie* [1998] ECR I-1931.

It has applied the same logic to prostitution,[82] and most famously to abortion, in *Grogan*. A group of students in Ireland distributed pamphlets providing information on how to get an abortion in the United Kingdom. Abortion is constitutionally prohibited in Ireland. The Irish authorities took steps to prohibit the distribution of the pamphlets, and the question was whether this amounted to a restriction on the free movement of services.

Case C-159/90 *Society for the Protection of the Unborn Child (SPUC)* v *Grogan* [1991] ECR I-4685

18. It must be held that termination of pregnancy, as lawfully practised in several Member States, is a medical activity which is normally provided for remuneration and may be carried out as part of a professional activity. In any event, the Court has already held in the judgment in *Luisi and Carbone* that medical activities fall within the scope of Article [57] of the Treaty.[83]

19. SPUC, however, maintains that the provision of abortion cannot be regarded as being a service, on the grounds that it is grossly immoral and involves the destruction of the life of a human being, namely the unborn child.

20. Whatever the merits of those arguments on the moral plane, they cannot influence the answer to the national court's first question. It is not for the Court to substitute its assessment for that of the legislature in those Member States where the activities in question are practised legally.

21. Consequently, the answer to the national court's first question must be that medical termination of pregnancy, performed in accordance with the law of the State in which it is carried out, constitutes a service within the meaning of Article [57] of the Treaty....

24. As regards, first, the provisions of Article [56] of the Treaty, which prohibit any restriction on the freedom to supply services, it is apparent from the facts of the case that the link between the activity of the students associations of which Mr Grogan and the other defendants are officers and medical terminations of pregnancies carried out in clinics in another Member State is too tenuous for the prohibition on the distribution of information to be capable of being regarded as a restriction within the meaning of Article [56] of the Treaty.

In fact, the Court managed to avoid a major conflict of values by finding that Article 56 did not apply because the students had no connection with the service providers.[84] They were acting out of non-commercial motives on their own initiative. The case implicitly introduces a 'directness' criterion into the concept of a restriction on services,[85] but the context was so politically sensitive and the facts so unusual that this extrapolation must remain uncertain.

However, the lasting importance of the case is in the confirmation that, however offensive or illegal a service may be in one state, if it is permitted in others then providers in those states can rely on Article 56. Had the Irish government taken sufficiently concrete steps to prevent Irish women going to the United Kingdom for paid abortions, Article 56 would have applied, the Irish Constitution notwithstanding.

[82] See also Case C-268/99 *Jany* v *Staatssecretaris van Justitie* [2001] ECR I-8615.

[83] Joined Cases 286/82 and 26/83 *Luisi and Carbone* v *Ministero del Tesoro* [1984] ECR 377, para. 16.

[84] See D. R. Phelan, 'The Right to Life of the Unborn v Promotion of Trade in Services: The European Court and the Normative Shaping of the European Union' (1992) 55 *MLR* 670. Shortly after this case a Protocol was adopted protecting the Irish ban on abortion from EU law. See C. Barnard, *The Substantive Law of the EU* (2nd edn, Oxford, Oxford University Press, 2007) 362–6.

[85] *Ibid.* 361.

This is not to say that national constitutional values will not be respected, or may not prevail. Both mandatory requirements and Treaty exceptions may justify a restriction on free movement and it is undoubtedly the case that where there is such strong national feeling as exists in Ireland over abortion, the Court will weigh this heavily.[86] However, the structure of the normative framework has been changed. After *Kohll*, *Grogan* and *Schindler*, moral, social and cultural perspectives are tested against economic rights, rather than economic rights being clearly subordinated to higher norms. This does not necessarily lead to different outcomes in cases, but it may encourage them: rhetorical reordering does influence the reasoning process, both in public debate and in judicial proceedings. As Hervey puts it:

> [T]he ability and indeed duty to apply EC law hinders national courts from explicitly approaching issues concerned with moral or ethical choices. Rather, the application of EC law may encourage or at least enable national courts to resolve cases by applying economic concepts, for example, relating to trade in goods and services. The EU legal order, with its underlying principles of market openness, and conceptualization of individuals as market actors, might aid this type of approach.[87]

(ii) The market society

The fundamental fear – for others the hope – is that Article 56 will create a market society, in Polanyi's famous term, which inverts the relationship between the market and society.[88] Instead of the economy being embedded in social relations, social relations are embedded in the economic system.

A feature of the market society is that the contract is the central social relation. The contract is not only legally protected by Article 56 through its protection of the freedom to transact. Many social relations are recast as contractual relations. The provision of a medical operation, for example, is not seen, under Article 56, in terms of the Hippocratic ideal, whereby the doctor commits herself to the unconditional alleviation of suffering and not to exploit the patient, and the patient commits herself to the professional expertise of the doctor and to the doctor's judgement on what is best. Instead, the terms of the relationship are to be determined by the contractual document. This allows more room for the patient's desires. She can look around for operations not considered suitable by some doctors. She can doubt the chosen doctor's judgement. Similarly, the responsibilities of the doctor have altered. She may want to weigh the possibility and type of treatment against the cost. She is, after all, in competition with other doctors. Finally, she is only committed to treat those with whom she has a contractual arrangement.

A second feature of the market society is that many collective goods become measured as a series of individual entitlements. Public health is no longer a public good, of which the level and distribution are to be decided collectively. As something which can be transacted, health becomes a series of individual rights.

Finally, the market society places a particular value on subjective preferences and desires. Subjective desire becomes a source of value. It is the justification for Article 56, which grants

---

[86] See p. 902.
[87] T. Hervey, 'Buy Baby: The European Union and the Regulation of Human Reproduction' (1998) 18 *OJLS* 207, 230.
[88] The term was first used in K. Polanyi, *The Great Transformation* (2nd edn, Boston, Beacon, 2001).

the individual a prima facie right to transact for what she desires. A desire will only be refused where the activity threatens some external good, which is seen as having a greater value. The prohibition of the selling of certain forms of other drugs, such as heroin or cocaine, is prohibited, therefore, precisely because the importance of maintaining public order and public health are seen to outweigh the value of the enjoyment the user derives from the drugs. The market society, however, does not attribute equal value to the desires of all individuals. The desire of the homeless to have a warm home is not accorded any value. Instead, value is only attached to preferences insofar as one is a market actor and can pay the market price for realisation of those preferences.

(iii) Article 56 TFEU and the welfare state

If the processes above are to be observed, then the most promising context is where Article 56 has interacted with the welfare state, and in particular health care.[89] This is the area where the law has intruded the furthest into a sensitive service area, embodying many non-economic values. The cases show, as suggested above, an increasing centrality for individual transactions and preferences above systemic considerations.[90] However, they also show pragmatism and compromise, and a willingness at least to listen to Member State fears, if not always to accept them. Nor can they be seen as a simple triumph of economic freedom over other values: in most cases, states oppose the use of Article 56 on largely budgetary (economic) grounds, while individuals plead for free movement using a normative and non-economic language in which their personal and medical circumstances are more central than any notion of economic liberty. Perhaps the far-reaching scope of the health care cases has been partly possible because it is the patients, rather than the providers, who have led the litigation, and have more easily claimed the moral high ground than a commercial service provider could have done.

In any event, the judgments discussed below are leading to a reorganising of welfare structures and a redrawing of the boundaries of solidarity.[91] Individuals have been granted rights to exit their national system and receive services in other Member States, with consequences for the budgets of their home state and the state they travel to. As well as this, institutions have also been granted the right to offer welfare services in other Member States, with consequences for the integrity and stability of pre-existing national institutions. This is primarily an issue of establishment, and is dealt with in Chapter 20.[92] What follows focuses on the rights of individuals to seek services such as health care and education abroad.

---

[89] See e.g. G. de Búrca (ed.), *EU Law and the Welfare State* (Oxford, Oxford University Press, 2005); M. Dougan and E. Spaventa, *Social Welfare and EU Law* (Oxford, Hart, 2005); E. Spaventa, 'Public Services and European Law: Looking for Boundaries' (2002) *CYELS* 271; G. Davies, *The Process and Side-effects of Harmonisation of European Welfare States*, Jean Monnet Working Paper No. 2/06 (2006).

[90] See C. Newdick, 'Citizenship, Free Movement and Healthcare: Cementing Individual Rights by Corroding Social Solidarity' (2006) 43 *CMLRev.* 1645.

[91] See e.g. D. S. Martinsen and V. Vrangbaek, 'The Europeanisation of Health Care Governance: Implementing the Market Imperatives of Europe' (2008) 86 *Public Administration* 169; Davies, above n. 88; J. Montgomery, 'The Impact of European Union Law on English Healthcare Law' in M. Dougan and E. Spaventa, *Social Welfare and EU Law* (Oxford, Hart, 2005) 145; M. Ferrera, 'Towards an Open Social Citizenship? The New Boundaries of Welfare in the European Union' in G. de Búrca (ed.), *EU Law and the Welfare State* (Oxford, Oxford University Press, 2005) 11.

[92] See p. 842.

This right took some time to emerge. Many public services are provided free and the Court has found these not to be remunerated, and so not to be Treaty services.[93] This was enough to prevent Article 56 and the welfare state meeting, and to raise a perception that this meeting would not occur.

One reason that this has changed in recent years is that public institutions such as schools, universities and hospitals are increasingly funded by private insurance or by the consumers of their services, so that Article 56 applies to at least some of their activities. Yet another reason, which has been more important in the case law, is that the type of migration has changed: instead of individuals going abroad to receive free public services, in recent years individuals have been exiting their (free) domestic systems in order to pay for services abroad. Instead of the non-economic welfare state being a destination, it has become a hindrance.

This creates a role for Article 56. Whatever the character of the domestic welfare state, economic or not, where migrants pay for services abroad there is obviously a remunerated cross-border service in issue. The nature of the domestic system becomes quite irrelevant to this point. For example, in *Commission v Germany*, the Commission challenged German rules which made school fees tax deductible, but only if the school was in Germany.[94] This, of course, discouraged the sending of children to schools abroad. Germany argued that school education was not a service.

Case C–318/05 *Commission v Germany* [2007] ECR I-6957

71. It is undisputed that, in parallel with schools belonging to a public educational system whereby the State performs its task in the social, educational and cultural areas, the financing of which is essentially from public funds, there are schools in certain Member States which do not belong to such a system of public education and which are financed essentially from private funds.

72. The education provided by such schools must be regarded as a service provided for remuneration.

73. It should be added that, for the purposes of determining whether Article [56 TFEU] applies to the national legislation at issue, it is irrelevant whether or not the schools established in the Member State of the user of the service – in this case the Federal Republic of Germany – which are approved, authorised or recognised in that Member State within the meaning of that legislation, provide services within the meaning of the first paragraph of Article [57 TFEU]. All that matters is that the private school established in another Member State may be regarded as providing services for remuneration.

The logic applied above has been used more frequently and has been even more important in the context of health care. The Dutch and UK governments have both argued in the past that Article 56 could not be used by patients who wished to leave the Netherlands or United Kingdom for health care abroad, because those countries provided health care to their citizens within a non-remunerated framework to which Article 56 did not apply (this has now changed in the Netherlands). In both cases, this argument was just as irrelevant as above.[95]

---

[93] See pp. 790–2.

[94] See also Case C-76/05 *Schwarz and Gootjes-Schwarz v Finanzamt Bergisch Gladbach* [2007] ECR I-6849.

[95] Case C-157/99 *Geraets-Smits v Stichting Ziekenfonds; Peerbooms v Stichting CZ Groep Zorgverzekeringen* [2001] ECR I-5473; Case C-372/04 *Watts v Bedford Primary Care Trust* [2006] ECR I-4325.

A right to go abroad for health care is, however, only half the story. The real question is what kind of national measures will be seen as impeding this right. In particular, most national health systems or insurers have traditionally only paid for health care at home, and refused to cover the cost of treatment abroad, except perhaps in exceptional situations. A policy such as this discourages patients from exiting the system and encourages them to receive their health care at home. Is that sufficient to say that not paying for foreign treatment is a restriction on services?

In *Kohll*, the Court ruled that this is the case. Kohll, a Luxembourgeois national, applied for his daughter to have dental treatment in Germany. Under Luxembourg law, such treatment could be received free if provided in Luxembourg, but required prior authorisation from the sickness insurance fund if it were to be provided outside the country. Authorisation was refused on the grounds that the treatment was not urgent and could, in any case, be provided within Luxembourg. Kohll argued that this breached Article 56 as the dental treatment constituted a service under that provision.

Case C‑158/96 *Kohll* v *Union des Caisses de Maladie* [1998] ECR I‑1931

32. The Member States which have submitted observations consider, on the contrary, that the rules at issue do not have as their purpose or effect to restrict freedom to provide services, but merely lay down the conditions for the reimbursement of medical expenses.

33. It should be noted that, according to the Court's case law, [Article [56 TFEU]] precludes the application of any national rules which have the effect of making the provision of services between Member States more difficult than the provision of services purely within one Member State (Case C‑381/93 *Commission* v *France* [1994] ECR I‑5145, paragraph 17).

34. While the national rules at issue in the main proceedings do not deprive insured persons of the possibility of approaching a provider of services established in another Member State, they do nevertheless make reimbursement of the costs incurred in that Member State subject to prior authorisation, and deny such reimbursement to insured persons who have not obtained that authorisation. Costs incurred in the State of insurance are not, however, subject to that authorisation.

35. Consequently, such rules deter insured persons from approaching providers of medical services established in another Member State and constitute, for them and their patients, a barrier to freedom to provide services...

The practical consequences of this judgment are displayed in the series of post-*Kohll* cases on health care, which are likely to culminate in the near future in a Directive on patients' rights. These confirm a patient's right to exit the national system of health care and choose treatment abroad, subject to certain limitations.[96]

---

[96] See V. Hatzopoulos, 'Killing National Health and Insurance Systems but Healing Patients? The European Market for Health Care Services after the Judgments of the ECJ in *Van Braekel* and *Peerbooms*' (2002) 39 *CMLRev*. 683; M. Flear, 'Note on Müller‑Fauré' (2004) 41 *CMLRev*. 209; M. Cousins, 'Patient Mobility and National Health Systems' (2007) 34 *LIEI* 183; K. Stoger, 'Freedom of Establishment and the Market Access of Hospital Operators' (2006) *EBLRev*. 1545; V. Hatzopoulos, 'Health Law and Policy: The Impact of the EU' in G. de Búrca (ed.), *EU Law and the Welfare State* (Oxford, Oxford University Press, 2005) 111; P. Koutrakos, 'Healthcare as an Economic Service under EC Law' in M. Dougan and E. Spaventa, *Social Welfare and EU Law* (Oxford, Hart, 2005) 105; Davies, above n. 28.

The three best-known cases, *Geraerts-Smits and Peerbooms*, *Müller-Fauré* and *Watts*, share essentially the same fact pattern as *Kohll*.[97] A patient (Dutch in the first two cases, British in the third) approached their health insurer or health authority to ask for authorisation to go abroad for treatment, to ask for confirmation that the insurer or authority would pay the costs. This was refused in each case, whereupon the patient went anyway, and submitted the bill. The insurers or authorities refused to pay, the patient litigated, and the Court of Justice was ultimately asked to adjudicate on exactly when a state or insurer was permitted to refuse payment for treatment abroad and exactly when a patient could obtain it.

In all of these cases, the Member States argued that restrictions on treatment abroad could be justified by public health reasons. They claimed that the cost increases which might result from patient migration could be so dramatic that the stability and sustainability of the public health system would be threatened.

The reasons why costs might increase are several. First, the costs of treatment abroad may be higher than the cost of equivalent treatment domestically. Secondly, patients may go abroad for treatment that is not in fact medically effective, following their whims rather than medical science. Thirdly, a good domestic health system requires the maintenance of an expensive medical infrastructure. For the most efficient use of this there must be a stable and continuous flow of clients. If patients can go abroad then domestic hospitals may run at less than full capacity. Yet, states cannot close them, because each state wants to maintain the domestic capacity to treat its citizens. Hence, states may be forced to effectively pay twice, once for the unused domestic capacity, and once for the actual treatment abroad.

In all of the cases, the Court took the same approach: merely budgetary or economic arguments do not justify a restriction on free movement.[98] However, if states could show that the financial consequences would be so great that they would indeed threaten the stability and quality of the system, then this would justify restrictions. The question is when this would be the case.

The first two arguments for cost increase – expensive foreign treatment and luxury treatment – have not been accepted. The Court has noted that Member States are free to define the scope of health care for which their system will pay, and the rates that they will pay.[99] Provided they do this in a non-discriminatory, transparent and rational way, the existence of a defined health package will not in itself contravene Article 56.[100] These limits then apply equally to treatment abroad, so that the cost risk is avoided. If states determine that a hip operation costs €3,000 in their domestic system, they may, for example, rule that they will pay a maximum of €3,000 for the same operation abroad. They must not have a lower reimbursement tariff for foreign treatment, but it need not be higher.

---

[97] Case C-157/99 *Geraets-Smits v Stichting Ziekenfonds; Peerbooms v Stichting CZ Groep Zorgverzekeringen* [2001] ECR I-5473; Case C-385/99 *Müller-Fauré v Onderlinge Waarborgmaatschappij OZ Zorgverzekeringen* [2003] ECR I-4509; Case C-372/04 *Watts v Bedford Primary Care Trust* [2006] ECR I-4325; see also Case C-8/02 *Leichtle v Bundesanstalt für Arbeit* [2004] ECR I-2641; Case C-368/98 *Vanbraekel v ANMC* [2001] ECR I-5363; Case C-444/05 *Stamatelaki v OAEE* [2007] ECR I-3185; Case C-56/01 *Inizan v Caisse Primaire d'Assurance Maladie des Hauts-de-Seine* [2003] ECR I-12403.

[98] See pp. 875–7.

[99] Case C-157/99 *Geraets-Smits v Stichting Ziekenfonds; Peerbooms v Stichting CZ Groep Zorgverzekeringen* [2001] ECR I-5473; Case C-385/99 *Müller-Fauré v Onderlinge Waarborgmaatschappij OZ Zorgverzekeringen* [2003] ECR I-4509; Case C-372/04 *Watts v Bedford Primary Care Trust* [2006] ECR I-4325.

[100] See cases above n. 99.

This sounds reasonable, but defining the domestic health care package imposes considerable administrative burdens on states.[101] In *Geraets-Smits and Peerbooms*, a Dutch coma patient was refused authorisation for a treatment in Austria on the grounds that it was experimental and had not been proven to be effective. The Dutch system only paid for treatment that was considered 'normal'. Even after the patient had been cured by the Austrian treatment, the Dutch insurance fund continued to refuse reimbursement on this ground. They lost before the Court because the definition of 'normal' treatment appeared to be one deriving exclusively from domestic medical practice, rather than from medical science, which, as the Court noted, is inherently international. 'Only an interpretation on the basis of what is sufficiently tried and tested by international medical science' was compatible with Article 56. Thus, states which wish to effectively limit the treatment their patients can receive abroad must define the scope of their domestic care with reasonable precision and care.

This applies also to costs. Treatment abroad may be limited to the costs of equivalent domestic care, but this requires establishing what domestic care actually costs. In many systems, this is no easy task. Where hospitals receive lump-sum funding, or a mix of lump-sum funding and per-patient or per-treatment funding, establishing what a given operation or treatment costs is extremely difficult, and any sum is likely to be open to legal challenge. If it is artificially low it will prevent patients going abroad, but attract foreign patients, burdening the domestic system. If it is artificially high, then patients will be able to accumulate large bills abroad. States are also likely to find that as they establish transparent price lists and lists of available treatment, this has considerable domestic political effects. It will reveal the efficiencies and weaknesses of the system, and enable international comparison.

The third argument for cost increase – the cost of infrastructure – has been recognised by the Court. In *Müller-Fauré*, it made a distinction between hospital care and non-hospital care.[102] Where non-hospital care is concerned, it ruled that the infrastructure argument did not apply, and there is no justification for restricting foreign treatment. EU patients may now go wherever they want in the European Union for their consultations or minor treatments and expect costs to be covered by their domestic system just as if they had had the treatment at home.

By contrast, where hospital care is concerned the Court conceded that the potential cost risks were indeed far greater. It found that states could justify certain restrictions on treatment abroad. Article 56 only requires them to pay for treatment abroad, the Court found, if the necessary treatment cannot be provided domestically without 'undue delay'.

This ruling is particularly important because the most common reason for patient migration is not to receive better or different treatment but to avoid domestic waiting lists. States have a particular objection to this which is not to do with absolute cost increases, but to do with cost control. The UK government position in *Watts*, and as intervener in *Müller-Fauré*, was that it had a finite annual health care budget, and so needed to control the rate of treatment. If patients could avoid waiting lists, then apart from this being unethical (queue jumping) it would make this annual budget control impossible. It would also undermine planning: with a finite budget the state may wish to determine which treatments get priority, and make hip

---

[101] G. Davies, 'The Effect of Mrs Watts' Trip to France on the National Health Service' (2007) 18 *Kings Law Journal* 158.

[102] For a definition of the difference, see article 8(1) of the proposed Directive on patients' rights in cross-border health care, COM(2008)414 final.

patients wait longer than heart patients, for example. Waiting lists, in the view of the United Kingdom, were part of a fair and effective health care system.[103]

The Court accepted that making patients wait could be a legitimate part of health care system-management, but found in both *Watts* and *Müller-Fauré*, that this could only justify restricting authorisation where the waiting time in question was not 'undue'. The phrase 'undue delay' now marks the line between reasonable planning and waiting times, which may serve overall patient welfare, and a failing health care system, which clearly does not.

The question of when a waiting time is 'undue' is thus very much at the heart of the law and policy. States, for the reasons in the paragraphs above, would like to define this purely by reference to prevailing national norms: if the waiting period for treatment is no longer than is normal in that state – no longer than other patients have to wait – then it is not undue. The Court, however, making one of its most important decisions on health care and Article 56, has categorically rejected this. Undue delay is a concept to be decided primarily by looking at the concerns of the patient, not of the health care system.

Case C-385/99 *Müller-Fauré* v *Onderlinge Waarborgmaatschappij OZ Zorgverzekeringen* [2003] ECR I-4509

90. In order to determine whether treatment which is equally effective for the patient can be obtained without undue delay in an establishment having an agreement with the insured person's fund, the national authorities are required to have regard to all the circumstances of each specific case and to take due account not only of the patient's medical condition at the time when authorisation is sought and, where appropriate, of the degree of pain or the nature of the patient's disability which might, for example, make it impossible or extremely difficult for him to carry out a professional activity, but also of his medical history...

The fact that the effect of illness on the patient's broader health, and on their career, is relevant to undue delay renders this a fluid and contestable concept. Each case has to be looked at on its own facts, and it is no longer possible for states or insurers to decide authorisation applications purely by looking at a tariff or standard times.[104] This means that the acceptability of a waiting period is often at the centre of patient-insurer disputes over treatment abroad, which makes the Court's procedural requirements concerning authorisation of particular importance. While states may have authorisation procedures, it must not be the case that treatment abroad can effectively be blocked by dragging patients into a slow, expensive and ineffective bureaucratic procedure.

Case C-157/99 *Geraets-Smits* v *Stichting Ziekenfonds; Peerbooms* v *Stichting CZ Groep Zorgverzekeringen* [2001] ECR I-5473

90. ... a scheme of prior authorisation cannot legitimise discretionary decisions taken by the national authorities which are liable to negate the effectiveness of provisions of Community law, in particular those relating to a fundamental freedom such as that at issue in the main proceedings... Therefore, in order for a prior administrative authorisation scheme to be justified even though it derogates from such a

---

[103] See Newdick, above n. 90.
[104] Davies, above n. 101.

fundamental freedom, it must, in any event, be based on objective, non-discriminatory criteria which are known in advance, in such a way as to circumscribe the exercise of the national authorities' discretion, so that it is not used arbitrarily... Such a prior administrative authorisation scheme must likewise be based on a procedural system which is easily accessible and capable of ensuring that a request for authorisation will be dealt with objectively and impartially within a reasonable time and refusals to grant authorisation must also be capable of being challenged in judicial or quasi-judicial proceedings.

As ever, the Court is concerned not just with abstract principle but with the effectiveness of EU law. States are likely to be just as concerned about these procedural demands as about the substantive rights of patients. As long as the number of patients migrating is small the issue is manageable, but the requirement for quick, objective and transparent decision-making is precisely what may make the right to receive medical services abroad a reality for the many rather than the few. Whether this will happen continues to be the object of research. The factors which are likely to influence this include cultural and linguistic barriers (border areas between states sharing a language may see significant cross-border health care), physical distance (distant states such as the United Kingdom or Greece may see less for this reason), but also the presence of domestic waiting lists (so states with national health systems, which tend to have waiting lists, may have the greatest outflow). Views on the likely extent of patient migration in the future vary widely and remain speculative.[105]

The law developed above needs to be seen alongside Regulation 1408/71/EC on social security coordination.[106] This Regulation provides a right for patients to receive health care in another Member State where it cannot be provided without undue delay at home. The patients in *Watts* and *Müller-Fauré* used this Regulation alongside Article 56. However, the secondary legislation provides for a specific reimbursement regime which can be less advantageous than direct reliance on the Treaty. The Regulation requires patients to be reimbursed at the rate and tariff applicable in the state of treatment. By contrast, Article 56 is concerned primarily to ensure that the patient is no worse off than she would be if she had stayed at home, so it is the domestic tariff and system which is the basis for calculation.

(iv) The proposed Directive on patients' rights

At the time of writing this chapter, a proposed Directive on patient's rights in cross-border health care was nearing adoption. It largely consolidates and embodies the principles of the case law above.[107]

---

[105] See the special edition of the *European Journal of Public Health* on cross-border health care: (1997) 7 *EJPub Health Supplement* 3, 1–50; see e.g. G. France, 'Cross-border Flows of Italian Patients within the European Union' (1997) 7 *EJPub Health Supplement* 3, 18 (Italians were then the largest group of users of cross-border health care in the Union).

[106] See D. Sjindberg Martinsen, 'Social Security Regulation in the EU: The De-Territorialization of Welfare?' in G. de Búrca (ed.), *EU Law and the Welfare State* (Oxford, Oxford University Press, 2005) 89; A. Dawes, 'Bonjour Herr Doctor: National Healthcare Systems, the Internal Market, and Cross-Border Healthcare within the European Union' (2006) 33 *LIEI* 67.

[107] Commission Communication of 2 July 2008, Proposal for a Directive on the application of patients' rights in cross-border health care, COM(2008)414 final. See W. Sauter, 'The Proposed Patients' Rights Directive and the Reform of (Cross-border) Healthcare in the EU' (2009) 36 *LIEI* 109. See also amendments proposed by the Parliament after its first reading in Interinstitutional File 2008/0142 (COD), 30 April 2009.

The Directive addresses different aspects of the rights of patients who wish to receive treatment abroad. Its provisions can be broadly assessed in four groups. First, it provides rights of exit, permitting patients to leave their domestic system. Secondly, it provides rights of entry, ensuring that patients will not be excluded by foreign health providers. Thirdly, it contains facilitating provisions, making movement easier by addressing, for example, the provision of information to patients. Fourthly, it contains a small amount of substantive harmonisation of aspects of health care.

An oddity of the Directive is that it is not to apply to situations to which Regulation 1408/71/EC would apply. This means that where domestic treatment is not available in due time, the Regulation, and Article 56, will apply, not the Directive. The Directive is therefore limited to situations where a patient could be treated within a reasonable time at home, but nevertheless wishes to go abroad. Since the case law prima facie permits a state to refuse authorisation for such treatment, at least when it is hospital treatment, it is not clear how much the Directive will add to the law. Yet, while the Directive adopts the general approach to authorisation that the Court has developed, it appears to have a slightly stricter tone, as if authorisation for treatment abroad may be a little harder to restrict. Articles 7 and 8 set out the principles.

Proposed Directive on patients' rights in cross-border health care, articles 7, 8

Article 7, Non–hospital care
The Member State of affiliation shall not make the reimbursement of the costs of non-hospital care provided in another Member State subject to prior authorisation, where the cost of that care, if it had been provided in its territory, would have been paid for by its social security system.

Article 8

...

3. The Member State of affiliation may provide for a system of prior authorisation for reimbursement by its social security system of the cost of hospital care provided in another Member State where the following conditions are met:
   (a) had the health care been provided in its territory, it would have been assumed by the Member State's social security system; and
   (b) the purpose of the system is to address the consequent outflow of patients due to the implementation of the present Article and to prevent it from seriously undermining, or being likely to seriously undermine:
      (i) the financial balance of the Member State's social security system; and/or
      (ii) the planning and rationalisation carried out in the hospital sector to avoid hospital overcapacity, imbalance in the supply of hospital care and logistical and financial wastage, the maintenance of a balanced medical and hospital service open to all, or the maintenance of treatment capacity or medical competence on the territory of the concerned Member State.
4. The prior authorisation system shall be limited to what is necessary and proportionate to avoid such impact, and shall not constitute a means of arbitrary discrimination.
5. The Member State shall make publicly available all relevant information on the prior authorisation systems introduced pursuant to the provisions of paragraph 3.

These articles reflect the cases, but article 8 seems to highlight the obligation on states to provide evidence that their authorisation schemes really are necessary, as if the evidential threshold is being raised. This raises the possibility that an authorisation scheme might be permitted in one state, which can perhaps show that large number of patients are migrating, while not in another, where distance or language may limit migrant patient numbers.

Rights of entry are addressed primarily in article 5, notably in paragraph (1)(g), which provides that 'patients from other Member States shall enjoy equal treatment with the nationals of the Member State of treatment, including the protection against discrimination provided for according to Community law and national legislation in force in the Member State of treatment'. The Parliament has proposed amending this so that the ban on discrimination against foreign patients covers also discrimination on grounds of racial or ethnic origin, sex, religion or belief, disability, age or sexual orientation.[108] This would be a very powerful amendment that would raise complicated issues. When is the provision of care to be seen as discriminating on one of these grounds? Could it be argued that funding or liberalisation of certain diseases or facilities amounts to discrimination on grounds of sex or sexuality, for example? And would the inclusion of religion and disability require some states to rethink the terms of access to their health care? Everything from female circumcision to transport for patients might conceivably be addressed within such a provision.

Articles 6 and 9 are about the facilitation of migration. They address the procedural and information issues which make rights practical and enforceable. They stick very closely to the judgments of the Court. Article 6 provides that patients will be reimbursed for health care received abroad where they would have had a right to similar health care at home, and that the tariff for reimbursement will reflect the level of costs which would have been assumed by the domestic system. Article 6 also provides that the information on these tariffs will be made clearly available in advance, so that patients can know what their rights are.

Article 9 sets out the procedures applicable to authorisation schemes.

Proposed Directive on patients' rights in cross-border health care, article 9

1. The Member State of affiliation shall ensure that administrative procedures regarding the use of health care in another Member State related to any prior authorisation...are based on objective, non-discriminatory criteria which are published in advance, and which are necessary and proportionate to the objective to be achieved...

2. Any such procedural systems shall be easily accessible and capable of ensuring that requests are dealt with objectively and impartially within time limits set out and made public in advance by the Member States.

3. Member States shall specify in advance and in a transparent way the criteria for refusal of the prior authorisation referred to in Article 8(3).

4. Member States shall, when setting out the time limits within which requests for the use of health care in another Member State must be dealt with, take into account:
   (a) the specific medical condition,
   (b) the patient's degree of pain,

---

[108] Amendments proposed by the Parliament after its first reading, in Interinstitutional File 2008/0142 (COD), 30 April 2009.

(c) the nature of the patient's disability, and

(d) the patient's ability to carry out a professional activity.

5. Member States shall ensure that any administrative decisions regarding the use of health care in another Member State are subject to administrative review and also capable of being challenged in judicial proceedings, which include provision for interim measures.

Finally, article 5 contains a few aspects which can only be seen as limited, but not trivial, harmonisation of the law on health care. It requires Member States to define and enforce clear quality and safety standards for health care on their territory, ensure that providers inform patients about prices, prognoses and risks, and that patients have effective remedies and compensation when things go wrong. Some of these may be more controversial than they seem: patient expectations of information in particular vary from state to state, and demands for information which may seem reasonable to some will be at odds with the prevailing medical culture elsewhere.[109]

7 THE SERVICES DIRECTIVE

Directive 2006/123/EC on services in the internal market ('Services Directive') is the product of one of the most publicised and controversial legislative processes that the Union has enjoyed.[110] The aim of the Directive, which was due to be implemented by 28 December 2009, is to finally break down the many barriers to interstate service provision and establishment. There is a perception that the complexity and sensitivity of many services has meant that case law has not succeeded in this task. States continue to rely on mandatory requirements to obstruct services, and providers must fight for their rights on a case-by-case basis. Yet, the original draft proclaimed its goals too proudly for the Parliament and many Europeans and was not adopted. It explicitly chose a widely applicable country of origin principle as the foundation of the European services market, effectively abolishing the possibility of relying on mandatory requirements to impose restrictions. The spectre of uncontrolled regulatory competition was raised, and of economic interests trampling on non-economic concerns, and in the same period where the Union was struggling with its proposed Constitution this was a step too far for the legislator as well as for the public.[111]

The final version applies to a narrower range of services, with the most sensitive, such as health care, excluded. Moreover, it does not use the words 'country of origin'. However, as will be seen, in substance it does apply such a principle to the services within its scope, and does

---

[109] H. Leenan, *The Rights of Patients in Europe* (The Hague, Kluwer Law and Taxation, 1993), chs. 4, 8 and 9, especially 41–5.

[110] See C. Barnard, 'Unravelling the Services Directive' (2008) 41 *CMLRev.* 323; V. Hatzopoulos, 'Assessing the Services Directive' in C. Barnard (ed.) (2007–08) 10 *CYELS* 215; U. Neergaard, R. Nielsen and L. M. Roseberry (eds.), *The Services Directive: Consequences for the Welfare State and the European Social Model* (Copenhagen, DJØF Publishing, 2008); G. Davies, 'The Services Directive: Extending the Country of Origin Principle and Reforming Public Administration' (2007) 32 *ELRev.* 232.

[111] B. De Witte, *Setting the Scene: How Did Services Get to Bolkestein and Why?*, Mitchell Working Paper No. 3/2007 (2007).; C. Barnard, 'Unravelling the Services Directive' (2008) 41 *CMLRev.* 323, 329–30.

abolish mandatory requirements. The regulatory approach chosen differs from the original version more in rhetoric than in substance.[112]

The Services Directive has three aspects. First, it regulates the administrative and bureaucratic procedures relevant to services and establishment. Secondly, it elaborates the scope of the rights to provide and receive services and to establish in another Member State. Thirdly, it contains coordination provisions allowing and requiring states to exchange the information necessary for an effective regulation of service providers.

(i) Scope of application of the Services Directive

The Directive applies to all services except those specifically excluded. However, these exclusions are so impressively numerous that it is almost easier to think about what the Directive does apply to. A list of examples is provided in recital 33: management consultancy; facilities management; advertising; recruitment services; real estate services; legal and fiscal advice; car rental; travel agencies; and tourism services such as those provided by tour guides or amusement parks.

By contrast, it does not apply to financial services, electronic communications services, transport services, temporary work agencies, health care services, gambling, private security, most social services such as social housing or child care, notaries and bailiffs, or audio-visual services.[113] In addition, there are specific exclusions relating only to services, but not to establishment.[114] These include waste treatment, posted workers, social security, water distribution and the registration of vehicles in other states.

There are also several areas upon which the Services Directive is said not to impinge or not to affect or not to concern; taxation, labour law, fundamental rights, criminal law, cultural or linguistic diversity and the liberalisation of services of general economic interest or private international law.[115] As a description of the Directive, these provisions are rather dubious. It is quite imaginable that the rest of the Directive could have significant implications for these matters. Education provided for remuneration, by example, is not excluded, and the free movement of educational services has obvious implications for cultural diversity. If these provisions are to have meaning, then presumably where the application of the Directive would have implications for e.g. labour law or fundamental rights, this would be a reason to set the Directive aside, or to interpret it differently.

In addition, the Services Directive is expressed to be residual. Article 3(1) provides that if it conflicts with other EU legislation concerning a specific service activity, the specific legislation will take precedence. Examples given include legislation on posted workers, social security and television broadcasting.

The Services Directive's limited scope means that services now fall broadly into one of three categories: those governed by the Directive, those governed by specific legislation and those governed by the case law and Article 56 directly. However, the situation is actually

---

[112] R. Craufurd Smith, *Old Wine in New Bottles? From the 'Country of Origin Principle' to 'Freedom to Provide Services' in the European Community Directive on Services in the Internal Market*, Mitchell Working Paper No. 6/2007 (2007).
[113] Directive 2006/123/EC ('Services Directive'), article 2.
[114] *Ibid.* article 17.
[115] *Ibid.* articles 1–3.

more complex than this. Even if a service falls within the Directive, then it will be necessary to look at the particular measure which is being challenged. It may be that this is addressed by the Directive, in which case that will apply and the case law will be of purely interpretative or contextual relevance. On the other hand, it may be that a service is involved which in itself is within the Directive (say management consultancy), but the measure being challenged involves labour law or taxation or the registration of a vehicle abroad, or is addressed by specific legislation, so that the Directive cannot be relied upon and the cases or the specific legislation are the proper source of law. Given that many cases involve a long list of measures which impede a particular services activity, it is quite likely that some will fall within the Directive and some without, so that we will see a body of case law in which the Directive and Article 56 are used alongside each other. This only increases the likelihood that they will exert an interpretative influence on each other.

(ii) Administrative simplification

Bureaucratic and administrative procedures have long been identified as a major obstacle to the free movement of services. A Commission survey of small and medium-sized enterprises found that 91 per cent of these believed that the highest priority should be given to simplification of these.[116] The time taken to complete the certification of translation, the fees, the non-constructive attitude of the authorities and the difficulties in lodging appeals were all seen as hindering the provision of services.[117]

Article 5(1) of the Services Directive accordingly provides that:

Member States shall examine the procedure and formalities applicable to access to a service activity and to the exercise thereof. Where procedures and formalities examined under this paragraph are not sufficiently simple, Member States shall simplify them.

Articles 6, 7 and 8 go on to provide that service providers must be able to complete all formalities and procedures via a single point of contact, and that this must be possible electronically and at a distance. Thus, the vision of the Directive is that where an activity is legitimately regulated and service providers must complete formalities, instead of going from office to office filling in forms they can simply visit a single website or office and complete everything once.

It is not entirely clear what formalities are included here. 'Access to a service activity' could simply cover explicit authorisations to engage in that activity, for example, the obtaining of a licence or the membership of a professional regulatory body. However, the exercise of a service may involve renting premises, making noise and waste, or using transport and distributing advertising, all of which might involve other authorisations or procedures. Are they all covered? It is even arguable that 'access to a service activity' should be interpreted in the light of the case law to include any formality or procedure which may hinder market access. That could stretch from procedures associated with the buying of a house to those linked to the presence of family members.[118]

---

[116] European Commission, Internal Market and Services Directorate-General, *Internal Market Scoreboard November 2000* (Brussels, 2000) 10–12.
[117] European Commission, *The State of the Internal Market for Services*, COM(2004)441 final, 18.
[118] See Barnard, above n. 110, 336–40.

It appears that these provisions do not just apply to foreign service providers or established persons, but also to the national starting a business in her own state.[119] She is also engaging in a service activity in that state. In any case, even if this is not the case as a matter of law it will be as a matter of practice. States are unlikely to introduce a new streamlined bureaucracy for foreigners while imposing the old model on their own citizens. These provisions are therefore a limited harmonisation of the government-citizen relationship, changing the balance of power towards the citizen, and moving the mode of interaction from face-to-face towards the electronic.[120]

(iii) Right to provide and receive services

The Services Directive has a Chapter on establishment and one on services. The establishment provisions are discussed in Chapter 20.[121] The central provision on the free movement of services is article 16.

Services Directive, article 16

Freedom to provide services

1. Member States shall respect the right of providers to provide services in a Member State other than that in which they are established. The Member State in which the service is provided shall ensure free access to and free exercise of a service activity within its territory.

   Member States shall not make access to or exercise of a service activity in their territory subject to compliance with any requirements which do not respect the following principles:
   (a) non-discrimination: the requirement may be neither directly nor indirectly discriminatory with regard to nationality or, in the case of legal persons, with regard to the Member State in which they are established;
   (b) necessity: the requirement must be justified for reasons of public policy, public security, public health or the protection of the environment;
   (c) proportionality: the requirement must be suitable for attaining the objective pursued, and must not go beyond what is necessary to attain that objective...

Examples of prohibited requirements are included in article 16(2) and include the obligation to have an establishment within the Member State, to register with a professional body in that state, or to possess an identity document issued by that state.

This article therefore applies to any public measure imposing conditions on access to or exercise of a service activity. It seems plausible that this should be understood to encompass the same public measures which are considered to be 'restrictions on the free movement of services' in the Court's case law.[122] In that case, article 16 reproduces the case law with one striking difference: restrictions may only be justified by public policy, security, health or the environment. Other possible justifications, such as consumer protection, are no longer possible.

---

[119] Davies, above n. 110. See also Barnard, above n. 110, 341–2.
[120] Davies, above n. 110.
[121] See pp. 867–9.
[122] Barnard, above n. 110; see pp. 792–7.

This is not entirely certain. In fact, article 16 largely reproduces the words of the Treaty, which also does not mention mandatory requirements. This did not prevent the Court discovering them to be implicit. Why should it not do the same here? This is certainly a possibility, but article 16 needs to be contrasted with article 9 on establishment, which specifically includes the possibility to restrict establishment for an 'overriding reason relating to the public interest'. This suggests persuasively that article 16 is intended to be narrower, and not to encompass public interest derogations beyond the short list in article 16(1)(b).

The impact of this may be put in perspective: state attempts to rely on mandatory requirements usually fail except where the issue is serious, in which case public policy can usually be invoked. However, it remains the case that article 16 establishes a strong country of origin principle, with very limited exceptions, despite the political fears which this has always attracted, and despite the fact that the Court has never felt able to go quite so far.[123] The greatest substantive innovation of the Services Directive is that the judicially created doctrine of mandatory requirements is legislatively abolished as far as the free movement of services is concerned.

(iv) Administrative cooperation

The risks to the consumer which home state regulation entails are twofold. One is that the consumer will contract with a foreign provider, not realising that this provider is subject to laxer regulation than providers established in the consumer's home state. They may not receive the quality of service they expect from the type of provider they expected. The second risk is that providers in fact slip through the supervisory net. Their home state regulators have little idea exactly what the provider is doing when providing services abroad, and may not be very interested, while host state regulators are prohibited from interfering and imposing their own rules.

These fears are addressed by the later parts of the Services Directive. The Chapter on quality of services requires Member States to ensure that providers make a range of information available to service recipients, from the legal form and address of the provider to their indemnity insurance, where relevant, so that the recipient can have a clear idea of exactly what she is paying for, and from whom.[124] It also, quietly but importantly, requires Member States to remove all total prohibitions on commercial communication (broadly, advertising) by the regulated professions, although it permits continued regulation of this.[125] The philosophy is, just as with the Court's consumer case law, that consumer protection should primarily be achieved by clear and fair communication between all parties.[126]

Chapter VI of the Services Directive addresses administrative cooperation between national supervisory authorities. It requires these bodies to communicate with each other about service providers, providing information on those who might be a threat to recipients, for example because they are struck off or convicted or bankrupt.[127] This may raise human rights issues where concerns are communicated that later turn out to be misplaced: getting off the watchlist in other Member States will probably be harder than getting onto it. There is also a specific

---

[123] Cf. Hatzopoulos, above n. 110.
[124] Services Directive, article 22.
[125] *Ibid.* article 24.
[126] See pp. 768–9.
[127] Services Directive, articles 28–33.

obligation on authorities not to relax their supervision of those established in their state merely because services are being provided in another state.[128] The logic of home state regulation requires that national authorities now protect the interests of consumers in other states.

The supervisory challenge raised by cross-border services is also addressed by a special emergency procedure, provided for in articles 18 and 35. This permits host states to take measures necessary for the safety of consumers, in exceptional circumstances. However, rather than acting unilaterally against service providers, they are to follow a mutual assistance procedure in which they ask the state of establishment to investigate the service provider and take appropriate measures. The state of establishment is obliged to do this 'within the shortest possible period'.[129] The host state may then take additional measures, but only if it can show that the measures taken by the state of establishment are insufficient. The Commission is to be informed, and will take a decision either confirming or rejecting the host state measures.

This procedure is an attempt to reconcile the country of origin principle with high levels of service safety. It concedes that host states need to be able to guarantee service safety on their territory, but creates a communicative and cooperative mechanism which attempts to achieve this goal as much as possible via home state control.

FURTHER READING

M. Andenas and W.-H. Roth (eds.), *Services and Free Movement in EU Law* (Oxford, Oxford University Press, 2002)

C. Barnard, 'Unravelling the Services Directive' (2008) 41 *Common Market Law Review* 323 *Employment Rights, Free Movement under the EC Treaty and the Services Directive*, Mitchell Working Paper No. 5/08 (2008)

A. Biondi, 'Recurring Cycles in the Internal Market: Some Reflections on the Free Movement of Services' in A. Arnull, P. Eeckhout and T. Tridimas (eds.), *Continuity and Change in EU Law* (Oxford, Oxford University Press, 2008) 228

G. Davies, *The Process and Side-effects of Harmonisation of European Welfare States*, Jean Monnet Working Paper No. 02/06 (2006)

T. Do and V. Hatzopoulos, 'The Case Law of the ECJ Concerning the Free Movement of Services 2000–2005' (2006) 43 *Common Market Law Review* 923

V. Hatzopoulos, 'Killing National Health Systems but Healing Patients?' (2002) 39 *Common Market Law Review* 683

T. Hervey, 'Buy Baby: The European Union and Regulation of Human Reproduction' (1998) 18 *Oxford Journal of Legal Studies* 207

G. Marenco, 'The Notion of Restriction on the Freedom of Establishment and Provision of Services in the Case-law of the Court' (1991) 11 *Yearbook of European Law* 111

J. Snell, *Goods and Services in EC Law: A Study of the Relationship Between the Freedoms* (Oxford, Oxford University Press, 2002)

B. De Witte, *Setting the Scene: How Did Services Get to Bolkestein and Why?*, Mitchell Working Paper No. 3/07 (2007)

---

[128] *Ibid.* article 30.
[129] *Ibid.* article 35(2).

20

The Pursuit of an Occupation in Another Member State

CONTENTS

1 INTRODUCTION

This chapter is about the right to pursue an occupation in another Member State. It is organised as follows.

Section 2 outlines the scope of this right. Article 45 TFEU provides a right to work in other Member States, while Article 49 TFEU provides a right to self-employment in other

Member States. While these are separate Treaty provisions, the Court of Justice increasingly interprets them in parallel. Beneficiaries are EU citizens (and companies in the case of Article 49) who engage in a more than marginal economic activity with some cross-border element. If the subject lives in one state and works in another, this is sufficiently cross-border.

Section 3 considers national measures which restrict access to an occupation. In the past, certain professions were often restricted to nationals, but more recent cases tend to concern refusals to recognise foreign qualifications, or measures which make establishment of a business or professional practice subject to various requirements: these may be to do with the legal form of the business, the qualifications of the owner or shareholders, local economic need, or limits on the number of establishments which one person or company may run. The Court's approach, as ever, is to permit only those justified by the public interest and proportionate. However, because access restrictions have the effect of excluding some people from labour and business markets, the Court has been strict, and has been prepared to review even non-discriminatory national rules.

Section 4 analyses restrictions on the exercise of an occupation. Discrimination in pay and conditions, in union rights and in tax benefits, are all prohibited by case law and secondary legislation. The Court also examines measures critically for proportionality where they are equally applicable but tend to protect incumbents and disadvantage market entrants. However, it has been reluctant to engage with national measures whose only effect is to hinder economic effect generally, without any inequality in their impact.

Section 5 discusses the free movement of companies. Freedom of establishment enables companies to incorporate in one state while doing all their business in another. They can then avoid burdensome company laws in their state of business. Member States have argued that this is an abuse of free movement, but the Court disagrees. It is part of free movement that economic actors can choose to establish themselves in the jurisdiction most advantageous for them. This raises considerable risks of a company law 'race to the bottom'.

Section 6 is about the Services Directive, which also addresses establishment. Its Chapter on establishment addresses a limited number of national measures, but takes a similar approach to the case law; states may not discriminate, and measures restricting the business activities of established persons must be justified and proportionate. However, it appears that the Directive applies these principles not only where the measures impact on cross-border establishment, but generally, so that those starting a business in their own state will also benefit.

2 TAKING UP AND PURSUIT OF AN OCCUPATION IN ANOTHER MEMBER STATE

A central feature of any market is the possibility for individuals and companies to relocate to any part of its territory which offers them economic opportunities. Two economic freedoms in EU law are pivotal to the realisation of this. The first is free movement of workers, for which the central provision is Article 45 TFEU.

Article 45 TFEU

1. Freedom of movement for workers shall be secured within the Union.
2. Such freedom of movement shall entail the abolition of any discrimination based on nationality between workers of the Member States as regards employment, remuneration and other conditions of work and employment.
3. It shall entail the right, subject to limitations justified on grounds of public policy, public security or public health:
   (a) to accept offers of employment actually made;
   (b) to move freely within the territory of Member States for this purpose;
   (c) to stay in a Member State for the purpose of employment in accordance with the provisions governing the employment of nationals of that State laid down by law, regulation or administrative action;
   (d) to remain in the territory of a Member State after having been employed in that State, subject to conditions which shall be embodied in regulations to be drawn up by the Commission.
4. The provisions of this Article shall not apply to employment in the public service.

The second freedom is that of establishment. The central provision governing this is Article 49 TFEU.

Article 49 TFEU

Within the framework of the provisions set out below, restrictions on the freedom of establishment of nationals of a Member State in the territory of another Member State shall be prohibited. Such prohibition shall also apply to restrictions on the setting-up of agencies, branches or subsidiaries by nationals of any Member State established in the territory of any Member State.

Freedom of establishment shall include the right to take up and pursue activities as self-employed persons and to set up and manage undertakings, in particular companies or firms within the meaning of the second paragraph of Article 54, under the conditions laid down for its own nationals by the law of the country where such establishment is effected, subject to the provisions of the Chapter relating to capital.

An important difference between the Articles is that Article 45 only applies to natural persons, whereas Article 49 also applies to legal persons such as companies.

Regarding natural persons, the reason for treating the employed and self-employed separately is not obvious, and this chapter will suggest that the two groups are best considered in parallel. Their separateness in the Treaty is a historical artefact which does not fully correspond to the current state of the law or of society.

The origins of the distinction lie in the circumstances surrounding the original EEC Treaty. At a time of full employment, there were no concerns about the labour market and thus an assumption that free movement of labour was unproblematic. By contrast, there was concern that free movement might undermine professionals, such as lawyers, accountants and doctors, much of whose activity was carried out on a self-employed basis. Legislative harmonisation was thus seen as a precondition for free movement of the self-employed, and provision was made in the EEC Treaty for the Commission to propose a General Programme for the Abolition of Restrictions on Freedom of Establishment,[1] and for legislation to be adopted allowing for mutual recognition of diplomas.[2]

However, in today's world the distinction appears anachronistic. People move interchangeably between employment and self-employment, each being economically substitutable for the other. In addition, companies have a range of contracts with individuals working for them, of which only some fit easily into the traditional model of the contract of employment.

Moreover, the legal distinctiveness of the two categories has been eroded by EU citizenship. Regulation 1612/68/EEC confers on workers certain advantages and restrictions, most notably in the field of social benefits, but does not extend these to the self-employed.[3] These rights provided the most significant added value to the status of worker. However, both workers and the self-employed are EU citizens, and this fact has been used in recent years by both the Court of Justice and the EU legislator to assimilate their rights. In particular, the Citizenship Directive ensures that rights of entry, residence and expulsion, and rights to social benefits, are now the same for all categories of economically active migrant.[4] The distinction between economically active and non-active is more important today than the distinction between employed and self-employed.

This constitutional and social convergence of the worker and the self-employed person may have influenced the Court. A central argument of this chapter is that Articles 45 and 49 are being interpreted in a similar manner, and using the same concepts and limits. In particular, both these provisions are being interpreted as being part of a more general right to pursue an occupation in another Member State.

Nevertheless, the free movement of persons, established or employed, cannot be understood in isolation from the free movement of services. The situations to which they are relevant often overlap: a measure which makes service provision from state X to other states harder will deter establishment in state X, and vice versa. Unsurprisingly, therefore, the Court has interpreted the law on services, establishment and workers largely in parallel. This chapter is therefore complemented by the chapter on free movement of services. In particular, the discussion of horizontal application of Article 56 is just as relevant to Articles 45 and 49,[5] while the discussion of abuse later in this chapter is applicable to the law on services.[6]

(i) Employment and self-employment

Article 45 governs movement of the employed, whereas Article 49 performs the same function for the self-employed. The distinction between the two was explored in some depth in *Trojani*. Trojani, a French man, was given accommodation in a Salvation Army hostel in Brussels and some pocket money, in return for which he carried out approximately thirty hours of work each week for the hostel. This arrangement had a social purpose, as it was perceived to be

---

[1] Article 50 TFEU. The programme is contained in OJ Spec. edn, Second Series, IX, 7.
[2] Article 53 TFEU.
[3] [1968] OJ Spec. edn L257/2, 475.
[4] See p. 448.
[5] See pp. 797–803.
[6] See p. 852.

a rehabilitation programme. After two years, Trojani approached the Belgian authorities for social assistance. On refusal, he argued that he was a worker under Article 45 and therefore entitled to social assistance.

Case C-456/02 *Trojani v Centre public d'aide sociale* [2004] ECR 1–7573

15. ... the concept of 'worker' within the meaning of Article [45 TFEU] has a specific Community meaning and must not be interpreted narrowly. Any person who pursues activities which are real and genuine, to the exclusion of activities on such a small scale as to be regarded as purely marginal and ancillary, must be regarded as a 'worker'. The essential feature of an employment relationship is, according to that case law, that for a certain period of time a person performs services for and under the direction of another person in return for which he receives remuneration ...

16. Moreover, neither the *sui generis* nature of the employment relationship under national law, nor the level of productivity of the person concerned, the origin of the funds from which the remuneration is paid or the limited amount of the remuneration can have any consequence in regard to whether or not the person is a worker for the purposes of Community law ...

17. With respect more particularly to establishing whether the condition of the pursuit of real and genuine activity for remuneration is satisfied, the national court must base its examination on objective criteria and make an overall assessment of all the circumstances of the case relating to the nature both of the activities concerned and of the employment relationship at issue ...

18. In this respect, the Court has held that activities cannot be regarded as a real and genuine economic activity if they constitute merely a means of rehabilitation or reintegration for the persons concerned ...

19. However, that conclusion can be explained only by the particular characteristics of the case in question,[7] which concerned the situation of a person who, by reason of his addiction to drugs, had been recruited on the basis of a national law intended to provide work for persons who, for an indefinite period, are unable, by reason of circumstances related to their situation, to work under normal conditions ...

20. In the present case, as is apparent from the decision making the reference, Mr Trojani performs, for the Salvation Army and under its direction, various jobs for approximately 30 hours a week, as part of a personal reintegration programme, in return for which he receives benefits in kind and some pocket money.

21. Under the relevant provisions [the national law] the Salvation Army has the task of receiving, accommodating and providing psycho-social assistance appropriate to the recipients in order to promote their autonomy, physical well-being and reintegration in society. For that purpose it must agree with each person concerned a personal reintegration programme setting out the objectives to be attained and the means to be employed to attain them.

22. Having established that the benefits in kind and money provided by the Salvation Army to Mr Trojani constitute the consideration for the services performed by him for and under the direction of the hostel, the national court has thereby established the existence of the constituent elements of any paid employment relationship, namely subordination and the payment of remuneration.

23. For the claimant in the main proceedings to have the status of worker, however, the national court, in the assessment of the facts which is within its exclusive jurisdiction, would have to establish that the paid activity in question is real and genuine.

---

[7] Case 344/87 *Bettray* v *Staatssecretaris van Justitie* [1989] ECR 1621.

24. The national court must in particular ascertain whether the services actually performed by Mr Trojani are capable of being regarded as forming part of the normal labour market.

For that purpose, account may be taken of the status and practices of the hostel, the content of the social reintegration programme, and the nature and details of performance of the services. ...

27. ... the freedom of establishment provided for in Articles [49 TFEU] to [54 TFEU] includes only the right to take up and pursue all types of self-employed activity, to set up and manage undertakings, and to set up agencies, branches or subsidiaries ... Paid activities are therefore excluded.

Trojani provides a useful and oft-cited summary of the preceding case law on the application of Article 45. The extract above should also be read alongside the following section.

The judgment makes clear that where a migrant works under the direction of another person in return for payment, she is regarded as an employee and falls under Article 45. The essence of a worker is that she has a boss and a wage. By contrast, if she earns her living independently through supplying goods or services to other persons, she is treated as self-employed and falls under Article 49.

(ii) Performance of significant economic activity in another Member State

To fall within either Articles 45 or 49, the migrant must be engaging in activity which is economic in nature. Economic activity involves her 'satisfying a request by the beneficiary in return for consideration'.[8] In the case of employment, the migrant will be receiving consideration from the employer and providing services under the direction of the employer. In the case of the self-employed, the remuneration is usually received from the customer for whom the service is carried out.

The Court of Justice has enlarged this notion of economic activity in two ways. In *Steynmann*, a migrant lived in a Bhagwan community and received food and lodging and pocket money in return for doing tasks and duties within the community. The Court accepted that remuneration need not be financial, but could be in kind, so that Steynmann was a worker in the Treaty sense.[9]

Relationships involving an element of guardianship or social welfare may also constitute economic activity. Training will be considered economic activity if it is regarded as practical preparation directly related to the actual pursuit of an occupation, and the training period itself takes the form of economic activity.[10] Similarly, jobs which would otherwise be unviable, sponsored with public funds to enable individuals to enter or re-enter working life, have been classified as economic activity.[11] Within such schemes, however, the person must have been chosen on the basis of their ability to perform a particular activity. In *Bettray*,[12] a Dutch

---

[8] Case C-268/99 *Jany* v *Staatssecretaris van Justitie* [2001] ECR I-8615.

[9] Case 196/87 *Steymann* v *Staatssecretaris van Justitie* [1988] ECR 6159. See also Case C-456/02 *Trojani* v *Centre public d'aide sociale* [2004] ECR 1-7573.

[10] Case C-109/04 *Kranemann* v *Land Nordrhein-Westfalen* [2005] ECR I-2421.

[11] Case C-1/97 *Birden* v *Stadtgemeinde Bremen* [1998] ECR I-7747.

[12] Case 344/87 *Bettray* v *Staatssecretaris van Justitie* [1989] ECR 1621.

drug rehabilitation scheme which offered individuals employment as part of the treatment of weaning them off drugs was not considered economic activity. It was regarded instead as a form of treatment because the jobs were adapted to the physical and mental capabilities of each person.

In *Raccanelli*, the Court found that a PhD student may or may not be a worker.[13] It depends on whether the key elements of the worker relationship are present: remuneration and subordination. A grant may count as remuneration, but whether the researcher is under the direction of the faculty in question, or is independent in their activities, is a question of fact for the national court.

To fall within the provisions, the degree of economic activity must be more than minimal. In *Levin*, the Court ruled that to fall within Article 45 a migrant had to pursue 'effective and genuine activities, to the exclusion of activities on such a small scale as to be purely marginal and ancillary'.[14] But this does not exclude work under a short-term contract,[15] part-time work or low-paid work. In the same case the Court offered an interpretation of Article 45 in its broader context which still stands:

> 15. ... Since part-time employment, although it may provide an income lower than what is considered to be the minimum required for subsistence, constitutes for a large number of persons an effective means of improving their living conditions, the effectiveness of Community law would be jeopardized if the enjoyment of rights conferred by the principle of freedom of movement for workers were reserved solely to persons engaged in full-time employment and earning, as a result, a wage at least equivalent to the guaranteed minimum wage in the sector under consideration.

Following this, in *Kempf*,[16] the Court held that a part-time music teacher who gave twelve hours of lessons a week was doing sufficient work to be covered by Article 45, even though she earned so little that she was forced to apply for benefits.

The minimum threshold for engaging Article 49 is a little more complex. In some cases the question may be whether an individual is established in a host state or providing services, and the intensity and scale of their economic activity will be relevant to this determination. This was discussed in Chapter 19.[17] However, if an individual is resident in a host state, so that there is no question that this is the centre of her activities, then the question may arise, as with Article 45, whether those activities are of a sufficient scale to classify her as economically active. The only words of guidance that the Court has provided are in *Gebhard*, in which it said that:

> 25. The concept of establishment within the meaning of the Treaty is therefore a very broad one, allowing a Community national to participate, on a stable and continuous basis, in the economic life of a Member State other than his State of origin and to profit therefrom, so contributing to economic and social interpenetration within the Community in the sphere of activities as self-employed persons ... [18]

---

[13] Case C-94/07 *Raccanelli v Max-Planck-Gesellschaft zur Förderung der Wissenschaften* [2008] ECR I-5939.
[14] Case 53/81 *Levin v Staatssecretaris van Justitie* [1982] ECR 1035.
[15] Case C-413/01 *Franca Ninni-Orasche v Bundesminister für Wissenschaft, Verkehr und Kunst* [2003] ECR I-13187.
[16] Case 139/85 *Kempf v Staatssecretaris van Justitie* [1986] ECR 1741.
[17] See pp. 787–8.
[18] Case C-55/94 *Gebhard v Consiglio dell'ordine degli avvocati e procuratori di Milano* [1995] ECR1-4165.

This was intended to distinguish establishment from services, but may also indicate the minimum criteria for establishment per se. There must be some non-trivial stability and continuity in the activities: one job performed for one client is not enough. In substance, it is suggested that the minimum level of economic activity will be interpreted in the same way as for Article 45.

(iii) The cross-border element

In an analogous manner to the other freedoms, Articles 45 and 49 apply only to work or establishment with a cross-border aspect.[19] The usual situation is where the individual physically relocates to another Member State. However, Article 45 also includes the situation where the worker works in their home state, but lives in another. In *Hartmann*, a German worker living and working in Germany moved house, but not job, to France. The Court found that this was enough to give him the status of migrant worker.[20] In similar fashion, the Court has stated that where the economic activity of a person or company based in one Member State is entirely or principally directed towards the territory of another Member State, they fall within Article 49.[21]

The cross-border economic activity need not already be underway to engage Articles 45 and 49. Measures which prevent it starting are also caught, provided their effect is not too hypothetical.[22] These Articles therefore involve not merely the right to pursue an occupation in another Member State but also the right to *take up* that occupation. Article 45 therefore protects both workers and work-seekers.[23] In like vein, Article 49 covers restrictions on those who are self-employed as well as restrictions preventing EU citizens wishing to take up self-employment, but not yet self-employed. For example, in *Reyners*,[24] a Dutch national successfully challenged a Belgian measure permitting only Belgian nationals to practise as advocates in Belgium, which was preventing him practising as a lawyer in that state.

(iv) Towards an overarching right to pursue an occupation in another Member State

The common themes present in employment and self-employment, and the Court's clear inclination towards parallel development of the four freedoms,[25] suggest room for an explicit overarching right to take up and pursue an occupation in another Member State, which encompasses and structures both Articles 45 and 49. Such reasoning is present in the recent case of *Danish Company Cars*.[26] To avoid tax evasion, Denmark prohibited Danish residents

---

[19] Case 175/78 *Saunders* [1979] ECR 1129; Case C-65/96 *Uecker and Jacquet* [1997] ECR I-3171; Case C-107/94 *Asscher* [1994] ECR I-1137. See also pp. 462–4, 755–6 and 788–90.

[20] Case C-212/05 *Hartmann v Freistaat Bayern* [2007] ECR I-6303; see also Case C-336/96 *Gilly v Directeur des services fiscaux du Bas-Rhin* [1998] ECR I-2793; Case C-213/03 *Geven v Land Nordrhein-Westfalen* [2007] ECR I-6347; A. Tryonidou, 'In Search of the Aim of the EC Free Movement of Persons Provisions: Has the Court of Justice Missed the Point?' (2009) 46 *Common Market Law Review* 1591.

[21] Case 205/84 *Commission v Germany (German insurance)* [1986] ECR 3755.

[22] See pp. 839–44.

[23] Case 53/81 *Levin v Staatssecretaris van Justitie* [1982] ECR 1035; Case C-281/98 *Roman Angonese v Cassa di Risparmio di Bolzano SpA* [2000] ECR I-4139.

[24] Case 2/74 *Reyners v Belgium* [1974] ECR 631.

[25] See A. Tryfonidou, 'Further Steps on the Road to Convergence Among the Market Freedoms' (2010) 35 *ELRev.* 35.

[26] For similar reasoning in respect of Article 56 TFEU, see Case 143/87 *Stanton v INASTI* [1988] ECR 3877, paras. 13 and 14.

from using company cars registered abroad for private purposes in Denmark. The Commission considered this to penalise those working abroad and therefore to breach Article 45, as Danish residents could use company cars registered in Denmark for private purposes. The Danish government argued that the measure fell outside Article 45 as this article related solely to conditions of employment.

Case C-464/02 *Commission v Denmark (Danish Company Cars)* [2005] ECR I-7929

34. The provisions of the Treaty on freedom of movement for persons are intended to facilitate the pursuit by Community citizens of occupational activities of all kinds throughout the Community, and preclude measures which might place Community citizens at a disadvantage when they wish to pursue an economic activity in the territory of another Member State ...

35. Provisions which preclude or deter a national of a Member State from leaving his country of origin in order to exercise his right to freedom of movement therefore constitute an obstacle to that freedom even if they apply without regard to the nationality of the workers concerned ...

36. However, in order to be capable of constituting such an obstacle, they must affect access of workers to the labour market ...

37. The manner in which an activity is pursued is liable also to affect access to that activity. Consequently, legislation which relates to the conditions in which an economic activity is pursued may constitute an obstacle to freedom of movement within the meaning of that case law.

38. It follows that the Danish legislation at issue in this case is not excluded from the outset from the scope of Article [45 TFEU].

The case is, like *Alpine Investments, Ruffler, Bosman*[27] and the case law on Article 35, about a restriction on exit, imposed by the home state. These are legally interesting because they can rarely be seen in terms of nationality discrimination. As a result, the Court is often forced into innovative legal formulations, usually relying on the fact that a measure makes cross-border movement less attractive than staying at home.[28] Accordingly, in the extract above the central objection is that the measure discouraged Danes from going abroad to work, since a job abroad would be relatively less advantageous for them. In paragraph 34, the Court places this in a cross-category context. The extract implies a right to pursue an occupation abroad which encompasses both Articles 45 and 49, and extends beyond mere equal treatment.

As a matter of convenience, the right to pursue an occupation abroad can be considered to have two aspects: the right to *take up* economic activities and the right to *pursue* these activities. This distinction often occurs in the language of the Court,[29] and is useful in understanding the kinds of situations which may arise.

---

[27] Case C-384/93 *Alpine Investments v Minister van Financiën* [1995] ECR I-1141; Case C-544/07 *Rüffler*, Judgment of 23 April 2009; Case C-415/93 *Union Royale Belge des Sociétés de Football Association and Others v Bosman and Others* [1995] ECR I-4921.

[28] See pp. 460–2, 780–2 and 793.

[29] Case 197/84 *Steinhauser v City of Biarritz* [1985] ECR 1819; Case C-311/06 *Consiglio Nazionale degli Ingegneri v Ministero della Giustizia and Marco Cavallera*, Judgment of 29 January 2009; Case C-464/02 *Commission v Denmark (Danish Company Cars)* [2005] ECR I-7929.

The right to take up activities concerns entry onto the market of another Member State. At its crudest, this would capture restrictions on residence in another Member State. It would also comprise anything that might prevent the migrant from commencing activity in that Member State. This would include restrictions on secondary establishment, which prevent traders with a central place of business opening up branches, agencies or subsidiaries in other Member States, restrictions on entering the labour market, such as prerequisites that one have a licence or join a trade union, which may be difficult to meet or, finally, requirements that a migrant have a qualification before she can pursue a particular activity. Any of these deny the migrant entry on to the market.

Restrictions on the pursuit of economic activity are restrictions on activities of the migrant once she is on the market of the host Member State. They might involve discriminatory conditions of employment, discriminatory planning restrictions for the location of a business, or discrimination in the tax system or in access to credit. They may also include non-discriminatory regulation of economic activity which, because it imposes disproportionate burdens, hinders that activity.[30]

The distinction between restrictions on the taking up of activities and restrictions on the pursuit of activities is not always clear-cut. There are restrictions on the taking up of an activity that also apply to the pursuit of that activity. Qualifications are a case in point. They are necessary for entry onto a market as certain activities cannot be taken up without them. Yet, possession of qualifications will often also go to the pursuit of economic activity as they strengthen the trader's position in the marketplace by demonstrating recognition of a particular expertise. In a corollary manner, as *Danish Company Cars* suggests, restrictions on the pursuit of economic activity may be so onerous for the trader that they make it unviable for her to enter the market, and so perform the same role as restrictions on the taking up of activity.

These arguments should not be allowed to disguise the fact that in most cases the distinction is real and useful. It is different to be told by a state 'You cannot practise that profession' than to be permitted to do so but to find that some of the state's regulation is burdensome. The first is directed at the actor, the second at the activity. More important, the first kind of restriction is far more exclusionary. A measure which prevents the taking up of an occupation is therefore something that justifies intensive judicial scrutiny. Indeed, measures which exclude some players from the market have always concerned the Court, as the case law on goods and services also shows.[31]

Moreover, restrictions on taking up an occupation do not always lend themselves to a discrimination-based analysis. A comparison with other market participants is not always useful nor is it appropriate for an actor who cannot participate herself, while a comparison with other potential market participants is often far-fetched or evidentially challenging. There is thus a particularly strong case for restrictions on the right to take up activities falling within Articles 45 and 49 even where no discrimination has been shown.

The non-discrimination principle does become central, however, where restrictions on the pursuit of economic activities are concerned. It protects the competitive position of the migrant within the host state by ensuring that she is treated in a neutral manner vis-à-vis a state's own nationals. The non-discrimination principle safeguards the ideal that the migrant should

---

[30] See pp. 853–60.
[31] See pp. 774 and 795–6.

prosper or fail in a single market only on the basis of the competitiveness of her activities. The application of the Treaty provisions to discriminatory restrictions on the pursuit of economic activity is, therefore, also uncontentious. By contrast, the arguments about whether Articles 45 and 49 should cover non-discriminatory restrictions on the pursuit of economic activity are more finely balanced. Such restrictions go not to market access or the competitive position of non-nationals, but to the general level of regulation within a Member State, and whether this is compatible with the Treaty. Extending Articles 45 and 49 to cover such measures would have significant market liberalising effects, but would also result in the extension of the reach of these Articles into almost all areas of regulation of economic life. Legislation as diverse as that covering general labour, the environment, consumers and health and safety could all be challenged on the grounds that it limits in some way the economic activity pursued by a migrant in the host state. There is a significant danger of overreaching here, with EU law being perceived, particularly from a local perspective, as being both excessively deregulatory and excessively intrusive. For this reason, the Court of Justice has found it fairly easy to deal with the first two types of restriction: non-discriminatory restrictions on the taking up of activity and discriminatory restrictions on the pursuit of activity. By contrast, as we shall see, its case law on non-discriminatory restrictions on the pursuit of economic activity has been contradictory and uncertain. We now turn to each of these lines of reasoning.

3 RESTRICTIONS ON THE TAKING UP OF AN OCCUPATION

(i) Discriminatory restrictions on the taking up of an activity

In some instances, Member States have reserved certain occupations to their own nationals. Because of the obvious discriminatory intent of such measures, the Court has chosen to strike them down as a violation of the non-discrimination principle. In *Reyners*,[32] a Belgian requirement that one have Belgian nationality to practise as an advocate was therefore condemned as a breach of Article 49 on the grounds that it discriminated against other EU nationals. Similar reasoning has been applied to companies,[33] and in respect of Article 45. In *French Merchant Navy*,[34] a French restriction limiting the proportion of non-national French merchant navy employees was found to breach Article 45 on the grounds of its discriminatory nature. In *Angonese*, a bank in the German-speaking part of Italy made employment conditional upon a particular local certificate of bilingualism, refusing to accept other evidence.[35] The Court found this a violation of Article 45 because of its discriminatory effect on access to the posts, notwithstanding that instead of a public measure, a rule imposed by a private company was in issue. Article 45 is general, and applies equally to private and public employers and measures.

In addition, Regulation 1612/68/EC, article 3(1) declares Member State laws or practices invalid whose exclusive aim or effect is to limit the access of non-nationals to employment.[36] The provision nuances this prohibition, however, by explicitly permitting language requirements

---

[32] Case 2/74 *Reyners v Belgium* [1974] ECR 631.
[33] Case C-299/02 *Commission v Netherlands* [2004] ECR I-9761.
[34] Case 167/73 *Commission v France (French Merchant Navy)* [1974] ECR 359.
[35] Case C-281/98 *Roman Angonese v Cassa di Risparmio di Bolzano SpA* [2000] ECR I-4139.
[36] Cf. posted workers in a recent situation: C. Barnard, '"British Jobs for British Workers": The Lindsey Oil Refinery Dispute and the Future of Local Labour Clauses in an Integrated EU Market' (2009) 38 *ILJ* 245.

where the linguistic knowledge is required by reason of the nature of the post. Although these may adversely affect foreign applicants, they will not be treated as prohibited discrimination. In *Groener*,[37] a Dutch teacher challenged an Irish requirement that all full-time teachers in Irish state colleges were proficient in the Irish language. She argued that this did not fall within the exception, as teaching could be done in English. The Court nevertheless found the requirement to be lawful. It stated that any requirement of linguistic proficiency would be lawful if it was necessary for the implementation of a policy to protect and promote a language which is both the national language and the first official language, and the restriction was neither disproportionate to the aim pursued nor unnecessarily discriminatory towards other Member State nationals. In this case, the restriction was not disproportionate, as education was seen by the Court as central to the implementation of such a policy. In this instance, education included not merely teaching but also participation in the daily life of the school and the forging of relations with pupils. In such circumstances, the Court considered that even though teaching did not have to be done in Irish, the language could be central to other parts of school life.[38]

The vast majority of restrictions on the taking up of activity in another Member State are not explicitly directed at foreigners. In such instances, the Court looks at the restrictive effects of the measure rather than its discriminatory effects. We look at these below.

(ii) Restrictions on access to occupational activities and labour markets

Outside the small world of EU lawyers, arguably the most famous case in the history of EU law is that of *Bosman*, which revolutionalised the football industry. Bosman played football for Liège in Belgium. Following the end of his contract, relations between him and the club broke down. Under the footballing rules of the time, the club held on to the registration card that entitled him to play as a footballer. They sought to transfer him, with his consent, to Dunkerque in France. The sale broke down because there were doubts about Dunkerque's solvency and its ability to pay the transfer fee demanded by Liège. Despite his being out of contract, Liège refused to allow Bosman to move to Dunkerque until its demand for a transfer fee had been met. Bosman was therefore unable to work as a footballer: Liège would not use him, but they would not let him go to another team. He challenged the transfer system operating in football, which allowed clubs to restrict the movement of players post-contract by holding on to their registration card, arguing it violated Article 45.

Case C-415/93 Union Royale Belge des Sociétés de Football Association and Others v Bosman and Others [1995] ECR 1-4921

94. … the provisions of the Treaty relating to freedom of movement for persons are intended to facilitate the pursuit by Community citizens of occupational activities of all kinds throughout the Community, and preclude measures which might place Community citizens at a disadvantage when they wish to pursue an economic activity in the territory of another Member State …

---

[37] Case 379/87 *Groener v Minister for Education and the City of Dublin Vocational Educational Committee* [1989] ECR 3967.

[38] See also Case C-424/97 *Salomone Haim v Kassenzahnärztliche Vereinigung Nordrhein* [2000] ECR I-5123; Case C-506/04 *Wilson v Ordre des avocats du barreau de Luxembourg* [2006] ECR I-8613.

95. In that context, nationals of Member States have in particular the right, which they derive directly from the Treaty, to leave their country of origin to enter the territory of another Member State and reside there in order there to pursue an economic activity ...

96. Provisions which preclude or deter a national of a Member State from leaving his country of origin in order to exercise his right to freedom of movement therefore constitute an obstacle to that freedom even if they apply without regard to the nationality of the workers concerned ...

97. The Court has also stated in [Case 81/87 *Daily Mail*] that even though the Treaty provisions relating to freedom of establishment are directed mainly to ensuring that foreign nationals and companies are treated in the host Member State in the same way as nationals of that State, they also prohibit the Member State of origin from hindering the establishment in another Member State of one of its nationals or of a company incorporated under its legislation which comes within the definition contained in Article [54 TFEU]. The rights guaranteed by Article [49 TFEU] *et seq.* of the Treaty would be rendered meaningless if the Member State of origin could prohibit undertakings from leaving in order to establish themselves in another Member State. The same considerations apply, in relation to Article [45 TFEU], with regard to rules which impede the freedom of movement of nationals of one Member State wishing to engage in gainful employment in another Member State.

98. It is true that the transfer rules in issue in the main proceedings apply also to transfers of players between clubs belonging to different national associations within the same Member State and that similar rules govern transfers between clubs belonging to the same national association.

99. However ... those rules are likely to restrict the freedom of movement of players who wish to pursue their activity in another Member State by preventing or deterring them from leaving the clubs to which they belong even after the expiry of their contracts of employment with those clubs.

100. Since they provide that a professional footballer may not pursue his activity with a new club established in another Member State unless it has paid his former club a transfer fee agreed upon between the two clubs or determined in accordance with the regulations of the sporting associations, the said rules constitute an obstacle to freedom of movement for workers. ...

103. It is sufficient to note that, although the rules in issue in the main proceedings apply also to transfers between clubs belonging to different national associations within the same Member State and are similar to those governing transfers between clubs belonging to the same national association, they still directly affect players' access to the employment market in other Member States and are thus capable of impeding freedom of movement for workers. They cannot, thus, be deemed comparable to the rules on selling arrangements for goods which in *Keck and Mithouard* were held to fall outside the ambit of Article [34 TFEU].

104. Consequently, the transfer rules constitute an obstacle to freedom of movement for workers prohibited in principle by Article [45 TFEU]. It could only be otherwise if those rules pursued a legitimate aim compatible with the Treaty and were justified by pressing reasons of public interest. But even if that were so, application of those rules would still have to be such as to ensure achievement of the aim in question and not go beyond what is necessary for that purpose.

The Court went on to find that the rules could not be justified by the need to maintain the financial and competitive balance between clubs, nor by the need to find and support young talent. These were good goals, but the Court was convinced they could be achieved by means less restrictive of free movement.

Bosman applies the same logic to Articles 45 and 49[39] as has been applied, since *Cassis de Dijon*, to the case law on free movement of goods and freedom to provide services.[40] The provisions will not only catch measures which distinguish between nationals of different Member States. They will also catch certain equally applicable restrictions on employment and establishment. In cases where such a measure falls within either provision, it will only be lawful if it meets a number of conditions. It must be justified in the public interest; it must be applied in a non-discriminatory manner, it must be suitable for securing the attainment of the objective pursued and it must not go beyond what is necessary to attain this objective.[41]

The same reasoning has been applied in the context of Article 49 in *Gebhard*, where the Court pronounced that any measure 'liable to hinder or make less attractive the exercise of fundamental freedoms' would be prohibited, unless it complied with the same justificatory requirements outlined in *Bosman*.[42] In *Gebhard*, as in *Bosman*, the reasoning was expressed to be general, applying to restrictions on the pursuit of an occupation as much as to restrictions on taking up an occupation. However, *Gebhard* concerned the right to use the title 'avvocato' in Italy, and a prohibition imposed upon Mr Gebhard from 'pursuing his professional activity' in Milan. As such it was about access to an activity, as was *Bosman*. The facts of these cases are somewhat narrower than the Court's conclusions. This is relevant because, as will be seen below, where restrictions on pursuit of an occupation are concerned it is not clear that the full potential scope of these judgments has actually been realised: in fact the Court does seem to use non-discrimination as a guiding and limiting idea.[43]

The application of Article 45 to equally applicable measures has, as with the other freedoms, been a powerful tool for opening up regulated professions to new competition. In *Hartlauer*, an Austrian rule made the setting up of an outpatient dental clinic conditional upon local 'need', which was determined by the relevant authority.[44] This was found to be a restriction on establishment which ultimately, because of various arbitrary elements in the authorisation procedure, was not justified. Similarly, rules in Greece permitting opticians to own only one shop, and Italian laws which prohibited either companies or non-pharmacists from owning pharmacies, were both found to comprise restrictions on establishment, albeit in the latter case justified.[45]

As in *Bosman*, these cases concern rules which do not discriminate explicitly, and do not seem to have any greater effect on cross-border movement than domestic movement.[46] The only sense in which it could be argued that they are discriminatory is that they tend to entrench the status quo, and protect incumbents, who still tend to be disproportionately national

---

[39] Similar reasoning was first used in relation to Article 49 in Case 107/83 *Ordre des Avocats au Barreau de Paris* v *Klopp* [1984] ECR 2971.

[40] See pp. 763 and 803.

[41] Case C-55/94 *Gebhard* v *Consiglio dell'ordine degli avvocati e procuratori di Milano* [1995] ECR 1-4165; Case C-299/02 *Commission* v *Netherlands* [2004] ECR 1-9761.

[42] Case C-55/94 *Gebhard* v *Consiglio dell'ordine degli avvocati e procuratori di Milano* [1995] ECR 1-4165.

[43] See pp. 856–60.

[44] Case C-169/07 *Hartlauer Handelsgesellschaft mbH* v *Wiener Landesregierung, Oberösterreichische Landesregierung*, Judgment of 10 March 2009.

[45] Case C-140/03 *Commission* v *Greece* [2005] ECR I-3177; Case C-531/06 *Commission* v *Italy*, Judgment of 9 May 2009; see also Joined Cases C-171/07 and C-172/07 *Apothekerkammer des Saarlandes*, Judgment of 19 May 2009.

[46] See C. Costello, 'Market Access All Areas? The Treatment of Non-Discriminatory Barriers to the Free Movement of Workers' (2000) 27(3) *LIEI* 267.

in almost all industries, from new competition. Not that the Court uses this argument. Its objection is just that for some parties, establishment or employment will be hindered.

Bosman concerned a measure with a very direct and powerful effect. In *Graf*, the Court stated that measures affecting the taking up of economic activities in another Member State would not fall within Article 45 if their restrictive effects were too indirect or uncertain.[47] In that instance, an Austrian law entitling employees to two months' pay as compensation for loss of employment where they had been working for their employer for at least three years was challenged. This entitlement did not exist where it was the employee who gave notice. Graf left his company to work in Germany. He sued for the compensation, claiming that its absence acted as a disincentive to move job, and thus fell within Article 45. The Court disagreed.

Case C-190/98 *Graf v Filzmoser Maschinenbau* [2000] ECR I-493

22. Nationals of Member States have in particular the right, which they derive directly from the Treaty, to leave their country of origin to enter the territory of another Member State and reside there in order to pursue an economic activity …

23. Provisions which, even if they are applicable without distinction, preclude or deter a national of a Member State from leaving his country of origin in order to exercise his right to freedom of movement therefore constitute an obstacle to that freedom. However, in order to be capable of constituting such an obstacle, they must affect access of workers to the labour market.

24. Legislation of the kind at issue in the main proceedings is not such as to preclude or deter a worker from ending his contract of employment in order to take a job with another employer, because the entitlement to compensation on termination of employment is not dependent on the worker's choosing whether or not to stay with his current employer but on a future and hypothetical event, namely the subsequent termination of his contract without such termination being at his own initiative or attributable to him.

25. Such an event is too uncertain and indirect a possibility for legislation to be capable of being regarded as liable to hinder freedom of movement for workers where it does not attach to termination of a contract of employment by the worker himself the same consequence as it attaches to termination which was not at his initiative or is not attributable to him.

Graf may be contrasted with *Kranemann*,[48] where there was a challenge to the regulations governing travel expenses for trainee civil servants in the German state of Nordrhein-Westfalen. Travel expenses were reimbursed where the training was carried out within Germany, but not for that outside Germany. It was not clear whether this would dissuade many trainees from taking up training abroad. The Court, nevertheless, considered that the measure violated Article 45, as it considered that it might deter trainees with limited financial resources from taking up training abroad. Two sorts of measure are, therefore, caught under this case law. The first are measures, such as that in *Bosman*, which prevent access to the market. Regardless of their aim, their extreme restrictive effects lead to their falling within Article 45 or 49. The second are

---

[47] *Ibid.*
[48] Case C-109/04 *Kranemann v Land Nordrhein-Westfalen* [2005] ECR 1-2421.

measures such as those in *Graf* or *Kranemann*. The effect of such measures is not to prevent access to the market, but to deter an individual from taking up activities in another Member State because of the economic costs such activity would entail. In the latter case, *Graf* creates a *de minimis* rule, but *Kranemann* suggests that this will not be applied, or will be less rigorously applied, where the measure specifically targets movement between Member States.

(iii) Restrictions on secondary establishment

The taking up of business activity in another Member State can occur either through primary or secondary establishment. The former is where a trader relocates her central place of business to another Member State. By contrast, with secondary establishment, the trader remains in her home state, but sets up branches, agencies or subsidiaries in other Member States. Restrictions on secondary establishment inevitably prevent traders from other Member States setting up a business in the host state, as to do so would involve their having to abandon their place of business in their home state. This question was raised in *Klopp*, concerning a German lawyer practising law in Dusseldorf. He applied to register with the Paris Bar Council in order to practise in Paris, but was refused because of a general prohibition on anyone practising at the Paris Bar unless their principal office was in Paris and the other offices they worked from were in the environs of Paris.

Case 107/83 *Ordre des Avocats au Barreau de Paris* v *Klopp* [1984] ECR 2971

17. ... under [the second paragraph of Article 49 TFEU] freedom of establishment includes access to and the pursuit of the activities of self-employed persons 'under the conditions laid down for its own nationals by the law of the country where such establishment is effected'. It follows from that provision and its context that in the absence of specific Community rules in the matter each Member State is free to regulate the exercise of the legal profession in its territory.

18. Nevertheless that rule does not mean that the legislation of a Member State may require a lawyer to have only one establishment throughout the Community territory. Such a restrictive interpretation would mean that a lawyer once established in a particular Member State would be able to enjoy the freedom of the Treaty to establish himself in another Member State only at the price of abandoning the establishment he already had.

19. That freedom of establishment is not confined to the right to create a single establishment within the Community is confirmed by the very words of Article [49 TFEU], according to which the progressive abolition of the restrictions on freedom of establishment applies to restrictions on the setting up of agencies, branches or subsidiaries by nationals of any Member State established in the territory of another Member State. That rule must be regarded as a specific statement of a general principle, applicable equally to the liberal professions, according to which the right of establishment includes freedom to set up and maintain, subject to observance of the professional rules of conduct, more than one place of work within the Community.

20. In view of the special nature of the legal profession, however, the second Member State must have the right, in the interests of the due administration of justice, to require that lawyers enrolled at a bar in its territory should practise in such a way as to maintain sufficient contact with their clients and the judicial authorities and abide by the rules of the profession. Nevertheless such requirements must

not prevent the nationals of other Member States from exercising properly the right of establishment guaranteed them by the Treaty.

21. In that respect it must be pointed out that modern methods of transport and telecommunications facilitate proper contact with clients and the judicial authorities. Similarly, the existence of a second set of chambers in another Member State does not prevent the application of the rules of ethics in the host Member State.

The judgment suggests that it is unlikely that restrictions on secondary establishment can be justified. This position is supported by *Commission* v *France*,[49] where the French government attempted to justify a similar prohibition on secondary establishment for doctors and dentists, on the grounds that patients will often wish to have access to the same doctor. The Court was equally dismissive, stating that even in general practices, recent developments resulted in practitioners belonging to group practices with the consequence that a patient could never ensure access to a particular practitioner. The argument in *Klopp* that effective supervision does not in fact require physical presence has been reinforced in the context of taxation in *Commission* v *Denmark*, where the Court pointed out that a Directive existed specifically to regulate mutual assistance between national tax authorities.[50] Denmark made certain tax breaks conditional upon incorporation in Denmark, saying this was necessary to prevent fraud, because the authorities could not verify tax claims made by companies based abroad. In a judgment entirely consistent with its information-based approach to the internal market, and with the philosophy of the Services Directive, the Court found this to be disproportionate.[51] If checking of claims was necessary, Denmark should seek to find ways to do this abroad, with the help of local authorities, rather than washing its hands of the matter. The case shows that states should not regard foreign establishments as beyond the supervisory pale, but rather should engage with authorities in other states to obtain the information that they need.

Most cases have concerned more hidden restrictions on secondary establishment. In *Stanton*,[52] a challenge was made to a Belgian requirement for the self-employed to pay social security contributions unless they were also employed in Belgium. The Court considered that such an exemption penalised those who extended their business activities across more than one Member State and whilst it was not discriminatory, as more Belgians were affected by it than any other nationality, it was nevertheless illegal as it restricted free movement. More recently, in *Commission* v *Portugal*,[53] a Portuguese requirement that private security firms be legally incorporated in Portugal was held to be an illegal restriction on secondary establishment as it prevented natural persons from other Member States setting up in Portugal.

---

[49] Case 96/85 *Commission* v *France* [1986] ECR 1475. See also Case C-351/90 *Commission* v *Luxembourg* [1992] ECR 1-3945.

[50] Case C-150/04 *Commission* v *Denmark* [2007] ECR I-1163.

[51] See p. 827.

[52] Case 143/87 *Stanton* v *INASTI* [1988] ECR 3877. See also Joined Cases 154/87 and 155/87 *Rijksinstituut voor de sociale verzekering des zelfstandigen* v *Wolf* [1998] ECR 3897; Case C-53/95 *INASTI* v *Kammler* [1996] ECR I-703.

[53] Case C-171/02 *Commission* v *Portugal* [2004] ECR I-5645.

(iv) Restrictions on the use of diplomas and qualifications

By definition, professions deny access to an occupation, for they prevent that activity being pursued unless the individual submits to oversight of the professional body governing the activity in question and has the qualifications required for exercise of the profession. It might, therefore, be that the very presence of a profession is challenged under Articles 45 and 49 on the grounds that it prevents an individual taking up an economic activity. Early on, however, the Court of Justice ruled that Member States may be permitted to lay down professional rules relating to organisation, qualifications, professional ethics, supervision and liability,[54] and this has been repeated on a number of occasions since.[55] The Court has, instead, scrutinised the conditions imposed by these rules for the taking up of a profession, most notably the qualifications required before a migrant can enter a particular profession.

The central case is *Vlassopoulou*, concerning a Greek lawyer who completed her doctorate at the University of Tübingen, Germany, in 1982, and from 1983 until 1988 worked at a German law firm in Mannheim. In 1988 she applied to become a Rechtsanwalt, a German lawyer, but was refused on the grounds that she had neither studied law at a German university for two years, nor completed the First State exams, nor undergone the relevant period of training in Germany. She argued that this violated Article 49 as no account was taken of her Greek qualifications or her work experience in Germany.

Case C–340/89 *Vlassopoulou v Ministerium für Justiz Bundes- und Europaangelegenheiten Baden-Wurttemberg* [1991] ECR I–2357

14. ... insofar as Community law makes no special provision, the objectives of the Treaty, and in particular freedom of establishment, may be achieved by measures enacted by the Member States, which, under Article [4(3) TEU], must take 'all appropriate measures, whether general or particular, to ensure fulfilment of the obligations arising out of this Treaty or resulting from action taken by the institutions of the Community' and abstain from 'any measure which could jeopardize the attainment of the objectives of this Treaty'. [The wording of this provision has since been slightly amended by the Lisbon Treaty.]

15. It must be stated in this regard that, even if applied without any discrimination on the basis of nationality, national requirements concerning qualifications may have the effect of hindering nationals of the other Member States in the exercise of their right of establishment guaranteed to them by Article [49 TFEU]. That could be the case if the national rules in question took no account of the knowledge and qualifications already acquired by the person concerned in another Member State.

16. Consequently, a Member State which receives a request to admit a person to a profession to which access, under national law, depends upon the possession of a diploma or a professional qualification must take into consideration the diplomas, certificates and other evidence of qualifications which the person concerned has acquired in order to exercise the same profession in another Member State by making a comparison between the specialized knowledge and abilities certified by those diplomas and the knowledge and qualifications required by the national rules.

---

[54] Case 71/76 *Thieffry* v *Conseil de l'Ordre des Avocats à la Cour de Paris* [1977] ECR 765.
[55] Case 292/86 *Gullung* v *Conseil de l'Ordre des Avocats* [1988] ECR 111; Case C-55/94 *Gebhard* v *Consiglio dell'ordine degli avvocati e procuratori di Milano* [1995] ECR I-4165.

17. That examination procedure must enable the authorities of the host Member State to assure themselves, on an objective basis, that the foreign diploma certifies that its holder has knowledge and qualifications which are, if not identical, at least equivalent to those certified by the national diploma. That assessment of the equivalence of the foreign diploma must be carried out exclusively in the light of the level of knowledge and qualifications which its holder can be assumed to possess in the light of that diploma, having regard to the nature and duration of the studies and practical training to which the diploma relates …

18. In the course of that examination, a Member State may, however, take into consideration objective differences relating to both the legal framework of the profession in question in the Member State of origin and to its field of activity. In the case of the profession of lawyer, a Member State may therefore carry out a comparative examination of diplomas, taking account of the differences identified between the national legal systems concerned.

19. If that comparative examination of diplomas results in the finding that the knowledge and qualifications certified by the foreign diploma correspond to those required by the national provisions, the Member State must recognize that diploma as fulfilling the requirements laid down by its national provisions. If, on the other hand, the comparison reveals that the knowledge and qualifications certified by the foreign diploma and those required by the national provisions correspond only partially, the host Member State is entitled to require the person concerned to show that he has acquired the knowledge and qualifications which are lacking.

20. In this regard, the competent national authorities must assess whether the knowledge acquired in the host Member State, either during a course of study or by way of practical experience, is sufficient in order to prove possession of the knowledge which is lacking.

21. If completion of a period of preparation or training for entry into the profession is required by the rules applying in the host Member State, those national authorities must determine whether professional experience acquired in the Member State of origin or in the host Member State may be regarded as satisfying that requirement in full or in part.

22. Finally, it must be pointed out that the examination made to determine whether the knowledge and qualifications certified by the foreign diploma and those required by the legislation of the host Member State correspond must be carried out by the national authorities in accordance with a procedure which is in conformity with the requirements of Community law concerning the effective protection of the fundamental rights conferred by the Treaty on Community subjects. It follows that any decision taken must be capable of being made the subject of judicial proceedings in which its legality under Community law can be reviewed and that the person concerned must be able to ascertain the reasons for the decision taken in his regard.

There is a duty to take account of the qualifications and experience of the migrant in deciding whether to grant her access to the market. A question emerging from *Vlassopoulou* is that concerning the types of proof that may be furnished by the migrant in order to demonstrate that she meets the required standard. The host state can only refuse access to the profession if there are 'objective differences' between its qualifications and the practical experience and qualifications of the migrant. Such an approach assumes a substitutability of knowledge, whereby if the migrant has the requisite standard of knowledge, no matter the source, she should be allowed to practise.

Subsequent case law has expounded on which knowledge and training must be taken into account by the host state authorities. In *Hocsman*,[56] a Spaniard applied to practise as a doctor in France. All his university training was from Argentina, whose diplomas France did not recognise as equivalent to its own. He had, however, worked for a number of years as a doctor in Spanish hospitals and as a urologist in French hospitals. The Court of Justice held that in making their decision the French authorities should have considered all the practical experience acquired by Hocsman not only in France, but also in Spain. They were also required to take into account all the diplomas and qualifications that certified a specialised knowledge, notwithstanding that these came from outside the European Union. The test imposes severe demands on the professional bodies. It will be difficult to vet the quality of practical experience not gained on their territory. It is even more difficult to know how to evaluate certification of an expertise from an institution whose standards are not trusted. Finally, they are required to provide some overall assessment on what may be a set of heterogeneous and eclectic experiences. Any decision will be difficult for the authority to make. Such requirements are not necessarily advantageous to the migrant, as this complexity results in any decision being difficult to review as it is difficult to point to a clear standard which is being breached.

Professional qualifications also facilitate the pursuit of an activity by demonstrating certification of a skill, thereby making the holder more marketable. It would be extremely complicated if different constraints were to apply to how Member States regulated access to a profession and how they regulated the broader use of professional qualifications. The Court has, therefore, a similar logic on all non-discriminatory restrictions on the recognition of non-national professional qualifications. In *Kraus*,[57] a German, who had completed an LLM at Edinburgh University, challenged a German requirement that administrative authorisation was necessary for use of higher education titles acquired abroad. The Court noted that qualifications were necessary both for access to a profession and, more generally, to facilitate the exercise of economic activity. Any conditions on the use of a title which hindered or made more difficult the exercise of the economic freedoms fell, in its view, within Article 49 TFEU. It refused to draw a distinction between titles necessary for access to a profession and other titles, but held that Member States could impose non-discriminatory restrictions on the use of titles to prevent fraud. An administrative authorisation for these purposes was lawful provided it was accessible, susceptible to judicial review, reasons were given for any refusal to approve a title, the administrative costs charged were not excessive and any sanctions imposed for the use of the title without authorisation were not disproportionately heavy.

Vlassopoulou took place against a backdrop of legislative developments in this field. Initially, the Union had pursued a sectoral approach in which agreement would be reached on the minimum standard of education or training and two Directives would be adopted: one establishing the general level of training and the other listing the qualifications and diplomas awarded in the Member States which satisfied the conditions for recognition.[58] Such an

---

[56] Case C-238/98 *Hocsman* v *Ministre de l'Emploi et de la Solidarité* [2000] ECR I-6623.
[57] Case C-19/92 *Kraus* v *Land Baden-Württemberg* [1993] ECR I-1663.
[58] An early example of this approach can be found in relation to general practitioners. On recognition, see Directive 75/362/EC [1975] OJ L167/1. On training, see Directive 75/363/EC [1975] OJ L167/14.

approach makes deep inroads into the independence of national educational policy in relation to training curricula. Whilst a number of Directives were enacted, particularly in the medical professions, progress was slow, piecemeal and not a great success. Because of the slow development, in 1984 agreement was reached to adopt a different approach: the general horizontal approach. This imposed a qualified duty of mutual recognition on Member States, whereby, for whole swathes of regulated activities, they were to recognise the qualifications granted by other Member States. Three Directives were adopted under this approach, but these co-existed with rather than replaced the Directives which had adopted the sectoral approach.[59] The system has been rationalised by Directive 2005/36/EC on the recognition of professional qualifications.[60] This brings all the legislation under one umbrella, whilst internalising many of the differences in the previous legislation.

The Directive governs the pursuit, either in an employed or self-employed capacity, of a regulated profession by EU nationals in a Member State other than that where they acquired their qualifications.[61] The Directive gives a nigh exhaustive definition of regulated professions, taking these to include any professional activity access to or the pursuit of which is subject to the possession of specific professional qualifications.[62] These professional qualifications may be attested by formal qualifications, a confirmation of competence, or professional experience.[63] The central provision of the Directive, article 4(1), states that an EU national who has qualified abroad will have access to the host state market where her qualifications are recognised by that state.

Directive 2005/36/EC, article 4(1)

The recognition of professional qualifications by the host Member State allows the beneficiary to gain access in that Member State to the same profession as that for which he is qualified in the home Member State and to pursue it in the host Member State under the same conditions as its nationals.

Recognition is not acquired automatically. The Directive provides three routes to recognition, depending upon the professional activity being undertaken.

The first is the 'general system for the recognition of evidence of training'. This applies where access to or pursuit of a regulated profession in the host state is contingent upon possession

---

[59] Directive 89/48/EC establishing a general system for the recognition of higher education diplomas awarded on completion of professional education and training of at least three years' duration [1989] OJ L19/16; Directive 92/51/EC on a second general system for the recognition of professional education and training to supplement Directive 89/48/EC [1992] OJ L209/25; Directive 1999/42/EC establishing a mechanism for the recognition of qualifications in respect of the professional activities covered by the Directives on liberalisation and transitional measures and supplementing the general system for the recognition of qualifications [1999] OJ L201/77.

[60] [2005] OJ L255/22. The date of transposition for this was 20 October 2007.

[61] Ibid. article 2(1).

[62] Ibid. article 3(1). The Directive also applies to a large number of occupations not fitting neatly into this definition. These are set out in Annex I.

[63] Ibid. article 3(1)(b).

of specific qualifications. The basic principle for such activities is mutual recognition of qualifications.

Directive 2005/36/EC, article 13

1. If access to or pursuit of a regulated profession in a host Member State is contingent upon possession of specific professional qualifications, the competent authority of that Member State shall permit access to and pursuit of that profession, under the same conditions as apply to its nationals, to applicants possessing the attestation of competence or evidence of formal qualifications required by another Member State in order to gain access to and pursue that profession on its territory. Attestations of competence or evidence of formal qualifications shall satisfy the following conditions:
   (a) they shall have been issued by a competent authority in a Member State, designated in accordance with the legislative, regulatory or administrative provisions of that Member State;
   (b) they shall attest a level of professional qualification at least equivalent to the level immediately prior to that which is required in the host Member State ...

2. Access to and pursuit of the profession, as described in paragraph 1, shall also be granted to applicants who have pursued the profession referred to in that paragraph on a full-time basis for two years during the previous 10 years in another Member State which does not regulate that profession, provided they possess one or more attestations of competence or documents providing evidence of formal qualifications. Attestations of competence and evidence of formal qualifications shall satisfy the following conditions:
   (a) they shall have been issued by a competent authority in a Member State, designated in accordance with the legislative, regulatory or administrative provisions of that Member State;
   (b) they shall attest a level of professional qualification at least equivalent to the level immediately prior to that required in the host Member State ...
   (c) they shall attest that the holder has been prepared for the pursuit of the profession in question.

Member States may require applicants to take an aptitude test or complete an adaptation period of up to three years where the duration of the training undertaken is at least one year shorter than that in the host state, where the training is substantially different from that in the host state, or where the regulated profession in the host state comprises one or more regulated activities which do not exist in the corresponding home state and where the difference consists of specific training required by the host state which is substantially dissimilar to anything covered by the applicant's qualification. The applicant must be given the choice between either taking the aptitude test or undergoing the adaptation period except where the activity requires precise knowledge of national law, in which case the host state may choose which of the obligations to impose on the applicant.[64]

The second route concerns activities which require only general commercial or professional knowledge. These are listed in Annex IV of the Directive and include activities involving mainly industrial experience. Access to the market is premised upon mutual recognition of experience.

---

[64] *Ibid.* article 14.

> **Directive 2005/36/EC, article 16**
>
> If, in a Member State, access to or pursuit of one of the activities listed in Annex IV is contingent upon possession of general, commercial or professional knowledge and aptitudes, that Member State shall recognise previous pursuit of the activity in another Member State as sufficient proof of such knowledge and aptitudes.

The length of time depends on the activity in question and whether any prior training has been carried out. There is less protection for these activities than for those in the first category. There are no checks on the equivalence of the experience or any exceptions to this requirement of mutual recognition.

The third category covers those professionals (doctors, vets, nurses, midwives, pharmacists, architects and dentists) who were previously regulated by sectoral Directives. These require not only evidence of formal qualifications, but also evidence that the applicant has satisfied minimum training conditions which are set out in the Directive.[65] A good example is the requirements set out for basic medical training.

> **Directive 2005/36/EC, article 24(1)**
>
> 1. Admission to basic medical training shall be contingent upon possession of a diploma or certificate providing access, for the studies in question, to universities.
> 2. Basic medical training shall comprise a total of at least six years of study or 5,500 hours of theoretical and practical training provided by, or under the supervision of, a university ...
> 3. Basic medical training shall provide an assurance that the person in question has acquired the following knowledge and skills:
>   (a) adequate knowledge of the sciences on which medicine is based and a good understanding of the scientific methods including the principles of measuring biological functions, the evaluation of scientifically established facts and the analysis of data;
>   (b) sufficient understanding of the structure, functions and behaviour of healthy and sick persons, as well as relations between the state of health and physical and social surroundings of the human being;
>   (c) adequate knowledge of clinical disciplines and practices, providing him with a coherent picture of mental and physical diseases, of medicine from the points of view of prophylaxis, diagnosis and therapy and of human reproduction;
>   (d) suitable clinical experience in hospitals under appropriate supervision.

A different philosophy underlies each category. These may be described respectively as qualified mutual recognition, unqualified mutual recognition and unqualified mutual recognition combined with partial harmonisation. The presence of these different approaches is generated in part by the wide range of activities covered by the Directive. Nevertheless, the absence of a

---

[65] *Ibid.* article 21.

single ethos is unsettling. Why is a different regime applied to engineers (the first approach) than to architects (the third approach)? The variety of activities may be a partial answer to that question, but it attracts further criticism. The principles determining the allocation of activities to each approach are unclear and, in turn, each approach covers a sweeping range of activities, many of which have demands that are not readily comparable.

(v) Restrictions on grounds of abuse of free movement

In a number of situations individuals may be motivated to go abroad in order to avoid inconvenient rules in their home state. This occurs where individuals migrate in order to benefit from the family rights awarded to migrant citizens, and then come home at a later date, continuing to rely on their migrant status. It also occurs where companies relocate to a Member State with more convenient tax or incorporation rules, but continue to do business in their original state. In both these cases, the original state is inclined to regard the use of free movement as 'abusive' and to claim that reliance on free movement rights merely to avoid national law should not be permitted. As is discussed in Chapter 11, and below, the Court has not been sympathetic.[66] It is not abusive to allow the legal advantages of a particular location or relocation to influence decision-making.

The context where abuse arguments have been the most numerous, particularly in recent years, is that of education and training. An early example was *Knoors*, where a Dutch citizen worked as a plumber in Belgium, and on his return to the Netherlands applied to have his experience recognised as equivalent to the Dutch plumbing qualification, as the Directive then in force permitted. The Dutch government claimed that he had migrated purely to avoid having to study for the plumbing qualification which in the Netherlands was compulsory.

Case 115/78 J. Knoors v Staatssecretaris van Economische Zaken [1979] ECR 399

24. Although it is true that the provisions of the Treaty relating to establishment and the provision of services cannot be applied to situations which are purely internal to a Member State, the position nevertheless remains that the reference in Article [49 TFEU] to 'nationals of a Member State' who wish to establish themselves 'in the territory of another Member State' cannot be interpreted in such a way as to exclude from the benefit of Community law a given Member State's own nationals when the latter, owing to the fact that they have lawfully resided on the territory of another Member State and have there acquired a trade qualification which is recognized by the provisions of Community law, are, with regard to their state of origin, in a situation which may be assimilated to that of any other persons enjoying the rights and liberties guaranteed by the Treaty.

25. However, it is not possible to disregard the legitimate interest which a Member State may have in preventing certain of its nationals, by means of facilities created under the Treaty, from attempting wrongly to evade the application of their national legislation as regards training for a trade.

---

[66] See p. 172; see also K. Engsig Sørensen, 'Abuse of Rights in Community Law: A Principle of Substance or Merely Rhetoric?' (2006) 43 *CMLRev.* 423; A. Kjellgren, 'On the Border of Abuse: The Jurisprudence of the European Court of Justice on Circumvention, Fraud and Other Misuses of Community Law' (2000) 11 *EBLRev.* 179; M. Evers and A. de Graaf, 'Limiting Benefit Shopping: Use and Abuse of EC Law' (2009) 18 *EC Tax Review* 279; R. De La Feria, 'Prohibition of Abuse of (Community) Law: The Creation of a New General Principle of EC Law Through Tax' (2008) 45 *CMLRev.* 395.

The suggestion in this last paragraph, that there may be limits to the extent to which individuals can choose the jurisdiction that suits them best, has hardly been realised in practice. The Court continues to respect the individual freedom of choice which is inherent in free movement. In *Knoors*, the Court found that because the legislation then in force required a minimum period before work experience could be considered equivalent to a qualification, the risk of abuse was 'excluded'.

In recent years the situation has become a little more complex, as higher education institutions have become more entrepreneurial. The European School of Economics (ESE) was a UK institution which awarded degrees according to UK law, but which provided classes at a campus in Italy. Italian law, however, only recognised foreign degrees if the study for that degree had actually been undertaken in the degree-awarding state. In *Neri*, the Court found that this was an unlawful restriction on the freedom of establishment of the ESE.[67] In *Khatzithanasis* and *Commission* v *Spain*, the Court took the same approach in similar situations, ruling that a failure to recognise qualifications as an optician or engineer just because the actual study was done in the home state was contrary to the Directive on professional qualifications then in force.[68] The requirement to recognise qualifications awarded by bodies in other Member States is not subject to an exception or condition to do with the physical place of study.

A limit was, however, reached in *Cavallera*.[69] In Italy, one may practise as an engineer after a university course in engineering, and the taking of a state exam. In Spain, a university course in engineering suffices. Mr Cavallera attempted to leverage this difference: he had obtained a university degree in engineering in Italy, and successfully obtained recognition of this in Spain as equivalent to a Spanish degree. This entitled him to practise as an engineer in Spain and he obtained certification to this effect. He then returned to Italy and argued that since he was entitled to practise as an engineer in Spain, his Spanish authorisation should be recognised and translated to an authorisation to practise in Italy, pursuant to the Directive on professional qualifications then in force. He would then have successfully avoided the Italian state examination. However, he lost his case. The Court found that the Directive did not grant any right to rely on a certificate authorising a person to practise a profession when that certificate did not attest to any course of study or examination at an institution in that state.

4 RESTRICTIONS ON THE PURSUIT OF AN OCCUPATION

Restrictions on the pursuit of economic activity concern restrictions placed on the migrant, which occur once she has placed herself on the market of the host state, either through working for an employer or through self-employment within that state. Once on the market, it is particularly important that she suffer no discrimination in relation to that state's own nationals. Both overt (direct) and covert (indirect) discrimination are prohibited. Overt discrimination occurs where there is an express reference to nationality which disadvantages the migrant.

---

[67] Case C-153/02 *Neri* v *European School of Economics* [2003] ECR I-13555.
[68] Case C-151/07 *Theologos-Grigorios Khatzithanasis* v *Ypourgos Ygeias kai Koinonikis Allilengyis and Organismos Epangelmatikis Ekpaidefsis kai Katartisis (OEEK)*, Judgment of 4 December 2008; Case C-286/06 *Commission* v *Spain* [2008] ECR I-8025. See also Case C-274/05 *Commission* v *Greece* [2008] ECR I-7969.
[69] Case C-311/06 *Consiglio Nazionale degli Ingegneri* v *Ministero della Giustizia and Marco Cavallera*, Judgment of 29 January 2009.

Covert discrimination results where the conditions are on their face formally neutral, but are liable to adversely affect migrants to a disproportionate extent. This is considered to be the case where the conditions imposed essentially disadvantage migrant workers, or where they can more easily be satisfied by national workers than by migrant workers, or where there is a risk that they may operate to the particular detriment of migrant workers. In such circumstances, the measure will be illegal as a form of covert discrimination unless justified by some legitimate objective and proportionate to that objective.[70] Discrimination is considered pernicious in this field on two grounds. First, it places the migrant at a competitive disadvantage and thus acts to protect that state's market. Secondly, the migrant is not simply a business machine concerned with accumulating profit. She is also a human being and thus discrimination constitutes an affront to her dignity and acts as an obstacle to her integration into the host society.

(i) Discrimination in labour markets

Discrimination between workers as regards remuneration and other conditions of employment is expressly prohibited by Article 45(2) TFEU. Regulation 1612/68/EC reiterates and elaborates this, and also provides in article 7(4) that:

> Any clause of a collective or individual agreement or of any other collective regulation concerning eligibility for employment, employment, remuneration and other conditions of work or dismissal shall be null and void insofar as it lays down or authorises discriminatory conditions in respect of workers who are nationals of the other Member States.

A good example of discrimination in work is *Köbler*.[71] Austrian law granted university professors an increased salary once they had completed fifteen years' service in the Austrian university system. This was not available to university professors who had served part of that time at universities outside Austria. Köbler was denied the increase on the grounds that he had spent some of this period in a German university and, as the scheme was designed to reward loyalty to the Austrian university system, it was considered that this period away meant he did not qualify. The Court of Justice found the measure to be illegal, as it discriminated in two ways. First, it penalised non-Austrians who were likely to have spent some time in universities elsewhere in the European Union. Secondly, it discriminated against Austrians who had exercised their rights under Article 45 and spent time abroad. Similar failures to take account of experience abroad, when domestic experience is rewarded, have been repeatedly condemned by the Court.[72] A variation on this theme was found in *Delay*, where a failure to take into account years of experience in a particular domestic job was also discriminatory, where that job was one that was primarily done by foreigners.[73] The case concerned language assistants in Italian universities. If they were lucky enough to obtain a permanent post, their years as a

---

[70] Case C-237/94 *O'Flynn* v *Adjudication Officer* [1996] ECR I-2617.
[71] Case C-224/01 *Köbler* v *Austria* [2003] ECR I-10239.
[72] Case C-429/92 *Ingetraut Scholz* v *Opera Universitaria di Cagliari and Cinzia Porcedda* [1994] ECR I-505; Case C-371/04 *Commission* v *Italy* [2006] ECR I-10257.
[73] Case C-276/07 *Nancy Delay* v *Università degli studi di Firenze, Istituto nazionale della previdenza sociale* [2008] ECR I-3635.

language assistant did not count towards their seniority, whereas under the Italian university rules experience in other comparable posts would have done.

Several types of discrimination have been the recurring subject of litigation before the Court of Justice: trade union rights, tax advantages and social advantages. With regard to trade union rights, provision is made in article 8 of Regulation 1612/68/EC for migrants to enjoy equality of treatment in respect of both membership of trade unions and exercise of those trade union rights.[74] A broad interpretation has been taken, so this right to equal treatment applies not merely to formally recognised trade unions, but also to any body to which workers pay contributions in return for defence and representation of their interests.[75] It also confers the right not only to equal protection from the union, but also the equal opportunity to govern the trade union, by standing for election for office.[76]

The migrant is entitled, by virtue of both Article 45(2) TFEU and secondary legislation,[77] to the same tax benefits in a Member State as its nationals who are working there.[78] This principle has not proved straightforward to apply. Tax benefits are intended to compensate for or diminish tax burdens. However, individuals are usually taxed in their place of residence. As a result, tax benefits are often also awarded only to residents. Yet, this is likely to especially adversely affect migrant workers, particularly frontier workers, and so may be indirectly discriminatory.

The Court addressed this problem in *Schumacker*, and found that since, in general, residents and non-residents were in objectively different positions with regard to taxation, differences in treatment with regard to tax benefits were not generally wrongful.[79] However, they found that there could be exceptions to this rule. Mr Schumacker earned the major part of his income in Germany, and it was taxed in Germany, while he earned no significant income in Belgium, where he lived. In those circumstances he should have the right to the same tax benefits as a German resident. This lays down a rule of thumb for a particular problem, but serves more to demonstrate the complexities of taxation than to provide a general framework for addressing them.[80]

Regulation 1612/68/EC also prohibits discrimination in 'social advantages' and housing.[81] However, these clauses have become considerably less important since the development of citizenship. Those relying on Articles 45 and 49 are also EU citizens, and can rely on Article 18 TFEU and the Citizenship Directive to obtain equal treatment in matters relating to their life outside work.[82]

(ii) Discrimination in the pursuit of a business

Freedom of establishment includes the right to pursue business activities. The Court of Justice has understood this as involving anything connected with the running of the business. There must be no discrimination in anything which affects the running of the migrant's business in

---

[74] [1968] OJ Spec. edn L257/2, 475.

[75] Case C-213/90 *Association de Soutien aux Travailleurs Immigrés (ASTI)* v *Chambre des employés privés* [1991] ECR I-3507.

[76] *Ibid.*; Case C-465/01 *Commission* v *Austria* [2004] ECR I-8291.

[77] Regulation 1612/68/EC, article 7(2).

[78] Case 175/88 *Biehl* v *Administration des contributions du grand-duché de Luxembourg* [1990] ECR I-1779.

[79] Case C-279/93 *Finanzamt Köln-Altstadt* v *Schumacker* [1995] ECR I-225.

[80] I. Roxan, 'Assuring Real Freedom of Movement in EU Direct Taxation' (2000) 63 *MLR* 831, 847–50.

[81] Regulation 1612/68/EC, articles 7(3), 9. See e.g. Case 32/75 *Anita Cristini* v *Société nationale des chemins de fer français* [1975] ECR 1085.

[82] See Chapter 11.

any way at all. In *Steinhauser*,[83] a German artist living in Biarritz in France applied to rent a fisherman's shed from the local authority but was refused on the grounds that he was not a French national. In its reference the national court noted that the letting of premises did not relate to a specific business activity and, therefore, implicitly raised the question of whether it fell outside Article 49. The Court held that the measure constituted illegal discrimination within Article 49. It stated that as the renting of premises for business purposes furthers the pursuit of a business, it falls within Article 49. Insofar as the measure was discriminatory, it was illegal. The remit of Article 49 in particular is, therefore, very wide. Planning, tax, health and safety, environmental and labour laws all affect the running of business. They must all be couched and applied in a manner that does not discriminate against non-nationals or foreign companies.

The remit of the non-discrimination principle is also wide in another sense. Whilst differential treatment of the migrant, per se, is not illegal, it need only result in the slightest of disadvantages to constitute illegal discrimination. In *Halliburton*,[84] a German subsidiary of Halliburton, an American parent company, wished to sell its assets in the Netherlands to the Dutch subsidiary of Halliburton. Under Dutch law, such a sale would normally be exempt from tax on the grounds that it was part of an internal company reorganisation. This exemption did not apply here because the vendor, the German subsidiary, was not incorporated in the Netherlands. The tax was levied, however, on the purchaser, which was the Dutch subsidiary. This seemed to be an internal matter as it primarily concerned the Dutch taxing of a Dutch company, which would be paying more tax because the person from which it purchased the company was not Dutch. The Court considered, nevertheless, that this resulted in illegal discrimination against the German subsidiary under Article 49. It argued that the tax placed the vendor at a disadvantage as the terms of sale for potential purchasers were not so favourable. Such reasoning was particularly stretched in this case as the sale was not an arm's length market transaction, but a company reorganisation and it is difficult to believe that the tax featured heavily in the German subsidiary's decision to buy. There is, therefore, an implication that wherever the Court finds differential treatment, it will be quick to find illegal behaviour by the Member State in question.

(iii) Equally applicable restrictions on the pursuit of an occupation

As we mentioned earlier,[85] regulation of the pursuit of an occupation covers a multitude of regulatory activities. Taxation laws or employment laws affect the employment relationship, and can make employment either more or less attractive in a Member State. These laws, as well as health and safety, environmental and planning laws, all affect business costs and therefore can also make establishment in another Member State less attractive. However, challenging these under EU law would have a number of effects. It would increase substantially the power of the Court of Justice and national courts, which would be required to rule on the appropriate level of regulation in these fields. In a corresponding vein, it would reduce the power of national and local authorities, who would only be able to legislate within the parameters set

---

[83] Case 197/84 *Steinhauser v City of Biarritz* [1985] ECR 1819.
[84] Case C-1/93 *Halliburton Services v Staatssecretaris van Financiën* [1994] ECR I-1137.
[85] See p. 838.

for them by the Court of Justice. It would also create uncertainty, as it would be unclear which laws affected the pursuit of an occupation, which could be justified in the public interest and which were pursued in a proportionate way. Finally, allowing non-discriminatory restrictions on the pursuit of economic activity to be challenged would introduce a strong deregulatory bias into EU law, as it would never be individuals pleading for more regulation but would, in all cases, be individuals challenging regulation they disliked for whatever reason. For these reasons, the Court's case law has been hesitant on whether non-discriminatory restrictions on the pursuit of economic activity should fall within either Article 45 or 49.

The Article 45 case law on this question has been rather terse. One of the cases in which it nevertheless has been addressed is *Danish Company Cars*. It will be remembered that Denmark prohibited residents using company cars registered abroad in Denmark, to quell the fear that many of its residents would use this as a way of not paying Danish motor vehicle tax. Company cars are an employment benefit and therefore relate to the pursuit of employment rather than the taking up of employment. In the excerpt quoted earlier,[86] the Court stated that such restrictions could fall within Article 45 if they affected access to the labour market. It then considered whether this was the case.

Case C-464/02 Commission v Denmark (Danish Company Cars) [2005] ECR I-7929

45. It is settled case law that Article [45 TFEU] prohibits not only all discrimination, direct or indirect, based on nationality, but also national rules which are applicable irrespective of the nationality of the workers concerned but impede their freedom of movement.

46. It is clear that the original scheme, insofar as it remains applicable, could, on account of the obligation to register in Denmark a company car made available to the employee by an employer established in another Member State, deter such an employer from taking on an employee resident in Denmark for work which is not the employee's principal employment and, consequently, impede access to such employment by residents in Denmark.

47. As regards employees resident in Denmark who wish to pursue their principal employment in an undertaking established in another Member State, the amended scheme also impedes freedom of movement for those workers since it imposes additional costs in the form of a temporary registration tax.

48. Insofar as the undertaking established in another Member State bears those costs without being compensated, it is deterred from taking on an employee resident in Denmark in respect of whom the costs are higher than those borne for an employee who does not reside in that State.

49. It is true, as the Danish Government asserts, that the employer could attempt to adjust the salary of an employee resident in Denmark in order to offset the additional expense in question. In other words, he could try to pay to that employee a salary lower than that paid to an employee engaged in the same activity, but who resides in another Member State.

50. However, an employee resident in Denmark might already be deterred from seeking employment in another Member State faced with the prospect of receiving a salary lower than that of a comparable employee resident in that other Member State. As the Court ruled in paragraph 18 of Case 121/86

---

[86] See p. 837.

Ledoux [1988] ECR 3741, the fact that an employee is placed at a disadvantage in regard to working conditions compared to his colleagues residing in the country of their employer has a direct effect on the exercise of his right to freedom of movement within the Community ...

52. Consequently, it must be held that the Danish legislation, both in its original version and in its amended version, constitutes a restriction on freedom of movement for workers.

The same reasoning has been applied to an analogous rule in the context of self-employed workers in *Nadin*.[87] In neither case was it possible to speak of nationality discrimination, but rather discrimination against migrants, against those who had exercised their EU rights to engage in economic activity in another Member State. This has been the theme in most of the cases on equally applicable restrictions on employment and establishment.[88]

Yet, where this argument cannot be made the Court has been reluctant to find restrictions. For example, in *Fearon*,[89] the Court considered an Irish residence requirement, which provided for compulsory acquisition of land if a person owning the land or, in the case of companies the company directors, had not been resident for more than a year within three miles of that land. The measure was held to fall outside Article 49 purely on the grounds that it did not discriminate against other EU nationals. Although the judgment is quite old, it has been followed in a number of subsequent decisions,[90] most notably in *Sodemare*. Sodemare was a Luxembourg company, which, amongst other things, provided sheltered accommodation for elderly residents. It was refused approval to enter into contracts with public authorities in the region of Lombardy in Italy, which would have allowed it to be reimbursed for some of the health care services it provided. The reason was that under Lombard law, such contracts were only available to non-profit-making bodies. Sodemare challenged this, claiming that it violated Article 49 as it affected its ability to run its business in Italy.

Case C-70/95 *Sodemare v Regione Lombardia* [1997] ECR I-3395

32. ... as Community law stands at present, a Member State may, in the exercise of the powers it retains to organize its social security system, consider that a social welfare system of the kind at issue in this case necessarily implies, with a view to attaining its objectives, that the admission of private operators to that system as providers of social welfare services is to be made subject to the condition that they are non-profit-making.

33. Moreover, the fact that it is impossible for profit-making companies automatically to participate in the running of a statutory social welfare system of a Member State by concluding a contract which entitles them to be reimbursed by the public authorities for the costs of providing social welfare services of a

---

[87] Joined Cases C-151/04 and C-152/04 *Nadin, Nadin-Lux and Durré* [2005] ECR I-11203.

[88] See e.g. Case C-464/05 *Geurts and Vogten v Administratie van de BTW, registratie en domeinen, Belgische Staat* [2007] ECR I-9325.

[89] Case 182/83 *Fearon v Irish Land Commission* [1984] ECR 3677.

[90] See also Case 221/85 *Commission v Belgium (right of establishment: clinical biology laboratories)* [1987] ECR 719; Case 196/86 *Conradi and Others v Direction de la Concurrence et des Prix* [1987] ECR 4469.

health-care nature is not liable to place profit-making companies from other Member States in a less favourable factual or legal situation than profit-making companies in the Member State in which they are established.

34. In view of the foregoing, the non-profit condition cannot be regarded as contrary to Article [49 TFEU] ...

It has been argued, therefore, that Articles 45 and 49 TFEU are only concerned with prohibiting discrimination. Restrictions on the taking up of an activity are in reality forms of discrimination as, by preventing migrants entering the market, they protect the state's own nationals from competition. Restrictions on the pursuit of economic activity, on the other hand, should be seen as discriminatory either where they unjustifiably disadvantage nationals of other Member States, or where they unjustifiably disadvantage those who exercise their cross-border EU rights.[91] Despite varying judicial language, it was until recently possible to square this interpretation with the results of the cases.[92]

It is becoming less obvious that this is still true. In *Caixa Bank France*, a challenge was made by the subsidiary of a Spanish bank to a French prohibition on the offering of certain types of bank account. French law prohibited remuneration or interest being offered on 'sight accounts'. These are accounts that allow instant withdrawals. The restriction applied to all banks and although it did not prevent foreign banks setting up in France, it did prevent them from carrying out these types of activity.

Case C-442/02 *Caixa Bank France* v *Ministère de l'Économie, des Finances et de l'Industrie* [2004] ECR I-8961

11. Article [49 TFEU] requires the elimination of restrictions on the freedom of establishment. All measures which prohibit, impede or render less attractive the exercise of that freedom must be regarded as such restrictions.

12. A prohibition on the remuneration of sight accounts such as that laid down by the French legislation constitutes, for companies from Member States other than the French Republic, a serious obstacle to the pursuit of their activities via a subsidiary in the latter Member State, affecting their access to the market. That prohibition is therefore to be regarded as a restriction within the meaning of Article [49 TFEU].

13. That prohibition hinders credit institutions which are subsidiaries of foreign companies in raising capital from the public, by depriving them of the possibility of competing more effectively, by paying remuneration on sight accounts, with the credit institutions traditionally established in the Member State of establishment, which have an extensive network of branches and therefore greater opportunities than those subsidiaries for raising capital from the public.

[91] G. Marenco, 'The Notion of Restriction on the Freedom of Establishment and Provision of Services in the Case-law of the Court' (1991) 11 *YBEL* 111.

[92] G. Davies, *Nationality Discrimination in the European Internal Market* (The Hague, Kluwer Law International, 2003).

14. Where credit institutions which are subsidiaries of foreign companies seek to enter the market of a Member State, competing by means of the rate of remuneration paid on sight accounts constitutes one of the most effective methods to that end. Access to the market by those establishments is thus made more difficult by such a prohibition ...

17. It is clear from settled case law that where, as in the case at issue in the main proceedings, such a measure applies to any person or undertaking carrying on an activity in the territory of the host Member State, it may be justified where it serves overriding requirements relating to the public interest, is suitable for securing the attainment of the objective it pursues and does not go beyond what is necessary to attain it ...

The Court nevertheless found that the restriction could not be justified by the protection of consumers or the need to encourage long-term saving. These admirable goals, it asserted, could be met by less restrictive measures.

While the Court in *Caixa Bank France* speaks about foreign companies wishing to enter the French market, and the problems which the rule may cause them, the Court does not make it obvious that the rule would affect them more than it would an emerging French competitor. Nor does the Court make any such comparison part of its reasoning. The core of the objection is that the rule disadvantages would-be market entrants. This could be presented in terms of nationality discrimination, since incumbents are being protected and they are usually national. However, it seems that this is not the way the Court wants to frame the law.

The Court may therefore be moving towards a position that in substance is similar to its position concerning the free movement of goods. Restrictions which do not actually prevent an actor from entering the market are only likely to fall within Articles 45 and 49 if they discriminate against market entrants.[93] Equal impact market regulation will not be caught. In *Caixa Bank France*, therefore, offering rewards on a current account would be a central route for any new bank, be it foreign or French, to build up market share. The bank is denied this important marketing strategy, and in a market in which it cannot differentiate itself, it will struggle to win clients. The basis for such reasoning is that participation in the single market necessitates that Member States allow sufficiently vibrant competition on their markets. This is not unreasonable, but it is a very imprecise goal to realise. Secondly, measures will only actually violate Articles 45 and 49 if they are unjustifiably heavy-handed. Thus, *Caixa Bank France* involves a measure which deprives banks of an important marketing tool and element of a business model, namely the right to offer interest on current accounts, and the reasons given for the deprivation are fairly weak.

5 THE FREE MOVEMENT OF COMPANIES

(i) Discrimination and foreign companies

Freedom of establishment is granted not merely to EU citizens, but also to non-natural legal persons. In this respect, it is quite different from Article 45 on the free movement of workers. The beneficiaries of the right to establishment are set out in Article 54 TFEU.

---

[93] See Case C-405/98 *Konsumentombudsmannen (KO)* v *Gourmet International Products AB* [2001] ECR I-1795; see pp. 774–5.

Article 54 TFEU

Companies or firms formed in accordance with the law of a Member State and having their registered office, central administration or principal place of business within the Community shall, for the purposes of this Chapter, be treated in the same way as natural persons who are nationals of Member States.

'Companies or firms' means companies or firms constituted under civil or commercial law, including cooperative societies, and other legal persons governed by public or private law, save for those which are non-profit-making.

Companies have to be formed in accordance with the laws of one of the Member States and have their registered office, central administration or principal place of business within the European Union if they are to have the right to freedom of establishment. Therefore, whilst the prohibition on discrimination in Article 49 forbids discrimination on the grounds of nationality in the case of individuals, it forbids discrimination on the grounds of the place of registered office, central administration or principal place of business in the case of companies.[94] As Marenco has pointed out, there is, however, an important difference between these grounds of discrimination and that of nationality.

G. Marenco, 'The Notion of Restriction on the Freedom of Establishment and Provision of Services in the Case-law of the Court' (1991) 11 _Yearbook of European Law_ 111, 113–14

[T]here can never be more than a partial equivalence of the nationality condition and that of the company's registered office on a national territory. The former indeed uses a purely formal criterion, with no concrete or substantial content, to exclude equality of treatment. Thus it cannot be justified on economic grounds, which is where freedom of establishment operates. By contrast, the registered office as criterion of the connection of a company with a State is simultaneously a concrete situation which might justify a difference in treatment. Thus it cannot be equated purely and simply with nationality.

This emerges in Case 270/83 _Commission_ v _France_ [[1986] ECR 273], which dealt with a French tax provision that denied tax credits in respect of dividends on shares in French companies held by branches or agencies of companies, the registered office of which was in another Member State. The Court, having found that this provision led to a difference in treatment between French companies and those in other Member States, took into consideration the French Government's arguments that this difference in treatment was in the circumstances justified by objective differences in the situations of the two types of company. While in the end finding in favour of the Commission, the Court observed, in refuting the French Government's arguments, that 'the possibility cannot altogether be excluded that a distinction based on the location of the registered office of a company or the place of residence of a natural person may, under certain circumstances, be justified in an area such as tax law'. The registered office is thus compared first with the nationality of physical persons and then with their residence. This double comparison reveals that the registered office condition plays a role at once formal and substantial.

---

[94] Case 270/83 _Commission_ v _France_ [1986] ECR 273.

(ii) Relocation of company activity from one Member State to another

Companies may wish to move their principal place of business or head office to another Member State or to reincorporate in another Member State. This would seem the type of relocation of business activity that the single market is intended to stimulate. However, there is a double context which complicates matters.

The first difficulty is a formal legal one. The company's incorporation within its home Member State is the feature which allows it to claim rights under Article 49. If companies lose their legal personality within that state, either by dissolving or not meeting its corporate law requirements, they would lose their right to establish under Article 49.

The second is the policy context. Companies may wish to evade their fiscal and corporate responsibilities in states where they carry out their principal business by creating a legal shell in another Member State, which has lower fiscal obligations and less demanding corporate law (e.g. lower minimum capital requirements or less protection of minority shareholders). There are, moreover, incentives for states to attract these legal shells because, at very little cost to themselves, they can attract taxes that would otherwise go to the state where the company carries out its principal place of business. This can lead to a 'race to the bottom' where the tax base and basic company law requirements are eroded as states compete to attract investment.[95]

These issues were first addressed in the *Daily Mail* judgment. Under UK law, companies could not transfer their central management from the United Kingdom and still retain their legal personality without first obtaining the consent of the Treasury. The *Daily Mail* newspaper wished to transfer its central management to the Netherlands so that it might sell off some of its shares without being subject to UK capital gains tax. After negotiations with the Treasury broke down, it brought an action claiming that the UK regime breached Article 49. The case therefore raised both of the concerns outlined above.

The Court found that there was no violation of Article 49. The United Kingdom was not preventing the *Daily Mail* from emigrating and becoming a Dutch company, if it so wanted. Rather, the *Mail* wanted to remain a UK company, while moving its headquarters abroad, whereas UK law said that to be a UK company entailed that its headquarters were in the United Kingdom. Thus the case, in the view of the Court, was not so much about whether the *Mail* could move, as about the right of the United Kingdom to define what it meant to be a UK company. In the absence of harmonisation of the rules concerning incorporation, this was for the United Kingdom to decide.

Case 81/87 *R* v *HM Treasury, ex parte Daily Mail* [1988] ECR 5483

18. The provision of United Kingdom law at issue in the main proceedings imposes no restriction on transactions such as those described above [reincorporation in another Member State]. Nor does it stand in the way of a partial or total transfer of the activities of a company incorporated in the United Kingdom to a company newly incorporated in another Member State, if necessary after winding-up and,

---

[95] This is sometimes called the 'Delaware effect' after a so-called 'race to the bottom' in state company laws in the United States was believed to have been initiated by the State of Delaware in the 1960s. W. Gary, 'Federalism and Corporate Law: Reflections upon Delaware' (1974) 83 *Yale Law Journal* 663. On this within the European Union, see C. Barnard, 'Social Dumping and the Race to the Bottom: Some Lessons for the European Union from Delaware?' (2000) 25 *ELRev.* 57. See also pp. 706–8.

consequently, the settlement of the tax position of the United Kingdom company. It requires Treasury consent only where such a company seeks to transfer its central management and control out of the United Kingdom while maintaining its legal personality and its status as a United Kingdom company.

19. In that regard it should be borne in mind that, unlike natural persons, companies are creatures of the law and, in the present state of Community law, creatures of national law. They exist only by virtue of the varying national legislation which determines their incorporation and functioning.

20. As the Commission has emphasized, the legislation of the Member States varies widely in regard to both the factor providing a connection to the national territory required for the incorporation of a company and the question whether a company incorporated under the legislation of a Member State may subsequently modify that connecting factor. Certain States require that not merely the registered office but also the real head office, that is to say the central administration of the company, should be situated on their territory, and the removal of the central administration from that territory thus presupposes the winding-up of the company with all the consequences that winding-up entails in company law and tax law. The legislation of other states permits companies to transfer their central administration to a foreign country but certain of them, such as the United Kingdom, make that right subject to certain restrictions, and the legal consequences of a transfer, particularly in regard to taxation, vary from one Member State to another.

21. The Treaty has taken account of that variety in national legislation. In defining, in Article [54 TFEU], the companies which enjoy the right of establishment, the Treaty places on the same footing, as connecting factors, the registered office, central administration and principal place of business of a company …

22. It should be added that none of the Directives on the coordination of company law adopted under Article 54(3)(g) of the Treaty deal with the differences at issue here.

23. It must therefore be held that the Treaty regards the differences in national legislation concerning the required connecting factor and the question whether – and if so how – the registered office or real head office of a company incorporated under national law may be transferred from one Member State to another as problems which are not resolved by the rules concerning the right of establishment but must be dealt with by future legislation or conventions.

24. Under those circumstances, Articles [49 and 54 TFEU] cannot be interpreted as conferring on companies incorporated under the law of a Member State a right to transfer their central management and control and their central administration to another Member State while retaining their status as companies incorporated under the legislation of the first Member State.

Daily Mail has been recently confirmed in *Cartesio*. The facts were similar, but concerned Hungary and Italy rather than the United Kingdom and the Netherlands. The company Cartesio argued that *Daily Mail* was no longer good law in the light of subsequent cases, but the Court rejected this, repeating its arguments above in almost identical terms, and emphasising that it was for states to determine the conditions for incorporation in their jurisdiction, and the presence of headquarters was a perfectly legitimate condition. Nevertheless, although this did not arise in *Cartesio*, it would be wrong to think that conditions for incorporation are outside the scope of Article 49. If, for example, they discriminate, they will still violate the Treaty.[96]

[96] Case C-299/02 *Commission v Netherlands* [2004] ECR I-9761. See also H. Schneeweiss, 'Exit Taxation after *Cartesio*: The European Fundamental Freedom's Impact on Taxing Migrating Companies' (2009) 37 *Intertax* 363.

Most cases involve a different scenario: where a company is incorporated in state X, but does most of its business in state Y. The reason for such a construction is often to avoid strict rules on incorporation in Y, and for this same reason state Y is usually inclined to view the incorporation in X as an abusive attempt to avoid its rules. These cases raise the concerns about regulatory competition raised above.

This scenario was addressed in *Centros*. Two Danish nationals registered a company in the United Kingdom. Although it never traded from the United Kingdom, it was registered there because the UK authorities impose no minimum share capital requirement for companies whilst in Denmark there was a requirement of a minimum of 100,000 Danish kroner. They were refused permission to register a branch in Denmark and challenged this under Article 49. The Danish government argued that there was no violation as they were simply refusing the setting up of a primary establishment and not the setting up of a branch. The Court of Justice disagreed.

Case C–212/97 *Centros v Erhvervs-og Selskabsstyrelsen* [1999] ECR I–1459

21. Where it is the practice of a Member State, in certain circumstances, to refuse to register a branch of a company having its registered office in another Member State, the result is that companies formed in accordance with the law of that other Member State are prevented from exercising the freedom of establishment conferred on them by Articles [49 and 54 TFEU].

22. Consequently, that practice constitutes an obstacle to the exercise of the freedoms guaranteed by those provisions.

23. According to the Danish authorities, however, Mr and Mrs Bryde cannot rely on those provisions, since the sole purpose of the company formation which they have in mind is to circumvent the application of the national law governing formation of private limited companies and therefore constitutes abuse of the freedom of establishment. In their submission, the Kingdom of Denmark is therefore entitled to take steps to prevent such abuse by refusing to register the branch.

24. It is true that according to the case law of the Court a Member State is entitled to take measures designed to prevent certain of its nationals from attempting, under cover of the rights created by the Treaty, improperly to circumvent their national legislation or to prevent individuals from improperly or fraudulently taking advantage of provisions of Community law ...

25. However, although, in such circumstances, the national courts may, case by case, take account – on the basis of objective evidence – of abuse or fraudulent conduct on the part of the persons concerned in order, where appropriate, to deny them the benefit of the provisions of Community law on which they seek to rely, they must nevertheless assess such conduct in the light of the objectives pursued by those provisions ...

26. In the present case, the provisions of national law, application of which the parties concerned have sought to avoid, are rules governing the formation of companies and not rules concerning the carrying on of certain trades, professions or businesses. The provisions of the Treaty on freedom of establishment are intended specifically to enable companies formed in accordance with the law of a Member State and having their registered office, central administration or principal place of business within the Community to pursue activities in other Member States through an agency, branch or subsidiary.

27. That being so, the fact that a national of a Member State who wishes to set up a company chooses to form it in the Member State whose rules of company law seem to him the least restrictive and to set

up branches in other Member States cannot, in itself, constitute an abuse of the right of establishment. The right to form a company in accordance with the law of a Member State and to set up branches in other Member States is inherent in the exercise, in a single market, of the freedom of establishment guaranteed by the Treaty.

28. In this connection, the fact that company law is not completely harmonised in the Community is of little consequence. Moreover, it is always open to the Council, on the basis of the powers conferred upon it by Article [50(3)(g) TFEU], to achieve complete harmonisation.

29. In addition ... the fact that a company does not conduct any business in the Member State in which it has its registered office and pursues its activities only in the Member State where its branch is established is not sufficient to prove the existence of abuse or fraudulent conduct which would entitle the latter Member State to deny that company the benefit of the provisions of Community law relating to the right of establishment.

30. Accordingly, the refusal of a Member State to register a branch of a company formed in accordance with the law of another Member State in which it has its registered office on the grounds that the branch is intended to enable the company to carry on all its economic activity in the host State, with the result that the secondary establishment escapes national rules on the provision for and the paying-up of a minimum capital, is incompatible with Articles [49 and 54 TFEU], insofar as it prevents any exercise of the right freely to set up a secondary establishment which Articles [49 and 54 TFEU] are specifically intended to guarantee.

Centros reaffirms the right of companies to secondary establishment in other states. Whilst a company retains corporate status within its home Member State, other Member States must recognise it as validly incorporated under Article 54 and therefore entitled to the benefits of Article 49. Needless to say, this does not meet the policy concerns about regulatory competition whereby companies will simply incorporate in the state whose fiscal and corporate regime is most favourable to them. States have attempted to prevent this practice in a number of cases before the Court of Justice.

In *Überseering*,[97] a challenge was made to the German law which stated that a company's legal capacity is governed by the law of the territory in which its central place of administration is based. What this meant in substance was that German law would only recognise the existence of a company whose administration and incorporation were in the same state. Überseering, however, had its central administration in Germany, but was incorporated in the Netherlands. Dutch law permitted this, but when Überseering sought to bring legal action in Germany over a business dispute it discovered that it had no standing because in the eyes of German law it did not exist. The Court found this to be a violation of Article 49. Where a company is validly incorporated in one state according to the laws of that state, other states are required to recognise that incorporation, notwithstanding that their own conditions for incorporation may be different. Not to recognise Überseering's Dutch legal status would be to greatly deter establishment in the Netherlands.

In *Inspire Art*,[98] the Netherlands rather clumsily attempted to avoid *Centros*. Companies incorporated abroad, but which conducted almost all their business in the Netherlands

---

[97] Case C-208/00 *Überseering* v *NCC* [2002] ECR I-9919.
[98] Case C-167/01 *Kamer van Koophandel en Fabrieken voor Amsterdam* v *Inspire Art* [2003] ECR I-10195.

through branches or agencies, had to register their agencies or branches in the Netherlands as 'foreign companies'. These were then required to meet Dutch company law requirements on directors' duties and minimum share capital for companies. Inspire Art was a company which conducted almost all its business in objets d'art, but which had incorporated in the United Kingdom specifically to avoid these requirements. It challenged the obligation to satisfy them under Article 49. The Dutch government argued that Inspire Art was engaged in an abuse of Article 49 as it was deliberately incorporating in another Member State in which it did no business to evade and thereby undermine Dutch company law. The Court disagreed. It found that the formation of a company in one Member State for the sole purpose of enjoying the benefit of more favourable legislation was not abusive behaviour even where that company conducted all its activities in another Member State. Thus, insofar as the Dutch government was imposing restrictions on companies validly incorporated within the European Union and thereby preventing them from trading in the Netherlands unless they met certain conditions concerning directors' duties and minimum share capital, it was engaged in a breach of Article 49.[99]

This case law reflects two potent dangers between which it is difficult to navigate. On the one hand, if companies could only trade in another Member State where they met all that state's company law requirements, there would be a grinding halt to economic activity across the Union. In effect, no foreign companies could operate in the state with the most restrictive company law as they would not meet these standards. On the other hand, allowing foreign companies who do not meet the state's company law standards to operate on local markets has the effect of completely undermining local company and tax laws, as it is easy and inexpensive for companies to locate in the state with the least onerous requirements.

Deakin has noted that Centros creates a potent example of what he calls 'competitive federalism'. If the case is not balanced by other measures it will undermine national diversity. The regime most attractive to companies will become the default law for the European Union as either they will incorporate there or other states will be quick to adopt parallel laws to prevent this. The typical solution of competitive federalism is therefore to develop laws at a federal, or pan-European, level. But Deakin notes that this is just as restrictive of national diversity as regulatory competition and instead suggests an alternative, that of 'reflexive harmonisation'.[100] The starting point for this model is the assumption that competition between regimes will take place. What is important in such circumstances is to secure the terms of competition in order to ensure that they do not eliminate diversity or lead to clearly undesirable outcomes, but rather act as a positive force where regimes learn from each other and unsatisfactory regimes are jettisoned. The central pillars of such an approach are that EU law would provide a floor of rights which act to prevent outcomes collectively agreed as undesirable. Beyond that, this approach would require Member States to put in place institutions at local level which secure as wide a

---

[99] There is substantial literature on this case law. See particularly M. Siems, 'Convergence, Competition, Centros and Conflicts of Law: European Company Law in the 21st Century' (2002) 27 *ELRev.* 47; W.-H. Roth, 'From Centros to Überseering: Free Movement of Companies, Private International Law, and Community Law' (2003) 52 *ICLQ* 177; E. Micheler, 'Recognition of Companies Incorporated in Other EU Member States' (2003) 52 *ICLQ* 521; C. Kersting and C. Philipp Schindler, 'The ECJ's Inspire Art Decision of 30 September 2003 and its Effects on Practice' (2003) 4(12) *German Law Journal* 1277.

[100] See pp. 710–11.

scope for deliberation and interest representation as possible, so that outcomes are considered in the context of both the wider EU environment and broad internal social needs.[101]

S. Deakin, 'Two Types of Regulatory Competition: Competitive Federalism versus Reflexive Harmonisation: A Law and Economics Approach to *Centros*' (1999) 2 *Cambridge Yearbook of European Legal Studies* 231, 245–6

Reflexive law, therefore, has a procedural orientation. What this means, in the context of economic regulation, is that the preferred mode of intervention is for the law to underpin and encourage autonomous processes of adjustment, in particular by supporting mechanisms of group representation and participation, rather than to intervene by imposing particular distributive outcomes. This type of approach finds a concrete manifestation in legislation which seeks, in various ways, to devolve or confer rule-making powers to self-regulatory processes. Examples are laws which allow collective bargaining by trade unions and employers to make qualified exceptions to limits on working time or similar standards ...

The purpose of harmonisation would not be to substitute for state-level regulation; hence the transnational standard would not operate to 'occupy the field' ... Rather, transnational standards would seek to promote diverse, local-level approaches to regulatory problems by creating a space for autonomous solutions to emerge when, because of market failure, they would not otherwise do so. This may involve what some regard as a restriction of competition, in the sense of ruling out certain options which could be associated with a 'race to the bottom' whilst leaving others open. This is now a familiar technique within the European Community ... Directives in the areas of labour law, consumer protection and environmental law are mostly interpreted as setting basic standards in the form of a 'floor of rights'. Although 'downwards' derogation is prohibited, Member States are allowed and implicitly encouraged to improve on the standards set centrally. Far from being a 'straitjacket', then, which restricts local autonomy, Community-level intervention may be the precondition for local-level experimentation.

---

6 THE SERVICES DIRECTIVE AND FREEDOM OF ESTABLISHMENT

Directive 2006/123/EC ('Services Directive') applies not only to cross-border service provision but also to those establishing in a Member State. They benefit from the Directive's Chapter on establishment, as well as from its rules on administrative simplification. These latter, and the material scope of the Services Directive, were discussed in Chapter 19.[102]

The Chapter on freedom of establishment addresses three categories of national measures.[103] The first articles in this Chapter deal with authorisation schemes – rules which require that a person cannot establish or begin their activity without an authorisation. Such rules are fairly

---

[101] Some are sceptical whether, even with such safeguards, such experimentation could take off, arguing that the broader context is still one in which local communities are being forced into quick decisions by the demands of multinational enterprises. W. Scheuerman, 'Democratic Experimentalism or Capitalist Synchronization? Critical Reflections on Directly-Deliberative Polyarchy' (2004) 17 *Canadian Journal of Law and Jurisprudence* 101; C. Joerges, 'What is Left of the European Economic Constitution? A Melancholic Eulogy' (2005) 30 *ELRev.* 461, 482.

[102] See pp. 823–8.

[103] Directive 2006/123/EC on services in the internal market, articles 9–15.

common in some Member States. Article 9 provides that such schemes are only permitted where they are non-discriminatory, justified by a public interest objective, and the goal cannot be met by a less restrictive measure. As is evident, this is no more or less than the existing case law would suggest. However, articles 9 to 13 provide some detail on the operation of authorisation schemes, with procedural requirements aimed at ensuring that they function in an accessible, fair, transparent and non-discriminatory way.

Article 14 then lists certain kinds of measure concerning established persons which are prohibited. These include discriminatory requirements, requirements concerning the nationality of shareholders or company directors, restrictions on secondary establishment or requirements that the establishment in the state be the primary establishment and market-need based restrictions. The Court has tended to prohibit such restrictions anyway, but the absence of grounds for derogation may make the Directive stricter, although this has to be weighed against the many exclusions from the Directive's scope.

Finally, article 15 provides a list of 'requirements to be evaluated'. These include limits on employee numbers or tariffs, requirements to have a particular legal form, or 'quantitative or territorial restrictions'. Any such requirements are only permitted if they are non-discriminatory, justified and proportionate. Once again, the Directive follows the case law of the Court.

The establishment Chapter is apparently weaker than the services Chapter. It only applies to certain specifically listed national requirements, and, apart from article 14, it permits these to be justified by any good public interest objective. Its approach to the legality of national measures is essentially a summary of the case law.

This difference between the approach to service and establishment reflects their different roles in the wider structure of the internal market. Home state regulation, which is the philosophy of the cases and of the Directive, entails that requirements imposed on service providers by their host state should be the exception, and so are subject to strict limits. By contrast, the home state approach entails that the established person has in principle made a choice to subject herself to the rules of her state of new establishment, and EU intervention should confine itself to rooting out discrimination against her, or particularly obstructive and disproportionate rules.

However, the Chapter on establishment does add to the law in another way: it appears to apply to those establishing in their own state, as well as those coming from other states. Either might fall victim to many of the measures discussed (the authorisation requirements or rules on employee numbers or tariffs), and there is nothing in the Directive to suggest that only the cross-border person can rely on it. By contrast, that text appears to regulate the national measures in question in a general way. Thus, while the law on establishment is not made stricter by the Directive, it has been broadened. It is at least arguable that within the scope of the Directive's provisions on establishment, as is the case with the provisions on administrative simplification, wholly internal situations are no longer excluded. The defined group of national rules to which this Chapter applies is now subject to proportionality review at the request of any economic actor suffering disadvantage from them.

This is understandable. The alternative would be that the foreigner wishing to start his business would be exempted from all kinds of authorisation procedures and administrative requirements with which the national would still have to comply. This would create reverse discrimination. That may sometimes be an unavoidable side-effect of the case law, but it is bad policy to entrench it in legislation.[104] Secondly, any such entrenched distinction would create a motivation for artificial cross-border constructions: the Frenchman wanting to start a business in France would be better first starting a nominal business abroad and then coming home, or looking for a foreign 'partner'. As is usually the case with harmonising legislation, the Directive tries to avoid such problems by creating a uniform structure of rights for all economic actors, albeit within a limited sphere.

FURTHER READING

C. Costello, 'Market Access All Areas? The Treatment of Non-Discriminatory Barriers to the Free Movement of Workers' (2000) 27(3) *Legal Issues of Economic Integration* 267

S. Deakin, 'Reflexive Governance and European Company Law' (2009) 15 *European Law Journal* 224

A. Johnston and P. Syrpis, 'Regulatory Competition in European Company Law after *Cartesio*' (2009) 34 *European Law Review* 378

A. Kranz, 'The *Bosman* Case: The Relationship Between European Union Law and the Transfer System in European Football' (1999) 5 *Cambridge Journal of European Law* 431

G. Marenco, 'The Notion of Restriction on the Freedom of Establishment and Provision of Services in the Case-law of the Court' (1991) 11 *Yearbook of European Law* 111

C. O'Brien, 'Social Blind Spots and Monocular Policy Making: The ECJ's Migrant Worker Model' (2009) 46 *Common Market Law Review* 1107

A. Tryfonidou, 'In Search of the Aim of the EC Free Movement of Persons Provisions: Has the Court of Justice Missed the Point?' (2009) 46 *Common Market Law Review* 1591

R. White, *Workers, Establishment, and Services in the European Union* (Oxford, Oxford University Press, 2005)

---

[104] See G. Davies, *Services, Citizenship and the Country of Origin Principle*, Mitchell Working Paper No. 2/07 (2007).

21

Trade Restrictions and Public Goods

1 INTRODUCTION

This chapter is about derogations from free movement, and their review by the Court of Justice. These derogations exist to protect important national interests – public goods – but they can also be used to disguise protectionism, which is why they are usually quite strictly reviewed.

Section 2 provides an introduction to the themes and context of the Treaty derogations. These Articles are at the heart of one of the most important current debates: whether globalisation unavoidably threatens non-economic interests and values, or whether reconciliation or compromise is possible. The Court uses a range of ideas and principles, from transparency to a margin of appreciation, in its search for the right approach.

Section 3 addresses the range of public goods which the Treaty protects. The explicit derogations are brief and limited, but the Court has extended them with its invention of the mandatory requirement, or the general public interest objective. The range of justifications which may be relied upon to restrict movement is now very broad, and only protectionist reasons, or purely economic reasons, have been excluded. This latter category is problematic: the distinction between an economic and a non-economic interest is often not clear. For example, protecting national budgets protects the health of public institutions, and so also protects interests such as public health and public security.

Section 4 is about the principles governing derogations. The Court will critically examine whether they are truly necessary, or whether the goals could be achieved by less restrictive measures. In deciding necessity it is very influenced by the coherence of national policy: if the state shows itself to be inconsistent in protecting a particular interest then this undermines its claim that the threat is serious and action is necessary. This, however, ignores the political compromises which legislation and policy-making entail. Consistency may not always be a feasible governmental goal. In deciding whether less restrictive measures could be adopted the Court may itself investigate the question, or instruct the national court to, or it may adopt a procedural approach and ask whether the state adequately investigated other possibilities before it acted.

Sections 5 to 8 are about specific Treaty derogations and provide examples of how the Court applies them. It becomes apparent that while, for example, public health claims are often critically examined and tested strictly for proportionality, where public policy and security are involved the Court may be more deferential. Environmental reasons occupy their own unique position. The environment is not specifically mentioned in the Treaty derogations, but the Court is aware that current concerns require it to be taken seriously and measures protecting the environment are weighed heavily in the balance when they impact on trade.

2 BALANCING FREE MOVEMENT AGAINST OTHER INTERESTS

At the heart of many globalisation debates is the fear that we are living in a run-away world.[1] In this world, the free movement of different factors of production undermines local democracy. Investment and companies simply move elsewhere whenever faced with unattractive demands by the local population. The dedication to the pursuit of wealth means that insufficient attention is paid to damaging side-effects, such as harm to the environment, further impoverishment of poor regions or the marketing of unsafe food. Finally, local forms of culture become swamped by the pervasiveness of global branding. Such a view is a distortion of what generally takes place, yet, if there is a setting to provide a stage for these fears, it is that offered by the economic freedoms. These freedoms institutionalise such concerns by giving capital, goods, services and labour a legal right to move across borders. This is not an unfettered right. Even in the early EEC Treaty, there were a number of grounds on which Member States were permitted to restrict trade. As attitudes evolved and conflicts have become more diverse, the Court of Justice has extended the grounds on which Member States may restrict trade to include an extremely wide array of justifications. The accommodation of so many interests and values has prompted further challenges. Everything turns on the way the Court of Justice mediates between the economic freedom and the exception in question. As we shall see, it has used a few generic principles to do this. Measures must be effective. They must not arbitrarily

---

[1] See e.g. K. Ohmae, *The Borderless World: Power and Strategy in the Interlinked Economy* (New York, Harper, 1990); J. Habermas, *The Postnational Constellation* (London, Polity, 2001) ch. 4.

discriminate. They must take account of the regulatory requirements that have already been met in other Member States. They must be the least restrictive of trade necessary to secure their objectives. However, the sheer diversity of the disputes and issues involved has inevitably led to the partial breakdown of these general principles, so that they are applied in different ways in different areas and cases. This has generated its own uncertainties, leading to doubt about the relationship between the general principles that are supposed to apply across the board and the specialised case law that predominates in certain areas.

Alongside a substantive investigation, or instead of it, the Court increasingly relies on procedural principles to determine the legitimacy of derogations. The Court now regularly asks whether the state has taken appropriate measures in the process leading to its decision, and whether that decision is adequately open to challenge by those affected: Was there a detailed risk assessment? Was international scientific opinion taken into account? Are authorisation procedures transparent, quick and accessible, and can decisions be challenged in court? This proceduralisation reflects broader themes in market regulation, especially the ever more central role of risk management, and the emphasis of recent years on good governance.

In general, the trend in many technocratic areas of the internal market seems to be towards more intrusive review and a heavier evidential burden on Member States to prove their case. Yet, in more subjective and value-laden fields the notion of a national margin of appreciation has become ever more central. Here, the Court looks for signs of honest intent, but emphasises the continuing freedom of states to define their own values and public norms. Perhaps the broadest overarching theme is that within a framework of common principles, there is a differentiated approach to their application, and an ever greater repertoire of rules and ideas which the Court can use.

3 PUBLIC GOODS PROTECTED UNDER EU LAW

The TFEU makes only limited provision for the protection of public goods from free trade, such as the environment, public morality and public health. The most extensive provision is that in relation to free movement of goods.

Article 36 TFEU

The provisions of Articles 34 and 35 shall not preclude prohibitions or restrictions on imports, exports or goods in transit justified on grounds of public morality, public policy or public security; the protection of health and life of humans, animals or plants; the protection of national treasures possessing artistic, historic or archaeological value; or the protection of industrial and commercial property. Such prohibitions or restrictions shall not, however, constitute a means of arbitrary discrimination or a disguised restriction on trade between Member States.

In addition, Article 65 TFEU sets out circumstances in which Member States may derogate from Article 63, which provides for free movement of capital.

Article 65(1) TFEU

The provisions of Article 63 shall be without prejudice to the right of Member States:

(a) to apply the relevant provisions of their tax law which distinguish between taxpayers who are not in the same situation with regard to their place of residence or with regard to the place where their capital is invested;

(b) to take all requisite measures to prevent infringements of national law and regulations, in particular in the field of taxation and the prudential supervision of financial institutions, or to lay down procedures for the declaration of capital movements for purposes of administrative or statistical information, or to take measures which are justified on grounds of public policy or public security.

In both instances, the grounds on which Member States can restrict trade are fairly limited. They are, however, more extensive than those provided for the other economic freedoms. Derogations from the Articles on free movement of workers, establishment and services are only provided for on grounds of public policy, public security and public health.[2] These, however, have been used more commonly as a form of migration control, to prevent persons entering the territory, than to stop undesirable economic activities.

Two more derogations allow for the protection of the special link between a state and its own nationals, reserving them an exclusive role in some aspects of the business of government. With regard to workers, therefore:

Article 45(4) TFEU

The provisions of this Article shall not apply to employment in the public service.

A parallel provision exists for services and establishment.

Article 51 TFEU

The provisions of this chapter [on establishment] shall not apply, so far as any given Member State is concerned, to activities which in that State are connected, even occasionally, with the exercise of official authority.

All the provisions above are both limited and static. Largely unchanged since they were first introduced into the EEC Treaty in 1957, it has been left to the Court of Justice to protect the mixed economy in a dynamic fashion that takes account of the changing nature of the integration process, developments in political value and the challenges posed by new

---

[2] Articles 45(3), 52(1) and 62 TFEU.

technologies. In the *Cassis de Dijon* judgment, the Court of Justice indicated that a quid pro quo for the extension of the economic freedoms was an acceptance that Member States should be able to take measures to protect a wide array of public interests, which would otherwise be threatened by these provisions, on condition that the measures did not arbitrarily discriminate and were proportionate and necessary to securing the objective they pursued.[3] The 'mandatory requirements' established in *Cassis de Dijon* to protect these interests from erosion by Article 34 have been applied in various guises to all the other economic freedoms.[4] The array of interests that have been successfully invoked to safeguard national legislation, using Treaty exceptions or mandatory requirements, may be grouped for convenience under four headings.

Market externalities   Market externalities arise where a transaction fails to take account of somebody's interests and that person was not deemed to have a choice in the matter. Most obviously, these interests are third party interests, such as those of the wider public. Market externalities can also affect the interests of one of the parties directly involved in the transaction. The sale of a dangerous product is an example. In all cases, the transaction is associated with the risk of some undesirable physical impact. The Court of Justice has moved to protect against a wide variety of market externalities. These include damage to public health,[5] harm to the consumer,[6] destruction of the environment,[7] unfair competition, fraud,[8] abuse of creditors,[9] dangers to road safety,[10] violation of intellectual property rights,[11] harm to the health and safety of workers,[12] and damage to the national historic and artistic heritage and to cultural policy.[13]

Civil liberties   The Court of Justice has also moved to ensure that the economic freedoms do not compromise those political values which are central to protecting human dignity, autonomy and equality. In such circumstances, the Court is concerned not only with the material impacts of trade but also its symbolic impacts, namely whether it is seen to undermine the standing of important constitutional values. To this end, the Court has indicated that it will

---

[3] Case 120/78 *Rewe-Zentrale AG v Bundesmonopolverwaltung für Branntwein (Cassis de Dijon)* [1979] ECR 649.

[4] Case C-415/93 *Union Royale Belge des Sociétés de Football Association and Others v Bosman and Others* [1995] ECR I-4921 (workers); Case 205/84 *Commission v Germany (German insurance)* [1986] ECR 3755 (services); Case 107/83 *Ordre des Avocats au Barreau de Paris v Klopp* [1984] ECR 2971 (establishment); Joined Cases C-515/99 and C-527/99–540/99 *Reisch and Others v Bürgermeister der Landeshaupstadt Salzburg* [2002] ECR I-2157 (capital).

[5] See e.g. Case C-429/02 *Bacardi France v Télévision française 1* [2004] ECR I-6613.

[6] Case 220/83 *Commission v France* [1986] ECR 3663; Case C-262/02 *Commission v France* [2004] ECR I-6569.

[7] Case 302/86 *Commission v Denmark* [1988] ECR 4607; Case C-17/00 *De Coster v Collège des bourgmestre et échevins de Watermael-Boitsfort* [2001] ECR I-9445.

[8] Case C-243/01 *Gambelli* [2003] ECR I-13031.

[9] Case C-212/97 *Centros v Erhvervs- og Selskabsstyrelsen* [1999] ECR I-1459.

[10] Case C-55/93 *Van Schaik* [1994] ECR I-4837; Case C-451/99 *Cura Anlagen v Auto Service Leasing* [2002] ECR I-3193; Case C-110/05 *Commission v Italy*, Judgment of 10 February 2009.

[11] Case 262/81 *Coditel v Ciné-Vog Films* [1980] ECR 881.

[12] Case 155/80 *Oebel* [1981] ECR 1993; Case C-113/89 *Rush Portuguesa v Office national d'immigration* [1990] ECR I-1417; Case C-164/99 *Portugaia Construções* [2002] ECR I-787; Case C-445/03 *Commission v Luxembourg (employment of foreign workers)* [2004] ECR I-10191.

[13] Case C-180/89 *Commission v Italy* [1991] ECR I-709; Case C-200/96 *Metronome Musik v Music Point Hokamp* [1998] ECR I-1953.

allow derogations to protect human dignity,[14] freedom of expression,[15] freedom of assembly,[16] the sanctity of religious beliefs[17] and cultural pluralism.[18]

Socio-cultural preferences   A body of case law concerns the impact of free movement on collective preferences about the way society is organised. Many rules may reflect or embody societal and cultural preferences or traditions. For example, rules concerning the role of professional organisations in regulating local markets are not just about the maintenance of objective standards, but about the place of the skilled person and of non-governmental bodies in society.[19] Such rules are seen as contributing to trust and stability. Rules on the opening hours of shops, such as Sunday opening, are not just economic policy, but reflect choices about the place of economic activity in the national lifestyle.[20] The autonomy of sporting organisations and their freedom to determine rules is also the product of the particular role of sport in society and attitudes towards it,[21] just as the rules on ownership of land, which have often been the subject of litigation, have much to do with the societal desire to nurture rural communities and protect a particular quality of life.[22]

Preservation of the machinery of the state   The final category of cases relate to the state's capacity to supply the services that are necessary for the government of its territory. In such cases, the Court is not so much concerned to protect certain values or interests per se but, rather, it aims to safeguard the machinery of government that enables such protection. Member States may, therefore, keep in place measures derogating from the economic freedoms to maintain internal and external security,[23] cohesion of their tax systems,[24] the order in society,[25] their systems of administration of justice,[26] and financial balance in their systems of social security.[27]

There is one group of interests that the Court of Justice will not protect: interests of a purely economic nature. In numerous cases it has repeated that purely economic reasons cannot justify restrictions on free movement.[28] The implication is that the type of interests protected

---

[14] Case C-36/02 *Omega Spielhallen -und Automatenaufstellungs-GmbH* v *Oberbürgermeisterin der Bundesstadt Bonn* [2004] ECR I-9609.

[15] Case C-71/02 *Karner* v *Troostwijk* [2004] ECR I-3025.

[16] Case C-112/00 *Schmidberger* v *Republic of Austria* [2003] ECR I-5659.

[17] Case C-275/92 *HM Customs and Excise* v *Schindler* [1994] ECR I-1039.

[18] Case C-288/89 *Gouda* v *Commissariat voor de Media* [1991] ECR I-4007.

[19] Case 33/74 *Van Binsbergen* v *Bestuur van de Bedrijsvereniging voor de Metaalnijverheid* [1974] ECR 1299; Case C-71/76 *Thieffry* v *Conseil de l'Ordre des Avocats à la Cour de Paris* [1977] ECR 765; Case C-58/98 *Corsten* [2000] ECR I-7919; Case C-309/99 *Wouters and Others* v *Algemene Raad van de Nederlandse Orde van Advocaten* [2002] ECR I-1577.

[20] Case C-145/88 *Torfaen Borough Council* v *B & Q* [1989] ECR I-3851.

[21] Case C-415/93 *Union Royale Belge des Sociétés de Football Association and Others* v *Bosman and Others* [1995] ECR I-4921.

[22] Case C-370/05 *Festersen* [2007] ECR I-1129.

[23] Case 72/83 *Campus Oil* v *Minister for Industry and Energy* [1984] ECR 2727.

[24] Case C-204/90 *Bachmann* v *Belgian State* [1992] ECR I-249; Case C-300/90 *Commission* v *Belgium* [1992] ECR I-305.

[25] Case C-275/92 *HM Customs and Excise* v *Schindler* [1994] ECR I-1039.

[26] Case C-3/95 *Reisebüro Broede* v *Sandker* [1996] ECR I-6511.

[27] Case C-158/96 *Kohll* v *Union des Caisses de Maladie* [1998] ECR I-1931.

[28] Case 352/85 *Bond van Adverteerders* [1988] ECR 2085; Case C-158/96 *Kohll* v *Union des Caisses de Maladie* [1998] ECR I-1931; Case C-398/95 *Syndesmos ton en Elladi Touristikon kai Taxidiotikon Grafeion* v *Ypourgos Ergasias* [1997] ECR I3091; J. Snell, 'Economic Aims as Justifications for Restrictions on Free Movement' in A. Schrauwen, *The Rule of Reason: Rethinking Another Classic of Community Law* (Groningen, Europa Law Publishing, 2005) 37.

by free movement are qualitatively of a higher order than purely economic matters, so these latter can never serve to restrict the former. However, in practice the idea of a purely economic reason is not tidily defined, since money impacts on other interests. Indeed, since the state's capacity to carry out policy is dependent to a large extent on its budget, and since the wellbeing of its citizens is dependent to a large extent on the state of the national economy, any economic reason can be repackaged as being about other interests, such as good public services, employee protection, or even public order, as the cases below show.

Within the concept of the economic reason there are two distinct types of reason, both unacceptable. One reason sometimes put forward for a measure is the desire to protect local businesses or industry, or the national or local economy.[29] The main reason to object to such measures is that they are implicitly protectionist. They aim to ensure that national economic actors are protected from foreign intrusion. This aim is not legitimate in the context of a market where states have committed to openness and non-discrimination. However, there is a very fine line between a quasi-protectionist measure and one serving legitimate goals. For example, in *Wolff and Müller*, a German law requiring foreign service providers to pay their employees the German minimum wage whilst providing services in Germany was claimed to breach Article 56 TFEU.[30] The Explanatory Memorandum made clear that the purpose of the law was to protect small and medium-sized enterprises from cheap competition. Yet, the measure also protected the employees of the service providers, and employees on the German market in general. For this reason, the Court ruled the measure to be lawful. The fact that one justification – protection from cheap competition – fails, does not mean that another justification – employee protection – cannot be put forward.

The other type of economic interest is where the state is trying to protect its own budget. For example, in *Kranemann*, the German government paid travel expenses for trips taken by trainee civil servants only if these trips were within Germany, and claimed that this was necessary for budgetary reasons.[31] Similarly, in *Kohll* and the other health care cases governments have argued that restrictions on patient migration should be imposed to prevent strain on health care budgets.[32] Neither argument was acceptable as such, since they posed purely economic interests against a fundamental freedom. However, in *Kohll* the Court acknowledged that if the economic effects were such that the health care system was threatened, then the economic concern in fact became a public health concern, which would be a legitimate reason for a restriction.[33] Analogously, in *Campus Oil* the Court permitted the Irish government to require oil companies to purchase some of their oil from a national refinery.[34] This measure reduced imports, and its immediate reason was to ensure the viability of the state refinery – an economic reason. However, the Irish government successfully argued that keeping the refinery operating was of strategic and security importance – legitimate reasons – and such operation could only be guaranteed by ensuring customers. Other interests which have been used to make concerns about money acceptable by presenting them as social, systemic or moral concerns,

---

[29] Case C-367/98 *Commission v Portugal (free movement of capital)* [2002] ECR I-473; Case C-452/01 *Ospelt v Schössle Weissenberg Familienstiftung* [2003] ECR I-9743.

[30] Case C-60/03 *Wolff and Müller v Felix* [2004] ECR I-9553. See also Case C-370/05 *Festersen* [2007] ECR I-1129.

[31] Case C-109/04 *Kranemann v Land Nordrhein-Westfalen* [2005] ECR I-2421.

[32] Case C-158/96 *Kohll v Union des Caisses de Maladie* [1998] ECR I-1931. See pp. 815–20.

[33] *Ibid.* See also Case C-141/07 *Commission v Germany* [2008] ECR I-6935.

[34] Case 72/83 *Campus Oil v Minister for Industry and Energy* [1984] ECR 2727.

are the cohesion of the tax system, the protection of local agricultural communities and the effectiveness of fiscal supervision (prevention of tax avoidance).[35] The lack of clarity in all this is reflected in the Court's ruling that preventing a reduction in tax revenue is in pursuit of an economic interest and cannot, therefore, justify restrictions.[36]

4 PRINCIPLES MEDIATING CONFLICTS BETWEEN FREE MOVEMENT AND PUBLIC GOODS

When applying Treaty exceptions, the starting point is that these are to be strictly and narrowly interpreted, and that they are EU law concepts. States cannot play a Treaty exception as a trump card. By contrast, it is for national judges and ultimately the Court of Justice to assess the state measure in the light of the constraints imposed by EU law. These points were made clear in *Van Duyn*, in which the United Kingdom wished to restrict the entry of a Dutch national on the grounds that she was a scientologist, and therefore a threat to public policy.

Case 41/74 *Van Duyn* v *Home Office* [1974] ECR 1337

18. ...It should be emphasized that the concept of public policy in the context of the community and where, in particular, it is used as a justification for derogating from the fundamental principle of freedom of movement for workers, must be interpreted strictly, so that its scope cannot be determined unilaterally by each Member State without being subject to control by the institutions of the Community. Nevertheless, the particular circumstances justifying recourse to the concept of public policy may vary from one country to another and from one period to another, and it is therefore necessary in this matter to allow the competent national authorities an area of discretion within the limits imposed by the Treaty.

A strict review can only mean that the Court assesses the proportionality of the measure, rather than just looking at formal correctness. In that sense, *Van Duyn* embodies similar principles to those which *Gebhard* and other cases have applied to mandatory requirements. It will be remembered that in this latter context, the Court found that restrictions on free movement could be justified by public interest objectives provided that the measures were equally applicable and proportionate.[37]

The fundamental difference between relying on a Treaty exception and relying on a mandatory requirement/general public interest objective is therefore that mandatory requirements are only available for equally applicable measures, whereas Treaty exceptions do not have this restriction — although overt discrimination will still require explanation, which may be a significant hurdle.

---

[35] Case C-204/90 *Bachmann* [1992] ECR I-249; Case C-250/95 *Futura Participations and Singer* v *Administration des contributions* [1997] ECR I-2471; Case C-452/01 *Ospelt*, above n. 29.

[36] Case C-35/98 *Staatssecretaris van Financiën* v *Verkooijen* [2000] ECR I-4071; Case C-436/00 *X and Y* v *Riksskatteverket* [2002] ECR I-10829.

[37] See pp. 766 and 803.

This distinction is often regarded as somewhat arbitrary.[38] Why not just merge the two classes of exception into one? Advocates General have suggested this course of action. In *Danner*, a case concerning Finnish rules which applied a more generous fiscal regime to pension insurance schemes based in Finland, Advocate General Jacobs stated:

> Once it is accepted that justifications other than those set out in the Treaty may be invoked, there seems no reason to apply one category of justification to discriminatory measures and another category to non-discriminatory restrictions. Certainly the text of the Treaty provides no reason to do so: Article [56 TFEU] does not refer to discrimination but speaks generally of restrictions on freedom to provide services. In any event, it is difficult to apply rigorously the distinction between (directly or indirectly) discriminatory and non-discriminatory measures. Moreover, there are general interest aims not expressly provided for in the Treaty (e.g. protection of the environment, consumer protection) which may in given circumstances be no less legitimate and no less powerful than those mentioned in the Treaty. The analysis should therefore be based on whether the ground invoked is a legitimate aim of general interest and if so whether the restriction can properly be justified under the principle of proportionality. In any event, the more discriminatory the measure, the more unlikely it is that the measure complies with the principle of proportionality.[39]

This line of reasoning is present in a number of Advocate Generals' Opinions, although all are confined to the tax field.[40] However, the Court has not adopted that reasoning, in *Danner* or the other cases. Whilst others may regard the distinction between the application of Treaty justifications and that of the mandatory requirements as undesirable, it is still supported by the Court of Justice.

Usually this is of little importance: measures which are not equally applicable are very hard to justify anyway, so the theoretical possibility of relying on mandatory exceptions would be unlikely to change the outcome of many cases. Moreover, there is a good symbolic argument for restricting the justifications open to overtly discriminatory measures. These are, after all, an affront to the basic principles of the Union. It can hardly be claimed, as is sometimes the case with the justified equally applicable measure, that they are not to be seen as restrictions on movement at all. Yet, in some exceptional contexts an overt distinction between people, products or providers from different states may apparently serve a legitimate policy aim which is not comfortably within the Treaty exceptions. In these situations, the Court has been known to overlook its general rule and permit non-Treaty justifications to be invoked.[41]

---

[38] P. Oliver, 'Some Further Reflections on the Scope of Articles 28–30 (ex 30–36) EC' (1999) 36 *CMLRev.* 783, 804–5; N. Notaro, 'The New Generation of Case Law on Trade and the Environment' (2000) 25 *ELRev.* 467, 489–91.

[39] Case C-136/00 *Danner* [2002] ECR I-8147.

[40] Opinion of Advocate General Leger in Case C-80/94 *Wielockx v Inspecteur der Directe Belastingen* [1995] ECR I-2493; Opinion of Advocate General Tesauro in Case C-120/95 *Decker v Caisse de maladie des employés privés* [1998] ECR I-1831; Opinion of Advocate General Poiares Maduro in Case C-446/03 *Marks & Spencer v Halsey* [2005] ECR I-10837.

[41] Case C-2/90 *Commission v Belgium (Walloon Waste)* [1992] ECR I-4431; Case C-379/98 *PreussenElektra* [2001] ECR I-2099; Case C-203/96 *Chemische Afvalstoppen Dusseldorp BV and Others v Minister van Volkhuisvesting, Ruimtelijke Ordening en Milieubeheer* [1998] ECR I-4075; Case 113/80 *Commission v Ireland (Irish souvenirs)* [1981] ECR 1625; Case C-120/95 *Decker* [1998] ECR I-1831; Case C-158/96 *Kohll v Union des Caisses de Maladie* [1998] ECR I-1931.

(i) The measure must be necessary

Any measure must meet a real rather than imagined threat to the public good in question. In *Commission* v *Denmark*,[42] Denmark prohibited foods being enriched with vitamins and minerals unless there was a nutritional need on the part of the Danish population for these additives. The Court of Justice held that such a restriction would only be lawful if it could be shown that the products posed a real risk to public health. The Court ruled that without the presence of a prior risk assessment to appraise the probability of the danger to public health, the products could not be shown to pose a real risk to public health.

In many cases there may be genuine scientific uncertainty about whether protective measures are necessary. Numerous health cases have, like *Commission* v *Denmark*, concerned the addition of vitamins to food, about the safety of which opinions vary widely. In *Greenham and Abel*, the Court followed positions it had taken in *Commission* v *Denmark* and *Sandoz*, and confirmed that in a situation of scientific uncertainty states may take legitimately varying positions, but are not relieved of the obligation to provide evidence for the position they choose.[43]

Case C-95/01 *Greenham and Abel* [2004] ECR I-1333

37. It is of course for the Member States, in the absence of harmonisation and to the extent that there is still uncertainty in the current state of scientific research, to decide on the level of protection of human health and life they wish to ensure and whether to require prior authorisation for the marketing of foodstuffs, taking into account the requirements of the free movement of goods within the Community.

38. That discretion relating to the protection of public health is particularly wide where it is shown that there is still uncertainty in the current state of scientific research as to certain nutrients, such as vitamins, which are not as a general rule harmful in themselves but may have special harmful effects solely if taken to excess as part of the general diet, the composition of which cannot be foreseen or monitored.

39. However, in exercising their discretion relating to the protection of public health, the Member States must comply with the principle of proportionality. The means which they choose must therefore be confined to what is actually necessary to ensure the safeguarding of public health; they must be proportionate to the objective thus pursued, which could not have been attained by measures less restrictive of intra-Community trade.

40. Furthermore, since Article [36 TFEU] provides for an exception, to be interpreted strictly, to the rule of free movement of goods within the Community, it is for the national authorities which invoke it to show in each case, in the light of national nutritional habits and in the light of the results of international scientific research, that their rules are necessary to give effective protection to the interests referred to in that provision and, in particular, that the marketing of the products in question poses a real risk to public health.

41. A prohibition on the marketing of foodstuffs to which nutrients have been added must therefore be based on a detailed assessment of the risk alleged by the Member State invoking Article [36 TFEU].

---

[42] Case C-192/01 *Commission* v *Denmark* [2003] ECR I-9693.
[43] *Ibid.*; Case 174/82 *Sandoz* [1983] ECR 5094.

The judgment refers to public health, but the procedural and substantive principles above should apply to any area where the underlying issue is one of scientific fact, rather than preference. The details of the risk assessment process and its consequences are discussed in the section on public health, below.

By contrast, the question of necessity is less amenable to a scientific approach where moral or social values and interests are concerned. The central concept here is consistency. Where a state attempts to prevent the entry of goods or persons, claiming they are a threat to some domestic interest, but takes no measures against similar domestically made goods, or nationals with the same allegedly dangerous characteristic, then it undermines its own claim of a serious threat, and will no longer be taken seriously. In *Conegate*,[44] pornographic rubber dolls were seized under the Customs Consolidation Act 1976, which prohibited the importation of obscene or indecent articles. However, British law on their domestic equivalents varied. In the Isle of Man and Scotland, the manufacture, sale and distribution of such articles were prohibited. In England and Wales, however, neither the manufacture nor sale was prohibited. The only controls were that such items could not be sold through the post, could not be displayed in a public place and had to be sold from licensed premises.

Case 121/85 *Conegate* v *Customs and Excise Commissioners* [1986] ECR 1007

14. ... In principle it is for each Member State to determine in accordance with its own scale of values and in the form selected by it the requirements of public morality in its territory.

15. However, although Community law leaves the Member States free to make their own assessments of the indecent or obscene character of certain articles, it must be pointed out that the fact that goods cause offence cannot be regarded as sufficiently serious to justify restrictions on the free movement of goods where the Member State concerned does not adopt, with respect to the same goods manufactured or marketed within its territory, penal measures or other serious and effective measures intended to prevent the distribution of such goods in its territory.

16. It follows that a Member State may not rely on grounds of public morality in order to prohibit the importation of goods from other Member States when its legislation contains no prohibition on the manufacture or marketing of the same goods on its territory.

17. It is not for the Court ... to consider whether, and to what extent, the United Kingdom legislation contains such a prohibition. However, the question whether or not such a prohibition exists in a state comprised of different constituent parts which have their own internal legislation, can be resolved only by taking into consideration all the relevant legislation. Although it is not necessary, for the purposes of the application of the above-mentioned rule, that the manufacture and marketing of the products whose importation has been prohibited should be prohibited in the territory of all the constituent parts, it must at least be possible to conclude from the applicable rules, taken as a whole, that their purpose is, in substance, to prohibit the manufacture and marketing of those products.

The same logic has been applied in numerous cases, but with varying results. In *Henn and Darby*, the United Kingdom was able to restrict the import of pornographic magazines, because the Court took the view that production of similar domestic ones was also prohibited.[45]

[44] Case 121/85 *Conegate* v *Customs and Excise Commissioners* [1986] ECR 1007.
[45] Case 34/79 *R* v *Henn and Darby* [1979] ECR 3975.

However, in *Adoui and Cornaille*, Belgium could not deport French prostitutes because even though prostitution was illegal in Belgium, repressive measures were not in fact taken.[46] The comparison between the domestic and the foreign must clearly be one of substance, not just legal form. Yet, this does not mean they need to be treated identically. In *Van Duyn*, the Court pointed out that states could not deport their own nationals, so one could not demand identical treatment of foreign and domestic scientologists.[47] What is necessary, if the state is to make good its claim of a serious threat against which action is necessary, is evidence of a consistent policy reflecting that view.

Most recently, in a slight variation on this theme, in *Placanica*, the Court rejected Italian arguments that restrictions on those who could offer horse betting services could be justified by the desire to reduce gambling:

> 53. With regard to the first type of objective, it is clear from the case law that although restrictions on the number of operators are in principle capable of being justified, those restrictions must in any event reflect a concern to bring about a genuine diminution of gambling opportunities and to limit activities in that sector in a consistent and systematic manner.
>
> 54. It is, however, common ground in the present case, according to the case law of the Corte suprema di cassazione, that the Italian legislature is pursuing a policy of expanding activity in the betting and gaming sector, with the aim of increasing tax revenue, and that no justification for the Italian legislation is to be found in the objectives of limiting the propensity of consumers to gamble or of curtailing the availability of gambling.[48]

Here the comparison is not between national and foreign operators, but between different policy actions. However, the theme of consistency is similar to the earlier cases. Because the state actively pursued other policies inconsistent with its claimed desire to reduce gambling, that goal, otherwise legitimate, could not be taken seriously as a justification for the restriction in issue.

A conceptual issue arose in *Compassion in World Farming*.[49] The United Kingsom wished to restrict the export of young calves to Spain on grounds of animal welfare: they were destined to be reared in boxes for veal, which is prohibited in the United Kingdom. The United Kingdom lost because minimum conditions for the welfare of calves were laid down in secondary legislation, and Spain complied with this legislation. The United Kingdom was free to have stricter standards, but where legislation of this type exists a Member State must accept as adequate the standards of any Member State complying with it, notwithstanding that the first state may be stricter.

Yet, the case could have been resolved on other grounds: the threat to animal welfare was to occur in Spain, and was none of the United Kingdom's business. The Advocate General hinted at this, but the Court did not raise the issue, and implicitly accepted that in principle the threat against which action is necessary need not be domestic. This principle is of particular

---

[46] Joined Cases 115/81 and 116/81 *Adoui and Cornuaille v Belgian State and City of Liège* [1982] ECR 1665; see also Case C-268/99 *Jany v Staatssecretaris van Justitie* [2001] ECR I-8615.

[47] Case 41/74 *Van Duyn v Home Office* [1974] ECR 1337.

[48] Joined Cases C-338/04, C-359/04 and C-360/04 *Placanica, Palazzese and Soricchio* [2007] ECR I-1891.

[49] Case C-1/96 *Compassion in World Farming* [1998] ECR I-1251.

importance where environmental measures are concerned, and the Court has indeed accepted measures which aim to protect the environment in other Member States, as well as the global environment.[50] Action may be necessary to protect interests beyond the borders of the acting Member State.

(ii) Prohibition on arbitrary discrimination

Differentiation is not prohibited per se, but even where a Treaty exception is used it must be justified, if it is not to be arbitrary and prohibited. This is generally true, but is specifically provided with respect to the free movement of goods by Article 36 TFEU. It is, like the emphasis on consistency in the cases above, another tool to prevent Treaty derogations being diverted towards protectionist ends.[51]

Its use is illustrated by *Rewe*.[52] In this instance, apples imported into Germany were treated differently from German apples in that they were specifically required to undergo phytosanitary checks for San José Scale, an extremely contagious disease, whilst no similar requirement was imposed on German apples. For German apples, the apple trees instead were examined and, if the disease was found, the area was isolated. Rewe, a German trading company, claimed that the German regime arbitrarily discriminated against imports by imposing checks on imported apples but not on German apples.

Case 4/75 Rewe-Zentralfinanz GmbH v Landwirtschaftskammer Bonn [1975] ECR 843

6. Under the first sentence of [Article 36 TFEU], [Articles 34 to 35] are not to preclude restrictions on imports and, therefore, measures having equivalent effect, which are justified for reasons of protection of the health of plants. In the light of the current Community rules in this matter, a phytosanitary inspection carried out by a Member State on the importation of plant products constitutes, in principle, one of the restrictions on imports which are justified under the first sentence of [Article 36 TFEU] ...

8. However, the restrictions on imports referred to in the first sentence of [Article 36 TFEU] cannot be accepted under the second sentence of that article if they constitute a means of arbitrary discrimination. The fact that plant products imported from another Member State are subject to a phytosanitary inspection although domestic products are not subject to an equivalent examination when they are despatched within the Member State might constitute arbitrary discrimination within the meaning of the above-mentioned provision ... The different treatment of imported and domestic products, based on the need to prevent the spread of the harmful organism, could not, however, be regarded as arbitrary discrimination if effective measures are taken in order to prevent the distribution of contaminated domestic products and if there is reason to believe, in particular on the basis of previous experience, that there is a risk of the harmful organism's spreading if no inspection is held on importation.

---

[50] See pp. 894–8. See also G. Davies, 'Process and Production Method-based Restrictions on Trade in the EU' in C. Barnard (ed.), *Cambridge Yearbook of European Legal Studies* 2008 (Oxford, Hart, 2008) 69.
[51] Case 34/79 *R v Henn and Darby* [1979] ECR 3975.
[52] Case 4/75 *Rewe-Zentralfinanz GmbH v Landwirtschaftskammer Bonn* [1975] ECR 843. See also Case C-324/93 *Evans Medical* [1995] ECR I-563.

The test is not, therefore, whether the German and French apples were competing, but whether they were truly comparable from the perspective of the risk in question. On the facts this was not the case, so the difference was permitted. Where domestic apples were concerned it was possible to check the tree, whereas this was not possible for imports. Measures which were effective and appropriate to contain the threat from domestic apples were therefore not suitable for imported apples, and vice versa.

(iii) The measure must be effective

In addition, the measure must effectively protect the public good in question. The Court will generally not look to whether there are more effective instruments available but, rather, will be concerned merely that the measure contributes to protection of the public good. In *Commission v Belgium*, the Court of Justice ruled illegal a Belgian law stipulating that all goods to which nutrients had been added must be labelled with a notification number allocated to them by the Belgian authorities.[53] The Court contemplated that labelling a product with a notification number did not protect public health or the consumer as it did not inform the consumer of the nutritional content of the goods or whether the appropriate checks had been carried out. The measure was, measured against its stated goals, useless.[54]

A situation which has recurred in several cases is where a measure could be effective, but in fact is not, as a result of other aspects of national law and policy. For example, *Hartlauer* concerned Austrian rules which required new outpatient dental clinics to be authorised. This was said to be necessary to prevent an over-supply of dentists in a given area, which might have implications for quality and for local health budgets, and so ultimately for access to good dental care. However, the rules only applied to clinics which employed dentists, not to group practices, which were usually partnerships. The difference between a clinic and a partnership is one of business model — the employment model being traditionally regarded as threatening by professionals — but not of obvious importance to the customer.

Case C-169/07 *Hartlauer Handelsgesellschaft mbH v Wiener Landesregierung and Oberösterreichische Landesregierung*, Judgment of 10 March 2009

50. Consequently, it must be ascertained whether the restrictions at issue in the main proceedings are appropriate for ensuring attainment of the objectives of maintaining a balanced high-quality medical service open to all and preventing the risk of serious harm to the financial balance of the social security system. [*The Court then accepted that a planning and authorisation system could in principle be a part of achieving these goals.*] ...

54. In the present case, however, two series of considerations prevent the legislation in question from being accepted as appropriate for ensuring attainment of the above objectives.

55. First, it must be recalled that national legislation is appropriate for ensuring attainment of the objective pursued only if it genuinely reflects a concern to attain it in a consistent and systematic manner.

56. However, it follows from [*national law*], that a prior authorisation based on an assessment of the needs of the market is required for setting up and operating new independent outpatient dental clinics,

---

[53] Case C-217/99 *Commission v Belgium* [2000] ECR I-10251.
[54] See also Case C-55/99 *Commission v France* [2000] ECR I-11499.

whatever their size, and that the setting up of new group practices, by contrast, is not subject to any system of authorisation, regardless of their size.

57. Yet it appears from the order for reference that the premises and equipment of group practices and those of outpatient dental clinics may have comparable features and that in many cases the patient will not notice any difference between them.

58. Moreover, group practices generally offer the same medical services as outpatient dental clinics and are subject to the same market conditions.

59. Similarly, group practices and outpatient dental clinics may have comparable numbers of practitioners. It is true that the practitioners who provide medical services within group practices have the status of personally liable partner and are authorised to practise independently as dental practitioners, whereas the practitioners in an outpatient clinic have the status of employee. However, the documents before the Court do not show that that circumstance has any definite effect on the nature or volume of the services provided.

60. Since those two categories of providers of services may have comparable features and a comparable number of practitioners and provide medical services of equivalent volume, they may therefore have a similar impact on the market in medical services, and are thus liable to affect in an equivalent manner the economic situation of contractual practitioners in certain geographical areas and, in consequence, the attainment of the planning objectives pursued by the competent authorities.

61. That inconsistency also affects the attainment of the objective of preventing a risk of serious harm to the financial balance of the national social security system. Even supposing that the uncontrolled establishment of independent outpatient dental clinics may lead to a considerable increase in the volume of medical services at constant prices to be paid for by that system, the Austrian Government has not put forward anything capable of explaining why the establishment of those clinics but not of group practices could have such an effect.

62. Moreover, the provision of dental care in those independent outpatient clinics is liable to prove more rational, in view of the way they are organised, the fact of having several practitioners, and the use in common of medical installations and equipment, which enable them to reduce their operating costs. They will thus be able to provide medical services in conditions that are less costly than those, in particular, of independent practitioners who do not have such opportunities. The provision of care services by those institutions may have the consequence of more efficient use of the public funds allocated to the statutory health insurance system.

63. In those circumstances, it must be concluded that the national legislation at issue in the main proceedings does not pursue the stated objectives in a consistent and systematic manner, since it does not make the setting up of group practices subject to a system of prior authorisation, as is the case with new outpatient dental clinics.

Hartlauer, with its emphasis on consistency, is very close in principle to *Adoui* and *Conegate*, and particularly to *Placanica*, which was cited. However, the Court's argument is slightly different. In this case it does not regard inconsistency as demonstrating that there is no real problem to be addressed, but rather that the measure is not actually going to effectively achieve its goal. *Hartlauer* shows the Court engaging in a moderately penetrating review of the broader policy context.

A similar level of intensity was shown by the Court in *Festersen*. Danish law required owners of agricultural property to live on the property. If they did not, within a certain period of buying it, they could be required by law to sell the land. This is a restriction on the free movement of capital, because it discourages investment in land and property. However, the aim was stated to be to protect agricultural communities, the risk being that urban people, or foreigners, would buy up the houses and old farms and use them as holiday homes, so that traditional agricultural activities, and much of the local economy, would die out. This has arisen in several cases, and the Court acknowledges the Member State concerns.[55] Nevertheless, in *Festersen* it considered critically whether the measures taken were actually suitable to meet the stated goals.

Case C-370/05 *Festersen* [2007] ECR I-1129

27. As regards the condition relating to the pursuance of an objective in the public interest, the Danish Government submits that the national legislation seeks, first, to preserve the farming of agricultural land by means of owner-occupancy, which constitutes one of the traditional forms of farming in Denmark, and to ensure that agricultural property be occupied and farmed predominantly by the owners, second, as a town and country planning measure, to preserve a permanent agricultural community and, third, to encourage a reasonable use of the available land by resisting pressure on land.

28. Such objectives are themselves in the public interest and are capable of justifying restrictions to the free movement of capital. In addition, as the Danish Government and the Commission of the European Communities maintain, those objectives are consistent with those of the common agricultural policy which, under Article [39(1)(b) TFEU] aims 'to ensure a fair standard of living for the agricultural community' in the working-out of which, according to Article [33(2)(a) TFEU], account must be taken 'of the particular nature of agricultural activity, which results from the social structure of agriculture and from structural and natural disparities between the various agricultural regions'.

29. As regards the condition of proportionality, it is necessary to check whether the requirement that the acquirer take up his fixed residence on the agricultural property acquired constitutes, as submitted by the Danish and Norwegian Governments, an appropriate and necessary measure for the attainment of the objectives mentioned in paragraph 27 above.

30. As regards whether the national measure at issue in the main proceedings is appropriate, it must be observed that it contains only a residence requirement and is not coupled, for an acquirer of an agricultural property of less than 30 hectares, with a requirement to farm the property personally. Such a measure thus does not appear, in itself, to ensure the attainment of the alleged objective seeking to preserve the traditional form of farming by owner-occupiers.

31. It is true that, as regards the second aim assigned to the Law on agriculture, the residence requirement is likely to contribute, by definition, to preserving an agricultural community and it can be met even further by farmers who, in accordance with one of the general objectives of the Law on agriculture seeking to encourage the owner-occupancy form of farming, personally farm their own land.

32. However, in the light of the phenomena of both reduction of the number of farms and regrouping of farms, as is apparent from the written observations lodged before the Court, and which were not challenged at the hearing, the objective of preserving an agricultural community cannot be met where the acquisition is made by a farmer who is already resident on another farm. In such a situation, the residence requirement does not guarantee the attainment of that objective, and thus it does not appear that that requirement is, in actual fact, appropriate, in itself, for the purpose of attaining such an objective.

---

[55] Case C-302/97 *Konle* [1999] ECR I-3099; Joined Cases C-515/99 and C-527–C-540/99 *Reisch and Others* v *Bürgermeister der Landeshaupstadt Salzburg* [2002] ECR I-2157; Case C-452/01 *Ospelt* v *Schössle Weissenberg Familienstiftung* [2003] ECR I-9743.

33. In relation to the third aim which the Law on agriculture seeks to attain, it must be found that the residence requirement can reduce the number of potential acquirers of agricultural property and, consequently, it is capable of reducing the pressure on that land. It can therefore be accepted that national legislation containing such a requirement, which seeks to avoid the acquisition of agricultural land for purely speculative reasons, and which is thus likely to facilitate the preferential appropriation of that land by persons wishing to farm it does pursue a public interest objective in a Member State in which agricultural land is, and this is not challenged, a limited natural resource.

The Court concludes that since there is only an obligation to live on the land, not to farm it, the measure is not suitable for protecting agricultural activities. Moreover, since the land might be bought by another farmer, as part of a consolidation of farms, a residence requirement here would also serve no purpose. However, the Court concedes that the residence rule will discourage some buyers, and this in itself might reduce pressure on agricultural land and make it easier for locals to buy and farm it.

Festersen and *Hartlauer* both concern policy areas which are dominated neither by science, as in food safety, nor by sensitive values, as where morality arguments are made. Rather, they are practical, reasonably comprehensible policy fields which lie within the judicial comfort zone, so we see the Court engaging in a factual analysis, and conclusion, which is slightly at odds with its role in the reference procedure. There is a risk with these apparently accessible national policy areas that the common sense judicial approach does not do justice to the full complexity of the policy and the factors involved.

(iv) Mutual recognition

The principle of equivalence or mutual recognition prevents the importing state duplicating measures which have already been taken by the exporting state. This principle was confirmed in *Biologische Producten*,[56] where a Dutch law requiring prior authorisation for the marketing of all toxic plant protection products by the Dutch authorities was challenged on the grounds that the product in question had already been subject to extensive laboratory analyses in France.

Case 272/80 *Frans-Nederlandse Maatschappij voor Biologische Producten* [1981] ECR 3277

14. Whilst a Member State is free to require a product of the type in question, which has already received approval in another Member State, to undergo a fresh procedure of examination and approval, the authorities of the Member States are nevertheless required to assist in bringing about a relaxation of the controls existing in intra-Community trade. It follows that they are not entitled unnecessarily to require technical or chemical analyses or laboratory tests where those analyses and tests have already been carried out in another Member State and their results are available to those authorities, or may at their request be placed at their disposal.

---

[56] Case 272/80 *Frans-Nederlandse Maatschappij voor Biologische Producten* [1981] ECR 3277. See also Case C-432/03 *Commission v Portugal* [2005] ECR I-9665.

15. For the same reasons, a Member State operating an approval procedure must ensure that no unnecessary control expenses are incurred if the practical effects of the control carried out in the Member State of origin satisfy the requirements of the protection of public health in the importing Member State. On the other hand, the mere fact that those expenses weigh more heavily on a trader marketing small quantities of an approved product than on his competitor who markets much greater quantities, does not justify the conclusion that such expenses constitute arbitrary discrimination or a disguised restriction within the meaning of [Article 30].

The requirement to accept foreign tests as adequate is premised on them being equivalent to the national ones. This may not always be so. If the state can establish that there are important differences, so that the tests do not in fact satisfy the – legitimate and proportionate – domestic needs, then they may impose additional tests. But while this is simple in principle it may be complex in practice.[57] The procedures used by different Member States will rarely be identical. Thus, establishing equivalence between different standards in often highly complex and technical areas will be difficult.[58] The principle of equivalence places an exacting burden on the national judge. This is not only true where product standards are concerned, but also where the adequacy of supervision by other Member State regulatory authorities is in issue. Member States should regard supervision by the home state as rendering their own supervision superfluous unless they can show that it leaves gaps in protection which must be filled, but this is once again often a complex matter.[59]

More recently, instead of concentrating exclusively on whether or not there is substantive equivalence, the Court of Justice has sought to proceduralise the equivalence principle, so that it becomes one of good governance.[60] In *French Vitamins*, the Commission challenged French legislation which provided that food containing added nutrients, that were not on an approved list endorsed by the French authorities, had to be subject to a procedure of prior authorisation before they could be marketed. The procedure for this authorisation was often lengthy and took no account of regulatory tests carried out in other Member States.

Case C–24/00 *Commission v France (French Vitamins)* [2004] ECR I–1277

24. It [the French legislation] does not contain any provision ensuring the free movement of fortified foodstuffs lawfully manufactured and/or marketed in another Member State and for which a level of human health protection equivalent to that ensured in France is guaranteed, even if such products do not wholly satisfy the requirements of that legislation.

25. However, the Court has held that national legislation which makes the addition of a nutrient to a foodstuff lawfully manufactured and/or marketed in other Member States subject to prior authorisation is not, in principle, contrary to Community law, provided that certain conditions are satisfied...

---

[57] See pp. 698–700.

[58] European Commission, *Second Biennial Report on the Application of the Principle of Mutual Recognition in the Single Market*, COM(2002)419 final, 17–21.

[59] Case C-243/01 *Gambelli* [2003] ECR I-13031; Case C-393/05 *Commission v Austria* [2007] ECR I-10195; Case C-404/05 *Commission v Germany* [2007] ECR I-10239.

[60] S. Prechal, 'Free Movement and Procedural Requirements: Proportionality Reconsidered' (2008) 35 *LIEI* 201.

26. First, such legislation must make provision for a procedure enabling economic operators to have that nutrient included on the national list of authorised substances. The procedure must be one which is readily accessible and can be completed within a reasonable time, and, if it leads to a refusal, the decision of refusal must be open to challenge before the courts...

27. Secondly, an application to obtain the inclusion of a nutrient on the national list of authorised substances may be refused by the competent national authorities only if such substance poses a genuine risk to public health...

36. As is clear from paragraph 26 of this judgment, a procedure which requires prior authorisation, in the interest of public health, for the addition of a nutrient authorised in another Member State complies with Community law only if it is readily accessible and can be completed within a reasonable time and if, when it is refused, the refusal can be challenged before the courts.

37. As regards first the accessibility of the procedure in question in this case, a Member State's obligation to provide for such a procedure in the case of any national rule which on grounds of public health makes the addition of nutrients subject to authorisation cannot be fulfilled if that procedure is not expressly provided for in a measure of general application which is binding on the national authorities...

38. By stating in their reply of 31 December 1998 to the reasoned opinion their intention of clarifying the French legislation by setting out in a legislative text the procedure for authorising the use of nutrients, the French authorities have recognised that, at least at the end of the period prescribed by the reasoned opinion, the national legislation did not formally provide for that procedure.

39. Whilst the French Government has prepared a notice to economic operators on the detailed rules for incorporating nutrients in foodstuffs for daily consumption which, it submits, fulfils that function, it is not apparent from the documents before the Court that such notice, assuming that it meets the requirements of Community law, was in force at the end of the period prescribed by the reasoned opinion.

40. Secondly, the examples provided by the Commission in its application reveal that applications for authorisation submitted by economic operators were not dealt with either within a reasonable period or according to a procedure which was sufficiently transparent as regards the possibility of challenging refusal to authorise before the courts.

41. Thus, in the case of the application for authorisation relating to the drink Red Bull, the applicant waited nearly seven months for acknowledgement of receipt of its application and more than two years to be informed of the decision to refuse it.

French Nutrients suggests that the equivalence principle entails some general principles of administrative due process, such as duties of transparency, efficiency and judicial accountability. The value of these is that they provide extra safeguards to ensure equitable treatment of the import. They should, however, be viewed as no more than that. If they become the test of whether an import has been lawfully treated, there is the danger of substituting empty proceduralism for substance.

(v) The measure must be the least restrictive option

Finally, measures must be the least restrictive necessary to secure their objectives. A well-known example of this is *De Peijper*.[61] In this case, any pharmaceutical marketed in the Netherlands had to present a file to the authorities setting out details of its composition,

---

[61] Case 104/75 *Officier van Justitie* v *De Peijper* [1976] ECR 613.

packaging and preparation. This file had to be certified by the manufacturer. Centrafarm was importing valium from the United Kingdom, which was produced by Hoffman La Roche. Hoffman La Roche refused to give Centrafarm the documentation, as it also sold valium on the Dutch market. When Centrafarm was prosecuted, it argued that although the Dutch authorities were entitled to take measures to protect public health, the requirement for it to obtain documentation from a competitor was unnecessarily restrictive.

Case 104/75 *Officier van Justitie* v *De Peijper* [1976] ECR 613

17. National rules or practices do not fall within the exception specified in [Article 36 TFEU] if the health and life of humans can be as effectively protected by measures which do not restrict intra-Community trade so much.

18. In particular [Article 36 TFEU] cannot be relied on to justify rules or practices which, even though they are beneficial, contain restrictions which are explained primarily by a concern to lighten the administration's burden or reduce public expenditure, unless, in the absence of the said rules or practices, this burden or expenditure clearly would exceed the limits of what can reasonably be required...

23. With regard to the documents relating to a specific batch of a medicinal preparation imported at a time when the public health authorities of the Member State of importation already have in their possession a file relating to this medicinal preparation, these authorities have a legitimate interest in being able at any time to carry out a thorough check to make certain that the said batch complies with the particulars on the file.

24. Nevertheless, having regard to the nature of the market for the pharmaceutical product in question, it is necessary to ask whether this objective cannot be equally well achieved if the national administrations, instead of waiting passively for the desired evidence to be produced to them — and in a form calculated to give the manufacturer of the product and his duly appointed representatives an advantage — were to admit, where appropriate, similar evidence and, in particular, to adopt a more active policy which could enable every trader to obtain the necessary evidence.

25. This question is all the more important because parallel importers are very often in a position to offer the goods at a price lower than the one applied by the duly appointed importer for the same product, a fact which, where medicinal preparations are concerned, should, where appropriate, encourage the public health authorities not to place parallel imports at a disadvantage, since the effective protection of health and life of humans also demands that medicinal preparations should be sold at reasonable prices.

26. National authorities possess legislative and administrative methods capable of compelling the manufacturer or his duly appointed representative to supply particulars making it possible to ascertain that the medicinal preparation which is in fact the subject of parallel importation is identical with the medicinal preparation in respect of which they are already informed.

27. Moreover, simple co-operation between the authorities of the Member States would enable them to obtain on a reciprocal basis the documents necessary for checking certain largely standardized and widely distributed products.

28. Taking into account all these possible ways of obtaining information the national public health authorities must consider whether the effective protection of health and life of humans justifies a presumption of the non-conformity of an imported batch with the description of the medicinal preparation, or whether on the contrary it would not be sufficient to lay down a presumption of

conformity with the result that, in appropriate cases, it would be for the administration to rebut this presumption.

29. Finally, even if it were absolutely necessary to require the parallel importer to prove this conformity, there would in any case be no justification under [Article 36 TFEU] for compelling him to do so with the help of documents to which he does not have access, when the administration, or as the case may be, the Court, finds that the evidence can be produced by other means.

The Court here accepts that Member States may need information on products which might be a risk to health, but points out that there may well be different ways of achieving this goal, and it is not legitimate for states to simply choose the method which imposes the least financial or administrative burden on them. The Court considers critically whether the various aspects of the Dutch scheme could not be made less burdensome for importers: Is it necessary to ask for documents when similar documents are already on file? Is it reasonable to expect an importer to obtain information from a competitor, when the state could obtain that information from authorities in other states? *De Peijper* is an example of the 'least restrictive option' rule being applied literally and thoroughly. As will be discussed below, this is not always the case.

The degree to which the Court can engage in *De Peijper*-like correction of the legislator depends on the complexity and subjectivity of the facts, but also on more subtle governance considerations. The principle that a measure must be the least restrictive option assumes a distinction between the objectives of a measure and the means used to pursue those objectives. The principle is not used to control the former. It does not decide on the level of protection, but is used instead to assess the latter by evaluating whether the means were the least restrictive necessary to secure these ends. Such analysis relies on the identification of a coherent series of ends or functions for the legislation, which the administration is assumed to be pursuing. The assumption of coherent or unitary objectives ignores the possibility of intra-institutional conflicts within ministries, and inter-institutional conflicts between different arms of government. The purpose of legislation may simply be to broker a compromise between different objectives; it may be deliberately contradictory. There is a danger that a judge may ignore this balance, by focusing on just one aim of the legislation and then declaring other aspects of the legislation unnecessary to that aim, and therefore illegal. Such analysis also obscures the distinction between policies and decisions. Whilst decisions are taken with regard to a particular factual situation, policies extend beyond the immediate scenario and deal with scenarios where facts are uncertain, and risk endemic. It may not be appropriate to attribute fixed objectives to them as circumstances change.

These tensions have led the Court of Justice not to apply the principle mechanistically. The intensity and form of the review has varied according to the type of subject matter reviewed.[62]

The Court has been most faithful to the strict *De Peijper* approach in its treatment of market externalities. In this field, one tends to find that the Court examines with some thoroughness whether the adopted measure was the least restrictive of trade necessary to secure its objectives.[63] It is here, therefore, that one finds most judicial intrusion into national

[62] G. de Búrca, 'The Principle of Proportionality and Its Application in EC Law' (1993) 13 *YBEL* 105.
[63] Case 124/81 *Commission v United Kingdom* [1983] ECR 203; Case C-67/97 *Bluhme* [1998] ECR I-8033.

policy-making.[64] The difficulty in distinguishing between ends and means has led the Court of Justice to curtail many policy options and set out fairly strict parameters as to what policy objectives are permissible in these fields. It is also in this field that its procedural bent has come most to the fore, as the section on public health below shows, and where it most explicitly puts the evidential burden on the restricting state. In *Leichtle*, concerning health care rules which impacted on free movement of services, the Court said that 'the reasons which may be invoked by a Member State by way of justification must be accompanied by an analysis of the appropriateness and proportionality of the restrictive measure adopted by that State' and went on in the next paragraph to find that the state had failed to supply evidence demonstrating the necessity of its measures.[65]

The position is more complicated with regard to measures protecting local socio-cultural preferences and traditions. These are often quirky and particularistic. Their value lies not so much in realising some general goal, but in reinforcing the identity of a community or region. As a consequence, it is very difficult to separate the institutions and legislation protecting these traditions and preferences from the tradition itself. It is also very difficult for the Court to provide a general statement about the nature and value of the tradition to act as a standard for review. This has led to an inconsistency in the Court's reasoning. In many cases in this field, the Court of Justice still applies an unadorned proportionality test: that the measure must be the least restrictive necessary to secure its objectives.[66] In others, a more layered or marginal standard of review is adopted. In *UTECA*, concerning Spanish rules requiring film companies to reserve a percentage of their income for financing films in local languages, the Court asked itself whether the measure went beyond what was necessary to protect 'Spanish multilingualism' and noted '[t]he documents submitted to the Court do not contain any material which might lead to the conclusion that such a percentage is disproportionate in relation to the objective pursued', an apparent reversal of the usual burden of proof.[67] A similar approach was taken in *Ahokainen*, on Finnish laws which severely restricted the import of extremely strong (80 per cent) alcohol. Although the primary derogations relied upon were public health and public order, these do not capture the character of the measure entirely. It was placed clearly in the context of a consistent national policy aimed at combating alcoholism, particularly among the young, and was part of an attempt by the state to define and protect a certain kind of national environment, reflecting certain values. In that sense it was not so different from *UTECA*.

By contrast, in the gambling cases the Court has been quite intrusive. It has found that administrations have a margin of appreciation because of the particular moral, social and cultural features associated with gambling.[68] Yet, it has often found national measures to be unduly restrictive. Part of the problem is that regulation of gambling serves multiple functions. Partly

---

[64] See e.g. Case C-322/01 *Deutscher Apothekerverband v DocMorris* [2003] ECR I-14887; Joined Cases C-338/04, C-359/04 and C-360/04 *Placanica, Palazzese and Soricchio* [2007] ECR I-1891; Case C-143/06 *Ludwigs–Apotheke München Internationale Apotheke v Juers Pharma Import-Export GmbH* [2007] ECR I-9623.

[65] Case C-8/02 *Leichtle v Bundesanstalt für Arbeit* [2004] ECR I-2641.

[66] Case C-452/01 *Ospelt v Schössle Weissenberg Familienstiftung* [2003] ECR I-9743; Case C-415/93 *Union Royale Belge des Sociétés de Football Association and Others v Bosman and Others* [1995] ECR I-4921.

[67] See e.g. Case C-434/04 *Ahokainen* [2006] ECR I-9171; Case C-192/01 *Commission v Denmark* [2003] ECR I-9693.

[68] Case C-275/92 *HM Customs and Excise v Schindler* [1994] ECR I-1039; Case C-124/97 *Läärä v Kihlakunnansyyttäjä* [1999] ECR I-6067; Case C-67/98 *Questore di Verona v Zenatti* [1999] ECR I-7289; Joined Cases C-338/04, C-359/04 and C-360/04 *Placanica, Palazzese and Soricchio* [2007] ECR I-1891; Case C-42/07 *Liga Portuguesa de Futebol Profissional and Bwin International Ltd v Departamento de Jogos da Santa Casa da Misericórdia de Lisboa*, Judgment of 8 September 2009.

it serves subtle social, cultural and policy goals. The presence of a national lottery monopoly, for example, may mean that the government can exert influence over marketing and other commercial behaviour, as well as contributing to social cohesion. The fragmentation of the industry might result in both upscale and distinctly down-market gambling businesses emerging, which in the long-term could present a regulatory and social challenge. Yet, states have not shown themselves to be good at explaining such things, and tend to focus before the Court on the more measurable and objective goals of their regulation, such as the prevention of fraud and crime. This has the effect of rendering the policy field less value laden, so that the Court is prepared to engage in more intensive review. In *Gambelli*,[69] Italian legislation granted a monopoly in the making of sporting bets to a state enterprise, CONI. Gambelli was prosecuted for breaching this monopoly by taking sporting bets for Stanley, an English bookmaker. In Italy, such activity was illegal and was punishable by a term of imprisonment of between six months and three years.

Case C-243/01 *Gambelli* [2003] ECR I-13031

72. Finally, the restrictions imposed by the Italian legislation must not go beyond what is necessary to attain the end in view. In that context the national court must consider whether the criminal penalty imposed on any person who from his home connects by Internet to a bookmaker established in another Member State is not disproportionate in the light of the Court's case law... especially where involvement in betting is encouraged in the context of games organised by licensed national bodies.

73. The national court will also need to determine whether the imposition of restrictions, accompanied by criminal penalties of up to a year's imprisonment, on intermediaries who facilitate the provision of services by a bookmaker in a Member State other than that in which those services are offered by making an Internet connection to that bookmaker available to bettors at their premises is a restriction that goes beyond what is necessary to combat fraud, especially where the supplier of the service is subject in his Member State of establishment to a regulation entailing controls and penalties, where the intermediaries are lawfully constituted, and where, before the statutory amendments effected by Law No. 388/00, those intermediaries considered that they were permitted to transmit bets on foreign sporting events.

74. As to the proportionality of the Italian legislation ... even if the objective of the authorities of a Member State is to avoid the risk of gaming licensees being involved in criminal or fraudulent activities, to prevent capital companies quoted on regulated markets of other Member States from obtaining licences to organise sporting bets, especially where there are other means of checking the accounts and activities of such companies, may be considered to be a measure which goes beyond what is necessary to check fraud.

The final field concerns the protection of the machinery of the state. This raises institutionally sensitive matters, as the economic freedoms are being invoked to challenge the national government's right and capacity to govern. The position of the Court of Justice depends on the sensitivity of the matter. In areas perceived to be less sensitive and where the government is capable of reorganising itself to realise the same goals, such as protection of the coherence

---

[69] Case C-243/01 *Gambelli* [2003] ECR I-13031.

of the fiscal system, the Court just looks at whether the measure is the least restrictive necessary to secure its objectives. In areas which are both more sensitive and where judicial intervention is less frequent, such as national security, a more marginal form of review is taken. The Court does not look to see whether the measure is the least restrictive necessary so much as at the bona fides of the measure. In *Campus Oil*, the Irish government required importers of petroleum to obtain a minimum of 35 per cent of their needs from the one Irish refinery, which had been set up to ensure an orderly supply of petrol onto the Irish market.[70] The Court of Justice found this minimum purchasing requirement to be lawful on the grounds that securing non-interruption of petrol supplies was essential to a state's security. It had been argued, however, that refineries could not secure a supply of oil, and maintenance of reserves would be a less restrictive way of securing this. A less onerous system of supporting the refinery than through a purchasing commitment might have been for the Irish government to subsidise the refinery directly. The Court was dismissive of these arguments. It noted that having an independent refining capacity prevented a state being dependent upon foreign refineries and thus removed one threat to its security. This does not give Member States a *carte blanche*. In *Commission* v *Greece*, the Court examined a Greek obligation on those marketing petrol to hold minimum stocks of petrol. It was unimpressed by a provision that allowed companies to transfer these obligations to refineries, so long as they had purchased petrol from those refineries in the last year.[71] The Court found that this requirement of prior purchase was not the least restrictive means available to secure petrol supply and was therefore illegal. The explanation for this stricter measure of review can be found in the sheer protectionist nature of the measure and its lack of relationship to public security. It had less to do with ensuring stocks were maintained than with providing a subsidy to those who purchased petrol from Greek refineries.

There is one final caveat with regard to all the above for measures taken by Member States to transpose EU legislation. The Court of Justice has developed a different test for national measures in such circumstances. In *Bellamy*, a Belgian law transposing Directive 79/112/EEC on the labelling and advertising of foodstuffs prohibited food from omitting the name under which the good was usually marketed.[72] Bellamy, an English woman, was prosecuted for selling milk as 'Breakfast Milk' and omitting to state that it was 'fresh, whole, pasteurised milk' as all other similar Belgian milk described itself. In the absence of the Directive, the measure would clearly have fallen within Article 34 TFEU. The Court held, however, that measures correctly transposing valid EU legislation could not be held to violate the Treaty.

An obvious criticism of the proportionality principle is the lack of consistency and predictability with which it is applied. Although this criticism is well-founded, it is inevitable that the interface between the economic freedoms and a great many diverse public interests will generate heterogeneous tensions. Inconsistency may be a price worth paying if the alternative is insensitivity to national concerns. A more defining criticism is that the case law is too 'decisionistic', in that it is too preoccupied with outcomes.[73]

---

[70] Case 72/83 *Campus Oil* v *Minister for Industry and Energy* [1984] ECR 2727.
[71] Case C-398/98 *Commission* v *Greece* [2001] ECR I-7915.
[72] Case C-123/00 *Bellamy and English Shop Wholesale* [2001] ECR I-2795.
[73] For more specific arguments that EU law should be concerned with process in this field, see J. Scott, 'Of Kith and Kine (and Crustaceans): Trade and Environment in the EU and WTO' in J. Weiler (ed.), *The EU, NAFTA and the WTO: Towards a Common Law of International Trade* (Oxford, Oxford University Press, 2000).

G. Majone, *Evidence, Argument and Persuasion in the Policy Process* (New Haven, CT, Yale University Press, 1989) 17–18

A... limitation of decisionism is its exclusive preoccupation with outcomes and lack of concern for the processes whereby the outcomes are produced. A lack of concern for process is justified in some situations. If the correctness or fairness of the outcome can be determined unambiguously, the manner in which the decision is made is often immaterial; only results count. But when the factual or value premises are moot, when there are no generally accepted criteria of rightness, the procedure of decision-making acquires special significance and cannot be treated as purely instrumental.

Even in formal decision analysis the explicit recognition of uncertainty forces a significant departure from a strict orientation toward outcomes. Under conditions of uncertainty different alternatives correspond to different probability distributions of the consequences, so that it is no longer possible to determine unambiguously what the optimal decision is. Hence, the usual criterion of rationality – according to which an action is rational if it can be explained as the choosing of the best means to achieve given objectives – is replaced by the weaker notion of consistency. The rational decision maker is no longer an optimiser, strictly speaking. All that is required now, and all that the principle of maximising expected utility guarantees, is that the choice be consistent with the decision maker's valuations of the probability and utility of the various consequences. Notice that consistency is a procedural, not a substantive, criterion.

Exclusive preoccupation with outcomes is a serious limitation of decisionism, since social processes seldom have only instrumental value for the people who engage in them. In most areas of social activity, the processes and rules that constitute the enterprise and define the roles of its participants matter quite apart from any identifiable 'end state' that is ultimately produced. Indeed in many cases it is the process itself that matters most to those who take part in it.

5 ENVIRONMENTAL PROTECTION

Protection of the environment has been used to justify a number of types of national restriction.[74] Member States are permitted to take measures prohibiting environmentally harmful activities where the ecological costs of an activity are obvious and high. A French prohibition on the burning of waste oils was, therefore, found to be compatible with Article 56 TFEU on the grounds that it protected the environment. In like vein, the Court of Justice has approved measures that ban chlorofluorocarbons or other ozone-depleting substances.[75] Member States must still show, however, that there are no other, less restrictive means of protecting the environment. In *Aher-Waggon*, a challenge was made to German restrictions on permissible noise emissions from aircraft.[76] These measures were stricter than those permitted by EU legislation. It was argued that there were less restrictive means of limiting noise, such as restricting the amount of flights or planning restrictions on the sites of airports. The Court, nevertheless, upheld the German restriction because it was convinced that these other options were not in fact feasible.

---

[74] See pp. 771–3.

[75] Case C-341/95 *Bettati* v *Safety Hi-Tech* [1998] ECR I-4355; Case C-284/95 *Safety Hi-Tech* v *S and T* [1998] ECR I-4301.

[76] Case C-389/96 *Aher-Waggon* v *Federal Republic of Germany* [1998] ECR I-4473.

Member States can also take measures to protect biodiversity. The most interesting case is *Bluhme*.[77] The case suggests that biodiversity is to be protected under the heading of protection of the health of animals rather than that of protection of the environment, and that Member States are to be given considerable leeway to protect fauna or flora. It concerned a Danish law allowing only Laesø brown bees to be kept on the island of Laesø in Denmark. Bluhme argued that this restriction, which was in order to protect the dissolution of the local brown bee population through mating with other bees, could not be justified ecologically as the brown bee was not a distinct species in its own right.

Case C-67/97 *Bluhme* [1998] ECR I-8033

33. … the Court considers that measures to preserve an indigenous animal population with distinct characteristics contribute to the maintenance of biodiversity by ensuring the survival of the population concerned. By so doing, they are aimed at protecting the life of those animals and are capable of being justified under Article [36 TFEU].

34. From the point of view of such conservation of biodiversity, it is immaterial whether the object of protection is a separate subspecies, a distinct strain within any given species or merely a local colony, so long as the populations in question have characteristics distinguishing them from others and are therefore judged worthy of protection either to shelter them from a risk of extinction that is more or less imminent, or, even in the absence of such risk, on account of a scientific or other interest in preserving the pure population at the location concerned.

35. It does, however, have to be determined whether the national legislation was necessary and proportionate in relation to its aim of protection, or whether it would have been possible to achieve the same result by less stringent measures …

36. Conservation of biodiversity through the establishment of areas in which a population enjoys special protection, which is a method recognised in the Rio Convention, especially Article 8a thereof, is already put into practice in Community law [in particular, by means of the special protection areas provided for in Council Directive 79/409/EEC of 2 April 1979 on the conservation of wild birds [1979] OJ L103/1, or the special conservation areas provided for in Directive 92/43/EC].

37. As for the threat of (the disappearance) of the Læsø brown bee, it is undoubtedly genuine in the event of mating with golden bees by reason of the recessive nature of the genes of the brown bee. The establishment by the national legislation of a protection area within which the keeping of bees other than Læsø brown bees is prohibited, for the purpose of ensuring the survival of the latter, therefore constitutes an appropriate measure in relation to the aim pursued.

The judgment is unusual in placing the Member State restriction in the context of international conventions. Environmental protection is an atypical ground for derogation because it is also an EU goal. There is not always a simple balance to be made between the Union interest in movement and the national interest in a restriction. Rather, the Union may have as great an interest as the state in the restriction, particularly where the environmental concerns are not strictly local as is the case with biodiversity and climate change.

---

[77] Case C-67/97 *Bluhme* [1998] ECR I-8033.

An example of this latter goal justifying an apparently discriminatory measure is *Preuss-enElektra*. The German government required electricity retailers to buy a proportion of their electricity from wind farms in Germany, the aim being to stimulate such farms and make them viable, and so reduce global warming. Such a measure is clearly both protectionist and directly discriminatory, but it is also, arguably, one of the most practical ways of stimulating a domestic green energy sector, particularly since the law on state aids imposes constraints on direct subsidy. The Court's judgment was, like that in *Bluhme*, notably context-aware and discursive. The cases suggest that where current environmental crises are in issue, the Court may take a less hostile approach to Member State derogations than is normally the case.

Case C-379/98 *PreussenElektra* [2001] ECR I-2099

70. Secondly, the case law of the Court also shows that an obligation placed on traders in a Member State to obtain a certain percentage of their supplies of a given product from a national supplier limits to that extent the possibility of importing the same product by preventing those traders from obtaining supplies in respect of part of their needs from traders situated in other Member States. ...

72. However, in order to determine whether such a purchase obligation is nevertheless compatible with Article [34 TFEU], account must be taken, first, of the aim of the provision in question, and, second, of the particular features of the electricity market.

73. The use of renewable energy sources for producing electricity, which a statute such as the amended Stromeinspeisungsgesetz is intended to promote, is useful for protecting the environment insofar as it contributes to the reduction in emissions of greenhouse gases which are amongst the main causes of climate change which the European Community and its Member States have pledged to combat.

74. Growth in that use is amongst the priority objectives which the Community and its Member States intend to pursue in implementing the obligations which they contracted by virtue of the United Nations Framework Convention on Climate Change, approved on behalf of the Community by Council Decision 94/69/EC of 15 December 1993 (OJ 1994 L 33, p. 11), and by virtue of the Protocol of the third conference of the parties to that Convention, done in Kyoto on 11 December 1997, signed by the European Community and its Member States on 29 April 1998 (see inter alia Council Resolution 98/C 198/01 of 8 June 1998 on renewable sources of energy (OJ 1998 C 198, p. 1), and Decision No. 646/2000/EC of the European Parliament and of the Council of 28 February 2000 adopting a multiannual programme for the promotion of renewable energy sources in the Community (Altener) (1998 to 2002) (OJ 2000 L 79, p. 1)).

75. It should be noted that that policy is also designed to protect the health and life of humans, animals and plants.

76. Moreover, as stated in the third sentence of the first subparagraph of Article [11 TFEU], environmental protection requirements must be integrated into the definition and implementation of other Community policies ...

77. In addition, the 28th recital in the preamble to Directive 96/92 expressly states that it is 'for reasons of environmental protection' that the latter authorises Member States in Articles 8(3) and 11(3) to give priority to the production of electricity from renewable sources.

78. It should also be noted that, as stated in the 39th recital in its preamble, the directive constitutes only a further phase in the liberalisation of the electricity market and leaves some obstacles to trade in electricity between Member States in place.

79. Moreover, the nature of electricity is such that, once it has been allowed into the transmission or distribution system, it is difficult to determine its origin and in particular the source of energy from which it was produced.

80. In that respect, the Commission took the view, in its Proposal for a Directive 2000/C 311 E/22 of the European Parliament and of the Council on the promotion of electricity from renewable energy sources in the internal electricity market (OJ 2000 C 311 E, p. 320), submitted on 10 May 2000, that the implementation in each Member State of a system of certificates of origin for electricity produced from renewable sources, capable of being the subject of mutual recognition, was essential in order to make trade in that type of electricity both reliable and possible in practice.

81. Having regard to all the above considerations, the answer to the third question must be that, in the current state of Community law concerning the electricity market, legislation such as the amended Stromeinspeisungsgesetz is not incompatible with Article [34 TFEU].

It is not clear from the judgment whether a Treaty derogation or a mandatory requirement is being relied upon. This is partly because the Treaty does not in fact contain an environmental exception, the free movement of goods derogation referring instead to the life and health of humans, animals and plants. This could be interpreted to cover all kinds of environmental harm, but it is sometimes an uncomfortable stretch, leading the Court in this case to choose studied ambiguity. The absence of a clear naming of the environment in Article 36 is distinctly old-fashioned, but the Court is clearly not going to allow this to have undesirable consequences.

Another type of environmental restriction which has been considered by the Court of Justice concerns the transportation of waste. In *Walloon Waste*, the Court considered a Wallonian ban on the import of waste from anywhere outside that region of Belgium.[78] The Court accepted the measure was justified on the basis of the proximity principle, namely that waste should be disposed of as close to the place of production as possible. The ecological basis for such a principle is that it avoids the environmental costs and risks of transporting the waste and establishes a principle of environmental equity. Clean places are not to bear the environmental costs generated by dirty places. However, the judgment is contentious. The reach of the proximity principle is unclear. *Walloon Waste* covered a regional restriction, but it is far harder to justify a similar national restriction, as that would permit waste to be transported over long distances. More fundamentally, the principle is unsatisfactory as an instrument for allocating environmental costs.[79] Most industrial waste is produced in locations far away from where the good is consumed and, in an integrated European economy, it is not really fair to expect the people who live close to the factory to bear the full cost of disposal. The inevitable duplication of facilities associated with such a principle, in addition, increases the risk of waste facilities being placed in locations which, in ecological terms, are far from ideal and deprives operators of the most suitable sites for waste disposal.

The operation of the proximity principle is made more difficult by the use of different reasoning for waste for recovery. In *Afvalstoffen Dusseldorp*,[80] an application to export two

[78] Case C-2/90 *Commission v Belgium (Walloon Waste)* [1992] ECR I-4431.

[79] P. von Wilmowsky, 'Waste Disposal in the Internal Market: The State of Play after the ECJ's Ruling on the Walloon Import Ban' (1993) 30 *CMLRev.* 541, 547–7; D. Chalmers, 'Community Policy on Waste Management: Managing Environmental Decline Gently' (1994) 14 *YBEL* 257, 280–4.

[80] Case C-203/96 *Chemische Afvalstoppen Dusseldorp BV and Others v Minister van Volkhuisvesting, Ruimtelijke Ordening en Milieubeheer* [1998] ECR I-4075.

loads of oil filters for processing was refused by the Dutch authorities on the grounds that, under Dutch law, export of waste for recovery was only permitted if there were superior processing techniques abroad or there was insufficient capacity in the Netherlands. The Court of Justice noted that such an export restriction provided an advantage for national facilities. It enabled the Dutch undertaking, AVR Chemie, which recovered the waste, to operate in a profitable manner and to use the filters as a cheap source of fuel. The Court found that there was no evidence of a health risk resulting from transport, and so no justification for the restriction on export of waste with an economic value. From an ecological perspective, however, the transport risks for both forms of waste are the same, and there is still the danger of dirty regions offloading waste onto clean regions. Advocates of the proximity principle have therefore been highly critical of *Dusseldorp*.[81] It may be that the reasons for the distinction are more pragmatic, economic ones. Waste for recovery is a large and growing industry. Preventing its development on a European scale might bring some environmental benefits, but would also bring significant economic costs.[82]

6 PUBLIC HEALTH

The exception most frequently invoked before the Court of Justice is that of public health. In its initial case law, the Court simply looked at the answers provided by international science. If there was doubt or international science ruled something unsafe, a Member State would be justified in banning the product. Increasingly, this test appeared unsatisfactory.[83] In many scenarios knowledge developed, so what had formerly appeared certain was now less so. In other scenarios, it would be unrealistic to assume zero risk as this would be something that science could never certify. Therefore, the Court of Justice has increasingly moved towards a proceduralist test of whether a sufficiently rigorous risk assessment has been carried out. An example of this new approach is *Dutch Vitamins*.[84] With a couple of exceptions, Dutch legislation prohibited the addition of a number of vitamins to foods. The Dutch argument was not that these vitamins were dangerous in themselves, but that ingestion of excess quantities could be dangerous. In this, they relied on general studies. There was no study that estimated the likelihood of risk. For this reason, the Court found the Dutch legislation to be illegal. It stated its general approach in the following manner.

Case C-41/02 *Commission v Netherlands (Dutch Vitamins)* [2004] ECR I-11375

45. It is clear from [Article 191 TFEU] that the protection of human health is one of the objectives of the Community policy on the environment, that that policy aims at a high level of protection and is to be based inter alia on the precautionary principle, and that the requirements of that policy must

---

[81] N. Notaro, 'The New Generation Case Law on Trade and Environment' (2000) 25 *ELRev.* 467.
[82] Movements of waste within the European Union are now governed exclusively by Regulation 259/93/EEC on the supervision and control of shipments of waste [1993] OJ L30/11. This retains the distinction made in the case law, however: Case C-324/99 *DaimlerChrysler v Land Baden-Württemberg* [2001] ECR I-9897. For discussion, see G. van Calster, 'The Free Movement of Waste after *DaimlerChrysler*' (2002) 27 *ELRev.* 610.
[83] Case 272/80 *Frans-Nederlandse Maatschappij voor Biologische Producten* [1981] ECR 3277.
[84] Case C-41/02 *Commission v Netherlands (Dutch Vitamins)* [2004] ECR I-11375. See also Case C-319/05 *Commission v Germany* [2007] ECR I-9811; Case C-88/07 *Commission v Spain*, Judgment of 5 March 2009.

be integrated into the definition and implementation of other Community policies. In addition, it follows from the case law of the Court that the precautionary principle may also apply in policy on the protection of human health which, according to [Article 168 TFEU] likewise aims at a high level of protection …

46. However, in exercising their discretion relating to the protection of public health, the Member States must comply with the principle of proportionality. The means which they choose must therefore be confined to what is actually necessary to ensure the safeguarding of public health; they must be proportional to the objective thus pursued, which could not have been attained by measures which are less restrictive of intra-Community trade.

47. Furthermore, since [Article 36 TFEU] provides for an exception, to be interpreted strictly, to the rule of free movement of goods within the Community, it is for the national authorities which invoke it to show in each case, in the light of national nutritional habits and in the light of the results of international scientific research, that their rules are necessary to give effective protection to the interests referred to in that provision and, in particular, that the marketing of the products in question poses a real risk for public health …

48. A prohibition on the marketing of foodstuffs to which nutrients have been added must therefore be based on a detailed assessment of the risk alleged by the Member State invoking [Article 36 TFEU] …

49. A decision to prohibit the marketing of a fortified foodstuff, which indeed constitutes the most restrictive obstacle to trade in products lawfully manufactured and marketed in other Member States, can be adopted only if the real risk for public health alleged appears sufficiently established on the basis of the latest scientific data available at the date of the adoption of such decision. In such a context, the object of the risk assessment to be carried out by the Member State is to appraise the degree of probability of harmful effects on human health from the addition of certain nutrients to foodstuffs and the seriousness of those potential effects …

50. In assessing the risk in question, it is not only the particular effects of the marketing of an individual product containing a definite quantity of nutrients which are relevant. It could be appropriate to take into consideration the cumulative effect of the presence on the market of several sources, natural or artificial, of a particular nutrient and of the possible existence in the future of additional sources which can reasonably be foreseen …

51. In a number of cases, the assessment of those factors will demonstrate that there is much uncertainty, in science and in practice, in that regard. Such uncertainty, which is inseparable from the precautionary principle, affects the scope of the Member State's discretion and thus also the manner in which the precautionary principle is applied.

52. It must therefore be accepted that a Member State may, in accordance with the precautionary principle, take protective measures without having to wait until the existence and gravity of those risks become fully apparent … However, the risk assessment cannot be based on purely hypothetical considerations …

53. A proper application of the precautionary principle requires, in the first place, the identification of the potentially negative consequences for health of the proposed addition of nutrients, and, secondly, a comprehensive assessment of the risk for health based on the most reliable scientific data available and the most recent results of international research …

54. Where it proves to be impossible to determine with certainty the existence or extent of the alleged risk because of the insufficiency, inconclusiveness or imprecision of the results of studies conducted, but the likelihood of real harm to public health persists should the risk materialise, the precautionary principle justifies the adoption of restrictive measures.

Dutch Vitamins suggests that, following a risk assessment, if the Member State finds a likelihood of real harm then, based on the precautionary principle, it can ban the good.

This leaves open the question whether Member States may impose restrictions for reasons of nutrition. This is a particular concern as the dangers posed by obesity mount in the European population. In *Sandoz*, permission was sought to market muesli bars to which vitamins A and D had been added. Authorisation was refused on the grounds that although these vitamins were necessary for a healthy life, too much of them could be dangerous. The Court of Justice held that Member States could ban a substance if there was a danger that it could be taken to excess as part of the general nutrition, and the individual amounts consumed could neither be monitored nor foreseen.[85] In *French Vitamins*, a broader ban was involved. The French authorities refused to allow vitamins or nutrients to be added to food unless there was a nutritional need.[86] The Court found this restriction to be unlawful. The blanket ban was not based on specific dangers, but just on the general view that such additives were not necessary. This fact could not, in itself, justify a ban. Even very small concrete risks can justify measures, but purely nutritional aspects of food are reserved to the sovereignty of the consumer.[87]

Restrictions on nutritional content can only be imposed, therefore, if the nutritional content of the good is felt to lead to some harm or be part of some threat to public health. An argument to this effect could certainly be made with respect to fat or carbohydrate levels in food, and it would not be difficult to produce relevant scientific evidence. The approach in *Sandoz* could be used to justify regulation of food aimed at combating obesity. Just like vitamins A and D, fats and carbohydrates are essential in some quantities, and dangerous in excess. Nevertheless, the politics and economics of such regulation would clearly be quite different, as the rules would have a far broader effect, and would also be difficult to adopt in a coherent and consistent way – many traditional and natural foods are as fatty as processed ones. The Court has not closed the door to the use of food law to attack obesity, but the demands of proportionality and consistency would make such a policy challenging.

A criticism of the case law is that it is too narrow. By focusing exclusively on demonstrable threats it chooses a test that is different from that chosen by many consumers when they decide whether food is safe or not. The latter weave in considerations such as how the food is produced, by whom and the effect on the environment. Trust in the producer, ideas about naturalness and purity, and mistrust of scientific progress, may all influence the consumer in her judgments about the risks food poses to her.[88] These may not be factors for which expert evidence can be produced, but they are relevant to consumers, so should they not be relevant to the law?

---

[85] Case 174/82 *Sandoz* [1983] ECR 5094.

[86] Case C-24/00 *Commission v France ('French Nutrients')* [2004] ECR I-1277. See also Case C-192/01 *Commission v Denmark* [2003] ECR I-9693.

[87] For a measure held lawful that constituted a minuscule risk to health, see Case C-121/00 *Hahn* [2002] ECR I-9193.

[88] See G. Davies, 'Morality Clauses and Decision-making in Situations of Scientific Uncertainty: The Case of GMOs' (2007) 6 *World Trade Review* 249.

B. Wynne, 'Scientific Knowledge and the Global Environment' in M. Redclift and T. Benton (eds.), *Social Theory and the Global Environment* (London, Routledge, 1994) 169, 175–6

[I]t is now commonplace to find the inevitable limitations of scientific knowledge recognized as a fact of life which policy-makers and publics should learn to accept. Thus scientific uncertainty is widely discussed as the cross which policy-makers have to bear, and the main obstacle to better and more consensual or authoritative policies. Yet much of this debate still assumes that if only scientific knowledge could develop enough to reduce the technical uncertainty, then basic social consensus would follow, assuming that people could be educated into the truth as revealed by science.

There are two main sociological strands of criticism of this dominant conventional perspective. The interests-oriented strand would note that even within the constraints of an accepted natural knowledge consensus, legitimate social interests — and hence favoured policies — can be in conflict. A perspective from the sociology of knowledge would go further, to argue that dominant interests control expertise and hence shape the available knowledge to reinforce their interests.

A more radical strand would suggest that beneath the level of conflicting explicit preferences or interests lies a deeper sense in which scientific knowledge tacitly reflects and reproduces normative models of social relations, cultural and moral identities, as if these are natural. Thus, for example, the level of intellectual aggregation of environmental data and variables such as radio caesium in the environment, when used to establish and justify restrictions on farmers operating in that environment, is effectively prescribing that degree of social or administrative standardization of the farmers. In other words, at a deeper level than explicit interests the form in which scientific knowledge is practically articulated prescribes important aspects of their social relations and identities. In research on the interactions of scientists and farmers after Chernobyl, this point came out as the farmers' detailed and differentiated local knowledge of the environment and what it meant for optimal farming methods, even in the same valley, were denied by scientific knowledge whose 'natural' form aggregated and deleted them into single, uniform data categories combining and homogenising several different valleys and many farmers. As one farmer caught by the Chernobyl restrictions lamented in this respect: 'this is what they can't understand; they think a farm is a farm and a ewe is a ewe. They think we just stamp them off a production line or something.'

The other question to arise is one concerning the administration of health restrictions. Whilst sampling of imports will often be permitted on grounds of public health, the Court of Justice has shown itself to be unsympathetic to systematic analysis. It was held disproportionate, in the absence of fraud or irregularities, for the French authorities to inspect three out of four consignments of Italian wine, and the Court, in its interim measures, ordered the French to inspect no more than 15 per cent of the consignments.[89] Conversely, a Directive authorising national authorities to check one in three consignments was not considered to be disproportionate.[90] This is an area, however, where there can clearly be very little certainty, as the number of inspections that may be permissible will depend upon the nature of the goods and other circumstances, such as whether there has been a recent outbreak of a particular disease.

[89] Case 42/82 *Commission* v *France* [1983] ECR 1013.
[90] Case 37/83 *Rewe-Zentrale* v *Landwirtschaftskammer Rheinland* [1984] ECR 1229.

Other areas where public health has recently become important are the distance selling of pharmaceuticals and policies combating alcohol misuse. In *Ahokkainen*, the Court faced the difficult question whether restrictions on certain alcohol imports were in fact necessary to combat the health and policy harm caused by alcohol misuse.[91] It referred this back to the national court to decide, but instructed them to examine the effects of the measures to see whether they had been effective, and also to consider what other measures might be possible but less restrictive of trade. The Court does not have the factual or investigative capacity to decide such matters – nor the competence – but most national courts will be shy of second-guessing the legislator. Therefore, the Court effectively instructs the national court on its function in the national judicial review process, giving it a more intrusive and intensive remit than national law would probably provide, in order to ensure that the EU interest in free movement is adequately protected.

In *DocMorris*, the Court was faced with a ban on distance sales of pharmaceuticals.[92] The risks of unregulated access to dangerous drugs are real, but so is the unequal impact of such a measure. It prevents cross-border retail supply of medical drugs, and primarily protects local pharmacies. Moreover, where the Internet pharmacies concerned were in other Member States, the presumption should be that they were adequately regulated by their host state, so that the risk of irresponsible supply without a prescription should not arise. By contrast with *Ahokkainen*, the Court went into the factual and policy context in some detail, before concluding that restrictions were nevertheless justified where prescription drugs were concerned, but not for non-prescription drugs.

7 PUBLIC POLICY, PUBLIC SECURITY AND PUBLIC MORALITY

Public policy, public security and public morality are treated as separate headings in the Treaty. Historically, they have also been treated differently in the case law. Public policy and public security have been treated, on the one hand, as interchangeably protecting the fundamental interests of a society.[93] Public morality has been concerned to secure the central values of a society.[94] However, there is no morality exception provided except for free movement of goods, so where morals questions arise in other fields they are treated as public policy matters. *Omega*[95] concerned a German prohibition on a laser game, where people simulated killing each other, on the grounds that it violated the German constitutional provision protecting human dignity. The measure was concerned with the protection of a fundamental value and was essentially about the moral standards of society. The Court, nevertheless, treated the matter as one of public policy, showing the fluidity and interchangeability of the concepts. Commentators have talked, in the meantime, of a more generalised move to create a 'European public order' exception whereby Member States are free to take measures to protect the central interests, symbols and values of their societies, and the Court engages in a more marginal form of appraisal.[96] There

---

[91] Case C-434/04 *Ahokkainen* [2006] ECR I-9171. See also Case C-170/04 *Klas Rosengren and Others* v *Riksåklagaren* [2007] ECR I-4071.

[92] Case C-322/01 *Deutscher Apothekerverband* v *DocMorris* [2003] ECR I-14887.

[93] Case C-100/01 *Ministre de l'Intérieur* v *Olazabal* [2002] ECR I-10981.

[94] Case 34/79 *R* v *Henn and Darby* [1979] ECR 3975.

[95] Case C-36/02 *Omega Spielhallen- und Automatenaufstellungs* v *Oberbürgermeisterin der Bundesstadt Bonn* [2004] ECR I-9609.

[96] G. Straetmans, 'Note on Case C-124/97 *Läärä* & Case C-67/98 *Zenatti*' (2000) 37 *CMLRev.* 991, 1002–5.

are still, however, certain constraints which Member States must observe. The central issues are usually the necessity of the measure, and the coherence of the national policy, as discussed above. *Conegate, Adoui, Van Duyn, Henn and Darby* and the gambling cases were all about public policy or morality.[97]

Public security is an even stronger governmental card, which judges are traditionally shy of challenging. The Court of Justice is primarily concerned to establish that the measure actually serves the right aim. In *Commission* v *Greece*, a challenge was brought to Greek rules on the storage of petroleum.[98] Oil companies operating in Greece were required to maintain a store of petroleum in Greece, which was justified by the national security interest in a domestic oil reserve. However, they could also transfer this reserve to a national refinery (that is to say, the refinery would maintain a store on their behalf) but only if and to the extent that they had purchased oil from this refinery in the last year. The Court was comfortable with the obligation to maintain national stores, but the creation of a system which protected and benefited national refineries appeared to have nothing to do with the storage goal, and could not be justified by Article 36.

In *Commission* v *France*, public policy was used, unusually, to justify inaction rather than action. French farmers had blocked cross-border roads and ports to prevent imports of agricultural products, which they regarded as unfair, or at any rate undesirable, competition. The French government, to the despair of its trading partners, did nothing. The blockages happened several times over a period of years, sometimes going on for weeks at a time, and occasionally involving eruptions of violence against foreign trucks, goods and drivers. One of the arguments put forward by the French government in its defence was that public feeling was so strong, particularly among the farmers but also in the general population, that if it were to use the police to clear roads and re-open ports this might lead to a breakdown of public order. The government was afraid of provoking demonstrations and riots and losing control.

Having found that the French government had not taken sufficient measures to guarantee the free movement of goods, the Court went on to consider whether these arguments in defence could be accepted.

Case C-265/95 *Commission* v *France (Spanish strawberries)* [1997] ECR I-6959

54. The above finding is in no way affected by the French Government's argument that the situation of French farmers was so difficult that there were reasonable grounds for fearing that more determined action by the competent authorities might provoke violent reactions by those concerned, which would lead to still more serious breaches of public order or even to social conflict.

55. Apprehension of internal difficulties cannot justify a failure by a Member State to apply Community law correctly.

56. It is for the Member State concerned, unless it can show that action on its part would have consequences for public order with which it could not cope by using the means at its disposal, to adopt all appropriate measures to guarantee the full scope and effect of Community law so as to ensure its proper implementation in the interests of all economic operators.

---

[97] See pp. 880–1 and 891–2.
[98] Case C-398/98 *Commission* v *Greece* [2001] ECR I-7915.

57. In the present case the French Government has adduced no concrete evidence proving the existence of a danger to public order with which it could not cope.

58. Moreover, although it is not impossible that the threat of serious disruption to public order may, in appropriate cases, justify non-intervention by the police, that argument can, on any view, be put forward only with respect to a specific incident and not, as in this case, in a general way covering all the incidents cited by the Commission.

59. As regards the fact that the French Republic has assumed responsibility for the losses caused to the victims, this cannot be put forward as an argument by the French Government in order to escape its obligations under Community law.

60. Even though compensation can provide reparation for at least part of the loss or damage sustained by the economic operators concerned, the provision of such compensation does not mean that the Member State has fulfilled its obligations.

The Court of Justice suggests that if feeling on an issue is sufficiently strong that a state is essentially unable to enforce EU law, or would be unable to deal with the consequences of such enforcement, this might justify non-action. The same could presumably be translated to positive acts: if a Member State takes measures restricting free movement because it otherwise fears consequences with which it cannot cope, this could also be legitimate. However, the judgment shows that such arguments will be regarded with great suspicion, and measures will be very strictly limited to what is necessary. Such a breakdown of order justification will be truly exceptional.

Part of the reason for such strictness is not just the cost for EU policy of national derogations, but the cost for individuals. Free movement is presented as a 'fundamental freedom' of Europeans which must be valued, but traditional human rights can be equally relevant. Where Member States do derogate, a condition for the legitimacy of their action is that any measure should respect both fundamental rights[99] and general principles of law. This is often particularly relevant to procedural questions, where states make exercise of EU rights conditional upon procedures which may be inaccessible, arbitrary or otherwise unfair.

In *Église de Scientologie de Paris*,[100] French law required any direct foreign investment, subject to highly limited exceptions, to have prior authorisation from the French authorities. The French government argued that this was necessary on grounds of public policy. The French authorities were accused, however, of exercising their discretion in an arbitrary manner.

Case C-54/99 *Église de Scientologie de Paris v Prime Minister* [2000] ECR I-1335

17. ... while Member States are still, in principle, free to determine the requirements of public policy and public security in the light of their national needs, those grounds must, in the Community context and, in particular, as derogations from the fundamental principle of free movement of capital, be interpreted strictly, so that their scope cannot be determined unilaterally by each Member State without any control by the Community institutions ... Thus, public policy and public security may be relied on only if

---

[99] Case C-112/00 *Schmidberger v Republic of Austria* [2003] ECR I-5659.
[100] Case C-54/99 *Église de Scientologie de Paris v Prime Minister* [2000] ECR I-1335.

there is a genuine and sufficiently serious threat to a fundamental interest of society ... Moreover, those derogations must not be misapplied so as, in fact, to serve purely economic ends ... Further, any person affected by a restrictive measure based on such a derogation must have access to legal redress ...

18. Second, measures which restrict the free movement of capital may be justified on public-policy and public-security grounds only if they are necessary for the protection of the interests which they are intended to guarantee and only insofar as those objectives cannot be attained by less restrictive measures ...

19. However, although the Court has held, in Joined Cases C-358/93 and C-416/93 *Bordessa and others* [1995] ECR I-361 ... which concerned the exportation of currency, that systems of prior authorisation were not, in the circumstances particular to those cases, necessary in order to enable the national authorities to carry out checks designed to prevent infringements of their laws and regulations and that such systems consequently constituted restrictions contrary to [Article 63 TFEU], it has not held that a system of prior authorisation can never be justified, particularly where such authorisation is in fact necessary for the protection of public policy or public security ...

20. In the case of direct foreign investments, the difficulty in identifying and blocking capital once it has entered a Member State may make it necessary to prevent, at the outset, transactions which would adversely affect public policy or public security. It follows that, in the case of direct foreign investments which constitute a genuine and sufficiently serious threat to public policy and public security, a system of prior declaration may prove to be inadequate to counter such a threat.

21. In the present case, however, the essence of the system in question is that prior authorisation is required for every direct foreign investment which is such as to represent a threat to public policy [and] public security, without any more detailed definition. Thus, the investors concerned are given no indication whatever as to the specific circumstances in which prior authorisation is required.

22. Such lack of precision does not enable individuals to be apprised of the extent of their rights and obligations deriving from [Article 63 TFEU]. That being so, the system established is contrary to the principle of legal certainty.

Analogous reasoning is found in a large number of cases concerning investment restrictions.[101] Concern over who may own or influence strategic industries is justifiable, but measures must be proportionate. This means that it must be possible that the criteria limiting investment must not go beyond what is necessary; for example, a general authorisation procedure for foreign investors will be unacceptable. Moreover, the criteria must be known in advance and authorisations must be accessible and speedy, and open to challenge in court.[102]

8 PUBLIC SERVICE AND OFFICIAL AUTHORITY

The exclusion of public service and the exercise of official authority from the free movement of workers, services and establishment may originally have been intended to have the scope that it now has: applying to functions which go to the heart of public power, and which

---

[101] Case C-222/97 *Trummer and Mayer* [1999] ECR I-1661; Case C-483/99 *Commission v France* [2002] ECR I-4781; Case C-503/99 *Commission v Belgium* [2002] ECR I-4809; Case C-174/04 *Commission v Italy (free movement of capital)* [2005] ECR -4933; Joined Cases C-282/04 and C-283/04 *Commission v Netherlands (direct and portfolio investments)* [2006] ECR I-9141; Case C-567/09 *Woningstichting Sint Servatius*, Judgment of 1 October 2009.
[102] *Ibid.*

demand a particular loyalty to the state, such as the judiciary, armed forces, and senior or sensitive posts in the national or regional administration.[103] However, the growth of welfare states meant that in most Member States a large proportion of the workforce was in some sense a state employee. Member States made opportunistic arguments for a formalist approach to the exclusions, catching all those paid by the state, however menial or non-sensitive their role. The Court of Justice consistently rejected this. The attraction for states of a broad exclusion was partly that some public service functions have traditionally been used to manage unemployment, an increase in the number of state functionaries being a politically acceptable way to provide jobs. In some cases, such jobs were part of broader social engineering. State employees may be posted to various areas of the state, so that public jobs were not only about reducing unemployment but also about redeploying the population to areas where their social or economic impact might be more beneficial, for example, taking unemployed urban youth and transferring them to aging and underpopulated rural areas. States therefore wanted to keep as much control as possible over their employees and employment policies.[104] Nevertheless, the very fact of the scope and size of the modern state meant that bowing to a broad interpretation of the exclusion would do significant, perhaps fatal, harm to the concept of a single market for occupational activity.

As well as restricting the core concept of public service and official authority, which are interpreted in parallel, the Court of Justice has made clear that they must be applied to specific functions, rather than to institutions as a whole. *Commission* v *Italy* concerned the Italian national research centre, in which all posts were reserved for Italians.[105] Part of the justification was that senior and management posts involved advising the government and contributing to policy formation. The Court accepted this, but found that it did not justify extending the exclusion to all researchers. The judgment had the consequence that foreign researchers might come up against a ceiling to their career, since unlike their Italian colleagues they could be legitimately denied promotion to the reserved senior posts. However, the Court emphasised that such discrimination must be kept to a minimum, and did not justify, for example, only employing foreigners on short-term contracts. Where foreigners were employed they were entitled to equality of conditions, and this must be reconciled with their more limited promotion prospects to the greatest extent possible.

Finally, the concept of public service may include work for private employers, if these are engaged in the service of the state and exercising public law powers.[106] The privatisation of public functions adds another layer of complexity to this particular derogation. The emphasis on the importance of the function for the state and its interests, rather than on the technical employment status, is consistent, however, with the ruling in *Bosman* that public policy derogation from free movement could, in principle, be relied upon by private parties.[107]

---

[103] Cf. Case 149/79 *Commission* v *Belgium (No. 2)* [1982] ECR 1845. See also [1988] OJ C72/2.
[104] See Case 149/79 *Commission* v *Belgium (No. 2)* [1982] ECR 1845.
[105] Case 225/85 *Commission* v *Italy* [1987] ECR 2625.
[106] Case C-47/02 *Anker* [2003] ECR I-10447; Case C-405/01 *Colegio de Oficiales de la Marina Mercante Española* v *Administración del Estado* [2003] ECR I-10391.
[107] Case C-415/93 *Union Royale Belge des Sociétés de Football Association and Others* v *Bosman and Others* [1995] ECR I-4921.

FURTHER READING

A. Arcuri, *The Case for a Procedural Version of the Precautionary Principle: Erring on the Side of Environmental Protection*, Global Law Working Paper 10/04 (New York, Hauser Global Law School, 2004)

C. Barnard, 'Derogations, Justifications and the Four Freedoms: Is State Interest Really Protected?' in C. Barnard and O. Odudu, *The Outer Limits of European Law* (Oxford, Hart, 2009)

G. Davies, 'Process and Production Method-based Restrictions on Trade in the EU' in C. Barnard (ed.), *Cambridge Yearbook of European Legal Studies* (Oxford, Hart, 2008)

N. Georgiadis, *Derogation Clauses: The Protection of National Interests in EC Law* (Brussels, Bruylant, 2006)

C. Macmaolain, 'Free Movement of Foodstuffs, Quality Requirements and Consumer Protection: Have the Court and the Commission Both Got it Wrong?' (2001) 26 *European Law Review* 413

J. Scott, 'Of Kith and Kine (and Crustaceans): Trade and Environment in the EU and WTO' in J. Weiler (ed.), *The EU, NAFTA and the WTO: Towards a Common Law of International Trade* (Oxford, Oxford University Press, 2000)

'Mandatory or Imperative Requirements in the EU and WTO' in C. Barnard and J. Scott, *The Law of the European Single Market: Unpacking the Premises* (Oxford, Hart, 2002)

J. Snell, 'Economic Aims as Justifications for Restrictions on Free Movement' in A. Schrauwen, *The Rule of Reason: Rethinking Another Classic of Community Law* (Groningen, Europa Law Publishing, 2005)

P. Wattel, 'Red Herrings in Direct Tax Cases Before the Court' (2004) 31(2) *Legal Issues of Economic Integration* 81

S. Weatherill, 'The Evolution of European Consumer Law and Policy: From Well Informed Consumer to Confident Consumer' in H. Micklitz, *Rechtseinheit order Rechtsvielfalt in Europa?* (Baden-Baden, Nomos, 1996)

22

EU Competition Law: Function and Enforcement

CONTENTS

1 INTRODUCTION

This section of the book contains a survey of the main competition law provisions, whose principal task is to regulate the behaviour of firms in the market. For example, competition law forbids price fixing cartels among competitors and other agreements that restrict competition

(Article 101 TFEU (ex Article 81 EC)) and prohibits monopolies from charging excessive prices (Article 102 TFEU (ex Article 82 EC)). Firms that infringe these rules may be fined by the Commission, indicating that competition law is designed principally to deter anti-competitive conduct. These two Treaty provisions are discussed in Chapter 23. Competition law also monitors Member States' regulation of markets and can prohibit anti-competitive legislation as well as promote competition in markets where national law has prevented competition. Here, law is enforced not merely to deter anti-competitive action, but also to open markets to competition. This function is analysed in Chapter 24. Finally, competition law monitors mergers to prevent those that restrict competition when it is feared that the merger gives the newly formed entity too much power. *This is discussed in Chapter 25, which is available as a supplement online.*

When the EEC Treaty was negotiated, there was considerable pressure from Americans, but also by segments of Europe's academic community, that competition law should be included in the Treaty.[1] However, at that time, the 'culture of competition' had yet to emerge in most Member States, who traditionally favoured cartel arrangements, state intervention and the promotion of national champions.[2] Indeed, some Member States only introduced national competition laws as late as the 1990s.[3] Thus, when provisions were first introduced to curb restrictive practices in the coal and steel sector (by Articles 65 and 66 of the ECSC Treaty), these were an innovation for the Member States.[4] Originally the purpose of introducing competition law into the EC Treaty was to complement the internal market rules by preventing businesses from partitioning the internal market and by encouraging competition across borders.[5] However today, the need for EU competition law as a means of securing economic welfare is widely accepted and the rules are enforced robustly.

The present chapter considers why competition law is important and how it is enforced. It is organised as follows.

Section 2 is a review of the debates about the objectives of EU competition law. It shows that there are divided opinions on two fronts: first, between those who consider that the application of competition law would benefit from a greater reliance on economic analysis and those who take the view that competition law is about the pursuit of economic and non-economic considerations; and secondly that even among those who think that economics offers a superior paradigm for applying competition law, there are differences of opinion about how best to deploy economic thinking. This section of the chapter is essential reading for an understanding of the subject, because, as will be seen in Chapter 23, these differences can have a significant impact on how competition law is applied and enforced.

---

[1] D. J. Gerber, *Law and Competition in Twentieth Century Europe* (Oxford, Oxford University Press, 1998) ch. 9.

[2] H. G. Schröter, 'Cartelization and Decartelization in Europe, 1870–1995: Rise and Decline of an Economic Institution' (1996) 25 *Journal of European Economic History* 129. An exception was West Germany's competition law drafted in 1957.

[3] For example, Ireland and Italy in 1990, the Netherlands in 1997, Luxemburg in 2004.

[4] Jean Monnet, *Mèmoires* (Paris, Fayard, 1976) 356–7, 411–13 (also noting US pressure to implement anti-cartel laws).

[5] G. Marenco, 'The Birth of Modern Competition Law in Europe' in A. von Bogdandy, P. Mavroidis and Y. Mény, (eds.), *European Integration and International Coordination: Studies in Transnational Economic Law in Honour of C-D Ehlermann* (The Hague, Kluwer, 2002) especially 297–8.

Section 3 examines the enforcement powers of the European Commission: it explains how the Commission investigates cases, the procedures for reaching a decision, and the penalties that may be imposed if an infringement is found. Attention is given to the effectiveness of the enforcement scheme as well as to its legitimacy, judged by how well it safeguards the fundamental rights of those under investigation.

Section 4 considers the significance of Regulation 1/2003/EC. This Regulation 'entrusted the national competition authorities with a key role in ensuring that the EU competition rules are applied effectively and consistently, in conjunction with the Commission'.[6] It was a significant and controversial measure. It gave greater prominence to national competition authorities, who are now primary enforcers of EU competition law, and changed the role of the Commission.

Section 5 reviews the rules relating to the private enforcement of EU competition law. It considers the contribution of the Court of Justice and the legislative proposals made by the Commission, and assesses the value and role of private enforcement.

2 AIMS OF EU COMPETITION LAW

There is considerable debate regarding the functions of competition law. Today, the majority view is that competition law should be enforced against firms whose behaviour harms consumers. Against this, there are two alternative views. One is that competition law should not be concerned with an outcome (efficiency) but with maintaining the competitive process. Another alternative view is that competition law can be enforced to attain a wider set of economic and non-economic ambitions; for example, it may be enforced to promote national industries, to safeguard employment, or to protect the environment. In (i) below, we sketch a justification of the role of competition law derived from the discipline of economics, which supports the majority view. In some jurisdictions (most notably the United States), scholars argue that competition law should be interpreted solely according to what economic theory dictates.[7] In (ii), we consider the alternative points of view. In (iii), we turn to explore how far these competing approaches have influenced EU competition policy.

(i) The economics of competition

From an economic perspective, competition law should prohibit commercial practices that damage the operation of markets and promote activities that yield economic benefits. Accordingly, the principal measuring stick of a good competition law is how well it sustains an efficient economic order. From the perspective of an economist, competition law is as important as the right to property and freedom of contract in guaranteeing efficiency. Efficiency is a multilayered term.

---

[6] European Commission, *Report on the Functioning of Regulation 1/2003*, COM(2009)206 final, para. 28.
[7] R. H. Bork, *The Antitrust Paradox* (New York, The Free Press, 1978, reprinted 1993); R. A. Posner, *Antitrust Law* (2nd edn, Chicago, IL, University of Chicago Press, 2000).

Miguel de la Mano, *For the Customer's Sake: The Competitive Effects of Efficiencies in European Merger Control*, Enterprise Papers No. 11 (2002 Enterprise Directorate-General) 8–14

Economists generally distinguish between three broad classes of efficiencies all of which are relevant for the analysis of competition: allocative, productive (or technical) and dynamic (or innovation) efficiency.

Allocative efficiency: Allocative efficiency is achieved when the existing stock of (final and intermediate) goods are allocated through the price system to those buyers who value them most, in terms of willingness to pay or willingness to forego other consumption possibilities. At an allocatively efficient outcome, market prices are equal to the real resource costs of producing and supplying the products.

Productive (or technical) efficiency: Productive efficiency is a narrower concept than allocative efficiency, and focuses on a particular firm or industry. It addresses the question of whether any given level of output is being produced by that firm/industry at least cost or, alternatively, whether any given combination of inputs is producing the maximum possible output. Productive efficiency depends on the existing technology and resource prices. The state of technology determines what alternative combinations of resources can produce a given amount of output. Resource prices determine which combination of resources is the most efficient one in that it gives rise to the lowest production cost. Productive efficiency is achieved when output is produced in plants of optimal scale (or minimum efficient scale) given the relative prices of production inputs.

Dynamic (or innovation) efficiency: Allocative and productive efficiency are static notions concerned with the performance of an economy, industry or firm at a given point in time, for a given technology and level of existing knowledge. Dynamic efficiency in antitrust economics is connected to whether appropriate incentives and ability exist to increase productivity and engage in innovative activity over time, which may yield cheaper or better goods or new products that afford consumers more satisfaction than previous consumption choices.

The distinction between static (allocative or productive) efficiency and dynamic efficiency is based on the idea that the latter leads to improvements in the available technology or the discovery of new production processes or products. In other words, dynamic efficiency is related to the ability of a firm, industry or economy to exploit its potential to innovate, develop new technologies and thus expand its production possibility frontier.

These definitions provide us with the main tools to evaluate the performance of industry. One approach that can be used to apply the above concepts is to suggest that there is a close relationship between a market's structure and its economic performance. Two extreme market structures can be identified: perfect competition is found when an industry is made up of many firms producing homogeneous products, where new firms can enter and existing firms exit with ease and where consumers are fully informed (a fruit stall in a market comes close: there are many competitors, consumers can shop around for the best price, and the goods sold are broadly comparable). At the other extreme, a monopoly is an industry with only one supplier, where there are no close substitutes and where it is very difficult for another firm to enter (Microsoft, with an 80 per cent share of the market for PC compatible operating systems, comes close).[8] The significance of these models is that in the former one can predict that there

---

[8] See further D. Begg, S. Fischer and R. Dornbusch, *Economics* (9th edn, London, McGraw Hill, 2008) ch. 8.

will be allocative and productive efficiency: consumers dissatisfied with one firm's prices or quality will switch to others. In contrast the monopolist is not responsive to consumer demand: it will set high prices, reducing the amount of goods consumers are able to buy, thus lowering allocative efficiency. Moreover, the monopolist wastes resources in a more harmful way, as de la Mano explains.

Miguel de la Mano, *For the Customer's Sake: The Competitive Effects of Efficiencies in European Merger Control*, Enterprise Papers No. 11 (2002 Enterprise Directorate-General) 8–14

Further, monopoly rents will tend to be dissipated as firms, in order to establish or defend a dominant position, are willing to spend anything up to the value of their monopoly profits. Such expenditures may take various forms: excess advertising, research and development (R&D), investment in excess capacity or brand proliferation in order to deter entry from rival firms, lobbying to secure government quotas or licences, etc. Often this expenditure is in itself entirely unproductive (e.g. lobbying) although other expenditures may partly lead to consumer benefits (as in the case of R&D that results in innovations). These examples imply that the costs of market power through weakened productive efficiency may be at least as important as its adverse impact on allocative efficiency.

The upshot is that competition law should be mostly concerned with manifestations of monopoly power. These may occur either when one firm dominates a market or when all competitors enter into a cartel to fix prices, so that collectively they act like a monopolist, or when firms merge creating a new firm that holds monopoly power.

Two qualifications should be borne in mind. First, perfect competition and monopoly are mere models and the majority of industry structures fall in between these extremes. And here, making predictions based on the structure of the market is less straightforward. For example, an oligopoly market structure is one where the firms are few in numbers and entry barriers high (e.g. the car manufacturing or soft drinks markets). Here, either one may find considerable rivalry between firms, or the firms might realise that there is no point competing among themselves and tacitly coordinate behaviour. 'Truly, almost anything does and can happen under oligopoly.'[9] Secondly, while these models help in focusing competition law enforcement towards firms that have market power approximating that found in monopoly, it should be recalled that in certain circumstances monopoly supply may be efficient, for instance where a single firm can produce all of the goods that society demands at a lower cost than if a large number of firms each produced a portion of the goods (where the sole industry player holds a natural monopoly).

Having made these qualifications, in the 1960s, some economists believed that there was a direct causal relation between market structure and economic performance, whereby the fewer

---

[9] W. J. Baumol and A. S. Blinder, *Economics: Principles and Policy* (10th edn, Mason, OH, Thomson South-Western, 2006) 238.

the firms (and thus the more concentrated the market), the less competitive the industry. This view (often labelled the 'Harvard School' view, as the main proponents were Harvard economists) influenced the development of US antitrust law (called antitrust rather than competition law, as its earliest actions were against cartels established in the form of trusts) until the 1970s, when the economic mood swung away from this exclusively structural understanding of markets.[10]

In the 1970s, the 'Chicago School' championed a different set of opinions about how markets worked and advocated a more lax degree of scrutiny than the Harvard School.[11] Their arguments can be summarised in the following manner. First, while it is true that a firm with a large market share may be tempted to behave anti-competitively by reducing output and increasing prices, this kind of behaviour will send a signal to other market players that there is unmet demand in the market, and invite the entry of new firms. This new entry will bring prices down and reintroduce the degree of competition necessary to satisfy consumer desires. In other words, while acknowledging that market structure may affect economic performance, the Chicago School added the rider that if economic performance led to unmet consumer demand, this would cause the entry of other firms. This economic dynamic meant that competition law was largely unnecessary unless new entry was hampered, and the greatest reason why entry was hampered was national legislation limiting business freedom, not the anti-competitive behaviour of business. Absent barriers for new competitors, the market would heal itself. Secondly, while the Harvard School lamented the increasing concentration of firms, the Chicago School argued that concentrated markets were more efficient because firms would be able to exploit economies of scale (that is, it is relatively cheaper for one firm to manufacture millions of cars than for several firms to manufacture a thousand cars each). Thirdly, the Chicagoans believed that law enforcers were more likely to damage the competitive process by their intervention because of their ignorance about how markets worked.

The Chicago and Harvard views can diverge significantly in their prescriptions for competition law enforcement. For example, a Harvard School approach would suggest that high prices by a monopoly are illegal but a Chicago School approach would indicate that high prices invite new entry, which would render the market competitive in the long run.

The Chicago School is probably the most influential school of thought in competition law. It placed economics at the centre of its analysis of competition law and set out a coherent view of competition law enforcement, embedded in confidence that markets work best without excessive regulation by states or courts. However, the Chicago School model is currently contested by 'post-Chicago' economic theories.[12]

---

[10] F. M. Scherer and G. Ross, *Industrial Market Structure and Economic Performance* (3rd edn, Boston, MA, Houghton Mifflin, 1990); see ch. 1 for a review.

[11] H. Hovenkamp, 'Antitrust Policy After Chicago' (1986) 84 *Michigan Law Review* 213; F. H. Easterbrook, 'Workable Antitrust Policy' (1986) 84 *Michigan Law Review* 1696; B. Hawk, 'The American Antitrust Revolution: Lessons for the EEC?' (1988) *ECLR* 53.

[12] See H. Hovenkamp, 'Post-Chicago Antitrust: A Review and Critique' (2001) *Colum. Bus. L Rev.* 257; L. A. Sullivan and W. S. Grimes, *The Law of Antitrust: An Integrated Handbook* (St Paul, MN, West Publishing, 2000), a textbook written taking into account many post-Chicago insights; R. Pitofsky (ed.), *How the Chicago School Overshot the Mark* (Oxford, Oxford University Press, 2008).

**Michael S. Jacobs, 'An Essay on the Normative Foundations of Antitrust Economics'
(1995–96) 74 *North Carolina Law Review* 219, 222–5**

A post-Chicago School of economics has arisen, working within the efficiency model, but starting from
assumptions and ending with an enforcement methodology markedly different from Chicago's ... Both
agree that economics is 'the essence of antitrust' and that protecting consumer welfare, conceived in
allocative efficiency terms, should be the exclusive goal of competition law. Both eschew the subjective
inquiries that they ascribe to the overtly political approaches of the past, and both assert that unless
business conduct raises prices or reduces output it should be left alone, regardless of the political or
distributive consequences.

The new debate involves contending visions of the workings of the market mechanism and of the
proper model for antitrust enforcement. Chicagoans believe that markets tend toward efficiency, that
market imperfections are normally transitory, and that judicial enforcement should proceed cautiously,
lest it mistakenly proscribe behavior that promotes consumer welfare. Post-Chicagoans, by contrast,
believe that market failures are not necessarily self-correcting, and that firms can therefore take
advantage of imperfections, such as information gaps or competitors' sunk costs, to produce inefficient
results even in ostensibly competitive markets. They argue that the distortions to competition made
possible by market imperfections should prompt enforcement authorities to scrutinize a wider variety of
conduct than Chicagoans would examine. On the doctrinal level, this debate has produced conflicting
answers to some of antitrust's most pressing questions: the relevant measures of market power, the
competitive effects of tying arrangements and other vertical restraints, the economic plausibility of
predatory pricing schemes, and the durability of cartels and oligopolies.

On its surface, the nature of this debate confirms the view that antitrust analysis has taken a
decidedly technological turn ... What apparently divide the parties are not their political ideologies or
interpretations of history, but differing evaluations of the efficiency implications of their respective
theories and methodologies. Indeed, some post-Chicagoans characterize their work not as an alternative
to Chicago thinking but as a refinement of it, an effort to provide decisionmakers with a more accurate
picture of the marketplace and more sensitive tools for detecting inefficient behavior.

These appearances, however, are deceptive. The parties' shared commitment to efficiency and
the debate's specialized vocabulary mask deep divisions regarding the normative assumptions most
appropriate to competition policy. The contending economic models reflect very different views of
human nature, firm behavior, and judicial competence. While Chicagoans assume that the desire to
maximize profits drives firms to compete away market imperfections and destabilizes collusive activity,
post-Chicagoans believe that strategizing firms can create or perpetuate market imperfections that can
seriously hamper competitive balance. Similarly, while Chicagoans presuppose that markets promote
efficient business behavior and that judges untrained in economics are ill-equipped to identify and
measure market imperfections, post-Chicagoans have less trust in markets and more confidence in the
judiciary's ability to distinguish between competitive and anticompetitive conduct. Post-Chicagoans
have shown that the neoclassical price model [based on assumptions that individuals have rational
preferences and act based on all relevant information to maximise income (firms) or utility (consumers)]
is not the only method for analyzing the efficiency questions central to antitrust. They have
demonstrated that economists equally loyal to the goal of consumer welfare can disagree markedly with
price theorists about the means most conducive to allocative efficiency. In doing so, however, they have
revealed, albeit unintentionally, the inability of economics to furnish empirical or theoretical criteria for
resolving the differences between their model and Chicago's. Their work has produced a stalemate in

economic theory that effectively requires antitrust decisionmakers, most of whom accept the legitimacy of the economic model, to probe the technocratic surface of the current debate and evaluate the conflicting beliefs about firms, markets, and governments embedded in its foundation. Ironically, far from having marginalized the role of value choice in antitrust discourse, the ascendancy of economic models underscores its enduring importance.

The post-Chicago approach leads to suggestions for competition law enforcement that are different from the Chicago model. For example, under a Chicago approach, predatory pricing (that is, prices set at a level below the cost of production) is only unlawful when the predator is able to cause all rivals to exit and so monopolise the market. In contrast, under post-Chicago theories, predatory pricing can be held to be unlawful even if the predator does not monopolise the market. Instead, predatory pricing may be a way of hurting competitors to 'discipline' them (for example, if a firm is well established in the United Kingdom and its competitor mainly sells in Germany, predatory pricing might be used by the UK firm should the German firm try to penetrate the UK market, the aim being not the destruction of the German competitor, but the maintenance of separate markets) or to establish a reputation as a tough competitor (for example, in a market where entry is relatively easy, one bout of predatory pricing against a new entrant may discourage other firms from entering, even when it might be economically rational to enter).[13] Jacobs suggests that these differences of opinion about what is economically rational belie a series of value assumptions about how markets work. Therefore, competition law cannot be founded upon economics; rather it is premised upon the assumptions we make about how market players operate. On this argument, a competition authority chooses an economic theory that supports those assumptions.

So far we have outlined economic debates where the major concern is an improvement in allocative and/or productive efficiency. Integrating dynamic efficiency is more problematic. We might object to the pharmaceutical sector being monopolised by one firm, but what if this is the only way to concentrate enough resources to obtain life-saving drugs in the future? How much can we suffocate competition today in favour of greater consumer benefits tomorrow? Some have taken the view that innovation occurs so frequently that competition law should not be overly concerned about firms that monopolise a high technology market, while others have taken the view that innovation can only take place if new entrants are protected by competition law regulating the firms that monopolise the market.[14] There is no consensus on the best competition policy to facilitate innovation, although 'antitrust economists recognise that dynamic net efficiency gains from continuing innovation may far outweigh the static gains from marginal-cost pricing'.[15] Having said that, competition authorities have tended to

---

[13] A. Kate and G. Neils, 'On the Rationality of Predatory Pricing: The Debate Between Chicago and Post-Chicago' (2002) *Antitrust Bulletin* 1.

[14] See D. S. Evans and R. Schmalensee, 'Some Economic Aspects of Antitrust Analysis in Dynamically Competitive Industries' in A. B. Jae, J. Lerner and S. Stern (eds.), *Innovation Policy and the Economy*, vol. II (Cambridge, MA, NBER and MIT Press, 2002); G. Monti, 'Article 82 EC and New Economy Markets' in C. Graham and F. Smith, *Competition, Regulation and the New Economy* (Oxford, Hart, 2004); J. D. Balto and R. Pitofsky, 'Challenges of the New Economy: Issues at the Intersection of Antitrust and the New Economy' (2001) 68 *Antitrust Bulletin* 913.

[15] M. de la Mano, *For the Customer's Sake: The Competitive Effects of Efficiencies in European Merger Control*, Enterprise Papers No. 11 (2002 Enterprise Directorate-General) 14.

focus on allocative and productive efficiency; intellectual property law is more focused on safeguarding dynamic efficiency.[16]

(ii) The politics of competition law

The debates about the economics of competition law often seem technical and non-political. However, as Jacobs argued above, there is an inherent political dimension to competition law, even when analysed through an economic perspective. Debates about the role of competition law run through the history of US competition law.

Eleanor M. Fox and Lawrence A. Sullivan, 'Antitrust – Retrospective and Prospective: Where are We Coming From? Where are We Going?' (1987) 62 *New York University Law Review* 936, 942, 956–9

Through many of the years of antitrust, some supporters of aggressive enforcement closely linked high concentration in markets and sectors with lessened competition. Many perceived that when few sellers dominate a market, consumers are worse off because they have fewer options, thus less choice. Moreover, prices are likely to be high, perhaps because competitive pressures are less intense; perhaps because costs are not effectively controlled. As a result, consumers are exploited for the profit or ease of producers. When the few sellers are also industrial behemoths, many concluded, small and aspiring sellers as well as the citizens of our political democracy are worse off. Entrepreneurs, especially creative and efficient ones, are likely to be the targets of strategic exclusionary prices. Moreover, the political process is manipulated, predominantly in the interests of the large corporations. When, in addition, it is difficult for new sellers to establish themselves in the market, the social, political, and economic costs are magnified. Consumers, entrepreneurs, and the public are the losers.

Many economists, especially those with Chicago leanings, think that because antitrust is about markets, as is microeconomics, antitrust law should be economics. They react as though the law is out of kilter whenever it diverges from their particular economic insight; and they so react regardless of whether the law diverges because empirical processes have not validated factual assumptions, or because the law has identified social goals other than or in addition to allocative efficiency.

Law is not economics. Nor were the antitrust laws adopted to squeeze the greatest possible efficiency out of business.

Finally, the producer-plus-consumer-welfare paradigm presses the analyst to think only in terms of aggregate outcomes or wealth of the nation. But this concept is static and outcome-oriented, while the antitrust laws are dynamic and process-oriented. They protect not an outcome, but a process – competition. Antitrust laws set fair rules of the game. They give rights of access and opportunity. The antitrust laws preserve and foster dynamic interactions among those in the market. They deal not with aggregate national wealth, but with the expectations and behavior of the people who participate in the markets.

---

[16] Although dynamic efficiency considerations played a role in the *Microsoft* Decision where the firm indicated the risk that the European Commission's action would undermine dynamic efficiency (summary at [2007] OJ L32/23; full text available at http://ec.europa.eu/competition/index_en.html); and in Joined Cases C-501/06 P, C-513/06 P, C-515/06 P and C-519/06 P *GlaxoSmithKline Services Unlimited* v *Commission*, Judgment of 6 October 2009, where the Court of Justice confirmed that dynamic efficiencies may be pleaded under Article 101(3) TFEU.

The American debate is particularly instructive in setting out the competing values that animate competition policy. In particular, the views of Fox and Sullivan also suggest that a total commitment to economic values is unnecessary, and that wider political interests may justifiably affect competition law decisions. More specifically, Fox and Sullivan locate competition law within the perspective of a liberal economic order, which has a particular affinity to the origins of EU competition law. In its early years, EU competition law was influenced by German scholarship and German officials played a key role in the development of competition law. Underpinning the German approach to competition was a unique economic philosophy: ordoliberalism.[17]

Wernhard Möschel, 'Competition Policy from an Ordo Point of View' in A. Peacock and H. Willgerodt, *German Neo-liberals and the Social Market Economy* (London, Macmillan, 1989) 146

The actual goal of the competition policy of Ordo-liberalism lies in the protection of individual economic freedom of action as a value in itself, or vice versa, in the restraint of undue economic power. Franz Böhm once illuminated this idea by the aphoristic formula, 'the one who has power has no right to be free and the one who wants to be free should have no power'. Economic efficiency as a generic term for growth, for the encouragement and development of technical progress and for allocative efficiency, is but an indirect and derived goal. It results generally from the realisation of individual freedom of action in a market system ...

This is contrary to the various concepts of utilitarianism. In this respect the Ordo-liberal competition policy is obviously related to the intellectual traditions of idealist German philosophy, particularly that of Immanuel Kant ... Modern currents in the American anti-trust law which lean directly upon wealth maximisation, [like] Richard Posner's constrained utilitarianism ... are obviously incompatible with the Ordo-liberal system of values. Ordo-liberalism treats individuals as ends in themselves and not as means of another's welfare.

The Ordoliberal's dislike of market power is not based on fears of inefficiency, rather on concerns that firms with market power can stifle the freedom of other economic operators. Like Fox and Sullivan, the process of competition, favouring access and opportunities for new businesses, is valued. This vision has had a strong influence in the development of EU competition law.[18] Under this theory, concern about economic power should lead a competition authority to intervene even if this would not result in the most efficient outcome. This view still has supporters (mainly in Germany), but as seen below, the Commission is now committed to using an economic approach. Those that support the old policy have three major concerns: first, the absence of any debate at EU level about the choice to abandon the model of competition based on safeguarding the competitive process and favouring an economic approach; secondly, that an economic approach may lead to reduced enforcement, especially against the most powerful

---

[17] See also D. J. Gerber, *Law and Competition in Twentieth Century Europe* (Oxford, Oxford University Press, 1998) ch. 7; W. Moschel, 'The Proper Scope of Government Viewed from an Ordoliberal Perspective: The Example of Competition Policy' (2001) 157(1) *Journal of Institution and Theoretical Economics* 3.

[18] D. Gerber, 'Constitutionalising the Economy: German Neo-Liberalism, Competition Law and the "New" Europe' (1994) 42 *American Journal of Comparative Law* 25, 69–74.

firms, while harming smaller players; and thirdly, that an economic approach focuses on allocative efficiency (i.e. measuring the direct impact on consumers today) at the expense of promoting dynamic efficiency.[19]

However, once one believes that competition law can serve a sole political objective (the preservation of the competitive process, or the protection of economic freedom), it is a short step to argue that other goals might be obtained by enforcing competition law. As we shall see below, this is what has occurred in EU competition law.

(iii) Aims of EU competition policy

As suggested above, ordoliberalism played an important role in the early development of competition law in the European Union, but it was only in the late 1980s that EU competition policy took shape. This happened as a result of five factors. First, the neoliberal economic policies championed by Reagan in the United States and Thatcher in the United Kingdom began to affect governments and industries across Europe, and the economic liberalisation called for by the Single European Act necessitated a stronger role for competition law to ensure that the transformation from a mixed economy to a free market occurred smoothly. Secondly, the Court of Justice, since the 1960s, had ruled on a number of competition law cases and established strong precedents that consolidated the Commission's powers. Thirdly, staff morale at the Directorate-General for Competition (charged with enforcing competition law in the Union) was considerably strengthened by the economic and legal backing that emerged in the 1980s. Fourthly, the personalities of the competition Commissioners were instrumental in strengthening this Directorate-General. Two competition Commissioners, Peter Sutherland (1985–89) and Sir Leon Brittan (1989–93), in particular, were instrumental in pursuing and extending the free market logic, often leading to clashes between the views espoused by DG Competition and those of the Commission President, Jacques Delors. Finally, in 1990, the Commission obtained powers to regulate mergers in the Union. With the economic restructuring that was taking place as a result of economic liberalisation, this placed EU competition law at the heart of the Union's transformation to a neoliberal market economy.[20]

Two aspects of this evolution are worthy of note. First, the increased emphasis on the benefits of efficient markets undermined ordoliberal concerns about economic power and economic freedom that were seminal in the early development of EU competition law. Secondly, there is the significance of the Commissioner for competition policy. He or she can have a direct role in influencing the general direction of competition policy. For instance, Sir Leon Brittan's advocacy of free markets was instrumental in the early success of the implementation of the merger rules. His successor, Karel van Miert (1993–99), however, was less convinced than his predecessor about grounding competition law in free market terms, as this quotation from one of his speeches indicates:

---

[19] I. L. O. Schmidt, 'The Suitability of the More Economic Approach for Competition Policy: Dynamic vs. Static Efficiency' (2007) *ECLR* 408; Bundeskartellamt/Competition Law Forum, 'A Bundeskartellamt/Competition Law Forum Debate on Reform of Article 82: A Dialectic on Competing Approaches' (2006) 2 *ECJ* 211; R. Zäch and A. Künzler, 'Freedom to Compete or Consumer Welfare: The Goal of Competition Law according to Constitutional Law' in R. Zäch, A. Heinemann and A. Kellerhals (eds.), *The Development of Competition Law* (Cheltenham, Edward Elgar, 2009).

[20] L. McGowan, 'Safeguarding the Economic Constitution: The Commission and Competition Policy' in N. Nugent, *At the Heart of the Union: Studies of the European Commission* (2nd edn, Basingstoke, Macmillan Press, 2000) 151–3.

Let me make one thing clear straight away: the application of competition principles is not an end in itself. Competition policy is a tool which can be used to help achieve the fundamental aims of the Community. The Commission's competition policy does not operate in a vacuum. It has to take account of its repercussions in other areas of Commission policy, such as industrial policy, regional policy, social policy and the environment. But this is not a one way process. Competition policy also makes its own contribution to the formulation and implementation of policy in those areas. The point is sometimes overlooked by those who criticize the institutional framework of European competition policy, such as the advocates of a European Cartel Office.[21]

Under his leadership, one would have expected more compromises between the economic and non-economic objectives. His replacement, Mario Monti (1999–2004), an economics professor, steered competition policy back along the lines taken by Sutherland and Brittain.

Mario Monti, 'European Competition for the 21st Century' (2001) *Fordham Corporate Law Institute* (B. Hawk (ed.) 2000) 257–8

Since its adoption more than 40 years ago, the Treaty acknowledges the fundamental role of the market and of competition in guaranteeing consumer welfare, in encouraging the optimal allocation of resources, and in granting to economic agents the appropriate incentives to pursue productive efficiency, quality, and innovation.

I personally believe that this principle of an open market economy does not imply an attitude of unconditional faith with respect to the operation of market mechanisms. On the contrary, it requires a serious commitment as well as self restraint by public powers, aimed at preserving those mechanisms … I consider all these legal instruments – antitrust rules, merger control and State aid provisions – as different tools at our disposal to achieve a single aim: to maintain a vibrant and competitive economy in Europe. The modernisation of our economy, as underlined by the European Heads of States and Governments in the Lisbon summit last spring, requires speeding up the processes of liberalisation and structural reforms in order to make our markets function smoothly. As Commissioner in charge of Competition Policy, I am determined to contribute to this aim by a strict application of all the legal tools under my responsibility.

The combination of liberalisation processes and strict enforcement of competition rules is indeed bringing benefits to European consumers. Just one example: thanks to liberalisation and competition, residential telephone tariffs for international calls fell, on average, by 40% between 1997 and 1999 in most Member States. Not only did competition result in lower prices; it also gave rise to a considerable increase in the supply of new and efficient services. I do not believe that these developments are the natural and inevitable consequence of technological development. I am convinced that without a firm liberalising attitude and the careful competition scrutiny of these processes, we would not have achieved such downward pressure on tariffs, or such upward growth in quality, variety and innovation.

Competition policy is also strictly connected with another of the fundamental objectives of the Treaty, namely the creation of the Single Market. After having painstakingly dismantled the barriers to trade represented by the national laws and regulations, we must be watchful for them not to be replaced by market segmentations introduced by firms.

---

[21] Karel van Miert, 'The Competition Policy of the New Commission', EGKartellrechtsforum der Studienvereinigung Kartellrecht Brussels 11/5/1995, available at http://europa.eu.int/comm/competition/index_en.html.

In my first term of office, over the last five years, as Commissioner for the Single Market, I have been deeply committed to pursue State measures which prevented the Single Market from becoming a reality. Now, my attention has turned to the practices of economic operators ... that have the same effect or distort the functioning of the Single Market in those sectors where it already has been or it is being achieved.

To give you a concrete example, having overseen the removal of many of the State barriers which stood in the way of consumers wishing to purchase a motor car in the Member State of their choice, I am not amused to find that some car producers have been seeking to prevent such transactions by way of agreement with their distributors. The Commission has already imposed substantial fines on car producers which engaged in such practices (Volkswagen, Opel) and is presently investigating several others. The elimination of the practices by firms that prevent the Single Market from becoming a reality continues to be one of my main goals.

While Monti speaks the language of economics, he also refers to two policies that animate EU competition law – market integration and the development of healthy European industry – which are said to complement competition policy.[22] But a closer study of the development of the Community shows that an even broader range of objectives have influenced EU competition law.

Rein Wesseling, *The Modernisation of EC Antitrust Law* (Oxford and Portland, Hart, 2000) 48–9

Initially, the antitrust law provisions were inserted into the Treaty in view of their role in the process of market integration. The antitrust rules were no more than the private counterpart to the rules, enshrined in Arts 28–30 EC, which guaranteed freedom to trade across borders without hindrance from the Community's Member States. The framers of the Treaty wanted to preclude private undertakings replacing the prohibited public obstacles to inter-state trade. The first period of Community antitrust policy [1958–1973][23] saw the Commission enforcing the rules with constant reference to ensuring the free flow of goods, thus promoting market integration.

Subsequently, in the second period [1973–1985], antitrust policy was employed to establish a broader Community industrial policy. Exemptions for the antitrust rules were granted to forms of (trans-national) co-operation between undertakings which the Commission considered desirable, to promote either integration (Eurocheque) or broader Community policy aims (for example employment in crisis sectors). Thus, a Community industrial policy was gradually developed on the basis of the Treaty's antitrust rules.

The momentum generated by the Commission's '1992 programme' then provided the occasion for expanding the scope of Community antitrust policy even further [in the third period commencing in 1985]. With continued reference to the needs of market integration, the Commission acquired powers under the Merger Regulation to regulate the structure of markets. Furthermore it extended the enforcement of the antitrust rules to the public sectors of the various Member States. While reference

---

[22] European Commission, *A Pro-active Competition Policy for a Competitive Europe*, COM(2004)293 final, especially ch. 2.

[23] The author uses the same time periods as J. Weiler, 'The Transformation of Europe' (1991) 100 *Yale Law Journal* 2403.

was still made to the underpinning of Community antitrust law in economic integration, the socio-political implications of integration by competition (law) became ever more apparent. In this respect the control of corporate mergers and the gradual liberalisation of public economic sectors, both highly political exercises, which commenced by the end of the 1980s, symbolise the altered character of Community antitrust law enforcement.

Although the system was originally devised for promoting market integration, antitrust policy is now also – and mainly – directed at promoting the various objectives of the Community enshrined in Article 2 EC. Absent a clear hierarchy between those objectives, priorities are selected on a case by case basis. Agreements between undertakings have been exempted from the prohibition in Article 81(1) EC when their negative effect on the intensity of competition on the relevant market was outweighed by positive consequences for European industry's competitiveness, or for social and economic cohesion. Likewise, mergers are sometimes held compatible with the common market, in spite of the significant reduction in the degree of competition they engender, when the Commission considers that they may contribute to one or more of the objectives laid down in Article 2 EC. While it is not submitted that the majority of antitrust issues is settled on the basis of extra-competition elements, it is evident from the Commission decisions, endorsed by the European Courts, that the Commission is able to pursue 'flanking' policies on the basis of its enforcement of the antitrust rules.

This review suggests that a wide range of policy issues affect competition law decisions, and that competition law objectives might at times take second place to other Community values. On the one hand, we might be sympathetic to the use of competition law to sustain other Community policies, but this would be to forget that there are other, direct means to achieve them, and that using competition law may not be the most effective means. Secondly, legal certainty for market participants is undermined if competition law is modified to achieve other objectives. Lastly, there is a risk that by securing other policies, markets may not develop efficiently and thereby harm consumers. These concerns, among others, led the Commission to try and concentrate on regulating markets only when there was harm to consumer welfare.

Recently, two events have challenged the Commission's current commitment to enforcing competition primarily to promote consumer welfare: the Treaty of Lisbon and the severe recession that began soon after the Treaty was signed.

No reform of the rules of competition law had been envisaged when the Treaties were being revised, but in June 2007 the newly elected French President insisted on an amendment to one of the foundational Treaty Articles to remove the word 'competition'. In the EC Treaty, Article 4(1) EC referred to the activities of the Member States and the Community, which included the adoption of an economic policy 'conducted in accordance with the principle of an open market economy with free competition'. In the new Treaty Article identifying the activities of the European Union, the reference to competition was deleted and relegated to a Protocol.

Article 3(3) TEU

The Union shall establish an internal market. It shall work for the sustainable development of Europe based on balanced economic growth and price stability, a highly competitive social market economy, aiming at full employment and social progress, and a high level of protection and improvement of the quality of the environment. It shall promote scientific and technological advance.

Protocol on the internal market and competition

The High Contracting Parties, considering that the internal market as set out in Article 2 of the Treaty on European Union includes a system ensuring that competition is not distorted, have agreed that:

to this end, the Union shall, if necessary, take action under the provisions of the Treaties, including under Article 308 of the Treaty on the Functioning of the European Union.

The Protocol is the compromise accepted by Member States who did not favour the French position and is designed for two purposes: first, to keep the focus on EU competition policy, and secondly, to ensure that the Union has legislative competence to use Article 253 TFEU (ex Article 308 EC) to enact legislation in the field of competition (this Article was used, for example to give a legal basis to the EC Merger Regulation).[24]

When this amendment was announced, the press and some commentators reacted with fear that competition as a key principle had been lost, and the Competition Commissioner responded with anger, suggesting that in her view the amendments were insignificant.[25] Both exaggerated responses are unwarranted. It is highly unlikely that the Commission's powers in enforcing Articles 101 and 102 TFEU or the merger rules will be affected in any significant way. Nevertheless, while the Lisbon Treaty continues to grant the Union legislative competence over competition law, the Union's role in using competition policy as a principle underpinning its initiatives is undermined. It is likely that the main objective that the French had in mind in securing this amendment was to slow down the liberalisation of utilities, in particular in the energy sector. It remains to be seen how far progress in this field is affected.[26] It is also possible that in individual decisions some Commissioners might feel emboldened to exempt agreements or authorise mergers that contribute to creating 'European champions' given Article 3(3) TFEU's reference to a high level of competitiveness; however, this already happens under the existing rules.[27]

The Union courts might be affected in two ways. First, it is well known that teleological reasoning forms a key part of its interpretative techniques and this has been used to develop competition law.[28] Perhaps the Court of Justice will not feel so bold in the future, seeing that the legislative intention is to give less priority to competition law. A second, related objective is that the Court might be more willing to exclude the application of competition law from certain practices when it judges there are valid reasons to do this. Whatever the practical significance that this amendment will have, it shows that there is still controversy among Member States as to the role of competition law in regulating markets. One of the main reasons that the Constitutional Treaty was not accepted in some Member States is said to be the concern that it favoured an Anglo-Saxon conception of capitalism. In this light, the amendment can be said

---

[24] Regulation 139/2004/EC on the control of concentrations between undertakings [2004] OJ L24/22, based on Articles 83 and 308 EC.

[25] Statement by European Commissioner for Competition Neelie Kroes on results of June 21–22 European Council, Protocol on Internal Market and Competition, Memo 07/250, 27 June 2007.

[26] Legislation has only recently been agreed, which is not as pro-market as originally proposed by the Commission in 2007. Directive 2009/72/EC of the European Parliament and of the Council of 13 July 2009 concerning common rules for the internal market in electricity and repealing Directive 2003/54/EC [2009] OJ L211/55.

[27] G. Monti, 'Merger Defences' in G. Amato and C.-D. Ehlermann (eds.), *EC Competition Law: A Critical Assessment* (Oxford, Hart, 2007).

[28] Most notably in Case 6/72 *Europemballage Corp. and Continental Can Co. Inc.* v *Commission* [1972] ECR 215.

to be a change to assure certain Member States that the Union's markets are not going to be transformed radically as a result of the new Treaty.

Potentially, the economic recession the world has found itself in since 2008 places more severe pressure on competition law, as Member States are tempted to deploy protectionist policies to safeguard jobs and prestigious national industries, and as firms tend to engage in cartels as one way of combating a decrease in demand. The present Commissioner has issued a strongly worded statement that the recession is not a reason for reducing competition law scrutiny:

Neelie Kroes, 'Competition, the Crisis and the Road to Recovery', address at Economic Club of Toronto, 30 March 2009 (Speech/09/152)

Why we need competition policy

While I have been a lifelong capitalist, I could never accept that laissez faire is a good solution for a society. It was John Ralston Saul who said that 'unregulated competition is just a naïve metaphor for anarchy' – we don't need that. What we need are regulated markets. And the challenge is to maximise our prosperity by finding the most efficient ways to regulate them. Competition in markets and competition policy enforcement are at the top of that list of effective market regulations. Intervention is limited to where it is necessary – getting rid of the few rotten apples in the basket, while allowing the millions of good apples to get on with business. In my opinion these forces have a natural home in advanced social market economies such as ours. Today, Canada and the EU prosper from open competitive markets and the high level of skills of our people. One of the core ingredients making this possible is competition policy ...

Competition encourages the innovations that create jobs. It keeps a lid on prices. It reminds us that we have to work hard if we want to succeed. And that all adds up to the understanding that competition policy is part of the solution to our economic needs. In good times and bad times we need it ...

Tackling the current crisis

Aside from the European Commission having the crucial power to control national government subsidies, we have spent the last five years developing, updating and streamlining our competition systems. Now we are cashing in on them as their efficiency and flexibility help us to cope with the current volatile market conditions. These reforms cover subsidy controls, cartels, mergers, antitrust and all the tools we possess to make markets work better. After four years – when the financial and then economic crisis hit – the systems were lean and fast and ready to deal with a moving target ...

In my field of competition policy the best thing we can do is be very clear about how and why our rules should be followed, and what we can do to help companies and governments work within those boundaries ... For example, we are crystal clear that cartels are harmful no matter what current economic growth rates are. They cause billions of dollars of direct harm in both our economies, and by cracking down hard on one cartel we estimate that we stop another five. So we can't go soft on them. More than that, if we went easy on cartels, a culture of 'anything goes' would quickly develop... and that's the same sort of risky, complacent culture that fostered this wider crisis. The story is similar for merger control. We have a Merger Regulation that can handle the complex cases that will no doubt be thrown at it. We aren't about to let EU Member States create inefficient national champions so they can patch up their pride. Nor do we want to see two struggling banks cripple each other through a botched merger, or create another bank that is 'too big to fail'. So it is business as usual in merger control – for all our sakes.

If that sounds like 'tough love' – it is. It is better to have clear and strong rules in the first place and then stick to them – it lifts standards and markets know what to expect.

The next few years will test how far the Commission and national competition authorities will display tough love or feel compelled to tolerate some restrictions of competition to mitigate the harsh economic climate.

3 ENFORCEMENT BY THE COMMISSION

To date, the Commission has been the principal enforcer of the competition rules (a task envisaged by Article 103 TFEU (ex Article 83 EC)) via the Directorate-General for Competition (formerly DG IV). The Commission's powers were originally set out in Regulation 17/62/EEC, which was in force between 1962 and 2004, and have been expanded by Regulation 1/2003/EC, which is in force from 1 May 2004.[29]

The cases the Commission takes up have two sources. First, the Commission may start an investigation on its own initiative, triggered by press reports, or its investigation of an economic sector under the powers provided in Regulation 1/2003, article 17. Secondly, some cases arise from complaints made by private parties or 'confessions' made by undertakings that have infringed the rules. However, the Commission has no obligation to reach a Decision for every complaint or confession it receives: it may prioritise cases on the basis of whether there is a Union interest.[30] There is deemed to be a Union interest in situations where the parties commit important violations, where the case gives rise to novel points of law, or where the practices in question have a significant effect on market integration.[31] In line with the desire to increase competition law enforcement at national level, fewer cases will be considered to be of Union interest in the future.

The enforcement procedure, which is administrative in character, is divided into two stages.[32] In the first stage, the Commission gathers evidence to determine whether there has been an infringement. In the second stage, it makes its concerns known to the parties being investigated and after a hearing issues a Decision.[33]

(i) First stage: investigation

In order to obtain information to determine whether an undertaking has infringed competition law, the Commission has two powers. First, it may require undertakings to hand over information and carry out interviews, and secondly, it has power to inspect business premises and private homes to seize relevant documents.

---

[29] Regulation 17/62/EC, First Regulation implementing Articles 81 and 82 EC [1959] OJ Spec. edn 062, 57; Regulation 1/2003/EC on the implementation of the rules on competition laid down in Articles 81 and 82 EC [2003] OJ L1/1.

[30] Case T-24/90 *Automec Srl v Commission (Automec II)* [1992] ECR II-2223.

[31] Commission Notice on cooperation within the Network of Competition Authorities [2004] OJ C101/42, paras. 14, 15 and 54.

[32] For a detailed exposition, see C. S. Kerse and N. Kahn, *EC Antitrust Procedure* (5th edn, London, Sweet & Maxwell 2005). See also Commission Regulation 773/2004/EC of 7 April 2004 relating to the conduct of proceedings by the Commission pursuant to Articles 81 and 82 EC [2004] OJ L123/18, setting out in more detail the practicalities of the proceedings.

[33] Joined Cases C-238/99 P, C-244/99 P, C-245/99 P, C-247/99 P, C-250/99 P, C-252/99 P and C-254/99 P *Limburgse Vinyl Maatschappij NV and Others v Commission* [2002] ECR I-8375, paras. 181–3.

(a) Requests for information and interviews

Article 18(1) of Regulation 1/2003 empowers the Commission to require undertakings to hand over information, but only that which is related to the infringement.[34] The Commission may make a simple request (to which reply is not compulsory, but a fine is payable if incorrect information is supplied intentionally or negligently),[35] or issue a decision requiring information to be provided. The information normally consists of documents setting out how the undertaking has acted. The Commission had also recently begun to rely on statements made to it by the parties.[36] Regulation 1/2003 codifies this practice in article 19(1), which empowers the Commission to interview any person who consents to be interviewed, but there are no penalties if the information provided is incorrect or misleading.

In supplying information, there is a risk that the undertaking is providing proof that it has infringed competition law. This would run counter to the undertaking's right against self-incrimination and in a challenge against a request for information by the Commission, the Court of Justice recognised this right in part. First, the right not to incriminate oneself only applies to requests where the addressee is required to reply, under pain of a fine; in cases of a simple request, this protection is not available, because the undertaking has no duty to reply.[37] Secondly, even in cases of requests made under pain of a fine, the right is limited.

Case 374/87 *Orkem v Commission* [1989] ECR 3283

28. In the absence of any right to remain silent expressly embodied in Regulation No. 17 [now Regulation 1/2003], it is appropriate to consider whether and to what extent the general principles of Community law, of which fundamental rights form an integral part and in the light of which all Community legislation must be interpreted, require, as the applicant claims, recognition of the right not to supply information capable of being used in order to establish, against the person supplying it, the existence of an infringement of the competition rules …

33. In that connection, the Court observed recently that whilst it is true that the rights of the defence must be observed in administrative procedures which may lead to the imposition of penalties, it is necessary to prevent those rights from being irremediably impaired during preliminary inquiry procedures which may be decisive in providing evidence of the unlawful nature of conduct engaged in by undertakings and for which they may be liable. Consequently, although certain rights of the defence relate only to contentious proceedings which follow the delivery of the statement of objections, other rights must be respected even during the preliminary inquiry.

34. Accordingly, whilst the Commission is entitled, in order to preserve the useful effect of [article 18 of Regulation 1/2003], to compel an undertaking to provide all necessary information concerning such facts as may be known to it and to disclose to it, if necessary, such documents relating thereto as are in its possession, even if the latter may be used to establish, against it or another undertaking, the existence of anti-competitive conduct, it may not, by means of a decision calling for information, undermine the rights of defence of the undertaking concerned.

35. Thus, the Commission may not compel an undertaking to provide it with answers which might involve an admission on its part of the existence of an infringement which it is incumbent upon the Commission to prove.

---

[34] Case C-36/92 P *SEP v Commission* [1994] ECR I-1911, para. 21.
[35] Regulation 1/2003/EC, article 23(1).
[36] For example, *Pre-Insulated Pipe Cartel* [1999] OJ L24/1, para. 24; *Zinc Phosphate* [2003] OJ L153/1, paras. 57 and 59.
[37] Case C-407/04 P *Dalmine SpA v Commission* [2007] ECR I-835, paras. 33–6.

On the facts of the case, the Court held that some of the information sought by the Commission infringed the applicant's rights.

Case 374/87 *Orkem* v *Commission* [1989] ECR 3283

39. ... By requiring disclosure of the 'details of any system or method which made it possible to attribute sales targets or quotas to the participants' and details of 'any method facilitating annual monitoring of compliance with any system of targets in terms of volume or quotas', the Commission endeavoured to obtain from the applicant an acknowledgment of its participation in an agreement intended to limit or control production or outlets or to share markets.

Likewise, the Commission cannot ask parties how many meetings they had with their competitors that infringed Article 101 TFEU. However, it is possible to obtain documentary information concerning agreements entered into, or factual information, for example about which undertakings were present in certain meetings.[38] Following *Orkem*, parties have challenged the Commission's requests for information as infringing the privilege against self-incrimination, with occasional success.[39] The Court has not changed the position taken in *Orkem*, which has been defended by Advocate General Geelhoed in the following terms:

the interplay between the fundamental rights of legal persons and competition enforcement remains a balancing exercise: at stake are the protection of fundamental rights versus effective enforcement of Community competition law. Article [101 TFEU] is a fundamental provision which is essential for the accomplishment of the tasks entrusted to the Community and, in particular, for the functioning of the internal market. Article [101 TFEU] forms part of public policy. If the Commission is no longer empowered to request the production of documents its enforcement of competition law in the Community legal order will become heavily dependent on either voluntary cooperation or on the use of other means of coercion as for example dawn raids. It is self-evident that the effective enforcement with reasonable means of the basic tenets of the Community public legal order should remain possible, just as it is evident that the rights of the defence should be respected too. In my view, the latter is the case. As case law now stands, a defendant is still able, either during the administrative procedure or in the proceedings before the Community courts, to contend that the documents produced have a different meaning from that ascribed to them by the Commission.[40]

And while the General Court considers that the approach reflects the jurisprudence of the European Court of Human Rights (ECtHR) on the right against self-incrimination, commentators have been less convinced.[41]

---

[38] *Austrian Banks* [2002] OJ L56/1, para. 488.

[39] See e.g. Case T-112/98 *Mannesmannröhren-Werke AG* v *Commission* [2001] ECR II-729, para. 71.

[40] Case C-301/04 P *Commission* v *SGL Carbon* [2006] ECR I-5915, Opinion of Advocate General Geelhoed, para. 67. The Court of Justice took the same view: see paras. 39–49 of the judgment.

[41] See Case T-112/98 *Mannesmannröhren-Werke AG* v *Commission* [2001] ECR II-729, para. 77. The leading cases are *Funke* v *France* [1993] 16 EHRR 297; *Saunders* v *United Kingdom* (1997) 23 EHRR 313. For comment see P. R. Willis, '"You Have the Right to Remain Silent ..." or Do You? The Privilege Against Self-incrimination following *Mannesmannröhren* and Other Recent Decisions' (2001) *ECLR* 313; I. van Bael and J.-F. Bellis, *Competition Law of the European Community* (4th edn, The Hague, Kluwer Law International, 2005) 107, opining that national courts which are signatories to the ECHR might interpret the ECHR more strictly than the Court of Justice; A. McCulloch 'The Privilege Against Self-incrimination in Competition Investigations' (2006) 26(2) *Legal Studies* 211, criticising the distinction between factual questions and admissions of infringement.

The Court of Justice also protects the privacy of communications between an undertaking and its lawyers, and information passing between lawyer and client need not be disclosed. This rule is justified by the view that the lawyer collaborates in the administration of justice and is required to provide, independently and confidentially, any legal assistance the client needs.[42] However, the Court curtails lawyer-client privilege in one way: it only protects communication by independent lawyers, not in-house lawyers. The rationale for this is that in many Member States in-house lawyers are not subject to professional codes of discipline.[43] Furthermore, the information that is privileged only extends to matters linked with the subject matter of the investigation, which will normally be material written after the investigation.[44] It may include working documents prepared by the undertaking to aid the lawyers in preparing the defence.[45]

(b) Inspections

The Commission's most draconian means to secure information about a possible competition law infringement are its powers to enter business premises of the parties under investigation and seize the relevant information. These procedures are colloquially referred to as 'dawn raids'.[46]

Regulation 1/2003/EC, article 20

1. In order to carry out the duties assigned to it by this Regulation, the Commission may conduct all necessary inspections of undertakings and associations of undertakings.
2. The officials and other accompanying persons authorised by the Commission to conduct an inspection are empowered:
   (a) to enter any premises, land and means of transport of undertakings and associations of undertakings;
   (b) to examine the books and other records related to the business, irrespective of the medium on which they are stored;
   (c) to take or obtain in any form copies of or extracts from such books or records;
   (d) to seal any business premises and books or records for the period and to the extent necessary for the inspection;
   (e) to ask any representative or member of staff of the undertaking or association of undertakings for explanations on facts or documents relating to the subject-matter and purpose of the inspection and to record the answers ...

---

[42] Case 155/79 *AM & S Europe Ltd v Commission* [1982] ECR 1575, para. 24. See generally J. Faull, 'Legal Professional Privilege: The Commission Proposes International Negotiations' (1985) 10 *ELRev.* 119.

[43] While the President of the Court of Justice (Case C-7/04 P(R)) noted that given changes in the regulation of the profession in many Member States, the exclusion may be obsolete (paras. 125–6), the General Court has confirmed the approach of the Court of Justice in Joined Cases T-125/03 and T-253/03 *Akzo Nobel Chemicals Ltd and Akcros Chemicals Ltd v Commission* [2007] ECR II-3523.

[44] See Case 155/79 *AM&S Europe Ltd v Commission* [1982] ECR 1575.

[45] *Akzo* [2007] ECR II-3523, paras. 123, 124.

[46] J. Joshua, 'The Element of Surprise' (1983) 8 *ELRev.* 3.

Article 21

1. If a reasonable suspicion exists that books or other records related to the business and to the subject-matter of the inspection, which may be relevant to prove a serious violation of Article [101 TFEU] or Article [102 TFEU], are being kept in any other premises, land and means of transport, including the homes of directors, managers and other members of staff of the undertakings and associations of undertakings concerned, the Commission can by decision order an inspection to be conducted in such other premises, land and means of transport.

The Commission must specify the subject matter and purpose of its investigation 'not merely to show that the proposed entry onto the premises of the undertakings concerned is justified but also to enable those undertakings to assess the scope of their duty to cooperate whilst at the same time safeguarding their rights of defence'.[47] Article 21 is an innovation and provides for searches into private homes, but these require prior authorisation from a national court where the premises are located.

The Commission's power to search premises is controversial when judged against fundamental rights standards. Article 8 of the European Convention of Human Rights (ECHR) incorporates a right to private and family life. A derogation from this right is specified in Article 8(2) ECHR, which states that infringements of privacy are justified only when necessary, inter alia, for the economic wellbeing of the country or the prevention of crime. To benefit from the derogation in Article 8(2), the interference with the right to privacy must be based on accessible legal rules, the interference must have a legitimate aim, and there must be effective protection against abuse by the investigators.[48] The Court of Justice originally held that privacy rights recognised by the ECHR only applied to searches of private homes, not business premises, although a similar right to privacy of business premises was held to exist as a general principle of Community law which protects all private persons against 'arbitrary or disproportionate intervention by public authorities'.[49]

This narrow interpretation of an undertaking's right to privacy under Community law must now be reconsidered as a result of two developments in the case law of the ECtHR. First, in *Niemetz* v *Germany*, the ECtHR held that the right to private life does not merely encompass private homes but also business premises, when this is necessary to protect the individual against arbitrary interference by public authorities.[50] Secondly, in *Société Colas Est and Others* v *France*, the ECtHR held that in competition cases, prior judicial authorisation is required when conducting inspections so as to afford adequate and effective safeguards against abuse.[51]

Applied to EU competition law, the *Niemetz* case suggests that Article 8 rights can no longer be distinguished on the basis that they only apply to private homes. This means that inspections are only lawful if they benefit from the derogation in Article 8(2). Articles 20 and 21 inspections normally satisfy the first two requirements established by the ECtHR for

---

[47] Joined Cases 46/87 and 227/88 *Hoechst AG* v *Commission* [1989] ECR 2859, para. 19.
[48] Kerse and Kahn, above n. 32, 166; *Société Colas Est and Others* v *France* (2004) 39 EHRR 17.
[49] C-94/00 *Roquette Frères* v *Directeur général de la concurrence, de la consommation et de la répression des fraudes* [2002] ECR I-9011.
[50] *Niemetz* v *Germany* [1993] 16 EHRR 97, para. 31; *Veeber* v *Estonia (No. 1)* (2004) 39 EHRR 6.
[51] *Société Colas Est and Others* v *France* (Application no. 37971/97) 16 April 2002 [2002] ECHR 418, para. 49.

Article 8(2) (the rules are transparent and the purpose is the suppression of anti-competitive behaviour). However, the principal doubt about the legality of the Commission's inspection procedures is whether there is effective protection against abuse, particularly in light of the *Société Colas Est* ruling. However, the Court of Justice in *Roquette Frères* did not consider judicial authorisation to be necessary, unless the Member State where the inspection is due to take place requires judicial authorisation. The main justification for not requiring prior judicial authorisation is that it is possible to seek judicial review after the event, on the grounds that, in the circumstances, a dawn raid was arbitrary, disproportionate or excessive.[52] If the Court of Justice agrees with the applicant that the Commission abused its powers, then the Commission would be prevented from using, for the purposes of proceedings in respect of an infringement of the Community competition rules, any documents or evidence which it might have obtained in the course of that investigation.[53] The Court of Justice's ruling was later codified in Regulation 1/2003.

Regulation 1/2003/EC, article 20

6. Where the officials and other accompanying persons authorised by the Commission find that an undertaking opposes an inspection ordered pursuant to this Article, the Member State concerned shall afford them the necessary assistance, requesting where appropriate the assistance of the police or of an equivalent enforcement authority, so as to enable them to conduct their inspection.

7. If the assistance provided for in paragraph 6 requires authorisation from a judicial authority according to national rules, such authorisation shall be applied for. Such authorisation may also be applied for as a precautionary measure.

8. Where authorisation as referred to in paragraph 7 is applied for, the national judicial authority shall control that the Commission decision is authentic and that the coercive measures envisaged are neither arbitrary nor excessive having regard to the subject matter of the inspection. In its control of the proportionality of the coercive measures, the national judicial authority may ask the Commission, directly or through the Member State competition authority, for detailed explanations in particular on the grounds the Commission has for suspecting infringement of Articles [101 TFEU] and [102 TFEU], as well as on the seriousness of the suspected infringement and on the nature of the involvement of the undertaking concerned. However, the national judicial authority may not call into question the necessity for the inspection nor demand that it be provided with the information in the Commission's file. The lawfulness of the Commission decision shall be subject to review only by the Court of Justice.

However, it has been argued that this falls short of the requirements for derogation stipulated by the ECtHR's case law because a judicial warrant need not be obtained in all cases, and the scope for judicial scrutiny by the national judge in article 20(8) is limited.[54] Accordingly, dawn raids may be challenged, either at national level, questioning national courts' authorisations of

---

[52] Joined Cases 97–99/87 *Dow Chemical Ibérica and Others v Commission* [1989] ECR 3165, para. 16.

[53] Case C-94/00 *Roquette Frères v Directeur général de la concurrence, de la consommation et de la répression des fraudes* [2002] ECR I-9011, para. 49.

[54] A. Riley, 'The ECHR Implications of the Investigation Provisions of the Draft Competition Regulation' (2002) 51 *ICLQ* 55, 76–7.

Commission inspections,[55] or at Community level, for compatibility with the protection of the undertaking's fundamental rights in the absence of judicial authorisation.

(ii) Second stage: adjudication

Once the information is gathered, two steps precede the Commission's Decision. First, the Commission issues a statement of objections and the parties have access to the Commission's file to see the evidence upon which the allegations are based. Secondly, the parties have the right to a hearing. The rationale for these procedures is to guarantee the parties' rights to defend themselves.

(a) Statement of objections and access to the file

After proceedings have begun, the Commission must notify the parties of the infringements that it believes have been committed. This document is known as the statement of objections.

Regulation 1/2003/EC, article 27

1. Before taking decisions … the Commission shall give the undertakings or associations of undertakings which are the subject of the proceedings conducted by the Commission the opportunity of being heard on the matters to which the Commission has taken objection. The Commission shall base its decisions only on objections on which the parties concerned have been able to comment. Complainants shall be associated closely with the proceedings.

As the final sentence of article 27(1) makes clear, the Commission can only issue a Decision on grounds set out in the statement of objections. Originally, the Commission would only allow the defendants access to incriminating evidence, which was unsatisfactory because the parties would not be able to see documents that would have been useful for their defence. However, in 1982, the Commission developed a practice to give access to all the documents it used in preparing the case (except for documents containing business secrets of other undertakings, other confidential information and internal documents of the Commission)[56] which was made compulsory by the General Court.[57] Following this judgment, the rights to access were specified in a notice,[58] and now the right to access the file is enshrined in article 27(2) of Regulation 1/2003:[59]

---

[55] As in Case C-94/00 *Roquette Frères v Directeur général de la concurrence, de la consommation et de la répression des fraudes* [2002] ECR I-9011, appeal against an order of a local judge to empower the Commission to conduct an investigation on the appellant's premises.

[56] Case T-23/99 *LR af 1998 A/S v Commission* [2002] ECR II-1705, para. 170.

[57] Case T-7/89 *Hercules v Commission* [1991] ECR II-1711, paras. 52–3.

[58] In 1997; the current version is Commission Notice on the internal rules of procedure for processing requests for access to the file in cases pursuant to Articles 81 and 82 EC [2005] OJ C325/7.

[59] And recognised by the Court of Justice: see e.g. Joined Cases 204/00 P etc. *Aalborg Portland A/S and Others v Commission*, Judgment of 7 January 2004, paras. 68–77.

The rights of defence of the parties concerned shall be fully respected in the proceedings. They shall be entitled to have access to the Commission's file, subject to the legitimate interest of undertakings in the protection of their business secrets. The right of access to the file shall not extend to confidential information and internal documents of the Commission or the competition authorities of the Member States. In particular, the right of access shall not extend to correspondence between the Commission and the competition authorities of the Member States, or between the latter. Nothing in this paragraph shall prevent the Commission from disclosing and using information necessary to prove an infringement.

A key principle of EU law is 'equality of arms': the party accused of an infringement has access to the Commission's entire file (save for the documents protected by article 27(2)) and it is not for the Commission to decide which documents to pass on.[60]

(b) Oral hearing

Hearings are normally attended by the following: the parties accused, complainants, Commission representatives and representatives of the national competition authorities. They are moderated by a Hearing Officer. This Commission official is independent of DG Competition and reports directly to the Commissioner for Competition. He or she is not involved in the preparation of the case and has the task of ensuring 'that the hearing is properly conducted and contributes to the objectivity of the hearing itself and of any decision taken subsequently'.[61]

The hearing is composed of arguments by Commission and accused, and followed by questions from those present.[62] Before the hearing the defendant will have had several exchanges of view with DG Competition. However, it has been said that the hearing is useful because it is the only time for the defendant to set out its case to the national authorities, to the Commission's legal service, and to representatives of other Directorates-General.[63]

After the hearings, the Commission prepares a Decision acting as a collegiate body. Draft decisions are reviewed by the Advisory Committee which is composed of representatives of Member States' competition authorities.[64] The Commission must take the 'utmost account' of the Committee's views but is not bound to follow them.[65] For most competition cases, the Commission operates with a 'written procedure' whereby the draft Decision is circulated to all Commissioners and is adopted if there are no objections.[66] For controversial cases, however, there are debates among the Commissioners, and lobbying is not uncommon.[67] The decisions must be fully reasoned to allow the parties to see which findings of fact and of law led the Commission to its conclusion.[68] This is necessary to afford the parties the opportunity of challenging the Commission's Decision in the courts.

---

[60] Case T-30/91 *Solvay SA* v *Commission* [1995] ECR II-1775, paras. 81–3. For a critique see C. D. Ehlermann and B. J. Drijber, 'Legal Protection of Enterprises: Administrative Procedure, in Particular Access to the File and Confidentiality' (1996) *ECLR* 375.

[61] Commission Decision on the terms of reference of Hearing Officers in certain competition proceedings, article 5 [2001] OJ L162/21.

[62] For detail see Regulation 773/2004/EC [2004] OJ L123/18.

[63] Van Bael and Bellis, above n. 41, 1096.

[64] Regulation 1/2003/EC, article 14.

[65] *Ibid.* article 14(5).

[66] Van Bael and Bellis, above n. 41, 1103.

[67] 'Brussels Braces for a Lobbying Invasion', *The Financial Times*, 3 October 2005.

[68] Case 41/69 *ACF Chemiefarma* v *Commission* [1970] ECR 661, paras. 76–81.

(iii) Penalties for infringement

Once an infringement is established, the Commission has a wide range of powers, which may be divided into two categories. First, the Commission has powers to bring the infringement to a close and to remedy the anti-competitive effects of the anti-competitive practice.

Regulation 1/2003/EC, article 7(1)

Where the Commission, acting on a complaint or on its own initiative, finds that there is an infringement of Article [101 TFEU] or of Article [102 TFEU], it may by decision require the undertakings and associations of undertakings concerned to bring such infringement to an end. For this purpose, it may impose on them any behavioural or structural remedies which are proportionate to the infringement committed and necessary to bring the infringement effectively to an end. Structural remedies can only be imposed either where there is no equally effective behavioural remedy or where any equally effective behavioural remedy would be more burdensome for the undertaking concerned than the structural remedy. If the Commission has a legitimate interest in doing so, it may also find that an infringement has been committed in the past.

In a cartel case, for example, the Commission will normally demand that the undertakings bring the agreement to an end so that the damage to competition does not continue. It may also order parties to change their behaviour vis-à-vis competitors, a sanction which has been imposed upon dominant undertakings to oblige them to supply competitors.[69] However, the Commission cannot impose obligations that are not necessary to bring the infringement to an end. In one case the General Court held that requiring members of a cartel to stop fixing prices was legitimate, but asking them to inform customers that they may renegotiate the contracts that had been signed when the cartel inflated prices was unnecessary, because the contracts in question were only of a year's duration and because if consumers suffer losses, this is a matter to be addressed by the national court.[70]

Article 7 adds a novel remedy: empowering the Commission to impose 'structural remedies'. This can entail a demand that a company be broken up into two or more smaller units – a remedy so draconian it is likely to be used sparingly. The final sentence of article 7 allows the Commission to make decisions against infringements that have occurred in the past but only if there is a legitimate interest: for example, clarifying a point of law or issuing a decision to facilitate follow-on damages claims.[71]

The category of powers the Commission has is to penalise the undertaking for breaching competition law. Fines not exceeding 1 per cent of the undertaking's turnover may be imposed for procedural infringements (for example, supplying incorrect or misleading information),[72] and fines not exceeding 10 per cent of the undertaking's turnover may be imposed for intentional or negligent infringements of Articles 101 and 102 TFEU.[73] The Commission's approach

---

[69] See e.g. Case T-201/04 R *Microsoft* v *Commission* [2007] ECR II-3601.
[70] Case T-395/94 *Atlantic Container Line* v *Commission* [2002] ECR II-875, paras. 410–16.
[71] Case 7/82 *GVL* v *Commission* [1983] ECR 483, para. 24.
[72] Regulation 1/2003, article 23(1).
[73] *Ibid.* article 23(2).

to fines should be read together with its policy on leniency applications and settlements. In this way, we can gain a sense of the Commission's enforcement strategy as a whole.

(a) Fining policy

In the early days, the fines were fairly low but have increased gradually. In 1980, the Commission declared that fines would be increased as a means of deterring undertakings,[74] and in 1991, it announced that in appropriate cases it would apply the highest penalty possible: 10 per cent of the undertaking's turnover.[75] The gradual increase can be seen as a sensible policy in that, in the early years, undertakings were unfamiliar with their obligations under the competition rules, but as the culture of competition spread, and as the deadline for achieving a single market neared, the fines were increased. The current policy targeting cartels has led to ever greater fines. Between 2004 and January 2009, the Commission imposed fines under Article 101 that totalled over €8.5 billion.[76] The highest fines to date (€1,383,896,000) were imposed in 2008 on undertakings that took part in a cartel in the car glass market.[77]

However, the Commission is often criticised for imposing fines arbitrarily. Article 23(3) of Regulation 1/2003 merely provides: 'in fixing the amount of the fine, regard shall be had both to the gravity and duration of the infringement'. The General Court held that the Commission had a margin of discretion,[78] but also warned that an undertaking was entitled 'to be able to determine in detail ... the method of calculation of the fine imposed upon them'.[79]

In response to calls for greater transparency, the Commission issued guidelines on the method of setting fines in 1998, which were updated in 2006.[80] The current guidelines reflect the Commission's practice and take into account the rulings of the Court of Justice;[81] but also aim to provide for tougher fines to deter the undertaking in question as well as all undertakings in the market. The guidelines indicate that the Commission will first determine a 'basic amount' for the fine, which is then adjusted by considering aggravating or mitigating circumstances. We consider these two steps in turn.

The basic amount is set by reference to the value of the sales of the goods to which the infringement relates, having regard to the gravity of the infringement. For 'very serious' infringements (e.g. price fixing and market sharing) the basic amount will be up to 30 per cent of the value of the sales. Under the 2006 guidelines, this figure is then multiplied by the number of years that the undertaking has infringed competition law.[82] Under the 1998 guidelines, in

---

[74] *Pioneer* [1980] OJ L60/21; affirmed in Joined Cases 100/80–103/80 *Musique diffusion française and Others* v *Commission* [1983] ECR 1825, paras. 105–9.

[75] European Commission, *Twenty-first Report on Competition Policy*, para. 139 (e.g. *Fine Art Auction Houses* [2005] OJ L200/92 (but here Christie's escaped without a fine because of its cooperation and Sotheby's fines were reduced by 40 per cent because of its cooperation)); *Pre-Insulated Pipe Cartel* [1999] OJ L24/1, para. 176.

[76] Source: http://ec.europa.eu/competition/cartels/statistics/statistics.pdf (before the parties appealed against the fine, the precise figure was €8,860,794,200; the figure after the appeals that have been heard was €8,639,338,200).

[77] 'Commission fines car glass producers over €1.3 billion for market sharing cartel', Press Release IP 08/1685, 12 November 2008.

[78] Case T-150/89 *Martinelli* v *Commission* [1995] ECR II-1165, para. 59.

[79] Case T-148/89 *Tréfilunion SA* v *Commission* [1995] ECR II-1063, para. 142.

[80] Guidelines on the method of setting fines imposed pursuant to article 23(2)(a) of Regulation 1/2003 [2006] OJ C210/2.

[81] See further P. Manzini, 'European Antitrust in Search of the Perfect Fine' (2008) 31(1) *World Competition* 3; C. Veljanovski, 'Cartel Fines in Europe: Law, Practice and Deterrence' (2007) 30(1) *World Competition* 65.

[82] Guidelines, above n. 80, para. 19.

contrast, an addition was made depending on the duration of the agreement. The change is significant in two respects. First, it places greater emphasis on the duration of the cartel, and secondly, it serves to raise the fine considerably. For example, under the old guidelines, in a cartel lasting three years where the basic amount was €20 million, the Commission would add 50 per cent for duration, making the total fine €30 million. Under the new guidelines, the same infringement would lead to a fine of €60 million (€20 million × 3). In addition, an 'entry fee' is added to the basic amount (of between 15 and 25 per cent of the value of sales) to cartels that involve price-fixing, market-sharing or output limitation, irrespective of duration.[83]

The basic amount is adjusted (a) upwards if there are aggravating circumstances (for example, repeated infringements, for which the fine will be increased by 100 per cent for each previous infringement,[84] refusal to cooperate with the investigation, instigating the infringement), or (b) downwards in the presence of attenuating circumstances (for example, a passive role in the infringement, termination as soon as the investigation begins, the existence of reasonable doubt as to the legality of the practice).[85]

Two themes can be detected in the Commission's fining guidelines. Deterrence features most prominently. The second theme focuses on sales as a proxy for how much each member stood to gain from the cartel, thereby imposing a more accurate fine on each member of the cartel. It can thus be said to lead to fairer fines as between cartel members. This is in response to one frequent ground on which fines are appealed: discrimination between cartel offenders.[86]

The Court of Justice has repeatedly upheld the legality of the Commission's guidelines, and the General Court has scrutinised closely the extent to which the Commission exercised its discretion appropriately.[87] The key legal principles were confirmed in an appeal against fines imposed against a member of a cartel in the market for industrial copper tubes. The Commission's Decision was reached before 2004, so the procedures are those found in Regulation 17, and the 1998 guidelines were followed, but similar principles are likely to be followed with the new guidelines, although the Court is not bound to approve the new guidelines as it did in *Wieland-Werke AG* v *Commission* (see paragraph 31).

Case T–116/04 *Wieland-Werke AG* v *Commission*, Judgment of 9 May 2009

28. As regards the pleas concerning the calculation of the amount of the fine, it should be noted, first, that, as appears from recitals 290 to 387 of the contested decision, the fines which the Commission imposed for the infringement were imposed by virtue of Article 15(2) of Regulation No. 17, and, secondly, that, although the Commission does not expressly refer to the Guidelines on the method of setting fines imposed pursuant to Article 15(2) of Regulation No. 17 and Article 65(5) [CS] (OJ 1998 C 9, p. 3, 'the Guidelines'), it is undisputed that it determined the amount of the fines by applying the methodology defined in those guidelines.

---

[83] *Ibid.* para. 25.

[84] *Ibid.* para. 28.

[85] For an example of the application of the previous guidelines, see Joined Cases T–236/01, T–239/01, T–244/01– T–246/01, T–251/01 and T–252/01 *Tokai Carbon Co. Ltd and Others* v *Commission* [2004] ECR II–1181, paras. 291–315.

[86] For example, in Case T–18/03 *CD Contact Data GmbH* v *Commission*, Judgment of 30 April 2009, the fine imposed was reduced to ensure compliance with the principle of equal treatment.

[87] See e.g. Joined Cases T–101/05 and T–111/05 *BASF AG and UCB SA* v *Commission*, Judgment of 12 December 2007.

29. Whilst the Guidelines may not be regarded as rules of law, they nevertheless form rules of practice from which the Commission may not depart in an individual case without giving reasons.

30. It is therefore for the Court to verify, when reviewing the legality of the fines imposed by the contested decision, whether the Commission exercised its discretion in accordance with the method set out in the Guidelines and, should it be found to have departed from that method, to verify whether that departure is justified and supported by sufficient legal reasoning. In that regard, it should be noted that the Court of Justice has confirmed the validity, first, of the very principle of the Guidelines, and, secondly, the method which is there indicated.

31. The self-limitation on the Commission's discretion arising from the adoption of the Guidelines is not incompatible with the Commission's maintaining a substantial margin of discretion. The Guidelines display flexibility in a number of ways, enabling the Commission to exercise its discretion in accordance with the provisions of Regulation No. 17, as interpreted by the Court of Justice.

32. Moreover, in areas such as determination of the amount of a fine imposed pursuant to Article 15(2) of Regulation No. 17, where the Commission has a discretion, for example, as regards the amount of increase for the purposes of deterrence, review of the legality of those assessments is limited to determining the absence of manifest error of assessment.

33. Nor, in principle, does the discretion enjoyed by the Commission and the limits which it has imposed in that regard prejudge the exercise by the Community judicature of its unlimited jurisdiction, which empowers it to annul, increase or reduce the fine imposed by the Commission.

The confirmation of the Commission's powers is a boost in its fight against cartels because these powers allow it to design a fining policy that it considers necessary to deter undertakings to create cartels. However, the Commission's wide discretion has led to criticism that the notice on the method of setting fines does little to increase transparency and consistency.[88] Moreover, some commentators consider that the current policy may not do enough to deter. Most cartels that are caught are on the verge of breaking up, so the more stable cartels remain undetected. Further, the number of investigations is still too low, so while the fine is high, the probability of being subject to the fine remains low. One study of US antitrust, where discovery and penalties are stronger than those in the Union, estimated that only one out of six cartels are detected.[89] In these circumstances it still pays to engage in restrictive practices.[90]

(b) Leniency policy

Pursuant to the Commission's leniency policy, the first undertaking that informs the Commission of the existence of an anti-competitive practice of which it is a member, and whose information allows the Commission to carry out an inspection or find an infringement under Article 101, obtains an immunity from any fine. However, if an undertaking collaborates with the Commission during the investigation by providing important evidence that strengthens the Commission's case, this may result in a reduction in the fine of between 20 and 50 per cent, the

---

[88] R. Richardson, 'Guidance Without Guidance: A European Revolution in Fining Policy?' (1999) *ECLR* 360.

[89] P. G. Bryant and E. W. Eckard, 'Price Fixing: The Probability of Getting Caught' (1991) 73 *Review of Economics and Statistics* 531.

[90] M. P. Schinkel, 'Effective Cartel Enforcement in Europe' (2007) 30 *World Competition* 539.

reduction being more significant for those who collaborate first.[91] The aim of this policy is to give members of a cartel the incentive to bring the existence of cartels to the attention of the Commission.[92] The prize for being the first to do so is designed to encourage cartel members to blow the whistle, which can save Commission resources, as it may be able to rely solely on the evidence supplied by the 'whistleblower' to reach a decision that competition law has been infringed. The policy began in 1996 and has been effective in increasing the number of successful cartel infringement Decisions brought by the Commission, if judged by the number of times fines have been reduced.[93] A significant proportion of cartel cases have been initiated by a leniency application (over half of the cartel cases decided between 2005 and 2008),[94] although the Commission stresses that it does not depend solely on leniency applications to uncover cartels.[95] These results match those of a comparable US programme, which has been described as 'the single greatest investigative tool available to anti-cartel enforcers'.[96]

Two factors that may undermine the initial success of the Commission's leniency policy have been addressed recently.[97] First, national competition authorities can enforce EU competition law, and Member States have different (or no) leniency policies.[98] If an undertaking provides evidence of a cartel to one competition authority, but the cartel is then prosecuted by a competition authority without a leniency programme or one with less generous reductions in fines, the benefits of confessing vanish. This may deter parties from stepping forward.[99] This has been tackled by the European Competition Network designing a Model Leniency Programme, and a significant number of Member States have used (or are planning to use) this model as a basis for designing national leniency policies.[100] Secondly, leniency policies do not affect the quantum of damages payable if cartel members are sued by undertakings harmed by the infringement of competition law. Confession raises the chances of liability, and if private litigation increases in the Union, this may deter parties from coming forward. The money saved by confessing to the existence of a cartel, which might never have been discovered by competition authorities, can be lost when the undertaking is sued for damages.[101] This has been addressed in the 2006 Leniency Notice by providing that a corporate statement made by

---

[91] Notice on immunity from fines and reduction of fines in cartel cases [2006] OJ C298/17. For comment on earlier drafts of this document, see J. Arp and C. Swaak, 'A Tempting Offer: Immunity from Fines for Cartel Conduct under the European Commission's New Leniency Notice' (2003) *ECLR* 9; N. Levy and R. O'Donoghue, 'The EU Leniency Programme Comes of Age' (2004) 27 *World Competition* 75.

[92] And some have gone even further, suggesting that the Commission should pay whistleblowers. See A. Riley, 'Beyond Leniency: Enhancing Enforcement in EC Antitrust Law' (2005) 28 *World Competition* 377.

[93] Kerse and Kahn, above n. 32, 417, report that since 1998 the leniency notice was applied in eighteen out of twenty cartel decisions.

[94] *Report on Competition Policy 2005*, SEC(2006)761 final, para. 174; *Report on Competition Policy 2006*, COM(2007)358 final, para. 8; *Report on Competition Policy 2007*, COM(2008)368 final, para. 6.

[95] *Report on Competition Policy 2007*, COM(2008)368 final, para. 6.

[96] S. D. Hammond, 'When Calculating the Cost and Benefits of Applying for Corporate Amnesty, How Do You Put a Price Tag on an Individual's Freedom?', 8 March 2001, www.usdoj.gov/atr.

[97] For a critical account, see P. Billiet 'How Lenient is the EC Leniency Policy? A Matter of Certainty and Predictability' (2009) *ECLR* 14.

[98] See L. Brokx, 'A Patchwork of Leniency Programmes' (2001) *ECLR* 35.

[99] The Commission suggests this is not a significant problem. S. Blake and D. Schnichels, 'Leniency Following Modernisation: Safeguarding Europe's Leniency Programmes' (2004) 2 *Competition Policy Newsletter* 7.

[100] Commission Staff Working Document, Annex to *Commission Report on Competition Policy 2007*, SEC(2008)2038, para. 449.

[101] P. C. Zane, 'The Price Fixer's Dilemma: Applying Game Theory to the Decision of Whether to Plead Guilty to Antitrust Crimes' (2003) *Antitrust Bulletin* 1.

a leniency applicant, which sets out the undertaking's knowledge of the cartel and its role in it, is protected from discovery in civil actions for damages. While this still leaves all undertakings that are found to have infringed Article 101 open to follow-on damages claims once the Commission makes a Decision, it protects those who make leniency applications from being targeted specifically because of the confession evidence they have provided.[102]

(iv) Commitment Decisions and settlements

Over 90 per cent of competition cases are closed without a formal Decision.[103] Settlements arise either because the parties stop what they are doing or agree to modify their behaviour to conform to EU competition law, or the Commission decides there is no infringement. Originally, there was little transparency in settlements. The Commission had considerable discretion in deciding whether to settle or press on with a final Decision, and it has been criticised for not exercising this discretion in a predictable manner.[104] For undertakings, settlements have the obvious advantage that fines and the publicity of an investigation (which may give rise to private litigation) are avoided, but the disadvantages are over-enforcement, on the one hand (e.g. without a full hearing the Commission may abuse its powers by accusing parties of a non-existing infringement); or under-enforcement on the other (settlements avoid the imposition of fines and are privately negotiated between parties and the Commission).[105] In an attempt to increase transparency of its settlements practice, the Council recently formalised this practice.

> ### Regulation 1/2003/EC, article 9(1)
>
> Where the Commission intends to adopt a decision requiring that an infringement be brought to an end and the undertakings concerned offer commitments to meet the concerns expressed to them by the Commission in its preliminary assessment, the Commission may by decision make those commitments binding on the undertakings. Such a decision may be adopted for a specified period and shall conclude that there are no longer grounds for action by the Commission.

Proposed Decisions to accept commitments must be published, inviting comments from third parties as a way of gaining information about the competitive impact of the commitment[106] and consulting the Advisory Committee.[107] Increased transparency and consultation may lead to more predictable use of settlement procedures. The legal status of a commitment Decision is as 'a substitute for a prohibition decision and not for an exemption decision. The commitment decision is a

---

[102] Given the rules on joint and several liability, making leniency statements discoverable would have made leniency applicants liable for all the losses, even those inflicted by other members of the cartel.

[103] In 2000, there were 38 formal Decisions and 362 settlements; in 2001, 54 Decisions and 324 settlements; in 2002, 33 Decisions and 363 settlements; and in 2003, 24 Decisions and 295 settlements (*Twenty-third Report on Competition Policy* (2003) 62). For a review of the settlement practice under Regulation 17/62/EC, see I. Van Bael, 'The Antitrust Settlement Practice of the EC Commission' (1986) 23 *CMLRev.* 61.

[104] Kerse and Kahn, above n. 32, 357.

[105] For a discussion of these concerns, see G. Bruzzone and G. Boccaccio, 'Taking Care of Modernisation After the Startup: A View from a Member State' (2008) 31 *World Competition* 89.

[106] Regulation 1/03, article 27(4).

[107] *Ibid.* article 14(1) (the composition of the committee is described above at p. 931).

formal settlement solicited by a company under investigation and agreed by the Commission where its enforcement priorities justify this choice.'[108] This means that national competition authorities are free to investigate the same practice and impose penalties for an infringement for past behaviour, and third parties may seek damages even in the presence of a commitment Decision.[109]

Commitment Decisions are only available for infringements that are not serious. Members of a cartel are unable to benefit from article 9.[110] But in 2008, the Commission introduced a policy that allows cartel members to settle.[111] Essentially, the Commission would approach parties after having concluded an investigation and invite them to settle, avoiding the lengthy procedures in exchange for a discount on the fine. The aim is not deterrence but saving in administrative costs, allowing the Commission to use its limited resources to tackle more infringements, and reducing appeals. Two issues arise: first, whether this policy will be effective. According to the American Bar Association, a sound settlement system relies upon four key principles: transparency (so that the defendant knows what the benefits are); generosity (the reduction in fine should be substantial); legal certainty (the person settling should be clear that his offer to settle will be accepted); and confidentiality (preventing disclosure of the settlement which might expose the applicant to claims in other jurisdictions). The argument is that, absent these features, there is a risk that parties have no incentive to settle.[112] Judged against these standards, the Leniency Notice provides detailed information of the procedures to be followed, and it guarantees confidentiality. However, the Commission retains much discretion whether to proceed with settlements, and it looks as if a settlement may only reduce the fine by 10 per cent, which is not particularly generous. It should be noted that the Commission's intention is for settlement and leniency policies to work hand in hand: leniency is available to those who help the Commission find an infringement, settlements are designed to save resources involved in prosecuting the parties. Accordingly, parties may well wish to benefit from fine reductions under both instruments.

(v) The Commission's procedures: an assessment

The vast powers, which we have reviewed, were conferred on the Commission as far back as 1962. They were remarkable especially because of the potential for the Commission to impose fines on any undertaking, regardless of national interests. The Commission benefited from the support of the Court of Justice, whose judgments ratified many of the Commission's Decisions, enabling the strengthening of competition enforcement. The Court has also endeavoured to bring the Commission's procedures in line with fundamental rights, although there is some doubt about whether the procedures are entirely compatible with the ECHR.[113] An additional criticism of the Commission's procedures is the potentially political nature of the decision-making process.

---

[108] Commission MEMO/04/217, Commitment Decisions, 17 September 2004.

[109] M. S. Ferro, 'Committing to Commitment Decisions: Unanswered Questions on Article 9 Decisions' (2005) *ECLR* 451.

[110] Regulation 1/2003, recital 13. Cf. Case T-170/06 *Alrosa v Commission* [2007] ECR II-2601 where the underlying infringement appears to be a cartel.

[111] Commission Regulation 622/2008/EC of 30 June 2008 amending Regulation 773/2004/EC as regards the conduct of settlement procedures in cartel cases [2008] OJ L171/3.

[112] These comments are available at http://ec.europa.eu/comm/competition/cartels/legislation/leniency_legislation. html.

[113] A. Riley, 'The ECHR Implications of the Investigation Provisions of the Draft Competition Regulation' (2002) 51 *ICLQ* 55; A. Andreangeli, 'Toward an EU Competition Court: "Article-6-Proofing" Antitrust Proceedings Before the Commission?' (2007) 30 *World Competition* 595.

Laraine Laudati, 'The European Commission as Regulator: The Uncertain Pursuit of the Competitive Market' in G. Majone (ed.), *Regulating Europe* (London, Routledge, 1996) 231, 235–6

The degree of independence of an antitrust enforcement institution is determined by two elements: the structural independence from political authority, and separation of investigatory, prosecutorial and decision-making functions. The Community antitrust enforcement has a low level of independence in both respects ...

When the Community system was established, it was believed that placing the powers to execute the competition laws in the hands of the Commission would minimize political interference with enforcement by the Member States. The Commission has, however, become a highly political body, and political considerations play a significant role in its competition enforcement decisions. National antitrust officials acknowledge that pressure from national governments may influence the Commission's decisions because the Commission must have the cooperation of national governments in order to fulfil its mission. Thus the Commission exerts considerable effort to reconcile national policies with Community policy.

Moreover, DG IV [now DG Competition] cannot act independently of the other DGs since final decisions are made by the full Commission. Political pressure from other DGs is felt constantly, owing to the broad economic implications of competition decisions. Such pressure, in general, runs against the negative decisions by DG IV, particularly with regard to mergers. Moreover, it forces DG IV to take account of policy considerations other than competition policy ... This type of pressure has grown in recent years owing to the increasingly important role of competition law, and the economic recession and high levels of unemployment throughout the Community.

For instance, DG III (industrial policy) and DG IV (social policy) frequently take positions at odds with those of DG IV. Other DGs likely to intervene regulate specific sectors of the economy, for example DG XIII (telecommunications) and DG XVII (energy). This does not mean that all communication among the DGs is contentious. Rather, collaboration and consultation regularly occur between rapporteurs of DG IV and those of other DGs, especially DG III, because of their familiarity with the various sectors. But if DG III staff believe that a merger should be cleared and their counterparts believe the opposite, the staff members of each DG must convince their Commissioner of the merits of their position. Commissioners themselves then resolve the dispute.

Another fault of the system is that it requires Commissioners with no expertise in competition law and severe time constraints to apply complex laws and economic analysis to facts in all cases, then make the final decision. It is doubtful whether all Commissioners are professionally qualified to perform this function. Critics point out that, in practice, most competition decisions are adopted with little or no debate, as written proposed decisions are circulated to each cabinet of each Commissioner and considered to be adopted if no objections are made within a limited period.

An additional problem results from a lack of clarity as to the standards being applied in deciding antitrust cases. As stated above, policy areas other than competition are considered, especially industrial and social policy. However, parties with competition matters before the Commission have no substantive or procedural rules to follow regarding the presentation of evidence on such policy issues, even though these matters could have significant impact on the outcome of their cases. This raises due process concerns.

Laudati's comments strengthen the views of Wesseling (discussed above) by noting how the interference of other Community objectives is inevitable, given both the institutional make-up of the Commission, and the Commission's own political energies and understanding of how the Community project impacts upon the development of competition law. Of course, not every competition Decision is keenly debated by the College of Commissioners: much competition law enforcement is the routine supervision of business practices where wider Community interests are affected marginally; but in significant cases that establish a new precedent or apply to novel markets, other Commissioners' views (whether based upon their portfolio or their national interests) become more prominent.

One key weakness identified by Laudati and many other commentators is that the Commission is the investigator, prosecutor and judge: it carries out the fact-finding exercises, it then issues a statement of objections to the parties it accuses of having infringed competition law; a hearing of the parties is subsequently held in front of a member of the Commission (the Hearing Officer) where members of DG Competition present the case; and the Commission imposes the final remedy. While the Decision is that of the College of Commissioners, the DG competition staff members in charge of investigating the case prepare the draft Decision to be discussed by the College of Commissioners.[114] This raises the question as to whether the procedures as a whole deny defendants their right (under Article 6 ECHR) to a hearing before an impartial tribunal. The Court of Justice has said, however, that the Article 6 ECHR right only applies to criminal proceedings and competition proceedings are not of a criminal nature (confirmed by Regulation 1/2003, article 23(5)). Therefore the Commission is entitled to exercise investigative and decision-making functions.[115] Moreover, even if this argument is not wholly satisfactory (because the penalties imposed by the Commission may be said to be criminal sanctions in nature),[116] parties accused of infringing competition law are able to appeal against the Decision to the Union courts. In this context the establishment of the General Court is of particular importance. In the first judgment of the General Court, Advocate General Vesterdorf set out the role of the Court in these terms:

> the very creation of the Court of First Instance as a court of both first and last instance for the examination of facts in the cases brought before it is an invitation to undertake an intensive review in order to ascertain whether the evidence on which the Commission relies in adopting a contested decision is sound.[117]

The importance of judicial review may be evidenced by the fact that between 1998 and 2002, ninety appeals were made, and fines of €665 million were reduced by €185 million, with 70 per cent of appeals successful in securing a partial reduction in the fine imposed by

---

[114] For criticism see A. Pera and M. Tondino, 'Enforcement of EC Competition Rules: Need for a Reform?' (1996) *FCLI* 125; F. Montag, 'The Case for Radical Reform of the Infringement Procedure under Regulation 17' (1998) *ECLR* 428.

[115] Observations repeated regularly by the courts: see e.g. Joined Cases T-25/95 etc. *Cimenteries CBR SA and Others v Commission* [2000] ECR II-700, paras. 713–19.

[116] For example, in *Société Stenuit v France* (1992) 14 EHRR 509, the European Commission on Human Rights held that French competition law was criminal in nature and the Court has held in other contexts that the imposition of fines to deter and sanction a person indicate that the proceedings are criminal in nature (e.g. *Bendenoun v France* (1994) 18 EHRR 54). Kerse and Kahn, above, n. 32, 129, suggest that the Court has implicitly accepted this in Case C-235/92 P *Montecatini v Commission* [1999] ECR I-4539, para. 176. See K. Lenartes and J. Vanhamme, 'Procedural Rights of Private Parties in the Community Administrative Process' (1997) 34 *CMLRev.* 531, 557.

[117] Joined Cases T-1/89–T-15/89 *Rhône-Poulenc SA and Others v Commission* [1991] ECR II-867, 908.

the Commission (normally because the Commission failed to prove precisely the duration of the infringement).[118] Therefore, it may be argued that even if proceedings before the Commission are not compatible with Article 6 ECHR, the possibility for judicial review guarantees the defendant's right to a hearing by an impartial tribunal.[119] More generally, the Courts' contribution to the development of competition law and procedures cannot be underestimated.

> **Christopher Harding and Julian Joshua, *Regulating Cartels in Europe: A Study of Legal Control of Corporate Delinquency* (Oxford, Oxford University Press, 2003) 201 and 204–5**
>
> It would not be an exaggeration to say that the [General Court] has for practical purposes almost turned itself into a trial court in this context, especially considering that a large number of its own decisions are in turn appealed to the ECJ. To put the matter another way, without formally amending the Commission's procedure ... there has nonetheless been a de facto separation of functions and an introduction of a distinct judicial trial authority... In effect, therefore, the separation of powers complaint ... has been addressed. In the majority of cartel cases, the Commission's formal decision has evolved into a summative statement of the case for the prosecution, which is then judicially tested before the [General Court]. Since the dust has settled on this development, from the middle of the 1990s both the Commission and the Court appear to have settled into a comfortable relationship, within which the former prepares its cases carefully, and the latter confirms most of the prosecution case.

However, Harding and Joshua are concerned with the fact that this legal development has occurred as a result of powerful corporate actors, who have explored the judicial process in the light of clear infringements of EU competition law. And while the appeals by these large firms have led to the creation of considerable procedural safeguards for their interests, the Court has had little opportunity to explain what rights those injured by anti-competitive behaviour have. This suggests that there is an imbalance between the rights of corporate actors and those of consumers, which competition law is designed to safeguard. Perhaps the way to reduce this imbalance is to increase enforcement efforts, and to enhance the role of those injured by infringement of competition laws. This is what the Commission planned in its modernisation policy, to which we now turn.

4 RESETTLEMENT OF COMPETITION REGULATORY AUTHORITY

(i) Modernisation

Concentrating the task of enforcement with the Commission brought certain advantages: a single regulator, a uniform approach to competition (although stricter national competition laws could still apply provided the Commission had not acted),[120] and DG Competition gained experience in handling disputes. However, there were two drawbacks in concentrating enforcement

---

[118] Van Bael and Bellis, above n. 41, 1163.

[119] *Le Compte, Van Leuven and De Meyere* v *Belgium* A/43 (1981) 23, para. 51; *Öztürk* v *Germany* A/73 (1984) 21–2, para. 56.

[120] Case 14/68 *Walt Wilhelm* v *Bundeskartellamt* [1969] ECR 1. On the difficulties of this, see R. Wesseling, 'Subsidiarity in Community Competition Law over National Law' (1997) 22 *ELRev.* 19.

in the hands of the Commission. The first, as we saw above, is that the Commission could act in a politically motivated manner. In the mid-1990s it was argued that competition enforcement should be delegated to a separate 'European Cartel Office' to enhance the independence of the decision-making process, but this suggestion is now unlikely to be implemented.[121] The second problem is that the Commission's limited resources soon became insufficient to deal with all competition problems coming to its attention. The principal reasons for the Commission's high workload lie in the substantive and procedural applications of Article 101 TFEU. We consider the problems of Article 101 in detail in Chapter 23 but a brief account is necessary to understand the significance of the reforms.

Article 101 TFEU regulates anti-competitive agreements. It is subdivided into three paragraphs: Article 101(1) prohibits agreements that restrict competition; Article 101(2) declares that agreements which restrict competition are automatically void; Article 101(3) provides that restrictive agreements may be exempted if they confer certain benefits, i.e. an improvement in the production or distribution of goods or the promotion of technical or economic progress. Article 101(1) and (2) have direct effect and can be applied in national courts,[122] while Article 101(3) exemptions, under the system that operated from 1962 to 2004, could only be granted by the Commission if it was notified of the agreement.[123] The result was that undertakings wishing to be certain that their contract was not void notified their agreements *en masse* to the Commission, even when it was unlikely the agreement would harm competition.[124] The Commission lacked the resources to review these expeditiously and it was unable to pursue its enforcement policy as actively as it wished. This enforcement pattern was neither in the interest of business nor in the interests of the proper enforcement of competition law.

Since the 1970s, the Commission attempted to ameliorate this, first by issuing comfort letters. These were administrative letters written in response to a notified agreement indicating that the Commission did not think the agreement restricted competition. The comfort letter was not a formal Decision and thus could be issued more quickly. However, its non-binding character gave parties little legal security where the agreement was challenged in national courts. The second solution was to draft Block Exemption Regulations. These provide that if an agreement meets certain specified criteria, it benefits from automatic exemption, without notification. The weakness of this approach is that it creates a straitjacket effect: the parties use the relevant Block Exemption as the basis for their contractual relations and structure the agreement according to its terms, which might skew their commercial desires. Requiring parties to sacrifice commercial practicality in order to gain legal security seemed to some too high a price to pay.[125]

In the early 1990s, the Commission attempted a third solution, often referred to as a programme of decentralisation. It encouraged national competition authorities to enforce EU competition law and invited private parties to use national courts to enforce competition law. The Commission argued that national competition authorities had a common task of protecting

---

[121] S. Wilks and L. McGowan, 'Disarming the Commission: The Debate over a European Cartel Office' (1995) 32 *Journal of Common Market Studies* 259.

[122] Regulation 17/62/EEC, First Regulation implementing Articles 85 and 86 EC, article 1 [1962] OJ Spec. edn, 204/62, 87; Case 127/73 *BRT v SABAM* [1974] ECR 62, para. 16.

[123] Regulation 17/62, articles 4(1) (notification) and 9(1) (Commission's sole power to exempt).

[124] 40,000 notifications were received. *Ninth Report on Competition Policy* (1979) 15–16.

[125] The first Block Exemption was implemented in 1967: Regulation 67/67/EEC on exclusive purchase agreements [1967] OJ L84/67.

competition and the national authorities should use EU competition law to regulate markets, allowing the Commission to take action in cases of particular significance to the Community.[126] However, encouraging decentralised enforcement though soft law notices failed to galvanise national authorities and courts and the Commission still had a worryingly heavy caseload, due to increase with impending enlargement, preventing it from setting its enforcement priorities. More drastic reforms were needed.

In 1999, the Commission published a White Paper on Modernisation, which proposed reform along the following lines: to abolish the system of notification, to declare Article 101(3) directly effective, and to compel national competition authorities to apply EU competition law.[127] These significant changes were agreed by the Council and came into effect on 1 May 2004 through Regulation 1/2003/EC.[128]

Regulation 1/2003/EC, article 1

1. Agreements, decisions and concerted practices caught by Article [101(1) TFEU] which do not satisfy the conditions of Article [101(3) TFEU] shall be prohibited, no prior decision to that effect being required.
2. Agreements, decisions and concerted practices caught by Article [101(1) TFEU] which satisfy the conditions of Article [101(3) TFEU] shall not be prohibited, no prior decision to that effect being required.

The implication of article 1 is profound: parties who before would have submitted a request for exemption and had to wait endlessly for a response must now decide for themselves whether their agreement infringes the competition rules. This represents a switch from an ex ante notification-based system of competition enforcement to an ex post deterrence-based system. Abolishing the right of parties to notify an agreement means that the Commission is now free to focus on the more serious infringements. However, some have queried whether a declaration that Article 101(3) has direct effect is in fact lawful given its discretionary character.[129]

The other plank of the reform is to require national competition authorities to enforce EU competition law, thereby decentralising enforcement of EU competition law.

Regulation 1/2003/EC, article 3

1. Where the competition authorities of the Member States or national courts apply national competition law to agreements, decisions by associations of undertakings or concerted practices within the meaning of Article [101(1) TFEU] which may affect trade between Member States within the meaning of that provision, they shall also apply Article [101 TFEU] to such agreements, decisions or concerted practices.

---

[126] Commission Notice on cooperation between national competition authorities and the Commission in handling cases falling within the scope of Articles [101 TFEU] and [102 TFEU] [1997] OJ C313/1; Commission Notice on cooperation between national courts and the Commission in applying Articles [101 TFEU] and [102 TFEU] [1993] OJ C39/6.

[127] White Paper on modernisation of the rules implementing Articles [101 TFEU] and [102 TFEU] [1999] OJ C132/1.

[128] Regulation 1/2003/EC on the implementation of the rules on competition laid down in Articles 81 and 82 EC [2003] OJ L1/1.

[129] W. Moschel, 'Guest Editorial: Change of Policy in European Competition Law?' (2000) 37 *CMLRev.* 495.

Where the competition authorities of the Member States or national courts apply national competition law to any abuse prohibited by Article [102 TFEU], they shall also apply Article [102 TFEU].

2. The application of national competition law may not lead to the prohibition of agreements, decisions by associations of undertakings or concerted practices which may affect trade between Member States but which do not restrict competition within the meaning of Article [101(1) TFEU], or which fulfil the conditions of Article [101(3) TFEU] or which are covered by a Regulation for the application of Article [101(3) TFEU]. Member States shall not under this Regulation be precluded from adopting and applying on their territory stricter national laws which prohibit or sanction unilateral conduct engaged in by undertakings.

3. Without prejudice to general principles and other provisions of Community law, paragraphs 1 and 2 do not apply when the competition authorities and the courts of the Member States apply national merger control laws nor do they preclude the application of provisions of national law that predominantly pursue an objective different from that pursued by Articles [101 TFEU] and [102 TFEU].

This provision obliges national competition authorities (NCAs) to apply Articles 101 and 102 and to give EU competition law priority over national competition law. 'Enforcement of Articles [101 and 102 TFEU] is now a shared responsibility, not just in theory but in practice. At both political and practical level the modernisation regime requires Member States to adopt a commitment to the enforcement of Community law in this area far in excess of anything to date.'[130] In effect, Regulation 1/2003 turns the NCA into a Community competition authority. There are three exceptions to the obligation of the NCA to give priority to EU competition law. The first is in the final sentence of article 3(2), which allows the authority to apply stricter national competition law that regulates unilateral behaviour. As we will see in the following two chapters, EU competition law only regulates unilateral behaviour when the firm has a dominant position. In contrast, some Member States have competition laws that are wider in scope. The second exception is that national merger law is unaffected. The final exception is that national laws which pursue non-competition objectives may be enforced to prohibit a practice which is unobjectionable from a competition perspective, for example, consumer protection legislation.

From the perspective of undertakings, Regulation 1/2003 reduces compliance costs. The same rules apply across the Union. Therefore, their practices will be scrutinised uniformly regardless of which competition authority handles the investigation. From the perspective of the Commission, this creates a battalion of competition authorities with ample resources, thereby improving the enforcement of competition law.

(ii) The Commission's new role

The Commission no longer has to review every agreement notified to it. It can now set its own agenda in a legal environment where the majority of competition enforcement will be carried out by national authorities. The Commission has carried out three main tasks.

First, the Commission has increased enforcement against cartels which operate internationally, as well as focusing on industries where a few firms hold market power. This is significant

---

[130] Kerse and Khan, above n. 32, 47.

because in the past the Commission was criticised for focusing on harmless business conduct that was notified to it,[131] whereas now it can direct enforcement in line with economic theory and focus on the more important infringements.[132]

The second task for the Commission is to provide guidance in novel cases to facilitate the work of national competition authorities. The Commission will continue the process of drafting notices and guidelines (begun in the late 1990s), which are not binding but are an expression of how the Commission would handle a case and are bound to influence the national authorities. These instruments will be of increasing importance for undertakings because they are now unable to notify agreements to gain exemption and require as much information as possible to determine for themselves whether their planned business practices are lawful. In exceptional circumstances, however, parties may be able to obtain individual guidance from the Commission.

Regulation 1/2003/EC, recital 38

Legal certainty for undertakings operating under the Community competition rules contributes to the promotion of innovation and investment. Where cases give rise to genuine uncertainty because they present novel or unresolved questions for the application of these rules, individual undertakings may wish to seek informal guidance from the Commission. This Regulation is without prejudice to the ability of the Commission to issue such informal guidance.

The Commission's powers to grant this guidance are not expressly provided for in the Regulation, and a Notice on Informal Guidance has been published, which suggests that guidance will be offered when parties engage in business practices where there is no precedent or other informal guidance to help the undertakings determine whether their proposed action infringes EU competition law.[133] Guidance letters resemble comfort letters which were issued under the old regime, but these new letters will only be issued sparingly. In addition to soft law measures, the Commission may also take formal Decisions.

Regulation 1/2003/EC, article 10

Where the Community public interest relating to the application of Articles [101 TFEU] and [102 TFEU] so requires, the Commission, acting on its own initiative, may by decision find that Article [101 TFEU] is not applicable to an agreement, a decision by an association of undertakings or a concerted practice, either because the conditions of Article [101(1) TFEU] are not fulfilled, or because the conditions of Article [101(3) TFEU] are satisfied.

The Commission may likewise make such a finding with reference to Article [102 TFEU].

There is a risk that article 10 could be used for reasons other than merely clarifying the law. The provision is triggered by the need to serve the *Community's public interest*. This is

---

[131] D. Neven, P. Papandropoulos and P. Seabright, *Trawling for Minnows: European Competition Policy and Agreements Between Firms* (London, CEPR, 1998).

[132] M. Monti, 'European Competition Policy: Quo Vadis?', 10 April 2003 http://europa.eu.int/comm/competition/index_en.html.

[133] [2004] OJ C101/78.

sufficiently wide to allow the Commission to decide that a particular practice does not in-fringe Article 101 because of some public policy reason unrelated to competition law. Given the institutional make-up of the Commission, the risk is present, even though the recitals to the Regulation suggest that the purpose of article 10 is to shed light on areas where the law is unclear.[134] To date, no decision has been issued under article 10.

The Commission's third task is to coordinate the network of national competition authori-ties, and we consider this novel role in the following section.

(iii) The European Competition Network

To ensure the successful functioning of national enforcement, each Member State must desig-nate the competition authority responsible for the application of Articles 101 and 102 TFEU,[135] and the NCA must have the following powers:[136]

(a) requiring that an infringement be brought to an end;
(b) ordering interim measures;
(c) accepting commitments;
(d) imposing fines, periodic penalty payments or any other penalty provided for in their national law.

This harmonises the sanctions of all NCAs to guarantee the effective enforcement of EU com-petition law. However, in addition to empowering each NCA, successful enforcement requires considerable coordination among the twenty-five NCAs and the Commission. Therefore, as early as 2002 the European Competition Network (ECN) was created, comprising all NCAs and the Com-mission. The ECN is not a competition authority, but a forum for cooperation for the NCAs. Its principal tasks are the following: first, to coordinate enforcement so that there is an efficient allo-cation of cases among the network, and secondly, to develop mechanisms for cooperation during investigations and means of ensuring consistency in the application of competition rules.

(a) Case allocation

Regulation 1/2003 envisaged that each case should be handled by a single authority,[137] but the detailed implementation was left to soft law instruments, setting out in detail how cases may be allocated. Three alternatives are envisaged: enforcement by one NCA, enforcement by several NCAs, or enforcement by the Commission.

Commission Notice on cooperation within the Network of Competition Authorities [2004] OJ C101/43

6. In most instances the authority that receives a complaint or starts an ex-officio procedure will remain in charge of the case. Re-allocation of a case would only be envisaged at the outset of a procedure where either that authority considered that it was not well placed to act or where other authorities also considered themselves well placed to act.

---

[134] Regulation 1/2003, recital 14.
[135] *Ibid.* article 35(1).
[136] *Ibid.* article 5.
[137] *Ibid.* recital 18.

7. Where re-allocation is found to be necessary for an effective protection of competition and of the Community interest, network members will endeavour to re-allocate cases to a single well placed competition authority as often as possible. In any event, re-allocation should be a quick and efficient process and not hold up ongoing investigations.

8. An authority can be considered to be well placed to deal with a case if the following three cumulative conditions are met:

    1. the agreement or practice has substantial direct actual or foreseeable effects on competition within its territory, is implemented within or originates from its territory;

    2. the authority is able to effectively bring to an end the entire infringement, i.e. it can adopt a cease-and-desist order the effect of which will be sufficient to bring an end to the infringement and it can, where appropriate, sanction the infringement adequately;

    3. it can gather, possibly with the assistance of other authorities, the evidence required to prove the infringement.

9. The above criteria indicate that a material link between the infringement and the territory of a Member State must exist in order for that Member State's competition authority to be considered well placed. It can be expected that in most cases the authorities of those Member States where competition is substantially affected by an infringement will be well placed provided they are capable of effectively bringing the infringement to an end through either single or parallel action unless the Commission is better placed to act.

10. It follows that a single NCA is usually well placed to deal with agreements or practices that substantially affect competition mainly within its territory ...

11. Furthermore single action of an NCA might also be appropriate where, although more than one NCA can be regarded as well placed, the action of a single NCA is sufficient to bring the entire infringement to an end ...

12. Parallel action by two or three NCAs may be appropriate where an agreement or practice has substantial effects on competition mainly in their respective territories and the action of only one NCA would not be sufficient to bring the entire infringement to an end and/or to sanction it adequately ...

13. The authorities dealing with a case in parallel action will endeavour to coordinate their action to the extent possible. To that effect, they may find it useful to designate one of them as a lead authority and to delegate tasks to the lead authority such as for example the coordination of investigative measures, while each authority remains responsible for conducting its own proceedings.

14. The Commission is particularly well placed if one or several agreement(s) or practice(s), including networks of similar agreements or practices, have effects on competition in more than three Member States (cross-border markets covering more than three Member States or several national markets).

15. Moreover, the Commission is particularly well placed to deal with a case if it is closely linked to other Community provisions which may be exclusively or more effectively applied by the Commission, if the Community interest requires the adoption of a Commission decision to develop Community competition policy when a new competition issue arises or to ensure effective enforcement.

The notice departs slightly from the intention of Regulation 1/2003 by providing for the possibilities of parallel investigations by more than one NCA. This creates risks of inconsistent decisions between NCAs.

(b) Cooperation within the network

Cooperation among NCAs is necessary both before the initiation of proceedings, so as to determine which competition authority will deal with the case, and during the proceedings, so that other NCAs are able to assist the authority in charge.

Regulation 1/2003/EC, article 11

3. The competition authorities of the Member States shall, when acting under Article [101 TFEU] or Article [102 TFEU], inform the Commission in writing before or without delay after commencing the first formal investigative measure. This information may also be made available to the competition authorities of the other Member States ...

6. The initiation by the Commission of proceedings for the adoption of a decision shall relieve the competition authorities of the Member States of their competence to apply Articles [101 TFEU] and [102 TFEU]. If a competition authority of a Member State is already acting on a case, the Commission shall only initiate proceedings after consulting with that national competition authority.

The purpose of article 11(3) is to trigger the case allocation procedures we discussed above. The network is made aware of each NCA's intention and discussions can be held, before proceedings are brought, to determine the best placed NCA. Once a draft Decision is ready, article 11(4) obliges the NCA to inform the Commission of any planned Decision. This is designed to allow other NCAs to express their views on the Decision and, more significantly, it is a way for the Commission to check that the NCA does not use the law in a political manner to favour national industry. As an additional safeguard against national bias in a planned decision, article 11(6) allows the Commission to remove the case from the NCA and decide it itself, although this power has yet to be deployed.

In addition to consultation, competition authorities may share information relevant to the dispute. Article 11(2) provides for important information obtained by the Commission to be transferred to the NCA, but more significant information-sharing powers exist.

Regulation 1/2003/EC, article 12

1. For the purpose of applying Articles [101 and 102 TFEU] the Commission and the competition authorities of the Member States shall have the power to provide one another with and use in evidence any matter of fact or of law, including confidential information.

2. Information exchanged shall only be used in evidence for the purpose of applying Article [101 TFEU] or Article [102 TFEU] and in respect of the subject-matter for which it was collected by the transmitting authority. However, where national competition law is applied in the same case and in parallel to Community competition law and does not lead to a different outcome, information exchanged under this Article may also be used for the application of national competition law.

3. Information exchanged pursuant to paragraph 1 can only be used in evidence to impose sanctions on natural persons where:

– the law of the transmitting authority foresees sanctions of a similar kind in relation to an infringement of Article [101 TFEU] or Article [102 TFEU] or, in the absence thereof,

– the information has been collected in a way which respects the same level of protection of the rights of defence of natural persons as provided for under the national rules of the receiving authority. However, in this case, the information exchanged cannot be used by the receiving authority to impose custodial sanctions.

The aim of article 12 is to allow for the exchange of information that can be used as evidence to apply EU competition law. This could be evidence gathered by one NCA before the case was reallocated to another, or information obtained by one NCA while assisting another in its investigation.[138] Considerable safeguards have been set up in article 12: paragraph 2 limits the use to which the information can be put, and paragraph 3 is designed to protect undertakings in those Member States where competition law enforcement can be criminal in nature (for example, the United Kingdom). One additional danger in allowing the transfer of evidence is that the procedures for obtaining evidence may differ between the Member State that obtained the evidence and the Member State wishing to receive it. In particular, what if the means by which the first state obtained the information is not available under the evidence rules of the state wishing to receive the evidence? If such evidence were to be held admissible, it would mean that an NCA wishing to obtain information could circumvent national law (designed to protect the accused) and request another authority to obtain it. Therefore, it has been argued that an NCA may only use evidence transmitted to it in circumstances where it would have been entitled, under its rules of evidence, to obtain that information.[139] However, the Regulation does not require this limitation and it has thus been argued that it is skewed in favour of facilitating the exchange of information to enhance enforcement of competition law by NCAs at the expense of the undertaking's rights to defence.[140]

(iv) Assessment

Decentralising enforcement was a bold step, laden with several risks. First, the Commission may have to make regular use of articles 10 and 11(6) of Regulation 1/2003 to monitor NCAs. Secondly, NCAs would apply Articles 101 and 102 TFEU in divergent ways. Thirdly, some NCAs have little experience in competition law, and some have larger budgets and are better staffed than others, so the quality and quantity of the work done may differ among the agencies. Fourthly, Regulation 1/2003 does not prevent multiple litigation, so an undertaking may be the subject of multiple investigations, perhaps even after one NCA has granted it an informal settlement.[141] Fifthly, further legislative intervention to harmonise procedures in competition cases among the Member States may be necessary to ensure the system works

---

[138] *Ibid.* article 22(1).

[139] Kerse and Kahn, above n. 32, 270.

[140] D. Reichelt, 'To What Extent does the Co-operation within the European Competition Network Protect the Rights of Undertakings?' (2005) 42 *CMLRev.* 745.

[141] See Van Bael and Bellis, above n. 41, 1034–5. For a more optimistic assessment see D. Cahill (ed.), *The Modernisation of EU Competition Law Enforcement in the European Union*, FIDE 2004 National Reports, available at www.FIDE2004.org.

well.[142] Moreover, some have suggested that the effect of modernisation is more pernicious because by compelling NCAs to adopt EU competition law, this reinforces the dominance of the European Commission, of EU law and of the Union's economic policy at the expense of national interests.[143] The Commission's first review of Regulation 1/2003 suggests that, while there is scope for improvement, decentralised enforcement has been a success.[144]

European Commission, *Report on the Functioning of Regulation 1/2003* COM(2009)206 final

24. Enforcement of the EC competition rules has vastly increased since the entry into application of Regulation 1/2003. By the end of March 2009, more than 1,000 cases have been pursued on the basis of the EC competition rules in a wide variety of sectors.

25. Work sharing between the enforcers in the network has generally been unproblematic. Five years of experience have confirmed that the flexible and pragmatic arrangements introduced by Regulation 1/2003 and the Network Notice work well. Discussions on case-allocation have come up in very few cases and have been resolved swiftly.

26. Cooperation mechanisms for fact-finding purposes within the ECN have worked well overall. The possibility to exchange and use information gathered by another competition authority enhances the overall efficiency within the network and is a pre-condition for a flexible case-allocation system. Moreover, the power of national competition authorities to carry out inspections or other fact-finding measures on behalf of another national competition authority, while encountering some limitations as a result of the diversity of national procedures, has been used actively in appropriate cases and has contributed to effective enforcement ...

28. By the end of the reporting period, the Commission had been informed of more than 300 envisaged decisions by the national competition authorities on the basis of Article 11(4). None of these cases resulted in the Commission initiating proceedings pursuant to Article 11(6) to relieve a national competition authority of its competence for reasons of coherent application. Experience indicates that national competition authorities are generally highly committed to ensuring consistency and efforts undertaken in the ECN have successfully contributed to this aim. Pursuant to Article 11(4), a practice of informally discussing the national authority's proposed course of action at services' level and within the confines of confidentiality in the network has been developed. Stakeholders are largely satisfied with the results of application of the EC competition rules within the ECN.

29. The ECN has proven to be a successful forum to discuss general policy issues. Constant dialogue between the network members on all levels over the last years has significantly contributed to coherent application of the EC competition rules.

30. While Regulation 1/2003 does not compel Member States to adopt a specific institutional framework for the implementation of EC competition rules, many Member States have reinforced or reviewed their enforcement structures to optimise their effectiveness.

---

[142] C. Gauer, 'Does the Effectiveness of the EU Network of Competition Authorities Require a Certain Degree of Harmonisation of National Procedures and Sanctions?' in C.-D. Ehlermann and I. Atanasiu (eds.), *European Competition Law Annual 2002: Constructing the EU Network of Competition Authorities* (Oxford, Hart, 2004).

[143] S. Wilks, 'Agency Escape: Decentralization or Dominance of the European Commission in the Modernization of Competition Policy?' (2005) 18 *Governance* 431.

[144] For a more critical assessment, see G. Bruzzone and G. Boccaccio, 'Taking Care of Modernisation After the Startup: A View from a Member State' (2008) 31 *World Competition* 89.

31. Regulation 1/2003 does not formally regulate or harmonise the procedures of national competition authorities, meaning that they apply the same substantive rules according to divergent procedures and they may impose a variety of sanctions. Regulation 1/2003 accommodates this diversity. It has also given rise to a significant degree of voluntary convergence of Member States' laws that has been supported by policy work in the ECN.

32. The ECN Model Leniency Programme illustrates how the ECN is able to combine its forces and jointly develop a new vision to address real and perceived deficits in the existing system. The work within the ECN has been a major catalyst in encouraging Member States and/or national competition authorities to introduce and develop their own leniency policies and in promoting convergence between them. Today, only two Member States do not have any kind of leniency policy in place. The Model Programme foresees that the ECN will evaluate the state of convergence of the leniency programmes by the end of 2008. The assessment will form the basis for a reflection on whether further action is needed in this field.

33. Notwithstanding, divergences of Member States' enforcement systems remain on important aspects such as fines, criminal sanctions, liability in groups of undertakings, liability of associations of undertakings, succession of undertakings, prescription periods and the standard of proof, the power to impose structural remedies, as well as the ability of Member States' competition authorities to formally set enforcement priorities. This aspect may merit further examination and reflection.

According to Giandomenico Majone, the success of a network rests on three factors. First, there has to be a high level of trust among the NCAs. Secondly, each NCA must be independent of government interference. Thirdly, there must be a common regulatory philosophy. In his view, the existence of the network can serve as a mechanism that, in the long term, enhances these three attributes. 'This is because the agency executives have an incentive to maintain their reputation in the eyes of their international colleagues. Unprofessional, self-seeking, poor politically motivated behaviour would compromise their international reputation and make co-operation more difficult to achieve in the future.'[145] To date, peer pressure has been sufficient to avoid serious disagreements within the network. However, each NCA remains independent in law,[146] and potentially able to enforce the law when it has concerns that another NCA would not safeguard competition effectively. More positively, the ECN's cooperation on leniency models suggests that the network has enormous potential to enhance both the harmonisation and the effectiveness of decentralised enforcement.[147] Conversely, some argue that there is no substitute for more legislative measures to ensure cases are allocated to only one authority, to harmonise leniency policies and to safeguard the rights of undertakings under investigation.[148]

[145] G. Majone, 'The Credibility Crisis of Community Regulation' (2000) 38(2) *Journal of Common Market* Studies 273, 297–8.

[146] 'All competition authorities within the Network are independent from one another. Cooperation between NCAs and with the Commission takes place on the basis of equality, respect and solidarity.' Council of the European Union, Doc. 15435/02 ADD 1 of 10 December 2002, para. 7, available at http://register.consilium.eu.int.

[147] K. Dekeyser and M. Jaspers, 'A New Era of ECN Cooperation' (2007) 30 *World Competition* 3. For a more theoretical analysis, see I. Maher, 'Regulation and Modes of Governance in EC Competition Law: What is New in Enforcement?' (2007–08) 31 *Fordham International Law Journal* 1713.

[148] A. Schwab and C. Steinle, 'Pitfalls of the European Competition Network: Why Better Protection of Leniency Applicants and Legal Regulation of Case Allocation is Needed' (2008) *ECLR* 523; A. Andreangeli, 'The Impact of the Modernisation Regulation on the Guarantees of Due Process in Competition Proceedings' (2006) *ELRev.* 342.

5 PRIVATE ENFORCEMENT

It has been argued that private litigation in competition law should be welcomed for two reasons: first, victims of competition law infringements are compensated (public law enforcement merely prevents further harm); secondly, private litigants increase the number of enforcement actions, widening the application of competition law.[149] The European Commission has long campaigned for private parties to bring competition cases in national courts, originally as a means of reducing the Commission's heavy caseload.[150] Recently, private enforcement (especially damages claims against undertakings who infringe EU competition law) has been promoted in an effort to complement the Commission's deterrence-based enforcement strategy. We begin by explaining the contribution of the Court of Justice in galvanising damages claims before turning to the legislative efforts that the Commission is seeking to implement.

(i) An EU right to damages

It has long been clear that Articles 101(1) TFEU and 102 TFEU have direct effect,[151] opening the way for parties to seek damages. However, there was very little litigation because of uncertainties about the nature of a claim for damages and because a national court could not decide on the application of Article 101(3) (which left it with little room for applying Article 101). The second problem, as we saw above, was resolved by Regulation 1/2003, which establishes the direct effect of Article 101(3), and the first was resolved in 2001 by the Court of Justice in a dispute that arose from a pub lease. Mr Crehan made a contract with Inntrepreneur for the lease of two pubs. The lease contract included a beer tie, providing that Crehan would buy his beer exclusively from Courage. The business was unsuccessful and Crehan abandoned the leases. He sought damages for the loss of a business from Inntrepreneur on the basis that the beer tie prevented him from buying cheaper beer which would have allowed him to make a profit. In the English courts, doubts arose as to whether a party privy to an anti-competitive agreement could claim damages. The Court of Justice enthusiastically affirmed that Crehan could claim damages. When the case returned to the English courts, the Court of Appeal awarded Crehan £131,336 in damages for the losses he suffered, but on appeal to the House of Lords the claim failed.[152]

Case C-453/99 *Courage Ltd* v *Crehan* [2001] ECR I-6314

24. ... any individual can rely on a breach of Article [101(1) TFEU] before a national court even where he is a party to a contract that is liable to restrict or distort competition within the meaning of that provision.

25. As regards the possibility of seeking compensation for loss caused by a contract or by conduct liable to restrict or distort competition, it should be remembered from the outset that ... the national courts whose task it is to apply the provisions of Community law in areas within their jurisdiction must ensure that those rules take full effect and must protect the rights which they confer on individuals.

---

[149] White Paper, *Productivity and Enterprise: A World Class Competition Regime*, Cm 5233 (2001) ch. 8.
[150] European Commission, *Thirteenth Report on Competition Policy* (1983) paras. 217–18; Commission Notice of 23 December 1992 on cooperation between national courts and the Commission in applying Articles 85 and 86 EC [1993] OJ C39/6.
[151] Case 127/73 *BRT* v *SABAM* [1974] ECR 313.
[152] *Crehan* v *Inntrepreneur* [2004] EWCA Civ 637; *Inntrepreneur Pub Company (CPC) and Others* v *Crehan* [2006] UKHL 38.

26. The full effectiveness of Article [101 TFEU] and, in particular, the practical effect of the prohibition laid down in Article [101(1) TFEU] would be put at risk if it were not open to any individual to claim damages for loss caused to him by a contract or by conduct liable to restrict or distort competition.

27. Indeed, the existence of such a right strengthens the working of the Community competition rules and discourages agreements or practices, which are frequently covert, which are liable to restrict or distort competition. From that point of view, actions for damages before the national courts can make a significant contribution to the maintenance of effective competition in the Community.

28. There should not therefore be any absolute bar to such an action being brought by a party to a contract which would be held to violate the competition rules.

29. However, in the absence of Community rules governing the matter, it is for the domestic legal system of each Member State to designate the courts and tribunals having jurisdiction and to lay down the detailed procedural rules governing actions for safeguarding rights which individuals derive directly from Community law, provided that such rules are not less favourable than those governing similar domestic actions (principle of equivalence) and that they do not render practically impossible or excessively difficult the exercise of rights conferred by Community law (principle of effectiveness).

30. In that regard, the Court has held that Community law does not prevent national courts from taking steps to ensure that the protection of the rights guaranteed by Community law does not entail the unjust enrichment of those who enjoy them.

31. Similarly, provided that the principles of equivalence and effectiveness are respected, Community law does not preclude national law from denying a party who is found to bear significant responsibility for the distortion of competition the right to obtain damages from the other contracting party. Under a principle which is recognised in most of the legal systems of the Member States and which the Court has applied in the past, a litigant should not profit from his own unlawful conduct, where this is proven.

32. In that regard, the matters to be taken into account by the competent national court include the economic and legal context in which the parties find themselves and, as the United Kingdom Government rightly points out, the respective bargaining power and conduct of the two parties to the contract.

33. In particular, it is for the national court to ascertain whether the party who claims to have suffered loss through concluding a contract that is liable to restrict or distort competition found himself in a markedly weaker position than the other party, such as seriously to compromise or even eliminate his freedom to negotiate the terms of the contract and his capacity to avoid the loss or reduce its extent, in particular by availing himself in good time of all the legal remedies available to him.

This judgment should be studied from two perspectives. From a narrow perspective focusing on the facts of the case, it should be noted that the English courts had never doubted that a right to damages for breach of competition law was available.[153] Rather, the question that had been referred to the Court of Justice was whether a party privy to an anti-competitive

---

[153] In the United Kingdom, for example, the House of Lords in *Garden Cottage Foods* v *Milk Marketing Board* [1984] AC 130 assumed damages to be available.

agreement should be able to seek compensation, because the principle of illegality in English law meant that those implicated in an illegal venture lost the right to damages for loss suffered. Only paragraph 33 addresses this point and it suggests that the illegality defence in English law is too wide. However, it is not particularly clear how to identify when a party finds itself in a 'significantly weaker position' than the other. From this angle, it might be questioned whether the claim has much merit, as it may allow opportunistic behaviour on the part of businesses that have entered into a bad bargain.[154]

From a wider perspective, the judgment must be seen as a general statement establishing a Community right to damages. This is significant because it gives the European and national courts a shared role in shaping the law. The most helpful analysis has been provided by A. P. Komninos, who has elaborated a framework developed by former Advocate General van Gerven.[155] He distinguishes three elements of a damages claim: constitutive, executive and procedural. The first relate to the nature of the claim itself, which must be identical among the Member States and which are shaped by the Court of Justice. Executive elements include matters like the test for causation, defences and damages. The rules pertaining to these issues can be designed by national courts and legislatures subject to two principles of EU law: first, that the rules are effective to safeguard the right, and secondly, that they are equivalent to comparable claims that are made in national law. Procedural matters (e.g. limitation periods and rules of evidence) can also be designed by national courts subject to a more lenient scrutiny under EU law.[156]

In *Manfredi*, the Court of Justice took further steps to explain the right to damages and the role of national courts relating to the executive and procedural conditions. This was a damages claim by Italian consumers who had purchased liability insurance for motor vehicles at inflated prices after insurers had colluded. This was a follow-on claim after the Italian competition authority had found an infringement of Italian competition law (the wording of which was very close to Article 81). However, the plaintiff claimed damages based on Article 81 because a claim for damages for breaches of Italian competition law rested with the Court of Appeal, while a claim under Article 81 could be taken to a small claims court, which was less formal, cheaper and quicker at delivering judgment. The Court of Justice agreed that it was plausible to find that the cartel affected trade between Member States, allowing the application of Article 101. It then gave some guidance on the role of national courts, suggesting that in the absence of Community rules on matters such as the jurisdiction of national courts, limitation periods, and the measure of damages, it was up to Member States to ensure that plaintiffs received adequate safeguards 'provided that such rules are not less favourable than those governing similar domestic actions (principle of equivalence) and that they do not render practically impossible or excessively difficult the exercise of rights conferred by Community law (principle of effectiveness)'.[157] The Court elaborated somewhat on the measure of damages.

[154] G. Monti, 'Anticompetitive Agreements: The Innocent Party's Right to Damages' (2002) 27 *ELRev.* 282.
[155] W. Van Gerven, 'Of Rights, Remedies and Procedures' (2000) 37 *CMLRev.* 501.
[156] A. P. Komninos, *EC Private Antitrust Enforcement* (Oxford, Hart, 2008) 170–6.
[157] Joined Cases C-295/04–C-298/04 *Vincenzo Manfredi and Others v Lloyd Adriatico Assicurazioni SpA and Others* [2006] ECR I-6619, para. 62.

Joined Cases C-295/04–C-298/04 *Vincenzo Manfredi and Others* v *Lloyd Adriatico Assicurazioni SpA and Others* [2006] ECR I-6619

93. ... in accordance with the principle of equivalence, it must be possible to award particular damages, such as exemplary or punitive damages, pursuant to actions founded on the Community competition rules, if such damages may be awarded pursuant to similar actions founded on domestic law.

94. However, it is settled case law that Community law does not prevent national courts from taking steps to ensure that the protection of the rights guaranteed by Community law does not entail the unjust enrichment of those who enjoy them.

95. Secondly, it follows from the principle of effectiveness and the right of any individual to seek compensation for loss caused by a contract or by conduct liable to restrict or distort competition that injured persons must be able to seek compensation not only for actual loss (*damnum emergens*) but also for loss of profit (*lucrum cessans*) plus interest.

96. Total exclusion of loss of profit as a head of damage for which compensation may be awarded cannot be accepted in the case of a breach of Community law since, especially in the context of economic or commercial litigation, such a total exclusion of loss of profit would be such as to make reparation of damage practically impossible.

The relevant Italian court has now rendered a judgment that among other matters awards the claimant 'double damages' as a means of giving effect to the Court of Justice's judgment, but it has been suggested that this is not what the Court intended.[158] Further guidance is probably needed on the quantum of damages, and it is significant that the Court of Justice suggests that claimants have a right to seek damages for loss of profit as well, although the difficulties in showing a causal link between an infringement of competition law and the loss of a chance to make profit seem insurmountable, and it is likely that most claimants will settle for a claim of actual loss (i.e. the overcharge caused by the cartel).[159]

According to Komninos, the Court in *Manfredi* also set out the constitutive conditions of the claim.

Joined Cases C-295/04–C-298/04 *Vincenzo Manfredi and Others* v *Lloyd Adriatico Assicurazioni SpA and Others* [2006] ECR I-6619

60. Next, as regards the possibility of seeking compensation for loss caused by a contract or by conduct liable to restrict or distort competition, it should be recalled that the full effectiveness of Article [101 TFEU] and, in particular, the practical effect of the prohibition laid down in Article [101(1) TFEU] would be put at risk if it were not open to any individual to claim damages for loss caused to him by a contract or by conduct liable to restrict or distort competition.

61. It follows that any individual can claim compensation for the harm suffered where there is a causal relationship between that harm and an agreement or practice prohibited under Article [101 TFEU].

---

[158] P. Nebbia, 'So What Happened to *Manfredi*?' (2007) *ECLR* 591, for a strong critique of the Italian court's decision.
[159] See e.g. *Devenish Nutrition Ltd and Others* v *Sanofi and Others* [2007] EWHC 2394 (Ch).

In his view, paragraph 61 means that the right to damages is available to any individual, when there is harm, a competition law violation and a causal link between the violation and the harm.[160] If this is correct, then two consequences follow. First, there is no need for the plaintiff to prove fault (liability is strict). Secondly, and more significantly, it means that both direct and indirect buyers may claim damages. Think, for example, of a cartel in the market for MP3 players sold by manufacturers to high street shops. The high street shop pays an inflated price, and as a result, they try and pass on some of that higher cost to consumers in the form of higher prices. It appears that a claim for damages may be brought by the shops (direct purchasers) and each individual buyer (indirect purchasers).

While the Court of Justice has made a major contribution in establishing certain elements to facilitate damages claims, the Commission has taken the view that further legislative efforts are required to ensure that the right to damages is exercised widely.

(ii) Legislative initiatives

Regulation 1/2003 envisages an increased role for private litigation, noting that 'national courts have an essential part to play in applying the Community competition rules'.[161] But only article 16 of Regulation 1/2003 facilitates private litigation. It provides that if the Commission brings a successful action against an anti-competitive practice, then this Decision binds national courts. Thus, the plaintiff does not have to prove the infringement again, only that she has suffered damage as a result. This saves considerable resources for litigants in what are often complex cases.[162]

A blueprint for more extensive legislative action is the White Paper on Damages Actions for Breach of the EC Antitrust Rules.[163] It begins by recalling the findings of the 2005 Green Paper that the dearth of private litigation is caused by 'legal and procedural hurdles' in Member States. The primary objective of the White Paper is suggested to be to lower these hurdles, guided by three principles: full compensation;[164] that the legal framework should be based on a genuinely European approach, so the proposals are 'balanced measures that are rooted in European legal culture and traditions';[165] and to preserve strong public enforcement so that damages actions complement public enforcement. A brief comment on these three principles is warranted before considering the proposals.

First, the principles confirm the views of some scholars that the action for damage is premised primarily upon the principle of corrective justice and not on optimal deterrence. This

---

[160] Komninos, above n. 156, 175.
[161] Regulation 1/2003, recital 7.
[162] Likewise for investigations by NCAs, e.g. UK Competition Act 1998, s. 58(1) provides that findings of *fact* by the Office of Fair Trading (OFT) are binding in court proceedings; s. 58A (inserted by Enterprise Act 2002, s. 20) provides that findings of *infringements* of the Competition Act or of Articles 101 and 102 TFEU are binding on courts; s. 47A (inserted by Enterprise Act 2002, s. 18) provides for a follow-on action for damages in the Competition Appeals Tribunal where there has been a finding of an infringement of UK or EU competition law by the OFT or the European Commission; this is without prejudice to bringing an action in the normal courts.
[163] COM(2008)165. It is accompanied by a more detailed Commission Staff Working Paper, *Damages Actions for Breach of the EC Antitrust Rules*, SEC(2008)404 and an Impact Assessment Report, SEC(2008)405. All three documents are available at http://ec.europa.eu/comm/competition/antitrust/actionsdamages/documents.html.
[164] COM(2008)165, 1–2.
[165] *Ibid.* 2.

means that preference is given to allow as many claims as possible rather than restricting claims to those plaintiffs whose lawsuits are most likely to deter future anti-competitive conduct.[166] Secondly, these principles are designed to allay fears of a US-style approach, so there are no proposals for punitive damages, class actions, contingency fees or other procedures that would jar with established civil law cultures. Thirdly, these principles recognise that too much private enforcement can undermine the Commission's leniency programme; if a firm applies for leniency but is then liable to pay considerable sums in damages, it may decide to keep its involvement in cartels secret.

The White Paper addresses a wide range of issues, but two in particular merit detailed discussion: managing claims by direct and indirect purchasers and collective redress.

(a) Direct and indirect purchasers

The White Paper states that indirect purchasers have standing to seek damages because this is now part of the acquis communautaire.[167] In claims by direct purchasers, the defendant should benefit from the passing-on defence so that a claimant who has bought goods from a cartel at a higher price but has mitigated this loss by passing the excess price to downstream buyers would see his damages claim reduced, otherwise he would be unjustly enriched. For example, if the cartel causes the price to rise by €2 and the claimant resells the goods to the indirect purchaser at a price that is €1 higher than before the cartel, he has passed on half of the overcharge, so damages would be €1, not €2. The burden of proof should be on the defendant to show that the claimant has passed on (some of) the overcharge, which seems a tricky burden to satisfy. To facilitate claims by indirect purchasers, these 'should be able to rely on a rebuttable presumption that the illegal overcharge was passed on to them in its entirety'.[168] On the example above, therefore, the indirect purchaser is entitled to make a claim of €2 even if only a €1 overcharge was passed on to it. This is justified by indicating that indirect purchasers would otherwise find it too hard to prove the existence and extent of the passing on. It is not particularly fair to ask the defendant to show how much of the higher costs were absorbed by the direct purchaser, so this proposal seems to lead to overcompensation of indirect purchasers. These two proposals have been criticised for overburdening the defendant: the risk is that if both direct and indirect purchasers seek damages based on the overcharge, it means the defendant will pay €4 when he only increased prices by €2.

An alternative approach to that proposed by the White Paper, and one which is applied in US federal law, is to grant a right to damages to the direct purchaser with no deduction for losses that have been passed on, and to ban claims by indirect purchasers.[169] It is claimed that the advantage of this approach is that it does not create an accumulation of claims for the same infringement (which would penalise the infringer excessively) and it compensates the person

---

[166] W. M. Landes and R. A. Posner, 'Should Indirect Purchasers have Standing to Sue under the Antitrust Laws? An Economic Analysis of the Rule in Illinois Brick' (1979) 46 *University of Chicago Law Review* 602 (banning indirect purchaser suits enhances deterrence).

[167] *Manfredi*, above n. 157.

[168] COM(2008)165, 8.

[169] *Hanover Shoe Inc.* v. *Shoe Machinery Corp.*, 392 US 481 (1968) (rejecting passing on as a defence); *Illinois Brick Co.* v *Illinois*, 431 US 720 (1977) (barring claims by indirect purchasers). For discussion see Sullivan and Grimes, above n. 12, 926–34.

who is directly injured by the anti-competitive conduct.[170] One of the advantages of this approach is that it gives direct purchasers a good incentive to seek damages, so that it enhances the deterrence value of damages claims. However, this perspective is controversial among Member States, who prefer to see damages claims serving the aim of corrective justice; and at Community level, there is an interest in ensuring that final consumers are protected.[171]

(b) Collective redress

That compensation is valued more highly than deterrence is also confirmed by the wish to facilitate collective redress. Two mechanisms are proposed: (i) representative actions brought by qualified entities (e.g. consumer associations), and (ii) opt-in collective actions whereby plaintiffs can decide to combine their claims in one single action. What is not proposed is an 'opt-out' system of collective redress whereby a person may launch a representative action for a group without each member of the group needing to agree, but each member is free to opt out of the lawsuit. These schemes operate in the United States but it is feared that Member States may be reluctant to agree to this measure. The European Parliament is not in favour of a distinct legal instrument of collective redress for competition law infringement, noting that legislative efforts are afoot for collective redress for breaches of consumer law, and favours a single instrument. It has also suggested that procedures to facilitate out-of-court settlements should be considered.[172]

(c) Further legislative initiatives

In addition, the following measures were proposed.

(i) To facilitate access to evidence national courts should be empowered to order the defendant to disclose certain evidence (only when specific conditions are met, for example, where there is an inability to secure the evidence by other means, specific categories of evidence are identified and the disclosure is relevant to the case, necessary and proportionate). This should be coupled with penalties if the defendant refuses to comply, including the option to draw adverse inferences from the refusal.

(ii) National courts should be bound by findings of any national competition authority in the European Competition Network. This would allow a follow-on claim, for example, in a Slovenian court after the UK competition authority reached a final decision.

(iii) A defendant should be liable for damages unless he proves that the breach was caused by a 'genuinely excusable error'. An error is excusable if 'a reasonable person applying a high standard of care could not have been aware that the conduct restricted competition'. This is designed to harmonise different approaches in Member States as to the presence of a fault requirement and is said to be in line with the principle of effectiveness.

---

[170] N. Reich, 'The "Courage" Doctrine: Encouraging or Discouraging Compensation for Antitrust Injuries?' (2005) 35 CMLRev. 35.

[171] For a good overview, see C. Petrucci, 'The Issues of the Passing-on Defence and Indirect Purchasers' Standing in European Competition Law' (2008) ECLR 33.

[172] European Parliament resolution of 26 March 2009 on the White Paper on damages actions for breach of the EC antitrust rules, P6_TA-PROV(2009)0187. The Parliament also disagreed with a number of other proposals in the White Paper.

(iv) Codification of the scope of damages is recommended, to clarify that damages can be claimed for: (a) actual loss, and (b) loss of profits resulting from any reduction in sales. Further, a soft law instrument is proposed with 'pragmatic guidance' to quantify damages with simplified rules on estimating loss.

(v) There are two proposals on limitation periods. The most significant is that in cases where anti-competitive activity is subject to public enforcement, a new limitation period of at least two years starts once the competition authority's infringement decision becomes final. The second is that a limitation period in other instances should not begin to run before the day on which the infringement ceases (even in cases of continuous or repeated infringement) and not before the victim can reasonably be expected to have knowledge of the infringement and of the harm it caused. The duration of this limitation period is not harmonised.

(vi) Member States should reconsider their cost allocation rules to ensure that these do not put off meritorious cases; settlements should be considered, as well as limits on court fees, and cost orders that do not always make the losing party bear all the costs of the winning party.

(vii) To safeguard the attraction of leniency programmes, the Commission considers that those who receive immunity should only face claims from direct and indirect contractual partners, so that by reducing the financial impact of damages claims leniency applications continue to be made. Two comments are warranted on the second proposal: first, this qualifies the Court of Justice case law giving anyone a right to damages in all cases; secondly, given that the defendant is liable to both direct and indirect purchasers (and so merely avoids claims by competitors), it is hard to see that this proposal actually reduces the amount of damages that the defendant would pay.

(d) Assessment

These proposals may be appraised from a number of perspectives. First, it will have become apparent that the White Paper is not a blueprint for a single legislative instrument. Some of the proposals are recommendations for Member State action (on costs), some are suggestions for soft law instruments (on calculating damages), and some are suggestions for discrete legislative tools, whether Directives (on representative actions) or Regulations (on the function of the passing on defence and the fault requirement).[173] The legal base for any legislative measure is not yet determined, so one might doubt how far the Community is able to legislate in this field.[174]

Secondly, the proposals have been criticised both by those who think they are not sufficiently bold and by those who consider that they are excessive. For example, it has been suggested that the White Paper does not propose three measures that the Commission considered to be those most likely to lead to an effective private enforcement regime: double damages, lax discovery rules and giving national courts the power to issue cost orders to favour losing plaintiffs.[175] On the other hand, Member States have expressed concerns about the creation

---

[173] A. P. Komninos, 'Enter the White Paper for Damages Actions: A First Selective Appraisal', 4 April 2008, available at www.globalcompetitionpolicy.org.

[174] *Ibid.*

[175] Editorial Comments, 'A Little More Action Please! The White Paper on Damages Actions for Breach of the EC Antitrust Rules' (2008) 45 *Common Market Law* Review 609.

of special damages rules for victims of competition law infringements. This is a valid point: why facilitate rules for victims of economic losses and not victims of, say, cancer caused by exposure to asbestos? Furthermore, there is a concern that the Commission wishes to enhance private litigation as a means of boosting the deterrent role of competition law, while Member States take the view that private litigation should serve only to compensate victims, rejecting an instrumentalist view of tort law.[176]

Thirdly, one might doubt whether damages actions are desirable in competition law at all. Insofar as the aim of deterrence is concerned, public enforcement is a superior form of deterrence for a number of reasons. First, antitrust authorities have more effective investigatory and sanctioning powers, in particular with the network of NCAs being developed. Secondly, private plaintiffs are motivated by profit and not necessarily motivated to bring claims against practices that injure the public interest, whereas NCAs will tend to bring claims of most value to the economy. Thirdly, private enforcement is more costly because NCAs are repeat players, who specialise in competition law and thus the marginal cost of additional actions is lower.[177] But this view has come under fire: the argument that NCAs are superior has been questioned on the basis that while private enforcement is imperfect, it is not an argument against allowing those who are able to mount an action to do so, and the risk that private parties will litigate unmeritorious claims is one which affects all private litigation, and which can be tempered by judges striking out worthless claims.[178] However, the Commission's justification seems to be that the estimated cost to antitrust victims ranges between €25 to €69 billion,[179] and that 'EU-wide infringements are becoming more and more frequent'.[180] However, don't these findings suggest that there is a failure of public enforcement? And if so, might resources not be better allocated at that end?

FURTHER READING

G. Amato, *Antitrust and the Bounds of Power* (Oxford, Hart, 1997)

A. Andreangeli, 'The Impact of the Modernisation Regulation on the Guarantees of Due Process in Competition Proceedings' (2006) 31 *European Law Review* 342

S. Bishop and M. Walker, *The Economics of EC Competition Law* (2nd edn, London, Sweet & Maxwell, 2002)

S. Brammer, 'Concurrent Jurisdiction under Regulation 1/2003 and the Issue of Case Allocation' (2005) 42 *Common Market Law Review* 1383

A. Burnside, 'Cooperation in Competition: A New Era' (2005) 30 *European Law Review* 234

D. J. Gerber, *Law and Competition in Twentieth Century Europe* (Oxford, Oxford University Press, 1998)

'Two Forms of Modernization in European Competition Law' (2008) *Fordham International Law Journal* 1235

---

[176] J. S. Kortmann and C. R. A. Swaak, 'The EC White Paper on Antitrust Damage Actions: Why the Member States are (Right to Be) Less Than Enthusiastic' (2009) *ECLR* 340.

[177] W. P. J. Wils, 'Should Private Antitrust Enforcement be Encouraged in Europe?' (2003) 26 *World Competition* 473.

[178] C. A. Jones, 'Private Antitrust Enforcement in Europe: A Policy Analysis and a Reality Check' (2004) 27 *World Competition* 13.

[179] Impact Assessment Report, above n. 163, paras. 42–3.

[180] *Ibid.* para. 32.

C. S. Kerse and N. Kahn, *EC Antitrust Procedure* (5th edn, London, Sweet & Maxwell, 2005)

A. P. Komninos, *EC Private Antitrust Enforcement* (Oxford, Hart, 2008)

E. J. Mestmäcker, 'The Commission's Modernisation of Competition Policy: A Challenge to the Community's Constitutional Order' (2000) *European Business Organisation Review* 401

M. Motta, *Competition Policy* (Cambridge, Cambridge University Press, 2004)

D. Neven, 'Competition Economics and Antitrust in Europe' (2006) *Economic policy* 741

W. Sauter, *Competition Law and Industrial Policy in the EU* (Oxford, Oxford University Press, 1997)

J. S. Venit, 'Brave New World: The Modernization and Decentralization of Enforcement under Articles 81 and 82 of the EC Treaty' (2003) 40 *Common Market Law Review* 545

S. B. Völker, 'Rough Justice? An Analysis of the European Commission's New Fining Guidelines' (2007) 44 *Common Market Law Review* 1285

R. Wesseling, *The Modernization of EC Antitrust Law* (Oxford and Portland, Hart, 2000)

S. Wilks, 'Agency Escape: Decentralization or Dominance of the European Commission in the Modernization of Competition Policy?' (2005) 18 *Governance* 431

W. P. J. Wils, 'Should Private Antitrust Enforcement be Encouraged in Europe?' (2003) 26 *World Competition* 473

23

Antitrust and Monopolies

1 INTRODUCTION

In this chapter we review the two principal provisions that implement the competition policy the aims and enforcement structure of which were discussed in Chapter 22: Articles 101 and 102 TFEU. Article 101 applies to agreements between undertakings and declares these agreements void when they are found to restrict competition; Article 102 TFEU applies to dominant undertakings and forbids them from abusing their position. Since the end of the 1990s, the

Commission has been engaged in a series of reform initiatives to the application of competition law, in response to criticisms that its approach was insufficiently grounded in economics and was overly aggressive. Explaining and evaluating this process of reform is the central theme of this chapter, which is organised in the following way.

Section 2 covers three legal issues that are common to both Articles: the meaning of an undertaking, the concept of an effect on trade between Member States and judge-made rules that exclude the application of competition law.

Section 3 is a review of the key issues that have arisen in the application of Article 101. It is divided into three parts. First, we explore how this provision applies to activities that undermine the key aims of EU competition law (the protection of the consumer and the integration of markets). In particular we study how this provision tackles cartels, whose agreements cause them to act as a monopoly and reduce consumer welfare. The former Competition Commissioner characterised them as 'cancers on the open market economy'.[1] Catching and punishing cartels is at the heart of the functions of all competition authorities.[2] This part of the chapter should be read together with section 3 of Chapter 22 which explains the powers the Commission has to find cartels and to penalise them. The task in this chapter is to examine how widely the meaning of the concepts of agreement and concerted practice have been used to catch collusion. Secondly, we consider how the Commission and Union courts determine whether agreements that are not obviously anti-competitive (for example, joint ventures and distribution agreements) are evaluated under Article 101(1) and consider different views on what the legal or economic standard for assessment is. Thirdly, we study how Article 101(3) is applied to exempt anti-competitive agreements and explores the debate between a narrow and a wide interpretation of this exemption. The bulk of the Commission's energies over the past forty years of competition law enforcement have been devoted to Article 101 cases, and a daunting number of Decisions have been published. However, in this chapter we will limit ourselves to analysing a small representative sample of Decisions in close detail.

Section 4 examines Article 102 TFEU by first discussing the concept of abuse in general terms, followed by a case study on predatory pricing. The key points are the breadth of the concept of dominance, and the policy underpinning the abuse doctrine. The Court of Justice's approach is to impose on dominant undertakings a special responsibility not to distort competition, but it seems to place little emphasis on testing whether a suspected abuse is successful in harming competition or in causing harm to economic welfare. This part of the section begins by explaining how the current approach to Article 102 may be justified before examining how the Commission intends to reform its enforcement strategy with respect to abuse of dominance.

Section 5 contains a brief overview of common themes that underpin the development of competition law enforcement under these two key provisions. It indicates that while there has been some convergence in the way the Commission has interpreted the two provisions, there are tensions between the reasoning of the Court and that of the Commission arising from the more economics-based approach pursued by the latter.

---

[1] M. Monti, 'Fighting Cartels Why and How?', speech 11–12 September 2000, available on the Commission's website under 'Speeches and articles': http://europa.eu.int/comm/competition/index_en.html.

[2] OECD, 'Hard Core Cartels: Recent Progress and Challenges Ahead' (OECD, 2003); European Commission, *Report on Competition Policy 2004*, SEC(2005)805 final, 29.

2 SCOPE OF APPLICATION OF EU COMPETITION LAW

(i) Undertakings

EU competition law applies to 'undertakings', a term that 'encompasses every entity engaged in an economic activity, regardless of the legal status of the entity or the way in which it is financed'.[3] Its meaning is independent of any national law definitions of what constitutes a company. Rather, it is effects-based: the question is whether the entity in question, when doing a specific task, has an economic impact on the market by offering goods or services. Inventors,[4] opera singers,[5] barristers,[6] sporting associations,[7] agricultural cooperatives[8] and multinational corporations can all act as undertakings. Employees, however, are not undertakings,[9] nor are agents who operate on behalf of their principal and take no financial risk.[10] In recent years, as governments have increasingly contracted out the provision of public services, questions have arisen as to whether entities engaged in the provision of these types of services (for example, emergency ambulance services and air traffic control) should be regulated by competition law. This issue is discussed in Chapter 24.

Subsidiaries may have independent legal personality, but for the purposes of competition law a subsidiary is treated as a single economic entity along with the parent company where the subsidiary has no ability to determine its conduct on the market.[11] Whether parent and subsidiary constitute a single economic entity is a question of fact. Relevant considerations include the number of shares that the parent has in the subsidiary (where a majority shareholding will give rise to a presumption that the parent controls the subsidiary),[12] the composition of the board of directors, and whether the subsidiary carries out the parent's instructions. Whether parent and subsidiary are one undertaking or two has considerable practical implications: first, if they are two undertakings then Article 101 applies, while if there is one undertaking, it is classified as an intra-firm agreement, to which Article 101 does not apply. As a result, an undertaking may evade the application of Article 101 by buying firms with whom it would normally contract if it finds that the burden of complying with Article 101 is too onerous. Parker Pen embarked on this strategy, owning all its distributors in certain Member States and orchestrating distribution through them. The effect of this was to partition the market, as each subsidiary was only allowed to sell in the territory allocated to it by Parker Pen. Viho (a Dutch wholesaler) complained because it wished to buy Parker products in Germany for resale in The Netherlands, but was unsuccessful in obtaining the goods from Parker's German subsidiary. Had Parker prohibited an independent distributor in Germany from selling to Viho, this would have constituted an agreement in breach of Article 101, but as it was an internal measure, the Court of Justice held that it was not caught by Article 101.

---

[3] Case C-41/90 *Klaus Höfner and Fritz Elser* v *Macrotron GmbH* [1991] ECR I-1979, para. 21.

[4] *Reuter/BASF* [1976] OJ L254/40.

[5] *RAI/UNITEL* [1978] OJ L157/39.

[6] Case C-309/99 *Wouters and Others* v *Algemene Raad van de Nederlandse Orde van Advocaten* [2002] ECR I-1577.

[7] *Distribution of Package Tours during the 1990 World Cup* [1992] OJ L326/31.

[8] Case C-250/92 *Gøttrup-Klim and Others Grovvareforeninger* v *Dansk Landbrugs Grovvareselskab AmbA* [1994] ECR I-5641.

[9] Case C-22/98 *Becu* [1999] ECR I-5665.

[10] See Guidelines on vertical restraints [2000] OJ C291/1, paras. 12–20.

[11] Case C-73/95 P *Viho Europe BV* v *Commission* [1996] ECR I-5457.

[12] Compare *Viho, ibid.* (100 per cent shareholding meant the parent and subsidiary was a single economic entity) with *Gosmé/Martell-DMP* [1991] OJ L185/23 (50 per cent ownership of a joint venture insufficient to treat the two as a single entity) and Case T-228/97 *Irish Sugar plc* v *Commission* [1999] ECR II-2696 (subsidiary in which Irish Sugar held 51 per cent of the shares held to be a separate undertaking).

Case C–73/95P *Viho Europe BV* v *Commission* [1996] ECR I–5457

15. It should be noted, first of all, that it is established that Parker holds 100% of the shares of its subsidiaries in Germany, Belgium, Spain, France and the Netherlands and that the sales and marketing activities of its subsidiaries are directed by an area team appointed by the parent company and which controls, in particular, sales targets, gross margins, sales costs, cash flow and stocks. The area team also lays down the range of products to be sold, monitors advertising and issues directives concerning prices and discounts.

16. Parker and its subsidiaries thus form a single economic unit within which the subsidiaries do not enjoy real autonomy in determining their course of action in the market, but carry out the instructions issued to them by the parent company controlling them.

17. In those circumstances, the fact that Parker's policy of referral, which consists essentially in dividing various national markets between its subsidiaries, might produce effects outside the ambit of the Parker group which are capable of affecting the competitive position of third parties cannot make Article [101(1) TFEU] applicable, even when it is read in conjunction with Article 2 and Article [3(1)(c) and (g) TFEU].[13] On the other hand, such unilateral conduct could fall under Article [102 TFEU] if the conditions for its application, as laid down in that article, were fulfilled.

18. The [General Court] was therefore fully entitled to base its decision solely on the existence of a single economic unit in order to rule out the application of Article [101(1) TFEU] to the Parker group.

Parker's strategy had been the result of an earlier Commission Decision (spurred by an earlier complaint from Viho) that its contracts with an independent distributor in Germany infringed Article 101 by prohibiting the German distributor from exporting Parker products.[14] In response, Parker Pen established its own distribution network, avoiding the finding of an agreement but dividing the market, thereby undermining one central aim of EU competition law.

A second significant reason for determining whether parents and subsidiaries are a single economic unit is that a parent is responsible for acts by its wholly owned subsidiary. This rule was used in *ICI* v *Commission* (*Dyestuffs*) to impose a penalty on foreign parents for a cartel carried out in the Union by subsidiaries even if the parent company had no presence in the Union.[15] Thirdly, a number of crucial determinations in competition law proceedings depend upon calculating the turnover or market shares of the undertaking concerned. For instance, a fine is calculated in part based upon the turnover of the undertaking (and this figure will include the turnover of the entire economic entity);[16] the application of certain regulations is based upon a calculation of market shares (which includes the market shares of the entire

---

[13] These provisions have been rearranged and modified slightly in the current version: see Article 3 TEU and Articles 3(1)(b) and 4(2)(a) TFEU. For discussion of the significance of the amendment in Article 3 TEU, see pp. 921–2.

[14] *Viho/Parker Pen* [1992] OJ L233/27; affirmed in Case T-66/92 *Herlitz* v *Commission* [1994] ECR II-531 and Case T-77/92 *Parker* v *Commission* [1994] ECR II-549.

[15] Joined Cases 48/69–57/69 *ICI* v *Commission* (*Dyestuffs*) [1972] ECR 619. This approach may be criticised because the Court merely considered whether the parent was able to exercise control over the subsidiary, and not whether it had in fact exercised control. See D. G. Goyder, *EC Competition Law* (4th edn, Oxford, Oxford University Press, 2003) 499–500.

[16] Regulation 1/2003/EC on the implementation of the rules on competition laid down in Articles 81 and 82 of the Treaty, article 23(2) [2003] OJ L1/1.

entity);[17] and the determination of whether two undertakings are competitors is based upon an evaluation of the activities of the whole corporate group, not merely upon the two firms that enter into the agreement.[18]

(ii) Effect on trade between Member States

EU competition law does not apply unless the practice in question has an appreciable effect on trade between Member States. The Court set out a wide definition of 'effect on trade', which corresponds to the test deployed in disputes concerning the internal market generally.[19]

Case 56/65 *Société Technique Minière* v *Maschinenbau Ulm GmbH* [1966] ECR 234, 249

For this requirement to be fulfilled it must be possible to foresee with a sufficient degree of probability on the basis of a set of objective factors of law or of fact that the agreement in question may have an influence, direct or indirect, actual or potential, on the pattern of trade between Member States. Therefore, in order to determine whether an agreement which contains a clause 'granting an exclusive right of sale' comes within the field of application of Article [101 TFEU], it is necessary to consider in particular whether it is capable of bringing about a partitioning of the market in certain products between Member States and thus rendering more difficult the interpenetration of trade which the Treaty is intended to create.

Two weeks after this judgment the Court expanded this formula by holding that determining whether an agreement has an effect on trade does not require an evaluation as to whether the effect is positive or negative. Even agreements which increase trade are caught.[20] The aim of the 'effect on trade between Member States' phrase is purely to determine whether EU law applies, and is not used to appraise the agreement. The test is extremely broad: agreements within one Member State may affect trade, for instance, a cartel among Dutch roofing felt manufacturers was held to affect trade between Member States because it restricted the ability of exporters to penetrate the Dutch market;[21] an agreement concerning goods that are not traded across borders may have a potential effect on trade if there is evidence to suggest that cross-border trade will increase;[22] an effect may be indirect when an agreement fixes prices for a raw material which is not exported but which is used in the manufacture of a product which is exported;[23] or when a product is sold with a warranty that is only valid in the Member State where the product is bought.[24] Lastly, an effect on trade may also arise when the agreement relates to trade outside the European Union. Thus, a distribution agreement whereby Yves Saint

---

[17] See e.g. Regulation 2790/1999/EC on the application of Article 81(3) to categories of vertical agreements and concerted practices, articles 3 and 11 [1999] OJ L336/21.

[18] See e.g. *ibid.* article 2(4).

[19] For an overview, see J. Faull, 'Effect on Trade Between Member States' (1999) *Fordham Corporate Law Institute* 481.

[20] Joined Cases 54/64 and 58/64 *Consten and Grundig* v *Commission* [1966] ECR 299.

[21] Case 246/86 *Belasco and Others* v *Commission* [1989] ECR 2117, paras. 33–8.

[22] Case 107/82 *AEG Telefunken* v *Commission* [1983] ECR 3151, para. 60.

[23] Case 123/83 *BNIC* v *Clair* [1983] ECR 391, para. 29.

[24] *Re Zanussi SpA Guarantee* [1978] OJ L322/26.

Laurent contracted with a firm to distribute its goods in Russia, Ukraine and Slovenia (at the time not a Member State) and prohibited the distributor from re-importing them into the Union could have an 'appreciable effect on the pattern of trade between the Member States such as to undermine attainment of the objectives of the common market'.[25]

On the one hand, the Commission welcomed this wide definition of an effect on trade as it extended the reach of EU competition law, but on the other hand, it also posed a risk because it meant that every agreement, even with players of insignificant size, would fall under Article 101, which would prevent the Commission from dealing with the more serious infringements. The Court attempted to unburden the Commission by holding that Article 101 would only apply if the effect on trade was appreciable, thus an agreement with undertakings that have small market shares would not be subject to Article 101 because its interstate effects are *de minimis*.[26] In 2004, in order to ensure consistency among national authorities in their determination of when to apply EU competition law, the Commission published a notice on the effect of trade between Member States that establishes the 'NAAT test' (no appreciable affectation of trade test).[27] According to this test, agreements are incapable of appreciably affecting trade when the parties' aggregate market share does not exceed 5 per cent, and in horizontal agreements the turnover of both parties is less than €40 million, while for vertical agreements the turnover of the supplier does not exceed €40 million. The Commission will not institute proceedings in these cases and the intention of the notice is to influence national authorities to follow suit. However, agreements below these thresholds may still be caught by national competition law.[28]

(iii) Excluded agreements

All economic activities fall to be regulated by EU competition law, but the Treaty provides for certain exceptions: for example, national security,[29] agriculture,[30] and providers entrusted with the provision of services of general economic interest.[31]

Alongside the economic sectors where exclusion was a matter of legislative choice, the Court of Justice has also identified certain fields where EU competition law is excluded. Agreements resulting from negotiations between employers and workers in the context of collective bargaining are excluded.[32] In the seminal case establishing this exclusion, a

---

[25] Case C-306/96 *Javico International and Javico AG* v *Yves Saint Laurent Parfums SA* [1998] ECR I-1983, para. 25.

[26] Case 5/69 *Völk* v *Vervaecke* [1969] ECR 295.

[27] Commission Notice, Guidelines on the effect on trade concept contained in Articles 81 and 82 of the Treaty [2004] OJ C101/81, para. 2.4.

[28] It is not clear why the Commission invented this test since agreements between operators with little market power are already, in certain circumstances, excluded from the application of Article 101 when deemed to be of minor importance on the basis that they are incapable of damaging competition substantially. See Commission Notice on agreements of minor importance which do not appreciably restrict competition under Article 81(1) [2001] OJ C368/13.

[29] Article 346 TFEU (ex Article 296 EC) (a provision invoked in mergers in the defence sector).

[30] Article 42 TFEU (ex Article 36 EC) provides that agriculture is covered to the extent that the Council determines, taking into account the aims of the Common Agricultural Policy. See Regulation 26/62/EC [1959–62] OJ Spec. edn, 129. The provisions of the exclusions in this Regulation have been read restrictively: see e.g. Case 71/74 *FRUBO* v *Commission* [1975] ECR 563.

[31] Article 106(2) TFEU (ex Article 86(2) EC). See Chapter 24 for discussion.

[32] See also Case C-67/96 *Albany International BV* v *Stichting Bedrijfspensioenfonds Textielindustrie* [1999] ECR I-5751, paras. 52–60; Case C-219/97 *Maatschappij Drijvende Bokken BV* v *Stichting Pensioenfonds voor de Vervoer- en Havenbedrijven* [1999] ECR I-6121, paras. 40–7.

decision was taken by an organisation representing employers and workers in the whole-sale trade of building materials in the Netherlands to establish a single pension fund for all employees in that sector. The fund would be responsible for managing the employees' supplementary pension scheme. The organisation of these supplementary funds was approved by Dutch law but the defendants, undertakings operating in the relevant sector, refused to make the relevant contributions. They had obtained a more advantageous private pension scheme, and considered that the decision by the employers and workers to make affiliation to a fund compulsory was restrictive of competition in two ways: it prevented undertakings from finding alternative pension schemes, and excluded insurers from the relevant market. In spite of the anti-competitive effects, the Court ruled that the agreement fell outside the scope of Article 101(1). The basis for this reasoning was that the Union is tasked with both ensuring competition and also developing a policy in the social sphere, and these two conflicting objectives had to be balanced. The Court found that restrictions of competition would be inherent in collective agreements between organisations representing employers and workers and that the application of competition law would damage collective attempts to improve the conditions of employment.[33] The judgment can be praised for consistency with the so-called 'European social model'. This imprecisely defined phrase is often used to explain that the Union's internal market project is not merely about the creation of economic wealth, but also about safeguarding the interests of employees. However, the Court does not subject the pension scheme in question to a proportionality test; it does not consider whether this kind of pension arrangement is the least restrictive way of achieving the improvement of working conditions, nor does the Court take into consideration the possibility that Article 101(3) could have exempted these agreements.[34] Instead, the social policy considerations trump the competition policy considerations.

This ruling seemed an exceptional scenario where the application of EU competition law was excluded to give way to another Treaty objective. However, the matter was to reoccur, only a few years later, in *Wouters*. The Dutch Bar Association prohibited partnerships between lawyers and accountants ('multidisciplinary partnerships') by the '1993 Regulation'. The 1993 Regulation (which was characterised as a decision by an association of undertakings) was challenged by lawyers wishing to work for an accountancy firm. It clearly restricted competition by preventing the creation of a new form of business. However, the Court held that Article 101(1) was not infringed because the restriction on competition was necessary to ensure the proper practice of the legal profession. In particular, the rule banning multidisciplinary practices was necessary to ensure that lawyers served their clients with no conflict of interest, and observed professional secrecy. The Dutch Bar Association considered that multidisciplinary practices threatened the obligations of professional conduct because, unlike lawyers, accountants had an obligation to audit clients and report their results to interested third parties. Thus, the professional obligations of the two professions clashed.

---

[33] Joined Cases C-115/97, C-116/97 and C-117/97 *Brentjens' Handelsonderneming BV* [1999] ECR I-6025, paras. 55–61.

[34] Advocate General Jacobs in this case (para. 193) had in fact acknowledged that the Court and Commission had in the past taken employment considerations into account in Article 81(3) (referring to Case 26/76 *Metro SB-Großmärkte GmbH & Co KG* v *Commission (No. 1)* [1977] ECR 1875, para. 43; Case 42/84 *Remia* [1985] ECR 2545, para. 42; *Synthetic Fibres* [1984] OJ L207/17, para. 37; and *Ford/Volkswagen* [1993] OJ L20/14, para. 23) while the Commission in its submissions insisted that such considerations were irrelevant in deciding on the application of the exemption.

Case C–309/99 *Wouters and Others* v *Algemene Raad van de Nederlandse Orde van Advocaten* [2002] ECR I-1577

105. The aim of the 1993 Regulation is therefore to ensure that, in the Member State concerned, the rules of professional conduct for members of the Bar are complied with, having regard to the prevailing perceptions of the profession in that State. The Bar of the Netherlands was entitled to consider that members of the Bar might no longer be in a position to advise and represent their clients independently and in the observance of strict professional secrecy if they belonged to an organisation which is also responsible for producing an account of the financial results of the transactions in respect of which their services were called upon and for certifying those accounts.

106. Moreover, the concurrent pursuit of the activities of statutory auditor and of adviser, in particular legal adviser, also raises questions within the accountancy profession itself ...

107. A regulation such as the 1993 Regulation could therefore reasonably be considered to be necessary in order to ensure the proper practice of the legal profession, as it is organised in the Member State concerned.

108. Furthermore, the fact that different rules may be applicable in another Member State does not mean that the rules in force in the former State are incompatible with Community law. Even if multi-disciplinary partnerships of lawyers and accountants are allowed in some Member States, the Bar of the Netherlands is entitled to consider that the objectives pursued by the 1993 Regulation cannot, having regard in particular to the legal regimes by which members of the Bar and accountants are respectively governed in the Netherlands, be attained by less restrictive means.

109. In light of those considerations, it does not appear that the effects restrictive of competition such as those resulting for members of the Bar practising in the Netherlands from a regulation such as the 1993 Regulation go beyond what is necessary in order to ensure the proper practice of the legal profession.

110. Having regard to all the foregoing considerations, the answer to be given to the second question must be that a national regulation such as the 1993 Regulation adopted by a body such as the Bar of the Netherlands does not infringe Article [101(1) TFEU], since that body could reasonably have considered that that regulation, despite the effects restrictive of competition that are inherent in it, is necessary for the proper practice of the legal profession, as organised in the Member State concerned.

The Court returned to consider the scope of application of competition law in a dispute that arose between two swimmers, on the one hand, and the International Olympic Committee (IOC) and international swimming federation (FINA), on the other. The swimmers were given a two-year ban because a drugs test revealed that they had taken a banned substance, nandrolone, but they considered the anti-doping rules were too strict and argued that the IOC's decision setting out the doping rules was restrictive of competition.

Case C–519/04 P *Meca Medina and Majcen* v *Commission* [2006] ECR I-6991

42. ... [T]he compatibility of rules with the Community rules on competition cannot be assessed in the abstract. Not every agreement between undertakings or every decision of an association of undertakings which restricts the freedom of action of the parties or of one of them necessarily falls within the prohibition laid down in Article [101(1) TFEU]. For the purposes of application of that provision to a

particular case, account must first of all be taken of the overall context in which the decision of the association of undertakings was taken or produces its effects and, more specifically, of its objectives. It has then to be considered whether the consequential effects restrictive of competition are inherent in the pursuit of those objectives and are proportionate to them.

43. As regards the overall context in which the rules at issue were adopted, the Commission could rightly take the view that the general objective of the rules was, as none of the parties disputes, to combat doping in order for competitive sport to be conducted fairly and that it included the need to safeguard equal chances for athletes, athletes' health, the integrity and objectivity of competitive sport and ethical values in sport.

44. In addition, given that penalties are necessary to ensure enforcement of the doping ban, their effect on athletes' freedom of action must be considered to be, in principle, inherent itself in the anti-doping rules.

45. Therefore, even if the anti-doping rules at issue are to be regarded as a decision of an association of undertakings limiting the appellants' freedom of action, they do not, for all that, necessarily constitute a restriction of competition incompatible with the common market, within the meaning of Article [101(1) TFEU], since they are justified by a legitimate objective. Such a limitation is inherent in the organisation and proper conduct of competitive sport and its very purpose is to ensure healthy rivalry between athletes. ...

47. It must be acknowledged that the penal nature of the anti-doping rules at issue and the magnitude of the penalties applicable if they are breached are capable of producing adverse effects on competition because they could, if penalties were ultimately to prove unjustified, result in an athlete's unwarranted exclusion from sporting events, and thus in impairment of the conditions under which the activity at issue is engaged in. It follows that, in order not to be covered by the prohibition laid down in Article [101(1) TFEU], the restrictions thus imposed by those rules must be limited to what is necessary to ensure the proper conduct of competitive sport.

48. Rules of that kind could indeed prove excessive by virtue of, first, the conditions laid down for establishing the dividing line between circumstances which amount to doping in respect of which penalties may be imposed and those which do not, and second, the severity of those penalties.

Applying this standard the Court concluded that banning nandrolone was justified and that banning athletes whose tests reveal a nandrolone content higher than 2 nanogrammes per millilitre of urine was a practice that did not go beyond that which was necessary to ensure that sporting events take place and function properly.[35]

These cases present a puzzle: how widely should they be construed? At its most restrictive, it may be said that these cases are about excluding ethical rules from the scope of competition law.[36] Alternatively, it has been suggested that these cases identify certain restrictions of competition that are ancillary to the main regulatory function of the body whose decision is being questioned.[37] A third, broader, interpretation is that these judgments exclude certain

---

[35] S. Weatherill, 'Anti-Doping Revisited: The Demise of the Rule of "Purely Sporting Interest"' (2006) *ECLR* 645; another example may be found in a decision of the New Zealand Commerce Commission, Decision 580 New Zealand Rugby Football Union Incorporated (2 July 2006) available at www.comcom.govt.nz. For comment, see R. Adhar, 'Professional Rugby, Competitive Balance and Competition Law' (2007) *ECLR* 36.

[36] E. Loozen, 'Professional Ethics and Restraints of Competition' (2006) 31 *ELRev.* 28.

[37] R. Whish, *Competition Law* (6th edn, Oxford, Oxford University Press, 2008) 126–32.

restrictive agreements when there are valid public policy reasons for so doing.[38] On the latter view, an agreement among pubs to eliminate 'happy hours' when alcohol is cheaper as a means of protecting public health might be justified. This wider interpretation draws legitimacy from the realities of self-regulation in modern society, when private bodies are often encouraged or even required to take the public interest into account when making commercial decisions. Further judicial refinement is required to establish the appropriate limits of this strand of case law, not least because it blurs the line between Article 101(1) and the exemption provision in Article 101(3).[39] However, the cases are problematic: on the one hand, the competition rules are a fundamental building block of the European Union's 'economic constitution' and should only be displaced exceptionally, by primary legislation, not by judges. On the other hand, recent revisions of the Treaty have widened the non-economic interests pursued by the Union (e.g. environmental protection and the protection of services of general interest) so that the judiciary plays a key role in balancing the relationship between competing values, and these judgments afford it the ability to balance competing objectives. To date, the case law has focused on Article 101, but there is nothing to prevent these principles from applying in cases falling under Article 102.

3 ARTICLE 101 TFEU: RESTRICTIVE PRACTICES

Article 101 TFEU

1. The following shall be prohibited as incompatible with the common market: all agreements between undertakings, decisions by associations of undertakings and concerted practices which may affect trade between Member States and which have as their object or effect the prevention, restriction or distortion of competition within the common market, and in particular those which:
   (a) directly or indirectly fix purchase or selling prices or any other trading conditions;
   (b) limit or control production, markets, technical development, or investment;
   (c) share markets or sources of supply;
   (d) apply dissimilar conditions to equivalent transactions with other trading parties, thereby placing them at a competitive disadvantage;
   (e) make the conclusion of contracts subject to acceptance by the other parties of supplementary obligations which, by their nature or according to commercial usage, have no connection with the subject of such contracts.
2. Any agreements or decisions prohibited pursuant to this article shall be automatically void.
3. The provisions of paragraph 1 may, however, be declared inapplicable in the case of:
   - any agreement or category of agreements between undertakings,
   - any decision or category of decisions by associations of undertakings,
   - any concerted practice or category of concerted practices,
   which contributes to improving the production or distribution of goods or to promoting technical or economic progress, while allowing consumers a fair share of the resulting benefit, and which does not:

---

[38] G. Monti, *EC Competition Law* (Cambridge, Cambridge University Press, 2007) 110–20.

[39] See A. P. Komninos, *Non-competition Concerns: Resolution of Conflicts in the Integrated Article 81*, EC Working Paper (L)08/05 (Oxford Centre for Competition Law & Policy), part IV, available at www.competition-law.ox.ac.uk/competition/portal.php; G. Monti, 'Article 81 EC and Public Policy' (2002) 39 *CMLRev.* 1057, 1086–90.

(a) impose on the undertakings concerned restrictions which are not indispensable to the attainment of these objectives;

(b) afford such undertakings the possibility of eliminating competition in respect of a substantial part of the products in question.

We provide a thumbnail sketch of this Article before considering it in more detail in the sections that follow. Paragraphs (1) and (3) should be read successively. Thus, while paragraph (1) declares that agreements which restrict competition are unlawful, this is subject to the exception in paragraph (3) which provides that anti-competitive agreements that yield certain benefits may be lawful. As we saw in Chapter 22, under Regulation 17/62/EEC only the Commission could decide whether an agreement could benefit from the exemption in Article 101(3).[40] After the coming into force of Regulation 1/2003/EC, Article 101(3) may be applied by national courts and national competition authorities.[41]

If an agreement restricts competition under paragraph (1) and is not exempted under paragraph (3) then, following paragraph (2), it is automatically void. Under EU law, agreements in breach of Article 101 are prohibited.[42] The Commission may require the undertakings to bring the infringement to an end,[43] and impose fines.[44] At national level, parties to a void agreement are unable to enforce the agreement in national courts[45] and may be sued for damages by parties who suffer harm as a result of anti-competitive practices.[46]

(i) Agreements, decisions and concerted practices

Three distinct types of cooperation fall under Article 101. An *agreement* represents a consensus between parties to act in a certain manner; it need not be inscribed in a binding contract,[47] and need not be in writing.[48] A *concerted practice* is a term used to catch forms of collusion that fall short of agreement, but where the parties substitute practical cooperation for the risks of competition, affecting the conditions of competition on the market.[49] An example is a situation where undertakings meet to exchange information about the prices they intend to charge and their sales volumes, information which makes coordination of behaviour likely because

---

[40] Regulation 17/62/EEC, First Regulation implementing Articles 81 and 82 of the Treaty, article 9(1), [1962] OJ Spec. edn, 204/62, 87.

[41] See Regulation 1/2003/EC on the implementation of the rules on competition laid down in Articles 81 and 82 of the Treaty, recital 4 and articles 1, 5, and 6 [2003] OJ L1/1.

[42] *Ibid.* article 1.

[43] *Ibid.* article 7.

[44] *Ibid.* article 23(2).

[45] Case C-126/97 *Eco Swiss China Time Ltd* v *Benetton* [1999] ECR I-3055, a precedent which allows a party in breach to avoid paying damages where the agreement is held to infringe Article 101 TFEU (the so-called 'Euro-defence'). See R. Whish, *Competition Law* (5th edn, London, Lexis Nexis Butterworths, 2003) 286–304.

[46] Case C-453/99 *Courage Ltd* v *Crehan* [2001] ECR I-6297.

[47] See the 'gentlemen's agreement' in Joined Cases 41/69, 44/69 and 45/69 *ACF Chemiefarma NV* v *Commission* [1970] ECR 661.

[48] *Polypropylene* [1986] OJ L230/1, para. 81.

[49] The seminal authorities defining concerted practices are Joined Cases 48/69–57/69 *ICI* v *Commission* (*Dyestuffs*) [1972] ECR 619, para. 64; Joined Cases 40–48, 50, 54–56, 111, 113 and 114/73 *Coöperatiëve Vereniging 'Suiker Unie' UA* v *Commission* [1975] ECR 1663.

after the meeting each player takes into consideration what others have disclosed when planning their strategy. There is no agreement because specific conduct has not been determined, but the post-market behaviour of each is influenced by the information received and it is likely that prices are higher and output less than if each had determined their business conduct independently. Often, cartels operate over a long period of time and are sustained by a mixture of agreements and concerted practices, whereby targets are agreed upon and then regular meetings are held where key information is disclosed to 'oil' the operation of the agreement. For example, in the polypropylene cartel investigated by the Commission, there was a period during which no definite agreement on the sales quotas for each party had been reached, but the sales of each cartel member were reported and monitored, facilitating coordination.[50] Thus, concerted practices differ in form from agreements because of their intensity, but both are collusive devices having the same effect: coordinating the behaviour of the participants.

A trade association is designed to protect the interests of its members. A *decision* by an association is a provision in the rules of a trade association or a decision reached by a trade association, which affects the members. For example, the Law Society of a Member State may decide to fix the remuneration for lawyers, or an agricultural association may coordinate prices on behalf of its members.[51] In appropriate circumstances, a non-binding recommendation (for example, on prices to be charged by members of the association) may also constitute a decision where it is likely to affect members' pricing determinations.[52]

(a) Cartels

There are four conditions for a successful cartel: the major suppliers of the product in question take part; they agree on how to coordinate their behaviour (for example, by agreeing upon how to set prices or allocating geographical markets to each other); there is a mechanism to detect and punish cartel members who 'cheat' by cutting prices below the cartel price; there are high entry barriers to prevent competitors entering the market thereby reducing the cartel's profitability.[53] With these factors present, the cartel is able to behave like a monopoly, reducing output and increasing prices. There is evidence that some cartels have broken down because parties were unable to agree or coordinate behaviour,[54] but when there is a high level of trust among members, cartels can last for a considerable length of time. As we saw in Chapter 22, EU competition law creates an additional source of instability for cartels: leniency programmes give incentives for cartel members to expose the existence of a cartel as a way of escaping the Commission's significant penalties.[55] Cartel-busting is a core activity for the Commission and the Union courts have facilitated this task in two ways: first, by setting out wide definitions of the terms 'agreement' and 'concerted practice'; secondly, by allowing the Commission to consider the pattern of collusion by several undertakings over a period of time as being a single infringement characterised in part by agreements and partly by concerted practices.

---

[50] *Polypropylene* [1986] OJ L230/1, para. 87.

[51] See e.g. Case C-309/99 *Wouters and Others v Algemene Raad van de Nederlandse Orde van Advocaten* [2002] ECR I-1577; Case C-250/92 *Gøttrup-Klim and Others Grovvareforeninger v Dansk Landbrugs Grovvareselskab AmbA* [1994] ECR I-5641.

[52] *Fenex* [1996] OJ L181/28, paras. 32–42.

[53] On the economics of cartels, see M. Motta, *Competition Policy* (Cambridge, Cambridge University Press, 2004) ch. 4.

[54] See e.g. *Zinc Producer Group* [1984] OJ L220/27 for a partial breakdown, and D. T. Armentano, *Antitrust and Monopoly: Anatomy of a Policy Failure* (New York, John Wiley and Sons, 1982) ch. 5.

[55] See Chapter 21.

The Court of Justice consolidated these methods in a series of judgments resulting from the polypropylene cartel Decision where the Commission found that several undertakings active in the European petrochemical industry had participated in a cartel between 1977 and 1983. The parties had set up a system of target prices and devised a system to limit output to share the market according to agreed quotas. One cartel member, Anic, held a market share between 2.7 and 4.2 per cent and was fined 750,000 ecu. The Commission appealed against the decision to the General Court, which annulled the Commission's Decision in part, on the basis that the Commission had failed to establish the correct duration of Anic's involvement in the cartel and had reduced the fine accordingly. Anic cross-appealed seeking further reduction or an annulment of the Decision in its entirety, inter alia, on the basis that the Commission had failed to characterise the infringement either as an agreement or as a concerted practice. In affirming the General Court's Decision, the Court established several important criteria for identifying agreements and concerted practices. These principles have continued to inform the Commission's cartel enforcement strategy since then.

Case C–49/92 Commission v Anic Partecipazioni SpA [1999] ECR I–4125

108. The list in Article [101(1) TFEU] is intended to apply to all collusion between undertakings, whatever the form it takes. There is continuity between the cases listed. The only essential thing is the distinction between independent conduct, which is allowed, and collusion, which is not, regardless of any distinction between types of collusion. Anic's argument would break down the unity and generality of the prohibited phenomenon and would remove from the ambit of the prohibition, without any reason, certain types of collusion which are no less dangerous than others. ...

109. The Court observes first of all that ... the [General Court] held that the Commission was entitled to categorise as agreements certain types of conduct on the part of the undertakings concerned, and, in the alternative, as concerted practices certain other forms of conduct on the part of the same undertakings. The [General Court] held that Anic had taken part in an integrated set of schemes constituting a single infringement which progressively manifested itself in both unlawful agreements and unlawful concerted practices. ...

112. Secondly, it must be observed that, if Article [101 TFEU] distinguishes between 'concerted practices', 'agreements between undertakings' and 'decisions by associations of undertakings', the aim is to have the prohibitions of that article catch different forms of coordination and collusion between undertakings.

113. It does not, however, follow that patterns of conduct having the same anti-competitive object, each of which, taken in isolation, would fall within the meaning of 'agreement', 'concerted practice' or 'a decision by an association of undertakings', cannot constitute different manifestations of a single infringement of Article [101(1) TFEU].

114. The [General Court] was therefore entitled to consider that patterns of conduct by several undertakings were a manifestation of a single infringement, corresponding partly to an agreement and partly to a concerted practice.

115. Thirdly, it must be borne in mind that a concerted practice, within the meaning of Article [101(1) TFEU], refers to a form of coordination between undertakings which, without having been taken to a stage where an agreement properly so called has been concluded, knowingly substitutes for the risks of competition practical cooperation between them.

116. The Court of Justice has further explained that criteria of coordination and cooperation must be understood in the light of the concept inherent in the provisions of the Treaty relating to competition, according to which each economic operator must determine independently the policy which he intends to adopt on the market.

117. According to that case law, although that requirement of independence does not deprive economic operators of the right to adapt themselves intelligently to the existing and anticipated conduct of their competitors, it does however strictly preclude any direct or indirect contact between such operators, the object or effect whereof is either to influence the conduct on the market of an actual or potential competitor or to disclose to such a competitor the course of conduct which they themselves have decided to adopt or contemplate adopting on the market, where the object or effect of such contact is to create conditions of competition which do not correspond to the normal conditions of the market in question, regard being had to the nature of the products or services offered, the size and number of the undertakings and the volume of the said market.

118. It follows that, as is clear from the very terms of Article [101(1) TFEU], a concerted practice implies, besides undertakings' concerting together, conduct on the market pursuant to those collusive practices, and a relationship of cause and effect between the two.

119. The [General Court] therefore committed an error of law in relation to the interpretation of the concept of concerted practice in holding that the undertakings' collusive practices had necessarily had an effect on the conduct of the undertakings which participated in them.

120. It does not, however, follow that the cross-appeal should be upheld. As the Court of Justice has repeatedly held, if the grounds of a judgment of the [General Court] reveal an infringement of Community law but the operative part appears well founded on other legal grounds, the appeal must be dismissed.

121. For one thing, subject to proof to the contrary, which it is for the economic operators concerned to adduce, there must be a presumption that the undertakings participating in concerted arrangements and remaining active on the market take account of the information exchanged with their competitors when determining their conduct on that market, particularly when they concert together on a regular basis over a long period, as was the case here, according to the findings of the [General Court].

122. For another, a concerted practice, as defined above, falls under Article [101(1) TFEU] even in the absence of anti-competitive effects on the market.

123. First, it follows from the actual text of Article [101(1) TFEU] that, as in the case of agreements between undertakings and decisions by associations of undertakings, concerted practices are prohibited, regardless of their effect, when they have an anti-competitive object.

124. Next, although the concept of a concerted practice presupposes conduct of the participating undertakings on the market, it does not necessarily imply that that conduct should produce the concrete effect of restricting, preventing or distorting competition.

125. Lastly, that interpretation is not incompatible with the restrictive nature of the prohibition laid down in Article [101(1) TFEU] since, far from extending its scope, it corresponds to the literal meaning of the terms used in that provision.

126. The [General Court] therefore rightly held, despite faulty legal reasoning, that, since the Commission had established to the requisite legal standard that Anic had participated in collusion for the purpose of restricting competition, it did not have to adduce evidence that the collusion had manifested itself in conduct on the market. ...

130. Fourthly, it is clear from the settled case law of the Court of Justice that an agreement within the meaning of Article [101(1) TFEU] arises from an expression, by the participating undertakings, of their joint intention to conduct themselves on the market in a specific way.

131. A comparison between that definition of agreement and the definition of a concerted practice shows that, from the subjective point of view, they are intended to catch forms of collusion having the same nature and are only distinguishable from each other by their intensity and the forms in which they manifest themselves.

132. It follows that, whilst the concepts of an agreement and of a concerted practice have particularly different elements, they are not mutually incompatible. Contrary to Anic's allegations, the [General Court] did not therefore have to require the Commission to categorise either as an agreement or as a concerted practice each form of conduct found but was right to hold that the Commission had been entitled to characterise some of those forms of conduct as principally 'agreements' and others as 'concerted practices'.

133. Fifthly, it must be pointed out that this interpretation is not incompatible with the restrictive nature of the prohibition laid down in Article [101(1) TFEU]. Far from creating a new form of infringement, the arrival at that interpretation merely entails acceptance of the fact that, in the case of an infringement involving different forms of conduct, these may meet different definitions whilst being caught by the same provision and being all equally prohibited.

134. Sixthly, it must be observed that, contrary to Anic's allegations, such an interpretation does not have an unacceptable effect on the question of proof and does not infringe the rights of defence of the undertakings concerned.

135. On the one hand, the Commission must still establish that each form of conduct found falls under the prohibition laid down in Article [101(1) TFEU] as an agreement, a concerted practice or a decision by an association of undertakings.

136. On the other hand, the undertakings charged with having participated in the infringement have the opportunity of disputing, for each form of conduct, the characterisation or the characterisations applied by the Commission by contending that the Commission has not adduced proof of the constituent elements of the various forms of infringement alleged.

These passages consolidate the definitions of agreement and concerted practice. The Court of Justice eases the Commission's burden of proof significantly in the context of concerted practices by holding that it can presume that a concerted practice has been implemented, and there is no need to prove anti-competitive effects resulting from the concerted practice. Moreover, several important consequences materialise as a result of the ruling that collusion constitutes a single infringement. The first is that the Commission is allowed to escape the limitation period of five years, which runs from the day when the infringement ceases.[56] Had each bout of collusion constituted a separate infringement, all acts would not have been punished and the deterrence value of competition law would have been dented. The second consequence is that the Commission's evidentiary burden is lightened significantly by not having to define each element of coordination as an agreement or a concerted practice. However, as the passages above make clear, the Commission must establish evidence of each instance of collusion and must allow the undertaking to respond and dispute the Commission's finding. The third consequence is that by characterising the infringement as a single conspiracy, a participant is responsible for all of the cartel's actions, even if it did not take part in all of them. This means that a cartel

[56] Regulation 1/2003, article 25(1).

is a 'conspiracy' by its members, and as a result even those with small market shares, whose participation is limited, contribute to the overall conspiracy.[57] Even Anic, with a small market share, contributed to the conspiracy. However, the Commission must prove that the undertaking intended to contribute to the common objectives pursued by all participants and that it was aware of the conduct planned by them or that it could have foreseen such conduct.[58]

These principles should not be taken to mean that an undertaking can never escape liability when it is involved in a long-running cartel but does not participate in all the cartel's actions. Recently the General Court in *BASF* had an opportunity to give guidance on how to apply Article 101 to long-running cartels. This concerned collusion in the market for chlorine chloride: a global cartel to fix prices and allocate territories between 1992 and 1994, and a European cartel designed to continue the global cartel between 1994 and 1998. The Commission's Decision treated the two parts of the cartel as a single infringement because if the two were separate agreements then the global cartel would not have been caught, as it had ended five years before the investigation started and fell outside the limitation period. As a result, the parties' fines would have been reduced. On appeal, the parties questioned the Commission's characterisation of the two agreements as a single infringement and the General Court found that while the global agreement involved North American manufacturers and was designed to divide the US and European markets, the European agreement did not involve the North American firms and was designed to divide the European market. Nor was there any evidence that the effect of the global agreement continued beyond the date when it had formally ceased.[58a] Accordingly, there had been two separate infringements.

Julian Joshua, 'Single Continuous Infringement of Article 81 EC: Has the Commission Stretched the Concept Beyond the Limit of Its Logic?' (2009) 5(2) *European Competition Journal* **451, 471–2**

The [General Court] concluded that, to establish a single violation, (i) there had to be a common plan or economic aim and (ii) the arrangements had to be 'complementary', in the sense of interacting to realise the intended set of anti-competitive effects within the framework of a single objective. For the Court, the European and global infringements were each continuous infringements on their own. To justify combining them into one, account had to be taken of all the circumstances, such as period of application, the content and methodology of the agreements and, 'correlatively', their objective. In the [General Court]'s judgment, the Commission had failed to demonstrate sufficient interdependence between the global and the later EU cartel: the Europeans had not adhered to the global arrangement in order to divide up the EEA market, the control methods were dissimilar and they only began to allocate the European market amongst themselves after the global arrangement had failed. ... Durable as the single infringement concept has proved, it was certainly never intended as a slogan to substitute for robust legal or factual assessment. Nor, without more detailed analysis, is it determinative of the issue of whether a given course of conduct constitutes a single conspiracy or multiple conspiracies. But if

---

[57] The treatment of cartel members is analogous to that of members of a criminal conspiracy: see e.g. UK Criminal Law Act 1977, s. 1(1) (as amended by the Criminal Attempts Act 1981) and *R v Anderson* [1986] AC 27. See e.g. Case T-23/99 *LR AF 1998 A/S v Commission* [2002] ECR II-1705, where an infringement was found even though the undertaking took no active role.

[58] Case C-49/92 *Commission v Anic Partecipazioni SpA* [1999] ECR I-4125, paras. 87 and 203–7.

[58a] Joined Cases T-101/05 and T-111/05 *BASF AG v Commission* [2007] ECR II-4949.

the distinction between a single and many conspiracies is clear enough conceptually, its empirical application is beset with difficulty. Overturning the decision on the facts, the Court basically confirmed the generic 'totality of the evidence' approach of the previous case law. Although the CFI has made it clear in *BASF* that meeting the interdependency requirement is not going to be a walkover for the Commission, it would be helpful to have some workable guidance. The assessment is an empirical one, but it should not be left to the Commission's discretion how to treat a given set of facts. An objective rule would free the Commission from suspicion that the approach it takes is driven by the desired outcome.

In sum, the policy behind the Court's case law is to send a message to parties to a cartel that once they agree to conspire against the interests of the Community, they will be held responsible for the entirety of the conduct to which they have assented. The aim is to maximise the deterrence of competition law. The only way out for an undertaking is either to make a leniency application confessing the presence of the agreement, or to publicly distance itself from what has been agreed, but then risk retaliation from the undertakings. The sole consolation for a minor participant is that the fact that it has not taken part in all aspects of an anticompetitive agreement, or that it played a minor role, will be taken into consideration when calculating the fine.[59]

So far we have considered the definition of agreements and concerted practices. It is also important to bear in mind the evidence that may be used to establish the existence of cooperation. In the majority of cases, the Commission obtains hard evidence in the form of memos or recordings of conversations that prove collusion. However, collusion can be established by inference from the conduct of the parties. The Court approved of this method early on,[60] and the limits upon the use of indirect evidence were set out in the *Wood Pulp* case.[61] The Commission decided that forty producers of wood pulp had colluded to fix prices between 1975 and 1981. For some aspects of the cartel, collusion was proven by documentary evidence of the undertakings' membership of certain trade associations, but for some, no documentary evidence supported a finding of collusion. The Court ruled that in principle a cartel could be inferred from the way undertakings behave only if their common behaviour has no other explanation than that the parties must have come to an agreement to behave in that way. However, on the facts, the Court refused to infer that the parties had colluded. Relying on a report carried out by two court-appointed experts, the Court found that the parallel behaviour by the undertakings could be explained by reasons other than a pre-existing agreement to align their commercial strategies. Since *Wood Pulp*, the Commission has not used economic evidence to infer the existence of an agreement, but has relied upon tangible evidence seized during searches of the cartel members' premises. While documents are hard to find, it is preferable for the Commission to bring a case based on hard evidence rather than having to argue that it can infer an agreement

---

[59] *Ibid.* para. 90.

[60] Joined Cases 48/69–57/69 *ICI v Commission (Dyestuffs)* [1972] ECR 619: while the Commission's Decision was also based on concrete evidence of collusion the Court focused solely on the circumstances of the market. See also Case 172/80 *Züchner v Bayerische Vereinsbank* [1981] ECR 2021.

[61] Joined Cases C-89/85, C-104/85, C-114/85, C-116/85, C-117/85 and C-125/85–C-129/85 *A. Ahlström Osakeyhtiö and Others v Commission (Wood Pulp)* [1993] ECR I-1307, paras. 70–2. A. Jones, 'Woodpulp: Concerted Practice and/or Conscious Parallelism?' (1993) *ECLR* 273.

from the way parties behave on the market. This is because it would have to show that the parallel behaviour has no other explanation except prior collusion, and alternative plausible reasons for parallel behaviour can often be found.

(b) Distinguishing between agreement and unilateral action

A key aim of EU competition law has been market integration. The paradigmatic example of how this is implemented is the early decision in *Consten and Grundig*. Grundig wished to distribute its electric goods in France and appointed Consten as exclusive distributor for that territory and took steps to guarantee that no other wholesaler was able to sell into France. An economist would justify Grundig's actions on the basis of the free-rider rationale: Consten's isolation gives it an incentive to market the goods aggressively knowing that it can recoup the promotional costs, as free-riders (who would wait for Consten to promote the goods and then sell them in France at prices lower than those which Consten would set, since they would not have to recover any promotional costs) could be kept out. Moreover, the distribution system could have enhanced inter-brand competition (that is, competition between Grundig's electronic goods and those of other brands). However, neither the Commission nor the Court accepted this argument, considering it more important that parallel imports (i.e. goods flowing from one state to another) should be allowed.

> ### Joined Cases 54/64 and 58/64 *Consten and Grundig v Commission* [1966] ECR 299, 340
>
> An agreement between producer and distributor which might tend to restore the national divisions in trade between Member States might be such as to frustrate the most fundamental [objectives] of the Community. The Treaty, whose preamble and content aim at abolishing the barriers between States, and which in several provisions gives evidence of a stern attitude with regard to their reappearance, could not allow undertakings to reconstruct such barriers. Article [101(1) TFEU] is designed to pursue this aim, even in the case of agreements between undertakings placed at different levels of the distribution process.

The Court emphatically rejected the applicants' arguments that the economics of the free-rider were relevant, in stark contrast to the US courts, which have embraced the free-rider rationale.[62] Gyselen explains and critiques the EU position.

> ### Luc Gyselen, 'Vertical Restraints in the Distribution Process: Strength and Weakness of the Free Rider Rationale under EEC Competition Law' (1984) *Common Market Law Review* 646, 666–7
>
> The free rider rationale is for EEC competition lawyers certainly the most intriguing one among the available defences of vertical restraints because it is conceptually antithetical to the parallel importer rationale, which has dominated the assessment of the restraints on competition in a distribution network ever since *Grundig Consten*. Parallel imports may indeed give rise to free rides from one

---

[62] *Continental TV v GTE Sylvania*, 433 US 36, 54–5 (1977).

exporting dealer to the promotional or servicing efforts of one local dealer. In the EEC Commission's eyes, however, the free rider is a hero because his sales foster the free movement of the brand within the common market and thus contribute to market integration. Consequently, restraints which limit his room for manoeuvre are subject to close scrutiny and will often fail to qualify for an exemption under Art [101(3) TFEU]. Ever more frequently the Commission is urged to alleviate its sacred parallel importer rationale and to give appropriate weight to the free rider rationale. ...

One could argue that the Commission should not be so much concerned with the free movement of one brand but rather with the free movement of all branded goods constituting one relevant market. Does not the establishment of a Common Market also, and in particular, mean more intense interbrand competition on the larger scale of ten [now twenty-five] composite territories, even at the price of reduced transfrontier traffic of the individual brands which are launched on the Common Market?

The Commission's interference with a brand's price levels in the distinct national markets, out of a concern for price harmonisation, has also been criticised as being *ultra vires*. The Commission is said to seek the achievement of so-called 'positive' integration goals ... by means of 'negative' integration instruments. This raises the quasi-constitutional question whether antitrust promotion of parallel imports, which aims at evening out price differentials, amounts to undue pre-emption of sovereign national powers in the price policy area.

If one were to discount the single market concerns, an economic appraisal would suggest that while there are some risks from vertical restraints, these tend to arise when the manufacturer or distributor has market power. The risk of retailers providing unnecessary pre-sale services only arises if the consumer has little choice (if one manufacturer were to offer too many services at a high price, a competitor might sell its goods with a more basic sales service outlet at a lower price); tacit collusion requires an oligopoly market, and foreclosure can only arise if the manufacturer ties up a large number of distribution outlets. This suggests that an economically sensible policy would be to treat vertical restraints as lawful except where market power suggests that consumers may suffer harm, and in case of market power, balance the pro- and anti-competitive risks posed by the agreement.

However, in line with its desire to promote parallel trade, the Commission has often interpreted the concept of agreement widely to catch commercial arrangements that segment markets. We can distinguish between two strands in the case law.

In the first, manufacturers sent notices to their distributors exhorting them not to export,[63] or printing the words 'export prohibited' on invoices.[64] These requests were not part of the distribution contract and the parties argued they were unilateral requests. However, it was held that these tactics constitute export bans that are part of the agreement between manufacturers and distributors and which were tacitly accepted by the distributor

---

[63] See e.g. Joined Cases 32/78 and 36/78–82/78 *BWM Belgium v Commission* [1979] ECR 2435; *Bayo-n-ox* [1990] OJ L21/71; *Volkswagen* [1998] OJ L124/60, affirmed by the General Court, Case T-62/98 *Volkswagen AG v Commission* [2000] ECR II-2707 and Court of Justice, Case C-338/00 P *Volkswagen AG v Commission* [2003] ECR I-9189.

[64] *Sandoz Prodotti Farmaceutici SpA* [1987] OJ L222/28, paras. 25–6, upheld in Case 227/87 *Sandoz v Commission* [1990] ECR I-45. See also *Tipp-Ex* [1987] OJ L222/1, upheld in Case 279/87 *Tipp-Ex v Commission* [1990] ECR 261 and J. E. Thompson, 'Case note on *Sandoz* and *Tipp-Ex*' (1990) 27 *CMLRev.* 589.

continuing to buy goods from the manufacturer.[65] This case law has been criticised in that payment of an invoice does not necessarily represent an agreement by the distributor, but the Court 'glosses over' such technicalities to apply Article 101 to secure an integrated market.[66]

The second set of cases is well illustrated by *Ford v Commission*.[67] Ford originally supplied both right- and left-hand drive cars to its German distributors; then, in an effort to prevent British purchasers from importing lower priced cars from Germany into the United Kingdom, it ceased to supply right-hand drive cars in Germany. Ford insisted that the fact that it ceased selling right-hand drive cars in Germany was merely a unilateral act on its part, but the Court held that the decision to withdraw right-hand drive cars was part of the contractual relations between Ford and its dealers. Thus, to be admitted into the Ford network in Germany a dealer would be required to accept Ford's policy, including its policy on preventing parallel imports.[68] The ruling in *Ford* may be criticised in that the dealers in Germany objected to the decision, but continued their commercial relations with Ford because it would have been commercially impossible to terminate the contract with Ford given the vast sums expended in developing the dealer network.[69] In these circumstances, it seems inappropriate to speak of an agreement between Ford and its dealers.[70]

In the first type of case, the Court read the manufacturer's action as a demand for a particular line of conduct by the distributors, while in the second, it interpreted the distribution network as a whole and found that the measures designed to prevent parallel trade were part of the agreement. In both, the Commission stretched the meaning of agreement to prevent restrictions on parallel trade. However, the limits of the Commission's ability to stretch the scope of Article 101 were limited by the Court's *Bayer* judgment. Bayer AG is the parent company of one of the main European chemical and pharmaceutical groups. It manufactured a drug to treat cardio-vascular disease (Adalat), sold by its wholly owned subsidiaries in the Member States. National health authorities fix the price of medicines and at the time of the dispute the price fixed by the Spanish and French health authorities was 40 per cent lower than the prices in the United Kingdom. As a result, wholesalers in Spain and France exported Adalat to the United Kingdom, causing considerable losses for Bayer UK. In response, the Bayer group changed its delivery policy, ceasing to fulfil all the large orders placed by wholesalers in Spain and France. The Commission ruled that Bayer France and Bayer Spain had made an agreement with the wholesalers in France and Spain providing for an export ban. Bayer disputed this, acknowledging that it had embarked on a policy to restrict sales from Spain and France to the United Kingdom, but denying that this policy was implemented by any agreement with the wholesalers. The Court agreed with Bayer.

---

[65] See e.g. *Konica* [1988] OJ L78/34, paras. 34–6.

[66] J. Shaw, 'The Concept of an Agreement in Article 85 EEC' (1991) *ELRev*. 262.

[67] Joined Cases 25/84 and 26/84 *Ford v Commission* [1985] ECR 2725; see also Case 107/82 *AEG Telefunken* v *Commission* [1983] ECR 3135 and *Tipp-Ex* [1987] OJ L222/1.

[68] Joined Cases 25/84 and 26/84 *Ford v Commission* [1985] ECR 2725, para. 21.

[69] P. Jakobsen and M. Broberg, 'The Concept of Agreement in Article 81 EC: On the Manufacturers' Right to Prevent Parallel Trade within the European Community' (2002) 23 *ECLR* 128, 130.

[70] C. Brown, '*Bayer* v *Commission*, the ECJ Agrees' (2004) 25 *ECLR* 388, arguing that after *Bayer*, the correctness of *Ford* can be questioned.

Joined Cases C–2/01 P and C–3/01 P *Bundesverband der Arzneimittel-Importeure eV and Commission* v *Bayer* [2004] 4 CMLR 13

97.   ... the [General Court] set out from the principle that the concept of an agreement within the meaning of Article [101(1) TFEU] centres around the existence of a concurrence of wills between at least two parties, the form in which it is manifested being unimportant so long as it constitutes the faithful expression of the parties' intention. The Court further recalled ... that for there to be an agreement within the meaning of Article [101(1) TFEU] it is sufficient that the undertakings in question should have expressed their common intention to conduct themselves on the market in a specific way.

98.   Since, however, the question arising in this case is whether a measure adopted or imposed apparently unilaterally by a manufacturer in the context of the continuous relations which it maintains with its wholesalers constitutes an agreement within the meaning of Article [101(1) TFEU], the [General Court] examined the Commission's arguments ... to the effect that Bayer infringed that article by imposing an export ban as part of the ... continuous commercial relations [of Bayer France and Bayer Spain] with their customers, and that the wholesalers' subsequent conduct reflected an implicit acquiescence in that ban. ...

100. Concerning the appellants' arguments that the [General Court] should have acknowledged that the manifestation of Bayer's intention to restrict parallel imports could constitute the basis of an agreement prohibited by Article [101(1) TFEU], it is true that the existence of an agreement within the meaning of that provision can be deduced from the conduct of the parties concerned.

101. However, such an agreement cannot be based on what is only the expression of a unilateral policy of one of the contracting parties, which can be put into effect without the assistance of others. To hold that an agreement prohibited by Article [101(1) TFEU] may be established simply on the basis of the expression of a unilateral policy aimed at preventing parallel imports would have the effect of confusing the scope of that provision with that of Article [102 TFEU].

102. For an agreement within the meaning of Article [101(1) TFEU] to be capable of being regarded as having been concluded by tacit acceptance, it is necessary that the manifestation of the wish of one of the contracting parties to achieve an anti-competitive goal constitute an invitation to the other party, whether express or implied, to fulfil that goal jointly, and that applies all the more where, as in this case, such an agreement is not at first sight in the interests of the other party, namely the wholesalers.

103. Therefore, the [General Court] was right to examine whether Bayer's conduct supported the conclusion that the latter had required of the wholesalers, as a condition of their future contractual relations, that they should comply with its new commercial policy.

The Commission's approach in these cases characterises the most unusual feature of EU competition law: the way the Commission uses it as a tool to sustain the single market. Parallel imports lead to lower prices throughout the Community and create incentives for manufacturers to harmonise prices. However, price uniformity in a diverse Union is a dangerous aspiration, as the purchasing power of a person resident in the United Kingdom or Germany is likely to be higher than that of a person in Poland or Portugal. If price homogeneity leads to a convergence towards the average price, goods in poorer countries will become unaffordable.[71] The *Bayer* judgment is significant because while in the past the Court had supported the increasingly wide meaning that the Commission gave to the notion of 'agreement', it has now said that enough

---

[71] B. Bishop, 'Price Discrimination under Article 86: Political Economy in the European Court' (1981) 44 *MLR* 282.

is enough and retreated from a teleological approach to a formalist, literal interpretation of the meaning of 'agreement'. The Court is willing to widen the meaning of Treaty Articles, but not to breaking point. It is also part of a pattern in the relationship between the Commission and the Court of Justice: while in the early years, the Court supported the Commission's bold interpretations, more recently, in particular since the creation of the General Court, both courts have interpreted the Treaty more literally and subjected the Commission to stricter review.[72]

(ii) Object or effect the restriction, distortion or prevention of competition

(a) Background to the controversy

The case law on parallel trade in pharmaceuticals is also useful in examining the Court of Justice's stance on what agreements harm competition. In *GlaxoSmithKline* ('GSK') we find a clear divergence between the General Court and the Court of Justice on this key question. The dispute arose when GSK, a producer of pharmaceuticals, inserted a clause in its contracts with Spanish wholesalers to ensure that they did not export the medicines to other Member States. The commercial rationale for GSK's practice is that medicines are bought by national health authorities and these buy medicines at different prices: in some, like Spain, the price is low because the government wants to guarantee availability of medicines, while in the United Kingdom, the price is higher because the government wishes to reward pharmaceutical firms and encourage future innovation. Given low transport costs, there is a clear incentive for wholesalers in Spain to export to the United Kingdom, and an obvious interest in GSK to prevent these exports because they harm profits in the UK market. The Commission found the agreement had as its object the restriction of competition, a result which was to be expected given that the agreement served to partition the internal market.[73] From an economic perspective, the parallel trader does not bring any benefits to consumers. In fact, by reducing the revenue to the pharmaceutical companies, their research and development strategies are hindered. On this basis, the Commission's policy harms the development of new drugs.[74] On appeal, the General Court ruled that the prevention of parallel trade was not sufficient to find a restriction of competition.

Case T-168/01 *GlaxoSmithKline Services Unlimited v Commission* [2006] ECR II-2969

118. In effect, the objective assigned to Article [101(1) TFEU], which constitutes a fundamental provision indispensable for the achievement of the missions entrusted to the Community, in particular for the functioning of the internal market, is to prevent undertakings, by restricting competition between themselves or with third parties, from reducing the welfare of the final consumer of the products in question. At the hearing, in fact, the Commission emphasised on a number of occasions that it was

---

[72] Case T-77/92 *Parker Pen v Commission* [1994] ECR II-549 is another illustration of the General Court refusing to adopt an expansive interpretation of the reach of competition law, and after *Bayer* the Court quashed another decision that took too expansive a view of the notion of agreement, Case T-208/01 *Volkswagen AG v Commission* [2003] ECR II-5141. See generally A. Arnull, *The European Union and its Court of Justice* (Oxford, Oxford University Press, 1999).

[73] *Glaxo Wellcome* [2001] OJ L302/1.

[74] For greater detail see P. Rey and J. S. Venit, 'Parallel Trade and Pharmaceuticals: A Policy in Search of Itself' (2004) 29 *ELRev.* 176.

from that perspective that it had carried out its examination in the present case, initially concluding that the General Sales Conditions clearly restricted the welfare of consumers, then considering whether that restriction would be offset by increased efficiency which would itself benefit consumers.

119. Consequently, the application of Article [101(1) TFEU] to the present case cannot depend solely on the fact that the agreement in question is intended to limit parallel trade in medicines or to partition the common market, which leads to the conclusion that it affects trade between Member States, but also requires an analysis designed to determine whether it has as its object or effect the prevention, restriction or distortion of competition on the relevant market, to the detriment of the final consumer ...[T]hat analysis, which may be abridged when the clauses of the agreement reveal in themselves the existence of an alteration of competition, as the Commission observed at the hearing, must, on the other hand, be supplemented, depending on the requirements of the case, where that is not so. ...

121. While it has been accepted since then that parallel trade must be given a certain protection, it is therefore not as such but, as the Court of Justice held, insofar as it favours the development of trade, on the one hand, and the strengthening of competition, on the other hand, that is to say, in this second respect, insofar as it gives final consumers the advantages of effective competition in terms of supply or price. Consequently, while it is accepted that an agreement intended to limit parallel trade must in principle be considered to have as its object the restriction of competition, that applies insofar as the agreement may be presumed to deprive final consumers of those advantages.

However, on appeal, the Court of Justice returned to the position it took in *Consten and Grundig* (which we discussed above). The Court ruled that nothing in the case law or in the text of Article 101 supported its position.

Joined Cases C–501/06 P, C–513/06 P, C–515/06 P and C–519/06 P *GlaxoSmithKline Services Unlimited* v *Commission*, Judgment of 6 October 2009

63. First of all, there is nothing in that provision to indicate that only those agreements which deprive consumers of certain advantages may have an anti-competitive object. Secondly, it must be borne in mind that the Court has held that, like other competition rules laid down in the Treaty, Article [101 TFEU] aims to protect not only the interests of competitors or of consumers, but also the structure of the market and, in so doing, competition as such. Consequently, for a finding that an agreement has an anti-competitive object, it is not necessary that final consumers be deprived of the advantages of effective competition in terms of supply or price.

64. It follows that, by requiring proof that the agreement entails disadvantages for final consumers as a prerequisite for a finding of anti-competitive object and by not finding that that agreement had such an object, the General Court committed an error of law.

The debate between the two courts is illustrative of the current controversy over the standard by which one assesses the anti-competitive nature of agreements. According to the General Court, a consumer welfare standard is preferred. This is in line with the Commission's current policy as well. In contrast, the Court of Justice's position reflects a different understanding of competition. The Court's statement that one is engaged in protecting 'competition as such' is opaque and leads to two competing interpretations. On the one hand, it may be that the Court is using Article 101(1) to safeguard the economic freedom of market participants.[75] On the other hand, the Court may have taken the view that when the competitive process is stifled, this is likely to have harmful effects on economic welfare. From this perspective, the difference between the two courts is not one of perspective, but of method: the General Court wishes to see proof of the likely economic impact of the agreement, while the Court of Justice considers that predicting the future in such a deterministic way is risky, and prefers to base its analysis on the premise that action that restricts economic freedom is likely to reduce efficiency.

This debate between the Union courts has important practical implications: having to establish that a practice is likely to cause harm to consumer welfare raises the amount of evidence needed by the Commission to establish an infringement, because it is not enough for the Commission to show that the agreement hampers the free movement of goods, or stifles the economic activities of one of the parties.

(b) Agreements restrictive of competition by object

Once we have determined that there is an agreement to which Article 101 applies,[76] we must evaluate whether it should be prohibited or allowed. Article 101 distinguishes between agreements whose *object* is the restriction of competition and those which have as an *effect* the restriction of competition.[77] It also sets out a non-exhaustive list of agreements which may be prohibited.

In considering infringements by object, two distinct considerations need to be kept in mind. The first is the definition of a restriction by object. It includes agreements which 'by their very nature' are 'injurious to the proper functioning of normal competition'.[78] Some of the agreements which are covered by this can be derived from the Court of Justice's analysis in the cases discussed above: agreements that fix prices or facilitate other forms of collusion with similar repercussions, and agreements that serve to partition the market.[79] The second question is about how one goes about establishing that an agreement has in fact an anti-competitive object, and here the Court's statements have been far from illuminating. In *T-Mobile*, the issue arose in the context of a concerted practice which arose after a single meeting of operators of mobile phones in the Netherlands, where they discussed reducing the remunerations paid to dealers for certain mobile phone contracts. In addition to confirming that there was no need to show consumer harm to establish that the agreement restricts competition, the Court had this to say about the concept of agreements restrictive by object.

---

[75] This is the view suggested by one of the co-authors of this book. G. Monti, *EC Competition Law* (Cambridge, Cambridge University Press, 2007).

[76] For convenience we will henceforth only refer to 'agreements' but the analysis applies to all forms of cooperation.

[77] Agreements may 'restrict, distort or eliminate' competition but the analysis is the same for all three effects.

[78] Case C-8/08 *T-Mobile Netherlands BV* v *Raad van bestuur van de Nederlandse Mededingingsautoriteit*, Judgment of 4 June 2009, para. 29.

[79] Joined Cases C-501/06 P, C-513/06 P, C-515/06 P and C-519/06 P *GlaxoSmithKline Services Unlimited* v *Commission*, Judgment 6 October 2009, paras. 60–1.

Case C–8/08 *T-Mobile Netherlands BV v Raad van bestuur van de Nederlandse Mededingingsautoriteit*, **Judgment of 4 June 2009**

27. With regard to the assessment as to whether a concerted practice is anti-competitive, close regard must be paid in particular to the objectives which it is intended to attain and to its economic and legal context. Moreover, while the intention of the parties is not an essential factor in determining whether a concerted practice is restrictive, there is nothing to prevent the Commission of the European Communities or the competent Community judicature from taking it into account.

28. As regards the distinction to be drawn between concerted practices having an anti-competitive object and those with anti-competitive effects, it must be borne in mind that an anti-competitive object and anti-competitive effects constitute not cumulative but alternative conditions in determining whether a practice falls within the prohibition in Article [101(1) TFEU]. It has … been settled case law that the alternative nature of that requirement, indicated by the conjunction 'or', means that it is necessary, first, to consider the precise purpose of the concerted practice, in the economic context in which it is to be pursued. Where, however, an analysis of the terms of the concerted practice does not reveal the effect on competition to be sufficiently deleterious, its consequences should then be considered and, for it to be caught by the prohibition, it is necessary to find that those factors are present which establish that competition has in fact been prevented or restricted or distorted to an appreciable extent.

29. Moreover, in deciding whether a concerted practice is prohibited by Article 101 TFEU, there is no need to take account of its actual effects once it is apparent that its object is to prevent, restrict or distort competition within the common market. The distinction between 'infringements by object' and 'infringements by effect' arises from the fact that certain forms of collusion between undertakings can be regarded, by their very nature, as being injurious to the proper functioning of normal competition …

30. Accordingly, contrary to what the referring court claims, there is no need to consider the effects of a concerted practice where its anti-competitive object is established.

31. With regard to the assessment as to whether a concerted practice, such as that at issue in the main proceedings, pursues an anti-competitive object, it should be noted … that in order for a concerted practice to be regarded as having an anti-competitive object, it is sufficient that it has the potential to have a negative impact on competition. In other words, the concerted practice must simply be capable in an individual case, having regard to the specific legal and economic context, of resulting in the prevention, restriction or distortion of competition within the common market. Whether and to what extent, in fact, such anti-competitive effects result can only be of relevance for determining the amount of any fine and assessing any claim for damages.

These paragraphs are very difficult to interpret. Paragraph 31 is perhaps the most illuminating because it suggests that the assessment is about the capacity of the agreement to have an anti-competitive effect. This explains why some economic analysis is required: an agreement is restrictive by object because it is capable of having an anti-competitive effect. On the facts of the case, it is significant, for example, that all major providers had conspired, which is necessary for a successful horizontal cartel. It follows that, as Odudu has remarked, a finding that an agreement is restrictive by object merely generates a presumption of illegality because the parties may deny the claim that in the economic context the agreement will necessarily have harmful effects.[80] If the parties are successful in rebutting the presumption, it follows from paragraph 28 that the plaintiff may still prevail if it shows that the agreement has in fact caused harmful effects. If this interpretation is correct, then some of the Court's statements are misleading; in particular, while the Court is keen to distinguish the concepts of object and effect, it is best to see them as interlinked because when analysing a restriction by object one is always considering the capacity for anti-competitive harm.

(c) Agreements having an anti-competitive effect

The methodology for determining whether an agreement has an anti-competitive effect is also problematic because the Commission has been too quick to find anti-competitive effects. The *Télévision par satellite* (TPS) decision is an illustration of the approach that has been criticised.[81] Six undertakings (including some French TV broadcasters) established a partnership (TPS) to launch a digital platform for the distribution of satellite pay-TV programmes in France. The agreement contained three contentious clauses: first, a non-competition clause whereby the parties agreed not to become involved in other digital pay-TV ventures in France for the duration of the agreement. Secondly, in order to supply TPS with the programmes it required, the parties agreed to give TPS first refusal in respect of the programmes or services which they themselves operated or over which they had effective control within the producing company, and in respect of the programmes and services which they produced. Thirdly, the general interest channels produced by the parent companies would be transmitted exclusively by TPS. The Commission held that the three clauses were in breach of Article 101(1) on the grounds that a third TV operator would have been unable to buy the programmes sold by the broadcasters party to the joint venture for the duration of the agreement (without evidence that any such third party was likely to emerge). However, the Commission granted an exemption because the agreement created considerable benefits to consumers by facilitating the entry of a new competitor in a market dominated by Canal + (the existing pay-TV operator that dominated the market in France). The Commission concluded, surprisingly in the light of its first finding that the agreement infringed Article 101(1), that:

> Far from eliminating competition, the TPS agreements are pro-competitive. Development of the pay-TV market has been strongly stimulated, particularly through the emergence of keen competition between CanalSatellite and TPS ...[82]

This Decision epitomises the key substantive and procedural problems with Article 101. If the agreement had been evaluated from an economic perspective, one would have balanced the fact that the agreement did make entry of a third broadcaster more difficult (although one would also have to consider whether a third pay-TV station could have obtained attractive content elsewhere), with the gains that consumers would make with the entry of a new competitor (TPS) in a market dominated by Canal +. On balance, as the Commission concluded above, the agreement benefits consumers. If so, why rule that the agreement's effects restrict competition?

---

[80] O. Odudu, 'Restriction of Competition by Object: What's the Beef?' (2008) *Competition Law* 11.
[81] *Télévision par satellite* [1999] OJ L90/6.
[82] *Ibid.* para. 135.

The reason is that the Commission sees a restriction on the conduct of undertakings as a restriction of competition. Thus, as soon as it saw that the contract might have made entry by a third party more difficult, it declared that the agreement's effects were anti-competitive. The restriction of the economic freedom of market participants is the reason why the agreement restricts competition. This is an unnecessarily wide interpretation of Article 101(1), whereby even agreements that are not harmful to consumer welfare are caught. Moreover, under the 'old' regime of Regulation 17/62, the impact of this approach also had major adverse procedural effects: parties were required to notify agreements in order to secure exemptions. However, most notified agreements were not exempted formally, the Commission replying with a 'comfort letter', which is a statement that in its opinion there is no problem under EU competition law. This letter provides little comfort as the agreement remains vulnerable to a challenge before national courts, which treat the Commission's comfort letter as persuasive but not binding.[83] The upshot in these cases is a high degree of legal uncertainty. TPS was lucky enough to obtain a Decision rather than a comfort letter, but one which undermined the original agreement by cutting short the term of the contracts, and the delay in the Decision was such that the duration was curtailed to a few months following the Decision![84] This can have serious repercussions for the parties to the contract because the Commission's rewriting of the agreement can alter the commercial objectives, perhaps fatally.

These procedural and substantive flaws undermined the development of sound commercial practices, and some went so far as to suggest that parties might consider not notifying their agreements and hope that the Commission with its few resources would not have the opportunity to investigate.[85] However, most commentators suggested a less cynical route, drawing upon one of the most widely discussed aspects of US antitrust doctrine: the rule of reason.[86] The gist of the argument was this: in the United States, the courts distinguish between agreements which are per se anti-competitive and are prohibited without any detailed analysis (for example, price fixing cartels), and agreements which may be anti-competitive but require detailed economic assessment to decide whether on balance the agreement promotes consumer welfare. This balancing analysis is known as a *rule of reason*. It was argued that the rule of reason analysis could be carried out in the European Union as a means of determining whether an agreement infringed Article 101(1).[87] If this were done, then agreements like those in *TPS* would be deemed not to infringe Article 101(1) and thus be lawful without the need for notification and exemption, because a rule of reason analysis would force the Commission to balance the anti-competitive risks of the agreement (the foreclosure of other pay-TV providers)

---

[83] Joined Cases 253/78 and 1/79–3/79 *Procureur de la République* v *Giry and Guérlain* [1980] ECR 2327, para. 13. See V. Korah, 'Comfort Letters: Reflections on the Perfume Cases' (1981) 6 *ELRev*. 14.

[84] The Decision is dated 3 March 1999, and the contract terms were to expire by 15 December 1999.

[85] C. Bright, 'EU Competition Policy: Rules, Objectives and Deregulation' (1996) 16 *OJLS* 535; A. Brown, 'Notification of Agreements to the EC Commission: Whether to Submit to a Flawed System' (1992) 17 *ELRev*. 323.

[86] For a modern judicial restatement, see *National Society of Professional Engineers* v *United States*, 435 US 679 (1978). For commentary see T. Calvani, 'Some Thoughts on the Rule of Reason' (2001) *ECLR* 201; P. Manzini, 'The European Rule of Reason: Crossing the Sea of Doubt' (2002) *ECLR* 392.

[87] The seminal contribution is R. Joliet, *The Rule of Reason in Antitrust Law: American, German and Common Market Laws in Comparative Perspective* (The Hague, Faculté de Droit and Martinus Nijhoff, 1967). See also V. Korah, 'The Rise and Fall of Provisional Validity: The Need for a Rule of Reason in EEC Antitrust' (1981) *Northwest Journal of International Law and Business* 320; I. Forrester and C. Norall, 'The Laicization of Community Competition Law: Self-Help and the Rule of Reason' (1984) 21 *CMLRev*. 11. For a contrary view see R. Whish and B. Sufrin, 'Article 85 and the Rule of Reason' (1987) 7 *YEL* 12.

with the benefits of the agreement (the entry of a new broadcaster to challenge the incumbent monopoly). Thus, on balance the agreement improved consumer welfare. The Court rejected this approach as early as 1966,[88] but advocates of a rule of reason maintained the pressure on the Commission, relying on a number of judgments where the Court seemed to adopt a more refined approach to determining whether there was a breach of Article 101(1), requiring that reference be had to the relevant *economic and legal context* of the agreement under scrutiny in order to determine the effects of an agreement.[89] To many this sounded like a call for the adoption of the rule of reason. However, the Union courts have rejected this approach.[90] The main reason for this is that any balance of pro- and anti-competitive effects of an agreement is to be carried out under Article 101(3). However, this response is not satisfactory because it places the onus on the parties to the agreement to show its beneficial effects in situations where there are no harmful effects.

These problems have been addressed in three different ways by three different actors.

First, the Council of Ministers issued Regulation 1/2003/EC: it abolished the procedure of notification and exemption and held that Article 101(3) had direct effect. In practical terms, if an agreement like that in *TPS* were to be entered into today, the parties would have to determine on their own whether their proposed course of action would be held lawful under Article 101. They will be able to implement this agreement without the need for scrutiny or exemption from the Commission. From a practical perspective it means that there is no need to notify an agreement in order to benefit from Article 101(3), and it is unlikely that the Commission would challenge practices that clearly benefit from Article 101(3). This procedural solution means that the overly broad interpretation of Article 101(1) is less problematic.

Secondly, the Commission published guidelines on the application of Article 81(3) (now 101(3) TFEU). These suggest that an economic appraisal will be carried out to determine whether an agreement has the effect of increasing prices or harming consumers in other ways. The intention of the guidelines is to indicate that henceforth a narrower interpretation of Article 101(1) will be followed. However, this approach has left commentators confused, some arguing that the Commission intends to carry out a detailed economic balance of the pro- and anti-competitive effects of an agreement under Article 101(1), leaving only borderline cases for evaluation under Article 101(3),[91] but others suggesting that an agreement will infringe Article 101(1) when the agreement gives the undertakings market power which may be used to harm consumers.[92] In sum, *some* economic analysis must be performed before determining that an agreement has anti-competitive effects, but we are still uncertain as to how much is needed before the burden shifts to the defendant to justify the practice under Article 101(3).

Thirdly, the General Court has stepped in with a significant judgment that requires the party alleging an infringement of Article 101(1) to provide more refined evidence of the

---

[88] Joined Cases 56/64 and 58/64 *Consten and Grundig v Commission* [1966] ECR 299.

[89] See e.g. Case 56/65 *Société Technique Minière v Maschinenbau Ulm GmbH* [1966] ECR 235; Case 26/76 *Metro SB-Großmärkte GmbH & Co KG v Commission (No. 1)* [1977] ECR 1875; Case 258/78 *Nungesser v Commission* [1982] ECR 2015; Case 161/84 *Pronuptia de Paris GmbH v Schilgallis* [1986] ECR 353; Case C-234/89 *Delimitis v Henninger Bräu AG* [1991] ECR I-935; Case C-250/92 *Gøttrup-Klim and Others Grovvareforeninger v Dansk Landbrugs Grovvareselskab AmbA* [1994] ECR I-5641; Case C-306/96 *Javico International and Javico AG v Yves Saint Laurent Parfums SA* [1998] ECR I-1983.

[90] Case T-112/99 *Métropole télévision (M6) and Others v Commission* [2001] ECR II-2459, paras. 74–7.

[91] J. Bourgeois and J. Bocken, 'Guidelines on the Application of Article 81(3) of the EC Treaty, or How to Restrict a Restriction' (2005) 32 *LIEI* 111.

[92] P. Nicolaides, 'The Balancing Myth: The Economics of Article 81(1) and (3)' (2005) 32 *LIEI* 123.

anti-competitive effects than the Commission has provided in some cases to date. At issue was a 'roaming' agreement between O2 and T-Mobile which was designed to help O2 secure a foothold in the German market while it was constructing its own network. As with *TPS*, the Commission first found that this restricted competition at wholesale and retail level, but when examining the agreement under Article 101(3) it found that the agreement would improve competition in the relevant markets. It exempted the agreement but for a period shorter than that which the parties had originally stipulated, so they sought (and obtained) annulment of the Commission's Decision. The significance of this judgment is the legal standard set by the Court.

Case T–328/03 *O2 (Germany) GmbH & Co. OHG v Commission* [2006] ECR II–1231

68. [I]n a case such as this, where it is accepted that the agreement does not have as its object a restriction of competition, the effects of the agreement should be considered and for it to be caught by the prohibition it is necessary to find that those factors are present which show that competition has in fact been prevented or restricted or distorted to an appreciable extent. The competition in question must be understood within the actual context in which it would occur in the absence of the agreement in dispute; the interference with competition may in particular be doubted if the agreement seems really necessary for the penetration of a new area by an undertaking.

69. Such a method of analysis, as regards in particular the taking into account of the competition situation that would exist in the absence of the agreement, does not amount to carrying out an assessment of the pro- and anti-competitive effects of the agreement and thus to applying a rule of reason, which the Community judicature has not deemed to have its place under Article [101(1) TFEU].

70. In this respect, to submit, as the applicant does, that the Commission failed to carry out a full analysis by not examining what the competitive situation would have been in the absence of the agreement does not mean that an assessment of the positive and negative effects of the agreement from the point of view of competition must be carried out at the stage of Article [101(1) TFEU]. Contrary to the defendant's interpretation of the applicant's arguments, the applicant relies only on the method of analysis required by settled case law.

71. The examination required in the light of Article [101(1) TFEU] consists essentially in taking account of the impact of the agreement on existing and potential competition and the competition situation in the absence of the agreement, those two factors being intrinsically linked.

Applied to the facts of the case, the General Court found first that the Commission had failed to examine the competitive effects without the agreement.

Case T–328/03 *O2 (Germany) GmbH & Co. OHG v Commission* [2006] ECR II–1231

77. Working on the assumption that O2 was present on the mobile communications market, the Commission did not therefore deem it necessary to consider in more detail whether, in the absence of the agreement, O2 would have been present on the 3G market. It must be held that that assumption is not supported in the Decision by any analysis or justification showing that it is correct, a finding that, moreover, the defendant could only confirm at the hearing. Given that there was no such objective examination of the competition situation in the absence of the agreement, the Commission could not have properly assessed the extent to which the agreement was necessary for O2 to penetrate the

3G mobile communications market. The Commission therefore failed to fulfil its obligation to carry out an objective analysis of the impact of the agreement on the competitive situation.

78. That lacuna cannot be deemed to be without consequences. It is apparent from the considerations set out in the Decision in the analysis of the agreement in the light of the conditions laid down in Article [101(3) TFEU] as regards whether it was possible to grant an exemption that, even in the Commission's view, it was unlikely that O2 would have been able, individually, without the agreement, to ensure from the outset better coverage, quality and transmission rates for 3G services, to roll out a network and launch 3G services rapidly, to penetrate the relevant wholesale and retail markets and therefore be an effective competitor (recitals 122 to 124, 126 and 135). It was because of those factors that the Commission considered that the agreement was eligible for exemption.

79. Such considerations, which imply some uncertainty concerning the competitive situation and, in particular, as regards O2's position in the absence of the agreement, show that the presence of O2 on the 3G communications market could not be taken for granted, as the Commission had assumed, and that an examination in this respect was necessary not only for the purposes of granting an exemption but, prior to that, for the purposes of the economic analysis of the effects of the agreement on the competitive situation determining the applicability of Article [101 TFEU].

The key insight from this judgment is that the Commission's evidentiary burden is raised: it is insufficient for it to show that the agreement affects the economic freedom of one of the parties, one has to demonstrate a causal link between the agreement and subsequent restrictions of competition. The General Court says this is not a rule of reason approach, but not everyone has been convinced by that denial.

Mel Marquis, 'O2 (Germany) v Commission and the Exotic Mysteries of Article 81(1) EC' (2007) European Law Review 27, 44–5

[I]t is questionable whether the nature of the counterfactual test is truly different from an analysis that 'weighs' the agreement's pro-competitive and anti-competitive effects... One could argue that the counterfactual test loses its meaning if the pro-competitive impact of the agreement cannot be weighed against its anti-competitive effects. What is to be compared with the counterfactual, *non-agreement* scenario if it is not the agreement's *net* impact on competition (or more precisely, its net impact on price and output)? If account is not taken of the agreement's pro-competitive effects as well as its restrictive effects, then the comparison becomes distorted and illogical.

The good news is that, regardless of the 'no balancing' doctrine, the CFI appears willing or indeed eager to apply an analysis under Art. 81(1) that is economically rigorous and commercially realistic. Thus, for example, the Commission's view that national roaming agreements restricted competition 'by definition' was rejected as a generalisation that had no specific bearing on the agreement at issue. Furthermore, the Court took very seriously – within the context of Art. 81(1), and consistently with *Société Technique Minière* – the structure of the market and the prospect that roaming could enhance O2's competitive position vis-à-vis the incumbent. This approach has important implications for the network industries, where liberalisation has resulted in lopsided competitive conditions, and above all for rapidly evolving sectors such as electronic communications, where the legacy of a dominant incumbent may potentially distort the development of emerging markets.

In short, the CFI seems to be applying the kind of searching inquiry that it applied in *European Night Services*, and it seems to be carrying out an assessment that looks suspiciously like balancing. Whatever it is called, it is a positive development, and the CFI's judgment provides further confirmation of what the ECJ has often asserted over the last 40 years, namely that there are boundaries to the concept of 'restriction of competition'. To be regretted is the lingering confusion – in the CFI's jurisprudence and in the Commission's Art. 81(3) Guidelines – regarding the division of labour between Art. 81(1) and 81(3). Much clarity could be achieved if the European Courts explicitly embraced the distinction described earlier between a consumer welfare test under Art. 81(1) and an assessment of productive/dynamic efficiency gains under Art. 81(3).

Taking these three developments collectively, one can suggest that the effects-based analysis is today less problematic than it used to be, but as Marquis concludes, a more forceful judgment of the Court is required to draw a precise line between the analysis required under Article 101(1) and (3). However, as we discuss below, Marquis' suggestion that Article 101(3) is only about efficiencies can be contested.

(iii) Role of Article 101(3) TFEU

As indicated above, the procedure whereby exemption decisions were the exclusive competence of the Commission and were only available if the agreement was notified has come to an end with Regulation 1/2003. Now exemption decisions are not issued by anyone: neither the Commission, nor national competition authorities, nor the courts. The effect of this reform is that Article 101 changed from a provision enforced primarily via an ex ante notification system to one that is enforced ex post and is based on deterrence: parties must assess for themselves whether the agreement falls foul of competition law. It follows that when a competition authority or a claimant challenges a restrictive practice, they have the burden of proving that the agreement infringes Article 101(1), and the defendant has the burden of proof in relation to Article 101(3).

(a) Individual exemptions

Four conditions must be satisfied for an agreement to benefit from an exemption: (1) it must improve the production and distribution of goods or promote technical and economic progress; (2) consumers must receive a fair share of the benefits identified in (1); (3) the restrictions of competition must be necessary to achieve the said benefits; (4) the agreement must not eliminate competition on the market. In theory, all agreements can qualify.[93] It is unlikely that a cartel would be exempted, although the Commission has in times of recession exempted 'crisis cartels' that are designed to soften the economic impact of the economic downturn affecting certain industries.[94]

The first condition is the most controversial because its scope is uncertain: does it mean that an agreement is exempted because it yields economic efficiency (the narrow view), or does

---

[93] Case T-17/93 *Matra Hachette v Commission* [1994] ECR II-595.
[94] See e.g. *Synthetic Fibres* [1984] OJ L207/17.

it also mean that an agreement may be exempted if it makes a contribution to other matters of interest to the Community (the wide view)?[95] For example, can the fact that an agreement enhances employment in a poor European region be a relevant consideration in determining whether it can be exempted? Or an agreement that strengthens a weak European industry against strong rivals from overseas? Neither the Decisions of the Commission, nor the Court's judgments, have provided an unambiguous answer to this question, although most commentators have suggested that non-economic factors play some role in influencing the decision to exempt an agreement, and others have also insisted that this is correct as a matter of law.[96] However, as a result of Regulation 1/2003 the Commission has been forced to give a direct answer to the scope of the first condition of Article 101(3) because it is now applied by national competition authorities and courts; thus consistency is necessary. The Commission has indicated that Article 101(3) can only serve agreements which enhance economic efficiency, and that it is not to be used to exempt agreements that support other Community interests. This position is somewhat out of line with the approach that has been taken to date, but is the result of the decentralisation in the enforcement of Regulation 1/2003 because it narrows down the discretion that national authorities have. From a practical perspective, then, a 'narrow' reading of Article 101(3) is desirable, although this approach may not necessarily be the correct legal interpretation of the provision. Moreover, the Commission's formal position is out of line with its practice. In *CECED*, for example, the Conseil Européen de la Construction d'Appareils Domestiques (CECED), an association representing manufacturers of domestic appliances, including washing machines, agreed to phase out from the market certain types of washing machines with low energy efficiency. The agreement was found anti-competitive by object because it prevented parties from manufacturing or exporting certain types of washing machines and thus restricted consumer choice. The agreement would also raise production costs for those manufacturers who had not yet developed more energy efficient models. However, the Commission found the following reasons for exempting the agreement.

CECED [2000] OJ L187/47

47. The agreement is designed to reduce the potential energy consumption of new washing machines by at least 15 to 20% (relative to 1994 data on models of washing machines) …

48. Washing machines which, other factors being constant, consume less electricity are objectively more technically efficient. Reduced electricity consumption indirectly leads to reduced pollution from electricity generation. The future operation of the total of installed machines providing the same service with less indirect pollution is more economically efficient than without the agreement. …

51. CECED estimates the pollution avoided at 3.5 million tons of carbon dioxide, 17,000 tons of sulphur dioxide and 6,000 tons of nitrous oxide per year in 2010, working on the basis of average emission values. Although such emissions are more efficiently tackled at the stage of electricity generation, the agreement is likely to deliver both individual and collective benefits for users and consumers.

---

[95] For detail on the differences between these two, see R. Whish, *Competition Law* (6th edn, Oxford, Oxford University Press, 2008) 151–7.

[96] R. B. Bouterse, *Competition and Integration: What Goals Count?* (The Hague, Kluwer Law International, 1994) chs. 1–4; and W. Sauter, *Competition Law and Industrial Policy in the EU* (Oxford, Oxford University Press, 1997) ch. 4, R. Wesseling, *The Modernisation of EC Antitrust Law* (Oxford, Hart, 2000) esp. 105–12.

(a) Individual economic benefits

52. The level at which the minimum performance standard is set provides a fair return within reasonable pay-back periods to a typical consumer for higher initial purchase costs derived from the more stringent standard in fact set out by CECED. Savings on electricity bills allow recouping of increased costs of upgraded, more expensive machines within nine to 40 months, depending mainly on frequency of use and electricity prices.

(b) Collective environmental benefits

56. The Commission reasonably estimates the saving in marginal damage from (avoided) carbon dioxide emissions (the so-called 'external costs') at EUR 41 to 61 per ton of carbon dioxide. On a European scale, avoided damage from sulphur dioxide amounts to EUR 4,000 to 7,000 per ton and EUR 3,000 to 5,000 per ton of nitrous oxide. On the basis of reasonable assumptions, the benefits to society brought about by the CECED agreement appear to be more than seven times greater than the increased purchase costs of more energy-efficient washing machines. Such environmental results for society would adequately allow consumers a fair share of the benefits even if no benefits accrued to individual purchasers of machines.

This Decision gives a wide interpretation of economic efficiency, noting that the considerable environmental benefits which the agreement generates are enough to exempt the agreement. On the one hand, the Decision may be read as suggesting that other Community policies affected the Decision to exempt (see in particular paragraph 56). On the other hand, the Decision might simply be read as stating that because the agreement reduces energy bills, consumers are better off because even though the price of washing machines rises, the electricity bills are low enough to compensate for this (see paragraph 52). Thus, it can be read as espousing both the wide and narrow interpretation of Article 101(3). This ambiguity also characterises earlier Decisions which suggest that a Decision to exempt may be influenced by a range of non-efficiency related competition factors, for example, relieving unemployment,[97] promoting environmental goals,[98] and helping the creation of stronger European industry in the face of competition from firms in the United States and Japan.[99]

CECED is also interesting for its interpretation of the second condition in Article 101(3): that consumers should benefit. On the one hand, the benefits should accrue to those who buy the goods, and thus gain directly by the agreement. In this respect, the word 'consumer' is misleading and a better translation would be 'user' because anyone who purchases the good or services from the undertakings that benefit from the exemption is treated as a consumer. However, in *CECED* the Commission was willing to consider collective benefits to society as a whole as 'consumer benefits', which is an overly wide interpretation. Another interesting analysis of the consumer benefit criteria was offered by the Court of Justice in *Asnef-Equifax* v *Ausbanc*.[100]

---

[97] See e.g. *Stichting Baksteen* [1994] OJ L131/15, paras. 27–8; *Synthetic Fibres* [1984] OJ L207/17, para. 37.

[98] See e.g. *Philips/Osram* [1994] OJ L378/37.

[99] See e.g. *Optical Fibres* [1986] OJ L236/30; *Olivetti/Canon* [1988] OJ L52/60; *Bayer/BPCL* [1988] OJ L150/35. See Bouterse, above n. 96.

[100] Case C-238/05 *Asnef-Equifax, Servicios de Información sobre Solvencia y Crédito, SL* v *Asociación de Usuarios de Servicios Bancarios (Ausbanc)* [2006] ECR I-11125.

Spanish banks agreed to set up an electronic register of credit information that would disclose the credit history of potential customers. The effect was that each bank was aware of each potential client's credit history and took this into account when negotiating further loans. The Court held that it was unlikely that this agreement would restrict competition, but also added some reflections on how one might go about analysing the consumer benefit test in Article 101(3). It suggested that two groups of consumers benefit: those who get loans on better terms, and those who do not get loans because of their bad credit scores, and this is a benefit because it avoids over-indebtedness. That persons who are unable to obtain a service as a result of an anti-competitive agreement can be seen as deriving a benefit requires further reflection: would one for example say that a cartel to fix the prices of cigarettes benefits smokers who therefore smoke less?

The third condition is that the agreement must only contain restrictions that are indispensable to achieve the benefits identified by the first two criteria. This means that if the benefits can be achieved in a less restrictive way, then an exemption will not be granted. In *CECED*, for example, the Commission considered whether there were any other ways of reducing energy consumption. One less restrictive alternative could have been for the parties to agree to inform consumers in more detail about the energy costs of each washing machine and allow the consumer to make the choice. This would be less restrictive of competition than withdrawing certain models. However, the Commission decided that informing the consumer would not have been as effective. Thus, the restriction agreed by the parties was necessary to achieve the relevant benefits.

The relevance of the final criteria is explained by the Commission: 'Ultimately, the protection of rivalry and the competitive process is given priority over potentially pro-competitive efficiency gains which could result from restrictive agreements.'[101] Therefore, if an agreement were to result in the parties not competing at all, then an exemption would not be granted. In *CECED*, there was no elimination of competition because the parties were able to compete on features like price, brand image and technical performance.[102]

(b) Block exemptions

As we explained above, until 1 May 2004 only the Commission could grant individual exemptions, which placed a considerable burden on it as thousands of agreements were notified. The principal solution was to issue 'block exemption' regulations which provided that all agreements meeting certain predefined criteria would merit exemption as a group. The 'old style' block exemptions defined a type of agreement and provided lists of clauses which parties were allowed to insert in the agreement (white lists) and lists of clauses which if present would deny the agreement the benefit of a block exemption (black lists).[103] The advantage of falling within the scope of a block exemption was that the parties did not need to notify the agreement, but this was at the expense of flexibility resulting from long black lists. Moreover, some block exemptions were said to be commercially unrealistic and to have been of no use in structuring certain types of agreement. The Commission has now redesigned block exemptions to make these more business friendly and more effectively based upon economic analysis. The

---

[101] Guidelines on Article 81(3), para. 105.
[102] *CECED* [2000] OJ L187/47, para. 64.
[103] See e.g. Regulation 1983/83/EC on exclusive distribution [1983] OJ L173/1.

first block exemption to be drafted in this way is that for vertical restraints, and a brief over-view is provided below.[104]

Vertical restraints are agreements between undertakings operating at different levels of trade (for example, a distribution contract between a manufacturer and a retailer), which restrict the parties' behaviour. For example a manufacturer of plasma TVs may decide to sell these only to a selected type of retail outlet whose staff are competent to give consumers advice. These contracts may restrict the number of outlets selling the plasma TVs (and so stifle intra-brand competition among retail outlets) but their redeeming virtue is that the selected retailers are better placed to satisfy consumer demand by providing valued pre-sale service. Provided there is healthy competition among rival brands of TV sets (inter-brand competition), then vertical restraints will enhance consumer welfare.[105] There may, however, be three anti-competitive risks that materialise with vertical restraints: first, if all manufacturers use similar distribution contracts this may facilitate collusion among them because they can monitor each other's prices more easily; secondly, vertical restraints that encourage unnecessary promotion by re-tailers may reduce consumer welfare;[106] and thirdly, vertical restraints might foreclose market access for new entrants (say because the new entrant finds that there are no more outlets will-ing to distribute his goods).[107]

Anti-competitive risks tend to arise when there is market power, and the Block Exemption Regulation is designed with this in mind.[108] Parties may benefit from the block exemption only if they meet the condition specified in article 3: that the market share held by the sup-plier or the buyer does not exceed 30 per cent of the relevant market on which the supplier sells or the buyer purchases the contract goods or services. Parties that fall within this threshold are free to enter into whichever distribution contracts they wish save for a small number of 'black listed' clauses set out in articles 4 and 5. For instance, the manufacturer cannot impose a minimum price at which distributors may sell the goods (which might facilitate collusion), and the manufacturer cannot prevent the dealer from selling the contract goods in question in another Member State when these are ordered by a customer there (this is based on the crucial importance of the market integration goal). Finally, the Regulation provides a safe-guard clause which allows the Commission (or a national competition authority) to remove the benefit of the block exemption if the benefits to consumers do not materialise. While this has hardly been used, it is a helpful mechanism to regulate vertical restraints that do not live up to their promise. The Regulation is accompanied by guidelines that explain how the Com-mission will apply Article 101 to agreements that fall outside the scope of the block exemption

---

[104] The Commission's earlier approach to regulating vertical restraints had been criticised harshly. See B. E. Hawk, 'System Failure: Vertical Restraints and EC Competition Law' (1995) 32 *CMLRev.* 973; D. Neven, P. Papan-dropolous and P. Seabright, *Trawling for Minnows: European Competition Policy and Agreements Between Firms* (London, CEPR, 1998) 42–3.

[105] For a detailed account of the economics see M. Motta, *Competition Policy* (Cambridge, Cambridge University Press, 2004) ch. 6; P. W. Dobson and M. Waterson, *Vertical Restraints and Competition Policy* (OFT, 1996); L. G. Tesler, 'Why Should Manufacturers Want Fair Trade?' (1960) 3 *Journal of Law and Economics* 86.

[106] W. S. Comanor, 'Vertical Price-Fixing, Vertical Market Restrictions, and the New Antitrust Policy' (1985) 98 *Harvard Law Review* 983, esp. 991–2 and 1000–2.

[107] Stephen C. Salop, 'Analysis of Foreclosure in the EC Guidelines on Vertical Restraints' (2000) *Fordham Corporate Law Institute* (B. Hawk (ed.) 2001) 177, 191–2.

[108] Commission Regulation 2790/1999/EC of 22 December 1999 on the application of Article 81(3) of the Treaty to categories of vertical agreements and concerted practices [1999] OJ L336/1; Guidelines on vertical restraints [2000] OJ C291/1.

(e.g. when the market share threshold is not met) and these provide for an economics-based appraisal of vertical restraints.

This Block Exemption Regulation has been very successful in limiting the intervention of competition law in this field.[109] While it is currently under review, only marginal amendments are being proposed: most significantly, that the market share threshold of 30 per cent should be applied to both the seller and buyer for the block exemption to apply. This is likely to yield a more precise measure of the anti-competitive risks, but may create a major burden on a seller with multiple distributors who has to calculate the market share of each one in their relevant geographical markets.

4 ARTICLE 102 TFEU: ABUSE OF A DOMINANT POSITION

Enterprises holding significant market power should receive considerable scrutiny by competition authorities. From an economic perspective, firms that dominate a market have the kind of economic power that normally reduces efficiency because there are no competitive pressures to prevent dominant firms from raising prices and reducing output.[110] Moreover, large firms may exercise market power to consolidate their dominance, or even to expand their influence into the political domain.[111]

Article 102 TFEU

Any abuse by one or more undertakings of a dominant position within the common market or in a substantial part of it shall be prohibited as incompatible with the common market insofar as it may affect trade between Member States.

Such abuse may, in particular, consist in:

- directly or indirectly imposing unfair purchase or selling prices or other unfair trading conditions;
- limiting production, markets or technical development to the prejudice of consumers;
- applying dissimilar conditions to equivalent transactions with other trading parties, thereby placing them at a competitive disadvantage;
- making the conclusion of contracts subject to acceptance by the other parties of supplementary obligations which, by their nature or according to commercial usage, have no connection with the subject of such contracts.

When the Commission seeks to establish an infringement of Article 102, it must show the following: that an undertaking is dominant in a given market; that it has abused its dominant position; that the abuse has an effect on trade between Member States; and the absence of any objective justification for the abuse.[112] Four examples of abuse are listed in Article 102 TFEU,

---

[109] V. Korah and D. O'Sullivan, *Distribution Agreements under the EC Competition Rules* (Oxford, Hart, 2002) ch. 8.
[110] See Chapter 22 for a review of the economic analysis underlying this.
[111] See R. A. Posner, 'The Social Costs of Monopoly and Regulation' (1975) 83 *Journal of Political Economy* 807; R. Pitofsky, 'The Political Content of Antitrust' (1979) 127 *U Penn. L Rev.* 105; G. Amato, *Antitrust and the Bounds of Power* (Oxford, Hart, 1997) ch. 7.
[112] The interpretation of the requirement of an effect on trade between Member States is considered in Chapter 22, and the same approach is taken in Article 102 TFEU.

but this list is not an exhaustive catalogue of what behaviour is considered abusive. As will be seen, the Commission and Court of Justice have found an ever-increasing number of practices abusive.

Compared to the voluminous case law under Article 101, the abuse prohibition has been applied relatively infrequently (around sixty decisions by the Commission) but the Commission and the Court's case law has received the most scathing criticism for fettering the economic freedom of dominant firms unnecessarily.[113] In response to the latter criticism, and in line with the more economics-oriented approach of contemporary competition law, the Commission has issued a document designed to redirect its enforcement strategy.[114] We start by considering the current case law and the criticisms it has elicited before turning to examining the new approach.

(i) Dominance

A dominant undertaking need not monopolise the entire market. Such an extreme degree of dominance is possible when an undertaking is given a monopoly by the state, for instance if the state grants the right to operate job centres exclusively to one undertaking.[115] But the concept of dominance is much wider.[116]

> **John Temple Lang, 'Some Aspects of Abuse of a Dominant Position in EC Antitrust Law' (1979) 3 *Fordham International Law Forum* 1, 9–12**
>
> A dominant position exists when the dominant enterprise is able to use its economic power to obtain benefits or to practise behaviour which it could not obtain or practise in conditions of reasonably effective competition, i.e., that dominant power is power of which unfair advantage can be taken, or power which is great enough to be 'abused'. ... This principle also implies a link between the concept of dominance and the concept of abuse. ...
>
> It is the ability to contain competition, not the ability to ignore it, which is characteristic of dominance. Dominant firms can overcome competition, but very few of them can disregard it. The power to plan and choose a controlled response to competitors' efforts, sufficient to ensure no significant long term loss of market share, is typical of dominant firms. As market leader a dominant firm is often able to adopt a strategy advantageous to itself and disadvantageous for the rest of the industry, without using overtly exclusionary practices, which will maintain its market in spite of some competition. Such a strategy may be adopted on the dominant firm's own initiative or in response to competitors' actions. Since dominance does not mean absence of competition, or even absence of effective competition, clearly it does not mean freedom to disregard competition. It follows that dominance can exist even if the dominant firm is compelled to react to its competitors' activities.

---

[113] V. Korah, *An Introductory Guide to EC Competition Law and Practice* (7th edn, Oxford, Hart, 2000); B. Sher, 'The Last of the Steam Powered Trains: Modernising Article 82' (2004) 25 *ECLR* 243.

[114] P. Lowe, 'DG Competition's Review of the Policy on Abuse of Dominance' (2003) *Fordham Corporate Law Institute* 163 (B. Hawk (ed.) 2004).

[115] Case C-41/90 *Klaus Höfner and Fritz Elser v Macrotron GmbH* [1991] ECR I-1979.

[116] The Court's definition is: 'A position of economic strength enjoyed by an undertaking which enables it to prevent effective competition being maintained on the relevant market by giving it the power to behave to an appreciable extent independently of its competitors, customers and ultimately of its consumers.' Case 27/76 *United Brands Company v Commission* [1978] ECR 207, para. 65.

Accordingly, dominance means that an undertaking has the power to harm the competitive process, either by harming consumers (for example, through higher prices) or by harming competitors (for example, by offering discounts to customers who would otherwise buy the competitor's goods). From this perspective, it can be said that there are different degrees of dominance: some undertakings are so powerful that they face no competitive constraint, while some dominant undertakings may face competition from others, but are strong enough to keep the smaller competitors at bay. Regardless of the degree, the Court measures dominance, first, by considering the undertaking's market share, and secondly, by other factors used to determine the undertaking's position vis-à-vis its competitors, customers and consumers.[117]

(a) Market shares

Market shares are used as a preliminary filter to determine whether there is dominance. Their significance was explored in *Hoffmann-La Roche*.[118] The Commission found that Roche held a dominant position in a number of vitamin markets and had abused it by entering into distribution contracts that granted purchasers fidelity rebates if they bought their vitamin requirements exclusively or almost exclusively from Roche, thereby excluding other vitamin suppliers. The Court confirmed that Roche was dominant, noting that holding a substantial market share for some time, when its smaller competitors are unable to meet the demand of Roche's customers, is dominance because Roche was free to act independently of competitors. Subsequent case law suggests that a market share of 50 per cent can give rise to a presumption of dominance.[119] In many cases the dominant firm has held market shares in excess of 50 per cent while its competitors all have had considerably smaller market shares.[120] However, a market share between 40 and 50 per cent has also been sufficient to identify a dominant position once other factors were taken into consideration, for instance where there were significant barriers to entry.[121]

(b) Barriers to/ease of entry

Dominance does not exist if entry is easy. A firm with a 90 per cent share of the market is not dominant if, as soon as it raised the price of its goods, other firms would enter its market and sell their goods at more competitive prices. As a result, a definition of dominance requires an analysis of whether there are any barriers to entry. But this notion is not without controversy. Economists have been divided between those who take a wide conception of entry barriers (any factor that allows the existing company to raise price), and a narrower conception of entry barriers (only those costs that a new entrant must incur that were not faced by the existing firms).[122] The wider the concept used, the more likely it is that one finds dominance. However

---

[117] Case 322/81 *Nederlandsche Banden-Industrie Michelin NV* v *Commission* [1983] ECR 3461, para. 31.

[118] Case 85/76 *Hoffmann-La Roche & Co. AG* v *Commission* [1979] ECR 461, paras. 39–41.

[119] Case 62/86 *AKZO Chemie BV* v *Commission* [1991] ECR I-3359, para. 60.

[120] See e.g. Case 322/81 *Nederlandsche Banden-Industrie Michelin NV* v *Commission* [1983] ECR 3461 (dominant firm with a market share of approximately 57–60 per cent and the others with market shares between 4 and 8 per cent).

[121] Case 27/76 *United Brands* v *Commission* [1978] ECR 207, paras. 109–10; Case T-219/99 *British Airways* v *Commission* [2003] ECR II-5917, paras. 211–24.

[122] Richard Schmalensee, 'Ease of Entry: Has the Concept been Applied Too Readily?' (1987) 56 *Antitrust Law Journal* 41; P. Geroski and A. Jacquemin, 'Industrial Change, Barriers to Mobility and European Industrial Policy' (1985) 1 *Economic Policy* 170, 182–3.

the application of this debate in competition law has been criticised: '[w]hat matters … is not what might happen in some year far off in the future but what will actually happen now and in the near future. Rather than focusing on whether an "entry barrier" exists according to some definition, analysts should explain how the industry will behave over the next several years.'[123] In this light, the wide range of factors identified by the Court of Justice as indicators of dominance can be explained by the Court's concern about whether in the relatively short term other firms can enter to compete against the dominant undertaking. In *Michelin*, the Court approved the Commission's Decision that Michelin held a dominant position in the market for new tyres for certain types of vehicles. It found that this position was abused because Michelin entered into distribution agreements with tyre retailers in the Netherlands which restricted the retailer's freedom to source tyres from competitors because it was given financial incentives in the form of quantity rebates if it purchased more Michelin tyres. The appellant's challenge against the finding of dominance was rejected by the Court.

Case 322/81 *Nederlandsche Banden-Industrie Michelin NV v Commission* [1983] ECR 3461

55. … it should first be observed that in order to assess the relative economic strength of Michelin NV and its competitors on the Netherlands market the advantages which those undertakings may derive from belonging to groups of undertakings operating throughout Europe or even the world must be taken into consideration. Amongst those advantages, the lead which the Michelin group has over its competitors in the matters of investment and research and the special extent of its range of products, to which the Commission referred in its Decision, have not been denied. In fact in the case of certain types of tyre the Michelin group is the only supplier on the market to offer them in its range.

56. That situation ensures that on the Netherlands market a large number of users of heavy-vehicle tyres have a strong preference for Michelin tyres. As the purchase of tyres represents a considerable investment for a transport undertaking and since much time is required in order to ascertain in practice the cost-effectiveness of a type or brand of tyre, Michelin NV therefore enjoys a position which renders it largely immune to competition. As a result, a dealer established in the Netherlands normally cannot afford not to sell Michelin tyres.

57. It is not possible to uphold the objections made against those arguments by Michelin NV, supported on this point by the French government, that Michelin NV is thus penalized for the quality of its products and services. A finding that an undertaking has a dominant position is not in itself a recrimination but simply means that, irrespective of the reasons for which it has such a dominant position, the undertaking concerned has a special responsibility not to allow its conduct to impair genuine undistorted competition on the common market.

58. Due weight must also be attached to the importance of Michelin NV's network of commercial representatives, which gives it direct access to tyre users at all times. Michelin NV has not disputed the fact that in absolute terms its network is considerably larger than those of its competitors or challenged the description, in the Decision at issue, of the services performed by its network whose efficiency and quality of service are unquestioned. The direct access to users and the standard of service which the network can give them enables Michelin NV to maintain and strengthen its position on the market and to protect itself more effectively against competition.

---

[123] D. E. Carlton, 'Why Barriers to Entry are Barriers to Understanding' (2004) 94 *American Economic Review* 466, 469.

59. As regards the additional criteria and evidence to which Michelin NV refers in order to disprove the existence of a dominant position, it must be observed that temporary unprofitability or even losses are not inconsistent with the existence of a dominant position. By the same token, the fact that the prices charged by Michelin NV do not constitute an abuse and are not even particularly high does not justify the conclusion that a dominant position does not exist. Finally, neither the size, financial strength and degree of diversification of Michelin NV's competitors at the world level nor the counterpoise arising from the fact that buyers of heavy-vehicle tyres are experienced trade users are such as to deprive Michelin NV of its privileged position on the Netherlands market.

The judgment provides an extensive list of factors that contributed to give Michelin a competitive advantage over its rivals. In addition, the Court has found that a dominant position might be protected by ownership of intellectual property rights (which prevent others from duplicating the dominant undertaking's products),[124] by access to capital, by considerable costs of entry, by economies of scale necessary to penetrate the market,[125] or by a well organised distribution system, advertising and brand recognition.[126] The criticism that by considering these factors one is merely describing the efficiency of the dominant firm, and using those efficiencies as a means to determine dominance, is rejected by the Court at paragraph 57 of *Michelin*: dominance is not unlawful, but dominant undertakings have a *special responsibility* not to hinder competition. But this has not assuaged those who think that the too-wide definition of dominance, combined with this passage, places a Damoclean sword over dominant undertakings whose commercial freedom is detrimentally affected by this obligation, paradoxically restricting the very kind of competition that dominant firms are said to endanger.[127]

(ii) Abuse of dominance: general principles

The Commission has indicated that the list of abuses in Article 102 is not exhaustive. In a seminal judgment, *Continental Can*, the Court of Justice set out three key principles that have informed the application of this provision.[128] First, the method by which novel categories of abuse are established is through teleological interpretation, i.e. whether by classifying a practice as an abuse one is contributing to the aims of the Treaty. Secondly, the Court does not require that the dominant firm uses its dominance to achieve the abuse, so long as the dominant firm's actions have anti-competitive effects. Third is the Court's subtle reinterpretation of the TFEU's focus on ensuring that competition is not distorted. The Court reads this as a provision which aims at sustaining an effective competition structure. The emphasis thus is on ensuring that markets are populated by a sufficient number of market players. This is akin to the Harvard School's structural paradigm and closely related to the ordoliberal views.[129]

---

[124] See e.g. Case 22/78 *Hugin Kassaregister AB* v *Commission* [1979] ECR 1869; Case T-30/89 *Hilti* v *Commission* [1991] ECR II-1439 (affirmed in Case C-53/92 P *Hilti* v *Commission* [1994] ECR I-667).

[125] Case 27/76 *United Brands Company* v *Commission* [1978] ECR 207.

[126] Case T-203/01 *Michelin* v *Commission* [2003] ECR II-4071.

[127] S. Turnbull, 'Barriers to Entry, Article 86 and the Abuse of a Dominant Position' (1996) *ECLR* 96.

[128] Case 6/72 *Europemballage Corp and Continental Can Co. Inc.* v *Commission* [1973] ECR 215.

[129] See Chapter 21 at pp. 917–18.

While these principles allow for a wide scope for the meaning of abuse, the *types* of abuse may be classified in two categories: exploitative and exclusionary. The first includes abuses that aim to harm the customer of the dominant undertaking (for example, excessive prices). However, the Commission has shown little interest in punishing exploitative abuses. The major reason for not intervening against firms that exploit market power is that it is difficult to identify the parameters for intervention. In any market where an undertaking has *some* market power, prices are higher than marginal cost.[130] However, if EU competition law were to apply to all prices above marginal cost, virtually all undertakings would be subject to scrutiny. Clearly, only exorbitantly high prices require regulation, although the Court's case law has provided little clear guidance to identify what constitutes an excessive price. In *United Brands*, the Court of Justice suggested that a price is excessive when it bears no reasonable relation to the economic value of the product in question. This could be measured by comparing the selling price with the cost of production.[131] This standard suggests that dominant firms are entitled to sell at a price somewhat above the cost of production, but not excessively beyond it. Quite how the line between a reasonably high and an unreasonably high price is to be drawn is not explained. As a result the Commission has not prioritised exploitative abuses in its enforcement plans.[132] That said, the Commission has initiated investigations over excessive prices in economic sectors that have only been recently liberalised, where the transition to a competitive market is also monitored by national regulators that have the power to control prices. These investigations have often resulted in informal settlements and price adjustments monitored by national regulators.[133]

The second category of abuse, exclusionary, contains abuses that are designed to impact negatively on rivals. There are two justifications for extending the application of Article 102 to exclusionary abuses.[134] On the one hand, these abusive practices are designed to safeguard the undertaking's dominant position and to facilitate subsequent exploitation of dominance.[135] For instance, United Brands, dominant in the market for bananas, fought to exclude other banana manufacturers from the European market as a way of maintaining its power over customers. Another justification for treating exclusionary abuses as anti-competitive is that by eliminating or weakening competitors, the dominant firm denies the opportunities of other economic actors to participate in the market. This justification is not based upon the inefficiency of exclusionary abuses, but merely upon the denial of the right to market access of other market players, consistent with the rationale in *Continental Can* discussed above. The Commission's approach to these kinds of abuse, however, appears to be designed to protect smaller undertakings rather than consumers. This is so for two reasons: the first is that a finding of an infringement is made very easy by the Court's case law (there is no need to show likely consumer harm, nor indeed a need to show that the exclusionary tactic was or will

---

[130] See S. Bishop and M. Walker, *The Economics of EC Competition Law* (2nd edn, London, Sweet and Maxwell, 2002) 43–4.

[131] Case 27/76 *United Brands Company v Commission* [1978] ECR 207, paras. 250–2.

[132] European Commission, *Twenty-fourth Report on Competition Policy* (1994) part 207.

[133] Most recently, see Case COMP/39.388 *German Electricity Wholesale Market*, Decision of 26 November 2008; Case COMP/39.402 *RWE Gas Foreclosure*, Decision of 19 March 2009.

[134] But some see no good reason for applying Article 102 TFEU to exclusionary abuses, notably R. Joliet, *Monopolization and Abuse of Dominant Position* (Liège, Université de Liège, 1970).

[135] T. G. Kattenmaker and S. C. Salop, 'Anticompetitive Exclusion: Raising Rivals' Costs to Achieve Power over Price' (1986) 96 *Yale Law Journal* 20.

be successful), and the second is that the undertakings under scrutiny find it difficult to justify their actions once these have been judged to constitute an abuse.

The controversial judgment in *British Airways* serves as a clear example of what many see as the overly aggressive approach adopted by the Union.[136] The Commission had condemned BA's strategy of offering travel agents extra commissions when they promoted BA tickets on the basis that this was discriminatory, designed to induce loyalty and served to exclude competing airlines.[137]

Case C-95/04 P *British Airways plc* v *Commission* [2007] ECR I-2331

Criteria for assessing exclusionary effects

68. It follows that in determining whether, on the part of an undertaking in a dominant position, a system of discounts or bonuses which constitute neither quantity discounts or bonuses nor fidelity discounts or bonuses within the meaning of the judgment in *Hoffmann-La Roche* constitutes an abuse, it first has to be determined whether those discounts or bonuses can produce an exclusionary effect, that is to say whether they are capable, first, of making market entry very difficult or impossible for competitors of the undertaking in a dominant position and, secondly, of making it more difficult or impossible for its co-contractors to choose between various sources of supply or commercial partners.

69. It then needs to be examined whether there is an objective economic justification for the discounts and bonuses granted. In accordance with the analysis carried out by the [General Court] ... an undertaking is at liberty to demonstrate that its bonus system producing an exclusionary effect is economically justified.

70. With regard to the first aspect, the case law gives indications as to the cases in which discount or bonus schemes of an undertaking in a dominant position are not merely the expression of a particularly favourable offer on the market, but give rise to an exclusionary effect.

71. First, an exclusionary effect may arise from goal-related discounts or bonuses, that is to say those the granting of which is linked to the attainment of sales objectives defined individually. ...

73. It is also apparent from the case law that the commitment of co-contractors towards the undertaking in a dominant position and the pressure exerted upon them may be particularly strong where a discount or bonus does not relate solely to the growth in turnover in relation to purchases or sales of products of that undertaking made by those co-contractors during the period under consideration, but extends also to the whole of the turnover relating to those purchases or sales. In that way, relatively modest variations – whether upwards or downwards – in the turnover figures relating to the products of the dominant undertaking have disproportionate effects on co-contractors. ...

75. Finally, the Court took the view that the pressure exerted on resellers by an undertaking in a dominant position which granted bonuses with those characteristics is further strengthened where that undertaking holds a very much larger market share than its competitors. It held that, in those

---

[136] For strong critique of the policy towards these practices, see J. Kallaugher and B. Sher, 'Rebates Revisited: Anti-competitive Effects and Exclusionary Abuse under Article 82' (2004) 25 *ECLR* 263; for a defence of these cases see L. Gyselen, 'Rebates: Competition on the Merits or Exclusionary Practice?' in C.-D. Ehlermann and I. Atanasiu (eds.), *European Competition Law Annual: What is an Abuse of a Dominant Position?* (Oxford and Portland, Hart, 2006).

[137] *Virgin/British Airways* [2000] OJ L30/1; affirmed by the CFI Case T-219/99 *British Airways* v *Commission* [2003] ECR II-5917. See further: G. Monti, *EC Competition Law* (Cambridge, Cambridge University Press, 2007) 162–72 and O. Odudu, 'Case Note on *BA* v *Commission*' (2007) 44 *CM Rev.* 1781.

circumstances, it is particularly difficult for competitors of that undertaking to outbid it in the face of discounts or bonuses based on overall sales volume. By reason of its significantly higher market share, the undertaking in a dominant position generally constitutes an unavoidable business partner in the market. Most often, discounts or bonuses granted by such an undertaking on the basis of overall turnover largely take precedence in absolute terms, even over more generous offers of its competitors. In order to attract the co-contractors of the undertaking in a dominant position, or to receive a sufficient volume of orders from them, those competitors would have to offer them significantly higher rates of discount or bonus. ...

Objective economic justification

86. Assessment of the economic justification for a system of discounts or bonuses established by an undertaking in a dominant position is to be made on the basis of the whole of the circumstances of the case. It has to be determined whether the exclusionary effect arising from such a system, which is disadvantageous for competition, may be counterbalanced, or outweighed, by advantages in terms of efficiency which also benefit the consumer. If the exclusionary effect of that system bears no relation to advantages for the market and consumers, or if it goes beyond what is necessary in order to attain those advantages, that system must be regarded as an abuse.

Applying these standards to the facts of the case, the Court of Justice confirmed that BA had abused its dominant position: the bonuses were drawn up individually for each travel agent; they were based upon the total number of tickets sold, and not on those sold over a given level, so selling extra BA tickets meant a significant increase in bonus payments, so that it was often more worthwhile selling a few extra BA tickets than selling some other airlines' tickets; BA's size was such that other competitors lacked 'a sufficiently broad financial base to allow them effectively to establish a reward scheme similar to BA's'.[138] It may be argued that this is insufficient to sustain a finding of abuse; for instance, there was no evidence that BA's scheme meant that its prices were below cost, in which case BA was simply more efficient than its rivals, or at least lucky to have been the first on the market and benefited from a statutory monopoly for several years, giving it a significant advantage over new entrants.

The Court's approach to objective justification should be welcomed, but it must be noted that no dominant firm has yet succeeded in showing that its behaviour is justified once it has been shown that the rebate scheme has exclusionary effects.[139]

The Court's preference for a more structurally based approach to competition, whereby the presence of competitors is necessary for a competitive market, does little to reduce the criticisms that EU competition law protects competitors, and not competition,[140] but there is a rational basis for this approach, as Professor Fox has indicated: 'It is a principle of freedom of non-dominant firms to trade without artificial obstacles constructed by dominant firms, and carries an assumption that preserving this freedom is important to the legitimacy of the

---

[138] Case C-95/04 P *British Airways plc* v *Commission* [2007] ECR I-2331, para. 76.

[139] E. Rousseva, 'Abuse of Dominant Position Defences' in G. Amato and C.-D. Ehlermann (eds.), *EC Competition Law: A Critical Assessment* (Oxford, Hart, 2007).

[140] But see H. Schweitzer, 'Parallels and Differences in the Attitudes Towards and Rules Regarding Market Power: What are the Reasons?' in C.-D. Ehlermann and M. Marquis (eds.), *European Competition Law Annual 2007: A Reformed Approach to Article 82 EC* (Oxford, Hart, 2008).

competition process and is likely to inure to the benefit of all market players, competitors and consumers.'[141] The reader should note the similarity between the Court's appraisal here and that which it takes in Article 101 cases like *GlaxoSmithKline* and *T-Mobile*, discussed earlier: in both instances, the Court is committed to safeguarding the competitive process, not solely competitive outcomes. As will be seen below, this places the Court of Justice in tension with the Commission's current strategy.

(iii) Predatory pricing

The tension between penalising dominant firms because of the possible harm they might cause to the competitive process and the possible benefits of certain forms of behaviour by dominant undertakings is particularly poignant in the context of below cost predatory pricing. Below cost pricing can be a benevolent strategy to enter a market, by reducing prices so as to invite customers, but it may also constitute a predatory strategy designed to drive other competitors out of the market, whereby the predator endures losses until the prey exits the market. Below cost pricing is often practised selectively, targeting those customer groups where the benefits of below cost pricing is greatest. The leading predatory pricing case concerns Akzo, a dominant manufacturer of benzonyl peroxide (a chemical used in two lines of business, flour additives and plastics). It became concerned that one of its competitors, ECS, who had originally sold benzonyl peroxide in the flour sector, was expanding its sales in the plastics sector. Intent on safeguarding its profits, Akzo threatened ECS with retaliation, sold benzonyl peroxide at very low prices to ECS's customers in the flour market, while maintaining a higher price for its regular customers, and engaged in other commercial tactics designed to woo customers away from ECS in an effort to persuade ECS to abandon the plastics sector. The Court established the parameters to determine when low prices are to be deemed predatory.

Case C–62/86 *Akzo Chemie BV v Commission* [1991] ECR I–3359

71. Prices below average variable costs (that is to say, those which vary depending on the quantities produced) by means of which a dominant undertaking seeks to eliminate a competitor must be regarded as abusive. A dominant undertaking has no interest in applying such prices except that of eliminating competitors so as to enable it subsequently to raise its prices by taking advantage of its monopolistic position, since each sale generates a loss, namely the total amount of the fixed costs (that is to say, those which remain constant regardless of the quantities produced) and, at least, part of the variable costs relating to the unit produced.

72. Moreover, prices below average total costs, that is to say, fixed costs plus variable costs, but above average variable costs, must be regarded as abusive if they are determined as part of a plan for eliminating a competitor. Such prices can drive from the market undertakings which are perhaps as efficient as the dominant undertaking but which, because of their smaller financial resources, are incapable of withstanding the competition waged against them.

---

[141] Eleanor M. Fox, 'What is Harm to Competition? Exclusionary Practices and Anticompetitive Effect' (2002) 70 *Antitrust Law Journal* 37, 395.

While more complex theories of predatory pricing suggest that price predation is possible, the Court's approach appears too wide-ranging.[142] First, it does not take into account that below cost pricing can be a pro-competitive strategy when a firm is entering a new product market, where low prices are necessary to generate initial sales.[143] Secondly, the judgment may dent dominant firms' competitive edge: why should Akzo not be entitled to increase its market share? Thirdly, intention was inferred by internal memoranda indicating the desire to undercut ECS, but the desire to undermine competitors is the prime instinct of any company, dominant or not, so the probative value of this approach to intention is unclear. Fourthly, the judgment requires no showing that the predatory pricing campaign is likely to be successful.[144]

In a recent application of these principles by the Commission, WIN (Wanadoo Interactive which, following a merger, was at that time a part of France Télécom) was found to have set predatory prices 'as part of a plan to pre-empt the market in high-speed Internet access during a key phase in its development'.[145] On appeal to the Court of Justice, the parties claimed that a finding of predatory pricing should only succeed if there is proof that the predator is able to recoup the losses incurred during the predatory pricing campaign. While the Advocate General was sympathetic, the Court confirmed that there was no need to establish recoupment.

Case C-202/07 P *France Télécom SA* v *Commission*, Judgment of 2 April 2009

110. Accordingly, contrary to what the appellant claims, it does not follow from the case law of the Court that proof of the possibility of recoupment of losses suffered by the application, by an undertaking in a dominant position, of prices lower than a certain level of costs constitutes a necessary precondition to establishing that such a pricing policy is abusive. In particular, the Court has taken the opportunity to dispense with such proof in circumstances where the eliminatory intent of the undertaking at issue could be presumed in view of that undertaking's application of prices lower than average variable costs.

111. That interpretation does not, of course, preclude the Commission from finding such a possibility of recoupment of losses to be a relevant factor in assessing whether or not the practice concerned is abusive, in that it may, for example where prices lower than average variable costs are applied, assist in excluding economic justifications other than the elimination of a competitor, or, where prices below average total costs but above average variable costs are applied, assist in establishing that a plan to eliminate a competitor exists.

112. Moreover, the lack of any possibility of recoupment of losses is not sufficient to prevent the undertaking concerned reinforcing its dominant position, in particular, following the withdrawal from the market of one or a number of its competitors, so that the degree of competition existing on the market, already weakened precisely because of the presence of the undertaking concerned, is further reduced and customers suffer loss as a result of the limitation of the choices available to them.

---

[142] See P. Bolton, J. F. Brodley and M. H. Riordan, 'Predatory Pricing: Strategic Theory and Legal Policy' (2000) 88 *Georgetown Law Journal* 2239; A. Kate and G. Niels, 'On the Rationality of Predatory Pricing' (2002) *Antitrust Bulletin* 1.

[143] The point was recognised in theory in Case T-83/91 *Tetra Pak* v *Commission* [1994] ECR II-755, para. 147, but the scope for justification is very narrow.

[144] Case C-333/94 P *Tetra Pak* v *Commission* [1996] ECR I-5951, para. 44.

[145] Case COMP/38.233 *Wanadoo Interactive*, Decision of 16 July 2003, article 1.

Since *Akzo*, the Court has failed to explain how a dominant undertaking may justify an aggressive price strategy when its dominant position is challenged by competitors. The General Court has suggested that a dominant firm may respond aggressively with price cuts that are not below cost, provided that the prices are (1) the result of a decision to protect one's position, (2) based on efficiencies, and (3) are in the interest of consumers.[146] However, the application of this standard is difficult. The Court suggests that the dominant firm may merely protect its position and not improve it, although it will be difficult to foresee whether a defensive practice leads the dominant firm to increase its market share (if you cut prices to save your sales you might also attract new customers). The condition that the dominant undertaking's practice must be efficient is not easy to prove, and it is not clear in the case law why low prices are not seen as beneficial to consumers. Thus, dominant undertakings may respond to 'meet competition' but the circumstances in which a dominant firm will succeed in justifying its practices are extremely limited.[147] Perhaps asking whether dominant undertakings can benefit from a meeting competition defence is to approach the abuse doctrine in Article 102 TFEU from the wrong perspective. A meeting competition defence is appropriate if the aim is to promote economic efficiency, thereby allowing dominant firms to defend themselves when they are able to exclude less efficient rivals.[148]

(iv) Reform

Practitioners have regularly criticised the jurisprudence under Article 102: first, the abuse case law has arisen pragmatically in response to individual disputes and without a systematic enforcement policy. As a result, the Commission and Court of Justice in individual cases have operated without 'any clear general analytical or intellectual framework'.[149] Secondly, the case law does not establish a comprehensive abuse doctrine because litigation is reactive. Therefore, only the discrete points that are raised have been considered. Thirdly, the influence of economic thinking, which has increasingly affected other areas of competition law, has not had the same impact on the application of Article 102. However, reviewing the case law from a historical perspective, David Gerber suggests that the jurisprudence is not without wealth or value.[150]

David J. Gerber, 'Law and the Abuse of Economic Power in Europe' (1987) 62 *Tulane Law Review* 57, 100–5

A. Conceptual Structure

In Community law the broad principle of competitive distortion is the central mechanism for giving content to the abuse concept. It is generally applied, however, according to a developing set of case-law principles fashioned to protect particular interests. These application principles protect, for example, the interests of consumers and small and medium-sized firms. They also protect dominant enterprises

---

[146] Case T-228/97 *Irish Sugar plc* v *Commission* [1999] ECR II-2969, para. 189.
[147] P. Andrews, 'Is Meeting Competition a Defence to Predatory Pricing?' (1998) *ECLR* 9; D. Ridyard, 'Domco's Dilemma: When is Price Competition Anti-Competitive?' (1999) *ECLR* 345.
[148] E. Elhauge, 'Why Above-Cost Price Cuts to Drive Out Entrants are Not Predatory: and the Implications for Defining Costs and Market Power' (2002) 112 *Yale Law Journal* 681.
[149] J. T. Lang, R. O'Donoghue, 'Defining Legitimate Competition: How to Clarify Pricing Abuses under Article 82 EC' (2002) 26 *Fordham International Law Journal* 83.
[150] *Ibid.*

by providing that conduct which otherwise would be a violation of [Article 102 TFEU] may be justified under certain circumstances. Analysis generally begins, therefore, with the issue of whether conduct 'distorts competition' and then turns to case law to determine whether the competitive distortion harms interests whose protection is required under existing guidelines ...

B. The Application of Abuse Law Concepts

Both systems [German and European] have also identified competitive unfairness as a category of abuse. Here the abuse concept is used to prevent dominant firms from using their power to achieve an unfair advantage in competition with other firms, such as, for example, through predatory pricing. In German law competitive unfairness is included within the concept of impediment abuse, whereas the European Commission applies [Article 102 TFEU] to such conduct because it distorts competition to the detriment of smaller competitors and, in the long run, consumers.

Both systems have encountered, however, significant difficulties in conceptualizing competitive unfairness for purposes of judicial application. Each has turned primarily to the intuitively appealing idea of competition on the merits in order to provide a fairness standard, but this method of giving content to the abuse concept has not been finally accepted in either system, and there are many who doubt its viability. These doubts relate to whether the merit competition notion has sufficient analytical power to make justifiable and reasonably predictable distinctions among the various types of conduct available to economically powerful firms. Neither system has yet had sufficient experience with this concept to warrant final conclusions about its effectiveness. Nevertheless, the fact that both systems have chosen to rely on it in using the abuse concept to combat competitive unfairness means that the future of the idea of unfairness as part of abuse law may well depend on the amenability to judicial application of the concept of merit competition.

A third category of practices that are considered abusive in both systems includes those by which dominant producers exercise control over firms that distribute their products. In both systems loyalty rebates, exclusive dealing contracts, and similar control measures may be abusive... Under Community law, such control mechanisms are found abusive when they distort competition to the detriment of consumers and interfere with the freedom of small and medium-sized firms. This analysis refers directly to the power that a dominant producer may have over distributors as well as to its effects. The result has been the development of flexible and judicially applicable principles to guide business behaviour ...

C. Methods of Interpretation

In Community law the decision in *Continental Can* to interpret abuse teleologically – i.e., by reference to the objectives of the Community – has determined the structure and development of abuse law, because it established the concept of competitive distortion as the analytical starting point. In addition, the court often fashions its application principles according to its perception of the systemic needs of the Community. For example, the court's application of the abuse concept to loyalty rebates is based on the perceived need to protect the structure of competition by protecting the competitive freedom of small and medium-sized firms. Although the court occasionally also finds guidance by analogizing to the examples provided in article 86, the teleological method has been the dominant means of ascribing meaning to abuse in Community law.

Despite criticism for failure fully to utilize more predictable methods of interpretation, the European Court has fashioned a body of legal principles with sufficient integrity and coherence to have achieved general acceptance. Its success in doing so is clearly related, however, to a general consensus concerning the basic objectives of [Articles 101 and 102 TFEU] – principally, the elimination of barriers to trade within the Community – as well as to the articulation of Community objectives in the governing treaty ...

D. The Process of Legal Development

... Although basic principles of analysis in Community abuse law were provided through the authority of outside experts,[151] the subsequent development of the law has been primarily the product of adjudication by the European Court. The court has established a basic framework for giving content to the abuse concept and has consistently applied this framework and the ideas generated thereby to new fact situations. Consequently, it is the court's central role that has dominated the developmental process.

The Commission has shaped this development through both policy and enforcement decisions. Its identification and articulation of Community policy goals has been particularly influential because of the court's focus on using the abuse concept to achieve the fundamental objectives of the Community. Moreover, not only has the Commission's enforcement policy determined the fact situations which would reach the court, but its decisions have also established lines of conceptual development which the court has later adopted.

One helpful lesson which we might draw from Gerber's analysis is that to understand the law in this field, less attention should be paid to legal nuances and to economic edicts, but greater focus should be placed upon matching the abuse doctrine to Community policies, with an understanding that the Commission has regularly used Article 102 as a tool to achieve a vast array of Community objectives, and the Court of Justice gave this approach unstinting support in the early years but has since the 1990s exercised a more stringent form of judicial review.[152] From this angle, a richer synthesis of abuse might be attained by matching the decisions with Community policies: cases which support the aims of safeguarding small and medium-sized undertakings and of market integration are both seen as engines for developing, in the long term, the interests of consumers.

In late 2005, DG Competition published a discussion paper on exclusionary abuse which indicated that it sought to redirect its policy by using a more economics-oriented framework.[153] This stimulated a lively debate among competition scholars and practitioners.[154] The outcome of these reflections is a paper issued in 2009 entitled 'Guidance on the Commission's enforcement priorities in applying Article 82 of the EC Treaty (now Article 102 TFEU) to abusive exclusionary conduct by dominant undertakings'.[155] This paper should be studied from two angles.[156]

---

[151] This alludes to a report prepared by academics for the Commission: *Memorandum sur le Problème de la Concentration dans le Marché Commun* (1 December 1965), reprinted in (1966) *Revue trimestrielle de droit européen* 651.

[152] See generally A. Arnull, *The European Union and Its Court of Justice* (Oxford, Oxford University Press, 1999) noting a general trend whereby the Court of Justice supports the expansion of EC competition law doctrines in the early years but applies a stricter approach from the mid-1980s.

[153] Discussion Paper on the application of Article 82 of the Treaty to exclusionary abuses (December 2005), available at http://ec.europa.eu/comm/competition/antitrust/art82/index.html.

[154] See e.g. the 2006 special issue of the *European Competition Journal*; C.-D. Ehlermann and I. Atanasiu (eds.), *European Competition Law Annual 2003: What is an Abuse of a Dominant Position?* (Oxford, Hart, 2004); Ehlermann and Marquis, above n. 141; R. O'Donoghue and A. J. Padilla, *The Law and Economics of Article 82 EC* (Oxford, Hart, 2006); J. Vickers, 'Abuse of Market Power' (2005) 115 *The Economic Journal* F244. See also EAGCP, 'An Economic Approach to Article 82', July 2005, available at http://europa.eu.int/comm/competition/publications/studies/eagcp_july_21_05.pdf.

[155] [2009] OJ C45/7.

[156] For some early assessments, see G. Monti, 'Article 82 EC: What Future for the Effects-Based Approach?' (2010) *Journal of European Competition Law and Practice* 2; H. Schweitzer, 'Recent Developments in EU Competition Law (2006–2008): Single-Firm Dominance and the Interpretation of Article 82' (2009) *European Review of Contract Law* 175.

First, it is designed to set the tone for the Commission's overall enforcement strategy, which will focus on behaviour likely to harm consumers and indicates a shift away from merely protecting competition as such. If so, then it appears that the Commission is on a collision course with the Court, as only the latter can determine the scope of Article 102. However, the way the Commission avoids this clash is not by denying the correctness of the case law, but by saying that while potentially more abuse cases could be brought, the Commission will exercise its prosecutorial discretion by only taking those cases where, in addition to establishing abuse under the legal parameters set out by the Court, the Commission also finds that the abuse harms a competitor as efficient as the dominant firm, and is likely to result in consumer harm. For example, in the *Intel* Decision the Commission established that the rebates in question were abusive in line with the Court's indications in *British Airways*, but then went on to discuss in detail how the rebates were likely to foreclose market access and harm consumer welfare.[157] From this perspective, the title of the Guidance is somewhat misleading: the paper does not list priority cases, rather it sets out an enforcement principle which allows the Commission to select those cases where enforcement is warranted. This is a very astute move from the Commission: incapable of overruling the Court's case law, it supplements the current elements of abuse (harm to the competitive process) with new ones (likely foreclosure of competitors and likely consumer harm). In the long run, the Union courts may feel compelled to endorse these new elements and so incrementally a novel abuse doctrine will materialise. It is less easy to see a scenario where the Court will be asked to reject the enforcement standard being proposed by the Commission. Parties who are condemned will more likely question the evidence of consumer harm (as Intel did), and the victims of those dominant undertakings who escape conviction are unlikely to be able to use the Court to require the Commission to ascertain an infringement absent likely consumer harm given the Commission's wide prosecutorial discretion. That said, national courts may continue to follow the precedents set by the Court of Justice and so there may be a tension between the interpretation of abuse at national and EU level.

The second perspective through which to study the Guidance is to test how far the Commission is true to its commitment to search for likely consumer harm. For instance, in considering predatory pricing abuses, one might reasonably conclude that the new approach would hinge on proving that the predator will be able to gain from this strategy by raising prices. However, the Commission's approach is somewhat broader.

Guidance on the Commission's enforcement priorities in applying Article 82 of the EC Treaty [now Article 102 TFEU] to abusive exclusionary conduct by dominant undertakings [2009] OJ C45/7

69. The Commission does not consider that it is necessary to show that competitors have exited the market in order to show that there has been anticompetitive foreclosure. The possibility cannot be excluded that the dominant undertaking may prefer to prevent the competitor from competing vigorously and have it follow the dominant undertaking's pricing, rather than eliminate it from the market altogether. Such disciplining avoids the risk inherent in eliminating competitors, in particular the risk that the assets of the competitor are sold at a low price and stay in the market, creating a new low cost entrant.

---

[157] Case COMP/37.990 *Intel*, Decision of 13 May 2009.

70. Generally speaking, consumers are likely to be harmed if the dominant undertaking can reasonably expect its market power after the predatory conduct comes to an end to be greater than it would have been had the undertaking not engaged in that conduct in the first place, that is to say, if the undertaking is likely to be in a position to benefit from the sacrifice.

71. This does not mean that the Commission will only intervene if the dominant undertaking would be likely to be able to increase its prices above the level persisting in the market before the conduct. It is sufficient, for instance, that the conduct would be likely to prevent or delay a decline in prices that would otherwise have occurred. Identifying consumer harm is not a mechanical calculation of profits and losses, and proof of overall profits is not required. Likely consumer harm may be demonstrated by assessing the likely foreclosure effect of the conduct, combined with consideration of other factors, such as entry barriers. In this context, the Commission will also consider possibilities of re-entry.

These passages indicate that the Commission will consider the likely effect of predatory pricing on consumer welfare, but without requiring proof that prices will rise, allowing the predator to recover the costs incurred. While some may challenge this as being out of line with economics, it may be defended in that jurisdictions that require proof of recoupment have found it impossible to convict undertakings engaging in predatory pricing.

5 CONVERGENCE

It is too early to say how the Commission's enforcement of Article 102 TFEU will develop and how the Court of Justice will respond, but the new stance allows us to conclude this chapter by drawing together common themes that underpin the interpretation of Articles 101 and 102 TFEU.

First, the Court has taken the opportunity, in a number of recent cases extracted in this chapter, to restate its commitment to the protection of competition, as opposed to the protection of consumer welfare. Accordingly, the process of competition is at the forefront of its interpretation of these rules. This contrasts with the Commission's emphasis on safeguarding consumer welfare. However, the difference between these two approaches may be less pronounced than appears because even the Commission is unlikely to allow practices that damage the structure of the market significantly. Thus, exemptions under Article 101(3) TFEU may not be granted if they would eliminate all competition; and there is still reluctance in affording dominant undertakings a defence once abuse has been established.

Secondly, there may be a more pronounced tension between the Court and Commission with respect to the role of non-economic factors. While the Commission wishes to narrow the scope of Article 101(3) TFEU to an efficiency defence, the Court's recent case law indicates both a wider role for exemptions and also the possibility of excluding the application of competition law when other public interest considerations merit protection.

Thirdly, there is now a shared analytical method in the application of both Articles. Save in cases where there is an anti-competitive object under Article 101(1), the Commission will begin its analysis with a definition of the relevant market (previously avoided in Article 101 cases), and an examination of market power. Absent a high level of market power, competition law will probably not apply. With market power, the Commission will then test to what extent the activities under scrutiny are likely to harm consumer welfare and will enforce competition law only if there is proof of such harm, while allowing the undertakings under investigation the chance of establishing that the agreement has certain benefits that outweigh the losses identified by the Commission. A shared analytical approach is to be welcomed given that these two provisions have the same objective.

Finally, now that the Commission is freed of the burdens that resulted from notification, it is in a better position to prioritise its enforcement strategies. In this light the Commission's recent guidance on Article 102 TFEU is best read in the light of the overall enforcement priorities that DG Competition sets for itself. The former Director-General, for instance, has recently indicated that the Commission uses the following criteria to determine its priorities: selecting certain sectors where anti-competitive effects are more pronounced (currently telecommunications and energy); focusing on practices that cause the most harm to consumers (which explains the emphasis on cartel cases, the new approach to exclusionary abuse and the less intrusive regulation of vertical restraints); and considering how far competition law is the best mechanism for addressing a given market failure.[158]

FURTHER READING

C.-D. Ehlermann and M. Marquis (eds.), *European Competition Law Annual 2007: A Reformed Approach to Article 82 EC* (Oxford, Hart, 2008)

T. Eilmansberger, 'How to Distinguish Good from Bad Competition under Article 82 EC: In Search of Clearer and More Coherent Standards for Anti-competitive Abuses' (2005) 42 *CMLRev.* 129

D. J. Gerber, 'Law and the Abuse of Economic Power in Europe' (1987) 62 *Tulane Law Review* 57

G. Van Gerven and E. Navarro Varona, 'The Wood Pulp Case and the Future of Concerted Practices' (1994) 31 *CMLRev.* 575

C. Harding and J. Joshua, *Regulating Cartels in Europe: A Study of Legal Control of Corporate Delinquency* (Oxford, Oxford University Press, 2003)

P. Jebsen and R. Stevens, 'Assumptions, Goals and Dominant Undertakings: The Regulation of Competition under Article 86' (1996) 64 *Antitrust Law Journal* 443

L. Kjølbe, 'The New Commission Guidelines on the Application of Article 81(3): An Economic Approach to Article 81' (2004) *ECLR* 566

G. Monti, *EC Competition Law* (Cambridge, Cambridge University Press, 2007)

M. Motta, *Competition Policy* (Cambridge, Cambridge University Press, 2004)

P. Nicolaides, 'The Balancing Myth: The Economics of Article 81(1) and (3)' (2005) 32 *LIEI* 123

R. O'Donoghue and A. J. Padilla, *The Law and Economics of Article 82 EC* (Oxford, Hart, 2006)

O. Odudu, *The Boundaries of EC Competition Law* (Oxford, Oxford University Press, 2006)

P. Rey and J. S. Venit, 'Parallel Trade and Pharmaceuticals: A Policy in Search of Itself' (2004) 29 *ELRev.* 176

C. Townley, *Article 81 EC and Public Policy* (Oxford, Hart, 2009)

J. Vickers, 'Abuse of Market Power' (2005) 115 *The Economic Journal* F244

R. Wesseling, *The Modernisation of EC Antitrust Law* (Oxford, Hart, 2000)

---

[158] P. Lowe, 'The Design of Competition Policy Institutions for the Twenty-first Century' in X. Vives (ed.), *Competition Policy in the EU* (Oxford, Oxford University Press, 2009).

24

State Regulation and EU Competition Law

CONTENTS

1 INTRODUCTION

In this chapter we consider the application of EU competition law to the regulation of markets by Member States. Enforcement of competition law in this field was slow to emerge.[1] The reason for the belated, and so far relatively cautious, intervention is threefold. First, there was change in the European Union's economic policy at the time of the Single European Act, favouring greater liberalisation of the economy. State intervention changed from a field where the Union did not venture, to being inherently suspect.[2] Secondly, regulating sovereign states is more politically sensitive than regulating private firms; thus the Commission and Union courts had to move with more caution. Thirdly, there is a tension between the Union's aims of competition and liberalisation, on the one hand, and the duties that Member States owe to their citizens, in particular the duty to ensure the availability of certain services (e.g. water,

---

[1] The regulation of state aid, the obligation to adjust national monopolies and public procurement are not covered in this chapter.

[2] A. Gardner, 'The Velvet Revolution: Article 90 and the Triumph of the Free Market in Europe's Regulated Sectors' (1995) *ECLR* 78, 79.

telecommunications, energy, postal services), on the other. The Member States' concern is that competition may undermine the provision of these services.

Initially, it fell to individuals, wishing to take advantage of increasingly liberalised markets, to challenge anti-competitive state regulation, which led to the Court of Justice becoming involved in determining how far markets should be liberalised (a process which may be labelled 'negative integration'). While this approach may result in some markets being opened, liberalisation of economic sectors is necessarily random and guided by private interests. Subsequently, the Community gradually began to take legislative steps to liberalise major industries formerly under state control or ownership, in particular the network industries (for example, telecommunications, transport, energy and postal services), as part of the Community's single market programme which sees network industries as a catalyst to generate increased competitiveness in the EU economy as a whole ('positive integration'). To reflect these developments, the chapter is organised in the following manner.

Section 2 is a review of how the Court of justice has interpreted two key Treaty provisions: Articles 4(3) TEU (ex Article 10 EC) and 106(1) TFEU (ex Article 86(1) EC). The Court has used these rules to put pressure on Member States to open markets. While these Treaty provisions could have been applied much more aggressively against Member States, the Court shied away from doing so.

Section 3 examines the tension between opening markets, on the one hand, and the provision of public services, on the other. We begin by examining two methods by which the Court has attempted to take into consideration Member States' claims that the need to ensure the provision of certain public services justifies the non-application of competition law: first, the Court has found that the providers of certain social security benefits were not 'undertakings', and so competition law did not apply to their actions even if they stifled competition; secondly, the Court has interpreted Article 106(2) TFEU (ex Article 86(2) EC) (which allows for the non-application of the Treaty rules as a whole when a Member State entrusts an undertaking with the performance of a service of general interest) in a generous way to protect the provision of certain public services. Then, we study successive amendments to the Treaties to explain how the Union has become increasingly sensitive to the demands of Member States, even though little concrete progress has been made.

Section 4 reviews measures of 'positive integration', that is, EU secondary legislation that liberalises markets, on the one hand, and creates EU-wide public service obligations, on the other. We use the liberalisation of the postal sector as an example to illustrate this process.

Section 5 closes by evaluating the legal developments discussed in this chapter from two perspectives: first, by considering what the economic impact has been: are markets more competitive as a result of EU law? Secondly, by considering the issue from a political science perspective, by questioning how far there has been harmonisation in these economic sectors, on the one hand, and by exploring how far the Union has used its powers to extend the reach and legitimacy of EU law, on the other.

2 ANTI-COMPETITIVE STATE REGULATION

(i) A general obligation

Member States have a general obligation to cooperate with the European Union to facilitate the objectives of the Treaty on the Functioning of the European Union.

Article 4(3) TEU

Pursuant to the principle of sincere cooperation, the Union and the Member States shall, in full mutual respect, assist each other in carrying out tasks which flow from the Treaties.

The Member States shall take any appropriate measure, general or particular, to ensure fulfilment of the obligations arising out of the Treaties or resulting from the acts of the institutions of the Union.

The Member States shall facilitate the achievement of the Union's tasks and refrain from any measure which could jeopardise the attainment of the Union's objectives.

In an adventurous spate of decisions from the late 1970s to the mid-1980s, the Court of Justice held that on the basis of Article 4(3) TEU, Member States could not maintain in force legislation that allowed an undertaking to infringe EU competition law because such legislation deprived competition law of its *effet utile*.[3] For example, in *van Vlaamse*, the Union of Belgian Travel Agents had set up a code of conduct prohibiting discounts, clearly a price fixing agreement contrary to Article 101 TFEU. The code was then incorporated in a Royal Decree and became compulsory. One travel agent infringed the code and was challenged by the Flemish Travel Agents Association; in his defence he claimed that the code was contrary to EU law. In a reference from the Belgian court, the Court of Justice held that the Belgian law reinforced the private agreement (in effect sanctioning a cartel) and as such the law was inconsistent with Article 4(3) TEU, read in conjunction with Article 101 TFEU.[4] The Court consolidated this approach in *Van Eycke*, which codifies the basis upon which state regulation will fall foul of EU competition law: a state measure would be incompatible with Articles 4(3) TEU read together with Articles 101 or 102 TFEU if it 'were to require or favour the adoption of agreements, decisions or concerted practices contrary to [Article 101 TFEU], or to reinforce their effects, or to deprive its own legislation of its official character by delegating to private traders responsibility for taking decisions affecting the economic sphere'.[5] In each of the circumstances identified in this passage, the Court seeks a causal link between a state measure and conduct by private undertakings which infringes Article 101 TFEU. Without an infringement of competition law by the undertakings (whether entered into before a state measure that reinforces its effects, or after a state measure delegates the creation of a restrictive agreement to the undertakings) Article 4(3) TEU on its own does not apply.[6] The ruling in *Meng* can serve to explain the significance of this limitation: an insurance agent was prosecuted by state officials for violation of a German regulation preventing insurance agents from passing on to their customers commissions or other financial advantages. The court found no evidence of a previous agreement by the insurance undertakings to restrict the commissions paid to

---

[3] In EU law, *effet utile* finds no easy English translation. It refers to the effectiveness of a rule of law. In this context it indicates that if states could legislate to legitimise anti-competitive behaviour the effectiveness of Articles 101 and 102 TFEU would be lost, as undertakings could merely lobby governments to shield their anti-competitive agreements with legislation preventing the application of EU competition law. The approach was first canvassed in Case 13/77 *GB-INNO-BM SA* v *Association des détaillants en tabac (ATAB)* [1977] ECR 2115.

[4] Case 311/85 *Vereniging van Vlaamse Reisbureaus* v *ASBL Sociale Dienst van de Plaatselijke en Gewestelijke Overheidsdiensten* [1987] ECR 3801.

[5] Case 267/86 *Pascal Van Eycke* v *ASPA NV* [1988] ECR 4769, para. 16.

[6] However, some case law had suggested that Article 10 EC (now Article 4(3) TEU) might apply without anti-competitive behaviour by private undertakings, notably *Association des Centres Distributeurs Leclerc* v *SARL 'Au Blé Vert'* [1985] ECR 1.

clients, nor of state law compelling insurers to enter into such agreements, nor of a delegation by the state. As a result the state law, whilst restricting price competition, was not in breach of Article 4(3) TEU and 101 TFEU.[7] However, the effect of the German legislation in *Meng* is identical to the effect of the law in *van Vlaamse*: in both cases the law causes a misallocation of economic resources by removing price competition. Not only that, but if the reason for the Court's approach in *van Vlaamse* is to maintain the effectiveness of competition law, then that consideration should apply also in the *Meng* case and allow the Court to declare state law incompatible with competition law if it has anti-competitive effects.[8] It fell to Advocate General Tesauro to explain why the state action doctrine did not apply absent an agreement by the undertakings.

Case C–2/91 *Criminal Proceedings Against Wolf W. Meng* [1993] ECR I–5751, Opinion of Advocate General Tesauro

25. ... I do not consider it permissible to criticize the possible and indirect anti-competitive effect of State measures when that effect has no link with the conduct of undertakings or in fact with Article [101 TFEU], that is to say when it does not in any way cloak, directly or indirectly, conduct ... on the part of the undertakings.

    Otherwise, the alleged illegality of the State measure would have to be based solely on the combined provisions of [Article 3(1)(b) TFEU] and [Article 4(3) TEU]: the first of course no longer being seen as an objective to be attained under the conditions laid down in the Treaty but rather as a fundamental and independent principle to which the competition provisions are merely ancillary. Moreover, that interpretation, although on a systematic reading of the Treaty, appearing somewhat improbable, would of course raise the not inconsiderable problem of the effect of such a principle on the legal position of individuals: it should not be forgotten that in this case it is an individual who has claimed before the national court a subjective legal position accorded to him, in his view, by Community law and denied him by national law. However, it seems to me that there can be no question of attributing direct effect to Article [3(1)(b) TFEU], even when read in conjunction with Article [4(3) TEU]. ...

27. ... Moreover, a solution based solely on the anti-competitive effect of national legislation displays numerous disadvantages, insofar as the Court may be called upon to examine every national measure affecting the business activity of the undertakings, and most importantly, because of the legal uncertainty that would arise regarding the type of State measures that are incompatible with the competition rules. Even if the review of measures of that kind were merely marginal and limited to the appropriateness of the measure, examining the extent to which the means adopted were consonant with the aims pursued in the public interest, the fact remains that the very possibility of verifying whether the choice made by the legislator is justified by reasons relating to the public interest, and above all the question whether or not such an interest takes precedence over the anti-competitive effect of the legislation in question, might lead to arbitrary solutions in the absence of any yardstick for the appraisal of legality.

---

[7] Case C–2/91 *Criminal Proceedings Against Wolf W. Meng* [1993] ECR I–5751.

[8] R. Joliet, 'National Anti-competitive Legislation and Community Law' in (1998) *Fordham Corporate Law Institute* 16 (B. Hawk (ed.) 1989). Some argued that *Meng* should be read as part of a general pattern of the Court's jurisprudence at that time, i.e. a retreat from the doctrine of *effet utile* and the adoption of a formalist approach. N. Reich, 'The "November Revolution" of the European Court of Justice: *Keck*, *Meng* and *Audi* Revisited' (1994) 31 *CMLRev*. 459, 465.

28. Admittedly, a solution based exclusively on the existence of a link between the State legislation and the anti-competitive conduct on the part of individuals may appear unsatisfactory, since it is quite possible that in certain cases an agreement between undertakings may prove to be of only formal significance This situation might arise in cases where a state measure has affected competition in the market in a manner substantially in harmony with the wishes expressed by the economic agents concerned. However, it must be borne in mind, first, that the influence of private individuals in the process of drafting legal provisions is an established fact in modern legal systems; and, secondly, that in practice it is not easy to determine whether the state measure concerned actually reflects courses of action advocated by private individuals, which may well coincide with the public interest pursued by the legislature. …

30. In any event, it does not seem to me that the approach so far taken by the Court is such as to afford immunity for measures whose sole aim is to evade the competition rules. I would point out that the cases in which it seems necessary to have recourse to Articles [4(3) TEU, 3(1)(b) and 101 TFEU] in order to declare unlawful national legislation having the same effects as an agreement prohibited by Article [101 TFEU] are purely residual. Most 'anti-competitive' economic measures in fact affect the Community rules on the common market in the areas covered by Article [34 TFEU] or Article [56 TFEU] … The application of [Article 34 TFEU] or [Article 56 TFEU] does not call for an artificial interpretation: they are provisions addressed to the Member States, which must be strictly interpreted and facilitate review of the State measure in question on the basis of clear and precise criteria.

While the Advocate General, on the one hand, warns of the 'floodgates' risk of applying Article 4(3) TEU to every legislative act that has anti-competitive effects, he notes that other Treaty provisions might apply to regulate anti-competitive state action. But if anti-competitive legislation can be caught by other means, this undermines the floodgates argument and begs the question of why the Court should preclude the application of Article 4(3) TEU in the way it has. The answer seems to be that at the time *Meng* was decided, it was uncertain whether the state would be able to provide a public interest defence if the court were to find that state law infringed the competition rules, while in the free movement context states can try to argue that national anti-competitive legislation is justified.[9] In the Article 101 context, exemptions are available under Article 101(3), but it is not clear how far non-economic considerations can serve to justify anti-competitive agreements.[10] However, even this rationalisation points to a gap: if anti-competitive state legislation falls outside the Article 4(3) TEU doctrine and is also not covered by the free movement laws, then some anti-competitive state action is possible, compromising the Treaty's ambition to create an economy based on market principles.[11]

From another perspective, the case law throws up a different problem: if we agree that the scope of the Article 4(3) TEU doctrine is limited to cases where there is a causal connection between the law and an agreement by the undertakings subject to the law, is the state always in breach of EU law? Is there no scope to justify anti-competitive state regulation even if this could be in the public interest? For instance, a Member State may want to regulate the price of

[9] See Chapters 16–21.
[10] K. Bacon, 'State Regulation of the Market and EC Competition Rules: Articles 85 and 86 Compared' (1997) *ECLR* 283, 288.
[11] A. F. Gagliardi, 'United States and European Union Antitrust versus State Regulation of the Economy: Is there a Better Test?' (2000) 25 *ELRev.* 353, 367.

certain goods to make sure that they are available for all citizens at reasonable prices, and may thus allow the sellers to agree a price. The Court's answer to date seems to be that while states are unable to give substantive policy reasons why their actions do not infringe competition law, they may avoid the application of competition law if procedures are in place to show that the state is not merely ratifying anti-competitive agreements but is regulating the economy in cooperation with relevant stakeholders and is thus acting in the public interest. This position can be inferred from the Court's jurisprudence.[12] In *Reiff*, the Court found that members of the German tariff board that fixed road haulage tariffs under the supervision of the ministry were not representatives of interested undertakings. Thus, the state was found not to have infringed Article 4(3) TEU because it had not delegated its legislative powers to private undertakings (the third limb of the *Van Eycke* test). Formalistically, the Court simply ruled that state law did not lead to any agreement contrary to Article 101 TFEU, but in order to reach this conclusion, the Court observed that there were two procedural safeguards to ensure that the state had not merely relinquished the regulation of the economy to private interests. First, members of the tariff board were experts nominated by members of the industry, but they were not bound by instructions from the undertakings. Secondly, the ministry had the final say on the composition of the board and the discretion to set its own tariffs if it felt the board's decisions went against the public interest.[13] Contrast this with the facts in *Commission v Italy*.[14] Italy appealed against a Commission declaration that an Italian law which empowered the National Council of Customs Agents to adopt a decision to fix compulsory tariffs for all customs agents infringed Italy's obligations under Articles 4(3) TEU and 101 TFEU. In contrast to the composition of the tariff board in *Reiff*, here the Council members 'are the representatives of professional customs agents and nothing in the national legislation concerned prevents the [Council] from acting in the exclusive interest of the profession'.[15] Nor was there any rule obliging or encouraging the Council to take the public interest into consideration when fixing tariffs. Thus, the state had relinquished its role as economic regulator to the industry, supporting a cartel agreement. While superficially the two cases can be distinguished on the basis that, in *Reiff*, there was no delegation of legislative power while there was such a delegation in *Commission v Italy*, Harm Schepel notes a potentially deeper grounding for the Court's approach.

> **Harm Schepel, 'Delegation of Regulatory Powers to Private Parties under EC Competition Law: Towards a Procedural Public Interest Test' (2002) 39 *Common Market Law Review* 31**
>
> Where the public authorities make use of committees of financially interested parties unencumbered by serious public interest obligations, it is perfectly proper for the Court to insist that these authorities consult affected parties and retain and exercise the power to reject or amend proposals made by those

---

[12] See I. Van Bael and J.-F. Bellis, *Competition Law of the European Community* (4th edn, The Hague, Kluwer Law International, 2004) 988–90.

[13] Case C-185/91 *Reiff* [1993] ECR I-5801, paras. 17–22. Similar safeguards were found in Case C-96/94 *Centro Servizi Spediporto Srl v Spedizione Marittima del Golfo Srl* [1995] ECR I-2883 and Case C-35/99 *Criminal Proceedings against Manuele Arduino* [2002] ECR I-1529; Joined Cases C-94/04 and C-202/04 *Federico Cipolla and Others v Rosaria Fazari, née Portolese and Roberto Meloni*, Judgment of 6 December 2006.

[14] Case C-35/96 *Commission v Italy (customs agents)* [1998] ECR I-3851.

[15] *Ibid.* para. 41.

committees. It should just not pretend that the committee is not an 'association of undertakings'. Where the public authorities delegate regulatory powers to self-regulatory bodies, it is perfectly proper for the Court to insist that these bodies have balanced interest representation and internal decision-making procedures that ensure that all concerned third parties have the chance to voice their opinions and have these taken into due account. It should just not pretend that the authorities have not 'delegated' decision-making power. And where, as in *Reiff*, there are doubts on both scores, it should not pretend to settle two different issues but should consider whether all elements combined – from the status of individual members as 'independent experts' to the obligation incumbent on the committee as a whole to take the 'public interest' into account and to consult affected third parties, to the provision granting the Minister at least the theoretical possibility to reject the committee's proposals – are sufficient to pass the test of public-regarding legislation.

Self-regulatory arrangements are to be protected from antitrust if they can make a plausible claim to put the 'public interest' over narrow private interests. The 'public interest' is defined neither substantively nor institutionally: the 'public interest' is defined procedurally. The test recognizes on the one hand that the public interest is a matter of political choice, and is not necessarily best served by the substantive norm of undistorted competition. On the other hand, it also recognizes that the public interest is not necessarily best served by the institutional norm of public status. That norm implies deference to public authorities which impoverishes the notion of the public interest and reduces the idea of democratic governance to formal structures of accountability and constitutional hierarchy. Moreover, by insisting on public power over the economy, it holds on to the territorial frame of State and market and has no way of addressing transnational governance regimes.

Albeit very implicitly, the Court has fashioned a public interest test that transforms Community competition law into a rudimentary set of procedural norms of good governance for private regulation. It is a set of norms that recognizes that the legitimacy of economic self-regulation depends on procedures that ensure the meaningful participation of all concerned parties rather than on hierarchical structures of formal political accountability. In that sense, the 'delegation' test contributes to the constitutionalization of private governance.

From a practical perspective, this approach avoids any substantive assessment of the public policy considerations that the state takes into account, with the safeguard that the state has the obligation to institute a procedure whereby it is seen to be regulating the economy in the public interest rather than succumbing to lobbying by interested parties. A French commentator noted a paradox in this approach: on the one hand, the basis for condemning the state is precisely its regulation of the market. However, the *Reiff* approach suggests that the state's involvement in securing that private actors work for the public interest is the reason for not applying competition law![16] Moreover, this procedural defence might not be as effective as confronting more directly whether the public policy invoked by the state is legitimate and whether the particular form of state regulation invoked is proportionate to the goal being sought, something which the Court may be more willing to consider today in the aftermath of the *Wouters* decision (which we considered in Chapter 23) where it held that EU competition law would not apply when it would conflict with the protection of a legitimate interest.[17]

---

[16] C. Leroy, 'L'intérêt général comme régulateur des marchés' (2001) 37 *Revue Trimestrielle de Droit Européen* 49.

[17] Case C-309/99 *Wouters and Others* v *Algemene Raad van de Nederlandse Orde van Advocaten* [2002] ECR I-1577. In Case C-202/04 *Cipolla*, above n. 13, the Court did not address this issue but it considered public interest defences when examining the fixing of lawyers' fees under the internal market rules.

One final consideration relates to enforcement of the state's obligations under Article 4(3) TEU. The Commission has only once (in *Commission* v *Italy*) issued a reasoned opinion that state law infringed this doctrine; the remainder of the case law is the result of national litigation where a person infringing national law uses Article 4(3) TEU to claim that national law is contrary to EU law and should be set aside. It must be recalled that the consequences of a national court setting aside national legislation because it is in breach of normatively superior EU law will not just aid the private litigant but will expose the state to damages claims if the legislation is not amended and harm is caused. This creates a strong, albeit indirect and haphazard, incentive upon states to remove anti-competitive legislation. More systematic challenges to anti-competitive state action might result from the Court's ruling in *Consorzio Industrie Fiammiferi* v *Autorità Garante della Concorrenza e del Mercato*.[18] Here, the Italian Competition Authority acted on a complaint from a German match manufacturer who considered that Italian legislation regulating a consortium of Italian match manufacturers had anti-competitive effects which hindered the export of matches into Italy. The Court of Justice seized on this eagerly and affirmed the Italian Competition Authority's duty to declare unlawful and disapply state law that facilitated or obliged private parties to enter into anti-competitive agreements contrary to Article 4(3) TEU read together with Article 101 TFEU. This adds an additional layer of enforcement and, according to the Italian Competition Authority, while 'the duties to disapply a law occur only exceptionally, the Court's judgment will have a more general effect, favouring the introduction of regulations that are more concerned about safeguarding the general interest and less focused on protectionist requests'.[19] To further strengthen the enforcement of competition law, the Court, in *Fiammiferi*, also held that liability in damages may be available against undertakings which act on the encouragement of state legislation, thereby furthering the Commission's policy of promoting private enforcement of EU competition law.[20] The effect of this judgment is that national competition authorities (NCAs) may be encouraged to review anti-competitive state regulation more systematically. It has been suggested that this could lead to a division of labour whereby the Commission deregulates the economy in sectors of general EU importance (electricity, telecommunications, postal services) while NCAs contribute to liberalisation by prohibiting state measures that affect local economies.[21]

(ii) A specific obligation

Imposing an obligation on Member States on the basis of Article 4(3) TEU was potentially a comprehensive way of regulating anti-competitive state regulation of the economy. However, the Court of Justice, respectful of state sovereignty, narrowed the application of the duty in Article 4(3) TEU to cases where state law is causally connected to an agreement in breach of Article 101 (or theoretically to an abuse of Article 102, although this has only been considered once).[22]

---

[18] Case C-198/01 *Consorzio Industrie Fiammiferi (CIF)* v *Autorità Garante della Concorrenza e del Mercato* [2003] ECR I-8055.

[19] *Relazione sull'attività svolta nel 2003*, 30 April 2004, available at www.agcm.it.

[20] With the significant limitation that if state law *requires* anti-competitive conduct, then the undertakings are immune from liability until the time when the disapplication of state law becomes 'definitive'. However, the Court did not establish how the criteria of definitiveness should be interpreted.

[21] P. Nebbia, 'Case Note on *Fiammiferi*' (2004) 41 *CMLRev.* 839.

[22] The application of the Article 4(3) TEU obligation to Article 102 TFEU is clear from Case 13/77 *GB-INNO-BM SA* v *Association des détaillants en tabac (ATAB)* [1977] ECR 2115.

Instead, the application of EU competition law to anti-competitive state regulation has been carried out under Article 106 TFEU (ex Article 86 EC) the remit of which is narrower than Article 4(3) TEU, but its effects considerably more significant.

Article 106 TFEU

1. In the case of public undertakings and undertakings to which Member States grant special or exclusive rights, Member States shall neither enact nor maintain in force any measure contrary to the rules contained in this Treaty, in particular to those rules provided for in Article 18 and Articles 101 to 109.
2. Undertakings entrusted with the operation of services of general economic interest or having the character of a revenue-producing monopoly shall be subject to the rules contained in this Treaty, in particular to the rules on competition, insofar as the application of such rules does not obstruct the performance, in law or in fact, of the particular tasks assigned to them. The development of trade must not be affected to such an extent as would be contrary to the interests of the Community.
3. The Commission shall ensure the application of the provisions of this Article and shall, where necessary, address appropriate directives or decisions to Member States.

This is an extraordinarily ambiguous provision and before exploring how it has been applied, we outline its constituent elements and compare it with Article 4(3) TEU.

First, note how the duty on Member States in paragraph 1 is to respect *the entirety* of their obligations under the TFEU by not enacting or maintaining in force any measure contrary to them. The specific reference to competition law obligations is not exhaustive, in fact in many instances the state legislation under scrutiny is also challenged on grounds that it contravenes the free movement rules.[23] In this respect, the obligation in Article 106(1) is similar to that in Article 4(3) TEU, which we saw above: the state will only infringe EU law if its acts are contrary to Article 106(1) read together with another Treaty obligation.

Secondly, the difference between Articles 4(3) TEU and 106 TFEU is that while Article 4(3) is potentially of general application, Article 106 obligations only apply vis-à-vis three types of undertakings: public undertakings (in which the state exercises a dominant influence, for example, by owning a majority of the shares),[24] undertakings to which the state has granted exclusive rights (which have a legal monopoly over the provision of a particular service, for example, an exclusive franchise to provide ambulance services in a city), and undertakings to which the state has granted special rights (that is, rights to operate in a particular economic sector which the state confers on a limited number of undertakings, for example, a concession to two airlines giving them rights to offer passenger services between two airports).[25] All these privileges share one feature: they restrict competition in the market to one or a small number of players.

[23] See e.g. Case C-157/94 *Commission v Netherlands* [1997] ECR 5699.
[24] See Directive 2006/111/EC on the transparency of financial relations between Member States and public undertakings as well as on financial transparency within certain undertakings, article 2 [2006] OJ L318/17.
[25] The Court has not yet articulated a clear distinction between special and exclusive rights. Three entities authorised to collect waste in Copenhagen were held to have exclusive rights, when it would have been more natural to say their rights were 'special' (Case C-209/98 *Entreprenørforeningens Affalds/Miljøsektion (FFAD) v Københavns Kommune* [2000] ECR I-3743, para. 37).

Thirdly, Article 106 does not state that granting special or exclusive rights, or creating public undertakings, is unlawful; it is neutral as to their existence.[26] This is consistent with Article 345 TFEU (ex Article 295 EC) according to which 'The Treaties shall in no way prejudice the rules in Member States governing the system of property ownership.' This provision was inserted in the original Treaty in 1957 to allow Member States to nationalise industries. However, while the existence of state-granted monopolies is tolerated, the exercise of these rights must not undermine the Treaty's objectives.

Fourthly, Article 106(2) TFEU provides states with the possibility of derogating from the obligations set out in paragraph (1) when the state is regulating the behaviour of certain undertakings.

Fifthly, unlike Article 4(3) TEU, the Commission has, on the basis of Article 106(3) TFEU, the power to issue decisions against Member States (rather than just issue a reasoned opinion) and also legislative powers to ensure states comply with Article 106(1).

Article 106(1) remained virtually dormant until private litigation brought this provision to the Court of Justice, whose judgments revealed the possibilities of using EU law to liberalise economic sectors that Member States had shielded from competition. The timing of these cases was opportune in that after the Single European Act, the Union was taking the first tentative steps towards the liberalisation of state-owned industries and the Court's case law gave the Union much needed support in designing its programme of liberalisation. In a quartet of decisions in 1991, the Court cast the scope of application of Article 106 very widely, and the last judgment of the series illustrates the Court's policy.[27] It involved a challenge to a Belgian law where a public undertaking, the Régie des télégraphes et des téléphones (RTT), was responsible for the establishment and the operation of the public telephone network (where it had a legal monopoly) and also enjoyed the exclusive power to grant type-approval to telephone equipment manufactured by other firms who wished to sell this equipment in Belgium and must have it approved to ensure it could be connected to the network. A dispute arose when GB-Inno-BM (GB) sold non-approved telephones at prices far lower than those charged by RTT for its telephones. Relying on Belgian law, RTT sought an order demanding that GB should only sell its phones if it informed customers that the telephones had not been approved by RTT (a notice which would have significantly dented GB's profits). In its defence, GB argued that the Belgian law's type-approval procedure was illegal and that RTT's action, if successful, would favour the sale of RTT's own, self-certified, equipment. The Belgian court referred questions to the Court of Justice about the compatibility of Belgian law both with Article 34 and Article 102, read in conjunction with Article 106 TFEU.

Case 18/88 *Régie des télégraphes et des téléphones* v *GB-Inno-BM SA* [1991] ECR 5941

17. The Court has consistently held that an undertaking vested with a legal monopoly may be regarded as occupying a dominant position within the meaning of [Article 102 TFEU] and that the territory of a Member State to which that monopoly extends may constitute a substantial part of the common market.

---

[26] Case 155/73 *Giuseppe Sacchi* [1974] ECR 409, para. 14, interpreting Article 106(1) as permitting the grant of special or exclusive rights.

[27] The three other cases are Case C-41/90 *Klaus Höfner and Fritz Elser* v *Macrotron GmbH* [1991] ECR I-1979; Case C-260/89 *Elliniki Radiophonia Tiléorassi AE and Others* v *Dimotiki Etairia Pliroforissis* [1991] ECR I-5941; Case C-179/90 *Merci convenzionali porto di Genova SpA* v *Siderurgica Gabrielli SpA* [1991] ECR 5889.

18. The Court has also held that an abuse within the meaning of [Article 102 TFEU] is committed where, without any objective necessity, an undertaking holding a dominant position on a particular market reserves to itself an ancillary activity which might be carried out by another undertaking as part of its activities on a neighbouring but separate market, with the possibility of eliminating all competition from such undertaking.

19. Therefore the fact that an undertaking holding a monopoly in the market for the establishment and operation of the network, without any objective necessity, reserves to itself a neighbouring but separate market, in this case the market for the importation, marketing, connection, commissioning and maintenance of equipment for connection to the said network, thereby eliminating all competition from other undertakings, constitutes an infringement of [Article 102 TFEU].

20. However, [Article 102 TFEU] applies only to anti-competitive conduct engaged in by undertakings on their own initiative, not to measures adopted by States. As regards measures adopted by States, it is [Article 106(1) TFEU] that applies. Under that provision, Member States must not, by laws, regulations or administrative measures, put public undertakings and undertakings to which they grant special or exclusive rights in a position which the said undertakings could not themselves attain by their own conduct without infringing [Article 102 TFEU].

21. Accordingly, where the extension of the dominant position of a public undertaking or undertaking to which the State has granted special or exclusive rights results from a State measure, such a measure constitutes an infringement of [Article 106 TFEU] in conjunction with [Article 102 TFEU]. ...

23. According to the RTT, there could be a finding of an infringement of [Article 106(1) TFEU] only if the Member State had favoured an abuse that the RTT itself had in fact committed, for example by applying the provisions on type-approval in a discriminatory manner. It emphasizes, however, that the order for reference does not state that any abuse has actually taken place, and that the mere possibility of discriminatory application of those provisions by reason of the fact that the RTT is designated as the authority for granting approval and is competing with the undertakings that apply for approval cannot in itself amount to an abuse within the meaning of [Article 102 TFEU].

24. That argument cannot be accepted. It is sufficient to point out in this regard that it is the extension of the monopoly in the establishment and operation of the telephone network to the market in telephone equipment, without any objective justification, which is prohibited as such by [Article 102 TFEU], or by [Article 106(1) TFEU] in conjunction with [Article 102 TFEU], where that extension results from a measure adopted by a State. As competition may not be eliminated in that manner, it may not be distorted either.

25. A system of undistorted competition, as laid down in the Treaty, can be guaranteed only if equality of opportunity is secured as between the various economic operators. To entrust an undertaking which markets terminal equipment with the task of drawing up the specifications for such equipment, monitoring their application and granting type-approval in respect thereof is tantamount to conferring upon it the power to determine at will which terminal equipment may be connected to the public network, and thereby placing that undertaking at an obvious advantage over its competitors.

26. In those circumstances, the maintenance of effective competition and the guaranteeing of transparency require that the drawing up of technical specifications, the monitoring of their application, and the granting of type-approval must be carried out by a body which is independent of public or private undertakings offering competing goods or services in the telecommunications sector.

27. Moreover, the provisions of the national regulations at issue in the main action may influence the imports of telephone equipment from other Member States, and hence may affect trade between Member States within the meaning of [Article 102 TFEU].

28. Accordingly, it must first be stated, in reply to the national court's questions, that [Articles 3(1)(b), 106 and 102 TFEU] preclude a Member State from granting to the undertaking which operates the public telecommunications network the power to lay down standards for telephone equipment and to check that economic operators meet those standards when it is itself competing with those operators on the market for that equipment.

The practical consequences of a judgment of this nature is that the national court is bound to set aside national law which is incompatible with EU law, placing considerable pressure on the state to amend its law, thereby facilitating market access by GB-INNO and other undertakings wishing to provide telephonic equipment. Markets previously closed by the protection afforded to the public undertaking are now opened up to competition. The judgment does not call into question the public ownership of RTT, but it cuts down the amount of activities that the public undertaking can carry out: in this context, RTT is free to run the telephone network, but cannot also control the approval activity for equipment. Thus, while the Treaty does not compel privatisation of state monopolies, it controls their scope.

The most significant contribution of this case law is that the Court took a more aggressive stance under Article 106 TFEU than it did under Article 4(3) TEU, where an anti-competitive agreement caused or legitimised by national law is necessary for the state to be found in breach of EU law. In this case, however, as Kelyn Bacon put it, the Court has 'apparently been willing to apply Article [102 TFEU] where there is no effective abuse by undertakings of a dominant position, but where a State measure produces the same effects as the abuse'.[28] Therefore, under certain circumstances, the grant of a special or exclusive right may be declared unlawful, even if it does not result in an abuse of dominance by the privileged undertaking. In an attempt to identify the limits of Article 106 after these judgments, Edward and Hoskins suggested that this provision should be read as an attempt to balance the Union's interest in creating competitive markets with national sovereign rights to restrict the extension of competition to certain economic sectors for public interest reasons.[29] In their view, the case law 'restricts sovereignty' to the extent that state measures are unlawful where they place private undertakings in a position in which they cannot avoid abusing their dominant position. For instance, in *Höfner*, the undertaking granted the exclusive right to operate recruitment offices was manifestly unable to meet demand so that some job-seekers were forced to look elsewhere for employment service providers (an abuse under Article 102(b) TFEU). And *RTT* cuts even further into state sovereignty by indicating that the risk of an abuse may render the grant of an exclusive right unlawful. These decisions suggest that if the state wishes to reserve the provision of a service to a particular undertaking (in order for instance to ensure that all citizens are able to gain access to it), then it has an obligation under EU law to ensure that the service works efficiently. Importantly, the state has an obligation to review the performance of economic sectors where it has excluded competition and to ensure that they perform adequately in response to changing market conditions. On the other hand, Edward and Hoskins note that the Court's case law also places a limit on the reach of competition as Article 106(2) allows states to depart from competition norms when necessary to safeguard the provision of a service of general economic

---

[28] K. Bacon, 'State Regulation of the Market and EC Competition Rules' (1997) *ECLR* 283.
[29] D. Edward and M. Hoskins, 'Article 90 [now Article 106 TFEU], Deregulation and EC Law' (1995) 32 *CMLRev.* 157.

interest. While this classification helps to explain the diverse interests to be balanced, it fails to yield a precise answer to the question of *when* states are in breach of Article 106(1).

A helpful assessment of the circumstances when a breach of Article 106(1) may be found was canvassed by Advocate General Jacobs, who identified three types of cases.[30] The first is when the state grants exclusive rights in too many markets, whereby the holder is induced to abuse the dominant position by exploiting the exclusive rights in one market to strengthen his dominance in other markets; *RTT* falls within this category. Here, there is no need to show the abuse of dominance by the undertaking, but merely the *potential* for an abuse caused by state law. The second category instead covers the grant of an exclusive right in one market only. Here, the grant cannot be challenged ex ante, rather only if there is a systemic failure by the state to create conditions whereby supply of the relevant service can meet demand. Accordingly, the Court adopts a significantly more severe assessment when the state grants exclusive rights in more than one market, and a more lax standard when there is the grant of an exclusive right in one relevant market. This is an efficient way of balancing the EU competition goal with the state's public policies: if there is a market where the state decides, in the public interest, that competition will be excluded, the state cannot also exclude competition from related markets and expand the reach of that monopoly. However, even when the grant is only of a monopoly in the market where the public interest demands the grant of an exclusive right, the state has an obligation (under EU law) to deliver the service efficiently.[31] The third category is where the Court goes straight to Article 106(2) without explaining the grounds on which there is an infringement. This might simply be done for convenience in that, if there is a justification, there is no need to show an infringement; or perhaps the Court takes the view that if a statutory monopoly granted to provide services of general economic interest goes beyond that which may be justified under Article 106(2), then *a fortiori* there is an infringement of Article 106(1).[32] However, many are unconvinced by this rationalisation and take the view that the Court may challenge the existence of exclusive rights, contradicting its oft-repeated view that the creation of dominance by state action is not in itself a breach of EU law.[33]

While doctrinal analysis may explain the Court's methods, it must not be forgotten that the Court of Justice is not immune from taking policy considerations into account at the expense of doctrinal purity. Hence, Leigh Hancher has noted that the Court's stance depends on the market under consideration: the Court is stricter when the protected market is not one providing public services (for example, in cases about dock work the Court applied a strict approach) than in cases where it is called upon to examine measures that are central to the provision of a public service (for example, the Court's reluctance to intervene in cases on the supply of gas and electricity).[34] Moreover, the Court applies a strict approach when the service in question is provided in competitive conditions in other Member States.[35] According to this view, the Court will apply Article 106(1) more aggressively in those cases where it perceives states have no

---

[30] Case C-67/96 *Albany International BV v Stichting Bedrijfspensioenfonds Textielindustrie* [1999] ECR I-5751, paras. 388–439.

[31] For a different view see Advocate General Tesauro in Case C-320/91 *Criminal proceedings against Paul Corbeau* [1993] ECR 2533, para. 16.

[32] W. Sauter and H. Schepel, *State and Market in European Union Law* (Cambridge, Cambridge University Press, 2009) 161.

[33] See e.g. R. Whish, *Competition Law* (6th edn, Oxford, Oxford University Press, 2008) 228.

[34] Case C-157/94 *Commission v Netherlands* [1997] ECR I-5699.

[35] L. Hancher, 'Community, State and Market' in P. Craig and G. de Búrca (eds.), *The Evolution of EU Law* (Oxford, Oxford University Press, 1998) 721, 731–5.

good reason for wishing to protect certain economic sectors, while it will limit the expansion of competition to sectors where there seem to be good public interest justifications.

3 SERVICES OF GENERAL INTEREST

There are 'good' and 'bad' reasons for state regulation of the economy. For a number of economic sectors, the 'bad' reason which seems to underpin much state regulation is the desire to protect national industries from competition for political reasons, whether to protect employment or safeguard an industry deemed to be of national importance. It is such protectionism that the European Union has sought to eliminate. On the other hand, one 'good' reason for state regulation is that certain goods or services should be distributed fairly among all citizens rather than allocated by the market system. As noted above, in certain cases the Court may apply the obligations in Article 106(1) more lightly when considering these services, but there are two formal routes that are deployed to allow states to regulate these markets without the duty to open them to competition: by declaring that the services are not provided by 'undertakings', thereby excluding the application of the competition rules, and by applying Article 106(2), which sets out a derogation from the application of EU law obligations.

(i) Definition of undertakings

The Union courts have excluded two types of activities from the scope of EU competition law by declaring that those who provide these services are not 'undertakings' and thereby not subject to competition law: (1) those where the Member State exercises sovereign powers, and (2) those where the activity in question is governed by the principle of solidarity. In crafting these exclusions, the Court has devised principles that qualify the functional approach to defining an undertaking, which we saw in Chapter 23. The functional approach asks whether the activity in question could be carried out by a private enterprise, i.e. whether there is a market for the provision of the service in question that undertakings may wish to tap into. The difficulty of this approach is that virtually all services might be provided by the market, as the British reforms of public services amply demonstrate.

The first qualification to the effects-based approach is where the Court focuses on the public interest of a particular activity and notes that the task is part of the 'essential function of the state' and the powers granted to the operator are typically those of a public authority. Within this remit come operators that are entrusted by the state to control and supervise the air space of a country, or anti-pollution surveillance authorities that protect the state's waters. While these operators may be private firms, they 'are the instruments of a policy in the (general) public interest and enjoy prerogatives of the public authority, that is to say bodies that exercise an activity typical of a public authority'.[36] As a result, those economic activities are excluded from the application of EU competition law.[37] Note, however, that the question whether a person is acting as an undertaking relates to each distinct activity. Therefore, it may be that a person

---

[36] Case C-343/95 *Diego Cali & Figli Srl v Servizi ecologici porto di Genova SpA (SEPG)* [1997] ECR I-1547 (Opinion of Advocate General Cosmas, para. 41).

[37] According to Advocate General Tesauro (in Case C-364/92 *SAT Fluggesellschaft v Eurocontrol* [1994] ECR I-43), it is also arguable that these kinds of activities are natural monopolies where competition is deemed undesirable for the effective performance of the activity in question.

who is in charge of supervising air safety and also manufactures aircraft may be deemed to be acting as an undertaking with regard to aircraft manufacture even if his activities in the field of air safety are outside the scope of competition law.[38]

The second qualification is more significant but less well defined and mostly applies to state regulation of social security insurance schemes. Schemes made compulsory by national law are being challenged by persons wishing to buy insurance elsewhere and who wish to stop making contributions to the national scheme. In *INAIL*, the managing partner of a company challenged a claim for unpaid national insurance contributions by arguing that the state's compulsory insurance scheme for accidents at work and occupational disease (the operation of which is entrusted to INAIL, a public-service providing body, subject to supervision by the Ministry of Employment and Social Security) was contrary to competition law and he was entitled to secure insurance elsewhere. The argument was premised on INAIL being an undertaking to which the state had granted an exclusive right to operate on the market for occupational insurance. Had his challenge been successful, he and other employers would have been able to opt out of the state scheme and seek better insurance contracts elsewhere. However, the Court held that INAIL was not an undertaking when implementing this scheme because the national scheme operated according to the principle of solidarity. As a result the challenge failed.

Case C-218/00 *Cisal di Battistello Venanzio & C. Sas v Istituto nazionale per l'assicurazione contro gli infortuni sul lavoro (INAIL)* [2002] ECR I-691

31. According to settled case law, Community law does not affect the power of the Member States to organise their social security systems.

32. In particular, the covering of risks of accidents at work and occupational diseases has for a long time been part of the social protection which Member States afford to all or part of their population. ...

34. The statutory scheme providing insurance against accidents at work and occupational diseases in question in the main proceedings, insofar as it provides for compulsory social protection for all non-salaried workers in the non-agricultural professions who carry out an activity classified as a risk activity by the law, pursues a social objective.

35. Such a scheme is intended to provide all the persons protected with cover against the risks of accidents at work and occupational diseases, irrespective of any fault which may have been committed by the victim, or by the employer, and therefore without any need for civil liability to be incurred by the person drawing benefits in respect of the risk activity.

36. Furthermore, the social aim of that insurance scheme is highlighted by the fact that benefits are paid even when the contributions due have not been paid, which obviously contributes to the protection of all insured workers against the economic consequences of accidents at work or occupational diseases. Even after the 1997 reform, which abolished that automatic cover for self-employed workers, benefits may still be paid in the event of regularisation, even after contributions have not been paid in good time.

---

[38] In Case C-113/07 P *SELEX Sistemi Integrati SpA v Commission*, Judgment of 26 March 2009, the Court of Justice was asked to consider how far certain ancillary services offered by Eurocontrol (e.g. preparing standards) could be held separable from its core task of air space management and maintaining the safety of air navigation (activities which are not of an economic nature by virtue of the exercise of public powers). It held that the ancillary activities were inseparable from the core task, so Eurocontrol could not be considered an undertaking for those services.

37. However, as is clear from the case law of the Court, the social aim of an insurance scheme is not in itself sufficient to preclude the activity in question from being classified as an economic activity. In that regard, two other aspects deserve attention.

38. In the first place, a number of elements tend to demonstrate that the insurance scheme in question in the main proceedings applies the principle of solidarity.

39. The insurance scheme is financed by contributions the rate of which is not systematically proportionate to the risk insured. For example, it is clear from the case-file that the rate may not exceed a maximum ceiling, even where the activity carried out entails a high risk, the balance of financing being born by all the undertakings in the same category as regards the risk run. Furthermore, contributions are calculated not only on the basis of the risk linked to the activity of the undertaking concerned but also according to the insured persons' earnings.

40. Second, the amount of benefits paid is not necessarily proportionate to the insured persons' earnings, since, for the calculation of pensions, only salaries situated between a minimum and a maximum corresponding to the average nationwide salary, decreased or increased by 30%, may be taken into consideration.

41. In those circumstances ... the payment of high contributions may give rise only to the grant of capped benefits, where the salary in question exceeds the maximum laid down by decree and, inversely, relatively low contributions, calculated on the basis of the statutory minimum wage, afford entitlement to benefits calculated according to earnings higher than that threshold, corresponding to the average salary decreased by 30%.

42. The absence of any direct link between the contributions paid and the benefits granted thus entails solidarity between better paid workers and those who, given their low earnings, would be deprived of proper social cover if such a link existed.

43. In the second place, it is clear from the case-file that the activity of the INAIL, entrusted by law with management of the scheme in question, is subject to supervision by the State and that the amount of benefits and of contributions is, in the last resort, fixed by the State. The amount of benefits is laid down by law and they may be paid regardless of the contributions paid and the financial results of the investments made by the INAIL. Second, the amount of contributions, upon which the INAIL deliberates, must be approved by ministerial decree, the competent minister having the power to reject the scales proposed and to invite the INAIL to submit to him a new proposal taking account of certain information.

44. In summary, it is clear from the foregoing that the amount of benefits and the amount of contributions, which are two essential elements of the scheme managed by the INAIL, are subject to supervision by the State and that the compulsory affiliation which characterises such an insurance scheme is essential for the financial balance of the scheme and for application of the principle of solidarity, which means that benefits paid to insured persons are not strictly proportionate to the contributions paid by them.

45. In conclusion, it may be stated that in participating in this way in the management of one of the traditional branches of social security, in this case insurance against accidents at work and occupational diseases, the INAIL fulfils an exclusively social function. It follows that its activity is not an economic activity for the purposes of competition law and that this body does not therefore constitute an undertaking within the meaning of Articles [101 and 102 TFEU].

The Court's analysis is based on two considerations: first, it will look to see whether there is a sufficiently high degree of solidarity, and then it will consider whether the restriction of competition (i.e. the compulsory nature of contributions) is necessary to guarantee the solidarity inherent in the scheme. It is not clear why the Court did not just declare that social security operators are undertakings subject to competition law, but that the restriction of competition may be justified under Article 106(2); after all, the provision of social security benefits premised upon notions of solidarity seems to be a quintessential service of general economic interest.

Moreover, the solidarity test is not carried out with much precision. The Court seems to measure the degree of solidarity in the scheme and declares the operator of the scheme not to be an undertaking only when a certain level of solidarity is achieved. For instance, in *Albany International*, a compulsory sectoral pension fund which constituted an element of the Dutch system of social protection and which embodied certain solidarity principles (for example, the acceptance by the fund of all workers without a prior medical examination, the accrual of pension rights even for those rendered unable to work through incapacity, the absence of equivalence between the contributions paid and the pension rights) was deemed to be an undertaking because the amount of benefits paid depended on the financial results achieved by the fund in the light of its investments. It thus operated like an insurance undertaking. Moreover, the fund was not compulsory as certain (limited) opt-outs were available suggesting that there was not complete solidarity among the workers in the sector. The manifestations of solidarity were deemed 'not sufficient' even though the Court acknowledged that the solidarity within the scheme rendered the fund less competitive compared to other insurance companies.[39]

In some recent cases, the Court has extended the solidarity approach to exclude certain commercial decisions made by bodies carrying out public service tasks. In *FENIN*, the bodies managing the Spanish health system were accused of abusing their monopsony power by delaying payment to suppliers of medical goods and equipment.[40] In *AOK Budesverband*, sickness funds were accused of colluding to fix the amount of money they would pay to insured patients when the latter purchased medicines.[41] In both cases, the body in question was not acting as an undertaking in the delivery of its core task (respectively, providing health care and managing sickness funds), but the question arose whether commercial activities that they did engage in could be challenged under EU competition law. The Court held that in purchasing medical equipment to perform their public service missions, and in fixing the prices, the defendants were not behaving as undertakings, thus excluding them from the scope of application of competition law. In *FENIN*, the Court excluded the application of competition law because the medical equipment was not purchased to operate an economic activity, but to offer a public service based upon national solidarity, and thus was not subject to EU competition law.[42] In reaching the same conclusion, the Court of Justice, in *AOK Bundesverband*, adopted a clearer criterion, concluding that the fixing of payment amounts was 'integrally connected' with the funds' public service activity.[43] Read jointly, these decisions are a significant widening of the solidarity doctrine in that the Court extends the latter beyond the provision of the services, to the commercial transactions that are connected with the provision of such services. In so doing, the Court is unconcerned with the degree to which competition is distorted and is willing

---

[39] Case C-67/96 *Albany International BV v Stichting Bedrijfspensioenfonds Textielindustrie* [1999] ECR I-5751, paras. 73–87.

[40] Case T-319/99 *Federación Nacional de Empresas de Instrumentación Científica, Médica, Técnica y Dental (FENIN) v Commission* [2003] ECR II-357.

[41] Joined Cases C-264/01, C-306/01, C-354/01 and C-355/01 *AOK Bundesverband and Others v Ichthyol-Gesellschaft Cordes, Hermani & Co.* [2004] ECR I-2493.

[42] Case T-319/99 *FENIN*, above n. 40, paras. 36–40; on appeal Case C-205/03 P *FENIN v Commission* [2006] ECR I-6295.

[43] *AOK Bundesverband*, above n. 41, para. 63.

to tolerate even price-fixing agreements. This seems undesirable. The purchasing power of state-wide providers of health care is considerable; accordingly, the potential anti-competitive effects of the exercise of this power cannot be underestimated.[44]

(ii) Application of Article 106(2) TFEU

A more explicit route to avoiding the application of competition law in order to safeguard the provision of services of general economic interest (SGEIs) is the derogation in Article 106(2). States and undertakings may justify the non-application of EU law obligations when the following three criteria are met: first, undertakings have been entrusted by the state with the operation of an SGEI; secondly, the application of competition law would obstruct the performance of undertakings entrusted with the operation of an SGEI;[45] thirdly, one must also show that the restriction of competition is not contrary to the interests of the Union. This final proviso has yet to receive detailed scrutiny by the Court, although it clearly demands more than proof that the state measures affect trade between Member States. On the other hand, it cannot be read so widely as to render the derogation redundant, thus some negative effects on trade may be tolerated.[46] As Article 106(2) is a derogation from the state's Treaty obligations in their entirety, it is strictly constructed.[47] Our focus here is on the first and second criteria.

The first criterion is that an undertaking must be 'entrusted' by the state[48] with the provision of an SGEI. Typical services of general economic interest include providing energy, telecommunications or transport networks.[49] The determination of what constitutes an SGEI is a matter over which states have considerable latitude,[50] as has been explained by the General Court in *BUPA*. At stake were the Irish government's arrangements in the health sector. Private medical insurance (PMI) was originally only offered by the Voluntary Health Insurance Board. In opening this market to competition, the Irish legislation also designed a risk equalisation scheme. The scheme meant that new entrants who insured healthier and younger patients would have to pay a levy to the Health Insurance Authority who would redistribute this money to those insurers whose clients were at higher risk. The upshot was that a new entrant like BUPA would be compensating the former monopoly provider. Ireland notified this scheme to the Commission as it considered it might be seen as constituting state aid. The Commission, however, said that the scheme was not state aid because (applying the standard set in a major judgment of the Court of Justice, *Altmark*) it was designed to compensate PMI insurers for providing services of general economic interest.[51] BUPA appealed against this decision, giving the General Court an opportunity to define the concept of SGEI.

---

[44] The position in EU law is in contrast with that in Germany and the United Kingdom. See, respectively, J. Winterstein, 'Nailing the Jellyfish: Social Security and Competition Law' (1999) *ECLR* 324, 333 and *Bettercare Group Ltd v Director General of Fair Trading* [2002] CAT 7.

[45] Article 106(2) TFEU also applies to revenue-producing monopolies; see above n. 34.

[46] In Case C-157/94 *Commission v Netherlands* [1997] ECR I-5699, paras 66–71, the Court rebuked the Commission for failure to show what adverse effects resulted, noting that trade between Member States was increasing.

[47] *Ibid.* para. 37.

[48] Case C-203/96 *Chemische Afvalstoffen Dusseldorp BV and Others v Minister van Volkshuisvesting, Ruimtelijke Ordening en Milieubeheer* [1998] ECR I-4075, Opinion of Advocate General Jacobs, para. 103.

[49] Communication from the Commission, Services of general interest in Europe, Annex II [2001] OJ C17/4.

[50] Though it is a Community concept: Case 10/71 *Ministère Public du Luxembourg v Muller* [1971] ECR 723, paras. 14–15.

[51] State Aid No. 46/2003, Ireland, 13 May 2003; applying the principles in Case C-280/00 *Altmark Trans GmbH v Nahverkehrsgesellschaft Altmark GmbH* [2003] ECR I-7747.

Case T-289/03 *British United Provident Association Ltd (BUPA) v Commission* [2008] ECR II-81

172. ... [E]ven though the Member State has a wide discretion when determining what it regards as an SGEI, that does not mean that it is not required, when it relies on the existence of and the need to protect an SGEI mission, to ensure that that mission satisfies certain minimum criteria common to every SGEI mission within the meaning of the [TFEU], as explained in the case law, and to demonstrate that those criteria are indeed satisfied in the particular case. These are, notably, the presence of an act of the public authority entrusting the operators in question with an SGEI mission and the universal and compulsory nature of that mission. Conversely, the lack of proof by the Member State that those criteria are satisfied, or failure on its part to observe them, may constitute a manifest error of assessment, in which case the Commission is required to make a finding to that effect, failing which the Commission itself makes a manifest error. Furthermore, it follows from the case law on [Article 106(2) TFEU] that the Member State must indicate the reasons why it considers that the service in question, because of its specific nature, deserves to be characterised as an SGEI and to be distinguished from other economic activities. In the absence of such reasons, even a marginal review by the Community institutions on the basis of both the first *Altmark* condition and [Article 106(2) TFEU] with respect to the existence of a manifest error by the Member State in the context of its discretion would not be possible. ...

179. On the other hand, the recognition of an SGEI mission does not necessarily presume that the operator entrusted with that mission will be given an exclusive or special right to carry it out. It follows from a reading of paragraph 1 together with paragraph 2 of [Article 106 TFEU] that a distinction must be drawn between a special or exclusive right conferred on an operator and the SGEI mission which, where appropriate, is attached to that right. The grant of a special or exclusive right to an operator is merely the instrument, possibly justified, which allows that operator to perform an SGEI mission. ...

186. As regards the universal nature of the PMI services, it must be noted at the outset that, contrary to the theory put forward by the applicants, it does not follow from Community law that, in order to be capable of being characterised as an SGEI, the service in question must constitute a universal service in the strict sense, such as the public social security scheme. In effect, the concept of universal service, within the meaning of Community law, does not mean that the service in question must respond to a need common to the whole population or be supplied throughout a territory ... [A]lthough those characteristics correspond to the classical type of SGEI, and the one most widely encountered in Member States, that does not preclude the existence of other, equally lawful, types of SGEIs which the Member States may validly choose to create in the exercise of their discretion.

187. Accordingly, the fact that the SGEI obligations in question have only a limited territorial or material application or that the services concerned are enjoyed by only a relatively limited group of users does not necessarily call in question the universal nature of an SGEI mission within the meaning of Community law. It follows that the applicants' restrictive understanding of the universal nature of an SGEI, based on certain Commission reports or documents, the content of which, moreover, is not legally binding, is not compatible with the scope of the discretion which Member States have when defining an SGEI mission. Consequently, that argument must be rejected as unfounded. ...

189. Contrary to the applicants' opinion, however, the binding nature of the SGEI mission does not presuppose that the public authorities impose on the operator concerned an obligation to provide a service having a clearly predetermined content ... In effect, the compulsory nature of the SGEI mission does not preclude a certain latitude being left to the operator on the market, including in relation to the content and pricing of the services which it proposes to provide. In those circumstances, a minimum of

freedom of action on the part of operators and, accordingly, of competition on the quality and content of the services in question is ensured, which is apt to limit, in the community interest, the scope of the restriction of competition which generally results from the attribution of an SGEI mission, without any effect on the objectives of that mission.

190. It follows that, in the absence of an exclusive or special right, it is sufficient, in order to conclude that a service is compulsory, that the operator entrusted with a particular mission is under an obligation to provide that service to any user requesting it. In other words, the compulsory nature of the service and, accordingly, the existence of an SGEI mission are established if the service-provider is obliged to contract, on consistent conditions, without being able to reject the other contracting party. That element makes it possible to distinguish a service forming part of an SGEI mission from any other service provided on the market and, accordingly, from any other activity carried out in complete freedom.

It is beyond the scope of this book to assess the impact of this case on the rules on state aid, but for our purposes it is worth noting that while the Court gives considerable latitude to Member States in determining what an SGEI is, it also suggests that there is an emerging set of EU-wide criteria for SGEIs.[52] In this judgment, these include the universal and compulsory nature of the service. Moreover, the state has an obligation to indicate why the service in question merits being labelled of general interest and so escaping from its Treaty obligations.

The second criterion is that, if a provider of an SGEI infringes EU law, it must show that a derogation from its EU law obligations is necessary to ensure that the service can be provided. Reading Article 106(2) literally, the defendant should have to show that without the derogation there would be no provision of the SGEI (because competition would 'obstruct' the performance of the service). However, the Court has taken a more lenient stance.[53] The rationale for the derogation in Article 106(2) is that the types of services in question are unlikely to be provided by the private sector because they are unprofitable,[54] so the state may have to offer some financial advantage to the undertaking obliged to provide the SGEI, the effect of which is to restrict competition. The Irish scheme described above, for example, ensures that those who provide insurance for high risk clients are compensated by those who insure low risk clients. The anti-competitive risks that arise can also be seen by considering the Court of Justice's analysis of arrangements for the provision of ambulance services in Germany, which is organised at regional level. In brief, the Rheinland-Pfalz Land wished to ensure the operation of an emergency ambulance service in its territory. However, this service is not profitable, so the operators were also given an exclusive right over the provision of another profitable service: non-emergency transport. Ambulanz Glockner wished to offer non-emergency transport in competition with the medical aid organisations, and sought to annul the grant of exclusive rights to its competitors. The Court agreed that the national law could be incompatible with Article 106(1), as in the *RTT* case, in that the law which had conferred a special or exclusive right on medical aid organisations for the provision of emergency services has the effect of 'reserving to those medical aid organisations an ancillary transport activity which could be carried on by independent operators', i.e. the market for non-emergency transport. The Court then went on to consider the application of Article 106(2).

---

[52] See further M. Ross, 'A Healthy Approach to Services of General Economic Interest? The *BUPA* Judgment of the Court of First Instance' (2009) *ELRev.* 127.

[53] The early case law adopted a stricter approach: see *NAVEWA-ANSEAU* [1982] OJ L167/39, para. 48.

[54] Case C-203/96 *Chemische Afvalstoffen Dusseldorp BV*, above n. 48, Opinion of Advocate General Jacobs, para. 39.

Case C–475/99 *Ambulanz Glöckner* v *Landkreis Südwestpfalz* [2001] ECR I–8089

52. [The defendant and others argued that] some measure of protection of the public ambulance service against competition from independent operators is necessary, even on the non-emergency transport market.

53. They argue that emergency transport services, which must be provided 24 hours a day throughout the territory, require costly investments in equipment and qualified personnel. It is necessary to avoid a situation in which those costs cannot be offset, at least partially, by revenue from non-emergency transport. Not only does the very presence of independent operators in this market have the effect of reducing revenue from the public ambulance service, but it is also to be expected that those operators, seeking profits, will prefer to concentrate their services in densely populated areas or on short distances, so that, besides emergency transport, the medical aid organisations would be left only with non-emergency transport in remote areas. The Austrian Government also points out that, since the public ambulance service is financed ultimately either through taxes or through health insurance contributions, there is a serious risk that the inevitable losses of the public ambulance service will be socialised, whilst its potential profits will go to the independent operators.

54. They also contend that it is likewise in the general interest for prices not to vary according to the areas served.

55. With regard to those arguments, the medical aid organisations are incontestably entrusted with a task of general economic interest, consisting in the obligation to provide a permanent standby service of transporting sick or injured persons in emergencies throughout the territory concerned, at uniform rates and on similar quality conditions, without regard to the particular situations or to the degree of economic profitability of each individual operation.

56. However, [Article 106(2) TFEU], read in conjunction with paragraph (1) of that provision, allows Member States to confer, on undertakings to which they entrust the operation of services of general economic interest, exclusive rights which may hinder the application of the rules of the Treaty on competition insofar as restrictions on competition, or even the exclusion of all competition, by other economic operators are necessary to ensure the performance of the particular tasks assigned to the undertakings holding the exclusive rights.

57. The question to be determined, therefore, is whether the restriction of competition is necessary to enable the holder of an exclusive right to perform its task of general interest in economically acceptable conditions. The Court has held that the starting point in making that determination must be the premise that the obligation, on the part of the undertaking entrusted with such a task, to perform its services in conditions of economic equilibrium presupposes that it will be possible to offset less profitable sectors against the profitable sectors and hence justifies a restriction of competition from individual undertakings in economically profitable sectors.

58. In the case before the national court ... it appears that the system put in place by the [state law] is such as to enable the medical aid organisations to perform their task in economically acceptable conditions. In particular, the evidence placed before the Court shows that the revenue from non-emergency transport helps to cover the costs of providing the emergency transport service. ...

61. ... the extension of the medical aid organisations' exclusive rights to the non-emergency transport sector does indeed enable them to discharge their general-interest task of providing emergency transport in conditions of economic equilibrium. The possibility which would be open to private operators to concentrate, in the non-emergency sector, on more profitable journeys could affect the degree of economic viability of the service provided by the medical aid organisations and, consequently, jeopardise the quality and reliability of that service.

62. However, as the Advocate General explains in point 188 of his Opinion, it is only if it were established that the medical aid organisations entrusted with the operation of the public ambulance service were manifestly unable to satisfy demand for emergency ambulance services and for patient transport at all times that the justification for extending their exclusive rights, based on the task of general interest, could not be accepted. ...

64. It is for the national court to determine whether the medical aid organisations which occupy a dominant position on the markets in question are in fact able to satisfy demand and to fulfil not only their statutory obligation to provide the public emergency ambulance services in all situations and 24 hours a day but also to offer efficient patient transport services.

65. Consequently, [the relevant law] is justified under [Article 106(2) TFEU] provided that it does not bar the grant of an authorisation to independent operators where it is established that the medical aid organisations entrusted with the operation of the public ambulance service are manifestly unable to satisfy demand in the area of emergency transport and patient transport services.

The facts illustrate a common means by which public services are financed: the state imposes a public service obligation in one market (which is usually unprofitable), but also grants those undertakings an exclusive right in a related, profitable sector which does not constitute an SGEI so that the losses in one are offset by the gains in the other. The upshot is that competition is eliminated in both the market for the public service and that of the profitable sector. As the Land noted in this case, without this arrangement, the provision of the public service would lead to greater taxation (because the alternative means of financing the public service is through direct cash injections from the state), while the present system allows for private sector involvement in the provision of public services and (so the ideology goes) private sector provision is more efficient and hence less costly than public sector, tax-funded, supply.

The judgment confirms the Court's recent jurisprudence that in order to prove that the non-application of competition law is necessary for the provision of the SGEI, there is no need to show that there is no other way to perform the task, only that the way the market is organised allows the provider of the SGEI to operate under economically acceptable conditions.[55] This standard leaves Member States free to determine the most appropriate way of financing a service of general economic interest.[56] But the Court inserts a new condition: if it is found that the undertaking is manifestly unable to satisfy demand on the reserved markets, then the derogation cannot be granted. Thus, the national public policy derogation in Article 106(2) is qualified by an EU law obligation to ensure that the markets where competition is eliminated so as to guarantee an SGEI operate efficiently.

[55] Case 157/94 *Commission v Netherlands* [1997] ECR I-5699, paras. 56–8.
[56] P. J. Slot, 'Note on the Energy Cases and Franzen' (1998) *CMLRev.* 1183, 1200. But in some cases the Court deploys a tougher proportionality standard, demanding proof that there is no less restrictive manner of preserving the SGEI, e.g. Case C-203/96 *Chemische Afvalstoffen Dusseldorp BV*, above n. 48, para. 67. The test set out in the main text has the advantage of being preferred by states and others who participated in a Community-wide consultation (see *Report on the Public Consultation on the Green Paper on Services of General Interest*, SEC(2004)362, 15 March 2004).

(iii) An EU approach to SGEIs?

Increasingly, EU law has impacted on the way in which SGEIs are financed and provided, insisting on competition and efficiency. For instance, while states may choose how to provide SGEIs, if the public authority entrusts the provision to a third party, it must respect the European Union's public procurement rules, which guarantee freedom to provide services, ensure transparency and equal treatment.[57] The procurement Directives ensure that states select the most efficient provider, allowing recipients to enjoy high quality services.[58] Moreover, state law designed to ensure the operation of SGEIs under the derogation of Article 106(2) is only available on the condition that the relevant service is provided in an efficient manner; if not, the state may be in breach of its obligations under Article 106(1). This is an indirect requirement upon states to monitor the performance of SGEI providers holding exclusive rights, which is supplemented by the Commission's monitoring of the performance of all SGEI providers to ascertain that they meet the needs of users.[59] Moreover, the derogation applied to state legislation does not remove the undertakings' duties to act compatibly with EU competition law. Lastly, in the context of Directives to liberalise certain economic sectors (one of which is considered below), the Union has 'Europeanised' the provision of SGEIs by listing a number of services (so-called universal services) that must be 'made available at a specified quality to all consumers and users throughout the territory of a Member State, independent of geographical location, and … at an affordable price',[60] thereby imposing on states obligations to provide a common range of SGEIs. The progressive 'Communitarisation' of SGEIs was consolidated by a novel provision, added by the Treaty of Amsterdam, and expanded by the Lisbon Treaty.[61]

Article 14 TFEU

Without prejudice to Article 4 of the Treaty on European Union or to Articles 93, 106 and 107 of this Treaty, and given the place occupied by services of general economic interest in the shared values of the Union as well as their role in promoting social and territorial cohesion, the Union and the Member States, each within their respective powers and within the scope of application of the Treaties, shall take care that such services operate on the basis of principles and conditions, particularly economic and financial conditions, which enable them to fulfil their missions. The European Parliament and the Council, acting by means of regulations in accordance with the ordinary legislative procedure, shall establish these principles and set these conditions without prejudice to the competence of Member States, in compliance with the Treaties, to provide, to commission and to fund such services.

---

[57] Directive 2004/18/EC on the coordination of procedures for the award of public works contracts and public service contracts [2004] OJ L134/1; Directive 2004/17 coordinating the procurement procedures of entities operating the water, energy, transport and postal services sectors [2004] OJ L134/114.

[58] European Commission, *Report to the Laeken European Council: Services of General Interest*, COM(2001)598 final, paras. 33–9.

[59] *Ibid.* paras. 41–7.

[60] European Commission, Green Paper on Services of General Interest, COM(2003)270 final, para. 50.

[61] See also Charter of Fundamental Rights of the European Union, Article 36 [2000] OJ C364/1.

The Lisbon Treaty amended this Article in two ways. First, it did so by underscoring the importance of ensuring that providers of these services are afforded 'economic and financial conditions' to carry out their tasks. Secondly, the final sentence gives the Union legislative competence; and by providing that secondary legislation is to be by way of regulations, this would undermine the state's autonomy to design services of general interest. Running contrary to this, however, is Protocol No. 26 on services of general interest which was introduced by the Lisbon Treaty. It contains two declarations. Article 1, regarding services of general *economic* interest (e.g. provision of electricity, telecommunications, water), notes 'the essential role and the wide discretion of national, regional and local authorities in providing, commissioning and organising services of general economic interest as closely as possible to the needs of the users; the diversity between various services of general economic interest and the differences in the needs and preferences of users that may result from different geographical, social or cultural situations; a high level of quality, safety and affordability, equal treatment and the promotion of universal access and of user rights'. Article 2 regarding *non-economic* services of general interest (e.g. police, social security benefits), declares that the Treaty does not affect the 'competence of Member States to provide, commission and organise' such services.

These amendments pit the Commission's liberalisation drive, which it believes is compatible with the delivery of public services, against a policy premised upon the reduction in the scope of competition law to ensure the Union and Member States fulfil their duties to the citizens. A clash between these two visions on how to deliver public services is likely, as the Commission's Communication reflecting on the Treaty amendments suggests that it is satisfied with the present rules and its plans are merely to inform parties what the rules are, to ensure that the liberalisation of utilities continues, and to monitor the effects of liberalisation.[62] Member States and the European Parliament are likely to want a stronger commitment to services of general interest.[63]

Until the Union chooses to legislate, the focus of analysis will remain on the first sentence of Article 14 and its possible impact. The key point to note is that this Article imposes an obligation upon both states and the Union to ensure that SGEIs fulfil their functions. The Commission's view is that SGEIs are 'an essential element of the European model of society'. Much is made of the value they play in a *social* sense (by enhancing the quality of life of the European citizen) and in an *economic* sense (the efficiency and quality of these services is seen as a key to increasing competitiveness by attracting investment in less developed regions of the Union).[64] Cynics have argued that the insertion of this Article was at the insistence of certain states who, concerned about the Union's expansive liberalisation of economic sectors, sought to protect national public services. In this view, the text is a political compromise of no consequence.[65] Others, like Advocate General Maduro, have suggested that the first sentence of Article 14 merely provides a point of reference for interpreting Article 106(2).[66] In a more optimistic light, Malcolm Ross argues that Article 14 has elevated the importance of these services and is potentially an 'upgraded endorsement of social objectives' within the European

---

[62] European Commission, *Services of General Interest, including Social Services of General Interest: A New European Commitment*, COM(2007)725 final.

[63] See generally M. G. Ross, 'Promoting Solidarity: From Public Services to a European Model of Competition?' (2007) 44 *CMLRev.* 1057; N. Boeger, 'Solidarity and EC Competition Law' (2007) 32 *ELRev.* 319.

[64] Green Paper, above n. 60, para. 2.

[65] A. Duff (ed.), *The Treaty of Amsterdam* (London, Federal Trust, 1997) 84.

[66] Case T-319/99 *FENIN*, above n. 40.

Union.[67] Moreover, he suggests that an EU concept of SGEI can galvanise the sense of European citizenship.[68] More broadly, Schwintoski suggests that Article 14 TFEU complements the Union's economic constitution.

Hans-Peter Schwintowski, 'The Common Good, Public Subsistence and the Functions of Public Undertakings in the European Internal Market' (2003) 4 *European Business Organization Law Review* 353, 371–2

Despite the fact that ours are market societies, the common good – *bonum commune* – plays a surprisingly important role, not only in the Member States of the European Union but also in Community law. As stated in the Communication from the Commission of 20 September 2000, services of public interest are a key element in the European model of society ... Article 16 EC [now Article 14 TFEU] now confirms their place among the shared values of the Union and their role in promoting social and territorial cohesion. On the other hand, as the Community is committed to the principle of free and fair competition, there is bound to be at least a certain tension between this principle and the concepts of common good or public subsistence. ...

This raises the question of whether there can be a true osmosis between internal market and common good, or whether what we are witnessing is merely an attempt on the part of certain forces to promote their own interests under the cover of the common good. The answer is that there can be room for the concept of common good in a free and social market economy to the extent that the market displays signs of *imperfection* – in economic terms we speak of a *market failure*. ...

In our search for the rationale behind the compensatory function of the concept of 'public good in the case of market imperfections', our very first, fundamental step must be to point to the decision of the citizens of Europe to favour a market economy over a planned economy. This embodies the principle of freedom as the absolute and fundamental control mechanism in Europe. The EC Treaty and the legal systems of the Member States provide the framework where freedom can evolve in an environment ruled by law – a situation that corresponds to *Kant's* ideas in his definition of ideal law. In a similar manner, modern *normative institutional economics* is based on the *autonomy of the players' individual preferences* (concept of 'normative individualism'). ...

In combination with [Article 106(2), Article 14 TFEU] is limited to the *compensation of partial market failures*. This is in accordance with the principle of the *subsidiarity* of state action in competitive markets: regulatory intervention can and should take place only where the market is imperfect, in other words where it fails. The difficulties associated with precisely defining the phenomenon of market failure are well known, and there is no need to discuss them in depth here. The point is that [Article 14 TFEU] does not provide for market-wide regulatory competence, for instance in the sense of the traditional French 'service public', but rather that it limits the state to the correction of market imperfections on the one hand and to the provision of an appropriate legal framework on the other (ensuring state). With regard to universal services in the area of telecommunications, or to energy connection and supply, it is therefore the market that has the primary task of satisfying demand for services. It is not until market supply fails, in other words not until the remote farmhouse or the North Sea islet can no longer be supplied with telecommunications services or with energy, that the state needs to step in as regulator. ...

---

[67] In the state aid field this is possibly reflected in Case C-280/00 *Altmark*, above n. 51.

[68] M. G. Ross, 'Article 16 EC and Services of General Interest: From Derogation to Obligation?' (2000) 25 *ELRev.* 22 and see the references to citizenship in the White Paper on Services of General Interest, COM(2004)734 final.

When a company provides a service of general economic interest — thus compensating a fundamental or a partial market failure — the state is fulfilling its mission to ensure the good function of the internal market in accordance with the aims of [Article 3(3) TEU and Articles 14 and 106 TFEU]. To be precise, the state, with these measures, is actually implementing the concept of functioning competition, because this concept intrinsically includes market imperfections such as externalities or asymmetrical information. Elimination of market imperfections is thus a component of the concept of competition per se — and in this sense competition and regulation are two sides of the same coin. One of the main reasons for this is that competition theory has long moved away from its unrealistic *price-analysis* equilibrium models and instead views market inequalities and imperfections as components of the competitive process itself ... state intervention, by eliminating market imperfections, ensures that competition actually works.

This position embraces an ordoliberal view of the market economy, whereby the safeguard of public services is a necessary corollary to the success of a free market economy. With this reading, Article 14 challenges the current interpretation of Article 106(2): it is not the case that social objectives are traded off against competition goals, rather the restriction of competition to safeguard SGEIs should be allowed only when the continued existence of these services enhances the market economy.

As we explain below, the Union has begun to harmonise the provision of SGEIs by identifying certain universal services that are deemed essential, and to which everyone has a right to access, throughout the European Union, at affordable prices. Part of the reason why there has not been more activity is the tension between those favouring a market-based approach to the provision of public services, seeking to deliver public services via competitive markets,[69] and others who prefer a less market-oriented approach to the supply of SGEIs and invoke subsidiarity as a justification for retaining national regulatory mechanisms.[70]

4 POSITIVE INTEGRATION: THE LIBERALISATION OF NETWORK INDUSTRIES

The case law discussed above is in large part the result of businesses seeking to participate in markets sealed off by anti-competitive state measures. By challenging restrictions on market access in fields as varied as telecommunications, postal services, harbour facilities, ambulance services, broadcasting and social security benefits, they forced the Court of Justice to apply the Treaty's pro-market provisions to liberalise a wide range of economic sectors. But such episodic and indirect pressures to facilitate market access cannot create the best conditions for competition in an economic sector, nor will they lead to a harmonised approach across the Union: positive integration measures were required. In the past two decades, the Commission has worked hard to press for EU legislation to open markets in network industries (e.g. energy, telecommunications and postal services) because these industries form the backbone of a number of other economic activities and creating more efficient European networks would improve the competitiveness of Europe's industry more generally.[71] Initially, the Commission

---

[69] E. Szyszczak, 'Public Service Provision in Competitive Markets' (2001) 20 *YBEL* 35.

[70] *Report on the Public Consultation on the Green Paper on Services of General Interest*, SEC(2004)362, 15 March 2004.

[71] *A Single Market for 21st Century Europe*, COM(2007)724 final.

met national reluctance to agree to such legislation by using its powers of legislation under Article 106(3) TFEU (which allows the Commission to issue Directives, eschewing the traditional law-making channel of Article 114 TFEU).[72] The Commission's legislative initiatives were a challenge to Member States who, fearful of uncontrolled, Commission-led initiatives,[73] were persuaded to negotiate liberalisation within the procedures in Article 95, which left them political space to advance liberalisation while allowing them some scope to safeguard national interests. The drawback, at least from the Commission's perspective, is that while in some economic sectors (notably telecommunications) liberalisation has been successful, political foot-dragging has meant that in other sectors (notably postal services and energy), the degree of market opening has been less pronounced. Occasionally, the Commission has threatened to revert to using Article 106(3) to liberalise certain economic sectors when Member States try to stall the legislative process.[74] The liberalisation of the postal sector is a representative case study of the Union's approach.

(i) Postal services liberalisation: the first phase

The Commission's interest in liberalising the postal sector began in the late 1980s, as private parcel firms that had begun to operate in the United States and the United Kingdom began to lobby for access to European markets, where national legislation prohibited access by couriers.[75] The courier companies allied themselves with DG Competition, which played a determinative role in the Green Paper on Postal Services,[76] and initiated action challenging state laws that reserved value-added services to one undertaking.[77] In response, national postal service providers (who were, in most Member States, public undertakings) argued in favour of their privileged position by indicating that competition law would dent the provision of a high quality, universal postal service that benefited all citizens. These positions set the tone for subsequent negotiations, the key question being: how far can one inject competition without compromising the provision of an efficient universal postal service?

The facts of the controversial *Corbeau* judgment show the main method that the European Union used to address this question. Mr Corbeau wished to operate a rapid delivery service, but this infringed the Belgian postal monopoly that granted the Régie des Postes the exclusive right to operate all postal services. In answering the Belgian court's question on the application of Article 106, the Court of Justice held that this kind of legislation would be contrary to

---

[72] See C. Scott, 'Changing Patterns of European Community Utilities Law and Policy: An Institutional Hypothesis' in J. Shaw and G. More, *New Legal Dynamics of European Union* (Oxford, Oxford University Press, 1995) 208–10.

[73] Especially as the Court confirmed the Commission's powers: Case C-202/88 *France* v *Commission* [1991] ECR I-1223.

[74] See e.g. in the run up to the amendment of the Gas and Electricity Directives: the Commission threatened the use of Article 106(3) (Press Release IP(01)872 of 20 June 2001).

[75] J. I. Campbell, Jr, 'Couriers and the European Postal Monopolies: Policy Challenges of a Newly Emerging Industry' in R. H. Pedlar and M. P. C. M. Van Schendelen (eds.), *Lobbying in the European Union* (Dartmouth, Aldershot, 1994).

[76] Green Paper on the Development of the Single Market for Postal Services, COM(91)476, 11 June 1992.

[77] *Dutch PTT* [1990] OJ L10/47, challenging a law excluding access for express delivery services (Joined Cases 48/90 and 60/90 *Netherlands and Koninklijke PTT Nederland NV and PTT Post BV* v *Commission* [1992] ECR 565, overruling the Commission on procedural grounds, but agreeing that the Commission was empowered under Article 106(3) to decide that national law was incompatible with Article 106(1)); *Spanish International Express Courier Services* [1990] OJ L233/19, challenging a law prohibiting competition for letters below 2kg and prohibiting private couriers from market access.

Article 106 when the postal service markets granted to the monopoly undertaking were excessive and unnecessary to guarantee the provision of the service of general economic interest. The gist of the Court's analysis is that postal services comprise a variety of markets, some of which should be operated by the state in order to guarantee that every citizen can use the post, but that other value-added services that are used by businesses (for example, same-day delivery) should be operated by many competitors so as to give consumers increased choice. The Court acknowledged that the operator subject to public service obligations could be granted the exclusive right to operate in other, profitable, markets to offset the losses arising from the supply of the service of general economic interest:

> The starting point ... must be the premise that the obligation on the part of the undertaking entrusted with that task to perform its services in conditions of economic equilibrium presupposes that it will be possible to offset less profitable sectors against the profitable sectors and hence justifies a restriction of competition from individual undertakings where economically profitable sectors are concerned.
>
> Indeed, to authorise individual undertakings to compete with the holder of the exclusive rights in the sectors of their choice corresponding to those rights would make it possible for them to concentrate on the economically profitable operations and to offer more advantageous tariffs than those adopted by the holders of the exclusive rights since, unlike the latter, they are not bound for economic reasons to offset losses in the unprofitable sectors against profits in the more profitable sectors.[78]

The upshot is that while value-added services can be offered across the Union, *Corbeau* guarantees that a core of economic sectors can be reserved to the national postal operator to finance the operation of the SGEIs.[79] The facts of *Corbeau* also indicate that certain postal services should be available universally, and that any EU law initiative should not only increase competition but safeguard, across the Union, the provision of a common set of universal services. The spirit of the Court's approach was followed in Directive 97/67/EC ('First Postal Directive') in 1997. It identified a range of universal services and provided that Member States had an obligation to ensure that these services were provided. The list of universal services has evolved as the First Directive was amended in 2002 and in 2008.

Directive 97/67/EC on common rules for the development of the internal market of Community postal services and the improvement of quality of service [1998] OJ L15/14 (as amended by Directive 2002/39/EC [2002] OJ L176/21 and Directive 2008/6/EC [2008] OJ L52/3)

Article 3
1. Member States shall ensure that users enjoy the right to a universal service involving the permanent provision of a postal service of specified quality at all points in their territory at affordable prices for all users.

---

[78] Case C-320/91 *Criminal proceedings against Paul Corbeau* [1993] ECR I-2533.
[79] For a critique see D. Geradin and C. Humpe, 'The Liberalisation of Postal Services in the European Union: An Analysis of Directive 97/67' in D. Geradin (ed.), *The Liberalization of Postal Services in the European Union* (The Hague, Kluwer Law International, 2002) 96–9.

2. To this end, Member States shall take steps to ensure that the density of the points of contact and of the access points takes account of the needs of users.

3. Member States shall take steps to ensure that the universal service is guaranteed not less than five working days a week, save in circumstances or geographical conditions deemed exceptional, and that it includes as a minimum:
   - one clearance,
   - one delivery to the home or premises of every natural or legal person or, by way of derogation, under conditions at the discretion of the national regulatory authority, one delivery to appropriate installations.

   Any exception or derogation granted by a national regulatory authority in accordance with this paragraph must be communicated to the Commission and to all national regulatory authorities.

4. Each Member State shall adopt the measures necessary to ensure that the universal service includes the following minimum facilities:
   - the clearance, sorting, transport and distribution of postal items up to two kilograms,
   - the clearance, sorting, transport and distribution of postal packages up to 10 kilograms,
   - services for registered items and insured items.

5. The national regulatory authorities may increase the weight limit of universal service coverage for postal parcels to any weight not exceeding 20 kilograms and may lay down special arrangements for the door-to-door delivery of such parcels.

   Notwithstanding the weight limit of universal service coverage for postal parcels established by a given Member State, Member States shall ensure that postal parcels received from other Member States and weighing up to 20 kilograms are delivered within their territory.

6. The minimum and maximum dimensions for the postal items in question shall be those as laid down in the relevant provisions adopted by the Universal Postal Union.

Article 4

1. Each Member State shall ensure that the provision of the universal service is guaranteed and shall notify the Commission of the steps it has taken to fulfil this obligation. The Committee referred to in Article 21 shall be informed of the measures established by Member States to ensure the provision of the universal service.

2. Member States may designate one or more undertakings as universal service providers in order that the whole of the national territory can be covered. Member States may designate different undertakings to provide different elements of universal service and/or to cover different parts of the national territory. When they do so, they shall determine in accordance with Community law the obligations and rights assigned to them and shall publish these obligations and rights. In particular, Member States shall take measures to ensure that the conditions under which universal services are entrusted are based on the principles of transparency, non-discrimination and proportionality, thereby guaranteeing the continuity of the universal service provision, by taking into account the important role it plays in social and territorial cohesion.

   Member States shall notify the Commission of the identity of the universal service provider(s) they designate. The designation of a universal service provider shall be subject to a periodic review and be examined against the conditions and principles set out in this Article. However, Member States shall ensure that the duration of this designation provides a sufficient period for return on investments.

The impact of article 3 is to 'Europeanise' universal services, by obliging Member States to harmonise the entitlements for all citizens across the Union. Article 4 is significant in that it anticipates competition even in the provision of universal service provision, questioning the grant of exclusive rights in this sector. In this respect, Directive 2008/6/EC ('Third Postal Directive') differs from the First Postal Directive of 1997 and Directive 2002/39/EC ('Second Postal Directive') of 2002: these had also (in line with the approach in *Corbeau*) identified a 'reserved sector' that the universal service providers may be granted so that the profits from it can offset the losses incurred in the provision of the universal service.[80] There was some debate as to whether this method of financing universal services is the most effective,[81] and there were also debates over the size of the reserved sector necessary to guarantee the continued provision of universal services. The debates centred upon a trade-off between allowing greater entry in the market which would yield efficiencies, and the cost of allowing too much competition so that the universal services could not be financed.[82] In the context of the Union, the size of the reserved sector was not merely based upon this trade-off, but also a political compromise whereby those states unwilling to expose national postal services to the full effects of competition are able to have more time to adjust their markets.

The Union was conscious of the political delicacy of reform and the Second Postal Directive merely set out a 'timetable for a gradual and controlled opening of the letters market to competition which allows all universal service providers sufficient time to put in place the further measures of modernisation and restructuring required to ensure their long-term viability under the new market conditions'.[83] Market opening occurred by gradually shrinking the size of the reserved sector. The First Directive (in 1997) only liberalised 3 per cent of the market (although the market for value-added services had already been rendered competitive by DG Competition's actions)[84] and the Second Directive (in 2002) opened up to competition a slice of the letter market, which comprises 16 per cent of postal revenues.[85] Accordingly, states were successful in protecting national postal providers, a politically important sector given the high level of employment.[86]

(ii) Postal services liberalisation: Commission monitoring

Transition to the partial level of liberalisation provided by the first two Directives has been slow and required Commission supervision under Article 106(3) TFEU when certain states protected

---

[80] First and Second Postal Directives, article 7.

[81] For a dissenting voice, see M. Griffiths, 'Failing to Install Effective Competition in Postal Services: The Limited Impact of EC Law' (2000) *ECLR* 399, 400.

[82] See M. A. Crew and P. R. Kleindorfer, 'Efficient Entry, and Universal Service Obligation in Postal Service' (1988) 14 *Journal of Regulatory Economics* 103 (in favour of a reserved sector) and Geradin and Humpe, above n. 79, 97–101 (against). An alternative way of financing the universal services is through the creation of a fund where postal service undertakings who do not offer universal services contribute to a fund to compensate the undertaking(s) operating the universal services: article 9(4). For an unsuccessful implementation of a compensation fund, see Case C-340/99 *TNT Traco v Poste Italiane* [2001] ECR I-4109.

[83] Second Postal Directive, recital 14.

[84] 'Europe's Last Post', *The Economist*, 13 May 2000.

[85] Second Postal Directive, recital 17.

[86] *Report on the Application of the Postal Directive*, COM(2002)632 final (25 November 2002), estimating that 1.2 million persons are employed by universal service providers. The number of persons employed in the postal sector was 1.6 million in 2006 (*Report on the Application of the Postal Directive*, COM(2008)884 final).

the national operator. France allowed the national post office, La Poste, to also participate in the market for mail preparation (i.e. sorting and packaging letters before delivery) where other firms also competed, and gave La Poste the right to control access to its network, thereby creating a risk that it would favour its mail preparation arm at the expense of competitors.[87] Italy attempted to extend the monopoly to a non-reserved sector in breach of Article 106(1).[88] At the same time, the providers of the universal services had undergone considerable transformation: in some states they were privatised, and in many instances began to respond to the entry of new service providers by competing against them, either by protecting their own markets, or by expanding in other postal markets beyond those reserved to them. The result was that DG Competition was obliged to enforce competition law in response against unfair methods of competition. In applying Article 102 TFEU to firms that have a guaranteed monopoly by virtue of their control over a reserved sector, the scope of the abuse doctrine expanded, in particular because the Commission was concerned about the use of profits made in the reserved sector being used to finance anti-competitive practices in the non-reserved sector.[89] A dramatic example of the Commission's powers under Article 102 TFEU in the context of liberalised sectors was the *Deutsche Post I* decision.[90] The Commission responded to a complaint from UPS (one of the private parcel firms that had pressed for market opening since the 1980s) that Deutsche Post was using revenue from its reserved sector to finance a predatory pricing campaign in the market for business parcel services and was also offering fidelity rebates to major customers who agreed to use it for the majority of their mail order needs. These two strategies raised entry barriers to potential competitors in a non-reserved market and threatened the liberalisation of the market. Upon a finding that these two abuses did exist, the Commission ordered a structural separation whereby Deutsche Post undertook to create a separate legal entity to provide the parcel service, thereby preventing any future cross-subsidisation between the profits from the reserved sector and other markets. Given the Commission's concern over the use of funds from the reserved sector to finance exclusionary behaviour in competitive markets, it is surprising that the Commission approved a joint venture between Deutsche Post and DHL. UPS, relying on earlier case law, opposed the joint venture, suggesting that the funds obtained in the reserved sector could only be used to finance the universal services and not be used to expand into other markets, but the General Court affirmed the Commission's clearance:

> [I]n the absence of any evidence to show that the funds used by [Deutsche Post] for the acquisition in question derived from abusive practices on its part in the reserved letter market, the mere fact that it used those funds to acquire joint control of an undertaking active in a neighbouring market open to competition does not, in itself, even if the source of those funds

---

[87] *La Poste* [2002] OJ L120/19.

[88] COMP/39.562 *Hybrid Mail* [2001] OJ L63/59.

[89] J.-F. Pons and T. Lüder, 'La politique européenne de la concurrence dans les services postaux hors monopole' (2001) *Competition Policy Newsletter* No. 3. The 2002 amendment of the Directive responds to this by also prohibiting the cross-subsidisation of universal services outside the reserved sector out of services in the reserved sector unless this is necessary to guarantee the universal service obligations (article 12). For a review of the anti-competitive risks, see R. R. Geddes, *Competing with the Government: Anticompetitive Behavior and Public Enterprises* (Stanford, CA, Hoover Institution Press, 2004) chs. 1 and 4, available at www-hoover.stanford.edu/publications/books/compgov.html.

[90] *Deutsche Post* [2001] OJ L125/27. The general principles were set out in the Notice from the Commission on the application of the competition rules to the postal sector and on the assessment of certain state measures relating to postal services, part 3 [1998] OJ C39/2.

was the reserved market, raise any problem from the standpoint of the competition rules and cannot therefore constitute an infringement of Article [102 TFEU] or give rise to an obligation on the Commission to examine the source of those funds in the light of that article.[91]

Perhaps the Court was reassured by the undertaking given by Deutsche Post to the Commission that after the acquisition it would not use revenues in the reserved sector to subsidise the operational costs of DHL, but this promise seems hard to enforce.[92] An alternative explanation for the Commission's leniency might be that the former postal monopolies, faced with increased competition, have embarked on a process of mergers and acquisition to diversify their businesses.[93] Lenient treatment of this process of consolidation facilitates the adjustment of the industry and perhaps serves to justify the elimination of a reserved sector, as the providers of the universal services will have a sufficiently diversified portfolio to make the universal service obligations sustainable without the need for monopoly profits.

(iii) Postal services liberalisation: full competition

The Third Postal Directive was enacted on 20 February 2008, and it provides for the removal of all special and exclusive rights by 31 December 2010 for most Member States and by 2012 for the others (mostly those who joined the European Union in 2004),[94] rendering the market fully open to competition.[95] This is a controversial move, not least because as we saw above the rationale behind the grant of exclusive rights is to allow the holder to use the revenue generated in that segment of the market to finance the provision of universal postal services.[96] In justifying this radical proposal, the Commission noted first that the current system gives the incumbent monopolies a reserved area, which overcompensates them for carrying out universal services obligations. This has two adverse effects: incumbents have no incentive to rationalise their business or develop new products, and entry is discouraged. Secondly, the Commission argued that today's postal operators are complex, multiproduct firms offering a range of services, and 87.5 per cent of all mail originates from business.[97] Accordingly, entry of more competitors is required to satisfy demand and to overcome the remaining inefficiencies in the marketplace. The Commission maintains that competitive pressure will lead universal service providers to adapt by becoming more efficient, diversifying their business and reducing costs. In addition, the efficient provision of universal services can be ensured by empowering national regulatory authorities to monitor the performance of operators, to grant new entrants access to the incumbent's delivery network in high cost areas (so injecting competition in the provision of universal services), to use licences imposing certain obligations and price caps to protect consumers from excessive charges, and possibly removing the obligations to set uniform tariffs so that prices are based on cost. If competition and regulation are insufficient to ensure that

---

[91] Case T-175/99 *UPS Europe v Commission* [2002] ECR II-1915, para. 66.

[92] Case IV/M.1168 *DHL/Deutsche Post*, para. 33; (1998) 6 *Bulletin of the European Union* para. 1.3.48.

[93] *Report from the Commission to the European Parliament and Council on the Application of the Postal Directive*, COM(2002)632 final, 27.

[94] Third Postal Directive, articles 2 and 3.

[95] See also Proposal for a Directive of the European Parliament and Council amending Directive 97/67/EC concerning the full accomplishment of the internal market of Community postal services, COM(2006)594 final.

[96] It is based on the *Corbeau* judgment discussed at p. 1040.

[97] European Commission, *Prospective Study on the Impact on Universal Service of the Full Accomplishment of the Postal Internal Market in 2009*, COM(2006)596 final, 3–4.

the providers of universal services have the resources to deliver, then EU law provides 'a set of alternative options to the reserved area ... to provide for compensation (state aid, sector fees or compensation fund) or to find alternative ways to provide the service (public tendering, imposing universal service obligations on other operators)'.[98] The removal of the reserved area and details of these alternative means of finance are provided in article 7 of the Directive.

Directive 2008/6/EC of 20 February 2008 amending Directive 97/67/EC with regard to the full accomplishment of the internal market of Community postal services, article 7 [2008] OJ L52/3

1. Member States shall not grant or maintain in force exclusive or special rights for the establishment and provision of postal services. Member States may finance the provision of universal services in accordance with one or more of the means provided for in paragraphs 2, 3 and 4, or in accordance with any other means compatible with the Treaty.

2. Member States may ensure the provision of universal services by procuring such services in accordance with applicable public procurement rules and regulations, including, as provided for in Directive 2004/17/EC of the European Parliament and of the Council of 31 March 2004 coordinating the procurement procedures of entities operating in the water, energy, transport and postal services, competitive dialogue or negotiated procedures with or without publication of a contract notice.

3. Where a Member State determines that the universal service obligations, as provided for in this Directive, entail a net cost, calculated taking into account Annex I, and represent an unfair financial burden on the universal service provider(s), it may introduce:
   (a) a mechanism to compensate the undertaking(s) concerned from public funds; or
   (b) a mechanism for the sharing of the net cost of the universal service obligations between providers of services and/or users.

4. Where the net cost is shared in accordance with paragraph 3(b), Member States may establish a compensation fund which may be funded by service providers and/or users' fees, and is administered for this purpose by a body independent of the beneficiary or beneficiaries. Member States may make the granting of authorisations to service providers under Article 9(2) subject to an obligation to make a financial contribution to that fund or to comply with universal service obligations. The universal service obligations of the universal service provider(s) set out in Article 3 may be financed in this manner.

5. Member States shall ensure that the principles of transparency, non-discrimination and proportionality are respected in establishing the compensation fund and when fixing the level of the financial contributions referred to in paragraphs 3 and 4. Decisions taken in accordance with paragraphs 3 and 4 shall be based on objective and verifiable criteria and be made public.

The choice to delay the timing of liberalisation is designed to afford Member States the time to alleviate the social impact that liberalisation will bring.[99] Two brief comments can be offered at this early stage. First, it is questionable whether opening the letter market will cause new entry. In Sweden and the United Kingdom, where the market is already liberalised, the

---

[98] *Ibid.* 9.
[99] Common Position adopted by the Council on 8 November 2007 with a view to the adoption of a Directive of the European Parliament and of the Council amending Directive 97/67/EC with regard to the full accomplishment of the internal market of Community postal services, 8 November 2007 (available at http://register.consilium.europa. eu/pdf/en/07/st13/st13593-re06.en07.pdf).

incumbent has retained over 90 per cent of the letter market,[100] so removing the reserved area need not inject those competitive pressures that are said to be necessary to create incentives to invest and reduce costs. Secondly, the view that universal services can be provided through competitive markets and subjected to public regulation and consumer redress seems to leave little scope for developing an alternative approach to universal services that the draftsman of the Lisbon Treaty envisaged. Instead, more attention has been paid to improving the competitiveness of the postal sector, to achieve the goals of the Lisbon competitiveness agenda.[101] The tension between the Union's role in strengthening the economy, on the one hand, and ensuring its citizens access to universal services, on the other, remains.

5 EVALUATION

Two major themes underpin the legal developments in this chapter. The first is an economic theme whereby targeting anti-competitive state action is said to be necessary to achieve the economic ambitions of the EU Treaties and where the Commission is portrayed as fighting a battle with protectionist Member States who wish to safeguard national industries. Jacques Pelkmans suggests that there are some fundamental weaknesses with the European Union's liberalisation project.[102] First, the deregulation of industries was not part of the Single European Act or of the 1992 project for completing the internal market. This meant that the Union took an ad hoc approach to liberalisation. This left the door open to lobbying that slowed down liberalisation. Secondly, national governments and civil servants working in the Union had ambivalent views about liberalisation which slowed down the rate of reform. In these conditions, it is unlikely that the benefits of liberalisation would materialise. Thus, even in a sector like telecommunications, where liberalisation has gone furthest, it is legitimate to question how far the lower costs and availability of mobile phones is down to competition law, as technological development is likely to have made a comparable contribution to improving consumer welfare.[103]

This pessimistic view is confirmed by the Commission's latest report on the operation of the Postal Directive: 'the development of competition with its benefits for businesses and consumers — although emerging — remains slower than expected'.[104] For example, in the four countries where 'end-to-end' competition is most developed (that is, where a competitor competes by collecting, transporting and delivering post), the market shares of new entrants are small (8 per cent in Spain, 9 per cent in Sweden, 10 per cent in Germany and 14 per cent in the Netherlands in 2007).[105] In part this is attributed to the presence of a reserved sector (and the Commission considers the Third Postal Directive abolishing the reserved sector a 'unique opportunity' to inject more competition), but also to the presence of a number of other barriers to entry to be addressed in various ways: EU legislation, Commission monitoring of Member

---

[100] *Study on the Evolution of the Regulatory Model for Postal Services* (WIK Consult, July 2005), available at http://ec.europa.eu/internal_market/post/studies_en.htm.

[101] 'Commission welcomes the adoption of the EU Postal Directive; market opening brings clear benefits for postal users', Press Release IP/08/163.

[102] J. Pelkmans, 'Making EU Network Markets Competitive' (2001) 17(3) *Oxford Review of Economic Policy* 432, 453.

[103] See J. Pelkmans, *European Integration: Methods and Economic Analysis* (Harlow, Financial Times and Prentice Hall, 2006) ch. 8.

[104] *Report on the Application of the Postal Directive*, COM(2008)884 final, 7.

[105] *Ibid.* 6.

States, and regulation by national regulatory authorities, whose role has been strengthened by the Third Postal Directive.[106]

While from an economic perspective the picture looks gloomy, from a policy perspective, the Union's achievements can be assessed in a more positive light: the Commission seized upon the case law of the Court of Justice, and the pioneering liberalisation of UK industry in the 1980s, to create a momentum for EU legislative action in the period after the Single European Act, even when the legal tools to achieve market opening were not perfect. Further, as Mark Thatcher notes, the impact of the Postal Directive was a varied range of incentives and threats for postal operators.

Mark Thatcher, *Internationalisation and Economic Institutions: Comparing European Perspectives* (Oxford, Oxford University Press, 2007) 246–7

EU regulation was central to overcoming opposition in France and Italy. First, liberalisation and re-regulatory rules in France and Italy were undertaken to transpose the 1997 Postal Directive. The Commission put pressure on Member States to correctly transpose directives. Thus after complaints that the French state was abusing its dominant position since it both fixed postal tariffs and supervised La Poste, the European Commission opened an inquiry and proceedings against France. It began proceedings against other Member States (beginning with Belgium) over the lack of separation of postal services and regulation, placing pressure on France to alter the allocation of regulatory powers and triggering reform in 2005 (although EU law did not require the creation of a sectoral independent regulatory agency). The Commission also took action against Italy ... a Commission Decision in 2000 led Italy to alter domestic legislation to reduce Poste Italiane's monopoly.

Second, EU regulation set the pace for liberalisation. For France and Italy, this occurred as they only liberalised when required to do so by EU law. For Germany, the effect was the converse, slowing up reform. The 1996 Postreforem planned to introduce full competition in 2002. However, the Social Democratic-Green government that came into office in 1998 sought to protect Deutsche Post's domestic position ... The government was able to justify its refusal to extend liberalisation by the fear that other European suppliers would enter the German market but that without EU regulation, the same would not be available to Deutsche Post ... Instead, the government decided to follow the EU's timetable for liberalisation, and hence delayed the end of Deutsche Post's monopoly from 2002 to 2007.

A third effect of EU liberalisation was to increase pressures and opportunities for change which were often desired both because of EU regulation and for other reasons. With respect to the latter, traditional postal services were growing slowly by the 1990s and faced competition from other cheaper telephone and electronic communications. In addition, postal organisations faced the weight of historically-imposed high labour costs. Their senior managers sought to make them more efficient and to diversify into fast-growing markets such as financial services and email. EU regulation provided justifications and increased incentives for new strategies based on more efficient working practices, reducing labour costs and international expansion. Thus, for instance, German policy makers sought to make Deutsche Post an international company ... By 2000, no less than 29% of its turnover came from abroad. Similar patterns were seen in France and Italy ... Thus EU regulation aided a switch in strategies of policy makers towards making postal operators commercial and internationally-competitive organisations, through transformation into corporations and privatisation.

---

[106] Third Postal Directive, article 22.

The significance of these findings is how EU law achieves similar outcomes (liberalised postal markets) even though the role of the Union varies: it had no impact on the United Kingdom's market opening agenda, it slowed down Germany's reform, while legal pressure was necessary to cajole France and Italy into action. In addition, the Union also seized upon Member States' concerns about public services to 'Europeanise' SGEIs, renaming these 'universal services'. The upshot was that the Union was able to press for greater liberalisation while at the same time guaranteeing the social protection for all citizens through the creation of universal service obligations. This was a masterful approach, for it assuaged states fearful of a European Union fully predicated upon economic liberalism, introducing other non-economic values held in high esteem by several states. Accordingly, while Pelkmans is right to state that progress has been painfully slow, if one considers the limited Treaty resources and the political controversies the Union has had to surmount, the strategy deployed by the Union for creating the current framework for liberalising markets whilst preserving services of general interest can be viewed in a more positive light: enhancing the legitimacy of EU action by bringing Europe closer to its citizens through the creation of an EU-wide conception of the general interest.

C. Boutayeb, 'Une recherche sur la place et les functions de l'intérêt general en droit communautaire' (2003) *Revue Trimestrielle de Droit Européen* 587,607–8 (translated by Giorgio Monti)

The simple reference or appeal to the general interest by the community legislator can be said to serve two distinct functions according to their nature: on the one hand, the general interest allows the Community legislator to ascertain the legitimacy of his action and from them his own legitimacy by responding to a clearly identified and especially undisputed collective need. In this case, the general interest becomes a condition of legality for the Community's legislative intervention and as such exercises a passive legislative function. On the other hand, the appeal to the general interest allows the Community to show to the citizens that, through the non-negligible advancement of considerations linked to the general interest, the Community is increasingly active in the domains which affect their daily lives. This gives the Community institutions a democratic legitimacy in the implementation of their actions. By thus regaining legitimacy, the EC authorities reply to the acidic critiques tied to its 'representativeness'. In this interpretation, the Community legislator establishes himself alongside the national legislator as guardian and guarantor of the general interest.

With this wide lens, Article 14 TFEU is part of a broader pattern of the European Union's evolution from a purely economic community concerned with the management of a borderless economy, into a Union which aspires to a European model of society premised upon a wider conception of the citizen's interests: 'a highly competitive *social* market economy'.[107] This discourse reveals a Union that is slowly developing a distinctive public policy dimension alongside its role as an engine for economic deregulation and integration. This is in large part the result of national interests in preserving public services being recast as interests to be addressed at transnational level.[108] Whether this is indeed a legitimate role for the European Union remains an open question, and whether it is a role it can carry out successfully will serve as a litmus test for the success of the Treaty of Lisbon.

---

[107] Article 3(3) TEU.
[108] A. Héritier, 'Market Integration and Social Cohesion: The Politics of Public Services in European Regulation' (2001) 8 *JEPP* 825.

FURTHER READING

V. Auricchio, 'Services of General Economic Interest and the Application of EC Competition Law' (2001) 24 *World Competition* 65

J. L. Buendia Sierra, *Exclusive Rights and State Monopolies under EC Law: Article 86 (formerly Article 90) of the EC Treaty* (Oxford, Oxford University Press, 1999)

G. T. Davies, 'Article 86 EC, the EC's Economic Approach to Competition Law and the General Interest' (2009) 5 *European Competition Journal* 549

D. Edward and M. Hoskins, 'Deregulation and EC Law: Reflections Arising from the XVI Fide Conference' (1995) 32 *Common Market Law Review* 157

L. Flynn and C. Rizza, 'Postal Services and Competition Law: A Review and Analysis of the EC Case-Law' (2001) 24 *World Competition* 475

A. Gardner, 'The Velvet Revolution: Article 90 and the Triumph of the Free Market in Europe's Regulated Sectors' (1995) *European Competition Law Review* 78

D. Geradin (ed.), *The Liberalisation of State Monopolies in the European Union and Beyond* (The Hague and Boston, Kluwer Law International, 2000)

L. Hancher, 'Community, State and Market' in P. Craig and G. de Búrca (eds.), *The Evolution of EU Law* (Oxford, Oxford University Press, 1999)

A. Héritier, 'Market Integration and Social Cohesion: The Politics of Public Services in European Regulation' (2001) 8 *Journal of European Public Policy* 825

J. Holmes, 'Fixing the Limits of EC Competition Law: State Action and the Accommodation of the Public Services' (2004) 57 *Current Legal Problems* 149

T. Prosser, *The Limits of Competition Law: Markets and Public Services* (Oxford, Oxford University Press, 2005)

M. G. Ross, 'Article 16 EC and Services of General Interest: From Derogation to Obligation?' (2000) 25 *European Law Review* 22

W. Sauter and H. Schepel, *State and Market in European Union Law: The Public and Private Spheres of the Internal Market Before the EU Courts* (Cambridge, Cambridge University Press, 2009)

E. Szyszczak, *The Regulation of the State in Competitive Markets in the EU* (Oxford, Hart, 2007)

J. Winterstein, 'Nailing the Jellyfish: Social Security and Competition Law' (1999) *European Competition Law Review* 324

Index